Lisa A. Urry • Michael L. Cain • Steven A. Wasserman
Peter V. Minorsky • Jane B. Reece

# Campbell Biology

Custom Edition for the University of Denver

Taken from:
*Campbell Biology*, Eleventh Edition
by Lisa A. Urry, Michael L. Cain, Steven A. Wasserman,
Peter V. Minorsky, and Jane B. Reece

Cover Art: Courtesy of Photodisc/Getty Images.

Taken from:

*Campbell Biology*, Eleventh Edition
by Lisa A. Urry, Michael L. Cain, Steven A. Wasserman,
Peter V. Minorsky, and Jane B. Reece
Copyright © 2017, 2014, 2011 by Pearson Education, Inc.
New York, NY 10013

This special edition published in cooperation with Pearson Education, Inc.

All trademarks, service marks, registered trademarks, and registered service marks are the
property of their respective owners and are used herein for identification purposes only.

Pearson Education, Inc., 330 Hudson Street, New York, New York 10013
A Pearson Education Company
www.pearsoned.com

Printed in the United States of America

1  17

000200010272083813

EF

ISBN 10: 1-323-64204-8
ISBN 13: 978-1-323-64204-7

# Brief Contents

# Detailed Contents

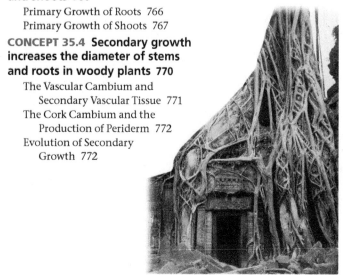

# 42 Circulation and Gas Exchange 919

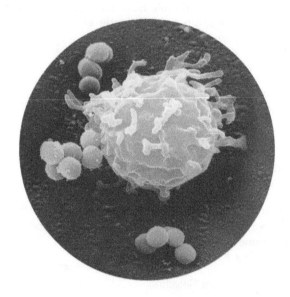

# 43 The Immune System 950

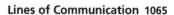

# UNIT 6 PLANT FORM AND FUNCTION

Philip N. Benfey is an authority on the developmental biology of plant root systems. After majoring in biology at the University of Paris, he learned the techniques of genetic engineering while doing his Ph.D. research on mammalian cell lines at Harvard Medical School. As a postdoctoral fellow at Rockefeller University, he began his studies of plant root development. He is an HHMI Investigator and the Paul Kramer Professor of Biology at Duke University. He has also founded two plant biotechnology companies.

## An Interview with Philip N. Benfey

### How did you begin your career path?

I felt lost as a college freshman, so after a year I dropped out to become a writer. To gain real-world experiences, I hitchhiked around the world. I worked in the iron mines in Australia, in the film industry in the Philippines, and for a gardening company in Japan. Eventually, I took the Trans-Siberian railroad across Russia and wound up in France, where I worked as a carpenter by day and tried my hand as a fiction writer by night. Many rejection letters later (and six years after graduating from high school), I decided to return to college.

### Did your parents support this detour in your life journey?

They did, and I am grateful to them. I think they were wise in allowing me to explore different directions. But I will always remember the letter that my mother wrote when I announced I was going back to school to study biology. She reported that my father, an organic chemistry professor, danced a jig on the table, which gave me some sense of what their true expectations and hopes were.

### How did you become interested in biology, particularly in plants?

I was, and remain to this day, very interested in the process of how a single cell becomes a multicellular organism. In the mid-1980s, I wanted to find a less-explored model system than *Drosophila*. Scientists at that time had just figured out how to genetically engineer plants. From a developmental perspective, plants were attractive because they have fewer cell types and are organized in straightforward ways.

### And why plant roots?

Roots have complex physiologies, yet they're formed in a really simple way: They're essentially rings of concentric cylinders, but each of those rings is carrying out a different function. Moreover, all the cells in a root are generated from stem cells at the tip of the root.

### Twenty-five years later, do you still think plants are simple?

Plants are incredibly complex in their metabolism and all sorts of things. But from a purely developmental perspective, they are simpler than animals, and the developmental simplicity of roots has allowed us to address questions that would have been much harder to do in any other system, including other parts of the plant.

### Is it a problem that roots are generally studied growing outside the soil?

Soil is among the most complex ecosystems in the world. According to soil scientists, there are 22,000 soil types, and those are just the combinations of clay, sandy, and loamy soil, the inorganic parts. Then add in the incredible diversity of bacteria and other organisms that are there. You will never be looking at the same thing at two different places, no matter how hard you try. Recently, we have been using X-rays to image root systems in different soil types and comparing how they look in the artificial gel matrix we had been using to grow roots. We can then add in various soil components and ask, as we change one or two things at a time, how does that change the root structure?

### Why is plant biology a good career to pursue?

Most of the major issues that are facing the world today—such as renewable energy, food security, and climate change—relate back to plants. Therefore, applying your energies and talents to the study of plants could change the future.

> ## "Most of the major issues that are facing the world today—such as renewable energy, food security, and climate change—relate back to plants."

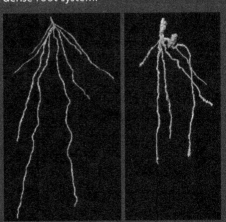

▼ X-rays of roots of two rice varieties. An Asian variety (left) that grows in paddies has long, fibrous roots. A Brazilian variety (right) that grows in soil has a short, dense root system.

# Vascular Plant Structure, Growth, and Development

# 35

▲ Figure 35.1 **Computer art?**

## KEY CONCEPTS

**35.1** Plants have a hierarchical organization consisting of organs, tissues, and cells

**35.2** Different meristems generate new cells for primary and secondary growth

**35.3** Primary growth lengthens roots and shoots

**35.4** Secondary growth increases the diameter of stems and roots in woody plants

**35.5** Growth, morphogenesis, and cell differentiation produce the plant body

## Are Plants Computers?

The object in **Figure 35.1** is not the creation of a computer genius with a flair for the artistic. It is a head of romanesco, an edible relative of broccoli. Romanesco's mesmerizing beauty is attributable to the fact that each of its smaller buds resembles in miniature the entire vegetable (shown below). (Mathematicians refer to such repetitive patterns as *fractals*.) If romanesco looks as if it were generated by a computer, it's because its growth pattern follows a repetitive sequence of instructions. As in most plants, the growing shoot tips lay down a pattern of stem … leaf … bud, over and over again. These repetitive developmental patterns are genetically determined and subject to natural selection. For example, a mutation that shortens the stem segments between leaves will generate a bushier plant. If this altered architecture enhances the plant's ability to access resources such as light and, by doing so, to produce more offspring, then this trait will occur more frequently in later generations—the population will have evolved.

Romanesco is unusual in adhering so rigidly to its basic body organization. Most plants show much greater diversity in their individual forms because the growth of most plants, much more than in animals, is affected by local environmental conditions. All adult lions, for example, have four legs and are of roughly the same size, but oak trees vary in the number and arrangement of their branches. This is because plants respond to challenges and opportunities in their local environment by altering

---

When you see this blue icon, log in to **MasteringBiology** and go to the Study Area for digital resources.

 Get Ready for This Chapter

their growth. (In contrast, animals typically respond by movement.) Illumination of a plant from the side, for example, creates asymmetries in its basic body plan. Branches grow more quickly from the illuminated side of a shoot than from the shaded side, an architectural change of obvious benefit for photosynthesis. Changes in growth and development facilitate a plant's ability to acquire resources from its local environment.

Chapters 29 and 30 provided an overview of plant diversity, including both nonvascular and vascular plants. In Unit Six, we'll focus on vascular plants, especially angiosperms because flowering plants are the primary producers in many terrestrial ecosystems and are of great agricultural importance. This chapter mainly explores nonreproductive growth—roots, stems, and leaves—and focuses primarily on the two main groups of angiosperms: eudicots and monocots (see Figure 30.16). Later, in Chapter 38, we'll examine angiosperm reproductive growth: flowers, seeds, and fruits.

# CONCEPT 35.1

## Plants have a hierarchical organization consisting of organs, tissues, and cells

Plants, like most animals, are composed of cells, tissues, and organs. A **cell** is the fundamental unit of life. A **tissue** is a group of cells consisting of one or more cell types that together perform a specialized function. An **organ** consists of several types of tissues that together carry out particular functions. As you learn about each of these levels of plant structure, keep in mind how natural selection has produced plant forms that fit plant function at all levels of organization. We begin by discussing plant organs because their structures are most familiar.

## Basic Vascular Plant Organs: Roots, Stems, and Leaves

**EVOLUTION** The basic morphology of vascular plants reflects their evolutionary history as terrestrial organisms that inhabit and draw resources from two very different environments—below the ground and above the ground. They must absorb water and minerals from below the ground surface and $CO_2$ and light from above the ground surface. The ability to acquire these resources efficiently is traceable to the evolution of roots, stems, and leaves as the three basic organs. These organs form a **root system** and a **shoot system**, the latter consisting of stems and leaves (**Figure 35.2**). Vascular plants, with few exceptions, rely on both systems for survival. Roots are almost never photosynthetic; they starve unless *photosynthates*, the sugars and the other carbohydrates produced during photosynthesis, are imported from the shoot

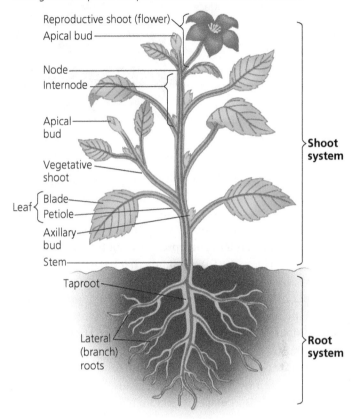

▼ **Figure 35.2 An overview of a flowering plant.** The plant body is divided into a root system and a shoot system, connected by vascular tissue (purple strands in this diagram) that is continuous throughout the plant. The plant shown is an idealized eudicot.

Reproductive shoot (flower)
Apical bud
Node
Internode
Apical bud
Vegetative shoot
Leaf { Blade
Petiole
Axillary bud
Stem
Taproot
Lateral (branch) roots
Shoot system
Root system

system. Conversely, the shoot system depends on the water and minerals that roots absorb from the soil.

### Roots

A **root** is an organ that anchors a vascular plant in the soil, absorbs minerals and water, and often stores carbohydrates and other reserves. The *primary root*, originating in the seed embryo, is the first root (and the first organ) to emerge from a germinating seed. It soon branches to form **lateral roots** (see Figure 35.2) that can also branch, greatly enhancing the ability of the root system to anchor the plant and to acquire resources such as water and minerals from the soil.

Tall, erect plants with large shoot masses generally have a *taproot system*, consisting of one main vertical root, the **taproot**, which usually develops from the primary root. In taproot systems, the role of absorption is restricted largely to the tips of lateral roots. A taproot, although energetically expensive to make, facilitates the anchorage of the plant in the soil. By preventing toppling, the taproot enables the plant to grow taller, thereby giving it access to more favorable light conditions and, in some cases, providing an advantage for pollen and seed dispersal. Taproots can also be specialized for food storage.

> **Figure 35.3 Root hairs of a radish seedling.** Root hairs grow by the thousands just behind the tip of each root. By increasing the root's surface area, they greatly enhance the absorption of water and minerals from the soil.

 Video: Root Growth in a Radish Seedling

Small vascular plants or those that have a trailing growth habit are particularly susceptible to grazing animals that can potentially uproot the plant and kill it. Such plants are most efficiently anchored by a *fibrous root system*, a thick mat of slender roots spreading out below the soil surface (see Figure 30.16). In plants that have fibrous root systems, including most monocots, the primary root dies early on and does not form a taproot. Instead, many small roots emerge from the stem. Such roots are said to be *adventitious*, a term describing a plant organ that grows in an unusual location, such as roots arising from stems or leaves. Each root forms its own lateral roots, which in turn form their own lateral roots. Because this mat of roots holds the topsoil in place, plants such as grasses that have dense fibrous root systems are especially good at preventing soil erosion.

In most plants, the absorption of water and minerals occurs primarily near the tips of elongating roots, where vast numbers of **root hairs**, thin, finger-like extensions of root epidermal cells, emerge and increase the surface area of the root enormously **(Figure 35.3)**. Most root systems also form *mycorrhizal associations*, symbiotic interactions with soil fungi that increase a plant's ability to absorb minerals (see Figure 31.15). The roots of many plants are adapted for specialized functions **(Figure 35.4)**.

◀ **Figure 35.4 Evolutionary adaptations of roots.**

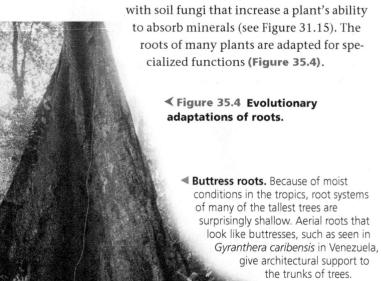

◀ **Buttress roots.** Because of moist conditions in the tropics, root systems of many of the tallest trees are surprisingly shallow. Aerial roots that look like buttresses, such as seen in *Gyranthera caribensis* in Venezuela, give architectural support to the trunks of trees.

▲ **Prop roots.** The aerial, adventitious roots of maize (corn) are prop roots, so named because they support tall, top-heavy plants. All roots of a mature maize plant are adventitious whether they emerge above or below ground.

▲ **Storage roots.** Many plants, such as the common beet, store food and water in their roots.

▲ **Pneumatophores.** Also known as air roots, pneumatophores are produced by trees such as mangroves that inhabit tidal swamps. By projecting above the water's surface at low tide, they enable the root system to obtain oxygen, which is lacking in the thick, waterlogged mud.

▶ **"Strangling" aerial roots.** Strangler fig seeds germinate in the crevices of tall trees. Aerial roots grow to the ground, wrapping around the host tree and objects such as this Cambodian temple. Shoots grow upward and shade out the host tree, killing it.

## Stems

A **stem** is a plant organ bearing leaves and buds. Its chief function is to elongate and orient the shoot in a way that maximizes photosynthesis by the leaves. Another function of stems is to elevate reproductive structures, thereby facilitating the dispersal of pollen and fruit. Green stems may also perform a limited amount of photosynthesis. Each stem consists of an alternating system of **nodes**, the points at which leaves are attached, and **internodes**, the stem segments between nodes (see Figure 35.2). Most of the growth of a young shoot is concentrated near the growing shoot tip or **apical bud**. Apical buds are not the only types of buds found in shoots. In the upper angle (axil) formed by each leaf and the stem is an **axillary bud**, which can potentially form a lateral branch or, in some cases, a thorn or flower.

Some plants have stems with alternative functions, such as food storage or asexual reproduction. Many of these modified stems, including rhizomes, stolons, and tubers, are often mistaken for roots **(Figure 35.5)**.

▼ Figure 35.5 **Evolutionary adaptations of stems.**

◀ **Rhizomes.** The base of this iris plant is an example of a rhizome, a horizontal shoot that grows just below the surface. Vertical shoots emerge from axillary buds on the rhizome.

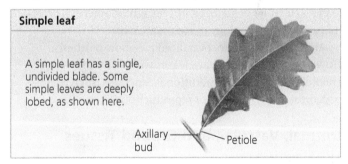

▶ **Stolons.** Shown here on a strawberry plant, stolons are horizontal shoots that grow along the surface. These "runners" enable a plant to reproduce asexually, as plantlets form at nodes along each runner.

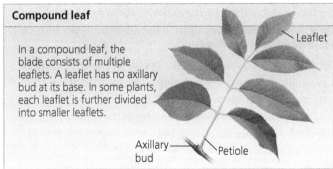

◀ **Tubers.** Tubers, such as these potatoes, are enlarged ends of rhizomes or stolons specialized for storing food. The "eyes" of a potato are clusters of axillary buds that mark the nodes.

## Leaves

In most vascular plants, the **leaf** is the main photosynthetic organ. In addition to intercepting light, leaves exchange gases with the atmosphere, dissipate heat, and defend themselves from herbivores and pathogens. These functions may have conflicting physiological, anatomical, or morphological requirements. For example, a dense covering of hairs may help repel herbivorous insects but may also trap air near the leaf surface, thereby reducing gas exchange and, consequently, photosynthesis. Because of these conflicting demands and trade-offs, leaves vary extensively in form. In general, however, a leaf consists of a flattened **blade** and a stalk, the **petiole**, which joins the leaf to the stem at a node (see Figure 35.2). Grasses and many other monocots lack petioles; instead, the base of the leaf forms a sheath that envelops the stem.

Monocots and eudicots differ in the arrangement of **veins**, the vascular tissue of leaves. Most monocots have parallel major veins of equal diameter that run the length of the blade. Eudicots generally have a branched network of veins arising from a major vein (the *midrib*) that runs down the center of the blade (see Figure 30.16).

In identifying angiosperms according to structure, taxonomists rely mainly on floral morphology, but they also use variations in leaf morphology, such as leaf shape, the branching pattern of veins, and the spatial arrangement of leaves. **Figure 35.6** illustrates a difference in leaf shape: simple versus compound. Compound leaves may withstand strong wind with less tearing. They may also confine some pathogens that invade the leaf to a single leaflet, rather than allowing them to spread to the entire leaf.

▼ Figure 35.6 **Simple versus compound leaves.**

**Simple leaf**

A simple leaf has a single, undivided blade. Some simple leaves are deeply lobed, as shown here.

Axillary bud — Petiole

**Compound leaf**

In a compound leaf, the blade consists of multiple leaflets. A leaflet has no axillary bud at its base. In some plants, each leaflet is further divided into smaller leaflets.

Leaflet

Axillary bud — Petiole

## Figure 35.7 Evolutionary adaptations of leaves.

▶ **Tendrils.** The tendrils by which this pea plant clings to a support are modified leaves. After it has "lassoed" a support, a tendril forms a coil that brings the plant closer to the support. Tendrils are typically modified leaves, but some tendrils are modified stems, as in grapevines.

◀ **Spines.** The spines of cacti, such as this prickly pear, are actually leaves; photosynthesis is carried out by the fleshy green stems.

◀ **Storage leaves.** Bulbs, such as this cut onion, have a short underground stem and modified leaves that store food.

Plantlet
Storage leaves
Stem

◀ **Reproductive leaves.** The leaves of some succulents, such as *Kalanchoë daigremontiana*, produce adventitious plantlets, which fall off the leaf and take root in the soil.

The morphological features of leaves are often products of genetic programs that are tweaked by environmental influences. Interpret the data in the **Scientific Skills Exercise** to explore the roles of genetics and the environment in determining leaf morphology in red maple trees.

Almost all leaves are specialized for photosynthesis. However, some species have leaves with adaptations that enable them to perform additional functions, such as support, protection, storage, or reproduction (**Figure 35.7**).

## Dermal, Vascular, and Ground Tissues

All three basic vascular plant organs—roots, stems, and leaves—are composed of three fundamental tissue types: dermal, vascular, and ground tissues. Each of these general types forms a **tissue system** that is continuous throughout the plant, connecting all the organs. However, specific characteristics of the tissues and the spatial relationships of tissues to one another vary in different organs (**Figure 35.8**).

The **dermal tissue system** serves as the outer protective covering of the plant. Like our skin, it forms the first line of defense against physical damage and pathogens. In nonwoody plants, it is usually a single tissue called the **epidermis**, a layer

# SCIENTIFIC SKILLS EXERCISE

## *Using Bar Graphs to Interpret Data*

**Nature Versus Nurture: Why Are Leaves from Northern Red Maples "Toothier" Than Leaves from Southern Red Maples?** Not all leaves of the red maple (*Acer rubrum*) are the same. The "teeth" along the margins of leaves growing in northern locations differ in size and number from those of their southern counterparts. (The leaf seen here has an intermediate appearance.) Are these morphological differences due to genetic differences between northern and southern *Acer rubrum* populations, or do they arise from environmental differences between northern and southern locations, such as average temperature, that affect gene expression?

**How the Experiment Was Done** Seeds of *Acer rubrum* were collected from four latitudinally distinct sites: Ontario (Canada), Pennsylvania, South Carolina, and Florida. The seeds from the four sites were then grown in a northern location (Rhode Island) and a southern location (Florida). After a few years of growth, leaves were harvested from the four sets of plants growing in the two locations. The average area of single teeth and the average number of teeth per leaf area were determined.

**Data from the Experiment**

| Seed Collection Site | Average Area of a Single Tooth (cm²) | | Number of Teeth per cm² of Leaf Area | |
|---|---|---|---|---|
| | Grown in Rhode Island | Grown in Florida | Grown in Rhode Island | Grown in Florida |
| Ontario (43.32°N) | 0.017 | 0.017 | 3.9 | 3.2 |
| Pennsylvania (42.12°N) | 0.020 | 0.014 | 3.0 | 3.5 |
| South Carolina (33.45°N) | 0.024 | 0.028 | 2.3 | 1.9 |
| Florida (30.65°N) | 0.027 | 0.047 | 2.1 | 0.9 |

**Data from** D. L. Royer et al., Phenotypic plasticity of leaf shape along a temperature gradient in *Acer rubrum*, *PLoS ONE* 4(10):e7653 (2009).

**INTERPRET THE DATA**

1. Make a bar graph for tooth size and a bar graph for number of teeth. (For information on bar graphs, see the Scientific Skills Review in Appendix F and the Study Area in MasteringBiology.) From north to south, what is the general trend in tooth size and number of teeth in leaves of *Acer rubrum*?

2. Based on the data, would you conclude that leaf tooth traits in the red maple are largely determined by genetic heritage (genotype), by the capacity for responding to environmental change within a single genotype (phenotypic plasticity), or by both? Make specific reference to the data in answering the question.

3. The "toothiness" of leaf fossils of known age has been used by paleoclimatologists to estimate past temperatures in a region. If a 10,000-year-old fossilized red maple leaf from South Carolina had an average of 4.2 teeth per square centimeter of leaf area, what could you infer about the temperature of South Carolina 10,000 years ago compared with the temperature today? Explain your reasoning.

 **Instructors:** A version of this Scientific Skills Exercise can be assigned in MasteringBiology.

The dermal tissue system (blue) provides a protective cover for the entire body of a plant. The vascular tissue system (purple), which transports materials between the root and shoot systems, is also continuous throughout the plant but is arranged differently in each organ. The ground tissue system (yellow), which is responsible for most of the metabolic functions, is located between the dermal tissue and the vascular tissue in each organ.

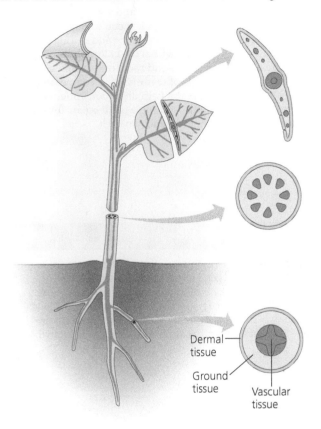

Dermal tissue

Ground tissue

Vascular tissue

▼ **Figure 35.9 Trichome diversity on the surface of a leaf.** Three types of trichomes are found on the surface of marjoram (*Origanum majorana*). Spear-like trichomes help hinder the movement of crawling insects, while the other two types of trichomes secrete oils and other chemicals involved in defense (colorized SEM).

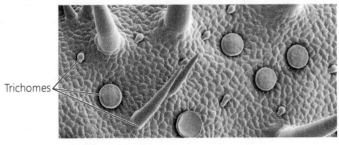

Trichomes

300 μm

stored—usually roots and sites of growth, such as developing leaves and fruits. The vascular tissue of a root or stem is collectively called the **stele** (the Greek word for "pillar"). The arrangement of the stele varies, depending on the species and organ. In angiosperms, for example, the root stele is a solid central **vascular cylinder** of xylem and phloem, whereas the stele of stems and leaves consists of *vascular bundles*, separate strands containing xylem and phloem (see Figure 35.8). Both xylem and phloem are composed of a variety of cell types, including cells that are highly specialized for transport or support.

Tissues that are neither dermal nor vascular are part of the **ground tissue system**. Ground tissue that is internal to the vascular tissue is known as **pith**, and ground tissue that is external to the vascular tissue is called **cortex**. Ground tissue is not just filler: It includes cells specialized for functions such as storage, photosynthesis, support, and short-distance transport.

## Common Types of Plant Cells

In a plant, as in any multicellular organism, cells undergo cell *differentiation*; that is, they become specialized in structure and function during the course of development. Cell differentiation may involve changes both in the cytoplasm and its organelles and in the cell wall. **Figure 35.10**, on the next two pages, focuses on the major types of plant cells. Notice the structural adaptations that make specific functions possible. You may also wish to review basic plant cell structure (see Figures 6.8 and 6.28).

(MB) BioFlix® Animation: Tour of a Plant Cell

### CONCEPT CHECK 35.1

1. How does the vascular tissue system enable leaves and roots to function together in supporting growth and development of the whole plant?

2. **WHAT IF?** ➤ If humans were photoautotrophs, making food by capturing light energy for photosynthesis, how might our anatomy be different?

3. **MAKE CONNECTIONS** ➤ Explain how central vacuoles and cellulose cell walls contribute to plant growth (see Concepts 6.4 and 6.7).

*For suggested answers, see Appendix A.*

of tightly packed cells. In leaves and most stems, the **cuticle**, a waxy epidermal coating, helps prevent water loss. In woody plants, protective tissues called **periderm** replace the epidermis in older regions of stems and roots. In addition to protecting the plant from water loss and disease, the epidermis has specialized characteristics in each organ. In roots, water and minerals absorbed from the soil enter through the epidermis, especially in root hairs. In shoots, specialized epidermal cells called **guard cells** are involved in gaseous exchange. Another class of highly specialized epidermal cells found in shoots consists of outgrowths called **trichomes**. In some desert species, hairlike trichomes reduce water loss and reflect excess light. Some trichomes defend against insects through shapes that hinder movement or glands that secrete sticky fluids or toxic compounds **(Figure 35.9)**.

The chief functions of the **vascular tissue system** are to facilitate the transport of materials through the plant and to provide mechanical support. The two types of vascular tissues are xylem and phloem. **Xylem** conducts water and dissolved minerals upward from roots into the shoots. **Phloem** transports sugars, the products of photosynthesis, from where they are made (usually the leaves) to where they are needed or

## Parenchyma Cells

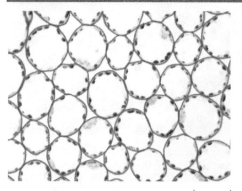

Mature **parenchyma cells** have primary walls that are relatively thin and flexible, and most lack secondary walls. (See Figure 6.27 to review primary and secondary cell walls.) When mature, parenchyma cells generally have a large central vacuole. Parenchyma cells perform most of the metabolic functions of the plant, synthesizing and storing various organic products. For example, photosynthesis occurs within the chloroplasts of parenchyma cells in the leaf. Some parenchyma cells in stems and roots have colorless plastids called amyloplasts that store starch. The fleshy tissue of many fruits is composed mainly of parenchyma cells. Most parenchyma cells retain the ability to divide and differentiate into other types of plant cells under particular conditions—during wound repair, for example. It is even possible to grow an entire plant from a single parenchyma cell.

**Parenchyma cells** in a privet
(*Ligustrum*) leaf (LM)      25 μm

## Collenchyma Cells

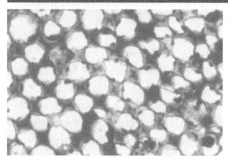

Grouped in strands, **collenchyma cells** (seen here in cross section) help support young parts of the plant shoot. Collenchyma cells are generally elongated cells that have thicker primary walls than parenchyma cells, though the walls are unevenly thickened. Young stems and petioles often have strands of collenchyma cells just below their epidermis. Collenchyma cells provide flexible support without restraining growth. At maturity, these cells are living and flexible, elongating with the stems and leaves they support—unlike sclerenchyma cells, which we discuss next.

**Collenchyma cells**
(in *Helianthus* stem) (LM)      5 μm

## Sclerenchyma Cells

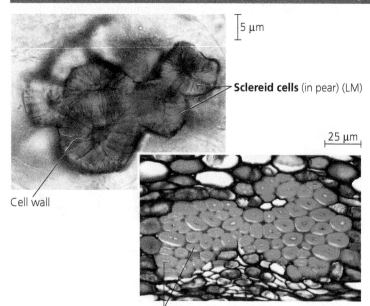

5 μm

Sclereid cells (in pear) (LM)

25 μm

Cell wall

Fiber cells (cross section from ash tree) (LM)

**Sclerenchyma cells** also function as supporting elements in the plant but are much more rigid than collenchyma cells. In sclerenchyma cells, the secondary cell wall, produced after cell elongation has ceased, is thick and contains large amounts of **lignin**, a relatively indigestible strengthening polymer that accounts for more than a quarter of the dry mass of wood. Lignin is present in all vascular plants but not in bryophytes. Mature sclerenchyma cells cannot elongate, and they occur in regions of the plant that have stopped growing in length. Sclerenchyma cells are so specialized for support that many are dead at functional maturity, but they produce secondary walls before the protoplast (the living part of the cell) dies. The rigid walls remain as a "skeleton" that supports the plant, in some cases for hundreds of years.

Two types of sclerenchyma cells, known as **sclereids** and **fibers**, are specialized entirely for support and strengthening. Sclereids, which are boxier than fibers and irregular in shape, have very thick, lignified secondary walls. Sclereids impart the hardness to nutshells and seed coats and the gritty texture to pear fruits. Fibers, which are usually grouped in strands, are long, slender, and tapered. Some are used commercially, such as hemp fibers for making rope and flax fibers for weaving into linen.

## Water-Conducting Cells of the Xylem

The two types of water-conducting cells, **tracheids** and **vessel elements**, are tubular, elongated cells that are dead and lignified at functional maturity. Tracheids occur in the xylem of all vascular plants. In addition to tracheids, most angiosperms, as well as a few gymnosperms and a few seedless vascular plants, have vessel elements. When the living cellular contents of a tracheid or vessel element disintegrate, the cell's thickened walls remain behind, forming a nonliving conduit through which water can flow. The secondary walls of tracheids and vessel elements are often interrupted by pits, thinner regions where only primary walls are present (see Figure 6.27 to review primary and secondary walls). Water can migrate laterally between neighboring cells through pits.

Tracheids are long, thin cells with tapered ends. Water moves from cell to cell mainly through the pits, where it does not have to cross thick secondary walls.

Vessel elements are generally wider, shorter, thinner walled, and less tapered than the tracheids. They are aligned end to end, forming long pipes known as vessels that in some cases are visible with the naked eye. The end walls of vessel elements have perforation plates that enable water to flow freely through the vessels.

The secondary walls of tracheids and vessel elements are hardened with lignin. This hardening provides support and prevents collapse under the tension of water transport.

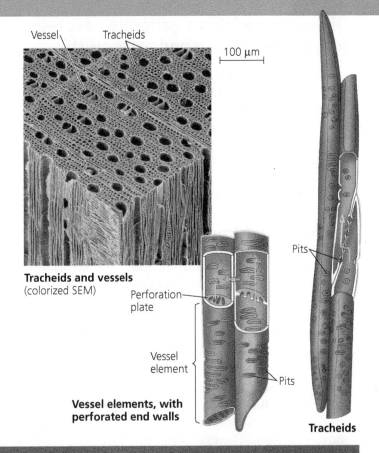

**Tracheids and vessels** (colorized SEM)

Perforation plate

Vessel element

Pits

**Vessel elements, with perforated end walls**

Pits

**Tracheids**

## Sugar-Conducting Cells of the Phloem

Unlike the water-conducting cells of the xylem, the sugar-conducting cells of the phloem are alive at functional maturity. In seedless vascular plants and gymnosperms, sugars and other organic nutrients are transported through long, narrow cells called sieve cells. In the phloem of angiosperms, these nutrients are transported through sieve tubes, which consist of chains of cells that are called **sieve-tube elements**, or sieve-tube members.

Though alive, sieve-tube elements lack a nucleus, ribosomes, a distinct vacuole, and cytoskeletal elements. This reduction in cell contents enables nutrients to pass more easily through the cell. The end walls between sieve-tube elements, called **sieve plates**, have pores that facilitate the flow of fluid from cell to cell along the sieve tube. Alongside each sieve-tube element is a nonconducting cell called a **companion cell**, which is connected to the sieve-tube element by numerous plasmodesmata (see Figure 6.27). The nucleus and ribosomes of the companion cell serve not only that cell itself but also the adjacent sieve-tube element. In some plants, the companion cells in leaves also help load sugars into the sieve-tube elements, which then transport the sugars to other parts of the plant.

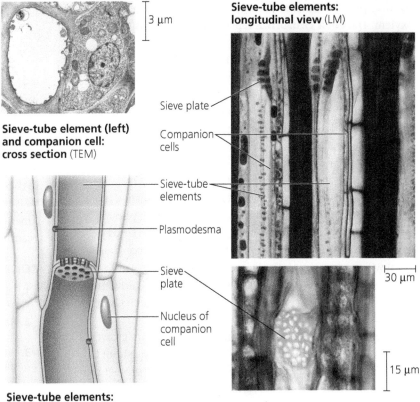

**Sieve-tube element (left) and companion cell: cross section** (TEM)

Sieve plate

Companion cells

Sieve-tube elements

Plasmodesma

Sieve plate

Nucleus of companion cell

**Sieve-tube elements: longitudinal view**

**Sieve-tube elements: longitudinal view** (LM)

**Sieve plate with pores** (LM)

## CONCEPT 35.2

## Different meristems generate new cells for primary and secondary growth

A major difference between plants and most animals is that plant growth is not limited to an embryonic or juvenile period. Instead, growth occurs throughout the plant's life, a process called **indeterminate growth**. Plants can keep growing because they have undifferentiated tissues called **meristems** containing cells that can divide, leading to new cells that elongate and become differentiated (**Figure 35.11**). Except for dormant periods, most plants grow continuously. In contrast, most animals and some plant organs—such as leaves, thorns, and flowers—undergo **determinate growth**; they stop growing after reaching a certain size.

There are two main types of meristems: apical meristems and lateral meristems. **Apical meristems**, located at root and shoot tips, provide cells that enable **primary growth**, growth in length. Primary growth allows roots to extend throughout the soil and shoots to increase exposure to light. In herbaceous (nonwoody) plants, it produces all, or almost all, of the plant body. Woody plants, however, also grow in circumference in the parts of stems and roots that no longer grow in length. This growth in thickness, known as **secondary growth**, is made possible by **lateral meristems**: the vascular cambium and cork cambium. These cylinders of dividing cells extend along the length of roots and stems. The **vascular cambium** adds vascular tissue called secondary xylem (wood) and secondary phloem. Most of the thickening is from secondary xylem. The **cork cambium** replaces the epidermis with the thicker, tougher periderm.

Cells in apical and lateral meristems divide frequently during the growing season, generating additional cells. Some new cells remain in the meristem and produce more cells, while others differentiate and are incorporated into tissues and organs. Cells that remain as sources of new cells have traditionally been called *initials* but are increasingly being called *stem cells* to correspond to animal stem cells that also divide and remain functionally undifferentiated.

Cells displaced from the meristem may divide several more times as they differentiate into mature cells. During primary growth, these cells give rise to three tissues called **primary meristems**—the *protoderm*, *ground meristem*, and *procambium*—that will produce, respectively, the three mature tissues of a root or shoot: the dermal, ground, and vascular tissues. The lateral meristems in woody plants also have stem cells, which give rise to all secondary growth.

The relationship between primary and secondary growth is seen in the winter twig of a deciduous tree. At the shoot tip is the dormant apical bud, enclosed by scales that protect its apical meristem (**Figure 35.12**). In spring, the bud sheds its scales and begins a new spurt of primary growth, producing a series of nodes and internodes. On each growth segment,

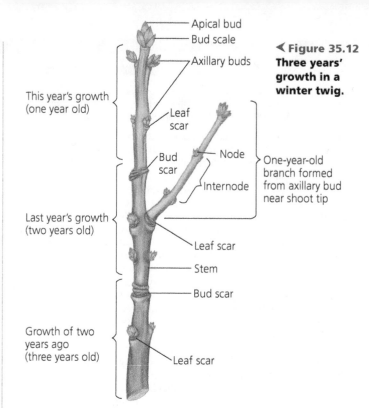

◄ **Figure 35.12**
**Three years' growth in a winter twig.**

nodes are marked by scars left when leaves fell. Leaf scars are prominent in many twigs. Above each scar is an axillary bud or a branch formed by an axillary bud. Farther down are bud scars from whorls of scales that enclosed the apical bud during the previous winter. In each growing season, primary growth extends shoots, and secondary growth increases the diameter of parts formed in previous years.

Although meristems enable plants to grow throughout their lives, plants do die, of course. Based on the length of their life cycle, flowering plants can be categorized as annuals, biennials, or perennials. *Annuals* complete their life cycle—from germination to flowering to seed production to death—in a single year or less. Many wildflowers are annuals, as are most staple food crops, including legumes and cereal grains such as wheat and rice. Dying after seed and fruit production is a strategy that enables plants to transfer the maximum amount of energy to production. *Biennials*, such as turnips, generally require two growing seasons to complete their life cycle, flowering and fruiting only in their second year. *Perennials* live many years and include trees, shrubs, and some grasses. Some buffalo grass of the North American plains is thought to have been growing for 10,000 years from seeds that sprouted at the close of the last ice age.

## CONCEPT CHECK 35.2

1. Would primary and secondary growth ever occur simultaneously in the same plant?

2. Roots and stems grow indeterminately, but leaves do not. How might this benefit the plant?

3. **WHAT IF?** ➤ After growing carrots for one season, a gardener decides that the carrots are too small. Since carrots are biennials, the gardener leaves the crop in the ground for a second year, thinking the carrot roots will grow larger. Is this a good idea? Explain.

*For suggested answers, see Appendix A.*

All vascular plants have primary growth: growth in length. Woody plants also have secondary growth: growth in thickness. As you study the diagrams, visualize how shoots and roots grow longer and thicker.

## Overview

**Primary growth** (growth in length) is made possible by apical meristems at the tips of shoots and roots.

**Secondary growth** (growth in thickness) is made possible by two lateral meristems extending along the length of a shoot or root where primary growth has ceased.

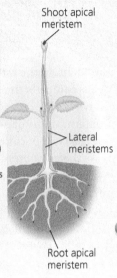

Shoot apical meristem

Lateral meristems

Root apical meristem

## Primary Growth (growth in length)

**Cutaway view of primary growth in a shoot tip**

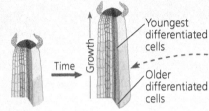

Leaf primordia

Shoot apical meristem

Primary meristems

Mature tissues

Dermal   Ground   Vascular

Cell division in apical meristem

Daughter cell in primary meristem

Cell division in primary meristem

Growing cells in primary meristem

Differentiated cells (for example, vessel elements)

Apical meristem cells in a shoot tip or root tip are undifferentiated. When they divide, some daughter cells remain in the apical meristem, ensuring a continuing population of undifferentiated cells. Other daughter cells become partly differentiated as primary meristem cells. After dividing and growing in length, they become fully differentiated cells in the mature tissues.

**①** *A root apical meristem is protected by a thimble-like root cap. Draw and label a simple outline of a root divided into four sections: root cap (at the bottom), root apical meristem, primary meristems, and mature tissues.*

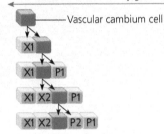

Time → Growth

Youngest differentiated cells

Older differentiated cells

The addition of elongated, differentiated cells lengthens a stem or root.

## Secondary Growth (growth in thickness)

The lateral meristems, called the vascular cambium and cork cambium, are cylinders of dividing cells that are one cell thick.

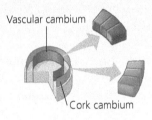

Vascular cambium

Cork cambium

**Increased circumference:** When a cambium cell divides, sometimes both daughter cells remain in the cambium and grow, increasing the cambium circumference.

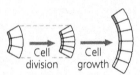

Cell division   Cell growth

**Addition of secondary xylem and phloem cells:** When a vascular cambium cell divides, sometimes one daughter cell becomes a secondary xylem cell (X) to the inside of the cambium or a secondary phloem cell (P) to the outside. Although xylem and phloem cells are shown being added equally here, usually many more xylem cells are produced.

**Addition of cork cells:** When a cork cambium cell divides, sometimes one daughter cell becomes a cork cell (C) to the outside of the cambium.

Direction of secondary growth

Vascular cambium cell

Time

X1
X1   P1
X1 X2   P1
X1 X2   P2 P1

Direction of secondary growth

Cork cambium cell

Time

C1
C2 C1

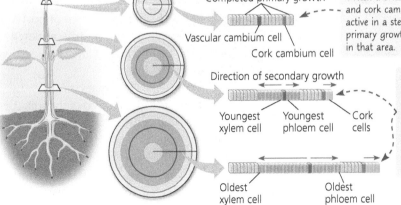

Completed primary growth

Vascular cambium cell

Cork cambium cell

Direction of secondary growth

Youngest xylem cell   Youngest phloem cell   Cork cells

Oldest xylem cell   Oldest phloem cell

When the vascular cambium and cork cambium become active in a stem or root, primary growth has ceased in that area.

A stem or root thickens as secondary xylem, secondary phloem, and cork cells are added. Most of the cells are secondary xylem (wood).

**②** *Show the sequence of secondary growth by drawing the row of cells from the boxed area below and labeling the vascular cambium cell (V), 5 xylem cells from oldest (X1) to youngest (X5), and 3 phloem cells (P1 to P3). Show what happens after growth continues by drawing and labeling a row with twice as many xylem and phloem cells. How does the vascular cambium's location change?*

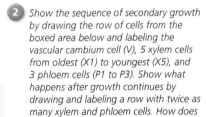

**Instructors:** Additional questions related to this Visualizing Figure can be assigned in MasteringBiology.

**Animation:** Primary and Secondary Growth

**765**

# CONCEPT 35.3

## Primary growth lengthens roots and shoots

Primary growth arises directly from cells produced by apical meristems. In herbaceous plants, almost the entire plant consists of primary growth, whereas in woody plants only the nonwoody, more recently formed parts of the plant represent primary growth. Although both roots and shoots lengthen as a result of cells derived from apical meristems, the details of their primary growth differ in many ways.

### Primary Growth of Roots

The entire biomass of a primary root is derived from the root apical meristem. The root apical meristem also makes a thimble-like **root cap**, which protects the delicate apical meristem as the root pushes through the abrasive soil. The root cap secretes a polysaccharide slime that lubricates the soil around the tip of the root. Growth occurs just behind the tip in three overlapping zones of cells at successive stages of primary growth. These are the zones of cell division, elongation, and differentiation (**Figure 35.13**).

The *zone of cell division* includes the stem cells of the root apical meristem and their immediate products. New root cells are produced in this region, including cells of the root cap.

▼ **Figure 35.13 Primary growth of a eudicot root.** In the micrograph, mitotic cells in the apical meristem are revealed by staining for cyclin, a protein involved in cell division (LM).

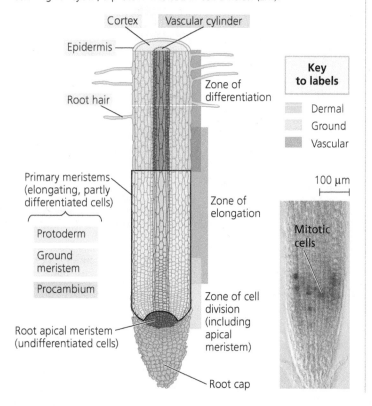

Typically, a few millimeters behind the tip of the root is the *zone of elongation*, where most of the growth occurs as root cells elongate—sometimes to more than ten times their original length. Cell elongation in this zone pushes the tip farther into the soil. Meanwhile, the root apical meristem keeps adding cells to the younger end of the zone of elongation. Even before the root cells finish lengthening, many begin specializing in structure and function. As this occurs, the three primary meristems—the protoderm, ground meristem, and procambium—become evident. In the *zone of differentiation*, or zone of maturation, cells complete their differentiation and become distinct cell types.

The protoderm, the outermost primary meristem, gives rise to the epidermis, a single layer of cuticle-free cells covering the root. Root hairs are the most prominent feature of the root epidermis. These modified epidermal cells function in the absorption of water and minerals. Root hairs typically only live a few weeks but together make up 70–90% of the total root surface area. It has been estimated that a 4-month-old rye plant has about 14 billion root hairs. Laid end to end, the root hairs of a single rye plant would cover 10,000 km, one-quarter the length of the equator.

Sandwiched between the protoderm and the procambium is the ground meristem, which gives rise to mature ground tissue. The ground tissue of roots, consisting mostly of parenchyma cells, is found in the cortex, the region between the vascular tissue and epidermis. In addition to storing carbohydrates, cells in the cortex transport water and salts from the root hairs to the center of the root. The cortex also allows for *extracellular* diffusion of water, minerals, and oxygen from the root hairs inward because there are large spaces between cells. The innermost layer of the cortex is called the **endodermis**, a cylinder one cell thick that forms the boundary with the vascular cylinder. The endodermis is a selective barrier that regulates passage of substances from the soil into the vascular cylinder (see Figure 36.8).

The procambium gives rise to the vascular cylinder, which consists of a solid core of xylem and phloem tissues surrounded by a cell layer called the **pericycle**. In most eudicot roots, the xylem has a starlike appearance in cross section, and the phloem occupies the indentations between the arms of the xylem "star" (**Figure 35.14a**). In many monocot roots, the vascular tissue consists of a core of undifferentiated parenchyma cells surrounded by a ring of alternating xylem and phloem tissues (**Figure 35.14b**).

By increasing the length of roots, primary growth facilitates their penetration and exploration of the soil. If a resource-rich pocket is located in the soil, the branching of roots may be stimulated. Branching, too, is a form of primary growth. Lateral (branch) roots arise from meristematically active regions of the pericycle, the outermost cell layer in the vascular cylinder, which is adjacent to and just inside the endodermis (see Figure 35.14). The emerging lateral

**▼ Figure 35.14 Organization of primary tissues in young roots.** Parts **(a)** and **(b)** show cross sections of the roots of a *Ranunculus* (buttercup) species and *Zea mays* (maize), respectively. These represent two basic patterns of root organization, of which there are many variations, depending on the plant species (all LMs).

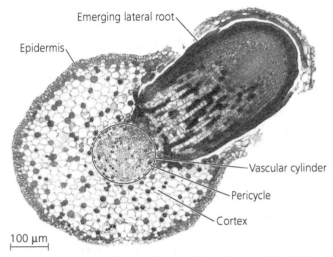

**▼ Figure 35.15 The formation of a lateral root.** A lateral root originates in the pericycle, the outermost layer of the vascular cylinder of a root, and destructively pushes through the outer tissues before emerging. In this light micrograph, the view of the original root is a cross section, but the view of the lateral root is a longitudinal section (a view along the length of the lateral root).

- Emerging lateral root
- Epidermis
- Vascular cylinder
- Pericycle
- Cortex

100 μm

**DRAW IT ▶** *Draw what the original root and lateral root would look like when viewed from the side, labeling both roots.*

roots destructively push through the outer tissues until they emerge from the established root **(Figure 35.15)**.

## Primary Growth of Shoots

The entire biomass of a primary shoot—all its leaves and stems—derives from its shoot apical meristem, a dome-shaped mass of dividing cells at the shoot tip **(Figure 35.16)**. The shoot apical meristem is a delicate structure protected by the leaves of the apical bud. These young leaves are spaced close together because the internodes are very short. Shoot

- Epidermis
- Cortex
- Endodermis
- Vascular cylinder
- Pericycle
- Xylem
- Phloem

100 μm

**(a) Root with xylem and phloem in the center (typical of eudicots).** In the roots of typical gymnosperms and eudicots, as well as some monocots, the stele is a vascular cylinder appearing in cross section as a lobed core of xylem with phloem between the lobes.

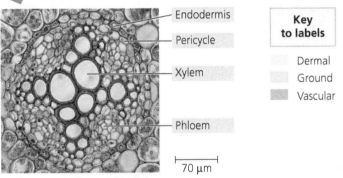

- Endodermis
- Pericycle
- Xylem
- Phloem

**Key to labels**

- ☐ Dermal
- ☐ Ground
- ☐ Vascular

70 μm

**▼ Figure 35.16 The shoot tip.** Leaf primordia arise from the flanks of the dome of the apical meristem. This is a longitudinal section of the shoot tip of *Coleus* (LM).

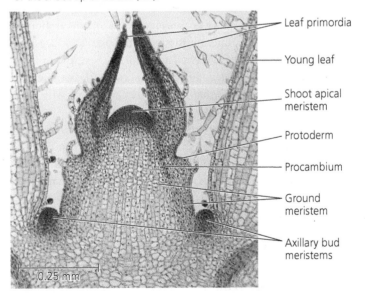

- Leaf primordia
- Young leaf
- Shoot apical meristem
- Protoderm
- Procambium
- Ground meristem
- Axillary bud meristems

0.25 mm

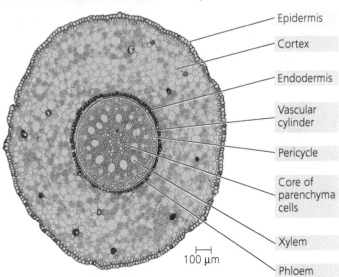

- Epidermis
- Cortex
- Endodermis
- Vascular cylinder
- Pericycle
- Core of parenchyma cells
- Xylem
- Phloem

100 μm

**(b) Root with parenchyma in the center (typical of monocots).** The stele of many monocot roots is a vascular cylinder with a core of parenchyma surrounded by a ring of xylem and a ring of phloem.

(MB) Animation: Root Cross Sections

elongation is due to the lengthening of internode cells below the shoot tip. As with the root apical meristem, the shoot apical meristem gives rise to three types of primary meristems in the shoot—the protoderm, ground meristem, and procambium. These three primary meristems in turn give rise to the mature primary tissues of the shoot.

The branching of shoots, which is also part of primary growth, arises from the activation of axillary buds, each of which has its own shoot apical meristem. Because of chemical communication by plant hormones, the closer an axillary bud is to an active apical bud, the more inhibited it is, a phenomenon called **apical dominance**. (The specific hormonal changes underlying apical dominance are discussed in Concept 39.2.) If an animal eats the end of the shoot or if shading results in the light being more intense on the side of the shoot, the chemical communication underlying apical dominance is disrupted. As a result, the axillary buds break dormancy and start to grow. Released from dormancy, an axillary bud eventually gives rise to a lateral shoot, complete with its own apical bud, leaves, and axillary buds. When gardeners prune shrubs and pinch back houseplants, they are reducing the number of apical buds a plant has, thereby allowing branches to elongate and giving the plants a fuller, bushier appearance.

## Stem Growth and Anatomy

The stem is covered by an epidermis that is usually one cell thick and covered with a waxy cuticle that prevents water loss. Some examples of specialized epidermal cells in the stem include guard cells and trichomes.

The ground tissue of stems consists mostly of parenchyma cells. However, collenchyma cells just beneath the epidermis strengthen many stems during primary growth. Sclerenchyma cells, especially fiber cells, also provide support in those parts of the stems that are no longer elongating.

Vascular tissue runs the length of a stem in vascular bundles. Unlike lateral roots, which arise from vascular tissue deep within a root and disrupt the vascular cylinder, cortex, and epidermis as they emerge (see Figure 35.15), lateral shoots develop from axillary bud meristems on the stem's surface and do not disrupt other tissues (see Figure 35.16). Near the soil surface, in the transition zone between shoot and root, the bundled vascular arrangement of the stem converges with the solid vascular cylinder of the root.

The vascular tissue of stems in most eudicot species consists of vascular bundles arranged in a ring (**Figure 35.17a**). The xylem in each vascular bundle is adjacent to the pith, and the phloem in each bundle is adjacent to the cortex. In most monocot stems, the vascular bundles are scattered throughout the ground tissue rather than forming a ring (**Figure 35.17b**).

## Leaf Growth and Anatomy

**Figure 35.18** provides an overview of leaf anatomy. Leaves develop from **leaf primordia** (singular, *primordium*), projections shaped like a cow's horns that emerge along the sides of

▼ **Figure 35.17 Organization of primary tissues in young stems.**

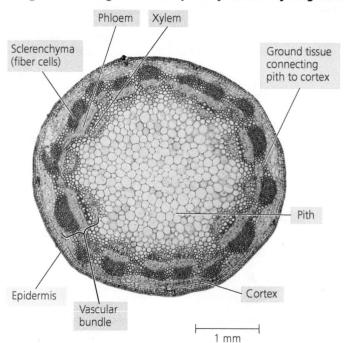

Phloem    Xylem

Sclerenchyma (fiber cells)

Ground tissue connecting pith to cortex

Pith

Epidermis

Cortex

Vascular bundle

1 mm

**(a) Cross section of stem with vascular bundles forming a ring (typical of eudicots).** Ground tissue toward the inside is called pith, and ground tissue toward the outside is called cortex (LM).

| Key to labels | |
| --- | --- |
| | Dermal |
| | Ground |
| | Vascular |

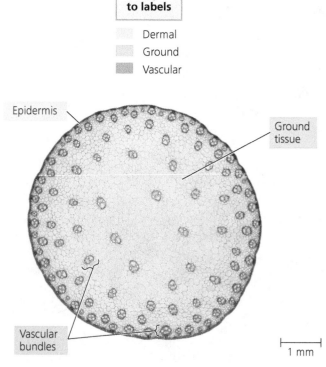

Epidermis

Ground tissue

Vascular bundles

1 mm

**(b) Cross section of stem with scattered vascular bundles (typical of monocots).** In such an arrangement, ground tissue is not partitioned into pith and cortex (LM).

**VISUAL SKILLS ➤** *Compare the locations of the vascular bundles in eudicot and monocot stems. Then explain why the terms* pith *and* cortex *are not used in describing the ground tissue of monocot stems.*

 **Animation: Stem Cross Sections**

**▼ Figure 35.18 Leaf anatomy.**

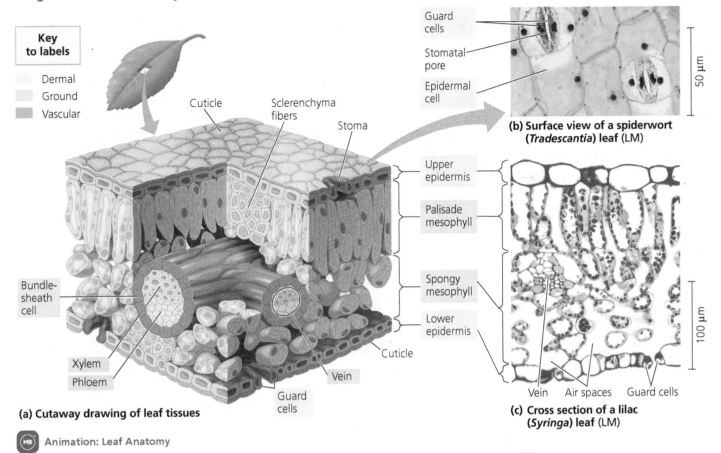

**Key to labels**

- Dermal
- Ground
- Vascular

Cuticle
Sclerenchyma fibers
Stoma
Bundle-sheath cell
Xylem
Phloem
Guard cells
Vein
Cuticle

**(a) Cutaway drawing of leaf tissues**

Guard cells
Stomatal pore
Epidermal cell

50 µm

**(b) Surface view of a spiderwort (*Tradescantia*) leaf (LM)**

Upper epidermis
Palisade mesophyll
Spongy mesophyll
Lower epidermis

Vein    Air spaces    Guard cells

100 µm

**(c) Cross section of a lilac (*Syringa*) leaf (LM)**

(MB) Animation: Leaf Anatomy

the shoot apical meristem (see Figure 35.16). Unlike roots and stems, secondary growth in leaves is minor or nonexistent. As with roots and stems, the three primary meristems give rise to the tissues of the mature organ.

The leaf epidermis is covered by a waxy cuticle except where it is interrupted by **stomata** (singular, *stoma*), which allow exchange of $CO_2$ and $O_2$ between the surrounding air and the photosynthetic cells inside the leaf. In addition to regulating $CO_2$ uptake for photosynthesis, stomata are major avenues for the evaporative loss of water. The term *stoma* can refer to the stomatal pore or to the entire stomatal complex consisting of a pore flanked by the two specialized epidermal cells known as guard cells, which regulate the opening and closing of the pore. (We will discuss stomata in detail in Concept 36.4.)

The leaf's ground tissue, called the **mesophyll** (from the Greek *mesos*, middle, and *phyll*, leaf), is sandwiched between the upper and lower epidermal layers. Mesophyll consists mainly of parenchyma cells specialized for photosynthesis. The mesophyll in many eudicot leaves has two distinct layers: palisade and spongy. *Palisade mesophyll* consists of one or more layers of elongated parenchyma cells on the upper part of the leaf. *Spongy mesophyll* is below the palisade mesophyll. These parenchyma cells are more loosely arranged, with a labyrinth of air spaces through which $CO_2$ and $O_2$ circulate around the cells and up to the palisade region. The air spaces

are particularly large in the vicinity of stomata, where $CO_2$ is taken up from the outside air and $O_2$ is released.

The vascular tissue of each leaf is continuous with the vascular tissue of the stem. Veins subdivide repeatedly and branch throughout the mesophyll. This network brings xylem and phloem into close contact with the photosynthetic tissue, which obtains water and minerals from the xylem and loads its sugars and other organic products into the phloem for transport to other parts of the plant. The vascular structure also functions as a framework that reinforces the shape of the leaf. Each vein is enclosed by a protective *bundle sheath*, a layer of cells that regulates the movement of substances between the vascular tissue and the mesophyll. Bundle-sheath cells are very prominent in leaves of species that carry out $C_4$ photosynthesis (see Concept 10.4).

## CONCEPT CHECK 35.3

1. Contrast primary growth in roots and shoots.
2. **WHAT IF?** ▶ If a plant species has vertically oriented leaves, would you expect its mesophyll to be divided into spongy and palisade layers? Explain.
3. **MAKE CONNECTIONS** ▶ How are root hairs and microvilli analogous structures? (See Figure 6.8 and the discussion of analogy in Concept 26.2.)

*For suggested answers, see Appendix A.*

# CONCEPT 35.4

## Secondary growth increases the diameter of stems and roots in woody plants

Many land plants display secondary growth, the growth in thickness produced by lateral meristems. The advent of secondary growth during plant evolution allowed the production of novel plant forms ranging from massive forest trees to woody vines. All gymnosperm species and many eudicot species undergo secondary growth, but it is unusual in monocots. It occurs in stems and roots of woody plants, but rarely in leaves.

Secondary growth consists of the tissues produced by the vascular cambium and cork cambium. The vascular cambium adds secondary xylem (wood) and secondary phloem, thereby increasing vascular flow and support for the shoots. The cork cambium produces a tough, thick covering of waxy cells that protect the stem from water loss and from invasion by insects, bacteria, and fungi.

In woody plants, primary growth and secondary growth occur simultaneously. As primary growth adds leaves and lengthens stems and roots in the younger regions of a plant, secondary growth increases the diameter of stems and roots in older regions where primary growth has ceased. The process is similar in shoots and roots. **Figure 35.19** provides an overview of growth in a woody stem.

▼ **Figure 35.19 Primary and secondary growth of a woody stem.**

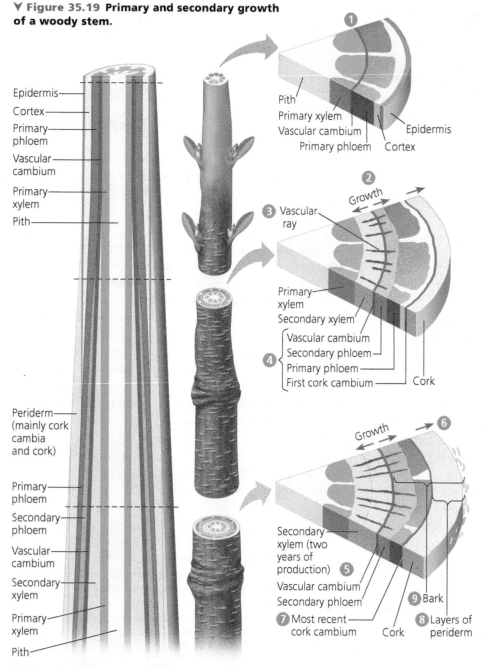

**1** Primary growth from the activity of the apical meristem is nearing completion. The vascular cambium has just formed.

**2** Although primary growth continues in the apical bud, only secondary growth occurs in this region. The stem thickens as the vascular cambium forms secondary xylem to the inside and secondary phloem to the outside.

**3** Some stem cells of the vascular cambium give rise to vascular rays.

**4** As the vascular cambium's diameter increases, the secondary phloem and other tissues external to the cambium can't keep pace because their cells no longer divide. As a result, these tissues, including the epidermis, will eventually rupture. A second lateral meristem, the cork cambium, develops from parenchyma cells in the cortex. The cork cambium produces cork cells, which replace the epidermis.

**5** In year 2 of secondary growth, the vascular cambium produces more secondary xylem and phloem. Most of the thickening is from secondary xylem. Meanwhile, the cork cambium produces more cork.

**6** As the stem's diameter increases, the outermost tissues exterior to the cork cambium rupture and are sloughed off.

**7** In many cases, the cork cambium re-forms deeper in the cortex. When none of the cortex is left, the cambium develops from phloem parenchyma cells.

**8** Each cork cambium and the tissues it produces form a layer of periderm.

**9** Bark consists of all tissues exterior to the vascular cambium.

 **Animation: Secondary Growth**

**VISUAL SKILLS** ➤ *Based on the diagram, explain how the vascular cambium causes some tissues to rupture.*

## The Vascular Cambium and Secondary Vascular Tissue

The vascular cambium, a cylinder of meristematic cells only one cell thick, is wholly responsible for the production of secondary vascular tissue. In a typical woody stem, the vascular cambium is located outside the pith and primary xylem and to the inside of the primary phloem and the cortex. In a typical woody root, the vascular cambium forms exterior to the primary xylem and interior to the primary phloem and pericycle.

In cross section, the vascular cambium appears as a ring of meristematic cells (see step 4 of Figure 35.19). As these cells divide, they increase the cambium's circumference and add secondary xylem to the inside and secondary phloem to the outside. Each ring is larger than the previous ring, increasing the diameter of roots and stems.

Some of the stem cells in the vascular cambium are elongated and oriented with their long axis parallel to the axis of the stem or root. The cells they produce give rise to mature cells such as the tracheids, vessel elements, and fibers of the xylem, as well as the sieve-tube elements, companion cells, axially oriented parenchyma, and fibers of the phloem. Other stem cells in the vascular cambium are shorter and are oriented perpendicular to the axis of the stem or root: they give rise to *vascular rays*—radial files of mostly parenchyma cells that connect the secondary xylem and phloem (see step 3 of Figure 35.19). These cells move water and nutrients between the secondary xylem and phloem, store carbohydrates and other reserves, and aid in wound repair.

As secondary growth continues, layers of secondary xylem (wood) accumulate, consisting mainly of tracheids, vessel elements, and fibers (see Figure 35.10). In most gymnosperms, tracheids are the only water-conducting cells. Most angiosperms also have vessel elements. The walls of secondary xylem cells are heavily lignified, giving wood its hardness and strength.

In temperate regions, wood that develops early in the spring, known as early (or spring) wood, usually has secondary xylem cells with large diameters and thin cell walls **(Figure 35.20)**.

This structure maximizes delivery of water to leaves. Wood produced later in the growing season is called late (or summer) wood. It has thick-walled cells that do not transport as much water but provide more support. Because there is a marked contrast between the large cells of the new early wood and the smaller cells of the late wood of the previous growing season, a year's growth appears as a distinct *growth ring* in cross sections of most tree trunks and roots. Therefore, researchers can estimate a tree's age by counting growth rings. *Dendrochronology* is the science of analyzing tree growth ring patterns. Growth rings vary in thickness, depending on seasonal growth. Trees grow well in wet and warm years but may grow hardly at all in cold or dry years. Since a thick ring indicates a warm year and a thin ring indicates a cold or dry one, scientists use ring patterns to study climate changes **(Figure 35.21)**.

As a tree or woody shrub ages, older layers of secondary xylem no longer transport water and minerals (a solution

▼ **Figure 35.21**

### Research Method Using Dendrochronology to Study Climate

**Application** Dendrochronology, the science of analyzing growth rings, is useful in studying climate change. Most scientists attribute recent global warming to the burning of fossil fuels and release of $CO_2$ and other greenhouse gases, whereas a small minority think it is a natural variation. Studying climate patterns requires comparing past and present temperatures, but instrumental climate records span only the last two centuries and apply only to some regions. By examining growth rings of Mongolian conifers dating back to the mid-1500s, Gordon C. Jacoby and Rosanne D'Arrigo, of the Lamont-Doherty Earth Observatory, and colleagues sought to learn whether Mongolia has experienced similar warm periods in the past.

**Technique** Researchers can analyze patterns of rings in living and dead trees. They can even study wood used for building long ago by matching samples with those from naturally situated specimens of overlapping age. Core samples, each about the diameter of a pencil, are taken from the bark to the center of the trunk. Each sample is dried and sanded to reveal the rings. By comparing, aligning, and averaging many samples from the conifers, the researchers compiled a chronology. The trees became a chronicle of environmental change.

**Results** This graph summarizes a composite record of the ring-width indexes for the Mongolian conifers from 1550 to 1993. The higher indexes indicate wider rings and higher temperatures.

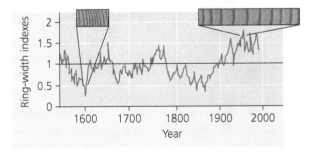

Data from G. C. Jacoby et al., Mongolian tree rings and 20th-century warming, *Science* 273:771–773 (1996).

**INTERPRET THE DATA** ➤ *What does the graph indicate about environmental change during the period 1550–1993?*

▼ **Figure 35.20 Cross section of a three-year-old *Tilia* (linden) stem (LM).**

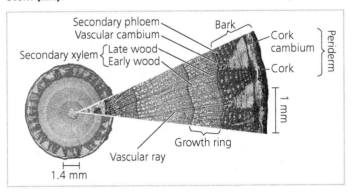

called xylem sap). These layers are called *heartwood* because they are closer to the center of a stem or root **(Figure 35.22)**. The newest, outer layers of secondary xylem still transport xylem sap and are therefore known as *sapwood*. Sapwood allows a large tree to survive even if the center of its trunk is hollow **(Figure 35.23)**. Because each new layer of secondary xylem has a larger circumference, secondary growth enables the xylem to transport more sap each year, supplying an increasing number of leaves. Heartwood is generally darker than sapwood because of resins and other compounds that permeate the cell cavities and help protect the core of the tree from fungi and wood-boring insects.

▼ **Figure 35.22 Anatomy of a tree trunk.**

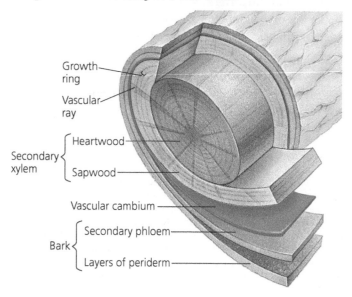

- Growth ring
- Vascular ray
- Secondary xylem { Heartwood
- Sapwood }
- Vascular cambium
- Bark { Secondary phloem
- Layers of periderm }

◄ **Figure 35.23 Is this tree living or dead?** The Wawona Sequoia tunnel in Yosemite National Park in California was cut in 1881 as a tourist attraction. This giant sequoia (*Sequoiadendron giganteum*) lived for another 88 years before falling during a severe winter. It was 71.3 m tall and estimated to be 2,100 years old. Though conservation policies today would forbid the mutilation of such an important specimen, the Wawona Sequoia did teach a valuable botanical lesson: Trees can survive the excision of large portions of their heartwood.

**VISUAL SKILLS** ➤ *Name in sequence the tissues that were destroyed as the lumberjacks excavated through the base of the tree to its center. Refer also to Figure 35.19.*

Only the youngest secondary phloem, closest to the vascular cambium, functions in sugar transport. As a stem or root increases in circumference, the older secondary phloem is sloughed off, which is one reason secondary phloem does not accumulate as extensively as secondary xylem.

## The Cork Cambium and the Production of Periderm

During the early stages of secondary growth, the epidermis is pushed outward, causing it to split, dry, and fall off the stem or root. It is replaced by tissues produced by the first cork cambium, a cylinder of dividing cells that arises in the outer cortex of stems (see Figure 35.19) and in the pericycle in roots. The cork cambium gives rise to *cork cells* that accumulate to the outside of the cork cambium. As cork cells mature, they deposit a waxy, hydrophobic material called *suberin* in their walls before dying. Because cork cells have suberin and are usually compacted together, most of the periderm is impermeable to water and gases, unlike the epidermis. Cork thus functions as a barrier that helps protect the stem or root from water loss, physical damage, and pathogens. It should be noted that "cork" is commonly and incorrectly referred to as "bark." In plant biology, **bark** includes all tissues external to the vascular cambium. Its main components are the secondary phloem (produced by the vascular cambium) and, external to that, the most recent periderm and all the older layers of periderm (see Figure 35.22). As this process continues, older layers of periderm are sloughed off, as evident in the cracked, peeling exteriors of many tree trunks.

How can living cells in the interior tissues of woody organs absorb oxygen and respire if they are surrounded by a waxy periderm? Dotting the periderm are small, raised areas called **lenticels**, in which there is more space between cork cells, enabling living cells within a woody stem or root to exchange gases with the outside air. Lenticels often appear as horizontal slits, as shown on the stem in Figure 35.19.

Figure 35.24 summarizes the relationships between the primary and secondary tissues of a woody shoot.

## Evolution of Secondary Growth

**EVOLUTION** Surprisingly, some insights into the evolution of secondary growth have been achieved by studying the herbaceous plant *Arabidopsis thaliana*. Researchers have found that they can stimulate some secondary growth in *Arabidopsis* stems by adding weights to the plant. These findings suggest that weight carried by the stem activates a developmental program leading to wood formation. Moreover, several developmental genes that regulate shoot apical meristems in *Arabidopsis* have been found to regulate vascular cambium activity in poplar (*Populus*) trees. This suggests that the processes of primary and secondary growth are evolutionarily more closely related than was previously thought.

**▼ Figure 35.24 A summary of primary and secondary growth in a woody shoot.** The same meristems and tissues are present in woody roots. However, the ground tissue of a root is not divided into pith and cortex, and the cork cambium arises instead from the pericycle, the outermost layer of the vascular cylinder.

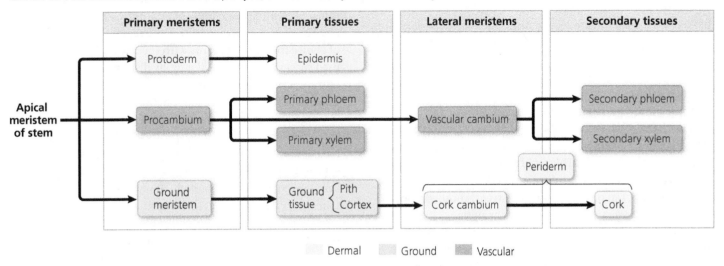

| Primary meristems | Primary tissues | Lateral meristems | Secondary tissues |
|---|---|---|---|

Apical meristem of stem → Protoderm → Epidermis

Procambium → Primary phloem, Primary xylem → Vascular cambium → Secondary phloem, Secondary xylem

Ground meristem → Ground tissue { Pith, Cortex } → Cork cambium → Cork

Periderm

Dermal    Ground    Vascular

## CONCEPT CHECK 35.4

1. A sign is hammered into a tree 2 m from the tree's base. If the tree is 10 m tall and elongates 1 m each year, how high will the sign be after ten years?

2. Stomata and lenticels are both involved in exchange of $CO_2$ and $O_2$. Why do stomata need to be able to close, but lenticels do not?

3. Would you expect a tropical tree to have distinct growth rings? Why or why not?

4. **WHAT IF?** ▶ If a complete ring of bark is removed from around a tree trunk (a technique called girdling), would the tree die slowly (in weeks) or quickly (in days)? Explain why.

*For suggested answers, see Appendix A.*

# CONCEPT 35.5

## Growth, morphogenesis, and cell differentiation produce the plant body

The specific series of changes by which cells form tissues, organs, and organisms is called **development**. Development unfolds according to the genetic information that an organism inherits from its parents but is also influenced by the external environment. A single genotype can produce different phenotypes in different environments. For example, the aquatic plant called the fanwort (*Cabomba caroliniana*) forms two very different types of leaves, depending on whether the shoot apical meristem is submerged (**Figure 35.25**). This ability to alter form in response to local environmental conditions is called *developmental plasticity*. Dramatic examples of plasticity, as in *Cabomba,* are much more common in plants than in animals and may help compensate for plants' inability to escape adverse conditions by moving.

**▼ Figure 35.25 Developmental plasticity in the aquatic plant *Cabomba caroliniana*.** The underwater leaves of *Cabomba* are feathery, an adaptation that protects them from damage by lessening their resistance to moving water. In contrast, the surface leaves are pads that aid in flotation. Both leaf types have genetically identical cells, but their different environments result in the turning on or off of different genes during leaf development.

The three overlapping processes involved in the development of a multicellular organism are growth, morphogenesis, and cell differentiation. *Growth* is an irreversible increase in size. *Morphogenesis* (from the Greek *morphê*, shape, and *genesis*, creation) is the process that gives a tissue, organ, or organism its shape and determines the positions of cell types. *Cell differentiation* is the process by which cells with the same genes become different from one another. We'll examine these three processes in turn, but first we'll discuss how applying techniques of modern molecular biology to model organisms, particularly *Arabidopsis thaliana*, has revolutionized the study of plant development.

## Model Organisms: Revolutionizing the Study of Plants

As in other branches of biology, techniques of molecular biology and a focus on model organisms such as *Arabidopsis thaliana* have catalyzed a research explosion in the last few decades. *Arabidopsis*, a tiny weed in the mustard family, has no inherent agricultural value but is a favored model organism of plant geneticists and molecular biologists for many reasons. It is so small that thousands of plants can be cultivated in a few square meters of lab space. It also has a short generation time, taking about six weeks for a seed to grow into a mature plant that produces more seeds. This rapid maturation enables biologists to conduct genetic cross experiments in a relatively short time. One plant can produce over 5,000 seeds, another property that makes *Arabidopsis* useful for genetic analysis.

Beyond these basic traits, the plant's genome makes it particularly well suited for analysis by molecular genetic methods. The *Arabidopsis* genome, which includes about 27,000 protein-encoding genes, is among the smallest known in plants. Furthermore, the plant has only five pairs of chromosomes, making it easier for geneticists to locate specific genes. Because *Arabidopsis* has such a small genome, it was the first plant to have its entire genome sequenced.

The natural range of *Arabidopsis* includes varied climates and elevations, from the high mountains of Central Asia to the European Atlantic coast, and from North Africa to the Arctic Circle. These local varieties can differ markedly in outward appearance **(Figure 35.26)**. Genome-sequencing efforts are being expanded to include hundreds of populations of *Arabidopsis* from throughout its natural range in Eurasia. Contained in the genomes of these populations is information about evolutionary adaptations that enabled *Arabidopsis* to expand its range into new environments following the retreat of the last ice age. This information may provide plant breeders with new insights and strategies for crop improvement.

▼ **Figure 35.26 Variations in leaf arrangement, leaf shape, and shoot growth between different populations of *Arabidopsis thaliana.*** Information in the genomes of these populations may provide insights into strategies for expanding crop production into new environments.

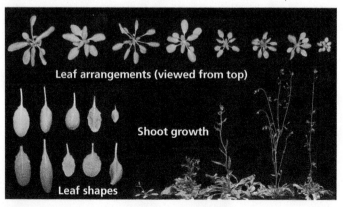

Leaf arrangements (viewed from top)

Shoot growth

Leaf shapes

Another property that makes *Arabidopsis* attractive to molecular biologists is that its cells can be easily transformed with *transgenes*, genes from a different organism that are stably introduced into the genome of another. CRISPR technology (see Figure 20.14), which is rapidly becoming the technique of choice for creating plants with specific mutations, has been used successfully in *Arabidopsis*. By disrupting or "knocking out" a specific gene, scientists can garner important information about the gene's normal function.

Large-scale projects are under way to determine the function of every gene in *Arabidopsis*. By identifying each gene's function and tracking every biochemical pathway, researchers aim to determine the blueprints for plant development, a major goal of systems biology. It may one day be possible to make a computer-generated "virtual plant" that enables researchers to visualize which genes are activated in different parts of the plant as the plant develops.

Basic research involving model organisms such as *Arabidopsis* has accelerated the pace of discovery in the plant sciences, including the identification of the complex genetic pathways underlying plant structure. As you read more about this, you'll be able to appreciate not just the power of studying model organisms but also the rich history of investigation that underpins all modern plant research.

 Interview with Joanne Chory: Sequencing the *Arabidopsis* genome

## Growth: Cell Division and Cell Expansion

Cell division enhances the potential for growth by increasing the number of cells, but plant growth itself is brought about by cell enlargement. The process of plant cell division is described more fully in Chapter 12 (see Figure 12.10), and Chapter 39 discusses the process of cell elongation (see Figure 39.7). Here we are concerned with how cell division and enlargement contribute to plant form.

### The Plane and Symmetry of Cell Division

The new cell walls that bisect plant cells during cytokinesis develop from the cell plate (see Figure 12.10). The precise plane of cell division, determined during late interphase, usually corresponds to the shortest path that will halve the volume of the parent cell. The first sign of this spatial orientation is rearrangement of the cytoskeleton. Microtubules in the cytoplasm become concentrated into a ring called the *preprophase band* **(Figure 35.27)**. The band disappears before metaphase but predicts the future plane of cell division.

It had long been thought that the plane of cell division provides the foundation for the forms of plant organs, but studies of an internally disorganized maize mutant called *tangled-1* now indicate that this is not the case. In wild-type maize plants, leaf cells divide either transversely (crosswise) or longitudinally relative to the axis of the parent cell. Transverse divisions precede leaf elongation, and longitudinal divisions precede leaf broadening. In *tangled-1* leaves,

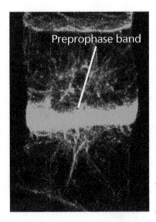

**Figure 35.27 The preprophase band and the plane of cell division.** The location of the preprophase band predicts the plane of cell division. In this light micrograph, the preprophase band has been stained with green fluorescent protein bound to a microtubule-associated protein.

Preprophase band

7 μm

transverse divisions are normal, but most longitudinal divisions are oriented abnormally, leading to cells that are crooked or curved **(Figure 35.28)**. However, these abnormal cell divisions do not affect leaf shape. Mutant leaves grow more slowly than wild-type leaves, but their overall shapes remain normal, indicating that leaf shape does not depend solely on precise spatial control of cell division. In addition, recent evidence suggests that the shape of the shoot apex in *Arabidopsis* depends not on the plane of cell division but on microtubule-dependent mechanical stresses stemming from the "crowding" associated with cell proliferation and growth.

An important feature of cell division that does affect plant development is the *symmetry* of cell division—the distribution of cytoplasm between daughter cells. Although chromosomes are allocated to daughter cells equally during mitosis, the cytoplasm may sometimes divide asymmetrically. *Asymmetrical cell division*, in which one daughter cell receives more cytoplasm than the other during mitosis, usually signals a key event in development. For example, the formation of guard cells typically involves both an asymmetrical cell division and a change in the plane of cell division. An epidermal cell divides asymmetrically, forming a large cell that remains an undifferentiated epidermal

**Figure 35.28 Cell division patterns in wild-type and mutant maize plants.** Compared with the epidermal cells of wild-type maize plants (left), the epidermal cells of the *tangled-1* mutant of maize (right) are highly disordered. Nevertheless, *tangled-1* maize plants produce normal-looking leaves.

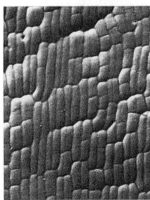

30 μm

Leaf epidermal cells of wild-type maize (SEM)

Leaf epidermal cells of *tangled-1* maize mutant (SEM)

**Figure 35.29 Asymmetrical cell division and stomatal development.** An asymmetrical cell division precedes the development of epidermal guard cells, the cells that border stomata (see Figure 35.18).

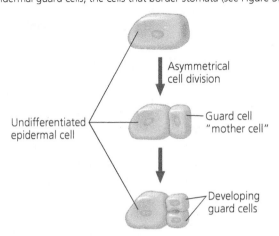

Undifferentiated epidermal cell

Asymmetrical cell division

Guard cell "mother cell"

Developing guard cells

cell and a small cell that becomes the guard cell "mother cell." Guard cells form when this small mother cell divides in a plane perpendicular to the first cell division **(Figure 35.29)**. Thus, asymmetrical cell division generates cells with different fates— that is, cells that mature into different types.

Asymmetrical cell divisions also play a role in the establishment of **polarity**, the condition of having structural or chemical differences at opposite ends of an organism. Plants typically have an axis, with a root end and a shoot end. Such polarity is most obvious in morphological differences, but it is also apparent in physiological properties, including the movement of the hormone auxin in a single direction and the emergence of adventitious roots and shoots from "cuttings." In a stem cutting, adventitious roots emerge from the end that was nearest the root; in a root cutting, adventitious shoots arise from the end that was nearest the shoot.

The first division of a plant zygote is normally asymmetrical, initiating polarization of the plant body into shoot and root. This polarity is difficult to reverse experimentally, indicating that the proper establishment of axial polarity is a critical step in a plant's morphogenesis. In the *gnom* (from the German for a dwarf and misshapen creature) mutant of *Arabidopsis*, the establishment of polarity is defective. The first cell division of the zygote is abnormal because it is symmetrical, and the resulting ball-shaped plant has neither roots nor leaves **(Figure 35.30)**.

**Figure 35.30 Establishment of axial polarity.** The normal *Arabidopsis* seedling (left) has a shoot end and a root end. In the *gnom* mutant (right), the first division of the zygote was not asymmetrical; as a result, the plant is ball-shaped and lacks leaves and roots. The defect in *gnom* mutants has been traced to an inability to transport the hormone auxin in a polar manner.

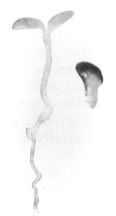

 Interview with Philip Benfey: Studying root development (see the interview before Chapter 35)

## Orientation of Cell Expansion

Before discussing how cell expansion contributes to plant form, it is useful to consider the difference in cell expansion between plants and animals. Animal cells grow mainly by synthesizing protein-rich cytoplasm, a metabolically expensive process. Growing plant cells also produce additional protein-rich material in their cytoplasm, but water uptake typically accounts for about 90% of expansion. Most of this water is stored in the large central vacuole. The vacuolar solution, or *vacuolar sap*, is very dilute and nearly devoid of the energetically expensive macromolecules that are found in great abundance in the rest of the cytoplasm. Large vacuoles are therefore a "cheap" way of filling space, enabling a plant to grow rapidly and economically. Bamboo shoots, for instance, can elongate more than 2 m per week. Rapid and efficient extensibility of shoots and roots was an important evolutionary adaptation that increased their exposure to light and soil.

Plant cells rarely expand equally in all directions. Their greatest expansion is usually oriented along the plant's main axis. For example, cells near the tip of the root may elongate up to 20 times their original length, with relatively little increase in width. The orientation of cellulose microfibrils in the innermost layers of the cell wall causes this differential growth. The microfibrils do not stretch, so the cell expands mainly perpendicular to the main orientation of the microfibrils, as shown in **Figure 35.31**. A leading hypothesis proposes that microtubules positioned just beneath the plasma membrane organize the cellulose-synthesizing enzyme complexes and guide their movement through the plasma membrane as they create the microfibrils that form much of the cell wall.

## Morphogenesis and Pattern Formation

A plant's body is more than a collection of dividing and expanding cells. During morphogenesis, cells acquire different identities in an ordered spatial arrangement. For example, dermal tissue forms on the exterior and vascular tissue in the interior—never the other way around. The development of specific structures in specific locations is called **pattern formation**.

Two types of hypotheses have been put forward to explain how the fate of plant cells is determined during pattern formation. Hypotheses based on *lineage-based mechanisms* propose that cell fate is determined early in development and that cells pass on this destiny to their progeny. In this view, the basic pattern of cell differentiation is mapped out according to the directions in which meristematic cells divide and expand. On the other hand, hypotheses based on *position-based mechanisms* propose that the cell's final position in an emerging organ determines what kind of cell it will become. In support of this view, experiments in which neighboring cells have been destroyed with lasers have demonstrated that a plant cell's fate is established late in the cell's development and largely depends on signaling from its neighbors.

▼ **Figure 35.31 The orientation of plant cell expansion.** Growing plant cells expand mainly through water uptake. In a growing cell, enzymes weaken cross-links in the cell wall, allowing it to expand as water diffuses into the vacuole by osmosis; at the same time, more microfibrils are made. The orientation of the cell expansion is mainly perpendicular to the orientation of cellulose microfibrils in the wall. The orientation of microtubules in the cell's outermost cytoplasm determines the orientation of cellulose microfibrils (fluorescent LM). The microfibrils are embedded in a matrix of other (noncellulose) polysaccharides, some of which form the cross-links visible in the TEM.

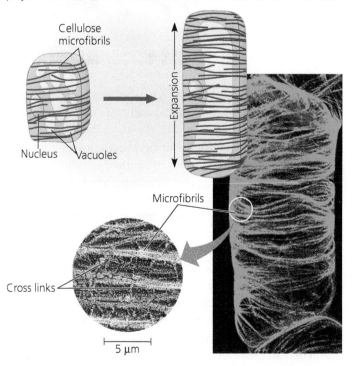

In contrast, cell fate in animals is largely determined by lineage-dependent mechanisms involving transcription factors. The homeotic (*Hox*) genes that encode such transcription factors are critical for the proper number and placement of embryonic structures, such as legs and antennae, in the fruit fly *Drosophila* (see Figure 18.19). Interestingly, maize has a homolog of *Hox* genes called *KNOTTED-1*, but unlike its counterparts in the animal world, *KNOTTED-1* does not affect the number or placement of plant organs. As you will see, an unrelated class of transcription factors called *MADS-box* proteins plays that role in plants. *KNOTTED-1* is, however, important in the development of leaf morphology, including the production of compound leaves. If the *KNOTTED-1* gene is expressed in greater quantity than normal in the genome of tomato plants, the normally compound leaves will then become "super-compound" **(Figure 35.32)**.

## Gene Expression and the Control of Cell Differentiation

The cells of a developing organism can synthesize different proteins and diverge in structure and function even though they share a common genome. If a mature cell removed from a root or leaf can dedifferentiate in tissue culture and give rise to the

**▼ Figure 35.32 Overexpression of a *Hox*-like gene in leaf formation.** *KNOTTED-1* is a gene that is involved in leaf and leaflet formation. An increase in its expression in tomato plants results in leaves that are "super-compound" (right) compared with normal leaves (left).

diverse cell types of a plant, then it must possess all the genes necessary to make any kind of cell in the plant. Therefore, cell differentiation depends, to a large degree, on the control of gene expression—the regulation of transcription and translation, resulting in the production of specific proteins.

Evidence suggests that the activation or inactivation of specific genes involved in cell differentiation results largely from cell-to-cell communication. Cells receive information about how they should specialize from neighboring cells. For example, two cell types arise in the root epidermis of *Arabidopsis*: root hair cells and hairless epidermal cells. Cell fate is associated with the position of the epidermal cells. The immature epidermal cells that are in contact with two underlying cells of the root cortex differentiate into root hair cells, whereas the immature epidermal cells in contact with only one cell in the cortex differentiate into mature hairless cells. The differential expression of a homeotic gene called *GLABRA-2* (from the Latin *glaber*, bald) is needed for proper distribution of root hairs **(Figure 35.33)**. Researchers have demonstrated this requirement by coupling the *GLABRA-2* gene to a "reporter gene" that causes every cell expressing *GLABRA-2* in the root to turn pale blue following a certain protocol. The *GLABRA-2* gene is normally expressed only in epidermal cells that will not develop root hairs.

## Shifts in Development: Phase Changes

Multicellular organisms generally pass through developmental stages. In humans, these are infancy, childhood, adolescence, and adulthood, with puberty as the dividing line between the nonreproductive and reproductive stages. Plants also pass through stages, developing from a juvenile stage to an adult vegetative stage to an adult reproductive stage. In animals, the developmental changes take place throughout the entire organism, such as when a larva develops into an adult animal. In contrast, plant developmental stages, called *phases*, occur within a single region, the shoot apical meristem. The morphological changes that arise from these transitions in shoot apical meristem activity are called **phase changes**. In the transition from

**▼ Figure 35.33 Control of root hair differentiation by a homeotic gene (LM).**

Cortical cells

When an epidermal cell borders a single cortical cell, the homeotic gene *GLABRA-2* is expressed, and the cell remains hairless. (The blue color indicates cells in which *GLABRA-2* is expressed.)

Here an epidermal cell borders two cortical cells. *GLABRA-2* is not expressed, and the cell will develop a root hair.

20 μm

The root cap cells external to the epidermal layer will be sloughed off before root hairs emerge.

**WHAT IF ➤** *What would the roots look like if* GLABRA-2 *were rendered dysfunctional by a mutation?*

a juvenile phase to an adult phase, some species exhibit some striking changes in leaf morphology **(Figure 35.34)**. Juvenile nodes and internodes retain their juvenile status even after the shoot continues to elongate and the shoot apical meristem has changed to the adult phase. Therefore, any *new* leaves that develop on branches that emerge from axillary buds at juvenile

**▼ Figure 35.34 Phase change in the shoot system of *Acacia koa*.** This native of Hawaii has compound juvenile leaves, consisting of many small leaflets, and simple mature leaves. This dual foliage reflects a phase change in the development of the apical meristem of each shoot. Once a node forms, the developmental phase—juvenile or adult—is fixed; compound leaves do not mature into simple leaves.

Leaves produced by adult phase of apical meristem

Leaves produced by juvenile phase of apical meristem

nodes will also be juvenile, even though the apical meristem of the stem's main axis may have been producing mature nodes for years.

If environmental conditions permit, an adult plant is induced to flower. Biologists have made great progress in explaining the genetic control of floral development—the topic of the next section.

## Genetic Control of Flowering

Flower formation involves a phase change from vegetative growth to reproductive growth. This transition is triggered by a combination of environmental cues, such as day length, and internal signals, such as hormones. (You will learn more about the roles of these signals in flowering in Concept 39.3.) Unlike vegetative growth, which is indeterminate, floral growth is usually determinate: The production of a flower by a shoot apical meristem generally stops the primary growth of that shoot. The transition from vegetative growth to flowering is associated with the switching on of floral **meristem identity genes**. The protein products of these genes are transcription factors that regulate the genes required for the conversion of the indeterminate vegetative meristems to determinate floral meristems.

When a shoot apical meristem is induced to flower, the order of each primordium's emergence determines its development into a specific type of floral organ—a sepal, petal, stamen, or carpel (see Figure 30.8 to review basic flower structure). These floral organs form four whorls that can be described roughly as concentric "circles" when viewed from above. Sepals form the first (outermost) whorl; petals form the second; stamens form the third; and carpels form the fourth (innermost) whorl. Plant biologists have identified several **organ identity genes** belonging to the *MADS-box* family that encode transcription factors that regulate the development of this characteristic floral pattern. Positional information determines which organ identity genes are expressed in a particular floral organ primordium. The result is the development of an emerging floral primordium into a specific floral organ. A mutation in a plant organ identity gene can cause abnormal floral development, such as petals growing in place of stamens **(Figure 35.35)**. Some homeotic mutants with increased petal numbers produce showier flowers that are prized by gardeners.

By studying mutants with abnormal flowers, researchers have identified and cloned three classes of floral organ identity genes, and their studies are beginning to reveal how these genes function. **Figure 35.36a** shows a simplified version of the **ABC hypothesis** of flower formation, which proposes that three classes of genes direct the formation of the four types of floral organs. According to the ABC hypothesis, each class of organ identity genes is switched on in two specific whorls of the floral meristem. Normally, *A* genes are switched on in the two outer whorls (sepals and petals); *B* genes are switched on in the two middle whorls (petals and stamens); and *C* genes are switched on in the two inner whorls (stamens and carpels). Sepals arise from those parts of floral meristems

▼ **Figure 35.35 Organ identity genes and pattern formation in flower development.**

▲ **Normal *Arabidopsis* flower.** *Arabidopsis* normally has four whorls of flower parts: sepals (Se), petals (Pe), stamens (St), and carpels (Ca).

▶ **Abnormal *Arabidopsis* flower.** Researchers have identified several mutations of organ identity genes that cause abnormal flowers to develop. This flower has an extra set of petals in place of stamens and an internal flower where normal plants have carpels.

**MAKE CONNECTIONS** ➤ *Provide another example of a homeotic gene mutation that leads to organs being produced in the wrong place (see Concept 18.4).*

in which only *A* genes are active; petals arise where *A* and *B* genes are active; stamens where *B* and *C* genes are active; and carpels where only *C* genes are active. The ABC hypothesis can account for the phenotypes of mutants lacking *A*, *B*, or *C* gene activity, with one addition: Where *A* gene activity is present, it inhibits *C*, and vice versa. If either the *A* gene or *C* gene is suppressed, the other gene is expressed. **Figure 35.36b** shows the floral patterns of mutants lacking each of the three classes of organ identity genes and depicts how the hypothesis accounts for the floral phenotypes. By constructing such hypotheses and designing experiments to test them, researchers are tracing the genetic basis of plant development.

In dissecting the plant to examine its parts, as we have done in this chapter, we must remember that the whole plant functions as an integrated organism. Plant structures largely reflect evolutionary adaptations to the challenges of a photoautotrophic existence on land.

(MB) Interview with Virginia Walbot: Researching plant genetics and development

## CONCEPT CHECK 35.5

1. How can two cells in a plant have vastly different structures even though they have the same genome?

2. What are three differences between animal development and plant development?

3. **WHAT IF?** ➤ In some species, sepals look like petals, and both are collectively called "tepals." Suggest an extension to the ABC hypothesis that could account for tepals.

*For suggested answers, see Appendix A.*

## ▼ Figure 35.36 The ABC hypothesis for the functioning of organ identity genes in flower development.

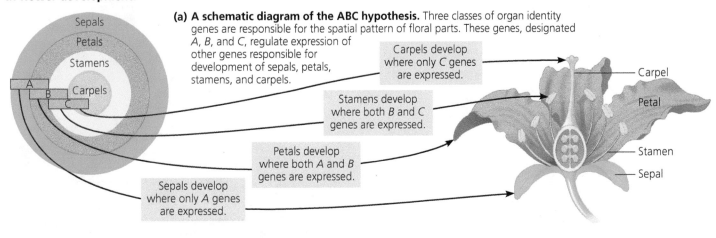

**(a) A schematic diagram of the ABC hypothesis.** Three classes of organ identity genes are responsible for the spatial pattern of floral parts. These genes, designated *A*, *B*, and *C*, regulate expression of other genes responsible for development of sepals, petals, stamens, and carpels.

Carpels develop where only *C* genes are expressed.

Stamens develop where both *B* and *C* genes are expressed.

Petals develop where both *A* and *B* genes are expressed.

Sepals develop where only *A* genes are expressed.

Carpel

Petal

Stamen

Sepal

Stamen   Carpel

Petal

Sepal

Wild type

Mutant with *A* gene suppressed (only carpels and stamens)

Mutant with *B* gene suppressed (only sepals and carpels)

Mutant with *C* gene suppressed (only sepals and petals)

**(b) Side view of wild type flower and flowers with organ identity mutations.** The phenotype of mutants lacking a functional *A*, *B*, or *C* organ identity gene can be explained by the model in part (a) and the observation that if either the *A* gene or *C* gene is suppressed, the other gene is expressed in that whorl. For example, if the *A* gene is suppressed in a mutant, the *C* gene is expressed where the *A* gene would normally be expressed. Therefore, carpels (*C* gene expressed) develop in the outermost whorl, and stamens (*B* and *C* genes expressed) develop in the next whorl.

**DRAW IT** ➤ *(a) For each mutant, draw a "bull's eye" diagram like the one in part (a), labeling the type of organ and gene(s) expressed in each whorl. (b) Draw and label a "bull's-eye" diagram for a mutant flower in which the A and B genes were suppressed.*

---

# 35 Chapter Review

Go to **MasteringBiology®** for Videos, Animations, Vocab Self-Quiz, Practice Tests, and more in the Study Area.

## SUMMARY OF KEY CONCEPTS

### CONCEPT 35.1

**Plants have a hierarchical organization consisting of organs, tissues, and cells** (pp. 757–763)

**VOCAB SELF-QUIZ** goo.gl/6u55ks

- Vascular plants have shoots consisting of **stems, leaves**, and, in angiosperms, flowers. **Roots** anchor the plant, absorb and conduct water and minerals, and store food. Leaves are attached to stem **nodes** and are the main **organs** of photosynthesis. The **axillary buds**, in axils of leaves and stems, give rise to branches. Plant organs may be adapted for specialized functions.
- Vascular plants have three **tissue systems**—dermal, vascular, and ground—which are continuous throughout the plant. The

**dermal tissue** is a continuous layer of cells that covers the plant exterior. **Vascular tissues** (**xylem** and **phloem**) facilitate the long-distance transport of substances. **Ground tissues** function in storage, metabolism, and regeneration.

- **Parenchyma cells** are relatively undifferentiated and thin-walled cells that retain the ability to divide; they perform most of the metabolic functions of synthesis and storage. **Collenchyma cells** have unevenly thickened walls; they support young, growing parts of the plant. **Sclerenchyma cells**—**sclereids** and **fibers**—have thick, lignified walls that help support mature, nongrowing parts of the plant. **Tracheids** and **vessel elements**, the water-conducting cells of xylem, have thick walls and are dead at functional maturity. **Sieve-tube elements** are living but highly modified cells that are largely devoid of internal organelles; they function in the transport of sugars through the phloem of angiosperms.

? *Describe at least three specializations in plant organs and plant cells that are adaptations to life on land.*

## CONCEPT 35.2

### Different meristems generate new cells for primary and secondary growth (pp. 764–765)

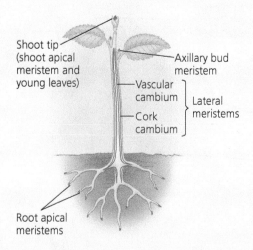

Shoot tip (shoot apical meristem and young leaves)

Axillary bud meristem

Vascular cambium

Cork cambium

Lateral meristems

Root apical meristems

**?** *What is the difference between primary and secondary growth?*

## CONCEPT 35.3

### Primary growth lengthens roots and shoots (pp. 766–769)

- The root **apical meristem** is located near the tip of the root, where it generates cells for the growing root axis and the **root cap**.
- The apical meristem of a shoot is located in the **apical bud**, where it gives rise to alternating **internodes** and leaf-bearing nodes.
- Eudicot stems have vascular bundles in a ring, whereas monocot stems have scattered vascular bundles.
- **Mesophyll** cells are adapted for photosynthesis. **Stomata**, epidermal pores formed by pairs of **guard cells**, allow for gaseous exchange and are major avenues for water loss.

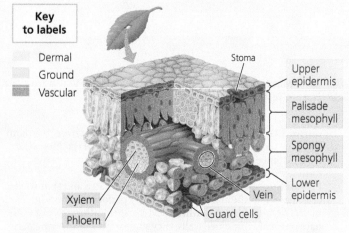

| Key to labels |
| --- |
| Dermal |
| Ground |
| Vascular |

Stoma

Upper epidermis

Palisade mesophyll

Spongy mesophyll

Lower epidermis

Xylem

Phloem

Vein

Guard cells

**?** *How does branching differ in roots versus stems?*

## CONCEPT 35.4

### Secondary growth increases the diameter of stems and roots in woody plants (pp. 770–773)

- The **vascular cambium** is a meristematic cylinder that produces secondary xylem and secondary phloem during **secondary growth**. Older layers of secondary xylem (heartwood) become inactive, whereas younger layers (sapwood) still conduct water.

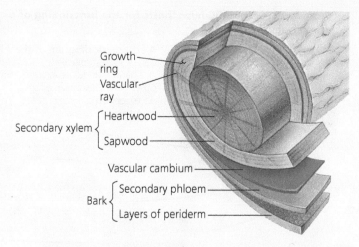

Growth ring

Vascular ray

Secondary xylem { Heartwood / Sapwood }

Vascular cambium

Bark { Secondary phloem / Layers of periderm }

- The **cork cambium** gives rise to a thick protective covering called the periderm, which consists of the cork cambium plus the layers of cork cells it produces.

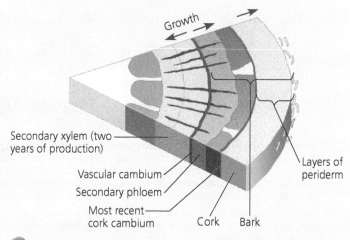

Growth

Secondary xylem (two years of production)

Vascular cambium

Secondary phloem

Most recent cork cambium

Cork

Bark

Layers of periderm

**?** *What advantages did plants gain from the evolution of secondary growth?*

## CONCEPT 35.5

### Growth, morphogenesis, and cell differentiation produce the plant body (pp. 773–779)

- Cell division and cell expansion are the primary determinants of growth. A preprophase band of microtubules determines where a cell plate will form in a dividing cell. Microtubule orientation also affects the direction of cell elongation by controlling the orientation of cellulose microfibrils in the cell wall.
- Morphogenesis, the development of body shape and organization, depends on cells responding to positional information from their neighbors.
- Cell differentiation, arising from differential gene activation, enables cells within the plant to assume different functions despite having identical genomes. The way in which a plant cell differentiates is determined largely by the cell's position in the developing plant.
- Internal or environmental cues may cause a plant to switch from one developmental stage to another—for example, from developing juvenile leaves to developing mature leaves. Such morphological changes are called **phase changes**.
- Research on **organ identity genes** in developing flowers provides a model system for studying **pattern formation**. The **ABC hypothesis** identifies how three classes of organ identity genes control formation of sepals, petals, stamens, and carpels.

**?** *By what mechanism do plant cells tend to elongate along one axis instead of expanding in all directions?*

## Level 1: Knowledge/Comprehension

**1.** Most of the growth of a plant body is the result of
(A) cell differentiation.
(B) morphogenesis.
(C) cell division.
(D) cell elongation.

**2.** The innermost layer of the root cortex is the
(A) core.
(B) pericycle.
(C) endodermis.
(D) pith.

**3.** Heartwood and sapwood consist of
(A) bark.
(B) periderm.
(C) secondary xylem.
(D) secondary phloem.

**4.** The phase change of an apical meristem from the juvenile to the mature vegetative phase is often revealed by
(A) a change in the morphology of the leaves produced.
(B) the initiation of secondary growth.
(C) the formation of lateral roots.
(D) the activation of floral meristem identity genes.

## Level 2: Application/Analysis

**5.** Suppose a flower had normal expression of genes *A* and *C* and expression of gene *B* in all four whorls. Based on the ABC hypothesis, what would be the structure of that flower, starting at the outermost whorl?
(A) carpel-petal-petal-carpel
(B) petal-petal-stamen-stamen
(C) sepal-carpel-carpel-sepal
(D) sepal-sepal-carpel-carpel

**6.** Which of the following arise(s), directly or indirectly, from meristematic activity?
(A) secondary xylem
(B) leaves
(C) dermal tissue
(D) all of the above

**7.** Which of the following would not be seen in a cross section through the woody part of a root?
(A) sclerenchyma cells
(B) parenchyma cells
(C) sieve-tube elements
(D) root hairs

**8.** **DRAW IT** On this cross section from a woody eudicot, label a growth ring, late wood, early wood, and a vessel element. Then draw an arrow in the pith-to-cork direction.

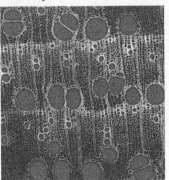

## Level 3: Synthesis/Evaluation

**9.** **EVOLUTION CONNECTION** Evolutionary biologists have coined the term *exaptation* to describe a common occurrence in the evolution of life: A limb or organ evolves in a particular context but over time takes on a new function (see Concept 25.6). What are some examples of exaptations in plant organs?

**10.** **SCIENTIFIC INQUIRY** Grasslands typically do not flourish when large herbivores are removed. Instead, grasslands are replaced by broad-leaved herbaceous eudicots, shrubs, and trees. Based on your knowledge of the structure and growth habits of monocots versus eudicots, suggest a reason why.

**11.** **SCIENCE, TECHNOLOGY, AND SOCIETY** Hunger and malnutrition are urgent problems for many poor countries, yet plant biologists in wealthy nations have focused most of their research efforts on *Arabidopsis thaliana*. Some people have argued that if plant biologists are truly concerned about fighting world hunger, they should study cassava and plantain because these two crops are staples for many of the world's poor. If you were an *Arabidopsis* researcher, how might you respond to this argument?

**12.** **WRITE ABOUT A THEME: ORGANIZATION** In a short essay (100–150 words), explain how the evolution of lignin affected vascular plant structure and function.

**13.** **SYNTHESIZE YOUR KNOWLEDGE**

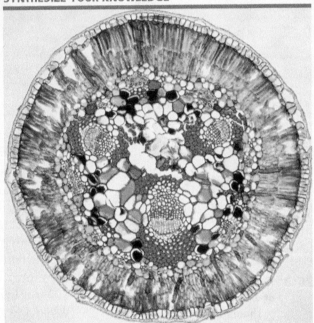

This stained light micrograph shows a cross section through a plant organ from *Hakea purpurea*, a shrub native to some arid regions of Australia. (a) Review Figures 35.14, 35.17, and 35.18 to identify whether this is a root, stem, or leaf. Explain your reasoning. (b) How might this organ be an adaptation for dry conditions?

*For selected answers, see Appendix A.*

**MB** For additional practice questions, check out the **Dynamic Study Modules** in MasteringBiology. You can use them to study on your smartphone, tablet, or computer anytime, anywhere!

# Resource Acquisition and Transport in Vascular Plants

# 36

▲ Figure 36.1 **Why do aspens quake?**

## KEY CONCEPTS

**36.1** Adaptations for acquiring resources were key steps in the evolution of vascular plants

**36.2** Different mechanisms transport substances over short or long distances

**36.3** Transpiration drives the transport of water and minerals from roots to shoots via the xylem

**36.4** The rate of transpiration is regulated by stomata

**36.5** Sugars are transported from sources to sinks via the phloem

**36.6** The symplast is highly dynamic

## A Whole Lot of Shaking Going On

If you walk amidst an aspen (*Populus tremuloides*) forest on a clear day, you will be treated to a fantastic light display **(Figure 36.1)**. Even on a day with little wind, the trembling of leaves causes shafts of brilliant sunlight to dapple the forest floor with ever-changing flecks of radiance. The mechanism underlying these passive leaf movements is not difficult to discern: The petiole of each leaf is flattened along its sides, permitting the leaf to flop only in the horizontal plane. Perhaps more curious is why this peculiar adaptation has evolved in *Populus*.

Many hypotheses have been put forward to explain how leaf quaking benefits *Populus*. Old ideas that leaf trembling helps replace the $CO_2$-depleted air near the leaf surface, or deters herbivores, have not been supported by experiments. The leading hypothesis is that leaf trembling increases the photosynthetic productivity of the whole plant by allowing more light to reach the lower leaves of the tree. If not for the shafts of transient sunlight provided by leaf trembling, the lower leaves would be too shaded to photosynthesize sufficiently.

In this chapter, we'll examine various adaptations that help plants acquire resources such as water, minerals, carbon dioxide, and light more efficiently. We'll look at what nutrients plants require and how plant nutrition often involves other organisms. The acquisition of these resources, however, is just the beginning of the story. Resources must be transported to where they are needed. Thus, we will also examine how water, minerals, and sugars are transported through the plant.

When you see this blue icon, log in to **MasteringBiology** and go to the Study Area for digital resources.

 Get Ready for This Chapter

# CONCEPT 36.1

## Adaptations for acquiring resources were key steps in the evolution of vascular plants

**EVOLUTION**  Most plants grow in soil and therefore inhabit two worlds—above ground, where shoots acquire sunlight and $CO_2$, and below ground, where roots acquire water and minerals. The successful colonization of the land by plants depended on adaptations that allowed early plants to acquire resources from these two different settings.

The algal ancestors of plants absorbed water, minerals, and $CO_2$ directly from the water in which they lived. Transport in these algae was relatively simple because every cell was close to the source of these substances. The earliest plants were nonvascular and produced photosynthetic shoots above the shallow fresh water in which they lived. These leafless shoots typically had waxy cuticles and few stomata, which allowed them to avoid excessive water loss while still permitting some exchange of $CO_2$ and $O_2$ for photosynthesis. The anchoring and absorbing functions of early plants were assumed by the base of the stem or by threadlike rhizoids (see Figure 29.6).

As plants evolved and increased in number, competition for light, water, and nutrients intensified. Taller plants with broad, flat appendages had an advantage in absorbing light. This increase in surface area, however, resulted in more evaporation and therefore a greater need for water. Larger shoots also required stronger anchorage. These needs favored the production of multicellular, branching roots. Meanwhile, as greater shoot heights further separated the top of the photosynthetic shoot from the nonphotosynthetic parts below ground, natural selection favored plants capable of efficient long-distance transport of water, minerals, and products of photosynthesis.

The evolution of vascular tissue consisting of xylem and phloem made possible the development of extensive root and shoot systems that carry out long-distance transport (see Figure 35.10). The **xylem** transports water and minerals from roots to shoots. The **phloem** transports products of photosynthesis from where they are made or stored to where they are needed. **Figure 36.2** provides an overview of resource acquisition and transport in an actively photosynthesizing plant.

## Shoot Architecture and Light Capture

Because most plants are photoautotrophs, their success depends ultimately on their ability to photosynthesize.

▼ **Figure 36.2 An overview of resource acquisition and transport in a vascular plant during the day.**

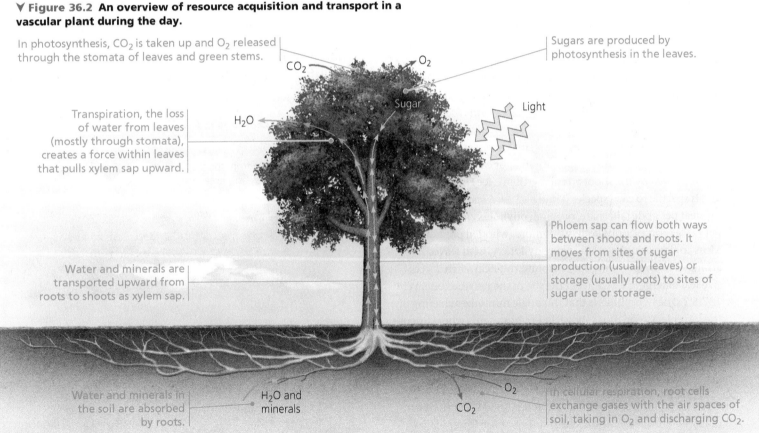

In photosynthesis, $CO_2$ is taken up and $O_2$ released through the stomata of leaves and green stems.

Sugars are produced by photosynthesis in the leaves.

Transpiration, the loss of water from leaves (mostly through stomata), creates a force within leaves that pulls xylem sap upward.

Phloem sap can flow both ways between shoots and roots. It moves from sites of sugar production (usually leaves) or storage (usually roots) to sites of sugar use or storage.

Water and minerals are transported upward from roots to shoots as xylem sap.

Water and minerals in the soil are absorbed by roots.

$H_2O$ and minerals

In cellular respiration, root cells exchange gases with the air spaces of soil, taking in $O_2$ and discharging $CO_2$.

$CO_2$  $O_2$

**MAKE CONNECTIONS** ➤ *When photosynthesis stops at night, cellular respiration continues. Explain how this affects gas exchange in leaf cells at night. See Figure 10.23 to review gas exchange between chloroplasts and mitochondria.*

Over the course of evolution, plants have developed a wide variety of shoot architectures that enable each species to compete successfully for light absorption in the ecological niche it occupies. For example, the lengths and widths of stems, as well as the branching pattern of shoots, are all architectural features affecting light capture.

Stems serve as supporting structures for leaves and as conduits for the transport of water and nutrients. Plants that grow tall avoid shading from neighboring plants. Most tall plants require thick stems, which enable greater vascular flow to and from the leaves and stronger mechanical support for them. Vines are an exception, relying on other objects (usually other plants) to support their stems. In woody plants, stems become thicker through secondary growth (see Figure 35.11). Branching generally enables plants to harvest sunlight for photosynthesis more effectively. However, some species, such as the coconut palm, do not branch at all. Why is there so much variation in branching patterns? Plants have only a finite amount of energy to devote to shoot growth. If most of that energy goes into branching, there is less available for growing tall, and the risk of being shaded by taller plants increases. Conversely, if most of the energy goes into growing tall, the plants are not optimally harvesting sunlight.

Leaf size and structure account for much of the outward diversity in plant form. Leaves range in length from 1.3 mm in the pygmyweed (*Crassula connata*), a native of dry, sandy regions in the western United States, to 20 m in the palm *Raphia regalis*, a native of African rain forests. These species represent extreme examples of a general correlation observed between water availability and leaf size. The largest leaves are typically found in species from tropical rain forests, whereas the smallest are usually found in species from dry or very cold environments, where liquid water is scarce and evaporative loss is more problematic.

The arrangement of leaves on a stem, known as **phyllotaxy**, is an architectural feature important in light capture. Phyllotaxy is determined by the shoot apical meristem (see Figure 35.16) and is specific to each species **(Figure 36.3)**. A species may have one leaf per node (alternate, or spiral, phyllotaxy), two leaves per node (opposite phyllotaxy), or more (whorled phyllotaxy). Most angiosperms have alternate phyllotaxy, with leaves arranged in an ascending spiral around the stem, each successive leaf emerging 137.5° from the site of the previous one. Why 137.5°? One hypothesis is that this angle minimizes shading of the lower leaves by those above. In environments where intense sunlight can harm leaves, the greater shading provided by oppositely arranged leaves may be advantageous.

The total area of the leafy portions of all the plants in a community, from the top layer of vegetation to the bottom layer, affects the productivity of each plant. When there are many layers of vegetation, the shading of the lower leaves is so great that they photosynthesize less than they respire. When this happens, the nonproductive leaves or branches

▼ **Figure 36.3 Emerging phyllotaxy of Norway spruce.** This SEM, taken from above a shoot tip, shows the pattern of emergence of leaves. The leaves are numbered, with 1 being the youngest. (Some numbered leaves are not visible in the close-up.)

**VISUAL SKILLS ➤** *With your finger, trace the progression of leaf emergence, moving from leaf number 29 to 28 and so on. What is the pattern? Based on this pattern of phyllotaxy, predict between which two developing leaf primordia the next primordium will emerge.*

undergo programmed cell death and are eventually shed, a process called *self-pruning*.

Plant features that reduce self-shading increase light capture. A useful measurement in this regard is the *leaf area index*, the ratio of the total upper leaf surface of a single plant or an entire crop divided by the surface area of the land on which the plant or crop grows **(Figure 36.4)**. Leaf area index values

▼ **Figure 36.4 Leaf area index.** The leaf area index of a single plant is the ratio of the total area of the top surfaces of the leaves to the area of ground covered by the plant, as shown in this illustration of two plants viewed from the top. With many layers of leaves, a leaf area index value can easily exceed 1.

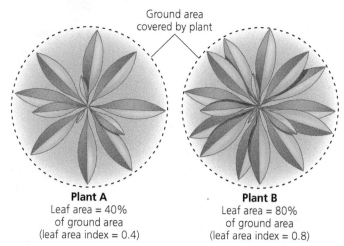

Ground area covered by plant

**Plant A**
Leaf area = 40% of ground area
(leaf area index = 0.4)

**Plant B**
Leaf area = 80% of ground area
(leaf area index = 0.8)

? *Would a higher leaf area index always increase the amount of photosynthesis? Explain.*

of up to 7 are common for many mature crops, and there is little agricultural benefit to leaf area indexes higher than this value. Adding more leaves increases shading of lower leaves to the point that self-pruning occurs.

Another factor affecting light capture is leaf orientation. Some plants have horizontally oriented leaves; others, such as grasses, have leaves that are vertically oriented. In low-light conditions, horizontal leaves capture sunlight much more effectively than vertical leaves. In grasslands or other sunny regions, however, horizontal orientation may expose upper leaves to overly intense light, injuring leaves and reducing photosynthesis. But if a plant's leaves are nearly vertical, light rays are essentially parallel to the leaf surfaces, so no leaf receives too much light, and light penetrates more deeply to the lower leaves.

### The Photosynthesis–Water Loss Compromise

The broad surface of most leaves favors light capture, while open stomatal pores allow for the diffusion of $CO_2$ into the photosynthetic tissues. Open stomatal pores, however, also promote evaporation of water from the plant. Over 90% of the water lost by plants is by evaporation from stomatal pores. Consequently, shoot adaptations represent compromises between enhancing photosynthesis and minimizing water loss, particularly in environments where water is scarce. Later in the chapter, we'll discuss the mechanisms by which plants enhance $CO_2$ uptake and minimize water loss by regulating the opening of stomatal pores.

### Root Architecture and Acquisition of Water and Minerals

Just as carbon dioxide and sunlight are resources exploited by the shoot system, soil contains resources mined by the root system. Plants rapidly adjust the architecture and physiology of their roots to exploit patches of available nutrients in the soil. The roots of many plants, for example, respond to pockets of low nitrate availability in soils by extending straight through the pockets instead of branching within them. Conversely, when encountering a pocket rich in nitrate, a root will often branch extensively there. Root cells also respond to high soil nitrate levels by synthesizing more proteins involved in nitrate transport and assimilation. Thus, not only does the plant devote more of its mass to exploiting a nitrate-rich patch, but the cells also absorb nitrate more efficiently.

The efficient absorption of limited nutrients is also enhanced by reduced competition within the root system. For example, cuttings taken from stolons of buffalo grass (*Buchloe dactyloides*) develop fewer and shorter roots in the presence of cuttings from the same plant than they do in the presence of cuttings from another buffalo grass plant. Researchers are trying to uncover how the plant distinguishes self from nonself.

Plant roots also form mutually beneficial relationships with microorganisms that enable the plant to exploit soil resources more efficiently. For example, the evolution of mutualistic associations between roots and fungi called **mycorrhizae** was a critical step in the successful colonization of land by plants. Mycorrhizal hyphae indirectly endow the root systems of many plants with an enormous surface area for absorbing water and minerals, particularly phosphate. The role of mycorrhizae in plant nutrition will be examined in Concept 37.3.

Once acquired, resources must be transported to other parts of the plant that need them. In the next section, we examine the processes and pathways that enable resources such as water, minerals, and sugars to be transported throughout the plant.

### CONCEPT CHECK 36.1

1. Why is long-distance transport important for vascular plants?
2. Some plants can detect increased levels of light reflected from leaves of encroaching neighbors. This detection elicits stem elongation, production of erect leaves, and reduced lateral branching. How do these responses help the plant compete?
3. WHAT IF? ➤ If you prune a plant's shoot tips, what will be the short-term effect on the plant's branching and leaf area index?

*For suggested answers, see Appendix A.*

## CONCEPT 36.2

# Different mechanisms transport substances over short or long distances

Given the diversity of substances that move through plants and the great range of distances and barriers over which such substances must be transported, it is not surprising that plants employ a variety of transport processes. Before examining these processes, however, we'll look at the two major pathways of transport: the apoplast and the symplast.

### The Apoplast and Symplast: Transport Continuums

Plant tissues have two major compartments—the apoplast and the symplast. The **apoplast** consists of everything external to the plasma membranes of living cells and includes cell walls, extracellular spaces, and the interior of dead cells such as vessel elements and tracheids (see Figure 35.10). The **symplast** consists of the entire mass of cytosol of all the living cells in a plant, as well as the plasmodesmata, the cytoplasmic channels that interconnect them.

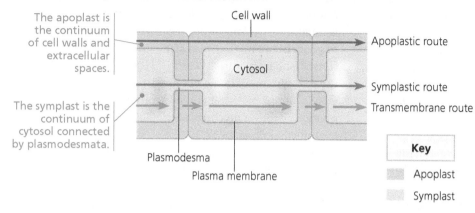

The apoplast is the continuum of cell walls and extracellular spaces.

The symplast is the continuum of cytosol connected by plasmodesmata.

Cell wall

Cytosol

Apoplastic route

Symplastic route

Transmembrane route

Plasmodesma

Plasma membrane

**Key**

Apoplast

Symplast

The compartmental structure of plants provides three routes for transport within a plant tissue or organ: the apoplastic, symplastic, and transmembrane routes **(Figure 36.5)**. In the *apoplastic route*, water and solutes (dissolved chemicals) move along the continuum of cell walls and extracellular spaces. In the *symplastic route*, water and solutes move along the continuum of cytosol. This route requires substances to cross a plasma membrane once, when they first enter the plant. After entering one cell, substances can move from cell to cell via plasmodesmata. In the *transmembrane route*, water and solutes move out of one cell, across the cell wall, and into the neighboring cell, which may pass them to the next cell in the same way. The transmembrane route requires repeated crossings of plasma membranes as substances exit one cell and enter the next. These three routes are not mutually exclusive, and some substances may use more than one route to varying degrees.

## Short-Distance Transport of Solutes Across Plasma Membranes

In plants, as in any organism, the selective permeability of the plasma membrane controls the short-distance movement of substances into and out of cells (see Concept 7.2). Both active and passive transport mechanisms occur in plants, and plant cell membranes are equipped with the same *general* types of pumps and transport proteins (channel proteins, carrier proteins, and cotransporters) that function in other cells. There are, however, *specific* differences between the membrane transport processes of plant and animal cells. In this section, we'll focus on some of those differences.

Unlike in animal cells, hydrogen ions ($H^+$) rather than sodium ions ($Na^+$) play the primary role in basic transport processes in plant cells. For example, in plant cells the membrane potential (the voltage across the membrane) is established mainly through the pumping of $H^+$ by proton pumps **(Figure 36.6a)**, rather than the pumping of $Na^+$ by sodium-potassium pumps. Also, $H^+$ is most often cotransported in plants, whereas $Na^+$ is typically cotransported in animals. During cotransport, plant cells use the energy in the $H^+$ gradient and membrane potential to drive the active transport of many different solutes. For instance, cotransport with $H^+$ is responsible for absorption of neutral solutes, such as the sugar sucrose, by phloem cells and other plant cells. An $H^+$/sucrose cotransporter couples movement of sucrose against its concentration gradient with movement of $H^+$ down its electrochemical gradient **(Figure 36.6b)**. Cotransport with $H^+$ also facilitates movement of ions, as in the uptake of nitrate ($NO_3^-$) by root cells **(Figure 36.6c)**.

The membranes of plant cells also have ion channels that allow only certain ions to pass **(Figure 36.6d)**. As in animal cells, most channels are gated, opening or closing in response to stimuli such as chemicals, pressure, or voltage. Later in this chapter, we'll discuss how potassium ion channels in guard cells function in opening and closing stomata. Ion channels are also involved in producing electrical signals analogous to the action potentials of animals (see Concept 48.2). However, these signals are 1,000 times slower and employ $Ca^{2+}$-activated anion channels rather than the sodium ion channels used by animal cells.

## Short-Distance Transport of Water Across Plasma Membranes

The absorption or loss of water by a cell occurs by **osmosis**, the diffusion of free water—water that is not bound to solutes or surfaces—across a membrane (see Figure 7.12). The physical property that predicts the direction in which water will flow is called **water potential**, a quantity that includes the effects of solute concentration and physical pressure. Free water moves from regions of higher water potential to regions of lower water potential if there is no barrier to its flow. The word *potential* in the term *water potential* refers to water's potential energy—water's capacity to perform work when it moves from a region of higher water potential to a region of lower water potential. For example, if a plant cell or seed is immersed in a solution that has a higher water potential, water will move into the cell or seed, causing it to expand. The expansion of plant cells and seeds can be a powerful force: The expansion of cells in tree roots can break concrete sidewalks, and the swelling of wet grain seeds within the holds of damaged ships can produce catastrophic hull failure and sink the ships. Given the strong forces generated by swelling seeds, it is interesting to consider whether water uptake by seeds is an active process.

## ▼ Figure 36.6 Solute transport across plant cell plasma membranes.

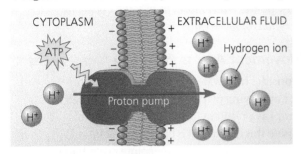

CYTOPLASM                    EXTRACELLULAR FLUID

**(a) H⁺ and membrane potential.** The plasma membranes of plant cells use ATP-dependent proton pumps to pump H⁺ out of the cell. These pumps contribute to the membrane potential and the establishment of a pH gradient across the membrane. These two forms of potential energy can drive the transport of solutes.

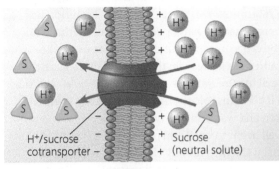

H⁺/sucrose cotransporter —     Sucrose (neutral solute)

**(b) H⁺ and cotransport of neutral solutes.** Neutral solutes such as sugars can be loaded into plant cells by cotransport with H⁺ ions. H⁺/sucrose cotransporters, for example, play a key role in loading sugar into the phloem prior to sugar transport throughout the plant.

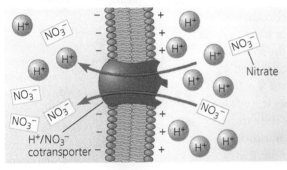

H⁺/NO₃⁻ cotransporter —          Nitrate

**(c) H⁺ and cotransport of ions.** Cotransport mechanisms involving H⁺ also participate in regulating ion fluxes into and out of cells. For example, H⁺/NO₃⁻ cotransporters in the plasma membranes of root cells are important for the uptake of NO₃⁻ by plant roots.

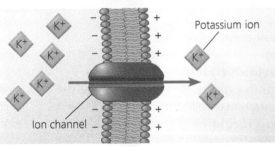

Ion channel                  Potassium ion

**(d) Ion channels.** Plant ion channels open and close in response to voltage, stretching of the membrane, and chemical factors. When open, ion channels allow specific ions to diffuse across membranes. For example, a K⁺ ion channel is involved in the release of K⁺ from guard cells when stomata close.

**?** *Assume that a plant cell has all four of the plasma membrane transport proteins shown above and that you have a specific inhibitor for each protein. Predict the effect of each inhibitor on the cell's membrane potential.*

This question is examined in the **Scientific Skills Exercise**, which explores the effect of temperature on this process.

Water potential is abbreviated by the Greek letter $\Psi$ (psi, pronounced "sigh"). Plant biologists measure $\Psi$ in a unit of pressure called a **megapascal** (abbreviated MPa). By definition, the $\Psi$ of pure water in a container open to the atmosphere under standard conditions (at sea level and at room temperature) is 0 MPa. One MPa is equal to about 10 times atmospheric pressure at sea level. The internal pressure of a living plant cell due to the osmotic uptake of water is approximately 0.5 MPa, about twice the air pressure inside an inflated car tire.

## How Solutes and Pressure Affect Water Potential

Solute concentration and physical pressure are the major determinants of water potential in hydrated plants, as expressed in the water potential equation:

$$\Psi = \Psi_S + \Psi_P$$

where $\Psi$ is the water potential, $\Psi_S$ is the solute potential (osmotic potential), and $\Psi_P$ is the pressure potential. The **solute potential** ($\Psi_S$) of a solution is directly proportional to its molarity. Solute potential is also called *osmotic potential* because solutes affect the direction of osmosis. The solutes in plants are typically mineral ions and sugars. By definition, the $\Psi_S$ of pure water is 0. When solutes are added, they bind water molecules. As a result, there are fewer free water molecules, reducing the capacity of the water to move and do work. In this way, an increase in solute concentration has a negative effect on water potential, which is why the $\Psi_S$ of a solution is always expressed as a negative number. For example, a 0.1 $M$ solution of a sugar has a $\Psi_S$ of −0.23 MPa. As the solute concentration increases, $\Psi_S$ will become more negative.

**Pressure potential** ($\Psi_P$) is the physical pressure on a solution. Unlike $\Psi_S$, $\Psi_P$ can be positive or negative relative to atmospheric pressure. For example, when a solution is being withdrawn by a syringe, it is under negative pressure; when it is being expelled from a syringe, it is under positive pressure. The water in living cells is usually under positive pressure due to the osmotic uptake of water. Specifically, the **protoplast** (the living part of the cell, which also includes the plasma membrane) presses against the cell wall, creating what is known as **turgor pressure**. This pushing effect of internal pressure, much like the air in an inflated tire, is critical for plant function because it helps maintain the stiffness of plant tissues and also serves as the driving force for cell elongation. Conversely, the water in the hollow nonliving xylem cells (tracheids and vessel elements) of a plant is often under a negative pressure potential (tension) of less than −2 MPa.

## Calculating and Interpreting Temperature Coefficients

**Does the Initial Uptake of Water by Seeds Depend on Temperature?** One way to answer this question is to soak seeds in water at different temperatures and measure the rate of water uptake at each temperature. The data can be used to calculate the temperature coefficient, $Q_{10}$, the factor by which a physiological reaction (or process) rate increases when the temperature is raised by 10°C:

$$Q_{10} = \left(\frac{k_2}{k_1}\right)^{\frac{10}{t_2-t_1}}$$

where $t_2$ is the higher temperature (°C), $t_1$ is the lower temperature, $k_2$ is the reaction (or process) rate at $t_2$, and $k_1$ is the reaction (or process) rate at $t_1$. (If $t_2 - t_1 = 10$, as here, the math is simplified.)

$Q_{10}$ values may be used to make inferences about the physiological process under investigation. Chemical (metabolic) processes involving large-scale protein shape changes are highly dependent on temperature and have higher $Q_{10}$ values, closer to 2 or 3. In contrast, many, but not all, physical parameters are relatively independent of temperature and have $Q_{10}$ values closer to 1. For example, the $Q_{10}$ of the change in the viscosity of water is 1.2–1.3. In this exercise, you will calculate $Q_{10}$ using data from radish seeds (*Raphanus sativum*) to assess whether the initial uptake of water by seeds is more likely to be a physical or a chemical process.

**How the Experiment Was Done** Samples of radish seeds were weighed and placed in water at four different temperatures. After 30 minutes, the seeds were removed, blotted dry, and reweighed. The researchers then calculated the percent increase in mass due to water uptake for each sample.

### Data from the Experiment

| Temperature | % Increase in Mass Due to Water Uptake after 30 Minutes |
|:---:|:---:|
| 5°C | 18.5 |
| 15°C | 26.0 |
| 25°C | 31.0 |
| 35°C | 36.2 |

**Data from** J. D. Murphy and D. L. Noland, Temperature effects on seed imbibition and leakage mediated by viscosity and membranes, *Plant Physiology* 69:428–431 (1982).

#### INTERPRET THE DATA

1. Based on the data, does the initial uptake of water by radish seeds vary with temperature? What is the relationship between temperature and water uptake?

2. (a) Using the data for 35°C and 25°C, calculate $Q_{10}$ for water uptake by radish seeds. Repeat the calculation using the data for 25°C and 15°C and the data for 15°C and 5°C. (b) What is the average $Q_{10}$? (c) Do your results imply that the uptake of water by radish seeds is mainly a physical process or a chemical (metabolic) process? (d) Given that the $Q_{10}$ for the change in the viscosity of water is 1.2–1.3, could the slight temperature dependence of water uptake by seeds be a reflection of the slight temperature dependence of the viscosity of water?

3. Besides temperature, what other independent variables could you alter to test whether radish seed swelling is essentially a physical process or a chemical process?

4. Would you expect plant growth to have a $Q_{10}$ closer to 1 or 3? Why?

 **Instructors:** A version of this Scientific Skills Exercise can be assigned in MasteringBiology.

---

As you learn to apply the water potential equation, keep in mind the key point: *Water moves from regions of higher water potential to regions of lower water potential.*

### Water Movement Across Plant Cell Membranes

Now let's consider how water potential affects absorption and loss of water by a living plant cell. First, imagine a cell that is **flaccid** (limp) as a result of losing water. The cell has a $\Psi_P$ of 0 MPa. Suppose this flaccid cell is bathed in a solution of higher solute concentration (more negative solute potential) than the cell itself **(Figure 36.7a)**. Since the external solution has the lower (more negative) water potential, water diffuses out of the cell. The cell's protoplast undergoes **plasmolysis**—that is, it shrinks and pulls away from the cell wall. If we place the same flaccid cell in pure water ($\Psi = 0$ MPa) **(Figure 36.7b)**, the cell, because it contains solutes, has a lower water potential than the water, and water enters the cell by osmosis. The contents of the cell begin to swell and press the plasma membrane against the cell wall. The partially elastic wall, exerting turgor pressure, confines the pressurized protoplast. When this pressure is enough to offset the tendency for water to enter because of the solutes in the cell, then $\Psi_P$ and $\Psi_S$ are equal, and $\Psi = 0$. This matches the water potential of the extracellular environment— in this example, 0 MPa. A dynamic equilibrium has been reached, and there is no further *net* movement of water.

Turgid

Wilted

In contrast to a flaccid cell, a walled cell with a greater solute concentration than its surroundings is **turgid**, or very firm. When turgid cells in a nonwoody tissue push against each other, the tissue is stiffened. The effects of turgor loss are seen during **wilting**, when leaves and stems droop as a result of cells losing water.

### Aquaporins: Facilitating Diffusion of Water

A difference in water potential determines the *direction* of water movement across membranes, but how do water molecules actually cross the membranes? Water molecules are small enough to diffuse across the phospholipid bilayer, even though the bilayer's interior is hydrophobic. However, their movement across biological membranes is too rapid to be explained by unaided diffusion. Transport proteins called

In these experiments, flaccid cells (cells in which the protoplast contacts the cell wall but lacks turgor pressure) are placed in two environments. The blue arrows indicate initial net water movement.

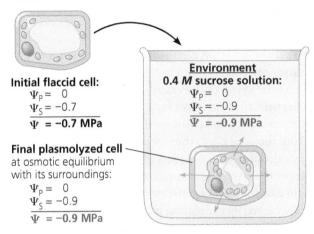

**Initial flaccid cell:**
$\Psi_P = 0$
$\Psi_S = -0.7$
$\overline{\Psi = -0.7 \text{ MPa}}$

**Environment**
**0.4 *M* sucrose solution:**
$\Psi_P = 0$
$\Psi_S = -0.9$
$\overline{\Psi = -0.9 \text{ MPa}}$

**Final plasmolyzed cell**
at osmotic equilibrium
with its surroundings:
$\Psi_P = 0$
$\Psi_S = -0.9$
$\overline{\Psi = -0.9 \text{ MPa}}$

**(a) Initial conditions: cellular $\Psi$ > environmental $\Psi$.** The protoplast loses water, and the cell plasmolyzes. After plasmolysis is complete, the water potentials of the cell and its surroundings are the same.

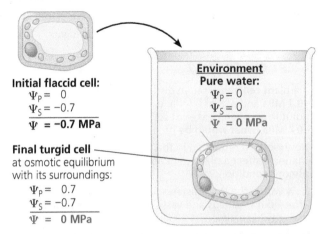

**Initial flaccid cell:**
$\Psi_P = 0$
$\Psi_S = -0.7$
$\overline{\Psi = -0.7 \text{ MPa}}$

**Environment**
**Pure water:**
$\Psi_P = 0$
$\Psi_S = 0$
$\overline{\Psi = 0 \text{ MPa}}$

**Final turgid cell**
at osmotic equilibrium
with its surroundings:
$\Psi_P = 0.7$
$\Psi_S = -0.7$
$\overline{\Psi = 0 \text{ MPa}}$

**(b) Initial conditions: cellular $\Psi$ < environmental $\Psi$.** There is a net uptake of water by osmosis, causing the cell to become turgid. When this tendency for water to enter is offset by the back pressure of the elastic wall, water potentials are equal for the cell and its surroundings. (The volume change of the cell is exaggerated in this diagram.)

(MB) Video: Plasmolysis

**aquaporins** (see Figure 7.1 and Concept 7.2) facilitate the transport of water molecules across plant cell plasma membranes. Aquaporin channels, which can open and close, affect the *rate* at which water moves osmotically across the membrane. Their permeability is decreased by increases in cytosolic $Ca^{2+}$ or decreases in cytosolic pH.

## Long-Distance Transport: The Role of Bulk Flow

Diffusion is an effective transport mechanism over the spatial scales typically found at the cellular level. However, diffusion is much too slow to function in long-distance transport within a plant. Although diffusion from one end of a cell to the other takes just seconds, diffusion from the roots to the top of a giant redwood would take several centuries. Instead, long-distance transport occurs through **bulk flow**, the movement of liquid in response to a pressure gradient. The bulk flow of material always occurs from higher to lower pressure. Unlike osmosis, bulk flow is independent of solute concentration.

Long-distance bulk flow occurs within specialized cells in the vascular tissue, namely, the tracheids and vessel elements of the xylem and the sieve-tube elements of the phloem. In leaves, the branching of veins ensures that no cell is more than a few cells away from the vascular tissue **(Figure 36.8)**.

The structures of the conducting cells of the xylem and phloem facilitate bulk flow. Mature tracheids and vessel elements are dead cells and therefore have no cytoplasm, and the cytoplasm of sieve-tube elements (also called sieve-tube members) is almost devoid of organelles (see Figure 35.10). If you have dealt with a partially clogged drain, you know that

the volume of flow depends on the pipe's diameter. Clogs reduce the effective diameter of the drainpipe. Such experiences help us understand how the structures of plant cells specialized for bulk flow fit their function. Like unclogging a drain, the absence or reduction of cytoplasm in a plant's "plumbing" facilitates bulk flow through the xylem and phloem. Bulk flow is also enhanced by the perforation plates at the ends of vessel elements and the porous sieve plates connecting sieve-tube elements.

Diffusion, active transport, and bulk flow act in concert to transport resources throughout the whole plant. For example, bulk flow due to a pressure difference is the mechanism of

▼ **Figure 36.8 Venation in an aspen leaf.** The finer and finer branching of leaf veins in eudicot leaves ensures that no leaf cell is far removed from the vascular system.

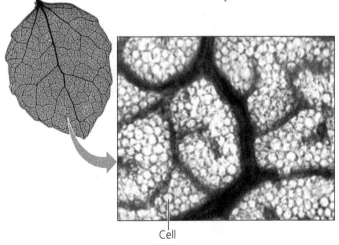

Cell

**VISUAL SKILLS** ➤ *In this leaf, what is the maximum number of cells any mesophyll cell is from a vein?*

long-distance transport of sugars in the phloem, but active transport of sugar at the cellular level maintains this pressure difference. In the next three sections, we'll examine in more detail the transport of water and minerals from roots to shoots, the control of evaporation, and the transport of sugars.

# CONCEPT 36.3

## Transpiration drives the transport of water and minerals from roots to shoots via the xylem

Picture yourself struggling to carry a 19-liter (5-gallon) container of water weighing 19 kilograms (42 pounds) up several flights of stairs. Imagine doing this 40 times a day. Then consider the fact that an average-sized tree, despite having neither heart nor muscle, transports a similar volume of water effortlessly on a daily basis. How do trees accomplish this feat? To answer this question, we'll follow each step in the journey of water and minerals from roots to leaves.

## Absorption of Water and Minerals by Root Cells

Although all living plant cells absorb nutrients across their plasma membranes, the cells near the tips of roots are particularly important because most of the absorption of water and minerals occurs there. In this region, the epidermal cells are permeable to water, and many are differentiated into root hairs, modified cells that account for much of the absorption of water by roots (see Figure 35.3). The root hairs absorb the soil solution, which consists of water molecules and dissolved mineral ions that are not bound tightly to soil particles. The soil solution is drawn into the hydrophilic walls of epidermal cells and passes freely along the cell walls and the extracellular spaces into the root cortex. This flow enhances the exposure of the cells of the cortex to the soil solution, providing a much greater membrane surface area for absorption than the surface area of the epidermis alone. Although the soil solution usually has a low mineral concentration, active transport enables roots to accumulate essential minerals, such as K⁺, to concentrations hundreds of times greater than in the soil.

## Transport of Water and Minerals into the Xylem

Water and minerals that pass from the soil into the root cortex cannot be transported to the rest of the plant until they enter the xylem of the vascular cylinder, or stele. The **endodermis**, the innermost layer of cells in the root cortex, functions as a last checkpoint for the selective passage of minerals from the cortex into the vascular cylinder **(Figure 36.9)**. Minerals already in the symplast when they reach the endodermis continue through the plasmodesmata of endodermal cells and pass into the vascular cylinder. These minerals were already screened by the plasma membrane they had to cross to enter the symplast in the epidermis or cortex.

Minerals that reach the endodermis via the apoplast encounter a dead end that blocks their passage into the vascular cylinder. This barrier, located in the transverse and radial walls of each endodermal cell, is the **Casparian strip**, a belt made of suberin, a waxy material impervious to water and dissolved minerals (see Figure 36.9). Because of the Casparian strip, water and minerals cannot cross the endodermis and enter the vascular cylinder via the apoplast. Instead, water and minerals that are passively moving through the apoplast must cross the *selectively permeable* plasma membrane of an endodermal cell before they can enter the vascular cylinder. In this way, the endodermis transports needed minerals from the soil into the xylem and keeps many unneeded or toxic substances out. The endodermis also prevents solutes that have accumulated in the xylem from leaking back into the soil solution.

The last segment in the soil-to-xylem pathway is the passage of water and minerals into the tracheids and vessel elements of the xylem. These water-conducting cells lack protoplasts when mature and are therefore parts of the apoplast. Endodermal cells, as well as living cells within the vascular cylinder, discharge minerals from their protoplasts into their own cell walls. Both diffusion and active transport are involved in this transfer of solutes from the symplast to the apoplast, and the water and minerals can now enter the tracheids and vessel elements, where they are transported to the shoot system by bulk flow.

## Bulk Flow Transport via the Xylem

Water and minerals from the soil enter the plant through the epidermis of roots, cross the root cortex, and pass into the vascular cylinder. From there the **xylem sap**, the water and dissolved minerals in the xylem, is transported long distances by bulk flow to the veins that branch throughout each leaf. As noted earlier, bulk flow is much faster than diffusion or active transport. Peak velocities in the transport of xylem sap can range from 15 to 45 m/hr for trees with wide vessel elements. The stems and leaves depend on this rapid delivery system for their supply of water and minerals.

## ▼ Figure 36.9 Transport of water and minerals from root hairs to the xylem.

**VISUAL SKILLS ▶** *After studying the figure, explain how the Casparian strip forces water and minerals to pass through the plasma membranes of endodermal cells.*

**Figure Walkthrough**
**BioFlix® Animation: Water Transport from Soil into Roots**

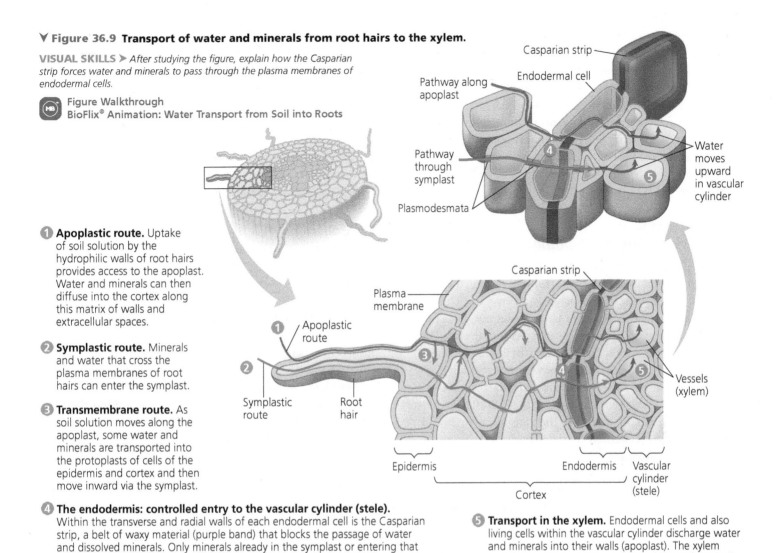

**❶ Apoplastic route.** Uptake of soil solution by the hydrophilic walls of root hairs provides access to the apoplast. Water and minerals can then diffuse into the cortex along this matrix of walls and extracellular spaces.

**❷ Symplastic route.** Minerals and water that cross the plasma membranes of root hairs can enter the symplast.

**❸ Transmembrane route.** As soil solution moves along the apoplast, some water and minerals are transported into the protoplasts of cells of the epidermis and cortex and then move inward via the symplast.

**❹ The endodermis: controlled entry to the vascular cylinder (stele).** Within the transverse and radial walls of each endodermal cell is the Casparian strip, a belt of waxy material (purple band) that blocks the passage of water and dissolved minerals. Only minerals already in the symplast or entering that pathway by crossing the plasma membrane of an endodermal cell can detour around the Casparian strip and pass into the vascular cylinder (stele).

**❺ Transport in the xylem.** Endodermal cells and also living cells within the vascular cylinder discharge water and minerals into their walls (apoplast). The xylem vessels then transport the water and minerals by bulk flow upward into the shoot system.

---

The process of transporting xylem sap involves the loss of an astonishing amount of water by **transpiration**, the loss of water vapor from leaves and other aerial parts of the plant. A single maize plant, for example, transpires 60 L of water (the equivalent of 170 12-ounce bottles) during a growing season. A maize crop growing at a typical density of 60,000 plants per hectare transpires almost 4 million L of water per hectare (about 400,000 gallons of water per acre) every growing season. If the transpired water is not replaced by water transported up from the roots, the leaves will wilt, and the plants will eventually die.

Xylem sap rises to heights of more than 120 m in the tallest trees. Is the sap mainly *pushed* upward from the roots, or is it mainly *pulled* upward? Let's evaluate the relative contributions of these two mechanisms.

### Pushing Xylem Sap: Root Pressure

At night, when there is almost no transpiration, root cells continue actively pumping mineral ions into the xylem of the vascular cylinder. Meanwhile, the Casparian strip of the endodermis prevents the ions from leaking back out into the cortex and soil. The resulting accumulation of minerals lowers the water potential within the vascular cylinder. Water flows in from the root cortex, generating **root pressure**, a push of xylem sap. The root pressure sometimes causes more water to enter the leaves than is transpired, resulting in **guttation**, the exudation of water droplets that can be seen in the morning on the tips or edges of some plant leaves (**Figure 36.10**). Guttation fluid should not be confused with dew, which is condensed atmospheric moisture.

**▶ Figure 36.10**
**Guttation.** Root pressure is forcing excess water from this strawberry leaf.

In most plants, root pressure is a minor mechanism driving the ascent of xylem sap, pushing water only a few meters at most. The positive pressures produced are simply too weak to overcome the gravitational force of the water column in the xylem, particularly in tall plants. Many plants do not generate any root pressure or do so only during part of the growing season. Even in plants that display guttation, root pressure cannot keep pace with transpiration after sunrise. For the most part, xylem sap is not pushed from below by root pressure but is pulled up.

## Pulling Xylem Sap: The Cohesion-Tension Hypothesis

As we have seen, root pressure, which depends on the active transport of solutes by plants, is only a minor force in the ascent of xylem sap. Far from depending on the metabolic activity of cells, most of the xylem sap that rises through a tree does not even require living cells to do so. As demonstrated by Eduard Strasburger in 1891, leafy stems with their lower end immersed in toxic solutions of copper sulfate or acid will readily draw these poisons up if the stem is cut below the surface of the liquid. As the toxic solutions ascend, they kill all living cells in their path, eventually arriving in the transpiring leaves and killing the leaf cells as well. Nevertheless, as Strasburger noted, the uptake of the toxic solutions and the loss of water from the dead leaves can continue for weeks.

In 1894, a few years after Strasburger's findings, two Irish scientists, John Joly and Henry Dixon, put forward a hypothesis that remains the leading explanation of the ascent of xylem sap. According to their **cohesion-tension hypothesis**, transpiration provides the pull for the ascent of xylem sap, and the cohesion of water molecules transmits this pull along the entire length of the xylem from shoots to roots. Hence, xylem sap is normally under negative pressure, or tension. Since transpiration is a "pulling" process, our exploration of the rise of xylem sap by the cohesion-tension mechanism begins not with the roots but with the leaves, where the driving force for transpirational pull begins.

**Transpirational Pull** Stomata on a leaf's surface lead to a maze of internal air spaces that expose the mesophyll cells to the $CO_2$ they need for photosynthesis. The air in these spaces is saturated with water vapor because it is in contact with the moist walls of the cells. On most days, the air outside the leaf is drier; that is, it has lower water potential than the air inside the leaf. Therefore, water vapor in the air spaces of a leaf diffuses down its water potential gradient and exits the leaf via the stomata. It is this loss of water vapor by diffusion and evaporation that we call transpiration.

But how does loss of water vapor from the leaf translate into a pulling force for upward movement of water through a plant? The negative pressure potential that causes water to move up through the xylem develops at the surface of mesophyll cell walls in the leaf (**Figure 36.11**). The cell wall acts like a very thin capillary network. Water adheres to the cellulose microfibrils and other hydrophilic components of the cell wall.

▼ **Figure 36.11 Generation of transpirational pull.** Negative pressure (tension) at the air-water interface in the leaf is the basis of transpirational pull, which draws water out of the xylem.

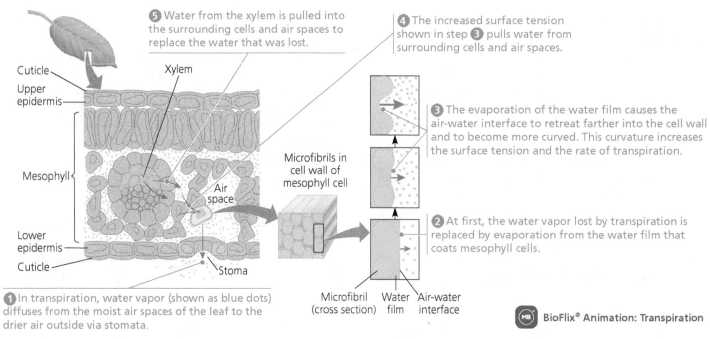

**5** Water from the xylem is pulled into the surrounding cells and air spaces to replace the water that was lost.

**4** The increased surface tension shown in step **3** pulls water from surrounding cells and air spaces.

**3** The evaporation of the water film causes the air-water interface to retreat farther into the cell wall and to become more curved. This curvature increases the surface tension and the rate of transpiration.

**2** At first, the water vapor lost by transpiration is replaced by evaporation from the water film that coats mesophyll cells.

**1** In transpiration, water vapor (shown as blue dots) diffuses from the moist air spaces of the leaf to the drier air outside via stomata.

Cuticle
Upper epidermis
Xylem
Mesophyll
Air space
Lower epidermis
Cuticle
Stoma
Microfibrils in cell wall of mesophyll cell
Microfibril (cross section)
Water film
Air-water interface

(MB) **BioFlix® Animation: Transpiration**

As water evaporates from the water film that covers the cell walls of mesophyll cells, the air-water interface retreats farther into the cell wall. Because of the high surface tension of water, the curvature of the interface induces a tension, or negative pressure potential, in the water. As more water evaporates from the cell wall, the curvature of the air-water interface increases and the pressure of the water becomes more negative. Water molecules from the more hydrated parts of the leaf are then pulled toward this area, reducing the tension. These pulling forces are transferred to the xylem because each water molecule is cohesively bound to the next by hydrogen bonds. Thus, transpirational pull depends on several of the properties of water discussed in Concept 3.2: adhesion, cohesion, and surface tension.

The role of negative pressure potential in transpiration is consistent with the water potential equation because negative pressure potential (tension) *lowers* water potential. Because water moves from areas of higher water potential to areas of lower water potential, the more negative pressure potential at the air-water interface causes water in xylem cells to be "pulled" into mesophyll cells, which lose water to the air spaces, the water diffusing out through stomata. In this way, the negative water potential of leaves provides the "pull" in transpirational pull. The transpirational pull on xylem sap is transmitted all the way from the leaves to the young roots and even into the soil solution (Figure 36.12).

## Cohesion and Adhesion in the Ascent of Xylem Sap

Cohesion and adhesion facilitate the transport of water by bulk flow. Cohesion is the attractive force between molecules of the same substance. Water has an unusually high cohesive force due to the hydrogen bonds each water molecule can potentially make with other water molecules. Water's cohesive force within the xylem gives it a tensile strength equivalent to that of a steel wire of similar diameter. The cohesion of water makes it possible to

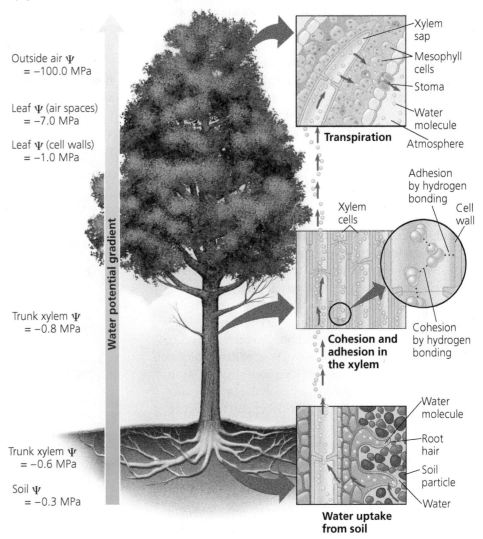

▼ **Figure 36.12 Ascent of xylem sap.** Hydrogen bonding forms an unbroken chain of water molecules extending from leaves to the soil. The force driving the ascent of xylem sap is a gradient of water potential (Ψ). For bulk flow over long distance, the Ψ gradient is due mainly to a gradient of the pressure potential ($Ψ_P$). Transpiration results in the $Ψ_P$ at the leaf end of the xylem being lower than the $Ψ_P$ at the root end. The Ψ values shown at the left are a "snapshot." They may vary during daylight, but the direction of the Ψ gradient remains the same.

Outside air Ψ = −100.0 MPa

Leaf Ψ (air spaces) = −7.0 MPa

Leaf Ψ (cell walls) = −1.0 MPa

Trunk xylem Ψ = −0.8 MPa

Trunk xylem Ψ = −0.6 MPa

Soil Ψ = −0.3 MPa

Water potential gradient

Xylem sap
Mesophyll cells
Stoma
Water molecule
Atmosphere
**Transpiration**

Adhesion by hydrogen bonding
Cell wall
Xylem cells
Cohesion by hydrogen bonding
**Cohesion and adhesion in the xylem**

Water molecule
Root hair
Soil particle
Water
**Water uptake from soil**

BioFlix® Animation: Transpiration-Cohesion-Tension Mechanism
Animation: Transport of Xylem Sap

pull a column of xylem sap from above without the water molecules separating. Water molecules exiting the xylem in the leaf tug on adjacent water molecules, and this pull is relayed, molecule by molecule, down the entire column of water in the xylem. Meanwhile, the strong adhesion of water molecules (again by hydrogen bonds) to the hydrophilic walls of xylem cells helps offset the downward force of gravity.

The upward pull on the sap creates tension within the vessel elements and tracheids, which are like elastic pipes. Positive pressure causes an elastic pipe to swell, whereas tension pulls the walls of the pipe inward. On a warm day, a decrease in the diameter of a tree trunk can even be measured.

As transpirational pull puts the vessel elements and tracheids under tension, their thick secondary walls prevent them from collapsing, much as wire rings maintain the shape of a vacuum-cleaner hose. The tension produced by transpirational pull lowers water potential in the root xylem to such an extent that water flows passively from the soil, across the root cortex, and into the vascular cylinder.

Transpirational pull can extend down to the roots only through an unbroken chain of water molecules. Cavitation, the formation of a water vapor pocket, breaks the chain. It is more common in wide vessel elements than in tracheids and can occur during drought stress or when xylem sap freezes in winter. The air bubbles resulting from cavitation expand and block water channels of the xylem. The rapid expansion of air bubbles produces clicking noises that can be heard by placing sensitive microphones at the surface of the stem.

The interruption of xylem sap transport by cavitation is not always permanent. The chain of water molecules can detour around the air bubbles through pits between adjacent tracheids or vessel elements (see Figure 35.10). Moreover, root pressure enables small plants to refill blocked vessel elements. Recent evidence suggests that cavitation may even be repaired when the xylem sap is under negative pressure, although the mechanism by which this occurs is uncertain. In addition, secondary growth adds a layer of new xylem each year. Only the youngest, outermost secondary xylem layers transport water. Although the older secondary xylem no longer transports water, it does provide support for the tree (see Figure 35.22).

Researchers have recently discovered that cavitation in trees can be avoided in some cases by transfer of water from the phloem to the xylem. Using a fluorescent dye as a proxy for water molecules, researchers concluded that water can move symplastically at significant rates from the xylem to the phloem and back again through parenchyma cells in vascular rays (see Figure 35.20). Water is more likely to travel from the xylem into the phloem at night, when more water is available. It is then temporarily stored in the phloem until the tree needs it, at which point it moves back to the xylem.

## Xylem Sap Ascent by Bulk Flow: *A Review*

The cohesion-tension mechanism that transports xylem sap against gravity is an excellent example of how physical principles apply to biological processes. In the long-distance transport of water from roots to leaves by bulk flow, the movement of fluid is driven by a water potential difference at opposite ends of xylem tissue. The water potential difference is created at the leaf end of the xylem by the evaporation of water from leaf cells. Evaporation lowers the water potential at the air-water interface, thereby generating the negative pressure (tension) that pulls water through the xylem.

Bulk flow in the xylem differs from diffusion in some key ways. First, it is driven by differences in pressure potential ($\psi_P$); solute potential ($\psi_S$) is not a factor. Therefore, the water potential gradient within the xylem is essentially a pressure gradient. Also, the flow does not occur across plasma membranes of living cells, but instead within hollow, dead cells. Furthermore, it moves the entire solution together—not just water or solutes—and at much greater speed than diffusion.

The plant expends no energy to lift xylem sap by bulk flow. Instead, the absorption of sunlight drives most of transpiration by causing water to evaporate from the moist walls of mesophyll cells and by lowering the water potential in the air spaces within a leaf. Thus, the ascent of xylem sap, like the process of photosynthesis, is ultimately solar powered.

 BioFlix® Animation: Water Transport in Plants

### CONCEPT CHECK 36.3

1. A horticulturalist notices that when *Zinnia* flowers are cut at dawn, a small drop of water collects at the surface of the rooted stump. However, when the flowers are cut at noon, no drop is observed. Suggest an explanation.

2. **WHAT IF?** ➤ Suppose an *Arabidopsis* mutant lacking functional aquaporin proteins has a root mass three times greater than that of wild-type plants. Suggest an explanation.

3. **MAKE CONNECTIONS** ➤ How are the Casparian strip and tight junctions similar (see Figure 6.30)?

*For suggested answers, see Appendix A.*

## CONCEPT 36.4

# The rate of transpiration is regulated by stomata

Leaves generally have large surface areas and high surface-to-volume ratios. The large surface area enhances light absorption for photosynthesis. The high surface-to-volume ratio aids in $CO_2$ absorption during photosynthesis as well as in the release of $O_2$, a by-product of photosynthesis. Upon diffusing through the stomata, $CO_2$ enters a honeycomb of air spaces formed by the spongy mesophyll cells (see Figure 35.18). Because of the irregular shapes of these cells, the leaf's internal surface area may be 10 to 30 times greater than the external surface area.

Although large surface areas and high surface-to-volume ratios increase the rate of photosynthesis, they also increase water loss by way of the stomata. Thus, a plant's tremendous requirement for water is largely a consequence of the shoot system's need for ample exchange of $CO_2$ and $O_2$ for photosynthesis. By opening and closing the stomata, guard cells help balance the plant's requirement to conserve water with its requirement for photosynthesis **(Figure 36.13)**.

**Figure 36.13 An open stoma (left) and closed stoma (SEMs).**

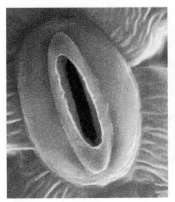 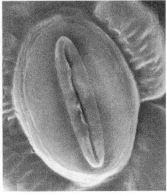

(MB) BioFlix® Animation: Water Transport from Roots to Leaves

## Stomata: Major Pathways for Water Loss

About 95% of the water a plant loses escapes through stomata, although these pores account for only 1–2% of the external leaf surface. The waxy cuticle limits water loss through the remaining surface of the leaf. Each stoma is flanked by a pair of guard cells. Guard cells control the diameter of the stoma by changing shape, thereby widening or narrowing the gap between the guard cell pair. Under the same environmental conditions, the amount of water lost by a leaf depends largely on the number of stomata and the average size of their pores.

The stomatal density of a leaf, which may be as high as 20,000 per square centimeter, is under both genetic and environmental control. For example, as a result of evolution by natural selection, desert plants are genetically programmed to have lower stomatal densities than do marsh plants. Stomatal density, however, is a developmentally plastic feature of many plants. High light exposures and low $CO_2$ levels during leaf development lead to increased density in many species. By measuring the stomatal density of leaf fossils, scientists have gained insight into the levels of atmospheric $CO_2$ in past climates. A recent British survey found that stomatal density of many woodland species has decreased since 1927, when a similar survey was made. This observation is consistent with other findings that atmospheric $CO_2$ levels increased dramatically during the late 20th century.

## Mechanisms of Stomatal Opening and Closing

When guard cells take in water from neighboring cells by osmosis, they become more turgid. In most angiosperm species, the cell walls of guard cells are uneven in thickness, and the cellulose microfibrils are oriented in a direction that causes the guard cells to bow outward when turgid (Figure 36.14a). This bowing outward increases the size of the pore between the

guard cells. When the cells lose water and become flaccid, they become less bowed, and the pore closes.

The changes in turgor pressure in guard cells result primarily from the reversible absorption and loss of $K^+$. Stomata open when guard cells actively accumulate $K^+$ from neighboring epidermal cells (Figure 36.14b). The flow of $K^+$ across the plasma membrane of the guard cell is coupled to the generation of a membrane potential by proton pumps (see Figure 36.6a). Stomatal opening correlates with active transport of $H^+$ out of the guard cell. The resulting voltage (membrane potential) drives $K^+$ into the cell through specific membrane channels. The absorption of $K^+$ causes the water potential to become more negative within the guard cells, and the cells become more turgid as water enters by osmosis. Because most of the $K^+$ and water are stored in the vacuole, the vacuolar membrane also plays a role in regulating guard cell dynamics. Stomatal closing results from a loss of $K^+$ from guard cells to neighboring

▼ **Figure 36.14 Mechanisms of stomatal opening and closing.**

**Guard cells turgid/Stoma open**     **Guard cells flaccid/Stoma closed**

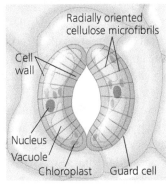 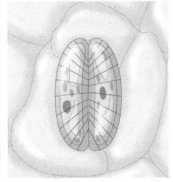

**(a) Changes in guard cell shape and stomatal opening and closing (surface view).** Guard cells of a typical angiosperm are illustrated in their turgid (stoma open) and flaccid (stoma closed) states. The radial orientation of cellulose microfibrils in the cell walls causes the guard cells to increase more in length than width when turgor increases. Since the two guard cells are tightly joined at their tips, they bow outward when turgid, causing the stomatal pore to open.

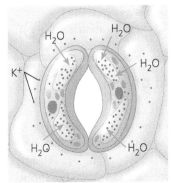 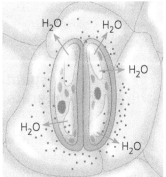

**(b) Role of potassium ions ($K^+$) in stomatal opening and closing.** The transport of $K^+$ (symbolized here as red dots) across the plasma membrane and vacuolar membrane causes the turgor changes of guard cells. The uptake of anions, such as malate and chloride ions (not shown), also contributes to guard cell swelling.

cells, which leads to an osmotic loss of water. Aquaporins also help regulate the osmotic swelling and shrinking of guard cells.

## Stimuli for Stomatal Opening and Closing

In general, stomata are open during the day and mostly closed at night, preventing the plant from losing water under conditions when photosynthesis cannot occur. At least three cues contribute to stomatal opening at dawn: light, $CO_2$ depletion, and an internal "clock" in guard cells.

Light stimulates guard cells to accumulate $K^+$ and become turgid. This response is triggered by illumination of blue-light receptors in the plasma membrane of guard cells. Activation of these receptors stimulates the activity of proton pumps in the plasma membrane of the guard cells, in turn promoting absorption of $K^+$.

Stomata also open in response to depletion of $CO_2$ within the leaf's air spaces as a result of photosynthesis. As $CO_2$ concentrations decrease during the day, the stomata progressively open if sufficient water is supplied to the leaf.

An internal "clock" in the guard cells ensures that stomata continue their daily rhythm of opening and closing. This rhythm occurs even if a plant is kept in a dark location. All eukaryotic organisms have internal clocks that regulate cyclic processes. Cycles with intervals of approximately 24 hours are called **circadian rhythms** (which you'll learn more about in Concept 39.3).

Drought stress can also cause stomata to close. A hormone called **abscisic acid (ABA),** which is produced in roots and leaves in response to water deficiency, signals guard cells to close stomata. This response reduces wilting but also restricts $CO_2$ absorption, thereby slowing photosynthesis. ABA also directly inhibits photosynthesis. Water availability is closely tied to plant productivity not because water is needed as a substrate in photosynthesis, but because freely available water allows plants to keep stomata open and take up more $CO_2$.

Guard cells control the photosynthesis-transpiration compromise on a moment-to-moment basis by integrating a variety of internal and external stimuli. Even the passage of a cloud or a transient shaft of sunlight through a forest can affect the rate of transpiration.

## Effects of Transpiration on Wilting and Leaf Temperature

As long as most stomata remain open, transpiration is greatest on a day that is sunny, warm, dry, and windy because these environmental factors increase evaporation. If transpiration cannot pull sufficient water to the leaves, the shoot becomes slightly wilted as cells lose turgor pressure. Although plants respond to such mild drought stress by rapidly closing stomata, some evaporative water loss still occurs through the cuticle. Under prolonged drought conditions, leaves can become severely wilted and irreversibly injured.

Transpiration also results in evaporative cooling, which can lower a leaf's temperature by as much as 10°C compared with the surrounding air. This cooling prevents the leaf from reaching temperatures that could denature enzymes involved in photosynthesis and other metabolic processes.

## Adaptations That Reduce Evaporative Water Loss

Water availability is a major determinant of plant productivity. The main reason water availability is tied to plant productivity is not related to photosynthesis's direct need for water as a substrate but rather because freely available water allows plants to keep stomata open and take up more $CO_2$. The problem of reducing water loss is especially acute for desert plants. Plants adapted to arid environments are called **xerophytes** (from the Greek *xero*, dry).

Many species of desert plants avoid drying out by completing their short life cycles during the brief rainy seasons. Rain comes infrequently in deserts, but when it arrives, the vegetation is transformed as dormant seeds of annual species quickly germinate and bloom, completing their life cycle before dry conditions return.

Other xerophytes have unusual physiological or morphological adaptations that enable them to withstand harsh desert conditions. The stems of many xerophytes are fleshy because they store water for use during long dry periods. Cacti have highly reduced leaves that resist excessive water loss; photosynthesis is carried out mainly in their stems. Another adaptation common in arid habitats is crassulacean acid metabolism (CAM), a specialized form of photosynthesis found in succulents of the family Crassulaceae and several other families (see Figure 10.21). Because the leaves of CAM plants take in $CO_2$ at night, the stomata can remain closed during the day, when evaporative stresses are greatest. Other examples of xerophytic adaptations are discussed in **Figure 36.15**.

 MP3 Tutor: Transpiration

### CONCEPT CHECK 36.4

1. What are the stimuli that control the opening and closing of stomata?
2. The pathogenic fungus *Fusicoccum amygdali* secretes a toxin called fusicoccin that activates the plasma membrane proton pumps of plant cells and leads to uncontrolled water loss. Suggest a mechanism by which the activation of proton pumps could lead to severe wilting.
3. **WHAT IF?** ➤ If you buy cut flowers, why might the florist recommend cutting the stems underwater and then transferring the flowers to a vase while the cut ends are still wet?
4. **MAKE CONNECTIONS** ➤ Explain why the evaporation of water from leaves lowers their temperature (see Concept 3.2).

*For suggested answers, see Appendix A.*

▼ **Figure 36.15 Some xerophytic adaptations.**

► Ocotillo (*Fouquieria splendens*) is common in the southwestern region of the United States and northern Mexico. It is leafless during most of the year, thereby avoiding excessive water loss (right). Immediately after a heavy rainfall, it produces small leaves (below and inset). As the soil dries, the leaves quickly shrivel and die.

▼ Oleander (*Nerium oleander*), shown in the inset, is commonly found in arid climates. Its leaves have a thick cuticle and multiple-layered epidermal tissue that reduce water loss. Stomata are recessed in cavities called "crypts," an adaptation that reduces the rate of transpiration by protecting the stomata from hot, dry wind. Trichomes help minimize transpiration by breaking up the flow of air, allowing the chamber of the crypt to have a higher humidity than the surrounding atmosphere (LM).

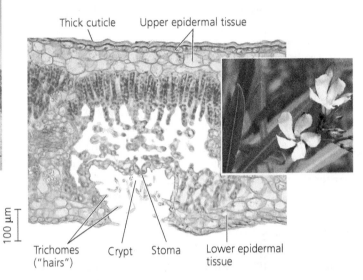

Thick cuticle      Upper epidermal tissue

100 μm

Trichomes ("hairs")      Crypt      Stoma      Lower epidermal tissue

► The long, white hairlike bristles along the stem of the old man cactus (*Cephalocereus senilis*) help reflect the intense sunlight of the Mexican desert.

# CONCEPT 36.5

## Sugars are transported from sources to sinks via the phloem

The unidirectional flow of water and minerals from soil to roots to leaves through the xylem is largely in an upward direction. In contrast, the movement of photosynthates often runs in the opposite direction, transporting sugars from mature leaves to lower parts of the plant, such as root tips that require large amounts of sugars for energy and growth. The transport of the products of photosynthesis, known as **translocation**, is carried out by another tissue, the phloem.

## Movement from Sugar Sources to Sugar Sinks

Sieve-tube elements are specialized cells in angiosperms that serve as conduits for translocation. Arranged end to end, they form long sieve tubes (see Figure 35.10). Between these cells are sieve plates, structures that allow the flow of sap along the sieve tube. **Phloem sap**, the aqueous solution that flows through sieve tubes, differs markedly from the xylem sap that is transported by tracheids and vessel elements. By far the most prevalent solute in phloem sap is sugar, typically sucrose in most species. The sucrose concentration may be as high as 30% by weight, giving the sap a syrupy thickness. Phloem sap may also contain amino acids, hormones, and minerals.

In contrast to the unidirectional transport of xylem sap from roots to leaves, phloem sap moves from sites of sugar production to sites of sugar use or storage (see Figure 36.2). A **sugar source** is a plant organ that is a net producer of sugar, by photosynthesis or by breakdown of starch. In contrast, a **sugar sink** is an organ that is a net consumer or depository of sugar. Growing roots, buds, stems, and fruits are sugar sinks. Although expanding leaves are sugar sinks, mature leaves, if well illuminated, are sugar sources. A storage organ, such as a tuber or a bulb, may be a source or a sink, depending on the season. When stockpiling carbohydrates in the summer, it is a sugar sink. After breaking dormancy in the spring, it is a sugar source because its starch is broken down to sugar, which is carried to the growing shoot tips.

Sinks usually receive sugar from the nearest sugar sources. The upper leaves on a branch, for example, may export sugar to the growing shoot tip, whereas the lower leaves may export sugar to the roots. A growing fruit may monopolize the sugar sources that surround it. For each sieve tube, the direction of transport depends on the locations of the sugar source and sugar sink that are connected by that tube. Therefore, neighboring sieve tubes may carry sap in opposite directions if they originate and end in different locations.

Sugar must be transported, or loaded, into sieve-tube elements before being exported to sugar sinks. In some species, it moves from mesophyll cells to sieve-tube elements via the symplast, passing through plasmodesmata. In other species, it moves by symplastic and apoplastic pathways. In maize leaves, for example, sucrose diffuses through the symplast from photosynthetic mesophyll cells into small veins. Much of it then moves into the apoplast and is accumulated by nearby sieve-tube elements, either directly or, as shown in **Figure 36.16a**,

through companion cells. In some plants, the walls of the companion cells feature many ingrowths, enhancing solute transfer between apoplast and symplast.

In many plants, sugar movement into the phloem requires active transport because sucrose is more concentrated in sieve-tube elements and companion cells than in mesophyll. Proton pumping and H⁺/sucrose cotransport enable sucrose to move from mesophyll cells to sieve-tube elements or companion cells **(Figure 36.16b)**.

Sucrose is unloaded at the sink end of a sieve tube. The process varies by species and organ. However, the concentration of free sugar in the sink is always lower than in the sieve tube because the unloaded sugar is consumed during growth and metabolism of the cells of the sink or converted to insoluble polymers such as starch. As a result of this sugar concentration gradient, sugar molecules diffuse from the phloem into the sink tissues, and water follows by osmosis.

## Bulk Flow by Positive Pressure: The Mechanism of Translocation in Angiosperms

Phloem sap flows from source to sink at rates as great as 1 m/hr, much faster than diffusion or cytoplasmic streaming. Researchers have concluded that phloem sap moves through the sieve tubes of angiosperms by bulk flow driven by positive pressure, known as *pressure flow* **(Figure 36.17)**. The building of pressure at the source and reduction of that pressure at the sink cause sap to flow from source to sink.

The pressure-flow hypothesis explains why phloem sap flows from source to sink, and experiments build a strong case for pressure flow as the mechanism of translocation in

▼ **Figure 36.16 Loading of sucrose into phloem.**

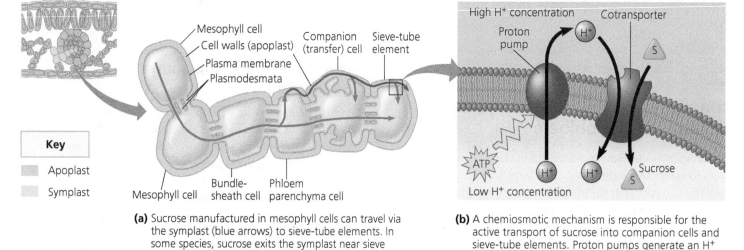

**(a)** Sucrose manufactured in mesophyll cells can travel via the symplast (blue arrows) to sieve-tube elements. In some species, sucrose exits the symplast near sieve tubes and travels through the apoplast (red arrow). It is then actively accumulated from the apoplast by sieve-tube elements and their companion cells.

**(b)** A chemiosmotic mechanism is responsible for the active transport of sucrose into companion cells and sieve-tube elements. Proton pumps generate an H⁺ gradient, which drives sucrose accumulation with the help of a cotransport protein that couples sucrose transport to the diffusion of H⁺ back into the cell.

▼ **Figure 36.17 Bulk flow by positive pressure (pressure flow) in a sieve tube.**

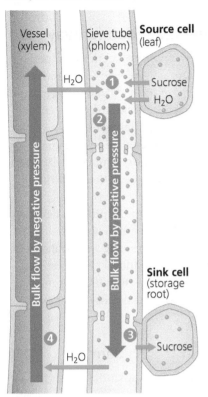

Vessel (xylem) | Sieve tube (phloem) | **Source cell** (leaf)

Bulk flow by negative pressure

Bulk flow by positive pressure

H₂O

Sucrose

H₂O

**Sink cell** (storage root)

Sucrose

H₂O

**1** Loading of sugar (green dots) into the sieve tube at the source (in this example, a mesophyll cell in a leaf) reduces water potential inside the sieve-tube elements. This causes the tube to take up water by osmosis.

**2** This uptake of water generates a positive pressure that forces the sap to flow along the tube.

**3** The pressure is relieved by the unloading of sugar and the consequent loss of water at the sink.

**4** In leaf-to-root translocation, xylem recycles water from sink to source.

 **Animation: Phloem Transport**

angiosperms (**Figure 36.18**). However, studies using electron microscopes suggest that in nonflowering vascular plants, the pores between phloem cells may be too small or obstructed to permit pressure flow.

Sinks vary in energy demands and capacity to unload sugars. Sometimes there are more sinks than can be supported by sources. In such cases, a plant might abort some flowers, seeds, or fruits—a phenomenon called *self-thinning*. Removing sinks can also be a horticulturally useful practice. For example, since large apples command a much better price than small ones, growers sometimes remove flowers or young fruits so that their trees produce fewer but larger apples.

**CONCEPT CHECK 36.5**

1. Compare and contrast the forces that move phloem sap and xylem sap over long distances.
2. Identify plant organs that are sugar sources, organs that are sugar sinks, and organs that might be either. Explain.
3. Why can xylem transport water and minerals using dead cells, whereas phloem requires living cells?
4. **WHAT IF?** ➤ Apple growers in Japan sometimes make a nonlethal spiral slash around the bark of trees that are destined for removal after the growing season. This practice makes the apples sweeter. Why?

*For suggested answers, see Appendix A.*

▼ **Figure 36.18**

**Inquiry** Does phloem sap contain more sugar near sources than near sinks?

**Experiment** The pressure-flow hypothesis predicts that phloem sap near sources should have a higher sugar content than phloem sap near sinks. To test this idea, researchers used aphids that feed on phloem sap. An aphid probes with a hypodermic-like mouthpart called a stylet that penetrates a sieve-tube element. As sieve-tube pressure forced out phloem sap into the stylets, the researchers separated the aphids from the stylets, which then acted as taps exuding sap for hours. Researchers measured the sugar concentration of sap from stylets at different points between a source and sink.

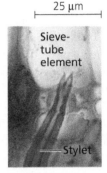

25 μm

Sieve-tube element

Stylet

Sap droplet

Sap droplet

Aphid feeding | Stylet in sieve-tube element | Separated stylet exuding sap

**Results** The closer the stylet was to a sugar source, the higher its sugar concentration was.

**Conclusion** The results of such experiments support the pressure-flow hypothesis, which predicts that sugar concentrations should be higher in sieve tubes closer to sugar sources.

**Data from** S. Rogers and A. J. Peel, Some evidence for the existence of turgor pressure in the sieve tubes of willow (*Salix*), *Planta* 126:259–267 (1975).

**WHAT IF?** ➤ *Spittlebugs (Clasirptora sp.) are xylem sap feeders that use strong muscles to pump xylem sap through their guts. Could you isolate xylem sap from the excised stylets of spittlebugs?*

# CONCEPT 36.6

## The symplast is highly dynamic

Although we have been discussing transport in mostly physical terms, almost like the flow of solutions through pipes, plant transport is a dynamic and finely tuned process that changes during development. A leaf, for example, may begin as a sugar sink but spend most of its life as a sugar source. Also, environmental changes may trigger responses in plant transport processes. Water stress may activate signal transduction pathways that greatly alter the membrane transport proteins governing the overall transport of water and minerals. Because the symplast is living tissue, it is largely responsible for the dynamic changes in plant transport processes. We'll look now at some other examples: changes in plasmodesmata, chemical signaling, and electrical signaling.

## Changes in Plasmodesmatal Number and Pore Size

Based mostly on the static images provided by electron microscopy, biologists formerly considered plasmodesmata to be unchanging, pore-like structures. More recent studies, however, have revealed that plasmodesmata are highly dynamic. They can open or close rapidly in response to changes in turgor pressure, cytosolic $Ca^{2+}$ levels, or cytosolic pH. Although some plasmodesmata form during cytokinesis, they can also form much later. Moreover, loss of function is common during differentiation. For example, as a leaf matures from a sink to a source, its plasmodesmata either close or are eliminated, causing phloem unloading to cease.

Early studies by plant physiologists and pathologists came to differing conclusions regarding pore sizes of plasmodesmata. Physiologists injected fluorescent probes of different molecular sizes into cells and recorded whether the molecules passed into adjacent cells. Based on these observations, they concluded that the pore sizes were approximately 2.5 nm—too small for macromolecules such as proteins to pass. In contrast, pathologists provided electron micrographs showing evidence of the passage of virus particles with diameters of 10 nm or greater (Figure 36.19).

Subsequently, it was learned that plant viruses produce *viral movement proteins* that cause the plasmodesmata to dilate, enabling the viral RNA to pass between cells. More recent evidence shows that plant cells themselves regulate plasmodesmata as part of a communication network. The viruses can subvert this network by mimicking the cell's regulators of plasmodesmata.

A high degree of cytosolic interconnectedness exists only within certain groups of cells and tissues, which are known as *symplastic domains*. Informational molecules, such as proteins and RNAs, coordinate development between cells within each symplastic domain. If symplastic communication is disrupted, development can be grossly affected.

## Phloem: An Information Superhighway

In addition to transporting sugars, the phloem is a "superhighway" for the transport of macromolecules and viruses. This transport is systemic (throughout the body), affecting many or all of the plant's systems or organs. Macromolecules translocated through the phloem include proteins and various types of RNA that enter the sieve tubes through plasmodesmata. Although they are often likened to the gap junctions between animal cells, plasmodesmata are unique in their ability to traffic proteins and RNA.

Systemic communication through the phloem helps integrate the functions of the whole plant. One classic example is the delivery of a flower-inducing chemical signal from leaves to vegetative meristems. Another is a defensive response to localized infection, in which chemical signals traveling through the phloem activate defense genes in noninfected tissues.

## Electrical Signaling in the Phloem

Rapid, long-distance electrical signaling through the phloem is another dynamic feature of the symplast. Electrical signaling has been studied extensively in plants that have rapid leaf movements, such as the sensitive plant (*Mimosa pudica*) and Venus flytrap (*Dionaea muscipula*). However, its role in other species is less clear. Some studies have revealed that a stimulus in one part of a plant can trigger an electrical signal in the phloem that affects another part, where it may elicit a change in gene transcription, respiration, photosynthesis, phloem unloading, or hormonal levels. Thus, the phloem can serve a nerve-like function, allowing for swift electrical communication between widely separated organs.

The coordinated transport of materials and information is central to plant survival. Plants can acquire only so many resources in the course of their lifetimes. Ultimately, the successful acquisition of these resources and their optimal distribution are the most critical determinants of whether the plant will compete successfully.

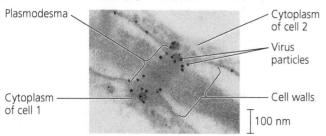

∨ **Figure 36.19 Virus particles moving cell to cell through plasmodesma connecting turnip leaf cells (TEM).**

Plasmodesma

Cytoplasm of cell 2

Virus particles

Cytoplasm of cell 1

Cell walls

100 nm

MB Interview with Patricia Zambryski: Exploring the dynamics of plasmodesmata

## CONCEPT CHECK 36.6

1. How do plasmodesmata differ from gap junctions?
2. Nerve-like signals in animals are thousands of times faster than their plant counterparts. Suggest a behavioral reason for the difference.
3. **WHAT IF?** ➤ Suppose plants were genetically modified to be unresponsive to viral movement proteins. Would this be a good way to prevent the spread of infection? Explain.

*For suggested answers, see Appendix A.*

# 36 Chapter Review

## SUMMARY OF KEY CONCEPTS

### CONCEPT 36.1

**Adaptations for acquiring resources were key steps in the evolution of vascular plants** (pp. 783–785)

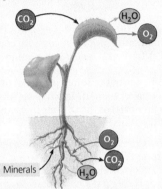

- Leaves typically function in gathering sunlight and $CO_2$. Stems serve as supporting structures for leaves and as conduits for the long-distance transport of water and nutrients. Roots mine the soil for water and minerals and anchor the whole plant.
- Natural selection has produced plant architectures that optimize resource acquisition in the ecological niche in which the plant species naturally exists.

**?** *How did the evolution of xylem and phloem contribute to the successful colonization of land by vascular plants?*

### CONCEPT 36.2

**Different mechanisms transport substances over short or long distances** (pp. 785–790)

- The selective permeability of the plasma membrane controls the movement of substances into and out of cells. Both active and passive transport mechanisms occur in plants.
- Plant tissues have two major compartments: the **apoplast** (everything outside the cells' plasma membranes) and the **symplast** (the cytosol and connecting plasmodesmata).
- Direction of water movement depends on the **water potential**, a quantity that incorporates solute concentration and physical pressure. The **osmotic** uptake of water by plant cells and the resulting internal pressure that builds up make plant cells **turgid**.
- Long-distance transport occurs through **bulk flow**, the movement of liquid in response to a pressure gradient. Bulk flow occurs within the tracheids and vessel elements of the **xylem** and within the sieve-tube elements of the **phloem**.

**?** *Is xylem sap usually pulled or pushed up the plant?*

### CONCEPT 36.3

**Transpiration drives the transport of water and minerals from roots to shoots via the xylem** (pp. 790–794)

- Water and minerals from the soil enter the plant through the epidermis of roots, cross the root cortex, and then pass into the vascular cylinder by way of the selectively permeable cells of the **endodermis**. From the vascular cylinder, the **xylem sap** is transported long distances by bulk flow to the veins that branch throughout each leaf.
- The **cohesion-tension hypothesis** proposes that the movement of xylem sap is driven by a water potential difference created at the leaf end of the xylem by the evaporation of water from leaf cells. Evaporation lowers the water potential at the air-water interface, thereby generating the negative pressure that pulls water through the xylem.

**?** *Why is the ability of water molecules to form hydrogen bonds important for the movement of xylem sap?*

### CONCEPT 36.4

**The rate of transpiration is regulated by stomata** (pp. 794–797)

- **Transpiration** is the loss of water vapor from plants. **Wilting** occurs when the water lost by transpiration is not replaced by absorption from roots. Plants respond to water deficits by closing their stomata. Under prolonged drought conditions, plants can become irreversibly injured.
- Stomata are the major pathway for water loss from plants. A stoma opens when guard cells bordering the stomatal pore take up $K^+$. The opening and closing of stomata are controlled by light, $CO_2$, the drought hormone **abscisic acid**, and a **circadian rhythm**.
- **Xerophytes** are plants that are adapted to arid environments. Reduced leaves and CAM photosynthesis are examples of adaptations to arid environments.

**?** *Why are stomata necessary?*

### CONCEPT 36.5

**Sugars are transported from sources to sinks via the phloem** (pp. 797–799)

- Mature leaves are the main **sugar sources**, although storage organs can be seasonal sources. Growing organs such as roots, stems, and fruits are the main **sugar sinks**. The direction of phloem transport is always from sugar source to sugar sink.
- Phloem loading depends on the active transport of sucrose. Sucrose is cotransported with $H^+$, which diffuses down a gradient generated by proton pumps. Loading of sugar at the source and unloading at the sink maintain a pressure difference that keeps **phloem sap** flowing through a sieve tube.

**?** *Why is phloem transport considered an active process?*

### CONCEPT 36.6

**The symplast is highly dynamic** (pp. 799–800)

- Plasmodesmata can change in permeability and number. When dilated, they provide a passageway for the symplastic transport of proteins, RNAs, and other macromolecules over long distances. The phloem also conducts nerve-like electrical signals that help integrate whole-plant function.

**?** *By what mechanisms is symplastic communication regulated?*

## TEST YOUR UNDERSTANDING

### Level 1: Knowledge/Comprehension

PRACTICE TEST
goo.gl/CUYGKD

1. Which of the following is an adaptation that enhances the uptake of water and minerals by roots?
   (A) mycorrhizae
   (B) pumping through plasmodesmata
   (C) active uptake by vessel elements
   (D) rhythmic contractions by cells in the root cortex

2. Which structure or compartment is part of the symplast?
   (A) the interior of a vessel element
   (B) the interior of a sieve tube
   (C) the cell wall of a mesophyll cell
   (D) an extracellular air space

3. Movement of phloem sap from a source to a sink
   (A) occurs through the apoplast of sieve-tube elements.
   (B) depends ultimately on the activity of proton pumps.
   (C) depends on tension, or negative pressure potential.
   (D) results mainly from diffusion.

### Level 2: Application/Analysis

4. Photosynthesis ceases when leaves wilt, mainly because
   (A) the chlorophyll in wilting leaves is degraded.
   (B) accumulation of $CO_2$ in the leaf inhibits enzymes.
   (C) stomata close, preventing $CO_2$ from entering the leaf.
   (D) photolysis, the water-splitting step of photosynthesis, cannot occur when there is a water deficiency.

5. What would enhance water uptake by a plant cell?
   (A) decreasing the $\Psi$ of the surrounding solution
   (B) positive pressure on the surrounding solution
   (C) the loss of solutes from the cell
   (D) increasing the $\Psi$ of the cytoplasm

6. A plant cell with a $\Psi_S$ of −0.65 MPa maintains a constant volume when bathed in a solution that has a $\Psi_S$ of −0.30 MPa and is in an open container. The cell has a
   (A) $\Psi_P$ of +0.65 MPa.
   (B) $\Psi$ of −0.65 MPa.
   (C) $\Psi_P$ of +0.35 MPa.
   (D) $\Psi_P$ of 0 MPa.

7. Compared with a cell with few aquaporin proteins in its membrane, a cell containing many aquaporin proteins will
   (A) have a faster rate of osmosis.
   (B) have a lower water potential.
   (C) have a higher water potential.
   (D) accumulate water by active transport.

8. Which of the following would tend to increase transpiration?
   (A) spiny leaves
   (B) sunken stomata
   (C) a thicker cuticle
   (D) higher stomatal density

### Level 3: Synthesis/Evaluation

9. EVOLUTION CONNECTION Large brown algae called kelps can grow as tall as 25 m. Kelps consist of a holdfast anchored to the ocean floor, blades that float at the surface and collect light, and a long stalk connecting the blades to the holdfast (see Figure 28.12). Specialized cells in the stalk, although nonvascular, can transport sugar. Suggest a reason why these structures analogous to sieve-tube elements might have evolved in kelps.

10. SCIENTIFIC INQUIRY • INTERPRET THE DATA A Minnesota gardener notes that the plants immediately bordering a walkway are stunted compared with those farther away. Suspecting that the soil near the walkway may be contaminated from salt added to the walkway in winter, the gardener tests the soil. The composition of the soil near the walkway is identical to that farther away except that it contains an additional 50 mM NaCl. Assuming that the NaCl is completely ionized, calculate how much it will lower the solute potential of the soil at 20°C using the *solute potential equation*:

$$\Psi_S = -iCRT$$

where *i* is the ionization constant (2 for NaCl), *C* is the molar concentration (in mol/L), *R* is the pressure constant [*R* = 0.00831 (L · MPa)/(mol · K)], and *T* is the temperature in Kelvin (273 + °C).

How would this change in the solute potential of the soil affect the water potential of the soil? In what way would the change in the water potential of the soil affect the movement of water in or out of the roots?

11. SCIENTIFIC INQUIRY Cotton plants wilt within a few hours of flooding of their roots. The flooding leads to low-oxygen conditions, increases in cytosolic $Ca^{2+}$ concentration, and decreases in cytosolic pH. Suggest a hypothesis to explain how flooding leads to wilting.

12. WRITE ABOUT A THEME: ORGANIZATION Natural selection has led to changes in the architecture of plants that enable them to photosynthesize more efficiently in the ecological niches they occupy. In a short essay (100–150 words), explain how shoot architecture enhances photosynthesis.

13. SYNTHESIZE YOUR KNOWLEDGE

Imagine yourself as a water molecule in the soil solution of a forest. In a short essay (100–150 words), explain what pathways and what forces would be necessary to carry you to the leaves of these trees.

*For selected answers, see Appendix A.*

 For additional practice questions, check out the **Dynamic Study Modules** in MasteringBiology. You can use them to study on your smartphone, tablet, or computer anytime, anywhere!

# Soil and Plant Nutrition

# 37

▲ Figure 37.1 **Does this plant have roots?**

## KEY CONCEPTS

**37.1** Soil contains a living, complex ecosystem

**37.2** Plant roots absorb essential elements from the soil

**37.3** Plant nutrition often involves relationships with other organisms

## The Corkscrew Carnivore

The pale, rootlike appendages of *Genlisea*, the wetland herb seen in **Figure 37.1**, are actually highly modified underground leaves adapted for trapping and digesting a variety of small soil inhabitants, including bacteria, algae, protozoa, nematodes, and copepods. But how do these trap-leaves work? Imagine twisting a narrow strip of paper to make a drinking straw. This is essentially the mechanism by which these corkscrew-shaped tubular leaves form. A narrow spiral slit runs along most of the trap-leaf's length; it is lined with curved hairs that allow microorganisms to enter the leaf tube but not exit. Once inside, prey find themselves traveling inexorably upward toward a small chamber lined with digestive glands that seal their fate. The inability of prey to backtrack is ensured by another set of curved hairs that allow only one-way passage (see micrograph at left). *Genlisea*'s carnivorous habit is a marvelous adaptation that enables the plant to supplement the meager mineral rations available from the boggy, nutrient-poor soils in which it grows with minerals released from its digested prey.

As discussed in Concept 36.1, plants obtain nutrients from both the atmosphere and the soil. Using sunlight as an energy source, they produce organic nutrients by reducing carbon dioxide to sugars through the process of photosynthesis. They also take up water and various inorganic nutrients from the soil through their root systems. This chapter focuses on plant nutrition, the study of the minerals necessary for plant growth. After discussing the physical properties of soils and the factors that govern soil quality,

When you see this blue icon, log in to **MasteringBiology** and go to the Study Area for digital resources.

 Get Ready for This Chapter

we explore why certain mineral nutrients are essential for plant function. Finally, we examine some nutritional adaptations that have evolved, often in relationships with other organisms.

# CONCEPT 37.1

## Soil contains a living, complex ecosystem

The upper layers of the soil, from which plants absorb nearly all of the water and minerals they require, contain a wide range of living organisms that interact with each other and with the physical environment. This complex ecosystem may take centuries to form but can be destroyed by human mismanagement in just a few years. To understand why soil must be conserved and why particular plants grow where they do, it is necessary to first consider the basic physical properties of soil: its texture and composition.

## Soil Texture

The texture of soil depends on the sizes of its particles. Soil particles can range from coarse sand (0.02–2 mm in diameter) to silt (0.002–0.02 mm) to microscopic clay particles (less than 0.002 mm). These different-sized particles arise ultimately from the weathering of rock. Water freezing in crevices of rocks causes mechanical fracturing, and weak acids in the soil break rocks down chemically. When organisms penetrate the rock, they accelerate breakdown by chemical and mechanical means. Roots, for example, secrete acids that dissolve the rock, and their growth in fissures leads to mechanical fracturing. Mineral particles released by weathering become mixed with living organisms and **humus**, the remains of dead organisms and other organic matter, forming **topsoil**. The topsoil and other soil layers are called **soil horizons (Figure 37.2)**. The topsoil, or A horizon, can range in depth from millimeters to meters. We focus mostly on properties of topsoil because it is generally the most important soil layer for plant growth.

The topsoils that are the most fertile—supporting the most abundant growth—are **loams**, which are composed of roughly equal amounts of sand, silt, and clay. Loamy soils have enough small silt and clay particles to provide ample surface area for the adhesion and retention of minerals and water.

Plants are actually nourished by the soil solution, which consists of the water and dissolved minerals in the pores between soil particles. After a heavy rain, water drains from the larger spaces in the soil, but smaller spaces retain water because water molecules are attracted to the negatively charged surfaces of clay and other particles. The large spaces between soil particles in sandy soils generally don't retain enough water to support vigorous plant growth, but they do enable efficient diffusion of oxygen to the roots. Clayey soils tend to retain too much water, and when soil does not

▼ Figure 37.2 **Soil horizons.**

The A horizon is the topsoil, a mixture of broken-down rock of various textures, living organisms, and decaying organic matter.

The B horizon contains much less organic matter than the A horizon and is less weathered.

The C horizon is composed mainly of partially broken-down rock. Some of the rock served as "parent" material for minerals that later helped form the upper horizons.

drain adequately, the air is replaced by water, and the roots suffocate from lack of oxygen. Typically, the most fertile topsoils have pores containing about half water and half air, providing a good balance between aeration, drainage, and water storage capacity. The physical properties of soils can be adjusted by adding soil amendments, such as peat moss, compost, manure, or sand.

## Topsoil Composition

A soil's composition encompasses its inorganic (mineral) and organic chemical components. The organic components include the many life-forms that inhabit the soil.

### Inorganic Components

The surface charges of soil particles determine their ability to bind many nutrients. Most of the soil particles in productive soils are negatively charged and therefore do not bind negatively charged ions (anions), such as the plant nutrients nitrate ($NO_3^-$), phosphate ($H_2PO_4^-$), and sulfate ($SO_4^{2-}$). As a result, these nutrients are easily lost by *leaching*, percolation of water through the soil. Positively charged ions (cations)—such as potassium ($K^+$), calcium ($Ca^{2+}$), and magnesium ($Mg^{2+}$)—adhere to negatively charged soil particles, so are less easily lost by leaching.

Roots, however, do not absorb mineral cations directly from soil particles; they absorb them from the soil solution. Mineral cations enter the soil solution by **cation exchange**, a process in which cations are displaced from soil particles by other cations, particularly $H^+$ **(Figure 37.3)**. Therefore, a soil's capacity to exchange cations is determined by the number of cation adhesion sites and by the soil's pH. In general, the

**▼ Figure 37.3 Cation exchange in soil.**

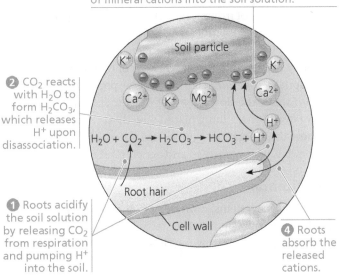

**❸** H⁺ ions in the soil solution neutralize the negative charge of soil particles, causing release of mineral cations into the soil solution.

**❷** CO₂ reacts with H₂O to form H₂CO₃, which releases H⁺ upon disassociation.

Soil particle

$K^+$   $K^+$   $Ca^{2+}$   $K^+$   $Mg^{2+}$   $Ca^{2+}$   $H^+$

$H_2O + CO_2 \rightarrow H_2CO_3 \rightarrow HCO_3^- + H^+$

Root hair

**❶** Roots acidify the soil solution by releasing CO₂ from respiration and pumping H⁺ into the soil.

Cell wall

**❹** Roots absorb the released cations.

**VISUAL SKILLS ➤** *Which are more likely to be leached from the soil by decreasing pH—cations or anions? Explain.*

  Animation: How Plants Obtain Minerals from Soil

more clay and organic matter in the soil, the higher the cation exchange capacity. The clay content is important because these small particles have a high ratio of surface area to volume, allowing for the ample binding of cations.

## *Organic Components*

The major organic component of topsoil is humus, which consists of organic material produced by the decomposition of fallen leaves, dead organisms, feces, and other organic matter by bacteria and fungi. Humus prevents clay particles from packing together and forms a crumbly soil that retains water but is still porous enough to aerate roots. Humus also increases the soil's capacity to exchange cations and is a reservoir of mineral nutrients that return gradually to the soil as microorganisms decompose the organic matter.

Topsoil is home to an astonishing number and variety of organisms. A teaspoon of topsoil has about 5 billion bacteria, which cohabit with fungi, algae and other protists, insects, earthworms, nematodes, and plant roots. The activities of all these organisms affect the soil's physical and chemical properties. Earthworms, for example, consume organic matter and derive their nutrition from the bacteria and fungi growing on this material. They excrete wastes and move large amounts of material to the soil surface. In addition, they move organic matter into deeper layers. Earthworms mix and clump the soil particles, allowing for better gaseous diffusion and water retention. Roots also affect soil texture and composition. For example, they reduce erosion by binding the soil, and they lower soil pH by excreting acids.

## Soil Conservation and Sustainable Agriculture

Ancient farmers recognized that crop yields on a particular plot of land decreased over the years. Moving to uncultivated areas, they observed the same pattern of reduced yields over time. Eventually, they realized that **fertilization**, the addition of mineral nutrients to the soil, could make soil a renewable resource that enabled crops to be cultivated season after season at a fixed location. This sedentary agriculture facilitated a new way of life. Humans began to build permanent dwellings—the first villages. They also stored food for use between harvests, and food surpluses enabled some people to specialize in nonfarming occupations. In short, soil management, by fertilization and other practices, helped prepare the way for modern societies.

Unfortunately, soil mismanagement has been a recurrent problem throughout human history, as exemplified by the American Dust Bowl, an ecological and human disaster that ravaged the southwestern Great Plains of the United States in the 1930s. This region suffered through devastating dust storms that resulted from a prolonged drought and decades of inappropriate farming techniques. Before the arrival of farmers, the Great Plains had been covered by hardy grasses that held the soil in place in spite of recurring droughts and torrential rains. But in the late 1800s and early 1900s, many homesteaders settled in the region, planting wheat and raising cattle. These land uses left the soil exposed to erosion by winds. A few years of drought made the problem worse. During the 1930s, huge quantities of fertile soil were blown away in "black blizzards," rendering millions of hectares of farmland useless **(Figure 37.4)**. In one of the worst dust storms, clouds of dust blew eastward to Chicago, where soil fell like snow, and even reached the Atlantic coast. Hundreds of thousands of people in the Dust Bowl region were forced to abandon their homes and land, a plight immortalized in John Steinbeck's novel *The Grapes of Wrath*.

**▼ Figure 37.4 A massive dust storm in the American Dust Bowl during the 1930s.**

**?** *Which soil horizon contributed to these dust clouds?*

Soil mismanagement continues to be a major problem to this day. More than 30% of the world's farmland has reduced productivity stemming from poor soil conditions, such as chemical contamination, mineral deficiencies, acidity, salinity, and poor drainage. As the world's population grows, the demand for food increases. Because soil quality greatly affects crop yield, soil resources must be managed prudently. Today, the most productive lands are already being used for agriculture, so there are no more frontiers for farmers to clear. Thus, it is critical that farmers embrace **sustainable agriculture**, a commitment to farming practices that are conservation minded, environmentally safe, and profitable. Sustainable agriculture includes the prudent use of irrigation and soil amendments, the protection of topsoil from salinization and erosion, and the restoration of degraded lands.

## Irrigation

Because water is often the limiting factor in plant growth, perhaps no technology has increased crop yield as much as irrigation. However, irrigation is a huge drain on freshwater resources. Globally, about 75% of all freshwater use is devoted to agriculture. Many rivers in arid regions have been reduced to trickles by the diversion of water for irrigation. The primary source of irrigation water, however, is not surface waters, such as rivers and lakes, but underground water reserves called *aquifers*. In some parts of the world, the rate of water removal is exceeding the natural refilling of the aquifers. The result is *land subsidence*, a gradual settling or sudden sinking of Earth's surface **(Figure 37.5)**. Land subsidence alters drainage patterns, causes damage to human-made structures, contributes to loss of underground springs, and increases the risk of flooding.

Irrigation, particularly from groundwater, can also lead to soil *salinization*—the addition of salts to the soil that make it too salty for cultivating plants. Salts dissolved in irrigation

▼ **Figure 37.5 Sudden land subsidence.** Overuse of groundwater for irrigation triggered formation of this sinkhole in Florida.

water accumulate in the soil as the water evaporates, making the water potential of the soil solution more negative. The water potential gradient from soil to roots is reduced, diminishing water uptake (see Figure 36.12).

Many forms of irrigation, such as the flooding of fields, are wasteful because much of the water evaporates. To use water efficiently, farmers must understand the water-holding capacity of their soil, the water needs of their crops, and the appropriate irrigation technology. One popular technology is *drip irrigation*, the slow release of water to soil and plants from perforated plastic tubing placed directly at the root zone. Because drip irrigation requires less water and reduces salinization, it is used mainly in arid agricultural regions.

## Fertilization

In natural ecosystems, mineral nutrients are usually recycled by the excretion of animal wastes and the decomposition of humus. Agriculture, however, is unnatural. The lettuce you eat, for example, contains minerals extracted from a farmer's field. As you excrete wastes, these minerals are deposited far from their original source. Over many harvests, the farmer's field will eventually become depleted of nutrients. Nutrient depletion is a major cause of global soil degradation. Farmers must reverse nutrient depletion by means of fertilization.

Today, most farmers in industrialized nations use fertilizers containing minerals that are either mined or prepared by energy-intensive processes. These fertilizers are usually enriched in nitrogen (N), phosphorus (P), and potassium (K)—the nutrients most commonly deficient in depleted soils. You may have seen fertilizers labeled with a three-number code, called the N–P–K ratio. A fertilizer marked "15–10–5," for instance, is 15% N (as ammonium or nitrate), 10% P (as phosphate), and 5% K (as the mineral potash).

Manure, fishmeal, and compost are called "organic" fertilizers because they are of biological origin and contain decomposing organic material. Before plants can use organic material, however, it must be decomposed into the inorganic nutrients that roots can absorb. Whether from organic fertilizer or a chemical factory, the minerals a plant extracts are in the same form. However, organic fertilizers release them gradually, whereas minerals in commercial fertilizers are immediately available but may not be retained by the soil for long. Minerals not absorbed by roots are often leached from the soil by rainwater or irrigation. To make matters worse, mineral run-off into lakes may lead to explosions in algal populations that can deplete oxygen levels and decimate fish populations.

## Adjusting Soil pH

Soil pH is an important factor that influences mineral availability by its effect on cation exchange and the chemical form of minerals. Depending on the soil pH, a particular mineral may be bound too tightly to clay particles or may be in a chemical form that the plant cannot absorb. Most plants prefer slightly acidic soil because the high $H^+$ concentrations can displace positively charged minerals from soil particles, making them more available for absorption. Adjusting soil pH is tricky because a change in $H^+$ concentration may make one mineral more available but another less available. At pH 8, for instance, plants can absorb calcium, but iron is almost unavailable. The soil pH should be matched to a crop's mineral needs. If the soil is too alkaline, adding sulfate will lower the pH. Soil that is too acidic can be adjusted by adding lime (calcium carbonate or calcium hydroxide).

When the soil pH dips to 5 or lower, toxic aluminum ions ($Al^{3+}$) become more soluble and are absorbed by roots, stunting root growth and preventing the uptake of calcium, a needed plant nutrient. Some plants can cope with high $Al^{3+}$ levels by secreting organic anions that bind $Al^{3+}$ and render it harmless. However, low soil pH and $Al^{3+}$ toxicity continue to pose serious problems, especially in tropical regions, where the pressure of producing food for a growing population is often most acute.

### Controlling Erosion

As happened most dramatically in the Dust Bowl, water and wind erosion can remove large amounts of topsoil. Erosion is a major cause of soil degradation because nutrients are carried away by wind and streams. To limit erosion, farmers plant rows of trees as windbreaks, terrace hillside crops, and cultivate crops in a contour pattern (**Figure 37.6**). Crops such as alfalfa and wheat provide good ground cover and protect the soil better than maize and other crops that are usually planted in more widely spaced rows.

Erosion can also be reduced by a plowing technique called **no-till agriculture**. In traditional plowing, the entire field is tilled, or turned over. This practice helps control weeds but disrupts the meshwork of roots that holds the soil in place, leading to increased surface runoff and erosion. In no-till agriculture, a special plow creates narrow furrows for seeds and fertilizer. In this way, the field is seeded with minimal disturbance to the soil, while also using less fertilizer.

### Phytoremediation

Some land areas are unfit for cultivation because toxic metals or organic pollutants have contaminated the soil or groundwater. Traditionally, soil remediation, the detoxification of contaminated soils, has focused on nonbiological technologies, such as removing and storing contaminated soil in landfills, but these techniques are costly and often disrupt the landscape. **Phytoremediation** is a nondestructive biotechnology that harnesses the ability of some plants to extract soil pollutants and concentrate them in portions of the plant that can be easily removed for safe disposal. For example, alpine pennycress (*Thlaspi caerulescens*) can accumulate zinc in its shoots at concentrations 300 times higher than most plants can tolerate. The shoots can be harvested and the zinc removed. Such plants show promise for cleaning up areas contaminated by smelters,

▼ **Figure 37.6 Contour tillage.** These crops are planted in rows that go around, rather than up and down, the hills. Contour tillage helps slow water runoff and topsoil erosion after heavy rains.

mines, or nuclear tests. Phytoremediation is a type of bioremediation, which also uses prokaryotes and protists to detoxify polluted sites (see Concepts 27.6 and 55.5).

We have discussed the importance of soil conservation for sustainable agriculture. Mineral nutrients contribute greatly to soil fertility, but which minerals are most important, and why do plants need them? These are the topics of the next section.

### CONCEPT CHECK 37.1

1. Explain how the phrase "too much of a good thing" can apply to watering and fertilizing plants.
2. Some lawn mowers collect clippings. What is a drawback of this practice with respect to plant nutrition?
3. WHAT IF? ➤ How would adding clay to loamy soil affect capacity to exchange cations and retain water? Explain.
4. MAKE CONNECTIONS ➤ Note three ways the properties of water contribute to soil formation. See Concept 3.2.

*For suggested answers, see Appendix A.*

## CONCEPT 37.2

## Plant roots absorb essential elements from the soil

Water, air, and soil minerals all contribute to plant growth. A plant's water content can be measured by comparing the mass before and after drying. Typically, 80–90% of a plant's fresh mass is water. Some 96% of the remaining dry mass consists of carbohydrates such as cellulose and starch that are produced by photosynthesis. Thus, the components of carbohydrates—carbon, oxygen, and hydrogen—are the most abundant elements in dried plant residue. Inorganic substances from the soil, although essential for plant survival, account for only about 4% of a plant's dry mass.

### Essential Elements

The inorganic substances in plants contain more than 50 chemical elements. In studying the chemical composition of plants, we must distinguish elements that are essential from those that are merely present in the plant. A chemical element is considered an **essential element** only if it is required for a plant to complete its life cycle and reproduce.

To determine which chemical elements are essential, researchers use **hydroponic culture**, in which plants are grown in mineral solutions instead of soil (**Figure 37.7**). Such studies have helped identify 17 essential elements needed by all plants. Hydroponic culture is also used on a small scale to grow some greenhouse crops.

Nine of the essential elements are called **macronutrients** because plants require them in relatively large amounts. Six of these are the major components of organic compounds forming a plant's structure: carbon, oxygen, hydrogen, nitrogen, phosphorus, and sulfur. The other three macronutrients are potassium, calcium, and magnesium. Of all the mineral nutrients, nitrogen contributes the most to plant growth and crop yields. Plants require nitrogen as a component of proteins, nucleic acids, chlorophyll, and other important organic molecules. **Table 37.1** summarizes the functions of the macronutrients.

The other essential elements are called **micronutrients** because plants need them in only tiny quantities. They are chlorine, iron, manganese, boron, zinc, copper, nickel, and molybdenum. Sodium is a ninth essential micronutrient for plants that use the $C_4$ or CAM pathways of photosynthesis (see Concept 10.4) because it is needed for the regeneration of phosphoenolpyruvate, the $CO_2$ acceptor used in these two types of carbon fixation.

Micronutrients function in plants mainly as cofactors, nonprotein helpers in enzymatic reactions (see Concept 8.4). Iron, for example, is a metallic component of cytochromes, the proteins in the electron transport chains of chloroplasts and mitochondria. It is because micronutrients generally play catalytic roles that plants need only tiny quantities. The requirement for molybdenum, for instance, is so modest that there is only one atom of this rare element for every 60 million atoms of hydrogen in dried plant material. Yet a deficiency of molybdenum or any other micronutrient can weaken or kill a plant.

## Symptoms of Mineral Deficiency

The symptoms of a deficiency depend partly on the mineral's function as a nutrient. For example, a deficiency of magnesium, a component of chlorophyll, causes *chlorosis*, yellowing of leaves. In some cases, the relationship between a deficiency and its symptoms is less direct. For instance, iron deficiency can cause chlorosis even though chlorophyll contains no iron, because iron ions are required as a cofactor in an enzymatic step of chlorophyll synthesis.

Mineral deficiency symptoms depend not only on the role of the nutrient but also on its mobility within the plant. If a nutrient moves about freely, symptoms appear first in older organs because young, growing tissues use more nutrients that are in short supply. For example, magnesium is relatively mobile and is shunted preferentially to young leaves. Therefore, a plant deficient in magnesium first shows signs of chlorosis in its older leaves. In contrast, a deficiency of a mineral that is relatively immobile affects young parts of the plant first. Older tissues may have adequate amounts that they retain during periods of short supply. For example, iron does not move freely within a plant, and an iron deficiency causes yellowing of young leaves before any effect on older leaves is visible. The mineral requirements of a plant may also change with the time of the year and the age of the plant. Young seedlings, for example, rarely show mineral deficiency symptoms because their mineral requirements are met largely by minerals released from stored reserves in the seeds themselves.

The symptoms of a mineral deficiency may vary between species but in a given plant are often distinctive enough to aid in diagnosis. Deficiencies of phosphorus, potassium, and nitrogen are most common, as in the example of maize leaves in **Figure 37.8**. In the **Scientific Skills Exercise**, you can diagnose a mineral deficiency in orange tree leaves. Micronutrient shortages are less common than macronutrient shortages and tend to occur in certain geographic regions because of differences in soil composition. One way to confirm a diagnosis is to analyze the mineral content of the plant or soil. The amount of a micronutrient needed to correct a deficiency is usually small. For example, a zinc deficiency in fruit trees can usually be cured by hammering a few zinc nails into each tree trunk.

▼ Figure 37.7

**Research Method Hydroponic Culture**

**Application** In hydroponic culture, plants are grown in mineral solutions without soil. One use of hydroponic culture is to identify essential elements in plants.

**Technique** Plant roots are bathed in aerated solutions of known mineral composition. Aerating the water provides the roots with oxygen for cellular respiration. (Note: The flasks would normally be opaque to prevent algal growth.) A mineral, such as iron, can be omitted to test whether it is essential.

**Control:** Solution containing all minerals     **Experimental:** Solution without iron

**Results** If the omitted mineral is essential, mineral deficiency symptoms occur, such as stunted growth and discolored leaves. By definition, the plant would not be able to complete its life cycle. Deficiencies of different elements may have different symptoms, which can aid in diagnosing mineral deficiencies in soil.

**Table 37.1** Macronutrients in Plants

| Element (Form Primarily Absorbed by Plants) | % Mass in Dry Tissue | Major Function(s) | Early Visual Symptom(s) of Nutrient Deficiencies |
|---|---|---|---|
| **Macronutrients** | | | |
| Carbon ($CO_2$) | 45% | Major component of plant's organic compounds | Poor growth |
| Oxygen ($CO_2$) | 45% | Major component of plant's organic compounds | Poor growth |
| Hydrogen ($H_2O$) | 6% | Major component of plant's organic compounds | Wilting, poor growth |
| Nitrogen ($NO_3^-$, $NH_4^+$) | 1.5% | Component of nucleic acids, proteins, and chlorophyll | Chlorosis at tips of older leaves (common in heavily cultivated soils or soils low in organic material) |
| Potassium ($K^+$) | 1.0% | Cofactor of many enzymes; major solute functioning in water balance; operation of stomata | Mottling of older leaves, with drying of leaf edges; weak stems; roots poorly developed (common in acidic or sandy soils) |
| Calcium ($Ca^{2+}$) | 0.5% | Important component of middle lamella and cell walls; maintains membrane function; signal transduction | Crinkling of young leaves; death of terminal buds (common in acidic or sandy soils) |
| Magnesium ($Mg^{2+}$) | 0.2% | Component of chlorophyll; cofactor of many enzymes | Chlorosis between veins, found in older leaves (common in acidic or sandy soils) |
| Phosphorus ($H_2PO_4^-$, $HPO_4^{2-}$) | 0.2% | Component of nucleic acids, phospholipids, ATP | Healthy appearance but very slow development; thin stems; purpling of veins; poor flowering and fruiting (common in acidic, wet, or cold soils) |
| Sulfur ($SO_4^{2-}$) | 0.1% | Component of proteins | General chlorosis in young leaves (common in sandy or very wet soils) |

**MAKE CONNECTIONS** ➤ *Explain why $CO_2$, rather than $O_2$, is the source of much of the dry mass oxygen in plants. See Concept 10.1.*

 Interview with Gloria Coruzzi: Assimilating more nitrogen into plants

▼ **Figure 37.8 The most common mineral deficiencies, as seen in maize leaves.** Mineral deficiency symptoms may vary in different species. In maize, nitrogen deficiency is evident in a yellowing that starts at the tip and moves along the center (midrib) of older leaves. Phosphorus-deficient maize plants have reddish purple margins, particularly in young leaves. Potassium-deficient maize plants exhibit "firing," or drying, along tips and margins of older leaves.

Healthy

Nitrogen-deficient

Phosphorus-deficient

Potassium-deficient

Moderation is important because overdoses of a micronutrient or macronutrient can be detrimental or toxic. Too much nitrogen, for example, can lead to excessive vine growth in tomato plants at the expense of good fruit production.

## Improving Plant Nutrition by Genetic Modification

In exploring plant nutrition so far, we have discussed how farmers use irrigation, fertilization, and other means to tailor soil conditions for a crop. An opposite approach is tailoring the plant by genetic engineering to better fit the soil. Here we highlight two examples of how genetic engineering improves plant nutrition and fertilizer usage.

### Resistance to Aluminum Toxicity

Aluminum in acidic soils damages roots and reduces crop yields. The major mechanism of aluminum resistance is secretion of organic acids (such as malic acid and citric acid) by roots. These acids bind to free aluminum ions and lower the levels of aluminum in the soil. Scientists have altered tobacco and papaya plants by introducing a citrate synthase gene from a bacterium into the plants' genomes. The resulting overproduction of citric acid increased aluminum resistance.

## Making Observations

**What Mineral Deficiency Is This Plant Exhibiting?** Plant growers often diagnose deficiencies in their crops by examining changes to the foliage, such as chlorosis (yellowing), death of some leaves, discoloring, mottling, scorching, or changes in size or texture. In this exercise, you will diagnose a mineral deficiency by observing a plant's leaves and applying what you have learned about symptoms from the text and Table 37.1.

**Data** The data for this exercise come from the photograph below of leaves on an orange tree exhibiting a mineral deficiency.

Older leaf

Young leaf

**INTERPRET THE DATA**

1. How do the young leaves differ in appearance from the older leaves?

2. In three words, what is the most prominent mineral deficiency symptom seen in this photo? List the three nutrients whose deficiencies give rise to this symptom. Based on the symptom's location, which one of these three nutrients can be ruled out, and why? What does the location suggest about the other two nutrients?

3. How would your hypothesis about the cause of this deficiency be influenced if tests showed that the soil was low in humus?

 **Instructors:** A version of this Scientific Skills Exercise can be assigned in MasteringBiology.

### Smart Plants

Agricultural researchers are developing ways to maintain crop yields while reducing fertilizer use. One approach is to genetically engineer "smart" plants that signal when a nutrient deficiency is imminent—but *before* damage has occurred. One type of smart plant takes advantage of a promoter (a DNA sequence indicating where the transcription of a gene starts) that more readily binds RNA polymerase (the transcription enzyme) when the phosphorus content of the plant's tissues begins to decline. This promoter is linked to a "reporter" gene that leads to production of a light blue

▼ **Figure 37.9 Deficiency warnings from "smart" plants.** Some plants have been genetically modified to signal an impending nutrient deficiency before irreparable damage occurs. For example, after laboratory treatments, the research plant *Arabidopsis* develops a blue color in response to an imminent phosphorus deficiency.

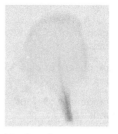  

| No phosphorus deficiency | Beginning phosphorus deficiency | Well-developed phosphorus deficiency |

pigment in the leaf cells (**Figure 37.9**). When leaves of these smart plants develop a blue tinge, the farmer knows it is time to add phosphorus-containing fertilizer.

So far, you have learned that soil, to support vigorous plant growth, must have an adequate supply of mineral nutrients, sufficient aeration, good water-holding capacity, low salinity, and a pH near neutrality. It must also be free of toxic concentrations of minerals and other chemicals. These physical and chemical features of soil, however, are just part of the story: We must also consider the living components of soil.

### CONCEPT CHECK 37.2

1. Are some essential elements more important than others? Explain.

2. **WHAT IF?** ➤ If an element increases the growth rate of a plant, can it be defined as an essential element?

3. **MAKE CONNECTIONS** ➤ Based on Figure 9.17, explain why hydroponically grown plants would grow much more slowly if they were not sufficiently aerated.

*For suggested answers, see Appendix A.*

# CONCEPT 37.3

## Plant nutrition often involves relationships with other organisms

To this point, we have portrayed plants as exploiters of soil resources, but plants and soil have a two-way relationship. Dead plants provide much of the energy needed by soil-dwelling bacteria and fungi. Many of these organisms also benefit from sugar-rich secretions produced by living roots. Meanwhile, plants derive benefits from their associations with soil bacteria and fungi. As shown in **Figure 37.10**, mutually beneficial relationships across kingdoms and domains are not rare in nature. However, they are of particular importance to plants. We'll explore some important *mutualisms* between plants and soil bacteria and fungi, as well as some unusual, nonmutualistic forms of plant nutrition.

# ▼ Figure 37.10 MAKE CONNECTIONS

## Mutualism Across Kingdoms and Domains

Some toxic species of fish don't make their own poison. How is that possible? Some species of ants chew leaves but don't eat them. Why? The answers lie in some amazing mutualisms, relationships between different species in which each species provides a substance or service that benefits the other (see Concept 54.1). Sometimes mutualisms occur within the same kingdom, such as between two species of animals. Many mutualisms, however, involve species from different kingdoms or domains, as in these examples.

### Fungus–Bacterium

A lichen is a mutualistic association between a fungus and a photosynthetic partner. In the lichen *Peltigera*, the photosynthetic partner is a species of cyanobacterium. The cyanobacterium supplies carbohydrates, while the fungus provides anchorage, protection, minerals, and water. (See Figure 31.22.)

The lichen *Peltigera*

A longitudinal section of the lichen *Peltigera* showing green photosynthetic bacteria sandwiched between layers of fungus

### Animal–Bacterium

Fugu is the Japanese name for puffer fish and the delicacy made from it, which can be deadly. Most species of puffer fish contain lethal amounts of the nerve toxin tetrodotoxin in their organs, especially the liver, ovaries, and intestines. Therefore, a specially trained chef must remove the poisonous parts. The tetrodotoxin is synthesized by mutualistic bacteria (various *Vibrio* species) associated with the fish. The fish gains a potent chemical defense, while the bacteria live in a high-nutrient, low-competition environment.

Puffer fish (fugu)

### Plant–Bacterium

The floating fern *Azolla* provides carbohydrates for a nitrogen-fixing cyanobacterium that resides in the air spaces of the leaves. In return, the fern receives nitrogen from the cyanobacterium. (See Concept 27.5.)

The floating fern *Azolla*

### Animal–Fungus

Leaf-cutter ants harvest leaves that they carry back to their nest, but the ants do not eat the leaves. Instead, a fungus grows by absorbing nutrients from the leaves, and the ants eat part of the fungus that they have cultivated.

Leaf-cutter ants bringing leaves to a nest

Ants tending a fungal garden in a nest

### Plant–Fungus

Most plant species have mycorrhizae, mutualistic associations between roots and fungi. The fungus absorbs carbohydrates from the roots. In return, the fungus's mycelium, a dense network of filaments called hyphae, increases the surface area for the uptake of water and minerals by the roots. (See Figure 31.4.)

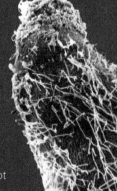

A fungus growing on the root of a sorghum plant (SEM)

### Plant–Animal

Some species of *Acacia* plants are aggressively defended from predators and competitors by ants that live within the plant's hollow thorns. The plant provides nourishment for the ants in the forms of protein-rich structures at the bases of leaves and carbohydrate-rich nectar. (See Figure 54.8.)

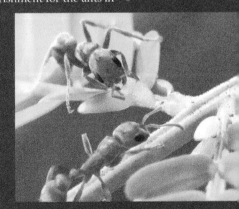

Protective ants harvesting protein-rich structures from an *Acacia* plant

**MAKE CONNECTIONS** ➤ *Describe three more examples of mutualisms. (See Figure 27.19, Figure 38.4, and Concept 41.4.)*

## Bacteria and Plant Nutrition

A variety of soil bacteria play roles in plant nutrition. Some engage in mutually beneficial chemical exchanges with plant roots. Others enhance the decomposition of organic materials and increase nutrient availability.

### Rhizobacteria

**Rhizobacteria** are bacteria that live either in close association with plant roots or in the **rhizosphere**, the soil closely surrounding plant roots. Many rhizobacteria form mutually beneficial associations with plant roots. Rhizobacteria depend on nutrients such as sugars, amino acids, and organic acids that are secreted by plant cells. Up to 20% of a plant's photosynthetic production may be used to fuel these complex bacterial communities. In return, plants reap many benefits from these mutualistic associations. Some rhizobacteria produce antibiotics that protect roots from disease. Others absorb toxic metals or make nutrients more available to roots. Still others convert gaseous nitrogen into forms usable by the plant or produce chemicals that stimulate plant growth. Inoculation of seeds with plant-growth-promoting rhizobacteria can increase crop yield and reduce the need for fertilizers and pesticides.

Some rhizobacteria are free-living in the rhizosphere, whereas other types of rhizobacteria are **endophytes** that live between cells within the plant. Both the intercellular spaces occupied by endophytic bacteria and the rhizosphere associated with each plant root system contain a unique and complex cocktail of root secretions and microbial products that differ from those of the surrounding soil. A recent metagenomics study revealed that the compositions of bacterial communities living endophytically and in the rhizosphere are not identical **(Figure 37.11)**. A better understanding of the types of bacteria within and around roots could potentially have profound agricultural benefits.

▼ **Figure 37.11**

### Inquiry  How variable are the compositions of bacterial communities inside and outside of roots?

**Experiment** The bacterial communities found within and immediately outside of root systems are known to improve plant growth. In order to devise agricultural strategies to increase the benefits of these bacterial communities, it is necessary to determine how complex they are and what factors affect their composition. A problem inherent in studying these bacterial communities is that a handful of soil contains as many as 10,000 types of bacteria, more than all the bacterial species that have been described. One cannot simply culture each species and use a taxonomic key to identify them; a molecular approach is needed.

Jeffery Dangl and his colleagues estimated the number of bacterial "species" in various samples using a technique called *metagenomics* (see Concept 21.1). The bacterial community samples they studied differed in location (endophytic, rhizospheric, or outside the rhizosphere), soil type (clayey or porous), and the developmental stage of the root system with which they were associated (old or young). The DNA from each sample was purified, and the polymerase chain reaction (PCR) was used to amplify the DNA that codes for the 16S ribosomal RNA subunits. Many thousands of DNA sequence variations were found in each sample. The researchers then lumped the sequences that were more than 97% identical into "taxonomic units" or "species." (The word *species* is in quotation marks because "two organisms having a single gene that is more than 97% identical" is not explicit in any definition of species.) Having established the types of "species" in each community, the researchers constructed a tree diagram showing the percent of bacterial "species" that were found in common in each community.

**Results** This tree diagram breaks down the relatedness of bacterial communities into finer and finer levels of detail. The two explanatory labels give examples of how to interpret the diagram.

▼ Bacteria (green) on surface of root (fluorescent LM)

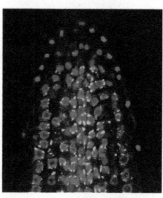

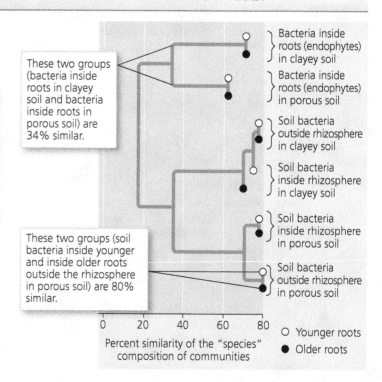

These two groups (bacteria inside roots in clayey soil and bacteria inside roots in porous soil) are 34% similar.

Bacteria inside roots (endophytes) in clayey soil

Bacteria inside roots (endophytes) in porous soil

Soil bacteria outside rhizosphere in clayey soil

Soil bacteria inside rhizosphere in clayey soil

Soil bacteria inside rhizosphere in porous soil

Soil bacteria outside rhizosphere in porous soil

These two groups (soil bacteria inside younger and inside older roots outside the rhizosphere in porous soil) are 80% similar.

0    20    40    60    80

Percent similarity of the "species" composition of communities

○ Younger roots
● Older roots

**Data from** D.S. Lundberg et al., Defining the core *Arabidopsis thaliana* root microbiome, *Nature* 488:86–94 (2012).

**Conclusion** The "species" composition of the bacterial communities varied markedly according to the location inside the root versus outside the root and according to soil type.

**INTERPRET THE DATA ➤ (a)** *Which of the three community locations was least like the other two?* **(b)** *Rank the three variables (community location, developmental stage of roots, and soil type) in terms of how strongly they affect the "species" composition of the bacterial communities.*

## Bacteria in the Nitrogen Cycle

Because nitrogen is required in large amounts for synthesizing proteins and nucleic acids, no mineral deficiency is more limiting to plant growth than a lack of nitrogen. The forms of nitrogen that plants can use include $NO_3^-$ and $NH_4^+$. Some soil nitrogen derives from the weathering of rocks, and lightning produces small amounts of $NO_3^-$ that get carried to the soil in rain. However, most of the nitrogen available to plants comes from the activity of bacteria **(Figure 37.12)**. This activity is part of the **nitrogen cycle**, a series of natural processes by which certain nitrogen-containing substances from the air and soil are made useful to living things, are used by them, and are returned to the air and soil (see Figure 55.14).

Plants commonly acquire nitrogen in the form of $NO_3^-$ (nitrate). Soil $NO_3^-$ is largely formed by a two-step process called *nitrification*, which consists of the oxidation of ammonia ($NH_3$) to nitrite ($NO_2^-$), followed by oxidation of $NO_2^-$ to $NO_3^-$. Different types of *nitrifying bacteria* mediate each step, as shown at the bottom of Figure 37.12. After the roots absorb $NO_3^-$, a plant enzyme reduces it back to $NH_4^+$, which other enzymes incorporate into amino acids and other organic compounds. Most plant species export nitrogen from roots to shoots via the xylem as $NO_3^-$ or as organic compounds synthesized in the roots. Some soil nitrogen is lost, particularly in anaerobic soils, when denitrifying bacteria convert $NO_3^-$ to $N_2$, which diffuses into the atmosphere.

In addition to $NO_3^-$, plants can acquire nitrogen in the form of $NH_4^+$ (ammonium) through two processes, as shown on the left in Figure 37.12. In one process, *nitrogen-fixing bacteria* convert gaseous nitrogen ($N_2$) to $NH_3$, which then picks up another $H^+$ in the soil solution, forming $NH_4^+$. In the other process, called ammonification, decomposers convert the organic nitrogen from dead organic material into $NH_4^+$.

## Nitrogen-Fixing Bacteria: A Closer Look

Although Earth's atmosphere is 79% nitrogen, plants cannot use free gaseous nitrogen ($N_2$) because there is a triple bond between the two nitrogen atoms, making the molecule almost inert. For atmospheric $N_2$ to be of use to plants, it must be reduced to $NH_3$ by a process known as **nitrogen fixation**. All nitrogen-fixing organisms are bacteria. Some nitrogen-fixing bacteria are free-living in the soil (see Figure 37.12), whereas others are rhizospheric. Among this latter group, members of the genus *Rhizobium* form efficient and intimate associations with the roots of legumes (such as beans, alfalfa, and peanuts), altering the structure of the hosts' roots markedly, as will be discussed shortly.

The multistep conversion of $N_2$ to $NH_3$ by nitrogen fixation can be summarized as follows:

$$N_2 + 8e^- + 8H^+ + 16\,ATP \rightarrow 2NH_3 + H_2 + 16\,ADP + 16\,\text{\textcircled{P}}_i$$

The reaction is driven by the enzyme complex *nitrogenase*. Because the process of nitrogen fixation requires 16 ATP

▼ **Figure 37.12 The roles of soil bacteria in the nitrogen nutrition of plants.** Ammonium is made available to plants by two types of soil bacteria: those that fix atmospheric $N_2$ (nitrogen-fixing bacteria) and those that decompose organic material (ammonifying bacteria). Although plants absorb some ammonium from the soil, they absorb mainly nitrate, which is produced from ammonium by nitrifying bacteria. Plants reduce nitrate back to ammonium before incorporating the nitrogen into organic compounds.

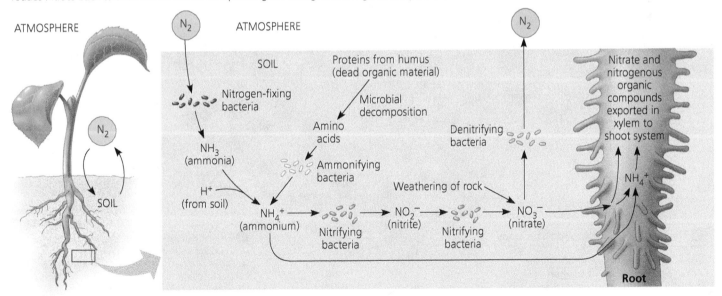

**VISUAL SKILLS** ➤ *If an animal died near a root, would the plant have greater access to ammonium, nitrate, or both?*

 Figure Walkthrough

molecules for every 2 NH₃ molecules synthesized, nitrogen-fixing bacteria require a rich supply of carbohydrates from decaying material, root secretions, or (in the case of the *Rhizobium* bacteria) the vascular tissue of roots.

The mutualism between *Rhizobium* ("root-living") bacteria and legume roots involves dramatic changes in root structure. Along a legume's roots are swellings called **nodules**, composed of plant cells "infected" by *Rhizobium* bacteria **(Figure 37.13)**.

> **Figure 37.13 Root nodules on a legume.** The spherical structures along this soybean root system are nodules containing *Rhizobium* bacteria. The bacteria fix nitrogen and obtain photosynthetic products supplied by the plant.

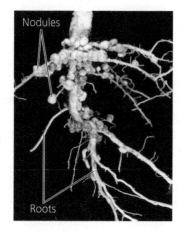

Nodules

Roots

 *How is the relationship between legume plants and* Rhizobium *bacteria mutualistic?*

Inside each nodule, *Rhizobium* bacteria assume a form called **bacteroids**, which are contained within vesicles formed in the root cells. Legume-*Rhizobium* relationships generate more usable nitrogen for plants than all industrial fertilizers used today—and at virtually no cost to the farmer.

Nitrogen fixation by *Rhizobium* requires an anaerobic environment, a condition facilitated by the location of the bacteroids inside living cells in the root cortex. The lignified external layers of root nodules also help to limit gas exchange. Some root nodules appear reddish because of a molecule called leghemoglobin (*leg-* for "legume"), an iron-containing protein that binds reversibly to oxygen (similar to the hemoglobin in human red blood cells). This protein is an oxygen "buffer," reducing the concentration of free oxygen and thereby providing an anaerobic environment for nitrogen fixation while regulating the oxygen supply for the intense cellular respiration required to produce ATP for nitrogen fixation.

Each legume species is associated with a particular strain of *Rhizobium* bacteria. **Figure 37.14** describes how a root nodule develops after bacteria enter through an "infection thread" in a root hair. The symbiotic relationship between a legume and

▼ **Figure 37.14 Development of a soybean root nodule.**

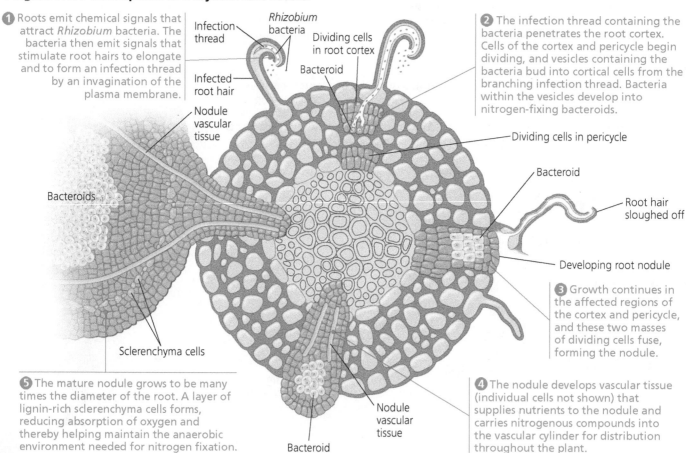

❶ Roots emit chemical signals that attract *Rhizobium* bacteria. The bacteria then emit signals that stimulate root hairs to elongate and to form an infection thread by an invagination of the plasma membrane.

❷ The infection thread containing the bacteria penetrates the root cortex. Cells of the cortex and pericycle begin dividing, and vesicles containing the bacteria bud into cortical cells from the branching infection thread. Bacteria within the vesicles develop into nitrogen-fixing bacteroids.

❸ Growth continues in the affected regions of the cortex and pericycle, and these two masses of dividing cells fuse, forming the nodule.

❹ The nodule develops vascular tissue (individual cells not shown) that supplies nutrients to the nodule and carries nitrogenous compounds into the vascular cylinder for distribution throughout the plant.

❺ The mature nodule grows to be many times the diameter of the root. A layer of lignin-rich sclerenchyma cells forms, reducing absorption of oxygen and thereby helping maintain the anaerobic environment needed for nitrogen fixation.

Infection thread
*Rhizobium* bacteria
Dividing cells in root cortex
Bacteroid
Infected root hair
Nodule vascular tissue
Bacteroids
Sclerenchyma cells
Dividing cells in pericycle
Bacteroid
Root hair sloughed off
Developing root nodule
Node vascular tissue
Bacteroid

**VISUAL SKILLS** ➤ *What plant tissue systems are modified by root nodule formation?*

nitrogen-fixing bacteria is mutualistic in that the bacteria supply the host plant with fixed nitrogen while the plant provides the bacteria with carbohydrates and other organic compounds. The root nodules use most of the ammonium produced to make amino acids, which are then transported up to the shoot through the xylem.

How does a legume species recognize a certain strain of *Rhizobium* among the many bacterial strains in the soil? And how does an encounter with that specific *Rhizobium* strain lead to development of a nodule? Each partner responds to chemical signals from the other by expressing certain genes whose products contribute to nodule formation. By understanding the molecular biology underlying the formation of root nodules, researchers hope to learn how to induce *Rhizobium* uptake and nodule formation in crop plants that do not normally form such nitrogen-fixing mutualistic relationships.

### Nitrogen Fixation and Agriculture

The benefits of nitrogen fixation underlie most types of **crop rotation**. In this practice, a nonlegume such as maize is planted one year, and the following year alfalfa or some other legume is planted to restore the concentration of fixed nitrogen in the soil. To ensure that the legume encounters its specific *Rhizobium* strain, the seeds are exposed to bacteria before sowing. Instead of being harvested, the legume crop is often plowed under so that it will decompose as "green manure," reducing the need for manufactured fertilizers.

Many plant families besides legumes include species that benefit from mutualistic nitrogen fixation. For example, red alder (*Alnus rubra*) trees host nitrogen-fixing actinomycete bacteria (see the gram-positive bacteria in Figure 27.16). Rice, a crop of great commercial importance, benefits indirectly from mutualistic nitrogen fixation. Rice farmers culture a free-floating aquatic fern, *Azolla*, which has mutualistic cyanobacteria that fix $N_2$. The growing rice eventually shades and kills the *Azolla*, and decomposition of this nitrogen-rich organic material increases the paddy's fertility. Ducks also eat the *Azolla*, providing the paddy with an extra source of manure and providing the farmers with an important source of meat.

## Fungi and Plant Nutrition

Certain species of soil fungi also form mutualistic relationships with roots and play a major role in plant nutrition. Some of these fungi are endophytic, but the most important relationships are **mycorrhizae** ("fungus roots"), the intimate mutualistic associations of roots and fungi (see Figure 31.14). The host plant provides the fungus with a steady supply of sugar. Meanwhile, the fungus increases the surface area for water uptake and also supplies the plant with phosphorus and other minerals absorbed from the soil. The fungi of mycorrhizae also secrete growth factors that stimulate roots to grow and branch, as well as antibiotics that help protect the plant from soil pathogens.

### Mycorrhizae and Plant Evolution

**EVOLUTION** Mycorrhizae are not oddities; they are formed by most plant species. In fact, this plant-fungus mutualism might have been one of the evolutionary adaptations that helped plants initially colonize land (see Concept 29.1). When the earliest plants, which evolved from green algae, began to invade the land 400 to 500 million years ago, they encountered a harsh environment. Although the soil contained mineral nutrients, it lacked organic matter. Therefore, rain probably quickly leached away many of the soluble mineral nutrients. The barren land, however, was also a place of opportunities because light and carbon dioxide were abundant, and there was little competition or herbivory.

Neither the early land plants nor early land fungi were fully equipped to exploit the terrestrial environment. The early plants lacked the ability to extract essential nutrients from the soil, while the fungi were unable to manufacture carbohydrates. Instead of the fungi becoming parasitic on the rhizoids of the evolving plants (roots or root hairs had not yet evolved), the two organisms formed mycorrhizal associations, a mutualistic symbiosis that allowed both of them to exploit the terrestrial environment. Fossil evidence supports the idea that mycorrhizal associations occurred in the earliest land plants. The small minority of extant angiosperms that are nonmycorrhizal probably lost this ability through gene loss.

### Types of Mycorrhizae

Mycorrhizae come in two forms called ectomycorrhizae and arbuscular mycorrhizae. **Ectomycorrhizae** form a dense sheath, or mantle, of mycelia (mass of branching hyphae; see Figure 31.2), over the *surface* of the root. Fungal hyphae extend from the mantle into the soil, greatly increasing the surface area for water and mineral absorption. Hyphae also grow into the root cortex. These hyphae do not penetrate the root cells but form a network in the apoplast, or extracellular space, which facilitates nutrient exchange between the fungus and the plant. Compared with "uninfected" roots, ectomycorrhizae are generally thicker, shorter, and more branched. They typically do not form root hairs, which would be superfluous given the extensive surface area of the fungal mycelium. Only about 10% of plant families have species that form ectomycorrhizae. The vast majority of these species are woody, including members of the pine, oak, birch, and eucalyptus families.

Unlike ectomycorrhizae, **arbuscular mycorrhizae** do not ensheath the root but are embedded within it. They start when microscopic soil hyphae respond to the presence of a root by growing toward it, establishing contact, and growing along its surface. The hyphae penetrate between epidermal

## ▼ Figure 37.15 Mycorrhizae.

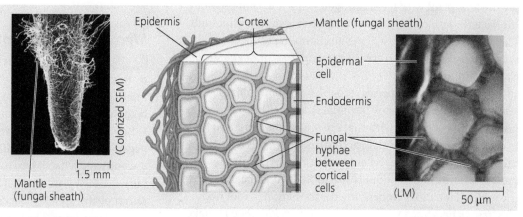

**Ectomycorrhizae.** The mantle of the fungal mycelium ensheathes the root. Fungal hyphae extend from the mantle into the soil, absorbing water and minerals, especially phosphorus. Hyphae also extend into the extracellular spaces of the root cortex, providing extensive surface area for nutrient exchange between the fungus and its host plant.

(Colorized SEM)

Mantle (fungal sheath)

1.5 mm

Epidermis · Cortex · Mantle (fungal sheath) · Epidermal cell · Endodermis · Fungal hyphae between cortical cells

(LM) · 50 μm

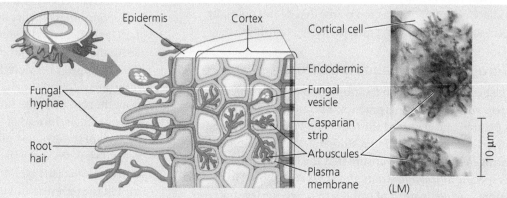

**Arbuscular mycorrhizae (endomycorrhizae).** No mantle forms around the root, but microscopic fungal hyphae extend into the root. Within the root cortex, the fungus makes extensive contact with the plant through branching of hyphae that form arbuscules, providing an enormous surface area for nutrient swapping. The hyphae penetrate the cell walls, but not the plasma membranes, of cells within the cortex.

Fungal hyphae · Root hair · Epidermis · Cortex · Cortical cell · Endodermis · Fungal vesicle · Casparian strip · Arbuscules · Plasma membrane

(LM) · 10 μm

---

cells and then enter the root cortex, where they digest small patches of the cell walls but don't pierce the plasma membrane. Instead of entering the cytoplasm, a hypha grows into a tube formed by invagination of the root cell's membrane. This invagination is like poking a finger gently into a balloon without popping it; your finger is like the fungal hypha, and the balloon skin is like the root cell's membrane. After the hyphae have penetrated in this way, some of them branch densely, forming structures called arbuscules ("little trees"), which are important sites of nutrient transfer between the fungus and the plant. Within the hyphae themselves, oval vesicles may form, possibly serving as food storage sites for the fungus. Arbuscular mycorrhizae are far more common than ectomycorrhizae, being found in over 85% of plant species, including most crops. About 5% of plant species don't form mycorrhizal associations. **Figure 37.15** provides an overview of mycorrhizae.

### Agricultural and Ecological Importance of Mycorrhizae

Good crop yields often depend on the formation of mycorrhizae. Roots can form mycorrhizal symbioses only if exposed to the appropriate species of fungus. In most ecosystems, these fungi are present in the soil, and seedlings develop mycorrhizae. But if crop seeds are collected in one environment and planted in foreign soil, the plants may show signs of malnutrition (particularly phosphorus deficiency), resulting from the absence of fungal partners. Treating seeds with spores of mycorrhizal fungi can help seedlings form mycorrhizae, facilitating recovery of damaged natural ecosystems (see Concept 55.5) or improving crop yield.

Mycorrhizal associations are also important in understanding ecological relationships. Arbuscular mycorrhizae fungi exhibit little host specificity; a single fungus may form a shared mycorrhizal network with several plants, even plants of different species. Mycorrhizal networks in a plant community may benefit one plant species more than another. Other examples of how mycorrhizae may affect the structures of plant communities come from studies of invasive plant species. For instance, garlic mustard (*Alliaria petiolata*), an exotic European species that has invaded woodlands throughout the eastern United States, does not form mycorrhizae but hinders the growth of other plant species by preventing the growth of arbuscular mycorrhizal fungi.

### Epiphytes, Parasitic Plants, and Carnivorous Plants

Almost all plant species have mutualistic relationships with soil fungi, bacteria, or both. Some plant species, including epiphytes, parasites, and carnivores, have unusual adaptations that facilitate exploiting other organisms (**Figure 37.16**).

## ▼ Figure 37.16 Exploring Unusual Nutritional Adaptations in Plants

### Epiphytes

An **epiphyte** (from the Greek *epi*, upon, and *phyton*, plant) is a plant that grows on another plant. Epiphytes produce and gather their own nutrients; they do not tap into their hosts for sustenance. Usually anchored to the branches or trunks of living trees, epiphytes absorb water and minerals from rain, mostly through leaves rather than roots. Some examples are staghorn ferns, bromeliads, and many orchids, including the vanilla plant.

▶ **Staghorn fern,** an epiphyte

### Parasitic Plants

Unlike epiphytes, parasitic plants absorb water, minerals, and sometimes products of photosynthesis from their living hosts. Many species have roots that function as haustoria, nutrient-absorbing projections that tap into the host plant. Some parasitic species, such as orange-colored, spaghetti-like dodder (genus *Cuscuta*), lack chlorophyll entirely, whereas others, such as mistletoe (genus *Phoradendron*), are photosynthetic. Still others, such as Indian pipe (*Monotropa uniflora*), absorb nutrients from the hyphae of mycorrhizae associated with other plants.

◀ **Mistletoe,** a photosynthetic parasite

▲ **Dodder,** a nonphoto-synthetic parasite (orange)

▲ **Indian pipe,** a nonphoto-synthetic parasite of mycorrhizae

### Carnivorous Plants

Carnivorous plants are photosynthetic but supplement their mineral diet by capturing insects and other small animals. They live in acid bogs and other habitats where soils are poor in nitrogen and other minerals. Pitcher plants such as *Nepenthes* and *Sarracenia* have water-filled funnels into which prey slip and drown, eventually to be digested by enzymes. Sundews (genus *Drosera*) exude a sticky fluid from tentacle-like glands on highly modified leaves. Stalked glands secrete sweet mucilage that attracts and ensnares insects, and they also release digestive enzymes. Other glands then absorb the nutrient "soup." The highly modified leaves of Venus flytrap (*Dionaea muscipula*) close quickly but partially when a prey hits two trigger hairs in rapid enough succession. Smaller insects can escape, but larger ones are trapped by the teeth lining the margins of the lobes. Excitation by the prey causes the trap to narrow more and digestive enzymes to be released.

▲ **Sundew**

◀ **Pitcher plants**

▼ **Venus flytraps**

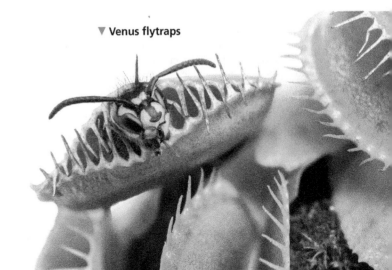

A recent study suggests that exploiting other organisms may be the norm. Chanyarat Paungfoo-Lonhienne and her colleagues at the University of Queensland in Australia have provided evidence that *Arabidopsis* and tomato can take up bacteria and yeast into their roots and digest them. Due to the small pore size of the cell wall (less than 10 nm) relative to the size of bacterial cells (about 1,000 nm), taking in microorganisms may depend on digestion of the cell wall. A study with wheat suggests that microorganisms provide only a tiny fraction of the plant's nitrogen needs, but this may not be true for all plants. These findings suggest that many plant species might engage in a limited amount of carnivory.

## CONCEPT CHECK 37.3

1. Why is the study of the rhizosphere critical to understanding plant nutrition?
2. How do soil bacteria and mycorrhizae contribute to plant nutrition?
3. **MAKE CONNECTIONS** ➤ What is a general term that is used to describe the strategy of using photosynthesis *and* heterotrophy for nutrition (see Concept 28.1)? What is a well-known class of protists that uses this strategy?
4. **WHAT IF?** ➤ A peanut farmer finds that the older leaves of his plants are turning yellow following a long period of wet weather. Suggest a reason why.

*For suggested answers, see Appendix A.*

# 37 Chapter Review

Go to **MasteringBiology**™ for Videos, Animations, Vocab Self-Quiz, Practice Tests, and more in the Study Area.

## SUMMARY OF KEY CONCEPTS

### CONCEPT 37.1

#### Soil contains a living, complex ecosystem (pp. 804–807)

VOCAB
SELF-QUIZ
goo.gl/6u55ks

- Soil particles of various sizes derived from the breakdown of rock are found in soil. Soil particle size affects the availability of water, oxygen, and minerals in the soil.
- A soil's composition encompasses its inorganic and organic components. **Topsoil** is a complex ecosystem teeming with bacteria, fungi, protists, animals, and the roots of plants.
- Some agricultural practices can deplete the mineral content of soil, tax water reserves, and promote erosion. The goal of soil conservation is to minimize this damage.

 *How is soil a complex ecosystem?*

### CONCEPT 37.2

#### Plant roots absorb essential elements from the soil (pp. 807–810)

- **Macronutrients**, elements required in relatively large amounts, include carbon, oxygen, hydrogen, nitrogen, and other major ingredients of organic compounds. **Micronutrients**, elements required in very small amounts, typically have catalytic functions as cofactors of enzymes.
- Deficiency of a mobile nutrient usually affects older organs more than younger ones; the reverse is true for nutrients that are less mobile within a plant. Macronutrient deficiencies are most common, particularly deficiencies of nitrogen, phosphorus, and potassium.
- Rather than tailoring the soil to match the plant, genetic engineers are tailoring the plant to match the soil.

 *Do plants need soil to grow? Explain.*

### CONCEPT 37.3

#### Plant nutrition often involves relationships with other organisms (pp. 810–818)

- **Rhizobacteria** derive their energy from the **rhizosphere**, a microorganism-enriched ecosystem intimately associated with roots. Plant secretions support the energy needs of the rhizosphere. Some rhizobacteria produce antibiotics, whereas others make nutrients more available for plants. Most are free-living, but some live inside plants. Plants satisfy most of their huge needs for nitrogen from the bacterial decomposition of **humus** and the fixation of gaseous nitrogen.

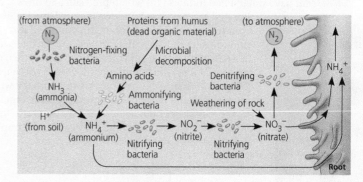

Nitrogen-fixing bacteria convert atmospheric $N_2$ to nitrogenous minerals that plants can absorb as a nitrogen source for organic synthesis. The most efficient mutualism between plants and nitrogen-fixing bacteria occurs in the **nodules** that are formed by *Rhizobium* bacteria growing in the roots of legumes. These bacteria obtain sugar from the plant and supply the plant with fixed nitrogen. In agriculture, legume crops are rotated with other crops to restore nitrogen to the soil.

- **Mycorrhizae** are mutualistic associations of fungi and roots. The fungal hyphae of mycorrhizae absorb water and minerals, which they supply to their plant hosts.

- **Epiphytes** grow on the surfaces of other plants but acquire water and minerals from rain. Parasitic plants absorb nutrients from host plants. Carnivorous plants supplement their mineral nutrition by digesting animals.

**?** *Do all plants gain energy directly from photosynthesis? Explain.*

## TEST YOUR UNDERSTANDING

### Level 1: Knowledge/Comprehension

1. The inorganic nutrient most often lacking in crops is
   (A) carbon.
   (C) phosphorus.
   (B) nitrogen.
   (D) potassium.

2. Micronutrients are needed in very small amounts because
   (A) most of them are mobile in the plant.
   (B) most serve mainly as cofactors of enzymes.
   (C) most are supplied in large enough quantities in seeds.
   (D) they play only a minor role in the growth and health of the plant.

3. Mycorrhizae enhance plant nutrition mainly by
   (A) absorbing water and minerals through the fungal hyphae.
   (B) providing sugar to root cells, which have no chloroplasts.
   (C) converting atmospheric nitrogen to ammonia.
   (D) enabling the roots to parasitize neighboring plants.

4. Epiphytes are
   (A) fungi that attack plants.
   (B) fungi that form mutualistic associations with roots.
   (C) nonphotosynthetic parasitic plants.
   (D) plants that grow on other plants.

5. Some of the problems associated with intensive irrigation include all of the following except
   (A) soil salinization.
   (C) land subsidence.
   (B) overfertilization.
   (D) aquifer depletion.

### Level 2: Application/Analysis

6. A mineral deficiency is likely to affect older leaves more than younger leaves if
   (A) the mineral is a micronutrient.
   (B) the mineral is very mobile within the plant.
   (C) the mineral is required for chlorophyll synthesis.
   (D) the mineral is a macronutrient.

7. The greatest difference in health between two groups of plants of the same species, one group with mycorrhizae and one group without mycorrhizae, would be in an environment
   (A) where nitrogen-fixing bacteria are abundant.
   (B) that has soil with poor drainage.
   (C) that has hot summers and cold winters.
   (D) in which the soil is relatively deficient in mineral nutrients.

8. Two groups of tomatoes were grown under laboratory conditions, one with humus added to the soil and one a control without humus. The leaves of the plants grown without humus were yellowish (less green) compared with those of the plants grown in humus-enriched soil. The best explanation is that
   (A) the healthy plants used the food in the decomposing leaves of the humus for energy to make chlorophyll.
   (B) the humus made the soil more loosely packed, so water penetrated more easily to the roots.
   (C) the humus contained minerals such as magnesium and iron needed for the synthesis of chlorophyll.
   (D) the heat released by the decomposing leaves of the humus caused more rapid growth and chlorophyll synthesis.

9. The specific relationship between a legume and its mutualistic *Rhizobium* strain probably depends on
   (A) each legume having a chemical dialogue with a fungus.
   (B) each *Rhizobium* strain having a form of nitrogenase that works only in the appropriate legume host.
   (C) each legume being found where the soil has only the *Rhizobium* specific to that legume.
   (D) specific recognition between chemical signals and signal receptors of the *Rhizobium* strain and legume species.

10. **DRAW IT** Draw a simple sketch of cation exchange, showing a root hair, a soil particle with anions, and a hydrogen ion displacing a mineral cation.

### Level 3: Synthesis/Evaluation

11. **EVOLUTION CONNECTION** Imagine taking the plant out of the picture in Figure 37.12. Write a paragraph explaining how soil bacteria could sustain the recycling of nitrogen *before* land plants evolved.

12. **SCIENTIFIC INQUIRY** Acid precipitation has an abnormally high concentration of hydrogen ions ($H^+$). One effect of acid precipitation is to deplete the soil of nutrients such as calcium ($Ca^{2+}$), potassium ($K^+$), and magnesium ($Mg^{2+}$). Suggest a hypothesis to explain how acid precipitation washes these nutrients from the soil. How might you test your hypothesis?

13. **SCIENCE, TECHNOLOGY, AND SOCIETY** In many countries, irrigation is depleting aquifers to such an extent that land is subsiding, harvests are decreasing, and it is becoming necessary to drill wells deeper. In many cases, the withdrawal of groundwater has now greatly surpassed the aquifers' rates of natural recharge. Discuss the possible consequences of this trend. What can society and science do to help alleviate this growing problem?

14. **WRITE ABOUT A THEME: INTERACTIONS** The soil in which plants grow teems with organisms from every taxonomic kingdom. In a short essay (100–150 words), discuss examples of how the mutualistic interactions of plants with bacteria, fungi, and animals improve plant nutrition.

15. **SYNTHESIZE YOUR KNOWLEDGE**

Making a footprint in the soil seems like an insignificant event. In a short essay (100–150 words), explain how a footprint would affect the properties of the soil and how these changes would affect soil organisms and the emergence of seedlings.

*For suggested answers, see Appendix A.*

 For additional practice questions, check out the **Dynamic Study Modules** in MasteringBiology. You can use them to study on your smartphone, tablet, or computer anytime, anywhere!

# Angiosperm Reproduction and Biotechnology

# 38

▲ Figure 38.1 **Why have blowflies laid their eggs on this flower?**

## KEY CONCEPTS

**38.1** Flowers, double fertilization, and fruits are key features of the angiosperm life cycle

**38.2** Flowering plants reproduce sexually, asexually, or both

**38.3** People modify crops by breeding and genetic engineering

## Flowers of Deceit

The only visible part of *Rhizanthes lowii*, a denizen of the rain forests of southeast Asia, is its large flesh-colored flower **(Figure 38.1)**. It derives all its energy from tapping into a species of tropical vine that it parasitizes. Its thieving ways also extend to its mode of pollination. Upon opening, a *Rhizanthes* flower emits a foul odor reminiscent of a decaying corpse. Female blowflies, insects that normally deposit their eggs on carrion, find the scent irresistible and lay their eggs on the flower. There, the blowflies are peppered with sticky pollen grains that adhere to their bodies. Eventually, the pollen-coated blowflies fly away, hopefully, from the plant's perspective, to another *Rhizanthes* flower.

An unusual aspect of the *Rhizanthes* example is that the insect does not profit from interacting with the flower. In fact, the blowfly maggots that emerge on *Rhizanthes* flowers find no carrion to eat and quickly perish. More typically, a plant lures an animal pollinator to its flowers not with offers of false carrion but with rewards of energy-rich nectar or pollen. Thus, both plant and pollinator benefit. Participating in such mutually beneficial relationships with other organisms is common in the plant kingdom. In fact, in recent evolutionary times, some flowering plants have formed relationships with an animal that not only disperses their seeds but also provides the plants with water and mineral nutrients and vigorously protects them from encroaching competitors, pathogens, and predators. In return for these favors, the animal typically gets to eat a fraction of some part of the plants, such as their seeds or fruits. These plants are called crops; the animals are humans.

---

When you see this blue icon, log in to **MasteringBiology** and go to the Study Area for digital resources.

 Get Ready for This Chapter

For over 10,000 years, plant breeders have genetically manipulated traits of a few hundred wild angiosperm species by artificial selection, transforming them into the crops we grow today. Genetic engineering has dramatically increased the variety of ways and the speed with which we can modify plants.

In Chapters 29 and 30, we approached plant reproduction from an evolutionary perspective, tracing the descent of land plants from algal ancestors. Because angiosperms are the most important group of plants in agricultural as well as most other terrestrial ecosystems, we'll explore their reproductive biology in detail in this chapter. After discussing the sexual and asexual reproduction of angiosperms, we'll examine the role of humans in genetically altering crop species, as well as the controversies surrounding modern plant biotechnology.

# CONCEPT 38.1

## Flowers, double fertilization, and fruits are key features of the angiosperm life cycle

The life cycles of all plants are characterized by an alternation of generations, in which multicellular haploid (*n*) and multicellular diploid (*2n*) generations alternately produce each other (see Figure 13.6b). The diploid plant, the *sporophyte*, produces haploid spores by meiosis. These spores divide by mitosis, giving rise to multicellular *gametophytes*, the male and female haploid plants that produce gametes (sperm and eggs). Fertilization, the fusion of gametes, results in a diploid zygote, which divides by mitosis and forms a new sporophyte. In angiosperms, the sporophyte is the dominant generation: It is larger, more conspicuous, and longer-lived than the gametophyte. The key traits of the angiosperm life cycle can be remembered as the

"three Fs"—*f*lowers, double *f*ertilization, and *f*ruits. We'll begin by discussing flowers.

## Flower Structure and Function

The **flower**, the sporophytic structure of angiosperms specialized for sexual reproduction, is typically composed of four types of floral organs: **carpels**, **stamens**, **petals**, and **sepals** (**Figure 38.2**). When viewed from above, these organs take the form of concentric whorls. Carpels form the first (innermost) whorl, stamens the second, petals the third, and sepals the fourth (outermost) whorl. All are attached to a part of the stem called the **receptacle**. Flowers are determinate shoots; they cease growing after the flower and fruit are formed.

Carpels and stamens are sporophylls—modified leaves specialized for reproduction (see Concept 30.1); sepals and petals are sterile modified leaves. A carpel (megasporophyll) has an **ovary** at its base and a long, slender neck called the **style**. At the top of the style is a sticky structure called the **stigma** that captures pollen. Within the ovary are one or more **ovules**, which become seeds if fertilized; the number of ovules depends on the species. The flower in Figure 38.2 has a single carpel, but many species have multiple carpels. In most species, the carpels are fused, resulting in a compound ovary with two or more chambers, each containing one or more ovules. The term **pistil** is sometimes used to refer to a single carpel or two or more fused carpels (**Figure 38.3**). A stamen (microsporophyll) consists of a stalk called the filament and a terminal structure called the **anther**; within the anther are chambers called microsporangia (pollen sacs) that produce pollen. Petals are typically more brightly colored than sepals and advertise the flower to insects and other animal pollinators. Sepals, which

▼ **Figure 38.3 The relationship between the terms *carpel* and *pistil*.** A simple pistil consists of a single, unfused carpel. A compound pistil consists of two or more fused carpels. Some types of flowers have only a single pistil, while other types have many pistils. In either case, the pistils may be simple or compound.

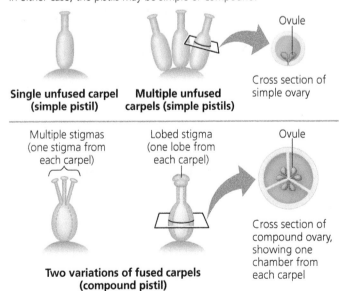

▼ **Figure 38.2 The structure of an idealized flower.**

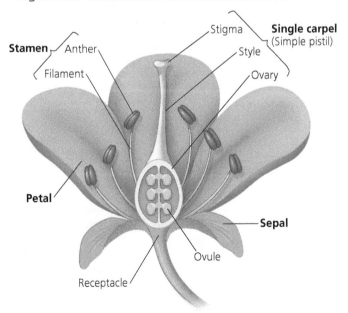

enclose and protect unopened floral buds, usually resemble leaves more than the other floral organs do.

**Complete flowers** have all four basic floral organs (see Figure 38.2). Some species have **incomplete flowers**, lacking sepals, petals, stamens, or carpels. For example, most grass flowers lack petals. Some incomplete flowers are sterile, lacking functional stamens and carpels; others are *unisexual*

(sometimes called *imperfect*), lacking either stamens or carpels. Flowers also vary in size, shape, color, odor, organ arrangement, and time of opening. Some are borne singly, while others are arranged in showy clusters called **inflorescences**. For example, a sunflower consists of a central disk composed of hundreds of tiny incomplete flowers, surrounded by sterile, incomplete flowers that look like yellow petals

## ▼ Figure 38.4 Exploring Flower Pollination

Most angiosperm species rely on a living (biotic) or nonliving (abiotic) pollinating agent that can move pollen from the anther of a flower on one plant to the stigma of a flower on another plant. Approximately 80% of all angiosperm pollination is biotic, employing animal go-betweens. Among abiotically pollinated species, 98% rely on wind and 2% on water. (Some angiosperm species can self-pollinate, but such species are limited to inbreeding in nature.)

### Abiotic Pollination by Wind

About 20% of all angiosperm species are wind-pollinated. Since their reproductive success does not depend on attracting pollinators, there has been no selective pressure favoring colorful or scented flowers. Accordingly, the flowers of wind-pollinated species are often small, green, and inconspicuous, and they produce neither scent nor the sugary solution called nectar. Most temperate trees and grasses are wind-pollinated. The flowers of hazel (*Corylus*

*avellana*) and many other temperate, wind-pollinated trees appear in the early spring, when there are no leaves to interfere with pollen movement. The relative inefficiency of wind pollination is compensated for by production of copious amounts of pollen grains. Wind tunnel studies reveal that wind pollination is often more efficient than it appears because floral structures can create eddy currents that aid in pollen capture.

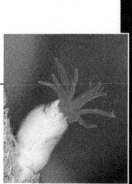

▲ Hazel carpellate flower (carpels only)

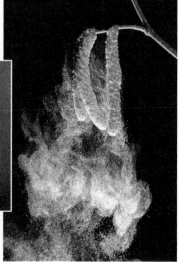

▲ Hazel staminate flowers (stamens only) releasing clouds of pollen

### Pollination by Bees

▲ Common dandelion under normal light

▲ Common dandelion under ultraviolet light

About 65% of all flowering plants require insects for pollination; the percentage is even greater for major crops. Bees are the most important insect pollinators, and there is great concern in Europe and North America that honeybee populations have shrunk. Pollinating bees depend on nectar and pollen for food. Typically, bee-pollinated flowers have a delicate, sweet

fragrance. Bees are attracted to bright colors, primarily yellow and blue. Red appears dull to them, but they can see ultraviolet radiation. Many species of bee-pollinated flowers, such as the common dandelion (*Taraxacum vulgare*), have ultraviolet markings called "nectar guides" that help insects locate the nectaries (nectar-producing glands) but are only visible to human eyes under ultraviolet light.

 **Video: Bee Colony Decline**

### Pollination by Moths and Butterflies

Moths and butterflies detect odors, and the flowers they pollinate are often sweetly fragrant. Butterflies perceive many bright colors, but moth-pollinated flowers are usually white or yellow, which stand out at night when moths are active. A yucca plant (shown here) is typically pollinated by a single species of moth with appendages that pack pollen onto the stigma. The moth then

deposits eggs directly into the ovary. The larvae eat some developing seeds, but this cost is outweighed by the benefit of an efficient and reliable pollinator. If a moth deposits too many eggs, the flower aborts and drops off, selecting against individuals that overexploit the plant.

**?** *What are the benefits and dangers to a plant of having a highly specific animal pollinator?*

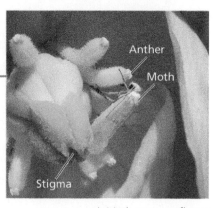

▲ Moth on yucca flower

(see Figure 40.23). Much of floral diversity represents adaptation to specific pollinators.

## Methods of Pollination

**Pollination** is the transfer of pollen to the part of a seed plant containing the ovules. In angiosperms, this transfer is from an anther to a stigma. Pollination can occur by wind, water, or animals **(Figure 38.4)**. In wind-pollinated species, including grasses and many trees, the release of enormous quantities of smaller-sized pollen compensates for the randomness of dispersal by the wind. At certain times of the year, the air is loaded with pollen grains, as anyone plagued with pollen allergies can attest. Some species of aquatic plants rely on water to disperse pollen. Most angiosperm species, however, depend on insects, birds, or other animal pollinators to transfer pollen directly from one flower to another.

**EVOLUTION** Animal pollinators are drawn to flowers for the food they provide in the form of pollen and nectar. Attracting pollinators that are loyal to a given plant species is an efficient way to ensure that pollen is transferred to another flower of the same species. Natural selection, therefore, favors deviations in floral structure or physiology that make it more likely for a flower to be pollinated regularly by an effective animal species. If a plant species develops traits that make its flowers more prized by pollinators, there is a selective pressure for pollinators to become adept at harvesting food from these flowers. The joint evolution of two interacting species, each in response to selection imposed by the other, is called **coevolution**. For example, some species have fused flower petals that form long, tubelike structures bearing nectaries tucked deep inside. Charles Darwin suggested that a race between flower and insect might lead to correspondences between the length of a floral tube and the length of an insect's proboscis, a straw-like mouthpart. Based on the length of a long, tubular flower that grows in Madagascar, Darwin predicted the existence of a pollinating moth with a 28-cm-long proboscis. Such a moth was discovered two decades after Darwin's death **(Figure 38.5)**.

Climate change may be affecting long-standing relationships between plants and animal pollinators. For example,

### Pollination by Bats

Bat-pollinated flowers, like moth-pollinated flowers, are light-colored and aromatic, attracting their nocturnal pollinators. The lesser long-nosed bat (*Leptonycteris curasoae yerbabuenae*) feeds on the nectar and pollen of agave and cactus flowers in the southwestern United States and Mexico. In feeding, the bats transfer pollen from plant to plant. Long-nosed bats are an endangered species.

▲ Long-nosed bat feeding on agave flowers at night

### Pollination by Flies

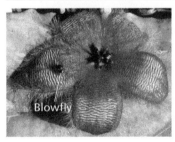

▲ Blowfly on carrion flower

Many fly-pollinated flowers are reddish and fleshy, with an odor like rotten meat. Blowflies visiting carrion flowers (*Stapelia* species) mistake the flower for a rotting corpse and lay their eggs on it. In the process, the blowflies become dusted with pollen that they carry to other flowers. When the eggs hatch, the larvae find no carrion to eat and die.

### Pollination by Birds

Bird-pollinated flowers, such as columbine flowers, are usually large and bright red or yellow, but they have little odor. Since birds often do not have a well-developed sense of smell, there has been no selective pressure favoring scent production. However, the flowers produce the sugary nectar that helps meet the high energy demands of the pollinating birds. The primary function of nectar, which is produced by nectaries at the base of many flowers, is to "reward" the pollinator. The petals of such flowers are often fused, forming a bent floral tube that fits the curved beak of the bird.

▶ Hummingbird drinking nectar of columbine flower

▼ **Figure 38.5 Coevolution of a flower and an insect pollinator.** The long floral tube of the Madagascar orchid *Angraecum sesquipedale* has coevolved with the 28-cm-long proboscis of its pollinator, the hawk moth *Xanthopan morganii praedicta*. The moth is named in honor of Darwin's prediction of its existence.

two species of Rocky Mountain bumblebees now have tongues that are about one-quarter shorter than those of bees of the same species 40 years ago. Flowers that require long-tongued pollinators have declined under the warmer conditions in the Rockies. As a result, there has been selective pressure favoring bumblebees with shorter tongues.

## The Angiosperm Life Cycle: An Overview

Pollination is one step in the angiosperm life cycle. **Figure 38.6** provides a complete overview of the life cycle, focusing on gametophyte development, sperm delivery by pollen tubes, double fertilization, and seed development.

Over the course of seed plant evolution, gametophytes became reduced in size and wholly dependent on the sporophyte for nutrients (see Figure 30.2). The gametophytes of angiosperms are the most reduced of all plants, consisting of only a few cells: They are microscopic, and their development is obscured by protective tissues.

### Development of Female Gametophytes (Embryo Sacs)

As a carpel develops, one or more ovules form deep within its ovary, its swollen base. A female gametophyte, also known as an **embryo sac**, develops inside each ovule. The process of embryo sac formation occurs in a tissue called the megasporangium ❶ within each ovule. Two *integuments* (layers of protective sporophytic tissue that will develop into the seed coat) surround each megasporangium, except at a gap called the *micropyle*. Female gametophyte development begins when one cell in the megasporangium of each ovule, the *megasporocyte* (or megaspore mother cell), enlarges and undergoes meiosis, producing four haploid **megaspores**. Only one megaspore survives; the others degenerate.

The nucleus of the surviving megaspore divides by mitosis three times without cytokinesis, resulting in one large cell with eight haploid nuclei. The multinucleate mass is then divided by membranes to form the embryo sac. Near the micropyle of the embryo sac, two cells called synergids flank the egg and help attract and guide the pollen tube to the embryo sac. At the opposite end of the embryo sac are three antipodal cells of unknown function. The other two nuclei, called polar nuclei, are not partitioned into separate cells but share the cytoplasm of the large central cell of the embryo sac. The mature embryo sac thus consists of eight nuclei contained within seven cells. The ovule, which will become a seed if fertilized, now consists of the embryo sac, enclosed by the megasporangium (which eventually withers) and two surrounding integuments.

### Development of Male Gametophytes in Pollen Grains

As the stamens are produced, each anther ❷ develops four microsporangia, also called pollen sacs. Within the microsporangia are many diploid cells called *microsporocytes,* or microspore mother cells. Each microsporocyte undergoes meiosis, forming four haploid **microspores**, ❸ each of which eventually gives rise to a haploid male gametophyte. Each microspore then undergoes mitosis, producing a haploid male gametophyte consisting of only two cells: the *generative cell* and the *tube cell*. Together, these two cells and the spore wall constitute a **pollen grain**. The spore wall, which consists of material produced by both the microspore and the anther, usually exhibits an elaborate pattern unique to the species. During maturation of the male gametophyte, the generative cell passes into the tube cell: The tube cell now has a completely free-standing cell inside it.

### Sperm Delivery by Pollen Tubes

After the microsporangium breaks open and releases the pollen, a pollen grain may be transferred to a receptive surface of a stigma—the act of pollination. At the time of pollination, the pollen grain typically consists of only the tube cell and the generative cell. It then absorbs water and germinates by producing a **pollen tube**, a long cellular protuberance that delivers sperm to the female gametophyte. As the pollen tube elongates through the style, the nucleus of the generative cell divides by mitosis and produces two sperm, which remain inside the tube cell. The tube nucleus leads ahead of the two sperm as the tip of the pollen tube grows toward the micropyle in response to chemical attractants produced by the synergids. The arrival of the pollen tube initiates the death of one of the two synergids, thereby providing a passageway into the embryo sac. The tube nucleus and the two sperm are then discharged from the pollen tube ❹ in the vicinity of the female gametophyte.

### Double Fertilization

**Fertilization**, the fusion of gametes, occurs after the two sperm reach the female gametophyte. One sperm fertilizes the egg, forming the zygote. The other sperm combines with the two polar nuclei, forming a triploid ($3n$) nucleus in the center of the large central cell of the female gametophyte. This cell will give rise to the **endosperm**, a food-storing tissue of the seed. ❺ The union of the two sperm cells with different nuclei of the female gametophyte is called **double fertilization**. Double fertilization ensures that endosperm develops only in ovules where the egg has been fertilized, thereby preventing angiosperms from squandering nutrients on infertile ovules. Near the time of double fertilization, the tube nucleus, the other synergid, and the antipodal cells degenerate.

### Seed Development

❻ After double fertilization, each ovule develops into a seed. Meanwhile, the ovary develops into a fruit, which encloses the seeds and aids in their dispersal by wind or animals. As the sporophyte embryo develops from the zygote, the seed stockpiles proteins, oils, and starch to varying degrees, depending on the species. This is why seeds are such a major nutrient drain. Initially, carbohydrates and other nutrients are stored in the seed's endosperm, but later, depending on the species, the swelling cotyledons (seed leaves) of the embryo may take over this function. When a seed germinates, ❼ the embryo develops into a new sporophyte. The mature

▼ **Figure 38.6 The life cycle of angiosperms.** For simplicity, a flower with a single carpel (simple pistil) is shown. Many species have multiple carpels, either separate or fused.

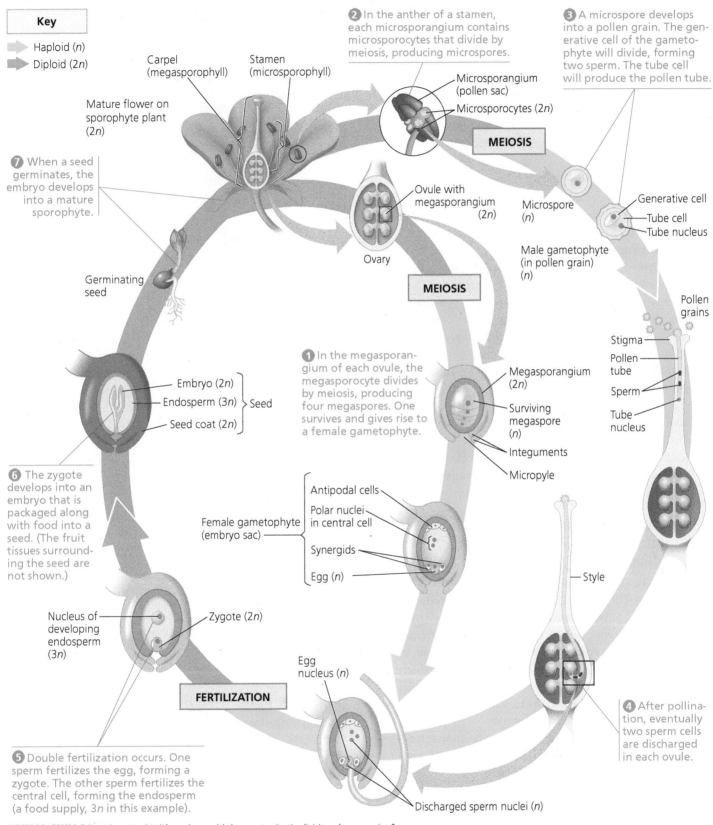

**Key**

Haploid (*n*)

Diploid (2*n*)

**2** In the anther of a stamen, each microsporangium contains microsporocytes that divide by meiosis, producing microspores.

**3** A microspore develops into a pollen grain. The generative cell of the gametophyte will divide, forming two sperm. The tube cell will produce the pollen tube.

Carpel (megasporophyll)

Stamen (microsporophyll)

Microsporangium (pollen sac)

Microsporocytes (2*n*)

Mature flower on sporophyte plant (2*n*)

**MEIOSIS**

**7** When a seed germinates, the embryo develops into a mature sporophyte.

Ovule with megasporangium (2*n*)

Microspore (*n*)

Generative cell

Tube cell

Tube nucleus

Ovary

Male gametophyte (in pollen grain) (*n*)

Germinating seed

**MEIOSIS**

Pollen grains

Stigma

Pollen tube

**1** In the megasporangium of each ovule, the megasporocyte divides by meiosis, producing four megaspores. One survives and gives rise to a female gametophyte.

Megasporangium (2*n*)

Surviving megaspore (*n*)

Sperm

Tube nucleus

Embryo (2*n*)

Endosperm (3*n*)       Seed

Seed coat (2*n*)

Integuments

Micropyle

Antipodal cells

**6** The zygote develops into an embryo that is packaged along with food into a seed. (The fruit tissues surrounding the seed are not shown.)

Polar nuclei in central cell

Female gametophyte (embryo sac)

Synergids

Style

Egg (*n*)

Nucleus of developing endosperm (3*n*)

Zygote (2*n*)

Egg nucleus (*n*)

**4** After pollination, eventually two sperm cells are discharged in each ovule.

**FERTILIZATION**

**5** Double fertilization occurs. One sperm fertilizes the egg, forming a zygote. The other sperm fertilizes the central cell, forming the endosperm (a food supply, 3*n* in this example).

Discharged sperm nuclei (*n*)

**VISUAL SKILLS ➤** *Where in this life cycle would the most mitotic divisions be occurring?*

MB  **Animation: Angiosperm Life Cycle**
**Animation: Sexual Reproduction in Angiosperms**
**Video: Flowering Plant Life Cycle**

sporophyte produces its own flowers and fruits: The life cycle is now complete, but it is necessary to examine more closely how an ovule develops into a mature seed.

## Seed Development and Structure: *A Closer Look*

After successful pollination and double fertilization, a seed begins to form. During this process, both the endosperm and the embryo develop. When mature, a **seed** consists of a dormant embryo surrounded by stored food and protective layers.

### *Endosperm Development*

Endosperm usually develops before the embryo does. After double fertilization, the triploid nucleus of the ovule's central cell divides, forming a multinucleate "supercell" that has a milky consistency. This liquid mass, the endosperm, becomes multicellular when cytokinesis partitions the cytoplasm by forming membranes between the nuclei. Eventually, these "naked" cells produce cell walls, and the endosperm becomes solid. Coconut "milk" and "meat" are examples of liquid and solid endosperm, respectively. The white fluffy part of popcorn is another example of endosperm. The endosperms of just three grains—wheat, maize, and rice—provide much of the food energy for human sustenance.

In grains and most other species of monocots, as well as many eudicots, the endosperm stores nutrients that can be used by the seedling after germination. In other eudicot seeds, the food reserves of the endosperm are completely exported to the cotyledons before the seed completes its development; consequently, the mature seed lacks endosperm.

### *Embryo Development*

The first mitotic division of the zygote is asymmetrical and splits the fertilized egg into a basal cell and a terminal cell **(Figure 38.7)**. The terminal cell eventually gives rise to most of the embryo. The basal cell continues to divide, producing a thread of cells called the suspensor, which anchors the embryo to the parent plant. The suspensor helps in transferring nutrients to the embryo from the parent plant and, in some species, from the endosperm. As the suspensor elongates, it pushes the embryo deeper into the nutritive and protective tissues. Meanwhile, the terminal cell divides several times and forms a spherical proembryo (early embryo) attached to the suspensor. The cotyledons begin to form as bumps on the proembryo. A eudicot embryo, with its two cotyledons, is heart-shaped at this stage.

Soon after the rudimentary cotyledons appear, the embryo elongates. Cradled between the two cotyledons is the embryonic shoot apex. At the opposite end of the embryo's axis, where the suspensor attaches, an embryonic root apex forms. After the seed germinates—indeed, for the rest of the plant's life—the apical meristems at the apices of shoots and roots sustain primary growth (see Figure 35.11).

**▼ Figure 38.7 The development of a eudicot plant embryo.** By the time the ovule becomes a mature seed and the integuments harden and thicken into the seed coat, the zygote has given rise to an embryonic plant with rudimentary organs.

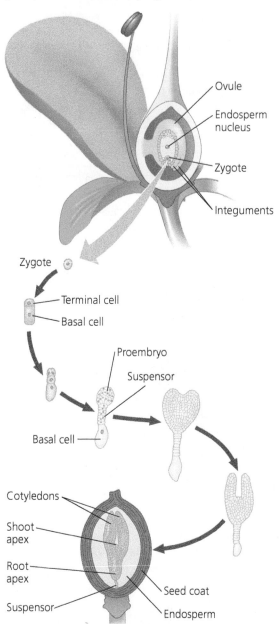

Ovule
Endosperm nucleus
Zygote
Integuments

Zygote

Terminal cell
Basal cell

Proembryo
Suspensor

Basal cell

Cotyledons
Shoot apex
Root apex
Suspensor
Seed coat
Endosperm

Ⓜ Animation: Embryo and Endosperm Development

### *Structure of the Mature Seed*

During the last stages of its maturation, the seed dehydrates until its water content is only about 5–15% of its weight. The embryo, which is surrounded by a food supply (cotyledons, endosperm, or both), enters **dormancy**; that is, it stops growing and its metabolism nearly ceases. The embryo and its food supply are enclosed by a hard, protective **seed coat** formed from the integuments of the ovule. In some species, dormancy is imposed by the presence of an intact seed coat rather than by the embryo itself.

If you split apart a seed of the garden bean, a type of eudicot, you can see that the embryo consists of an elongate structure, the embryonic axis, attached to two thick, fleshy cotyledons **(Figure 38.8a)**. Below where the cotyledons are attached, the embryonic axis is called the **hypocotyl** (from the Greek *hypo*, under). The hypocotyl terminates in the **radicle**, or embryonic root. The portion of the embryonic axis above where the cotyledons are attached and below the first pair of miniature leaves is the **epicotyl** (from the Greek *epi*, on, over). The epicotyl, young leaves, and shoot apical meristem are collectively called the *plumule*.

The cotyledons of the common garden bean are packed with starch before the seed germinates because they absorbed carbohydrates from the endosperm when the seed was developing. However, the seeds of some eudicot species, such as castor beans (*Ricinus communis*), retain their food supply in the endosperm and have very thin cotyledons. The cotyledons absorb nutrients from the endosperm and transfer them to the rest of the embryo when the seed germinates.

The embryos of monocots possess only a single cotyledon **(Figure 38.8b)**. Grasses, including maize and wheat, have a specialized cotyledon called a *scutellum* (from the Latin *scutella*, small shield, a reference to its shape). The scutellum, which has a large surface area, is pressed against the endosperm, from which it absorbs nutrients during germination. The embryo of a grass seed is enclosed within two protective sheathes: a **coleoptile**, which covers the young shoot, and a **coleorhiza**, which covers the young root. Both structures aid in soil penetration after germination.

### Seed Dormancy: An Adaptation for Tough Times

The environmental conditions required to break seed dormancy vary among species. Some seed types germinate as soon as they are in a suitable environment. Others remain dormant, even if sown in a favorable place, until a specific environmental cue causes them to break dormancy.

The requirement for specific cues to break seed dormancy increases the chances that germination will occur at a time and place most advantageous to the seedling. Seeds of many desert plants, for instance, germinate only after a substantial rainfall. If they were to germinate after a mild drizzle, the soil might soon become too dry to support the seedlings. Where natural fires are common, many seeds require intense heat or smoke to break dormancy; seedlings are therefore most abundant after fire has cleared away competing vegetation. Where winters are harsh, seeds may require extended exposure to cold before they germinate; seeds sown during summer or fall will therefore not germinate until the following spring, ensuring a long growth season before the next winter. Certain small seeds, such as those of some lettuce varieties, require light for germination and will break dormancy only if buried shallow enough for the seedlings to poke through the soil surface. Some seeds have coats that must be weakened by chemical attack as they pass through an animal's digestive tract and

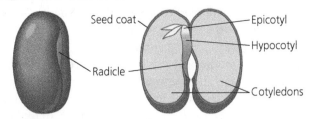

▼ **Figure 38.8 Seed structure.**

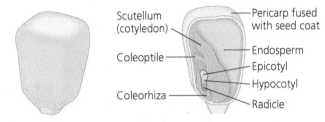

**(a) Common garden bean, a eudicot with thick cotyledons.** The fleshy cotyledons store food absorbed from the endosperm before the seed germinates.

**(b) Maize, a monocot.** Like all monocots, maize has only one cotyledon. Maize and other grasses have a large cotyledon called a scutellum. The rudimentary shoot is sheathed in a structure called the coleoptile, and the coleorhiza covers the young root.

**MAKE CONNECTIONS** ➤ *In addition to cotyledon number, how do the structures of monocots and eudicots differ? (See Figure 30.16.)*

**VISUAL SKILLS** ➤ *Which mature seed lacks an endosperm? What happened to it?*

thus are usually carried a long distance before germinating from feces.

The length of time a dormant seed remains viable and capable of germinating varies from a few days to decades or even longer, depending on the plant species and environmental conditions. The oldest carbon-14-dated seed that has grown into a viable plant was a 2,000-year-old date palm seed from Israel. Most seeds are durable enough to last a year or two until conditions are favorable for germinating. Thus, the soil has a bank of ungerminated seeds that may have accumulated for several years. This is one reason vegetation reappears so rapidly after an environmental disruption such as fire.

## Sporophyte Development from Seed to Mature Plant

When environmental conditions are conducive for growth, seed dormancy is lost and germination proceeds. Germination is followed by growth of stems, leaves, and roots, and eventually by flowering.

### Seed Germination

Seed germination is initiated by **imbibition**, the uptake of water due to the low water potential of the dry seed. Imbibition causes the seed to expand and rupture its coat and triggers changes in the embryo that enable it to resume growth. Following hydration, enzymes digest the storage materials of the endosperm or cotyledons, and the nutrients are transferred to the growing regions of the embryo.

The first organ to emerge from the germinating seed is the radicle, the embryonic root. The development of a root system anchors the seedling in the soil and supplies it with water necessary for cell expansion. A ready supply of water is a prerequisite for the next step, the emergence of the shoot tip into the drier conditions encountered above ground. In garden beans, for example, a hook forms in the hypocotyl, and growth pushes the hook above ground (**Figure 38.9a**). In response to light, the hypocotyl straightens, the cotyledons separate, and the delicate epicotyl, now exposed, spreads its first true leaves (as distinct from the cotyledons, or seed leaves). These leaves expand, become green, and begin making food by photosynthesis. The cotyledons shrivel and fall away, their food reserves having been exhausted by the germinating embryo.

Some monocots, such as maize and other grasses, use a different method for breaking ground when they germinate (**Figure 38.9b**). The coleoptile pushes up through the soil and into the air. The shoot tip grows through the tunnel provided by the coleoptile and breaks through the coleoptile's tip upon emergence.

▼ **Figure 38.9** **Two common types of seed germination.**

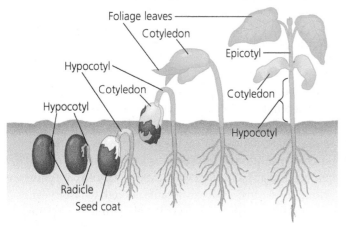

Foliage leaves
Cotyledon
Epicotyl
Hypocotyl
Cotyledon
Cotyledon
Hypocotyl
Hypocotyl
Radicle
Seed coat

(a) **Common garden bean.** In common garden beans, straightening of a hook in the hypocotyl pulls the cotyledons from the soil.

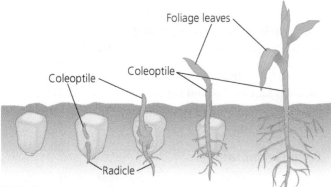

Foliage leaves
Coleoptile
Coleoptile
Radicle

(b) **Maize.** In maize and other grasses, the shoot grows straight up through the tube of the coleoptile.

**VISUAL SKILLS** ➤ *How do bean and maize seedlings protect their shoot systems as they push through the soil?*

 Animation: Seed Germination

### *Growth and Flowering*

Once a seed has germinated and started to photosynthesize, most of the plant's resources are devoted to the growth of stems, leaves, and roots (also known as *vegetative growth*). This growth, including both primary and secondary growth, arises from the activity of meristematic cells (see Concept 35.2). During this stage, usually the best strategy is to photosynthesize and grow as much as possible before flowering, the reproductive phase.

The flowers of a given plant species typically appear suddenly and simultaneously at a specific time of year. Such timing promotes outbreeding, the main advantage of sexual reproduction. Flower formation involves a developmental switch in the shoot apical meristem from a vegetative to a reproductive growth mode. This transition into a *floral meristem* is triggered by a combination of environmental cues (such as day length) and internal signals, as you'll learn in Concept 39.3. Once the transition to flowering has begun, the order of each organ's emergence from the floral meristem determines whether it will develop into a sepal, petal, stamen, or carpel (see Figure 35.36).

### Fruit Structure and Function

Before a seed can germinate and develop into a mature plant, it must be deposited in suitable soil. Fruits play a key role in this process. A **fruit** is the mature ovary of a flower. While the seeds are developing from ovules, the flower develops into a fruit (**Figure 38.10**). The fruit protects the enclosed seeds and, when mature, aids in their dispersal by wind or animals. Fertilization triggers hormonal changes that cause the ovary to begin its transformation into a fruit. If a flower has not been pollinated, fruit typically does not develop, and the flower usually withers and dies.

During fruit development, the ovary wall becomes the *pericarp*, the thickened wall of the fruit. In some fruits, such as soybean pods, the ovary wall dries out completely at maturity, whereas in other fruits, such as grapes, it remains fleshy. In still others, such as peaches, the inner part of the ovary

▼ **Figure 38.10** **The flower-to-fruit transition.** After flowers, such as those of the American pokeweed, are fertilized, stamens and petals fall off, stigmas and styles wither, and the ovary walls that house the developing seeds swell to form fruits. Developing seeds and fruits are major sinks for sugars and other carbohydrates.

**▼ Figure 38.11 Developmental origin of different classes of fruits.**

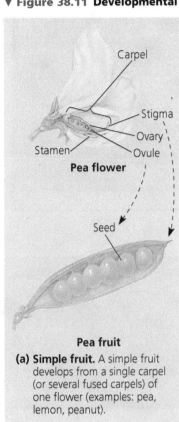

**Pea flower**

**Pea fruit**

**(a) Simple fruit.** A simple fruit develops from a single carpel (or several fused carpels) of one flower (examples: pea, lemon, peanut).

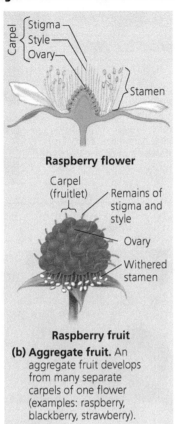

**Raspberry flower**

**Raspberry fruit**

**(b) Aggregate fruit.** An aggregate fruit develops from many separate carpels of one flower (examples: raspberry, blackberry, strawberry).

**Pineapple inflorescence**

Each segment develops from the carpel of one flower

**Pineapple fruit**

**(c) Multiple fruit.** A multiple fruit develops from many carpels of the many flowers that form an inflorescence (examples: pineapple, fig).

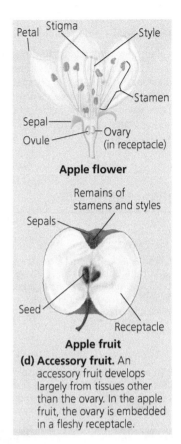

**Apple flower**

**Apple fruit**

**(d) Accessory fruit.** An accessory fruit develops largely from tissues other than the ovary. In the apple fruit, the ovary is embedded in a fleshy receptacle.

---

becomes stony (the pit) while the outer parts stay fleshy. As the ovary grows, the other parts of the flower usually wither and are shed.

Fruits are classified into several types, depending on their developmental origin. Most fruits are derived from a single carpel or several fused carpels and are called **simple fruits** (Figure 38.11a). An **aggregate fruit** results from a single flower that has more than one separate carpel, each forming a small fruit (Figure 38.11b). These "fruitlets" are clustered together on a single receptacle, as in a raspberry. A **multiple fruit** develops from an inflorescence, a group of flowers tightly clustered together. When the walls of the many ovaries start to thicken, they fuse together and become incorporated into one fruit, as in a pineapple (Figure 38.11c).

In some angiosperms, other floral parts contribute to what we commonly call the fruit. Such fruits are called **accessory fruits**. In apple flowers, the ovary is embedded in the receptacle, and the fleshy part of this simple fruit is derived mainly from the enlarged receptacle; only the apple core develops from the ovary (Figure 38.11d). Another example is the strawberry, an aggregate fruit consisting of an enlarged receptacle studded with tiny, partially embedded fruits, each bearing a single seed.

A fruit usually ripens about the same time that its seeds complete their development. Whereas the ripening of a dry fruit, such as a soybean pod, involves the aging and drying out of fruit tissues, the process in a fleshy fruit is more elaborate. Complex interactions of hormones result in an edible fruit that entices animals that disperse the seeds. The fruit's "pulp" becomes softer as enzymes digest components of cell walls. The color usually changes from green to another color, making the fruit more visible among the leaves. The fruit becomes sweeter as organic acids or starch molecules are converted to sugar, which may reach a concentration of 20% in a ripe fruit. Figure 38.12 examines some mechanisms of seed and fruit dispersal in more detail.

In this section, you have learned about the key features of sexual reproduction in angiosperms—flowers, double fertilization, and fruits. Next, we'll examine asexual reproduction.

## CONCEPT CHECK 38.1

1. Distinguish between pollination and fertilization.

2. **WHAT IF?** ➤ If flowers had shorter styles, pollen tubes would more easily reach the embryo sac. Suggest an explanation for why very long styles have evolved in most flowering plants.

3. **MAKE CONNECTIONS** ➤ Does the life cycle of humans have any structures analogous to plant gametophytes? Explain your answer. (See Figures 13.5 and 13.6.)

*For suggested answers, see Appendix A.*

**Exploring Fruit and Seed Dispersal**

A plant's life depends on finding fertile ground. But a seed that falls and sprouts beneath the parent plant will stand little chance of competing successfully for nutrients. To prosper, seeds must be widely dispersed. Plants use biotic dispersal agents as well as abiotic agents such as water and wind.

## Dispersal by Water

▶ Some buoyant seeds and fruits can survive months or years at sea. In coconut, the seed embryo and fleshy white "meat" (endosperm) are within a hard layer (endocarp) surrounded by a thick and buoyant fibrous husk.

## Dispersal by Wind

▶ With a wingspan of 12 cm, the giant seed of the tropical Asian climbing gourd *Alsomitra macrocarpa* glides through the air of the rain forest in wide circles when released.

▼ The winged fruit of a maple spins like a helicopter blade, slowing descent and increasing the chance of being carried farther by horizontal winds.

Dandelion fruit

▶ Tumbleweeds break off at the ground and tumble across the terrain, scattering their seeds.

▲ Some seeds and fruits are attached to umbrella-like "parachutes" that are made of intricately branched hairs and often produced in puffy clusters. These dandelion "seeds" (actually one-seeded fruits) are carried aloft by the slightest gust of wind.

## Dispersal by Animals

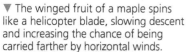

◀ The sharp, tack-like spines on the fruits of puncture vine (*Tribulus terrestris*) can pierce bicycle tires and injure animals, including humans. When these painful "tacks" are removed and discarded, the seeds are dispersed.

◀ Some animals, such as squirrels, hoard seeds or fruits in underground caches. If the animal dies or forgets the cache's location, the buried seeds are well positioned to germinate.

▶ Seeds in edible fruits are often dispersed in feces, such as the black bear feces shown here. Such dispersal may carry seeds far from the parent plant.

▶ Ants are chemically attracted to seeds with "food bodies" rich in fatty acids, amino acids, and sugars. The ants carry the seed to their underground nest, where the food body (the lighter-colored portion shown here) is removed and fed to larvae. Due to the seed's size, unwieldy shape, or hard coating, the remainder is usually left intact in the nest, where it germinates.

# CONCEPT 38.2

## Flowering plants reproduce sexually, asexually, or both

During **asexual reproduction**, offspring are derived from a single parent without any fusion of egg and sperm. The result is a clone, an individual genetically identical to its parent. Asexual reproduction is common in angiosperms, as well as in other plants, and for some species it is the main mode of reproduction.

## Mechanisms of Asexual Reproduction

Asexual reproduction in plants is typically an extension of the capacity for indeterminate growth. Plant growth can be sustained or renewed indefinitely by meristems, regions of undifferentiated, dividing cells (see Concept 35.2). In addition, parenchyma cells throughout the plant can divide and differentiate into more specialized types of cells, enabling plants to regenerate lost parts. Detached root or stem fragments of some plants can develop into whole offspring; for example, pieces of a potato with an "eye" (bud) can each regenerate a whole plant. Such **fragmentation**, the separation of a parent plant into parts that develop into whole plants, is one of the most common modes of asexual reproduction. The adventitious plantlets on *Kalanchoë* leaves exemplify an unusual type of fragmentation (see Figure 35.7). In other cases, the root system of a single parent, such as an aspen tree, can give rise to many adventitious shoots that become separate shoot systems (**Figure 38.13**). One aspen clone in Utah has been estimated to be composed of 47,000 stems of genetically identical trees. Although it is likely that some of the root system connections have been severed, making some of the trees isolated from the rest of the clone, each tree still shares a common genome.

A different mechanism of asexual reproduction has evolved in dandelions and some other plants. These plants can sometimes produce seeds without pollination or fertilization. This asexual production of seeds is called **apomixis** (from the Greek words meaning "away from the act of mixing") because there is no joining or, indeed, production of sperm and egg. Instead, a diploid cell in the ovule gives rise to the embryo, and the ovules mature into seeds, which in the dandelion are dispersed by windblown fruits. Thus, these plants clone themselves by an asexual process but have the advantage of seed dispersal, usually associated with sexual reproduction. Plant breeders are interested in introducing apomixis into hybrid crops because it would allow hybrid plants to pass desirable genomes intact to offspring.

## Advantages and Disadvantages of Asexual and Sexual Reproduction

**EVOLUTION** An advantage of asexual reproduction is that there is no need for a pollinator. This may be beneficial in situations where plants of the same species are sparsely distributed and unlikely to be visited by the same pollinator. Asexual reproduction also allows the plant to pass on all its genetic legacy intact to its progeny. In contrast, when reproducing sexually, a plant passes on only half of its alleles. If a plant is superbly suited to its environment, asexual reproduction can be advantageous. A vigorous plant can potentially clone many copies of itself, and if the environmental circumstances remain stable, these offspring will also be genetically well adapted to the same environmental conditions under which the parent flourished.

Asexual plant reproduction based on the vegetative growth of stems, leaves, or roots is known as **vegetative reproduction**. Generally, the progeny produced by vegetative reproduction are stronger than seedlings produced by sexual reproduction. In contrast, seed germination is a precarious stage in a plant's life. The tough seed gives rise to a fragile seedling that may face exposure to predators, parasites, wind, and other hazards. In the wild, few seedlings survive to become parents themselves. Production of enormous numbers of seeds compensates for the odds against individual survival and gives natural selection ample genetic variations to screen. However, this is an expensive means of reproduction in terms of the resources consumed in flowering and fruiting.

Because sexual reproduction generates variation in offspring and populations, it can be advantageous in unstable environments where evolving pathogens and other fluctuating conditions affect survival and reproductive success. In contrast, the genotypic uniformity of asexually produced plants puts them at great risk of local extinction if there is a catastrophic environmental change, such as a new strain of disease. Moreover, seeds (which are almost always produced sexually) facilitate the dispersal of offspring to more distant locations. Finally, seed dormancy allows growth to be suspended until environmental conditions become more

▼ **Figure 38.13 Asexual reproduction in aspen trees.** Some aspen groves, such as those shown here, consist of thousands of trees descended by asexual reproduction. Each grove of trees derives from the root system of one parent. Thus, the grove is a clone. Notice that genetic differences between groves descended from different parents result in different timing for the development of fall color.

## Using Positive and Negative Correlations to Interpret Data

**Do Monkey Flower Species Differ in Allocating Their Energy to Sexual Versus Asexual Reproduction?** Over the course of its life span, a plant captures only a finite amount of resources and energy, which must be allocated to best meet the plant's individual requirements for maintenance, growth, defense, and reproduction. Researchers examined how five species of monkey flower (genus *Mimulus*) use their resources for sexual and asexual reproduction.

**How the Experiment Was Done** After growing specimens of each species in separate pots in the open, the researchers determined averages for nectar volume, nectar concentration, seeds produced per flower, and the number of times the plants were visited by broad-tailed hummingbirds (*Selasphorus platycercus*, shown here). Using greenhouse-grown specimens, they determined the average number of rooted branches per gram fresh shoot weight for each of the species. The phrase *rooted branches* refers to asexual reproduction through horizontal shoots that develop roots.

### INTERPRET THE DATA

1. A correlation is a way to describe the relationship between two variables. In a positive correlation, as the values of one of the variables increase, the values of the second variable also increase. In a negative correlation, as the values of one of the variables increase, the values of the second variable decrease. Or there may be no correlation between two variables. If researchers know how two variables are correlated, they can make a prediction about one variable based on what they know about the other variable. (a) Which variable(s) is/are positively correlated with the volume of nectar production in this genus? (b) Which is/are negatively correlated? (c) Which show(s) no clear relationship?

2. (a) Which *Mimulus* species would you categorize as mainly asexual reproducers? Why? (b) Which species would you categorize as mainly sexual reproducers? Why?

3. (a) Which species would probably fare better in response to a pathogen that infects all *Mimulus* species? (b) Which species would fare better if a pathogen caused hummingbird populations to dwindle?

 **Instructors**: A version of this Scientific Skills Exercise can be assigned in MasteringBiology.

### Data from the Experiment

| Species | Nectar Volume (μL) | Nectar Concentration (% weight of sucrose/ total weight) | Seeds per Flower | Visits per Flower | Rooted Branches per Gram Shoot Weight |
|---|---|---|---|---|---|
| *M. rupestris* | 4.93 | 16.6 | 2.2 | 0.22 | 0.673 |
| *M. eastwoodiae* | 4.94 | 19.8 | 25 | 0.74 | 0.488 |
| *M. nelson* | 20.25 | 17.1 | 102.5 | 1.08 | 0.139 |
| *M. verbenaceus* | 38.96 | 16.9 | 155.1 | 1.26 | 0.091 |
| *M. cardinalis* | 50.00 | 19.9 | 283.7 | 1.75 | 0.069 |

**Data from** S. Sutherland and R. K. Vickery, Jr. Trade-offs between sexual and asexual reproduction in the genus *Mimulus*. *Oecologia* 76:330–335 (1998).

favorable. In the **Scientific Skills Exercise**, you can use data to determine which species of monkey flower are mainly asexual reproducers and which are mainly sexual reproducers.

Although sexual reproduction involving two genetically different plants produces the most genetically diverse offspring, some plants, such as garden peas, usually self-fertilize. This process, called "selfing," is a desirable attribute in some crop plants because it ensures that every ovule will develop into a seed. In many angiosperm species, however, mechanisms have evolved that make it difficult or impossible for a flower to fertilize itself, as we'll discuss next.

## Mechanisms That Prevent Self-Fertilization

The various mechanisms that prevent self-fertilization contribute to genetic variety by ensuring that the sperm and egg come from different parents. In the case of **dioecious** species, plants cannot self-fertilize because different individuals have either staminate flowers (lacking carpels) or carpellate flowers (lacking stamens) **(Figure 38.14a)**. Other plants have flowers with functional stamens and carpels that mature at different times or are structurally arranged in such a way that it is unlikely that an animal pollinator could transfer pollen from an anther to a stigma of the same flower **(Figure 38.14b)**. However, the most common anti-selfing mechanism in flowering plants is **self-incompatibility**, the ability of a plant to reject its own pollen and the pollen of closely related individuals. If a pollen grain lands on a stigma of a flower of the same plant or a closely related plant, a biochemical block prevents the pollen from completing its development and fertilizing an egg. This plant response is analogous to the immune response of animals because both are based on the ability to distinguish the cells of "self" from those of "nonself." The key difference is that the animal

**(a)** Some species, such as *Sagittaria latifolia* (common arrowhead), are dioecious, having plants that produce only staminate flowers (left) or carpellate flowers (right).

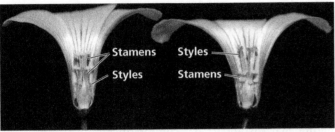

Thrum flower          Pin flower

**(b)** Some species, such as *Oxalis alpina* (alpine wood sorrel), produce two types of flowers on different individuals: "thrums," which have short styles and long stamens, and "pins," which have long styles and short stamens. An insect foraging for nectar would collect pollen on different parts of its body; thrum pollen would be deposited on pin stigmas, and vice versa.

immune system rejects nonself, as when the immune system mounts a defense against a pathogen or rejects a transplanted organ (see Concept 43.3). In contrast, self-incompatibility in plants is a rejection of self.

Researchers are unraveling the molecular mechanisms of self-incompatibility. Recognition of "self" pollen is based on genes called *S*-genes. In the gene pool of a population, there can be dozens of alleles of an *S*-gene. If a pollen grain has an allele that matches an allele of the stigma on which it lands, the pollen tube either fails to germinate or fails to grow through the style to the ovary. There are two types of self-incompatibility: gametophytic and sporophytic.

In gametophytic self-incompatibility, the *S*-allele in the pollen genome governs the blocking of fertilization. For example, an $S_1$ pollen grain from an $S_1S_2$ parental sporophyte cannot fertilize eggs of an $S_1S_2$ flower but can fertilize an $S_2S_3$ flower. An $S_2$ pollen grain cannot fertilize either flower. In some plants, this self-recognition involves the enzymatic destruction of RNA within a pollen tube. RNA-hydrolyzing enzymes are produced by the style and enter the pollen tube. If the pollen tube is a "self" type, they destroy its RNA.

In sporophytic self-incompatibility, fertilization is blocked by *S*-allele gene products in tissues of the parental sporophyte. For example, neither an $S_1$ nor an $S_2$ pollen grain from an $S_1S_2$ parental sporophyte can fertilize eggs of an $S_1S_2$ flower or an $S_2S_3$ flower, due to the $S_1S_2$ parental tissue attached to the pollen wall. Sporophytic incompatibility involves a signal transduction pathway in epidermal cells of the stigma that prevents germination of the pollen grain.

Research on self-incompatibility may have agricultural applications. Breeders often hybridize different genetic strains of a crop to combine the best traits of the two strains and to counter the loss of vigor that can often result from excessive inbreeding. To prevent self-fertilization within the two strains, breeders must either laboriously remove the anthers from the parent plants that provide the seeds (as Mendel did) or use male-sterile strains of the crop plant, if they exist. If self-compatibility can be genetically engineered back into domesticated plant varieties, these limitations to commercial hybridization of crop seeds could be overcome.

## Totipotency, Vegetative Reproduction, and Tissue Culture

In a multicellular organism, any cell that can divide and asexually generate a clone of the original organism is said to be **totipotent**. Totipotency is found in many plants, particularly but not exclusively in their meristematic tissues. Plant totipotency underlies most of the techniques used by humans to clone plants.

### Vegetative Propagation and Grafting

Vegetative reproduction occurs naturally in many plants, but it can often be facilitated or induced by humans, in which case it is called **vegetative propagation**. Most houseplants, landscape shrubs and bushes, and orchard trees are asexually reproduced from plant fragments called cuttings. In most cases, shoot cuttings are used. At the wounded end of the shoot, a mass of dividing, undifferentiated totipotent cells called a **callus** forms, and adventitious roots develop from the callus. If the shoot fragment includes a node, then adventitious roots form without a callus stage.

In grafting, a severed shoot from one plant is permanently joined to the truncated stem of another. This process, usually limited to closely related individuals, can combine the best qualities of different species or varieties into one plant. The plant that provides the roots is called the **stock**; the twig grafted onto the stock is known as the **scion**. For example, scions from varieties of vines that produce superior wine grapes are grafted onto rootstocks of varieties that produce inferior grapes but are more resistant to certain soil pathogens. The genes of the scion determine the quality of the fruit. During grafting, a callus first forms between the adjoining cut ends of the scion and stock; cell differentiation then completes the functional unification of the grafted individuals.

## Test-Tube Cloning and Related Techniques

Plant biologists have adopted *in vitro* methods to clone plants for research or horticulture. Whole plants can be obtained by culturing small pieces of tissue from the parent plant on an artificial medium containing nutrients and hormones. The cells or tissues can come from any part of a plant, but growth may vary depending on the plant part, species, and artificial medium. In some media, the cultured cells divide and form a callus of undifferentiated totipotent cells (**Figure 38.15a**). When the concentrations of hormones and nutrients are manipulated appropriately, a callus can sprout shoots and roots with fully differentiated cells (**Figure 38.15b and c**). If desired, the cloned plantlets can then be transferred to soil, where they continue their growth.

Plant tissue culture is important in eliminating weakly pathogenic viruses from vegetatively propagated varieties. Although the presence of weak viruses may not be obvious, yield or quality may be substantially reduced as a result of infection. Strawberry plants, for example, are susceptible to more than 60 viruses, and typically the plants must be replaced each year because of viral infection. However, since the apical meristems are often virus-free, they can be excised and used to produce virus-free material for tissue culture.

Plant tissue culture also facilitates genetic engineering. Most techniques for the introduction of foreign genes into plants require small pieces of plant tissue or single plant cells as the starting material. Test-tube culture makes it possible to regenerate genetically modified (GM) plants from a single plant cell into which the foreign DNA has been incorporated. The techniques of genetic engineering are discussed in more detail in Chapter 20. In the next section, we take a closer look at some of the promises and challenges surrounding the use of GM plants in agriculture.

▼ **Figure 38.15 Cloning a garlic plant. (a)** A root from a garlic clove gave rise to this callus culture, a mass of undifferentiated totipotent cells. **(b and c)** The differentiation of a callus into a plantlet depends on the nutrient levels and hormone concentrations in the artificial medium, as can be seen in these cultures grown for different lengths of time.

(a) (b) (c) Developing root

# CONCEPT 38.3

## People modify crops by breeding and genetic engineering

People have intervened in the reproduction and genetic makeup of plants since the dawn of agriculture. Maize, for example, owes its existence to humans. Left on its own in nature, maize would soon become extinct for the simple reason that it cannot spread its seeds. Maize kernels are not only permanently attached to the central axis (the "cob") but also permanently protected by tough, overlapping leaf sheathes (the "husk") (**Figure 38.16**). These attributes arose by artificial selection by humans. (See Concept 22.2 to review the basic concept of artificial selection.) Despite having no understanding of the scientific principles underlying plant breeding, early farmers domesticated most of our crop species over a relatively short period about 10,000 years ago.

▼ **Figure 38.16 Maize: a product of artificial selection.** Modern maize (bottom) was derived from teosinte (top). Teosinte kernels are tiny, and each row has a husk that must be removed to get at the kernel. The seeds are loose at maturity, allowing dispersal, which probably made harvesting difficult for early farmers. Neolithic farmers selected seeds from plants with larger cob and kernel size as well as the permanent attachment of seeds to the cob and the encasing of the entire cob by a tough husk.

 HHMI Video: Popped Secret: The Mysterious Origin of Corn

The natural genetic modification of plants began long before humans started altering crops by artificial selection. For example, researchers recently concluded that an early ancestor of the sweet potato (*Ipomoea batatas*) came into contact with the soil bacterium *Agrobacterium* (the vector commonly used to genetically engineer plants), upon which a horizontal gene transfer event (see Concept 26.6) occurred. Thus, sweet potato is a naturally genetically modified plant, a finding that adds to the controversies surrounding the regulation of genetically modified organisms, especially since plants that have been genetically engineered in the lab using *Agrobacterium* are currently subjected to heavy regulation. In a second example, the wheat species we rely on for much of our food evolved by natural hybridization between different species of grasses. Such hybridization is common in plants and has long been exploited by breeders to introduce genetic variation for artificial selection and crop improvement.

 Interview with Louis Herrera-Estrella: Using GMOs to help farmers

## Plant Breeding

Plant breeding is the art and science of changing the traits of plants in order to produce desired characteristics. Breeders scrutinize their fields carefully and travel far and wide searching for domesticated varieties or wild relatives with desirable traits. Such traits occasionally arise spontaneously through mutation, but the natural rate of mutation is too slow and unreliable to produce all the mutations that breeders would like to study. Breeders sometimes hasten mutations by treating large batches of seeds or seedlings with radiation or chemicals.

In traditional plant breeding, when a desirable trait is identified in a wild species, the wild species is crossed with a domesticated variety. Generally, those progeny that have inherited the desirable trait from the wild parent have also inherited many traits that are not desirable for agriculture, such as small fruits or low yields. The progeny that express the desired trait are again crossed with members of the domesticated species and their progeny examined for the desired trait. This process is continued until the progeny with the desired wild trait resemble the original domesticated parent in their other agricultural attributes.

While most breeders cross-pollinate plants of a single species, some breeding methods rely on hybridization between two distant species of the same genus. Such crosses sometimes result in the abortion of the hybrid seed during development. Often in these cases the embryo begins to develop, but the endosperm does not. Hybrid embryos are sometimes rescued by surgically removing them from the ovule and culturing them *in vitro*.

## Plant Biotechnology and Genetic Engineering

Plant biotechnology has two meanings. In the general sense, it refers to innovations in the use of plants (or substances obtained from plants) to make products of use to humans— an endeavor that began in prehistory. In a more specific sense, biotechnology refers to the use of GM organisms in agriculture and industry. Indeed, in the last two decades, genetic engineering has become such a powerful force that the terms *genetic engineering* and *biotechnology* have become synonymous in the media.

Unlike traditional plant breeders, modern plant biotechnologists, using techniques of genetic engineering, are not limited to the transfer of genes between closely related species or genera. For example, traditional breeding techniques could not be used to insert a desired gene from daffodil into rice because the many intermediate species between rice and daffodil and their common ancestor are extinct. In theory, if breeders had the intermediate species, over the course of several centuries they could probably introduce a daffodil gene into rice by traditional hybridization and breeding methods. With genetic engineering, however, such gene transfers can be done more quickly, more specifically, and without the need for intermediate species. The term **transgenic** is used to an organism that has been engineered to contain DNA from another organism of the same or a different species (see Concept 20.1 for a discussion of the methods underlying genetic engineering).

In the remainder of this chapter, we explore the prospects and controversies surrounding the use of GM crops. Advocates for plant biotechnology believe that the genetic engineering of crop plants is the key to overcoming some of the most pressing problems of the 21st century, including world hunger and fossil fuel dependency.

### Reducing World Hunger and Malnutrition

Although global hunger affects nearly a billion people, there is much disagreement about its causes. Some argue that food shortages arise from inequities in distribution and that the most poverty-stricken simply cannot afford food. Others regard food shortages as evidence that the world is overpopulated—that the human species has exceeded the carrying capacity of the planet (see Concept 53.3). Whatever the causes of malnutrition, increasing food production is a humane objective. Because land and water are the most limiting resources, the best option is to increase yields on already existing farmland. Indeed, there is very little "extra" land that can be farmed, especially if the few remaining pockets of wilderness are to be preserved. Based on conservative estimates of population growth, farmers will have to produce 40% more grain per hectare to feed the human population in 2030. Plant biotechnology can help make these crop yields possible.

Crops that have been genetically modified to express transgenes from *Bacillus thuringiensis,* a soil bacterium, require less pesticide. The "transgenes" involved encode a protein (*Bt* toxin)

**Figure 38.17 Non-*Bt* versus *Bt* maize.** Field trials reveal that non-*Bt* maize (left) is heavily damaged by insect feeding and *Fusarium* mold infection, whereas *Bt* maize (right) suffers little or no damage.

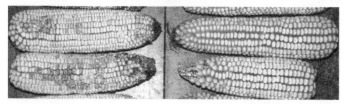

Non-*Bt* maize               *Bt* maize

that is toxic to many insect pests **(Figure 38.17)**. The *Bt* toxin used in crops is produced in the plant as a harmless protoxin that only becomes toxic if activated by alkaline conditions, such as in the guts of most insects. Because vertebrates have highly acidic stomachs, protoxin consumed by humans or livestock is rendered harmless by denaturation.

The nutritional quality of plants is also being improved. For example, some 250,000 to 500,000 children go blind each year because of vitamin A deficiencies. More than half of these children die within a year of becoming blind. In response to this crisis, genetic engineers created "Golden Rice," a transgenic variety supplemented with transgenes that enable it to produce grain with increased levels of beta-carotene, a precursor of vitamin A. The commercial release of Golden Rice has been delayed for over a decade by restrictions and regulations requiring further health and environmental safety tests. Another target for improvement by genetic engineering is cassava, a staple for 800 million of the poorest people on our planet **(Figure 38.18)**.

Researchers are also engineering plants with enhanced resistance to disease. In one case, a transgenic papaya that is resistant to a ring spot virus was introduced into Hawaii, thereby saving its papaya industry.

Considerable controversy has arisen concerning transgenic crops that are resistant to the herbicide glyphosate. Glyphosate is lethal to a wide variety of plants because it

**Figure 38.18 Fighting world hunger with transgenic cassava (*Manihot esculenta*).** This starchy root crop is the primary food for 800 million of the world's poor, but it does not provide a balanced diet. Moreover, it must be processed to remove chemicals that release cyanide, a toxin. Transgenic cassava plants have been developed with greatly increased levels of iron and beta-carotene (a vitamin A precursor). Researchers have also created cassava plants with root masses twice the normal size and others containing almost no cyanide-producing chemicals.

inhibits a key enzyme in a biochemical pathway that is found in plants (and most bacteria) but not in animals. Researchers discovered a bacterial strain that had undergone a mutation in the gene encoding this enzyme that rendered it glyphosate-resistant. When this mutated bacterial gene was spliced into the genome of various crops, these crops also became glyphosate-resistant. Farmers achieved almost total weed control by spraying glyphosate over their fields of glyphosate-resistant crops. Unfortunately, the overuse of glyphosate created a huge selective pressure on weed species, with the result that many have evolved resistance to glyphosate. There has also been a growing appreciation in recent decades of the role that gut bacteria play in animal and human health, and claims have been made that glyphosate may be having negative effects on the health of humans and livestock by interfering with beneficial gut bacteria. What's more, in 2015 the World Health Organization deemed glyphosate a probable cause of cancer.

### Reducing Fossil Fuel Dependency

Global sources of inexpensive fossil fuels, particularly oil, are rapidly being depleted. Moreover, most climatologists attribute global warming mainly to the rampant burning of fossil fuels, such as coal and oil, and the resulting release of the greenhouse gas $CO_2$. How can the world meet its energy demands in the 21st century in an economical and nonpolluting way? In certain localities, wind or solar power may become economically viable, but such alternative energy sources are unlikely to fill the global energy demands completely. Many scientists predict that **biofuels**—fuels derived from living biomass—could produce a sizable fraction of the world's energy needs in the not-too-distant future. **Biomass** is the total mass of organic matter in a group of organisms in a particular habitat. The use of biofuels from plant biomass would reduce the net emission of $CO_2$. Whereas burning fossil fuels increases atmospheric $CO_2$ concentrations, biofuel crops reabsorb by photosynthesis the $CO_2$ emitted when biofuels are burned, creating a cycle that is carbon neutral.

In working to create biofuel crops from wild precursors, scientists are focusing their domestication efforts on fast-growing plants, such as switchgrass (*Panicum virgatum*) and poplar (*Populus trichocarpa*), that can grow on soil that is too poor for food production. Scientists do not expect the plant biomass to be burned directly. Instead, the polymers in cell walls, such as cellulose and hemicellulose, which constitute the most abundant organic compounds on Earth, would be broken down into sugars by enzymatic reactions. These sugars, in turn, would be fermented into alcohol and distilled to yield biofuels. In addition to increasing plant polysaccharide content and overall biomass, researchers are trying to genetically engineer the cell walls of plants to increase the efficiency of the enzymatic conversion process.

# The Debate over Plant Biotechnology

Much of the debate about GM organisms (GMOs) in agriculture is political, social, economic, or ethical and therefore outside the scope of this book. But we *should* consider the biological concerns about GM crops. Some biologists, particularly ecologists, are concerned about the unknown risks associated with the release of GMOs into the environment. The debate centers on the extent to which GMOs could harm the environment or human health. Those who want to proceed more slowly with agricultural biotechnology (or end it) are concerned about the unstoppable nature of the "experiment." If a drug trial produces unanticipated harmful results, the trial is stopped. But we may not be able to stop the "trial" of introducing novel organisms into the biosphere. Here we examine some criticisms that have been leveled by opponents of GMOs, including the alleged effects on human health and nontarget organisms and the potential for transgene escape.

## Issues of Human Health

Many GMO opponents worry that genetic engineering may inadvertently transfer allergens, molecules to which some people are allergic, from a species that produces an allergen to a plant used for food. However, biotechnologists are already removing genes that encode allergenic proteins from soybeans and other crops. So far, there is no credible evidence that GM plants designed for human consumption have allergenic effects on human health. In fact, some GM foods are potentially healthier than non-GM foods. For example, *Bt* maize (the transgenic variety with the *Bt* toxin) contains 90% less of a fungal toxin that causes cancer and birth defects than non-*Bt* maize. Called fumonisin, this toxin is highly resistant to degradation and has been found in alarmingly high concentrations in some batches of processed maize products, ranging from cornflakes to beer. Fumonisin is produced by a fungus (*Fusarium*) that infects insect-damaged maize. Because *Bt* maize generally suffers less insect damage than non-GM maize, it contains much less fumonisin.

Assessing the impact of GMOs on human health also involves considering the health of farmworkers, many of whom were commonly exposed to high levels of chemical insecticides prior to the adoption of *Bt* crops. In India, for example, the widespread adoption of *Bt* cotton has led to a 41% decrease in insecticide use and an 80% reduction in the number of acute poisoning cases involving farmers.

## Possible Effects on Nontarget Organisms

Many ecologists are concerned that GM crops may have unforeseen effects on nontarget organisms. One laboratory study indicated that the larvae (caterpillars) of monarch butterflies responded adversely and even died after eating milkweed leaves (their preferred food) heavily dusted with pollen from transgenic *Bt* maize. This study has since been discredited,

affording a good example of the self-correcting nature of science. As it turns out, when the original researcher shook the male maize inflorescences onto the milkweed leaves in the laboratory, the filaments of stamens, opened microsporangia, and other floral parts also rained onto the leaves. Subsequent research found that it was these other floral parts, *not* the pollen, that contained *Bt* toxin in high concentrations. Unlike pollen, these floral parts would not be carried by the wind to neighboring milkweed plants when shed under natural field conditions. Only one *Bt* maize line, accounting for less than 2% of commercial *Bt* maize production (and now discontinued), produced pollen with high *Bt* toxin concentrations.

In considering the negative effects of *Bt* pollen on monarch butterflies, one must also weigh the effects of an alternative to the cultivation of *Bt* maize—the spraying of non-*Bt* maize with chemical pesticides. Subsequent studies have shown that such spraying is much more harmful to nearby monarch populations than is *Bt* maize production. Although the effects of *Bt* maize pollen on monarch butterfly larvae appear to be minor, the controversy has emphasized the need for accurate field testing of all GM crops and the importance of targeting gene expression to specific tissues to improve safety.

## Addressing the Problem of Transgene Escape

Perhaps the most serious concern raised about GM crops is the possibility of the introduced genes escaping from a transgenic crop into related weeds through crop-to-weed hybridization. The fear is that the spontaneous hybridization between a crop engineered for herbicide resistance and a wild relative might give rise to a "superweed" that would have a selective advantage over other weeds in the wild and would be much more difficult to control in the field. GMO advocates point out that the likelihood of transgene escape depends on the ability of the crop and weed to hybridize and on how the transgenes affect the overall fitness of the hybrids. A desirable crop trait—a dwarf phenotype, for example—might be disadvantageous to a weed growing in the wild. In other instances, there are no weedy relatives nearby with which to hybridize; soybean, for example, has no wild relatives in the United States. However, canola, sorghum, and many other crops do hybridize readily with weeds, and crop-to-weed transgene escape in a turfgrass has occurred. In 2003 a transgenic variety of creeping bentgrass (*Agrostis stolonifera*) genetically engineered to resist the herbicide glyphosate escaped from an experimental plot in Oregon following a windstorm. Despite efforts to eradicate the escapee, 62% of the *Agrostis* plants found in the vicinity three years later were glyphosate resistant. So far, the ecological impact of this event appears to be minor, but that may not be the case with future transgenic escapes.

Many strategies are being pursued with the goal of preventing transgene escape. For example, if male sterility could be engineered into plants, these plants would still produce seeds and fruit if pollinated by nearby nontransgenic plants, but they would produce no viable pollen. A second approach involves genetically engineering apomixis into transgenic crops. When a seed is produced by apomixis, the embryo and endosperm develop without fertilization. The transfer of this trait to transgenic crops would therefore minimize the possibility of transgene escape via pollen because plants could be male-sterile without compromising seed or fruit production. A third approach is to engineer the transgene into the chloroplast DNA of the crop. Chloroplast DNA in many plant species is inherited strictly from the egg, so transgenes in the chloroplast cannot be transferred by pollen. A fourth approach for preventing transgene escape is to genetically engineer flowers that develop normally but fail to open. Consequently, self-pollination would occur, but pollen would be unlikely to escape from the flower. This solution would require modifications to flower design. Several floral genes have been identified that could be manipulated to this end.

The continuing debate about GMOs in agriculture exemplifies one of this textbook's recurring ideas: the relationship of science and technology to society. Technological advances almost always involve some risk of unintended outcomes. In the case of genetically engineered crops, zero risk is probably unattainable. Therefore, scientists and the public must assess on a case-by-case basis the possible benefits of transgenic products versus the risks that society is willing to take. The best scenario is for these discussions and decisions to be based on sound scientific information and rigorous testing rather than on reflexive fear or blind optimism.

## CONCEPT CHECK 38.3

1. Compare traditional plant-breeding methods with genetic engineering.
2. Why does *Bt* maize have less fumonisin than non-GM maize?
3. **WHAT IF?** ➤ In a few species, chloroplast genes are inherited only from sperm. How might this influence efforts to prevent transgene escape?

*For suggested answers, see Appendix A.*

# 38 Chapter Review

 Go to **MasteringBiology**™ for Videos, Animations, Vocab Self-Quiz, Practice Tests, and more in the Study Area.

## SUMMARY OF KEY CONCEPTS

### CONCEPT 38.1

**Flowers, double fertilization, and fruits are key features of the angiosperm life cycle** (pp. 821–830)

**VOCAB SELF-QUIZ**
goo.gl/6u55ks

- Angiosperm reproduction involves an alternation of generations between a multicellular diploid sporophyte generation and a multicellular haploid gametophyte generation. **Flowers**, produced by the sporophyte, function in sexual reproduction.
- The four floral organs are sepals, petals, stamens, and carpels. **Sepals** protect the floral bud. **Petals** help attract pollinators. **Stamens** bear **anthers** in which haploid **microspores** develop into **pollen grains** containing a male gametophyte. **Carpels** contain **ovules** (immature seeds) in their swollen bases. Within the ovules, **embryo sacs** (female gametophytes) develop from **megaspores**.
- **Pollination**, which precedes **fertilization**, is the placing of pollen on the stigma of a carpel. After pollination, the **pollen tube** discharges two sperm into the female gametophyte. Two sperm are needed for **double fertilization**, a process in which one sperm fertilizes the egg, forming a zygote and eventually an embryo, while the other sperm

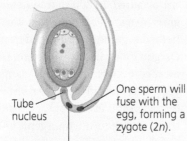

Tube nucleus

One sperm will fuse with the egg, forming a zygote (2*n*).

One sperm cell will fuse with the two polar nuclei, forming an endosperm nucleus (3*n*).

combines with the polar nuclei, giving rise to the food-storing endosperm.

- A **seed** consists of a dormant embryo along with a food supply stocked in either the **endosperm** or the **cotyledons**. Seed **dormancy** ensures that seeds germinate only when conditions for seedling survival are optimal. The breaking of dormancy often requires environmental cues, such as temperature or lighting changes.
- The **fruit** protects the enclosed seeds and aids in wind dispersal or in the attraction of seed-dispersing animals.

**?** *What changes occur to the four types of floral parts as a flower changes into a fruit?*

### CONCEPT 38.2

**Flowering plants reproduce sexually, asexually, or both** (pp. 831–834)

- **Asexual reproduction**, also known as **vegetative reproduction**, enables successful plants to proliferate quickly. Sexual reproduction generates most of the genetic variation that makes evolutionary adaptation possible.
- Plants have evolved many mechanisms to avoid self-fertilization, including having male and female flowers on different individuals, nonsynchronous production of male and female parts within a single flower, and **self-incompatibility** reactions in which pollen grains that bear an allele identical to one in the female are rejected.
- Plants can be cloned from single cells, which can be genetically manipulated before being allowed to develop into a plant.

**?** *What are the advantages of asexual and sexual reproduction?*

## CONCEPT 38.3

### People modify crops by breeding and genetic engineering (pp. 834–838)

- Hybridization of different varieties and even species of plants is common in nature and has been used by breeders, ancient and modern, to introduce new genes into crops. After two plants are successfully hybridized, plant breeders select those progeny that have the desired traits.

- In genetic engineering, genes from unrelated organisms are incorporated into plants. Genetically modified (GM) plants can increase the quality and quantity of food worldwide and may also become increasingly important as biofuels.

- There are concerns about the unknown risks of releasing GM organisms into the environment, but the potential benefits of **transgenic** crops need to be considered.

 *Give two examples of how genetic engineering has improved or might potentially improve food quality.*

## TEST YOUR UNDERSTANDING

### Level 1: Knowledge/Comprehension

**1.** A fruit is
 (A) a mature ovary.
 (B) a mature ovule.
 (C) a seed plus its integuments.
 (D) an enlarged embryo sac.

**2.** Double fertilization means that
 (A) flowers must be pollinated twice to yield fruits and seeds.
 (B) every egg must receive two sperm to produce an embryo.
 (C) one sperm is needed to fertilize the egg, and a second sperm is needed to fertilize the polar nuclei.
 (D) every sperm has two nuclei.

**3.** "*Bt* maize"
 (A) is resistant to various herbicides, making it practical to weed rice fields with those herbicides.
 (B) contains transgenes that increase vitamin A content.
 (C) includes bacterial genes that produce a toxin that reduces damage from insect pests.
 (D) is a "boron (B)-tolerant" transgenic variety of maize.

**4.** Which statement concerning grafting is correct?
 (A) Stocks and scions refer to twigs of different species.
 (B) Stocks and scions must come from unrelated species.
 (C) Stocks provide root systems for grafting.
 (D) Grafting creates new species.

### Level 2: Application/Analysis

**5.** Some dioecious species have the XY genotype for male and XX for female. After double fertilization, what would be the genotypes of the embryos and endosperm nuclei?
 (A) embryo XY/endosperm XXX or embryo XX/endosperm XXY
 (B) embryo XX/endosperm XX or embryo XY/endosperm XY
 (C) embryo XX/endosperm XXX or embryo XY/endosperm XYY
 (D) embryo XX/endosperm XXX or embryo XY/endosperm XXY

**6.** A small flower with green petals is most likely
 (A) bee-pollinated.
 (B) bird-pollinated.
 (C) bat-pollinated.
 (D) wind-pollinated.

**7.** The black dots that cover strawberries are actually fruits formed from the separate carpels of a single flower. The fleshy and tasty portion of a strawberry derives from the receptacle of a flower with many separate carpels. Therefore, a strawberry is
 (A) a simple fruit with many seeds.
 (B) both a multiple fruit and an accessory fruit.
 (C) both a simple fruit and an aggregate fruit.
 (D) both an aggregate fruit and an accessory fruit.

**8.** DRAW IT Draw and label the parts of a flower.

### Level 3: Synthesis/Evaluation

**9.** EVOLUTION CONNECTION With respect to sexual reproduction, some plant species are fully self-fertile, others are fully self-incompatible, and some exhibit a "mixed strategy" with partial self-incompatibility. These reproductive strategies differ in their implications for evolutionary potential. How, for example, might a self-incompatible species fare as a small founder population or remnant population in a severe population bottleneck (see Concept 23.3), as compared with a self-fertile species?

**10.** SCIENTIFIC INQUIRY Critics of GM foods have argued that transgenes may disturb cellular functioning, causing unexpected and potentially harmful substances to appear inside cells. Toxic intermediary substances that normally occur in very small amounts may arise in larger amounts, or new substances may appear. The disruption may also lead to loss of substances that help maintain normal metabolism. If you were your nation's chief scientific advisor, how would you respond to these criticisms?

**11.** SCIENCE, TECHNOLOGY, AND SOCIETY Humans have engaged in genetic manipulation for millennia, producing plant and animal varieties through selective breeding and hybridization that significantly modify genomes of organisms. Why do you think modern genetic engineering, which often entails introducing or modifying only one or a few genes, has met with so much opposition? Should some forms of genetic engineering be of greater concern than others? Explain.

**12.** WRITE ABOUT A THEME: ORGANIZATION In a short essay (100–150 words), discuss how a flower's ability to reproduce with other flowers of the same species is an emergent property arising from floral parts and their organization.

**13.** SYNTHESIZE YOUR KNOWLEDGE

This colorized SEM shows pollen grains from six plant species. Explain how a pollen grain forms, how it functions, and how pollen grains contributed to the dominance of angiosperms and other seed plants.

*For selected answers, see Appendix A.*

 For additional practice questions, check out the **Dynamic Study Modules** in MasteringBiology. You can use them to study on your smartphone, tablet, or computer anytime, anywhere!

# Plant Responses to Internal and External Signals

# 39

▲ Figure 39.1 A "vampire" plant?

## KEY CONCEPTS

**39.1** Signal transduction pathways link signal reception to response

**39.2** Plant hormones help coordinate growth, development, and responses to stimuli

**39.3** Responses to light are critical for plant success

**39.4** Plants respond to a wide variety of stimuli other than light

**39.5** Plants respond to attacks by pathogens and herbivores

## Stimuli and a Stationary Life

Slowly, the hunter slinks through the brush toward the shade, where its prey can best be found. It began its hunt with only a week of provisions. If it does not find food soon, it will perish. At long last, it detects a promising scent and steers toward the source. When it's within reach, it lassoes its quarry. Then it senses even better prey! It sets course for this new target, lassoes it, and taps into the vital juices of its nutritious victim.

The hunter is a parasitic, nonphotosynthetic flowering plant called dodder (*Cuscuta*). Upon germination, a dodder seedling, fueled by nutrients stored during embryo development, searches for a host plant (**Figure 39.1**). If a host is not found within a week or so, the seedling dies. Dodder attacks by sending out tendrils that coil around the host, as seen in the small photo. Within an hour, it either exploits the host or moves on. If it stays, it takes several days to tap into the host's phloem by means of feeding appendages called haustoria. Depending on how nutritious its host is, dodder grows more or fewer coils.

How does dodder locate its victims? Biologists have long known that it grows toward the shade (where better to find a stem?) but thought it just bumped into its victims. However, new studies reveal that chemicals released by a potential host plant attract dodder, causing it to rapidly set course in that direction.

Dodder's behavior is unusual, but photosynthetic plants also sense their environment, taking advantage of available sunlight and nutrient-rich patches

---

When you see this blue icon, log in to **MasteringBiology** and go to the Study Area for digital resources.

 Get Ready for This Chapter

in the soil. These behaviors involve signal transduction pathways not far removed from some pathways by which you interact with your environment. At the levels of signal reception and signal transduction, your cells are not that different from those of plants—the similarities far outweigh the differences. As an animal, however, your responses to environmental stimuli are generally quite different from those of plants. Animals commonly respond by movement; plants do so by altering growth and development.

Plants must also adjust to changes in time, such as the passage of seasons, to compete successfully. In addition, they interact with a wide range of organisms. All of these physical and chemical interactions involve complex signal transduction pathways. In this chapter, we focus on understanding the internal chemicals (hormones) that regulate plant growth and development and how plants perceive and respond to their environments.

# CONCEPT 39.1

## Signal transduction pathways link signal reception to response

Dodder plants receive specific signals from their environment and respond to them in ways that enhance survival and reproductive success, but dodder is not unique in this regard. Consider a more mundane example: a forgotten potato in the back corner of a kitchen cupboard. This modified underground stem, or tuber, has sprouted shoots from its "eyes" (axillary buds). These shoots, however, scarcely resemble those of a typical plant. Instead of sturdy stems and broad green leaves, this plant has ghostly pale stems and unexpanded leaves, as well as short, stubby roots **(Figure 39.2a)**. These morphological adaptations for growing in darkness, collectively referred to as **etiolation**, make sense if we consider that a young potato plant in nature usually encounters continuous darkness when sprouting underground. Under these circumstances, expanded leaves would be a hindrance to soil penetration and would be damaged as the shoots pushed through the soil. Because the leaves are unexpanded and underground, there is little evaporative loss of water and little requirement for an extensive root system to replace the water lost by transpiration. Moreover, the energy expended in producing green chlorophyll would be wasted because there is no light for photosynthesis. Instead, a potato plant growing in the dark allocates as much energy as possible to elongating its stems. This adaptation enables the shoots to break ground before the nutrient reserves in the tuber are exhausted. The etiolation response is one example of how a plant's morphology and physiology are tuned to its surroundings by complex interactions between environmental and internal signals.

▼ **Figure 39.2 Light-induced de-etiolation (greening) of dark-grown potatoes.**

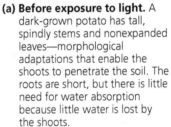

**(a) Before exposure to light.** A dark-grown potato has tall, spindly stems and nonexpanded leaves—morphological adaptations that enable the shoots to penetrate the soil. The roots are short, but there is little need for water absorption because little water is lost by the shoots.

**(b) After a week's exposure to natural daylight.** The potato plant begins to resemble a typical plant with broad green leaves, short sturdy stems, and long roots. This transformation begins with the reception of light by a specific pigment, phytochrome.

When a shoot reaches light, the plant undergoes profound changes, collectively called **de-etiolation** (informally known as greening). Stem elongation slows; leaves expand; roots elongate; and the shoot produces chlorophyll. In short, it begins to resemble a typical plant **(Figure 39.2b)**. In this section, we will use this de-etiolation response as an example of how a plant cell's reception of a signal—in this case, light—is transduced into a response (greening). Along the way, we will explore how studies of mutants provide insights into the molecular details of the stages of cell signal processing: reception, transduction, and response **(Figure 39.3)**.

▼ **Figure 39.3 Review of a general model for signal transduction pathways.** As discussed in Concept 11.1, a hormone or other kind of stimulus interacting with a specific receptor protein can trigger the sequential activation of relay proteins and also the production of second messengers that participate in the pathway. The signal is passed along, ultimately bringing about cellular responses. In this diagram, the receptor is on the surface of the target cell; in other cases, the stimulus interacts with receptors inside the cell.

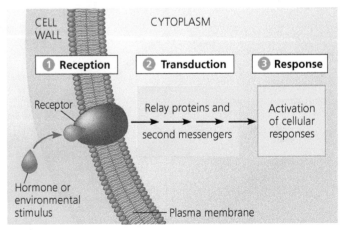

## Reception

Signals are first detected by receptors, proteins that undergo changes in shape in response to a specific stimulus. The receptor involved in de-etiolation is a type of *phytochrome*, a member of a class of photoreceptors that we'll discuss more fully later in the chapter. Unlike most receptors, which are built into the plasma membrane, the type of phytochrome that functions in de-etiolation is located in the cytoplasm. Researchers demonstrated the requirement for phytochrome in de-etiolation through studies of the tomato, a close relative of the potato. The *aurea* mutant of tomato, which has reduced levels of phytochrome, greens less than wild-type tomatoes when exposed to light. (*Aurea* is Latin for "gold." In the absence of chlorophyll, the yellow and orange accessory pigments called carotenoids are more obvious.) Researchers produced a normal de-etiolation response in individual *aurea* leaf cells by injecting phytochrome from other plants and then exposing the cells to light. Such experiments indicated that phytochrome functions in light detection during de-etiolation.

## Transduction

Receptors can be sensitive to very weak environmental or chemical signals. Some de-etiolation responses are triggered by extremely low levels of light, in certain cases as little as the equivalent of a few seconds of moonlight. The transduction of these extremely weak signals involves **second messengers**—small molecules and ions in the cell that amplify the signal and transfer it from the receptor to other proteins that carry out the response **(Figure 39.4)**. In Concept 11.3, we discussed several kinds of second messengers (see Figures 11.12 and 11.14). Here, we examine the particular roles of two types of second messengers in de-etiolation: calcium ions ($Ca^{2+}$) and cyclic GMP (cGMP).

Changes in cytosolic $Ca^{2+}$ levels play an important role in phytochrome signal transduction. The concentration of cytosolic $Ca^{2+}$ is generally very low (about $10^{-7}$ M), but phytochrome activation leads to the opening of $Ca^{2+}$ channels and a transient 100-fold increase in cytosolic $Ca^{2+}$ levels. In response to light, phytochrome undergoes a change in

▼ **Figure 39.4 An example of signal transduction in plants: the role of phytochrome in the de-etiolation (greening) response.**

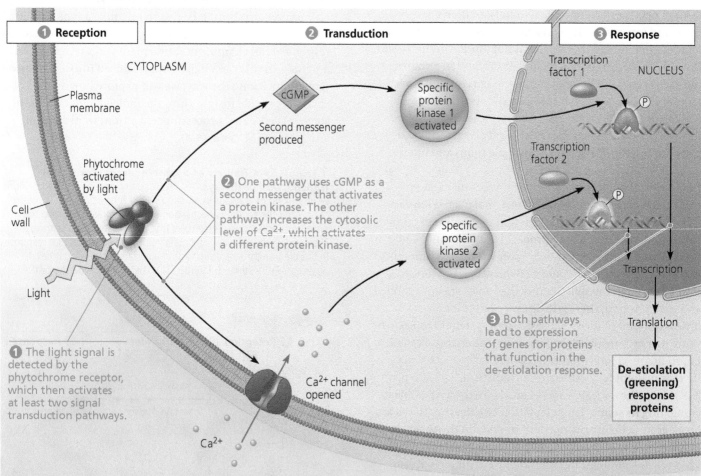

**MAKE CONNECTIONS** ➤ *Which panel in Figure 11.17 best exemplifies the phytochrome-dependent signal transduction pathway during de-etiolation? Explain.*

shape that leads to the activation of guanylyl cyclase, an enzyme that produces the second messenger cyclic GMP. Both $Ca^{2+}$ and cGMP must be produced for a complete de-etiolation response. The injection of cGMP into *aurea* tomato leaf cells, for example, induces only a partial de-etiolation response.

## Response

Ultimately, second messengers regulate one or more cellular activities. In most cases, these responses involve the increased activity of particular enzymes. There are two main mechanisms by which a signaling pathway can enhance an enzymatic step in a biochemical pathway: transcriptional regulation and post-translational modification. Transcriptional regulation increases or decreases the synthesis of mRNA encoding a specific enzyme. Post-translational modification activates preexisting enzymes.

### Post-translational Modification of Preexisting Proteins

In most signal transduction pathways, preexisting proteins are modified by the phosphorylation of specific amino acids, which alters the protein's hydrophobicity and activity. Many second messengers, including cGMP and $Ca^{2+}$, activate protein kinases directly. Often, one protein kinase will phosphorylate another protein kinase, which then phosphorylates another, and so on (see Figure 11.10). Such kinase cascades may link initial stimuli to responses at the level of gene expression, usually via the phosphorylation of transcription factors. As we'll discuss soon, many signal transduction pathways ultimately regulate the synthesis of new proteins by turning specific genes on or off.

Signal transduction pathways must also have a means for turning off when the initial signal is no longer present, such as when a sprouting potato is put back into the cupboard. Protein phosphatases, which are enzymes that dephosphorylate specific proteins, are important in these "switch-off" processes. At any particular moment, a cell's functioning depends on the balance of activity of many types of protein kinases and protein phosphatases.

### Transcriptional Regulation

As discussed in Concept 18.2, the proteins we call *specific transcription factors* bind to specific regions of DNA and control the transcription of specific genes (see Figure 18.10). In the case of phytochrome-induced de-etiolation, several such transcription factors are activated by phosphorylation in response to the appropriate light conditions. The activation of some of these transcription factors depends on their phosphorylation by protein kinases activated by cGMP or $Ca^{2+}$.

The mechanism by which a signal promotes developmental changes may depend on transcription factors that are activators (which *increase* transcription of specific genes) or repressors (which *decrease* transcription) or both. For example, some *Arabidopsis* mutants, except for their pale color, have a light-grown morphology when grown in the dark; they have expanded leaves and short, sturdy stems but are not green because the final step in chlorophyll production requires light directly. These mutants have defects in a repressor that normally inhibits the expression of other genes that are activated by light. When the repressor is eliminated by mutation, the pathway that is normally blocked proceeds. Thus, these mutants appear to have been grown in the light, except for their pale color.

### De-etiolation ("Greening") Proteins

What types of proteins are either activated by phosphorylation or newly transcribed during the de-etiolation process? Many are enzymes that function in photosynthesis directly; others are enzymes involved in supplying the chemical precursors necessary for chlorophyll production; still others affect the levels of plant hormones that regulate growth. For example, the levels of auxin and brassinosteroids, hormones that enhance stem elongation, decrease following the activation of phytochrome. That decrease explains the slowing of stem elongation that accompanies de-etiolation.

We have discussed the signal transduction involved in the de-etiolation response of a potato plant in some detail to give you a sense of the complexity of biochemical changes that underlie this one process. Every plant hormone and environmental stimulus will trigger one or more signal transduction pathways of comparable complexity. As in the studies on the *aurea* mutant tomato, the isolation of mutants (a genetic approach) and techniques of molecular biology are helping researchers identify these various pathways. But this recent research builds on a long history of careful physiological and biochemical investigations into how plants work. As you will read in the next section, classic experiments provided the first clues that transported signaling molecules called hormones are internal regulators of plant growth.

### CONCEPT CHECK 39.1

1. What are the morphological differences between dark- and light-grown plants? Explain how etiolation helps a seedling compete successfully.

2. Cycloheximide is a drug that inhibits protein synthesis. Predict what effect cycloheximide would have on de-etiolation.

3. **WHAT IF?** ➤ The sexual dysfunction drug Viagra inhibits an enzyme that breaks down cyclic GMP. If tomato leaf cells have a similar enzyme, would applying Viagra to these cells cause a normal de-etiolation of *aurea* mutant tomato leaves?

*For suggested answers, see Appendix A.*

# CONCEPT 39.2

## Plant hormones help coordinate growth, development, and responses to stimuli

A **hormone**, in the original meaning of the term, is a signaling molecule that is produced in low concentrations by one part of an organism's body and transported to other parts, where it binds to a specific receptor and triggers responses in target cells and tissues. In animals, hormones are usually transported through the circulatory system, a criterion often included in definitions of the term. Many modern plant biologists, however, argue that the hormone concept, which originated from studies of animals, is too limiting to describe plant physiological processes. For example, plants don't have circulating blood to transport hormone-like signaling molecules. Moreover, some signaling molecules that are considered plant hormones act only locally. Finally, there are some signaling molecules in plants, such as glucose, that typically occur in plants at concentrations that are thousands of times greater than a typical hormone. Nevertheless, they activate signal transduction pathways that greatly alter the functioning of plants in a manner similar to a hormone. Thus, many plant biologists prefer the broader term *plant growth regulator* to describe organic compounds, either natural or synthetic, that modify or control one or more specific physiological processes within a plant. At this point in time, the terms *plant hormone* and *plant growth regulator* are used about equally, but for historical continuity we will use the term *plant hormone* and adhere to the criterion that plant hormones are active at very low concentrations.

**Table 39.1** Overview of Plant Hormones

| Hormone | Where Produced or Found in Plant | Major Functions |
|---|---|---|
| Auxin (IAA) | Shoot apical meristems and young leaves are the primary sites of auxin synthesis. Root apical meristems also produce auxin, although the root depends on the shoot for much of its auxin. Developing seeds and fruits contain high levels of auxin, but it is unclear whether it is newly synthesized or transported from maternal tissues. | Stimulates stem elongation (low concentration only); promotes the formation of lateral and adventitious roots; regulates development of fruit; enhances apical dominance; functions in phototropism and gravitropism; promotes vascular differentiation; retards leaf abscission |
| Cytokinins | These are synthesized primarily in roots and transported to other organs, although there are many minor sites of production as well. | Regulate cell division in shoots and roots; modify apical dominance and promote lateral bud growth; promote movement of nutrients into sink tissues; stimulate seed germination; delay leaf senescence |
| Gibberellins (GA) | Meristems of apical buds and roots, young leaves, and developing seeds are the primary sites of production. | Stimulate stem elongation, pollen development, pollen tube growth, fruit growth, and seed development and germination; regulate sex determination and the transition from juvenile to adult phases |
| Abscisic acid (ABA) | Almost all plant cells have the ability to synthesize abscisic acid, and its presence has been detected in every major organ and living tissue; it may be transported in the phloem or xylem. | Inhibits growth; promotes stomatal closure during drought stress; promotes seed dormancy and inhibits early germination; promotes leaf senescence; promotes desiccation tolerance |
| Ethylene | This gaseous hormone can be produced by most parts of the plant. It is produced in high concentrations during senescence, leaf abscission, and the ripening of some types of fruits. Synthesis is also stimulated by wounding and stress. | Promotes ripening of many types of fruit, leaf abscission, and the triple response in seedlings (inhibition of stem elongation, promotion of lateral expansion, and horizontal growth); enhances the rate of senescence; promotes root and root hair formation; promotes flowering in the pineapple family |
| Brassinosteroids | These compounds are present in all plant tissues, although different intermediates predominate in different organs. Internally produced brassinosteroids act near the site of synthesis. | Promote cell expansion and cell division in shoots; promote root growth at low concentrations; inhibit root growth at high concentrations; promote xylem differentiation and inhibit phloem differentiation; promote seed germination and pollen tube elongation |
| Jasmonates | These are a small group of related molecules derived from the fatty acid linolenic acid. They are produced in several parts of the plant and travel in the phloem to other parts of the plant. | Regulate a wide variety of functions, including fruit ripening, floral development, pollen production, tendril coiling, root growth, seed germination, and nectar secretion; also produced in response to herbivory and pathogen invasion |
| Strigolactones | These carotenoid-derived hormones and extracellular signals are produced in roots in response to low phosphate conditions or high auxin flow from the shoot. | Promote seed germination, control of apical dominance, and the attraction of mycorrhizal fungi to the root |

Plant hormones are produced in very low concentrations, but a tiny amount of hormone can have a profound effect on plant growth and development. Virtually every aspect of plant growth and development is under hormonal control to some degree. Each hormone has multiple effects, depending on its site of action, its concentration, and the developmental stage of the plant. Conversely, multiple hormones can influence a single process. Plant hormone responses commonly depend on both the amounts of the hormones involved and their relative concentrations. It is often the interactions between different hormones, rather than hormones acting in isolation, that control growth and development. These interactions will become apparent in the following survey of hormone function.

## A Survey of Plant Hormones

**Table 39.1** previews the major types and actions of plant hormones, including auxin, cytokinins, gibberellins, abscisic acid, ethylene, brassinosteroids, jasmonates, and strigolactones.

### Auxin

The idea that chemical messengers exist in plants emerged from a series of classic experiments on how stems respond to light. As you know, the shoot of a houseplant on a windowsill grows toward light. Any growth response that results in plant organs curving toward or away from stimuli is called a **tropism** (from the Greek *tropos*, turn). The growth of a shoot toward light or away from it is called **phototropism**; the former is positive phototropism, and the latter is negative phototropism.

In natural ecosystems, where plants may be crowded, phototropism directs shoot growth toward the sunlight that powers photosynthesis. This response results from a differential growth of cells on opposite sides of the shoot; the cells on the darker side elongate faster than the cells on the brighter side.

Charles Darwin and his son Francis conducted some of the earliest experiments on phototropism in the late 1800s (**Figure 39.5**). They observed that a grass seedling ensheathed in its coleoptile (see Figure 38.9b) could bend toward light only if the tip of the coleoptile was present. If the tip was removed, the coleoptile did not curve. The seedling also failed to grow toward light if the tip was covered with an opaque cap, but neither a transparent cap over the tip nor an opaque shield placed below the coleoptile tip prevented the phototropic response. It was the tip of the coleoptile, the Darwins concluded, that was responsible for sensing light. However, they noted that the differential growth response that led to curvature of the coleoptile occurred some distance below the tip. The Darwins postulated that some signal was transmitted downward from the tip to the elongating region of the coleoptile. A few decades later, the Danish scientist Peter Boysen-Jensen demonstrated that the signal was a mobile chemical substance. He separated the tip from the remainder of the coleoptile by a cube of gelatin, which prevented cellular

**Inquiry** What part of a grass coleoptile senses light, and how is the signal transmitted?

**Experiment** In 1880, Charles and Francis Darwin removed and covered parts of grass coleoptiles to determine what part senses light. In 1913, Peter Boysen-Jensen separated coleoptiles with different materials to determine how the signal for phototropism is transmitted.

**Results**

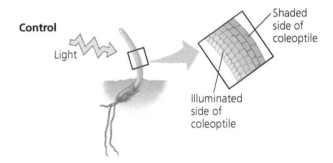

**Darwin and Darwin: Phototropism occurs only when the tip is illuminated.**

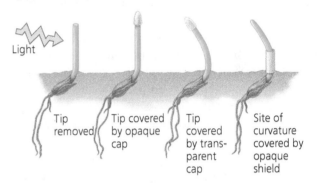

**Boysen-Jensen: Phototropism occurs when the tip is separated by a permeable barrier but not an impermeable barrier.**

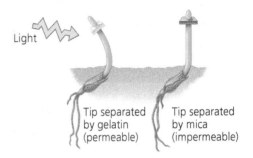

**Data from** C. R. Darwin, The power of movement in plants, John Murray, London (1880). P. Boysen-Jensen, Concerning the performance of phototropic stimuli on the Avenacoleoptile, *Berichte der Deutschen Botanischen Gesellschaft (Reports of the German Botanical Society)* 31:559–566 (1913).

**Conclusion** The Darwins' experiment suggested that only the tip of the coleoptile senses light. The phototropic bending, however, occurred at a distance from the site of light perception (the tip). Boysen-Jensen's results suggested that the signal for the bending is a light-activated mobile chemical.

**WHAT IF?** ➤ *How could you experimentally determine which colors of light cause the most phototropic bending?*

contact but allowed chemicals to pass through. These seedlings responded normally, bending toward light. However, if the tip was experimentally separated from the lower coleoptile by an impermeable barrier, such as the mineral mica, no phototropic response occurred.

Subsequent research showed that a chemical was released from coleoptile tips and could be collected by means of diffusion into agar blocks. Little cubes of agar containing this chemical could induce "phototropic-like" curvatures even in complete darkness if the agar cubes were placed off-center atop the cut surface of decapitated coleoptiles. Coleoptiles curve toward light because of a higher concentration of this growth-promoting chemical on the darker side of the coleoptile. Since this chemical stimulated growth as it passed down the coleoptile, it was dubbed "auxin" (from the Greek *auxein*, to increase). Auxin was later purified, and its chemical structure determined to be indoleacetic acid (IAA). The term **auxin** is used for any chemical substance that promotes elongation of coleoptiles, although auxins have multiple functions in flowering plants. The major natural auxin in plants is IAA, although several other compounds, including some synthetic ones, have auxin activity.

Auxin is produced predominantly in shoot tips and is transported from cell to cell down the stem at a rate of about 1 cm/hr. It moves only from tip to base, not in the reverse direction. This unidirectional transport of auxin is called *polar transport*. Polar transport is unrelated to gravity; experiments have shown that auxin travels upward when a stem or coleoptile segment is placed upside down. Rather, the polarity of auxin movement is attributable to the polar distribution of auxin transport protein in the cells. Concentrated at the basal end of a cell, the auxin transporters move the hormone out of the cell. The auxin can then enter the apical end of the neighboring cell **(Figure 39.6)**. Auxin has a variety of effects, including stimulating cell elongation and regulating plant architecture.

### The Role of Auxin in Cell Elongation

One of auxin's chief functions is to stimulate elongation of cells within young developing shoots. As auxin from the shoot apex moves down to the region of cell elongation (see Figure 35.16), the hormone stimulates cell growth, probably by binding to a receptor in the plasma membrane. Auxin stimulates growth only over a certain concentration range, from about $10^{-8}$ to $10^{-4}$ $M$. At higher concentrations, auxin may inhibit cell elongation by inducing production of ethylene, a hormone that generally hinders growth. We will return to this hormonal interaction when we discuss ethylene.

According to a model called the *acid growth hypothesis*, proton pumps play a major role in the growth response of cells to auxin. In a shoot's region of elongation, auxin stimulates the plasma membrane's proton ($H^+$) pumps. This pumping of $H^+$ increases the voltage across the membrane

▼ **Figure 39.6**

**Inquiry** What causes polar movement of auxin from shoot tip to base?

**Experiment** To investigate how auxin is transported unidirectionally, Leo Gälweiler and colleagues designed an experiment to identify the location of the auxin transport protein. They used a greenish yellow fluorescent molecule to label antibodies that bind to the auxin transport protein. Then they applied the antibodies to longitudinally sectioned *Arabidopsis* stems.

**Results** The light micrograph on the left shows that auxin transport proteins are not found in all stem tissues, but only in the xylem parenchyma. In the light micrograph on the right, a higher magnification reveals that these proteins are primarily localized at the basal ends of the cells.

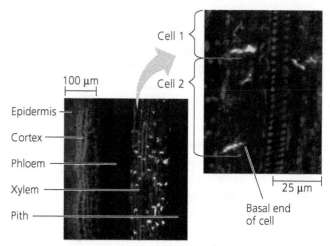

**Data from** L. Gälweiler et al., Regulation of polar auxin transport by AtPIN1 in *Arabidopsis* vascular tissue, *Science* 282:2226–2230 (1998).

**Conclusion** The results support the hypothesis that concentration of the auxin transport protein at the basal ends of cells mediates the polar transport of auxin.

**WHAT IF?** ➤ *If auxin transport proteins were equally distributed at both ends of the cells, would polar auxin transport still be possible? Explain.*

(membrane potential) and lowers the pH in the cell wall within minutes. Acidification of the wall activates proteins called **expansins** that break the cross-links (hydrogen bonds) between cellulose microfibrils and other cell wall constituents, loosening the wall's fabric **(Figure 39.7)**. Increasing the membrane potential enhances ion uptake into the cell, which causes osmotic uptake of water and increased turgor. Increased turgor and increased cell wall plasticity enable the cell to elongate.

Auxin also rapidly alters gene expression, causing cells in the region of elongation to produce new proteins within minutes. Some of these proteins are short-lived transcription factors that repress or activate the expression of other genes. For sustained growth after this initial spurt, cells must make more cytoplasm and wall material. In addition, auxin stimulates this sustained growth response.

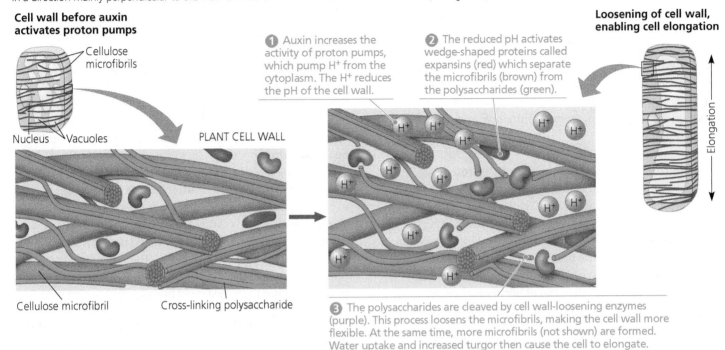

**▼ Figure 39.7 Cell elongation in response to auxin: the acid growth hypothesis.** The cell expands in a direction mainly perpendicular to the main orientation of the microfibrils in the cell wall (see Figure 35.31).

**Cell wall before auxin activates proton pumps**

Cellulose microfibrils

Nucleus  Vacuoles

PLANT CELL WALL

Cellulose microfibril  Cross-linking polysaccharide

**1** Auxin increases the activity of proton pumps, which pump H$^+$ from the cytoplasm. The H$^+$ reduces the pH of the cell wall.

**2** The reduced pH activates wedge-shaped proteins called expansins (red) which separate the microfibrils (brown) from the polysaccharides (green).

**Loosening of cell wall, enabling cell elongation**

Elongation

**3** The polysaccharides are cleaved by cell wall-loosening enzymes (purple). This process loosens the microfibrils, making the cell wall more flexible. At the same time, more microfibrils (not shown) are formed. Water uptake and increased turgor then cause the cell to elongate.

**Auxin's Role in Plant Development** The polar transport of auxin is a central element controlling the spatial organization, or *pattern formation*, of the developing plant. Auxin is synthesized in shoot tips, and it carries integrated information about the development, size, and environment of individual branches. This flow of information controls branching patterns. A reduced flow of auxin from a branch, for example, indicates that the branch is not being sufficiently productive: New branches are needed elsewhere. Thus, lateral buds below the branch are released from dormancy and begin to grow.

Transport of auxin also plays a key role in establishing *phyllotaxy* (see Figure 36.3), the arrangement of leaves on a stem. A leading model proposes that polar auxin transport in the shoot tip generates local peaks in auxin concentration that determine the site of leaf primordium formation and thereby the different phyllotaxies found in nature.

The polar transport of auxin from the leaf margin also directs the patterns of leaf veins. Inhibitors of polar auxin transport result in leaves that lack vascular continuity through the petiole and have broad, loosely organized main veins, an increased number of secondary veins, and a dense band of irregularly shaped vascular cells adjacent to the leaf margin.

The activity of the vascular cambium, the meristem that produces woody tissues, is also under the control of auxin transport. When a plant becomes dormant at the end of a growing season, there is a reduction in auxin transport capacity and the expression of genes encoding auxin transporters.

Auxin's effects on plant development are not limited to the familiar sporophyte plant that we see. Recent evidence suggests that the organization of the microscopic angiosperm female gametophytes is regulated by an auxin gradient.

**Practical Uses for Auxins** Auxins, both natural and synthetic, have many commercial applications. For example, the natural auxin indolebutyric acid (IBA) is used in the vegetative propagation of plants by cuttings. Treating a detached leaf or stem with powder containing IBA often causes adventitious roots to form near the cut surface.

Certain synthetic auxins are widely used as herbicides, including 2,4-dichlorophenoxyacetic acid (2,4-D). Monocots, such as maize and turfgrass, can rapidly inactivate such synthetic auxins. However, eudicots cannot and therefore die from hormonal overdose. Spraying cereal fields or turf with 2,4-D eliminates eudicot (broadleaf) weeds.

Developing seeds produce auxin, which promotes fruit growth. In tomato plants grown in greenhouses, often fewer seeds are produced, resulting in poorly developed tomato fruits. However, spraying synthetic auxins on greenhouse-grown tomato vines induces normal fruit development, making the greenhouse-cultivated tomatoes commercially viable.

### Cytokinins

Trial-and-error attempts to find chemical additives that would enhance the growth and development of plant cells in tissue culture led to the discovery of **cytokinins**. In the 1940s, researchers stimulated the growth of plant embryos in culture by adding coconut milk, the liquid endosperm of a coconut's giant seed. Subsequent researchers found that they could induce cultured tobacco cells to divide by adding degraded DNA samples. The active ingredients of both experimental additives turned out to be modified forms of adenine, a component of nucleic acids. These growth regulators were named cytokinins because they stimulate cytokinesis, or cell division. The most common natural cytokinin is zeatin, so named because it was discovered first in maize (*Zea mays*). The effects of cytokinins on cell division and differentiation, apical dominance, and aging are well documented.

### Control of Cell Division and Differentiation

Cytokinins are produced in actively growing tissues, particularly in roots, embryos, and fruits. Cytokinins produced in roots reach their target tissues by moving up the plant in the xylem sap. Acting in concert with auxin, cytokinins stimulate cell division and influence the pathway of differentiation. The effects of cytokinins on cells growing in tissue culture provide clues about how this class of hormones may function in an intact plant. When a piece of parenchyma tissue from a stem is cultured in the absence of cytokinins, the cells grow very large but do not divide. But if cytokinins are added along with auxin, the cells divide. Cytokinins alone have no effect. The ratio of cytokinins to auxin controls cell differentiation. When the concentrations of these two hormones are at certain levels, the mass of cells continues to grow, but it remains a cluster of undifferentiated cells called a callus (see Figure 38.15). If cytokinin levels increase, shoot buds develop from the callus. If auxin levels increase, roots form.

### Control of Apical Dominance

Apical dominance, the ability of the apical bud to suppress the development of axillary buds, is under the control of sugar and various plant hormones, including auxin, cytokinins, and strigolactones. The sugar demand of the shoot tip is critical for maintaining apical dominance. Cutting off the apical bud removes apical sugar demand and rapidly increases sugar (sucrose) availability to axillary buds. This increase of sugar is sufficient to initiate bud release. However, not all of the buds grow equally: Usually only one of the axillary buds closest to the cut surface will take over as the new apical bud.

Three plant hormones—auxin, cytokinins, and strigolactones—play a role in determining the extent to which specific axillary buds elongate (**Figure 39.8**). In an intact plant, auxin transported down the shoot from the apical bud *indirectly* inhibits axillary buds from growing,

causing a shoot to lengthen at the expense of lateral branching. The polar flow of auxin down the shoot triggers the synthesis of strigolactones, which *directly* repress bud growth. Meanwhile, cytokinins entering the shoot system from roots counter the action of auxin and strigolactones by signaling axillary buds to begin growing. Thus, in an intact plant, the cytokinin-rich axillary buds closer to the base of the plant tend to be longer than the auxin-rich axillary buds closer to the apical bud. Mutants that overproduce cytokinins or plants treated with cytokinins tend to be bushier than normal.

Removing the apical bud, a major site of auxin biosynthesis, causes the auxin and strigolactone levels in the stem to wane, particularly in those regions close to the cut surface (see Figure 39.8). This causes the axillary buds closest to the cut surface to grow most vigorously, and one of these axillary buds will eventually take over as the new apical bud. Applying auxin to the cut surface of the shoot tip resuppresses the growth of the lateral buds.

**Anti-aging Effects**   Cytokinins slow the aging of certain plant organs by inhibiting protein breakdown, stimulating RNA and protein synthesis, and mobilizing nutrients from surrounding tissues. If leaves removed from a plant are dipped in a cytokinin solution, they stay green much longer than otherwise.

### *Gibberellins*

In the early 1900s, farmers in Asia noticed that some rice seedlings in their paddies grew so tall and spindly that

▼ **Figure 39.8 Effects on apical dominance of removing the apical bud.** Apical dominance refers to the inhibition of the growth of axillary buds by the apical bud of a plant shoot. Removal of the apical bud enables lateral branches to grow. Multiple hormones play a role in this process, including auxin, cytokinin, and strigolactones.

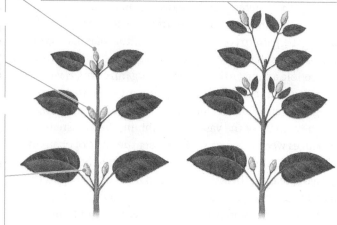

The apical bud is a preferred sugar sink and a major site of auxin biosynthesis.

Auxin moving downward from the apical bud produces strigolactones that repress the growth of axillary buds.

Cytokinin coming from the root antagonizes the actions of auxin and strigolactone, allowing for a limited amount of axillary bud growth. Therefore, the axillary buds farthest from the apex are increasingly elongated.

Removal of the apical bud allows remaining buds to receive more sugars for growth. Auxin and strigolactone levels also decline, particularly near the cut surface. This decline allows the topmost axillary buds in particular to grow and take over as the new apical bud.

Plant with apical bud intact      Plant with apical bud removed

they toppled over before they could mature. In 1926, it was discovered that a fungus of the genus *Gibberella* causes this "foolish seedling disease." By the 1930s, it was determined that the fungus causes hyperelongation of rice stems by secreting a chemical, which was given the name **gibberellin**. In the 1950s, researchers discovered that plants also produce gibberellins (GAs). Since that time, scientists have identified more than 100 different gibberellins that occur naturally in plants, although a much smaller number occur in each plant species. "Foolish rice" seedlings, it seems, suffer from too much gibberellin. Gibberellins have a variety of effects, such as stem elongation, fruit growth, and seed germination.

### Stem Elongation

The major sites of gibberellin production are young roots and leaves. Gibberellins are best known for stimulating stem and leaf growth by enhancing cell elongation *and* cell division. One hypothesis proposes that they activate enzymes that loosen cell walls, facilitating entry of expansin proteins. Thus, gibberellins act in concert with auxin to promote stem elongation.

The effects of gibberellins in enhancing stem elongation are evident when certain dwarf (mutant) varieties of plants are treated with gibberellins. For instance, some dwarf pea plants (including the variety Mendel studied; see Concept 14.1) grow tall if treated with gibberellins. But there is often no response if the gibberellins are applied to wild-type plants. Apparently, these plants already produce an optimal dose of the hormone. The most dramatic example of gibberellin-induced stem elongation is *bolting*, rapid growth of the floral stalk **(Figure 39.9a)**.

### Fruit Growth

In many plants, both auxin and gibberellins must be present for fruit to develop. The most important commercial application of gibberellins is in the spraying of Thompson seedless grapes **(Figure 39.9b)**. The hormone makes the individual grapes grow larger, a trait valued by the consumer. The gibberellin sprays also make the internodes of the grape bunch elongate, allowing more space for the individual grapes. By enhancing air circulation between the grapes, this increase in space also makes it harder for yeasts and other microorganisms to infect the fruit.

### Germination

The embryo of a seed is a rich source of gibberellins. After water is imbibed, the release of gibberellins from the embryo signals the seed to break dormancy and germinate. Some seeds that normally require particular

▽ **Figure 39.9 Effects of gibberellins on stem elongation and fruit growth.**

**(b)** The Thompson seedless grape bunch on the left is from an untreated control vine. The bunch on the right is growing from a vine that was sprayed with gibberellin during fruit development.

**(a)** Some plants develop in a rosette form, low to the ground with very short internodes, as in the *Arabidopsis* plant shown at the left. As the plant switches to reproductive growth, a surge of gibberellins induces bolting: Internodes elongate rapidly, elevating floral buds that develop at stem tips (right).

environmental conditions to germinate, such as exposure to light or low temperatures, break dormancy if they are treated with gibberellins. Gibberellins support the growth of cereal seedlings by stimulating the synthesis of digestive enzymes such as α-amylase that mobilize stored nutrients **(Figure 39.10)**.

▽ **Figure 39.10 Mobilization of nutrients by gibberellins during the germination of grain seeds such as barley.**

**1** After a seed imbibes water, the embryo releases gibberellin (GA), which sends a signal to the aleurone, the thin outer layer of the endosperm.

**2** The aleurone responds to GA by synthesizing and secreting digestive enzymes that hydrolyze nutrients stored in the endosperm. One example is α-amylase, which hydrolyzes starch.

**3** Sugars and other nutrients absorbed from the endosperm by the scutellum (cotyledon) are consumed during growth of the embryo into a seedling.

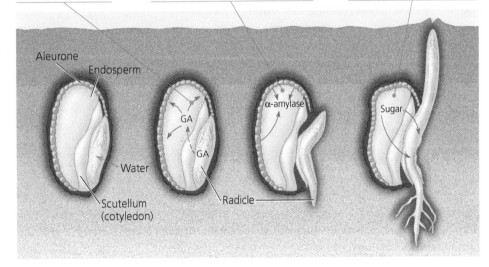

Aleurone
Endosperm
GA
Water
α-amylase
GA
Sugar
Scutellum (cotyledon)
Radicle

## Abscisic Acid

In the 1960s, one research group studying the chemical changes that precede bud dormancy and leaf abscission in deciduous trees and another team investigating chemical changes preceding abscission of cotton fruits isolated the same compound, **abscisic acid (ABA)**. Ironically, ABA is no longer thought to play a primary role in bud dormancy or leaf abscission, but it is very important in other functions. Unlike the growth-stimulating hormones we have discussed so far—auxin, cytokinins, gibberellins, and brassinosteroids—ABA *slows* growth. ABA often antagonizes the actions of growth hormones, and the ratio of ABA to one or more growth hormones determines the final physiological outcome. We will consider here two of ABA's many effects: seed dormancy and drought tolerance.

**Seed Dormancy** Seed dormancy increases the likelihood that seeds will germinate only when there are sufficient amounts of light, temperature, and moisture for the seedlings to survive (see Concept 38.1). What prevents seeds dispersed in autumn from germinating immediately, only to die in the winter? What mechanisms ensure that such seeds do not germinate until spring? For that matter, what prevents seeds from germinating in the dark, moist interior of the fruit? The answer to these questions is ABA. The levels of ABA may increase 100-fold during seed maturation. The high levels of ABA in maturing seeds inhibit germination and induce the production of proteins that help the seeds withstand the extreme dehydration that accompanies maturation.

Many types of dormant seeds germinate when ABA is removed or inactivated. The seeds of some desert plants break dormancy only when heavy rains wash ABA out of them. Other seeds require light or prolonged exposure to cold to inactivate ABA. Often, the ratio of ABA to gibberellins determines whether seeds remain dormant or germinate, and adding ABA to seeds that are primed to germinate makes them dormant again. Inactivated ABA or low levels of ABA can lead to precocious (early) germination **(Figure 39.11)**. For example, a maize mutant with grains that germinate while still on the cob lacks a functional transcription factor required for ABA to induce expression of certain genes. Precocious germination of red mangrove seeds, due to low ABA levels, is actually an adaptation that helps the young seedlings to plant themselves like darts in the soft mud below the parent tree.

**Drought Tolerance** ABA plays a major role in drought signaling. When a plant begins to wilt, ABA accumulates in the leaves and causes stomata to close rapidly, reducing transpiration and preventing further water loss. By affecting second messengers such as calcium, ABA causes potassium channels in the plasma membrane of guard cells

▼ **Figure 39.11 Precocious germination of wild-type mangrove and mutant maize seeds.**

◄ Red mangrove (*Rhizophora mangle*) seeds produce only low levels of ABA, and their seeds germinate while still on the tree. In this case, early germination is a useful adaptation. When released, the radicle of the dart-like seedling deeply penetrates the soft mudflats in which the mangroves grow.

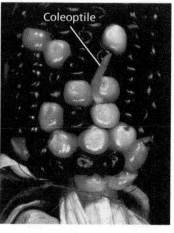

Coleoptile

▲ Precocious germination in this maize mutant is caused by lack of a functional transcription factor required for ABA action.

to open, leading to a massive loss of potassium ions from the cells. The accompanying osmotic loss of water reduces guard cell turgor and leads to closing of the stomatal pores (see Figure 36.14). In some cases, water shortage stresses the root system before the shoot system, and ABA transported from roots to leaves may function as an "early warning system." Many mutants that are especially prone to wilting are deficient in ABA production.

## Ethylene

During the 1800s, when coal gas was used as fuel for streetlights, leakage from gas pipes caused nearby trees to drop leaves prematurely. In 1901, the gas **ethylene** was demonstrated to be the active factor in coal gas. But the idea that it is a plant hormone was not widely accepted until the advent of a technique called gas chromatography simplified its identification.

Plants produce ethylene in response to stresses such as drought, flooding, mechanical pressure, injury, and infection. Ethylene is also produced during fruit ripening and programmed cell death and in response to high concentrations of externally applied auxin. Indeed, many effects previously ascribed to auxin, such as inhibition of root elongation, may be due to auxin-induced ethylene production. We will focus here on four of ethylene's many effects: response to mechanical stress, senescence, leaf abscission, and fruit ripening.

## The Triple Response to Mechanical Stress

Imagine a pea seedling pushing upward through the soil, only to come up against a stone. As it pushes against the obstacle, the stress in its delicate tip induces the seedling to produce ethylene. The hormone then instigates a growth maneuver known as the **triple response** that enables the shoot to avoid the obstacle. The three parts of this response are a slowing of stem elongation, a thickening of the stem (which makes it stronger), and a curvature that causes the stem to start growing horizontally. As the effects of the initial ethylene pulse lessen, the stem resumes vertical growth. If it again contacts a barrier, another burst of ethylene is released, and horizontal growth resumes. However, if the upward touch detects no solid object, then ethylene production decreases, and the stem, now clear of the obstacle, resumes its normal upward growth. It is ethylene that induces the stem to grow horizontally rather than the physical obstruction itself; when ethylene is applied to normal seedlings growing free of physical impediments, they still undergo the triple response **(Figure 39.12)**.

Studies of *Arabidopsis* mutants with abnormal triple responses are an example of how biologists identify a signal transduction pathway. Scientists isolated ethylene-insensitive (*ein*) mutants, which fail to undergo the triple response after

▼ Figure 39.12 **The ethylene-induced triple response.** In response to ethylene, a gaseous plant hormone, germinating pea seedlings grown in the dark undergo the triple response—slowing of stem elongation, stem thickening, and horizontal stem growth. The response is greater with increased ethylene concentration.

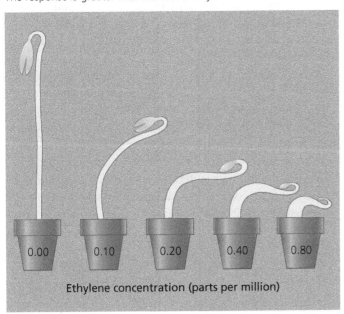

Ethylene concentration (parts per million)

**VISUAL SKILLS** ➤ *If the* ein *single mutation is combined with an ethylene-overproducing* (eto) *mutation, would the phenotype of the double mutant be different from that of the single mutant? Explain.*

▼ Figure 39.13 **Ethylene triple-response *Arabidopsis* mutants.**

*ein* mutant

*ctr* mutant

**(a)** *ein* **mutant.** An ethylene-insensitive (*ein*) mutant fails to undergo the triple response in the presence of ethylene.

**(b)** *ctr* **mutant.** A constitutive triple-response (*ctr*) mutant undergoes the triple response even in the absence of ethylene.

exposure to ethylene **(Figure 39.13a)**. Some types of *ein* mutants are insensitive to ethylene because they lack a functional ethylene receptor. Mutants of a different sort undergo the triple response even out of soil, in the air, where there are no physical obstacles. Some of these mutants have a regulatory defect that causes them to produce ethylene at rates 20 times normal. The phenotype of such ethylene-overproducing (*eto*) mutants can be restored to wild-type by treating the seedlings with inhibitors of ethylene synthesis. Other mutants, called constitutive triple-response (*ctr*) mutants, undergo the triple response in air but do not respond to inhibitors of ethylene synthesis **(Figure 39.13b)**. (Constitutive genes are genes that are continually expressed in all cells of an organism.) In *ctr* mutants, ethylene signal transduction is permanently turned on, even though ethylene is not present.

The affected gene in *ctr* mutants codes for a protein kinase. The fact that this mutation *activates* the ethylene response suggests that the normal kinase product of the wild-type allele is a *negative* regulator of ethylene signal transduction. Thus, binding of the hormone ethylene to the ethylene receptor normally leads to inactivation of the kinase, and the inactivation of this negative regulator allows synthesis of the proteins required for the triple response.

## Senescence

Consider the shedding of a leaf in autumn or the death of an annual after flowering. Or think about the final step in differentiation of a vessel element, when its living contents are destroyed, leaving a hollow tube behind. Such events involve **senescence**—the programmed death of certain cells or organs or the entire plant. Cells, organs, and plants genetically programmed to die on a schedule do not simply shut down cellular machinery and await death. Instead, at the molecular level, the onset of the programmed cell death called apoptosis is a very busy time in a cell's life, requiring new gene expression. During apoptosis, newly formed enzymes break down many chemical components, including chlorophyll, DNA, RNA, proteins, and membrane lipids. The plant salvages many of the breakdown products. A burst of ethylene is almost always associated with the apoptosis of cells during senescence.

**Leaf Abscission**  The loss of leaves from deciduous trees helps prevent desiccation during seasonal periods when the availability of water to the roots is severely limited. Before dying leaves abscise, many essential elements are salvaged from them and stored in stem parenchyma cells. These nutrients are recycled back to developing leaves during the following spring. The colors of autumn leaves are due to newly made red pigments as well as yellow and orange carotenoids (see Concept 10.2) that were already present in the leaves and are rendered visible by the breakdown of the dark green chlorophyll in autumn.

When an autumn leaf falls, it detaches from the stem at an abscission layer that develops near the base of the petiole (**Figure 39.14**). The small parenchyma cells of this layer have very thin walls, and there are no fiber cells around the vascular tissue. The abscission layer is further weakened when enzymes hydrolyze polysaccharides in the cell walls. Finally, the weight of the leaf, with the help of the wind, causes a separation within the abscission layer. Even before

▼ **Figure 39.14 Abscission of a maple leaf.** Abscission is controlled by a change in the ratio of ethylene to auxin. The abscission layer is seen in this longitudinal section as a vertical band at the base of the petiole. After the leaf falls, a protective layer of cork becomes the leaf scar that helps prevent pathogens from invading the plant (LM).

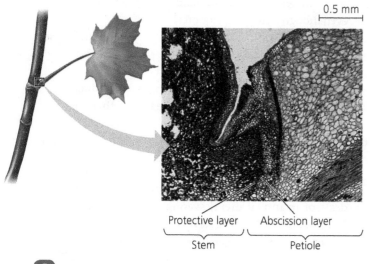

0.5 mm

Protective layer    Abscission layer

Stem    Petiole

Ⓜ️ Animation: Leaf Abscission

the leaf falls, a layer of cork forms a protective scar on the twig side of the abscission layer, preventing pathogens from invading the plant.

A change in the ratio of ethylene to auxin controls abscission. An aging leaf produces less and less auxin, rendering the cells of the abscission layer more sensitive to ethylene. As the influence of ethylene on the abscission layer prevails, the cells produce enzymes that digest the cellulose and other components of cell walls.

**Fruit Ripening**  Immature fleshy fruits are generally tart, hard, and green—features that help protect the developing seeds from herbivores. After ripening, the mature fruits help *attract* animals that disperse the seeds (see Figures 30.10 and 30.11). In many cases, a burst of ethylene production in the fruit triggers the ripening process. The enzymatic breakdown of cell wall components softens the fruit, and the conversion of starches and acids to sugars makes the fruit sweet. The production of new scents and colors helps advertise ripeness to animals, which eat the fruits and disperse the seeds.

A chain reaction occurs during ripening: Ethylene triggers ripening, and ripening triggers more ethylene production. The result is a huge burst in ethylene production. Because ethylene is a gas, the signal to ripen spreads from fruit to fruit. If you pick or buy green fruit, you may be able to speed ripening by storing the fruit in a paper bag, allowing ethylene to accumulate. On a commercial scale, many kinds of fruits are ripened in huge storage containers in which ethylene levels are enhanced. In other cases, fruit producers take measures to slow ripening caused by natural ethylene. Apples, for instance, are stored in bins flushed with carbon dioxide. Circulating the air prevents ethylene from accumulating, and carbon dioxide inhibits synthesis of new ethylene. Stored in this way, apples picked in autumn can still be shipped to grocery stores the following summer.

Given the importance of ethylene in the postharvest physiology of fruits, the genetic engineering of ethylene signal transduction pathways has potential commercial applications. For example, by engineering a way to block the transcription of one of the genes required for ethylene synthesis, molecular biologists have created tomato fruits that ripen on demand. These fruits are picked while green and will not ripen unless ethylene gas is added. As such methods are refined, they will reduce spoilage of fruits and vegetables, a problem that ruins almost half the produce harvested in the United States.

### *More Recently Discovered Plant Hormones*

Auxin, gibberellins, cytokinins, abscisic acid, and ethylene are often considered the five "classic" plant hormones. However, more recently discovered hormones have swelled the list of important plant growth regulators.

**Brassinosteroids** are steroids similar to cholesterol and the sex hormones of animals. They induce cell elongation and division in stem segments and seedlings at concentrations as low as $10^{-12}$ $M$. They also slow leaf abscission (leaf drop) and promote xylem differentiation. These effects are so qualitatively similar to those of auxin that it took years for plant physiologists to determine that brassinosteroids were not types of auxins.

The identification of brassinosteroids as plant hormones arose from studies of an *Arabidopsis* mutant that even when grown in the dark exhibited morphological features similar to plants grown in the light. The researchers discovered that the mutation affects a gene that normally codes for an enzyme similar to one involved in steroid synthesis in mammals. They also found that this brassinosteroid-deficient mutant could be restored to the wild-type phenotype by applying brassinosteroids.

**Jasmonates**, including *jasmonate* (JA) and *methyl jasmonate* (MeJA), are fatty acid–derived molecules that play important roles both in plant defense (see Concept 39.5) and, as discussed here, in plant development. Chemists first isolated MeJA as a key ingredient producing the enchanting fragrance of jasmine (*Jasminum grandiflorum*) flowers. Interest in jasmonates exploded when it was realized that jasmonates are produced by wounded plants and play a key role in controlling plant defenses against herbivores and pathogens. In studying jasmonate signal transduction mutants as well as the effects of applying jasmonates to plants, it soon became apparent that jasmonates and their derivatives regulate a wide variety of physiological processes in plants, including nectar secretion, fruit ripening, pollen production, flowering time, seed germination, root growth, tuber formation, mycorrhizal symbioses, and tendril coiling. In controlling plant processes, jasmonates also engage in crosstalk with phytochrome and various hormones, including GA, IAA, and ethylene.

**Strigolactones** are xylem-mobile chemicals that stimulate seed germination, suppress adventitious root formation, help establish mycorrhizal associations, and (as noted earlier) help control apical dominance. Their recent discovery relates back to studies of their namesake, *Striga*, a colorfully named genus of rootless parasitic plants that penetrate the roots of other plants, diverting essential nutrients from them and stunting their growth. (In Romanian legend, Striga is a vampire-like creature that lives for thousands of years, only needing to feed every 25 years or so.) Also known as witchweed, *Striga* may be the greatest obstacle to food production in Africa, infesting about two-thirds of the area devoted to cereal crops. Each *Striga* plant produces tens of thousands of tiny seeds that can remain dormant in the soil for many years until a suitable host begins to grow. Thus, *Striga* cannot be eradicated by growing non-grain crops for several years. Strigolactones, exuded by the host roots, were first identified as the chemical signals that stimulate the germination of *Striga* seeds.

## CONCEPT CHECK 39.2

1. Fusicoccin is a fungal toxin that stimulates the plasma membrane H$^+$ pumps of plant cells. How may it affect the growth of isolated stem sections?

2. **WHAT IF?** ➤ If a plant has the double mutation *ctr* and *ein*, what is its triple-response phenotype? Explain your answer.

3. **MAKE CONNECTIONS** ➤ What type of feedback process is exemplified by the production of ethylene during fruit ripening? Explain. (See Figure 1.10.)

*For suggested answers, see Appendix A.*

# CONCEPT 39.3

# Responses to light are critical for plant success

Light is an especially important environmental factor in the lives of plants. In addition to being required for photosynthesis, light triggers many key events in plant growth and development, collectively known as **photomorphogenesis**. Light reception also allows plants to measure the passage of days and seasons.

Plants detect not only the presence of light signals but also their direction, intensity, and wavelength (color). A graph called an **action spectrum** depicts the relative effectiveness of different wavelengths of radiation in driving a particular process, such as photosynthesis (see Figure 10.10b). Action spectra are useful in studying *any* process that depends on light. By comparing action spectra of various plant responses, researchers determine which responses are mediated by the same photoreceptor (pigment). They also compare action spectra with absorption spectra of pigments; a close correspondence for a given pigment suggests that the pigment is the photoreceptor mediating the response. Action spectra reveal that red and blue light are the most important colors in regulating a plant's photomorphogenesis. These observations led researchers to two major classes of light receptors: **blue-light photoreceptors** and **phytochromes**, photoreceptors that absorb mostly red light.

## Blue-Light Photoreceptors

Blue light initiates a variety of responses in plants, including phototropism, the light-induced opening of stomata (see Figure 36.13), and the light-induced slowing of hypocotyl elongation that occurs when a seedling breaks ground. The biochemical identity of the blue-light photoreceptor was so elusive that in the 1970s, plant physiologists began to call this receptor "cryptochrome" (from the Greek *kryptos*, hidden, and *chrom*, pigment). In the 1990s, molecular biologists analyzing *Arabidopsis* mutants found that plants use different types of pigments to detect blue light. *Cryptochromes*, molecular relatives of DNA repair enzymes, are involved in the blue-light-induced inhibition of stem elongation that occurs, for example, when a seedling first emerges from the soil. *Phototropin* is a protein kinase involved in mediating blue-light-mediated stomatal opening, chloroplast movements in response to light, and phototropic curvatures **(Figure 39.15)**, such as those studied by the Darwins.

▼ **Figure 39.15 Action spectrum for blue-light-stimulated phototropism in maize coleoptiles.** Phototropic bending toward light is controlled by phototropin, a photoreceptor sensitive to blue and violet light, particularly blue light.

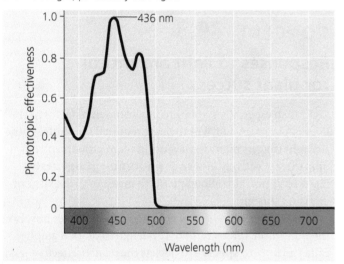

**(a)** This action spectrum illustrates that only light wavelengths below 500 nm (blue and violet light) induce curvature.

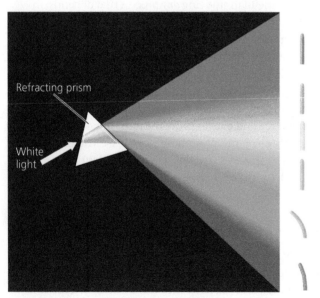

**(b)** When coleoptiles are exposed to light of various wavelengths as shown here, violet light induces slight curvature toward the light and blue light induces the most curvature. The other colors do not induce any curvature.

 Video: Phototropism

## Phytochrome Photoreceptors

When introducing signal transduction in plants earlier in the chapter, we discussed the role of the plant pigments called phytochromes in the de-etiolation process. Phytochromes are another class of photoreceptors that regulate many plant responses to light, including seed germination and shade avoidance.

### Phytochromes and Seed Germination

Studies of seed germination led to the discovery of phytochromes. Because of limited nutrient reserves, many types of seeds, especially small ones, germinate only when the light environment and other conditions are near optimal. Such seeds often remain dormant for years until light conditions change. For example, the death of a shading tree or the plowing of a field may create a favorable light environment for germination.

In the 1930s, scientists determined the action spectrum for light-induced germination of lettuce seeds. They exposed water-swollen seeds to a few minutes of single-colored light of various wavelengths and then stored the seeds in the dark. After two days, the researchers counted the number of seeds that had germinated under each light regimen. They found that red light of wavelength 660 nm increased the germination percentage of lettuce seeds maximally, whereas far-red light—that is, light of wavelengths near the upper edge of human visibility (730 nm)—*inhibited* germination compared with dark controls **(Figure 39.16)**. What happens when the lettuce seeds are subjected to a flash of red light followed by a flash of far-red light or, conversely, to far-red light followed by red light? The *last* flash of light determines the seeds' response: The effects of red and far-red light are reversible.

The photoreceptors responsible for the opposing effects of red and far-red light are phytochromes. So far, researchers have identified five phytochromes in *Arabidopsis*, each with a slightly different polypeptide component. In most phytochromes, the light-absorbing portion is photoreversible, converting back and forth between two forms, depending on the color of light to which it is exposed. In its red-absorbing form ($P_r$), a phytochrome absorbs red (r) light maximally and is converted to its far-red-absorbing form ($P_{fr}$); in its $P_{fr}$ form, it absorbs far-red (fr) light and is converted to its $P_r$ form **(Figure 39.17)**. This $P_r \leftrightarrow P_{fr}$ interconversion is a switching mechanism that controls various light-induced events in the life of the plant. $P_{fr}$ is the form of phytochrome that triggers many of a plant's developmental responses to light. For example, $P_r$ in lettuce seeds exposed to red light is converted to $P_{fr}$, stimulating the cellular responses that lead to germination. When red-illuminated seeds are then exposed to far-red light, the $P_{fr}$ is converted back to $P_r$, inhibiting the germination response.

## Inquiry  How does the order of red and far-red illumination affect seed germination?

**Experiment**  Scientists at the U.S. Department of Agriculture briefly exposed batches of lettuce seeds to red light or far-red light to test the effects on germination. After the light exposure, the seeds were placed in the dark, and the results were compared with control seeds that were not exposed to light.

**Results**  The bar below each photo indicates the sequence of red light exposure, far-red light exposure, and darkness. The germination rate increased greatly in groups of seeds that were last exposed to red light (left). Germination was inhibited in groups of seeds that were last exposed to far-red light (right).

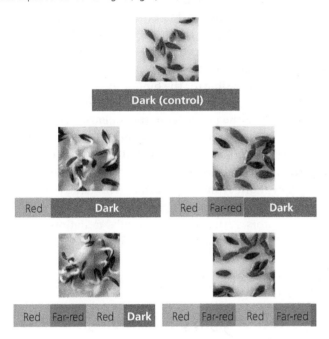

**Data from**  H. Borthwick et al., A reversible photoreaction controlling seed germination, *Proceedings of the National Academy of Sciences USA* 38:662–666 (1952).

**Conclusion**  Red light stimulates germination, and far-red light inhibits germination. The final light exposure is the determining factor. The effects of red and far-red light are reversible.

**WHAT IF?** ➤ *Phytochrome responds faster to red light than to far-red light. If the seeds had been placed in white light instead of the dark after their red light and far-red light treatments, would the results have been different?*

How does phytochrome switching explain light-induced germination in nature? Plants synthesize phytochrome as $P_r$, and if seeds are kept in the dark, the pigment remains almost entirely in the $P_r$ form (see Figure 39.17). Sunlight contains both red light and far-red light, but the conversion to $P_{fr}$ is faster than the conversion to $P_r$. Therefore, the ratio of $P_{fr}$ to $P_r$ increases in the sunlight. When seeds are exposed to adequate sunlight, the production and accumulation of $P_{fr}$ trigger their germination.

▼ **Figure 39.17  Phytochrome: a molecular switching mechanism.** The absorption of red light causes $P_r$ to change to $P_{fr}$. Far-red light reverses this conversion. In most cases, it is the $P_{fr}$ form of the pigment that switches on physiological and developmental responses in the plant.

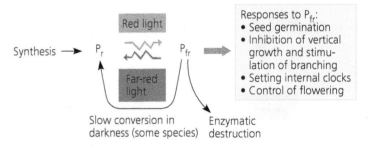

### Phytochromes and Shade Avoidance

The phytochrome system also provides the plant with information about the *quality* of light. Because sunlight includes both red and far-red radiation, during the day the $P_r \leftrightarrow P_{fr}$ interconversion reaches a dynamic equilibrium, with the ratio of the two phytochrome forms indicating the relative amounts of red and far-red light. This sensing mechanism enables plants to adapt to changes in light conditions. Consider, for example, the "shade avoidance" response of a tree that requires relatively high light intensity. If other trees in a forest shade this tree, the phytochrome ratio shifts in favor of $P_r$ because the forest canopy screens out more red light than far-red light. This is because the chlorophyll pigments in the leaves of the canopy absorb red light and allow far-red light to pass. The shift in the ratio of red to far-red light induces the tree to allocate more of its resources to growing taller. In contrast, direct sunlight increases the proportion of $P_{fr}$, which stimulates branching and inhibits vertical growth.

In addition to helping plants detect light, phytochrome helps a plant keep track of the passage of days and seasons. To understand phytochrome's role in these timekeeping processes, we must first examine the nature of the plant's internal clock.

## Biological Clocks and Circadian Rhythms

Many plant processes, such as transpiration and the synthesis of certain enzymes, undergo a daily oscillation. Some of these cyclic variations are responses to the changes in light levels and temperature that accompany the 24-hour cycle of day and night. We can control these external factors by growing plants in growth chambers under rigidly maintained conditions of light and temperature. But even under artificially constant conditions, many physiological processes in plants, such as the opening and closing of stomata and the production of photosynthetic enzymes, continue to oscillate with a frequency of about 24 hours. For example, many legumes lower their leaves in the evening and raise them in

The movements are caused by reversible changes in the turgor pressure of cells on opposing sides of the pulvini, motor organs of the leaf.

Noon                    10:00 PM

the morning (Figure 39.18). A bean plant continues these "sleep movements" even if kept in constant light or constant darkness; the leaves are not simply responding to sunrise and sunset. Such cycles, with a frequency of about 24 hours and not directly controlled by any known environmental variable, are called **circadian rhythms** (from the Latin *circa*, approximately, and *dies*, day).

Recent research supports the idea that the molecular "gears" of the circadian clock really are internal and not a daily response to some subtle but pervasive environmental cycle, such as geomagnetism or cosmic radiation. Organisms, including plants and humans, continue their rhythms even after being placed in deep mine shafts or when orbited in satellites, conditions that alter these subtle geophysical periodicities. However, daily signals from the environment can entrain (set) the circadian clock to a period of precisely 24 hours.

If an organism is kept in a constant environment, its circadian rhythms deviate from a 24-hour period (a period is the duration of one cycle). These free-running periods, as they are called, vary from about 21 to 27 hours, depending on the particular rhythmic response. The sleep movements of bean plants, for instance, have a period of 26 hours when the plants are kept in the free-running condition of constant darkness. Deviation of the free-running period from exactly 24 hours does not mean that biological clocks drift erratically. Free-running clocks are still keeping perfect time, but they are not synchronized with the outside world. To understand the mechanisms underlying circadian rhythms, we must distinguish between the clock and the rhythmic processes it controls. For example, the leaves of the bean plant in Figure 39.18 are the clock's "hands" but are not the essence of the clock itself. If bean leaves are restrained for several hours and then released, they will reestablish the position appropriate for the time of day. We can interfere with a biological rhythm, but the underlying clockwork continues to tick.

At the heart of the molecular mechanisms underlying circadian rhythms are oscillations in the transcription of certain genes. Mathematical models propose that the 24-hour period arises from negative-feedback loops involving the transcription of a few central "clock genes." Some clock genes may encode transcription factors that inhibit, after a time delay, the transcription of the gene that encodes the transcription factor itself. Such negative-feedback loops, together with a time delay, are enough to produce oscillations.

Researchers have used a novel technique to identify clock mutants of *Arabidopsis*. One prominent circadian rhythm in plants is the daily production of certain photosynthesis-related proteins. Molecular biologists traced the source of this rhythm to the promoter that initiates the transcription of the genes for these photosynthesis proteins. To identify clock mutants, scientists inserted the gene for an enzyme responsible for the bioluminescence of fireflies, called luciferase, to the promoter. When the biological clock turned on the promoter in the *Arabidopsis* genome, it also turned on the production of luciferase. The plants began to glow with a circadian periodicity. Clock mutants were then isolated by selecting specimens that glowed for a longer or shorter time than normal. The genes altered in some of these mutants affect proteins that normally bind photoreceptors. Perhaps these particular mutations disrupt a light-dependent mechanism that sets the biological clock.

 Interview with Ruth Satter: Investigating sleep movements in plants

## The Effect of Light on the Biological Clock

As we have discussed, the free-running period of the circadian rhythm of bean leaf movements is 26 hours. Consider a bean plant placed at dawn in a dark cabinet for 72 hours: Its leaves would not rise again until 2 hours after natural dawn on the second day, 4 hours after natural dawn on the third day, and so on. Shut off from environmental cues, the plant becomes desynchronized. Desynchronization happens to humans when we fly across several time zones; when we reach our destination, the clocks on the wall are not synchronized with our internal clocks. Most organisms are probably prone to jet lag.

The factor that entrains the biological clock to precisely 24 hours every day is light. Both phytochromes and blue-light photoreceptors can entrain circadian rhythms in plants, but our understanding of how phytochromes do this is more complete. The mechanism involves turning cellular responses on and off by means of the $P_r \leftrightarrow P_{fr}$ switch.

Consider again the photoreversible system in Figure 39.17. In darkness, the phytochrome ratio shifts gradually in favor of the $P_r$ form, partly as a result of turnover in the overall phytochrome pool. The pigment is synthesized in the $P_r$ form, and enzymes destroy more $P_{fr}$ than $P_r$. In some plant species, $P_{fr}$ present at sundown slowly converts to $P_r$. In darkness, there is no means for the $P_r$ to be reconverted to $P_{fr}$, but upon illumination, the $P_{fr}$ level suddenly increases again as $P_r$ is rapidly converted. This increase in $P_{fr}$ each day at dawn resets the biological clock: Bean leaves reach their most extreme night position 16 hours after dawn.

In nature, interactions between phytochrome and the biological clock enable plants to measure the passage of night and day. The relative lengths of night and day, however, change over the course of the year (except at the equator). Plants use this change to adjust activities in timing with the seasons.

## Photoperiodism and Responses to Seasons

Imagine the consequences if a plant produced flowers when pollinators were not present or if a deciduous tree produced leaves in the middle of winter. Seasonal events are of critical importance in the life cycles of most plants. Seed germination, flowering, and the onset and breaking of bud dormancy are all stages that usually occur at specific times of the year. The environmental cue that plants use to detect the time of year is the change in day length (*photoperiod*). A physiological response to specific night or day lengths, such as flowering, is called **photoperiodism**.

### Photoperiodism and Control of Flowering

An early clue to how plants detect seasons came from a mutant variety of tobacco, Maryland Mammoth, that grew tall but failed to flower during summer. It finally bloomed in a greenhouse in December. After trying to induce earlier flowering by varying temperature, moisture, and mineral nutrition, researchers learned that the shortening days of winter stimulated this variety to flower. Experiments revealed that flowering occurred only if the photoperiod was 14 hours or shorter. This variety did not flower during summer because at Maryland's latitude the photoperiods were too long.

The researchers called Maryland Mammoth a **short-day plant** because it apparently required a light period *shorter* than a critical length to flower. Chrysanthemums, poinsettias, and some soybean varieties are also short-day plants, which generally flower in late summer, fall, or winter. Another group of plants flower only when the light period is *longer* than a certain number of hours. These **long-day plants** generally flower in late spring or early summer. Spinach, for example, flowers when days are 14 hours or longer. Radishes, lettuce, irises, and many cereal varieties are also long-day plants. **Day-neutral plants**, such as tomatoes, rice, and dandelions, are unaffected by photoperiod and flower when they reach a certain stage of maturity, regardless of photoperiod.

**Critical Night Length** In the 1940s, researchers learned that flowering in short- and long-day plants is actually controlled by night length, not day length (photoperiod). Many of these scientists worked with cocklebur (*Xanthium strumarium*), a short-day plant that flowers only when days are 16 hours or shorter (and nights are at least 8 hours long). These researchers found that if the photoperiod is broken by a brief exposure to darkness, flowering proceeds. However, if the night length is interrupted by even a few minutes of dim light, cocklebur will not flower, and this turned out to be true for other short-day plants as well **(Figure 39.19a)**. Cocklebur is unresponsive to day length, but it requires at least 8 hours of continuous darkness to flower. Short-day plants are really long-night plants, but the older term is embedded firmly in the lexicon of plant physiology. Similarly, long-day plants are actually short-night plants. A long-day plant grown under long-night conditions that would not normally induce flowering will flower if the night length is interrupted by a few minutes of light **(Figure 39.19b)**.

Notice that long-day plants are *not* distinguished from short-day plants by an absolute night length. Instead, they are distinguished by whether the critical night length sets a *maximum* number of hours of darkness required for flowering (long-day plants) or a *minimum* number of hours of darkness required for flowering (short-day plants). In both cases, the actual number of hours in the critical night length is specific to each species of plant.

▼ **Figure 39.19 Photoperiodic control of flowering.**

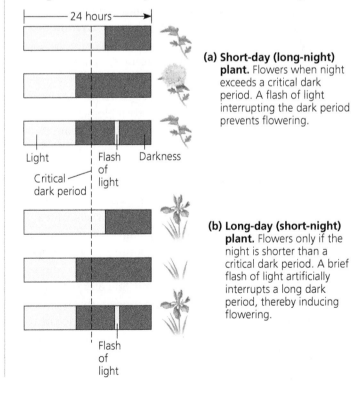

**(a) Short-day (long-night) plant.** Flowers when night exceeds a critical dark period. A flash of light interrupting the dark period prevents flowering.

**(b) Long-day (short-night) plant.** Flowers only if the night is shorter than a critical dark period. A brief flash of light artificially interrupts a long dark period, thereby inducing flowering.

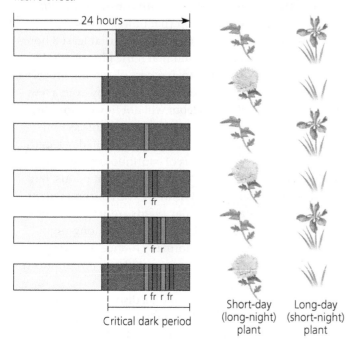

**▼ Figure 39.20 Reversible effects of red and far-red light on photoperiodic response.** A flash of red (r) light shortens the dark period. A subsequent flash of far-red (fr) light cancels the red flash's effect.

r

r fr

r fr r

r fr r fr

Critical dark period

Short-day (long-night) plant

Long-day (short-night) plant

**VISUAL SKILLS ➤** *Under long-day conditions (as in the top panel) or under short-day conditions (as in the second panel), how would a single flash of far-red light during the dark period affect flowering?*

Red light is the most effective color in interrupting the night length. Action spectra and photoreversibility experiments show that phytochrome is the pigment that detects the red light **(Figure 39.20)**. For example, if a flash of red light during the night length is followed by a flash of far-red light, then the plant detects no interruption of night length. As in the case of phytochrome-mediated seed germination, red/far-red photoreversibility occurs.

Plants measure night lengths very precisely; some short-day plants will not flower if night is even 1 minute shorter than the critical length. Some plant species always flower on the same day each year. It appears that plants use their biological clock, entrained by night length with the help of phytochrome, to tell the season of the year. The floriculture (flower-growing) industry applies this knowledge to produce flowers out of season. Chrysanthemums, for instance, are short-day plants that normally bloom in fall, but their blooming can be stalled until Mother's Day in May by punctuating each long night with a flash of light, thus turning one long night into two short nights.

Some plants bloom after a single exposure to the photoperiod required for flowering. Other species need several successive days of the appropriate photoperiod. Still others respond to a photoperiod only if they have been previously exposed to some other environmental stimulus, such as a period of cold. Winter wheat, for example, will not flower unless it has been exposed to several weeks of temperatures below 10°C. The use of pretreatment with cold to induce flowering is called **vernalization** (from the Latin for "spring"). Several weeks after winter wheat is vernalized, a long photoperiod (short night) induces flowering.

## A Flowering Hormone?

Although flowers form from apical or axillary bud meristems, it is leaves that detect changes in photoperiod and produce signaling molecules that cue buds to develop as flowers. In many short-day and long-day plants, exposing just one leaf to the appropriate photoperiod is enough to induce flowering. Indeed, as long as one leaf is left on the plant, photoperiod is detected and floral buds are induced. If all leaves are removed, the plant is insensitive to photoperiod.

Classic experiments revealed that the floral stimulus could move across a graft from an induced plant to a noninduced plant and trigger flowering in the latter. Moreover, the flowering stimulus appears to be the same for short-day and long-day plants, despite the different photoperiodic conditions required for leaves to send this signal **(Figure 39.21)**. The hypothetical signaling molecule for flowering, called **florigen**, remained unidentified for over 70 years as scientists focused on small hormone-like molecules. However, large macromolecules, such as mRNA and proteins, can move by the symplastic route via plasmodesmata and regulate plant development. It now appears that florigen is a protein. A gene called *FLOWERING LOCUS T (FT)* is activated in leaf cells during conditions favoring flowering, and the FT protein travels through the symplasm to the shoot apical meristem, initiating the transition of a bud's meristem from a vegetative to a flowering state.

**▼ Figure 39.21 Experimental evidence for a flowering hormone.** If grown individually under short-day conditions, a short-day plant will flower and a long-day plant will not. However, both will flower if grafted together and exposed to short days. This result indicates that a flower-inducing substance (florigen) is transmitted across grafts and induces flowering in both short-day and long-day plants.

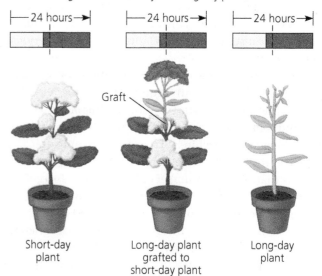

Graft

Short-day plant

Long-day plant grafted to short-day plant

Long-day plant

**WHAT IF? ➤** *If flowering were inhibited in both parts of the grafted plants, what would you conclude?*

1. If an enzyme in field-grown soybean leaves is most active at noon and least active at midnight, is its activity under circadian regulation?

2. **WHAT IF?** ➤ If a plant flowers in a controlled chamber with a daily cycle of 10 hours of light and 14 hours of darkness, is it a short-day plant? Explain.

3. **MAKE CONNECTIONS** ➤ Plants detect the quality of their light environment by using blue-light photoreceptors and red-light-absorbing phytochromes. After reviewing Figure 10.10, suggest a reason why plants are so sensitive to these colors of light.

*For suggested answers, see Appendix A.*

# CONCEPT 39.4

## Plants respond to a wide variety of stimuli other than light

Although plants are immobile, some mechanisms have evolved by natural selection that enable them to adjust to a wide range of environmental circumstances by developmental or physiological means. Light is so important in the life of a plant that we devoted the entire previous section to the topic of a plant's reception of and response to this particular environmental factor. In this section, we will examine responses to some of the other environmental stimuli that a plant commonly encounters.

## Gravity

Because plants are photoautotrophs, it is not surprising that mechanisms for growing toward light have evolved. But what environmental cue does the shoot of a young seedling use to grow upward when it is completely underground and there is no light for it to detect? Similarly, what environmental factor prompts the young root to grow downward? The answer to both questions is gravity.

Place a plant on its side, and it adjusts its growth so that the shoot bends upward and the root curves downward. In their responses to gravity, or **gravitropism**, roots display positive gravitropism **(Figure 39.22a)** and shoots exhibit negative gravitropism. Gravitropism occurs as soon as a seed germinates, ensuring that the root grows into the soil and the shoot grows toward sunlight, regardless of how the seed is oriented when it lands.

Plants may detect gravity by the settling of **statoliths**, dense cytoplasmic components that settle under the influence of gravity to the lower portions of the cell. The statoliths of vascular plants are specialized plastids containing dense starch grains **(Figure 39.22b)**. In roots, statoliths are located in certain cells of the root cap. According to one hypothesis, the aggregation of statoliths at the low points of these cells triggers a redistribution of calcium, which causes lateral

▼ **Figure 39.22 Positive gravitropism in roots: the statolith hypothesis.**

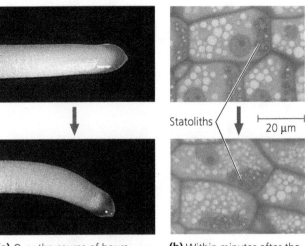

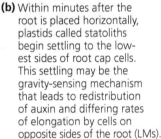

Statoliths   20 µm

**(a)** Over the course of hours, a horizontally oriented primary root of maize bends gravitropically until its growing tip becomes vertically oriented (LMs).

**(b)** Within minutes after the root is placed horizontally, plastids called statoliths begin settling to the lowest sides of root cap cells. This settling may be the gravity-sensing mechanism that leads to redistribution of auxin and differing rates of elongation by cells on opposite sides of the root (LMs).

Ⓜ Video: Gravitropism

transport of auxin within the root. The calcium and auxin accumulate on the lower side of the root's zone of elongation. At high concentration, auxin inhibits cell elongation, an effect that slows growth on the root's lower side. The more rapid elongation of cells on the upper side causes the root to grow straight downward.

Falling statoliths, however, may not be necessary for gravitropism. For example, there are mutants of *Arabidopsis* and tobacco that lack statoliths but are still capable of gravitropism, though the response is slower than in wild-type plants. It could be that the entire cell helps the root sense gravity by mechanically pulling on proteins that tether the protoplast to the cell wall, stretching the proteins on the "up" side and compressing the proteins on the "down" side of the root cells. Dense organelles, in addition to starch granules, may also contribute by distorting the cytoskeleton as they are pulled by gravity. Statoliths, because of their density, may enhance gravitational sensing by a mechanism that simply works more slowly in their absence.

## Mechanical Stimuli

Trees in windy environments usually have shorter, stockier trunks than a tree of the same species growing in more sheltered locations. The advantage of this stunted morphology is that it enables the plant to hold its ground against strong gusts of wind. The term **thigmomorphogenesis** (from the Greek *thigma*, touch) refers to the changes in form that result

▼ **Figure 39.23 Thigmomorphogenesis in *Arabidopsis*.** The shorter plant on the right was rubbed twice a day. The untouched plant (left) grew much taller.

from mechanical perturbation. Plants are very sensitive to mechanical stress: Even the act of measuring the length of a leaf with a ruler alters its subsequent growth. Rubbing the stems of a young plant a couple of times daily results in plants that are shorter than controls **(Figure 39.23)**.

Some plant species have become, over the course of their evolution, "touch specialists." Acute responsiveness to mechanical stimuli is an integral part of these plants' "life strategies." Most vines and other climbing plants have tendrils that coil rapidly around supports (see Figure 35.7). These grasping organs usually grow straight until they touch something; the contact stimulates a coiling response caused by differential growth of cells on opposite sides of the tendril. This directional growth in response to touch is called **thigmotropism**, and it allows the vine to take advantage of whatever mechanical supports it comes across as it climbs upward toward a forest canopy.

Other examples of touch specialists are plants that undergo rapid leaf movements in response to mechanical stimulation. For example, when the compound leaf of the sensitive plant *Mimosa pudica* is touched, it collapses and its leaflets fold together **(Figure 39.24)**. This response, which takes only a second or two, results from a rapid loss of turgor in cells within pulvini, specialized motor organs located at the joints of the leaf. The motor cells suddenly become flaccid after stimulation because they lose potassium ions, causing water to leave the cells by osmosis. It takes about 10 minutes for the cells to regain their turgor and restore the "unstimulated" form of the leaf. The function of the sensitive plant's behavior invites speculation. Perhaps the plant appears less leafy and

appetizing to herbivores by folding its leaves and reducing its surface area when jostled.

A remarkable feature of rapid leaf movements is the mode of transmission of the stimulus through the plant. If one leaflet on a sensitive plant is touched, first that leaflet responds, then the adjacent leaflet responds, and so on, until all the leaflet pairs have folded together. From the point of stimulation, the signal that produces this response travels at a speed of about 1 cm/sec. An electrical impulse traveling at the same rate can be detected when electrodes are attached to the leaf. These impulses, called **action potentials**, resemble nerve impulses in animals, though the action potentials of plants are thousands of times slower. Action potentials have been discovered in many species of algae and plants and may be used as a form of internal communication. For example, in the Venus flytrap (*Dionaea muscipula*), action potentials are transmitted from sensory hairs in the trap to the cells that respond by closing the trap (see Figure 37.16). In the case of *Mimosa pudica*, more violent stimuli, such as touching a leaf with a hot needle, causes *all* the leaves and leaflets to droop. This whole-plant response involves the spread of signaling molecules from the injured area to other parts of the shoot.

## Environmental Stresses

Environmental stresses, such as flooding, drought, or extreme temperatures, can have devastating effects on plant survival, growth, and reproduction. In natural ecosystems, plants that cannot tolerate an environmental stress either die or are outcompeted by other plants. Thus, environmental stresses are an important factor in determining the geographic ranges of plants. In the last section of this chapter, we will examine the defensive responses of plants to common **biotic** (living) stresses, such as herbivores and pathogens. Here we will consider some of the more common **abiotic** (nonliving) stresses that plants encounter. Since these abiotic factors are major determinants of crop yields, there is currently much interest in trying to project how global climate change will impact crop production (see the **Problem-Solving Exercise**).

▼ **Figure 39.24 Rapid turgor movements by the sensitive plant (*Mimosa pudica*).**

**(a) Unstimulated state (leaflets spread apart)**   **(b) Stimulated state (leaflets folded)**

 Video: *Mimosa* Leaves

# How will climate change affect crop productivity?

Plant growth is significantly limited by air temperature, water availability, and solar radiation. A useful parameter for estimating crop productivity is the number of days per year when these three climate variables are suitable for plant growth. Camilo Mora (University of Hawaii at Manoa) and his colleagues analyzed global climate models to project the effect of climate change on suitable days for plant growth by the year 2100.

In this exercise, you will examine projected effects of climate change on crop productivity and identify the resulting human impacts.

**Your Approach**  Analyze the map and table. Then answer the questions below.

**Your Data**  The researchers projected the annual changes in suitable days for plant growth for all three climate variables: temperature, water availability, and solar radiation. They did so by subtracting recent averages (1996–2005) from projected future averages (2091–2100). The map shows the projected changes if no measures are taken to reduce climate change. The numbers identify locations of the 15 most populous nations. The table identifies their economies as either mainly industrial (🏭) or agricultural (🌱) and their annual per capita income category.

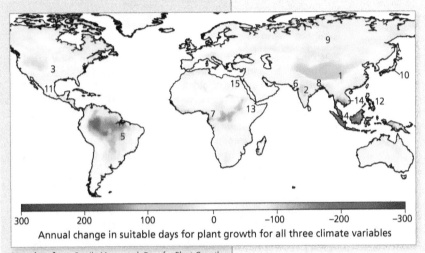

Annual change in suitable days for plant growth for all three climate variables

**Map data from** Camilo Mora, et al. Days for Plant Growth Disappear under Projected Climate Change: Potential Human and Biotic Vulnerability. *PLoS Biol* 13(6): e1002167 (2015).

| Nation | Map location | Estimated population in 2014 (millions) | Type of economy | Income category* |
|---|---|---|---|---|
| China | 1 | 1,350 | 🏭 | $$$ |
| India | 2 | 1,221 | 🌱 | $$ |
| United States | 3 | 317 | 🏭 | $$$$ |
| Indonesia | 4 | 251 | 🌱 | $ |
| Brazil | 5 | 201 | 🌱 | $$$ |
| Pakistan | 6 | 193 | 🌱 | $$ |
| Nigeria | 7 | 175 | 🌱 | $$ |
| Bangladesh | 8 | 164 | 🌱 | $ |
| Russia | 9 | 143 | 🏭 | $$$$ |
| Japan | 10 | 127 | 🏭 | $$$$ |
| Mexico | 11 | 116 | 🌱 | $$$ |
| Philippines | 12 | 106 | 🌱 | $$ |
| Ethiopia | 13 | 94 | 🌱 | $ |
| Vietnam | 14 | 92 | 🌱 | $ |
| Egypt | 15 | 85 | 🌱 | $$ |

*Based on World Bank categories: $ = low: < $1,035; $$ = lower middle: $1,036-$4,085; $$$ = upper middle: $4,086-$12,615; $$$$= high: > $12,615.

  **Instructors:** A version of this Problem-Solving Exercise can be assigned in MasteringBiology.

**Your Analysis**

1. Camilo Mora began the study as a result of talking with someone who claimed climate change improves plant growth because it increases the number of days above freezing. Based on the map data, how would you respond to this claim?

2. What does the table data indicate about the human impact of the projected changes?

## Drought

On a sunny, dry day, a plant may wilt because its water loss by transpiration exceeds water absorption from the soil. Prolonged drought, of course, will kill a plant, but plants have control systems that enable them to cope with less extreme water deficits.

Many of a plant's responses to water deficit help the plant conserve water by reducing the rate of transpiration. Water deficit in a leaf causes stomata to close, thereby slowing transpiration dramatically (see Figure 36.14). Water deficit stimulates increased synthesis and release of abscisic acid in the leaves; this hormone helps keep stomata closed by acting on guard cell membranes. Leaves respond to water deficit in several other ways. For example, when the leaves of grasses wilt, they roll into a tubelike shape that reduces transpiration by exposing less leaf surface to dry air and wind. Other plants, such as ocotillo (see Figure 36.15), shed their leaves in response to seasonal drought. Although these leaf responses conserve water, they also reduce photosynthesis, which is one reason why a drought diminishes crop yield. Plants can even take advantage of early warnings in the form of chemical signals from wilting neighbors and prime themselves to respond more readily and intensely to impending drought stress (see the **Scientific Skills Exercise**).

## Interpreting Experimental Results from a Bar Graph

**Do Drought-Stressed Plants Communicate Their Condition to Their Neighbors?** Researchers wanted to learn if plants can communicate drought-induced stress to neighboring plants and, if so, whether they use aboveground or belowground signals. In this exercise, you will interpret a bar graph concerning widths of stomatal openings to investigate whether drought-induced stress can be communicated from plant to plant.

**How the Experiment Was Done** Eleven potted pea plants (*Pisum sativum*) were placed equidistantly in a row. The root systems of plants 6–11 were connected to those of their immediate neighbors by tubes, which allowed chemicals to move from the roots of one plant to the roots of the next plant without moving through the soil. The root systems of plants 1–6 were not connected. Osmotic shock was inflicted on plant 6 using a highly concentrated solution of mannitol, a natural sugar commonly used to mimic drought stress in vascular plants.

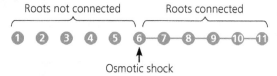

Fifteen minutes following the osmotic shock to plant 6, researchers measured the width of stomatal openings in leaves from all the plants. A control experiment was also done in which water was added to plant 6 instead of mannitol.

### INTERPRET THE DATA

1. How do the widths of the stomatal openings of plants 6–8 and plants 9 and 10 compare with those of the other plants in the experiment? What does this indicate about the state of plants 6–8 and 9 and 10? (For information about reading graphs, see the Scientific Skills Review in Appendix F and in the Study Area at www.masteringbiology.com.)

**Data from the Experiment**

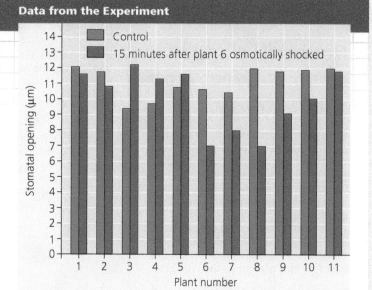

**Data from** O. Falik et al., Rumor has it …: Relay communication of stress cues in plants, *PLoS ONE* 6(11):e23625 (2011).

2. Do the data support the idea that plants can communicate their drought-stressed condition to their neighbors? If so, do the data indicate that the communication is via the shoot system or the root system? Make specific reference to the data in answering both questions.

3. Why was it necessary to make sure that chemicals could not move through the soil from one plant to the next?

4. When the experiment was run for 1 hour rather than 15 minutes, the results were about the same except that the stomatal openings of plants 9–11 were comparable to those of plants 6–8. Suggest a reason why.

5. Why was water added to plant 6 instead of mannitol in the control experiment? What do the results of the control experiment indicate?

**Instructors:** A version of this Scientific Skills Exercise can be assigned in MasteringBiology.

## Flooding

Too much water is also a problem for a plant. An overwatered houseplant may suffocate because the soil lacks the air spaces that provide oxygen for cellular respiration in the roots. Some plants are structurally adapted to very wet habitats. For example, the submerged roots of mangroves, which inhabit coastal marshes, are continuous with aerial roots exposed to oxygen (see Figure 35.4). But how do less specialized plants cope with oxygen deprivation in waterlogged soils? Oxygen deprivation stimulates the production of ethylene, which causes some cells in the root cortex to die. The destruction of these cells creates air tubes that function as "snorkels," providing oxygen to the submerged roots **(Figure 39.25)**.

▼ **Figure 39.25 A developmental response of maize roots to flooding and oxygen deprivation. (a)** A cross section of a control root grown in an aerated hydroponic medium. **(b)** A root grown in a nonaerated hydroponic medium. Ethylene-stimulated apoptosis (programmed cell death) creates the air tubes (SEMs).

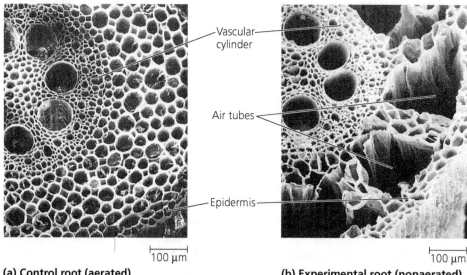

**(a) Control root (aerated)**  **(b) Experimental root (nonaerated)**

## Salt Stress

An excess of sodium chloride or other salts in the soil threatens plants for two reasons. First, by lowering the water potential of the soil solution, salt can cause a water deficit in plants even though the soil has plenty of water. As the water potential of the soil solution becomes more negative, the water potential gradient from soil to roots is lowered, thereby reducing water uptake (see Figure 36.12). Another problem with saline soil is that sodium and certain other ions are toxic to plants when their concentrations are too high. Many plants can respond to moderate soil salinity by producing solutes that are well tolerated at high concentrations: These mostly organic compounds keep the water potential of cells more negative than that of the soil solution without admitting toxic quantities of salt. However, most plants cannot survive salt stress for long. The exceptions are halophytes, salt-tolerant plants with adaptations such as salt glands that pump salts out across the leaf epidermis.

## Heat Stress

Excessive heat may harm and even kill a plant by denaturing its enzymes. Transpiration helps cool leaves by evaporative cooling. On a warm day, for example, the temperature of a leaf may be 3–10°C below the ambient air temperature. Hot, dry weather also tends to dehydrate many plants; the closing of stomata in response to this stress conserves water but then sacrifices evaporative cooling. This dilemma is one reason why very hot, dry days take a toll on most plants.

Most plants have a backup response that enables them to survive heat stress. Above a certain temperature—about 40°C for most plants in temperate regions—plant cells begin synthesizing **heat-shock proteins**, which help protect other proteins from heat stress. This response also occurs in heat-stressed animals and microorganisms. Some heat-shock proteins function in unstressed cells as temporary scaffolds that help other proteins fold into their functional shapes. In their roles as heat-shock proteins, perhaps these molecules bind to other proteins and help prevent their denaturation.

## Cold Stress

One problem plants face when the temperature of the environment falls is a change in the fluidity of cell membranes. When a membrane cools below a critical point, membranes lose their fluidity as the lipids become locked into crystalline structures. This alters solute transport across the membrane and also adversely affects the functions of membrane proteins. Plants respond to cold stress by altering the lipid composition of their membranes. For example, membrane lipids increase in their proportion of unsaturated fatty acids, which have shapes that help keep membranes more fluid at low temperatures. Such membrane modification requires from several hours to days, which is one reason why unseasonably cold temperatures are generally more stressful to plants than the more gradual seasonal drop in air temperature.

Freezing is another type of cold stress. At subfreezing temperatures, ice forms in the cell walls and intercellular spaces of most plants. The cytosol generally does not freeze at the cooling rates encountered in nature because it contains more solutes than the very dilute solution found in the cell wall, and solutes lower the freezing point of a solution. The reduction in liquid water in the cell wall caused by ice formation lowers the extracellular water potential, causing water to leave the cytoplasm. The resulting increase in the concentration of ions in the cytoplasm is harmful and can lead to cell death. Whether the cell survives depends largely on how well it resists dehydration. In regions with cold winters, native plants are adapted to cope with freezing stress. For example, before the onset of winter, the cells of many frost-tolerant species increase cytoplasmic levels of specific solutes, such as sugars, that are well tolerated at high concentrations and that help reduce the loss of water from the cell during extracellular freezing. The unsaturation of membrane lipids also increases, thereby maintaining proper levels of membrane fluidity.

**EVOLUTION** Many organisms, including certain vertebrates, fungi, bacteria, and many species of plants, have proteins that hinder ice crystals from growing, helping the organism escape freezing damage. First described in Arctic fish in the 1950s, these *antifreeze proteins* permit survival at temperatures below 0°C. They bind to small ice crystals and inhibit their growth or, in the case of plants, prevent the crystallization of ice. The five major classes of antifreeze proteins differ markedly in their amino acid sequences but have a similar three-dimensional structure, suggesting convergent evolution. Surprisingly, antifreeze proteins from winter rye are homologous to antifungal defense proteins, but they are produced in response to cold temperatures and shorter days, not fungal pathogens. Progress is being made in increasing the freezing tolerance of crop plants by engineering antifreeze protein genes into their genomes.

### CONCEPT CHECK 39.4

1. Thermal images are photographs of the heat emitted by an object. Researchers have used thermal imaging of plants to isolate mutants that overproduce abscisic acid. Suggest a reason why they are warmer than wild-type plants under conditions that are normally nonstressful.

2. A greenhouse worker finds that potted chrysanthemums nearest the aisles are often shorter than those in the middle of the bench. Explain this "edge effect," a common problem in horticulture.

3. **WHAT IF?** ➤ If you removed the root cap from a root, would the root still respond to gravity? Explain.

*For suggested answers, see Appendix A.*

## CONCEPT 39.5

# Plants respond to attacks by pathogens and herbivores

Through natural selection, plants have evolved many types of interactions with other species in their communities. Some interspecific interactions are mutually beneficial, such as the associations of plants with mycorrhizal fungi (see Figure 37.15) or with pollinators (see Figures 38.4 and 38.5). Many plant interactions with other organisms, however, do not benefit the plant. As primary producers, plants are at the base of most food webs and are subject to attack by a wide range of plant-eating (herbivorous) animals. A plant is also subject to infection by diverse viruses, bacteria, and fungi that can damage tissues or even kill the plant. Plants counter these threats with defense systems that deter animals and prevent infection or combat invading pathogens.

## Defenses Against Pathogens

A plant's first line of defense against infection is the physical barrier presented by the epidermis and periderm of the plant body (see Figure 35.19). This line of defense, however, is not impenetrable. The mechanical wounding of leaves by herbivores, for example, opens up portals for invasion by pathogens. Even when plant tissues are intact, viruses, bacteria, and the spores and hyphae of fungi can still enter the plant through natural openings in the epidermis, such as stomata. Once the physical lines of defense are breached, a plant's next lines of defense are two types of immune responses: PAMP-triggered immunity and effector-triggered immunity.

### PAMP-Triggered Immunity

When a pathogen succeeds in invading a host plant, the plant mounts the first of two lines of immune defense, which ultimately results in a chemical attack that isolates the pathogen and prevents its spread from the site of infection. This first line of immune defense, called *PAMP-triggered immunity*, depends on the plant's ability to recognize **pathogen-associated molecular patterns** (**PAMPs**; formerly called *elicitors*), molecular sequences that are specific to certain pathogens. For example, bacterial *flagellin,* a major protein found in bacterial flagella, is a PAMP. Many soil bacteria, including some pathogenic varieties, get splashed onto the shoots of plants by raindrops. If these bacteria penetrate the plant, a specific amino acid sequence within flagellin is perceived by a Toll-like receptor, a type of receptor also found in animals, where it plays a key role in the innate immune system (see Concept 43.1). The innate immune system is an evolutionarily old defense strategy and is the dominant immune system in plants, fungi, insects, and primitive multicellular organisms. Unlike vertebrates, plants do not have an adaptive immune system: Plants neither generate antibody or T cell responses nor possess mobile cells that detect and attack pathogens.

PAMP recognition in plants leads to a chain of signaling events that lead ultimately to the local production of broad-spectrum, antimicrobial chemicals called *phytoalexins,* which are compounds having fungicidal and bactericidal properties. The plant cell wall is also toughened, hindering further progress of the pathogen. Similar but even stronger defenses are initiated by the second plant immune response, effector-triggered immunity.

### Effector-Triggered Immunity

**EVOLUTION** Over the course of evolution, plants and pathogens have engaged in an arms race. PAMP-triggered immunity can be overcome by the evolution of pathogens that can evade detection by the plant. These pathogens deliver **effectors**, pathogen-encoded proteins that cripple the plant's innate immune system, directly into plant cells. For example, some bacteria deliver effectors inside the plant cell that block the perception of flagellin. Thus, these effectors allow the pathogen to redirect the host's metabolism to the pathogen's advantage.

The suppression of PAMP-triggered immunity by pathogen effectors led to the evolution of *effector-triggered immunity*. Because there are thousands of effectors, this plant defense is typically made up of hundreds of disease resistance (*R*) genes. Each *R* gene codes for an R protein that can be activated by a specific effector. Signal transduction pathways then lead to an arsenal of defense responses, including a local defense called the *hypersensitive response* and a general defense called *systemic acquired resistance*. Local and systemic responses to pathogens require extensive genetic reprogramming and commitment of cellular resources. Therefore, a plant activates these defenses only after detecting a pathogen.

**The Hypersensitive Response** The **hypersensitive response** refers to the local cell and tissue death that occurs at and near the infection site. In some cases, the hypersensitive response restricts the spread of a pathogen, but in other cases it appears to be merely a consequence of the overall defense response. As indicated in **Figure 39.26**, the hypersensitive response is initiated as part of effector-triggered immunity. The hypersensitive response is part of a complex defense that involves the production of enzymes and chemicals that impair the pathogen's cell wall integrity, metabolism, or reproduction. Effector-triggered immunity also stimulates the formation of lignin and the cross-linking of molecules within the plant cell wall, responses that hinder the spread of the pathogen to other parts of the plant. As shown in the upper right of the figure, the hypersensitive response results in localized lesions on a leaf. As "sick" as such a leaf appears, it will still survive, and its defensive response will help protect the rest of the plant.

### Systemic Acquired Resistance

The hypersensitive response is localized and specific. However, as noted previously, pathogen invasions can also produce signaling molecules that "sound the alarm" of infection to the whole plant. The resulting **systemic acquired resistance**

**▼ Figure 39.26 Defense responses against pathogens.** Plants can often prevent the systemic spread of infection by instigating a hypersensitive response. This response helps isolate the pathogen by producing lesions that form "rings of death" around the sites of infection.

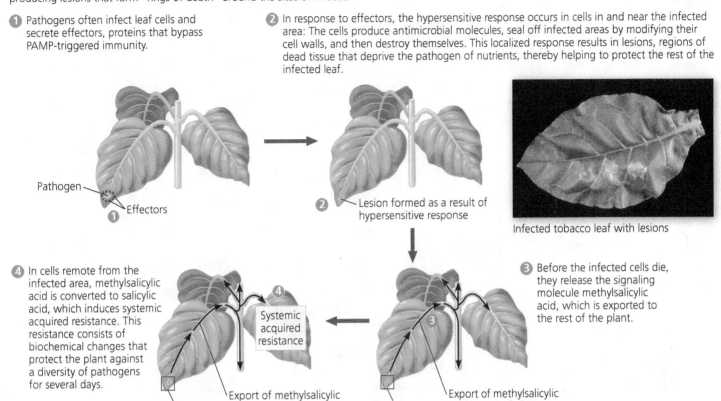

**1** Pathogens often infect leaf cells and secrete effectors, proteins that bypass PAMP-triggered immunity.

**2** In response to effectors, the hypersensitive response occurs in cells in and near the infected area: The cells produce antimicrobial molecules, seal off infected areas by modifying their cell walls, and then destroy themselves. This localized response results in lesions, regions of dead tissue that deprive the pathogen of nutrients, thereby helping to protect the rest of the infected leaf.

Pathogen
**1** Effectors

**2** Lesion formed as a result of hypersensitive response

Infected tobacco leaf with lesions

**4** In cells remote from the infected area, methylsalicylic acid is converted to salicylic acid, which induces systemic acquired resistance. This resistance consists of biochemical changes that protect the plant against a diversity of pathogens for several days.

**4** Systemic acquired resistance

**3** Before the infected cells die, they release the signaling molecule methylsalicylic acid, which is exported to the rest of the plant.

Infected area
Export of methylsalicylic acid to rest of plant

Infected area
Export of methylsalicylic acid to rest of plant

arises from the plant-wide expression of defense genes. It is nonspecific, providing protection against a diversity of pathogens that can last for days. A signaling molecule called methylsalicylic acid is produced around the infection site, carried by the phloem throughout the plant, and then converted to **salicylic acid** in areas remote from the sites of infection. Salicylic acid activates a signal transduction pathway that poises the defense system to respond rapidly to another infection (see step 4 of Figure 39.26).

Plant disease epidemics, such as the potato blight (see Concept 28.6) that caused the Irish potato famine of the 1840s, can lead to incalculable human misery. Other diseases, such as chestnut blight (see Concept 31.5) and sudden oak death (see Concept 54.5), can dramatically alter community structures. Plant epidemics are often the result of infected plants or timber being inadvertently transported around the world. As global commerce increases, such epidemics will become increasingly more common. To prepare for such outbreaks, plant biologists are stockpiling the seeds of wild relatives of crop plants in special storage facilities. Scientists hope that undomesticated relatives may have genes that will be able to curb the next plant epidemic.

## Defenses Against Herbivores

**Herbivory**, animals eating plants, is a stress that plants face in any ecosystem. The mechanical damage caused by

herbivores reduces the size of plants, hindering ability to acquire resources. It can restrict growth because many species divert some energy to defend against herbivores. Also, it opens portals for infection by viruses, bacteria, and fungi. Plants prevent excessive herbivory through methods that span all levels of biological organization (**Figure 39.27**, before the Chapter Review), including physical defenses, such as thorns and trichomes (see Figure 35.9), and chemical defenses, such as distasteful or toxic compounds.

## CONCEPT CHECK 39.5

1. What are some drawbacks of spraying fields with general-purpose insecticides?

2. Chewing insects mechanically damage plants and lessen the surface area of leaves for photosynthesis. In addition, these insects make plants more vulnerable to pathogen attack. Suggest a reason why.

3. Many fungal pathogens get food by causing plant cells to become leaky, releasing nutrients into the intercellular spaces. Would it benefit the fungus to kill the host plant in a way that results in all the nutrients leaking out?

4. **WHAT IF?** ➤ Suppose a scientist finds that a population of plants growing in a breezy location is more prone to herbivory by insects than a population of the same species growing in a sheltered area. Suggest a hypothesis to account for this observation.

*For suggested answers, see Appendix A.*

# ▼ Figure 39.27 MAKE CONNECTIONS

## Levels of Plant Defenses Against Herbivores

Herbivory, animals eating plants, is ubiquitous in nature. Plant defenses against herbivores are examples of how biological processes can be observed at multiple levels of biological organization: molecular, cellular, tissue, organ, organism, population, and community. (See Figure 1.3.)

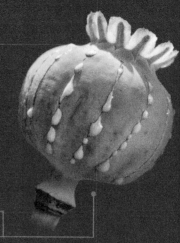

Opium poppy fruit

### Molecular-Level Defenses

At the molecular level, plants produce chemical compounds that deter attackers. These compounds are typically terpenoids, phenolics, and alkaloids. Some terpenoids mimic insect hormones and cause insects to molt prematurely and die. Some examples of phenolics are tannins, which have an unpleasant taste and hinder the digestion of proteins. Their synthesis is often enhanced following attack. The opium poppy (*Papaver somniferum*) is the source of the narcotic alkaloids morphine, heroin, and codeine. These drugs accumulate in secretory cells called laticifers, which exude a milky-white latex (opium) when the plant is damaged.

### Cellular-Level Defenses

Some plant cells are specialized for deterring herbivores. Trichomes on leaves and stems hinder the access of chewing insects. Laticifers and, more generally, the central vacuoles of plant cells may serve as storage depots for chemicals that deter herbivores. *Idioblasts* are specialized cells found in the leaves and stems of many species, including taro (*Colocasia esculenta*). Some idioblasts contain needle-shaped crystals of calcium oxalate called *raphides*. They penetrate the soft tissues of the tongue and palate, making it easier for an irritant produced by the plant, possibly a protease, to enter animal tissues and cause temporary swelling of the lips, mouth, and throat. The crystals act as a carrier for the irritant, enabling it to seep deeper into the herbivore's tissues. The irritant is destroyed by cooking.

Raphide crystals from taro plant

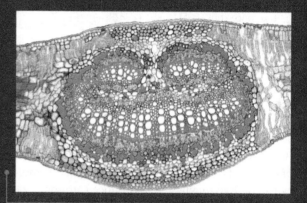

### Tissue-Level Defenses

Some leaves deter herbivores by being especially tough to chew as a result of extensive growth of thick, hardened sclerenchyma tissue. The bright red cells with thick cell walls seen in this cross section through the major vein of an olive leaf (*Olea europaea*) are tough sclerenchyma fibers.

### Organ-Level Defenses

The shapes of plant organs may deter herbivores by causing pain or making the plant appear unappealing. Spines (modified leaves) and thorns (modified stems) provide mechanical defenses against herbivores. Bristles on the spines of some cacti have fearsome barbs that tear flesh during removal. The leaf of the snowflake plant (*Trevesia palmata*) looks as if it has been partially eaten, perhaps making it less attractive. Some plants mimic the presence of insect eggs on their leaves, dissuading insects from laying eggs there. For example, the leaf glands of some species of *Passiflora* (passion flowers) closely imitate the bright yellow eggs of *Heliconius* butterflies.

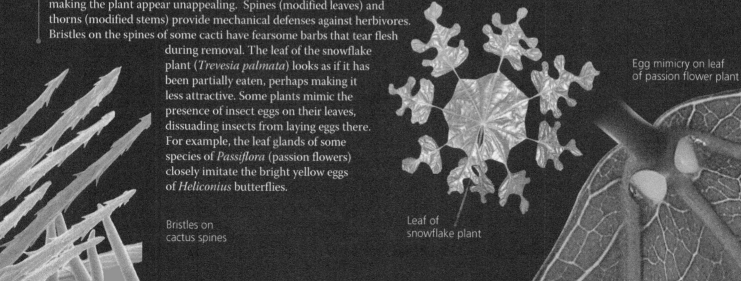

Bristles on cactus spines

Leaf of snowflake plant

Egg mimicry on leaf of passion flower plant

## Organismal-Level Defenses

Mechanical damage by herbivores can greatly alter a plant's entire physiology, deterring further attack. For example, a species of wild tobacco called *Nicotiana attenuata* changes the timing of its flowering as a result of herbivory. It normally flowers at night, emitting the chemical benzyl acetone, which attracts hawk-moths as pollinators. Unfortunately for the plant, the moths often lay eggs on the leaves as they pollinate, and the larvae are herbivores. When the plants become too larvae-infested, they stop producing the chemical and instead open their flowers at dawn, when the moths are gone. They are then pollinated by hummingbirds. Research has shown that oral secretions from the munching larvae trigger the dramatic shift in the timing of flower opening.

Hummingbird pollinating wild tobacco plant

## Population-Level Defenses

In some species, a coordinated behavior at the population level helps defend against herbivores. Some plants can communicate their distress from attack by releasing molecules that warn nearby plants of the same species. For example, lima bean (*Phaseolus lunatus*) plants infested with spider mites release a cocktail of chemicals that signal "news" of the attack to noninfested lima bean plants. In response, these neighbors instigate biochemical changes that make them less susceptible to attack. Another type of population-level defense is a phenomenon in some species called masting, in which a population synchronously produces a massive amount of seeds after a long interval. Regardless of environmental conditions, an internal clock signals each plant in the population that it is time to flower. Bamboo populations, for example, grow vegetatively for decades and suddenly flower en masse, set seed, and die. As much as 80,000 kg of bamboo seeds are released per hectare, much more than the local herbivores, mostly rodents, can eat. As a result, some seeds escape the herbivores' attention, germinate, and grow.

Flowering bamboo plants

## Community-Level Defenses

Some plant species "recruit" predatory animals that help defend the plant against specific herbivores. Parasitoid wasps, for example, inject their eggs into caterpillars feeding on plants. The eggs hatch within the caterpillars, and the larvae eat through their organic containers from the inside out. The larvae then form cocoons on the surface of the host before emerging as adult wasps. The plant has an active role in this drama. A leaf damaged by caterpillars releases compounds that attract parasitoid wasps. The stimulus for this response is a combination of physical damage to the leaf caused by the munching caterpillar and a specific compound in the caterpillar's saliva.

Parasitoid wasp cocoons on caterpillar host

Adult wasp emerging from a cocoon

**MAKE CONNECTIONS** ➤ *As with plant adaptations against herbivores, other biological processes can involve multiple levels of biological organization (Figure 1.3). Discuss examples of specialized photosynthetic adaptations involving modifications at the molecular (Concept 10.4), tissue (Concept 36.4), and organismal (Concept 36.1) levels.*

Go to **MasteringBiology**™ for Videos, Animations, Vocab Self-Quiz, Practice Tests, and more in the Study Area.

## SUMMARY OF KEY CONCEPTS

### CONCEPT 39.1

**Signal transduction pathways link signal reception to response** (pp. 841–843)

VOCAB
SELF-QUIZ
goo.gl/6u55ks

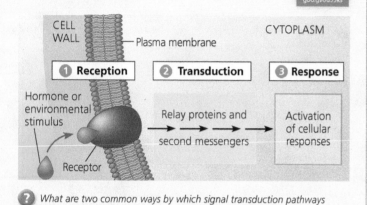

**?** *What are two common ways by which signal transduction pathways enhance the activity of specific enzymes?*

### CONCEPT 39.2

**Plant hormones help coordinate growth, development, and responses to stimuli** (pp. 844–853)

- **Hormones** control plant growth and development by affecting the division, elongation, and differentiation of cells. Some also mediate the responses of plants to environmental stimuli.

| Plant Hormone | Major Responses |
|---|---|
| Auxin | Stimulates cell elongation; regulates branching and organ bending |
| Cytokinins | Stimulate plant cell division; promote later bud growth; slow organ death |
| Gibberellins | Promote stem elongation; help seeds break dormancy and use stored reserves |
| Abscisic acid | Promotes stomatal closure in response to drought; promotes seed dormancy |
| Ethylene | Mediates fruit ripening and the triple response |
| Brassinosteroids | Chemically similar to the sex hormones of animals; induce cell elongation and division |
| Jasmonates | Mediate plant defenses against insect herbivores; regulate a wide range of physiological processes |
| Strigolactones | Regulate apical dominance, seed germination, and mycorrhizal associations |

**?** *Is there any truth to the old adage, "One bad apple spoils the whole bunch?" Explain.*

### CONCEPT 39.3

**Responses to light are critical for plant success** (pp. 853–859)

- **Blue-light photoreceptors** control hypocotyl elongation, stomatal opening, and phototropism.
- **Phytochromes** act like molecular "on-off" switches that regulate shade avoidance and germination of many seed types. Red light turns phytochrome "on," and far-red light turns it "off."

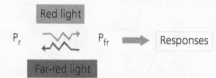

- Phytochrome conversion also provides information about the day length (photoperiod) and hence the time of year. **Photoperiodism** regulates the time of flowering in many species. **Short-day plants** require a night longer than a critical length to flower. **Long-day plants** need a night length shorter than a critical period to flower.
- Many daily rhythms in plant behavior are controlled by an internal circadian clock. Free-running **circadian rhythms** are approximately 24 hours long but are entrained to exactly 24 hours by dawn and dusk effects on phytochrome form.

**?** *Why did plant physiologists propose the existence of a mobile molecule (florigen) that triggers flowering?*

### CONCEPT 39.4

**Plants respond to a wide variety of stimuli other than light** (pp. 859–863)

- **Gravitropism** is bending in response to gravity. Roots show positive gravitropism, and stems show negative gravitropism. **Statoliths**, starch-filled plastids, enable roots to detect gravity.
- **Thigmotropism** is a growth response to touch. Rapid leaf movements involve transmission of electrical impulses.
- Plants are sensitive to environmental stresses, including drought, flooding, high salinity, and extremes of temperature.

| Environmental Stress | Major Response |
|---|---|
| Drought | ABA production, reducing water loss by closing stomata |
| Flooding | Formation of air tubes that help roots survive oxygen deprivation |
| Salt | Avoiding osmotic water loss by producing solutes tolerated at high concentrations |
| Heat | Synthesis of heat-shock proteins, which reduce protein denaturation at high temperatures |
| Cold | Adjusting membrane fluidity; avoiding osmotic water loss; producing antifreeze proteins |

**?** *Plants that have acclimated to drought stress are often more resistant to freezing stress as well. Suggest a reason why.*

## CONCEPT 39.5

### Plants respond to attacks by pathogens and herbivores (pp. 864–867)

- The **hypersensitive response** seals off an infection and destroys both pathogen and host cells in the region. **Systemic acquired resistance** is a generalized defense response in organs distant from the infection site.
- In addition to physical defenses such as thorns and trichomes, plants produce distasteful or toxic chemicals, as well as attractants that recruit animals that destroy herbivores.

 *How can insects make plants more susceptible to pathogens?*

## TEST YOUR UNDERSTANDING

### Level 1: Knowledge/Comprehension

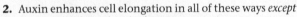

**PRACTICE TEST** goo.gl/CUYGKD

1. The hormone that helps plants respond to drought is
   (A) auxin.
   (B) abscisic acid.
   (C) cytokinin.
   (D) ethylene.

2. Auxin enhances cell elongation in all of these ways *except*
   (A) increased uptake of solutes.
   (B) gene activation.
   (C) acid-induced denaturation of cell wall proteins.
   (D) cell wall loosening.

3. Charles and Francis Darwin discovered that
   (A) auxin is responsible for phototropic curvature.
   (B) red light is most effective in shoot phototropism.
   (C) light destroys auxin.
   (D) light is perceived by the tips of coleoptiles.

4. How may a plant respond to *severe* heat stress?
   (A) by reorienting leaves to increase evaporative cooling
   (B) by creating air tubes for ventilation
   (C) by producing heat-shock proteins, which may protect the plant's proteins from denaturing
   (D) by increasing the proportion of unsaturated fatty acids in cell membranes, reducing their fluidity

### Level 2: Application/Analysis

5. The signaling molecule for flowering might be released earlier than usual in a long-day plant exposed to flashes of
   (A) far-red light during the night.
   (B) red light during the night.
   (C) red light followed by far-red light during the night.
   (D) far-red light during the day.

6. If a long-day plant has a critical night length of 9 hours, which 24-hour cycle would prevent flowering?
   (A) 16 hours light/8 hours dark
   (B) 14 hours light/10 hours dark
   (C) 4 hours light/8 hours dark/4 hours light/8 hours dark
   (D) 8 hours light/8 hours dark/light flash/8 hours dark

7. A plant mutant that shows normal gravitropic bending but does not store starch in its plastids would require a reevaluation of the role of _____ in gravitropism.
   (A) auxin
   (B) calcium
   (C) statoliths
   (D) differential growth

8. **DRAW IT** Indicate the response to each condition by drawing a straight seedling or one with the triple response.

| | Control | Ethylene added | Ethylene synthesis inhibitor |
|---|---|---|---|
| Wild-type | | | |
| Ethylene insensitive (*ein*) | | | |
| Ethylene overproducing (*eto*) | | | |
| Constitutive triple response (*ctr*) | | | |

### Level 3: Synthesis/Evaluation

9. **EVOLUTION CONNECTION** In general, light-sensitive germination is more pronounced in small seeds compared with germination of large seeds. Suggest a reason why.

10. **SCIENTIFIC INQUIRY** A plant biologist observed a peculiar pattern when a tropical shrub was attacked by caterpillars. After a caterpillar ate a leaf, it would skip over nearby leaves and attack a leaf some distance away. Simply removing a leaf did not deter caterpillars from eating nearby leaves. The biologist suspected that an insect-damaged leaf sent out a chemical that signaled nearby leaves. How could the researcher test this hypothesis?

11. **SCIENCE, TECHNOLOGY, AND SOCIETY** Describe how our knowledge about the control systems of plants is being applied to agriculture or horticulture.

12. **WRITE ABOUT A THEME: INTERACTIONS** In a short essay (100–150 words), summarize phytochrome's role in altering shoot growth for the enhancement of light capture.

13. **SYNTHESIZE YOUR KNOWLEDGE**

This mule deer is grazing on the shoot tips of a shrub. Describe how this event will alter the physiology, biochemistry, structure, and health of the plant, and identify which hormones and other chemicals are involved in making these changes.

*For selected answers, see Appendix A.*

 For additional practice questions, check out the **Dynamic Study Modules** in MasteringBiology. You can use them to study on your smartphone, tablet, or computer anytime, anywhere!

Born in 1936, Harald zur Hausen completed undergraduate and medical studies in his native Germany. He moved to Philadelphia for a three-year fellowship in molecular biology, studying how viruses induce chromosomal breaks. Upon returning to Germany, Dr. zur Hausen turned his attention to the idea that viruses might cause cervical cancer. He focused on the role of sexually transmitted viruses, in part inspired by an 1842 report noting that cervical cancer is absent among nuns. In 1983, he published a study linking cervical cancer to infection with certain types of human papilloma virus (HPV). This discovery provided the basis for the HPV vaccine, which can prevent cervical cancer as well as certain oral cancers in both men and women. In 2008, Dr. zur Hausen was honored as a recipient of the Nobel Prize in Physiology or Medicine.

## "Learn to be critical and not to trust all the dogmas."

▼ **Computer model of HPV**

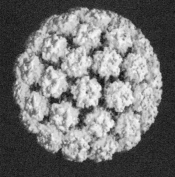

## An Interview with Harald zur Hausen

### Why as a young doctor did you set out to study the role of viruses in cancer?

During my medical training, I became aware of data on bacterial phages, showing that the phages left their genomes in the bacteria they infected and may have changed the properties of the bacteria. This triggered the idea that cancer might be the same kind of story: Normal cells would pick up a viral genome, and the viral genome would persist and subsequently contribute to the development of cancer. A little bit of a naïve idea, but it followed me through the more than 50 years of my career.

### Your model and your findings proved correct, but met with resistance along the way. Tell us a bit about that.

At the end of the 1960s the idea came up that the herpes simplex type 2 virus could play a role in cervical cancer. So we started to look in cervical cancer biopsies and tested close to 100 of them. Not in a single one was there any herpes simplex virus type 2 DNA. At a meeting in 1974, a well-known researcher claimed to have found a piece of herpes simplex type 2 DNA in one cervical cancer biopsy. I presented our work at the same meeting. Because I was supposed to be a medically trained person without a background in molecular biology, as some of the colleagues claimed, they simply didn't believe our negative results. I must say that meeting was, for me, the worst professional experience I ever had, even later in my life.

### How did the work on human papillomavirus (HPV) begin?

I came across a review on papillomavirus that described how papillomas, including genital warts, develop. I also found studies showing that genital warts occasionally converted to malignant tumors. That fascinated me. We initiated studies isolating viral DNA from individual warts. It took us about seven years before we had a specimen from which we could isolate sufficient DNA to use for labeling procedures. We saw that papillomavirus is indeed present in many genital warts, but to our disappointment we didn't find the genital wart virus in cervical cancer. However, using this material enabled us to isolate a related virus, which we named HPV-11.

### What was the path from this finding to the breakthrough?

Using HPV-11 DNA as a probe against biopsy material from cervical cancer, we saw a very faint signal in samples from a few tumors. That triggered the idea that there should be something not identical, but related, in those tumors. At that time I had several skillful students and co-workers in the lab. They quite quickly isolated DNA for HPV-16, which, it turns out, is found in 50% of all cervical cancer biopsies, and a bit later HPV-18, for which 20% of biopsies are positive. The papers were published in 1983 and 1984, the vaccine was licensed in 2006, and by now many millions of young people have been immunized.

### Looking back on your training and career, do you have any advice for our students?

Many talented young people stay in the same field as their mentors, a bit of scientific inbreeding. Look into other areas to see whether there is something which would fascinate you even more, using the expertise that you have. Also, learn to be critical and not to trust all the dogmas. Currently, for example, we are investigating whether single-stranded DNA viruses that we have isolated from cattle might contribute to the increased risk of colon cancer associated with consumption of red meat.

# Basic Principles of Animal Form and Function

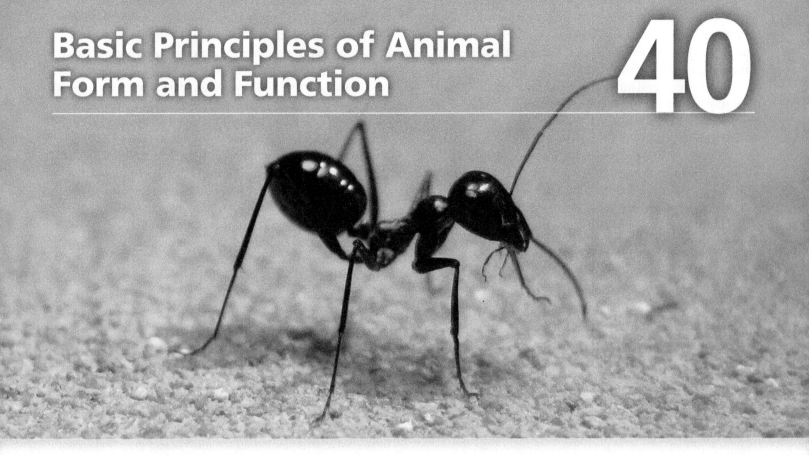

▲ Figure 40.1 **How do long legs help this scavenger survive in the scorching desert heat?**

## KEY CONCEPTS

**40.1** Animal form and function are correlated at all levels of organization

**40.2** Feedback control maintains the internal environment in many animals

**40.3** Homeostatic processes for thermoregulation involve form, function, and behavior

**40.4** Energy requirements are related to animal size, activity, and environment

## Diverse Forms, Common Challenges

The desert ant (genus *Cataglyphis*) in **Figure 40.1** scavenges insects that have succumbed to the daytime heat of the Sahara Desert. To gather corpses for feeding, the ant must forage when surface temperatures on the sunbaked sand exceed 60°C (140°F), well above the thermal limit for virtually all animals. How does the desert ant survive in these conditions? To address this question, we need to consider the relationship of **anatomy**, or biological form, to species survival.

In studying the desert ant, researchers noted that its stilt-like legs are disproportionately long. Elevated 4 mm above the sand by these legs, the ant's body is exposed to a temperature 6°C lower than that at ground level. Researchers have also found that a desert ant can use its long legs to run as fast as 1 m/sec, close to the top speed recorded for any running arthropod. Speedy sprinting minimizes the time that the ant is out of its nest and exposed to the sun. Thus, the long legs of the desert ant are adaptations that allow it to be active during the heat of the day, when competition for food and the risk of predation are lowest.

Over the course of its life, an ant faces the same fundamental challenges as any other animal, whether hydra, hawk, or human. All animals must obtain nutrients and oxygen, fight off infection, and produce offspring. Given that they share these and other basic requirements, why do species vary so enormously in organization and appearance? The answer lies in natural selection and adaptation.

When you see this blue icon, log in to **MasteringBiology** and go to the Study Area for digital resources.

 Get Ready for This Chapter

Natural selection favors those variations in a population that increase relative fitness (see Concept 23.4). The evolutionary adaptations that enable survival vary among environments and species but frequently result in a close match of form to function, as shown by the legs of the desert ant.

Because form and function are correlated, examining anatomy often provides clues to **physiology**—biological function. In this chapter, we'll begin our study of animal form and function by examining the levels of organization in the animal body and the systems for coordinating the activities of different body parts. Next, we'll use the example of body temperature regulation to illustrate how animals control their internal environment. Finally, we'll explore how anatomy and physiology relate to an animal's interactions with the environment and its management of energy use.

# CONCEPT 40.1

## Animal form and function are correlated at all levels of organization

An animal's size and shape are fundamental aspects of form that significantly affect the way the animal interacts with its environment. Although we may refer to size and shape as elements of a "body plan" or "design," this does not imply a process of conscious invention. The body plan of an animal is the result of a pattern of development programmed by the genome, itself the product of millions of years of evolution.

### Evolution of Animal Size and Shape

EVOLUTION Many different body plans have arisen during the course of evolution, but these variations fall within certain bounds. Physical laws that govern strength, diffusion, movement, and heat exchange limit the range of animal forms.

As an example of how physical laws constrain evolution, let's consider how some properties of water limit the possible shapes for animals that are fast swimmers. Water is about 1,000 times denser than air and also far more viscous. Therefore, any bump on an animal's body surface that causes drag impedes a swimmer more than it would a runner or flyer. Tuna and other fast ray-finned fishes can swim at speeds up to 80 km/hr (50 miles/hour). Sharks, penguins, dolphins, and seals are also relatively fast swimmers. As illustrated by the three examples in **Figure 40.2**, these animals all have a shape that is fusiform, meaning tapered on both ends. The similar

▼ **Figure 40.2 Convergent evolution in fast swimmers.**

Seal

Penguin

Tuna

streamlined shape found in these speedy vertebrates is an example of convergent evolution (see Concept 22.3). Natural selection often results in similar adaptations when diverse organisms face the same environmental challenge, such as overcoming drag during swimming.

Physical laws also influence animal body plans with regard to maximum size. As body dimensions increase, thicker skeletons are required to maintain adequate support. This limitation affects internal skeletons, such as those of vertebrates, as well as external skeletons, such as those of insects and other arthropods. In addition, as bodies increase in size, the muscles required for locomotion must represent an ever-larger fraction of the total body mass. At some point, mobility becomes limited. By considering the fraction of body mass in leg muscles and the effective force such muscles generate, scientists can estimate maximum running speed for a wide range of body plans. Such calculations indicate that the dinosaur *Tyrannosaurus rex*, which stood more than 6 m tall, probably could run at 30 km/hr (19 miles/hour), about as fast as the fastest humans today can run.

### Exchange with the Environment

Animals must exchange nutrients, waste products, and gases with their environment, and this requirement imposes an additional limitation on body plans. Exchange occurs as substances dissolved in an aqueous solution move across the plasma membrane of each cell. A single-celled organism, such as the amoeba in **Figure 40.3a**, has a sufficient membrane surface area in contact with its environment to carry out all necessary exchange. In contrast, an animal is composed of many cells, each with its own plasma membrane across which exchange must occur. The rate of exchange is proportional to the membrane surface area involved in exchange, whereas the amount of material that must be exchanged is proportional to the body volume. A multicellular organization therefore works only if every cell has access to a suitable aqueous environment, either inside or outside the animal's body.

Many animals with a simple internal organization have body plans that enable direct exchange between almost all their cells and the external environment. For example, a pond-dwelling hydra, which has a saclike body plan, has a body wall only two cell layers thick **(Figure 40.3b)**. Because its gastrovascular cavity opens to the external environment, both the outer and inner layers of cells are constantly bathed by pond water. Another common body plan that maximizes exposure to the surrounding medium is a flat shape. Consider, for instance, a parasitic tapeworm, which can reach several meters in length

## ▼ Figure 40.3 Direct exchange with the environment.

Exchange

0.1 mm

**(a) An amoeba, a single-celled organism**

Mouth

Gastrovascular cavity

Exchange

Exchange

1 mm

**(b) A hydra, an animal with two layers of cells**

(see Figure 33.12). A thin, flat shape places most cells of the worm in direct contact with its particular environment—the nutrient-rich intestinal fluid of a vertebrate host.

Our bodies and those of most other animals are composed of compact masses of cells, with an internal organization much more complex than that of a hydra or a tapeworm. For such a body plan, increasing the number of cells decreases the ratio of outer surface area to total volume. As an extreme comparison, the ratio of outer surface area to volume for a whale is hundreds of thousands of times smaller than that for a water flea. Nevertheless, every cell in the whale must be bathed in fluid and have access to oxygen, nutrients, and other resources. How is this accomplished?

In whales and most other animals, the evolutionary adaptations that enable sufficient exchange with the environment are specialized surfaces that are extensively branched or folded **(Figure 40.4)**. In almost all cases, these exchange surfaces lie within the body, an arrangement that protects their delicate tissues from abrasion or dehydration and allows for streamlined body contours. The branching or folding greatly increases surface area (see Figure 33.9). In humans, for example, the internal exchange surfaces for digestion, respiration, and circulation each have an area more than 25 times larger than that of the skin.

Internal body fluids link exchange surfaces to body cells. The spaces between cells are filled with fluid, known in many animals as **interstitial fluid** (from the Latin for "stand between"). Complex body plans also include a circulatory fluid, such as blood. Exchange between the interstitial fluid and the circulatory fluid enables cells throughout the body to obtain nutrients and get rid of wastes (see Figure 40.4).

## ▼ Figure 40.4 Internal exchange surfaces of complex animals.

Most animals have surfaces that are specialized for exchanging chemicals with the surroundings. These exchange surfaces are usually internal but are connected to the environment via openings on the body surface (the mouth, for example). The exchange surfaces are finely branched or folded, giving them a very large area. The digestive, respiratory, and excretory systems all have such exchange surfaces. The circulatory system carries chemicals transported across these surfaces throughout the body.

**VISUAL SKILLS ▶** *Using this diagram, explain how exchange carried out by animals can be described as both internal and external.*

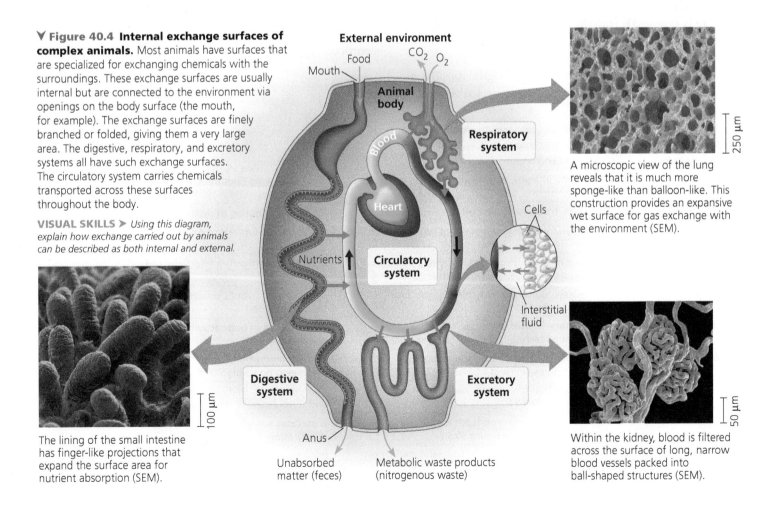

External environment

Food    CO₂   O₂

Mouth

Animal body

Blood

Respiratory system

Heart

Cells

Nutrients

Circulatory system

Interstitial fluid

Digestive system

Excretory system

Anus

Unabsorbed matter (feces)

Metabolic waste products (nitrogenous waste)

A microscopic view of the lung reveals that it is much more sponge-like than balloon-like. This construction provides an expansive wet surface for gas exchange with the environment (SEM). 250 μm

The lining of the small intestine has finger-like projections that expand the surface area for nutrient absorption (SEM). 100 μm

Within the kidney, blood is filtered across the surface of long, narrow blood vessels packed into ball-shaped structures (SEM). 50 μm

Despite the greater challenges of exchange with the environment, complex body plans have distinct benefits over simple ones. For example, an external skeleton can protect against predators, and sensory organs can provide detailed information on the animal's surroundings. Internal digestive organs can break down food gradually, controlling the release of stored energy. In addition, specialized filtration systems can adjust the composition of the internal fluid that bathes the animal's body cells. In this way, an animal can maintain a relatively stable internal environment despite the fact that it is living in a changeable external environment. A complex body plan is especially advantageous for animals living on land, where the external environment may be highly variable.

## Hierarchical Organization of Body Plans

Cells form a working animal body through their emergent properties, which arise from successive levels of structural and functional organization (see Chapter 1). Cells are organized into **tissues**, groups of cells with a similar appearance and a common function. Different types of tissues are further organized into functional units called **organs**. (The simplest animals, such as sponges, lack organs or even true tissues.) Groups of organs that work together, providing an additional level of organization and coordination, make up an **organ system (Table 40.1)**. Thus, for example, the skin is an organ of the integumentary system, which protects against infection and helps regulate body temperature.

Many organs have more than one physiological role. If the roles are distinct enough, we consider the organ to belong to more than one organ system. The pancreas, for instance, produces enzymes critical to the function of the digestive system but also regulates the level of sugar in the blood as a vital part of the endocrine system.

Just as viewing the body's organization from the "bottom up" (from cells to organ systems) reveals emergent properties, a "top-down" view of the hierarchy reveals the multilayered basis of specialization. Organ systems include specialized organs made up of specialized tissues and cells. For example, consider the human digestive system. Each organ has specific roles. In the case of the stomach, one role is to initiate protein breakdown. This process requires a churning motion powered by stomach muscles, as well as digestive juices secreted by the stomach lining. Producing digestive juices, in turn, requires highly specialized cell types: One cell type secretes a protein-digesting enzyme, a second generates concentrated hydrochloric acid, and a third produces mucus, which protects the stomach lining.

The specialized and complex organ systems of animals are built from a limited set of cell and tissue types. For example, lungs and blood vessels have different functions but are lined by tissues that are of the same basic type and therefore share many properties.

There are four main types of animal tissues: epithelial, connective, muscle, and nervous. **Figure 40.5** explores the structure and function of each type. In later chapters, we'll discuss how these tissue types contribute to the functions of particular organ systems.

 Animation: Overview of Animal Tissues

| Table 40.1 Organ Systems in Mammals | | |
|---|---|---|
| **Organ System** | **Main Components** | **Main Functions** |
| Digestive | Mouth, pharynx, esophagus, stomach, intestines, liver, pancreas, anus (See Figure 41.8.) | Food processing (ingestion, digestion, absorption, elimination) |
| Circulatory | Heart, blood vessels, blood (See Figure 42.5.) | Internal distribution of materials |
| Respiratory | Lungs, trachea, other breathing tubes (See Figure 42.24.) | Gas exchange (uptake of oxygen; disposal of carbon dioxide) |
| Immune and lymphatic | Bone marrow, lymph nodes, thymus, spleen, lymph vessels (See Figure 43.7.) | Body defense (fighting infections and virally induced cancers) |
| Excretory | Kidneys, ureters, urinary bladder, urethra (See Figure 44.12.) | Disposal of metabolic wastes; regulation of osmotic balance of blood |
| Endocrine | Pituitary, thyroid, pancreas, adrenal, and other hormone-secreting glands (See Figure 45.8.) | Coordination of body activities (such as digestion and metabolism) |
| Reproductive | Ovaries or testes and associated organs (See Figures 46.9 and 46.10.) | Gamete production; promotion of fertilization; support of developing embryo |
| Nervous | Brain, spinal cord, nerves, sensory organs (See Figure 49.6.) | Coordination of body activities; detection of stimuli and formulation of responses to them |
| Integumentary | Skin and its derivatives (such as hair, claws, sweat glands) (See Figure 50.5.) | Protection against mechanical injury, infection, dehydration; thermoregulation |
| Skeletal | Skeleton (bones, tendons, ligaments, cartilage) (See Figure 50.37.) | Body support, protection of internal organs, movement |
| Muscular | Skeletal muscles (See Figure 50.26.) | Locomotion and other movement |

## Epithelial Tissue

Occurring as sheets of cells, **epithelial tissues**, or **epithelia** (singular, *epithelium*), cover the outside of the body and line organs and cavities within the body. Because epithelial cells are closely packed, often with tight junctions, they function as a barrier against mechanical injury, pathogens, and fluid loss. Epithelia also form active interfaces with the environment. For example, the epithelium that lines the nasal passages is crucial for olfaction, the sense of smell. Note how different cell shapes and arrangements correlate with distinct functions.

 Animation:
Epithelial Tissue

### Stratified squamous epithelium

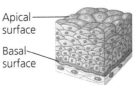

Apical surface

Basal surface

A stratified squamous epithelium is multilayered and regenerates rapidly. New cells formed by division near the basal surface (see micrograph below) push outward, replacing cells that are sloughed off. This epithelium is commonly found on surfaces subject to abrasion, such as the outer skin and the linings of the mouth, anus, and vagina.

### Cuboidal epithelium

A cuboidal epithelium, with dice-shaped cells specialized for secretion, makes up the epithelium of kidney tubules and many glands, including the thyroid gland and salivary glands.

### Simple columnar epithelium

The large, brick-shaped cells of simple columnar epithelia are often found where secretion or active absorption is important. For example, a simple columnar epithelium lines the intestines, secreting digestive juices and absorbing nutrients.

### Simple squamous epithelium

The single layer of platelike cells that form a simple squamous epithelium functions in the exchange of material by diffusion. This type of epithelium, which is thin and leaky, lines blood vessels and the air sacs of the lungs, where diffusion of nutrients and gases is critical.

### Pseudostratified columnar epithelium

A pseudostratified epithelium consists of a single layer of cells varying in height and the position of their nuclei. In many vertebrates, a pseudostratified epithelium of ciliated cells forms a mucous membrane that lines portions of the respiratory tract. The beating cilia sweep the film of mucus along the surface.

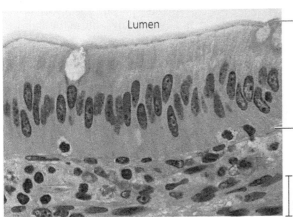

Lumen

Apical surface

Basal surface

10 μm

### Polarity of epithelia

All epithelia are polarized, meaning that they have two different sides. The *apical* surface faces the lumen (cavity) or outside of the organ and is therefore exposed to fluid or air. Specialized projections often cover this surface. For example, the apical surface of the epithelium lining the small intestine is covered with microvilli, projections that increase the surface area available for absorbing nutrients. The opposite side of each epithelium is the *basal* surface.

## Connective Tissue

**Connective tissue**, consisting of a sparse population of cells scattered through an extracellular matrix, holds many tissues and organs together and in place. The matrix generally consists of a web of fibers embedded in a liquid, jellylike, or solid foundation. Within the matrix are numerous cells called **fibroblasts**, which secrete fiber proteins, and **macrophages**, which engulf foreign particles and any cell debris by phagocytosis.

Connective tissue fibers are of three kinds: *Collagenous fibers* provide strength and flexibility,

*reticular fibers* join connective tissue to adjacent tissues, and *elastic fibers* make tissues elastic. If you pinch a fold of tissue on the back of your hand, the collagenous and reticular fibers prevent the skin from being pulled far from the bone, whereas the elastic fibers restore the skin to its original shape when you release your grip. Different mixtures of fibers and foundation form the major types of connective tissue shown below.

(MB) **Animation: Connective Tissue**

### Loose connective tissue

The most widespread connective tissue in the vertebrate body is *loose connective tissue,* which binds epithelia to underlying tissues and holds organs in place. Loose connective tissue gets its name from the loose weave of its fibers, which include all three types. It is found in the skin and throughout the body.

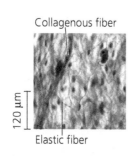

Collagenous fiber

120 μm

Elastic fiber

### Fibrous connective tissue

*Fibrous connective tissue* is dense with collagenous fibers. It is found in **tendons**, which attach muscles to bones, and in **ligaments**, which connect bones at joints.

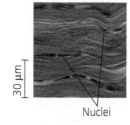

30 μm

Nuclei

### Bone

The skeleton of most vertebrates is made of **bone**, a mineralized connective tissue. Bone-forming cells called *osteoblasts* deposit a matrix of collagen. Calcium, magnesium, and phosphate ions combine into a hard mineral within the matrix. The microscopic structure of hard mammalian bone consists of repeating units called *osteons*. Each osteon has concentric layers of the mineralized matrix, which are deposited around a central canal containing blood vessels and nerves.

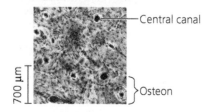

Central canal

700 μm

Osteon

### Adipose tissue

**Adipose tissue** is a specialized loose connective tissue that stores fat in adipose cells distributed throughout its matrix. Adipose tissue pads and insulates the body and stores fuel as fat molecules. Each adipose cell contains a large fat droplet that swells when fat is stored and shrinks when the body uses that fat as fuel.

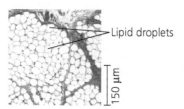

Lipid droplets

150 μm

### Blood

**Blood** has a liquid extracellular matrix called plasma, which consists of water, salts, and dissolved proteins. Suspended in plasma are erythrocytes (red blood cells), leukocytes (white blood cells), and cell fragments called platelets. Red cells carry oxygen, white cells function in defense, and platelets aid in blood clotting.

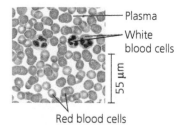

Plasma

White blood cells

55 μm

Red blood cells

### Cartilage

**Cartilage** contains collagenous fibers embedded in a rubbery protein-carbohydrate complex called chondroitin sulfate. Cells called *chondrocytes* secrete the collagen and chondroitin sulfate, which together make cartilage a strong yet flexible support material. The skeletons of many vertebrate embryos contain cartilage that is replaced by bone as the embryo matures. Cartilage remains in some locations, such as the disks that act as cushions between vertebrae.

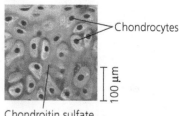

Chondrocytes

100 μm

Chondroitin sulfate

The tissue responsible for nearly all types of body movement is **muscle tissue**. All muscle cells consist of filaments containing the proteins actin and myosin, which together enable muscles to contract. There are three types of muscle tissue in the vertebrate body: skeletal, smooth, and cardiac.

 Animation: Muscle Tissue

### Skeletal muscle

Attached to bones by tendons, **skeletal muscle**, or *striated muscle*, is responsible for voluntary movements. Skeletal muscle consists of bundles of long cells that are called muscle fibers. During development, skeletal muscle fibers form by the fusion of many cells, resulting in multiple nuclei in each muscle fiber. The arrangement of contractile units, or sarcomeres, along the fibers gives the cells a striped (striated) appearance. In adult mammals, building muscle increases the size but not the number of muscle fibers.

### Smooth muscle

**Smooth muscle**, which lacks striations, is found in the walls of the digestive tract, urinary bladder, arteries, and other internal organs. The cells are spindle-shaped. Smooth muscles are responsible for involuntary body activities, such as churning of the stomach and constriction of arteries.

### Cardiac muscle

**Cardiac muscle** forms the contractile wall of the heart. It is striated like skeletal muscle and has similar contractile properties. Unlike skeletal muscle, however, cardiac muscle has branched fibers that interconnect via intercalated disks, which relay signals from cell to cell and help synchronize heart contraction.

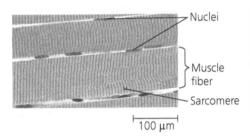

Nuclei
Muscle fiber
Sarcomere
100 μm

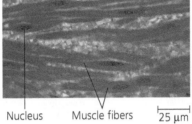

Nucleus    Muscle fibers    25 μm

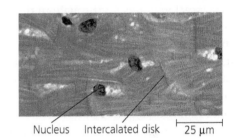

Nucleus    Intercalated disk    25 μm

**Nervous tissue** functions in the receipt, processing, and transmission of information. Nervous tissue contains **neurons**, or nerve cells, which transmit nerve impulses, as well as support cells called **glial cells**, or simply **glia**. In many animals, a concentration of nervous tissue forms a brain, an information-processing center.

 Animation: Nervous Tissue

### Neurons

Neurons are the basic units of the nervous system. A neuron receives nerve impulses from other neurons via its cell body and multiple extensions called dendrites. Neurons transmit impulses to neurons, muscles, or other cells via extensions called axons, which are often bundled together into nerves.

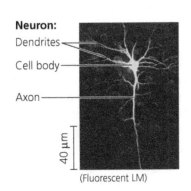

**Neuron:**
Dendrites
Cell body
Axon
40 μm
(Fluorescent LM)

### Glia

The various types of glia help nourish, insulate, and replenish neurons, and in some cases, modulate neuron function.

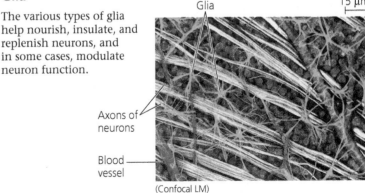

15 μm
Glia
Axons of neurons
Blood vessel
(Confocal LM)

## Coordination and Control

For an animal's tissues and organ systems to perform their specialized functions effectively, they must act in concert with one another. For example, when the wolf shown in Figure 40.5 hunts, blood flow is regulated to bring adequate nutrients and gases to its leg muscles, which in turn are activated by the brain in response to cues detected by the nose. What signals are used to coordinate activity? How do the signals move within the body?

Animals have two major systems for coordinating and controlling responses to stimuli: the endocrine and nervous systems (Figure 40.6). In the **endocrine system**, signaling molecules released into the bloodstream by endocrine cells are carried to all locations in the body. In the **nervous system**, neurons transmit signals along dedicated routes connecting specific locations in the body. In each system, the type of pathway used is the same regardless of whether the signal's ultimate target is at the other end of the body or just a few cell diameters away.

The signaling molecules that are broadcast throughout the body by the endocrine system are called **hormones**. Different hormones cause distinct effects, and only cells that have receptors for a particular hormone respond (Figure 40.6a). Depending on which cells have receptors for that hormone, the hormone may have an effect in just a single location or in sites throughout the body. For example, thyroid-stimulating hormone (TSH), which acts solely on thyroid cells, stimulates release of thyroid hormone, which acts on nearly every body tissue to increase oxygen consumption and heat production. It takes seconds for hormones to be released into the bloodstream and carried throughout the body. The effects are often long-lasting, however, because hormones can remain in the bloodstream for minutes or even hours.

In the nervous system, signals called nerve impulses travel to specific target cells along communication lines consisting mainly of axons (Figure 40.6b). Nerve impulses can act on other neurons, on muscle cells, and on cells and glands that produce secretions. Unlike the endocrine system, the nervous system conveys information by the particular *pathway* the signal takes. For example, a person can distinguish different musical notes because within the ear each note's frequency activates neurons that connect to slightly different locations in the brain.

Communication in the nervous system usually involves more than one type of signal. Nerve impulses travel along axons, sometimes over long distances, as changes in voltage. In contrast, passing information from one neuron to another often involves very short-range chemical signals. Overall, transmission in the nervous system is extremely fast; nerve impulses take only a fraction of a second to reach the target and last only a fraction of a second.

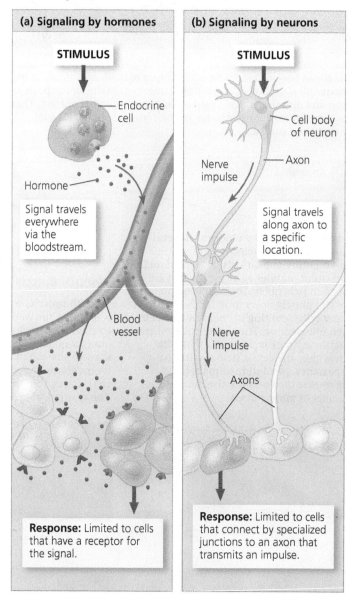

▼ **Figure 40.6 Signaling in the endocrine and nervous systems.**

**(a) Signaling by hormones**

STIMULUS

Endocrine cell

Hormone

Signal travels everywhere via the bloodstream.

Blood vessel

**Response:** Limited to cells that have a receptor for the signal.

**(b) Signaling by neurons**

STIMULUS

Cell body of neuron

Nerve impulse

Axon

Signal travels along axon to a specific location.

Nerve impulse

Axons

**Response:** Limited to cells that connect by specialized junctions to an axon that transmits an impulse.

**VISUAL SKILLS ➤** *After comparing the two diagrams, explain why a particular nerve impulse signal has only one physical pathway but a particular hormone molecule can have multiple physical pathways.*

Because the two major communication systems of the body differ in signal type, transmission, speed, and duration, it is not surprising that they are adapted to different functions. The endocrine system is especially well adapted for coordinating gradual changes that affect the entire body, such as growth, development, reproduction, metabolic processes, and digestion. The nervous system is well suited for directing immediate and rapid responses to the environment, such as reflexes and other rapid movements.

Although the functions of the endocrine and nervous systems are distinct, the two systems often work in close coordination. Both contribute to maintaining a stable internal environment, our next topic of discussion.

1. What properties do all types of epithelia share?

2. **VISUAL SKILLS** ➤ Consider the idealized animal in Figure 40.4. At which sites must oxygen cross a plasma membrane in traveling from the external environment to the cytoplasm of a body cell?

3. **WHAT IF?** ➤ Suppose you are standing at the edge of a cliff and suddenly slip, barely managing to keep your balance and avoid falling. As your heart races, you feel a burst of energy, due in part to a surge of blood into dilated (widened) vessels in your muscles and an upward spike in the level of glucose in your blood. Why might you expect that this "fight-or-flight" response requires both the nervous and endocrine systems?

*For suggested answers, see Appendix A.*

# CONCEPT 40.2

## Feedback control maintains the internal environment in many animals

Many organ systems play a role in managing an animal's internal environment, a task that can present a major challenge. Imagine if your body temperature soared every time you took a hot shower or drank a freshly brewed cup of coffee. Faced with environmental fluctuations, animals manage their internal environment by either regulating or conforming.

## Regulating and Conforming

Compare the two sets of data in **Figure 40.7**. The river otter's body temperature is largely independent of that of the surrounding water, whereas the largemouth bass's body warms or cools when the water temperature changes. We can convey these two trends by labeling the otter a regulator and the bass a conformer with regard to body temperature. An animal is a **regulator** for an environmental variable if it uses internal mechanisms to control internal change in the face of external fluctuation. In contrast, an animal is a **conformer** if it allows its internal condition to change in accordance with external changes in the particular variable.

An animal may regulate some internal conditions

while allowing others to conform to the environment. For instance, even though the bass conforms to the temperature of the surrounding water, it regulates the solute concentration in its blood and interstitial fluid. In addition, conforming does not always involve changes in an internal variable. For example, many marine invertebrates, such as spider crabs of the genus *Libinia*, let their internal solute concentration conform to the relatively stable solute concentration (salinity) of their ocean environment.

## Homeostasis

The steady body temperature of a river otter and the stable concentration of solutes in a freshwater bass are examples of **homeostasis**, which means the maintenance of internal balance. In achieving homeostasis, animals maintain a "steady state"—a relatively constant internal environment— even when the external environment changes significantly.

Many animals exhibit homeostasis for a range of physical and chemical properties. For example, humans maintain a fairly constant body temperature of about 37°C (98.6°F), a blood pH within 0.1 pH unit of 7.4, and a blood glucose concentration that is predominantly in the range of 70–110 mg of glucose per 100 mL of blood.

### Mechanisms of Homeostasis

Homeostasis requires a control system. Before exploring homeostasis in animals, let's get a basic picture of how a control system works by considering a nonliving example: the regulation of room temperature. Let's assume you want

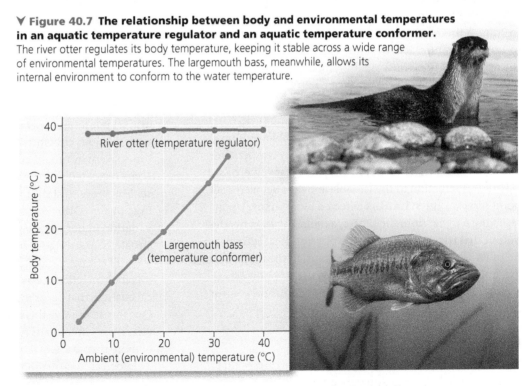

▼ **Figure 40.7 The relationship between body and environmental temperatures in an aquatic temperature regulator and an aquatic temperature conformer.** The river otter regulates its body temperature, keeping it stable across a wide range of environmental temperatures. The largemouth bass, meanwhile, allows its internal environment to conform to the water temperature.

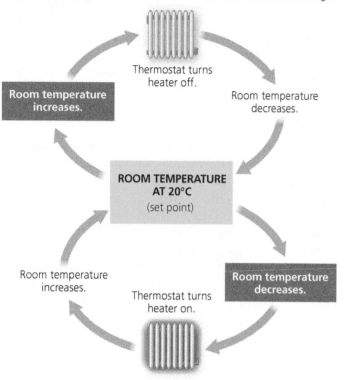

**DRAW IT ➤** *Label at least one stimulus, response, and sensor/control center in the figure. How would you modify the drawing to add an air conditioner to the system?*

to keep a room at 20°C (68°F), a comfortable temperature for normal activity. You set a control device—the thermostat—to 20°C. A thermometer in the thermostat monitors the room temperature. If the temperature falls below 20°C, the thermostat turns on a radiator, furnace, or other heater **(Figure 40.8)**. When the room exceeds 20°C, the thermostat switches off the heater. If the temperature then drifts below 20°C, the thermostat activates another heating cycle.

Like a home heating system, an animal achieves homeostasis by maintaining a variable, such as body temperature or solute concentration, at or near a particular value, or **set point**. A fluctuation in the variable above or below the set point serves as the **stimulus** detected by a **sensor**. Upon receiving a signal from the sensor, a *control center* generates output that triggers a **response**, a physiological activity that helps return the variable to the set point. In the home heating example, a drop in temperature below the set point acts as a stimulus, the thermostat serves as the sensor and control center, and the heater produces the response.

## Feedback Control in Homeostasis

If you examine the circuit in Figure 40.8, you can see that the response (the production of heat) reduces the stimulus

(a room temperature below the set point). The circuit thus displays **negative feedback**, a control mechanism that "damps" its stimulus (see Figure 1.10). This type of feedback regulation plays a major role in homeostasis in animals. For example, when you exercise vigorously, you produce heat, which increases your body temperature. Your nervous system detects this increase and triggers sweating. As you sweat, the evaporation of moisture from your skin cools your body, helping return your body temperature to its set point and eliminating the stimulus.

Homeostasis is a dynamic equilibrium, an interplay between external factors that tend to change the internal environment and internal control mechanisms that oppose such changes. Note that physiological responses to stimuli are not instantaneous, just as switching on a furnace does not immediately warm a room. As a result, homeostasis moderates but doesn't eliminate changes in the internal environment. Fluctuation is greater if a variable has a *normal range*—an upper and lower limit—rather than a set point. This is equivalent to a thermostat that turns on a heater when the room temperature drops to 19°C (66°F) and turns off the heater when the temperature reaches 21°C (70°F). Regardless of whether there is a set point or a normal range, homeostasis is enhanced by adaptations that reduce fluctuations, such as insulation in the case of temperature and physiological buffers in the case of pH.

Unlike negative feedback, **positive feedback** is a control mechanism that amplifies the stimulus. In animals, positive-feedback loops do not play a major role in homeostasis, but instead help drive processes to completion. During childbirth, for instance, the pressure of the baby's head against sensors near the opening of the mother's uterus stimulates the uterus to contract. These contractions result in greater pressure against the opening of the uterus, heightening the contractions and thereby causing even greater pressure, until the baby is born.

### Alterations in Homeostasis

The set points and normal ranges for homeostasis can change under various circumstances. In fact, *regulated changes* in the internal environment are essential to normal body functions. Some regulated changes occur during a particular stage in life, such as the radical shift in hormone balance that occurs during puberty. Other regulated changes are cyclic, such as the variation in hormone levels responsible for a woman's menstrual cycle (see Figure 46.14).

In all animals (and plants), certain cyclic alterations in metabolism reflect a **circadian rhythm**, a set of physiological changes that occur roughly every 24 hours **(Figure 40.9)**. One way to observe this rhythm is to monitor body temperature, which in humans typically undergoes a cyclic rise and fall of more than 0.6°C (1°F) in every 24-hour period. Remarkably, a biological clock maintains this rhythm even when variations in human activity, room temperature, and light levels

### Figure 40.9 Human circadian rhythm.

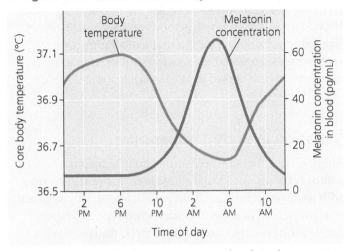

(a) **Variation in core body temperature and melatonin concentration in blood.** Researchers measured these two variables in resting but awake volunteers in an isolation chamber with constant temperature and low light. (Melatonin is a hormone that appears to be involved in sleep/wake cycles.)

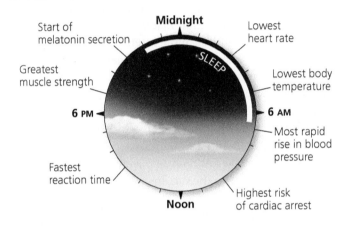

(b) **The human circadian clock.** Metabolic activities undergo daily cycles in response to the circadian clock. As illustrated for a typical individual who rises early in the morning, eats lunch around noon, and sleeps at night, these cyclic changes occur throughout a 24-hour day.

are minimized (see Figure 40.9a). A circadian rhythm is thus intrinsic to the body, although the biological clock is normally coordinated with the cycle of light and darkness in the environment (see Figure 40.9b). For example, the hormone melatonin is secreted at night, and more is released during the longer nights of winter. External stimuli can reset the biological clock, but the effect is not immediate. That is why flying across several time zones results in jet lag, a mismatch between the circadian rhythm and local environment that persists until the clock fully resets.

Homeostasis is sometimes altered by **acclimatization**, an animal's physiological adjustment to changes in its external environment. For instance, when an elk moves up into the

### Figure 40.10 Acclimatization by mountain climbers in the Himalayas.
To lessen the risk of altitude sickness when ascending a high peak, climbers acclimatize by camping partway up the mountain. Spending time at an intermediate altitude allows the circulatory and respiratory systems to become more efficient in capturing and distributing oxygen at a lower concentration.

mountains from sea level, the lower oxygen concentration in the high mountain air stimulates the animal to breathe more rapidly and deeply. As a result, more $CO_2$ is lost through exhalation, raising blood pH above its normal range. As the animal acclimatizes over several days, changes in kidney function cause it to excrete urine that is more alkaline, returning blood pH to its normal range. Other mammals, including humans, are also capable of acclimatizing to dramatic altitude changes **(Figure 40.10).**

Note that acclimatization, a temporary change during an animal's lifetime, should not be confused with adaptation, a process of change in a population brought about by natural selection acting over many generations.

### CONCEPT CHECK 40.2

1. **MAKE CONNECTIONS** ➤ How does negative feedback in thermoregulation differ from feedback inhibition in an enzyme-catalyzed biosynthetic process (see Figure 8.21)?

2. If you were deciding where to put the thermostat in a house, what factors would govern your decision? How do these factors relate to the fact that many homeostatic control sensors in humans are located in the brain?

3. **MAKE CONNECTIONS** ➤ Like animals, cyanobacteria have a circadian rhythm. By analyzing the genes that maintain biological clocks, scientists concluded that the 24-hour rhythms of humans and cyanobacteria reflect convergent evolution (see Concept 26.2). What evidence would have supported this conclusion? Explain.

*For suggested answers, see Appendix A.*

# CONCEPT 40.3

## Homeostatic processes for thermoregulation involve form, function, and behavior

In this section, we'll examine the regulation of body temperature as an example of how form and function work together in regulating an animal's internal environment. Later chapters in this unit will discuss other physiological systems involved in maintaining homeostasis.

**Thermoregulation** is the process by which animals maintain their body temperature within a normal range. Body temperatures outside the normal range can reduce the efficiency of enzymatic reactions, alter the fluidity of cellular membranes, and affect other temperature-sensitive biochemical processes, potentially with fatal results.

### Endothermy and Ectothermy

Heat for thermoregulation can come from either internal metabolism or the external environment. Humans and other mammals, as well as birds, are **endothermic**, meaning that they are warmed mostly by heat generated by metabolism. Some fishes and insect species and a few nonavian reptiles are also mainly endothermic. In contrast, amphibians, many nonavian reptiles and fishes, and most invertebrates are **ectothermic**, meaning that they gain most of their heat from external sources. Endothermy and ectothermy are not mutually exclusive, however. For example, a bird is mainly endothermic but may warm itself in the sun on a cold morning, much as an ectothermic lizard does.

Endotherms can maintain a stable body temperature even in the face of large fluctuations in the environmental temperature. In a cold environment, an endotherm generates enough heat to keep its body substantially warmer than its surroundings **(Figure 40.11a)**. In a hot environment, endothermic vertebrates have mechanisms for cooling their bodies, enabling them to withstand heat loads that are intolerable for most ectotherms.

Many ectotherms adjust their body temperature by behavioral means, such as seeking out shade or basking in the sun **(Figure 40.11b)**. Because their heat source is largely environmental, ectotherms generally need to consume much less food than endotherms of equivalent size—an advantage if food supplies are limited. Ectotherms also usually tolerate larger fluctuations in their internal temperature. Overall, ectothermy is an effective and successful strategy in most environments, as shown by the abundance and diversity of ectotherms.

### Variation in Body Temperature

Animals also differ in whether their body temperature is variable or constant. An animal whose body temperature varies with its environment is called a *poikilotherm* (from the Greek *poikilos*, varied). In contrast, a *homeotherm* has a relatively constant body temperature. For example, the largemouth bass is a poikilotherm, and the river otter is a homeotherm (see Figure 40.7).

From the descriptions of ectotherms and endotherms, it might seem that all ectotherms are poikilothermic and all endotherms are homeothermic. In fact, there is no fixed relationship between the source of heat and the stability of body temperature. Many ectothermic marine fishes and invertebrates inhabit waters with such stable temperatures that their body temperature varies less than that of mammals and other endotherms. Conversely, the body temperature of a few endotherms varies considerably. For example, the body temperature of some bats drops 40°C when they enter hibernation.

It is a common misconception that ectotherms are "cold-blooded" and endotherms are "warm-blooded." Ectotherms do not necessarily have low body temperatures. On the contrary, when sitting in the sun, many ectothermic lizards

▼ **Figure 40.11 Thermoregulation by internal or external sources of heat.** Endotherms obtain heat from their internal metabolism, whereas ectotherms rely on heat from their external environment.

**(a) A walrus, an endotherm**

**(b) A lizard, an ectotherm**

have higher body temperatures than mammals. Thus, the terms *cold-blooded* and *warm-blooded* are misleading and are avoided in scientific communication.

## Balancing Heat Loss and Gain

Thermoregulation depends on an animal's ability to control the exchange of heat with its environment. That exchange can occur by any of four processes: radiation, evaporation, convection, and conduction (**Figure 40.12**). Heat is always transferred from an object of higher temperature to one of lower temperature.

The essence of thermoregulation is maintaining a rate of heat gain that equals the rate of heat loss. Animals do this through mechanisms that either reduce heat exchange overall or favor heat exchange in a particular direction. In mammals, several of these mechanisms involve the **integumentary system**, the outer covering of the body, consisting of the skin, hair, and nails (claws or hooves in some species).

▼ **Figure 40.12  Heat exchange between an organism and its environment.**

**Radiation** is the emission of electromagnetic waves by all objects warmer than absolute zero. Here, a lizard absorbs heat radiating from the distant sun and radiates a smaller amount of energy to the surrounding air.

**Evaporation** is the removal of heat from the surface of a liquid that is losing some of its molecules as gas. Evaporation of water from a lizard's moist surfaces that are exposed to the environment has a strong cooling effect.

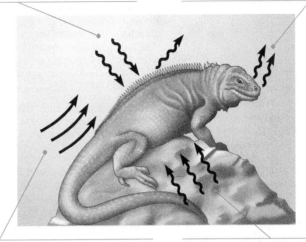

**Convection** is the transfer of heat by the movement of air or liquid past a surface, as when a breeze contributes to heat loss from a lizard's dry skin or when blood moves heat from the body core to the extremities.

**Conduction** is the direct transfer of thermal motion (heat) between molecules of objects in contact with each other, as when a lizard sits on a hot rock.

**VISUAL SKILLS** ➤ *If this figure showed a walrus (an endotherm) rather than an iguana, would any of the arrows point in a different direction? Explain.*

### Insulation

Insulation, which reduces the flow of heat between an animal's body and its environment, is a major adaptation for thermoregulation in both mammals and birds. Insulation is found both at the body surface—hair and feathers—and beneath—layers of fat formed by adipose tissue. In addition, some animals secrete oily substances that repel water, protecting the insulating capacity of feathers or fur. Birds, for example, secrete oils that they apply to their feathers during preening.

Often, animals can adjust their insulating layers to further regulate body temperature. Most land mammals and birds, for example, react to cold by raising their fur or feathers. This action traps a thicker layer of air, thereby increasing the effectiveness of the insulation. Lacking feathers or fur, humans must rely primarily on fat for insulation. We do, however, get "goose bumps," a vestige of hair raising inherited from our furry ancestors.

Insulation is particularly important for marine mammals, such as whales and walruses. These animals swim in water colder than their body core, and many species spend at least part of the year in nearly freezing polar seas. Furthermore, the transfer of heat to water occurs 50 to 100 times more rapidly than heat transfer to air. Survival under these conditions is made possible by an evolutionary adaptation called blubber, a very thick layer of insulating fat just under the skin. The insulation that blubber provides is so effective that marine mammals can maintain body core temperatures of about 36–38°C (97–100°F) without requiring much more energy from food than land mammals of similar size.

### Circulatory Adaptations

Circulatory systems provide a major route for heat flow between the interior and exterior of the body. Adaptations that regulate the extent of blood flow near the body surface or that trap heat within the body core play a significant role in thermoregulation.

In response to changes in the temperature of their surroundings, many animals alter the amount of blood (and hence heat) flowing between their body core and their skin. Nerve signals that relax the muscles of the vessel walls result in *vasodilation*, a widening of superficial blood vessels (those near the body surface). As a consequence of the increase in vessel diameter, blood flow in the skin increases. In endotherms, vasodilation usually increases the transfer of body heat to the environment by radiation, conduction, and convection (see Figure 40.12). The reverse process, *vasoconstriction*, reduces blood flow and heat transfer by decreasing the diameter of superficial vessels.

Like endotherms, some ectotherms control heat exchange by regulating blood flow. For example, when the marine iguana of the Galápagos Islands swims in the cold ocean, its superficial blood vessels undergo vasoconstriction. This process routes more blood to the body core, conserving body heat.

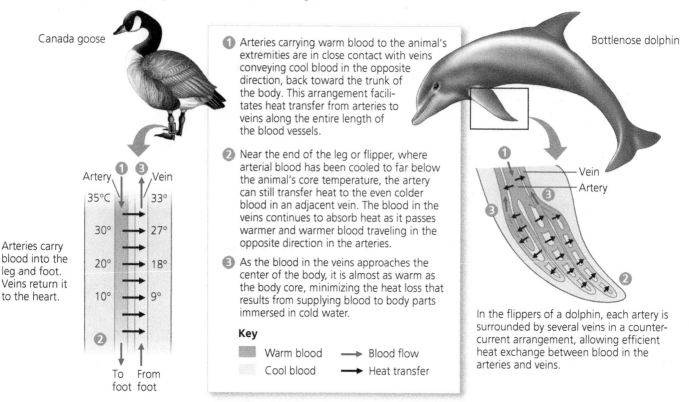

▼ **Figure 40.13 Countercurrent heat exchangers.** A countercurrent exchange system traps heat in the body core, thus reducing heat loss from the extremities, particularly when they are immersed in cold water or in contact with ice or snow. In essence, heat in the arterial blood emerging from the body core is transferred directly to the returning venous blood instead of being lost to the environment.

Canada goose

Bottlenose dolphin

❶ Arteries carrying warm blood to the animal's extremities are in close contact with veins conveying cool blood in the opposite direction, back toward the trunk of the body. This arrangement facilitates heat transfer from arteries to veins along the entire length of the blood vessels.

❷ Near the end of the leg or flipper, where arterial blood has been cooled to far below the animal's core temperature, the artery can still transfer heat to the even colder blood in an adjacent vein. The blood in the veins continues to absorb heat as it passes warmer and warmer blood traveling in the opposite direction in the arteries.

❸ As the blood in the veins approaches the center of the body, it is almost as warm as the body core, minimizing the heat loss that results from supplying blood to body parts immersed in cold water.

Artery ❶ ❸ Vein

35°C ... 33°

30° ... 27°

20° ... 18°

10° ... 9°

Arteries carry blood into the leg and foot. Veins return it to the heart.

To foot    From foot

Vein
Artery

**Key**

▨ Warm blood    → Blood flow
▨ Cool blood    ⟶ Heat transfer

In the flippers of a dolphin, each artery is surrounded by several veins in a countercurrent arrangement, allowing efficient heat exchange between blood in the arteries and veins.

In many birds and mammals, reducing heat loss from the body relies on **countercurrent exchange**, the transfer of heat (or solutes) between fluids that are flowing in opposite directions. In a countercurrent heat exchanger, arteries and veins are located adjacent to each other **(Figure 40.13)**. Because blood flows through the arteries and veins in opposite directions, this arrangement allows heat exchange to be remarkably efficient. As warm blood moves outward in the arteries from the body core, it transfers heat to the colder blood in the veins returning from the extremities. Most importantly, heat is transferred along the entire length of the exchanger, maximizing the rate of heat exchange and minimizing heat loss to the environment.

Certain sharks, fishes, and insects also use countercurrent heat exchange. Although most sharks and fishes are temperature conformers, countercurrent heat exchangers are found in some large, powerful swimmers, including great white sharks, bluefin tuna, and swordfish. By keeping the main swimming muscles warm, this adaptation enables vigorous, sustained activity. Similarly, many endothermic insects (bumblebees, honeybees, and some moths) have a countercurrent exchanger that helps maintain a high temperature in their thorax, where flight muscles are located.

### Cooling by Evaporative Heat Loss

Many mammals and birds live in places where regulating body temperature requires cooling at some times and warming at others. If environmental temperature is above body temperature, only evaporation can keep body temperature from rising. Water absorbs considerable heat when it evaporates (see Concept 3.2); this heat is carried away from the skin and respiratory surfaces with water vapor.

Some animals exhibit adaptations that greatly facilitate evaporative cooling. A few mammals, including horses and humans, have sweat glands **(Figure 40.14)**. In many other

▼ **Figure 40.14 Enhancing evaporative cooling.** Horses and humans are among the few animals for which sweat glands distributed across the body facilitate thermoregulation.

mammals, as well as in birds, panting is important. Some birds have a pouch richly supplied with blood vessels in the floor of the mouth; fluttering the pouch increases evaporation. Pigeons can use this adaptation to keep their body temperature close to 40°C (104°F) in air temperatures as high as 60°C (140°F), as long as they have sufficient water.

### Behavioral Responses

Ectotherms, and sometimes endotherms, control body temperature through behavioral responses to changes in the environment. When cold, they seek warm places, orienting themselves toward heat sources and expanding the portion of their body surface exposed to the heat source (see Figure 40.11b). When hot, they bathe, move to cool areas, or turn in another direction, minimizing their absorption of heat from the sun. For example, a dragonfly's "obelisk" posture is an adaptation that minimizes the amount of body surface exposed to the sun and thus to heating (Figure 40.15). Although these behaviors are relatively simple, they enable many ectotherms to maintain a nearly constant body temperature.

▼ Figure 40.15 **Thermoregulatory behavior in a dragonfly.** By orienting its body so that the narrow tip of its abdomen faces the sun, the dragonfly minimizes heating by solar radiation.

Honeybees use a thermoregulatory mechanism that depends on social behavior. In cold weather, they increase heat production and huddle together, thereby retaining heat. Individuals move between the cooler outer edges of the huddle and the warmer center, thus circulating and distributing the heat. Even when huddling, honeybees must expend considerable energy to keep warm during long periods of cold weather. (This is the main function of storing large quantities of fuel in the hive in the form of honey.) In hot weather, honeybees cool the hive by transporting water to the hive and fanning with their wings, promoting evaporation and convection. Thus, a honeybee colony uses many of the mechanisms of thermoregulation seen in individual animals.

### Adjusting Metabolic Heat Production

Because endotherms generally maintain a body temperature considerably higher than that of the environment, they must counteract continual heat loss. Endotherms can vary heat production—*thermogenesis*—to match changing rates of heat loss. Thermogenesis is increased by such muscle activity as moving or shivering. For example, shivering helps chickadees, birds with a body mass of only 20 g, remain active and hold their body temperature nearly constant at 40°C (104°F) in environmental temperatures as low as −40°C (−40°F).

The smallest endotherms—flying insects such as bees and moths—are also capable of varying heat production. Many endothermic insects warm up by shivering before taking off. As they contract their flight muscles in synchrony, only slight wing movements occur, but considerable heat is produced. Chemical reactions, and hence cellular respiration, accelerate in the warmed-up flight "motors," enabling these insects to fly even when the air is cold.

In some mammals, endocrine signals released in response to cold cause mitochondria to increase their metabolic activity and produce heat instead of ATP. This process, called *nonshivering thermogenesis,* takes place throughout the body. Some mammals also have a tissue called *brown fat* in their neck and between their shoulders that is specialized for rapid heat production. (The presence of extra mitochondria is what gives brown fat its characteristic color.) Brown fat is found in the infants of many mammals, representing about 5% of total body weight in human infants. Long known to be present in adult mammals that hibernate, brown fat has also recently been detected in human adults (Figure 40.16). There, the amount has been found to vary, with individuals exposed to a cool environment for a month having increased amounts of brown fat. Using these varied adaptations for thermogenesis, mammals and birds can increase their metabolic heat production by as much as five to ten times.

▼ Figure 40.16 **Brown fat activity during cold stress.** This PET scan shows metabolically active brown fat deposits (see arrows) surrounding the neck.

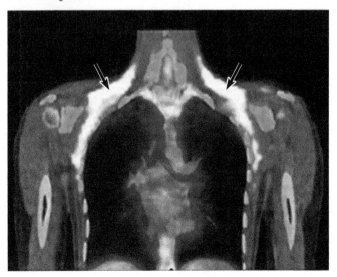

Among the nonavian reptiles, endothermy has been observed in some large species in certain circumstances. For example, researchers found that a female Burmese python (*Python molurus bivittatus*) incubating eggs maintained a body temperature roughly 6°C (11°F) above that of the surrounding air. Where did the heat come from? Further studies showed that such pythons, like birds, can raise their body temperature through shivering (**Figure 40.17**). Whether certain groups of

Mesozoic dinosaurs were similarly endothermic is a matter of active debate.

## Acclimatization in Thermoregulation

Acclimatization contributes to thermoregulation in many animal species. In birds and mammals, acclimatization to seasonal temperature changes often includes adjusting insulation—growing a thicker coat of fur in the winter and shedding it in the summer, for example. These changes help endotherms keep a constant body temperature year-round.

Acclimatization in ectotherms often includes adjustments at the cellular level. Cells may produce variants of enzymes that have the same function but different optimal temperatures. Also, the proportions of saturated and unsaturated lipids in membranes may change; unsaturated lipids help keep membranes fluid at lower temperatures (see Figure 7.5).

Remarkably, some ectotherms can survive subzero temperatures, producing "antifreeze" proteins that prevent ice formation in their cells. In the Arctic and Southern (Antarctic) Oceans, these proteins enable certain fishes to survive in water as cold as −2°C (28°F), a full degree Celsius below the freezing point of body fluids in other species.

## Physiological Thermostats and Fever

In humans and other mammals, the sensors responsible for thermoregulation are concentrated in the **hypothalamus**, the brain region that also controls the circadian clock. Within the hypothalamus, a group of nerve cells functions as a thermostat, responding to body temperatures outside the normal range by activating mechanisms that promote heat loss or gain (**Figure 40.18**).

Distinct sensors signal the hypothalamic thermostat when the temperature of the blood increases or decreases. At body temperatures below the normal range, the thermostat inhibits heat loss mechanisms while activating mechanisms that either save heat, including constriction of vessels in the skin, or generate heat, such as shivering. In response to elevated body temperature, the thermostat shuts down heat retention mechanisms and promotes cooling of the body by dilation of vessels in the skin, sweating, or panting.

In the course of certain bacterial and viral infections, mammals and birds develop *fever*, an elevated body temperature. A variety of experiments have shown that fever reflects an increase in the normal range for the biological thermostat. For example, artificially *raising* the temperature of the hypothalamus in an infected animal *reduces* fever in the rest of the body.

Among certain ectotherms, an increase in body temperature upon infection reflects what is called a behavioral fever.

▼ **Figure 40.17**

### Inquiry How does a Burmese python generate heat while incubating eggs?

**Experiment** Herndon Dowling and colleagues at the Bronx Zoo in New York observed that when a female Burmese python incubated eggs by wrapping her body around them, she raised her body temperature and frequently contracted the muscles in her coils. To learn if the contractions were elevating her body temperature, they placed the python and her eggs in a chamber. As they varied the chamber's temperature, they monitored the python's muscle contractions as well as her oxygen uptake, a measure of her rate of cellular respiration.

**Results** The python's oxygen consumption increased when the temperature in the chamber decreased. As shown in the graph, this increase in oxygen consumption paralleled an increase in the rate of muscle contraction.

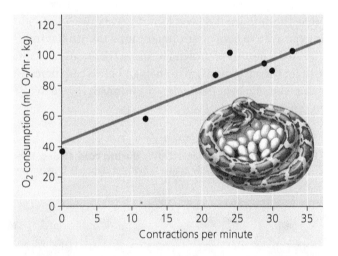

**Conclusion** Because oxygen consumption, which generates heat through cellular respiration, was correlated with the rate of muscle contraction, the researchers concluded that the muscle contractions, a form of shivering, were the source of the Burmese python's elevated body temperature.

**Data from** V. H. Hutchison, H. G. Dowling, and A. Vinegar, Thermoregulation in a brooding female Indian python, *Python molurus bivittatus, Science* 151:694–696 (1966).

**WHAT IF?** ➤ *Suppose you varied air temperature and measured oxygen consumption for a female Burmese python without a clutch of eggs. Since she would not show shivering behavior, how would you expect the snake's oxygen consumption to vary with environmental temperature?*

**WHAT IF?** ➤ *Suppose at the end of a hard run on a hot day you find that there are no drinks left in the cooler. If, out of desperation, you dunk your head into the cooler, how might the ice-cold water affect the rate at which your body temperature returns to normal?*

 **Figure Walkthrough**

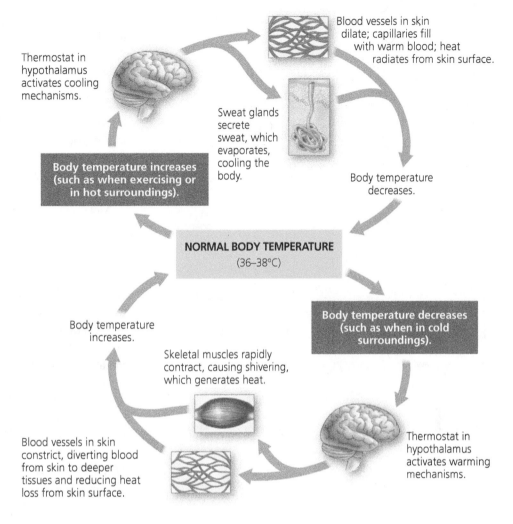

Thermostat in hypothalamus activates cooling mechanisms.

Blood vessels in skin dilate; capillaries fill with warm blood; heat radiates from skin surface.

Sweat glands secrete sweat, which evaporates, cooling the body.

Body temperature decreases.

**Body temperature increases (such as when exercising or in hot surroundings).**

**NORMAL BODY TEMPERATURE** (36–38°C)

**Body temperature decreases (such as when in cold surroundings).**

Body temperature increases.

Skeletal muscles rapidly contract, causing shivering, which generates heat.

Blood vessels in skin constrict, diverting blood from skin to deeper tissues and reducing heat loss from skin surface.

Thermostat in hypothalamus activates warming mechanisms.

---

For example, the desert iguana (*Dipsosaurus dorsalis*) responds to infection with certain bacteria by seeking a warmer environment and then maintaining a body temperature that is elevated by 2–4°C (4–7°F). Similar observations in fishes, amphibians, and even cockroaches indicate that fever is common to both endotherms and ectotherms.

Now that we have explored thermoregulation, we'll conclude our introduction to animal form and function by considering the different ways that animals allocate, use, and conserve energy.

### CONCEPT CHECK 40.3

1. What mode of heat exchange is involved in "wind chill," when moving air feels colder than still air at the same temperature? Explain.
2. Flowers differ in how much sunlight they absorb. Why might this matter to a hummingbird seeking nectar on a cool morning?
3. **WHAT IF?** ➤ Why is shivering likely during the onset of a fever?

*For suggested answers, see Appendix A.*

## CONCEPT 40.4

### Energy requirements are related to animal size, activity, and environment

One of the unifying themes of biology introduced in Concept 1.1 is that life requires energy transfer and transformation. Like other organisms, animals use chemical energy for growth, repair, activity, and reproduction. The overall flow and transformation of energy in an animal— its **bioenergetics**—determines nutritional needs and is related to the animal's size, activity, and environment.

### Energy Allocation and Use

Organisms can be classified by how they obtain chemical energy. Most *autotrophs*, such as plants, harness light energy to build energy-rich organic molecules and then use those molecules for fuel. Most *heterotrophs*, such as animals, obtain

## Figure 40.19 Bioenergetics of an animal: an overview.

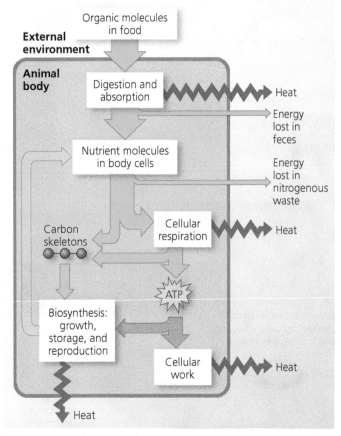

External environment

Animal body

Organic molecules in food

Digestion and absorption → Heat

Energy lost in feces

Nutrient molecules in body cells

Energy lost in nitrogenous waste

Carbon skeletons

Cellular respiration → Heat

ATP

Biosynthesis: growth, storage, and reproduction

Cellular work → Heat

Heat

**MAKE CONNECTIONS** ➤ *Use the idea of energy coupling to explain why heat is produced in the absorption of nutrients, in cellular respiration, and in the synthesis of biopolymers (see Concept 8.3).*

their chemical energy from food, which contains organic molecules synthesized by other organisms.

Animals use chemical energy harvested from the food they eat to fuel metabolism and activity. Food is digested by enzymatic hydrolysis (see Figure 5.2b), and nutrients are absorbed by body cells **(Figure 40.19)**. The ATP produced by cellular respiration and fermentation powers cellular work, enabling cells, organs, and organ systems to perform the functions that keep an animal alive. Other uses of energy in the form of ATP include biosynthesis, which is needed for body growth and repair, synthesis of storage material such as fat, and production of gametes. The production and use of ATP generate heat, which the animal eventually gives off to its surroundings.

## Quantifying Energy Use

How much of the total energy an animal obtains from food does it need just to stay alive? How much energy must

be expended to walk, run, swim, or fly from one place to another? What fraction of the energy intake is used for reproduction? Physiologists answer such questions by measuring the rate at which an animal uses chemical energy and how this rate changes in different circumstances.

The sum of all the energy an animal uses in a given time interval is called its **metabolic rate**. Energy is measured in joules (J) or in calories (cal) and kilocalories (kcal). (A kilocalorie equals 1,000 calories, or 4,184 joules. The unit Calorie, with a capital C, as used by many nutritionists, is actually a kilocalorie.)

Metabolic rate can be determined in several ways. Because nearly all of the chemical energy used in cellular respiration eventually appears as heat, metabolic rate can be measured by monitoring an animal's rate of heat loss. For this approach, researchers use a calorimeter, which is a closed, insulated chamber equipped with a device that records an animal's heat loss. Metabolic rate can also be determined from the amount of oxygen consumed or carbon dioxide produced by an animal's cellular respiration **(Figure 40.20)**. To calculate metabolic rate over longer periods, researchers record the rate of food consumption, the energy content of the food (about 4.5–5 kcal per gram of protein or carbohydrate and about 9 kcal per gram of fat), and the chemical energy lost in waste products (feces and urine or other nitrogenous wastes).

## Minimum Metabolic Rate and Thermoregulation

Animals must maintain a minimum metabolic rate for basic functions such as cell maintenance, breathing, and circulation. Researchers measure this minimum metabolic rate differently for endotherms and ectotherms. The minimum metabolic rate of a nongrowing endotherm that is at rest, has an empty stomach, and is not experiencing stress is called the **basal metabolic rate (BMR)**. BMR is measured under a

**Figure 40.20 Measuring the rate of oxygen consumption by a swimming shark.** A researcher monitors the decrease in oxygen level over time in the recirculating water of a juvenile hammerhead's tank.

"comfortable" temperature range—a range that requires only the minimum generation or shedding of heat. The minimum metabolic rate of ectotherms is determined at a specific temperature because changes in the environmental temperature alter body temperature and therefore metabolic rate. The metabolic rate of a fasting, nonstressed ectotherm at rest at a particular temperature is called its **standard metabolic rate (SMR)**.

Comparisons of minimum metabolic rates reveal the different energy costs of endothermy and ectothermy. The BMR for humans averages 1,600–1,800 kcal per day for adult males and 1,300–1,500 kcal per day for adult females. These BMRs are about equivalent to the rate of energy use by a 75-watt lightbulb. In contrast, the SMR of an American alligator is only about 60 kcal per day at 20°C (68°F). As this represents less than $\frac{1}{20}$ the energy used by a comparably sized adult human, it is clear that ectothermy has a markedly lower energetic requirement than endothermy.

## Influences on Metabolic Rate

Metabolic rate is affected by many factors other than an animal being an endotherm or an ectotherm. Some key factors are age, sex, size, activity, temperature, and nutrition. Here we'll examine the effects of size and activity.

### Size and Metabolic Rate

Larger animals have more body mass and therefore require more chemical energy. Remarkably, the relationship between overall metabolic rate and body mass is constant across a wide range of sizes and forms, as illustrated for various mammals in **Figure 40.21a**. In fact, for even more varied organisms ranging in size from bacteria to blue whales, metabolic rate remains roughly proportional to body mass to the three-quarter power ($m^{3/4}$). Scientists are still researching the basis of this relationship, which applies to ectotherms as well as endotherms.

The relationship of metabolic rate to size profoundly affects energy consumption by body cells and tissues. As shown in **Figure 40.21b**, the energy it takes to maintain each gram of body mass is inversely related to body size. Each gram of a mouse, for instance, requires about 20 times as many calories as a gram of an elephant, even though the whole elephant uses far more calories than the whole mouse. The smaller animal's higher metabolic rate per gram demands a higher rate of oxygen delivery. To meet this demand, the smaller animal must have a higher breathing rate, blood volume (relative to its size), and heart rate.

Thinking about body size in bioenergetic terms reveals how trade-offs shape the evolution of body plans. As body size decreases, each gram of tissue increases in energy cost. As body size increases, energy costs per gram of tissue decrease, but an ever-larger fraction of body tissue is required for exchange, support, and locomotion.

▼ **Figure 40.21** **The relationship of metabolic rate to body size.**

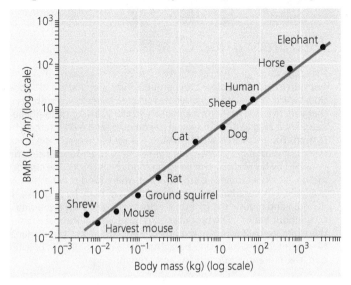

**(a)** Relationship of basal metabolic rate (BMR) to body size for various mammals. From shrew to elephant, size increases 1 millionfold.

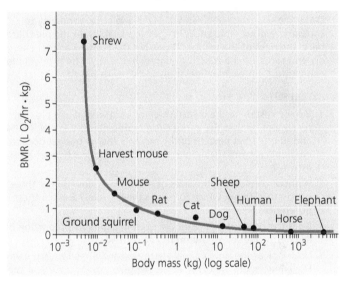

**(b)** Relationship of BMR per kilogram of body mass to body size for the same mammals as in (a).

**INTERPRET THE DATA** ➤ *Based on the graph in (a), one observer suggests that a group of 100 ground squirrels has the same basal metabolic rate as 1 dog. A second observer looking at the graph disagrees. Who is correct and why?*

### Activity and Metabolic Rate

For both ectotherms and endotherms, activity greatly affects metabolic rate. Even a person reading quietly at a desk or an insect twitching its wings consumes energy beyond the BMR or SMR. Maximum metabolic rates (the highest rates of ATP use) occur during peak activity, such as lifting a heavy object, sprinting, or swimming at high speed. In general, the maximum metabolic rate an animal can sustain is inversely related to the duration of activity.

For most terrestrial animals, the average daily rate of energy consumption is two to four times BMR (for endotherms) or

# Interpreting Pie Charts

**How Do Energy Budgets Differ for Three Terrestrial Vertebrates?** To explore bioenergetics in animal bodies, let's consider typical annual energy budgets for three terrestrial vertebrates that vary in size and thermoregulatory strategy: a 4-kg male Adélie penguin, a 25-g (0.025-kg) female deer mouse, and a 4-kg female ball python. The penguin is well-insulated against his Antarctic environment but must expend energy in swimming to catch food, incubating eggs laid by his partner, and bringing food to his chicks. The tiny deer mouse lives in a temperate environment where food may be readily available, but her small size causes rapid loss of body heat. Unlike the penguin and mouse, the python is ectothermic and keeps growing throughout her life. She produces eggs but does not incubate them. In this exercise, we'll compare the energy expenditures of these animals for five important functions: basal (standard) metabolism, reproduction, thermoregulation, activity, and growth.

**How the Data Were Obtained** Energy budgets were calculated for each of the animals based on measurements from field and laboratory studies.

**Data from the Experiments** Pie charts are a good way to compare *relative* differences in a set of variables. In the pie charts here, the sizes of the wedges represent the relative annual energy expenditures for the functions shown in the key. The total annual expenditure for each animal is given below its pie chart.

#### INTERPRET THE DATA

1. You can estimate the contribution of each wedge in a pie chart by remembering that the entire circle represents 100%, half is 50%, and so on. What percent of the mouse's energy budget goes to basal metabolism? What percent of the penguin's budget is for activity?

2. Without considering the sizes of the wedges, how do the three pie charts differ in which functions they include? Explain these differences.

3. Does the penguin or the mouse expend a greater proportion of its energy budget on thermoregulation? Why?

4. Now look at the *total* annual energy expenditures for each animal. How much more energy does the penguin expend each year compared to the similarly sized python?

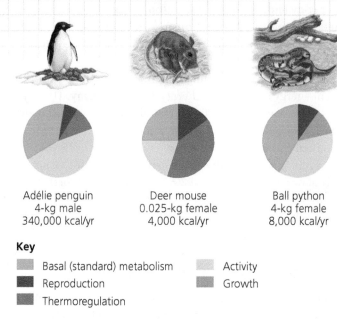

| Adélie penguin | Deer mouse | Ball python |
| --- | --- | --- |
| 4-kg male | 0.025-kg female | 4-kg female |
| 340,000 kcal/yr | 4,000 kcal/yr | 8,000 kcal/yr |

**Key**

- ▨ Basal (standard) metabolism
- ▨ Reproduction
- ▨ Thermoregulation
- ▨ Activity
- ▨ Growth

**Data from** M. A. Chappell et al., Energetics of foraging in breeding Adélie penguins, *Ecology* 74:2450–2461 (1993); M. A. Chappell et al., Voluntary running in deer mice: speed, distance, energy costs, and temperature effects, *Journal of Experimental Biology* 207:3839–3854 (2004); T. M. Ellis and M. A. Chappell, Metabolism, temperature relations, maternal behavior, and reproductive energetics in the ball python (*Python regius*), *Journal of Comparative Physiology B* 157:393–402 (1987).

5. Which animal expends the most kilocalories per year on thermoregulation?

6. If you monitored energy allocation in the penguin for just a few months instead of an entire year, you might find the growth category to be a significant part of the pie chart. Given that adult penguins don't grow from year to year, how would you explain this finding?

**ⓂⒷ** **Instructors:** A version of this Scientific Skills Exercise can be assigned in MasteringBiology.

---

SMR (for ectotherms). Humans in most developed countries have an unusually low average daily metabolic rate of about 1.5 times BMR—an indication of a relatively sedentary lifestyle.

The fraction of an animal's energy "budget" that is devoted to activity depends on many factors, including its environment, behavior, size, and thermoregulation. In the **Scientific Skills Exercise**, you'll interpret data on the annual energy budgets of three terrestrial vertebrates.

## Torpor and Energy Conservation

Despite their many adaptations for homeostasis, animals may encounter conditions that severely challenge their abilities to balance their heat, energy, and materials budgets. For example, at certain times of the day or year, their surroundings may be extremely hot or cold, or food may be unavailable. A major adaptation that enables animals to save energy in the face of such difficult conditions is **torpor**, a physiological state of decreased activity and metabolism.

Many birds and small mammals exhibit a daily torpor that is well adapted to feeding patterns. For instance, some bats feed at night and go into torpor in daylight. Similarly, chickadees and hummingbirds, which feed during the day, often go into torpor on cold nights.

All endotherms that exhibit daily torpor are relatively small; when active, they have high metabolic rates and thus very high rates of energy consumption. The changes in body temperature, and thus the energy savings, are often considerable: the body temperature of chickadees drops as much as 10°C (18°F) at night, and the core body temperature of a humming-bird can fall 25°C (45°F) or more.

**Hibernation** is long-term torpor that is an adaptation to winter cold and food scarcity. When a mammal enters hibernation, its body temperature declines as its body's thermostat is turned down. Some hibernating mammals cool to as low as 1–2°C (34–36°F), and at least one, the Arctic ground squirrel (*Spermophilus parryii*), can enter a supercooled (unfrozen) state in which its body temperature dips below 0°C (32°F). Periodically, perhaps every two weeks or so, hibernating animals undergo arousal, raising their body temperature and becoming active briefly before resuming hibernation.

Metabolic rates during hibernation can be 20 times lower than if the animal attempted to maintain normal body temperatures of 36–38°C (97–100°F). As a result, hibernators such as the ground squirrel can survive through the winter on limited supplies of energy stored in the body tissues or as food cached in a burrow. Similarly, the slow metabolism and inactivity of *estivation*, or summer torpor, enable animals to survive long periods of high temperatures and scarce water.

What happens to the circadian rhythm in hibernating animals? In the past, researchers reported detecting daily biological rhythms in hibernating animals. However, in some cases the animals were probably in a state of torpor from which they could readily arouse, rather than "deep" hibernation. More recently, a group of researchers in France addressed this question in a different way, examining the machinery of the biological clock rather than the rhythms it controls **(Figure 40.22)**. Working with the European hamster, they found that molecular components of the clock stopped oscillating during hibernation. These findings support the hypothesis that the circadian clock ceases operation during hibernation, at least in this species.

From tissue types to homeostasis, this chapter has focused on the whole animal. We also investigated how animals exchange materials with the environment and how size and activity affect metabolic rate. For much of the rest of this unit, we'll explore how specialized organs and organ systems enable animals to meet the basic challenges of life. In Unit 6, we investigated how plants meet the same challenges. **Figure 40.23**, on the next two pages, highlights some fundamental similarities and differences in the evolutionary adaptations of plants and animals. This figure is thus a review of Unit 6, an introduction to Unit 7, and, most importantly, an illustration of the connections that unify the myriad forms of life.

▼ **Hibernating dormouse**
(*Muscardinus avellanarius*)

▼ Figure 40.22

**Inquiry** What happens to the circadian clock during hibernation?

**Experiment** To determine whether the 24-hour biological clock continues to run during hibernation, Paul Pévet and colleagues at the University of Louis Pasteur in Strasbourg, France, studied molecular components of the circadian clock in the European hamster (*Cricetus cricetus*). The researchers measured RNA levels for two clock genes—*Per2* and *Bmal1*—during normal activity (euthermia) and during hibernation in constant darkness. The RNA samples were obtained from the suprachiasmatic nuclei (SCN), a pair of structures in the mammalian brain that control circadian rhythms.

**Results**

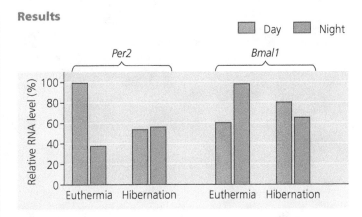

**Conclusion** Hibernation disrupted circadian variation in the hamster's clock gene RNA levels. Further experiments demonstrated that this disruption was not simply due to the dark environment during hibernation, since for nonhibernating animals RNA levels during a darkened daytime were the same as in daylight. The researchers concluded that the biological clock stops running in hibernating European hamsters and, perhaps, in other hibernators as well.

**Data from** F. G. Revel et al., The circadian clock stops ticking during deep hibernation in the European hamster, *Proceedings of the National Academy of Sciences USA* 104:13816–13820 (2007).

**WHAT IF** ➤ *Suppose you discovered a new hamster gene and found that the levels of RNA for this gene were constant during hibernation. What could you conclude about the day and night RNA levels for this gene during euthermia?*

 Interview with George Bartholomew: Exploring connections between animal physiology and the environment

## CONCEPT CHECK 40.4

1. If a mouse and a small lizard of the same mass (both at rest) were placed in experimental chambers under identical environmental conditions, which animal would consume oxygen at a higher rate? Explain.

2. Which animal must eat a larger proportion of its weight in food each day: a house cat or an African lion caged in a zoo? Explain.

3. **WHAT IF?** ➤ Suppose the animals at a zoo were resting comfortably and remained at rest while the nighttime air temperature dropped. If the temperature change were sufficient to cause a change in metabolic rate, what changes would you expect for an alligator and a lion?

*For suggested answers, see Appendix A.*

**MAKE CONNECTIONS**

# Life Challenges and Solutions in Plants and Animals

Multicellular organisms face a common set of challenges. Comparing the solutions that have evolved in plants and animals reveals both unity (shared elements) and diversity (distinct features) across these two lineages.

## Nutritional Mode

All living things must obtain energy and carbon from the environment to grow, survive, and reproduce. Plants are autotrophs, obtaining their energy through photosynthesis and their carbon from inorganic sources, whereas animals are heterotrophs, obtaining their energy and carbon from food. Evolutionary adaptations in plants and animals support these different nutritional modes. The broad surface of many leaves (left) enhances light capture for photosynthesis. When hunting, a bobcat relies on stealth, speed, and sharp claws (right). (See Figure 36.2 and Figure 41.16.)

## Growth and Regulation

The growth and physiology of both plants and animals are regulated by hormones. In plants, hormones may act in a local area or be transported in the body. They control growth patterns, flowering, fruit development, and more (left). In animals, hormones circulate throughout the body and act in specific target tissues, controlling homeostatic processes and developmental events such as molting (below). (See Figure 39.9 and Figure 45.12.)

 BioFlix® Animation: Homeostasis: Regulating Blood Sugar

## Environmental Response

All forms of life must detect and respond appropriately to conditions in their environment. Specialized organs sense environmental signals. For example, the floral head of a sunflower (left) and an insect's eyes (right) both contain photoreceptors that detect light. Environmental signals activate specific receptor proteins, triggering signal transduction pathways that initiate cellular responses coordinated by chemical and electrical communication. (See Figure 39.19 and Figure 50.15.)

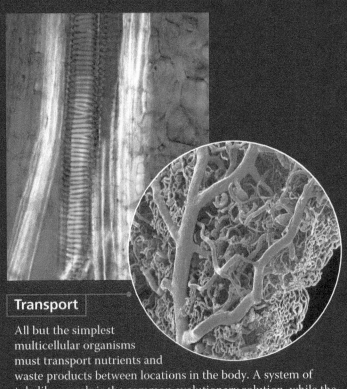

## Transport

All but the simplest
multicellular organisms
must transport nutrients and
waste products between locations in the body. A system of
tubelike vessels is the common evolutionary solution, while the
mechanism of circulation varies. Plants harness solar energy
to transport water, minerals, and sugars through specialized
tubes (left). In animals, a pump (heart) moves circulatory fluid
through vessels (right). (See Figure 35.10 and Figure 42.9.)

**MB** BioFlix® Animation: Water Transport in Plants

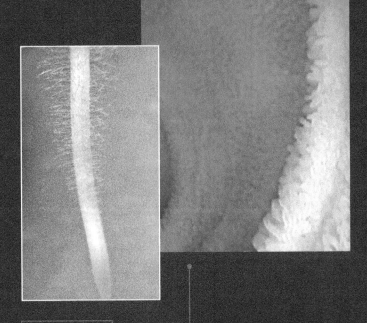

## Absorption

Organisms need to absorb nutrients. The root hairs
of plants (left) and the villi (projections) that line
the intestines of vertebrates (right) increase the
surface area available for absorption. (See Figure 35.3
and Figure 41.12.)

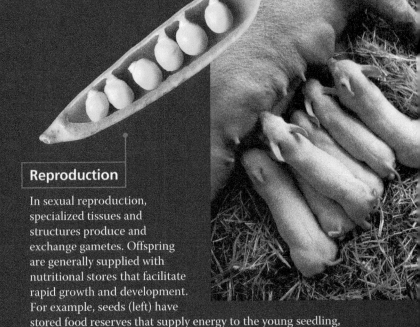

## Reproduction

In sexual reproduction,
specialized tissues and
structures produce and
exchange gametes. Offspring
are generally supplied with
nutritional stores that facilitate
rapid growth and development.
For example, seeds (left) have
stored food reserves that supply energy to the young seedling,
while milk provides sustenance for juvenile mammals (right).
(See Figure 38.8 and Figure 46.7.)

## Gas Exchange

The exchange of certain
gases with the environment
is essential for life.
Respiration by plants and
animals requires taking up
oxygen ($O_2$) and releasing carbon dioxide ($CO_2$). In photosynthesis,
net exchange occurs in the opposite direction: $CO_2$ uptake and $O_2$
release. In both plants and animals, highly convoluted surfaces that
increase the area available for gas exchange have evolved, such as
the spongy mesophyll of leaves (left) and the alveoli of lungs (right).
(See Figure 35.18 and Figure 42.24.)

**MB** BioFlix® Animation: Gas Exchange

**MAKE CONNECTIONS ➤** *Compare the adaptations that enable
plants and animals to respond to the challenges of living in hot
and cold environments. See Concepts 39.4 and 40.3.*

Go to **MasteringBiology**™ for Videos, Animations, Vocab Self-Quiz, Practice Tests, and more in the Study Area.

## SUMMARY OF KEY CONCEPTS

### CONCEPT 40.1

**Animal form and function are correlated at all levels of organization** (pp. 872–879)

VOCAB
SELF-QUIZ
goo.gl/6u55ks

- Physical laws constrain the evolution of an animal's size and shape. These constraints contribute to convergent evolution in animal body forms.
- Each animal cell must have access to an aqueous environment. Simple two-layered sacs and flat shapes maximize exposure to the surrounding medium. More complex body plans have highly folded internal surfaces specialized for exchanging materials.
- Animal bodies are based on a hierarchy of cells, **tissues, organs**, and **organ systems. Epithelial tissue** forms active interfaces on external and internal surfaces; **connective tissue** binds and supports other tissues; **muscle tissue** contracts, moving body parts; and **nervous tissue** transmits nerve impulses throughout the body.
- The **endocrine** and **nervous systems** are the two means of communication between different locations in the body. The endocrine system broadcasts signaling molecules called **hormones** everywhere via the bloodstream, but only certain cells are responsive to each hormone. The nervous system uses dedicated cellular circuits involving electrical and chemical signals to send information to specific locations.

? *For a large animal, what challenges would a spherical shape pose for carrying out exchange with the environment?*

### CONCEPT 40.2

**Feedback control maintains the internal environment in many animals** (pp. 879–881)

- An animal is a **regulator** if it controls an internal variable and a **conformer** if it allows an internal variable to vary with external changes. **Homeostasis** is the maintenance of a steady state despite internal and external changes.
- Homeostatic mechanisms are usually based on **negative feedback**, in which the **response** reduces the **stimulus**. In contrast, **positive feedback** involves amplification of a stimulus by the response and often brings about a change in state, such as the transition from pregnancy to childbirth.

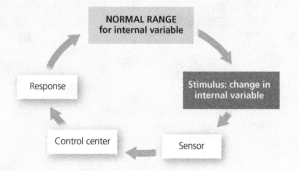

- Regulated change in the internal environment is essential to normal function. **Circadian rhythms** are daily fluctuations in metabolism and behavior tuned to the cycles of light and dark in the environment. Other environmental changes may trigger **acclimatization**, a temporary shift in the steady state.

? *Is it accurate to define homeostasis as a constant internal environment? Explain.*

### CONCEPT 40.3

**Homeostatic processes for thermoregulation involve form, function, and behavior** (pp. 882–887)

- An animal maintains its internal temperature within a tolerable range by **thermoregulation. Endothermic** animals are warmed mostly by heat generated by metabolism. **Ectothermic** animals get most of their heat from external sources. Endothermy requires a greater expenditure of energy. Body temperature may vary with environmental temperature, as in *poikilotherms*, or be relatively constant, as in *homeotherms*.
- In thermoregulation, physiological and behavioral adjustments balance heat gain and loss, which occur through radiation, evaporation, convection, and conduction. Insulation and **countercurrent exchange** reduce heat loss, whereas panting, sweating, and bathing increase evaporation, cooling the body. Many ectotherms and endotherms adjust their rate of heat exchange with their surroundings by vasodilation or vasoconstriction and by behavioral responses.
- Many mammals and birds adjust their amount of body insulation in response to changes in environmental temperature. Ectotherms undergo a variety of changes at the cellular level to acclimatize to shifts in temperature.
- The **hypothalamus** acts as the thermostat in mammalian regulation of body temperature. Fever reflects a resetting of this thermostat to a higher normal range in response to infection.

? *Given that humans thermoregulate, explain why your skin is cooler than your body core.*

### CONCEPT 40.4

**Energy requirements are related to animal size, activity, and environment** (pp. 887–893)

- Animals obtain chemical energy from food, storing it for short-term use in ATP. The total amount of energy used in a unit of time defines an animal's **metabolic rate**.
- Under similar conditions and for animals of the same size, the **basal metabolic rate** of endotherms is substantially higher than the **standard metabolic rate** of ectotherms. Minimum metabolic rate per gram is inversely related to body size among similar animals. Animals allocate energy for basal (or standard) metabolism, activity, homeostasis, growth, and reproduction.
- **Torpor**, a state of decreased activity and metabolism, conserves energy during environmental extremes. Animals may enter torpor according to a circadian rhythm (daily torpor), in winter (**hibernation**), or in summer (estivation).

? *Why do small animals breathe more rapidly than large animals?*

## Level 1: Knowledge/Comprehension

1. The body tissue that consists largely of material located outside of cells is
   (A) epithelial tissue.
   (B) connective tissue.
   (C) muscle tissue.
   (D) nervous tissue.

2. Which of the following would increase the rate of heat exchange between an animal and its environment?
   (A) feathers or fur
   (B) vasoconstriction
   (C) wind blowing across the body surface
   (D) countercurrent heat exchanger

3. Consider the energy budgets for a human, an elephant, a penguin, a mouse, and a snake. The _____ would have the highest total annual energy expenditure, and the _____ would have the highest energy expenditure per unit mass.
   (A) elephant; mouse
   (B) elephant; human
   (C) mouse; snake
   (D) penguin; mouse

## Level 2: Application/Analysis

4. Compared with a smaller cell, a larger cell of the same shape has
   (A) less surface area.
   (B) less surface area per unit of volume.
   (C) the same surface-area-to-volume ratio.
   (D) a smaller cytoplasm-to-nucleus ratio.

5. An animal's inputs of energy and materials would exceed its outputs
   (A) if the animal is an endotherm, which must always take in more energy because of its high metabolic rate.
   (B) if it is actively foraging for food.
   (C) if it is growing and increasing its mass.
   (D) never; due to homeostasis, these energy and material budgets always balance.

6. You are studying a large tropical reptile that has a high and relatively stable body temperature. How do you determine whether this animal is an endotherm or an ectotherm?
   (A) You know from its high and stable body temperature that it must be an endotherm.
   (B) You subject this reptile to various temperatures in the lab and find that its body temperature and metabolic rate change with the ambient temperature. You conclude that it is an ectotherm.
   (C) You note that its environment has a high and stable temperature. Because its body temperature matches the environmental temperature, you conclude that it is an ectotherm.
   (D) You measure the metabolic rate of the reptile, and because it is higher than that of a related species that lives in temperate forests, you conclude that this reptile is an endotherm and its relative is an ectotherm.

7. Which of the following animals uses the largest percentage of its energy budget for homeostatic regulation?
   (A) marine jelly (an invertebrate)
   (B) snake in a temperate forest
   (C) desert insect
   (D) desert bird

8. **DRAW IT** Draw a model of the control circuit(s) required for driving an automobile at a fairly constant speed over a hilly road. Indicate each feature that represents a sensor, stimulus, or response.

## Level 3: Synthesis/Evaluation

9. **EVOLUTION CONNECTION** In 1847, the German biologist Christian Bergmann noted that mammals and birds living at higher latitudes (farther from the equator) are on average larger and bulkier than related species found at lower latitudes. Suggest an evolutionary hypothesis to explain this observation.

10. **SCIENTIFIC INQUIRY** Eastern tent caterpillars (*Malacosoma americanum*) live in large groups in silk nests resembling tents, which they build in trees. They are among the first insects to be active in early spring, when daily temperature fluctuates from freezing to very hot. Over the course of a day, they display striking differences in behavior: Early in the morning, they rest in a tightly packed group on the tent's east-facing surface. In midafternoon, they are on its undersurface, each caterpillar hanging by a few of its legs. Propose a hypothesis to explain this behavior. How could you test it?

11. **SCIENCE, TECHNOLOGY, AND SOCIETY** Medical researchers are investigating artificial substitutes for various human tissues. Why might artificial blood or skin be useful? What characteristics would these substitutes need in order to function well in the body? Why do real tissues work better? Why not use the real tissues if they work better? What other artificial tissues might be useful? What problems do you anticipate in developing and applying them?

12. **WRITE ABOUT A THEME: ENERGY AND MATTER** In a short essay (about 100–150 words) focusing on energy transfer and transformation, discuss the advantages and disadvantages of hibernation.

13. **SYNTHESIZE YOUR KNOWLEDGE**

These macaques (*Macaca fuscata*) are partially immersed in a hot spring in a snowy region of Japan. What are some ways that form, function, and behavior contribute to homeostasis for these animals?

*For selected answers, see Appendix A.*

 For additional practice questions, check out the **Dynamic Study Modules** in MasteringBiology. You can use them to study on your smartphone, tablet, or computer anytime, anywhere!

# Animal Nutrition

# 41

▲ Figure 41.1 **How does a crab help an otter make fur?**

## KEY CONCEPTS

**41.1** An animal's diet must supply chemical energy, organic building blocks, and essential nutrients

**41.2** Food processing involves ingestion, digestion, absorption, and elimination

**41.3** Organs specialized for sequential stages of food processing form the mammalian digestive system

**41.4** Evolutionary adaptations of vertebrate digestive systems correlate with diet

**41.5** Feedback circuits regulate digestion, energy storage, and appetite

## The Need to Feed

Dinnertime has arrived for the sea otter in **Figure 41.1** (and for the crab, though in quite a different sense). The muscles and other tissues of the crab will be chewed into pieces, broken down by acid and enzymes in the otter's digestive system, and finally absorbed as small molecules into the body of the otter. Together, this is animal **nutrition**: food being taken in, taken apart, and taken up.

Although dining on fish, crabs, urchins, and abalone is the sea otter's specialty, all animals eat other organisms—dead or alive, piecemeal or whole. Unlike plants, animals must consume food for both energy and the organic molecules used to assemble new molecules, cells, and tissues. Despite this shared need, animals have diverse diets. **Herbivores**, such as cattle, sea slugs, and caterpillars, dine mainly on plants or algae. **Carnivores**, such as sea otters, hawks, and spiders, mostly eat other animals. Rats and other **omnivores** (from the Latin *omnis*, all) don't in fact eat everything, but they do regularly consume animals as well as plants or algae. We humans are typically omnivores, as are cockroaches and crows.

The terms *herbivore, carnivore,* and *omnivore* represent the kinds of food an animal usually eats. However, most animals are opportunistic feeders, eating foods outside their standard diet when their usual foods aren't available. For example, deer are herbivores, but in addition to feeding on grass and other plants, they occasionally eat insects, worms, or bird eggs. Note as well that microorganisms are an unavoidable "supplement" in every animal's diet.

When you see this blue icon, log in to **MasteringBiology** and go to the Study Area for digital resources.

 Get Ready for This Chapter

To survive and reproduce, animals must balance their consumption, storage, and use of food. Sea otters, for example, support a high rate of metabolism by eating up to 25% of their body mass each day. Eating too little food, too much food, or the wrong mixture of foods can endanger an animal's health. In this chapter, we'll examine the nutritional requirements of animals, explore diverse evolutionary adaptations for obtaining and processing food, and investigate the regulation of energy intake and expenditure.

# CONCEPT 41.1

## An animal's diet must supply chemical energy, organic building blocks, and essential nutrients

Overall, an adequate diet must satisfy three nutritional needs: chemical energy for cellular processes, organic building blocks for macromolecules, and essential nutrients.

The activities of cells, tissues, organs, and whole animals depend on sources of chemical energy in the diet. This energy is used to produce ATP, which powers processes ranging from DNA replication and cell division to vision and flight (see Concept 8.3). To meet the need for ATP, animals ingest and digest nutrients, including carbohydrates, proteins, and lipids, for use in cellular respiration and energy storage.

In addition to fuel for ATP production, an animal requires raw materials for biosynthesis. To build the complex molecules it needs to grow, maintain itself, and reproduce, an animal must obtain two types of organic molecules from its food: a source of organic carbon (such as sugar) and a source of organic nitrogen (such as protein). From these materials, animal cells can construct a great variety of organic molecules.

## Essential Nutrients

The third requirement of an animal's diet is to provide **essential nutrients**, substances that an animal requires but cannot assemble from simple organic molecules. Essential nutrients in the diet include essential amino acids, essential fatty acids, vitamins, and minerals. Essential nutrients have key functions in cells, including serving as substrates of enzymes, as coenzymes, and as cofactors in biosynthetic reactions **(Figure 41.2)**.

In general, an animal can obtain all essential amino acids and fatty acids, as well as vitamins and minerals, by feeding on plants or other animals. Needs for particular nutrients vary among species. For instance, some animals (including humans) must get ascorbic acid (vitamin C) from their diet, whereas most animals can synthesize it from other nutrients.

### Essential Amino Acids

All organisms require a standard set of 20 amino acids to make a complete set of proteins (see Figure 5.14). Plants and microorganisms normally can produce all 20. Most animals have the enzymes to synthesize about half of these amino acids, as long as their diet includes sulfur and organic nitrogen. The remaining amino acids must be obtained from the animal's food in prefabricated form and are therefore called **essential amino acids**. Many animals, including adult humans, require eight amino acids in their diet: isoleucine, leucine, lysine, methionine, phenylalanine, threonine, tryptophan, and valine. (Human infants also need a ninth, histidine.)

The proteins in animal products such as meat, eggs, and cheese are "complete," which means that they provide all the essential amino acids in their proper proportions. In contrast, most plant proteins are "incomplete," being deficient in one or more essential amino acids. Corn (maize), for example, is deficient in tryptophan and lysine, whereas beans are lacking in methionine. However, vegetarians can easily obtain all of the essential amino acids by eating a varied diet of plant proteins.

### Essential Fatty Acids

Animals require fatty acids to synthesize a variety of cellular components, including membrane phospholipids, signaling molecules, and storage fats.

▼ **Figure 41.2 Roles of essential nutrients.** This example of a biosynthetic reaction illustrates some common functions for essential nutrients. The conversion of linoleic acid to γ-linoleic acid by the enzyme fatty acid desaturase involves all four classes of essential nutrients, as labeled in blue. Note that almost all enzymes and other proteins in animals contain some essential amino acids, as indicated in the partial sequence shown for fatty acid desaturase.

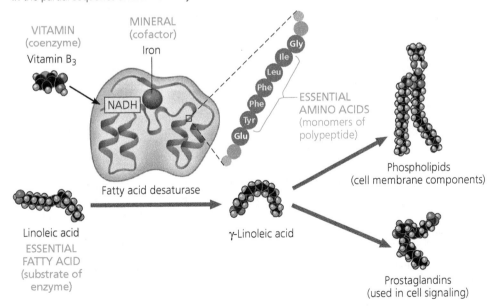

Although animals can synthesize many fatty acids, they lack the enzymes to form the double bonds found in certain required fatty acids. Instead, these molecules must be obtained from the diet and are considered **essential fatty acids**. In mammals, they include linoleic acid (see Figure 41.2). Animals typically obtain ample quantities of essential fatty acids from seeds, grains, and vegetables in their diet.

## Vitamins

As Albert Szent-Györgyi, the discoverer of vitamin C, once quipped, "A vitamin is a substance that makes you ill if you *don't* eat it." **Vitamins** are organic molecules that are required in the diet in very small amounts (0.01–100 mg per day, depending on the vitamin).

The 13 vitamins required by humans vary in both chemical properties and function **(Table 41.1)**. Vitamin $B_2$, for example, is a water-soluble vitamin that is converted in the body to FAD, a coenzyme used in many metabolic processes, including cellular respiration (see Figure 9.12). Vitamin C, which is required for the production of connective tissue, is also water-soluble.

Fat-soluble vitamins include vitamin A, which is incorporated into visual pigments of the eye, and vitamin D, which aids in calcium absorption and bone formation. Our dietary requirement for vitamin D, unlike other vitamins, turns out to be variable. Why? When our skin is exposed to sunlight, our bodies synthesize vitamin D, reducing our dietary need.

For people with imbalanced diets, taking supplements that provide vitamins at recommended daily levels is reasonable. It is far less clear that massive doses of vitamins confer any health benefits or are even safe. Moderate overdoses of water-soluble vitamins are probably harmless because excesses are excreted in urine. However, excesses of fat-soluble vitamins are deposited in body fat, so overconsumption may cause them to accumulate to toxic levels.

## Minerals

Dietary **minerals** are inorganic nutrients, such as iron and sulfur, that are usually required in small amounts—from less than 1 mg to about 2,500 mg per day. As shown in **Table 41.2**, minerals have diverse functions in animal physiology. Some are assembled into the structure of proteins; iron, for example,

**Table 41.1  Vitamin Requirements of Humans**

| Vitamin | Major Dietary Sources | Major Functions in the Body | Symptoms of Deficiency |
|---|---|---|---|
| **Water-Soluble Vitamins** | | | |
| $B_1$ (thiamine) | Pork, legumes, peanuts, whole grains | Coenzyme used in removing $CO_2$ from organic compounds | Beriberi (tingling, poor coordination, reduced heart function) |
| $B_2$ (riboflavin) | Dairy products, meats, enriched grains, vegetables | Component of coenzymes FAD and FMN | Skin lesions, such as cracks at corners of mouth |
| $B_3$ (niacin) | Nuts, meats, grains | Component of coenzymes $NAD^+$ and $NADP^+$ | Skin and gastrointestinal lesions, delusions, confusion |
| $B_5$ (pantothenic acid) | Meats, dairy products, whole grains, fruits, vegetables | Component of coenzyme A | Fatigue, numbness, tingling of hands and feet |
| $B_6$ (pyridoxine) | Meats, vegetables, whole grains | Coenzyme used in amino acid metabolism | Irritability, convulsions, muscular twitching, anemia |
| $B_7$ (biotin) | Legumes, other vegetables, meats | Coenzyme in synthesis of fat, glycogen, and amino acids | Scaly skin inflammation, neuromuscular disorders |
| $B_9$ (folic acid) | Green vegetables, oranges, nuts, legumes, whole grains | Coenzyme in nucleic acid and amino acid metabolism | Anemia, birth defects |
| $B_{12}$ (cobalamin) | Meats, eggs, dairy products | Production of nucleic acids and red blood cells | Anemia, numbness, loss of balance |
| C (ascorbic acid) | Citrus fruits, broccoli, tomatoes | Used in collagen synthesis; antioxidant | Scurvy (degeneration of skin and teeth), delayed wound healing |
| **Fat-Soluble Vitamins** | | | |
| A (retinol) | Dark green and orange vegetables and fruits, dairy products | Component of visual pigments; maintenance of epithelial tissues | Blindness, skin disorders, impaired immunity |
| D | Dairy products, egg yolk | Aids in absorption and use of calcium and phosphorus | Rickets (bone deformities) in children, bone softening in adults |
| E (tocopherol) | Vegetable oils, nuts, seeds | Antioxidant; helps prevent damage to cell membranes | Nervous system degeneration |
| K (phylloquinone) | Green vegetables, tea; also made by colon bacteria | Important in blood clotting | Defective blood clotting |

**Table 41.2** Mineral Requirements of Humans*

| Mineral | | Major Dietary Sources | Major Functions in the Body | Symptoms of Deficiency |
|---|---|---|---|---|
| More than 200 mg per day required | Calcium (Ca) | Dairy products, dark green vegetables, legumes | Bone and tooth formation, blood clotting, nerve and muscle function | Impaired growth, loss of bone mass |
| | Phosphorus (P) | Dairy products, meats, grains | Bone and tooth formation, acid-base balance, nucleotide synthesis | Weakness, loss of minerals from bone, calcium loss |
| | Sulfur (S) | Proteins from many sources | Component of certain amino acids | Impaired growth, fatigue, swelling |
| | Potassium (K) | Meats, dairy products, many fruits and vegetables, grains | Acid-base balance, water balance, nerve function | Muscular weakness, paralysis, nausea, heart failure |
| | Chlorine (Cl) | Table salt | Acid-base balance, formation of gastric juice, nerve function, osmotic balance | Muscle cramps, reduced appetite |
| | Sodium (Na) | Table salt | Acid-base balance, water balance, nerve function | Muscle cramps, reduced appetite |
| | Magnesium (Mg) | Whole grains, green leafy vegetables | Enzyme cofactor; ATP bioenergetics | Nervous system disturbances |
| Iron (Fe) | | Meats, eggs, legumes, whole grains, green leafy vegetables | Component of hemoglobin and of electron carriers; enzyme cofactor | Iron-deficiency anemia, weakness, impaired immunity |
| Fluorine (F) | | Drinking water, tea, seafood | Maintenance of tooth structure | Higher frequency of tooth decay |
| Iodine (I) | | Seafood, iodized salt | Component of thyroid hormones | Goiter (enlarged thyroid gland) |

*Additional minerals required in trace amounts include cobalt (Co), copper (Cu), manganese (Mn), molybdenum (Mo), selenium (Se), and zinc (Zn). All of these minerals, as well as those in the table, can be harmful in excess.

is incorporated into the oxygen carrier hemoglobin as well as some enzymes (see Figure 41.2). Others, such as sodium, potassium, and chloride, are important in the functioning of nerves and muscles and in maintaining osmotic balance between cells and the surrounding body fluid. In vertebrates, the mineral iodine is incorporated into thyroid hormone, which regulates metabolic rate. Vertebrates also require relatively large quantities of calcium and phosphorus for building and maintaining bone.

Ingesting too much of some minerals can upset homeostatic balance and cause health problems. For example, excess sodium can contribute to high blood pressure. This is a particular problem in the United States, where the typical person consumes enough salt (sodium chloride) to provide about 20 times the required amount of sodium. Processed foods often contain large amounts of sodium chloride, even if they do not taste salty.

## Dietary Deficiencies

A diet that lacks one or more essential nutrients or consistently supplies less chemical energy than the body requires results in *malnutrition*, a failure to obtain adequate nutrition. Malnutrition affects one out of four children worldwide, impairing health and often survival.

### Deficiencies in Essential Nutrients

Insufficient intake of essential nutrients can cause deformities, disease, and even death. For example, deer or other herbivores that feed on plants growing in phosphorus-deficient soil can develop fragile bones. In such environments, some grazing animals obtain missing nutrients by consuming concentrated sources of salt or other minerals **(Figure 41.3)**. Similarly, some birds supplement their diet with snail shells, and certain tortoises obtain minerals from stones they ingest.

Like other animals, humans sometimes have diets lacking in essential nutrients. A diet with insufficient amounts of one or more essential amino acids causes protein deficiency, the most common type of malnutrition among humans. In children, protein deficiency may arise if their diet shifts from breast milk to foods that contain relatively little protein, such as rice. Such children, if they survive infancy, often have impaired physical and mental development.

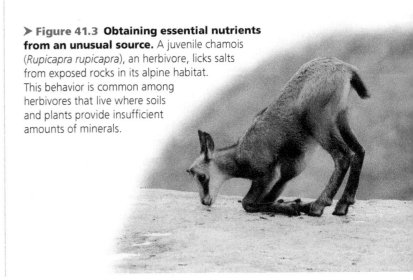

**➤ Figure 41.3 Obtaining essential nutrients from an unusual source.** A juvenile chamois (*Rupicapra rupicapra*), an herbivore, licks salts from exposed rocks in its alpine habitat. This behavior is common among herbivores that live where soils and plants provide insufficient amounts of minerals.

## Undernourishment

As mentioned earlier, malnutrition can also be caused by a diet that fails to provide enough chemical energy. In this situation, the body first uses up stored carbohydrates and fat. It then begins breaking down its own proteins for fuel: Muscles shrink, and the brain may become protein-deficient. If energy intake remains less than energy expenditures, the animal will eventually die. Even if a seriously undernourished animal survives, some of the damage may be irreversible.

Inadequate nourishment in humans is most common when drought, war, or another crisis severely disrupts the food supply. In sub-Saharan Africa, where the AIDS epidemic has crippled both rural and urban communities, approximately 200 million children and adults cannot obtain enough food.

Sometimes undernourishment occurs within well-fed human populations as a result of eating disorders. For example, in anorexia nervosa, weight loss to a level that is unhealthy for the individual's age and height may be related to a distorted body image.

## Assessing Nutritional Needs

Determining the ideal diet for the human population is an important but difficult problem for scientists. As objects of study, people present many challenges. Unlike laboratory animals, humans are genetically diverse. They also live in settings far more varied than the stable and uniform environment that scientists use to facilitate comparisons in laboratory experiments. Ethical concerns present an additional barrier. For example, it is not acceptable to investigate the nutritional needs of children in a way that might harm a child's growth or development.

Many insights into human nutrition have come from *epidemiology*, the study of human health and disease at the population level. In the 1970s, for instance, researchers discovered that children born to women of low socioeconomic status were more likely to have neural tube defects, which occur when tissue fails to enclose the developing brain and spinal cord (see Concept 47.2). The English scientist Richard Smithells thought that malnutrition among these women might be responsible. As described in **Figure 41.4**, he found that vitamin supplementation greatly reduced the risk of neural tube defects. In other studies, he obtained evidence that folic acid (vitamin $B_9$) was the specific vitamin responsible, a finding confirmed by other researchers. Based on this evidence, the United States in 1998 began to require that folic acid be added to enriched grain products used to make bread, cereals, and other foods. Follow-up studies have documented the effectiveness of this program in reducing the frequency of neural tube defects. Thus, at a time when microsurgery and sophisticated diagnostic imaging dominate the headlines, a simple dietary change such as folic acid supplementation may be among the greatest contributors to human health.

▼ Figure 41.4

**Inquiry** Can diet influence the frequency of birth defects?

**Experiment** Richard Smithells, of the University of Leeds, in England, examined the effect of vitamin supplementation on the risk of neural tube defects. Women who had had one or more babies with such a defect were put into two study groups. The experimental group consisted of those who were planning a pregnancy and began taking a multivitamin at least four weeks before attempting conception. The control group, who were not given vitamins, included women who declined them and women who were already pregnant. The numbers of neural tube defects resulting from the pregnancies were recorded for each group.

**Results**

| Group | Number of Infants/Fetuses Studied | Infants/Fetuses with a Neural Tube Defect |
|---|---|---|
| Vitamin supplements (experimental group) | 141 | 1 |
| No vitamin supplements (control group) | 204 | 12 |

**Data from** R. W. Smithells et al., Possible prevention of neural-tube defects by periconceptional vitamin supplementation, *Lancet* 315:339–340 (1980).

**Conclusion** This controlled study provided evidence that vitamin supplementation protects against neural tube defects, at least after the first pregnancy. Follow-up trials demonstrated that folic acid alone provided an equivalent protective effect.

**Inquiry in Action** Read and analyze the original paper in *Inquiry in Action: Interpreting Scientific Papers.*

**INTERPRET THE DATA ➤** *After folic acid supplementation became standard in the United States, the frequency of neural tube defects dropped to an average of just 1 in 5,000 live births. Propose two explanations why the observed frequency was much higher in the experimental group of the Smithells study.*

---

## CONCEPT CHECK 41.1

1. An animal requires 20 amino acids to make proteins. Why aren't all 20 essential to animal diets?

2. **MAKE CONNECTIONS ➤** Considering how enzymes function (see Concept 8.4), explain why vitamins are required in very small amounts.

3. **WHAT IF? ➤** If a zoo animal eating ample food shows signs of malnutrition, how might a researcher determine which nutrient is lacking in its diet?

*For suggested answers, see Appendix A.*

# CONCEPT 41.2

## Food processing involves ingestion, digestion, absorption, and elimination

In this section, we turn from nutritional requirements to the mechanisms by which animals process food. We will consider food processing in four stages: ingestion, digestion, absorption, and elimination.

Food processing begins with **ingestion**, the act of eating or feeding. As shown in **Figure 41.5**, the feeding mechanisms of most animal species can be grouped into four basic types.

**Exploring Four Main Feeding Mechanisms of Animals**

## Filter Feeding

Baleen

Many aquatic animals are **filter feeders**, which strain small organisms or food particles from the surrounding medium. The humpback whale, shown above, is one example. Attached to the whale's upper jaw are comblike plates called baleen, which remove small invertebrates and fish from enormous volumes of water and sometimes mud. Filter feeding in water is a type of suspension feeding, which also includes removing suspended food particles from the surrounding medium by capture or trapping mechanisms.

## Substrate Feeding

**Substrate feeders** are animals that live in or on their food source. This leaf miner caterpillar, the larva of a moth, is eating through the soft tissue of an oak leaf, leaving a dark trail of feces in its wake. Other substrate feeders include maggots (fly larvae), which burrow into animal carcasses.

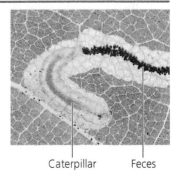

Caterpillar    Feces

## Fluid Feeding

**Fluid feeders** suck nutrient-rich fluid from a living host. This tsetse fly has pierced the skin of its human host with hollow, needle-like mouthparts and is consuming a blood meal. Similarly, aphids are fluid feeders that tap the phloem sap of plants. In contrast to such parasites, some fluid feeders actually benefit their hosts. For example, hummingbirds and bees move pollen between flowers as they fluid-feed on nectar.

## Bulk Feeding

Most animals, including humans, are **bulk feeders**, which eat relatively large pieces of food. Their adaptations include tentacles, pincers, claws, venomous fangs, jaws, and teeth that kill their prey or tear off pieces of meat or vegetation. In this amazing scene, a rock python is beginning to ingest a gazelle it has captured and killed. Snakes cannot chew their food into pieces and must swallow it whole—even if the prey is much bigger than the diameter of the snake. They can do so because the lower jaw is loosely hinged to the skull by an elastic ligament that permits the mouth and throat to open very wide. After swallowing its prey, which may take more than an hour, the python will spend two weeks or longer digesting its meal.

During **digestion**, the second stage of food processing, food is broken down into molecules small enough for the body to absorb. Both mechanical and chemical processes are typically required. Mechanical digestion, such as chewing or grinding, breaks food into smaller pieces, increasing surface area. The food particles then undergo chemical digestion, which cleaves large molecules into smaller components.

Chemical digestion is necessary because animals cannot directly use the proteins, carbohydrates, nucleic acids, fats, and phospholipids in food. These molecules are too large to pass through cell membranes and also are not all identical to those the animal needs for its particular tissues and functions. But when large molecules in food are broken down into their smaller components, the animal can use these products of digestion to assemble the large molecules it needs. For example, although the humpback whale and the tsetse fly in Figure 41.5 have very different diets, both break down proteins in their food to the same 20 amino acids from which they assemble all of the specific proteins in their bodies.

A cell makes a macromolecule or fat by linking together smaller components; it does so by removing a molecule of water for each new covalent bond formed. Chemical digestion by enzymes reverses this process by breaking bonds through the addition of water (see Figure 5.2). This splitting process is catalyzed by digestive enzymes and is called *enzymatic hydrolysis*. Polysaccharides and disaccharides are split into simple sugars as shown here for sucrose:

▼ **Enzymatic hydrolysis of a disaccharide**

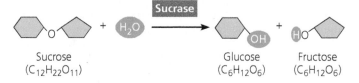

Sucrose ($C_{12}H_{22}O_{11}$)     Glucose ($C_6H_{12}O_6$)     Fructose ($C_6H_{12}O_6$)

Similarly, proteins are broken down into small peptides and amino acids; and nucleic acids are cleaved into nucleotides and their components. Enzymatic hydrolysis also releases fatty acids and other components from fats and phospholipids. In many animals, bacteria living in the digestive system carry out some chemical digestion.

The last two stages of food processing occur after the food is digested. In the third stage, **absorption**, the animal's cells take up (absorb) small molecules such as amino acids and simple sugars. **Elimination**, in which undigested material passes out of the digestive system, completes the process.

## Digestive Compartments

You have just read that digestive enzymes hydrolyze the same biological materials (such as proteins, fats, and carbohydrates) that make up the bodies of the animals themselves. How, then, are animals able to digest food without

digesting their own cells and tissues? The evolutionary adaptation that allows animals to avoid self-digestion is the processing of food within specialized intracellular or extracellular compartments.

### *Intracellular Digestion*

Food vacuoles—cellular organelles in which hydrolytic enzymes break down food—are the simplest digestive compartments. The hydrolysis of food inside vacuoles, called intracellular digestion, begins after a cell engulfs solid food by phagocytosis or liquid food by pinocytosis (see Figure 7.19). Newly formed food vacuoles fuse with lysosomes, organelles containing hydrolytic enzymes. This fusion of organelles brings food in contact with these enzymes, allowing digestion to occur safely within a compartment enclosed by a protective membrane. A few animals, such as sponges, digest all their food in this way (see Figure 33.4).

### *Extracellular Digestion*

In most animal species, hydrolysis occurs largely by extracellular digestion, the breakdown of food in compartments that are continuous with the outside of the animal's body. Having one or more extracellular compartments for digestion enables an animal to devour much larger pieces of food than can be ingested by phagocytosis.

Animals with relatively simple body plans typically have a digestive compartment with a single opening (**Figure 41.6**). This pouch, called a **gastrovascular cavity**, functions in

▼ **Figure 41.6 Digestion in a hydra.** Digestion begins in the gastrovascular cavity and is completed intracellularly after small food particles are engulfed by specialized cells of the gastrodermis.

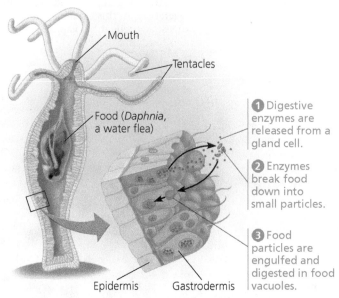

**DRAW IT** ➤ *Draw and label a simple diagram showing the pathway that nutrients follow from when food enters the hydra's mouth to when nutrients reach a cell on the outside of the tip of one of its tentacles.*

 Video: *Hydra* Eating *Daphnia*

digestion as well as in the distribution of nutrients throughout the body (hence the *vascular* part of the term). Small fresh-water cnidarians called hydras provide a good example of how a gastrovascular cavity works. The hydra—a carnivore—uses its tentacles to stuff captured prey through its mouth into its gastrovascular cavity. Specialized gland cells of the hydra's gastrodermis, the tissue layer that lines the cavity, then secrete digestive enzymes that break the soft tissues of the prey into tiny pieces. Other cells of the gastrodermis engulf these food particles, and most of the hydrolysis of macromolecules occurs intracellularly, as in sponges. After the hydra has digested its meal, undigested materials that remain in its gas-trovascular cavity, such as exoskeletons of small crustaceans,

▼ **Figure 41.7 Variation in alimentary canals.** These examples illustrate how the organization and structure of compartments for digestion, storage, and absorption differ among animals.

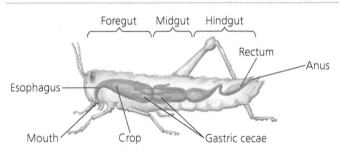

**(a) Earthworm.** The alimentary canal of an earthworm includes a muscular pharynx that sucks food in through the mouth. Food passes through the esophagus and is stored and moistened in the crop. Mechanical digestion occurs in the muscular gizzard, which pulverizes food with the aid of small bits of sand and gravel. Further digestion and absorption occur in the intestine.

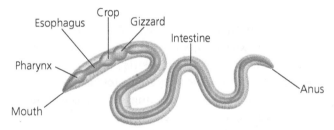

**(b) Grasshopper.** A grasshopper has several digestive chambers grouped into three main regions: a foregut, with an esophagus and crop; a midgut; and a hindgut. Food is moistened and stored in the crop, but most digestion occurs in the midgut. Pouches called gastric cecae (singular, *ceca*) extend from the beginning of the midgut and function in digestion and absorption.

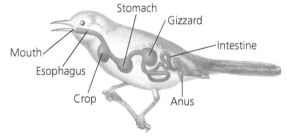

**(c) Bird.** Many birds have a crop for storing food and a stomach and gizzard for mechanically digesting it. Chemical digestion and absorption of nutrients occur in the intestine.

are eliminated through its mouth. Many flatworms also have a gastrovascular cavity (see Figure 33.10).

Rather than a gastrovascular cavity, animals with complex body plans have a digestive tube with two openings, a mouth and an anus (Figure 41.7). Such a tube is called a *complete digestive tract* or, more commonly, an **alimentary canal**. Because food moves along the alimentary canal in a single direction, the tube can be organized into specialized compart-ments that carry out digestion and nutrient absorption in a stepwise fashion. An animal with an alimentary canal can ingest food while earlier meals are still being digested, a feat that is likely to be difficult or inefficient for an animal with a gastrovascular cavity.

Because most animals, including mammals, have an alimentary canal, we'll use the mammalian digestive system in the next section to illustrate the general principles of food processing.

### CONCEPT CHECK 41.2

1. Distinguish the overall structure of a gastrovascular cav-ity from that of an alimentary canal.

2. In what sense are nutrients from a recently ingested meal not really "inside" your body prior to the absorption stage of food processing?

3. **WHAT IF?** ➤ Thinking in broad terms, what similarities can you identify between digestion in an animal body and the breakdown of gasoline in an automobile? (You don't have to know about auto mechanics.)

*For suggested answers, see Appendix A.*

## CONCEPT 41.3

# Organs specialized for sequential stages of food processing form the mammalian digestive system

In mammals, a number of accessory glands support food processing by secreting digestive juices through ducts into the alimentary canal. There are three pairs of salivary glands, as well as three individual glands: the pancreas, the liver, and the gallbladder. To explore the coordinated function of the accessory glands and alimentary canal, we'll consider the steps in food processing as a meal travels along the canal in a human.

### The Oral Cavity, Pharynx, and Esophagus

As soon as a bite of food enters your mouth, or **oral cavity**, food processing begins (Figure 41.8). Teeth with specialized shapes cut, mash, and grind, breaking the food into smaller pieces. This mechanical breakdown not only increases the surface area available for chemical breakdown but also facili-tates swallowing. Meanwhile, the anticipation or arrival of food in the oral cavity triggers the release of saliva by the **salivary glands**.

**▼ Figure 41.8 The human digestive system.** After food is chewed and swallowed, it takes 5–10 seconds for it to pass down the esophagus and into the stomach, where it spends 2–6 hours being partially digested. Further digestion and nutrient absorption occur in the small intestine over a period of 5–6 hours. Within 12–24 hours, any undigested material passes through the large intestine, and feces are expelled through the anus.

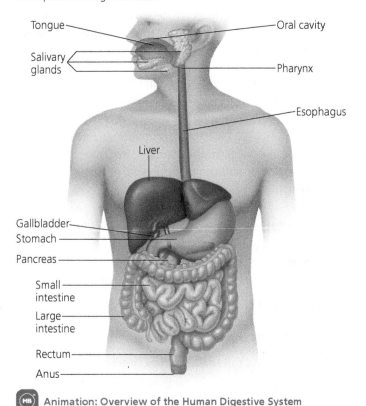

Tongue
Salivary glands
Liver
Gallbladder
Stomach
Pancreas
Small intestine
Large intestine
Rectum
Anus

Oral cavity
Pharynx
Esophagus

🔵 Animation: Overview of the Human Digestive System

**▼ Figure 41.9 Intersection of the human airway and digestive tract.** In humans, the pharynx connects to the trachea and the esophagus. **(a)** At most times, a contracted sphincter seals off the esophagus while the trachea remains open. **(b)** When a food bolus arrives at the pharynx, the swallowing reflex is triggered. Movement of the larynx, the upper part of the airway, tips a flap of tissue called the epiglottis down, preventing food from entering the trachea. At the same time, the esophageal sphincter relaxes, allowing the bolus to pass into the esophagus. The trachea then reopens, and peristaltic contractions of the esophagus move the bolus to the stomach.

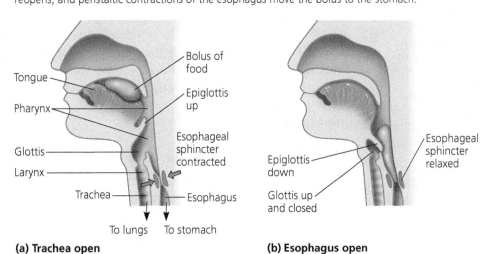

Tongue
Pharynx
Glottis
Larynx
Trachea

Bolus of food
Epiglottis up
Esophageal sphincter contracted
Esophagus

To lungs   To stomach

**(a) Trachea open**

Epiglottis down
Glottis up and closed

Esophageal sphincter relaxed

**(b) Esophagus open**

**VISUAL SKILLS ➤** *If you laugh while drinking water, the liquid may be ejected from your nostrils. Use this diagram to explain why this happens, taking into account that laughing involves exhaling.*

Saliva is a complex mixture of materials with a number of vital functions. One major component is **mucus**, a viscous mixture of water, salts, cells, and slippery glycoproteins (carbohydrate-protein complexes). Mucus lubricates food for easier swallowing, protects the gums against abrasion, and facilitates taste and smell. Saliva also contains buffers, which help prevent tooth decay by neutralizing acid, and antimicrobial agents (such as lysozyme; see Figure 5.16), which protect against bacteria that enter the mouth with food.

Scientists have long been puzzled by the fact that saliva contains a large amount of the enzyme **amylase**, which breaks down starch (a glucose polymer from plants) and glycogen (a glucose polymer from animals). Most chemical digestion occurs not in the mouth but in the small intestine, where amylase is also present. Why, then, does saliva contain so much amylase? A current hypothesis is that amylase in saliva releases food particles that are stuck to the teeth, thereby reducing the nutrients available to microorganisms living in the mouth.

The tongue also has important roles in food processing. Much as a doorman screens and assists people entering a fancy hotel, the tongue aids digestive processes by evaluating ingested material, distinguishing which foods should be processed further and then enabling their passage. (See Concept 50.4 for a discussion of the sense of taste.) After food is deemed acceptable and chewing begins, tongue movements manipulate the mixture of saliva and food, helping shape it into a ball called a **bolus (Figure 41.9).** During swallowing, the tongue provides further assistance, pushing the bolus to the back of the oral cavity and into the pharynx.

Each bolus of food is received by the **pharynx**, or throat region, which leads to two passageways: the esophagus and the trachea. The **esophagus** is a muscular tube that connects to the stomach; the trachea (windpipe) leads to the lungs. Swallowing must therefore be carefully choreographed to keep food and liquids from entering the trachea and causing choking, a blockage of the trachea. The resulting lack of airflow into the lungs can be fatal if the material is not dislodged by vigorous coughing, a series of back slaps, or a forced upward thrust of the diaphragm (the Heimlich maneuver).

Within the esophagus, food is pushed along by **peristalsis**, alternating waves of smooth muscle contraction and relaxation. Upon reaching the end of the esophagus, the bolus encounters a **sphincter**, a ringlike valve of muscle (**Figure 41.10**). Acting like a drawstring, the sphincter regulates passage of the ingested food into the next compartment, the stomach.

## Digestion in the Stomach

The **stomach**, which is located just below the diaphragm, plays two major roles in digestion. The first is storage. With accordion-like folds and a very elastic wall, the stomach can stretch to accommodate about 2 L of food and fluid. The second major function is to process food into a liquid suspension. As shown in Figure 41.10, the stomach secretes a digestive fluid called **gastric juice** and mixes it with the food through a churning action. This mixture of ingested food and gastric juice is called **chyme**.

### Chemical Digestion in the Stomach

Two components of gastric juice help liquefy food in the stomach. First, hydrochloric acid (HCl) disrupts the extracellular matrix that binds cells together in meat and plant material. The concentration of HCl is so high that the pH of gastric juice is about 2, acidic enough to dissolve iron nails (and to kill most bacteria). This low pH denatures (unfolds) proteins in food, increasing exposure of their peptide bonds. The exposed bonds are then attacked by the second component of gastric juice—a **protease**, or protein-digesting enzyme, called **pepsin**. Unlike most enzymes, pepsin is adapted to work best in a very acidic environment. By breaking peptide bonds, it cleaves proteins into smaller polypeptides and further exposes the contents of ingested tissues.

Two types of cells in the gastric glands of the stomach produce the components of gastric juice. *Parietal cells* use an ATP-driven pump to expel hydrogen ions into the lumen. At the same time, chloride ions diffuse into the lumen through specific membrane channels of the parietal cells. It is therefore only within the lumen that hydrogen and chloride ions combine to form HCl (see Figure 41.10). Meanwhile, *chief cells* release pepsin into the lumen in an inactive form called **pepsinogen**. HCl converts pepsinogen to active pepsin by clipping off a small portion of the molecule and exposing its active site. Through these processes, both HCl and pepsin form in the lumen (cavity) of the stomach, not within the cells of the gastric glands. As a result, the parietal and chief cells produce gastric juice but are not digested from within by its components.

After hydrochloric acid converts a small amount of pepsinogen to pepsin, pepsin itself helps activate the remaining pepsinogen. Pepsin, like HCl, can clip pepsinogen to expose the enzyme's active site. This generates more pepsin, which activates more pepsinogen. This series of events is an example of positive feedback (see Concept 40.2).

Why don't HCl and pepsin eat through the lining of the stomach? For one thing, mucus secreted by cells in gastric glands protects against self-digestion (see Figure 41.10).

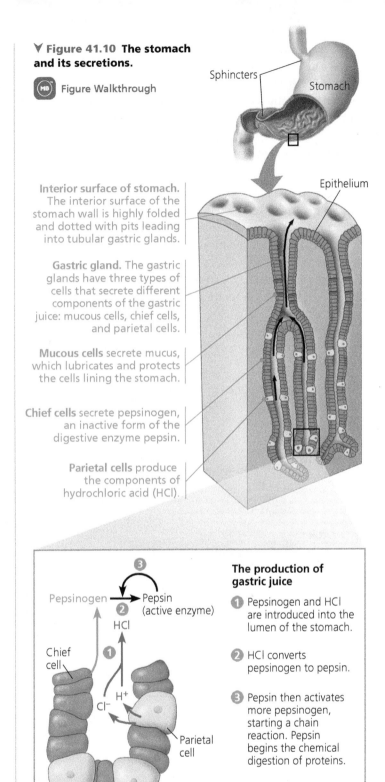

Sphincters

Stomach

Epithelium

**Interior surface of stomach.** The interior surface of the stomach wall is highly folded and dotted with pits leading into tubular gastric glands.

**Gastric gland.** The gastric glands have three types of cells that secrete different components of the gastric juice: mucous cells, chief cells, and parietal cells.

**Mucous cells** secrete mucus, which lubricates and protects the cells lining the stomach.

**Chief cells** secrete pepsinogen, an inactive form of the digestive enzyme pepsin.

**Parietal cells** produce the components of hydrochloric acid (HCl).

Pepsinogen → Pepsin (active enzyme)

HCl

Chief cell

$H^+$

$Cl^-$

Parietal cell

**The production of gastric juice**

1. Pepsinogen and HCl are introduced into the lumen of the stomach.

2. HCl converts pepsinogen to pepsin.

3. Pepsin then activates more pepsinogen, starting a chain reaction. Pepsin begins the chemical digestion of proteins.

In addition, cell division adds a new epithelial layer every three days, replacing cells before the lining is fully eroded by digestive juices. Under certain circumstances, however, damaged areas of the stomach lining called gastric ulcers can appear. It had been thought that they were caused by psychological stress and resulting excess acid secretion.

However, Australian researchers Barry Marshall and Robin Warren discovered that infection by the acid-tolerant bacterium *Helicobacter pylori* causes ulcers. They also demonstrated that an antibiotic could cure most gastric ulcers. For these findings, they were awarded the Nobel Prize in 2005.

## Stomach Dynamics

The breakdown of food by gastric juices is enhanced by muscular activity of the stomach. The coordinated series of muscle contractions and relaxations that we call "churning" mixes the stomach contents about every 20 seconds. Churning facilitates chemical digestion by bringing all of the food into contact with the gastric juices secreted by the lining of the stomach. As a result, what began as a recently swallowed meal becomes the acidic, nutrient-rich broth known as chyme.

Contractions of stomach muscles also help move material through the alimentary canal. In particular, peristaltic contractions typically move the contents of the stomach into the small intestine within 2–6 hours after a meal. The sphincter located where the stomach opens to the small intestine helps regulate passage into the small intestine, allowing only one squirt of chyme to enter at a time.

Occasionally, the sphincter at the top of the stomach allows a movement, or flux, of chyme from the stomach back into the lower end of the esophagus. The painful irritation of the esophagus that results from this process of acid reflux is commonly called "heartburn."

## Digestion in the Small Intestine

Although some chemical digestion begins in the oral cavity and stomach, most enzymatic hydrolysis of macromolecules from food occurs in the small intestine **(Figure 41.11)**. This organ's name refers to its small diameter compared to the large intestine, not to its length. The **small intestine** is in fact the alimentary canal's longest compartment—over

▼ **Figure 41.11 Chemical digestion in the human digestive system.** The timing and location of chemical breakdown are specific to each class of nutrients.

❓ *Pepsin is resistant to the denaturing effect of the low pH environment of the stomach. Thinking about the different digestive processes that occur in the small intestine, describe an adaptation shared by the digestive enzymes in that compartment.*

(MB) Animation: Digestive System Function

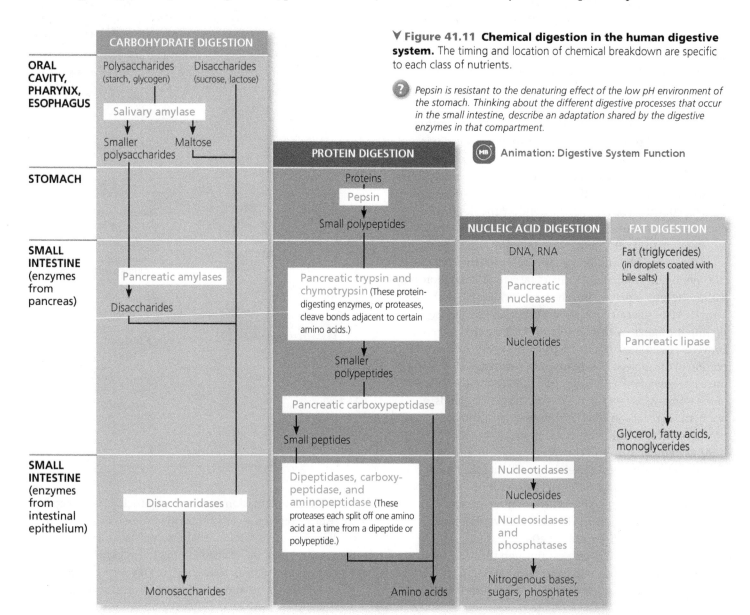

6 m (20 feet) long in humans. The first 25 cm (10 inches) or so of the small intestine forms the **duodenum**. It is here that chyme from the stomach mixes with digestive juices from the pancreas, liver, and gallbladder, as well as from gland cells of the intestinal wall itself. As you will read in Concept 41.5, hormones released by the stomach and duodenum control the digestive secretions into the alimentary canal.

The arrival of chyme in the duodenum triggers release of the hormone secretin, which stimulates the **pancreas** to secrete biocarbonate. Bicarbonate neutralizes the acidity of chyme and acts as a buffer for chemical digestion in the small intestine. The pancreas also secretes numerous digestive enzymes into the small intestine. These include the proteases trypsin and chymotrypsin, which are produced in inactive forms. In a chain reaction similar to that for pepsinogen, they are activated when safely located in the lumen of the duodenum.

The epithelial lining of the duodenum is the source of additional digestive enzymes. Some are secreted into the lumen of the duodenum, whereas others are bound to the surface of epithelial cells. Together with the enzymes from the pancreas, they complete most digestion in the duodenum.

Fats present a particular challenge for digestion. Insoluble in water, they form large globules that cannot be attacked efficiently by digestive enzymes. In humans and other vertebrates, fat digestion is facilitated by bile salts, which act as emulsifiers (detergents) that break apart fat and lipid globules. Bile salts are a major component of **bile**, a secretion of the **liver** that is stored and concentrated in the **gallbladder**.

Bile production contributes to another vital liver function: the destruction of red blood cells that are no longer fully functional. Pigments released during red blood cell disassembly are incorporated into bile pigments, which are eliminated from the body with the feces. In some liver and blood disorders, bile pigments accumulate in the skin, resulting in a yellowing called jaundice.

## Absorption in the Small Intestine

With digestion largely complete, the contents of the duodenum move by peristalsis into the *jejunum* and *ileum*, the remaining regions of the small intestine. There, nutrient absorption occurs across the lining of the intestine **(Figure 41.12)**. Large folds in the lining encircle the intestine and are studded with finger-shaped projections called **villi**. Within the villi, each epithelial cell has many microscopic projections, or **microvilli**, that face the intestinal lumen. The many side-by-side microvilli give cells of the intestinal epithelium a brush-like appearance that is reflected in the name *brush border*. Together, the folds, villi, and microvilli have a surface area of 200–300 m$^2$, roughly the size of a tennis court. This enormous surface area is an evolutionary adaptation that greatly increases the rate of nutrient absorption (see Figure 33.9 for more discussion and examples of maximizing surface area in diverse organisms).

Depending on the nutrient, transport across the epithelial cells can be passive or active (see Concepts 7.3 and 7.4). The sugar fructose, for example, moves by facilitated diffusion down its concentration gradient from the lumen of the small

▼ **Figure 41.12 Nutrient absorption in the small intestine.** Water-soluble nutrients, such as amino acids and sugars, enter the bloodstream, whereas fats are transported to the lymphatic system.

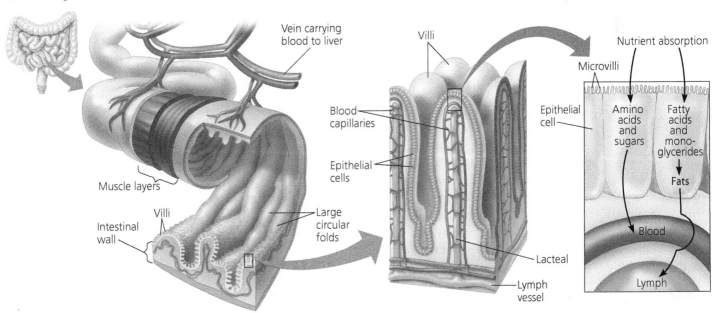

(?) *Tapeworms sometimes infect the human alimentary canal, anchoring themselves to the wall of the small intestine. Based on how digestion is compartmentalized along the mammalian alimentary canal, what digestive functions would you expect these parasites to have?*

BioFlix® Animation: Nutrient Transport Across Membranes

intestine into the epithelial cells. From there, fructose exits the basal surface and is absorbed into microscopic blood vessels, or capillaries, at the core of each villus. Other nutrients, including amino acids, small peptides, vitamins, and most glucose molecules, are pumped against concentration gradients into the epithelial cells of the villus. This active transport allows much more absorption of those nutrients than would be possible with passive diffusion alone.

The capillaries and veins that carry nutrient-rich blood away from the villi converge into the **hepatic portal vein**, a blood vessel that leads directly to the liver. From the liver, blood travels to the heart and then to other tissues and organs. This arrangement serves two major functions. First, it allows the liver to regulate the distribution of nutrients to the rest of the body. Because the liver converts many organic nutrients to different forms for use elsewhere, blood leaving the liver may have a very different nutrient balance than the blood that entered. Second, the arrangement allows the liver to remove toxic substances before they can circulate broadly. The liver is the primary site for detoxifying many organic molecules foreign to the body, such as drugs, and certain metabolic waste products.

Although many nutrients leave the small intestine through the bloodstream and pass through the liver for processing, some products of fat (triglyceride, also known as triacyl-glycerol) digestion take a different path (Figure 41.13). Hydrolysis of a fat by lipase in the small intestine generates fatty acids and a monoglyceride (glycerol joined to a fatty acid). These products are absorbed by epithelial cells and recombined into triglycerides. They are then coated with phospholipids, cholesterol, and proteins, forming globules called **chylomicrons**.

In exiting the small intestine, chylomicrons first enter a **lacteal**, a vessel at the core of each villus. Lacteals are part of the vertebrate lymphatic system, which is a network of vessels filled with a clear fluid called lymph. Starting at the lacteals, lymph containing the chylomicrons passes into the larger vessels of the lymphatic system and eventually into large veins that return the blood directly to the heart.

In addition to absorbing nutrients, the small intestine recovers water and ions. Each day a person consumes about 2 L of water and secretes another 7 L in digestive juices into the alimentary canal. Typically all but 0.1 L of the water is reabsorbed in the intestines, with most of the recovery occurring in the small intestine. There is no mechanism for active transport of water. Instead, water is reabsorbed by osmosis when sodium and other ions are pumped out of the lumen of the intestine.

## Processing in the Large Intestine

The alimentary canal ends with the **large intestine**, which includes the colon, cecum, and rectum. The small intestine connects to the large intestine at a T-shaped junction

▼ **Figure 41.13 Digestion and absorption of fats.** Fats, which are insoluble in water, are broken down in the lumen of the small intestine, reassembled in epithelial cells, and then transported in water-soluble globules called chylomicrons. The chylomicrons enter the lymph via narrow vessels called lacteals and are later transferred to the blood in large veins leading to the liver and heart.

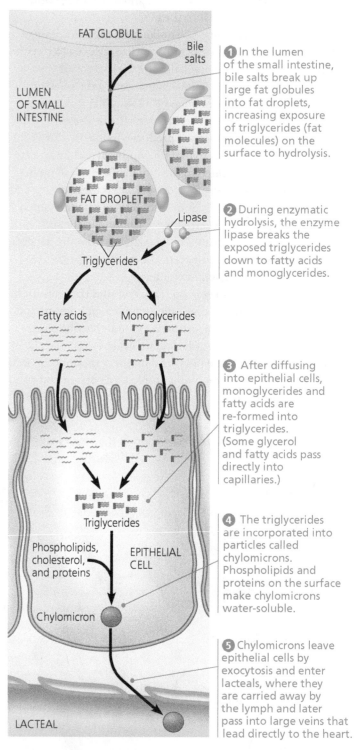

**①** In the lumen of the small intestine, bile salts break up large fat globules into fat droplets, increasing exposure of triglycerides (fat molecules) on the surface to hydrolysis.

**②** During enzymatic hydrolysis, the enzyme lipase breaks the exposed triglycerides down to fatty acids and monoglycerides.

**③** After diffusing into epithelial cells, monoglycerides and fatty acids are re-formed into triglycerides. (Some glycerol and fatty acids pass directly into capillaries.)

**④** The triglycerides are incorporated into particles called chylomicrons. Phospholipids and proteins on the surface make chylomicrons water-soluble.

**⑤** Chylomicrons leave epithelial cells by exocytosis and enter lacteals, where they are carried away by the lymph and later pass into large veins that lead directly to the heart.

**VISUAL SKILLS** ➤ *Two of the arrows in this figure indicate movement of materials between the cell and its surroundings. Does either require an input of energy? Explain.*

 HHMI Animation: The Fate of Fat

**(Figure 41.14).** One arm of the T is the 1.5-m-long **colon**, which leads to the rectum and anus. The other arm is a pouch called the **cecum**. The cecum is important for fermenting ingested material, especially in animals that eat large amounts of plant material. Compared with many other mammals, humans have a small cecum. The **appendix**, a finger-shaped extension of the human cecum, is thought

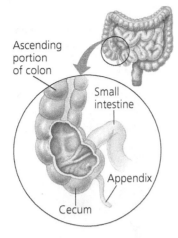

Ascending portion of colon

Small intestine

Appendix

Cecum

▲ **Figure 41.14 Junction of the small and large intestines.**

to serve as a reservoir for symbiotic microorganisms, which are discussed in Concept 41.4.

The colon completes the recovery of water that began in the small intestine. What remain are the **feces**, the wastes of the digestive system, which become increasingly solid as they are moved along the colon by peristalsis. It takes approximately 12–24 hours for material to travel the length of the colon. If the lining of the colon is irritated—by a viral or bacterial infection, for instance—less water than normal may be reabsorbed, resulting in diarrhea. The opposite problem, constipation, occurs when the feces move along the colon too slowly. Too much water is reabsorbed, and the feces become compacted.

The undigested material in feces includes cellulose fiber. Although it provides no caloric value (energy) to humans, it helps move food along the alimentary canal.

The community of bacteria living on unabsorbed organic material in the human colon contributes about one-third of the dry weight of feces. As by-products of their metabolism, many colon bacteria generate gases, including methane and hydrogen sulfide, the latter of which has an offensive odor. These gases and ingested air are expelled through the anus.

The terminal portion of the large intestine is the **rectum**, where the feces are stored until they can be eliminated. Between the rectum and the anus are two sphincters; the inner one is involuntary and the outer one is voluntary. Periodically, strong contractions of the colon create an urge to defecate. Because filling of the stomach triggers a reflex that increases the rate of contractions in the colon, the urge to defecate often follows a meal.

Having followed a meal through the alimentary canal, we'll look next at some adaptations of this general digestive plan in different animals.

**CONCEPT CHECK 41.3**

1. Explain why a proton pump inhibitor, such as the drug Prilosec, can relieve the symptoms of acid reflux.

2. Thinking about our nutritional needs and feeding behavior, propose an evolutionary explanation for why amylase, unlike other digestive enzymes, is secreted into the mouth.

3. **WHAT IF?** ➤ Predict what would happen if you mixed gastric juice with crushed food in a test tube.

*For suggested answers, see Appendix A.*

# CONCEPT 41.4

## Evolutionary adaptations of vertebrate digestive systems correlate with diet

**EVOLUTION** The digestive systems of vertebrates are variations on a theme, but there are many adaptations associated with the animal's diet. To highlight how form fits function, we'll examine a few of them.

### Dental Adaptations

Dentition, an animal's assortment of teeth, is one example of structural variation reflecting diet **(Figure 41.15).** The

▼ **Figure 41.15 Dentition and diet.**

| Carnivore | Herbivore | Omnivore |
|---|---|---|
| 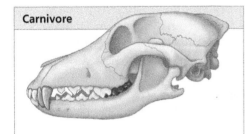 | 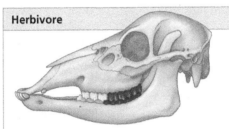 | 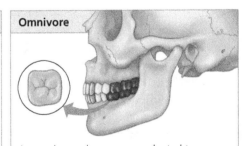 |
| Carnivores, such as members of the dog and cat families, generally have large, pointed incisors and canines that can be used to kill prey and rip or cut away pieces of flesh. The jagged premolars and molars crush and shred food. | Herbivores, such as horses and deer, usually have premolars and molars with broad, ridged surfaces that grind tough plant material. The incisors and canines are generally modified for biting off pieces of vegetation. In some herbivores, canines are absent. | As omnivores, humans are adapted to eating both plants and meat. Adults have 32 teeth. From front to back along either side of the mouth are four bladelike incisors for biting, a pair of pointed canines for tearing, four premolars for grinding, and six molars for crushing (see inset, top view). |

**Key** ■ Incisors ■ Canines ■ Premolars ■ Molars

evolutionary adaptation of teeth for processing different kinds of food is one of the major reasons mammals have been so successful. For example, the sea otter in Figure 41.1 uses its sharp canine teeth to tear apart prey such as crabs and its slightly rounded molars to crush their shells. Nonmammalian vertebrates generally have less specialized dentition, but there are interesting exceptions. Venomous snakes, such as rattlesnakes, have fangs, modified teeth that inject venom into prey. Some fangs are hollow, like syringes, whereas others drip the toxin along grooves on the surfaces of the teeth.

## Stomach and Intestinal Adaptations

Evolutionary adaptations to differences in diet are sometimes apparent as variations in the dimensions of digestive organs. For example, large, expandable stomachs are common in carnivorous vertebrates, which may wait a long time between meals and must eat as much as they can when they do catch prey. An expandable stomach enables a rock python to ingest a whole gazelle (see Figure 41.5) and a 200-kg African lion to consume 40 kg of meat in one meal!

Adaptation is also apparent in the length of the digestive system in different vertebrates. In general, herbivores and omnivores have longer alimentary canals relative to their body size than do carnivores **(Figure 41.16)**. Plant matter is more difficult to digest than meat because it contains cell walls. A longer digestive tract furnishes more time for digestion and more surface area for nutrient absorption. As an example, consider the coyote and koala. Although these two mammals are about the same size, the koala's intestines are much longer, enhancing the processing of fibrous, protein-poor eucalyptus leaves from which the koala obtains nearly all of its nutrients and water.

## Mutualistic Adaptations

An estimated 10–100 trillion bacteria live in the human digestive system. One bacterial inhabitant, *Escherichia coli*, is so common in the digestive system that its presence in lakes and streams is a useful indicator of contamination by untreated sewage.

The coexistence of humans and many intestinal bacteria is an example of mutualism, an interaction between two species that benefits both of them (see Concept 54.1). For example, some intestinal bacteria produce vitamins, such as vitamin K, biotin, and folic acid, that supplement our dietary intake when absorbed into the blood. Intestinal bacteria also regulate the development of the intestinal epithelium and the function of the innate immune system. The bacteria in turn receive a steady supply of nutrients and a stable host environment.

Recently, we have greatly expanded our knowledge of the **microbiome**, the collection of microorganisms living in and on the body, along with their genetic material. To study the

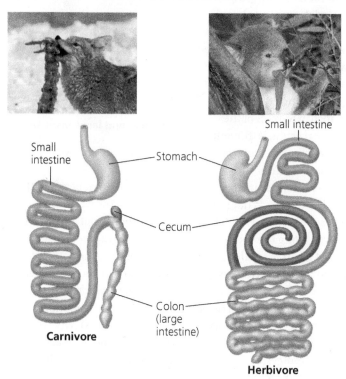

▼ **Figure 41.16 The alimentary canals of a carnivore (coyote) and herbivore (koala).** The relatively short digestive tract of the coyote is sufficient for digesting meat and absorbing its nutrients. In contrast, the koala's long alimentary canal is specialized for digesting eucalyptus leaves. Extensive chewing chops the leaves into tiny pieces, increasing exposure to digestive juices. In the long cecum and the upper portion of the colon, symbiotic bacteria further digest the shredded leaves, releasing nutrients that the koala can absorb.

Small intestine

Small intestine

Stomach

Cecum

Colon (large intestine)

**Carnivore**

**Herbivore**

microbiome, scientists are using a DNA sequencing approach based on the polymerase chain reaction (see Figure 20.8). They have found more than 400 bacterial species in the human digestive tract, a far greater number than had been identified through approaches relying on laboratory culture and characterization. Furthermore, researchers have found significant differences in the microbiome associated with diet, disease, and age **(Figure 41.17)**.

One microbiome study provided an important clue as to why the bacterium *H. pylori* can disrupt stomach health, leading to ulcers. After collecting stomach tissue from uninfected and *H. pylori*–infected adults, researchers identified all the bacterial species in each sample. What they found was remarkable: *H. pylori* infection led to the near-complete elimination from the stomach of all other bacterial species **(Figure 41.18)**. Such studies on differences in the microbiome associated with particular diseases hold promise for the development of new and more effective therapies.

There is now evidence that changes in the microbiome can play a role in obesity, nutritional deficiencies, diabetes, cardiovascular disease, and inflammatory diseases of the digestive system. There are even effects on brain function and mood. For example, eliminating microorganisms

## Figure 41.17 Variation in human gut microbiome at different life stages.

By copying and sequencing bacterial DNA in samples obtained from human intestinal tracts, researchers characterized the bacterial community that makes up the human gut.

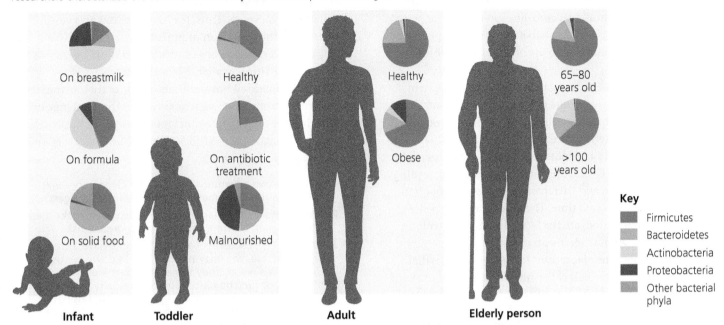

On breastmilk

On formula

On solid food

**Infant**

Healthy

On antibiotic treatment

Malnourished

**Toddler**

Healthy

Obese

**Adult**

65–80 years old

>100 years old

**Elderly person**

**Key**
- Firmicutes
- Bacteroidetes
- Actinobacteria
- Proteobacteria
- Other bacterial phyla

**INTERPRET THE DATA ➤** *Compare the relative abundance of Actinobacteria in the microbiome of a healthy adult's intestinal tract to that in a healthy stomach (see Figure 41.18). Suggest a possible explanation for why the microbiome composition in the two organs is different even through the intestine and stomach are directly connected.*

from the digestive system of mice causes the mice to have elevated blood concentrations of corticosterone, a stress hormone. Furthermore, such mice exhibit a greater stress response than control mice when their body movement is restricted.

The microbiome of a person's digestive system has more than 100 times as many genes as there are in one of his or her body cells. Given this enormous difference in gene number, many new and significant discoveries are likely to be made regarding the role of bacterial genes in the physiology of human health and disease.

## Mutualistic Adaptations in Herbivores

Mutualistic relationships with microorganisms are particularly important in herbivores. Much of the chemical energy in herbivore diets comes from the cellulose of plant cell walls, but animals do not produce enzymes that hydrolyze cellulose. Instead, many vertebrates (as well as termites, whose wooden diets consist largely of cellulose) host large populations of mutualistic bacteria and protists in fermentation chambers in their alimentary canals. These symbiotic microorganisms have enzymes that can digest cellulose to simple sugars and other compounds that the animal can absorb. In many cases, the microorganisms also use the sugars from digested cellulose in the production of a variety of essential nutrients, such as vitamins and amino acids.

## ▼ Figure 41.18 The stomach microbiome.

By copying and sequencing bacterial DNA in samples obtained from human stomachs, researchers characterized the bacterial community that makes up the stomach microbiome. In samples from individuals infected with *Helicobacter pylori*, more than 95% of the sequences were from that species, which belongs to the phylum Proteobacteria. The stomach microbiome in uninfected individuals was much more diverse.

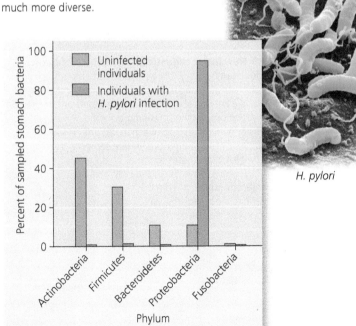

*H. pylori*

In horses, koalas, and elephants, symbiotic microorganisms are housed in a large cecum. In contrast, the hoatzin, an herbivorous bird found in South American rain forests, hosts microorganisms in a large, muscular crop (an esophageal pouch; see Figure 41.7). Hard ridges in the wall of the crop grind plant leaves into small fragments, and the microorganisms break down cellulose.

In rabbits and some rodents, mutualistic bacteria live in the large intestine as well as the cecum. Since most nutrients are absorbed in the small intestine, nourishing by-products of fermentation by bacteria in the large intestine are initially lost with the feces. Rabbits and rodents recover these nutrients by *coprophagy* (from the Greek, meaning "dung eating"), feeding on some of their feces and then passing the food through the alimentary canal a second time. The familiar rabbit "pellets," which are not reingested, are the feces eliminated after food has passed through the digestive tract twice.

The most elaborate adaptations for an herbivorous diet have evolved in the animals called *ruminants*, the cud-chewing animals that include deer, sheep, and cattle (Figure 41.19).

Although we have focused our discussion on vertebrates, adaptations related to digestion are also widespread among other animals. Some of the most remarkable examples are the giant tubeworms (over 3 m long) that live at pressures as high as 260 atmospheres around deep-sea hydrothermal vents (see Figure 52.15). These worms have no mouth or digestive system. Instead, they obtain all of their energy and nutrients from

▼ **Giant tubeworm**

mutualistic bacteria that live within their bodies. The bacteria carry out chemoautotrophy (see Concept 27.3) using the carbon dioxide, oxygen, hydrogen sulfide, and nitrate available at the vents. Thus, for invertebrates and vertebrates alike, the evolution of mutualistic relationships with symbiotic microorganisms is an adaptation that expands the sources of nutrition available to animals.

Having examined how animals optimize their extraction of nutrients from food, we'll next turn to the challenge of balancing the use of these nutrients.

## CONCEPT CHECK 41.4

1. What are two advantages of a longer alimentary canal for processing plant material that is difficult to digest?
2. What features of a mammal's digestive system make it an attractive habitat for mutualistic microorganisms?
3. **WHAT IF?** ➤ "Lactose-intolerant" people have a shortage of lactase, the enzyme that breaks down lactose in milk. As a result, they sometimes develop cramps, bloating, or diarrhea after consuming dairy products. Suppose such a person ate yogurt that contains bacteria that produce lactase. Why would eating yogurt likely provide at best only temporary relief of the symptoms?

*For suggested answers, see Appendix A.*

# CONCEPT 41.5

## Feedback circuits regulate digestion, energy storage, and appetite

To complete our consideration of animal nutrition, we'll explore the ways that obtaining and using nutrients are matched to an animal's circumstances and need for energy.

➤ **Figure 41.19 Ruminant digestion.** The stomach of a cow, a ruminant, has four chambers. ❶ Chewed food first enters the rumen and reticulum, where mutualistic microorganisms digest cellulose in the plant material. ❷ Periodically, the cow regurgitates and rechews "cud" from the reticulum, further breaking down fibers and thereby enhancing microbial action. ❸ The reswallowed cud passes to the omasum, where some water is removed. ❹ It then passes to the abomasum for digestion by the cow's enzymes. In this way, the cow obtains significant nutrients from both the grass and the mutualistic microorganisms, which maintain a stable population in the rumen.

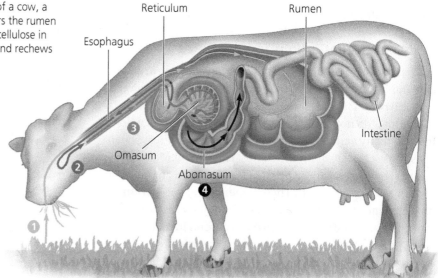

## Regulation of Digestion

Many animals face long gaps between meals. Under such circumstances, there is no need for their digestive systems to be active continuously. Instead, processing is activated stepwise. As food reaches each new compartment, it triggers the secretion of digestive juices for the next stage of processing. In addition, muscular contractions move the contents farther along the canal. For example, you learned earlier that nervous reflexes stimulate the release of saliva when food enters the oral cavity and orchestrate swallowing when a bolus of food reaches the pharynx. Similarly, the arrival of food in the stomach triggers churning and the release of gastric juices. These events, as well as peristalsis in the small and large intestines, are regulated by the *enteric nervous system*, a network of neurons dedicated to the digestive organs.

The endocrine system also plays a critical role in controlling digestion. As described in **Figure 41.20**, a series of hormones released by the stomach and duodenum help ensure that digestive secretions are present only when needed. Like all hormones, they are transported through the bloodstream. This is true even for the hormone gastrin, which is secreted by the stomach and targets that same organ.

## Regulation of Energy Storage

When an animal takes in more energy-rich molecules than it needs for metabolism and activity, it stores the excess energy (see Concept 40.4). In humans, liver and muscle cells serve as the primary sites for energy storage. In these cells, excess energy from the diet is stored in glycogen, a polymer made up of many glucose units (see Figure 5.6b). Once glycogen depots are full, any additional excess energy is usually stored in fat in adipose cells.

At times when fewer calories are taken in than are expended—perhaps because of sustained heavy exercise or lack of food—the human body generally expends liver glycogen first and then draws on muscle glycogen and fat. Fats are especially rich in energy; oxidizing a gram of fat liberates about twice the energy liberated from a gram of carbohydrate or protein. For this reason, adipose tissue provides the most space-efficient way for the body to store large amounts of energy. Most healthy people have enough stored fat to sustain them through several weeks without food.

### Glucose Homeostasis

The synthesis and breakdown of glycogen are central not only to energy storage, but also to maintaining metabolic balance through glucose homeostasis. In humans, the normal range for the concentration of glucose in the blood is 70–110 mg/100 mL. Because glucose is a major fuel for cellular respiration and a key source of carbon skeletons for biosynthesis, maintaining blood glucose concentrations near this normal range is essential.

▼ **Figure 41.20 Hormonal control of digestion.**

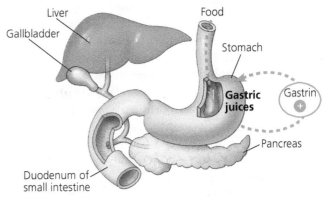

❶ As food arrives at the stomach, it stretches the stomach walls, triggering release of the hormone *gastrin*. Gastrin circulates via the bloodstream back to the stomach, where it stimulates production of gastric juices.

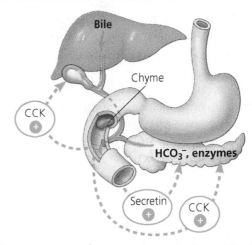

❷ Chyme—an acidic mixture of partially digested food—eventually passes from the stomach to the duodenum. The duodenum responds by releasing the digestive hormones cholecystokinin and secretin. *Cholecystokinin (CCK)* stimulates the release of digestive enzymes from the pancreas and of bile from the gallbladder. *Secretin* stimulates the pancreas to release bicarbonate ($HCO_3^-$), which neutralizes chyme.

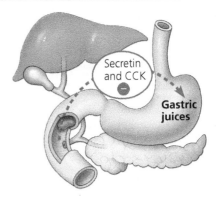

❸ If the chyme is rich in fats, the high levels of secretin and CCK released act on the stomach to inhibit peristalsis and secretion of gastric juices, thereby slowing digestion.

**Key**   Stimulation   Inhibition

Glucose homeostasis relies predominantly on the antagonistic (opposing) effects of two hormones, insulin and glucagon (**Figure 41.21**). When the blood glucose level rises above the normal range, the secretion of **insulin** triggers the uptake of glucose from the blood into body cells, decreasing the blood glucose concentration. When the blood glucose level drops below the normal range, the secretion of **glucagon** promotes the release of glucose into the blood from energy stores, such as liver glycogen, increasing the blood glucose concentration.

The liver is a key site of action for both insulin and glucagon. After a carbohydrate-rich meal, for example, the rising level of insulin promotes biosynthesis of glycogen from glucose entering the liver in the hepatic portal vein. Between meals, when blood in the hepatic portal vein has a much lower glucose concentration, glucagon stimulates the liver to break down glycogen, convert amino acids and glycerol to glucose, and release glucose into the blood. Together, these opposing effects of insulin and glucagon ensure that blood exiting the liver has a glucose concentration in the normal range at nearly all times.

Insulin also acts on nearly all body cells to stimulate glucose uptake from blood. A major exception is brain cells, which can take up glucose whether or not insulin is present. This evolutionary adaptation ensures that the brain almost always has access to circulating fuel, even if supplies are low.

Glucagon and insulin are both produced in the pancreas. Clusters of endocrine cells called pancreatic islets are scattered throughout this organ. Each islet has *alpha cells*, which make glucagon, and *beta cells*, which make insulin. Like all hormones, insulin and glucagon are secreted into the interstitial fluid and enter the circulatory system.

Overall, hormone-secreting cells make up only 1–2% of the mass of the pancreas. Other cells in the pancreas produce and secrete bicarbonate ions and the digestive enzymes active in the small intestine (see Figure 41.11). These secretions are released into small ducts that empty into the pancreatic duct, which leads to the small intestine. Thus, the pancreas has functions in both the endocrine and digestive systems.

## Diabetes Mellitus

In discussing the role of insulin and glucagon in glucose homeostasis, we have focused exclusively on a healthy metabolic state. However, a number of disorders can disrupt glucose homeostasis with potentially serious consequences, especially for the heart, blood vessels, eyes, and kidneys. The best known and most prevalent of these disorders is diabetes mellitus.

The disease **diabetes mellitus** is caused by a deficiency of insulin or a decreased response to insulin in target tissues. The blood glucose level rises, but cells are unable to take up enough glucose to meet metabolic needs. Instead, fat becomes the main substrate for cellular respiration.

> **Figure 41.21 Homeostatic regulation of cellular fuel.** After a meal is digested, glucose and other monomers are absorbed into the blood from the digestive tract. The human body regulates the use and storage of glucose, a major cellular fuel.

**MAKE CONNECTIONS** ➤ *What form of feedback control does each of these regulatory circuits reflect (see Concept 40.2)?*

 BioFlix® Animation: Homeostasis: Regulating Blood Sugar
Animation: Pancreatic Hormones Regulate Blood Glucose Level

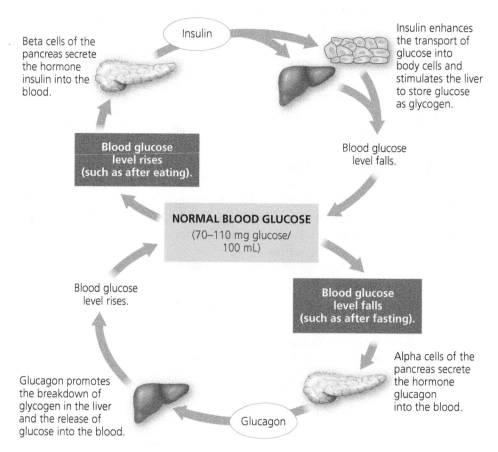

Beta cells of the pancreas secrete the hormone insulin into the blood.

Insulin

Insulin enhances the transport of glucose into body cells and stimulates the liver to store glucose as glycogen.

Blood glucose level rises (such as after eating).

Blood glucose level falls.

**NORMAL BLOOD GLUCOSE**
(70–110 mg glucose/
100 mL)

Blood glucose level rises.

Blood glucose level falls (such as after fasting).

Glucagon promotes the breakdown of glycogen in the liver and the release of glucose into the blood.

Glucagon

Alpha cells of the pancreas secrete the hormone glucagon into the blood.

In severe cases, acidic metabolites formed during fat breakdown accumulate in the blood, threatening life by lowering blood pH and depleting sodium and potassium ions from the body.

In people with diabetes mellitus, the level of glucose in the blood may exceed the capacity of the kidneys to reabsorb this nutrient. Glucose that remains in the kidney filtrate is excreted. For this reason, the presence of sugar in urine is one test for this disorder. As glucose is concentrated in the urine, more water is excreted along with it, resulting in excessive volumes of urine. *Diabetes* (from the Greek *diabainein*, to pass through) refers to this copious urination, and *mellitus* (from the Greek *meli*, honey) refers to the presence of sugar in urine.

There are two main types of diabetes mellitus: type 1 and type 2. Each is marked by high blood glucose levels, but with very different causes.

**Type 1 Diabetes** Also called insulin-dependent diabetes, *type 1 diabetes* is an autoimmune disorder in which the immune system destroys the beta cells of the pancreas. Type 1 diabetes, which usually appears during childhood, destroys the person's ability to produce insulin. Treatment consists of insulin injections, typically given several times daily. In the past, insulin was extracted from animal pancreases, but now human insulin can be obtained from genetically engineered bacteria, a relatively inexpensive source (see Figure 20.2). Stem cell research may someday provide a cure for type 1 diabetes by generating replacement beta cells that restore insulin production by the pancreas.

**Type 2 Diabetes** Non-insulin-dependent diabetes, or *type 2 diabetes,* is characterized by a failure of target cells to respond normally to insulin. Insulin is produced, but target cells fail to take up glucose from the blood, and blood glucose levels remain elevated. Although heredity can play a role in type 2 diabetes, excess body weight and lack of exercise significantly increase the risk of developing this disorder. This form of diabetes generally appears after age 40, but even children can develop the disease, particularly if they are overweight and sedentary. More than 90% of people with diabetes have type 2. Many can control their blood glucose levels with regular exercise and a healthy diet; some require medications. Nevertheless, type 2 diabetes is the seventh most common cause of death in the United States and a growing public health problem worldwide.

The resistance to insulin signaling in type 2 diabetes is sometimes due to a genetic defect in the insulin receptor or the insulin response pathway. In many cases, however, events in target cells suppress activity of an otherwise functional response pathway. One source of this suppression appears to be inflammatory signals generated by the innate immune system (see Concept 43.1). How obesity and inactivity relate to this suppression is being studied in both humans and laboratory animals.

 BioFlix® Animation: Diabetes

## Regulation of Appetite and Consumption

Consuming more calories than the body needs for normal metabolism, or *overnourishment*, can lead to obesity, the excessive accumulation of fat. Obesity, in turn, contributes to a number of health problems, including type 2 diabetes, cancer of the colon and breast, and cardiovascular disease that can result in heart attacks and strokes. It is estimated that obesity is a factor in 300,000 deaths per year in the United States alone.

Researchers have discovered several homeostatic mechanisms that operate as feedback circuits controlling the storage and metabolism of fat. A network of neurons relays and integrates information from the digestive system to regulate secretion of hormones that regulate long-term and short-term appetite. The target for these hormones is a "satiety center" in the brain **(Figure 41.22)**. For example, *ghrelin*, a hormone

▼ **Figure 41.22 A few of the appetite-regulating hormones.** Secreted by various organs and tissues, the hormones reach the brain via the bloodstream. These signals act on a region of the brain that in turn controls the "satiety center," which generates the nervous impulses that make us feel either hungry or satiated ("full"). The hormone ghrelin is an appetite stimulant; the other three hormones shown here are appetite suppressants.

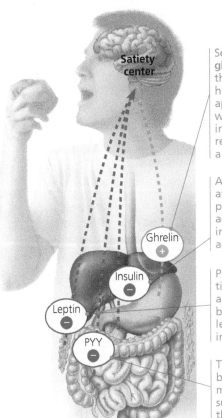

Secreted by the stomach wall, **ghrelin** is one of the signals that triggers feelings of hunger as mealtimes approach. In dieters who lose weight, ghrelin levels increase, which may be one reason it's so hard to stay on a diet.

A rise in blood sugar level after a meal stimulates the pancreas to secrete **insulin**. In addition to its other functions, insulin suppresses appetite by acting on the brain.

Produced by adipose (fat) tissue, **leptin** suppresses appetite. When the amount of body fat decreases, leptin levels fall, and appetite increases.

The hormone **PYY**, secreted by the small intestine after meals, acts as an appetite suppressant that counters the appetite stimulant ghrelin.

# Interpreting Data from Experiments with Genetic Mutants

**What Are the Roles of the *ob* and *db* Genes in Appetite Regulation?** A mutation that disrupts a physiological process is often used to study the normal function of the mutated gene. Ideally, researchers use a standard set of conditions and compare animals that differ genetically only in whether a particular gene is mutant (nonfunctional) or wild-type (normal). In this way, a difference in phenotype, the physiological property being measured, can be attributed to a difference in genotype, the presence or absence of the mutation. To study the role of specific genes in regulating appetite, researchers used laboratory animals with known mutations in those genes.

Mice in which recessive mutations inactivate both copies of either the *ob* gene or the *db* gene eat voraciously and grow much more massive than wild-type mice. In the photograph below, the mouse on the right is wild-type, whereas the obese mouse on the left has an inactivating mutation in both copies of the *ob* gene.

One hypothesis for the normal role of the *ob* and *db* genes is that they participate in a hormone pathway that suppresses appetite when caloric intake is sufficient. Before setting out to isolate the potential hormone, researchers explored this hypothesis genetically.

**How the Experiment Was Done** The researchers measured the mass of young subject mice of various genotypes and surgically linked the circulatory system of each one to that of another mouse. This procedure ensured that any factor circulating in the bloodstream of either mouse would be transferred to the other in the pair. After eight weeks, they again measured the mass of each subject mouse.

### Data from the Experiment

| | Genotype Pairing (red type indicates mutant genes) | | Average Change in Body Mass of Subject (g) |
|---|---|---|---|
| | **Subject** | **Paired with** | |
| (a) | *ob⁺/ob⁺, db⁺/db⁺* | *ob⁺/ob⁺, db⁺/db⁺* | 8.3 |
| (b) | *ob/ob, db⁺/db⁺* | *ob/ob, db⁺/db⁺* | 38.7 |
| (c) | *ob/ob, db⁺/db⁺* | *ob⁺/ob⁺, db⁺/db⁺* | 8.2 |
| (d) | *ob/ob, db⁺/db⁺* | *ob⁺/ob⁺, db/db* | −14.9* |

*Due to pronounced weight loss and weakening, subjects in this pairing were remeasured after less than eight weeks.

**Data from** D. L. Coleman, Effects of parabiosis of obese mice with diabetes and normal mice, *Diabetologia* 9:294–298 (1973).

### INTERPRET THE DATA

1. First, practice reading the genotype information given in the data table. For example, pairing (a) joined two mice that each had the wild-type version of both genes. Describe the two mice in pairing (b), pairing (c), and pairing (d). Explain how each pairing contributed to the experimental design.

2. Compare the results observed for pairing (a) and pairing (b) in terms of phenotype. If the results had been identical for these two pairings, what would that outcome have implied about the experimental design?

3. Compare the results observed for pairing (c) to those observed for pairing (b). Based on these results, does the *ob⁺* gene product appear to promote or suppress appetite? Explain your answer.

4. Describe the results observed for pairing (d). Note how these results differ from those for pairing (b). Suggest a hypothesis to explain this difference. How could you test your hypothesis using the kinds of mice in this study?

 **Instructors:** A version of this Scientific Skills Exercise can be assigned in MasteringBiology.

---

secreted by the stomach wall, triggers feelings of hunger before meals. In contrast, both insulin and *PYY*, a hormone secreted by the small intestine after meals, suppress appetite. *Leptin*, a hormone produced by adipose (fat) tissue, also suppresses appetite and appears to play a major role in regulating body fat levels. In the **Scientific Skills Exercise**, you'll interpret data from an experiment studying genes that affect leptin production and function in mice.

Obtaining food, digesting it, and absorbing nutrients are part of the larger story of how animals fuel their activities. Provisioning the body also involves distributing nutrients (circulation), and using nutrients for metabolism requires exchanging respiratory gases with the environment. These processes and the adaptations that facilitate such distribution and exchange are the focus of Chapter 42.

## CONCEPT CHECK 41.5

1. Explain how people can become obese even if their intake of dietary fat is relatively low compared with carbohydrate intake.

2. **WHAT IF?** ➤ Suppose you were studying two groups of obese people with genetic abnormalities in the leptin pathway. In one group, the leptin levels are abnormally high; in the other group, they are abnormally low. How would each group's leptin levels change if they ate a low-calorie diet for an extended period? Explain.

3. **WHAT IF?** ➤ An insulinoma is a cancerous mass of pancreatic beta cells that secrete insulin but do not respond to feedback mechanisms. How you would expect an insulinoma to affect blood glucose levels and liver activity?

*For suggested answers, see Appendix A.*

Go to **MasteringBiology**™ for Videos, Animations, Vocab Self-Quiz, Practice Tests, and more in the Study Area.

## SUMMARY OF KEY CONCEPTS

- Animals have diverse diets. **Herbivores** mainly eat plants; **carnivores** mainly eat other animals; and **omnivores** eat both. Animals must balance consumption, storage, and use of food.

**VOCAB SELF-QUIZ** goo.gl/6u55ks

### CONCEPT 41.1

**An animal's diet must supply chemical energy, organic building blocks, and essential nutrients** (pp. 897–900)

- Food provides animals with energy for ATP production, carbon skeletons for biosynthesis, and **essential nutrients**—nutrients that must be supplied in preassembled form. Essential nutrients include certain amino acids and fatty acids that animals cannot synthesize; **vitamins**, which are organic molecules; and **minerals**, which are inorganic substances.
- Malnutrition results from an inadequate intake of essential nutrients or a deficiency in sources of chemical energy. Studies of disease at the population level help researchers determine human dietary requirements.

**?** *How can an enzyme cofactor needed for an essential process be an essential nutrient for only some animals?*

### CONCEPT 41.2

**Food processing involves ingestion, digestion, absorption, and elimination** (pp. 900–903)

- Animals differ in the ways they obtain and ingest food. Many animals are **bulk feeders**, eating large pieces of food. Other strategies include **filter feeding**, **substrate feeding**, and **fluid feeding**.
- Compartmentalization is necessary to avoid self-digestion. In intracellular digestion, food particles are engulfed by phagocytosis and digested within food vacuoles that have fused with lysosomes. In extracellular digestion, which is used by most animals, enzymatic hydrolysis occurs outside cells in a **gastrovascular cavity** or **alimentary canal**.

**?** *Propose an artificial diet that would eliminate the need for one of the first three steps in food processing.*

### CONCEPT 41.3

**Organs specialized for sequential stages of food processing form the mammalian digestive system** (pp. 903–909)

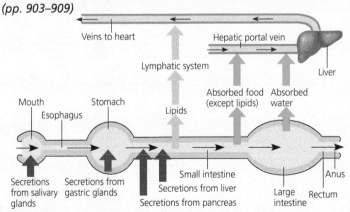

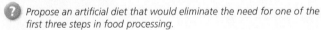

**?** *What structural feature of the small intestine makes it better suited for absorption of nutrients than the stomach?*

### CONCEPT 41.4

**Evolutionary adaptations of vertebrate digestive systems correlate with diet** (pp. 909–912)

- Vertebrate digestive systems display many evolutionary adaptations associated with diet. For example, the assortment of teeth (dentition) generally correlates with diet. Also, many herbivores have fermentation chambers where mutualistic microorganisms digest cellulose. In addition, herbivores usually have longer alimentary canals than carnivores, reflecting the longer time needed to digest vegetation.

**?** *How does human anatomy indicate that our primate ancestors were not strict vegetarians?*

### CONCEPT 41.5

**Feedback circuits regulate digestion, energy storage, and appetite** (pp. 912–916)

- Nutrition is regulated at multiple levels. Food intake triggers nervous and hormonal responses that cause secretion of digestive juices and promote movement of ingested material through the canal. The hormones **insulin** and **glucagon** control the synthesis and breakdown of glycogen, thereby regulating glucose availability.
- Vertebrates store excess calories in glycogen (in liver and muscle cells) and in fat (in adipose cells). These energy stores can be tapped when an animal expends more calories than it consumes. If, however, an animal consumes more calories than it needs for normal metabolism, the resulting overnourishment can cause obesity.
- Several hormones, including leptin and insulin, regulate appetite by affecting the brain's satiety center.

**?** *Explain why your stomach might make growling noises when you skip a meal.*

## TEST YOUR UNDERSTANDING

### Level 1: Knowledge/Comprehension

**PRACTICE TEST** goo.gl/CUYGKD

1. Fat digestion yields fatty acids and glycerol. Protein digestion yields amino acids. Both digestive processes
   (A) occur inside cells in most animals.
   (B) add a water molecule to break bonds.
   (C) require a low pH resulting from HCl production.
   (D) consume ATP.

2. The mammalian trachea and esophagus both connect to the
   (A) pharynx.      (C) large intestine.
   (B) stomach.      (D) rectum.

3. Which of the following organs is *incorrectly* paired with its function?
   (A) stomach—protein digestion
   (B) large intestine—bile production
   (C) small intestine—nutrient absorption
   (D) pancreas—enzyme production

4. Which of the following is *not* a major activity of the stomach?
   (A) storage
   (B) HCl production
   (C) nutrient absorption
   (D) enzyme secretion

## Level 2: Application/Analysis

5. If you put the following events in the order they occur in the human digestive system, the third event in the series would be
   (A) Cells in gastric pits secrete protons.
   (B) Pepsin activates pepsinogen.
   (C) HCl activates pepsinogen.
   (D) Partially digested food enters the small intestine.

6. After surgical removal of the gallbladder, a person might need to limit his or her dietary intake of
   (A) starch.
   (B) protein.
   (C) sugar.
   (D) fat.

7. If you were to jog 1 km a few hours after lunch, which stored fuel would you probably tap?
   (A) muscle proteins
   (B) muscle and liver glycogen
   (C) fat in the liver
   (D) fat in adipose tissue

## Level 3: Synthesis/Evaluation

8. **DRAW IT** Create a flowchart to summarize the events that occur after partially digested food leaves the stomach. Use the following terms: bicarbonate secretion, circulation, decrease in acidity, increase in acidity, secretin secretion, signal detection. Next to each term, indicate the compartment(s) involved. You may use terms more than once.

9. **EVOLUTION CONNECTION** Lizards and snakes cannot breathe while chewing food because the connection between their external nostrils and their esophagus is in the mouth. In contrast, mammals can continue breathing through the nostrils while chewing food in the mouth. However, choking sometimes occurs when the paths of air and food cross each other. Thinking about the high oxygen demand of active endotherms, explain how the concept of descent with modification explains this "imperfect" anatomy of some amniotes (see Figure 34.2 to review vertebrate phylogeny).

10. **SCIENTIFIC INQUIRY** In human populations of northern European origin, the disorder called hemochromatosis causes excess iron uptake from food and affects one in 200 adults. Among adults, men are ten times as likely as women to suffer from iron overload. Taking into account the existence of a menstrual cycle in humans, propose a hypothesis that explains this difference.

11. **WRITE ABOUT A THEME: ORGANIZATION** Hair is largely made up of the protein keratin. In a short essay (100–150 words), explain why a shampoo containing protein cannot replace the protein in damaged hair.

12. **SYNTHESIZE YOUR KNOWLEDGE**

Hummingbirds are well adapted to obtain sugary nectar from flowers, but they use some of the energy obtained from nectar when they forage for insects or spiders, as this individual is doing. Explain why this foraging is necessary.

*For selected answers, see Appendix A.*

 For additional practice questions, check out the **Dynamic Study Modules** in MasteringBiology. You can use them to study on your smartphone, tablet, or computer anytime, anywhere!

# Circulation and Gas Exchange  42

▲ Figure 42.1 **How does a feathery fringe help this animal survive?**

## KEY CONCEPTS

**42.1** Circulatory systems link exchange surfaces with cells throughout the body

**42.2** Coordinated cycles of heart contraction drive double circulation in mammals

**42.3** Patterns of blood pressure and flow reflect the structure and arrangement of blood vessels

**42.4** Blood components function in exchange, transport, and defense

**42.5** Gas exchange occurs across specialized respiratory surfaces

**42.6** Breathing ventilates the lungs

**42.7** Adaptations for gas exchange include pigments that bind and transport gases

## Trading Places

The animal in **Figure 42.1** may look like a creature from a science fiction film, but it's actually an axolotl, a salamander native to shallow ponds in central Mexico. The feathery red appendages jutting out from the head of this albino adult are gills. Although external gills are uncommon in adult animals, for the axolotl they help carry out a process common to all organisms—the exchange of substances between body cells and the environment.

The transfer of substances between an axolotl or any other animal and its surroundings ultimately occurs at the cellular level. Required resources, such as nutrients and oxygen ($O_2$), enter the cytoplasm by crossing the plasma membrane. Waste products, such as carbon dioxide ($CO_2$), exit the cell by crossing the same membrane. Unicellular organisms exchange materials directly with the external environment. For most multicellular organisms, however, direct exchange between every cell and the environment is not possible. Instead, we and most other animals rely on specialized respiratory systems for exchange with the environment and on circulatory systems for transport of materials between sites of exchange and the rest of the body.

The reddish color and the branching structure of the axolotl's gills reflect the intimate association between exchange and transport. Tiny blood vessels lie close to the surface of each filament in the gills. Across this surface, there is a net movement

---

When you see this blue icon, log in to **MasteringBiology** and go to the Study Area for digital resources.

 Get Ready for This Chapter

of $O_2$ from the surrounding water into the blood and of $CO_2$ from the blood into the water. The short distances involved allow diffusion to be rapid. The axolotl's heart pumps the oxygen-rich blood from the gill filaments to all other tissues of the body. There, more short-range exchange occurs, involving nutrients and $O_2$ as well as $CO_2$ and other wastes.

Because internal transport and gas exchange are functionally related in most animals, not just axolotls, we'll discuss circulatory and respiratory systems together in this chapter. By considering examples of these systems from a range of species, we'll explore the common elements as well as the remarkable variation in form and organization. We'll also highlight the roles of circulatory and respiratory systems in homeostasis, the maintenance of internal balance (see Concept 40.2).

## CONCEPT 42.1

### Circulatory systems link exchange surfaces with cells throughout the body

The molecular trade that an animal carries out with its environment—gaining $O_2$ and nutrients while releasing $CO_2$ and other waste products—must ultimately involve every cell in the body. Small molecules in and around cells, including $O_2$ and $CO_2$, undergo **diffusion**, which is random thermal motion (see Concept 7.3). When there is a difference in concentration, such as between a cell and its immediate surroundings, diffusion can result in net movement. But such movement is very slow for distances of more than a few millimeters. That's because the time it takes for a substance to diffuse from one place to another is proportional to the *square* of the distance. For example, a quantity of glucose that takes 1 second to diffuse 100 μm will take 100 seconds to diffuse 1 mm and almost 3 hours to diffuse 1 cm.

Given that net movement by diffusion is rapid only over very small distances, how does each cell of an animal participate in exchange? Natural selection has resulted in two basic adaptations that permit effective exchange for all of an animal's cells.

One adaptation for efficient exchange is a simple body plan that places many or all cells in direct contact with the environment. Each cell can thus exchange materials directly with the surrounding medium. Such an arrangement is characteristic of certain invertebrates, including cnidarians and flatworms. Animals that lack a simple body plan display an alternative adaptation for efficient exchange: a circulatory system. Such systems move fluid between each cell's immediate surroundings and the body tissues. As a result, exchange with the environment and exchange with body tissues both occur over very short distances.

### Gastrovascular Cavities

Let's begin by looking at some animals whose body shapes put many of their cells into contact with their environment, enabling them to live without a distinct circulatory system. In hydras, jellies, and other cnidarians, a central **gastrovascular cavity** functions in the distribution of substances throughout the body, as well as in digestion (see Figure 41.6). An opening at one end connects the cavity to the surrounding water. In a hydra, thin branches of the gastrovascular cavity extend into the animal's tentacles. In jellies and some other cnidarians, the gastrovascular cavity has a much more elaborate branching pattern (Figure 42.2a).

In animals with a gastrovascular cavity, fluid bathes both the inner and outer tissue layers, facilitating exchange

▼ **Figure 42.2 Internal transport in gastrovascular cavities.**

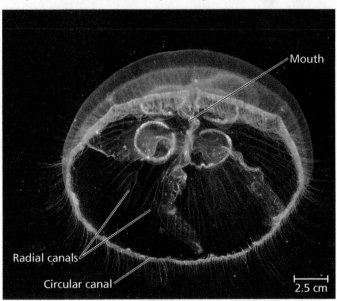

**(a) The moon jelly *Aurelia*, a cnidarian.** The jelly is viewed here from its underside (oral surface). The mouth leads to an elaborate gastrovascular cavity that consists of radial canals leading to and from a circular canal. Ciliated cells lining the canals circulate fluid within the cavity.

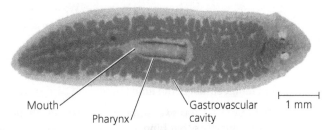

**(b) The planarian *Dugesia*, a flatworm.** The mouth and pharynx on the ventral side lead to the highly branched gastrovascular cavity, stained dark red in this specimen (LM).

**WHAT IF ➤** *Suppose a gastrovascular cavity were open at two ends, with fluid entering one end and leaving the other. How would this affect the cavity's functions in gas exchange and digestion?*

of gases and cellular waste. Only the cells lining the cavity have direct access to nutrients released by digestion. However, because the body wall is a mere two cells thick, nutrients only need to diffuse a short distance to reach the cells of the outer tissue layer.

Planarians and most other flatworms also survive without a circulatory system. Their combination of a gastrovascular cavity and a flat body is well suited for exchange with the environment **(Figure 42.2b)**. A flat body optimizes exchange by increasing surface area and minimizing diffusion distances.

## Open and Closed Circulatory Systems

A circulatory system has three basic components: a circulatory fluid, a set of interconnecting vessels, and a muscular pump, the **heart**. The heart powers circulation by using metabolic energy to elevate the circulatory fluid's hydrostatic pressure, the pressure the fluid exerts on surrounding vessels. The fluid then flows through the vessels and back to the heart.

By transporting fluid throughout the body, the circulatory system functionally connects the aqueous environment of the body cells to the organs that exchange gases, absorb nutrients, and dispose of wastes. In mammals, for example, $O_2$ from inhaled air diffuses across only two layers of cells in the lungs before reaching the blood. The circulatory system then carries the oxygen-rich blood to all parts of the body. As the blood passes throughout the body tissues in tiny blood vessels, $O_2$ in the blood diffuses only a short distance before entering the fluid that directly bathes the cells.

Circulatory systems are either open or closed. In an **open circulatory system**, the circulatory fluid, called **hemolymph**, is also the *interstitial fluid* that bathes body cells. Arthropods, such as grasshoppers, and some molluscs, including clams, have open circulatory systems. Contraction of the heart pumps the hemolymph through the circulatory vessels into interconnected sinuses, spaces surrounding the organs **(Figure 42.3a)**. Within the sinuses, the hemolymph and body cells exchange gases and other chemicals. Relaxation of the heart draws hemolymph back in through pores, which have valves that close when the heart contracts. Body movements periodically squeeze the sinuses, helping circulate the hemolymph. The open circulatory system of larger crustaceans, such as lobsters and crabs, includes a more extensive system of vessels as well as an accessory pump.

In a **closed circulatory system**, a circulatory fluid called **blood** is confined to vessels and is distinct from the interstitial fluid **(Figure 42.3b)**. One or more hearts pump blood into large vessels that branch into smaller ones that infiltrate the tissues and organs. Chemical exchange occurs between the blood and the interstitial fluid, as well as between the interstitial fluid and body cells. Annelids (including earthworms),

▼ **Figure 42.3 Open and closed circulatory systems.**

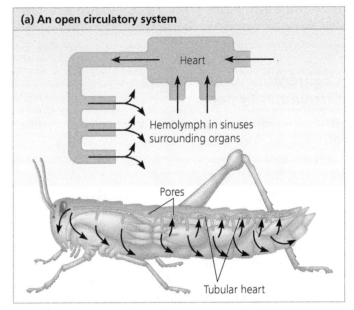

**(a) An open circulatory system**

Heart

Hemolymph in sinuses surrounding organs

Pores

Tubular heart

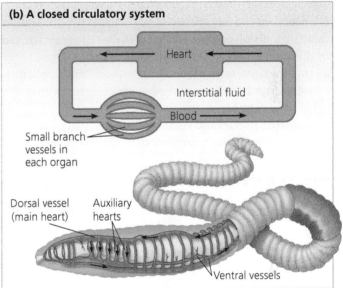

**(b) A closed circulatory system**

Heart

Interstitial fluid

Blood

Small branch vessels in each organ

Dorsal vessel (main heart)

Auxiliary hearts

Ventral vessels

cephalopods (including squids and octopuses), and all vertebrates have closed circulatory systems.

The fact that both open and closed circulatory systems are widespread among animals suggests that each system offers evolutionary advantages. The lower hydrostatic pressures typically associated with open circulatory systems allow them to use less energy than closed systems. In some invertebrates, open circulatory systems serve additional functions. For example, spiders use the hydrostatic pressure of their open circulatory system to extend their legs. The benefits of closed circulatory systems include blood pressure high enough to enable the effective delivery of $O_2$ and nutrients in larger and more active animals. Among the molluscs, for instance, closed circulatory systems are found in the largest and most active species, the squids and octopuses. Closed systems are also particularly well suited to regulating the distribution of blood to different organs, as you'll learn later in this chapter. We'll now examine closed circulatory systems in more detail, focusing on vertebrates.

## Organization of Vertebrate Circulatory Systems

The term **cardiovascular system** is often used to describe the heart and blood vessels in vertebrates. Blood circulates to and from the heart through an amazingly extensive network of vessels: The total length of blood vessels in an average human adult is twice Earth's circumference at the equator!

Arteries, veins, and capillaries are the three main types of blood vessels. Within each type, blood flows in only one direction. **Arteries** carry blood from the heart to organs throughout the body. Within organs, arteries branch into **arterioles**. These small vessels convey blood to **capillaries**, microscopic vessels with very thin, porous walls. Networks of capillaries, called **capillary beds**, infiltrate tissues, passing within a few cell diameters of every cell in the body. Across the thin walls of capillaries, dissolved gases and other chemicals are exchanged by diffusion between the blood and the interstitial fluid around the tissue cells. At their "downstream" end, capillaries converge into **venules**, and venules converge into **veins**, the vessels that carry blood back to the heart.

Note that arteries and veins are distinguished by the *direction* in which they carry blood, not by the $O_2$ content or other characteristics of the blood they contain. Arteries carry blood *away* from the heart toward capillaries, and veins return blood *toward* the heart from capillaries. The only exceptions are the portal veins, which carry blood between pairs of capillary beds. The hepatic portal vein, for example, carries blood from capillary beds in the digestive system to capillary beds in the liver.

The hearts of all vertebrates contain two or more muscular chambers. The chambers that receive blood entering the heart are called **atria** (singular, *atrium*). The chambers responsible for pumping blood out of the heart are called **ventricles**. The number of chambers and the extent to which they are separated from one another differ substantially among groups of vertebrates, as we'll discuss next. These important differences reflect the close fit of form to function that arises from natural selection.

### Single Circulation

In sharks, rays, and bony fishes, blood travels through the body and returns to its starting point in a single circuit (loop), an arrangement called **single circulation (Figure 42.4a)**. These animals have a heart that consists of two chambers: an atrium and a ventricle. Blood entering the heart collects in the atrium before transfer to the ventricle. Contraction of the ventricle pumps blood to a capillary bed in the gills, where there is a net diffusion of $O_2$ into the blood and of $CO_2$ out of the blood. As blood leaves the gills, the capillaries converge

▼ **Figure 42.4 Examples of vertebrate circulatory system organization.**

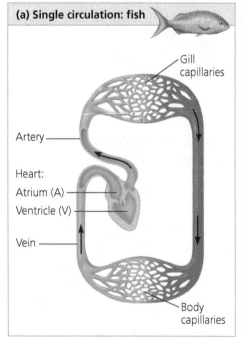

**(a) Single circulation: fish**

Gill capillaries

Artery

Heart:
Atrium (A)
Ventricle (V)

Vein

Body capillaries

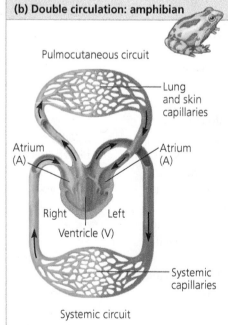

**(b) Double circulation: amphibian**

Pulmocutaneous circuit

Lung and skin capillaries

Atrium (A)

Atrium (A)

Right    Left
Ventricle (V)

Systemic capillaries

Systemic circuit

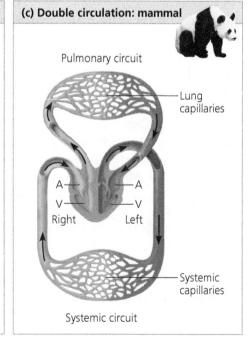

**(c) Double circulation: mammal**

Pulmonary circuit

Lung capillaries

A    A
V    V
Right    Left

Systemic capillaries

Systemic circuit

**Key**
■ Oxygen-rich blood
■ Oxygen-poor blood

(Note that circulatory systems are shown as if the body were facing you: The right side of the heart is shown on the left, and vice versa.)

into a vessel that carries oxygen-rich blood to capillary beds throughout the body. Following gas exchange in the capillary beds, blood enters veins and returns to the heart.

In single circulation, blood that leaves the heart passes through two capillary beds before returning to the heart. When blood flows through a capillary bed, blood pressure drops substantially, for reasons we'll explain later in the chapter. The drop in blood pressure in the gills limits the rate of blood flow in the rest of the animal's body. As the animal swims, however, the contraction and relaxation of its muscles help accelerate the relatively sluggish pace of circulation.

## Double Circulation

The circulatory systems of amphibians, reptiles, and mammals have two circuits of blood flow, an arrangement called **double circulation** (Figure 42.4b and c). In animals with double circulation, the pumps for the two circuits are combined into a single organ, the heart. Having both pumps within a single heart simplifies coordination of the pumping cycles.

In one circuit, the right side of the heart pumps oxygen-poor blood to the capillary beds of the gas exchange tissues, where there is a net movement of $O_2$ into the blood and of $CO_2$ out of the blood. In most vertebrates, including reptiles and mammals, this is called the *pulmonary circuit* (from the Latin *pulmo*, lung) because gas exchange takes place in the lungs. For many amphibians, it is called the *pulmocutaneous circuit* because gas exchange takes place in capillaries in both the lungs and the skin.

The other circuit, called the *systemic circuit*, begins with the left side of the heart pumping oxygen-enriched blood from the gas exchange tissues to capillary beds in organs and tissues throughout the body. Following the exchange of $O_2$ and $CO_2$, as well as nutrients and waste products, the now oxygen-poor blood returns to the heart, completing the circuit.

Double circulation provides a vigorous flow of blood to the brain, muscles, and other organs because the heart repressurizes the blood after it passes through the capillary beds of the lungs or skin. Indeed, blood pressure is often much higher in the systemic circuit than in the gas exchange circuit. By contrast, in single circulation the blood flows under reduced pressure directly from the gas exchange organs to other organs.

## Evolutionary Variation in Double Circulation

EVOLUTION  Some vertebrates with double circulation are intermittent breathers. For example, amphibians and many reptiles fill their lungs with air periodically, passing long periods either without gas exchange or by relying on another gas exchange tissue, typically the skin. A variety of adaptations found among intermittent breathers enable their circulatory systems to temporarily bypass the lungs in part or in whole:

- Frogs and other amphibians have a heart with three chambers—two atria and one ventricle (see Figure 42.4b). A ridge within the ventricle diverts most (about 90%) of the oxygen-rich blood from the left atrium into the systemic circuit and most of the oxygen-poor blood from the right atrium into the pulmocutaneous circuit. When a frog is underwater, it takes advantage of the incomplete division of the ventricle, largely shutting off blood flow to its temporarily ineffective lungs. Blood flow continues to the skin, which acts as the sole site of gas exchange while the frog is submerged.

- In the three-chambered heart of turtles, snakes, and lizards, an incomplete septum partially divides the single ventricle into right and left chambers. Two major arteries, called aortas, lead to the systemic circulation. As with amphibians, the circulatory system enables control of the relative amount of blood flowing to the lungs and the rest of the body.

- In alligators, caimans, and other crocodilians, the ventricles are divided by a complete septum, but the pulmonary and systemic circuits connect where the arteries exit the heart. This connection allows arterial valves to shunt blood flow away from the lungs temporarily, such as when the animal is underwater.

Double circulation in birds and mammals, which for the most part breathe continuously, differs from double circulation in other vertebrates. As shown for a panda in Figure 42.4c, the heart has two atria and two completely divided ventricles. The left side of the heart receives and pumps only oxygen-rich blood, while the right side receives and pumps only oxygen-poor blood. Unlike amphibians and many reptiles, birds and mammals cannot vary blood flow to the lungs without varying blood flow throughout the body in parallel.

How has natural selection shaped the double circulation of birds and mammals? As endotherms, they use about ten times as much energy as equal-sized ectotherms (see Concept 40.4). Their circulatory systems therefore need to deliver about ten times as much fuel and $O_2$ to their tissues and remove ten times as much $CO_2$ and other wastes. This large traffic of substances is made possible by the separate and independently powered systemic and pulmonary circuits and by large hearts. A powerful four-chambered heart arose independently in the distinct ancestors of birds and mammals and thus reflects convergent evolution (see Concept 22.3).

In the next section, we'll restrict our focus to circulation in mammals and to the anatomy and physiology of the key circulatory organ—the heart.

1. How is the flow of hemolymph through an open circulatory system similar to the flow of water through an outdoor fountain?

2. Three-chambered hearts with incomplete septa were once viewed as being less adapted to circulatory function than mammalian hearts. What advantage of such hearts did this viewpoint overlook?

3. **WHAT IF?** ➤ The heart of a normally developing human fetus has a hole between the left and right atria. In some cases, this hole does not close completely before birth. If the hole weren't surgically corrected, how would it affect the $O_2$ content of the blood entering the systemic circuit?

*For suggested answers, see Appendix A.*

# CONCEPT 42.2

## Coordinated cycles of heart contraction drive double circulation in mammals

The timely delivery of $O_2$ to the body's organs is critical. Some brain cells, for example, die if their $O_2$ supply is interrupted for even a few minutes. How does the mammalian cardiovascular system meet the body's continuous (although variable) demand for $O_2$? To answer this question, we must consider how the parts of the system are arranged and how each of these parts functions.

### Mammalian Circulation

Let's first examine the overall organization of the mammalian cardiovascular system, beginning with the pulmonary circuit. (The circled numbers refer to labeled structures in **Figure 42.5**.) Contraction of ❶ the right ventricle pumps blood to the lungs via ❷ the pulmonary arteries. As the blood flows through ❸ capillary beds in the left and right lungs, it loads $O_2$ and unloads $CO_2$. Oxygen-rich blood returns from the lungs via the pulmonary veins to ❹ the left atrium of the heart. Next, the oxygen-rich blood flows into ❺ the heart's left ventricle, which pumps the oxygen-rich blood out to body tissues through the systemic circuit. Blood leaves the left ventricle via ❻ the aorta, which conveys blood to arteries leading throughout the body. The first branches leading from the aorta are the coronary arteries (not shown), which supply blood to the heart muscle itself. Then branches lead to ❼ capillary beds in the head and arms (forelimbs). The aorta then descends into the abdomen, supplying oxygen-rich blood to arteries leading to ❽ capillary beds in the abdominal organs and legs (hind limbs). Within the capillaries, there is a net diffusion of $O_2$ from the blood to the tissues and of $CO_2$ (produced by cellular respiration) into the blood. Capillaries rejoin, forming venules, which convey blood to

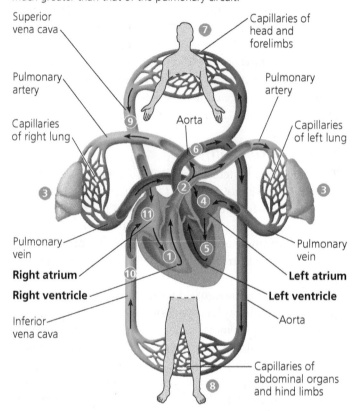

▼ **Figure 42.5** **The mammalian cardiovascular system: an overview.** Note that the dual circuits operate simultaneously, not in the serial fashion that the numbering in the diagram suggests. The two ventricles contract almost in unison and pump the same volume of blood. However, the total volume of the systemic circuit is much greater than that of the pulmonary circuit.

**VISUAL SKILLS** ➤ *If you trace the path of a molecule of carbon dioxide that starts in an arteriole in the right thumb and leaves the body in exhaled air, what is the minimum number of capillary beds the molecule encountered? Explain.*

**MB** Animation: The Human Heart and Circulation

veins. Oxygen-poor blood from the head, neck, and forelimbs is channeled into a large vein, ❾ the superior vena cava. Another large vein, ❿ the inferior vena cava, drains blood from the trunk and hind limbs. The two venae cavae empty their blood into ⓫ the right atrium, from which the oxygen-poor blood flows into the right ventricle.

### The Mammalian Heart: *A Closer Look*

Using the human heart as an example, let's now take a closer look at how the mammalian heart works (**Figure 42.6**). Located behind the sternum (breastbone), the human heart is about the size of a clenched fist and consists mostly of cardiac muscle (see Figure 40.5). The two atria have relatively thin walls and serve as collection chambers for blood returning to the heart from the lungs or other body tissues. Much of the blood that enters the atria flows into the ventricles while all four heart chambers are relaxed. The remainder is

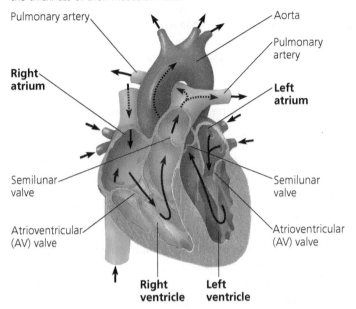

MB Animation: Structure of the Human Heart

▼ **Figure 42.7 The cardiac cycle.** For an adult human at rest with a heart rate of about 72 beats per minute, one complete cardiac cycle takes about 0.8 second. Note that during all but 0.1 second of the cardiac cycle, the atria are relaxed and are filling with blood returning via the veins.

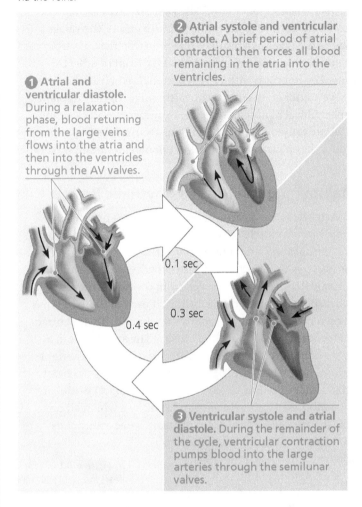

❶ **Atrial and ventricular diastole.** During a relaxation phase, blood returning from the large veins flows into the atria and then into the ventricles through the AV valves.

❷ **Atrial systole and ventricular diastole.** A brief period of atrial contraction then forces all blood remaining in the atria into the ventricles.

❸ **Ventricular systole and atrial diastole.** During the remainder of the cycle, ventricular contraction pumps blood into the large arteries through the semilunar valves.

transferred by contraction of the atria before the ventricles begin to contract. Compared with the atria, the ventricles have thicker walls and contract much more forcefully—especially the left ventricle, which pumps blood throughout the body via the systemic circuit. Although the left ventricle contracts with greater force than the right ventricle, it pumps the same volume of blood as the right ventricle during each contraction.

The heart contracts and relaxes in a rhythmic cycle. When it contracts, it pumps blood; when it relaxes, its chambers fill with blood. One complete sequence of pumping and filling is referred to as the **cardiac cycle**. The contraction phase of the cycle is called **systole**, and the relaxation phase is called **diastole (Figure 42.7).**

The volume of blood each ventricle pumps per minute is the **cardiac output**. Two factors determine cardiac output: the rate of contraction, or **heart rate** (number of beats per minute), and the **stroke volume**, the amount of blood pumped by a ventricle in a single contraction. The average stroke volume in humans is about 70 mL. Multiplying this stroke volume by a resting heart rate of 72 beats per minute yields a cardiac output of 5 L/min—about equal to the total volume of blood in the human body. During heavy exercise, the increased demand for $O_2$ is met by an increase in cardiac output that can be as much as fivefold.

Four valves in the heart prevent backflow and keep blood moving in the correct direction (see Figures 42.6 and 42.7). Made of flaps of connective tissue, the valves open when pushed from one side and close when pushed from the other. An **atrioventricular (AV) valve** lies between each atrium and ventricle. The AV valves are anchored by strong fibers that prevent them from turning inside out during ventricular systole. Pressure generated by the powerful contraction of the ventricles closes the AV valves, keeping blood from flowing back into the atria. **Semilunar valves** are located at the two exits of the heart: where the pulmonary artery leaves the right ventricle and where the aorta leaves the left ventricle. These valves are pushed open by the pressure generated during contraction of the ventricles. When the ventricles relax, blood pressure built up in the pulmonary artery and aorta closes the semilunar valves and prevents significant backflow.

You can follow the closing of the two sets of heart valves either with a stethoscope or by pressing your ear tightly against the chest of a friend (or a friendly dog). The sound pattern is "lub-dup, lub-dup, lub-dup." The first heart sound ("lub") is created by the recoil of blood against the closed AV valves. The second sound ("dup") is due to the vibrations caused by closing of the semilunar valves.

If blood squirts backward through a defective valve, it may produce an abnormal sound called a **heart murmur**. Some people are born with heart murmurs. In others, the valves may be damaged as a result of infection (for instance, from rheumatic fever, an inflammation of the heart or other tissues caused by infection with certain bacteria). When a valve defect is severe enough to endanger health, surgeons may implant a mechanical replacement valve. However, not all heart murmurs are caused by a defect, and most valve defects do not reduce the efficiency of blood flow enough to warrant surgery.

## Maintaining the Heart's Rhythmic Beat

In vertebrates, the heartbeat originates in the heart itself. Some cardiac muscle cells are autorhythmic, meaning they can contract and relax repeatedly without any signal from the nervous system. You can see these rhythmic contractions in tissue that has been removed from the heart and placed in a dish in the laboratory! Given that each of these cells has its own intrinsic contraction rhythm, how are their contractions coordinated in the intact heart? The answer lies in a group of autorhythmic cells located in the wall of the right atrium, near where the superior vena cava enters the heart. This cluster of cells is called the **sinoatrial (SA) node**, or *pacemaker*, and it sets the rate and timing at which all cardiac muscle cells contract. (In contrast, some arthropods have pacemakers located in the nervous system, outside the heart.)

The SA node produces electrical impulses much like those produced by nerve cells. Because cardiac muscle cells are electrically coupled through gap junctions (see Figure 6.30), impulses from the SA node spread rapidly within heart tissue. These impulses generate currents that can be measured when they reach the skin via body fluids. In an **electrocardiogram** (**ECG** or **EKG**, from the German spelling), electrodes placed on the skin record the currents, thus measuring electrical activity of the heart. The graph of current against time has a shape that represents the stages in the cardiac cycle (**Figure 42.8**).

Impulses from the SA node first spread rapidly through the walls of the atria, causing both atria to contract in unison. During atrial contraction, the impulses originating at the SA node

reach other autorhythmic cells located in the wall between the left and right atria. These cells form a relay point called the **atrioventricular (AV) node**. Here the impulses are delayed for about 0.1 second before spreading to the heart apex. This delay allows the atria to empty completely before the ventricles contract. Then the signals from the AV node are conducted to the heart apex and throughout the ventricular walls by specialized structures called bundle branches and Purkinje fibers.

Physiological cues alter heart tempo by regulating the pacemaker function of the SA node. Two portions of the nervous system, the sympathetic and parasympathetic divisions, are largely responsible for this regulation. They function like the accelerator and brake in a car. For example, when you stand up and start walking, the sympathetic division speeds up your pacemaker. The resulting increase in heart rate provides the additional $O_2$ needed by the muscles that are powering your activity. If you then sit down and relax, the parasympathetic division slows down your pacemaker, decreasing your heart rate and thus conserving energy. Hormones secreted into the blood also influence the pacemaker. For instance, epinephrine, the "fight-or-flight" hormone secreted by the adrenal glands, speeds up the pacemaker. A third type of input that affects the pacemaker is body temperature. An increase of only 1°C raises the heart rate by about 10 beats per minute. This is the reason your heart beats faster when you have a fever.

Having examined the operation of the circulatory pump, we turn in the next section to the forces and structures that influence blood flow in the vessels of each circuit.

▼ **Figure 42.8 The control of heart rhythm.** Electrical signals follow a set path through the heart in establishing the heart rhythm. The diagrams at the top trace the movement of these signals (yellow) during the cardiac cycle; specialized muscle cells involved in controlling of the rhythm are indicated in orange. Under each step, the corresponding portion of an electrocardiogram (ECG) is highlighted (yellow). In step 4, the portion of the ECG to the right of the "spike" represents electrical activity that reprimes the ventricles for the next round of contraction.

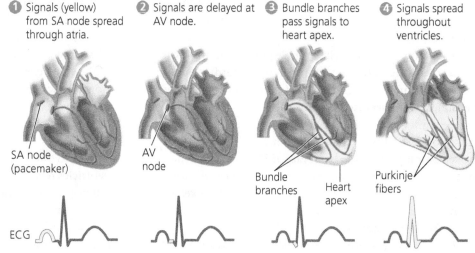

1. Signals (yellow) from SA node spread through atria.
2. Signals are delayed at AV node.
3. Bundle branches pass signals to heart apex.
4. Signals spread throughout ventricles.

SA node (pacemaker)

AV node

Bundle branches    Heart apex

Purkinje fibers

ECG

**WHAT IF?** ▶ *If your doctor gave you a copy of your ECG recording, how could you determine what your heart rate had been during the test?*

1. Explain why blood has a higher $O_2$ concentration in the pulmonary veins than in the venae cavae, which are also veins.

2. Why is it important that the AV node delay the electrical impulse moving from the SA node and the atria to the ventricles?

3. **WHAT IF?** ➤ Suppose that after you exercise regularly for several months, your resting heart rate decreases, but your cardiac output at rest is unchanged. Based on these observations, what other change in the function of your heart at rest likely occurred?

*For suggested answers, see Appendix A.*

# CONCEPT 42.3

## Patterns of blood pressure and flow reflect the structure and arrangement of blood vessels

To deliver oxygen and nutrients and remove wastes throughout the body, the vertebrate circulatory system relies on blood vessels that exhibit a close match of structure and function.

## Blood Vessel Structure and Function

All blood vessels contain a central lumen (cavity) lined with an **endothelium**, a single layer of flattened epithelial cells. Like the polished surface of a copper pipe, the smooth endothelial layer minimizes resistance to fluid flow. Surrounding the endothelium are tissue layers that differ among capillaries, arteries, and veins, reflecting distinct adaptations to the particular functions of these vessels **(Figure 42.9)**.

Capillaries are the smallest blood vessels, having a diameter only slightly greater than that of a red blood cell. Capillaries also have very thin walls, which consist of just an endothelium and a surrounding extracellular layer called the *basal lamina*. The exchange of substances between the blood and interstitial fluid occurs only in capillaries because only there are the vessel walls thin enough to permit this exchange.

In contrast to capillaries, both arteries and veins have walls that consist of two layers of tissue surrounding the endothelium. The outer layer is formed

by connective tissue that contains elastic fibers, which allow the vessel to stretch and recoil, and collagen, which provides strength. The layer next to the endothelium contains smooth muscle and more elastic fibers.

Arterial walls are thick, strong, and elastic. They can thus accommodate blood pumped at high pressure by the heart, bulging outward as blood enters and recoiling as the heart relaxes between contractions. As we'll discuss shortly, this behavior of arterial walls has an essential role in maintaining blood pressure and flow to capillaries.

The smooth muscles in the walls of arteries and arterioles help regulate the path of blood flow. Signals from the nervous system and circulating hormones act on the smooth muscle of these vessels, causing dilation or constriction that modulates blood flow to different parts of the body.

Because veins convey blood back to the heart at a lower pressure, they do not require thick walls. For a given blood vessel diameter, a vein has a wall only about a third as thick as that of an artery. Unlike arteries, veins contain valves,

▼ **Figure 42.9 The structure of blood vessels.**

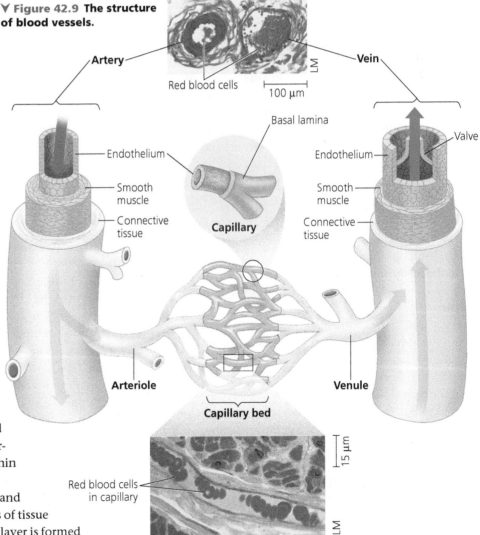

which maintain a unidirectional flow of blood despite the low blood pressure in these vessels.

We consider next how blood vessel diameter, vessel number, and blood pressure influence the speed at which blood flows in different locations within the body.

## Blood Flow Velocity

To understand how blood vessel diameter influences blood flow, consider how water flows through a thick-walled hose connected to a faucet. When the faucet is turned on, water flows at the same velocity at each point along the hose. What happens when a narrow nozzle is attached to the end of the hose? Because water doesn't compress under pressure, the volume of water moving through the nozzle in a given time must be the same as the volume moving through the rest of the hose. The cross-sectional area of the nozzle is smaller than that of the hose, so the water speeds up, exiting the nozzle at high velocity.

An analogous situation exists in the circulatory system, but blood *slows* as it moves from arteries to arterioles to the much narrower capillaries. Why? The number of capillaries is enormous, roughly 7 billion in a human body. Each artery conveys blood to so many capillaries that the *total* cross-sectional area is much greater in capillary beds than in the arteries or any other part of the circulatory system **(Figure 42.10)**. This enormous increase in cross-sectional area results in a dramatic decrease in velocity from the arteries to the capillaries: Blood travels 500 times more slowly in the capillaries (about 0.1 cm/sec) than in the aorta (about 48 cm/sec). After passing through the capillaries, the blood speeds up as it enters the venules and veins, which have smaller *total* cross-sectional areas.

## Blood Pressure

Blood, like all fluids, flows from areas of higher pressure to areas of lower pressure. Contraction of a heart ventricle generates blood pressure, which exerts a force in all directions. The part of the force directed lengthwise in an artery causes the blood to flow away from the heart, the site of highest pressure. The part of the force exerted sideways stretches the wall of the artery. Following ventricular contraction, the recoil of the elastic arterial walls plays a critical role in maintaining blood pressure, and hence blood flow, throughout the cardiac cycle. Once the blood enters the millions of tiny arterioles and capillaries, the narrow diameter of these vessels generates substantial resistance to flow. By the time the blood enters the veins, this resistance has dissipated much of the pressure generated by the pumping heart (see Figure 42.10).

### Changes in Blood Pressure During the Cardiac Cycle

Arterial blood pressure is highest when the heart contracts during ventricular systole. The pressure at this time is called

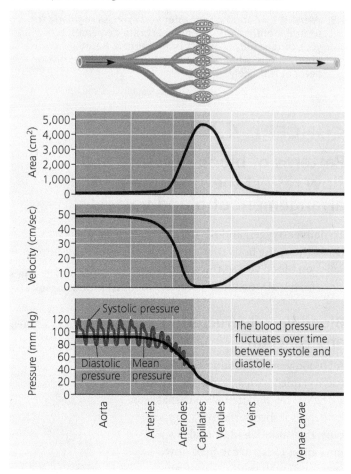

▼ **Figure 42.10 The interrelationship of cross-sectional area of blood vessels, blood flow velocity, and blood pressure.** As a result of an increase in total cross-sectional area, blood flow velocity decreases markedly in the arterioles and is lowest in the capillaries. Blood pressure, the main force driving blood from the heart to the capillaries, is highest in the aorta and other arteries.

**systolic pressure** (see Figure 42.10). Each ventricular contraction causes a spike in blood pressure that stretches the walls of the arteries. You can feel this **pulse**—the rhythmic bulging of the artery walls with each heartbeat—by placing the tips of your fingers on the inside of the opposite wrist. The pressure surge is partly due to the narrow openings of arterioles impeding the exit of blood from the arteries. When the heart contracts, blood enters the arteries faster than it can leave, and the vessels stretch to a wider diameter from the rise in pressure.

During diastole, the elastic walls of the arteries snap back. As a consequence, there is a lower but still substantial blood pressure when the ventricles are relaxed (**diastolic pressure**). Before enough blood has flowed into the arterioles to completely relieve pressure in the arteries, the heart contracts again. Because the arteries remain pressurized throughout the cardiac cycle (see Figure 42.10), blood continuously flows into arterioles and capillaries.

## Regulation of Blood Pressure

Homeostatic mechanisms regulate arterial blood pressure by altering the diameter of arterioles. If the smooth muscles in arteriole walls contract, the arterioles narrow, a process called **vasoconstriction**. Vasoconstriction increases blood pressure upstream in the arteries. When the smooth muscles relax, the arterioles undergo **vasodilation**, an increase in diameter that causes blood pressure in the arteries to fall.

Researchers have identified nitric oxide (NO), a gas, as a major inducer of vasodilation and endothelin, a peptide, as the most potent inducer of vasoconstriction. Cues from the nervous and endocrine systems regulate production of NO and endothelin in blood vessels, where their opposing activities provide homeostatic regulation of blood pressure.

Vasoconstriction and vasodilation are often coupled to changes in cardiac output that also affect blood pressure. This coordination of regulatory mechanisms maintains adequate blood flow as the body's demands on the circulatory system change. During heavy exercise, for example, the arterioles in working muscles dilate, causing a greater flow of oxygen-rich blood to the muscles. By itself, this increased flow to the muscles would cause a drop in blood pressure (and therefore blood flow) in the body as a whole. However, cardiac output increases at the same time, maintaining blood pressure and supporting the necessary increase in blood flow.

Interview with Masashi Yanagisawa: Discovering the key inducer of vasoconstriction

## Blood Pressure and Gravity

Blood pressure is generally measured for an artery in the arm at the same height as the heart (**Figure 42.11**). For a healthy 20-year-old human at rest, arterial blood pressure in the systemic circuit is typically about 120 millimeters of mercury (mm Hg) at systole and 70 mm Hg at diastole, expressed as 120/70. (Arterial blood pressure in the pulmonary circuit is six to ten times lower.)

Gravity has a significant effect on blood pressure. When you are standing, for example, your head is roughly 0.35 m higher than your chest, and the arterial blood pressure in your brain is about 27 mm Hg less than that near your heart. This relationship of blood pressure and gravity is the key to understanding fainting. The fainting response is triggered when the nervous system detects that the blood pressure in your brain is below the level needed to

provide adequate blood flow. By causing your body to collapse to the ground, fainting effectively places your head at the level of your heart, quickly increasing blood flow to your brain.

For animals with very long necks, the blood pressure required to overcome gravity is particularly high. A giraffe, for example, requires a systolic pressure of more than 250 mm Hg near the heart to get blood to its head. When a giraffe lowers its head to drink, one-way valves and sinuses, along with feedback mechanisms that reduce cardiac output, reduce blood pressure in the head, preventing brain damage. A dinosaur with a neck nearly 10 m long would have required even greater systolic pressure—nearly 760 mm Hg—to pump blood to its brain when its head was fully raised. However, calculations based on anatomy and inferred metabolic rate suggest that dinosaurs did not have a heart powerful enough to generate such high pressure. Based on this evidence as well as studies of neck bone structure, some biologists have concluded that the long-necked dinosaurs fed close to the ground rather than on high foliage.

Gravity is also a consideration for blood flow in veins, especially those in the legs. When you stand or sit, gravity draws blood downward to your feet and impedes its upward return to the heart. Because blood pressure in veins is relatively low, valves inside the veins have an important function in maintaining the unidirectional flow of blood within these vessels. The return of blood to the heart is further enhanced by rhythmic contractions of smooth muscles in the walls of venules

▼ **Figure 42.11 Measurement of blood pressure.** Blood pressure is recorded as two numbers separated by a slash. The first number is the systolic pressure; the second is the diastolic pressure.

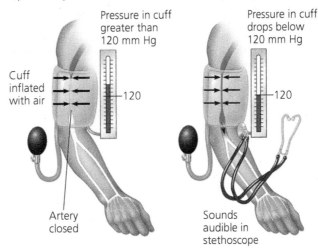
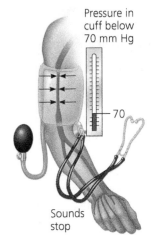
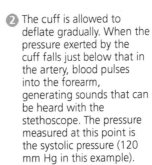

Pressure in cuff greater than 120 mm Hg

Cuff inflated with air

Artery closed

Pressure in cuff drops below 120 mm Hg

Sounds audible in stethoscope

Pressure in cuff below 70 mm Hg

Sounds stop

❶ A sphygmomanometer, an inflatable cuff attached to a pressure gauge, measures blood pressure in an artery. The cuff is inflated until the pressure closes the artery, so that no blood flows past the cuff. When this occurs, the pressure exerted by the cuff exceeds the pressure in the artery.

❷ The cuff is allowed to deflate gradually. When the pressure exerted by the cuff falls just below that in the artery, blood pulses into the forearm, generating sounds that can be heard with the stethoscope. The pressure measured at this point is the systolic pressure (120 mm Hg in this example).

❸ The cuff is allowed to deflate further, just until the blood flows freely through the artery and the sounds below the cuff disappear. The pressure at this point is the diastolic pressure (70 mm Hg in this example).

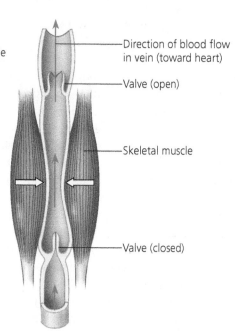

**▶ Figure 42.12**
**Blood flow in veins.** Skeletal muscle contraction squeezes and constricts veins. Flaps of tissue within the veins act as one-way valves that keep blood moving only toward the heart. If you sit or stand too long, the lack of muscular activity may cause your feet to swell as blood pools in your veins.

Direction of blood flow in vein (toward heart)

Valve (open)

Skeletal muscle

Valve (closed)

and veins and by the contraction of skeletal muscles during exercise (Figure 42.12).

In rare instances, runners and other athletes can suffer heart failure if they stop vigorous exercise abruptly. When the leg muscles suddenly cease contracting and relaxing, less blood returns to the heart, which continues to beat rapidly. If the heart is weak or damaged, this inadequate blood flow may cause the heart to malfunction. To reduce the risk of stressing the heart excessively, athletes are encouraged to follow hard exercise with moderate activity, such as walking, to "cool down" until their heart rate approaches its resting level.

## Capillary Function

At any given time, only about 5–10% of the body's capillaries have blood flowing through them. However, each tissue has many capillaries, so every part of the body is supplied with blood at all times. Capillaries in the brain, heart, kidneys, and liver are usually filled to capacity, but at many other sites the blood supply varies over time as blood is diverted from one destination to another. For example, blood flow to the skin is regulated to help control body temperature, and blood supply to the digestive tract increases after a meal. In contrast, blood is diverted from the digestive tract and supplied more generously to skeletal muscles and skin during strenuous exercise.

Given that capillaries lack smooth muscle, how is blood flow in capillary beds altered? One mechanism is constriction or dilation of the arterioles that supply capillary beds. A second mechanism involves precapillary sphincters, rings of smooth muscle located at the entrance to capillary beds (Figure 42.13). The opening and closing of these muscular rings regulates and redirects the passage of blood into particular sets of capillaries. The signals regulating blood flow by these mechanisms include nerve impulses, hormones traveling throughout the bloodstream, and chemicals produced

locally. For example, the chemical histamine released by cells at a wound site causes vasodilation. The result is increased blood flow and increased access of disease-fighting white blood cells to invading microorganisms.

As you have read, the critical exchange of substances between the blood and interstitial fluid takes place across the thin endothelial walls of the capillaries. How does exchange occur? A few macromolecules are carried across the endothelium in vesicles that form on one side by endocytosis and release their contents on the opposite side by exocytosis. Small molecules, such as $O_2$ and $CO_2$, simply diffuse across the endothelial cells or, in some tissues, through microscopic pores in the capillary wall. These openings also provide the route for transport of small solutes such as sugars, salts, and urea, as well as for bulk flow of fluid into tissues driven by blood pressure within the capillary.

Two opposing forces control the movement of fluid between the capillaries and the surrounding tissues: Blood pressure tends to drive fluid out of the capillaries, and the presence of blood

**▼ Figure 42.13 Blood flow in capillary beds.** Precapillary sphincters regulate the passage of blood into capillary beds. Some blood flows directly from arterioles to venules through capillaries called thoroughfare channels, which are always open.

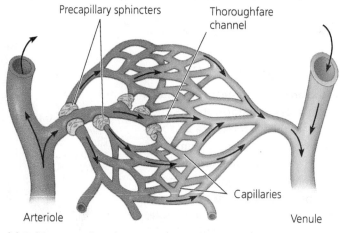

Precapillary sphincters

Thoroughfare channel

Capillaries

Arteriole

Venule

**(a) Sphincters relaxed**

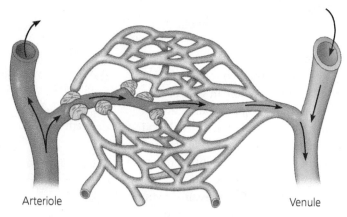

Arteriole

Venule

**(b) Sphincters contracted**

**▼ Figure 42.14 Fluid exchange between capillaries and the interstitial fluid.** This diagram shows a hypothetical capillary in which blood pressure exceeds osmotic pressure throughout the entire length of the capillary. In other capillaries, blood pressure may be lower than osmotic pressure along all or part of the capillary.

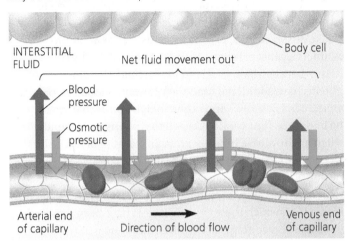

**▼ Figure 42.15 The close association of lymphatic vessels and blood capillaries.**

Fluid and proteins leak from the blood capillaries into the interstitial fluid.

Lymphatic vessels recover leaked fluid and proteins, carrying them to large veins at the base of the neck.

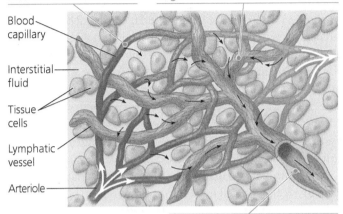

Valves in larger lymphatic vessels prevent the backflow of fluid.

proteins tends to pull fluid back **(Figure 42.14)**. Many blood proteins (and all blood cells) are too large to pass readily through the endothelium, so they remain in the capillaries. These dissolved proteins are responsible for much of the blood's *osmotic pressure* (the pressure produced by the difference in solute concentration across a membrane). The difference in osmotic pressure between the blood and the interstitial fluid opposes fluid movement out of the capillaries. On average, blood pressure is greater than the opposing forces, leading to a net loss of fluid from capillaries. The net loss is generally greatest at the arterial end of these vessels, where blood pressure is highest.

## Fluid Return by the Lymphatic System

Each day the adult human body loses approximately 4–8 L of fluid from capillaries to the surrounding tissues. There is also some leakage of blood proteins, even though the capillary wall is not very permeable to large molecules. The lost fluid and the proteins within it are recovered and returned to the blood via the **lymphatic system** (see Figure 43.6).

Fluid diffuses into the lymphatic system via a network of tiny vessels intermingled with capillaries **(Figure 42.15)**. The recovered fluid, called **lymph**, circulates within the lymphatic system before draining into a pair of large veins of the cardiovascular system at the base of the neck. This joining of the lymphatic and cardiovascular systems completes the recovery of fluid lost from capillaries as well as the transfer of lipids from the small intestine to the blood (see Figure 41.13).

The movement of lymph from peripheral tissues to the heart relies on many of the same mechanisms that assist blood flow in veins. Lymph vessels, like veins, have valves that prevent the backflow of fluid. Rhythmic contractions of the vessel walls help draw fluid into the small lymphatic vessels. In addition, skeletal muscle contractions play a role in moving lymph.

Disruptions in the movement of lymph often result in fluid accumulation, or edema, in affected tissues. In some circumstances, the consequence is severe. For example, certain species of parasitic worms that lodge in lymph vessels and thereby block lymph movement cause elephantiasis, a condition marked by extreme swelling in limbs or other body parts.

Along a lymph vessel are small, lymph-filtering organs called **lymph nodes**, which play an important role in the body's defense. Inside each lymph node is a honeycomb of connective tissue with spaces filled by white blood cells, which function in defense. When the body is fighting an infection, the white blood cells multiply rapidly, and the lymph nodes become swollen and tender. This is why your doctor may check for swollen lymph nodes in your neck, armpits, or groin when you feel sick. Because lymph nodes may also trap circulating cancer cells, doctors often examine the lymph nodes of cancer patients to detect the spread of the disease.

In recent years, evidence has surfaced demonstrating that the lymphatic system plays a role in harmful immune responses, such as those responsible for asthma. Because of these and other findings, the lymphatic system, largely ignored until the 1990s, has become a very active and promising area of biomedical research.

### CONCEPT CHECK 42.3

1. What is the primary cause of the low velocity of blood flow in capillaries?

2. What short-term changes in an animal's cardiovascular function might facilitate using skeletal muscles to escape from a dangerous situation?

3. **WHAT IF?** ➤ If you had additional hearts distributed throughout your body, what would be one likely advantage and one likely disadvantage?

*For suggested answers, see Appendix A.*

## CONCEPT 42.4

# Blood components function in exchange, transport, and defense

As you read in Concept 42.1, the fluid transported by an open circulatory system is continuous with the fluid that surrounds all of the body cells and thus has the same composition. In contrast, the fluid in a closed circulatory system can be much more specialized, as is the case for the blood of vertebrates.

## Blood Composition and Function

Vertebrate blood is a connective tissue consisting of cells suspended in a liquid matrix called **plasma**. Separating the components of blood using a centrifuge reveals that cellular elements (cells and cell fragments) occupy about 45% of the volume of blood (**Figure 42.16**). The remainder is plasma.

### Plasma

Dissolved in the plasma are ions and proteins that, together with the blood cells, function in osmotic regulation, transport, and defense. Inorganic salts in the form of dissolved ions are an essential component of the blood. Some buffer the blood, while others help maintaining osmotic balance. In addition, the concentration of ions in plasma directly affects the composition of the interstitial fluid, where many of these ions have a vital role in muscle and nerve activity. Serving all of these functions necessitates keeping plasma electrolytes within narrow concentration ranges.

Like dissolved ions, plasma proteins such as albumins act as buffers against pH changes and help maintain the osmotic balance between blood and interstitial fluid. Certain plasma proteins have additional functions. Immunoglobulins, or antibodies, combat viruses and other foreign agents that invade the body (see Figure 43.10). Apolipoproteins escort lipids, which are insoluble in water and can travel in blood only when bound to proteins. Additional plasma proteins include the fibrinogens, which are clotting factors that help plug leaks when blood vessels are injured. (The term *serum* refers to blood plasma from which these clotting factors have been removed.)

Plasma also contains many other substances in transit, including nutrients, metabolic wastes, respiratory gases, and hormones. Plasma has a much higher protein concentration than interstitial fluid, although the two fluids are otherwise similar. (Capillary walls, remember, are not very permeable to proteins.)

▼ **Figure 42.16 The composition of mammalian blood.** Centrifuged blood separates into three layers: plasma, leukocytes and platelets, and erythrocytes.

| Plasma 55% | |
|---|---|
| **Constituent** | **Major functions** |
| **Water** | Solvent |
| **Ions (blood electrolytes)** Sodium Potassium Calcium Magnesium Chloride Bicarbonate | Osmotic balance, pH buffering, and regulation of membrane permeability |
| **Plasma proteins** Albumin | Osmotic balance, pH buffering |
| Immunoglobulins (antibodies) | Defense |
| Apolipoproteins | Lipid transport |
| Fibrinogen | Clotting |
| **Substances transported by blood** Nutrients (such as glucose, fatty acids, vitamins), waste products of metabolism, respiratory gases ($O_2$ and $CO_2$), and hormones | |

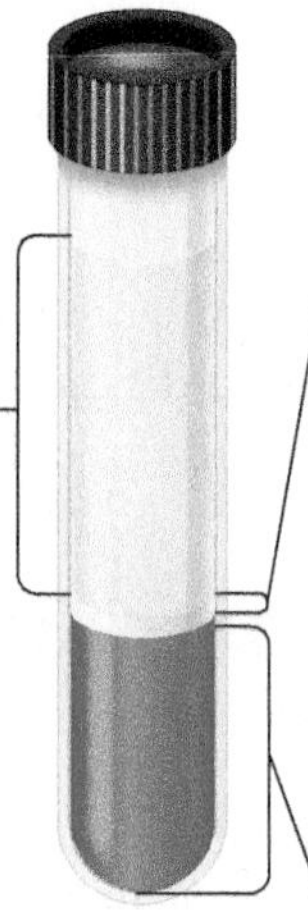

Separated blood elements

| Cellular elements 45% | | |
|---|---|---|
| **Cell type** | **Number per µL (mm$^3$) of blood** | **Functions** |
| **Leukocytes (white blood cells)** 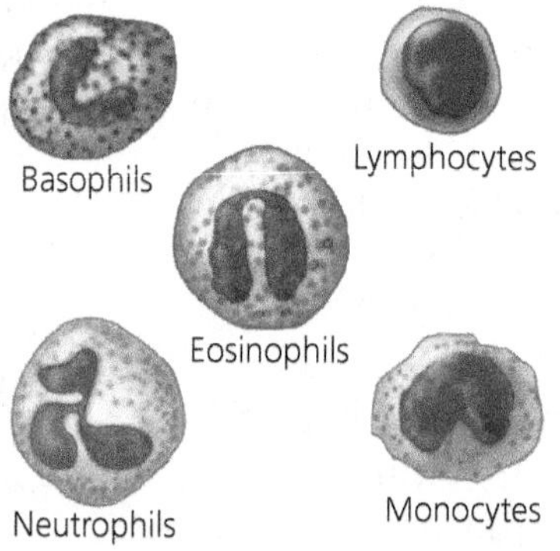 Basophils Lymphocytes Eosinophils Neutrophils Monocytes | 5,000–10,000 | Defense and immunity |
| **Platelets**  | 250,000–400,000 | Blood clotting |
| **Erythrocytes (red blood cells)**  | 5,000,000–6,000,000 | Transport of $O_2$ and some $CO_2$ |

## Cellular Elements

Blood contains two classes of cells: red blood cells, which transport $O_2$, and white blood cells, which function in defense (see Figure 42.16). Also suspended in blood plasma are **platelets**, cell fragments that are involved in the clotting process.

**Erythrocytes** Red blood cells, or **erythrocytes**, are by far the most numerous blood cells (see Figure 42.16). Their main function is $O_2$ transport, and their structure is closely related to this function. Human erythrocytes are small disks (7–8 μm in diameter) that are biconcave—thinner in the center than at the edges. This shape increases surface area, enhancing the rate of diffusion of $O_2$ across the plasma membrane. Mature mammalian erythrocytes lack nuclei. This unusual characteristic leaves more space in these tiny cells for **hemoglobin**, the iron-containing protein that transports $O_2$ (see Figure 5.18). Erythrocytes also lack mitochondria and generate their ATP exclusively by anaerobic metabolism. Oxygen transport would be less efficient if erythrocytes were aerobic and consumed some of the $O_2$ they carry.

Despite its small size, an erythrocyte contains about 250 million molecules of hemoglobin (Hb). Because each molecule of hemoglobin binds up to four molecules of $O_2$, one erythrocyte can transport about 1 billion $O_2$ molecules. As erythrocytes pass through the capillary beds of lungs, gills, or other respiratory organs, $O_2$ diffuses into the erythrocytes and binds to hemoglobin. In the systemic capillaries, $O_2$ dissociates from hemoglobin and diffuses into body cells.

In **sickle-cell disease**, an abnormal form of hemoglobin ($Hb^S$) polymerizes into aggregates. Because the concentration of hemoglobin in erythrocytes is so high, these aggregates are large enough to distort the erythrocyte into an elongated, curved shape that resembles a sickle. This abnormality results from an alteration in the amino acid sequence of hemoglobin at a single position (see Figure 5.19).

Sickle-cell disease significantly impairs the function of the circulatory system. Sickled cells often lodge in arterioles and capillaries, preventing delivery of $O_2$ and nutrients and removal of $CO_2$ and wastes. Blood vessel blockage and resulting organ swelling frequently result in severe pain. In addition, sickled cells frequently rupture, reducing the number of red blood cells available for transporting $O_2$. The average life span of a sickled erythrocyte is only 20 days—one-sixth that of a normal erythrocyte. The rate of erythrocyte loss outstrips their production rate. Short-term therapy includes replacement of erythrocytes by blood transfusion; long-term treatments are generally aimed at inhibiting aggregation of $Hb^S$.

**Leukocytes** The blood contains five major types of white blood cells, or **leukocytes**. Their function is to fight infections. Some are phagocytic, engulfing and digesting microorganisms and debris from the body's own dead cells. Other leukocytes, called lymphocytes, mount immune responses against foreign substances (as we'll discuss in Concepts 43.2 and 43.3). Normally, 1 μL of human blood contains about 5,000–10,000 leukocytes; their numbers increase temporarily whenever the body is fighting an infection. Unlike erythrocytes, leukocytes are also found outside the circulatory system, patrolling interstitial fluid and the lymphatic system.

**Platelets** Platelets are pinched-off cytoplasmic fragments of specialized bone marrow cells. They are about 2–3 μm in diameter and have no nuclei. Platelets serve both structural and molecular functions in blood clotting.

## Stem Cells and the Replacement of Cellular Elements

Erythrocytes, leukocytes, and platelets all develop from stem cells that are dedicated to replenishing the body's blood cell populations. As described in Concept 20.3, a **stem cell** can reproduce indefinitely, dividing mitotically to produce one daughter cell that remains a stem cell and another that adopts a specialized function. The stem cells that produce the cellular elements of blood cells are located in the red marrow inside bones, particularly the ribs, vertebrae, sternum, and pelvis. As they divide and self-renew, these stem cells give rise to two sets of progenitor cells with a more limited capacity for self-renewal **(Figure 42.17)**. One set, the lymphoid progenitors, produces

▼ **Figure 42.17 Differentiation of blood cells.** Cell divisions of stem cells in bone marrow give rise to two specialized sets of cells. The lymphoid progenitor cells give rise to immune cells called lymphocytes, primarily B and T cells. The myeloid progenitor cells give rise to other immune cells, red blood cells (erythrocytes), and cell fragments called platelets.

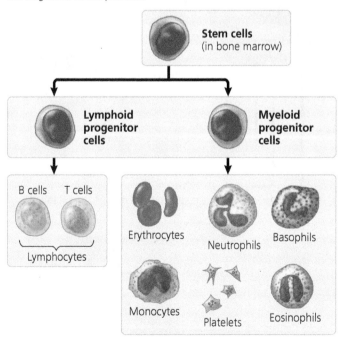

lymphocytes. The other set, the myeloid progenitors, produces all other white blood cells, red blood cells, and platelets.

Throughout a person's life, stem cells replace the worn-out cellular elements of blood. Erythrocytes are the shortest-lived, circulating for only 120 days on average before being replaced. A feedback mechanism sensitive to $O_2$ levels controls erythrocyte production. If $O_2$ levels fall, the kidneys synthesize and secrete a hormone called **erythropoietin (EPO)** that stimulates the generation of more erythrocytes.

Recombinant DNA technology is now used to synthesize EPO in cultured cells. Physicians use recombinant EPO to treat disorders such as *anemia*, a condition of lower-than-normal erythrocyte or hemoglobin levels that decreases the oxygen-carrying capacity of the blood. Some athletes inject themselves with EPO to increase their erythrocyte levels. Because this practice is outlawed by most major sports organizations, runners, cyclists, and other athletes caught using EPO-related drugs have forfeited their records and been banned from future competitions.

## Blood Clotting

When blood vessels are broken by an injury such as a small cut or scrape, a chain of events ensues that quickly seals the break, halting blood loss and exposure to infection. The key mechanical event in this response is coagulation, the conversion of the liquid components of blood into a solid—a blood clot.

In the absence of injury, the coagulant, or sealant, circulates in an inactive form called fibrinogen. Blood clotting begins when injury exposes the proteins in a broken blood vessel wall to blood constituents. The exposed proteins attract platelets, which gather at the site of injury and release clotting factors. These clotting factors trigger a cascade of reactions leading to the formation of an active enzyme, *thrombin*, from an inactive form, prothrombin **(Figure 42.18)**. Thrombin in turn converts fibrinogen to fibrin, which aggregates into threads that form the framework of the clot. Any mutation that blocks a step in the clotting process can cause hemophilia, a disease characterized by excessive bleeding and bruising from even minor cuts and bumps (see Concept 15.2).

As shown in Figure 42.18, clotting involves a positive feedback loop. Initially, the clotting reactions convert only some of the prothrombin at the clot site to thrombin. However, thrombin itself stimulates the enzymatic cascade, leading to more conversion of prothrombin to thrombin and thus driving clotting to completion.

▼ **Figure 42.18 Blood clotting.**

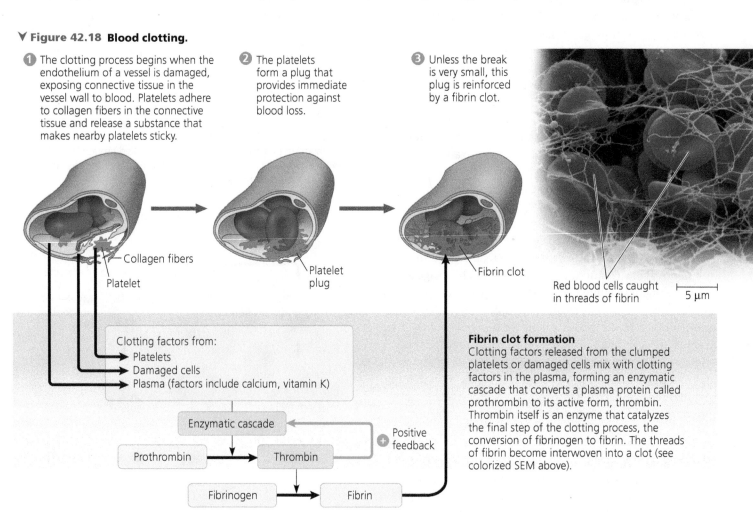

① The clotting process begins when the endothelium of a vessel is damaged, exposing connective tissue in the vessel wall to blood. Platelets adhere to collagen fibers in the connective tissue and release a substance that makes nearby platelets sticky.

② The platelets form a plug that provides immediate protection against blood loss.

③ Unless the break is very small, this plug is reinforced by a fibrin clot.

Collagen fibers

Platelet

Platelet plug

Fibrin clot

Red blood cells caught in threads of fibrin

5 μm

Clotting factors from:
- Platelets
- Damaged cells
- Plasma (factors include calcium, vitamin K)

Enzymatic cascade

Prothrombin → Thrombin

⊕ Positive feedback

Fibrinogen → Fibrin

**Fibrin clot formation**
Clotting factors released from the clumped platelets or damaged cells mix with clotting factors in the plasma, forming an enzymatic cascade that converts a plasma protein called prothrombin to its active form, thrombin. Thrombin itself is an enzyme that catalyzes the final step of the clotting process, the conversion of fibrinogen to fibrin. The threads of fibrin become interwoven into a clot (see colorized SEM above).

Anticlotting factors in the blood normally prevent spontaneous clotting in the absence of injury. Sometimes, however, clots form within a blood vessel, blocking the flow of blood. Such a clot is called a **thrombus** (plural, *thrombi*). We'll explore how thrombi form and the dangers that they pose shortly.

## Cardiovascular Disease

Each year, cardiovascular diseases—disorders of the heart and blood vessels—kill more than 750,000 people in the United States. These diseases range from minor disturbances of vein or heart valve function to life-threatening disruptions of blood flow to the heart or brain.

### Atherosclerosis, Heart Attacks, and Stroke

Healthy arteries have a smooth inner lining that reduces resistance to blood flow. However, damage or infection can roughen the lining and lead to **atherosclerosis**, the hardening of the arteries by accumulation of fatty deposits. A key player in the development of atherosclerosis is cholesterol, a steroid that is important for maintaining normal membrane fluidity in animal cells (see Figure 7.5). Cholesterol travels in blood plasma mainly in particles that consist of thousands of cholesterol molecules and other lipids bound to a protein. One type of particle—**low-density lipoprotein (LDL)**—delivers cholesterol to cells for membrane production. Another type—**high-density lipoprotein (HDL)**—scavenges excess cholesterol for return to the liver. Individuals with a high ratio of LDL to HDL are at substantially increased risk for atherosclerosis.

In atherosclerosis, damage to the arterial lining results in *inflammation*, the body's reaction to injury. Leukocytes are attracted to the inflamed area and begin to take up lipids, including cholesterol. A fatty deposit, called a plaque, grows steadily, incorporating fibrous connective tissue and additional cholesterol. As the plaque grows, the walls of the artery become thick and stiff, and the obstruction of the artery increases. If the plaque ruptures, a thrombus can form in the artery **(Figure 42.19)**, potentially triggering a heart attack or a stroke.

A **heart attack**, also called a *myocardial infarction*, is the damage or death of cardiac muscle tissue resulting from blockage of one or more coronary arteries, which supply oxygen-rich blood to the heart muscle. The coronary arteries are small in diameter and therefore especially vulnerable to obstruction by atherosclerotic plaques or thrombi. Such blockage can destroy cardiac muscle quickly because the constantly beating heart muscle requires a steady supply of $O_2$. If a large enough portion of the heart is affected, the heart will stop beating. Such cardiac arrest causes death if a heartbeat is not restored within minutes by cardiopulmonary resuscitation (CPR) or some other emergency procedure.

A **stroke** is the death of nervous tissue in the brain due to a lack of $O_2$. Strokes usually result from rupture or blockage of

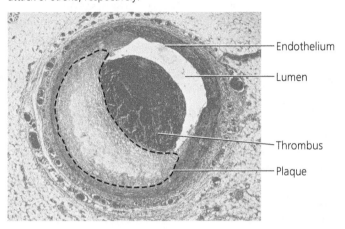

**Figure 42.19 Atherosclerosis.** In atherosclerosis, thickening of an arterial wall by plaque formation can restrict blood flow through the artery. If a plaque ruptures, a thrombus can form, further restricting blood flow. Fragments of a ruptured plaque can also travel via the bloodstream and become lodged in other arteries. If the blockage is in an artery that supplies the heart or brain, the result could be a heart attack or stroke, respectively.

arteries in the head. The effects of a stroke and the individual's chance of survival depend on the extent and location of the damaged brain tissue. If a stroke results from arterial blockage by a thrombus, rapid administration of a clot-dissolving drug may help limit the damage.

Although atherosclerosis often isn't detected until critical blood flow is disrupted, there can be warning signs. Partial blockage of the coronary arteries may cause occasional chest pain, a condition known as angina pectoris. The pain is most likely to be felt when the heart is laboring under stress, and it signals that part of the heart is not receiving enough $O_2$. An obstructed artery may be treated surgically, either by inserting a mesh tube called a stent to expand the artery **(Figure 42.20)** or by transplanting a healthy blood vessel from the chest or a limb to bypass the blockage.

**Figure 42.20 Inserting a stent to widen an obstructed artery.**

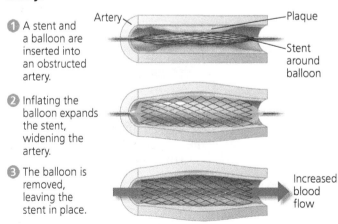

❶ A stent and a balloon are inserted into an obstructed artery.

❷ Inflating the balloon expands the stent, widening the artery.

❸ The balloon is removed, leaving the stent in place.

### Risk Factors and Treatment of Cardiovascular Disease

Although the tendency to develop particular cardiovascular diseases is inherited, it is also strongly influenced by lifestyle. For example, exercise decreases the LDL/HDL ratio, reducing the risk of cardiovascular disease. In contrast, consumption of certain processed vegetable oils called *trans fats* and smoking increase the LDL/HDL ratio. For many individuals at high risk, treatment with drugs called statins can lower LDL levels and thereby reduce the risk of heart attacks. In the **Scientific Skills Exercise**, you can interpret the effect of a genetic mutation on blood LDL levels.

 BBC Video: The Impact of Smoking

---

## SCIENTIFIC SKILLS EXERCISE

### *Making and Interpreting Histograms*

**Does Inactivating the PCSK9 Enzyme Lower LDL Levels?** Researchers interested in genetic factors affecting susceptibility to cardiovascular disease examined the DNA of 15,000 individuals. They found that 3% of the individuals had a mutation that inactivates one copy of the gene for PCSK9, a liver enzyme. Because mutations that *increase* the activity of PCSK9 are known to *increase* levels of LDL cholesterol in the blood, the researchers hypothesized that *inactivating* mutations in this gene would *lower* LDL levels. In this exercise, you will interpret the results of an experiment they carried out to test this hypothesis.

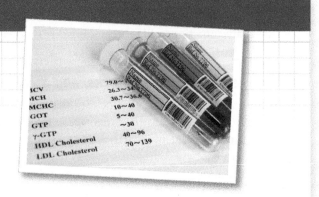

**How the Experiment Was Done** Researchers measured LDL cholesterol levels in blood plasma from 85 individuals with one copy of the *PCSK9* gene inactivated (the study group) and from 3,278 individuals with two functional copies of the gene (the control group).

**Data from the Experiment**

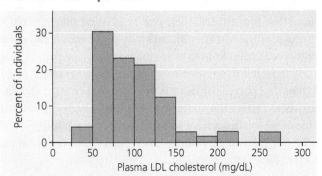

**Individuals with an inactivating mutation in one copy of *PCSK9* gene (study group)**

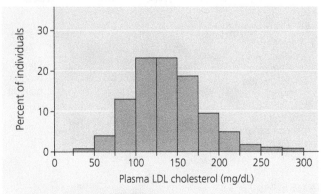

**Individuals with two functional copies of *PCSK9* gene (control group)**

**INTERPRET THE DATA**

1. The results are presented using a variant of a bar graph called a *histogram*. In a histogram, the variable on the *x*-axis is grouped into ranges. The height of each bar in this histogram reflects the percentage of samples that fall into the range specified on the *x*-axis for that bar. For example, in the top histogram, about 4% of individuals studied had plasma LDL cholesterol levels in the 25–50 mg/dL (milligrams per deciliter) range. Add the percentages for the relevant bars to calculate the percentage of individuals in the study and control groups that had an LDL level of 100 mg/dL or less. (For additional information about histograms, see the Scientific Skills Review in Appendix F and in the Study Area in MasteringBiology.)

2. Comparing the two histograms, do you find support for the researchers' hypothesis? Explain.

3. What if instead of graphing the data, the researchers had compared the range of concentrations for plasma LDL cholesterol (low to high) in the control and study groups? How would their conclusions have differed?

4. What does the fact that the two histograms overlap as much as they do indicate about the extent to which PCSK9 determines plasma LDL cholesterol levels?

5. Comparing these two histograms allowed researchers to draw a conclusion regarding the effect of PCSK9 mutations on LDL cholesterol levels in blood. Consider two individuals with a plasma LDL level cholesterol of 160 mg/dL, one from the study group and one from the control group. What do you predict regarding their relative risk of developing cardiovascular disease? Explain how you arrived at your prediction. What role did the histograms play in making your prediction?

 **Instructors:** A version of this Scientific Skills Exercise can be assigned in MasteringBiology.

**Data from** J. C. Cohen et al., Sequence variations in *PCSK9*, low LDL, and protection against coronary heart disease, *New England Journal of Medicine* 354:1264–1272 (2006).

The recognition that inflammation plays a central role in atherosclerosis and thrombus formation is also influencing the treatment of cardiovascular disease. For example, aspirin, which inhibits the inflammatory response, has been found to help prevent the recurrence of heart attacks and stroke.

**Hypertension** (high blood pressure) is yet another contributor to heart attack and stroke. According to one hypothesis, chronic high blood pressure damages the endothelium that lines the arteries, promoting plaque formation. The usual definition of hypertension in adults is a systolic pressure above 140 mm Hg or a diastolic pressure above 90 mm Hg. Fortunately, hypertension is simple to diagnose and can usually be controlled by dietary changes, exercise, medication, or a combination of these approaches.

### CONCEPT CHECK 42.4

1. Explain why a physician might order a white cell count for a patient with symptoms of an infection.

2. Clots in arteries can cause heart attacks and strokes. Why, then, does it make sense to treat people with hemophilia by introducing clotting factors into their blood?

3. **WHAT IF?** ➤ Nitroglycerin (the key ingredient in dynamite) is sometimes prescribed for heart disease patients. Within the body, nitroglycerin is converted to nitric oxide (see Concept 42.3). Why would you expect nitroglycerin to relieve chest pain caused by narrowing of the cardiac arteries?

4. **MAKE CONNECTIONS** ➤ How do stem cells from the bone marrow of an adult differ from embryonic stem cells (see Concept 20.3)?

*For suggested answers, see Appendix A.*

# CONCEPT 42.5

## Gas exchange occurs across specialized respiratory surfaces

In the remainder of this chapter, we will focus on the process of **gas exchange**. Although this process is often called respiratory exchange or respiration, it should not be confused with the energy transformations of cellular respiration. Gas exchange is the uptake of molecular $O_2$ from the environment and the discharge of $CO_2$ to the environment.

### Partial Pressure Gradients in Gas Exchange

To understand the driving forces for gas exchange, we must consider **partial pressure**, which is simply the pressure exerted by a particular gas in a mixture of gases. Determining partial pressures enables us to predict the net movement of a gas at an exchange surface: A gas always undergoes net diffusion from a region of higher partial pressure to a region of lower partial pressure.

To calculate partial pressures, we need to know the pressure that a gas mixture exerts and the fraction of the mixture represented by a particular gas. Let's consider $O_2$ as an example. At sea level, the atmosphere exerts a downward force equal to that of a column of mercury (Hg) 760 mm high. Atmospheric pressure at sea level is thus 760 mm Hg. Since the atmosphere is 21% $O_2$ by volume, the partial pressure of $O_2$ is $0.21 \times 760$, or about 160 mm Hg. This value is called the *partial pressure* of $O_2$ (abbreviated $P_{O_2}$) because it is the part of atmospheric pressure contributed by $O_2$. The partial pressure of $CO_2$ (abbreviated $P_{CO_2}$) is much, much less, only 0.29 mm Hg at sea level.

Partial pressures also apply to gases dissolved in a liquid, such as water. When water is exposed to air, an equilibrium state is reached such that the partial pressure of each gas in the water equals the partial pressure of that gas in the air. Thus, water exposed to air at sea level has a $P_{O_2}$ of 160 mm Hg, the same as in the atmosphere. However, the *concentrations* of $O_2$ in the air and water differ substantially because $O_2$ is much less soluble in water than in air (Table 42.1). Furthermore, the warmer and saltier the water is, the less dissolved $O_2$ it can hold.

| Table 42.1  Comparing Air and Water as Respiratory Media | | | |
|---|---|---|---|
| | Air (Sea Level) | Water (20°C) | Air-to-Water Ratio |
| $O_2$ Partial Pressure | 160 mm | 160 mm | 1:1 |
| $O_2$ Concentration | 210 ml/L | 7 ml/L | 30:1 |
| Density | 0.0013 kg/L | 1 kg/L | 1:770 |
| Viscosity | 0.02 cP | 1 cP | 1:50 |

### Respiratory Media

The conditions for gas exchange vary considerably, depending on whether the respiratory medium—the source of $O_2$—is air or water. As already noted, $O_2$ is plentiful in air, making up about 21% of Earth's atmosphere by volume. As shown in Table 42.1, air is much less dense and less viscous than water, so it is easier to move and to force through small passageways. As a result, breathing air is relatively easy and need not be particularly efficient. Humans, for example, extract only about 25% of the $O_2$ in inhaled air.

Water is a much more demanding gas exchange medium than air. The amount of $O_2$ dissolved in a given volume of water varies but is always less than in an equivalent volume of air. Water in many marine and freshwater habitats contains only about 7 mL of dissolved $O_2$ per liter, a concentration roughly 30 times less than in air. Water's lower $O_2$ content, greater density, and greater viscosity mean that aquatic animals such as fishes and lobsters must expend considerable energy to carry out gas exchange. In the context of these challenges, adaptations have evolved that enable most aquatic animals to be very efficient in gas exchange. Many of these adaptations involve the organization of the surfaces dedicated to exchange.

## Respiratory Surfaces

Specialization for gas exchange is apparent in the structure of the respiratory surface, the part of an animal's body where gas exchange occurs. Like all living cells, the cells that carry out gas exchange have a plasma membrane that must be in contact with an aqueous solution. Respiratory surfaces are therefore always moist.

The movement of $O_2$ and $CO_2$ across respiratory surfaces takes place by diffusion. The rate of diffusion is proportional to the surface area across which it occurs and inversely proportional to the square of the distance through which molecules must move. In other words, gas exchange is fast when the area for diffusion is large and the path for diffusion is short. As a result, respiratory surfaces tend to be large and thin.

In some relatively simple animals, such as sponges, cnidarians, and flatworms, every cell in the body is close enough to the external environment that gases can diffuse quickly between any cell and the environment. In many animals, however, the bulk of the body's cells lack immediate access to the environment. The respiratory surface in these animals is a thin, moist epithelium that constitutes a respiratory organ.

For earthworms, as well as some amphibians and other animals, the skin serves as a respiratory organ. A dense network of capillaries just below the skin facilitates the exchange of gases between the circulatory system and the environment. For most animals, however, the general body surface lacks sufficient area to exchange gases for the whole organism. The evolutionary solution to this limitation is a respiratory organ that is extensively folded or branched, thereby enlarging the available surface area for gas exchange. Gills, tracheae, and lungs are three such organs.

## Gills in Aquatic Animals

Gills are outfoldings of the body surface that are suspended in the water. As illustrated in **Figure 42.21** (and in Figure 42.1), the distribution of gills over the body can vary considerably.

▼ Figure 42.21 **Diversity in the structure of gills, external body surfaces that function in gas exchange.**

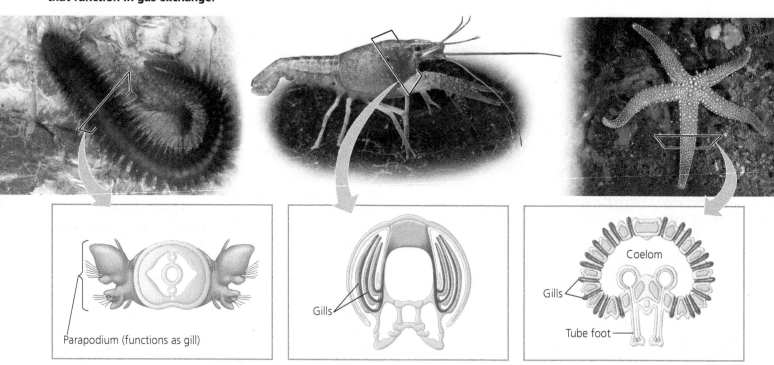

**(a) Marine worm.** Many polychaetes (marine worms of the phylum Annelida) have a pair of flattened appendages called parapodia (singular, *parapodium*) on each body segment. The parapodia serve as gills and also function in crawling and swimming.

**(b) Crayfish.** Crayfish and other crustaceans have long, feathery gills covered by the exoskeleton. Specialized body appendages drive water over the gill surfaces.

**(c) Sea star.** The gills of a sea star are simple tubular projections of the skin. The hollow core of each gill is an extension of the coelom (body cavity). Gas exchange occurs by diffusion across the gill surfaces, and fluid in the coelom circulates in and out of the gills, aiding gas transport. The tube feet surfaces also function in gas exchange.

Regardless of their distribution, gills often have a total surface area much greater than that of the rest of the body's exterior.

Movement of the respiratory medium over the respiratory surface, a process called **ventilation**, maintains the partial pressure gradients of $O_2$ and $CO_2$ across the gill that are necessary for gas exchange. To promote ventilation, most gill-bearing animals either move their gills through the water or move water over their gills. For example, crayfish and lobsters have paddle-like appendages that drive a current of water over the gills, whereas mussels and clams move water with cilia. Octopuses and squids ventilate their gills by taking in and ejecting water, with the significant side benefit of getting about by jet propulsion. Fishes use the motion of swimming or coordinated movements of the mouth and gill covers to ventilate their gills. In both cases, a current of water enters the mouth of the fish, passes through slits in the pharynx, flows over the gills, and then exits the body (Figure 42.22).

In fishes, the efficiency of gas exchange is maximized by **countercurrent exchange**, the exchange of a substance or heat between two fluids flowing in opposite directions. In a fish gill, the two fluids are blood and water. Because blood flows in the direction opposite to that of water passing over the gills, at each point in its travel blood is less saturated with $O_2$ than the water it meets (see Figure 42.22). As blood enters a gill capillary, it encounters water that is completing its passage through the gill. Depleted of much of its dissolved $O_2$, this water nevertheless has a higher $P_{O_2}$ than the incoming blood, and $O_2$ transfer takes place. As the blood continues its passage, its $P_{O_2}$ steadily increases, but so does that of the water it encounters, since each successive position in the blood's travel corresponds to an earlier position in the water's passage over the gills. The result is a partial pressure gradient that favors the diffusion of $O_2$ from water to blood along the entire length of the capillary.

Countercurrent exchange mechanisms are remarkably efficient. In the fish gill, more than 80% of the $O_2$ dissolved in the water is removed as the water passes over the respiratory surface. In other settings, countercurrent mechanisms contribute to temperature regulation and to the functioning of the mammalian kidney (see Concepts 40.3 and 44.4).

## Tracheal Systems in Insects

In most terrestrial animals, respiratory surfaces are enclosed within the body, exposed to the atmosphere only through narrow tubes. Although the most familiar example of such an arrangement is the lung, the most common is the insect **tracheal system**, a network of air tubes that branch throughout the body. The largest tubes, called tracheae,

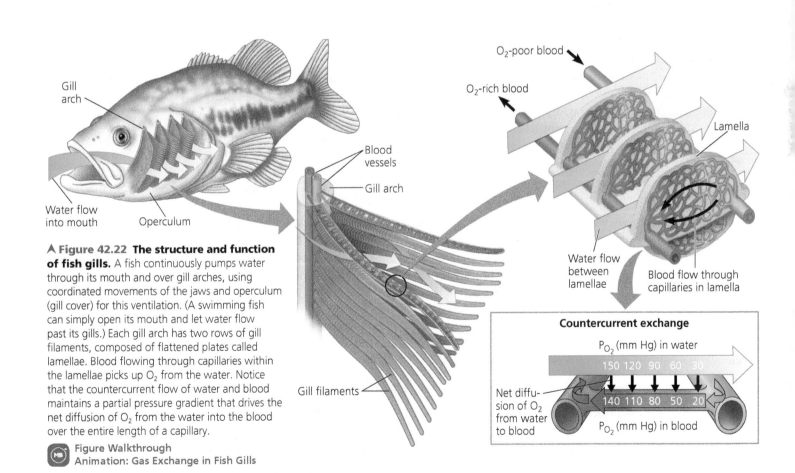

**⋏ Figure 42.22 The structure and function of fish gills.** A fish continuously pumps water through its mouth and over gill arches, using coordinated movements of the jaws and operculum (gill cover) for this ventilation. (A swimming fish can simply open its mouth and let water flow past its gills.) Each gill arch has two rows of gill filaments, composed of flattened plates called lamellae. Blood flowing through capillaries within the lamellae picks up $O_2$ from the water. Notice that the countercurrent flow of water and blood maintains a partial pressure gradient that drives the net diffusion of $O_2$ from the water into the blood over the entire length of a capillary.

Figure Walkthrough
Animation: Gas Exchange in Fish Gills

▼ **Figure 42.23** **A tracheal system.**

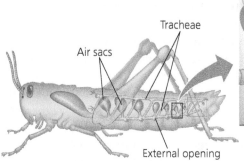

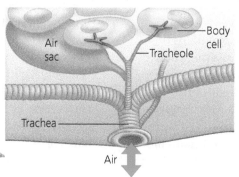

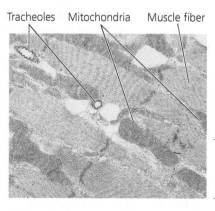

**(a)** The respiratory system of an insect consists of branched internal tubes. The largest tubes, called tracheae, connect to external openings spaced along the insect's body surface. Air sacs formed from enlarged portions of the tracheae are found near organs that require a large supply of oxygen.

**(b)** Rings of chitin keep the tracheae open, allowing air to enter and pass into smaller tubes called tracheoles. The branched tracheoles deliver air directly to cells throughout the body. Tracheoles have closed ends filled with fluid (blue-gray). When the animal is active and using more $O_2$, most of the fluid is withdrawn into the body. This increases the surface area of air-filled tracheoles in contact with cells.

**(c)** The TEM above shows cross sections of tracheoles in a tiny piece of insect flight muscle. Each of the numerous mitochondria in the muscle cells lies within about 5 μm of a tracheole.

open to the outside (**Figure 42.23**). At the tips of the finest branches, a moist epithelial lining enables gas exchange by diffusion. Because the tracheal system brings air within a very short distance of virtually every body cell in an insect, the efficient exchange of $O_2$ and $CO_2$ does not require the participation of the animal's open circulatory system.

Tracheal systems often exhibit adaptations directly related to bioenergetics. Consider, for example, a flying insect, which consumes 10 to 200 times more $O_2$ when in flight than it does at rest. In many flying insects, cycles of flight muscle contraction and relaxation pump air rapidly through the tracheal system. This pumping improves ventilation, bringing ample $O_2$ to the densely packed mitochondria that support the high metabolic rate of flight muscle (see Figure 42.23).

## Lungs

Unlike tracheal systems, which branch throughout the insect body, **lungs** are localized respiratory organs. Representing an infolding of the body surface, they are typically subdivided into numerous pockets. Because the respiratory surface of a lung is not in direct contact with all other parts of the body, the gap must be bridged by the circulatory system, which transports gases between the lungs and the rest of the body. Lungs have evolved both in organisms with open circulatory systems, such as spiders and land snails, and in vertebrates.

Among vertebrates that lack gills, the use of lungs for gas exchange varies. Amphibians rely heavily on diffusion across external body surfaces, such as the skin, to carry out gas exchange; lungs, if present, are relatively small. In contrast, most reptiles (including all birds) and all mammals depend entirely on lungs for gas exchange. Turtles are an exception; they supplement lung breathing with gas exchange across moist epithelial surfaces continuous with their mouth or anus. Lungs and air breathing have evolved in a few aquatic vertebrates as adaptations to living in oxygen-poor water or to spending part of their time exposed to air (for instance, when the water level of a pond recedes).

### *Mammalian Respiratory Systems:* A Closer Look

In mammals, branching ducts convey air to the lungs, which are located in the *thoracic cavity*, enclosed by the ribs and diaphragm. Air enters through the nostrils and is then filtered by hairs, warmed, humidified, and sampled for odors as it flows through a maze of spaces in the nasal cavity. The nasal cavity leads to the pharynx, an intersection where the paths for air and food cross (**Figure 42.24**). When food is swallowed, the **larynx** (the upper part of the respiratory tract) moves upward and tips the epiglottis over the glottis, which is the opening of the **trachea**, or windpipe. This allows food to go down the esophagus to the stomach (see Figure 41.9). The rest of the time, the glottis is open, enabling breathing.

From the larynx, air passes into the trachea. The cartilage that reinforces the walls of both the larynx and the trachea keeps this part of the airway open. Within the larynx of most mammals, the exhaled air rushes by a pair of elastic bands of muscle called vocal folds or, in humans, vocal cords. Sounds are produced when muscles in the larynx are tensed, stretching the cords so that they vibrate. High-pitched sounds result from tightly stretched cords vibrating rapidly; low-pitched sounds come from looser cords vibrating slowly.

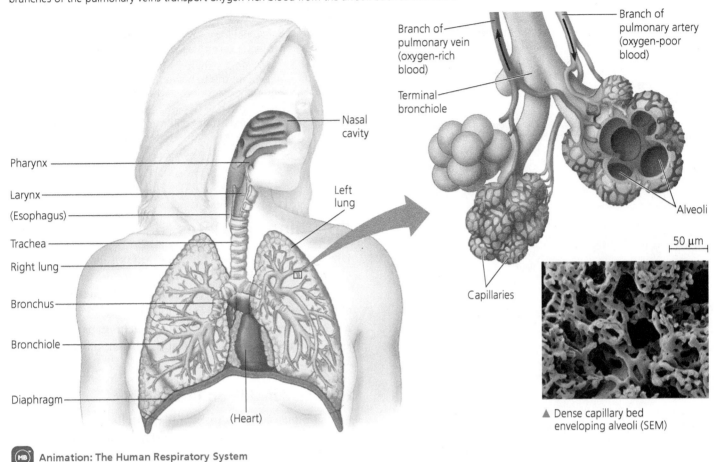

▼ **Figure 42.24 The mammalian respiratory system.** From the nasal cavity and pharynx, inhaled air passes through the larynx, trachea, and bronchi to the bronchioles, which end in microscopic alveoli lined by a thin, moist epithelium. Branches of the pulmonary arteries convey oxygen-poor blood to the alveoli; branches of the pulmonary veins transport oxygen-rich blood from the alveoli back to the heart.

Nasal cavity

Pharynx

Larynx

(Esophagus)

Trachea

Right lung

Bronchus

Bronchiole

Diaphragm

(Heart)

Left lung

Branch of pulmonary vein (oxygen-rich blood)

Terminal bronchiole

Branch of pulmonary artery (oxygen-poor blood)

Alveoli

Capillaries

50 μm

▲ Dense capillary bed enveloping alveoli (SEM)

(MB) Animation: The Human Respiratory System

The trachea branches into two **bronchi** (singular, *bronchus*), one leading to each lung. Within the lung, the bronchi branch repeatedly into finer and finer tubes called **bronchioles**. The entire system of air ducts has the appearance of an inverted tree, the trunk being the trachea. The epithelium lining the major branches of this respiratory tree is covered by cilia and a thin film of mucus. The mucus traps dust, pollen, and other particulate contaminants, and the beating cilia move the mucus upward to the pharynx, where it can be swallowed into the esophagus. This process, sometimes referred to as the "mucus escalator," plays a crucial role in cleansing the respiratory system.

Gas exchange in mammals occurs in **alveoli** (singular, *alveolus*; see Figure 42.24), air sacs clustered at the tips of the tiniest bronchioles. Human lungs contain millions of alveoli, which together have a surface area of about 100 m², 50 times that of the skin. Oxygen in the air entering the alveoli dissolves in the moist film lining their inner surfaces and rapidly diffuses across the epithelium into a web of capillaries that surrounds each alveolus. Net diffusion of carbon dioxide occurs in the opposite direction, from the capillaries across the epithelium of the alveolus and into the air space.

Lacking cilia or significant air currents to remove particles from their surface, alveoli are highly susceptible to contamination. White blood cells patrol the alveoli, engulfing foreign particles. However, if too much particulate matter reaches the alveoli, the defenses can be overwhelmed, leading to inflammation and irreversible damage. For example, particulates from cigarette smoke that enter alveoli can cause a permanent reduction in lung capacity. For coal miners, inhalation of large amounts of coal dust can lead to silicosis, a disabling, irreversible, and sometimes fatal lung disease.

The film of liquid that lines alveoli is subject to surface tension, an attractive force that has the effect of minimizing a liquid's surface area (see Concept 3.2). Given their tiny diameter (about 0.25 mm), alveoli would be expected to collapse under high surface tension. It turns out, however, that these air sacs produce a mixture of phospholipids and proteins called **surfactant**, for *surf*ace-*act*ive age*nt*, which coats the alveoli and reduces surface tension.

## ▼ Figure 42.25

### Inquiry What causes respiratory distress syndrome?

**Experiment** Mary Ellen Avery, a research fellow at Harvard University, hypothesized that a lack of surfactant caused respiratory distress syndrome (RDS) in preterm infants. To test this hypothesis, she obtained autopsy samples of lungs from infants who had died of RDS or from other causes. She extracted material from the samples and let it form a film on water. Avery then measured the tension (in dynes per centimeter) across the water surface and recorded the lowest surface tension observed for each sample.

**Results** Avery noted a pattern when she grouped the samples based on the body mass of the infant: less than 1,200 g (2.7 pounds) and 1,200 g or greater.

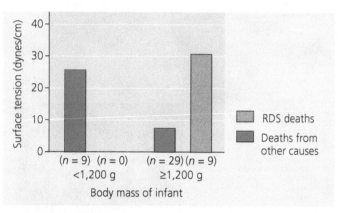

**Data from** M. E. Avery and J. Mead, Surface properties in relation to atelectasis and hyaline membrane disease, *American Journal of Diseases of Children* 97:517–523 (1959).

**Conclusion** For infants with a body mass of 1,200 g or greater, the material from those who had died of RDS exhibited much higher surface tension than the material from those who had died from other causes. Avery inferred that infants' lungs normally contain a surface-tension-reducing substance (now called surfactant) and that a lack of this substance was a likely cause of RDS. The results from infants with a body mass less than 1,200 g were similar to those from infants who had died from RDS, suggesting that surfactant is not normally produced until a fetus reaches this size.

**WHAT IF?** ▶ *If the researchers had measured the amount of surfactant in lung samples from the infants, what relationship would you expect between the amount of surfactant and infant body mass?*

In the 1950s, Mary Ellen Avery did the first experiment linking a lack of surfactant to *respiratory distress syndrome* (RDS), a disease common in infants born 6 weeks or more before their due dates (**Figure 42.25**). (The average full-term human pregnancy is 38 weeks.) Later studies revealed that surfactant typically appears in the lungs after 33 weeks of development. In the 1950s, RDS killed 10,000 infants annually in the United States, but artificial surfactants are now used successfully to treat early preterm infants. Treated babies with a body mass over 900 g (2 pounds) at birth usually survive without long-term health problems. For her contributions, Avery received the National Medal of Science.

Having surveyed the route that air follows when we breathe, we'll turn next to the process of breathing itself.

### CONCEPT CHECK 42.5

1. Why is an internal location for gas exchange tissues advantageous for terrestrial animals?

2. After a heavy rain, earthworms come to the surface. How would you explain this behavior in terms of an earthworm's requirements for gas exchange?

3. **MAKE CONNECTIONS** ▶ Describe similarities in the countercurrent exchange that facilitates respiration in fish and thermoregulation in geese (see Concept 40.3).

*For suggested answers, see Appendix A.*

# CONCEPT 42.6

## Breathing ventilates the lungs

Like fishes, terrestrial vertebrates rely on ventilation to maintain high $O_2$ and low $CO_2$ concentrations at the gas exchange surface. The process that ventilates lungs is **breathing**, the alternating inhalation and exhalation of air. A variety of mechanisms for moving air in and out of lungs have evolved, as we will see by considering breathing in amphibians, birds, and mammals.

### How an Amphibian Breathes

An amphibian such as a frog ventilates its lungs by **positive pressure breathing**, inflating the lungs with forced air-flow. Inhalation begins when muscles lower the floor of an amphibian's oral cavity, drawing in air through its nostrils. Next, with the nostrils and mouth closed, the floor of the oral cavity rises, forcing air down the trachea. Exhalation follows as air is expelled by the elastic recoil of the lungs and by compression of the muscular body wall. When male frogs puff themselves up in aggressive or courtship displays, they disrupt this breathing cycle, taking in air several times without allowing any release.

### How a Bird Breathes

When a bird breathes, it passes air over the gas exchange surface in only one direction. Air sacs situated on either side of the lungs act as bellows that direct air flow through the lungs. Within the lungs, tiny channels called *parabronchi* serve as the sites of gas exchange. Passage of air through the entire system—air sacs and lungs—requires two cycles of inhalation and exhalation (**Figure 42.26**).

Ventilation in birds is highly efficient. One reason is that birds pass air over the gas exchange surface in only one direction during breathing. In addition, incoming fresh air does not mix with air that has already carried out gas exchange, maximizing the partial pressure difference with blood flowing through the lungs.

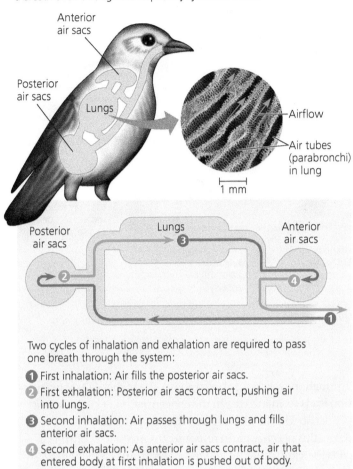

▼ **Figure 42.26 The avian respiratory system.** This diagram traces a breath of air through the respiratory system of a bird.

Anterior air sacs

Posterior air sacs

Lungs

Airflow

Air tubes (parabronchi) in lung

1 mm

Posterior air sacs

Lungs

Anterior air sacs

3

2

4

1

Two cycles of inhalation and exhalation are required to pass one breath through the system:

❶ First inhalation: Air fills the posterior air sacs.

❷ First exhalation: Posterior air sacs contract, pushing air into lungs.

❸ Second inhalation: Air passes through lungs and fills anterior air sacs.

❹ Second exhalation: As anterior air sacs contract, air that entered body at first inhalation is pushed out of body.

## How a Mammal Breathes

To understand how a mammal breathes, think about filling a syringe. By pulling back on the plunger, you lower the pressure in the syringe, drawing gas or fluid through the needle into the syringe chamber. Similarly, mammals employ **negative pressure breathing**—pulling, rather than pushing, air into their lungs **(Figure 42.27)**. Using muscle contraction to actively expand the thoracic cavity, mammals lower air pressure in their lungs below that of the air outside their body. Because gas flows from a region of higher pressure to a region of lower pressure, the lowered air pressure in the lungs causes air to rush through the nostrils and mouth and down the breathing tubes to the alveoli.

Expanding the thoracic cavity during inhalation involves the animal's rib muscles and the **diaphragm**, a sheet of skeletal muscle that forms the bottom wall of the cavity. Contracting the rib muscles pulls the ribs upward and the sternum outward. This has the effect of expanding the rib cage, the front wall of the thoracic cavity. At the same time, the diaphragm contracts, expanding the thoracic cavity downward. It is this descending movement of the diaphragm that is analogous to a plunger being drawn out of a syringe.

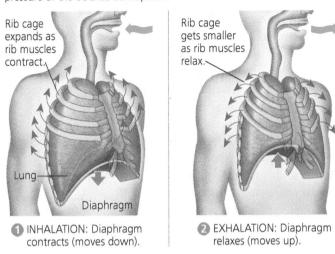

▼ **Figure 42.27 Negative pressure breathing.** A mammal breathes by changing the air pressure within its lungs relative to the pressure of the outside atmosphere.

Rib cage expands as rib muscles contract.

Rib cage gets smaller as rib muscles relax.

Lung

Diaphragm

❶ INHALATION: Diaphragm contracts (moves down).

❷ EXHALATION: Diaphragm relaxes (moves up).

**WHAT IF?** ➤ *The walls of alveoli contain elastic fibers that allow the alveoli to expand and contract with each breath. If the alveoli lost their elasticity, how would that affect gas exchange in the lungs?*

 **BioFlix Animation: Mechanics of Breathing**

Whereas inhalation is always active and requires work, exhalation is usually passive. During exhalation, the muscles controlling the thoracic cavity relax, and the volume of the cavity is reduced. The increased air pressure in the alveoli forces air up the breathing tubes and out of the body.

Within the thoracic cavity, a double membrane surrounds the lungs. The inner layer of this membrane adheres to the outside of the lungs, and the outer layer adheres to the wall of the thoracic cavity. A thin space filled with fluid separates the two layers. Surface tension in the fluid causes the two layers to stick together like two plates of glass separated by a film of water: The layers can slide smoothly past each other, but they cannot be pulled apart easily. Consequently, the volume of the thoracic cavity and the volume of the lungs change in unison.

The rib muscles and diaphragm are sufficient to change lung volume when a mammal is at rest. During exercise, other muscles of the neck, back, and chest increase the volume of the thoracic cavity by raising the rib cage. In kangaroos and some other mammals, locomotion causes a rhythmic movement of organs in the abdomen, including the stomach and liver. The result is a piston-like pumping motion that pushes and pulls on the diaphragm, further increasing the volume of air moved in and out of the lungs.

The volume of air inhaled and exhaled with each breath is called **tidal volume**. It averages about 500 mL in resting humans. The tidal volume during maximal inhalation and exhalation is the **vital capacity**, which is about 3.4 L and 4.8 L for college-age women and men, respectively. The air that remains after a forced exhalation is called the **residual volume**. With age, the lungs lose their resilience, and residual volume increases at the expense of vital capacity.

Because the lungs in mammals do not completely empty with each breath, and because inhalation occurs through the same airways as exhalation, each inhalation mixes fresh air with oxygen-depleted residual air. As a result, the maximum $P_{O_2}$ in alveoli is always considerably less than in the atmosphere. The maximum $P_{O_2}$ in lungs is also less for mammals than for birds, which have a unidirectional flow of air through the lungs. This is one reason why mammals function less well than birds at high altitude. For example, humans have great difficulty obtaining enough $O_2$ when climbing at high elevations, such as those in the Himalayas. However, bar-headed geese and several other bird species easily fly through high Himalayan passes during their migrations.

▼ **Figure 42.28** **Homeostatic control of breathing.**

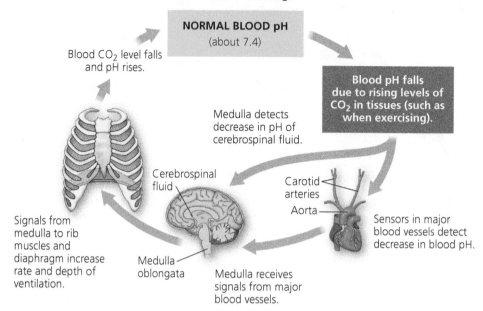

**VISUAL SKILLS ➤** *Suppose a person began breathing very rapidly while resting. Tracing a path along this negative-feedback control circuit, describe the effect on blood $CO_2$ levels and the steps by which homeostasis would be restored.*

## Control of Breathing in Humans

Although you can voluntarily hold your breath or breathe faster and deeper, most of the time your breathing is regulated by involuntary mechanisms. These control mechanisms ensure that gas exchange is coordinated with blood circulation and with metabolic demand.

The neurons mainly responsible for regulating breathing are in the medulla oblongata, near the base of the brain **(Figure 42.28)**. Neural circuits in the medulla form a pair of *breathing control centers* that establish the breathing rhythm. When you breathe deeply, a negative-feedback mechanism prevents the lungs from overexpanding: During inhalation, sensors that detect stretching of the lung tissue send nerve impulses to the control circuits in the medulla, inhibiting further inhalation.

In regulating breathing, the medulla uses the pH of the fluid in which it is bathed as an indicator of blood $CO_2$ concentration. The pH can be used in this way because blood $CO_2$ is the main determinant of the pH of cerebrospinal fluid, the fluid surrounding the brain and spinal cord. Carbon dioxide diffuses from the blood to the cerebrospinal fluid, where it reacts with water and forms carbonic acid ($H_2CO_3$). The $H_2CO_3$ can then dissociate into a bicarbonate ion ($HCO_3^-$) and a hydrogen ion ($H^+$):

$$CO_2 + H_2O \rightleftharpoons H_2CO_3 \rightleftharpoons HCO_3^- + H^+$$

Consider what happens when metabolic activity increases, for example, during exercise. Increased metabolism raises the concentration of $CO_2$ in the blood and cerebrospinal fluid.

Through the reactions shown above, the higher $CO_2$ concentration leads to an increase in the concentration of $H^+$, lowering pH. Sensors in the medulla as well as in major blood vessels detect this pH change. In response, the medulla's control circuits increase the depth and rate of breathing (see Figure 42.28). Both remain high until the excess $CO_2$ is eliminated in exhaled air and pH returns to a normal value.

The blood $O_2$ level usually has little effect on the breathing control centers. However, when the $O_2$ level drops very low (at high altitudes, for instance), $O_2$ sensors in the aorta and the carotid arteries in the neck send signals to the breathing control centers, which respond by increasing the breathing rate. The regulation of breathing is modulated by additional neural circuits, primarily in the pons, a part of the brain next to the medulla.

Breathing control is effective only if ventilation is matched to blood flow through alveolar capillaries. During exercise, for instance, such coordination couples an increased breathing rate, which enhances $O_2$ uptake and $CO_2$ removal, with an increase in cardiac output.

### CONCEPT CHECK 42.6

1. How does an increase in the $CO_2$ concentration in the blood affect the pH of cerebrospinal fluid?

2. A drop in blood pH causes an increase in heart rate. What is the function of this control mechanism?

3. **WHAT IF? ➤** If an injury tore a small hole in the membranes surrounding your lungs, what effect on lung function would you expect?

*For suggested answers, see Appendix A.*

# CONCEPT 42.7

## Adaptations for gas exchange include pigments that bind and transport gases

The high metabolic demands of many animals necessitate the exchange of large quantities of $O_2$ and $CO_2$. Here we'll examine how blood molecules called respiratory pigments facilitate this exchange through their interaction with $O_2$ and $CO_2$. We'll also investigate physiological adaptations that enable animals to be active under conditions of high metabolic load or very limiting $P_{O_2}$. As a basis for exploring these topics, let's summarize the basic gas exchange circuit in humans.

### Coordination of Circulation and Gas Exchange

To appreciate how the gas exchange and circulatory systems function together, let's track the variation in partial pressure for $O_2$ and $CO_2$ across these systems **(Figure 42.29)**. ❶ During inhalation, fresh air mixes with air remaining in the lungs. ❷ The resulting mixture formed in the alveoli has a higher $P_{O_2}$ than the blood flowing through the alveolar capillaries. Consequently, there is a net diffusion of $O_2$ down its partial pressure gradient from the air in the alveoli to the blood. Meanwhile, the presence of a $P_{CO_2}$ in the alveoli that is higher in the capillaries than in the air drives the net diffusion of $CO_2$ from blood to air. ❸ By the time the blood leaves the lungs in the pulmonary veins, its $P_{O_2}$ and $P_{CO_2}$ match the values for the air in alveoli. After returning to the heart, this blood is pumped through the systemic circuit.

❹ In the systemic capillaries, gradients of partial pressure favor the net diffusion of $O_2$ out of the blood and $CO_2$ into the blood. These gradients exist because cellular respiration in the mitochondria of cells near each capillary removes $O_2$ from and adds $CO_2$ to the surrounding interstitial fluid. ❺ Having unloaded $O_2$ and loaded $CO_2$, the blood is returned to the heart and pumped to the lungs again. ❻ There, exchange occurs across the alveolar capillaries, resulting in exhaled air enriched in $CO_2$ and partially depleted of $O_2$.

### Respiratory Pigments

The low solubility of $O_2$ in water (and thus in blood) poses a problem for animals that rely on the circulatory system to deliver $O_2$. For example, a person requires almost 2 L of $O_2$ per minute during intense exercise, and all of it must be carried in the blood from the lungs to the active tissues. At normal body temperature and air pressure, however, only 4.5 mL of $O_2$ can dissolve into a liter of blood in the lungs. Even if 80% of the dissolved $O_2$ were delivered to the tissues, the heart would still need to pump 555 L of blood per minute!

In fact, animals transport most of their $O_2$ bound to proteins called **respiratory pigments**. Respiratory pigments circulate with the blood or hemolymph and are often contained within specialized cells. The pigments greatly increase the amount of $O_2$ that can be carried in the circulatory fluid (from 4.5 to about 200 mL of $O_2$ per liter in mammalian blood). In our example of an exercising human with an $O_2$ delivery rate of 80%, the presence of a respiratory pigment reduces the cardiac output necessary for $O_2$ transport to a manageable 12.5 L of blood per minute.

A variety of respiratory pigments have evolved in animals. With a few exceptions, these molecules have a distinctive color (hence the term *pigment*) and consist of a metal bound to a protein. One example is the blue pigment *hemocyanin*, which has copper as its oxygen-binding component and is found in arthropods and many molluscs.

The respiratory pigment of many invertebrates and almost all vertebrates is hemoglobin. In vertebrates, it is contained in

▼ **Figure 42.29 Loading and unloading of respiratory gases.**

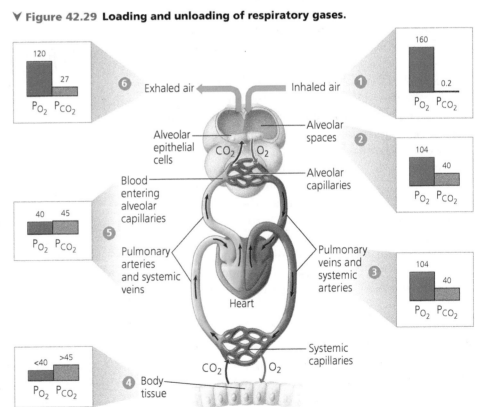

**WHAT IF?** *If you consciously forced more air out of your lungs each time you exhaled, how would that affect the values shown in the figure?*

(MB) BioFlix® Animation: Gas Exchange in the Human Body

erythrocytes and has four subunits. Each consists of a polypeptide and a heme group, a
cofactor that has an iron atom
at its center (**Figure 42.30**).
Each iron atom binds one
molecule of $O_2$, so a hemoglobin molecule can carry four $O_2$
molecules. Like all respiratory
pigments, hemoglobin binds
$O_2$ reversibly, loading $O_2$ in
the lungs or gills and unload-
ing it elsewhere in the body. This process is enhanced by
cooperativity between the hemoglobin subunits (see
Concept 8.5). When $O_2$ binds to one subunit, the others
change shape slightly, increasing affinity for $O_2$. When four
$O_2$ molecules are bound and one subunit unloads its $O_2$, the
other three subunits more readily unload $O_2$, as an associated
change in shape lowers their affinity for $O_2$.

Cooperativity in $O_2$ binding and release is evident in the
dissociation curve for hemoglobin (**Figure 42.31a**). Over the
range of $P_{O_2}$ where the dissociation curve has a steep slope,
even a slight change in $P_{O_2}$ causes hemoglobin to load or
unload a substantial amount of $O_2$. The steep part of the curve
corresponds to the range of $P_{O_2}$ found in body tissues. When
cells in a particular location begin working harder—during
exercise, for instance—$P_{O_2}$ dips in their vicinity as the $O_2$ is
consumed in cellular respiration. Because of subunit cooperativity, a slight drop in $P_{O_2}$ causes a relatively large increase in
the amount of $O_2$ the blood unloads.

Hemoglobin is especially efficient at delivering $O_2$ to tissues actively consuming $O_2$. However, this increased efficiency
results not from $O_2$ consumption, but rather from $CO_2$ production. As tissues consume $O_2$ in cell respiration, they also
produce $CO_2$. As we have seen, $CO_2$ reacts with water, forming
carbonic acid, which lowers the pH of its surroundings. Low
pH decreases the affinity of hemoglobin for $O_2$, an effect called
the **Bohr shift** (**Figure 42.31b**). Thus, where $CO_2$ production
is greater, hemoglobin releases more $O_2$, which can then be
used to support more cellular respiration.

Hemoglobin also assists in buffering the blood—that is,
preventing harmful changes in pH. In addition, it has a minor
role in $CO_2$ transport, the topic we'll explore next.

## Carbon Dioxide Transport

Only about 7% of the $CO_2$ released by respiring cells is transported in solution in blood plasma. The rest diffuses from
plasma into erythrocytes and reacts with water (assisted
by the enzyme carbonic anhydrase), forming $H_2CO_3$. The
$H_2CO_3$ readily dissociates into $H^+$ and $HCO_3^-$. Most $H^+$ binds
to hemoglobin and other proteins, minimizing change in
blood pH. Most $HCO_3^-$ diffuses out of the erythrocytes and is
transported to the lungs in the plasma. The remaining $HCO_3^-$,

▼ **Figure 42.30 Hemoglobin.**

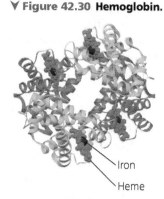

Iron

Heme

▼ **Figure 42.31 Dissociation curves for hemoglobin at 37°C.**

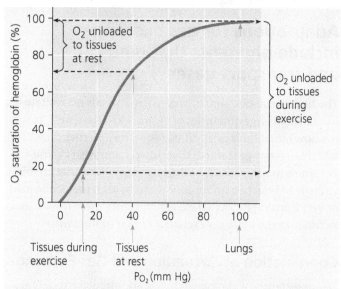

Tissues during
exercise

Tissues
at rest

Lungs

$P_{O_2}$ (mm Hg)

**(a) $P_{O_2}$ and hemoglobin dissociation at pH 7.4.** This dissociation
curve shows the relative amounts of $O_2$ bound to hemoglobin
exposed to solutions with different $P_{O_2}$. At a $P_{O_2}$ of 100 mm Hg,
typical in the lungs, hemoglobin is about 98% saturated with
$O_2$. At a $P_{O_2}$ of 40 mm Hg, common in resting tissues, hemoglobin is about 70% saturated, nearly a third of its $O_2$ having
been released by dissociation. As shown in the above graph,
hemoglobin can release much more $O_2$ to metabolically very
active tissues, such as muscle tissue during exercise.

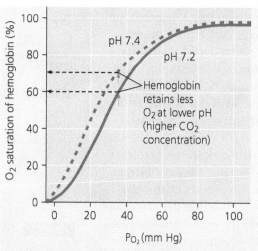

$P_{O_2}$ (mm Hg)

**(b) pH and hemoglobin dissociation.** In very active tissues, $CO_2$
from cellular respiration reacts with water to form carbonic acid,
decreasing pH. Because hydrogen ions affect hemoglobin shape,
a drop in pH shifts the $O_2$ dissociation curve toward the right (the
Bohr shift). For a given $P_{O_2}$, hemoglobin releases more $O_2$ at a
lower pH, supporting increased cellular respiration.

representing about 5% of the $CO_2$, binds to hemoglobin and
is transported in erythrocytes.

When blood flows through the lungs, the relative partial
pressures of $CO_2$ favor the net diffusion of $CO_2$ out of the
blood. As $CO_2$ diffuses into alveoli, the amount of $CO_2$ in the
blood decreases. This decrease shifts the chemical equilibrium
in favor of the conversion of $HCO_3^-$ to $CO_2$, enabling further

net diffusion of $CO_2$ into alveoli. Overall, the $P_{CO_2}$ gradient is sufficient to drive about a 15% reduction in $P_{CO_2}$ during passage of blood through the lungs.

 Animation: Transport of Respiratory Gases

## Respiratory Adaptations of Diving Mammals

**EVOLUTION** Animals vary greatly in their ability to spend time in environments in which there is no access to their normal respiratory medium—for example, when an air-breathing mammal swims underwater. Whereas most humans, even expert divers, cannot hold their breath longer than 2–3 minutes or swim deeper than 20 m, the Weddell seal of Antarctica routinely plunges to 200–500 m and remains there for a period ranging from 20 minutes to more than an hour. Another diving mammal, the Cuvier's beaked whale, can reach depths of 2,900 m—nearly 2 miles— and stay submerged for more than 2 hours! What enables these amazing feats?

One evolutionary adaptation of diving mammals to prolonged stays underwater is a capacity to store large amounts of $O_2$ in their bodies. The Weddell seal has about twice the volume of blood per kilogram of body mass as a human. Furthermore, the muscles of seals and other diving mammals contain a high concentration of an oxygen-storing protein called **myoglobin** in their muscles. As a result, the Weddell seal can store about twice as much $O_2$ per kilogram of body mass as can a human.

Diving mammals not only have a relatively large $O_2$ stockpile but also have adaptations that conserve $O_2$. They swim

▲ **Weddell seal**

with little muscular effort and glide passively for prolonged periods. During a dive, their heart rate and $O_2$ consumption rate decrease, and most blood is routed to vital tissues: the brain, spinal cord, eyes, adrenal glands, and, in pregnant seals, the placenta. Blood supply to the muscles is restricted or, during extended dives, shut off altogether. During these dives, a Weddell seal's muscles deplete the $O_2$ stored in myoglobin and then derive their ATP from fermentation instead of respiration (see Concept 9.5).

How did these adaptations arise over the course of evolution? All mammals, including humans, have a diving reflex triggered by a plunge or fall into water: When the face contacts cold water, the heart rate immediately decreases and blood flow to body extremities is reduced. Genetic changes that strengthened this reflex would have provided a selective advantage to seal ancestors foraging underwater. Also, genetic variations that increased traits such as blood volume or myoglobin concentration would have improved diving ability and therefore been favored during selection over many generations.

### CONCEPT CHECK 42.7

1. What determines whether $O_2$ and $CO_2$ undergo net diffusion into or out of capillaries? Explain.
2. How does the Bohr shift help deliver $O_2$ to very active tissues?
3. **WHAT IF?** ➤ A doctor might give bicarbonate ($HCO_3^-$) to a patient who is breathing very rapidly. What is the doctor assuming about the patient's blood chemistry?

*For suggested answers, see Appendix A.*

---

# 42 Chapter Review

 Go to **MasteringBiology**™ for Videos, Animations, Vocab Self-Quiz, Practice Tests, and more in the Study Area.

## SUMMARY OF KEY CONCEPTS

### CONCEPT 42.1

**Circulatory systems link exchange surfaces with cells throughout the body** (pp. 920–924)

**VOCAB SELF-QUIZ**
goo.gl/6u55ks

- In animals with simple body plans, a **gastrovascular cavity** mediates exchange between the environment and cells that can be reached by **diffusion**. Because diffusion is slow over long distances, most complex animals have a circulatory system that

moves fluid between cells and the organs that carry out exchange with the environment. Arthropods and most molluscs have an **open circulatory system**, in which **hemolymph** bathes organs directly. Vertebrates have a **closed circulatory system**, in which **blood** circulates in a closed network of pumps and vessels.

- The closed circulatory system of vertebrates consists of blood, **blood vessels**, and a two- to four-chambered **heart**. Blood pumped by a heart **ventricle** passes to **arteries** and then to the **capillaries**, sites of chemical exchange between blood and interstitial fluid. **Veins** return blood from capillaries to an **atrium**, which passes blood to a ventricle. Fishes, rays, and sharks have a single pump in their circulation. Air-breathing vertebrates have two pumps combined in a single heart. Variations in ventricle number and separation reflect adaptations to different environments and metabolic needs.

 *How does the flow of a fluid in a closed circulatory system differ from the movement of molecules between cells and their environment with regard to distance traveled, direction traveled, and driving force?*

CONCEPT 42.2

## Coordinated cycles of heart contraction drive double circulation in mammals (pp. 924–927)

- The right ventricle pumps blood to the lungs, where it loads $O_2$ and unloads $CO_2$. Oxygen-rich blood from the lungs enters the heart at the left atrium and is pumped to the body tissues by the left ventricle. Blood returns to the heart through the right atrium.

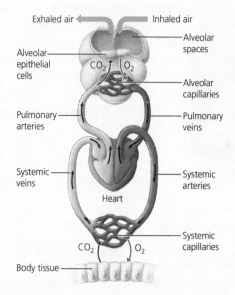

- The **cardiac cycle**, a complete sequence of the heart's pumping and filling, consists of a period of contraction, called **systole**, and a period of relaxation, called **diastole**. Heart function can be assessed by measuring the **pulse** (number of times the heart beats each minute) and **cardiac output** (volume of blood pumped by each ventricle per minute).
- The heartbeat originates with impulses at the **sinoatrial (SA) node** (pacemaker) of the right atrium. They trigger atrial contraction, are delayed at the **atrioventricular (AV) node**, and are then conducted along the bundle branches and Purkinje fibers, triggering ventricular contraction. The nervous system, hormones, and body temperature affect pacemaker activity.

 *What changes in cardiac function might you expect after surgical replacement of a defective heart valve?*

CONCEPT 42.3

## Patterns of blood pressure and flow reflect the structure and arrangement of blood vessels (pp. 927–931)

- Blood vessels have structures well adapted to function. Capillaries have narrow diameters and thin walls that facilitate exchange. The velocity of blood flow is lowest in the capillary beds as a result of their large total cross-sectional area. Arteries contain thick elastic walls that maintain blood pressure. Veins contain one-way valves that contribute to the return of blood to the heart. Blood pressure is altered by changes in cardiac output and by variable constriction of arterioles.

- Fluid leaks out of capillaries and is returned to blood by the **lymphatic system**, which also defends against infection.

 *If you placed your forearm on your head, how, if at all, would the blood pressure in that arm change? Explain.*

CONCEPT 42.4

## Blood components function in exchange, transport, and defense (pp. 932–937)

- Whole blood consists of cells and cell fragments (**platelets**) suspended in a liquid matrix called **plasma**. Plasma proteins influence blood pH, osmotic pressure, and viscosity, and they function in lipid transport, immunity (antibodies), and blood clotting (fibrinogen). Red blood cells, or **erythrocytes**, transport $O_2$. Five types of white blood cells, or **leukocytes**, function in defense against microorganisms and foreign substances in the blood. Platelets function in blood clotting, a cascade of reactions that converts plasma fibrinogen to fibrin.
- A variety of diseases impair function of the circulatory system. In **sickle-cell disease**, an aberrant form of **hemoglobin** disrupts erythrocyte shape and function, leading to blockage of small blood vessels and a decrease in the oxygen-carrying capacity of the blood. In cardiovascular disease, inflammation of the arterial lining enhances deposition of lipids and cells, resulting in the potential for life-threatening damage to the heart or brain.

 *In the absence of infection, what percentage of cells in human blood are leukocytes?*

CONCEPT 42.5

## Gas exchange occurs across specialized respiratory surfaces (pp. 937–942)

- At all sites of **gas exchange**, a gas undergoes net diffusion from where its **partial pressure** is higher to where it is lower. Air is more conducive to gas exchange than water because air has a higher $O_2$ content, lower density, and lower viscosity.
- The structure and organization of respiratory surfaces differ among animal species. Gills are outfoldings of the body surface specialized for gas exchange in water. The effectiveness of gas exchange in some gills, including those of fishes, is increased by **ventilation** and **countercurrent exchange** between blood and water. Gas exchange in insects relies on a **tracheal system**, a branched network of tubes that bring $O_2$ directly to cells. Spiders, land snails, and most terrestrial vertebrates have internal **lungs**. In mammals, air inhaled through the nostrils passes through the pharynx into the **trachea, bronchi, bronchioles**, and dead-end **alveoli**, where gas exchange occurs.

 *Why does altitude have almost no effect on an animal's ability to rid itself of $CO_2$ through gas exchange?*

CONCEPT 42.6

## Breathing ventilates the lungs (pp. 942–944)

- Breathing mechanisms vary substantially among vertebrates. An amphibian ventilates its lungs by **positive pressure breathing**, which forces air down the trachea. Birds use a system of air sacs as bellows to keep air flowing through the lungs in one direction only, preventing the mixing of incoming and outgoing air. Mammals ventilate their lungs by **negative pressure breathing**, which pulls air into the lungs when the rib muscles and **diaphragm** contract. Incoming and outgoing air mix, decreasing the efficiency of ventilation.
- Sensors detect the pH of cerebrospinal fluid (reflecting $CO_2$ concentration in the blood), and a control center in the brain adjusts breathing rate and depth to match metabolic demands.

Additional input to the control center is provided by sensors in the aorta and carotid arteries that monitor blood levels of $O_2$ as well as $CO_2$ (via blood pH).

 *How does air in the lungs differ from the fresh air that enters the body during inspiration?*

## CONCEPT 42.7

### Adaptations for gas exchange include pigments that bind and transport gases *(pp. 945–947)*

- In the lungs, gradients of partial pressure favor the net diffusion of $O_2$ into the blood and $CO_2$ out of the blood. The opposite situation exists in the rest of the body. **Respiratory pigments** such as hemocyanin and hemoglobin bind $O_2$, greatly increasing the amount of $O_2$ transported by the circulatory system.
- Evolutionary adaptations enable some animals to satisfy extraordinary $O_2$ demands. Deep-diving mammals stockpile $O_2$ in blood and other tissues and deplete it slowly.

? *How are the roles of a respiratory pigment and an enzyme similar?*

## TEST YOUR UNDERSTANDING

### Level 1: Knowledge/Comprehension

**PRACTICE TEST**
goo.gl/CUYGKD

1. Which of the following respiratory systems is not closely associated with a blood supply?
   (A) the lungs of a vertebrate
   (B) the gills of a fish
   (C) the tracheal system of an insect
   (D) the skin of an earthworm

2. Blood returning to the mammalian heart in a pulmonary vein drains first into the
   (A) left atrium.        (C) left ventricle.
   (B) right atrium.       (D) right ventricle.

3. Pulse is a direct measure of
   (A) blood pressure.
   (B) stroke volume.
   (C) cardiac output.
   (D) heart rate.

4. When you hold your breath, which of the following blood gas changes first leads to the urge to breathe?
   (A) rising $O_2$        (C) rising $CO_2$
   (B) falling $O_2$       (D) falling $CO_2$

5. One feature that amphibians and humans have in common is
   (A) the number of heart chambers.
   (B) a complete separation of circuits for circulation.
   (C) the number of circuits for circulation.
   (D) a low blood pressure in the systemic circuit.

### Level 2: Application/Analysis

6. If a molecule of $CO_2$ released into the blood in your left toe is exhaled from your nose, it must pass through all of the following except
   (A) the pulmonary vein.
   (B) the trachea.
   (C) the right atrium.
   (D) the right ventricle.

7. Compared with the interstitial fluid that bathes active muscle cells, blood reaching these cells in arterioles has a
   (A) higher $P_{O_2}$.
   (B) higher $P_{CO_2}$.
   (C) greater bicarbonate concentration.
   (D) lower pH.

## Level 3: Synthesis/Evaluation

8. **DRAW IT** Plot blood pressure against time for one cardiac cycle in humans, drawing separate lines for the pressure in the aorta, the left ventricle, and the right ventricle. Below the time axis, add a vertical arrow pointing to the time when you expect a peak in atrial blood pressure.

9. **EVOLUTION CONNECTION** One opponent of the movie monster Godzilla is Mothra, a mothlike creature with a wingspan of several dozen meters. The largest known insects were Paleozoic dragonflies with half-meter wingspans. Focusing on respiration and gas exchange, explain why giant insects are improbable.

10. **SCIENTIFIC INQUIRY**
    **INTERPRET THE DATA**
    The hemoglobin of a human fetus differs from adult hemoglobin. Compare the dissociation curves of the two hemoglobins in the graph at right. Describe how they differ, and propose a hypothesis to explain the benefit of this difference.

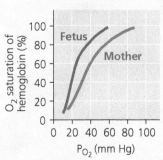

11. **SCIENCE, TECHNOLOGY, AND SOCIETY** Hundreds of studies have linked smoking with cardiovascular and lung disease. According to most health authorities, smoking is the leading cause of preventable, premature death in the United States. What are some arguments in favor of a total ban on cigarette advertising? What are arguments in opposition? Do you favor or oppose such a ban? Explain.

12. **WRITE ABOUT A THEME: INTERACTIONS** Some athletes prepare for competition at sea level by sleeping in a tent in which $P_{O_2}$ is kept low. When climbing high peaks, some mountaineers breathe from bottles of pure $O_2$. In a short essay (100–150 words), relate these behaviors to the mechanism of $O_2$ transport in the human body and to physiological interactions with our gaseous environment.

13. **SYNTHESIZE YOUR KNOWLEDGE**

The diving bell spider (*Argyroneta aquatica*) stores air underwater in a net of silk. Explain why this adaptation could be more advantageous than having gills, taking into account differences in gas exchange media and gas exchange organs among animals.

*For selected answers, see Appendix A.*

 For additional practice questions, check out the **Dynamic Study Modules** in MasteringBiology. You can use them to study on your smartphone, tablet, or computer anytime, anywhere!

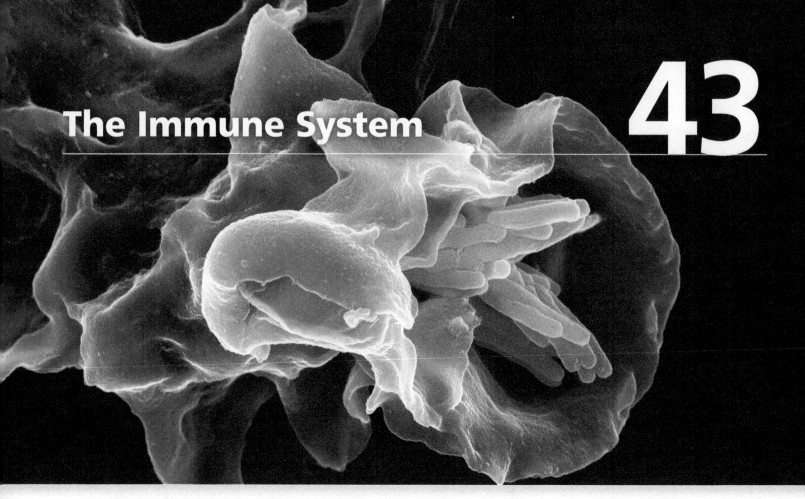

# The Immune System

▲ Figure 43.1 What triggered this attack by an immune cell on a clump of bacteria?

## KEY CONCEPTS

**43.1** In innate immunity, recognition and response rely on traits common to groups of pathogens

**43.2** In adaptive immunity, receptors provide pathogen-specific recognition

**43.3** Adaptive immunity defends against infection of body fluids and body cells

**43.4** Disruptions in immune system function can elicit or exacerbate disease

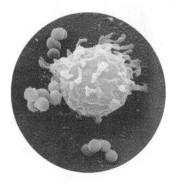

## Recognition and Response

For a **pathogen**—a bacterium, fungus, virus, or other disease-causing agent—the internal environment of an animal offers a ready source of nutrients, a protected setting, and a means of transport to new environments. From the perspective of a cold or flu virus, we are in many ways wonderful hosts. From our vantage point, the situation is not so ideal. Fortunately, adaptations have arisen over the course of evolution that protect animals against many pathogens.

Dedicated immune cells in the body fluids and tissues of most animals specifically interact with and destroy pathogens. In **Figure 43.1**, for example, an immune cell called a macrophage (brown) is engulfing rod-shaped bacteria (green). Some immune cells are types of white blood cells called lymphocytes (such as the one shown below with bacteria). Most lymphocytes recognize and respond to specific types of pathogens. Together, the body's defenses make up the **immune system**, which enables an animal to avoid or limit many infections. A foreign molecule or cell doesn't have to be pathogenic to elicit an immune response, but we'll focus in this chapter on the immune system's role in defending against pathogens.

The first lines of defense offered by immune systems help prevent pathogens from gaining entrance to the body. For example, an outer covering, such as a skin or shell, blocks entry by many pathogens. Sealing off the entire body surface is impossible, however, because gas exchange, nutrition, and reproduction require openings

---

When you see this blue icon, log in to **MasteringBiology** and go to the Study Area for digital resources.

 Get Ready for This Chapter

to the environment. Secretions that trap or kill pathogens guard the body's entrances and exits, while the linings of the digestive tract, airway, and other exchange surfaces provide additional barriers to infection.

If a pathogen breaches barrier defenses and enters the body, the problem of how to fend off attack changes substantially. Housed within body fluids and tissues, the invader is no longer an outsider. To fight infections, an animal's immune system must detect foreign particles and cells within the body. In other words, a properly functioning immune system distinguishes nonself from self. How is this accomplished? Immune cells produce receptor molecules that bind specifically to molecules from foreign cells or viruses and activate defense responses. The specific binding of immune receptors to foreign molecules is a type of *molecular recognition* and is the central event in identifying nonself molecules, particles, and cells.

Two types of molecular recognition provide the basis for the two types of immune defense found among animals: innate immunity, which is common to all animals, and adaptive immunity, which is found only in vertebrates. **Figure 43.2** summarizes these two types of immunity, highlighting fundamental similarities and differences.

In **innate immunity**, which includes barrier defenses, molecular recognition relies on a small set of receptor proteins that bind to molecules or structures that are absent from animal bodies but common to a group of viruses, bacteria, or other pathogens. Binding of an innate immune receptor to a foreign molecule activates internal defenses, enabling responses to a very broad range of pathogens.

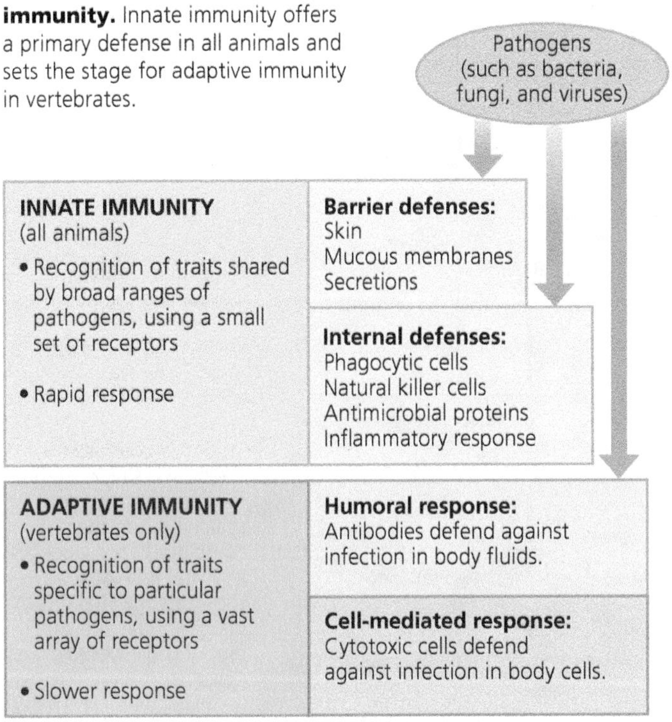

In **adaptive immunity**, molecular recognition relies on a vast arsenal of receptors, each of which recognizes a feature typically found only on a particular part of a particular molecule in a particular pathogen. As a result, recognition and response in adaptive immunity occur with remarkable specificity.

The adaptive immune response, also known as the acquired immune response, is activated after the innate immune response and develops more slowly. As reflected by the names *adaptive* and *acquired*, this immune response is enhanced by previous exposure to the infecting pathogen. Examples of adaptive responses include the synthesis of proteins that inactivate a bacterial toxin and the targeted killing of a virus-infected body cell.

In this chapter, we'll examine how each type of immunity protects animals from disease. We'll also investigate how pathogens can avoid or overwhelm the immune system and how defects in the immune system can imperil health.

# CONCEPT 43.1

## In innate immunity, recognition and response rely on traits common to groups of pathogens

Innate immunity is found in all animals (as well as in plants). In exploring innate immunity, we'll begin with invertebrates, which repel and fight infection with only this type of immunity. We'll then turn to vertebrates, in which innate immunity serves both as an immediate defense against infection and as the foundation for adaptive immune defenses.

### Innate Immunity of Invertebrates

The great success of insects in terrestrial and freshwater habitats teeming with diverse pathogens highlights the effectiveness of invertebrate innate immunity. In any environment, insects rely on their exoskeleton as a physical barrier against infection. Composed largely of the polysaccharide chitin, the exoskeleton provides an effective barrier defense against most pathogens. Chitin also lines the insect intestine, where it blocks infection by many pathogens ingested with food. **Lysozyme**, an enzyme that breaks down bacterial cell walls, further protects the insect digestive system.

Any pathogen that breaches an insect's barrier defenses encounters internal immune defenses. Insect immune cells produce a set of recognition proteins, each of which binds to a molecule common to a broad class of pathogens. Many of these molecules are components of fungal or bacterial cell walls. Because such molecules are not normally found in animal cells, they function as "identity tags" for pathogen recognition. Once bound to a pathogen molecule, a recognition protein triggers an innate immune response.

▼ **Figure 43.2 Overview of animal immunity.** Innate immunity offers a primary defense in all animals and sets the stage for adaptive immunity in vertebrates.

Pathogens (such as bacteria, fungi, and viruses)

| INNATE IMMUNITY (all animals) | Barrier defenses: |
|---|---|
| • Recognition of traits shared by broad ranges of pathogens, using a small set of receptors<br><br>• Rapid response | Skin<br>Mucous membranes<br>Secretions |
| | **Internal defenses:**<br>Phagocytic cells<br>Natural killer cells<br>Antimicrobial proteins<br>Inflammatory response |

| ADAPTIVE IMMUNITY (vertebrates only) | Humoral response: |
|---|---|
| • Recognition of traits specific to particular pathogens, using a vast array of receptors<br><br>• Slower response | Antibodies defend against infection in body fluids. |
| | **Cell-mediated response:**<br>Cytotoxic cells defend against infection in body cells. |

The major immune cells of insects are called *hemocytes*. Like amoebas, some hemocytes ingest and break down microorganisms, a process known as **phagocytosis** (**Figure 43.3**). One class of hemocytes produces a defense molecule that helps entrap large pathogens, such as *Plasmodium*, the single-celled parasite of mosquitoes that causes malaria in humans. Many other hemocytes release *antimicrobial peptides*, which circulate throughout the body of the insect and inactivate or kill fungi and bacteria by disrupting their plasma membranes.

The innate immune response of insects is specific for particular classes of pathogens. For example, if a fungus infects an insect, binding of recognition proteins to fungal cell wall molecules activates a transmembrane receptor called Toll. Toll in turn activates production and secretion of antimicrobial peptides that specifically kill fungal cells. Remarkably, phagocytic mammalian cells use receptor proteins very similar to the Toll receptor to recognize viral, fungal, and bacterial components, a discovery that was recognized with the Nobel Prize in Physiology or Medicine in 2011.

Insects also have specific defenses that protect against infection by viruses. Many viruses that infect insects have a genome consisting of a single strand of RNA. When the virus replicates in the host cell, this RNA strand is the template for synthesis of double-stranded RNA. Because animals do not produce double-stranded RNA, its presence can trigger a specific defense against the invading virus, as illustrated in **Figure 43.4**.

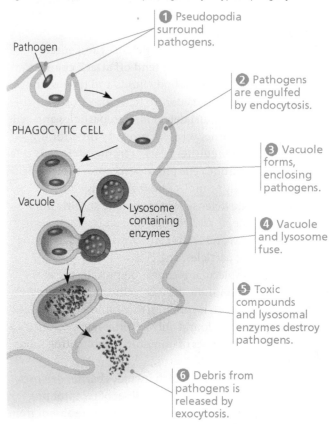

▼ **Figure 43.3 Phagocytosis.** This diagram depicts events in the ingestion and destruction of pathogens by a typical phagocytic cell.

Pathogen

PHAGOCYTIC CELL

Vacuole

Lysosome containing enzymes

❶ Pseudopodia surround pathogens.

❷ Pathogens are engulfed by endocytosis.

❸ Vacuole forms, enclosing pathogens.

❹ Vacuole and lysosome fuse.

❺ Toxic compounds and lysosomal enzymes destroy pathogens.

❻ Debris from pathogens is released by exocytosis.

▼ **Figure 43.4 Antiviral defense in insects.** In defending against an infecting RNA virus, an insect cell turns the viral genome against itself, cutting the viral genome into small fragments that it then uses as guide molecules to find and destroy viral messenger RNAs (mRNAs).

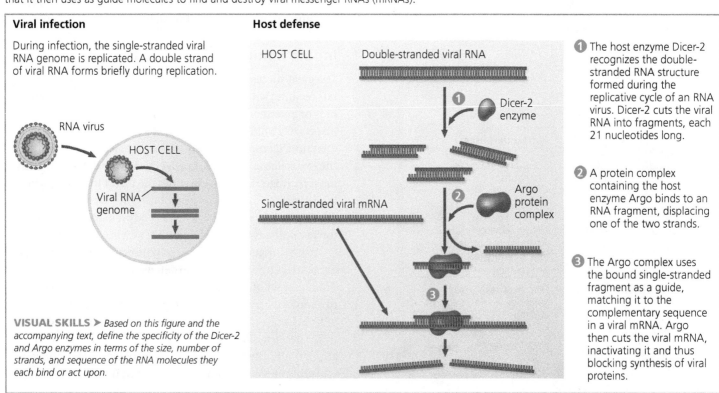

**Viral infection**

During infection, the single-stranded viral RNA genome is replicated. A double strand of viral RNA forms briefly during replication.

RNA virus

HOST CELL

Viral RNA genome

**VISUAL SKILLS ➤** *Based on this figure and the accompanying text, define the specificity of the Dicer-2 and Argo enzymes in terms of the size, number of strands, and sequence of the RNA molecules they each bind or act upon.*

**Host defense**

HOST CELL        Double-stranded viral RNA

❶ Dicer-2 enzyme

Single-stranded viral mRNA

❷ Argo protein complex

❸

❶ The host enzyme Dicer-2 recognizes the double-stranded RNA structure formed during the replicative cycle of an RNA virus. Dicer-2 cuts the viral RNA into fragments, each 21 nucleotides long.

❷ A protein complex containing the host enzyme Argo binds to an RNA fragment, displacing one of the two strands.

❸ The Argo complex uses the bound single-stranded fragment as a guide, matching it to the complementary sequence in a viral mRNA. Argo then cuts the viral mRNA, inactivating it and thus blocking synthesis of viral proteins.

## Innate Immunity of Vertebrates

In jawed vertebrates, innate immune defenses coexist with the more recently evolved system of adaptive immunity. Because most discoveries regarding vertebrate innate immunity have come from studies of mice and humans, we'll focus here on mammals. In this section, we'll consider first the innate defenses that are similar to those found among invertebrates: barrier defenses, phagocytosis, and antimicrobial peptides. We'll then examine some unique aspects of vertebrate innate immunity, such as natural killer cells, interferons, and the inflammatory response.

### Barrier Defenses

The barrier defenses of mammals, which block the entry of many pathogens, include the mucous membranes and skin. The mucous membranes that line the digestive, respiratory, urinary, and reproductive tracts produce *mucus*, a viscous fluid that traps pathogens and other particles. In the airway, ciliated epithelial cells sweep mucus and any entrapped material upward, helping prevent infection of the lungs. Saliva, tears, and mucous secretions that bathe various exposed epithelia provide a washing action that also inhibits colonization by fungi and bacteria.

Beyond their physical role in inhibiting microbial entry, body secretions create an environment that is hostile to many pathogens. Lysozyme in tears, saliva, and mucous secretions destroys the cell walls of susceptible bacteria as they enter the openings around the eyes or the upper respiratory tract. Pathogens in food or water and those in swallowed mucus must also contend with the acidic environment of the stomach (pH 2), which kills most of them before they can enter the intestines. Similarly, secretions from oil and sweat glands give human skin a pH ranging from 3 to 5, acidic enough to prevent the growth of many bacteria.

### Cellular Innate Defenses

In mammals, as in insects, there are innate immune cells dedicated to detecting, devouring, and destroying invading pathogens. In doing so, these cells often rely on a **Toll-like receptor (TLR)**, a mammalian recognition protein similar to the Toll protein of insects. Upon recognizing pathogens, TLR proteins produce signals that initiate responses tuned to the invading microorganism.

Each TLR protein binds to fragments of molecules characteristic of a set of pathogens **(Figure 43.5)**. For example, TLR3, on the inner surface of vesicles formed by endocytosis, binds to double-stranded RNA, a form of nucleic acid produced by certain viruses. Similarly, TLR4, located on immune cell plasma membranes, recognizes lipopolysaccharide, a type of molecule found on the surface of many bacteria, and TLR5 recognizes flagellin, the main protein of bacterial flagella.

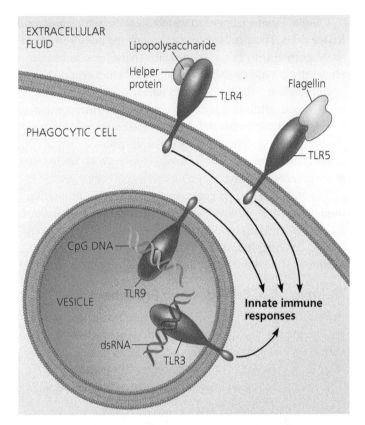

▲ **Figure 43.5 TLR signaling.** Each mammalian Toll-like receptor (TLR) recognizes a molecular pattern characteristic of a group of pathogens. Lipopolysaccharide, flagellin, CpG DNA (DNA containing unmethylated CG sequences), and double-stranded (ds) RNA are all found in bacteria, fungi, or viruses but not in animal cells. Together with other recognition and response factors, TLR proteins trigger internal innate immune defenses, including production of cytokines and antimicrobial peptides.

**VISUAL SKILLS** ➤ *Look at the locations of the TLR proteins and then suggest a possible benefit of their distribution.*

The two main types of phagocytic cells in the mammalian body are neutrophils and macrophages. **Neutrophils**, which circulate in the blood, are attracted by signals from infected tissues and then engulf and destroy the infecting pathogens. **Macrophages** ("big eaters"), like the one shown in Figure 43.1, are larger phagocytic cells. Some migrate throughout the body, whereas others reside permanently in organs and tissues where they are likely to encounter pathogens. For example, some macrophages are located in the spleen, where pathogens in the blood are often trapped.

Two other types of cells—dendritic cells and eosinophils—also have roles in innate defense. **Dendritic cells** mainly populate tissues, such as skin, that contact the environment. They stimulate adaptive immunity against pathogens that they encounter and engulf, as we'll explore shortly. *Eosinophils*, often found in tissues underlying an epithelium, are important in defending against multicellular invaders, such as parasitic worms. Upon encountering such parasites, eosinophils discharge destructive enzymes.

Cellular innate defenses in vertebrates also involve **natural killer cells**. These cells circulate through the body and detect the abnormal array of surface proteins characteristic of some virus-infected and cancerous cells. Natural killer cells do not engulf stricken cells. Instead, they release chemicals that lead to cell death, inhibiting further spread of the virus or cancer.

Many cellular innate defenses in vertebrates involve the lymphatic system, a network that distributes the fluid called lymph throughout the body (**Figure 43.6**). Some macrophages reside in lymph nodes, where they engulf pathogens that have entered the lymph from the interstitial fluid. Dendritic cells reside outside the lymphatic system but migrate to the lymph nodes after interacting with pathogens. Within the lymph nodes, dendritic cells interact with other immune cells, stimulating adaptive immunity.

### Antimicrobial Peptides and Proteins

In mammals, pathogen recognition triggers the production and release of a variety of peptides and proteins that attack pathogens or impede their reproduction. As in insects, some of these defense molecules function as antimicrobial peptides, damaging broad groups of pathogens by disrupting membrane integrity. Others, including the interferons and complement proteins, are unique to vertebrate immune systems.

**Interferons** are proteins that provide innate defense by interfering with viral infections. Virus-infected body cells secrete interferon proteins that induce nearby uninfected cells to produce substances that inhibit viral replication. In this way, these interferons limit the cell-to-cell spread of viruses in the body, helping control viral infections such as colds and influenza. Some white blood cells secrete a different type of interferon that helps activate macrophages, enhancing their phagocytic ability. Pharmaceutical companies now use recombinant DNA technology to mass-produce interferons to help treat certain viral infections, such as hepatitis C.

The infection-fighting **complement system** consists of roughly 30 proteins in blood plasma. These proteins circulate in an inactive state and are activated by substances on the surface of many pathogens. Activation results in a cascade of biochemical reactions that can lead to lysis (bursting) of invading cells. The complement system also functions in the inflammatory response, our next topic, as well as in the adaptive defenses discussed later in the chapter.

▼ **Figure 43.6 The human lymphatic system.** The lymphatic system consists of lymphatic vessels (shown in green), through which lymph travels, and structures that trap foreign substances. These structures include lymph nodes (orange) and lymphoid organs (yellow): the adenoids, tonsils, thymus, spleen, Peyer's patches, and appendix. Steps 1–4 trace the flow of lymph and illustrate the role of lymph nodes in activating adaptive immunity. (Concept 42.3 describes the relationship between the lymphatic and circulatory systems.)

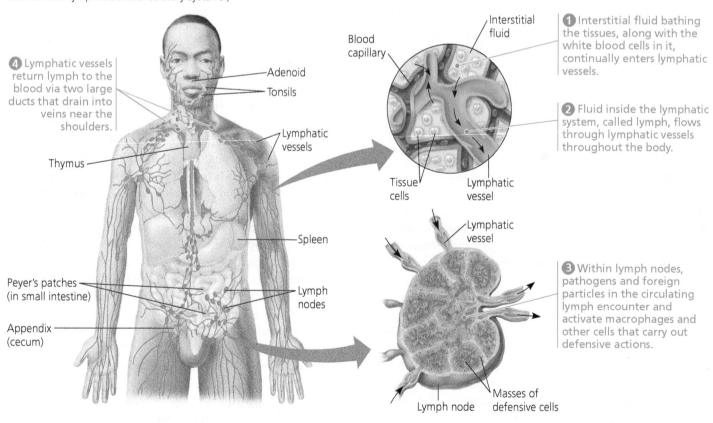

❹ Lymphatic vessels return lymph to the blood via two large ducts that drain into veins near the shoulders.

Adenoid

Tonsils

Lymphatic vessels

Thymus

Spleen

Peyer's patches (in small intestine)

Lymph nodes

Appendix (cecum)

Blood capillary

Interstitial fluid

❶ Interstitial fluid bathing the tissues, along with the white blood cells in it, continually enters lymphatic vessels.

Tissue cells

Lymphatic vessel

❷ Fluid inside the lymphatic system, called lymph, flows through lymphatic vessels throughout the body.

Lymphatic vessel

❸ Within lymph nodes, pathogens and foreign particles in the circulating lymph encounter and activate macrophages and other cells that carry out defensive actions.

Lymph node

Masses of defensive cells

## Inflammatory Response

When a splinter lodges under your skin, the surrounding area becomes swollen and warm to the touch. Both changes reflect a local **inflammatory response**, a set of events triggered by signaling molecules released upon injury or infection **(Figure 43.7)**. Activated macrophages discharge *cytokines*, signaling molecules that recruit neutrophils to the site of injury or infection. In addition, *mast cells*, immune cells found in connective tissue, release the signaling molecule **histamine** at sites of damage. Histamine triggers nearby blood vessels to dilate and become more permeable. The resulting increase in local blood supply produces the redness and increased skin temperature typical of the inflammatory response (from the Latin *inflammare*, to set on fire).

During inflammation, cycles of signaling and response transform the site of injury and infection. Activated complement proteins promote further release of histamine, attracting more phagocytic cells (see Figure 43.7) that carry out additional phagocytosis. At the same time, enhanced blood flow to the site helps deliver antimicrobial peptides. The result is an accumulation of *pus*, a fluid rich in white blood cells, dead pathogens, and debris from damaged tissue.

A minor injury or infection causes a local inflammatory response, but more extensive tissue damage or infection may lead to a response that is systemic (throughout the body). Cells in injured or infected tissue often secrete molecules that stimulate the release of additional neutrophils from the bone marrow. In the case of a severe infection, such as meningitis or appendicitis, the number of white blood cells in the bloodstream may increase several-fold within only a few hours.

A systemic inflammatory response sometimes involves fever. In response to certain pathogens, substances released by activated macrophages cause the body's thermostat to reset to a higher temperature (see Concept 40.3). There is good evidence that fever can be beneficial in fighting certain infections, although the underlying mechanism is still a subject of debate. One hypothesis is that an elevated body temperature may enhance phagocytosis and, by speeding up chemical reactions, accelerate tissue repair.

Certain bacterial infections can induce an overwhelming systemic inflammatory response, leading to a life-threatening condition known as *septic shock*. Characterized by very high fever, low blood pressure, and poor blood flow through capillaries, septic shock occurs most often in the very old and the very young. It is fatal in roughly one-third of cases and contributes to the death of more than 200,000 people each year in the United States alone.

Chronic (ongoing) inflammation can also threaten human health. For example, millions of individuals worldwide suffer from Crohn's disease and ulcerative colitis, often debilitating disorders in which an unregulated inflammatory response disrupts intestinal function.

▼ **Figure 43.7 Major events in a local inflammatory response.**

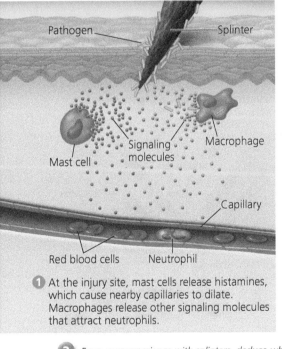

**1** At the injury site, mast cells release histamines, which cause nearby capillaries to dilate. Macrophages release other signaling molecules that attract neutrophils.

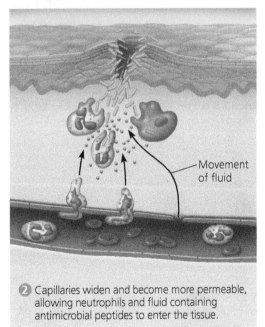

**2** Capillaries widen and become more permeable, allowing neutrophils and fluid containing antimicrobial peptides to enter the tissue.

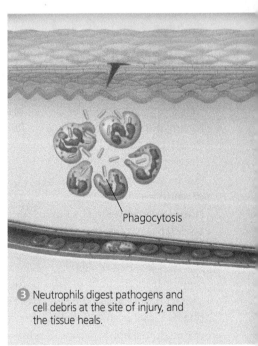

**3** Neutrophils digest pathogens and cell debris at the site of injury, and the tissue heals.

 *From your experience with splinters, deduce whether the signals mediating an inflammatory response are short- or long-lived. Explain your answer.*

**MB** Animation: Overview of the Inflammatory Response

## Evasion of Innate Immunity by Pathogens

Adaptations have evolved in some pathogens that enable them to avoid destruction by phagocytic cells. For example, the outer capsule that surrounds certain bacteria interferes with molecular recognition and phagocytosis. One such bacterium, *Streptococcus pneumoniae*, is a major cause of pneumonia and meningitis in humans (see Concept 16.1).

Some bacteria are recognized but resist breakdown after being engulfed by a host cell. One example is *Mycobacterium tuberculosis*, the bacterium shown in Figure 43.1. Rather than being destroyed, this bacterium grows and reproduces within host cells, effectively hidden from the body's immune defenses. The result of this infection is tuberculosis (TB), a disease that attacks the lungs and other tissues. Worldwide, TB kills more than 1 million people a year.

### CONCEPT CHECK 43.1

1. Pus is both a sign of infection and an indicator of immune defenses in action. Explain.

2. **MAKE CONNECTIONS** ➤ How do the molecules that activate the vertebrate TLR signal transduction pathway differ from the ligands in most other signaling pathways (see Concept 11.2)?

3. **WHAT IF?** ➤ Parasitic wasps inject their eggs into host larvae of other insects. If the host immune system doesn't kill the wasp egg, the egg hatches and the wasp larva devours the host larva as food. Why can some insect species initiate an innate immune response to a wasp egg, but others cannot?

*For suggested answers, see Appendix A.*

# CONCEPT 43.2

## In adaptive immunity, receptors provide pathogen-specific recognition

Vertebrates are unique in having both adaptive and innate immunity. The adaptive response relies on T cells and B cells, which are types of white blood cells called **lymphocytes** (Figure 43.8). Like all blood cells, lymphocytes originate from stem cells in the bone marrow. Some migrate from the bone marrow to the **thymus**, an organ in the thoracic cavity above the heart (see Figure 43.6). These lymphocytes mature into **T cells**. Lymphocytes that remain and mature in the bone marrow develop as **B cells**. (Lymphocytes of a third type remain in the blood and become the natural killer cells active in innate immunity.)

Any substance that elicits a B or T cell response is called an **antigen**. In adaptive immunity, recognition occurs when a

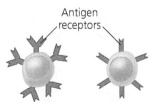
▼ **Figure 43.8 B and T lymphocytes.**

Antigen receptors

Mature B cell          Mature T cell

B cell or T cell binds to an antigen, such as a bacterial or viral protein, via a protein called an **antigen receptor**. Each antigen receptor binds to just one part of one molecule from a particular pathogen, such as a species of bacteria or strain of virus.

The cells of the immune system produce millions of different antigen receptors. A given lymphocyte, however, produces just one variety; all of the antigen receptors made by a single B or T cell are identical. Infection by a virus, bacterium, or other pathogen triggers activation of B and T cells with antigen receptors specific for parts of that pathogen. Although drawings of B and T cells typically include just a few antigen receptors, a single B or T cell actually has about 100,000 antigen receptors on its surface.

Antigens are usually large foreign molecules, either proteins or polysaccharides. Many antigens protrude from the surface of foreign cells or viruses. Other antigens, such as toxins secreted by bacteria, are released into the extracellular fluid.

The small, accessible portion of an antigen that binds to an antigen receptor is called an **epitope**. An example is a group of amino acids in a particular protein. A single antigen usually has several epitopes, each binding a receptor with a different specificity. Because all antigen receptors produced by a single B cell or T cell are identical, they bind to the same epitope. Each B or T cell thus displays *specificity* for a particular epitope, enabling it to respond to any pathogen that produces molecules containing that epitope.

The antigen receptors of B cells and T cells have similar components, but they encounter antigens in different ways. We'll consider the two processes in turn.

### Antigen Recognition by B Cells and Antibodies

Each B cell antigen receptor is a Y-shaped protein consisting of four polypeptide chains: two identical **heavy chains** and two identical **light chains**. Disulfide bridges link the chains together (Figure 43.9).

▼ **Figure 43.9 The structure of a B cell antigen receptor.**

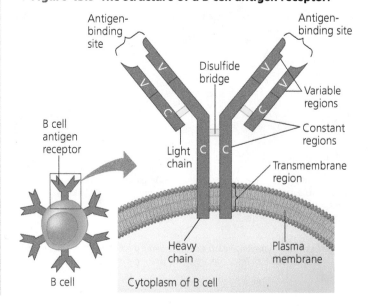

Each light chain or heavy chain has a *constant (C) region*, where amino acid sequences vary little among the receptors on different B cells. The constant region of heavy chains contains a transmembrane region, which anchors the receptor in the cell's plasma membrane. As shown in Figure 43.9, each light or heavy chain also has a *variable (V) region*, so named because its amino acid sequence varies extensively from one B cell to another. Together, parts of a heavy-chain V region and a light-chain V region form an asymmetric binding site for an antigen. Therefore, each B cell antigen receptor has two identical antigen-binding sites.

Binding of a B cell antigen receptor to an antigen is an early step in B cell activation, leading to formation of cells that secrete a soluble form of the receptor **(Figure 43.10a)**. This secreted protein is called an **antibody**, also known as an **immunoglobulin (Ig)**. Antibodies have the same Y-shaped structure as B cell antigen receptors but lack a membrane anchor. As you'll see later, antibodies provide a direct defense against pathogens in body fluids.

The antigen-binding site of a membrane-bound receptor or antibody has a unique shape that provides a lock-and-key fit for a particular epitope. This stable interaction involves any noncovalent bonds between an epitope and the surface of the binding site. Differences in the amino acid sequences of variable regions provide the variation in binding surfaces that enables binding to be highly specific.

B cell antigen receptors and antibodies bind to intact antigens in the blood and lymph. As illustrated in **Figure 43.10b** for antibodies, they can bind to antigens on the surface of pathogens or free in body fluids.

## Antigen Recognition by T Cells

For a T cell, the antigen receptor consists of two different polypeptide chains, an *α chain* and a *β chain*, linked by a disulfide bridge **(Figure 43.11)**. Near the base of the T cell antigen receptor (often called simply a T cell receptor) is a transmembrane region that anchors the molecule in the cell's plasma membrane. At the outer tip of the molecule, the variable (V) regions of the α and β chains together form a single antigen-binding site. The remainder of the molecule is made up of the constant (C) regions.

Whereas the antigen receptors of B cells bind to epitopes of *intact* antigens protruding from pathogens or circulating free in body fluids, antigen receptors of T cells bind only to fragments of antigens that are displayed, or presented, on the surface of host cells. The host protein that displays the antigen fragment on the cell surface is called a **major histocompatibility complex (MHC) molecule**. By displaying antigen fragments, MHC molecules are essential for antigen recognition by T cells.

▽ **Figure 43.10 Antigen recognition by B cells and antibodies.**

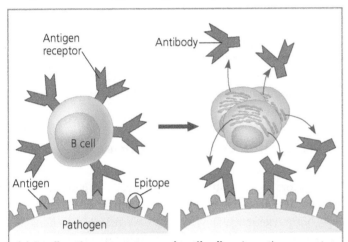

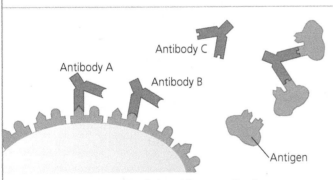

**(a) B cell antigen receptors and antibodies.** An antigen receptor of a B cell binds to an epitope, a particular part of an antigen. Following binding, the B cell gives rise to cells that secrete a soluble form of the antigen receptor. This soluble receptor, called an antibody, is specific for the same epitope as the original B cell.

**(b) Antigen receptor specificity.** Different antibodies can recognize distinct epitopes on the same antigen. Furthermore, antibodies can recognize free antigens as well as antigens on a pathogen's surface.

**MAKE CONNECTIONS** ➤ *The interactions depicted here involve a highly specific binding between antigen and receptor (see Figure 5.17). How is this similar to an enzyme-substrate interaction (see Figure 8.15)?*

▽ **Figure 43.11 The structure of a T cell antigen receptor.**

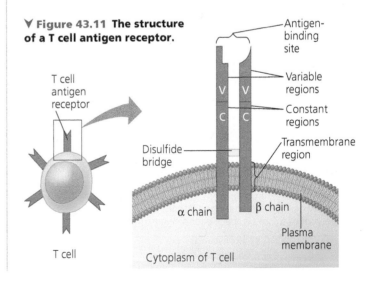

The display and recognition of protein antigens begin when a pathogen infects a cell of the animal host or parts of a pathogen are taken in by an immune cell **(Figure 43.12a)**. Inside the animal cell, enzymes cleave each antigen into antigen fragments, which are smaller peptides. Each antigen fragment binds to an MHC molecule, which transports the bound peptide to the cell surface. The result is **antigen presentation**, the display of the antigen fragment in an exposed groove of the MHC protein. **Figure 43.12b** shows a close-up view of antigen presentation, a process advertising the fact that a host cell contains a foreign substance. If the cell displaying an antigen fragment encounters a T cell with the right specificity, the antigen receptor on the T cell can bind to both the antigen fragment and the MHC molecule. This interaction of an MHC molecule, an antigen fragment, and an antigen receptor triggers an adaptive immune response, as we'll explore in Concept 43.3.

## B Cell and T Cell Development

Now that you know how B cells and T cells recognize antigens, let's consider four major characteristics of adaptive immunity. First, the immense repertoire of lymphocytes and receptors enables detection of antigens and pathogens never before encountered. Second, adaptive immunity normally has self-tolerance, the lack of reactivity against an animal's own molecules and cells. Third, cell proliferation triggered by activation greatly increases the number of B and T cells specific for an antigen. Fourth, there is a stronger and more rapid response to an antigen encountered previously, due to a feature known as *immunological memory*, which we'll explore later in the chapter.

Receptor diversity and self-tolerance arise as a lymphocyte matures. Proliferation of cells and the formation of immunological memory occur later, after a mature lymphocyte encounters and binds to a specific antigen. We'll consider these four characteristics in the order in which they develop.

### Generation of B Cell and T Cell Diversity

Each person makes more than 1 million different B cell antigen receptors and 10 million different T cell antigen receptors. Yet there are only about 20,000 protein-coding genes in the human genome. How, then, do we generate so many different antigen receptors? The answer lies in combinations. Think of selecting a cell phone that comes in three sizes and six colors. There are 18 (3 × 6) combinations to consider. Similarly, by combining variable elements, the immune system assembles millions of different receptors from a very small collection of parts.

To understand the origin of receptor diversity, let's consider an immunoglobulin (Ig) gene that encodes the light chain of both membrane-bound B cell antigen receptors and secreted antibodies (immunoglobulins). Although we'll analyze only a single Ig light-chain gene, all B and T cell antigen receptor genes undergo very similar transformations.

The capacity to generate diversity is built into the structure of Ig genes. A receptor light chain is encoded by three gene segments: a variable (V) segment, a joining (J) segment, and a constant (C) segment. The V and J segments together encode the variable region of the receptor chain, while the C segment encodes the constant region. The light-chain gene contains a single C segment, 40 different V segments, and 5 different J segments. The alternative copies of the V and J segments are arrayed along the

▼ **Figure 43.12 Antigen recognition by T cells.**

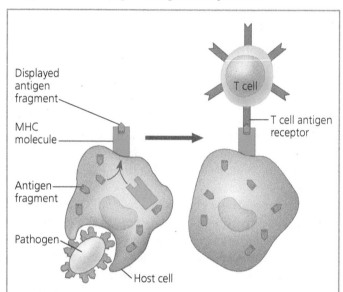

**(a) Antigen recognition by a T cell.** Inside the host cell, an antigen fragment from a pathogen binds to an MHC molecule and is brought up to the cell surface, where it is displayed. The combination of MHC molecule and antigen fragment is recognized by a T cell.

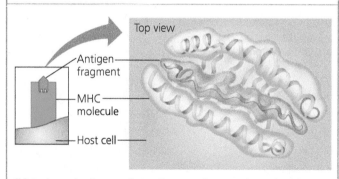

**(b) A closer look at antigen presentation.** As shown in this ribbon model, the top of the MHC molecule cradles an antigen fragment, like a bun holding a hot dog. An MHC molecule can display many different antigen fragments, but the antigen receptor of a T cell is specific for a single antigen fragment.

**▼ Figure 43.13 Immunoglobulin (antibody) gene rearrangement.** The joining of randomly selected *V* and *J* gene segments ($V_{39}$ and $J_5$ in the example shown) results in a functional gene that encodes the light-chain polypeptide of a B cell antigen receptor. Transcription, splicing, and translation result in a light chain that combines with a polypeptide produced from an independently rearranged heavy-chain gene to form a functional receptor. Mature B cells (and T cells) are exceptions to the generalization that all nucleated cells in the body have exactly the same DNA.

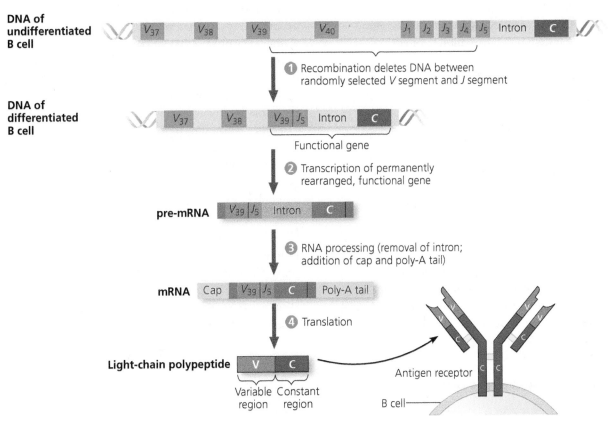

**MAKE CONNECTIONS** ➤ *Both alternative splicing and joining of V and J segments by recombination generate diverse gene products from a limited set of gene segments (see Figure 18.13). How do these processes differ?*

gene in a series **(Figure 43.13)**. Because a functional gene is built from one copy of each type of segment, the pieces can be combined in 200 different ways ($40\ V \times 5\ J \times 1\ C$). The number of different heavy-chain combinations is even greater, resulting in even more diversity.

Assembling a functional Ig gene requires rearranging the DNA. Early in B cell development, an enzyme complex called *recombinase* links one light-chain *V* gene segment to one *J* gene segment. This recombination event eliminates the long stretch of DNA between the segments, forming a single exon that is part *V* and part *J*.

Recombinase acts randomly, linking any one of the 40 *V* gene segments to any one of the 5 *J* gene segments. Heavy-chain genes undergo a similar rearrangement. In any given cell, however, only one allele of a light-chain gene and one allele of a heavy-chain gene are rearranged. Furthermore, the rearrangements are permanent and are passed on to the daughter cells when the lymphocyte divides.

After both a light-chain and a heavy-chain gene have been rearranged, antigen receptors can be synthesized.

The rearranged genes are transcribed, and the transcripts are processed for translation. Following translation, the light chain and heavy chain assemble together, forming an antigen receptor (see Figure 43.13). Each pair of randomly rearranged heavy and light chains results in a different antigen-binding site. For the total population of B cells in a human body, the number of such combinations has been calculated as $3.5 \times 10^6$. Furthermore, mutations introduced during *VJ* recombination add additional variation, making the number of antigen-binding specificities even greater.

### Origin of Self-Tolerance

In adaptive immunity, how does the body distinguish self from nonself? Because antigen receptor genes are randomly rearranged, some immature lymphocytes produce receptors specific for epitopes on the organism's own molecules. If these self-reactive lymphocytes were not eliminated or inactivated, the immune system could not distinguish self from nonself and would attack body proteins, cells, and tissues. Instead, as lymphocytes mature in the bone marrow or thymus, their antigen receptors are tested for self-reactivity. Some B and T cells with receptors specific for the body's own molecules are destroyed by *apoptosis*, which is a programmed cell death (see Concept 11.5). The remaining self-reactive lymphocytes are typically rendered nonfunctional, leaving only those that react to foreign molecules. Since the body normally lacks mature lymphocytes that can react against its own components, the immune system is said to exhibit *self-tolerance*.

## Proliferation of B Cells and T Cells

Despite the enormous variety of antigen receptors, only a tiny fraction are specific for a given epitope. How then does an effective adaptive response develop? To begin with, an antigen is presented to a steady stream of lymphocytes in the lymph nodes (see Figure 43.6) until a match is made. A successful match between an antigen receptor and an epitope initiates events that activate the lymphocyte bearing the receptor.

Once activated, a B cell or T cell undergoes multiple cell divisions. For each activated cell, the result of this proliferation is a clone, a population of cells that are identical to the original cell. Some cells from this clone become **effector cells**, mostly short-lived cells that take effect immediately against the antigen and any pathogens producing that antigen. For B cells, the effector forms are *plasma cells*, which secrete antibodies.

For T cells, the effector forms are helper T cells and cytotoxic T cells, whose roles we'll explore in Concept 43.3. The remaining cells in the clone become **memory cells**, long-lived cells that can give rise to effector cells if the same antigen is encountered later in the animal's life.

The proliferation of a B cell or T cell into a clone of cells occurs in response to a specific antigen and to immune cell signals. The process is called **clonal selection** because an encounter with an antigen *selects* which lymphocyte will divide to produce a *clonal* population of thousands of cells specific for a particular epitope. Cells that have antigen receptors specific for other antigens do not respond.

**Figure 43.14** summarizes the process of clonal selection, using the example of B cells, which generate memory cells and plasma cells. When T cells undergo clonal selection, they generate memory T cells and effector T cells (cytotoxic T cells and helper T cells).

## Immunological Memory

Immunological memory is responsible for the long-term protection that a prior infection provides against many diseases, such as chicken pox. This type of protection was noted almost 2,400 years ago by the Greek historian Thucydides. He observed that individuals who had recovered from the plague

∀ **Figure 43.14 Clonal selection of B cells.**

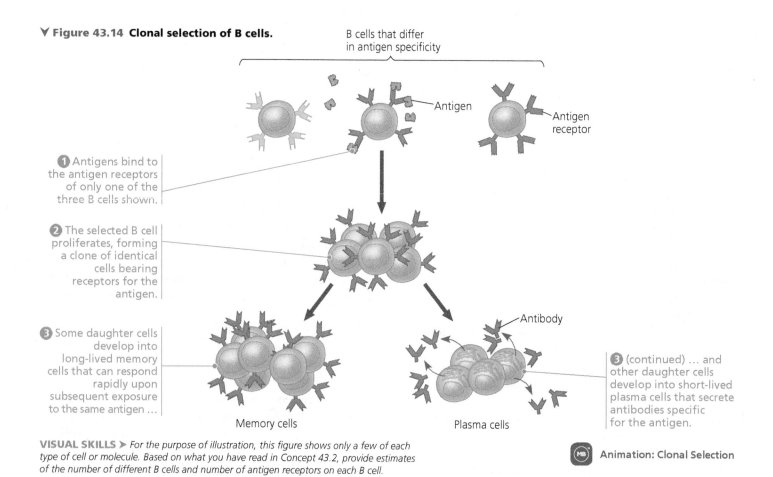

B cells that differ in antigen specificity

Antigen

Antigen receptor

1 Antigens bind to the antigen receptors of only one of the three B cells shown.

2 The selected B cell proliferates, forming a clone of identical cells bearing receptors for the antigen.

3 Some daughter cells develop into long-lived memory cells that can respond rapidly upon subsequent exposure to the same antigen ...

Memory cells

Antibody

Plasma cells

3 (continued) ... and other daughter cells develop into short-lived plasma cells that secrete antibodies specific for the antigen.

**VISUAL SKILLS ▶** *For the purpose of illustration, this figure shows only a few of each type of cell or molecule. Based on what you have read in Concept 43.2, provide estimates of the number of different B cells and number of antigen receptors on each B cell.*

(MB) **Animation: Clonal Selection**

could safely care for those who were sick or dying, "for the same man was never attacked twice—never at least fatally."

Prior exposure to an antigen alters the speed, strength, and duration of the immune response. The effector cells formed by clones of lymphocytes after an initial exposure to an antigen produce a **primary immune response**. The primary response peaks about 10–17 days after the initial exposure. If the same antigen is encountered again later, there is a **secondary immune response**, a response that is faster (typically peaking only 2–7 days after exposure), of greater magnitude, and more prolonged. These differences between primary and secondary immune responses are readily apparent in a graph of the concentrations of specific antibodies in blood over time **(Figure 43.15)**.

The secondary immune response relies on the reservoir of T and B memory cells generated upon initial exposure to an antigen. Because these cells are long-lived, they provide the basis for immunological memory, which can span many decades. (Most effector cells have much shorter life spans.) If an antigen is encountered again, memory cells specific for that antigen enable the rapid formation of clones of thousands of effector cells also specific for that antigen, thus generating a greatly enhanced immune defense.

Although the processes for antigen recognition, clonal selection, and immunological memory are similar for B cells

▼ **Figure 43.15 The specificity of immunological memory.** Long-lived memory cells that are generated in the primary response to antigen A give rise to a heightened secondary response to the same antigen but don't affect the primary response to another antigen (B).

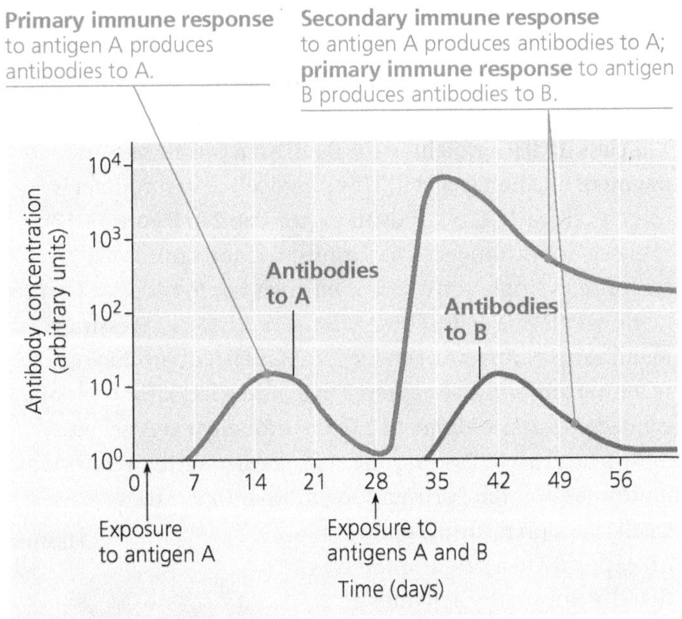

Primary immune response to antigen A produces antibodies to A.

Secondary immune response to antigen A produces antibodies to A; **primary immune response** to antigen B produces antibodies to B.

**INTERPRET THE DATA** ➤ *Assume that on average one out of every $10^5$ B cells in the body is specific for antigen A on day 16 and that the number of B cells producing a specific antibody is proportional to the concentration of that antibody. What would you predict is the frequency of B cells specific for antigen A on day 36?*

and T cells, these two classes of lymphocytes fight infection in different ways and in different settings, as we'll explore in Concept 43.3.

## CONCEPT CHECK 43.2

1. **DRAW IT** ➤ Sketch a B cell antigen receptor. Label the V and C regions of the light and heavy chains. Label the antigen-binding sites, disulfide bridges, and transmembrane region. Where are these features located relative to the V and C regions?

2. Explain two advantages of having memory cells when a pathogen is encountered for a second time.

3. **WHAT IF?** ➤ If both copies of a light-chain gene and a heavy-chain gene recombined in each (diploid) B cell, how would this affect B cell development and function?

*For suggested answers, see Appendix A.*

# CONCEPT 43.3

## Adaptive immunity defends against infection of body fluids and body cells

Having considered how clones of lymphocytes arise, we now explore how these cells help fight infections and minimize damage by pathogens. The defenses provided by B and T lymphocytes can be divided into humoral and cell-mediated immune responses. The **humoral immune response** occurs in the blood and lymph (once called body *humors*, or fluids). In this response, antibodies help neutralize or eliminate toxins and pathogens in body fluids. In the **cell-mediated immune response**, specialized T cells destroy infected host cells. Both humoral and cellular immunity can include a primary immune response and a secondary immune response, with memory cells enabling the secondary response.

## Helper T Cells: Activating Adaptive Immunity

A type of T cell called a **helper T cell** activates humoral and cell-mediated immune responses. Before this can happen, however, two conditions must be met. First, a foreign molecule must be present that can bind specifically to the antigen receptor of the helper T cell. Second, this antigen must be displayed on the surface of an **antigen-presenting cell**. An antigen-presenting cell can be a dendritic cell, macrophage, or B cell.

Like immune cells, infected cells can display antigens on their surface. What then distinguishes an antigen-presenting cell? The answer lies in the existence of two classes of MHC molecules. Most body cells have only the class I MHC molecules, but antigen-presenting cells have class I and class II MHC molecules. Class II molecules provide a molecular signature by which an antigen-presenting cell is recognized.

▼ **Figure 43.16 The central role of helper T cells in humoral and cell-mediated immune responses.** Here, a helper T cell responds to a dendritic cell displaying an antigen.

 **BioFlix® Animation: Activation of a Helper T Cell by a Dendritic Cell (Example: Infection by a Rhinovirus)**

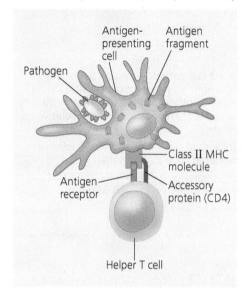

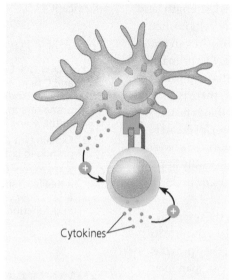

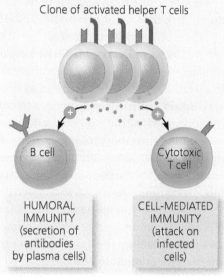

① An antigen-presenting cell engulfs a pathogen, degrades it, and displays antigen fragments complexed with class II MHC molecules on the cell surface. A specific helper T cell binds to this complex via its antigen receptor and an accessory protein called CD4.

② Binding of the helper T cell promotes secretion of cytokines by the antigen-presenting cell. These cytokines, along with cytokines from the helper T cell itself, activate the helper T cell and stimulate its proliferation.

③ Cell proliferation produces a clone of activated helper T cells. All cells in the clone have receptors for the same antigen fragment complex with the same antigen specificity. These cells secrete other cytokines, which help activate B cells and cytotoxic T cells.

A helper T cell and the antigen-presenting cell displaying its specific epitope have a complex interaction **(Figure 43.16)**. The antigen receptors on the surface of the helper T cell bind to the antigen fragment and to the class II MHC molecule displaying that fragment on the antigen-presenting cell. At the same time, an accessory protein called CD4 on the helper T cell surface binds to the class II MHC molecule, helping keep the cells joined. As the two cells interact, signals in the form of cytokines are exchanged. For example, the cytokines secreted from a dendritic cell act in combination with the antigen to stimulate the helper T cell, causing it to produce its own set of cytokines. Also, extensive contact between the cell surfaces enables further information exchange.

Antigen-presenting cells interact with helper T cells in several contexts. Antigen presentation by a dendritic cell or macrophage activates a helper T cell, which proliferates, forming a clone of activated cells. In contrast, B cells present antigens to *already* activated helper T cells, which in turn activate the B cells themselves. Activated helper T cells also help stimulate cytotoxic T cells, as you'll see shortly.

## B Cells and Antibodies: A Response to Extracellular Pathogens

Secretion of antibodies is the hallmark of the humoral immune response. It begins with activation of the B cells.

### Activation of B Cells

As illustrated in **Figure 43.17**, activation of B cells involves both helper T cells and proteins on the surface of pathogens.

Stimulated by both an antigen and cytokines, the B cell proliferates and differentiates into memory B cells and antibody-secreting plasma cells.

The pathway for antigen processing and display in B cells differs from that in other antigen-presenting cells. A macrophage or dendritic cell can present fragments from a wide variety of protein antigens, whereas a B cell presents only the antigen to which it specifically binds. When an antigen first binds to receptors on the surface of a B cell, the cell takes in a few foreign molecules by receptor-mediated endocytosis (see Figure 7.19). The class II MHC protein of the B cell then presents an antigen fragment to a helper T cell. This direct cell-to-cell contact is usually critical to B cell activation (see step 2 in Figure 43.17).

B cell activation leads to a robust humoral immune response: A single activated B cell gives rise to thousands of identical plasma cells. These plasma cells stop expressing a membrane-bound antigen receptor and begin producing and secreting antibodies (see step 3 in Figure 43.17). Each plasma cell secretes approximately 2,000 antibodies every second during its four- to five-day life span, nearly a trillion antibody molecules in total. Furthermore, most antigens recognized by B cells contain multiple epitopes. An exposure to a single antigen therefore normally activates a variety of B cells, which give rise to different plasma cells producing antibodies directed against different epitopes on the common antigen.

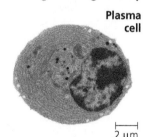

**Plasma cell**

2 µm

**▼ Figure 43.17 Activation of a B cell in the humoral immune response.** Most protein antigens require activated helper T cells to trigger a humoral response. A macrophage (shown here) or a dendritic cell can activate a helper T cell, which in turn can activate a B cell to give rise to antibody-secreting plasma cells.

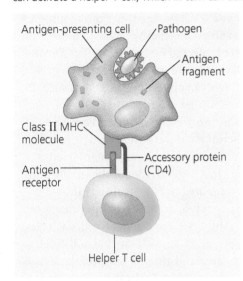
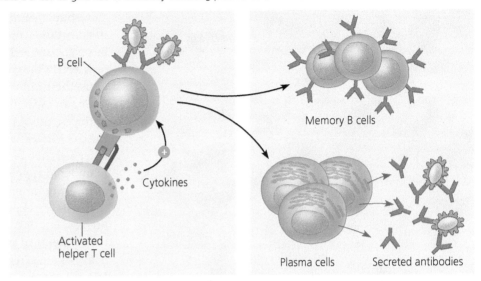

**❶** After an antigen-presenting cell engulfs and degrades a pathogen, it displays an antigen fragment complexed with a class II MHC molecule. A helper T cell that recognizes the complex is activated with the aid of cytokines secreted from the antigen-presenting cell.

**❷** When a B cell with receptors for the same epitope internalizes the antigen, it displays an antigen fragment on the cell surface in a complex with a class II MHC molecule. An activated helper T cell bearing receptors specific for the displayed fragment binds to and activates the B cell.

**❸** The activated B cell proliferates and differentiates into memory B cells and antibody-secreting plasma cells. The secreted antibodies are specific for the same antigen that initiated the response.

**?** *Looking at the steps in this figure, propose a function for the cell-surface antigen receptors of memory B cells.*

**MB** BioFlix® Animation: Adaptive Defenses: B Cells (Example: Infection by a Rhinovirus)

## Antibody Function

Antibodies do not directly kill pathogens, but by binding to antigens, they interfere with pathogen activity or mark pathogens in various ways for inactivation or destruction. Consider, for example, *neutralization*, a process in which antibodies bind to proteins on the surface of a virus **(Figure 43.18)**. The bound antibodies prevent infection of a host cell, thus neutralizing the virus. Similarly, antibodies sometimes bind to toxins released in body fluids, preventing the toxins from entering body cells.

In *opsonization*, antibodies that are bound to antigens on bacteria do not block infection, but instead present a readily recognized structure for macrophages or neutrophils,

thereby promoting phagocytosis **(Figure 43.19)**. Because each antibody has two antigen-binding sites, antibodies can also facilitate phagocytosis by linking bacterial cells, viruses, or other foreign substances into aggregates.

When antibodies facilitate phagocytosis, as in opsonization, they also help fine-tune the humoral immune response. Recall that phagocytosis enables macrophages and dendritic cells to present antigens to and stimulate helper T cells, which in turn stimulate the very B cells whose antibodies contribute to phagocytosis. This positive feedback between innate and adaptive immunity contributes to a coordinated, effective response to infection.

**▼ Figure 43.19 Opsonization**

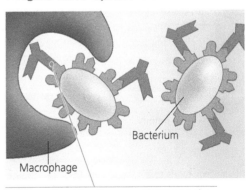

Binding of antibodies to antigens on the surface of bacteria promotes phagocytosis by macrophages and neutrophils.

**▼ Figure 43.18 Neutralization**

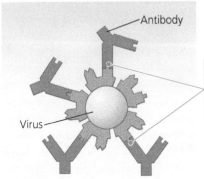

Antibodies bound to antigens on the surface of a virus neutralize it by blocking its ability to bind to a host cell.

**▼ Figure 43.20 Activation of complement system and pore formation.**

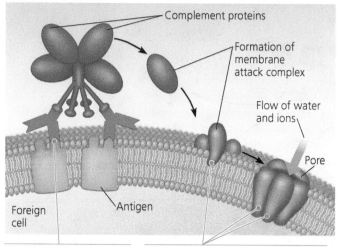

Complement proteins

Formation of membrane attack complex

Flow of water and ions

Pore

Foreign cell

Antigen

Binding of antibodies to antigens on the surface of a foreign cell activates the complement system.

After activation of the complement system, the membrane attack complex forms pores in the cell's membrane, allowing water and ions to rush in. The cell swells and lyses.

Antibodies sometimes work together with the proteins of the complement system (**Figure 43.20**). (The name *complement* reflects the fact that these proteins add to the effectiveness of antibody-directed attacks on bacteria.) Binding of a complement protein to an antigen-antibody complex on a foreign cell triggers the generation of a *membrane attack complex* that forms a pore in the membrane of the cell. Ions and water rush into the cell, causing it to swell and lyse. Whether activated as part of innate or adaptive defenses, this cascade of

complement protein activity results in the lysis of foreign cells and produces factors that promote inflammation or stimulate phagocytosis.

Although antibodies are the cornerstones of the response in body fluids, there is also a mechanism by which they can bring about the death of infected body cells. When a virus uses a cell's biosynthetic machinery to produce viral proteins, these viral products can appear on the cell surface. If antibodies specific for epitopes on these viral proteins bind to the exposed proteins, the presence of bound antibody at the cell surface can recruit a natural killer cell. The natural killer cell then releases proteins that cause the infected cell to undergo apoptosis. Thus the activities of the innate and adaptive immune systems are once again closely linked.

B cells can express five types, or *classes*, of immunoglobulin (IgA, IgD, IgE, IgG, and IgM). For a given B cell, each class has an identical antigen-binding specificity but a distinct heavy-chain C region. The B cell antigen receptor, known as IgD, is exclusively membrane bound. The other four classes have soluble forms, such as the antibodies found in blood, tears, saliva, and breast milk.

## Cytotoxic T Cells: A Response to Infected Host Cells

In the absence of an immune response, pathogens can reproduce in and kill infected cells (**Figure 43.21**). In the cell-mediated immune response, **cytotoxic T cells** use toxic proteins to kill cells infected by viruses or other intracellular pathogens before pathogens fully mature. To become active, cytotoxic T cells require signals from helper T cells and interaction with an antigen-presenting cell. Fragments of foreign

**▼ Figure 43.21 The killing action of cytotoxic T cells on an infected host cell.** An activated cytotoxic T cell releases molecules that make pores in an infected cell's membrane and enzymes that break down proteins, promoting the cell's death.

BioFlix® Animation: Adaptive Defenses: Cytotoxic T Cells (Example: Infection by a Rhinovirus)

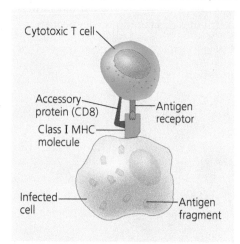

Cytotoxic T cell

Accessory protein (CD8)

Antigen receptor

Class I MHC molecule

Infected cell

Antigen fragment

❶ An activated cytotoxic T cell binds to a class I MHC–antigen fragment complex on an infected cell via its antigen receptor and an accessory protein called CD8.

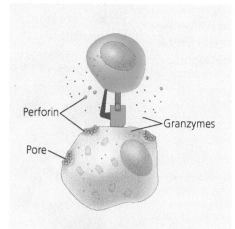

Perforin

Granzymes

Pore

❷ The T cell releases perforin molecules, which form pores in the infected cell membrane, and granzymes, enzymes that break down proteins. Granzymes enter the infected cell by endocytosis.

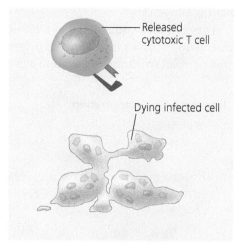

Released cytotoxic T cell

Dying infected cell

❸ The granzymes initiate apoptosis within the infected cell, leading to fragmentation of the nucleus and cytoplasm and eventual cell death. The released cytotoxic T cell can attack other infected cells.

proteins produced in infected host cells associate with class I MHC molecules and are displayed on the cell surface, where they can be recognized by cytotoxic T cells. As with helper T cells, cytotoxic T cells have an accessory protein that binds to the MHC molecule. This accessory protein, called CD8, helps keep the two cells in contact while the cytotoxic T cell is activated.

The targeted destruction of an infected host cell by a cytotoxic T cell involves the secretion of proteins that disrupt membrane integrity and trigger cell death (apoptosis; see Figure 43.21). The death of the infected cell not only deprives the pathogen of a place to multiply but also exposes cell contents to circulating antibodies, which mark released antigens for disposal.

## Summary of the Humoral and Cell-Mediated Immune Responses

As noted earlier, both humoral and cell-mediated immunity can include primary and secondary immune responses. Memory cells of each type—helper T cell, B cell, and cytotoxic T cell—enable the secondary response. For example, when body fluids are reinfected by a pathogen encountered previously, memory B cells and memory helper T cells initiate a secondary humoral response. **Figure 43.22** summarizes adaptive immunity, reviews the events that initiate humoral and cell-mediated immune responses, highlights the difference in response to pathogens in body fluids versus in body cells, and emphasizes the central role of the helper T cell.

▼ **Figure 43.22 An overview of the adaptive immune response.**

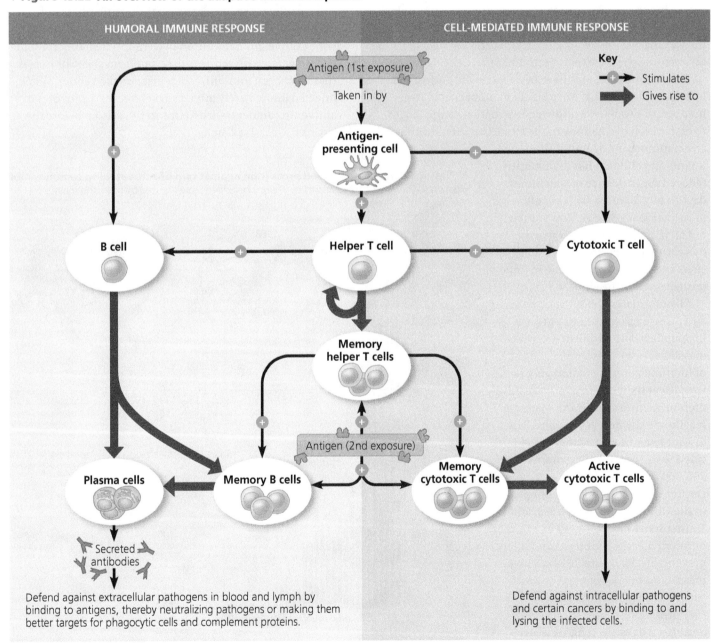

**VISUAL SKILLS** ➤ *Identify each arrow as representing part of the primary response or secondary response.*

BioFlix® Animation: Summary of the Adaptive Immune Response (Example: Infection by a Rhinovirus)

## Immunization

The protection provided by a second immune response provides the basis for **immunization**, the use of antigens artificially introduced into the body to generate an adaptive immune response and memory cell formation. In 1796, Edward Jenner noted that milkmaids who had cowpox, a mild disease usually seen only in cows, did not contract smallpox, a far more dangerous disease. In the first documented immunization (or *vaccination*, from the Latin *vacca*, cow), Jenner used the cowpox virus to induce adaptive immunity against the closely related smallpox virus. Today, immunizations are carried out with vaccines—preparations of antigen—obtained from many sources, including inactivated bacterial toxins, killed or weakened pathogens, and even genes encoding microbial proteins. Because all of these agents induce a primary immune response and immunological memory, an encounter with the pathogen from which the vaccine was derived triggers a rapid and strong secondary immune response (see Figure 43.15).

Vaccination programs have been successful against many infectious diseases that once killed or incapacitated large numbers of people. A worldwide vaccination campaign led to eradication of smallpox in the late 1970s. In industrialized nations, routine immunization of infants and children has dramatically reduced the incidence of sometimes devastating diseases, such as polio and measles **(Figure 43.23)**. Unfortunately, not all pathogens are easily managed by vaccination. Furthermore, some vaccines are not readily available in impoverished areas of the globe.

Misinformation about vaccine safety and disease risk has led to a growing public health problem. Consider measles as just one example. Side effects of immunization are remarkably rare, with fewer than one in a million children suffering a significant allergic reaction to the measles vaccine. The disease remains quite dangerous to this day, however, killing more than 200,000 people worldwide each year. Declines in vaccination rates in parts of the United Kingdom, Russia, and the United States have resulted in a number of recent measles outbreaks and many preventable deaths. In 2014–2015, a measles outbreak triggered by a visitor to a Disney theme park in Southern California spread to multiple states and affected people ranging in age from 6 weeks to 70 years.

## Active and Passive Immunity

The discussion of adaptive immunity has to this point focused on **active immunity**, the defenses that arise when a pathogen infection or immunization prompts an immune response. A different type of immunity results when the IgG antibodies in the blood of a pregnant female cross the placenta to her fetus. This protection is called **passive immunity** because the antibodies in the recipient (in this case, the fetus) are produced by another individual (the mother). IgA antibodies present in breast milk provide additional passive immunity to the infant's digestive tract while the infant's immune system develops. Because passive immunity does not involve the recipient's B and T cells, it persists only as long as the transferred antibodies last (a few weeks to a few months).

In artificial passive immunization, antibodies from an immune animal are injected into a nonimmune animal. For example, humans bitten by venomous snakes are sometimes treated with antivenin, serum from sheep or horses that have been immunized against a snake venom. When injected immediately after a snakebite, the antibodies in antivenin can neutralize toxins in the venom before the toxins do massive damage.

▼ **Figure 43.23 Vaccine-based protection against two life-threatening communicable diseases.** The graphs show deaths by year in the United States caused by polio and measles. The maps show examples of the global progress against these two diseases.

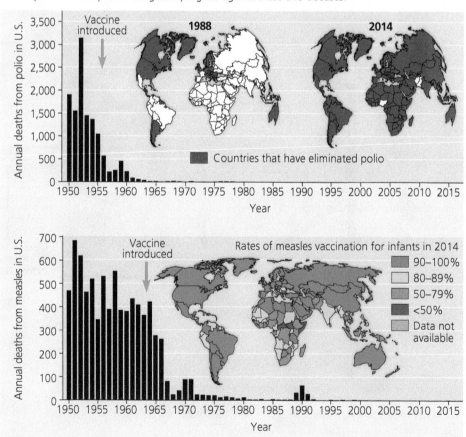

## Antibodies as Tools

Antibodies that an animal produces after exposure to an antigen are the products of many different clones of plasma cells, each specific for a different epitope. However, antibodies can also be prepared from a single clone of B cells grown in culture. The **monoclonal antibodies** produced by such a culture are identical and specific for the same epitope on an antigen.

Monoclonal antibodies have provided the basis for many recent advances in medical diagnosis and treatment. For example, home pregnancy test kits use monoclonal antibodies to detect human chorionic gonadotropin (hCG). Because hCG is produced as soon as an embryo implants in the uterus (see Concept 46.5), the presence of this hormone in a woman's urine is a reliable indicator for a very early stage of pregnancy. Monoclonal antibodies are injected as a therapy for a number of human diseases, including certain cancers.

One of the most recently developed antibody tools uses a single drop of blood to identify every virus that a person has encountered through infection or vaccination. To detect the antibodies formed against these viruses, researchers generate a set of nearly 100,000 bacteriophages, each of which displays a different peptide from one of the roughly 200 species of viruses that infect humans. **Figure 43.24** provides an overview of how this technique works.

## Immune Rejection

Like pathogens, cells from another person can be recognized as foreign and attacked by immune defenses. For example, skin transplanted from one person to a genetically nonidentical person will look healthy for a week or so but will then be destroyed (rejected) by the recipient's immune response. It turns out that MHC molecules are a primary cause of rejection. Why? Each of us expresses MHC proteins from more than a dozen different MHC genes. Furthermore, there are more than 100 different versions, or alleles, of human MHC genes. As a consequence, the sets of MHC proteins on cell surfaces are likely to differ between any two people, except identical twins. Such differences can stimulate an immune response in the recipient of a graft or transplant, causing rejection. To minimize rejection of a transplant or graft, surgeons use donor tissue bearing MHC molecules that match those of the recipient as closely as possible. In addition, the recipient takes medicines that suppress immune responses (but as a result leave the recipient more susceptible to infections).

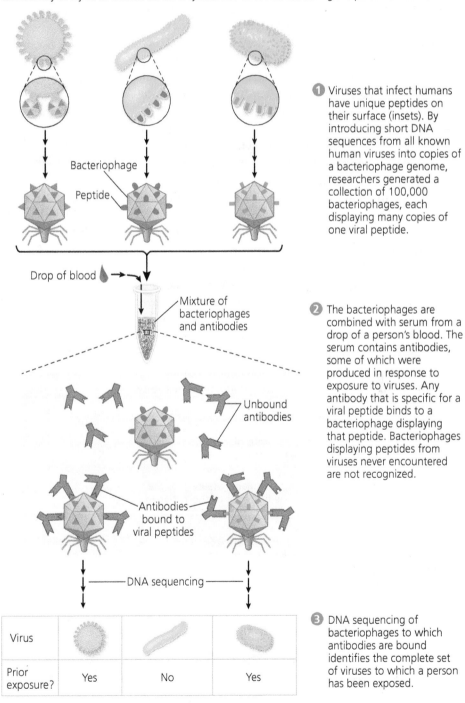

▼ **Figure 43.24 A comprehensive test for past viral encounters.** By combining the power of DNA sequencing with the specificity of antigen recognition by antibodies, researchers can identify every virus that an immune system has encountered during the person's lifetime.

**1** Viruses that infect humans have unique peptides on their surface (insets). By introducing short DNA sequences from all known human viruses into copies of a bacteriophage genome, researchers generated a collection of 100,000 bacteriophages, each displaying many copies of one viral peptide.

Bacteriophage

Peptide

Drop of blood

Mixture of bacteriophages and antibodies

**2** The bacteriophages are combined with serum from a drop of a person's blood. The serum contains antibodies, some of which were produced in response to exposure to viruses. Any antibody that is specific for a viral peptide binds to a bacteriophage displaying that peptide. Bacteriophages displaying peptides from viruses never encountered are not recognized.

Unbound antibodies

Antibodies bound to viral peptides

DNA sequencing

| Virus | | | |
|-------|-----|-----|-----|
| Prior exposure? | Yes | No | Yes |

**3** DNA sequencing of bacteriophages to which antibodies are bound identifies the complete set of viruses to which a person has been exposed.

**WHAT IF?** ➤ *All of the antibodies are shown with just one antigen binding site occupied. If a single antibody bound to two bacteriophages, how would this affect the results?*

## Blood Groups

In the case of blood transfusions, the recipient's immune system can recognize carbohydrates on the surface of blood cells as foreign, triggering an immediate and devastating reaction. To avoid this danger, the so-called ABO blood groups of the donor and recipient must be taken into account. Red blood cells are designated as type A if they have the A carbohydrate on their surface. Similarly, the B carbohydrate is found on the surface of type B red blood cells; both A and B carbohydrates are found on type AB red blood cells; and neither carbohydrate is found on type O red blood cells (see Figure 14.11).

Why does the immune system recognize particular sugars on red blood cells? It turns out that we are frequently exposed to certain bacteria that have epitopes very similar to the carbohydrates on blood cells. A person with type A blood will respond to the bacterial epitope similar to the B carbohydrate and make antibodies that will react with any B carbohydrate encountered upon a transfusion. However, that same person doesn't make antibodies against the bacterial epitope similar to the A carbohydrate because lymphocytes that would be reactive with the body's own cells and molecules were inactivated or eliminated during development.

To understand how ABO blood groups affect transfusions, let's consider further the example of a person with type A blood receiving a transfusion of type B blood. The person's anti-B antibodies would cause the transfused red blood cells to undergo lysis, triggering chills, fever, shock, and perhaps kidney malfunction. At the same time, anti-A antibodies in the donated type B blood would act against the recipient's red blood cells. Applying the same logic to a type O person, we can see that such interactions would cause a problem upon transfusion of any other blood type. Fortunately, the discovery of enzymes that can cleave the A and B carbohydrates from red blood cells may eliminate this problem in the future.

### CONCEPT CHECK 43.3

1. If a child were born without a thymus gland, what cells and functions of the immune system would be deficient? Explain.

2. Treatment of antibodies with a particular protease clips the heavy chains in half, releasing the two arms of the Y-shaped molecule. How might the antibodies continue to function?

3. **WHAT IF?** ➤ Suppose that a snake handler bitten by a particular venomous snake species was treated with antivenin. Why might the same treatment for a second such bite have a harmful side effect?

*For suggested answers, see Appendix A.*

## CONCEPT 43.4

### Disruptions in immune system function can elicit or exacerbate disease

Although adaptive immunity offers significant protection against a wide range of pathogens, it is not fail-safe. Here we'll first examine the disorders and diseases that arise when adaptive immunity is blocked or misregulated. We'll then turn to some of the evolutionary adaptations of pathogens that diminish the effectiveness of adaptive immune responses in the host.

### Exaggerated, Self-Directed, and Diminished Immune Responses

The highly regulated interplay among lymphocytes, other body cells, and foreign substances generates an immune response that provides extraordinary protection against many pathogens. When allergic, autoimmune, or immunodeficiency disorders disrupt this delicate balance, the effects are frequently severe.

### Allergies

Allergies are exaggerated (hypersensitive) responses to certain antigens called *allergens*. The most common allergies involve antibodies of the IgE class. Hay fever, for instance, occurs when plasma cells secrete IgE antibodies specific for antigens on the surface of pollen grains **(Figure 43.25)**. Some IgE antibodies attach by their base to mast cells in connective tissues. Pollen grains that enter the body later attach to the antigen-binding sites of these IgE antibodies.

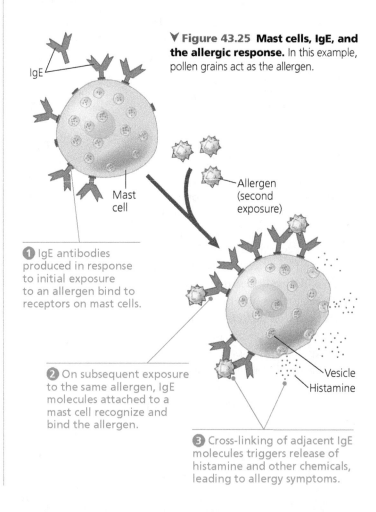

▼ **Figure 43.25 Mast cells, IgE, and the allergic response.** In this example, pollen grains act as the allergen.

IgE

Mast cell

Allergen (second exposure)

Vesicle
Histamine

❶ IgE antibodies produced in response to initial exposure to an allergen bind to receptors on mast cells.

❷ On subsequent exposure to the same allergen, IgE molecules attached to a mast cell recognize and bind the allergen.

❸ Cross-linking of adjacent IgE molecules triggers release of histamine and other chemicals, leading to allergy symptoms.

Such attachment cross-links adjacent IgE molecules, inducing the mast cell to release histamine and other inflammatory chemicals. Acting on a variety of cell types, these chemicals bring about the typical allergy symptoms: sneezing, runny nose, teary eyes, and smooth muscle contractions in the lungs that can inhibit effective breathing. Drugs known as antihistamines block receptors for histamine, diminishing allergy symptoms (and inflammation).

An acute allergic response sometimes leads to a life-threatening reaction called *anaphylactic shock*. Inflammatory chemicals released from immune cells trigger constriction of bronchioles and sudden dilation of peripheral blood vessels, which causes a precipitous drop in blood pressure. Death may occur within minutes due to the inability to breathe and lack of blood flow. Substances that can cause anaphylactic shock in allergic individuals include bee venom, penicillin, peanuts, and shellfish. People with severe hypersensitivities often carry an autoinjector containing the hormone epinephrine. An injection of epinephrine rapidly counteracts this allergic response, constricting peripheral blood vessels, reducing swelling in the throat, and relaxing muscles in the lungs to help breathing (see Figure 45.20b).

### Autoimmune Diseases

In some people, the immune system is active against particular molecules of the body, causing an **autoimmune disease**. Such a loss of self-tolerance has many forms. In systemic lupus erythematosus, commonly called *lupus*, the immune system generates antibodies against histones and DNA released by the normal breakdown of body cells. These self-reactive antibodies cause skin rashes, fever, arthritis, and kidney dysfunction. Other targets of autoimmunity include the insulin-producing beta cells of the pancreas (in type 1 diabetes) and the myelin sheaths that encase many neurons (in multiple sclerosis).

Heredity, gender, and environment all influence susceptibility to autoimmune disorders. For example, members of certain families show an increased susceptibility to particular autoimmune disorders. In addition, many autoimmune diseases afflict females more often than males. Women are nine times as likely as men to suffer from lupus and two to three times as likely to develop *rheumatoid arthritis*, a damaging and painful inflammation of the cartilage and bone in joints **(Figure 43.26)**. The causes of this sex bias, as well as the rise in autoimmune disease frequency in industrialized countries, are areas of active research and debate.

An additional focus of current research on autoimmune disorders is the activity of *regulatory T cells*, nicknamed Tregs. These specialized T cells help modulate immune system activity and prevent response to self-antigens.

### Exertion, Stress, and the Immune System

Many forms of exertion and stress influence immune system function. For example, moderate exercise improves

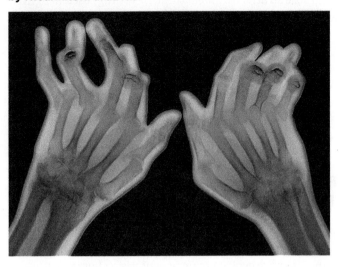

▼ **Figure 43.26 X-ray of hands that are deformed by rheumatoid arthritis.**

immune system function and significantly reduces susceptibility to the common cold and other infections of the upper respiratory tract. In contrast, exercise to the point of exhaustion leads to more frequent infections and more severe symptoms. Studies of marathon runners support the conclusion that exercise intensity is the critical variable. On average, such runners get sick less often than their more sedentary peers during training, a time of moderate exertion, but markedly more often in the period immediately following the grueling race itself. Similarly, psychological stress has been shown to disrupt immune system regulation by altering the interplay of the hormonal, nervous, and immune systems (see Figure 45.20). Research also confirms that rest is important for immunity: Adults who averaged fewer than 7 hours of sleep got sick three times as often when exposed to a cold virus as those who averaged at least 8 hours.

### Immunodeficiency Diseases

A disorder in which an immune system response to antigens is defective or absent is called an immunodeficiency. Whatever its cause and nature, an immunodeficiency can lead to frequent and recurrent infections and increased susceptibility to certain cancers.

An *inborn immunodeficiency* results from a genetic or developmental defect in the production of immune system cells or of specific proteins, such as antibodies or the proteins of the complement system. Depending on the specific defect, either innate or adaptive defenses—or both—may be impaired. In severe combined immunodeficiency (SCID), functional lymphocytes are rare or absent. Lacking an adaptive immune response, SCID patients are susceptible to infections that can cause death in infancy, such as pneumonia and meningitis. Treatments include bone marrow and stem cell transplantation.

Later in life, exposure to chemicals or biological agents can cause an *acquired immunodeficiency*. Drugs used to fight autoimmune diseases or prevent transplant rejection suppress the immune system, leading to an immunodeficient state. Certain cancers also suppress the immune system, especially Hodgkin's disease, which damages the lymphatic system. Acquired immunodeficiencies range from temporary states that may arise from physiological stress to the devastating disease AIDS (acquired immune deficiency syndrome), which we'll explore in the next section.

## Evolutionary Adaptations of Pathogens That Underlie Immune System Avoidance

**EVOLUTION** Just as immune systems that ward off pathogens have evolved in animals, mechanisms that thwart immune responses have evolved in pathogens. Using human pathogens as examples, we'll examine some common mechanisms: antigenic variation, latency, and direct attack on the immune system.

### Antigenic Variation

One mechanism for escaping the body's defenses is for a pathogen to alter how it appears to the immune system. Immunological memory is a record of the foreign epitopes an animal has encountered. If the pathogen that expressed those epitopes no longer does so, it can reinfect or remain in a host without triggering the rapid and robust response that memory cells provide. Such changes in epitope expression are called *antigenic variation*. The parasite that causes sleeping sickness (trypanosomiasis) provides an extreme example, periodically switching at random among 1,000 versions of the protein found over its entire surface. In the **Scientific Skills Exercise**, you'll interpret data on this form of antigenic variation and the body's response.

Antigenic variation is the main reason the influenza, or "flu," virus remains a major public health problem. As it replicates in one human host after another, the virus undergoes frequent mutations. Because any change that lessens recognition by the immune system provides a selective advantage, the virus steadily accumulates mutations that change its surface proteins, reducing the effectiveness of the host immune response. As a result, a new flu vaccine must be developed, produced, and distributed each year. In addition, the human influenza virus occasionally forms new strains by exchanging genes with influenza viruses that infect domesticated animals, such as pigs or chickens. When this exchange of genes occurs, the new strain may not be recognized by any of the memory cells in the human population. The resulting outbreak can be deadly: The 1918–1919 influenza outbreak killed more than 20 million people.

### Latency

Some viruses avoid an immune response by infecting cells and then entering a largely inactive state called *latency*. In latency, the production of most viral proteins and free viruses ceases; as a result, latent viruses do not trigger an adaptive immune response. Nevertheless, the viral genome persists in the nuclei of infected cells, either as a separate DNA molecule or as a copy integrated into the host genome. Latency typically persists until conditions arise that are favorable for viral transmission or unfavorable for host survival, such as when the host is infected by another pathogen. Such circumstances trigger the synthesis and release of free viruses that can infect new hosts.

Herpes simplex viruses, which establish themselves in human sensory neurons, provide a good example of latency. The type 1 virus causes most oral herpes infections, whereas the type 2 virus is responsible for most cases of genital herpes. Because sensory neurons express relatively few MHC I molecules, the infected cells are inefficient at presenting viral antigens to circulating lymphocytes. Stimuli such as fever, emotional stress, or menstruation reactivate the virus to replicate and infect surrounding epithelial tissues. Activation of the type 1 virus can result in blisters around the mouth that are called "cold" sores. The type 2 virus can cause genital sores, but people infected with either the type 1 or type 2 virus often have no symptoms. Infections of the type 2 virus, which is sexually transmitted, pose a serious threat to the babies of infected mothers and can increase transmission of the virus that causes AIDS.

### Attack on the Immune System: HIV

The **human immunodeficiency virus (HIV)**, the pathogen that causes AIDS, both escapes and attacks the adaptive immune response. Once introduced into the body, HIV infects helper T cells with high efficiency by binding specifically to the CD4 accessory protein (see Figure 43.17). HIV also infects some cell types that have low levels of CD4, such as macrophages and brain cells. Inside cells, the HIV RNA genome is reverse-transcribed, and the product DNA is integrated into the host cell's genome (see Figure 19.8). In this form, the viral genome can direct the production of new viruses.

Although the body responds to HIV with an immune response sufficient to eliminate most viral infections, some HIV invariably escapes. One reason HIV persists is that it has a very high mutation rate. Altered proteins on the surface of some mutated viruses reduce interaction with antibodies and cytotoxic T cells. Such viruses replicate and mutate further. HIV thus evolves within the body. The continued presence of HIV is also helped by latency while the viral DNA is integrated in the host cell's genome. This latent DNA is shielded from the immune system as well as from antiviral agents currently used against HIV, which attack only actively replicating viruses.

# SCIENTIFIC SKILLS EXERCISE

## Comparing Two Variables on a Common x-Axis

**How Does the Immune System Respond to a Changing Pathogen?** Natural selection favors parasites that are able to maintain a low-level infection in a host for a long time. *Trypanosoma*, the unicellular parasite that causes sleeping sickness, is one example. The glycoproteins covering a trypanosome's surface are encoded by a gene that is duplicated more than 1,000 times in the organism's genome. Each copy is slightly different. By periodically switching among these genes, the trypanosome can display a series of surface glycoproteins with different molecular structures. In this exercise, you will interpret two data sets to explore hypotheses about the benefits of the trypanosome's ever-shifting surface glycoproteins and the host's immune response.

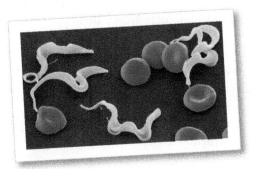

**Part A: Data from a Study of Parasite Levels** This study measured the abundance of parasites in the blood of one human patient during the first few weeks of a chronic infection.

| Day | Number of Parasites (in millions) per mL of Blood |
|---|---|
| 4 | 0.1 |
| 6 | 0.3 |
| 8 | 1.2 |
| 10 | 0.2 |
| 12 | 0.2 |
| 14 | 0.9 |
| 16 | 0.6 |
| 18 | 0.1 |
| 20 | 0.7 |
| 22 | 1.2 |
| 24 | 0.2 |

### Part A: Interpret The Data

1. Plot the data in the above table as a line graph. Which column is the independent variable, and which is the dependent variable? Put the independent variable on the *x*-axis. (For additional information about graphs, see the Scientific Skills Review in Appendix F.)

2. Visually displaying data in a graph can help make patterns in the data more noticeable. Describe any patterns revealed by your graph.

3. Assume that a drop in parasite abundance reflects an effective immune response by the host. Formulate a hypothesis to explain the pattern you described in question 2.

**Part B: Data from a Study of Antibody Levels** Many decades after scientists first observed the pattern of *Trypanosoma* abundance over the course of infection, researchers identified antibodies specific to different forms of the parasite's surface glycoprotein. The table below lists the relative abundance of two such antibodies during the early period of chronic infection, using an index ranging from 0 (absent) to 1.

| Day | Antibody Specific to Glycoprotein Variant A | Antibody Specific to Glycoprotein Variant B |
|---|---|---|
| 4 | 0 | 0 |
| 6 | 0 | 0 |
| 8 | 0.2 | 0 |
| 10 | 0.5 | 0 |
| 12 | 1 | 0 |
| 14 | 1 | 0.1 |
| 16 | 1 | 0.3 |
| 18 | 1 | 0.9 |
| 20 | 1 | 1 |
| 22 | 1 | 1 |
| 24 | 1 | 1 |

### Part B: Interpret The Data

4. Note that these data were collected over the same period of infection (days 4–24) as the parasite abundance data you graphed in part A. Therefore, you can incorporate these new data into your first graph, using the same *x*-axis. However, since the antibody level data are measured in a different way than the parasite abundance data, add a second set of *y*-axis labels on the right side of your graph. Then, using different colors or sets of symbols, add the data for the two antibody types. Labeling the *y*-axis two different ways enables you to compare how two dependent variables change relative to a shared independent variable.

5. Describe any patterns you observe by comparing the two data sets over the same period. Do these patterns support your hypothesis from part A? Do they prove that hypothesis? Explain.

6. Scientists can now also distinguish the abundance of trypanosomes recognized specifically by antibodies type A and type B. How would incorporating such information change your graph?

**Instructors**: A version of this Scientific Skills Exercise can be assigned in MasteringBiology.

**Data from** L. J. Morrison et al., Probabilistic order in antigenic variation of Trypanosoma brucei, *International Journal for Parasitology* 35:961–972 (2005); and L. J. Morrison et al., Antigenic variation in the African trypanosome: molecular mechanisms and phenotypic complexity, *Cellular Microbiology* 1:1724–1734 (2009).

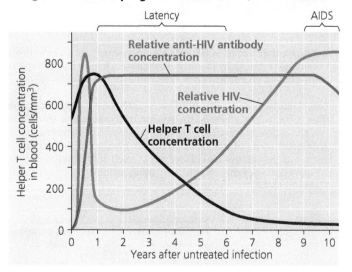

▼ **Figure 43.27 The progress of an untreated HIV infection.**

Latency | AIDS

Relative anti-HIV antibody concentration

Relative HIV concentration

**Helper T cell concentration**

Helper T cell concentration in blood (cells/mm³)

800
600
400
200
0

0  1  2  3  4  5  6  7  8  9  10

Years after untreated infection

Animation: HIV Reproductive Cycle
Interview with Flossie Wong-Staal: Characterizing HIV

Over time, an untreated HIV infection not only avoids the adaptive immune response but also abolishes it **(Figure 43.27)**. Viral replication and cell death triggered by the virus lead to loss of helper T cells, impairing both humoral and cell-mediated immune responses. The eventual result is **acquired immunodeficiency syndrome (AIDS)**, an impairment in immune responses that leaves the body susceptible to infections and cancers that a healthy immune system would usually defeat. For example, *Pneumocystis jirovecii*, a common fungus that does not cause disease in healthy individuals, can result in severe pneumonia in people with AIDS. Such opportunistic diseases, as well as nerve damage and body wasting, are the primary causes of death in AIDS patients, rather than HIV itself.

Transmission of HIV requires the transfer of virus particles or infected cells from person to person via body fluids such as semen, blood, or breast milk. Unprotected sex (that is, without using a condom) and transmission via HIV-contaminated needles (typically among intravenous drug users) cause the vast majority of HIV infections. The virus can enter the body through mucosal linings of the vagina, vulva, penis, or rectum during intercourse or via the mouth during oral sex. People infected with HIV can transmit the disease in the first few weeks of infection, *before* they produce HIV-specific antibodies that can be detected in a blood test. Currently, 10–50% of all new HIV infections appear to be caused by recently infected individuals. Although no cure has been found for HIV infection, drugs that can significantly slow HIV replication and the progression to AIDS have been developed.

## Cancer and Immunity

When adaptive immunity is inactivated, the frequency of certain cancers increases dramatically. For example, the risk of developing Kaposi's sarcoma is 20,000 times greater for untreated AIDS patients than for healthy people. This observation was at first puzzling. If the immune system recognizes only nonself, it should fail to recognize the uncontrolled growth of self cells that is the hallmark of cancer. It turns out, however, that viruses are involved in about 15–20% of all human cancers. Because the immune system can recognize viral proteins as foreign, it can act as a defense against viruses that can cause cancer and against cancer cells that harbor viruses. A vaccine introduced in 1986 for hepatitis B virus helps prevent liver cancer, the first cancer for which a human vaccine became available.

In the 1970s, Harald zur Hausen, working in Heidelberg, Germany, proposed that human papillomavirus (HPV) causes cervical cancer. Many scientists were skeptical that cancer could result from infection by HPV, the most common sexually transmitted pathogen. However, after more than a decade of work, zur Hausen isolated two particular types of HPV from patients with cervical cancer. He quickly made samples available to other scientists, leading in 2006 to the development of highly effective vaccines against HPV. The computer graphic image of an HPV particle in **Figure 43.28** illustrates the abundant copies of the capsid protein (yellow) that is used as the antigen in vaccination.

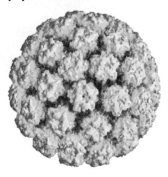

▼ **Figure 43.28 Human papillomavirus**

Cervical cancer kills more than 4,000 women annually in the United States and is the fifth-most common cause of cancer deaths among women worldwide. Administering an HPV vaccine, either Gardasil or Cervarix, to young adults greatly reduces their chance of being infected with the HPV viruses that cause cervical and oral cancers, as well as genital warts. In 2008, zur Hausen shared the Nobel Prize in Physiology or Medicine for his discovery.

Interview with Harald zur Hausen: Discovering the cause of cervical cancer (see the interview before Chapter 40)

### CONCEPT CHECK 43.4

1. In the muscular disease myasthenia gravis, antibodies bind to and block certain receptors on muscle cells, preventing muscle contraction. Is this disease best classified as an immunodeficiency disease, an autoimmune disease, or an allergic reaction? Explain.

2. People with herpes simplex type 1 viruses often get mouth sores when they have a cold or similar infection. How might this location benefit the virus?

3. **WHAT IF?** ➤ How would a macrophage deficiency likely affect a person's innate and adaptive defenses?

*For suggested answers, see Appendix A.*

# 43 Chapter Review

 Go to **MasteringBiology**™ for Videos, Animations, Vocab Self-Quiz, Practice Tests, and more in the Study Area.

## SUMMARY OF KEY CONCEPTS

### CONCEPT 43.1

**In innate immunity, recognition and response rely on traits common to groups of pathogens** (pp. 951–956)

VOCAB SELF-QUIZ
goo.gl/6u55ks

- In both invertebrates and vertebrates, **innate immunity** is mediated by physical and chemical barriers as well as cell-based defenses. Activation of innate immune responses relies on recognition proteins specific for broad classes of pathogens. Pathogens that penetrate barrier defenses are ingested by phagocytic cells, which in vertebrates include **macrophages** and **dendritic cells**. Additional cellular defenses include **natural killer cells**, which can induce the death of virus-infected cells. **Complement system** proteins, **interferons**, and other antimicrobial peptides also act against pathogens. In the **inflammatory response**, **histamine** and other chemicals that are released at the injury site promote changes in blood vessels that enhance immune cell access.
- Pathogens sometimes evade innate immune defenses. For example, some bacteria have an outer capsule that prevents recognition, while others are resistant to breakdown within lysosomes.

? *In what ways does innate immunity protect the mammalian digestive tract?*

### CONCEPT 43.2

**In adaptive immunity, receptors provide pathogen-specific recognition** (pp. 956–961)

- **Adaptive immunity** relies on two types of **lymphocytes** that arise from stem cells in the bone marrow: **B cells** and **T cells**. Lymphocytes have cell-surface **antigen receptors** for foreign molecules (**antigens**). All receptor proteins on a single B or T cell are the same, but there are millions of B and T cells in the body that differ in the foreign molecules that their receptors recognize. Upon infection, B and T cells specific for the pathogen are activated. Some T cells help other lymphocytes; others kill infected host cells. B cells called **plasma cells** produce soluble proteins called **antibodies**, which bind to foreign molecules and cells. Activated B and T cells called **memory cells** defend against future infections by the same pathogen.

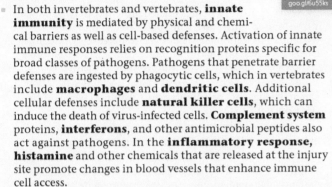

- Recognition of foreign molecules by B cells and T cells involves the binding of variable regions of receptors to an **epitope**, a small region of an antigen. B cells and antibodies recognize epitopes on the surface of antigens circulating in the blood or lymph. T cells recognize epitopes in small antigen fragments (peptides) that are presented on the surface of host cells by proteins called **major histocompatibility complex (MHC) molecules** This interaction activates a T cell, enabling it to participate in adaptive immunity.

- The four major characteristics of B and T cell development are the generation of cell diversity, self-tolerance, proliferation, and immunological memory. Proliferation and memory are both based on **clonal selection**, illustrated here for B cells:

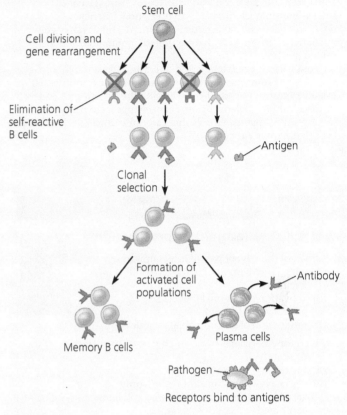

? *Why is the adaptive immune response to an initial infection slower than the innate response?*

### CONCEPT 43.3

**Adaptive immunity defends against infection of body fluids and body cells** (pp. 961–968)

- **Helper T cells** interact with antigen fragments displayed by class II MHC molecules on the surface of **antigen-presenting cells**: dendritic cells, macrophages, and B cells. Activated helper T cells secrete cytokines that stimulate other lymphocytes. In the **cell-mediated immune response**, activated **cytotoxic T cells** trigger destruction of infected cells. In the **humoral immune response**, antibodies help eliminate antigens by promoting phagocytosis and complement-mediated lysis.
- **Active immunity** develops in response to infection or to **immunization**. The transfer of antibodies in **passive immunity** provides immediate, short-term protection.
- Tissues or cells transferred from one person to another are subject to immune rejection. In tissue grafts and organ transplants, MHC molecules stimulate rejection. Lymphocytes in bone marrow transplants may cause a graft-versus-host reaction.

? *Is immunological memory after a natural infection fundamentally different from immunological memory after vaccination? Explain.*

## CONCEPT 43.4

### Disruptions in immune system function can elicit or exacerbate disease
(pp. 968–972)

- In allergies, such as hay fever, the interaction of antibodies and allergens triggers immune cells to release histamine and other mediators that cause vascular changes and allergic symptoms. Loss of self-tolerance can lead to **autoimmune diseases**, such as multiple sclerosis. Inborn immunodeficiencies result from defects that interfere with innate, humoral, or cell-mediated defenses. **AIDS** is an acquired immunodeficiency caused by **HIV**.

- Antigenic variation, latency, and direct assault on the immune system allow some pathogens to thwart immune responses. HIV infection destroys helper T cells, leaving the patient prone to disease. Immune defense against cancer appears to primarily involve action against viruses that can cause cancer and cancer cells that harbor viruses.

 *Is being infected with HIV the same as having AIDS? Explain.*

## TEST YOUR UNDERSTANDING

### Level 1: Knowledge/Comprehension

1. Which of these is *not* part of insect immunity?
   (A) enzyme activation of pathogen-killing chemicals
   (B) activation of natural killer cells
   (C) phagocytosis by hemocytes
   (D) production of antimicrobial peptides

2. An epitope associates with which part of an antigen receptor or antibody?
   (A) the tail
   (B) the heavy-chain constant regions only
   (C) variable regions of a heavy chain and light chain combined
   (D) the light-chain constant regions only

3. Which statement best describes the difference between responses of effector B cells (plasma cells) and those of cytotoxic T cells?
   (A) B cells confer active immunity; cytotoxic T cells confer passive immunity.
   (B) B cells respond the first time a pathogen is present; cytotoxic T cells respond subsequent times.
   (C) B cells secrete antibodies against a pathogen; cytotoxic T cells kill pathogen-infected host cells.
   (D) B cells carry out the cell-mediated response; cytotoxic T cells carry out the humoral response.

### Level 2: Application/Analysis

4. Which of the following statements is *not* true?
   (A) An antibody has more than one antigen-binding site.
   (B) A lymphocyte has receptors for multiple different antigens.
   (C) An antigen can have different epitopes.
   (D) A liver or muscle cell makes one class of MHC molecule.

5. Which of the following should be the same in identical twins?
   (A) the set of antibodies produced
   (B) the set of MHC molecules produced
   (C) the set of T cell antigen receptors produced
   (D) the set of immune cells eliminated as self-reactive

### Level 3: Synthesis/Evaluation

6. Vaccination increases the number of
   (A) different receptors that recognize a pathogen.
   (B) lymphocytes with receptors that can bind to the pathogen.
   (C) epitopes that the immune system can recognize.
   (D) MHC molecules that can present an antigen.

7. Which of the following would *not* help a virus avoid triggering an adaptive immune response?
   (A) having frequent mutations in genes for surface proteins
   (B) infecting cells that produce very few MHC molecules
   (C) producing proteins very similar to those of other viruses
   (D) infecting and killing helper T cells

8. **DRAW IT** Consider a pencil-shaped protein with two epitopes, Y (the "eraser" end) and Z (the "point" end). They are recognized by antibodies A1 and A2, respectively. Draw and label a picture showing the antibodies linking proteins into a complex that could trigger endocytosis by a macrophage.

9. **MAKE CONNECTIONS** Contrast clonal selection with Lamarck's idea for the inheritance of acquired characteristics (see Concept 22.1).

10. **EVOLUTION CONNECTION** Describe one invertebrate mechanism of defense against pathogens and discuss how it is an evolutionary adaptation retained in vertebrates.

11. **SCIENTIFIC INQUIRY** A major cause of septic shock is the presence of lipopolysaccharide (LPS) from bacteria in the blood. Suppose you have available purified LPS and several strains of mice, each with a mutation that inactivates a particular TLR gene. How might you use these mice to test the feasibility of treating septic shock with a drug that blocks TLR signaling?

12. **WRITE ABOUT A THEME: INFORMATION** Among all nucleated body cells, only B and T cells lose DNA during their development and maturation. In a short essay (100–150 words), discuss the relationship between this loss and DNA as heritable biological information, focusing on similarities between cellular and organismal generations.

13. **SYNTHESIZE YOUR KNOWLEDGE**

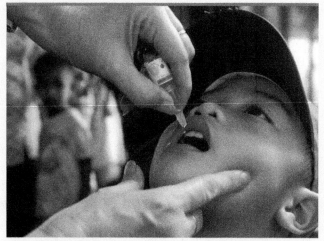

This photo shows a child receiving an oral vaccine against polio, a disease caused by a virus that infects neurons. Given that the body cannot readily replace most neurons, why is it important that a polio vaccine stimulate not only a cell-mediated response but also a humoral response?

*For selected answers, see Appendix A.*

 For additional practice questions, check out the **Dynamic Study Modules** in MasteringBiology. You can use them to study on your smartphone, tablet, or computer anytime, anywhere!

# Osmoregulation and Excretion 44

**Figure 44.1 How does an albatross drink salt water without ill effect?**

## KEY CONCEPTS

**44.1** Osmoregulation balances the uptake and loss of water and solutes

**44.2** An animal's nitrogenous wastes reflect its phylogeny and habitat

**44.3** Diverse excretory systems are variations on a tubular theme

**44.4** The nephron is organized for stepwise processing of blood filtrate

**44.5** Hormonal circuits link kidney function, water balance, and blood pressure

## A Balancing Act

At 3.5 m, the wingspan of a wandering albatross (*Diomedea exulans*) is the largest of any living bird. But the albatross commands attention for more than just its size. This massive bird remains at sea day and night throughout the year, returning to land only to reproduce. A human with only seawater to drink would die of dehydration, but faced with the same conditions, the albatross thrives **(Figure 44.1)**.

For both albatross and human, maintaining the fluid balance of their tissues requires that the relative concentrations of water and solutes be kept within fairly narrow limits. In addition, ions such as sodium and calcium must be maintained at concentrations that permit normal activity of muscles, neurons, and other body cells. Homeostasis thus requires **osmoregulation**, the general term for the processes by which animals control solute concentrations and balance water gain and loss.

A number of mechanisms for water and solute control have arisen during evolution, reflecting the varied and often severe osmoregulatory challenges presented by an animal's surroundings. Animals living in the arid conditions of a desert, for instance, can quickly lose body water. So too can albatrosses and other marine animals. Survival in these dehydrating environments depends on conserving body water and, for marine birds and fishes, eliminating excess salts. Freshwater animals face a distinct challenge: a watery environment that threatens

When you see this blue icon, log in to **MasteringBiology** and go to the Study Area for digital resources.

 Get Ready for This Chapter

to dilute their body fluids. These organisms survive by conserving solutes and absorbing salts from their surroundings.

In safeguarding their internal fluids, animals must deal with ammonia, a toxic metabolite produced by the dismantling of *nitrogenous* (nitrogen-containing) molecules, chiefly proteins and nucleic acids. Several mechanisms have evolved for ridding the body of nitrogenous metabolites and other metabolic waste products, a process called **excretion**. Because systems for excretion and osmoregulation are structurally and functionally linked in many animals, we'll consider both of these processes in this chapter.

# CONCEPT 44.1

## Osmoregulation balances the uptake and loss of water and solutes

Just as thermoregulation depends on balancing heat loss and gain (see Concept 40.3), regulating the chemical composition of body fluids depends on balancing the uptake and loss of water and solutes. If water uptake is excessive, animal cells swell and burst; if water loss is substantial, cells shrivel and die. Ultimately, the driving force for the movement of both water and solutes—in animals as in all other organisms—is a concentration gradient of one or more solutes across the plasma membrane.

### Osmosis and Osmolarity

Water enters and leaves cells by osmosis, which occurs when two solutions separated by a membrane differ in total solute concentration **(Figure 44.2)**. The unit of measurement for solute concentration is **osmolarity**, the number of moles of solute per liter of solution. The osmolarity of human blood is about 300 milliosmoles per liter (mOsm/L), whereas that of seawater is about 1,000 mOsm/L.

Two solutions with the same osmolarity are said to be *isoosmotic*. If a selectively permeable membrane separates the solutions, water molecules will continually cross the

membrane at equal rates in both directions. Thus, there is no *net* movement of water by osmosis between isoosmotic solutions. When two solutions differ in osmolarity, the solution with the higher concentration of solutes is said to be *hyperosmotic*, and the more dilute solution is said to be *hypoosmotic*. Water flows by osmosis from a hypoosmotic solution to a hyperosmotic one, thus reducing the concentration difference for both solutes and free water (see Figure 44.2).

In this chapter, we use the terms *isoosmotic, hypoosmotic,* and *hyperosmotic*, which refer specifically to osmolarity, instead of *isotonic, hypotonic,* and *hypertonic*. The latter set of terms applies to the response of animal cells—whether they swell or shrink—in solutions of known solute concentrations.

### Osmoregulatory Challenges and Mechanisms

An animal can maintain water balance in two ways. One is to be an **osmoconformer**: to be isoosmotic with its surroundings. All osmoconformers are marine animals. Because an osmoconformer's internal osmolarity is the same as that of its environment, there is no tendency to gain or lose water. Many osmoconformers live in water that has a stable composition and hence have a constant internal osmolarity.

The second way to maintain water balance is to be an **osmoregulator**: to control internal osmolarity independent of that of the external environment. Osmoregulation enables animals to live in environments that are uninhabitable for osmoconformers, such as freshwater and terrestrial habitats, or to move between marine and freshwater environments **(Figure 44.3)**.

In a hypoosmotic environment, an osmoregulator must discharge excess water. In a hyperosmotic environment, it must instead take in water to offset osmotic loss. Osmoregulation allows many marine animals to maintain an internal osmolarity different from that of seawater.

▼ **Figure 44.3 Sockeye salmon (*Oncorhynchus nerka*), osmoregulators that migrate between rivers and the ocean.**

▼ Figure 44.2 **Solute concentration and osmosis.**

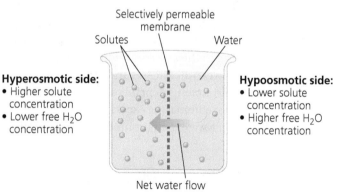

Selectively permeable membrane

Solutes

Water

**Hyperosmotic side:**
• Higher solute concentration
• Lower free H₂O concentration

**Hypoosmotic side:**
• Lower solute concentration
• Higher free H₂O concentration

Net water flow

Whether osmoconformers or osmoregulators, most animals cannot tolerate substantial changes in external osmolarity and are said to be *stenohaline* (from the Greek *stenos*, narrow, and *halos*, salt). In contrast, *euryhaline* animals (from the Greek *eurys*, broad) can survive large fluctuations in external osmolarity. Euryhaline osmoconformers include barnacles and mussels in estuaries that are alternately exposed to fresh and salt water; euryhaline osmoregulators include striped bass and the various species of salmon (see Figure 44.3).

Next we'll examine adaptations for osmoregulation that have evolved in marine, freshwater, and terrestrial animals.

## Marine Animals

Most marine invertebrates are osmoconformers. Their osmolarity is the same as that of seawater. Therefore, they face no substantial challenges in water balance. Nevertheless, they actively transport *specific* solutes that establish levels in hemolymph (circulatory fluid) different from those in the ocean. For example, homeostatic mechanisms in the Atlantic lobster (*Homarus americanus*) maintain a magnesium ion ($Mg^{2+}$) concentration of less than 9 m$M$ (millimolar, or $10^{-3}$ mol/L), far below the 50 m$M$ concentration of $Mg^{2+}$ in their environment.

Two osmoregulatory strategies evolved among marine vertebrates that address the challenges of a strongly dehydrating environment. One is found among marine "bony fishes," a group that includes ray-finned and lobe-finned fishes. The other is found in marine sharks and most other chondrichthyans (cartilaginous animals; see Concept 34.3).

Cod, shown in **Figure 44.4a**, and other marine bony fishes constantly lose water by osmosis. They balance water loss by drinking a lot of seawater. The excess salts ingested with seawater are eliminated through the gills and kidneys.

As noted earlier, osmoregulation is frequently coupled to elimination of nitrogenous waste products, such as urea.

Eliminating urea is important because high concentrations of urea can denature (unfold) proteins and thus disrupt cellular functions. Sharks, however, have a high concentration of urea in their body. Why isn't urea toxic for these animals? The answer lies in an organic molecule, trimethylamine oxide (TMAO), produced by shark tissues. TMAO protects proteins from the denaturing effect of urea.

TMAO has another function in sharks: osmoregulation. Like bony fishes, sharks have an internal salt concentration much lower than that of seawater. Thus, salt tends to diffuse from the water into their bodies, especially across their gills. However, the combination of TMAO with salts, urea, and other compounds results in a solute concentration in shark tissues that is actually somewhat higher than 1,000 mOsm/L. For this reason, water slowly *enters* the shark's body by osmosis and in food (sharks do not drink).

The small influx of water into the shark's body is disposed of in urine produced by the kidneys. The urine also removes some of the salt that diffuses into the shark's body; the rest is lost in feces or is secreted from a specialized gland.

## Freshwater Animals

The osmoregulatory problems of freshwater animals are the opposite of those of marine animals. The body fluids of freshwater animals must be hyperosmotic because animal cells cannot tolerate salt concentrations as low as that of lake or river water. Since freshwater animals have internal fluids with an osmolarity higher than that of their surroundings, they face the problem of gaining water by osmosis. In many freshwater animals, including bony fishes such as the perch, shown in **Figure 44.4b**, water balance relies on excreting large amounts of very dilute urine and drinking almost no water. In addition, salts lost by diffusion and in the urine are replenished by eating and by salt uptake across their gills.

▾ **Figure 44.4 Osmoregulation in marine and freshwater bony fishes: a comparison.**

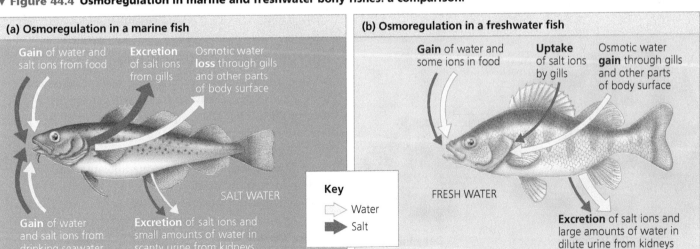

**(a) Osmoregulation in a marine fish**

**Gain** of water and salt ions from food

**Excretion** of salt ions from gills

Osmotic water **loss** through gills and other parts of body surface

**Gain** of water and salt ions from drinking seawater

**Excretion** of salt ions and small amounts of water in scanty urine from kidneys

SALT WATER

**Key**

▷ Water
➤ Salt

**(b) Osmoregulation in a freshwater fish**

**Gain** of water and some ions in food

**Uptake** of salt ions by gills

Osmotic water **gain** through gills and other parts of body surface

FRESH WATER

**Excretion** of salt ions and large amounts of water in dilute urine from kidneys

Salmon and other euryhaline fishes that migrate between fresh water and seawater undergo dramatic changes in osmoregulatory status. When living in rivers and streams, salmon osmoregulate like other freshwater fishes, producing large amounts of dilute urine and taking up salt from the dilute environment through their gills. When they migrate to the ocean, salmon acclimatize (see Concept 40.2). They produce more of the steroid hormone cortisol, which increases the number and size of specialized salt-secreting cells. As a result of these and other physiological changes, salmon in salt water excrete excess salt from their gills and produce only small amounts of urine—just like bony fishes that spend their entire lives in salt water.

### Animals That Live in Temporary Waters

Extreme dehydration, or *desiccation*, is fatal for most animals. However, a few aquatic invertebrates that live in temporary ponds and in films of water around soil particles can lose almost all their body water and survive. These animals enter a dormant state when their habitats dry up, an adaptation called **anhydrobiosis** ("life without water"). Among the most striking examples are the tardigrades, or water bears, tiny invertebrates less than 1 mm long (**Figure 44.5**). In their active, hydrated state, they contain about 85% water by weight, but they can dehydrate to less than 2% water and survive in an inactive state, dry as dust, for a decade or more. Just add water, and within hours the rehydrated tardigrades are moving about and feeding.

Anhydrobiosis requires adaptations that keep cell membranes intact. Researchers are just beginning to learn how tardigrades survive drying out, but studies of anhydrobiotic roundworms (phylum Nematoda; see Concept 33.4) show that desiccated individuals contain large amounts of sugars. In particular, a disaccharide called trehalose seems to protect the cells by replacing the water that is normally associated with proteins and membrane lipids. Many insects that survive freezing in the winter also use trehalose as a membrane protectant, as do some plants resistant to desiccation.

Recently, scientists began applying lessons learned from the study of anhydrobiosis to the preservation of biological materials. Traditionally, samples of protein, DNA, and cells have been kept in ultracold freezers (−80°C), consuming large amounts of energy and space. Now, however, the manufacture of materials modeled after the protectants found in anhydrobiotic species has enabled such samples to be stored in compact chambers at room temperature.

### Land Animals

The threat of dehydration is a major regulatory problem for terrestrial plants and animals. Adaptations that reduce water loss are key to survival on land. Much as a waxy cuticle contributes to the success of land plants, the body coverings of most terrestrial animals help prevent dehydration. Examples are the waxy layers of insect exoskeletons, the shells of land snails, and the layers of dead, keratinized skin cells covering most terrestrial vertebrates, including humans. Many terrestrial animals, especially desert-dwellers, are nocturnal, which reduces evaporative water loss because of the lower temperature and higher humidity of night air.

Despite these and other adaptations, most terrestrial animals lose water through many routes: in urine and feces, across the skin, and from the surfaces of gas exchange organs. Land animals maintain water balance by drinking and eating moist foods and by producing water metabolically through cellular respiration.

A number of desert animals are well enough adapted for minimizing water loss that they can survive for long periods of time without drinking. Camels, for example, tolerate a 7°C rise in body temperature, greatly reducing the amount of water lost in sweat production. Also, they can lose 25% of their body water and survive. (In contrast, a human who loses half this amount of body water will die from heart failure.) In the **Scientific Skills Exercise**, you can examine water balance in another desert species, the sandy inland mouse.

## Energetics of Osmoregulation

Maintaining an osmolarity difference between an animal's body and its external environment carries an energy cost. Because diffusion tends to equalize concentrations in a system, osmoregulators must expend energy to maintain the osmotic gradients that cause water to move in or out. They do so by using active transport to manipulate solute concentrations in their body fluids.

The energy cost of osmoregulation depends on how different an animal's osmolarity is from its surroundings, how easily water and solutes can move across the animal's surface, and how much work is required to pump solutes across the

▼ **Figure 44.5 Anhydrobiosis.** Tardigrades (SEM images) inhabit temporary ponds as well as droplets of water in soil and on moist plants.

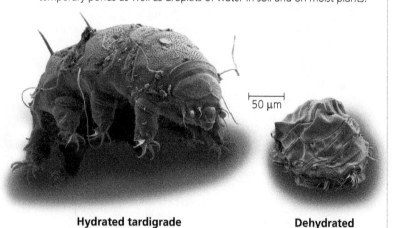

| Hydrated tardigrade | Dehydrated tardigrade |

50 μm

## Describing and Interpreting Quantitative Data

**How Do Desert Mice Maintain Osmotic Homeostasis?** The sandy inland mouse (now known as *Pseudomys hermannsburgensis*) is an Australian desert mammal that can survive indefinitely on a diet of dried seeds without drinking water. To study this species' adaptations to its arid environment, researchers conducted a laboratory experiment in which they controlled access to water. In this exercise, you will analyze some of the data from the experiment.

**How the Experiment Was Done** Nine captured mice were kept in an environmentally controlled room and given birdseed (10% water by weight) to eat. In part A of the study, the mice had unlimited access to tap water for drinking; in part B of the study, the mice were not given any drinking water for 35 days, similar to conditions in their natural habitat. At the end of parts A and B, the researchers measured the osmolarity and urea concentration of the urine and blood of each mouse. The mice were also weighed three times a week.

### Data from the Experiment

| Access to Water | Mean Osmolarity (mOsm/L) | | Mean Urea Concentration (mM) | |
|---|---|---|---|---|
| | Urine | Blood | Urine | Blood |
| Part A: Unlimited | 490 | 350 | 330 | 7.6 |
| Part B: None | 4,700 | 320 | 2,700 | 11 |

In part A, the mice drank about 33% of their body weight each day. The change in body weight during the study was negligible for all mice.

**INTERPRET THE DATA**

1. In words, describe how the data differ between the unlimited water and no-water conditions for the following: (a) osmolarity of urine, (b) osmolarity of blood, (c) urea concentration in urine, (d) urea concentration in blood. (e) Does this data set provide evidence of homeostatic regulation? Explain.

2. (a) Calculate the ratio of urine osmolarity to blood osmolarity for mice with unlimited access to water. (b) Calculate this ratio for mice with no access to water. (c) What conclusion would you draw from these ratios?

3. If the amount of urine produced were different in the two conditions, how would that affect your calculation? Explain.

 **Instructors:** A version of this Scientific Skills Exercise can be assigned in MasteringBiology.

**Data from** R. E. MacMillen et al., Water economy and energy metabolism of the sandy inland mouse, *Leggadina hermannsburgensis, Journal of Mammalogy* 53: 529–539 (1972).

---

membrane. Osmoregulation accounts for 5% or more of the resting metabolic rate of many fishes. For brine shrimp, small crustaceans that live in extremely salty lakes, the gradient between internal and external osmolarity is very large, and the cost of osmoregulation is correspondingly high—as much as 30% of the resting metabolic rate.

The energy cost to an animal of maintaining water and salt balance is minimized by having body fluids that are adapted to the salinity of the animal's habitat. Thus, the body fluids of most animals that live in fresh water (which has an osmolarity of 0.5–15 mOsm/L) have lower solute concentrations than the body fluids of their closest relatives that live in seawater (1,000 mOsm/L). For instance, whereas marine molluscs have body fluids with solute concentrations of approximately 1,000 mOsm/L, some freshwater molluscs maintain the osmolarity of their body fluids at just 40 mOsm/L. In each case, minimizing the osmotic difference between body fluids and the surrounding environment decreases the energy cost of osmoregulation.

## Transport Epithelia in Osmoregulation

The ultimate function of osmoregulation is to control solute concentrations in cells, but most animals do this indirectly by managing the solute content of an internal body fluid that bathes the cells. In insects and other animals with an open circulatory system, the fluid surrounding cells is hemolymph. In vertebrates and other animals with a closed circulatory system, the cells are bathed in an interstitial fluid that contains a mixture of solutes controlled indirectly by the blood. Maintaining the composition of such fluids depends on structures ranging from individual cells that regulate solute movement to complex organs such as the vertebrate kidney.

In most animals, osmoregulation and metabolic waste disposal rely on **transport epithelia**—one or more layers of epithelial cells specialized for moving particular solutes in controlled amounts in specific directions. Transport epithelia are typically arranged into tubular networks with extensive surface areas. Some transport epithelia face the outside environment directly, whereas others line channels connected to the outside by an opening on the body surface.

The transport epithelium that enables the albatross and other marine birds to survive on seawater remained undiscovered for many years. To explore this question, researchers gave captive marine birds only seawater to drink. Although very little salt appeared in the birds' urine, fluid dripping from the tip of their beaks was a concentrated solution of salt (NaCl). The source of this solution was a pair of nasal salt glands packed with transport epithelia (**Figure 44.6**). Salt glands, which are also found in sea turtles and marine iguanas, use active transport of ions to secrete a fluid much saltier than the ocean. Even though drinking seawater brings in a lot of salt, the salt gland enables these marine vertebrates to achieve a net gain of water. By contrast, humans who drink a given volume of seawater must use a *greater* volume of water to excrete the salt load, with the result that they become dehydrated.

Transport epithelia that function in maintaining water balance also often function in disposal of metabolic wastes. We'll see examples of this coordinated function in our upcoming consideration of earthworm and insect excretory systems as well as the vertebrate kidney.

▼ **Figure 44.6 Salt secretion in the nasal glands of a marine bird.** A transport epithelium moves salt from the blood into secretory tubules, which drain into central ducts leading to the nostrils.

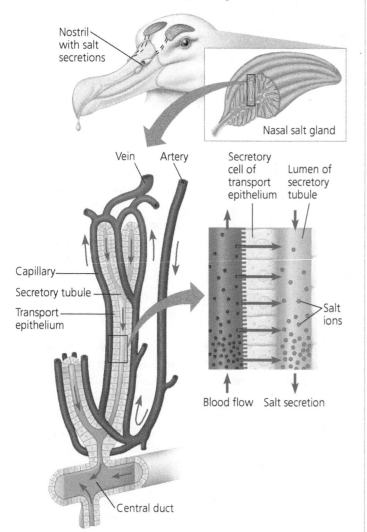

1. The movement of salt from the surrounding water to the blood of a freshwater fish requires the expenditure of energy in the form of ATP. Why?

2. Why aren't any freshwater animals osmoconformers?

3. **WHAT IF?** ➤ Researchers found that a camel in the sun required much more water when its fur was shaved off, although its body temperature was the same. What can you conclude about the relationship between osmoregulation and the insulation provided by fur?

*For suggested answers, see Appendix A.*

# CONCEPT 44.2

# An animal's nitrogenous wastes reflect its phylogeny and habitat

Because most metabolic wastes must be dissolved in water to be excreted from the body, the type and quantity of an animal's waste products may have a large impact on its water balance. In this regard, some of the most significant waste products are the nitrogenous breakdown products of proteins and nucleic acids. When proteins and nucleic acids are broken apart for energy or converted to carbohydrates or fats, enzymes remove nitrogen in the form of **ammonia** ($NH_3$). Ammonia is very toxic, in part because its ion, ammonium ($NH_4^+$), can interfere with oxidative phosphorylation. Although some animals excrete ammonia directly, many species expend energy to convert it to less toxic compounds prior to excretion.

## Forms of Nitrogenous Waste

Animals excrete nitrogenous wastes as ammonia, urea, or uric acid (**Figure 44.7**). These different forms vary significantly in their toxicity and the energy costs of producing them.

### Ammonia

Animals that excrete ammonia need access to lots of water because ammonia can be tolerated only at very low concentrations. Therefore, ammonia excretion is most common in aquatic species. The highly soluble ammonia molecules, which interconvert between $NH_3$ and $NH_4^+$ forms, easily pass through membranes and are readily lost by diffusion to the surrounding water. In many invertebrates, ammonia release occurs across the whole body surface.

### Urea

Although ammonia excretion works well in many aquatic species, it is much less suitable for land animals. Ammonia is so toxic that it can be safely transported through and excreted from the body only in large volumes of very dilute solutions. Most terrestrial animals and many marine species

## Figure 44.7 Variations in forms of nitrogenous waste among animal species.

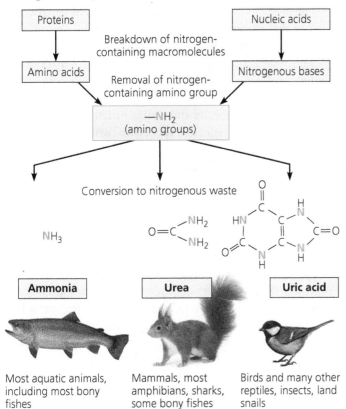

Most aquatic animals, including most bony fishes — **Ammonia** ($NH_3$)

Mammals, most amphibians, sharks, some bony fishes — **Urea**

Birds and many other reptiles, insects, land snails — **Uric acid**

simply do not have access to sufficient water to routinely excrete ammonia. Instead, they mainly excrete a different nitrogenous waste, **urea**. In vertebrates, urea is the product of an energy-consuming metabolic cycle that combines ammonia with carbon dioxide in the liver.

The main advantage of urea for nitrogenous waste excretion is its very low toxicity. The main disadvantage is its energy cost: Animals must expend energy to produce urea from ammonia. From a bioenergetic standpoint, we would predict that animals that spend part of their lives in water and part on land would switch between excreting ammonia (thereby saving energy) and excreting urea (reducing excretory water loss). Indeed, many amphibians excrete mainly ammonia when they are aquatic tadpoles and switch largely to urea excretion when they become land-dwelling adults.

### Uric Acid

Insects, land snails, and many reptiles, including birds, excrete **uric acid** as their primary nitrogenous waste. (Bird droppings, or *guano*, are a mixture of white uric acid and brown feces.) Uric acid is relatively nontoxic and does not readily dissolve in water. It therefore can be excreted as a semisolid paste with very little water loss. However, uric acid is even more energetically expensive than urea, requiring considerable ATP for synthesis from ammonia.

While not primarily uric acid producers, humans and some other animals generate a small amount of uric acid from metabolism. Diseases that alter this process reflect problems that can arise when a metabolic product is insoluble. For example, a genetic defect predisposes Dalmatian dogs to form uric acid stones in their bladder. In humans, adult males are particularly susceptible to *gout*, a painful joint inflammation caused by deposits of uric acid crystals. Some dinosaurs appear to have been similarly affected: Fossilized bones of *Tyrannosaurus rex* exhibit joint damage characteristic of gout.

## The Influence of Evolution and Environment on Nitrogenous Wastes

**EVOLUTION** As a result of natural selection, the type and amount of nitrogenous waste a species produces are matched to its environment. One key factor in a habitat is the availability of water. For example, terrestrial turtles (which often live in dry areas) excrete mainly uric acid, whereas aquatic turtles excrete both urea and ammonia.

In some cases, an animal's egg is the immediate environment of relevance to the type of nitrogenous waste excreted. In an amphibian egg, which lacks a shell, ammonia or urea can simply diffuse out of the egg. Similarly, soluble wastes produced by a mammalian embryo can be carried away by the mother's blood. In the case of birds and other reptiles, however, the egg is surrounded by a shell that is permeable to gases but not to liquids. As a result, any soluble nitrogenous wastes released by the embryo would be trapped within the egg and could accumulate to dangerous levels. For this reason, using uric acid as an insoluble waste product conveys a selective advantage in reptiles. Stored within the egg as a harmless solid, the uric acid is left behind when the animal hatches.

Regardless of the type of nitrogenous waste, the amount produced is coupled to the animal's energy budget. Endotherms, which use energy at high rates, eat more food and produce more nitrogenous waste than ectotherms. The amount of nitrogenous waste is also linked to diet. Predators, which derive much of their energy from protein, excrete more nitrogen than animals that rely mainly on lipids or carbohydrates as energy sources.

Having surveyed the forms of nitrogenous waste and their interrelationship with habitat and energy consumption, we'll turn next to the processes and systems animals use to excrete these and other wastes.

### CONCEPT CHECK 44.2

1. What advantage does uric acid offer as a nitrogenous waste in arid environments?

2. **WHAT IF?** ➤ Suppose a bird and a human both have gout. Why might reducing purine in their diets help the human much more than the bird?

*For suggested answers, see Appendix A.*

# CONCEPT 44.3

## Diverse excretory systems are variations on a tubular theme

Whether an animal lives on land, in salt water, or in fresh water, water balance depends on the regulation of solute movement between internal fluids and the external environment. Much of this movement is handled by excretory systems. These systems are central to homeostasis because they dispose of metabolic wastes and control body fluid composition.

### Excretory Processes

Animals across a wide range of species produce a fluid waste called urine through the basic steps shown in **Figure 44.8**. In the first step, body fluid (blood, coelomic fluid, or hemolymph) is brought in contact with the selectively permeable membrane of a transport epithelium. In most cases, hydrostatic pressure (blood pressure in many animals) drives a process of **filtration**. Cells, as well as proteins and other large molecules, cannot cross the epithelial membrane and remain in the body fluid. In contrast, water and small solutes, such as salts, sugars, amino acids, and nitrogenous wastes, cross the membrane, forming a solution called the **filtrate**.

The filtrate is converted to a waste fluid by the specific transport of materials into or out of the filtrate. The process of selective **reabsorption** recovers useful molecules and water from the filtrate and returns them to the body fluid. Valuable solutes—including glucose, certain salts, vitamins, hormones, and amino acids—are reabsorbed by active transport. Nonessential solutes and wastes are left in the filtrate or are added to it by selective **secretion**, which also occurs by active transport. The pumping of various solutes in turn determines whether water moves by osmosis into or out of the filtrate. In the last step—excretion—the processed filtrate containing nitrogenous wastes is released from the body as urine.

### Survey of Excretory Systems

The systems that perform the basic excretory functions vary widely among animal groups. However, they are generally built on a complex network of tubules that provide a large surface area for the exchange of water and solutes, including nitrogenous wastes. We'll examine the excretory systems of flatworms, earthworms, insects, and vertebrates as examples of evolutionary variations on tubule networks.

### Protonephridia

As illustrated in **Figure 44.9**, flatworms (phylum Platyhelminthes), which lack a coelom or body cavity, have excretory systems called **protonephridia** (singular, *protonephridium*).

▼ **Figure 44.8 Key steps of excretory system function: an overview.** Most excretory systems produce a filtrate by pressure-filtering body fluids and then modify the filtrate's contents. This diagram is modeled after the vertebrate excretory system.

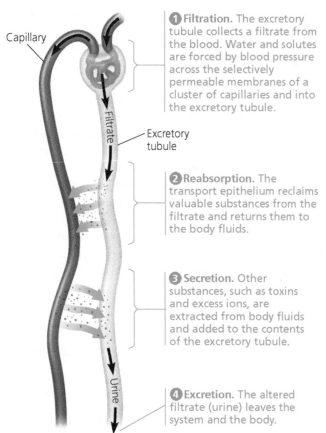

Capillary

Filtrate

**1 Filtration.** The excretory tubule collects a filtrate from the blood. Water and solutes are forced by blood pressure across the selectively permeable membranes of a cluster of capillaries and into the excretory tubule.

Excretory tubule

**2 Reabsorption.** The transport epithelium reclaims valuable substances from the filtrate and returns them to the body fluids.

**3 Secretion.** Other substances, such as toxins and excess ions, are extracted from body fluids and added to the contents of the excretory tubule.

Urine

**4 Excretion.** The altered filtrate (urine) leaves the system and the body.

▼ **Figure 44.9 Protonephridia in a planarian.**

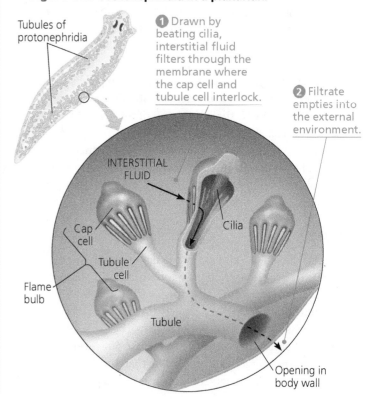

Tubules of protonephridia

**1** Drawn by beating cilia, interstitial fluid filters through the membrane where the cap cell and tubule cell interlock.

**2** Filtrate empties into the external environment.

INTERSTITIAL FLUID

Cap cell

Cilia

Tubule cell

Flame bulb

Tubule

Opening in body wall

Protonephridia consist of a network of dead-end tubules that branch throughout the body. Cellular units called flame bulbs cap the branches of each protonephridium. Each flame bulb, consisting of a tubule cell and a cap cell, has a tuft of cilia projecting into the tubule.

During filtration, the beating of the cilia draws water and solutes from the interstitial fluid through the flame bulb, releasing filtrate into the tubule network. (The name *flame bulb* derives from the moving cilia's resemblance to a flickering flame.) The processed filtrate moves outward through the tubules and empties as urine via external openings. Because the urine excreted by freshwater flatworms is low in solutes, its production helps to balance the osmotic uptake of water from the environment.

Protonephridia are also found in rotifers, some annelids, mollusc larvae, and lancelets (see Figure 34.4). In the freshwater flatworms, protonephridia serve chiefly in osmoregulation. Most metabolic wastes diffuse out of the animal across the body surface or are excreted into the gastrovascular cavity and eliminated through the mouth (see Figure 33.10). In contrast, parasitic flatworms that are isoosmotic to the surrounding fluids of their host organisms have protonephridia that primarily function in disposing of nitrogenous wastes. Natural selection has thus adapted protonephridia to different tasks in different environments.

## Metanephridia

Most annelids, such as earthworms, have **metanephridia** (singular, *metanephridium*), excretory organs that collect fluid directly from the coelom **(Figure 44.10)**. A pair of metanephridia are found in each segment of an annelid, where they are immersed in coelomic fluid and enveloped by a capillary network. A ciliated funnel surrounds the internal opening of each metanephridium. As the cilia beat, fluid is drawn into a collecting tubule, which includes a storage bladder that opens to the outside.

Earthworms inhabit damp soil and therefore usually experience a net uptake of water by osmosis through their skin. Their metanephridia balance the water influx by producing urine that is dilute (hypoosmotic to body fluids). In producing a hypoosmotic filtrate, the transport epithelium reabsorbs most solutes and returns them to the blood in the capillaries. Nitrogenous wastes, however, remain in the tubule and are excreted to the environment. The metanephridia of an earthworm thus serve both an excretory and an osmoregulatory function.

## Malpighian Tubules

Insects and other terrestrial arthropods have organs called **Malpighian tubules** that remove nitrogenous wastes and that also function in osmoregulation **(Figure 44.11)**. The Malpighian tubules extend from dead-end tips immersed in hemolymph to openings into the digestive tract. The filtration step common to other excretory systems is absent. Instead, the transport epithelium that lines the tubules secretes certain solutes, including nitrogenous wastes, from the hemolymph into the lumen of the tubule. Water follows the solutes into the tubule by osmosis.

▼ **Figure 44.11 Malpighian tubules of insects.** Malpighian tubules are outpocketings of the digestive tract that remove nitrogenous wastes and function in osmoregulation.

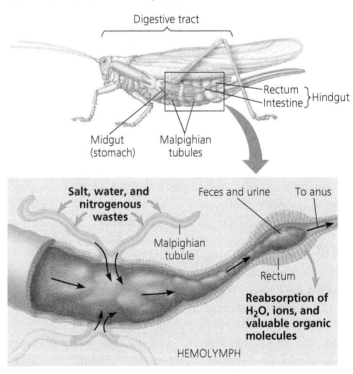

▼ **Figure 44.10 Metanephridia of an earthworm.** Each segment of the worm contains a pair of metanephridia, which collect coelomic fluid from the adjacent anterior segment. The region highlighted in yellow illustrates the organization of one metanephridium of a pair; the other would be behind it.

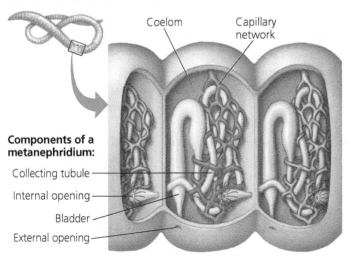

## ▼ Figure 44.12 Exploring The Mammalian Excretory System

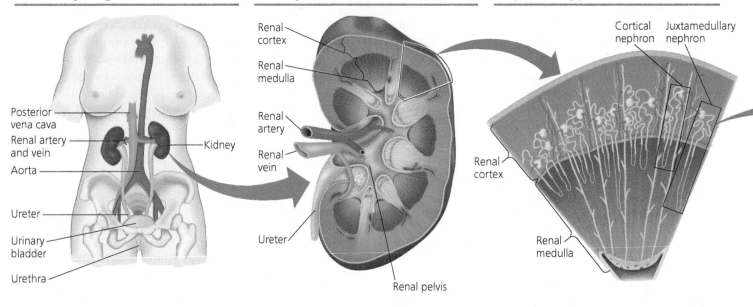

### Excretory Organs

In humans, the excretory system consists of **kidneys**, a pair of organs each about 10 cm in length, as well as organs for transporting and storing urine. Urine produced by each kidney exits through a duct called the **ureter**; the two ureters drain into a common sac called the **urinary bladder**. During urination, urine is expelled from the bladder through a tube called the **urethra**, which empties to the outside near the vagina in females and through the penis in males. Sphincter muscles near the junction of the urethra and bladder regulate urination.

### Kidney Structure

Each kidney has an outer **renal cortex** and an inner **renal medulla**. Both regions are supplied with blood by a renal artery and drained by a renal vein. Within the cortex and medulla lie tightly packed excretory tubules and associated blood vessels. The excretory tubules carry and process a filtrate produced from the blood entering the kidney. Nearly all of the fluid in the filtrate is reabsorbed into the surrounding blood vessels and exits the kidney in the renal vein. The remaining fluid leaves the excretory tubules as urine, is collected in the inner **renal pelvis**, and exits the kidney via the ureter.

### Nephron Types

Weaving back and forth across the renal cortex and medulla are the **nephrons**, the functional units of the vertebrate kidney. Of the roughly 1 million nephrons in a human kidney, 85% are **cortical nephrons**, which reach only a short distance into the medulla. The remainder, the **juxtamedullary nephrons**, extend deep into the medulla. Juxtamedullary nephrons are essential for production of urine that is hyperosmotic to body fluids, a key adaptation for water conservation in mammals.

 Animation: Kidney Structure

---

As fluid passes from the tubules into the rectum, most solutes are pumped back into the hemolymph; water reabsorption by osmosis follows. The nitrogenous wastes—mainly insoluble uric acid—are eliminated as nearly dry matter along with the feces. The insect excretory system is capable of conserving water very effectively, a key adaptation contributing to the tremendous success of insects on land.

### Kidneys

In vertebrates and some other chordates, a compact organ called the **kidney** functions in both osmoregulation and excretion. Like the excretory organs of most animal phyla, kidneys consist of tubules. The tubules of kidneys are arranged in a highly organized manner and are closely associated with a network of capillaries. The vertebrate excretory system also includes ducts and other structures that carry urine from the tubules out of the kidney and, eventually, the body.

Vertebrate kidneys are typically nonsegmented. However, hagfishes, which are jawless vertebrates (see Concept 34.2), have kidneys with segmentally arranged excretory tubules. Because hagfishes and other vertebrates share a common chordate ancestor, it is possible that the excretory structures of vertebrate ancestors were also segmented.

We conclude this introduction to excretory systems with an exploration of the anatomy of the mammalian kidney and associated structures **(Figure 44.12)**. Familiarizing yourself with the terms and diagrams in this figure will provide you with a solid foundation for learning about filtrate processing in the kidney, the focus of the next section of this chapter.

## Nephron Organization

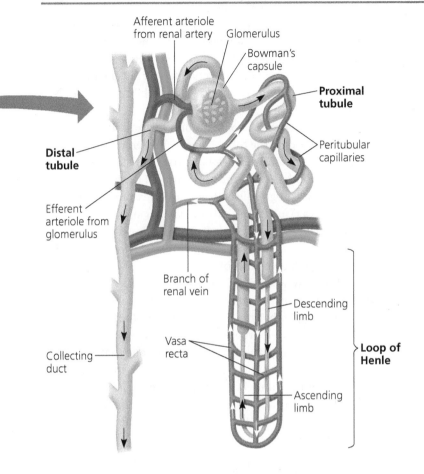

Afferent arteriole from renal artery
Glomerulus
Bowman's capsule
**Proximal tubule**
**Distal tubule**
Peritubular capillaries
Efferent arteriole from glomerulus
Branch of renal vein
Descending limb
Vasa recta
Collecting duct
Ascending limb
**Loop of Henle**

Each nephron consists of a single long tubule as well as a ball of capillaries called the **glomerulus**. The blind end of the tubule forms a cup-shaped swelling, called **Bowman's capsule**, which surrounds the glomerulus. Filtrate is formed when blood pressure forces fluid from the blood in the glomerulus into the lumen of Bowman's capsule. Processing occurs as the filtrate passes through three major regions of the nephron: the **proximal tubule**, the **loop of Henle** (a hairpin turn with a descending limb and an ascending limb), and the **distal tubule**. A **collecting duct** receives processed filtrate from many nephrons and transports it to the renal pelvis.

Each nephron is supplied with blood by an *afferent arteriole*, an offshoot of the renal artery that branches and forms the capillaries of the glomerulus. The capillaries converge as they leave the glomerulus, forming an *efferent arteriole*. Branches of this vessel form the **peritubular capillaries**, which surround the proximal and distal tubules. Other branches extend downward and form the **vasa recta**, hairpin-shaped capillaries that serve the renal medulla, including the long loop of Henle of juxtamedullary nephrons.

▶ In this SEM of densely packed blood vessels from a human kidney, arterioles and peritubular capillaries appear pink; the glomeruli appear yellow.

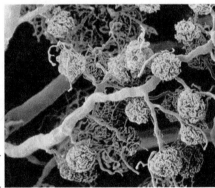

200 μm

---

### CONCEPT CHECK 44.3

1. Compare and contrast the ways that metabolic waste products enter the excretory systems of flatworms, earthworms, and insects.

2. Where and how does filtrate originate in the vertebrate kidney, and by what two routes do the components of the filtrate exit the kidney?

3. **WHAT IF?** ▶ Kidney failure is often treated by hemodialysis, in which blood diverted out of the body is filtered and then allowed to flow on one side of a semipermeable membrane. Fluid called dialysate flows in the opposite direction on the other side of the membrane. In replacing the reabsorption and secretion of solutes in a functional kidney, the makeup of the starting dialysate is critical. What initial solute composition would work well?

*For suggested answers, see Appendix A.*

# CONCEPT 44.4

## The nephron is organized for stepwise processing of blood filtrate

In the human kidney, filtrate forms when fluid passes from the bloodstream to the lumen of Bowman's capsule. The glomerular capillaries and specialized cells of Bowman's capsule retain blood cells and large molecules, such as plasma proteins, but are permeable to water and small solutes. Thus, the filtrate produced in the capsule contains salts, glucose, amino acids, vitamins, nitrogenous wastes, and other small molecules. Because such molecules pass freely between glomerular capillaries and Bowman's capsule, the concentrations of these substances in the initial filtrate are the same as those in blood plasma.

Under normal conditions, roughly 1,600 L of blood flows through a pair of human kidneys each day, yielding about 180 L of initial filtrate. Of this, about 99% of the water and nearly all of the sugars, amino acids, vitamins, and other organic nutrients are reabsorbed into the blood, leaving only about 1.5 L of urine to be transported to the bladder.

## From Blood Filtrate to Urine: *A Closer Look*

To explore how filtrate is processed into urine, we'll follow the filtrate along its path in the nephron (**Figure 44.13**). Each circled number refers to the processing in transport epithelia as the filtrate moves through the kidney cortex and medulla.

❶ **Proximal tubule.** Reabsorption in the proximal tubule is critical for the recapture of ions, water, and valuable nutrients from the huge volume of initial filtrate. NaCl (salt) in the filtrate enters the cells of the transport epithelium by facilitated diffusion and cotransport mechanisms and then is transferred to the interstitial fluid by active transport (see Concept 7.4). This transfer of positive charge out of the tubule drives the passive transport of $Cl^-$.

As salt moves from the filtrate to the interstitial fluid, water follows by osmosis, reducing filtrate volume considerably. The salt and water that exit the filtrate diffuse from the interstitial fluid into the peritubular capillaries. Glucose, amino acids, potassium ions ($K^+$), and other essential substances are also actively or passively transported from the filtrate to the interstitial fluid and then into the peritubular capillaries.

Processing of filtrate in the proximal tubule helps maintain a relatively constant pH in body fluids. Cells of the transport epithelium secrete $H^+$ into the lumen of the tubule but also synthesize and secrete ammonia, which acts as a buffer to trap $H^+$ in the form of ammonium ions ($NH_4^+$). The more acidic the filtrate is, the more ammonia the cells produce and secrete, and a mammal's urine usually contains some ammonia from this source (even though most nitrogenous waste is excreted as urea). The proximal tubules also reabsorb about 90% of the buffer bicarbonate ($HCO_3^-$) from the filtrate, contributing further to pH balance in body fluids.

As the filtrate passes through the proximal tubule, materials to be excreted become concentrated. Many wastes leave the body fluids during the nonselective filtration process and remain in the filtrate while water and salts are reabsorbed. Urea, for example, is reabsorbed at a much lower rate than are salt and water. In addition, some materials are actively secreted into the filtrate from surrounding tissues. For example, drugs and toxins that have been processed in the liver pass from the peritubular capillaries into the interstitial fluid. These molecules are then actively secreted by the transport epithelium into the lumen of the proximal tubule.

❷ **Descending limb of the loop of Henle.** Upon leaving the proximal tubule, filtrate enters the loop of Henle, which further reduces filtrate volume via distinct stages of water and salt movement. In the first portion of the loop, the descending limb, numerous water channels formed by **aquaporin** proteins make the transport epithelium freely permeable to water. In contrast, there are almost no channels for salt and other small solutes, resulting in very low permeability for these substances.

For water to move out of the tubule by osmosis, the interstitial fluid bathing the tubule must be hyperosmotic to the filtrate. This condition is met along the entire length of the descending limb because the osmolarity of the interstitial fluid increases progressively from the cortex through the medulla. As a result, the filtrate loses water and increases in solute concentration all along its journey down the descending limb. The highest osmolarity (about 1,200 mOsm/L) occurs at the elbow of the loop of Henle.

❸ **Ascending limb of the loop of Henle.** The filtrate reaches the tip of the loop and then returns to the cortex in the ascending limb. Unlike the descending limb, the ascending limb has a transport epithelium that lacks water channels. Consequently, the epithelial membrane that faces the filtrate in the ascending limb is impermeable to water.

The ascending limb has two specialized regions: a thin segment near the loop tip and a thick segment adjacent to the distal tubule. As filtrate ascends in the thin segment, NaCl, which became highly concentrated in the descending limb, diffuses out of the permeable tubule into the interstitial fluid. This movement of NaCl out of the tubule helps maintain the osmolarity of the interstitial fluid in the medulla.

In the thick segment of the ascending limb, the movement of NaCl out of the filtrate continues. Here, however, the epithelium actively transports NaCl into the interstitial fluid. As a result of losing salt but not water, the filtrate becomes progressively more dilute as it moves up to the cortex in the ascending limb of the loop.

❹ **Distal tubule.** The distal tubule plays a key role in regulating the $K^+$ and NaCl concentration of body fluids. This regulation involves variation in the amount of $K^+$ secreted into the filtrate as well as the amount of NaCl reabsorbed from the filtrate. The distal tubule also contributes to pH regulation by the controlled secretion of $H^+$ and reabsorption of $HCO_3^-$.

❺ **Collecting duct.** The collecting duct processes the filtrate into urine, which it carries to the renal pelvis (see Figure 44.12). As filtrate passes along the transport epithelium of the collecting duct, hormonal control of permeability and transport determines the extent to which the urine becomes concentrated.

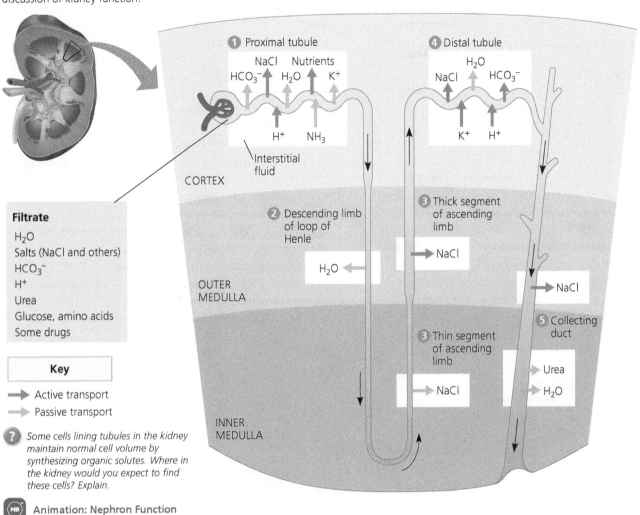

**Filtrate**

$H_2O$
Salts (NaCl and others)
$HCO_3^-$
$H^+$
Urea
Glucose, amino acids
Some drugs

**Key**

→ Active transport
→ Passive transport

? *Some cells lining tubules in the kidney maintain normal cell volume by synthesizing organic solutes. Where in the kidney would you expect to find these cells? Explain.*

MB **Animation: Nephron Function**

When the kidneys are conserving water, aquaporin channels in the collecting duct allow water molecules to cross the epithelium. At the same time, the epithelium remains impermeable to salt and, in the renal cortex, to urea. As the collecting duct traverses the gradient of osmolarity in the kidney, the filtrate becomes increasingly concentrated, losing more and more water by osmosis to the hyperosmotic interstitial fluid. In the inner medulla, the duct becomes permeable to urea. Because of the high urea concentration in the filtrate at this point, some urea diffuses out of the duct and into the interstitial fluid. Along with NaCl, this urea contributes to the high osmolarity of the interstitial fluid in the medulla. The net result is urine that is hyperosmotic to the general body fluids.

When producing dilute rather than concentrated urine, the collecting duct actively absorbs salts without allowing water to follow by osmosis. At these times, the epithelium lacks aquaporin channels, and NaCl is actively transported out of filtrate. As we'll see, the presence of water channels in the collecting duct epithelium is controlled by hormones that regulate blood pressure, volume, and osmolarity.

## Solute Gradients and Water Conservation

The ability of the mammalian kidney to conserve water is a key adaptation for terrestrial habitats. In humans, the osmolarity of blood is about 300 mOsm/L, but the kidney can excrete urine up to four times as concentrated—about 1,200 mOsm/L. Some mammals can do even better: Australian hopping mice, small marsupials that live in dry desert regions, can produce urine with an osmolarity of 9,300 mOsm/L, 25 times as concentrated as the animal's blood.

In a mammalian kidney, the production of hyperosmotic urine is possible only because considerable energy is expended for the active transport of solutes against concentration gradients. The nephrons—particularly the loops of Henle—can be thought of as energy-consuming machines that produce an osmolarity gradient suitable for extracting water from the filtrate in the collecting duct. The primary solutes affecting osmolarity are NaCl, which is concentrated in the renal medulla by the loop of Henle, and urea, which passes across the epithelium of the collecting duct in the inner medulla.

## Concentrating Urine in the Mammalian Kidney

To better understand the physiology of the mammalian kidney as a water-conserving organ, let's retrace the flow of filtrate through the excretory tubule. This time, let's focus on how juxtamedullary nephrons maintain an osmolarity gradient in the tissues that surround the loop of Henle and how they use that gradient to excrete hyperosmotic urine **(Figure 44.14)**. Filtrate passing from Bowman's capsule to the proximal tubule has about the same osmolarity as blood. A large amount of water *and* salt is reabsorbed from the filtrate as it flows through the proximal tubule in the renal cortex. As a result, the filtrate's volume decreases substantially, but its osmolarity remains about the same.

As the filtrate flows from cortex to medulla in the descending limb of the loop of Henle, water leaves the tubule by osmosis. Solutes, including NaCl, become more concentrated,

increasing the osmolarity of the filtrate. Diffusion of salt out of the tubule is maximal as the filtrate rounds the curve and enters the ascending limb, which is permeable to salt but not to water. NaCl diffusing from the ascending limb helps maintain a high osmolarity in the interstitial fluid of the renal medulla.

The loop of Henle and surrounding capillaries act as a type of countercurrent system to generate the steep osmotic gradient between the medulla and cortex. Recall that some endotherms have a countercurrent heat exchanger that reduces heat loss and that countercurrent gas exchange in fish gills maximizes oxygen absorption (see Figures 40.13 and 42.21). In those cases, the countercurrent mechanisms involve passive movement along either an oxygen concentration gradient or a heat gradient. In contrast, the countercurrent system of the loop of Henle involves active transport and thus an expenditure of energy. The active transport of NaCl from the filtrate in the upper part of the ascending limb of the loop maintains a high salt concentration in the interior of the kidney, enabling the kidney to form concentrated urine. Such countercurrent systems, which expend energy to create concentration gradients, are called **countercurrent multiplier systems**.

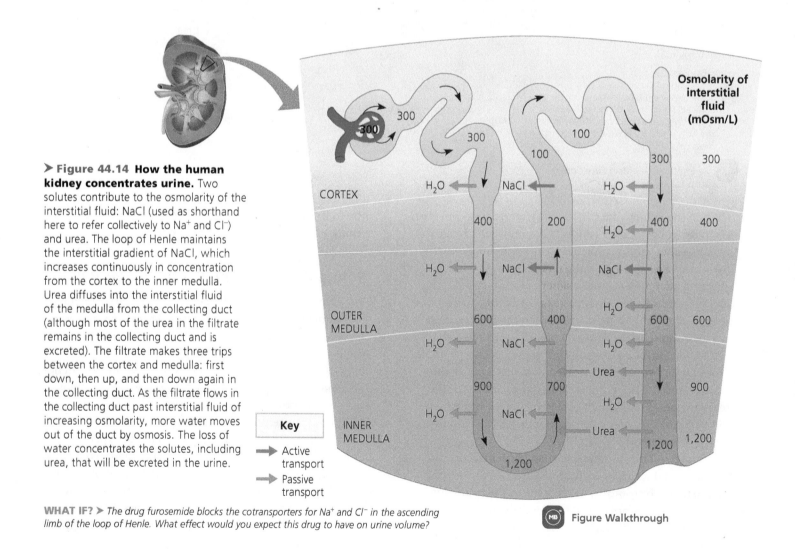

➤ **Figure 44.14 How the human kidney concentrates urine.** Two solutes contribute to the osmolarity of the interstitial fluid: NaCl (used as shorthand here to refer collectively to Na+ and Cl−) and urea. The loop of Henle maintains the interstitial gradient of NaCl, which increases continuously in concentration from the cortex to the inner medulla. Urea diffuses into the interstitial fluid of the medulla from the collecting duct (although most of the urea in the filtrate remains in the collecting duct and is excreted). The filtrate makes three trips between the cortex and medulla: first down, then up, and then down again in the collecting duct. As the filtrate flows in the collecting duct past interstitial fluid of increasing osmolarity, more water moves out of the duct by osmosis. The loss of water concentrates the solutes, including urea, that will be excreted in the urine.

**Key**

➡ Active transport

➡ Passive transport

**WHAT IF?** ➤ *The drug furosemide blocks the cotransporters for Na+ and Cl− in the ascending limb of the loop of Henle. What effect would you expect this drug to have on urine volume?*

(MB) Figure Walkthrough

What prevents the capillaries of the vasa recta from dissipating the gradient by carrying away the high concentration of NaCl in the medulla's interstitial fluid? As shown in Figure 44.12, the descending and ascending vessels of the vasa recta carry blood in opposite directions through the kidney's osmolarity gradient. As the descending vessel conveys blood toward the inner medulla, water is lost from the blood and NaCl is gained by diffusion. These net fluxes are reversed as blood flows back toward the cortex in the ascending vessel of the vasa recta, with water reentering the blood and salt diffusing out. Thus, the vasa recta can supply the kidney with nutrients and other important substances carried by the blood without interfering with the osmolarity gradient in the inner and outer medulla.

The countercurrent-like characteristics of the loop of Henle and the vasa recta help to generate the steep osmotic gradient between the medulla and cortex. However, diffusion will eventually eliminate any osmotic gradient within animal tissue unless energy is expended to maintain the gradient. In the kidney, this expenditure largely occurs in the thick segment of the ascending limb of the loop of Henle, where NaCl is actively transported out of the tubule. Even with the benefits of countercurrent exchange, this process—along with other renal active transport systems—consumes considerable ATP. Thus, for its size, the kidney has one of the highest metabolic rates of any organ.

As a result of active transport of NaCl out of the thick segment of the ascending limb, the filtrate is actually hypoosmotic to body fluids by the time it reaches the distal tubule. Next, the filtrate descends again toward the medulla, this time in the collecting duct, which is permeable to water but not to salt. Therefore, osmosis extracts water from the filtrate as it passes from cortex to medulla and encounters interstitial fluid of increasing osmolarity. This process concentrates salt, urea, and other solutes in the filtrate. Some urea passes out of the lower portion of the collecting duct and contributes to the high interstitial osmolarity of the inner medulla. (This urea is recycled by diffusion into the loop of Henle, but continual leakage from the collecting duct maintains a high interstitial urea concentration.) When the kidney concentrates urine maximally, the urine reaches 1,200 mOsm/L, the osmolarity of the interstitial fluid in the inner medulla. Although *isoosmotic* to the inner medulla's interstitial fluid, the urine is *hyperosmotic* to blood and interstitial fluid elsewhere in the body. This high osmolarity allows the solutes remaining in the urine to be excreted from the body with minimal water loss.

## Adaptations of the Vertebrate Kidney to Diverse Environments

**EVOLUTION** Vertebrates occupy habitats ranging from rain forests to deserts and from some of the saltiest bodies of water to the nearly pure waters of high mountain lakes. Comparing vertebrates across environments reveals adaptive variations in nephron structure and function. In the case of mammals, for example, the presence of juxtamedullary nephrons is a key adaptation that enables these terrestrial animals to shed salts and nitrogenous wastes without squandering water. Differences among species in the length of the loop of Henle in the juxtamedullary nephrons and in the relative numbers of juxtamedullary and cortical nephrons help to fine-tune osmoregulation to particular habitats.

### Mammals

Mammals that excrete the most hyperosmotic urine, such as Australian hopping mice, North American kangaroo rats, and other desert mammals, have many juxtamedullary nephrons with loops of Henle that extend deep into the medulla. Long loops maintain steep osmotic gradients in the kidney, resulting in urine becoming very concentrated as it passes from cortex to medulla in the collecting ducts.

In contrast, beavers, muskrats, and other aquatic mammals that spend much of their time in fresh water and rarely face problems of dehydration have mostly cortical nephrons, resulting in a much lower ability to concentrate urine. Terrestrial mammals living in moist conditions have loops of Henle of intermediate length and the capacity to produce urine intermediate in concentration to that produced by freshwater and desert mammals.

## Case Study: *Kidney Function in the Vampire Bat*

The South American vampire bat shown in **Figure 44.15** illustrates the versatility of the mammalian kidney. This species feeds at night on the blood of large birds and mammals. The bat uses its sharp teeth to make a small incision in the prey's skin and then laps up blood from the wound (the prey is typically not seriously harmed). Anticoagulants in the bat's saliva prevent the blood from clotting.

A vampire bat may search for hours and fly long distances to locate a suitable victim. When it does find prey, it benefits from consuming as much blood as possible. Often drinking more than half its body mass, the bat is at risk of becoming too

> **Figure 44.15** A vampire bat (*Desmodus rotundus*), a mammal with unique excretory challenges.

heavy to fly. As the bat feeds, however, its kidneys excrete large volumes of dilute urine, up to 24% of body mass per hour. Having lost enough weight to take off, the bat can fly back to its roost in a cave or hollow tree, where it spends the day.

In the roost, the vampire bat faces a different regulatory problem. Most of the nutrition it derives from blood comes in the form of protein. Digesting proteins generates large quantities of urea, but roosting bats lack access to the drinking water necessary to dilute it. Instead, their kidneys shift to producing small quantities of highly concentrated urine (up to 4,600 mOsm/L), an adjustment that disposes of the urea load while conserving as much water as possible. The vampire bat's ability to alternate rapidly between producing large amounts of dilute urine and small amounts of very hyperosmotic urine is an essential part of its adaptation to an unusual food source.

## Birds and Other Reptiles

Most birds, including the albatross (see Figure 44.1) and the ostrich (**Figure 44.16**), live in environments that are dehydrating. Like mammals but no other species, birds have kidneys with juxtamedullary nephrons. However, the nephrons of birds have loops of Henle that extend less far into the medulla than those of mammals. Thus, bird kidneys cannot concentrate urine to the high osmolarities achieved by mammalian kidneys. Although birds can produce hyperosmotic urine, their main water conservation adaptation is having uric acid as the nitrogenous waste molecule.

The kidneys of other reptiles have only cortical nephrons and produce urine that is isoosmotic or hypoosmotic to body fluids. However, the epithelium of the cloaca from which

▼ **Figure 44.16 An ostrich (*Struthio camelus*), an animal well adapted to its dry environment.**

urine and feces leave the body conserves fluid by reabsorbing water from these wastes. Like birds, most other reptiles excrete their nitrogenous wastes as uric acid.

## Freshwater Fishes and Amphibians

Hyperosmotic to their surroundings, freshwater fishes produce large volumes of very dilute urine. Their kidneys, which are packed with cortical nephrons, produce filtrate at a high rate. Salt conservation relies on the reabsorption of ions from the filtrate in the distal tubules.

Amphibian kidneys function much like those of freshwater fishes. When frogs are in fresh water, their kidneys excrete dilute urine while their skin accumulates certain salts from the water by active transport. On land, where dehydration is the most pressing problem of osmoregulation, frogs conserve body fluid by reabsorbing water across the epithelium of the urinary bladder.

## Marine Bony Fishes

Compared with freshwater fishes, marine fishes have fewer and smaller nephrons, and their nephrons lack a distal tubule. In addition, their kidneys have small glomeruli or lack glomeruli entirely. In keeping with these features, filtration rates are low and very little urine is excreted.

The main function of kidneys in marine bony fishes is to get rid of divalent ions (those with a charge of 2+ or 2−) such as calcium ($Ca^{2+}$), magnesium ($Mg^{2+}$), and sulfate ($SO_4^{2-}$). Marine fishes take in divalent ions by incessantly drinking seawater. They rid themselves of these ions by secreting them into the proximal tubules of the nephrons and excreting them in urine. Osmoregulation in marine bony fishes also relies on specialized *chloride cells* in the gills. By establishing ion gradients that enable secretion of salt (NaCl) into seawater, the chloride cells maintain proper levels of monovalent ions (charge of 1+ or 1−) such as $Na^+$ and $Cl^-$.

The generation of ion gradients and the movement of ions across membranes are central to salt and water balance in marine bony fishes. These events, however, are by no means unique to these organisms nor to homeostasis. As illustrated by the examples in **Figure 44.17**, osmoregulation by chloride cells is but one of many diverse physiological processes that are driven by the movement of ions across a membrane.

### CONCEPT CHECK 44.4

1. What do the number and length of nephrons in a fish's kidney indicate about the fish's habitat? How do they correlate with urine production?

2. Many medications make the epithelium of the collecting duct less permeable to water. How would taking such a medication affect kidney output?

3. **WHAT IF?** ➤ If blood pressure in the afferent arteriole leading to a glomerulus decreased, how would the rate of blood filtration within Bowman's capsule be affected? Explain.

*For suggested answers, see Appendix A.*

**MAKE CONNECTIONS**

# Ion Movement and Gradients

The transport of ions across the plasma membrane of a cell is a fundamental activity of all animals, and indeed of all living things. By generating ion gradients, ion transport provides the potential energy that powers processes ranging from an organism's regulation of salts and gases in internal fluids to its perception of and locomotion through its environment.

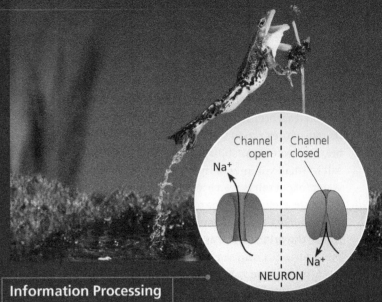

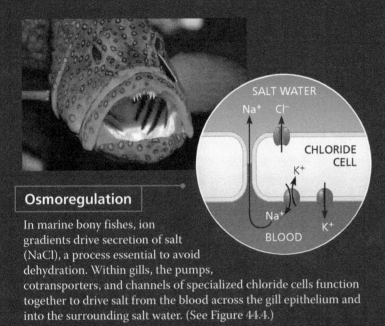

## Osmoregulation

In marine bony fishes, ion gradients drive secretion of salt (NaCl), a process essential to avoid dehydration. Within gills, the pumps, cotransporters, and channels of specialized chloride cells function together to drive salt from the blood across the gill epithelium and into the surrounding salt water. (See Figure 44.4.)

## Information Processing

In neurons, transmission of information as nerve impulses is made possible by the opening and closing of channels selective for sodium or other ions. These signals enable nervous systems to receive and process input and to direct appropriate output, such as this leap of a frog capturing prey. (See Concept 48.3 and Concept 50.5.)

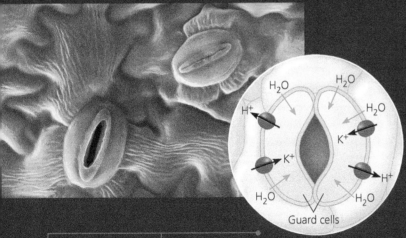

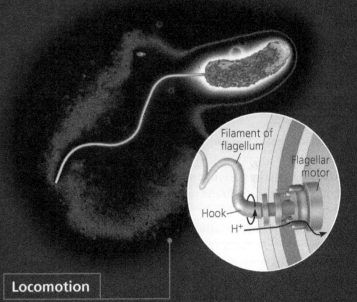

## Locomotion

A gradient of $H^+$ ions powers the bacterial flagellum. An electron transport chain generates this gradient, establishing a higher concentration of $H^+$ outside the bacterial cell. Protons reentering the cell provide a force that causes the flagellar motor to rotate. The rotating motor turns the curved hook, causing the attached filament to propel the cell. (See Concept 9.4 and Figure 27.7)

**MAKE CONNECTIONS ➤** *Explain why the set of forces driving ion movement across the plasma membrane of a cell is described as an electrochemical (electrical and chemical) gradient (see Concept 7.4).*

 **BioFlix® Animation: Membrane Transport**

## Gas Exchange

Ion gradients provide the basis for the opening of plant stomata by surrounding guard cells. Active transport of $H^+$ out of a guard cell generates a voltage (membrane potential) that drives inward movement of $K^+$ ions. This uptake of $K^+$ by guard cells triggers an osmotic influx of water that changes cell shape, bowing the guard cells outward and thereby opening the stoma. (See Concept 36.4.)

# CONCEPT 44.5

## Hormonal circuits link kidney function, water balance, and blood pressure

In mammals, both the volume and osmolarity of urine are adjusted according to an animal's water and salt balance and its rate of urea production. In situations of high salt intake and low water availability, a mammal can excrete urea and salt in small volumes of hyperosmotic urine with minimal water loss. If salt is scarce and fluid intake is high, the kidney can instead eliminate the excess water with little salt loss by producing large volumes of hypoosmotic urine. At such times, the urine can be as dilute as 70 mOsm/L, less than one-fourth the osmolarity of human blood.

How are urine volume and osmolarity regulated so effectively? As we'll explore in this final portion of the chapter, two major control circuits that respond to different stimuli together restore and maintain normal water and salt balance.

## Homeostatic Regulation of the Kidney

A combination of nervous and hormonal controls manages the osmoregulatory function of the mammalian kidney. Through their effects on the amount and osmolarity of urine, these controls contribute to homeostasis for both blood pressure and blood volume.

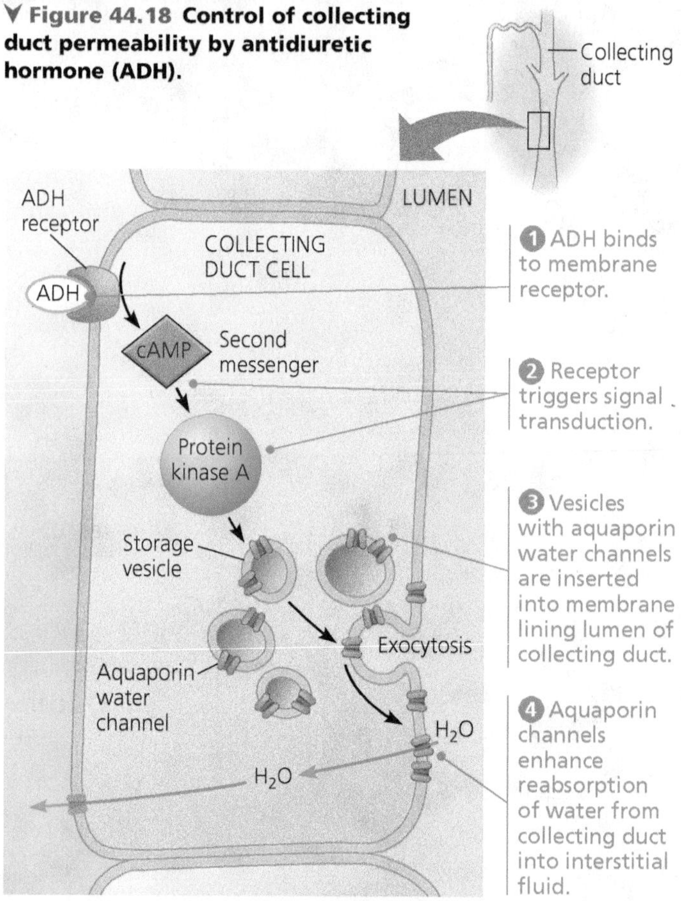

### Antidiuretic Hormone

One key hormone in of the kidney is **antidiuretic hormone (ADH)**, also called *vasopressin*. ADH molecules released from the posterior pituitary bind to and activate membrane receptors on the surface of collecting duct cells. The activated receptors initiate a signal transduction cascade that directs insertion of aquaporin proteins into the membrane lining the collecting duct (**Figure 44.18**). More aquaporin channels result in more water recapture, reducing urine volume. (A high level of urine production is called diuresis; ADH is therefore called *anti*diuretic hormone.)

To understand the regulatory circuitry based on ADH, let's consider first what occurs when blood osmolarity rises, such as after eating salty food or losing water through sweating (**Figure 44.19**). When osmolarity rises above the normal range (285–295 mOsm/L), osmoreceptor cells

▽ **Figure 44.18 Control of collecting duct permeability by antidiuretic hormone (ADH).**

Collecting duct

ADH receptor

LUMEN

COLLECTING DUCT CELL

ADH

❶ ADH binds to membrane receptor.

cAMP — Second messenger

❷ Receptor triggers signal transduction.

Protein kinase A

Storage vesicle

❸ Vesicles with aquaporin water channels are inserted into membrane lining lumen of collecting duct.

Exocytosis

Aquaporin water channel

$H_2O$

❹ Aquaporin channels enhance reabsorption of water from collecting duct into interstitial fluid.

$H_2O$

▽ **Figure 44.19 Regulation of fluid retention in the kidney.** Osmoreceptors in the hypothalamus monitor blood osmolarity via its effect on the net diffusion of water into or out of the receptor cells. When blood osmolarity increases, signals from the osmoreceptors trigger a release of ADH from the posterior pituitary and generate thirst. Water reabsorption in the collecting duct and water intake restore normal blood osmolarity, inhibiting further ADH secretion.

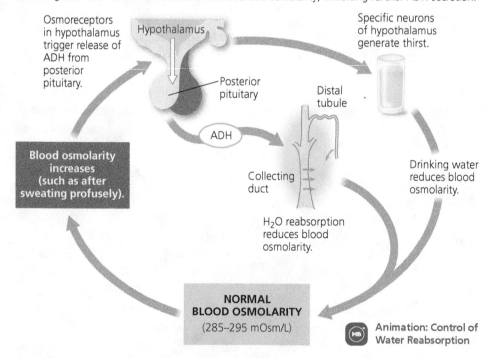

Osmoreceptors in hypothalamus trigger release of ADH from posterior pituitary.

Hypothalamus

Specific neurons of hypothalamus generate thirst.

Posterior pituitary

ADH

Distal tubule

Blood osmolarity increases (such as after sweating profusely).

Collecting duct

Drinking water reduces blood osmolarity.

$H_2O$ reabsorption reduces blood osmolarity.

**NORMAL BLOOD OSMOLARITY** (285–295 mOsm/L)

Animation: Control of Water Reabsorption

in the hypothalamus trigger increased release of ADH from the posterior pituitary. The resulting increase in water reabsorption in the collecting duct concentrates urine, reduces urine volume, and lowers blood osmolarity back toward the set point. As the osmolarity of the blood falls, a negative-feedback mechanism reduces the activity of osmoreceptor cells in the hypothalamus, and ADH secretion is reduced.

What happens if, instead of ingesting salt or sweating profusely, you drink a large amount of water? Blood osmolarity falls below the set point, causing a drop in ADH secretion to a very low level. The resulting decrease in permeability of the collecting ducts reduces water reabsorption, resulting in discharge of large volumes of dilute urine.

Contrary to common belief, caffeinated drinks increase urine production to no greater degree than water of comparable volume: Numerous studies of coffee and tea drinkers have found no diuretic effect for caffeine.

Blood osmolarity, ADH release, and water reabsorption in the kidney are normally linked in a feedback circuit that contributes to homeostasis. Anything that disrupts this circuit can interfere with water balance. For example, alcohol inhibits ADH release, leading to excessive urinary water loss and dehydration (which may cause some of the symptoms of a hangover).

Mutations that prevent ADH production or that inactivate the ADH receptor gene disrupt homeostasis by blocking the insertion of additional aquaporin channels in the collecting duct membrane. The resulting disorder can cause severe dehydration and solute imbalance due to production of copious dilute urine. These symptoms give the disorder its name: *diabetes insipidus* (from the Greek for "to pass through" and "having no flavor"). Could mutations in an aquaporin gene have a similar effect? **Figure 44.20** describes an experimental approach that addressed this question.

## The Renin-Angiotensin-Aldosterone System

The release of ADH is a response to an increase in blood osmolarity, as when the body is dehydrated from excessive water loss or inadequate water intake. However, an excessive loss of both salt and body fluids—caused, for example, by a major wound or severe diarrhea—will reduce blood volume *without* increasing osmolarity. Given that this will not affect ADH release, how does the body respond? It turns out that an endocrine circuit called the ***renin-angiotensin-aldosterone system (RAAS)*** also regulates kidney function. The RAAS responds to the drop in blood volume and pressure by increasing water and Na$^+$ reabsorption.

The RAAS involves the **juxtaglomerular apparatus (JGA)**, a specialized tissue consisting of cells of and around the afferent arteriole, which supplies blood to the glomerulus. When blood pressure or volume drops in the afferent arteriole (for instance, as a result of dehydration), the JGA releases the

**Inquiry** Can aquaporin mutations cause diabetes?

**Experiment** Researchers studied a diabetes insipidus patient with a normal ADH receptor gene but two mutant alleles (A and B) of the aquaporin-2 gene. The resulting changes are shown below in an alignment of protein sequences that includes other species.

| Source of Aquaporin-2 Gene Sequence | Amino Acids 183–191* in Encoded Protein | Amino Acids 212–220* in Encoded Protein |
|---|---|---|
| Frog (*Xenopus laevis*) | MNPARSFAP | GIFASLIYN |
| Lizard (*Anolis carolinensis*) | MNPARSFGP | AVVASLLYN |
| Chicken (*Gallus gallus*) | MNPARSFAP | AAAASIIYN |
| Human (*Homo sapiens*) | MNPARSLAP | AILGSLLYN |
| Conserved residues | MNPARSxxP | xxxxSxxYN |
| Patient's gene: allele A | MNPACSLAP | AILGSLLYN |
| Patient's gene: allele B | MNPARSLAP | AILGPLLYN |

*The numbering is based on the human aquaporin-2 protein sequence.

Each mutation changed the protein sequence at a highly conserved position. To test the hypothesis that the changes affect function, researchers used frog oocytes, cells that will express foreign messenger RNA and can be readily collected from adult female frogs.

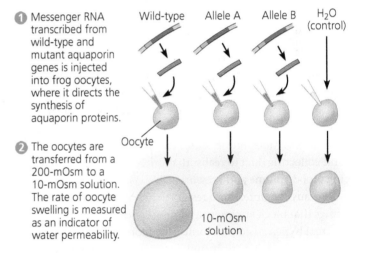

1 Messenger RNA transcribed from wild-type and mutant aquaporin genes is injected into frog oocytes, where it directs the synthesis of aquaporin proteins.

2 The oocytes are transferred from a 200-mOsm to a 10-mOsm solution. The rate of oocyte swelling is measured as an indicator of water permeability.

Wild-type   Allele A   Allele B   H$_2$O (control)

Oocyte

10-mOsm solution

**Results**

| Source of Injected mRNA | Rate of Swelling (μm/sec) |
|---|---|
| Human wild type | 196 |
| Patient's allele A | 17 |
| Patient's allele B | 18 |
| None (H$_2$O control) | 20 |

**Conclusion** Because each mutation renders aquaporin inactive as a water channel, researchers concluded that these mutations cause the disorder common to the patients.

**Data from** P. M. Deen et al., Requirement of human renal water channel aquaporin-2 for vasopressin-dependent concentration of urine, *Science* 264:92–95 (1994).

**WHAT IF?** ➤ *If you measured ADH levels in patients with ADH receptor mutations and in patients with aquaporin mutations, what would you expect to find, compared with wild-type subjects?*

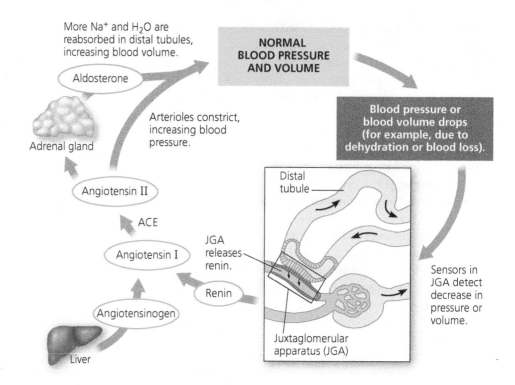

> **Figure 44.21 Regulation of blood volume and blood pressure by the renin-angiotensin-aldosterone system (RAAS).**

**VISUAL SKILLS** ➤ *Label each arrow that represents the secretion of a hormone.*

More Na⁺ and H₂O are reabsorbed in distal tubules, increasing blood volume.

Aldosterone

Adrenal gland

Arterioles constrict, increasing blood pressure.

Angiotensin II

ACE

Angiotensin I

Angiotensinogen

Liver

Renin

NORMAL BLOOD PRESSURE AND VOLUME

Blood pressure or blood volume drops (for example, due to dehydration or blood loss).

Distal tubule

JGA releases renin.

Sensors in JGA detect decrease in pressure or volume.

Juxtaglomerular apparatus (JGA)

enzyme renin. Renin initiates a sequence of steps that cleave a plasma protein called angiotensinogen, ultimately yielding a peptide called *angiotensin II* (**Figure 44.21**).

Functioning as a hormone, angiotensin II triggers vasoconstriction, increasing blood pressure and decreasing blood flow to capillaries in the kidney (and elsewhere). Angiotensin II also stimulates the adrenal glands to release a hormone called *aldosterone*. Aldosterone causes the nephrons' distal tubules and collecting duct to reabsorb more Na⁺ and water, increasing blood volume and pressure.

Because angiotensin II results in increased blood pressure, drugs that block angiotensin II production are widely used to treat hypertension (chronic high blood pressure). Many of these drugs are specific inhibitors of angiotensin converting enzyme (ACE), which catalyzes one of the steps in the production of angiotensin II.

The RAAS operates as a feedback circuit. A drop in blood pressure and blood volume triggers renin release. The resulting production of angiotensin II and release of aldosterone cause a rise in blood pressure and volume, reducing the release of renin from the JGA.

### Coordinated Regulation of Salt and Water Balance

Both ADH and RAAS increase water reabsorption in the kidney. However, whereas ADH alone would lower blood Na⁺ concentration via water reabsorption in the kidney, the RAAS helps maintain body fluid osmolarity at the set point by stimulating Na⁺ reabsorption.

Another hormone, **atrial natriuretic peptide (ANP)**, opposes the RAAS. The walls of the atria of the heart release ANP in response to an increase in blood volume and pressure. ANP inhibits the release of renin from the JGA, inhibits NaCl reabsorption by the collecting ducts, and reduces aldosterone release from the adrenal glands. These actions lower blood volume and pressure. Thus, ADH, the RAAS, and ANP provide an elaborate system of checks and balances that regulate the kidney's ability to control blood osmolarity, salt concentration, volume, and pressure.

Thirst plays an essential role in the control of water and salt balance. Recently, researchers have identified neurons in the hypothalamus dedicated to regulating thirst. Stimulating one set of neurons in mice causes intense drinking behavior, even if the animal is fully hydrated. Stimulating a second set causes an immediate halt in water consumption, even in dehydrated animals. Follow-up studies are focused on identifying the cellular and molecular pathways linking these neurons to the behavioral responses.

### CONCEPT CHECK 44.5

1. How does alcohol affect regulation of water balance in the body?

2. Why could it be dangerous to drink a very large amount of water in a short period of time?

3. **WHAT IF?** ➤ Conn's syndrome is a condition caused by tumors of the adrenal cortex that secrete high amounts of aldosterone in an unregulated manner. What would you expect to be the major symptom of this disorder?

*For suggested answers, see Appendix A.*

# 44 Chapter Review

Go to **MasteringBiology**™ for Videos, Animations, Vocab Self-Quiz, Practice Tests, and more in the Study Area.

## SUMMARY OF KEY CONCEPTS

### CONCEPT 44.1

**Osmoregulation balances the uptake and loss of water and solutes** (pp. 976–980)

VOCAB SELF-QUIZ
goo.gl/6u55ks

| Animal | Inflow/Outflow | Urine |
|---|---|---|
| **Freshwater fish.** Lives in water less concentrated than body fluids; fish tends to gain water, lose salt | Does not drink water<br>Salt in (active transport by gills)   H₂O in<br>Salt out   H₂O out | ▸ Large volume of urine<br>▸ Urine is less concentrated than body fluids |
| **Marine bony fish.** Lives in water more concentrated than body fluids; fish tends to lose water, gain salt | Drinks water<br>Salt in   H₂O out<br>Salt out (active transport by gills) | ▸ Small volume of urine<br>▸ Urine is slightly less concentrated than body fluids |
| **Terrestrial vertebrate.** Terrestrial environment; tends to lose body water to air | Drinks water<br>Salt in (by mouth)<br>H₂O and salt out | ▸ Moderate volume of urine<br>▸ Urine is more concentrated than body fluids |

- Cells balance water gain and loss through **osmoregulation**, a process based on the controlled movement of solutes between internal fluids and the external environment and on the movement of water, which follows by osmosis.
- **Osmoconformers** are isoosmotic with their marine environment and do not regulate their **osmolarity**. In contrast, **osmoregulators** control water uptake and loss in a hypoosmotic or hyperosmotic environment, respectively. Water-conserving excretory organs help terrestrial animals avoid desiccation, which can be life-threatening. Animals that live in temporary waters may enter a dormant state called **anhydrobiosis** when their habitats dry up.
- **Transport epithelia** contain specialized epithelial cells that control the solute movements required for waste disposal and osmoregulation.

? *Under what environmental conditions does water move into a cell by osmosis?*

### CONCEPT 44.2

**An animal's nitrogenous wastes reflect its phylogeny and habitat** (pp. 980–981)

- Protein and nucleic acid metabolism generates **ammonia**. Most aquatic animals excrete ammonia. Mammals and most adult amphibians convert ammonia to the less toxic **urea**, which is excreted with a minimal loss of water. Insects and many reptiles, including birds, convert ammonia to **uric acid**, a mostly insoluble waste excreted in a paste-like urine.
- The kind of nitrogenous waste excreted depends on an animal's habitat, whereas the amount excreted is coupled to the animal's energy budget and dietary protein intake.

**DRAW IT** ➤ *Construct a table summarizing the three major types of nitrogenous wastes and their relative toxicity, energy cost to produce, and associated water loss during excretion.*

### CONCEPT 44.3

**Diverse excretory systems are variations on a tubular theme** (pp. 982–985)

- Most excretory systems carry out **filtration, reabsorption, secretion**, and **excretion**. Invertebrate excretory systems include the **protonephridia** of flatworms, the **metanephridia** of earthworms, and the **Malpighian tubules** of insects. **Kidneys** function in both excretion and osmoregulation in vertebrates.
- Excretory tubules (consisting of **nephrons** and **collecting ducts**) and blood vessels pack the mammalian kidney. Blood pressure forces fluid from blood in the **glomerulus** into the lumen of **Bowman's capsule**. Following reabsorption and secretion, filtrate flows into a collecting duct. The **ureter** conveys urine from the **renal pelvis** to the **urinary bladder**.

? *What is the function of the filtration step in excretory systems?*

### CONCEPT 44.4

**The nephron is organized for stepwise processing of blood filtrate** (pp. 985–991)

- Within the nephron, selective secretion and reabsorption in the **proximal tubule** alter filtrate volume and composition. The *descending limb* of the **loop of Henle** is permeable to water but not salt; water moves by osmosis into the interstitial fluid. The *ascending limb* is permeable to salt but not water; salt leaves by diffusion and by active transport. The **distal tubule** and collecting duct regulate K⁺ and NaCl levels in body fluids.
- In mammals, **a countercurrent multiplier system** involving the loop of Henle maintains the gradient of salt concentration in the kidney interior. Urea exiting the collecting duct contributes to the osmotic gradient of the kidney.
- Natural selection has shaped the form and function of nephrons in various vertebrates to the osmoregulatory challenges of the animals' habitats. For example, desert mammals, which excrete the most hyperosmotic urine, have loops of Henle that extend deep into the **renal medulla**, whereas mammals in moist habitats have shorter loops and excrete more dilute urine.

? *How do cortical and juxtamedullary nephrons differ with respect to reabsorbing nutrients and concentrating urine?*

## CONCEPT 44.5

### Hormonal circuits link kidney function, water balance, and blood pressure (pp. 992–994)

- The posterior pituitary gland releases antidiuretic hormone (ADH) when blood osmolarity rises above a set point, such as when water intake is inadequate. ADH increases the permeability to water of the collecting ducts by increasing the number of epithelial **aquaporin** channels.
- When blood pressure or blood volume in the afferent arteriole drops, the **juxtaglomerular apparatus** releases renin. Angiotensin II formed in response to renin constricts arterioles and triggers release of the hormone aldosterone, raising blood pressure and reducing the release of renin. This **renin-angiotensin-aldosterone system** has functions that overlap with those of ADH and are opposed by **atrial natriuretic peptide**.

 *Why can only some patients with diabetes insipidus be treated effectively with ADH?*

## TEST YOUR UNDERSTANDING

### Level 1: Knowledge/Comprehension

1. *Unlike* an earthworm's metanephridia, a mammalian nephron
   - (A) is intimately associated with a capillary network.
   - (B) functions in both osmoregulation and excretion.
   - (C) receives filtrate from blood instead of coelomic fluid.
   - (D) has a transport epithelium.

2. Which process in the nephron is *least* selective?
   - (A) filtration
   - (B) reabsorption
   - (C) active transport
   - (D) secretion

3. Which of the following animals generally has the lowest volume of urine production?
   - (A) vampire bat
   - (B) salmon in fresh water
   - (C) marine bony fish
   - (D) freshwater flatworm

### Level 2: Application/Analysis

4. The high osmolarity of the renal medulla is maintained by all of the following *except*
   - (A) active transport of salt from the upper region of the ascending limb.
   - (B) the spatial arrangement of juxtamedullary nephrons.
   - (C) diffusion of urea from the collecting duct.
   - (D) diffusion of salt from the descending limb of the loop of Henle.

5. In which of the following species should natural selection favor the highest proportion of juxtamedullary nephrons?
   - (A) a river otter
   - (B) a mouse species living in a temperate broadleaf forest
   - (C) a mouse species living in a desert
   - (D) a beaver

6. African lungfish, which are often found in small stagnant pools of fresh water, produce urea as a nitrogenous waste. What is the advantage of this adaptation?
   - (A) Urea takes less energy to synthesize than ammonia.
   - (B) Small stagnant pools do not provide enough water to dilute ammonia, which is toxic.
   - (C) Urea forms an insoluble precipitate.
   - (D) Urea makes lungfish tissue hypoosmotic to the pool.

### Level 3: Synthesis/Evaluation

7. **INTERPRET THE DATA** Use the data below to draw four pie charts for water gain and loss in a kangaroo rat and a human.

| | Kangaroo Rat | Human |
|---|---|---|
| **Water Gain (mL)** | | |
| Ingested in food | 0.2 | 750 |
| Ingested in liquid | 0 | 1,500 |
| Derived from metabolism | 1.8 | 250 |
| **Water Loss (mL)** | | |
| Urine | 0.45 | 1,500 |
| Feces | 0.09 | 100 |
| Evaporation | 1.46 | 900 |

Which routes of water gain and loss make up a much larger share of the total in a kangaroo rat than in a human?

8. **EVOLUTION CONNECTION** Merriam's kangaroo rats (*Dipodomys merriami*) live in North American habitats ranging from moist, cool woodlands to hot deserts. Based on the hypothesis that there are adaptive differences in water conservation between *D. merriami* populations, predict how the rates of evaporative water loss would differ for populations that live in moist versus dry environments. Propose a test of your prediction, using a humidity sensor to detect evaporative water loss by kangaroo rats.

9. **SCIENTIFIC INQUIRY** You are exploring kidney function in kangaroo rats. You measure urine volume and osmolarity, as well as the amount of chloride (Cl⁻) and urea in the urine. If the water source provided to the animals were switched from tap water to a 2% NaCl solution, indicate what change in urine osmolarity you would expect. How would you determine if this change was more likely due to a change in the excretion of Cl⁻ or urea?

10. **WRITE ABOUT A THEME: ORGANIZATION** In a short essay (100–150 words), compare how membrane structures in the loop of Henle and collecting duct of the mammalian kidney enable water to be recovered from filtrate in the process of osmoregulation.

11. **SYNTHESIZE YOUR KNOWLEDGE**

The marine iguana (*Amblyrhynchus cristatus*), which spends long periods under water feeding on seaweed, relies on both salt glands and kidneys for homeostasis of its internal fluids. Describe how these organs together meet the particular osmoregulatory challenges of this animal's environment.

*For selected answers, see Appendix A.*

 For additional practice questions, check out the **Dynamic Study Modules** in MasteringBiology. You can use them to study on your smartphone, tablet, or computer anytime, anywhere!

# Hormones and the Endocrine System

# 45

▲ Figure 45.1 **What makes male and female elephant seals look so different?**

## KEY CONCEPTS

**45.1** Hormones and other signaling molecules bind to target receptors, triggering specific response pathways

**45.2** Feedback regulation and coordination with the nervous system are common in hormone pathways

**45.3** Endocrine glands respond to diverse stimuli in regulating homeostasis, development, and behavior

▼ **Male elephant seals sparring**

## The Body's Long-Distance Regulators

Although we often distinguish animals of different species by their appearance, in many species the females and males look quite different from each other. Such is the case for elephant seals (*Mirounga angustirostris*), shown in **Figure 45.1**. The male is much larger than the female, and only he has the prominent proboscis for which the species is named. Males are also far more territorial and aggressive than females. A sex-determining gene on the Y chromosome makes a seal embryo male. But how does the presence of this gene lead to male size, shape, and behavior? The answer to this and many other questions about biological processes involves signaling molecules called **hormones** (from the Greek *horman*, to excite).

In animals, hormones are secreted into the extracellular fluid, circulate in the blood (or hemolymph), and communicate regulatory messages throughout the body. In the case of the elephant seal, increased secretion of particular hormones at puberty triggers sexual maturation as well as the accompanying changes that result in *sexual dimorphism*, the distinct appearance of adult females and males. Hormones influence much more than sex and reproduction, however. For example, when seals, humans, and other mammals are stressed, are dehydrated, or have low blood sugar levels, hormones coordinate the physiological responses that restore balance in our bodies.

When you see this blue icon, log in to **MasteringBiology** and go to the Study Area for digital resources.

 Get Ready for This Chapter

Each hormone binds to specific receptors in the body. Although a given hormone can reach all cells of the body, only some cells have receptors for that hormone. A hormone elicits a response—such as a change in metabolism—in specific *target cells*, those that have the matching receptor. Cells lacking a receptor for that hormone are unaffected.

Chemical signaling by hormones is the function of the **endocrine system**, one of the two basic systems for communication and regulation in the animal body. The other major communication and control system is the **nervous system**, a network of specialized cells—neurons—that transmit signals along dedicated pathways. These signals in turn regulate neurons, muscle cells, and endocrine cells. Because signaling by neurons can regulate the release of hormones, the nervous and endocrine systems often overlap in function.

In this chapter, we'll begin with an overview of the different types of chemical signaling in animals. We'll then explore how hormones regulate target cells, how hormone secretion is regulated, and how hormones help maintain homeostasis. We'll also consider the ways in which endocrine and nervous system activities are coordinated as well as examine how hormones regulate growth and development.

# CONCEPT 45.1

## Hormones and other signaling molecules bind to target receptors, triggering specific response pathways

To begin, we'll examine the diverse ways that animal cells use chemical signals to communicate.

## Intercellular Communication

Communication between animal cells via secreted signals is often classified by two criteria: the type of secreting cell and the route taken by the signal in reaching its target. **Figure 45.2** illustrates five forms of signaling distinguished in this manner.

### Endocrine Signaling

In endocrine signaling (see Figure 45.2a), hormones secreted into extracellular fluid by endocrine cells reach target cells via the bloodstream (or hemolymph). One function of endocrine signaling is to maintain homeostasis. Hormones regulate properties that include blood pressure and volume, energy metabolism and allocation, and solute concentrations in body fluids. Endocrine signaling also mediates responses to environmental stimuli, regulates growth and development, and, as discussed above, triggers physical and behavioral changes underlying sexual maturity and reproduction.

▼ **Figure 45.2 Intercellular communication by secreted molecules.** In each type of signaling, secreted molecules (●) bind to a specific receptor protein (♥) expressed by target cells. Some receptors are located inside cells, but for simplicity, here all are drawn on the cell surface.

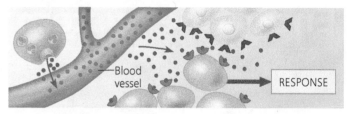

**(a)** In **endocrine signaling**, secreted molecules diffuse into the bloodstream and trigger responses in target cells anywhere in the body.

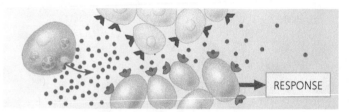

**(b)** In **paracrine signaling**, secreted molecules diffuse locally and trigger a response in neighboring cells.

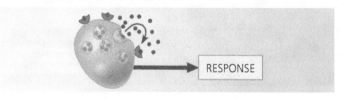

**(c)** In **autocrine signaling**, secreted molecules diffuse locally and trigger a response in the cells that secrete them.

**(d)** In **synaptic signaling**, neurotransmitters diffuse across synapses and trigger responses in cells of target tissues (neurons, muscles, or glands).

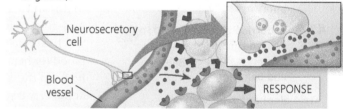

**(e)** In **neuroendocrine signaling**, neurohormones diffuse into the bloodstream and trigger responses in target cells anywhere in the body.

### Paracrine and Autocrine Signaling

Many types of cells produce and secrete **local regulators**, molecules that act over short distances, reach their target cells solely by diffusion, and act on their target cells within seconds or even milliseconds. Local regulators play roles in many physiological processes, including blood pressure regulation, nervous system function, and reproduction.

Depending on the target cell, signaling by local regulators can be either paracrine or autocrine. In **paracrine** signaling (from the Greek *para*, to one side of), target cells lie near the secreting cell (see Figure 45.2b). In **autocrine** signaling (from the Greek *auto*, self), the secreting cells themselves are the target cells (see Figure 45.2c).

One group of local regulators with diverse and widespread functions are the **prostaglandins**. In the immune system, for example, prostaglandins promote inflammation and the sensation of pain in response to injury. Drugs that block prostaglandin synthesis, such as aspirin and ibuprofen, prevent these activities, producing both anti-inflammatory and pain-relieving effects.

Prostaglandins also help regulate the aggregation of platelets, one step in the formation of blood clots. Because blood clots in vessels that supply the heart can block blood flow, causing a heart attack (see Concept 42.4), some physicians recommend that people at risk for a heart attack take aspirin on a regular basis.

### Synaptic and Neuroendocrine Signaling

Secreted molecules are essential for the function of the nervous system. Neurons communicate with target cells, such as other neurons and muscle cells, via specialized junctions called synapses. At most synapses, neurons secrete molecules called **neurotransmitters** that diffuse a very short distance (a fraction of a cell diameter) and bind to receptors on the target cells (see Figure 45.2d). Such *synaptic signaling* is central to sensation, memory, cognition, and movement (as we'll explore in Chapters 48–50).

In *neuroendocrine signaling*, neurons called neurosecretory cells secrete **neurohormones**, which diffuse from nerve cell endings into the bloodstream (see Figure 45.2e). One example of a neurohormone is antidiuretic hormone, which functions in kidney function and water balance as well as courtship behavior. Many neurohormones regulate endocrine signaling, as we'll discuss later in this chapter.

### Signaling by Pheromones

Not all secreted signaling molecules act within the body. Members of a particular animal species sometimes communicate with each other via **pheromones**, chemicals that are released into the external environment. For example, when a foraging ant discovers a new food source, it marks its path back to the nest with a pheromone. Ants also use pheromones for guidance when a colony migrates to a new location **(Figure 45.3)**.

Pheromones serve a wide range of functions that include defining territories, warning of predators, and attracting

▼ **Figure 45.3 Signaling by pheromones.** Using their lowered antennae, these Asian army ants (*Leptogenys distinguenda*) follow a pheromone-marked trail as they carry pupae and larvae to a new nest site.

potential mates. The polyphemus moth (*Antheraea polyphemus*) provides a noteworthy example: The sex pheromone released into the air by a female enables her to attract a male of the species from up to 4.5 km away. You'll read more about pheromone function when we take up the topic of animal behavior in Chapter 51.

## Chemical Classes of Local Regulators and Hormones

What kinds of molecules convey signals in animal bodies? Let's take a look.

### Classes of Local Regulators

Prostaglandins are modified fatty acids. Many other local regulators are polypeptides, including cytokines, which enable immune cell communication (see Figure 43.16 and Figure 43.17), and growth factors, which promote cell growth, division, and development. Some local regulators are gases.

**Nitric oxide (NO)**, a gas, functions in the body as both a local regulator and a neurotransmitter. When the level of oxygen in the blood falls, endothelial cells in blood vessel walls synthesize and release NO. After diffusing into the surrounding smooth muscle cells, NO activates an enzyme that relaxes the cells. The result is vasodilation, which increases blood flow to tissues.

In human males, NO's ability to promote vasodilation enables sexual function by increasing blood flow into the penis, producing an erection. The drug Viagra (sildenafil citrate), a treatment for male erectile dysfunction, sustains an erection by prolonging activity of the NO response pathway.

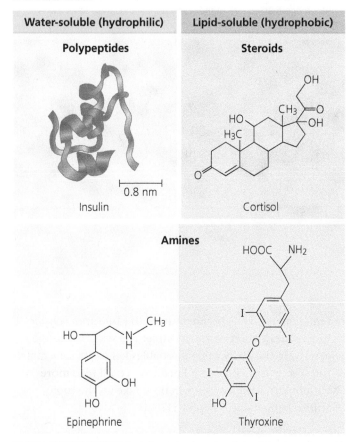

| Water-soluble (hydrophilic) | Lipid-soluble (hydrophobic) |
| --- | --- |
| **Polypeptides** | **Steroids** |

Insulin

0.8 nm

Cortisol

**Amines**

Epinephrine

Thyroxine

**MAKE CONNECTIONS** ➤ *Cells synthesize epinephrine from the amino acid tyrosine (see Figure 5.14). On the structure of epinephrine shown above, draw an arrow pointing to the position corresponding to the α carbon of tyrosine.*

## Classes of Hormones

Hormones fall into three major chemical classes: polypeptides, steroids, and amines **(Figure 45.4)**. The hormone insulin, for example, is a polypeptide that contains two chains in its active form. Steroid hormones, such as cortisol, are lipids that contain four fused carbon rings; all are derived from the steroid cholesterol (see Figure 5.12). Epinephrine and thyroxine are amine hormones, each synthesized from a single amino acid, either tyrosine or tryptophan.

As Figure 45.4 indicates, hormones vary in their solubility in aqueous and lipid-rich environments. Polypeptides and most amine hormones are water-soluble, whereas steroid hormones and other largely nonpolar (hydrophobic) hormones, such as thyroxine, are lipid-soluble.

## Cellular Hormone Response Pathways

Water-soluble and lipid-soluble hormones differ in their response pathways. One key difference is the location of the receptor proteins in target cells. Water-soluble hormones are secreted by exocytosis and travel freely in the bloodstream. Being insoluble in lipids, they cannot diffuse through the plasma membranes of target cells. Instead, these hormones

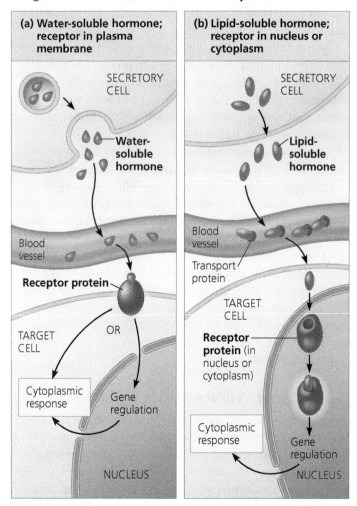

**(a) Water-soluble hormone; receptor in plasma membrane**

SECRETORY CELL

Water-soluble hormone

Blood vessel

Receptor protein

TARGET CELL

OR

Cytoplasmic response

Gene regulation

NUCLEUS

**(b) Lipid-soluble hormone; receptor in nucleus or cytoplasm**

SECRETORY CELL

Lipid-soluble hormone

Blood vessel

Transport protein

TARGET CELL

Receptor protein (in nucleus or cytoplasm)

Cytoplasmic response

Gene regulation

NUCLEUS

**WHAT IF?** ➤ *Suppose you are studying a cell's response to a particular hormone. You observe that the cell produces the same response to the hormone whether or not the cell is treated with a chemical that blocks transcription. What can you surmise about the hormone and its receptor?*

 Animation: Binding of Hormones

bind to cell-surface receptors, inducing changes in cytoplasmic molecules and sometimes altering gene transcription **(Figure 45.5a)**. In contrast, lipid-soluble hormones exit endocrine cells by diffusing out across the membranes. They then bind to transport proteins, which keep them soluble in blood. After circulating in the blood, they diffuse into target cells and typically bind to receptors in the cytoplasm or nucleus **(Figure 45.5b)**. The hormone-bound receptor then triggers changes in gene transcription.

To explore further the distinct cellular responses to water-soluble and lipid-soluble hormones, we'll examine the two response pathways in turn.

### Response Pathway for Water-Soluble Hormones

The binding of a water-soluble hormone to a cell-surface receptor protein triggers a cellular response. The response may be the activation of an enzyme, a change in the uptake or secretion of specific molecules, or a rearrangement of the cytoskeleton. In some cases, cell-surface receptors cause proteins in the cytoplasm to move into the nucleus and alter the transcription of specific genes.

The chain of events that converts the extracellular chemical signal to a specific intracellular response is called **signal transduction**. As an example, we'll consider one response to short-term stress. When you are in a stressful situation, perhaps running to catch a bus, the adrenal glands that lie atop your kidneys secrete the water-soluble hormone **epinephrine**, also known as *adrenaline*. Epinephrine regulates many organs, including the liver, where it binds to a G protein-coupled receptor in the plasma membrane of target cells. A shown in **Figure 45.6**, this interaction triggers a cascade of events involving synthesis of cyclic AMP (cAMP) as a short-lived *second messenger*. Activation of protein kinase A by cAMP leads to activation of an enzyme required for glycogen breakdown and inactivation of an enzyme needed for glycogen synthesis. The net result is that the liver releases glucose into the bloodstream, very quickly providing the body with extra fuel.

### Response Pathway for Lipid-Soluble Hormones

Intracellular receptors for lipid-soluble hormones perform the entire task of transducing a signal within a target cell. The hormone activates the receptor, which then directly triggers the cell's response. In most cases, the response to a lipid-soluble hormone is a change in gene expression.

Most steroid hormone receptors are located in the cytosol prior to binding to a hormone. Binding of a steroid hormone to its cytosolic receptor forms a complex that moves into the nucleus (see Figure 18.9). There, the receptor portion of the complex alters transcription of particular genes by interacting with a specific DNA-binding protein or response element in the DNA. (In some cell types, steroid hormones trigger additional responses by interacting with other kinds of receptor proteins located at the cell surface).

Among the best-characterized steroid hormone receptors are those that bind to estrogens, steroid hormones necessary for female reproductive function in vertebrates. For example, in female birds and frogs, estradiol, a form of estrogen, binds to a cytoplasmic receptor in liver cells. Binding of estradiol to this receptor activates transcription of the vitellogenin gene **(Figure 45.7)**. Following translation of the messenger RNA, vitellogenin protein is secreted and transported in the blood to the reproductive system, where it is used to produce egg yolk.

Thyroxine, vitamin D, and other lipid-soluble hormones that are not steroids typically have receptors in the nucleus. These receptors bind to hormone molecules that diffuse from the bloodstream across both the plasma membrane and nuclear envelope. Once bound to a hormone, the receptor binds to specific sites in the cell's DNA and stimulates the transcription of specific genes.

▼ Figure 45.6 **Signal transduction triggered by a cell-surface hormone receptor.**

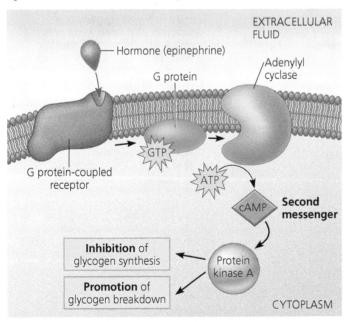

**VISUAL SKILLS** ➤ *A series of arrows represents the steps linking epinephrine to protein kinase A. How does the event represented by the arrow between ATP and cAMP differ from the other four?*

(MB) Animation: Water-Soluble Hormone Pathway

▼ Figure 45.7 **Direct regulation of gene expression by a steroid hormone receptor.**

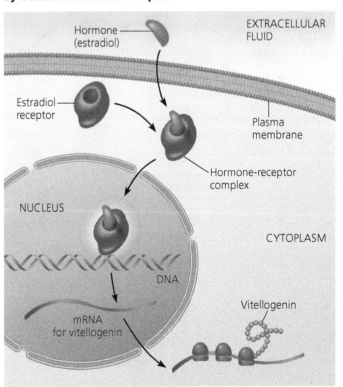

(MB) Animation: Steroid Hormone Pathway

## Multiple Responses to a Single Hormone

Although hormones bind to specific receptors, a particular hormone can vary in its effects. A hormone can elicit distinct responses in particular target cells if those cells differ in receptor type or in the molecules that produce the response. In this way a single hormone can trigger a range of activities that together bring about a coordinated response to a stimulus. For example, the multiple effects of epinephrine form the basis for the "fight-or-flight" response, a rapid response to stress that you'll read about in Concept 45.3.

## Endocrine Tissues and Organs

Some endocrine cells are found in organs that are part of other organ systems. For example, the stomach contains isolated endocrine cells that help regulate digestive processes by secreting the hormone gastrin. More often, endocrine cells are grouped in ductless organs called **endocrine glands**, such as the thyroid and parathyroid glands and the gonads, either testes in males or ovaries in females (**Figure 45.8**).

Note that endocrine glands secrete hormones directly into the surrounding fluid. In contrast, *exocrine glands* have ducts that carry secreted substances, such as sweat or saliva, onto body surfaces or into body cavities. This distinction is reflected in the glands' names: The Greek *endo* (within) and *exo* (out of) refer to secretion into or out of body fluids, while *crine* (from the Greek word meaning "separate") refers to movement away from the secreting cell. In the case of the pancreas, endocrine and exocrine tissues are found in the same gland: Ductless tissues secrete hormones, whereas tissues with ducts secrete enzymes and bicarbonate.

### CONCEPT CHECK 45.1

1. How do response mechanisms in target cells differ for water-soluble and lipid-soluble hormones?
2. What type of gland would you expect to secrete pheromones? Explain.
3. **WHAT IF?** ➤ Predict what would happen if you injected a water-soluble hormone into the cytosol of a target cell.

*For suggested answers, see Appendix A.*

▼ **Figure 45.8 Human endocrine glands and their hormones.** This figure highlights the location and primary functions of the major human endocrine glands. Endocrine tissues and cells are also located in the thymus, heart, liver, stomach, kidneys, and small intestine.

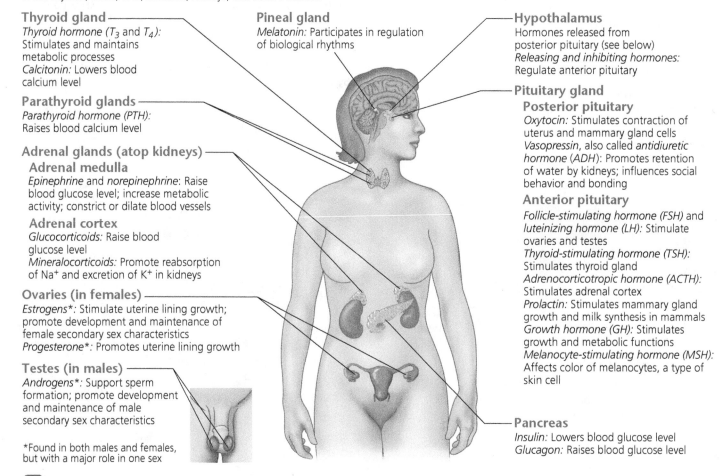

**Thyroid gland**
*Thyroid hormone ($T_3$ and $T_4$):* Stimulates and maintains metabolic processes
*Calcitonin:* Lowers blood calcium level

**Parathyroid glands**
*Parathyroid hormone (PTH):* Raises blood calcium level

**Adrenal glands (atop kidneys)**
**Adrenal medulla**
*Epinephrine* and *norepinephrine*: Raise blood glucose level; increase metabolic activity; constrict or dilate blood vessels
**Adrenal cortex**
*Glucocorticoids:* Raise blood glucose level
*Mineralocorticoids:* Promote reabsorption of $Na^+$ and excretion of $K^+$ in kidneys

**Ovaries (in females)**
*Estrogens*:* Stimulate uterine lining growth; promote development and maintenance of female secondary sex characteristics
*Progesterone*:* Promotes uterine lining growth

**Testes (in males)**
*Androgens*:* Support sperm formation; promote development and maintenance of male secondary sex characteristics

*Found in both males and females, but with a major role in one sex

**Pineal gland**
*Melatonin:* Participates in regulation of biological rhythms

**Hypothalamus**
Hormones released from posterior pituitary (see below)
*Releasing and inhibiting hormones:* Regulate anterior pituitary

**Pituitary gland**
**Posterior pituitary**
*Oxytocin:* Stimulates contraction of uterus and mammary gland cells
*Vasopressin*, also called *antidiuretic hormone (ADH)*: Promotes retention of water by kidneys; influences social behavior and bonding
**Anterior pituitary**
*Follicle-stimulating hormone (FSH)* and *luteinizing hormone (LH):* Stimulate ovaries and testes
*Thyroid-stimulating hormone (TSH):* Stimulates thyroid gland
*Adrenocorticotropic hormone (ACTH):* Stimulates adrenal cortex
*Prolactin:* Stimulates mammary gland growth and milk synthesis in mammals
*Growth hormone (GH):* Stimulates growth and metabolic functions
*Melanocyte-stimulating hormone (MSH):* Affects color of melanocytes, a type of skin cell

**Pancreas**
*Insulin:* Lowers blood glucose level
*Glucagon:* Raises blood glucose level

(MB) Animation: Endocrine System Anatomy

# CONCEPT 45.2

## Feedback regulation and coordination with the nervous system are common in hormone pathways

Having explored hormone structure, recognition, and response, we now consider how regulatory pathways controlling hormone secretion are organized.

### Simple Endocrine Pathways

In a *simple endocrine pathway*, endocrine cells respond directly to an internal or environmental stimulus by secreting a particular hormone. The hormone travels in the bloodstream to target cells, where it interacts with its specific receptors. Signal transduction within target cells brings about a physiological response.

The activity of endocrine cells in the duodenum, the first part of the small intestine, provides a useful example of a simple endocrine pathway. During digestion, the partially processed food that enters the duodenum contains highly acidic digestive juices secreted by the stomach. Before further digestion can occur, this acidic mixture must be neutralized. **Figure 45.9** outlines the simple endocrine pathway that ensures neutralization takes place.

▼ **Figure 45.9 A simple endocrine pathway.** Endocrine cells respond to a change in some internal or external variable—the stimulus—by secreting hormone molecules that trigger a specific response by target cells. In the case of secretin signaling, the simple endocrine pathway is self-limiting because the response to secretin (bicarbonate release) reduces the stimulus (low pH) through negative feedback.

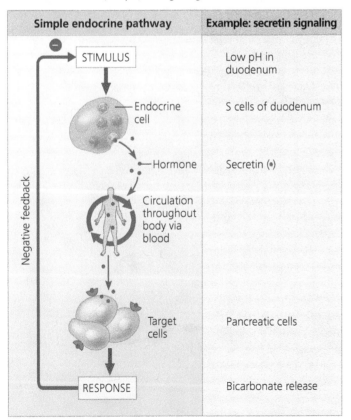

The low pH of partially digested food entering the small intestine is detected by S cells, which are endocrine cells in the lining of the duodenum. In response, the S cells secrete the hormone *secretin*, which diffuses into the blood. Traveling throughout the circulatory system, secretin reaches the pancreas. Target cells in the pancreas have receptors for secretin and respond by releasing bicarbonate into ducts that lead to the duodenum. In the last step of the pathway, the bicarbonate released into the duodenum raises the pH, neutralizing the stomach acid.

### Simple Neuroendocrine Pathways

In a *simple neuroendocrine pathway*, the stimulus is received by a sensory neuron rather than endocrine tissue. The sensory neuron in turn stimulates a neurosecretory cell. In response, the neurosecretory cell secretes a neurohormone. Like other hormones, the neurohormone diffuses into the bloodstream and travels in the circulation to target cells.

As an example of a simple neuroendocrine pathway, consider the regulation of milk release during nursing in mammals **(Figure 45.10)**. When an infant suckles, it stimulates

▼ **Figure 45.10 A simple neuroendocrine pathway.** Sensory neurons respond to a stimulus by sending nerve impulses to a neurosecretory cell, triggering secretion of a neurohormone. Upon reaching its target cells, the neurohormone binds to its receptor, triggering a specific response. In oxytocin signaling, the response increases the stimulus, forming a positive-feedback loop that amplifies signaling.

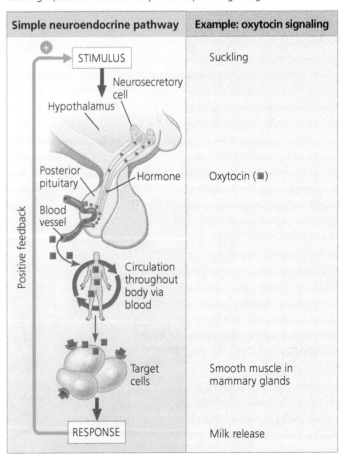

sensory neurons in the nipples, generating nerve impulses that reach the hypothalamus. This input triggers the secretion of the neurohormone **oxytocin** from the posterior pituitary gland. Oxytocin then causes contraction of mammary gland cells, forcing milk from reservoirs in the gland.

## Feedback Regulation

A feedback loop linking a response back to an initial stimulus is a feature of many control pathways. Often, this loop involves **negative feedback**, in which the response reduces the initial stimulus. For instance, bicarbonate released in response to secretin increases pH in the intestine, eliminating the stimulus and thereby shutting off secretin release (see Figure 45.9). By decreasing hormone signaling, negative-feedback regulation prevents excessive pathway activity.

Whereas negative feedback dampens a stimulus, **positive feedback** reinforces a stimulus, leading to an even greater response. For example, in the oxytocin pathway outlined in Figure 45.10, the mammary glands secrete milk in response to circulating oxytocin. The released milk in turn leads to more suckling and therefore more stimulation. Activation of the pathway is sustained until the baby stops suckling. Other functions of oxytocin, such as stimulating contractions of the uterus during birthing, also exhibit positive feedback.

Comparing negative and positive feedback, we see that only negative feedback helps restore a preexisting state. It is not surprising, therefore, that hormone pathways involved in homeostasis typically exhibit negative feedback. Often such pathways are paired, providing even more balanced control. For example, blood glucose levels are regulated by the opposing effects of insulin and glucagon (see Figure 41.21).

## Coordination of the Endocrine and Nervous Systems

In a wide range of animals, endocrine organs in the brain integrate function of the endocrine system with that of the nervous system. We'll explore the basic principles of such integration in invertebrates and vertebrates.

### Invertebrates

▼ **Figure 45.11 Larva of the giant silk moth.**

The control of development in a moth illustrates neuroendocrine coordination in invertebrates. A moth larva, such as the caterpillar of the giant silk moth (*Hyalophora cecropia*) shown in **Figure 45.11**, grows in stages. Because its exoskeleton cannot stretch, the larva must periodically molt, shedding the old exoskeleton and secreting a new one. The endocrine pathway that controls molting originates in the larval brain **(Figure 45.12)**. Neurosecretory cells in the brain produce PTTH, a polypeptide neurohormone. When PTTH reaches an endocrine organ called the prothoracic gland, it directs release of a

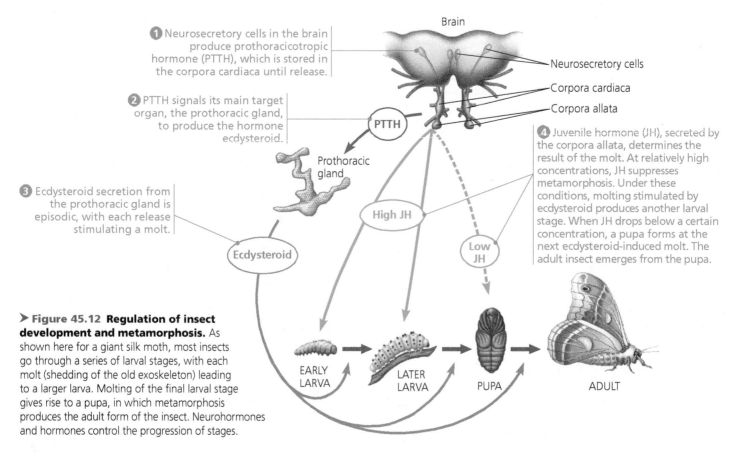

① Neurosecretory cells in the brain produce prothoracicotropic hormone (PTTH), which is stored in the corpora cardiaca until release.

② PTTH signals its main target organ, the prothoracic gland, to produce the hormone ecdysteroid.

③ Ecdysteroid secretion from the prothoracic gland is episodic, with each release stimulating a molt.

④ Juvenile hormone (JH), secreted by the corpora allata, determines the result of the molt. At relatively high concentrations, JH suppresses metamorphosis. Under these conditions, molting stimulated by ecdysteroid produces another larval stage. When JH drops below a certain concentration, a pupa forms at the next ecdysteroid-induced molt. The adult insect emerges from the pupa.

➤ **Figure 45.12 Regulation of insect development and metamorphosis.** As shown here for a giant silk moth, most insects go through a series of larval stages, with each molt (shedding of the old exoskeleton) leading to a larger larva. Molting of the final larval stage gives rise to a pupa, in which metamorphosis produces the adult form of the insect. Neurohormones and hormones control the progression of stages.

Brain — Neurosecretory cells — Corpora cardiaca — Corpora allata — PTTH — Prothoracic gland — Ecdysteroid — High JH — Low JH — EARLY LARVA — LATER LARVA — PUPA — ADULT

second hormone, *ecdysteroid*. Bursts of ecdysteroid trigger each successive molt.

Ecdysteroid also controls a remarkable change in form called metamorphosis. Within the larva lie islands of tissues that will become the eyes, wings, brain, and other adult structures. Once a plump, crawling larva becomes a stationary pupa, these islands of cells take over. They complete their program of development, while many larval tissues undergo programmed cell death. The end result is the transformation of the crawling caterpillar into a free-flying moth.

Given that ecdysteroid can cause either molting or metamorphosis, what determines which process takes place? The answer is another signal, juvenile hormone (JH), secreted by a pair of endocrine glands behind the brain. JH modulates ecdysteroid activity. When the level of JH is high, ecdysteroid stimulates molting (and thus maintains the "juvenile" larval state). When the JH level drops, ecdysteroid instead induces formation of a pupa, within which metamorphosis occurs.

Knowledge of the coordination between the nervous system and endocrine system in insects has provided a basis for novel methods of agricultural pest control. For example, one tool to control insect pests is a chemical that binds to the ecdysteroid receptor, causing insect larvae to molt prematurely and die.

## Vertebrates

In vertebrates, coordination of endocrine signaling relies heavily on the **hypothalamus (Figure 45.13)**. The hypothalamus receives information from nerves throughout the body and, in response, initiates neuroendocrine signaling appropriate to environmental conditions. In many vertebrates, for example, nerve signals from the brain pass sensory information to the hypothalamus about seasonal changes. The hypothalamus, in turn, regulates the release of reproductive hormones required during the breeding season.

Signals from the hypothalamus travel to the **pituitary gland**, a gland located at the base of the hypothalamus (see Figure 45.13). Roughly the size and shape of a lima bean, the pituitary is made up of two fused glands that form discrete posterior and anterior parts, or lobes, and perform very different functions. The **posterior pituitary** is an extension of the hypothalamus. Hypothalamic axons that reach into the posterior pituitary secrete neurohormones synthesized in the hypothalamus. In contrast, the **anterior pituitary** is an endocrine gland that synthesizes and secretes hormones in response to hormones from the hypothalamus.

**Posterior Pituitary Hormones**   Neurosecretory cells of the hypothalamus synthesize the two posterior pituitary hormones: antidiuretic hormone (ADH) and oxytocin. After traveling to the posterior pituitary within the long axons of the neurosecretory cells, these neurohormones are stored, to be released in response to nerve impulses transmitted by the hypothalamus **(Figure 45.14)**.

▼ **Figure 45.13 Endocrine glands in the human brain.** This side view of the brain indicates the position of the hypothalamus, the pituitary gland, and the pineal gland. (The pineal gland plays a role in regulating biological rhythms.)

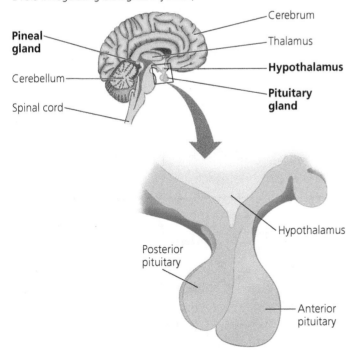

▼ **Figure 45.14 Production and release of posterior pituitary hormones.** The posterior pituitary gland is an extension of the hypothalamus. Certain neurosecretory cells in the hypothalamus make antidiuretic hormone (ADH) and oxytocin, which are transported to the posterior pituitary, where they are stored. Nerve signals from the brain trigger release of these neurohormones.

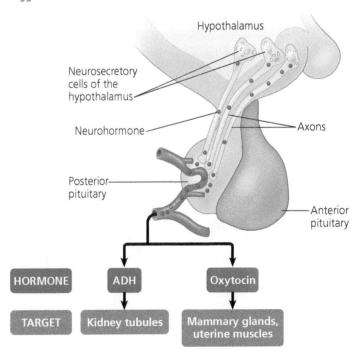

**Antidiuretic hormone (ADH)**, or *vasopressin*, regulates kidney function. Secretion of ADH increases water retention in the kidneys, helping maintain normal blood osmolarity (see Concept 44.5). ADH also has an important role in social behavior (see Concept 51.4).

Oxytocin has multiple functions related to reproduction. As we have seen, in female mammals oxytocin controls milk secretion by the mammary glands and regulates uterine contractions during birthing. In addition, oxytocin has targets in the brain, where it influences behaviors related to maternal care, pair bonding, and sexual activity.

**Anterior Pituitary Hormones**    Hormones secreted by the anterior pituitary control diverse processes in the human body, including metabolism, osmoregulation, and reproduction. As illustrated in **Figure 45.15**, many anterior pituitary hormones, but not all, regulate endocrine glands or tissues.

Hormones secreted by the hypothalamus control the release of all anterior pituitary hormones. Each hypothalamic hormone that regulates release of one or more hormones by the anterior pituitary is called a *releasing* or *inhibiting* hormone. *Prolactin-releasing hormone*, for example, is a hypothalamic hormone that stimulates the anterior pituitary to secrete **prolactin**, which has activities that include stimulating milk production. Each anterior pituitary hormone is controlled by at least one releasing hormone.

Some, such as prolactin, have both a releasing hormone and an inhibiting hormone.

The hypothalamic releasing and inhibiting hormones are secreted near capillaries at the base of the hypothalamus. The capillaries drain into short blood vessels, called portal vessels, which subdivide into a second capillary bed within the anterior pituitary. Releasing and inhibiting hormones thus have direct access to the gland they control.

In neuroendocrine pathways, sets of hormones from the hypothalamus, the anterior pituitary, and a target endocrine gland are often organized into a *hormone cascade*, a form of regulation in which multiple endocrine organs and signals act in series. Signals to the brain stimulate the hypothalamus to secrete a hormone that stimulates or inhibits release of a specific anterior pituitary hormone. The anterior pituitary hormone in turn stimulates another endocrine organ to secrete yet another hormone, which affects specific target tissues. In reproduction, for example, the hypothalamus signals the anterior pituitary to release the hormones FSH and LH, which in turn regulate hormone secretion by the gonads (ovaries or testes).

In a sense, hormone cascade pathways redirect signals from the hypothalamus to other endocrine glands. For this reason, the anterior pituitary hormones in such pathways are called *tropic* hormones and are said to have a *tropic* effect, from *tropos*, the Greek word meaning "bending" or "turning."

▶ **Figure 45.15 Production and release of anterior pituitary hormones.** The release of hormones synthesized in the anterior pituitary gland is controlled by hypothalamic releasing and inhibiting hormones. The hypothalamic hormones are secreted by neurosecretory cells and enter a capillary network within the hypothalamus. These capillaries drain into portal vessels that connect with a second capillary network in the anterior pituitary.

| HORMONE | FSH and LH | TSH | ACTH | Prolactin | MSH | GH |
|---------|------------|-----|------|-----------|-----|-----|
| TARGET | Testes or ovaries | Thyroid | Adrenal cortex | Mammary glands | Melanocytes | Liver, bones, other tissues |

**Tropic effects only**          **Nontropic effects only**     **Tropic and nontropic effects**

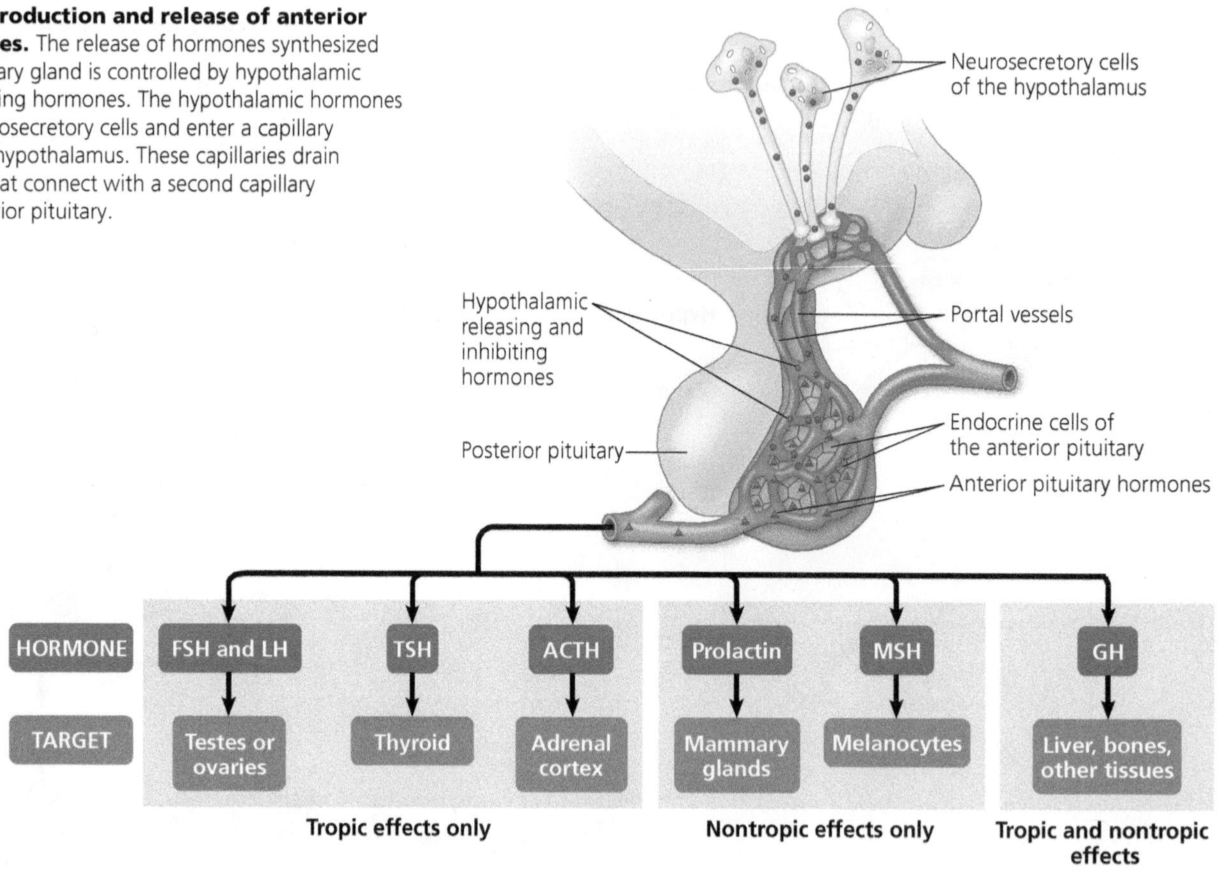

Thus, FSH and LH are gonadotropins because they convey signals from the hypothalamus to the gonads. To learn more about tropic hormones and hormone cascade pathways, we'll turn next to thyroid gland function and regulation.

## Thyroid Regulation: A Hormone Cascade Pathway

In mammals, **thyroid hormone** regulates bioenergetics; helps maintain normal blood pressure, heart rate, and muscle tone; and regulates digestive and reproductive functions. **Figure 45.16** provides an overview of the hormone cascade pathway that regulates thyroid hormone release. If the level of thyroid hormone in the blood drops, the hypothalamus secretes thyrotropin-releasing hormone (TRH), causing the anterior pituitary to secrete thyrotropin, a tropic hormone also known as thyroid-stimulating hormone (TSH). TSH in turn stimulates the **thyroid gland**, an organ in the neck consisting of two lobes on the ventral surface of the trachea. The thyroid gland responds by secreting thyroid hormone, which increases metabolic rate.

As with other hormone cascade pathways, feedback regulation often occurs at multiple levels. For example, thyroid hormone exerts negative feedback on the hypothalamus and on the anterior pituitary, in each case blocking release of the hormone that promotes its production (see Figure 45.16).

### Disorders of Thyroid Function and Regulation

Disruption of thyroid hormone production and regulation can result in serious disorders. One such disorder reflects the unusual chemical makeup of thyroid hormone, the only iodine-containing molecule synthesized in the body. *Thyroid hormone* is actually a pair of very similar molecules derived from the amino acid tyrosine. *Triiodothyronine* ($T_3$) contains three iodine atoms, whereas tetraiodothyronine, or *thyroxine* ($T_4$), contains four (see Figure 45.4).

Although iodine is readily obtained from seafood or iodized salt, people in many parts of the world lack enough iodine in their diet to synthesize adequate amounts of thyroid hormone. With only low blood levels of thyroid hormone, the pituitary receives no negative feedback and continues to secrete TSH. Elevated TSH levels in turn cause the thyroid gland to enlarge, resulting in goiter, a marked swelling of the neck. The **Problem-Solving Exercise** further explores thyroid regulation abnormalities in the context of a medical mystery.

## Hormonal Regulation of Growth

**Growth hormone (GH)**, which is secreted by the anterior pituitary, stimulates growth through both tropic and non-tropic effects. A major target, the liver, responds to GH by releasing *insulin-like growth factors* (IGFs), which circulate in the blood and directly stimulate bone and cartilage growth. (IGFs also appear to play a key role in aging in many animal

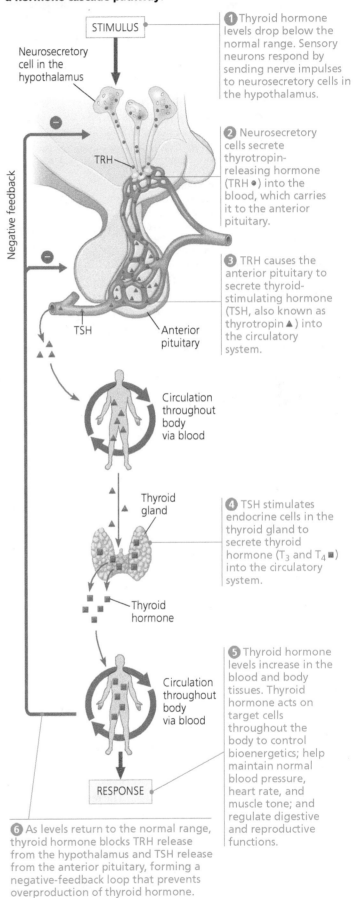

▼ **Figure 45.16 Regulation of thyroid hormone secretion: a hormone cascade pathway.**

STIMULUS

Neurosecretory cell in the hypothalamus

Negative feedback

TRH

TSH

Anterior pituitary

Circulation throughout body via blood

Thyroid gland

Thyroid hormone

Circulation throughout body via blood

RESPONSE

❶ Thyroid hormone levels drop below the normal range. Sensory neurons respond by sending nerve impulses to neurosecretory cells in the hypothalamus.

❷ Neurosecretory cells secrete thyrotropin-releasing hormone (TRH ●) into the blood, which carries it to the anterior pituitary.

❸ TRH causes the anterior pituitary to secrete thyroid-stimulating hormone (TSH, also known as thyrotropin ▲) into the circulatory system.

❹ TSH stimulates endocrine cells in the thyroid gland to secrete thyroid hormone ($T_3$ and $T_4$ ■) into the circulatory system.

❺ Thyroid hormone levels increase in the blood and body tissues. Thyroid hormone acts on target cells throughout the body to control bioenergetics; help maintain normal blood pressure, heart rate, and muscle tone; and regulate digestive and reproductive functions.

❻ As levels return to the normal range, thyroid hormone blocks TRH release from the hypothalamus and TSH release from the anterior pituitary, forming a negative-feedback loop that prevents overproduction of thyroid hormone.

# Is thyroid regulation normal in this patient?

Normal health requires proper regulation of the thyroid gland. Hypothyroidism, the secretion of too little thyroid hormone ($T_3$ and $T_4$) can cause weight gain, lethargy, and intolerance to cold in adults. In contrast, excessive secretion of thyroid hormone, known as hyperthyroidism, can lead to high body temperature, profuse sweating, weight loss, muscle weakness, irritability, and high blood pressure. Thyroid-stimulating hormone (TSH) stimulates the thyroid to release thyroid hormone. Testing for levels of $T_3$, $T_4$, and TSH in the blood can help diagnose various medical conditions.

In this exercise, you will determine whether a 35-year-old man who came to the emergency room with episodes of paralysis has thyroid problems.

**Your Approach**  As the emergency physician, you order a set of blood tests, including four that measure thyroid function. To determine whether the thyroid activity of your patient is normal, you will compare his blood test results with the normal range, as determined from a large set of healthy people.

**Your Data**

| # | Test | Patient | Normal Range | Comments |
|---|------|---------|--------------|----------|
| a. | Serum total $T_3$ | 2.93 nmol/L | 0.89–2.44 nmol/L | |
| b. | Free thyroxine ($T_4$) | 27.4 pmol/L | 9.0–21.0 pmol/L | |
| c. | TSH levels | 5.55 mU/L | 0.35–4.94 mU/L | |
| d. | TSH receptor autoantibody | 0.2 U/mL | 0–1.5 U/mL | |

**Your Analysis**

1. For each test, determine whether the patient's test value is high, low, or normal relative to the normal range. Then write *High*, *Low*, or *Normal* in the Comments column of the table.

2. Based on tests a–c, is your patient hypothyroid or hyperthyroid?

3. Test d measures the level of auto- (self-reactive) antibodies that bind to and activate the body's receptor for TSH. High levels of auto-antibodies cause sustained thyroid hormone production and the autoimmune disorder called Graves' disease. Is it likely that your patient has this disease? Explain.

4. A thyroid tumor increases the mass of cells producing $T_3$ and $T_4$, whereas a tumor in the anterior pituitary increases the mass of TSH-secreting cells. Would you expect either condition to result in the observed blood test values? Explain.

 **Instructors**: A version of this Problem-Solving Exercise can be assigned in MasteringBiology.

---

species.) In the absence of GH, the skeleton of an immature animal stops growing. GH also exerts diverse metabolic effects that tend to raise blood glucose levels, thus opposing the effects of insulin.

Abnormal production of GH in humans can result in several disorders, depending on when the problem occurs and whether it involves hypersecretion (too much) or hyposecretion (too little). Hypersecretion of GH during childhood can lead to gigantism, in which the person grows unusually tall but retains relatively normal body proportions **(Figure 45.17)**. Excessive GH production in adulthood stimulates bony growth in the few body parts that are still responsive to the hormone—predominantly the face, hands, and feet. The result is an overgrowth of the extremities called acromegaly (from the Greek *acros*, extreme, and *mega*, large).

Hyposecretion of GH in childhood retards long-bone growth and can lead to pituitary dwarfism. People with this disorder are for the most part properly proportioned but generally reach a height of only about 1.2 m (4 feet). If diagnosed before puberty, pituitary dwarfism can be treated with human GH (also called HGH). Treatment with HGH produced by recombinant DNA technology is common.

## CONCEPT CHECK 45.2

1. What are the roles of oxytocin and prolactin in regulating the mammary glands?

2. How do the two fused glands of the pituitary gland differ in function?

3. **WHAT IF?** ➤ Propose an explanation for why defects in a particular hormone cascade pathway observed in patients typically affect the final gland in the pathway rather than the hypothalamus or pituitary.

4. **WHAT IF?** ➤ Lab tests of two patients, each diagnosed with excessive thyroid hormone production, revealed elevated levels of TSH in one but not the other. Was the diagnosis of one patient necessarily incorrect? Explain.

*For suggested answers, see Appendix A.*

**▼ Figure 45.17 Effect of growth hormone overproduction.**
Shown here surrounded by his family, Robert Wadlow grew to a height of 2.7 m (8 feet 11 inches) by age 22, making him the tallest man in history. His height was due to excess secretion of growth hormone by his pituitary gland.

# CONCEPT 45.3

## Endocrine glands respond to diverse stimuli in regulating homeostasis, development, and behavior

In the remainder of this chapter, we'll focus on endocrine function in homeostasis, development, and behavior. We'll begin with another example of a simple hormone pathway, the regulation of calcium ion concentration in the circulatory system.

### Parathyroid Hormone and Vitamin D: Control of Blood Calcium

Because calcium ions ($Ca^{2+}$) are essential to the normal functioning of all cells, homeostatic control of blood calcium level is vital. If the blood $Ca^{2+}$ level falls substantially, skeletal muscles begin to contract convulsively, a potentially fatal condition. If the blood $Ca^{2+}$ level rises substantially, calcium phosphate can form precipitates in body tissues, leading to widespread organ damage.

In mammals, the **parathyroid glands**, a set of four small structures embedded in the posterior surface of the thyroid (see Figure 45.8), play a major role in blood $Ca^{2+}$ regulation. When the blood $Ca^{2+}$ level falls below a set point of about 10 mg/100 mL, these glands release **parathyroid hormone (PTH)**.

PTH raises the level of blood $Ca^{2+}$ through direct effects in bones and the kidneys and an indirect effect on the intestines (**Figure 45.18**). In bones, PTH causes the mineralized matrix to break down, releasing $Ca^{2+}$ into the blood. In the kidneys, PTH directly stimulates reabsorption of $Ca^{2+}$ through the renal tubules. In addition, PTH indirectly raises blood $Ca^{2+}$ levels by promoting production of vitamin D. A precursor form of vitamin D is obtained from food or synthesized by skin exposed to sunlight. Conversion of this precursor to active vitamin D begins in the liver. PTH acts in the kidney to stimulate completion of the conversion process. Vitamin D in turn acts on the intestines, stimulating the uptake of $Ca^{2+}$ from food. As the blood $Ca^{2+}$ level rises, a negative-feedback loop inhibits further release of PTH from the parathyroid glands (not shown in Figure 45.18).

The thyroid gland can also contribute to calcium homeostasis. If the blood $Ca^{2+}$ level rises above the set point, the thyroid gland releases **calcitonin**, a hormone that inhibits bone breakdown and enhances $Ca^{2+}$ excretion by the kidneys. In fishes, rodents, and some other animals, calcitonin is required for $Ca^{2+}$ homeostasis. In humans, however, calcitonin is apparently needed only during the extensive bone growth of childhood.

**▼ Figure 45.18 The roles of parathyroid hormone (PTH) in regulating blood calcium levels in mammals.**

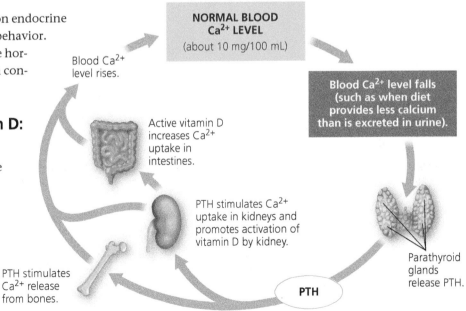

NORMAL BLOOD Ca²⁺ LEVEL (about 10 mg/100 mL)

Blood Ca²⁺ level rises.

Blood Ca²⁺ level falls (such as when diet provides less calcium than is excreted in urine).

Active vitamin D increases Ca²⁺ uptake in intestines.

PTH stimulates Ca²⁺ uptake in kidneys and promotes activation of vitamin D by kidney.

Parathyroid glands release PTH.

PTH

PTH stimulates Ca²⁺ release from bones.

## Adrenal Hormones: Response to Stress

The adrenal glands of vertebrates play a major role in the response to *stress*, a state of threatened homeostasis. Located atop the kidneys (the *renal* organs), each **adrenal gland** is actually made up of two glands with different cell types, functions, and embryonic origins: the adrenal *cortex*, the outer portion, and the adrenal *medulla*, the central portion. The adrenal cortex consists of true endocrine cells, whereas the secretory cells of the adrenal medulla develop from neural tissue. Thus, like the pituitary gland, each adrenal gland is a fused endocrine and neuroendocrine gland.

### The Role of the Adrenal Medulla

Imagine that while walking in the woods at night you hear a growling noise nearby. "A bear?" you wonder. Your heart beats faster, your breathing quickens, your muscles tense, and your thoughts speed up. These and other rapid responses to perceived danger comprise the "fight-or-flight" response. This coordinated set of physiological changes is triggered by two hormones of the adrenal medulla, epinephrine (adrenaline) and **norepinephrine** (also known as noradrenaline). Both are *catecholamines*, a class of amine hormones synthesized from the amino acid tyrosine. Both molecules also function as neurotransmitters, as you'll read in Concept 48.4.

As hormones, epinephrine and norepinephrine increase the amount of chemical energy available for immediate use **(Figure 45.19a)**. Both catecholamines increase the rate of glycogen breakdown in the liver and skeletal muscles and promote the release of glucose by liver cells and of fatty acids from fat cells. The released glucose and fatty acids circulate in the blood and can be used by body cells as fuel.

Catecholamines also exert profound effects on the cardiovascular and respiratory systems. For example, they increase heart rate and stroke volume and dilate the bronchioles in the lungs, actions that raise the rate of oxygen delivery to body cells. For this reason, doctors may prescribe epinephrine as a heart stimulant or to open the airways during an asthma attack. Catecholamines also alter blood flow, causing constriction of some blood vessels and dilation of others. The overall effect is to shunt blood away from the skin, digestive organs, and kidneys, while increasing the blood supply to the heart, brain, and skeletal muscles.

▼ **Figure 45.19 Stress and the adrenal gland.**

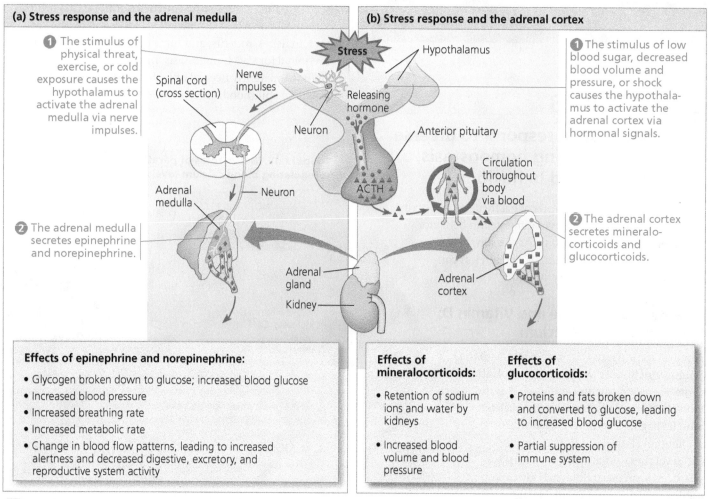

**(a) Stress response and the adrenal medulla**

❶ The stimulus of physical threat, exercise, or cold exposure causes the hypothalamus to activate the adrenal medulla via nerve impulses.

Spinal cord (cross section) — Nerve impulses — Neuron — Adrenal medulla — Neuron

❷ The adrenal medulla secretes epinephrine and norepinephrine.

Adrenal gland — Kidney

**Effects of epinephrine and norepinephrine:**
- Glycogen broken down to glucose; increased blood glucose
- Increased blood pressure
- Increased breathing rate
- Increased metabolic rate
- Change in blood flow patterns, leading to increased alertness and decreased digestive, excretory, and reproductive system activity

**(b) Stress response and the adrenal cortex**

Stress — Hypothalamus — Releasing hormone — Anterior pituitary — ACTH — Circulation throughout body via blood — Adrenal cortex

❶ The stimulus of low blood sugar, decreased blood volume and pressure, or shock causes the hypothalamus to activate the adrenal cortex via hormonal signals.

❷ The adrenal cortex secretes mineralocorticoids and glucocorticoids.

**Effects of mineralocorticoids:**
- Retention of sodium ions and water by kidneys
- Increased blood volume and blood pressure

**Effects of glucocorticoids:**
- Proteins and fats broken down and converted to glucose, leading to increased blood glucose
- Partial suppression of immune system

**MB** Animation: Hormonal Response to Stress

## Epinephrine's Multiple Effects: A Closer Look

How can epinephrine coordinate a response to stress that involves widely varying effects in individual tissues? We can answer that question by examining different response pathways **(Figure 45.20)** in a range of target cells:

- In liver cells, epinephrine binds to a β-type receptor in the plasma membrane. This receptor activates the enzyme protein kinase A, which in turn regulates enzymes of glycogen metabolism, causing release of glucose into the blood **(Figure 45.20a)**. Note that this is the signal transduction pathway illustrated in Figure 45.6.
- In the smooth muscle cells that line blood vessels supplying skeletal muscle, the same kinase activated by the same epinephrine receptor inactivates a muscle-specific enzyme. The result is smooth muscle relaxation, leading to vasodilation and hence increased blood flow to skeletal muscles **(Figure 45.20b)**.
- In the smooth muscle cells lining blood vessels of the intestines, epinephrine binds to an α-type receptor **(Figure 45.20c)**. Rather than activating protein kinase A, this receptor triggers a signaling pathway involving a different G protein and different enzymes. The result is smooth muscle contraction that brings about vasoconstriction, restricting blood flow to the intestines.

Thus, epinephrine elicits multiple responses if its target cells differ in their receptor type or if they differ in the molecules that produce the response. As illustrated in these examples, such variation in response plays a key role in enabling epinephrine to trigger a range of activities that together bring about a coordinated rapid response to stressful stimuli.

### The Role of the Adrenal Cortex

Like the adrenal medulla, the adrenal cortex mediates an endocrine response to stress **(Figure 45.19b)**. The two portions of the adrenal gland differ, however, in both the types of stress that trigger a response and the targets of the hormones that are released.

The adrenal cortex becomes active under stressful conditions that include low blood sugar, decreased blood volume and pressure, and shock. Such stimuli cause the hypothalamus to secrete a releasing hormone that stimulates the anterior pituitary to release adrenocorticotropic hormone (ACTH), a tropic hormone. When ACTH reaches the adrenal cortex via the bloodstream, it stimulates the endocrine cells to synthesize and secrete a family of steroids called *corticosteroids*. The two main types of corticosteroids in humans are glucocorticoids and mineralocorticoids.

**Glucocorticoids**, such as cortisol (see Figure 45.4), make more glucose available as fuel by promoting glucose synthesis from noncarbohydrate sources, such as proteins. Glucocorticoids also act on skeletal muscle, causing the breakdown of muscle proteins into amino acids. These are transported to the liver and kidneys, converted to glucose, and released into the blood. The synthesis of glucose upon the breakdown of muscle proteins provides circulating fuel when the body requires more glucose than the liver can mobilize from its glycogen stores.

If glucocorticoids are introduced into the body at levels above those normally present, they suppress certain components of the body's immune system. For this reason, glucocorticoids are sometimes used to treat inflammatory diseases such as arthritis. However, their long-term use can have serious side effects on metabolism. Nonsteroidal anti-inflammatory drugs (NSAIDs), such as aspirin and

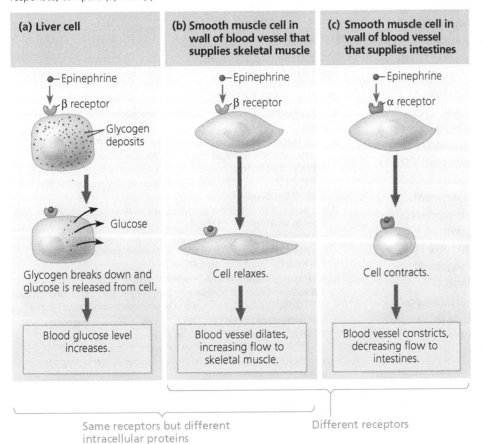

**▼ Figure 45.20 One hormone, different effects.** Epinephrine, the primary "fight-or-flight" hormone, produces different responses in different target cells. Target cells with the same receptor exhibit different responses if they have different signal transduction pathways or effector proteins; compare (a) with (b). Target cells with different receptors for the hormone often exhibit different responses; compare (b) with (c).

ibuprofen, are therefore generally preferred for treating chronic inflammatory conditions.

**Mineralocorticoids** act principally in maintaining salt and water balance. For example, the mineralocorticoid *aldosterone* functions in ion and water homeostasis of the blood (see Figure 44.21). Like glucocorticoids, mineralocorticoids not only mediate stress responses, but also participate in homeostatic regulation of metabolism. In the **Scientific Skills Exercise**, you can explore an experiment investigating changes in ACTH secretion as humans awaken from sleep.

## Sex Hormones

Sex hormones affect growth, development, reproductive cycles, and sexual behavior. Whereas the adrenal glands secrete small quantities of these hormones, the gonads (testes of males and ovaries of females) are their principal sources. The gonads produce and secrete three major types of steroid sex hormones: androgens, estrogens, and progesterone. All three types are found in both males and females but in different proportions.

The testes primarily synthesize **androgens**, the main one being **testosterone**. In humans, testosterone first functions before birth, promoting development of male reproductive structures (**Figure 45.21**). Androgens play a major role again at puberty, when they are responsible for the development of male secondary sex characteristics. High concentrations of androgens lead to lengthening and thickening of the vocal cords that lower the voice, male patterns of hair growth, and increases in muscle and bone mass. The muscle-building, or anabolic, action of testosterone and related steroids has enticed some athletes to take them as supplements, despite prohibitions against their use in nearly all sports. Use of anabolic steroids, while effective in increasing muscle mass, can cause severe acne outbreaks and liver damage, as well as significant decreases in sperm count and testicular size.

**Estrogens**, of which the most important is **estradiol**, are responsible for the maintenance of the female reproductive system and for the development of female secondary sex characteristics. In mammals, **progesterone** is involved in preparing and maintaining tissues of the uterus required to support the growth and development of an embryo.

Estrogens and other gonadal sex hormones are components of hormone cascade pathways. Synthesis of these hormones is primarily controlled by two gonadotropins from the anterior pituitary, follicle-stimulating hormone and luteinizing hormone (see Figure 45.15). Gonadotropin secretion is in turn controlled by GnRH (gonadotropin-releasing hormone) from the hypothalamus. We'll examine the feedback relationships that regulate gonadal hormone secretion in detail when we discuss animal reproduction in Chapter 46.

## SCIENTIFIC SKILLS EXERCISE

### Designing a Controlled Experiment

**How Is Nighttime ACTH Secretion Related to Expected Sleep Duration?** Humans secrete increasing amounts of adrenocorticotropic hormone (ACTH) during the late stages of normal sleep, with the peak secretion occurring at the time of spontaneous waking. Because ACTH is released in response to stressful stimuli, scientists hypothesized that ACTH secretion prior to waking might be an anticipatory response to the stress associated with transitioning from sleep to a more active state. If so, an individual's expectation of waking at a particular time might influence the timing of ACTH secretion. How can such a hypothesis be tested? In this exercise, you will examine how researchers designed a controlled experiment to study the role of expectation.

**How the Experiment Was Done** Researchers studied 15 healthy volunteers in their mid-20s over three nights. Each night, each subject was told when he or she would be awakened: 6:00 or 9:00 AM. The subjects went to sleep at midnight. Subjects in the "short" or "long" protocol group were awakened at the expected time (6:00 or 9:00 AM, respectively). Subjects in the "surprise" protocol group were told they would be awakened at 9:00 AM, but were actually awakened 3 hours early, at 6:00 AM. At set times, blood samples were drawn to determine plasma levels of ACTH. To determine the change (Δ) in ACTH concentration post-waking, the researchers compared samples drawn at waking and 30 minutes later.

**Data from the Experiment**

| Sleep Protocol | Expected Wake Time | Actual Wake Time | Mean Plasma ACTH Level (pg/mL) | | |
|---|---|---|---|---|---|
| | | | 1:00 AM | 6:00 AM | Δ in the 30 Minutes Post-waking |
| Short | 6:00 AM | 6:00 AM | 9.9 | 37.3 | 10.6 |
| Long | 9:00 AM | 9:00 AM | 8.1 | 26.5 | 12.2 |
| Surprise | 9:00 AM | 6:00 AM | 8.0 | 25.5 | 22.1 |

**Data from** J. Born et al., Timing the end of nocturnal sleep, *Nature* 397:29–30 (1999).

**INTERPRET THE DATA**

1. Describe the role of the "surprise" protocol in the experimental design.

2. Each subject was given a different protocol on each of the three nights, and the order of the protocols was varied among the subjects that so that one-third had each protocol each night. What factors were the researchers attempting to control for with this approach?

3. For subjects in the short protocol, what was the mean ACTH level at waking? Using the data in the last two columns, calculate the mean level 30 minutes later. Was the rate of change faster or slower in that 30-minute period than during the interval from 1:00 to 6:00 AM?

4. How does the change in ACTH level between 1:00 and 6:00 AM for the surprise protocol compare to that for the short and long protocols? Does this result support the hypothesis being tested? Explain.

5. Using the data in the last two columns, calculate the mean ACTH concentration 30 minutes post-waking for the surprise protocol and compare to your answer for question 3. What do your results suggest about a person's physiological response immediately after waking?

6. What are some variables that weren't controlled for in this experiment that could be explored in a follow-up study?

 **Instructors:** A version of this Scientific Skills Exercise can be assigned in MasteringBiology.

## Figure 45.21 Sex hormones regulate formation of internal reproductive structures in human development.

In a male (XY) embryo, the bipotential gonads (gonads that can develop into either of two forms) become the testes, which secrete testosterone and anti-Müllerian hormone (AMH). Testosterone directs formation of sperm-carrying ducts (vas deferens and seminal vesicles), while AMH causes the female ducts to degenerate. In the absence of these testis hormones, the male ducts degenerate and female structures form, including the oviduct, uterus, and vagina.

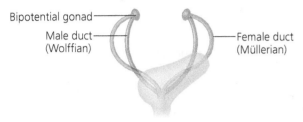

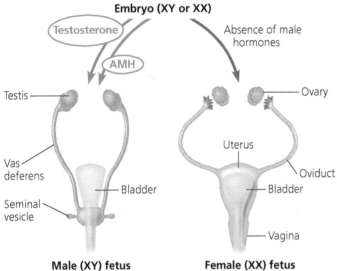

**VISUAL SKILLS ➤** *Looking at this figure, explain why the adjective* bipotential *is only used to describe the gonad.*

 BBC Video: Male, Female, or Intersex?

### *Endocrine Disruptors*

Between 1938 and 1971, some pregnant women at risk for pregnancy complications were prescribed a synthetic estrogen called diethylstilbestrol (DES). What was not known until 1971 was that exposure to DES can alter reproductive system development in the fetus. Daughters of women who took DES were more frequently afflicted with certain reproductive abnormalities, including vaginal and cervical cancer, structural changes in the reproductive organs, and increased risk of miscarriage (spontaneous abortion). DES is now recognized as an *endocrine disruptor*, a foreign molecule that interrupts the normal function of a hormone pathway.

In recent years, some scientists have hypothesized that molecules in the environment also act as endocrine disruptors. For example, bisphenol A, a chemical used in making some plastics, has been studied for potential interference with normal reproduction and development. In addition, it has been suggested that some estrogen-like molecules, such as those present in soybeans and other edible plant products, have the beneficial effect of lowering breast cancer risk. Sorting out such effects, whether harmful or beneficial, has proven quite difficult, in part because enzymes in the liver change the properties of any such molecules entering the body through the digestive system.

## Hormones and Biological Rhythms

There is still much to be learned about the hormone **melatonin**, a modified amino acid that regulates functions related to light and the seasons. Melatonin is produced by the **pineal gland**, a small mass of tissue near the center of the mammalian brain (see Figure 45.13).

Although melatonin affects skin pigmentation in many vertebrates, its primary effects relate to biological rhythms associated with reproduction and with daily activity levels (see Figure 40.9). Melatonin is secreted at night, and the amount released depends on the length of the night. In winter, for example, when days are short and nights are long, more melatonin is secreted. There is also good evidence that nightly increases in the levels of melatonin play a significant role in promoting sleep.

The release of melatonin by the pineal gland is controlled by a group of neurons in the hypothalamus called the suprachiasmatic nucleus (SCN). The SCN functions as a biological clock and receives input from specialized light-sensitive neurons in the retina of the eye. Although the SCN regulates melatonin production during the 24-hour light/dark cycle, melatonin also influences SCN activity. We'll consider biological rhythms further in Concept 49.2, where we analyze experiments on SCN function.

## Evolution of Hormone Function

**EVOLUTION** Over the course of evolution, the functions of a given hormone often diverge between species. An example is thyroid hormone, which across many evolutionary lineages plays a role in regulating metabolism (see Figure 45.16). In frogs, however, the thyroid hormone thyroxine ($T_4$) has taken on an apparently unique function: stimulating resorption of the tadpole's tail during metamorphosis **(Figure 45.22)**.

## ▼ Figure 45.22 Specialized role of a hormone in frog metamorphosis.
The hormone thyroxine is responsible for the resorption of the tadpole's tail as the frog develops into its adult form.

▲ Tadpole

▲ Adult frog

The hormone *prolactin* has an especially broad range of activities. Prolactin stimulates mammary gland growth and milk synthesis in mammals, regulates fat metabolism and reproduction in birds, delays metamorphosis in amphibians, and regulates salt and water balance in freshwater fishes. These varied roles indicate that prolactin is an ancient hormone with functions that have diversified during the evolution of vertebrate groups.

**Melanocyte-stimulating hormone (MSH)**, secreted by the anterior pituitary, provides another example of a hormone with distinct functions in different evolutionary lineages. In amphibians, fishes, and reptiles, MSH regulates skin color by controlling pigment distribution in skin cells called melanocytes. In mammals, MSH functions in hunger and metabolism in addition to skin coloration.

The specialized action of MSH that has evolved in the mammalian brain may prove to be of particular medical importance. Many patients with late-stage cancer, AIDS, tuberculosis, and certain aging disorders suffer from a devastating wasting condition called cachexia. Characterized by weight loss, muscle atrophy, and loss of appetite, cachexia responds poorly to existing therapies. However, it turns out that activation of a brain receptor for MSH produces some of the same changes seen in cachexia. Moreover, in experiments on mice with mutations that cause cancer and consequently cachexia, treatment with drugs that blocked the brain receptor for MSH prevented cachexia. Whether such drugs can be used to treat cachexia in humans is an area of active study.

## CONCEPT CHECK 45.3

1. If a hormone pathway produces a transient response to a stimulus, how would shortening the stimulus duration affect the need for negative feedback?

2. WHAT IF? ➤ Suppose you receive an injection of cortisone, a glucocorticoid, in an inflamed joint. What aspect of glucocorticoid activity would you be exploiting? If a glucocorticoid pill were also effective at treating the inflammation, why would it still be preferable to introduce the drug locally?

3. MAKE CONNECTIONS ➤ What parallels can you identify in the properties and effects of epinephrine and the plant hormone auxin (see Concept 39.2) with regard to their effects in different target tissues?

*For suggested answers, see Appendix A.*

# 45 Chapter Review

 Go to **MasteringBiology**™ for Videos, Animations, Vocab Self-Quiz, Practice Tests, and more in the Study Area.

## SUMMARY OF KEY CONCEPTS

### CONCEPT 45.1

**Hormones and other signaling molecules bind to target receptors, triggering specific response pathways** (pp. 998–1002)

VOCAB SELF-QUIZ
goo.gl/6u55ks

- The forms of signaling between animal cells differ in the type of secreting cell and the route taken by the signal to its target. **Endocrine** signals, or **hormones**, are secreted into the extracellular fluid by endocrine cells or ductless glands and reach target cells via circulatory fluids. There the binding of a hormone to a receptor specific for that particular hormone triggers a cellular response. **Paracrine** signals act on neighboring cells, whereas **autocrine** signals act on the secreting cell itself. **Neurotransmitters** also act locally, but **neurohormones** can act throughout the body. **Pheromones** are released into the environment for communication between animals of the same species.
- **Local regulators**, which carry out paracrine and autocrine signaling, include cytokines and growth factors (polypeptides), **prostaglandins** (modified fatty acids), and **nitric oxide** (a gas).
- Polypeptides, steroids, and amines comprise the major classes of animal hormones. Depending on whether they are water-soluble or lipid-soluble, hormones activate different response pathways. The endocrine cells that secrete hormones are often located in glands dedicated in part or in whole to endocrine signaling.

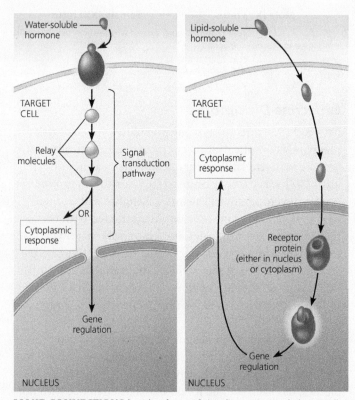

**MAKE CONNECTIONS** ➤ *What forms of signaling activate a helper T cell in immune responses (see Figure 43.16)?*

## CONCEPT 45.2

### Feedback regulation and coordination with the nervous system are common in hormone pathways *(pp. 1003–1009)*

- In a *simple endocrine pathway*, endocrine cells respond directly to a stimulus. By contrast, in a *simple neuroendocrine pathway* a sensory neuron receives the stimulus.
- Hormone pathways may be regulated by **negative feedback**, which dampens the stimulus, or **positive feedback**, which amplifies the stimulus and drives the response to completion.

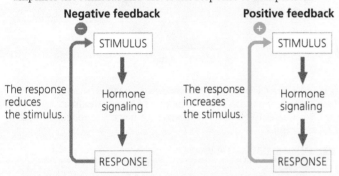

**Negative feedback**

The response reduces the stimulus.

STIMULUS → Hormone signaling → RESPONSE

**Positive feedback**

The response increases the stimulus.

STIMULUS → Hormone signaling → RESPONSE

- In insects, molting and development are controlled by three hormones: PTTH; ecdysteroid, whose release is triggered by PTTH; and juvenile hormone. Coordination of signals from the nervous and endocrine systems and modulation of one hormone activity by another bring about the sequence of developmental stages that lead to an adult form.
- In vertebrates, neurosecretory cells in the **hypothalamus** produce two hormones that are secreted by the **posterior pituitary** and that act directly on nonendocrine tissues: **oxytocin**, which induces uterine contractions and release of milk from mammary glands, and **antidiuretic hormone (ADH)**, which enhances water reabsorption in the kidneys.
- Other hypothalamic cells produce hormones that are transported to the **anterior pituitary**, where they stimulate or inhibit the release of particular hormones.
- Often, anterior pituitary hormones act in a cascade. For example, the secretion of thyroid-stimulating hormone (TSH) is regulated by thyrotropin-releasing hormone (TRH). TSH in turn induces the **thyroid gland** to secrete **thyroid hormone**, a combination of the iodine-containing hormones $T_3$ and $T_4$. Thyroid hormone stimulates metabolism and influences development and maturation.

**Hormone cascade**

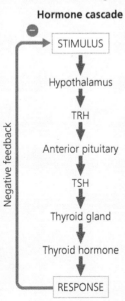

STIMULUS → Hypothalamus → TRH → Anterior pituitary → TSH → Thyroid gland → Thyroid hormone → RESPONSE

Negative feedback

- Most anterior pituitary hormones are tropic hormones, acting on endocrine tissues or glands to regulate hormone secretion. Tropic hormones of the anterior pituitary include TSH, follicle-stimulating hormone (FSH), luteinizing hormone (LH), and adrenocorticotropic hormone (ACTH). **Growth hormone** (GH) has both tropic and nontropic effects. It promotes growth directly, affects metabolism, and stimulates the production of growth factors by other tissues.

? *Which major endocrine organs described in Figure 45.8 are regulated independently of the hypothalamus and pituitary?*

## CONCEPT 45.3

### Endocrine glands respond to diverse stimuli in regulating homeostasis, development, and behavior *(pp. 1009–1014)*

- **Parathyroid hormone (PTH)**, secreted by the **parathyroid glands**, causes bone to release $Ca^{2+}$ into the blood and stimulates reabsorption of $Ca^{2+}$ in the kidneys. PTH also stimulates the kidneys to activate vitamin D, which promotes intestinal uptake of $Ca^{2+}$ from food. **Calcitonin**, secreted by the thyroid, has the opposite effects in bones and kidneys as PTH. Calcitonin is important for calcium homeostasis in adults of some vertebrates, but not humans.
- In response to stress, neurosecretory cells in the adrenal medulla release **epinephrine** and **norepinephrine**, which mediate various fight-or-flight responses. The adrenal cortex releases **glucocorticoids**, such as cortisol, which influence glucose metabolism and the immune system. It also releases **mineralocorticoids**, primarily aldosterone, which help regulate salt and water balance.
- Sex hormones regulate growth, development, reproduction, and sexual behavior. Although the adrenal cortex produces small amounts of these hormones, the gonads (testes and ovaries) serve as the major source. All three types—**androgens, estrogens**, and **progesterone**—are produced in males and females, but in different proportions.
- The **pineal gland**, located within the brain, secretes **melatonin**, which functions in biological rhythms related to reproduction and sleep. Release of melatonin is controlled by the SCN, the region of the brain that functions as a biological clock.
- Hormones have acquired distinct roles in different species over the course of evolution. **Prolactin** stimulates milk production in mammals but has diverse effects in other vertebrates. **Melanocyte-stimulating hormone (MSH)** influences fat metabolism in mammals and skin pigmentation in other vertebrates.

? *ADH and epinephrine act as hormones when released into the bloodstream and as neurotransmitters when released in synapses between neurons. What is similar about the endocrine glands that produce these two molecules?*

### TEST YOUR UNDERSTANDING

#### Level 1: Knowledge/Comprehension

1. Which of the following is *not* an accurate statement?
   - (A) Hormones are chemical messengers that travel to target cells through the circulatory system.
   - (B) Hormones often regulate homeostasis through antagonistic functions.
   - (C) Hormones of the same chemical class usually have the same function.
   - (D) Hormones are often regulated through feedback loops.

2. The hypothalamus
   (A) synthesizes all of the hormones produced by the pituitary gland.
   (B) influences the function of only one lobe of the pituitary gland.
   (C) produces only inhibitory hormones.
   (D) regulates both reproduction and body temperature.

3. Growth factors are local regulators that
   (A) are produced by the anterior pituitary.
   (B) are modified fatty acids that stimulate bone and cartilage growth.
   (C) are found on the surface of cancer cells and stimulate abnormal cell division.
   (D) bind to cell-surface receptors and stimulate growth and development of target cells.

4. Which hormone is *incorrectly* paired with its action?
   (A) oxytocin—stimulates uterine contractions during childbirth
   (B) thyroxine—inhibits metabolic processes
   (C) ACTH—stimulates the release of glucocorticoids by the adrenal cortex
   (D) melatonin—affects biological rhythms and seasonal reproduction

## Level 2: Application/Analysis

5. What do steroid and peptide hormones typically have in common?
   (A) their solubility in cell membranes
   (B) their requirement for travel through the bloodstream
   (C) the location of their receptors
   (D) their reliance on signal transduction in the cell

6. Which of the following is the most likely explanation for hypothyroidism in a patient whose iodine level is normal?
   (A) greater production of $T_3$ than of $T_4$
   (B) hyposecretion of TSH
   (C) hypersecretion of MSH
   (D) a decrease in the thyroid secretion of calcitonin

7. The relationship between the insect hormones ecdysteroid and PTTH is an example of
   (A) an interaction of the endocrine and nervous systems.
   (B) homeostasis achieved by positive feedback.
   (C) homeostasis maintained by antagonistic hormones.
   (D) competitive inhibition of a hormone receptor.

8. **DRAW IT** In mammals, milk production by mammary glands is controlled by prolactin and prolactin-releasing hormone. Draw a simple sketch of this pathway, including glands, tissues, hormones, routes for hormone movement, and effects.

## Level 3: Synthesis/Evaluation

9. **EVOLUTION CONNECTION** The intracellular receptors used by all the steroid and thyroid hormones are similar enough in structure that they are all considered members of one "superfamily" of proteins. Propose a hypothesis for how the genes encoding these receptors may have evolved. (*Hint*: See Figure 21.13.) Explain how you could test your hypothesis using DNA sequence data.

10. **SCIENTIFIC INQUIRY**
    **INTERPRET THE DATA** Chronically high levels of glucocorticoids can result in obesity, muscle weakness, and depression, a combination of symptoms called Cushing's syndrome. Excessive activity of either the pituitary or the adrenal gland can be the cause. To determine which gland has abnormal activity in a particular patient, doctors use the drug dexamethasone, a synthetic glucocorticoid that blocks ACTH release. Based on the graph, identify which gland is affected in patient X.

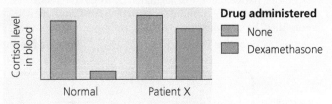

11. **WRITE ABOUT A THEME: INTERACTIONS** In a short essay (100–150 words), discuss the role of hormones in an animal's responses to changes in its environment. Use specific examples.

12. **SYNTHESIZE YOUR KNOWLEDGE**

The frog on the left was injected with MSH, causing a change in skin color within minutes due to a rapid redistribution of pigment granules in specialized skin cells. Using what you know about neuroendocrine signaling, explain how a frog could use MSH to match its skin coloration to that of its surroundings.

*For selected answers, see Appendix A.*

 For additional practice questions, check out the **Dynamic Study Modules** in MasteringBiology. You can use them to study on your smartphone, tablet, or computer anytime, anywhere!

# Animal Reproduction

# 46

▲ Figure 46.1 **What are the tiny orbs, and where are they going?**

## KEY CONCEPTS

**46.1** Both asexual and sexual reproduction occur in the animal kingdom

**46.2** Fertilization depends on mechanisms that bring together sperm and eggs of the same species

**46.3** Reproductive organs produce and transport gametes

**46.4** The interplay of tropic and sex hormones regulates reproduction in mammals

**46.5** In placental mammals, an embryo develops fully within the mother's uterus

## Let Me Count the Ways

Though you might guess that the tiny orbs in **Figure 46.1** are falling, they are in fact drifting up, not down. Each orb is packed with sperm and eggs, released from the pinkish orange coral polyps that dot the surface of this coral reef. Rising through the seawater, the eggs and sperm reach the surface, break free, and often fuse, forming embryos that become larvae that eventually drift back down to begin new colonies of coral.

As humans, we tend to think of reproduction in terms of the mating of males and females. Animal reproduction, however, takes many forms. There are species that can reproduce without any form of sex and species in which individuals change sex during their lifetime. There are also species, including certain corals, in which individuals have both male and female organs. Some social insects, such as honeybees, display a further variation, with reproduction involving only a few individuals in a large population.

A population outlives its members only by reproduction, the generation of new individuals from existing ones. In this chapter, we'll compare the diverse reproductive mechanisms that have evolved among animals. We'll then examine details of mammalian reproduction, with emphasis on the well-studied example of humans. We'll focus on reproduction mostly from the parents' perspective, deferring the details of embryonic development until the next chapter.

When you see this blue icon, log in to **MasteringBiology** and go to the Study Area for digital resources.

 Get Ready for This Chapter

# CONCEPT 46.1

## Both asexual and sexual reproduction occur in the animal kingdom

There are two modes of animal reproduction—sexual and asexual. In **sexual reproduction**, the fusion of haploid gametes forms a diploid cell, the **zygote**. The animal that develops from a zygote can in turn give rise to gametes by meiosis (see Figure 13.8). The female gamete, the **egg**, is large and nonmotile, whereas the male gamete, the **sperm**, is generally much smaller and motile. In **asexual reproduction**, new individuals are generated without the fusion of egg and sperm. For most asexual animals, reproduction relies entirely on mitotic cell division. Asexual and sexual reproduction are both common among animals.

## Mechanisms of Asexual Reproduction

Among animals, several simple forms of asexual reproduction are found exclusively in invertebrates. One of these is *budding*, in which new individuals arise from outgrowths of existing ones (see Figure 13.2). In stony corals, for example, buds form and remain attached to the parent. The eventual result is a colony more than 1 m across, consisting of thousands of connected individuals. Also common among invertebrates is **fission**, the splitting and separation of a parent organism into two individuals of approximately equal size.

One form of asexual reproduction is a two-step process: *fragmentation*, the breaking of the body into several pieces, followed by *regeneration*, regrowth of lost body parts. If more than one piece grows and develops into a complete animal, the effect is reproduction. For example, certain annelid worms can split into several fragments, each regenerating a complete worm in less than a week. Numerous corals, sponges, cnidarians, and tunicates also reproduce by fragmentation and regeneration.

A particularly intriguing form of asexual reproduction is **parthenogenesis**, in which an egg develops without being fertilized. Among invertebrates, parthenogenesis occurs in certain species of bees, wasps, and ants. The offspring can be either haploid or diploid. In the case of honeybees, males (drones) are fertile haploid adults that arise by parthenogenesis. In contrast, female honeybees, including both the sterile workers and the fertile queens, are diploid adults that develop from fertilized eggs.

Among vertebrates, parthenogenesis is thought to be a rare response to low population density. For example, for both the Komodo dragon and hammerhead shark, zookeepers observed that a female produced offspring when kept apart from males of its species. In 2015, DNA analysis revealed an example of vertebrate parthenogenesis in the wild, a group of female sawfish that were genetically completely identical to one another.

## Variation in Patterns of Sexual Reproduction

In many animal species, including humans, sexual reproduction involves the mating of a female and a male. For many sexual animals, however, finding a partner for reproduction can be challenging. Adaptations that arose during the evolution of some species meet this challenge by blurring the distinction between male and female. One such adaptation is particularly common among sessile (stationary) animals, such as barnacles, burrowing animals, such as clams, and some parasites, including tapeworms. These animals have a very limited opportunity to find a mate. The evolutionary solution in this case is **hermaphroditism**, in which each individual has both male and female reproductive systems (the term *hermaphrodite* merges the names Hermes and Aphrodite, a Greek god and goddess).

Because each hermaphrodite reproduces as both a male and a female, *any* two individuals can mate. Each animal donates and receives sperm during mating, as shown for a pair of sea slugs in **Figure 46.2**. In some species, including many corals, hermaphrodites can also self-fertilize, allowing a form of sexual reproduction that doesn't require any partner.

The bluehead wrasse (*Thalassoma bifasciatum*) provides an example of a quite different variation in sexual reproduction. These coral reef fish live in harems, each consisting of a single male and several females. When the lone male dies, the opportunity for sexual reproduction would appear to be lost. Instead, the largest female in the harem transforms into a male and within a week begins to produce sperm instead of eggs. What selective pressure in the evolution of the bluehead wrasse resulted in sex reversal for the female with the largest body? Because it is the male wrasse that defends a harem against intruders, a larger size may be particularly important for a male in ensuring successful reproduction.

Certain oyster species also undergo sex reversal. In this case, individuals reproduce as males and then later as females, when their size is greatest. Since the number of gametes produced generally increases with size much more for females than for males, sex reversal in this direction maximizes gamete production. The result is enhanced reproductive success: Because oysters are sedentary animals and release their gametes into the surrounding water rather than mating directly, releasing more gametes tends to result in more offspring.

▼ **Figure 46.2 Reproduction among hermaphrodites.** In this mating of sea slugs, or nudibranchs (*Nembrotha chamberlaini*), each hermaphrodite is providing sperm to fertilize the eggs of the other.

## Reproductive Cycles

Most animals, whether asexual or sexual, exhibit cycles in reproductive activity, often related to changing seasons. These cycles are controlled by hormones, whose secretion is in turn regulated by environmental cues. In this way, animals conserve resources, reproducing only when sufficient energy sources are available and when environmental conditions favor the survival of offspring. For example, ewes (female sheep) have a reproductive cycle lasting 15–17 days. **Ovulation**, the release of mature eggs, occurs at the midpoint of each cycle. For ewes, reproductive cycles generally occur only during fall and early winter, and the length of any pregnancy is five months. Thus, most lambs are born in the early spring, when their chances of survival are optimal.

Because seasonal temperature is often an important cue for reproduction, climate change can decrease reproductive success. Researchers have discovered such an effect on caribou (wild reindeer) in Greenland. In spring, caribou migrate to calving grounds to eat sprouting plants, give birth, and care for their calves. Prior to 1993, the arrival of the caribou at the calving grounds coincided with the brief period during which the plants were nutritious and digestible. By 2006, however, average spring temperatures in the calving grounds had increased by more than 4°C, and the plants sprouted two weeks earlier. Because caribou migration is triggered by day length, not temperature, there is a mismatch between the timing of new plant growth and caribou birthing. Without adequate nutrition for the nursing females, production of caribou offspring has declined by 75% since 1993. To learn more about the effects of climate change on caribou and other organisms, see Make Connections Figure 56.29.

Reproductive cycles are also found among animals that can reproduce both sexually and asexually. Consider, for instance, the water flea (genus *Daphnia*). A *Daphnia* female can produce eggs of two types. One type of egg requires fertilization to develop, but the other type does not and develops instead by parthenogenesis. *Daphnia* reproduce asexually when environmental conditions are favorable and sexually during times of environmental stress. As a result, the switch between sexual and asexual reproduction is roughly linked to season.

For some asexual whiptail lizards, a cycle of reproductive behavior appears to reflect a sexual evolutionary past. In these species of the genus *Aspidoscelis*, reproduction is exclusively asexual, and there are no males. Nevertheless, these lizards have courtship and mating behaviors very similar to those of sexual species of *Aspidoscelis*. During the breeding season, one female of each mating pair mimics a male (**Figure 46.3a**). Each member of the pair alternates roles two or three times during the season. An individual adopts female behavior when the level of the hormone estradiol is high, and it switches to male-like behavior when the level of the hormone progesterone is high (**Figure 46.3b**). A female is more likely to ovulate if she is mounted at a critical time of

**▼ Figure 46.3 Sexual behavior in parthenogenetic lizards.** The desert grassland whiptail lizard (*Aspidoscelis uniparens*) is an all-female species. These reptiles reproduce by parthenogenesis, the development of an unfertilized egg, but ovulation is stimulated by mating behavior.

**(a)** Both lizards in this photograph are *A. uniparens* females. The one on top is playing the role of a male. Individuals switch sex roles two or three times during the breeding season.

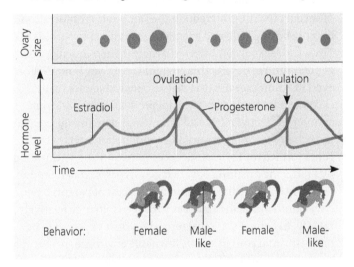

**(b)** The changes in sexual behavior of *A. uniparens* individuals are correlated with the cycles of ovulation and changing levels of the sex hormones estradiol and progesterone. These drawings track the changes in ovary size, hormone levels, and sexual behavior of one female lizard (shown in brown).

**INTERPRET THE DATA ➤** *If you plotted hormone levels for the lizard shown in gray, how would your graph differ from the graph in (b)?*

the hormone cycle; isolated lizards lay fewer eggs than those that go through the motions of sex. These findings support the hypothesis that these parthenogenetic lizards evolved from species having two sexes and still require certain sexual stimuli for maximum reproductive success.

## Sexual Reproduction: An Evolutionary Enigma

**EVOLUTION** Although our species and many others reproduce sexually, the existence of sexual reproduction is actually puzzling. To see why, imagine an animal population in which half the females reproduce sexually and half reproduce asexually. We'll assume that the number of offspring per female is a constant, two in this case. The two offspring of an asexual female will both be daughters that will each give birth

**Figure 46.4 The "reproductive handicap" of sex.** These diagrams contrast asexual versus sexual reproduction over four generations, assuming two surviving offspring per female.

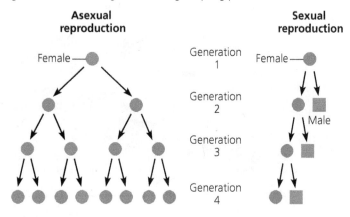

Asexual reproduction        Sexual reproduction

to two more reproductive daughters. In contrast, half of a sexual female's offspring will be male **(Figure 46.4)**. The number of sexual offspring will remain the same at each generation because both a male and a female are required to reproduce. Thus, the asexual condition will increase in frequency at each generation. Yet despite this "twofold cost," sex is maintained even in animal species that can also reproduce asexually.

What advantage does sexual reproduction provide that counteracts its twofold cost? The answer remains elusive. Most hypotheses focus on the unique combinations of parental genes formed during meiotic recombination and fertilization. By producing offspring of varied genotypes, sexual reproduction may enhance the reproductive success of parents when environmental factors, such as pathogens, change relatively rapidly. In contrast, asexual reproduction is expected to be most advantageous in stable, favorable environments because it perpetuates successful genotypes precisely.

There are a number of reasons why the unique gene combinations formed during sexual reproduction might be advantageous. One is that beneficial gene combinations arising through recombination might speed up adaptation. Although this idea appears straightforward, the theoretical advantage is significant only when the rate of beneficial mutations is high and population size is small. Another idea is that the shuffling of genes during sexual reproduction might allow a population to rid itself of sets of harmful genes more readily.

## CONCEPT CHECK 46.1

1. Compare and contrast the outcomes of asexual and sexual reproduction.

2. Parthenogenesis is the most common form of asexual reproduction in animals that at other times reproduce sexually. What characteristic of parthenogenesis might explain this observation?

3. **WHAT IF?** ➤ If a hermaphrodite self-fertilizes, will the offspring be identical to the parent? Explain.

4. **MAKE CONNECTIONS** ➤ What examples of plant reproduction are most similar to asexual reproduction in animals? (See Concept 38.2.)

*For suggested answers, see Appendix A.*

# CONCEPT 46.2

## Fertilization depends on mechanisms that bring together sperm and eggs of the same species

The union of sperm and egg—**fertilization**—can be external or internal. In species with *external fertilization*, the female releases eggs into the environment, where the male then fertilizes them **(Figure 46.5)**. In species with *internal fertilization*, sperm deposited in or near the female reproductive tract fertilize eggs within the tract. (We'll discuss cellular and molecular details of fertilization in Concept 47.1.)

A moist habitat is almost always required for external fertilization, both to prevent the gametes from drying out and to allow the sperm to swim to the eggs. Many aquatic invertebrates simply shed their eggs and sperm into the surroundings, and fertilization occurs without the parents making physical contact. However, timing is crucial to ensure that mature sperm and eggs encounter one another.

Among some species with external fertilization, individuals clustered in the same area release their gametes into the water at the same time, a process known as *spawning*. In some cases, chemical signals that one individual generates in releasing gametes trigger others to release gametes. In other cases, environmental cues, such as temperature or day length, cause a whole population to release gametes at one time. For example, the palolo worm of the South Pacific, like the coral in Figure 46.1, times its spawning to both the season and the lunar cycle. In spring, when the moon is in its last quarter, palolo worms break in half, releasing tail segments engorged with sperm or eggs. These packets rise

**Figure 46.5 External fertilization.** Many species of amphibians reproduce by external fertilization. In most of these species, behavioral adaptations ensure that a male is present when the female releases eggs. Here, a female frog (on bottom) has released a mass of eggs in response to being clasped by a male. The male released sperm (not visible) at the same time, and external fertilization has already occurred in the water.

to the ocean surface and burst in such vast numbers that the sea appears milky with gametes. The sperm quickly fertilize the floating eggs, and within hours the palolo's once-a-year reproductive frenzy is complete.

When external fertilization is not synchronous across a population, individuals may exhibit specific "courtship" behaviors leading to the fertilization of the eggs of one female by one male (see Figure 46.5). By triggering the release of both sperm and eggs, these behaviors increase the probability of successful fertilization.

Internal fertilization is an adaptation that enables sperm to reach an egg even when the external environment is dry. It typically requires sophisticated and compatible reproductive systems, as well as cooperative behavior that leads to copulation. The male copulatory organ delivers sperm, and the female reproductive tract often has receptacles for storage and delivery of sperm to mature eggs.

No matter how fertilization occurs, the mating animals may make use of *pheromones*, chemicals released by one organism that can influence the physiology and behavior of other individuals of the same species. Pheromones are small, volatile or water-soluble molecules that disperse into the environment and, like hormones, are active at very low concentrations (see Concept 45.1). Many pheromones function as mate attractants, enabling some female insects to be detected by males more than a kilometer away.

Evidence for human pheromones remains controversial. It was once argued that female roommates produce pheromones that trigger synchrony in menstrual cycles, but further statistical analyses have failed to support this finding.

## Ensuring the Survival of Offspring

Typically, animals that fertilize eggs internally produce fewer gametes than species with external fertilization, but a higher fraction of their zygotes survive. Better zygote survival is due in part to the fact that eggs fertilized internally are sheltered from potential predators. However, internal fertilization is also more often associated with mechanisms that provide greater protection of the embryos and parental care of the young. For example, the internally fertilized eggs of birds and other reptiles have shells and internal membranes that protect against water loss and physical damage during the eggs' external development (see Figure 34.26). In contrast, the eggs of fishes and amphibians have only a gelatinous coat and lack internal membranes.

Rather than secreting a protective eggshell, some animals retain the embryo for a portion of its development within the female's reproductive tract. The offspring of marsupial mammals, such as kangaroos and opossums, spend only a short period in the uterus as embryos; they then crawl out and complete development attached to a mammary gland in the mother's pouch. Embryos of eutherian (placental) mammals, such as sheep and humans, remain in the uterus throughout fetal development. There they are nourished by the mother's

**Figure 46.6 Parental care in an invertebrate.** Compared with many other insects, giant water bugs of the genus *Belostoma* produce relatively few offspring but offer much greater parental protection. Following internal fertilization, the female glues her fertilized eggs to the back of the male. The male (shown here) carries the eggs for days, frequently fanning water over them to keep them moist, aerated, and free of parasites.

blood supply through a temporary organ, the placenta. The embryos of some fishes and sharks also complete development internally.

When a caribou or kangaroo is born or when a baby eagle hatches out of an egg, the newborn is not yet capable of independent existence. Instead, mammals nurse their offspring, and adult birds feed their young. Examples of parental care are in fact widespread among animals, including some invertebrates **(Figure 46.6)**.

## Gamete Production and Delivery

Sexual reproduction in animals relies on sets of cells that are precursors for eggs and sperm. Cells dedicated to this function are often established early in the formation of the embryo and remain inactive while the body plan takes shape. Cycles of growth and mitosis then increase the number of cells available for making eggs or sperm.

In producing gametes from the precursor cells and making them available for fertilization, animals employ a variety of reproductive systems. **Gonads**, organs that produce gametes, are found in many but not all animals. Exceptions include the palolo, discussed above. The palolo and most other polychaete worms (phylum Annelida) have separate sexes but lack distinct gonads; rather, the eggs and sperm develop from undifferentiated cells lining the coelom (body cavity). As the gametes mature, they are released from the body wall and fill the coelom. Depending on the species, mature gametes in these worms may be shed through the excretory opening, or the swelling mass of eggs may split a portion of the body open, spilling the eggs into the environment.

More elaborate reproductive systems include sets of accessory tubes and glands that carry, nourish, and protect the gametes and sometimes the developing embryos. For example, fruit flies and most other insects have separate sexes with complex reproductive systems (**Figure 46.7**). In many insect species, the female reproductive system includes one or more **spermathecae** (singular, *spermatheca*), sacs in which sperm may be kept alive for extended periods, a year or more in some species. Because the female releases male gametes from the spermathecae and thus fertilizes her eggs only in response to the appropriate stimuli, fertilization occurs under conditions likely to be well suited to survival of offspring.

Vertebrate reproductive systems display limited but significant variations. In some vertebrates, the uterus is divided into two chambers; in others, including humans and birds, it is a single structure. In many nonmammalian vertebrates, the digestive, excretory, and reproductive systems have a common opening to the outside, the **cloaca**, a structure probably present in the ancestors of all vertebrates. Lacking a well-developed penis, males of these species instead release sperm by turning the cloaca inside out. In contrast, mammals generally lack a cloaca and have a separate opening for the digestive tract. In addition, most female mammals have separate openings for the excretory and reproductive systems.

Although fertilization involves the union of a single egg and sperm, animals often mate with more than one member of the other sex. Monogamy, the sustained sexual partnership of two individuals, is rare among animals, including most mammals. Mechanisms have evolved, however, that enhance the reproductive success of a male with a particular female and diminish the chance of that female mating successfully with another partner. For example, some male insects transfer secretions that make a female less receptive to courtship, reducing the likelihood of her mating again.

Can females also influence the relative reproductive success of their mates? This question intrigued two scientific collaborators working in Europe. Studying female fruit flies that copulated with one male and then another, the researchers traced the fate of sperm transferred in the first mating. As shown in **Figure 46.8**, females play a major role

▼ **Figure 46.7 An example of insect reproductive anatomy.** The circled numbers indicate sequences of sperm and egg movement.

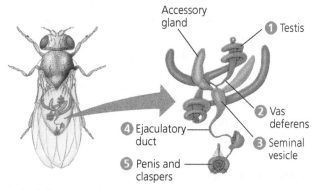

Accessory gland

**1** Testis

**2** Vas deferens

**4** Ejaculatory duct

**3** Seminal vesicle

**5** Penis and claspers

**(a) Male fruit fly.** Sperm form in the testes, pass through a sperm duct (vas deferens), and are stored in the seminal vesicles. The male ejaculates sperm along with fluid from the accessory glands. (Males of some species of insects and other arthropods have appendages called claspers that grasp the female during copulation.)

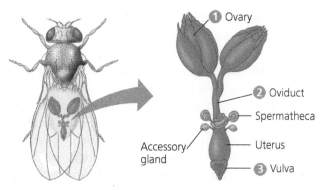

**1** Ovary

**2** Oviduct

Spermatheca

Accessory gland

Uterus

**3** Vulva

**(b) Female fruit fly.** Eggs develop in the ovaries and then travel through the oviducts to the uterus. After mating, sperm are stored in the spermathecae, which are connected to the uterus by short ducts. The female uses a stored sperm to fertilize each egg as it enters the uterus before she passes the egg out through the vulva.

**VISUAL SKILLS** ➤ *Study the two drawings and then describe the movement of fruit fly sperm from formation to fertilization.*

▼ **Figure 46.8**

**Inquiry** **Why is sperm usage biased when female fruit flies mate twice?**

**Experiment** When a female fruit fly mates twice, 80% of the offspring result from the second mating. Scientists had hypothesized that ejaculate from the second mating displaces sperm from the first mating. To test this hypothesis, Rhonda Snook, at the University of Sheffield, and David Hosken, at the University of Zurich, used mutant males with altered reproductive systems. "No-ejaculate" males mate but do not transfer sperm or fluid to females. "No-sperm" males mate and ejaculate but make no sperm. The researchers allowed females to mate first with wild-type males and then with wild-type males, no-sperm males, or no-ejaculate males. As a control, some females were mated only once (to wild-type males). The scientists then dissected each female under a microscope and recorded whether sperm were absent from the spermathecae, the major sperm storage organs.

**Results**

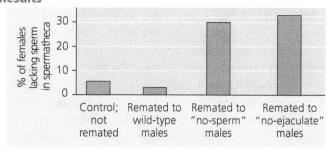

**Conclusion** Because remating reduces sperm storage when no sperm or fluids are transferred, the hypothesis that ejaculate from a second mating displaces stored sperm is incorrect. Instead, it appears females may get rid of stored sperm in response to remating, perhaps allowing for replacing stored sperm, possibly of diminished fitness, with fresh sperm.

**Data from** R. R. Snook and D. J. Hosken, Sperm death and dumping in *Drosophila*, *Nature* 428:939–941 (2004).

**WHAT IF?** ➤ *Suppose males in the first mating had a mutant allele that resulted in smaller eyes as a dominant trait (see Concept 14.1). What fraction of the females would produce some offspring with smaller eyes?*

in determining the outcome of multiple matings. The processes by which gametes and individuals compete during reproduction remain a vibrant research area.

## CONCEPT CHECK 46.2

1. How does internal fertilization facilitate life on land?
2. What mechanisms have evolved in animals with (a) external fertilization and (b) internal fertilization that help offspring survive to adulthood?
3. **MAKE CONNECTIONS** ➤ What are the shared and distinct functions of the uterus of an insect and the ovary of a flowering plant? (See Figure 38.6.)

*For suggested answers, see Appendix A.*

a *testicle*). In many rodents, the testes are drawn back into the cavity between breeding seasons, interrupting sperm maturation. Some mammals whose body temperature is low enough to allow sperm maturation—such as whales and elephants—retain the testes in the abdominal cavity at all times.

### Ducts

From the seminiferous tubules of a testis, the sperm pass into the coiled duct of an **epididymis**. In humans, it takes 3 weeks for sperm to travel the 6-m length of this duct, during which time the sperm complete maturation and become motile. During **ejaculation**, the sperm are propelled from each epididymis through a muscular duct, the **vas deferens**.

# CONCEPT 46.3

## Reproductive organs produce and transport gametes

Having surveyed some of the general features of animal reproduction, we'll focus in the rest of the chapter on humans, beginning with the reproductive anatomy of each sex.

## Human Male Reproductive Anatomy

The human male's external reproductive organs are the scrotum and penis. The internal reproductive organs consist of gonads that produce both sperm and reproductive hormones, accessory glands that secrete products essential to sperm movement, and ducts that carry the sperm and glandular secretions **(Figure 46.9)**.

### Testes

The male gonads, or **testes** (singular, *testis*), produce sperm in highly coiled tubes called **seminiferous tubules**. Most mammals produce sperm properly only when the testes are cooler than the rest of the body. In humans and many other mammals, testis temperature is maintained about 2°C below the core body temperature by the **scrotum**, a fold of the body wall.

The testes develop in the abdominal cavity and descend into the scrotum just before birth (a testis within a scrotum is

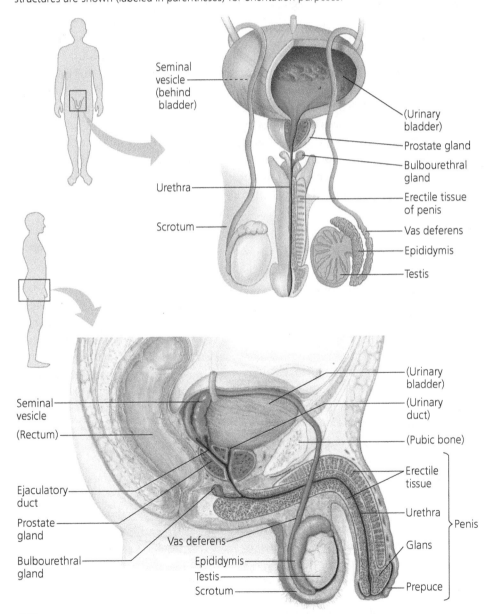

**▼ Figure 46.9 Reproductive anatomy of the human male.** Some nonreproductive structures are shown (labeled in parentheses) for orientation purposes.

Seminal vesicle (behind bladder)
(Urinary bladder)
Prostate gland
Bulbourethral gland
Urethra
Erectile tissue of penis
Scrotum
Vas deferens
Epididymis
Testis

(Urinary bladder)
(Urinary duct)
Seminal vesicle
(Rectum)
(Pubic bone)
Ejaculatory duct
Erectile tissue
Prostate gland
Urethra
Vas deferens
Penis
Glans
Bulbourethral gland
Epididymis
Testis
Scrotum
Prepuce

 Animation: Reproductive System of the Human Male

Each vas deferens (one from each epididymis) extends around and behind the urinary bladder, where it joins a duct from the seminal vesicle, forming a short *ejaculatory duct*. The ejaculatory ducts open into the **urethra**, the outlet tube for both the excretory system and the reproductive system. The urethra runs through the penis and opens to the outside at the tip of the penis.

### Accessory Glands

Three sets of accessory glands—the seminal vesicles, the prostate gland, and the bulbourethral glands—produce secretions that combine with sperm to form **semen**, the fluid that is ejaculated. Two **seminal vesicles** contribute about 60% of the volume of semen. The fluid from the seminal vesicles is thick, yellowish, and alkaline. It contains mucus, the sugar fructose (which provides most of the sperm's energy), a coagulating enzyme, ascorbic acid, and local regulators called prostaglandins (see Concept 45.1).

The **prostate gland** secretes its products directly into the urethra through small ducts. Thin and milky, the fluid from this gland contains anticoagulant enzymes and citrate (a sperm nutrient). The *bulbourethral glands* are a pair of small glands along the urethra below the prostate. Before ejaculation, they secrete clear mucus that neutralizes any acidic urine remaining in the urethra. There is evidence that bulbourethral fluid carries some sperm released before ejaculation, which may contribute to the high failure rate of the withdrawal method of birth control (coitus interruptus).

### Penis

The human **penis** contains the urethra as well as three cylinders of spongy erectile tissue. During sexual arousal, the erectile tissue fills with blood from the arteries. As this tissue fills, the increasing pressure seals off the veins that drain the penis, causing it to engorge with blood. The resulting erection enables the penis to be inserted into the vagina. Alcohol consumption, certain drugs, emotional issues, and aging all can cause an inability to achieve an erection (erectile dysfunction). For individuals with long-term erectile dysfunction, drugs such as Viagra promote the vasodilating action of the local regulator nitric oxide (NO; see Concept 45.1); the resulting relaxation of smooth muscles in the blood vessels of the penis enhances blood flow into the erectile tissues. Although all mammals rely on penile erection for mating, the penis of dogs, raccoons, walruses, and several other mammals also contains a bone, the baculum, which is thought to further stiffen the penis for mating.

The main shaft of the penis is covered by relatively thick skin. The head, or **glans**, of the penis has a much thinner outer layer and is consequently more sensitive to stimulation. The human glans is surrounded by a fold of skin called the **prepuce**, or foreskin, which is removed if a male is circumcised.

## Human Female Reproductive Anatomy

The human female's external reproductive structures are the clitoris and two sets of labia, which surround the clitoris and vaginal opening. The internal organs consist of gonads, which produce eggs and reproductive hormones, and a system of ducts and chambers, which receive and carry gametes and house the embryo and fetus **(Figure 46.10)**.

### Ovaries

The female gonads are a pair of **ovaries** that flank the uterus and are held in place in the abdominal cavity by ligaments. The outer layer of each ovary is packed with **follicles**, each consisting of an **oocyte**, a partially developed egg, surrounded by support cells. The surrounding cells nourish and protect the oocyte during much of its formation and development.

### Oviducts and Uterus

An **oviduct**, or fallopian tube, extends from the uterus toward a funnel-like opening at each ovary. The dimensions of this tube vary along its length, with the inside diameter near the uterus being as narrow as a human hair. Upon ovulation, cilia on the epithelial lining of the oviduct help collect the egg by drawing fluid from the body cavity into the oviduct. Together with wavelike contractions of the oviduct, the cilia convey the egg down the duct to the **uterus**, also known as the womb. The uterus is a thick, muscular organ that can expand during pregnancy to accommodate a 4-kg fetus. The inner lining of the uterus, the **endometrium**, is richly supplied with blood vessels. The neck of the uterus, called the **cervix**, opens into the vagina.

### Vagina and Vulva

The **vagina** is a muscular but elastic chamber that is the site for insertion of the penis and deposition of sperm during copulation. The vagina, which also serves as the birth canal through which a baby is born, opens to the outside at the **vulva**, the collective term for the external female genitalia.

A pair of thick, fatty ridges called the **labia majora** enclose and protect the rest of the vulva. The vaginal opening and the separate opening of the urethra are located within a cavity bordered by a pair of slender skin folds, the **labia minora**. A thin piece of tissue called the *hymen* partly covers the vaginal opening in humans at birth, but becomes thinner over time and typically wears away through physical activity. Located at the top of the labia minora, the **clitoris** consists of erectile tissue supporting a rounded glans, or head, covered by a small hood of skin, the prepuce. During sexual arousal, the clitoris, vagina, and labia minora all engorge with blood and enlarge. Richly supplied with nerve endings, the clitoris is one of the most sensitive points of sexual stimulation. Sexual arousal also induces the vestibular glands near the vaginal opening to secrete lubricating mucus, thereby facilitating intercourse.

## ▼ Figure 46.10 Reproductive anatomy of the human female.
Some nonreproductive structures are shown (labeled in parentheses) for orientation purposes.

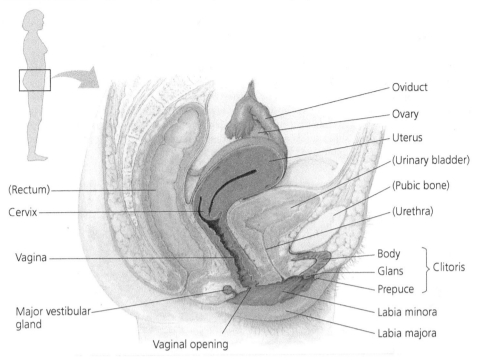

Oviduct
Ovary
Uterus
(Urinary bladder)
(Pubic bone)
(Urethra)
(Rectum)
Cervix
Vagina
Body
Glans
Prepuce } Clitoris
Major vestibular gland
Labia minora
Labia majora
Vaginal opening

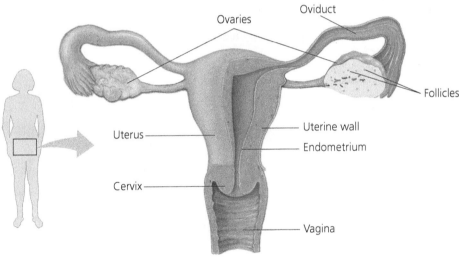

Ovaries
Oviduct
Uterus
Cervix
Vagina
Follicles
Uterine wall
Endometrium

 Animation: Reproductive System of the Human Female

### Mammary Glands

The **mammary glands** are present in both sexes, but they normally produce milk only in females. Though not part of the reproductive system, the female mammary glands are important to reproduction. Within the glands, small sacs of epithelial tissue secrete milk, which drains into a series of ducts that open at the nipple. The breasts contain connective and fatty (adipose) tissue in addition to the mammary glands.

## Gametogenesis

With this overview of anatomy in mind, we turn to **gametogenesis**, which is the production of gametes.

Figure 46.11 explores this process in human males and females, highlighting the close relationship between gonadal structure and function.

**Spermatogenesis**, the formation and development of sperm, is continuous and prolific in adult human males. Cell division and maturation occur throughout the seminiferous tubules coiled within the two testes, producing hundreds of millions of sperm each day. For a single sperm, the process takes about seven weeks from start to finish.

**Oogenesis**, the development of mature oocytes (eggs), is a prolonged process in the human female. Immature eggs form in the ovary of the female embryo but do not complete their development until years, and often decades, later.

Spermatogenesis and oogenesis differ in three significant ways:

- Only in spermatogenesis do all four products of meiosis develop into mature gametes. In oogenesis, cytokinesis during meiosis is unequal, with almost all the cytoplasm segregated to a single daughter cell. This large cell is destined to become the egg; the other products of meiosis, smaller cells known as polar bodies, degenerate.
- Spermatogenesis occurs throughout adolescence and adulthood. In contrast, the mitotic divisions that occur in oogenesis in human females are thought to be complete before birth, and the production of mature gametes ceases at about age 50.
- Spermatogenesis produces mature sperm from precursor cells in a continuous sequence, whereas there are long interruptions in oogenesis.

### CONCEPT CHECK 46.3

1. Why might frequent use of a hot tub make it harder for a couple to conceive a child?
2. The process of oogenesis is often described as the production of a haploid egg by meiosis, but in some animals, including humans, this description is not entirely accurate. Explain.
3. **WHAT IF?** ➤ If each vas deferens in a male was surgically sealed off, what changes would you expect in sexual response and ejaculate composition?

*For suggested answers, see Appendix A.*

## Spermatogenesis

Stem cells that give rise to sperm are situated near the outer edge of the seminiferous tubules. Their progeny move inward as they pass through the spermatocyte and spermatid stages, and sperm are released into the lumen (fluid-filled cavity) of the tubule. The sperm travel along the tubule into the epididymis, where they become motile.

(MB) Animation: Human Spermatogensis

The stem cells arise from division and differentiation of primordial germ cells in the embryonic testes. In mature testes, they divide mitotically to form **spermatogonia**, which in turn generate spermatocytes by mitosis. (Only a single product of each set of mitoses is shown below.) Each spermatocyte gives rise to four spermatids through meiosis, reducing the chromosome number from diploid ($2n = 46$ in humans) to haploid ($n = 23$). Spermatids undergo extensive changes in differentiating into sperm.

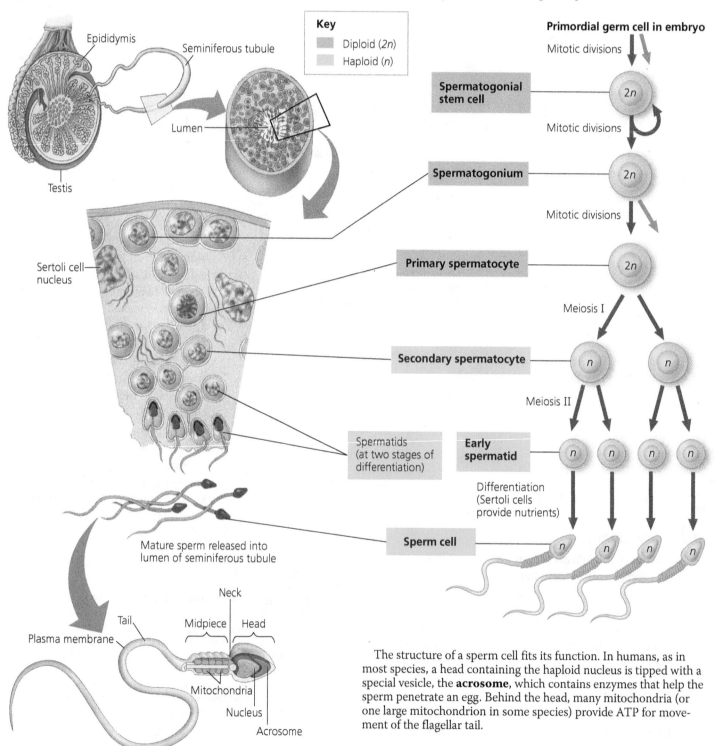

The structure of a sperm cell fits its function. In humans, as in most species, a head containing the haploid nucleus is tipped with a special vesicle, the **acrosome**, which contains enzymes that help the sperm penetrate an egg. Behind the head, many mitochondria (or one large mitochondrion in some species) provide ATP for movement of the flagellar tail.

## Oogenesis

Oogenesis begins in the female embryo with the production of **oogonia** from primordial germ cells. (Only a single product of each set of mitoses is shown below.) The oogonia divide by mitosis to form cells that begin meiosis, but stop the process at prophase I before birth. These developmentally arrested cells, which are **primary oocytes**, each reside within a small follicle, a cavity lined with protective cells. At birth, the ovaries together contain about 1–2 million primary oocytes, of which about 500 fully mature between puberty and menopause.

MB **Animation: Human Oogensis**

To the best of our current knowledge, women are born with all the primary oocytes they will ever have. It is worth noting, however, that a similar conclusion regarding most other mammals was overturned in 2004 when researchers discovered that the ovaries of adult mice contain multiplying oogonia that develop into oocytes. If the same turned out to be true of humans, it might be that the marked decline in fertility that occurs as women age results from both a depletion of oogonia and the degeneration of aging oocytes.

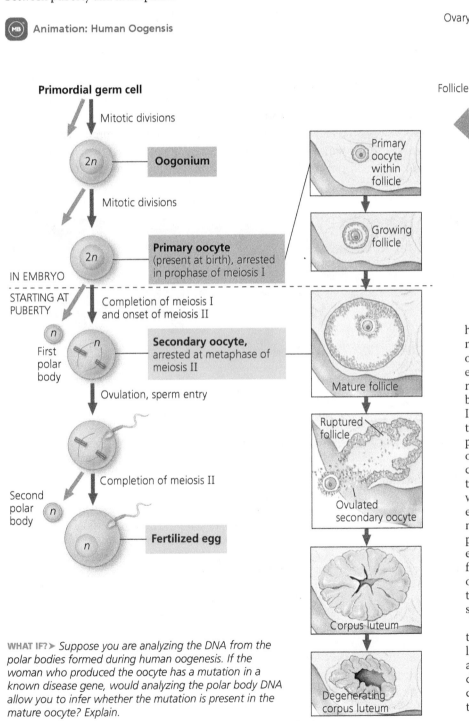

Beginning at puberty, follicle-stimulating hormone (FSH) periodically stimulates a small number of follicles to resume growth and development. Typically, only one follicle fully matures each month, with its primary oocyte completing meiosis I. The second meiotic division begins, but stops at metaphase. Thus arrested in meiosis II, the **secondary oocyte** is released at ovulation, when its follicle breaks open. Only if a sperm penetrates the oocyte does meiosis II resume. (In other animal species, the sperm may enter the oocyte at the same stage, earlier, or later.) Each of the two meiotic divisions involves unequal cytokinesis, with the smaller cells becoming polar bodies that eventually degenerate (the first polar body may or may not divide again). As a result, the functional product of complete oogenesis is a single mature egg containing a sperm head. Fertilization is defined strictly as the fusion of the haploid nuclei of the sperm and secondary oocyte, although the term is often used loosely to mean the entry of the sperm head into the egg.

The ruptured follicle left behind after ovulation develops into the **corpus luteum**. The corpus luteum secretes estradiol as well as progesterone, a hormone that helps maintain the uterine lining during pregnancy. If the egg is not fertilized, the corpus luteum degenerates, and a new follicle matures during the next cycle

**WHAT IF?** ► *Suppose you are analyzing the DNA from the polar bodies formed during human oogenesis. If the woman who produced the oocyte has a mutation in a known disease gene, would analyzing the polar body DNA allow you to infer whether the mutation is present in the mature oocyte? Explain.*

# CONCEPT 46.4

## The interplay of tropic and sex hormones regulates reproduction in mammals

Mammalian reproduction is governed by the coordinated actions of hormones from the hypothalamus, anterior pituitary, and gonads. Endocrine control of reproduction begins with the hypothalamus, which secretes *gonadotropin-releasing hormone* (GnRH). This hormone directs the anterior pituitary to secrete the gonadotropins **follicle-stimulating hormone (FSH)** and **luteinizing hormone (LH)** (see Figure 45.15). Both are tropic hormones, meaning that they regulate the activity of endocrine cells or glands. They are called *gonadotropins* because they act on the male and female gonads. FSH and LH support gametogenesis, in part by stimulating sex hormone production by the gonads.

The gonads produce and secrete three major types of steroid sex hormones: *androgens*, principally **testosterone**; *estrogens*, principally **estradiol**; and **progesterone**. All three hormones are found in both males and females, but at quite different concentrations. Testosterone levels in the blood are roughly ten times higher in males than in females. In contrast, estradiol levels are about ten times higher in females than in males; peak progesterone levels are also much higher in females. Although the gonads are the major source of sex hormones, the adrenal glands also secrete sex hormones in small amounts.

In mammals, sex hormone function in reproduction begins in the embryo. In particular, androgens produced in male embryos direct the appearance of the primary sex characteristics of males, the structures directly involved in reproduction. These include the seminal vesicles and associated ducts, as well as external reproductive structures. In the **Scientific Skills Exercise**, you can interpret the results of an experiment investigating the development of reproductive structures in mammals.

During sexual maturation, sex hormones in human males and females induce formation of secondary sex characteristics, the physical and behavioral differences between males and females that are not directly related to the reproductive system. Secondary sex characteristics often lead to sexual dimorphism, the difference in appearance between the male and

---

## SCIENTIFIC SKILLS EXERCISE

### Making Inferences and Designing an Experiment

**What Role Do Hormones Play in Making a Mammal Male or Female?** In non-egg-laying mammals, females have two X chromosomes, whereas males have one X chromosome and one Y chromosome. In the 1940s, French physiologist Alfred Jost wondered whether development of mammalian embryos as female or male in accord with their chromosome set requires instructions in the form of hormones produced by the gonads. In this exercise, you will interpret the results of an experiment that Jost performed to answer this question.

**How the Experiment Was Done** Working with rabbit embryos still in the mother's uterus at a stage before sex differences are observable, Jost surgically removed the portion of each embryo that would form the ovaries or testes. When the baby rabbits were born, he made note of their chromosomal sex and whether their genital structures were male or female.

**Data from the Experiment**

| | Appearance of Genitalia | |
|---|---|---|
| Chromosome Set | No Surgery | Embryonic Gonad Removed |
| XY (male) | Male | Female |
| XX (female) | Female | Female |

**Data from** A. Jost, Recherches sur la differenciation sexuelle de l'embryon de lapin (Studies on the sexual differentiation of the rabbit embryo), *Archives d'Anatomie Microscopique et de Morphologie Experimentale* 36:271–316 (1947).

**INTERPRET THE DATA**

1. This experiment is an example of a research approach in which scientists infer how something works normally based on what happens when the normal process is blocked. What normal process was blocked in Jost's experiment? From the results, what inference can you make about the role of the gonads in controlling the development of mammalian genitalia?

2. The data in Jost's experiment could be explained if some aspect of the surgery other than gonad removal caused female genitalia to develop. If you were to repeat Jost's experiment, how might you test the validity of such an explanation?

3. What result would Jost have obtained if female development also required a signal from the gonad?

4. Design another experiment to determine whether the signal that controls male development is a hormone. Make sure to identify your hypothesis, prediction, data collection plan, and controls.

 **Instructors**: A version of this Scientific Skills Exercise can be assigned in MasteringBiology.

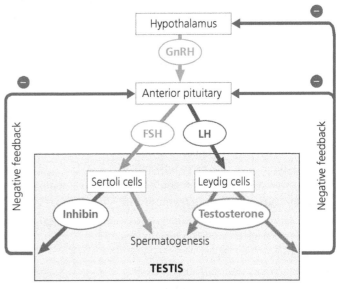

Animation: Hormonal Control of the Testes

female adults of a species **(Figure 46.12)**. When human males enter puberty, androgens cause the voice to deepen, facial and pubic hair to develop, and muscles to grow (by stimulating protein synthesis). Androgens also promote specific sexual behaviors and sex drive, as well as an increase in general aggressiveness. Estrogens similarly have multiple effects in females. At puberty, estradiol stimulates breast and pubic hair development. Estradiol also influences female sexual behavior, induces fat deposition in the breasts and hips, increases water retention, and alters calcium metabolism.

When mammals reach sexual maturity, the sex hormones and gonadotropins have essential roles in gametogenesis. In exploring this hormonal control of reproduction, we'll begin with the relatively simple system found in males.

## Hormonal Control of the Male Reproductive System

In directing spermatogenesis, FSH and LH act on two types of cells in the testis **(Figure 46.13)**. FSH stimulates *Sertoli cells*, located within the seminiferous tubules, to nourish developing sperm (see Figure 46.11). LH causes *Leydig cells*, scattered in connective tissue between the tubules, to produce testosterone and other androgens, which promote spermatogenesis in the tubules.

Two negative-feedback mechanisms control sex hormone production in males (see Figure 46.13). Testosterone regulates blood levels of GnRH, FSH, and LH through inhibitory effects on the hypothalamus and anterior pituitary. In addition, *inhibin*, a hormone that in males is produced by Sertoli cells, acts on the anterior pituitary gland to reduce FSH secretion. Together, these negative-feedback circuits maintain androgen levels in the normal range.

Leydig cells have other roles besides producing testosterone. They in fact secrete small quantities of many other hormones

and local regulators, including oxytocin, renin, angiotensin, corticotropin-releasing factor, growth factors, and prostaglandins. These signals coordinate the activity of reproduction with growth, metabolism, homeostasis, and behavior.

## Hormonal Control of Female Reproductive Cycles

Whereas sperm are produced continuously in human males, there are two closely linked reproductive cycles in human females. Both are controlled by cyclic patterns of endocrine signaling.

Cyclic events in the ovaries define the **ovarian cycle**: Once per cycle a follicle matures and an oocyte is released. Changes in the uterus define the **uterine cycle**, which in humans and some other primates is a menstrual cycle. In each **menstrual cycle**, the endometrium (lining of the uterus) thickens and develops a rich blood supply before being shed through the cervix and vagina if pregnancy does not occur. By linking the ovarian and uterine cycles, hormone activity synchronizes ovulation with the establishment of a uterine lining that can support embryo implantation and development.

If an oocyte is not fertilized and pregnancy does not occur, the uterine lining is sloughed off, and another pair of ovarian and uterine cycles begins. The cyclic shedding of the blood-rich endometrium from the uterus, a process that occurs in a flow through the cervix and vagina, is called **menstruation**. Menstrual cycles average 28 days but can range from about 20 to 40 days.

**Figure 46.14** outlines the major events of the female reproductive cycles, illustrating the close coordination across different tissues in the body.

## The Ovarian Cycle

In human females, as in males, the hypothalamus has a central role in regulating reproduction. The ovarian cycle begins ❶ when the hypothalamus releases GnRH, which stimulates the anterior pituitary to ❷ secrete small amounts of FSH and LH. ❸ Follicle-stimulating hormone stimulates follicle growth, aided by LH, and ❹ the follicles start to make estradiol. Estradiol concentration slowly rises during most of the *follicular phase*, when follicles grow and oocytes mature. (Several follicles begin to grow with each cycle, but usually only one matures; the others disintegrate.) Low levels of estradiol inhibit secretion of pituitary hormones, keeping levels of FSH and LH relatively low. In this portion of the cycle, regulation of hormones closely parallels the regulation in males.

❺ When estradiol secretion by the follicle begins to rise steeply, ❻ the FSH and LH levels increase markedly. Why? Whereas a low level of estradiol inhibits secretion of pituitary gonadotropins, a high concentration has the opposite effect: It stimulates gonadotropin secretion by causing the hypothalamus to increase output of GnRH. A high estradiol concentration also increases the GnRH sensitivity of LH-releasing cells in the pituitary, further increasing LH levels.

❼ The maturing follicle, containing a fluid-filled cavity, enlarges to form a bulge at the surface of the ovary. The follicular phase ends at ovulation, about a day after the LH surge. In response to FSH and the peak in LH level, the follicle and adjacent wall of the ovary rupture, releasing the secondary oocyte. At or near the time of ovulation, women may feel a pain in the lower abdomen, on the same side as the ovary that released the oocyte.

The *luteal phase* follows ovulation. ❽ Luteinizing hormone stimulates the remaining follicular tissue to form the corpus luteum, a glandular structure. Stimulated by LH, the corpus luteum secretes progesterone and estradiol, which in combination exert negative feedback on the hypothalamus and

▼ **Figure 46.14 The reproductive cycles of the human female.** This figure shows how **(c)** the ovarian cycle and **(e)** the uterine (menstrual) cycle are regulated by changing hormone levels in the blood, depicted in parts **(a)**, **(b)**, and **(d)**. The time scale at the bottom of the figure applies to parts **(b)–(e)**.

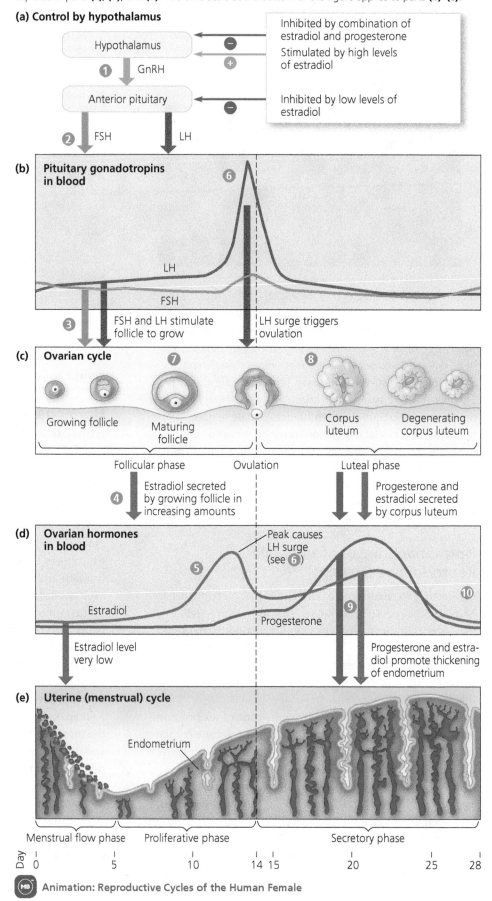

**Animation: Reproductive Cycles of the Human Female**

pituitary. This feedback greatly reduces LH and FSH secretion, preventing maturation of another egg when a pregnancy may be under way.

If pregnancy does not occur, low gonadotropin levels at the end of the luteal phase cause the corpus luteum to disintegrate, triggering a sharp decline in estradiol and progesterone concentrations. This decline liberates the hypothalamus and pituitary from negative feedback. The pituitary can then secrete enough FSH to stimulate the growth of new follicles, initiating the next ovarian cycle.

### The Uterine (Menstrual) Cycle

Prior to ovulation, ovarian steroid hormones stimulate the uterus to prepare for support of an embryo. Estradiol secreted in increasing amounts by growing follicles signals the endometrium to thicken. In this way, the follicular phase of the ovarian cycle is coordinated with the *proliferative phase* of the uterine cycle. After ovulation, ⑨ the estradiol and progesterone secreted by the corpus luteum stimulate maintenance and further development of the uterine lining, including enlargement of arteries and growth of endometrial glands. These glands secrete a nutrient fluid that can sustain an early embryo even before it implants in the uterine lining. Thus, the luteal phase of the ovarian cycle is coordinated with the *secretory phase* of the uterine cycle.

If an embryo has not implanted in the endometrium by the end of the secretory phase, the corpus luteum disintegrates. The resulting drop ⑩ in ovarian hormone levels causes arteries in the endometrium to constrict. Deprived of its circulation, the uterine lining largely disintegrates, releasing blood that is shed along with endometrial tissue and fluid. The result is menstruation—the *menstrual flow phase* of the uterine cycle. During this phase, which usually lasts a few days, a new set of ovarian follicles begin to grow. By convention, the first day of flow is designated day 1 of the new uterine (and ovarian) cycle.

About 7% of women of reproductive age suffer from a disorder called **endometriosis**, in which some cells of the uterine lining migrate to an abdominal location that is abnormal, or **ectopic** (from the Greek *ektopos*, away from a place). Having migrated to a location such as an oviduct, ovary, or large intestine, the ectopic tissue responds to hormones in the bloodstream. Like the uterine endometrium, the ectopic tissue swells and breaks down during each ovarian cycle, resulting in pelvic pain and bleeding into the abdomen. Researchers have not yet determined why endometriosis occurs, but hormonal therapy or surgery can be used to lessen discomfort.

### Menopause

After about 500 cycles, a woman undergoes **menopause**, the cessation of ovulation and menstruation. Menopause usually occurs between the ages of 46 and 54. During this interval, the ovaries lose their responsiveness to FSH and LH, resulting in a decline in estradiol production.

Menopause is an unusual phenomenon. In most other species, females and males can reproduce throughout life. Is there an evolutionary explanation for menopause? One intriguing hypothesis proposes that during early human evolution, undergoing menopause after bearing several children allowed a mother to provide better care for her children and grandchildren, thereby increasing the chances for survival of individuals who share much of her genetic makeup.

### Menstrual Versus Estrous Cycles

In all female mammals, the endometrium thickens before ovulation, but only humans and some other primates have menstrual cycles. In other mammals, both domesticated and wild, the uterus reabsorbs the endometrium in the absence of a pregnancy, and no extensive fluid flow occurs. For these animals, the cyclic changes in the uterus occur as part of an **estrous cycle** that also controls the sexual receptivity of females: Whereas human females may engage in sexual activity throughout the menstrual cycle, mammals with estrous cycles usually copulate only during the period surrounding ovulation. This period, called estrus (from the Latin *oestrus*, frenzy, passion), is the only time the female is receptive to mating. It is often called "heat," and the female's temperature does increase slightly.

The length, frequency, and nature of estrous cycles vary widely among mammals. Bears and wolves have one estrous cycle per year; elephants have several. Rats have estrous cycles throughout the year, each lasting just five days. Their nemesis, the household cat, ovulates only upon mating.

## Human Sexual Response

The arousal of sexual interest in humans is complex, involving a variety of psychological as well as physical factors. Although reproductive structures in the male and female differ in appearance, a number serve similar functions in arousal, reflecting their shared developmental origin. For example, the same embryonic tissues give rise to the scrotum and the labia majora, to the skin on the penis and the labia minora, and to the glans of the penis and the clitoris. Furthermore, the general pattern of human sexual response is similar in males and females. Two types of physiological reactions predominate in both sexes: *vasocongestion*, the filling of a tissue with blood, and *myotonia*, increased muscle tension.

The sexual response cycle can be divided into four phases: excitement, plateau, orgasm, and resolution. An important function of the excitement phase is to prepare the vagina and penis for *coitus* (sexual intercourse). During this phase, vasocongestion is particularly evident in erection of the penis and clitoris and in enlargement of the testicles, labia, and breasts. The vagina becomes lubricated, and myotonia may occur, as evident in nipple erection or tension of the limbs.

In the plateau phase, sexual responses continue as a result of direct stimulation of the genitalia. In females, the outer third of the vagina becomes vasocongested, while the inner two-thirds slightly expands. This change, coupled with the elevation of the uterus, forms a depression for receiving sperm at the back of the vagina. Breathing quickens and heart rate rises, sometimes to 150 beats per minute—not only in response to the physical effort of sexual activity, but also as an involuntary reaction to stimulation by the autonomic nervous system (see Figure 49.9).

*Orgasm* is characterized by rhythmic, involuntary contractions of the reproductive structures in both sexes. Male orgasm has two stages. The first, emission, occurs when the glands and ducts of the reproductive tract contract, forcing semen into the urethra. Expulsion, or ejaculation, occurs when the urethra contracts and the semen is expelled. During female orgasm, the uterus and outer vagina contract, but the inner two-thirds of the vagina does not. Orgasm is the shortest phase of the sexual response cycle, usually lasting only a few seconds. In both sexes, contractions occur at about 0.8-second intervals and may also involve the anal sphincter and several abdominal muscles.

The resolution phase completes the cycle and reverses the responses of the earlier stages. Vasocongested organs return to normal size and color, and muscles relax. Most of these changes are completed within 5 minutes, but some may take as long as an hour. Following orgasm, the male typically enters a refractory period, lasting from a few minutes to hours, when erection and orgasm cannot be achieved. Females do not have a refractory period, making possible multiple orgasms within a short period of time.

## CONCEPT CHECK 46.4

1. How are the functions of FSH and LH in females and males similar?
2. How does an estrous cycle differ from a menstrual cycle? In what animals are the two types of cycles found?
3. **WHAT IF?** ➤ If a human female begins taking estradiol and progesterone immediately after the start of a new menstrual cycle, how will ovulation be affected? Explain.
4. **MAKE CONNECTIONS** ➤ A coordination of events is characteristic of the reproductive cycle of a human female and the replicative cycle of an enveloped RNA virus (see Figure 19.7). What is the nature of the coordination in each of these cycles?

*For suggested answers, see Appendix A.*

# CONCEPT 46.5

## In placental mammals, an embryo develops fully within the mother's uterus

Having surveyed the ovarian and uterine cycles of human females, we turn now to reproduction itself, beginning with the events that transform an egg into a developing embryo.

## Conception, Embryonic Development, and Birth

During human copulation, the male delivers 2–5 mL of semen containing hundreds of millions of sperm. When first ejaculated, the semen coagulates, which likely keeps the ejaculate in place until sperm reach the cervix. Soon after, anticoagulants liquefy the semen, and the sperm swim through the cervix and oviducts. Fertilization—also called **conception** in humans—occurs when a sperm fuses with an egg (mature oocyte) in an oviduct (**Figure 46.15**).

▼ **Figure 46.15 Formation of a human zygote and early postfertilization events.**

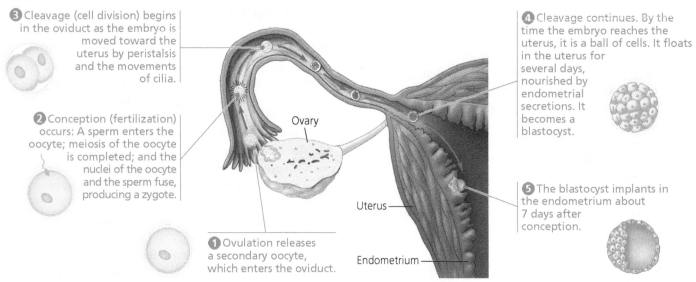

❸ Cleavage (cell division) begins in the oviduct as the embryo is moved toward the uterus by peristalsis and the movements of cilia.

❷ Conception (fertilization) occurs: A sperm enters the oocyte; meiosis of the oocyte is completed; and the nuclei of the oocyte and the sperm fuse, producing a zygote.

Ovary

❶ Ovulation releases a secondary oocyte, which enters the oviduct.

Uterus

Endometrium

❹ Cleavage continues. By the time the embryo reaches the uterus, it is a ball of cells. It floats in the uterus for several days, nourished by endometrial secretions. It becomes a blastocyst.

❺ The blastocyst implants in the endometrium about 7 days after conception.

**VISUAL SKILLS** ➤ *If a woman's eggs need to be fertilized in vitro, they can be readily introduced into the uterus but not the extremely narrow oviduct. Based on this drawing, propose conditions for culturing a fertilized egg that you predict will optimize the chance of a successful pregnancy.*

The zygote begins a series of cell divisions called cleavage about 24 hours after fertilization and after an additional 4 days produces a **blastocyst**, a sphere of cells surrounding a central cavity. A few days later, the embryo implants into the endometrium of the uterus. The condition of carrying one or more embryos in the uterus is called **pregnancy**, or **gestation**. Human pregnancy averages 266 days (38 weeks) from fertilization of the egg, or 40 weeks from the start of the last menstrual cycle. In comparison, gestation averages 21 days in many rodents, 280 days in cows, and more than 600 days in elephants. The roughly nine months of human gestation are divided into three *trimesters* of equal length.

## First Trimester

During the first trimester, the implanted embryo secretes hormones that signal its presence and regulate the mother's reproductive system. One embryonic hormone, *human chorionic gonadotropin (hCG)*, acts like pituitary LH in maintaining secretion of progesterone and estrogens by the corpus luteum through the first few months of pregnancy. Some hCG passes from the maternal blood to the urine, where it can be detected by the most common early pregnancy tests.

Not all embryos are capable of completing development. Many spontaneously stop developing as a result of chromosomal or developmental abnormalities. Much less often, a fertilized egg lodges in an oviduct (fallopian tube), resulting in a tubal, or ectopic, pregnancy. Such pregnancies cannot be sustained and may rupture the oviduct, resulting in serious internal bleeding. The risk of ectopic pregnancy increases if the oviduct is scarred by bacterial infections arising during childbirth, by medical procedures, or by a sexually transmitted disease.

During its first 2–4 weeks of development, the embryo obtains nutrients directly from the endometrium. Meanwhile, the outer layer of the blastocyst, which is called the **trophoblast**, grows outward and mingles with the endometrium, eventually helping form the **placenta**. This disk-shaped organ, containing both embryonic and maternal blood vessels, can weigh close to 1 kg at birth. Diffusion of material between the maternal and embryonic circulatory systems supplies nutrients, provides immune protection, exchanges respiratory gases, and disposes of metabolic wastes for the embryo. Blood from the embryo travels to the placenta through the arteries of the umbilical cord and returns via the umbilical vein **(Figure 46.16)**.

▼ **Figure 46.16 Placental circulation.**
From the 4th week of development until birth, the placenta, a combination of maternal and embryonic tissues, transports nutrients, respiratory gases, and wastes between the embryo or fetus and the mother. Maternal blood enters the placenta in arteries, flows through blood pools in the endometrium, and leaves via veins. Embryonic or fetal blood, which remains in vessels, enters the placenta through arteries and passes through capillaries in finger-like chorionic villi, where oxygen and nutrients are acquired. Fetal blood leaves the placenta through veins leading back to the fetus. Materials are exchanged by diffusion, active transport, and selective absorption between the fetal capillary bed and the maternal blood pools.

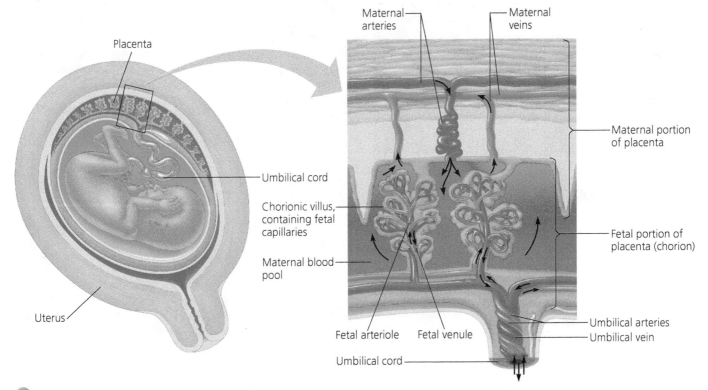

In a rare genetic disorder, the absence of a particular enzyme leads to increased testosterone production. When the fetus has this disorder, the mother develops a male-like pattern of body hair during the pregnancy. Explain why.

Occasionally, an embryo splits during the first month of development, resulting in identical, or *monozygotic* (one-egg), twins. Fraternal, or *dizygotic*, twins arise in a very different way: Two follicles mature in a single cycle, followed by independent fertilization and implantation of two genetically distinct embryos.

The first trimester is the main period of **organogenesis**, the development of the body organs **(Figure 46.17a)**. During organogenesis, the embryo is particularly susceptible to damage. For example, alcohol that passes through the placenta and reaches the developing central nervous system of the embryo can cause fetal alcohol syndrome, a disorder that can result in mental retardation and other serious birth defects. The heart begins beating by the 4th week; a heartbeat can be detected at 8–10 weeks. At 8 weeks, all the major structures of the adult are present in rudimentary form, and the embryo is called a **fetus**. At the end of the first trimester, the fetus, although well differentiated, is only 5 cm long.

Meanwhile, high levels of progesterone bring about rapid changes in the mother: Mucus in the cervix forms a plug that protects against infection, the maternal part of the placenta grows, the mother's breasts and uterus get larger, and both ovulation and menstrual cycling stop. About three-fourths of all pregnant women experience nausea, misleadingly called "morning sickness," during the first trimester.

## Second and Third Trimesters

During the second trimester, the fetus grows to about 30 cm in length. Development continues, including formation of fingernails, external sex organs, and outer ears **(Figure 46.17b)**. The mother may feel fetal movements as early as one month into the second trimester, and fetal activity is typically visible through the abdominal wall one to two months later. Hormone levels stabilize as hCG secretion declines; the corpus luteum deteriorates; and the placenta completely takes over the production of progesterone, the hormone that maintains the pregnancy.

During the third trimester, the fetus grows to about 3–4 kg in weight and 50 cm in length. Fetal activity may decrease as the fetus fills the available space. As the fetus grows and the uterus expands around it, the mother's abdominal organs become compressed and displaced, leading to digestive blockages and a need for frequent urination.

Childbirth begins with *labor*, a series of strong, rhythmic uterine contractions that push the fetus and placenta out of the body. Once labor begins, local regulators (prostaglandins)

▼ Figure 46.17 **Some stages of human development during the first and second trimesters.**

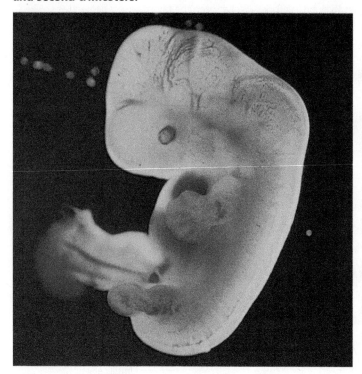

**(a) 5 weeks.** Limb buds, eyes, the heart, the liver, and rudiments of all other organs have started to develop in the embryo, which is only about 1 cm long.

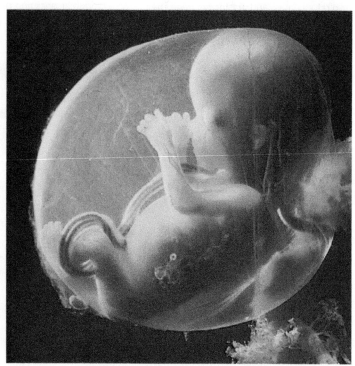

**(b) 14 weeks.** Growth and development of the offspring, now called a fetus, continue during the second trimester. This fetus is about 6 cm long.

## ▼ Figure 46.18 Positive feedback in labor.

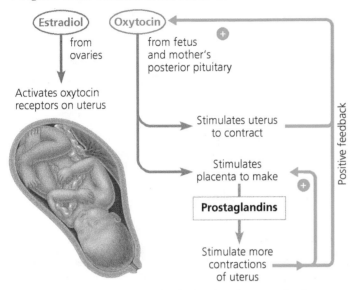

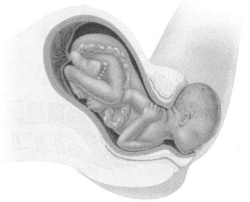

**VISUAL SKILLS** ➤ *Based on the feedback circuits shown, predict the effect of a single dose of oxytocin on a pregnant woman at the end of 39 weeks gestation.*

and hormones (chiefly estradiol and oxytocin) induce and regulate further contractions of the uterus **(Figure 46.18)**. Central to this regulation is a positive-feedback loop (see Concept 45.2) in which uterine contractions stimulate secretion of oxytocin, which in turn stimulates further contractions.

Labor is typically described as having three stages **(Figure 46.19)**. The first stage is the thinning and opening up (dilation) of the cervix. The second stage is the expulsion, or delivery, of the baby. Continuous strong contractions force the fetus out of the uterus and through the vagina. The final stage of labor is the delivery of the placenta.

One aspect of postnatal care unique to mammals is *lactation*, the production of mother's milk. In response to suckling by the newborn and changes in estradiol levels after birth, the hypothalamus signals the anterior pituitary to secrete prolactin, which stimulates the mammary glands to produce milk. Suckling also stimulates the secretion of oxytocin from the posterior pituitary, which triggers release of milk from the mammary glands (see Figure 45.14).

## Maternal Immune Tolerance of the Embryo and Fetus

Pregnancy is an immunological puzzle. Because half of the embryo's genes are inherited from the father, many of the chemical markers present on the surface of the embryo are foreign to the mother. Why, then, does the mother not reject the embryo as a foreign body, as she would a tissue or organ graft from another person? One intriguing clue comes from

## ▼ Figure 46.19 The three stages of labor.

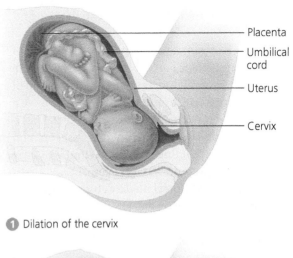

❶ Dilation of the cervix

❷ Expulsion: delivery of the infant

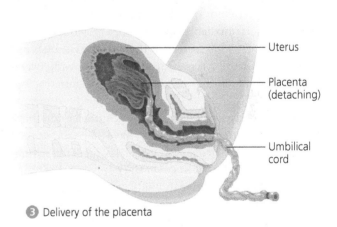

❸ Delivery of the placenta

the relationship between certain autoimmune disorders and pregnancy. For example, the symptoms of rheumatoid arthritis, an autoimmune disease of the joints, become less severe during pregnancy. Such observations suggest that the overall regulation of the immune system changes during pregnancy. Sorting out these changes and how they might protect the developing fetus is an active area of research for immunologists.

## Contraception and Abortion

**Contraception**, the deliberate prevention of pregnancy, can be achieved in a number of ways. Some contraceptive methods prevent gamete development or release from female or male gonads; others prevent fertilization by keeping sperm and egg apart; and still others prevent implantation of an embryo. For complete information on contraceptive methods, you should consult a health-care provider. The following brief introduction to the biology of the most common methods and the corresponding diagram in **Figure 46.20** make no pretense of being a contraception manual.

Fertilization can be prevented by abstinence from sexual intercourse or by any of several kinds of barriers that keep live sperm from contacting the egg. Temporary abstinence, sometimes called *natural family planning*, depends on refraining from intercourse when conception is most likely. Because the egg can survive in the oviduct for 24–48 hours and sperm for up to 5 days, a couple practicing temporary abstinence should not engage in intercourse for a significant number of days before and after ovulation. Contraceptive methods based on fertility awareness require knowledge of physiological indicators associated with ovulation, such as changes in cervical mucus. Note also that a pregnancy rate of 10–20% is typically reported for couples practicing natural family planning. (In this context, pregnancy rate is the percentage of women who become pregnant in one year while using a particular pregnancy prevention method.)

As a method of preventing fertilization, *coitus interruptus*, or withdrawal (removal of the penis from the vagina before ejaculation), is unreliable. Sperm from a previous ejaculate may be transferred in secretions that precede ejaculation. Furthermore, a split-second lapse in timing or willpower can result in tens of millions of sperm being transferred before withdrawal.

Used properly, several methods of contraception that block sperm from meeting the egg have pregnancy rates of less than 10%. The *condom* is a thin, latex rubber or natural membrane sheath that fits over the penis to collect the semen. For sexually active individuals, latex condoms are the only contraceptives that are highly effective in preventing the spread of AIDS and other *sexually transmitted diseases* (*STDs*), also known as *sexually transmitted infections* (*STIs*). This protection is not absolute, however. Another common barrier device is the *diaphragm*, a dome-shaped rubber cap inserted into the upper portion of the vagina before intercourse. Both of these devices have lower pregnancy rates when used in conjunction with a spermicidal (sperm-killing) foam or jelly. Other barrier devices include the vaginal pouch, or "female condom."

Except for complete abstinence from sexual intercourse or sterilization (discussed later), the most effective means of birth control are the intrauterine device (IUD) and

▼ **Figure 46.20 Mechanisms of several contraceptive methods.** Red arrows indicate where these methods, devices, or products interfere with events from the production of sperm and primary oocytes to implantation of a developing embryo.

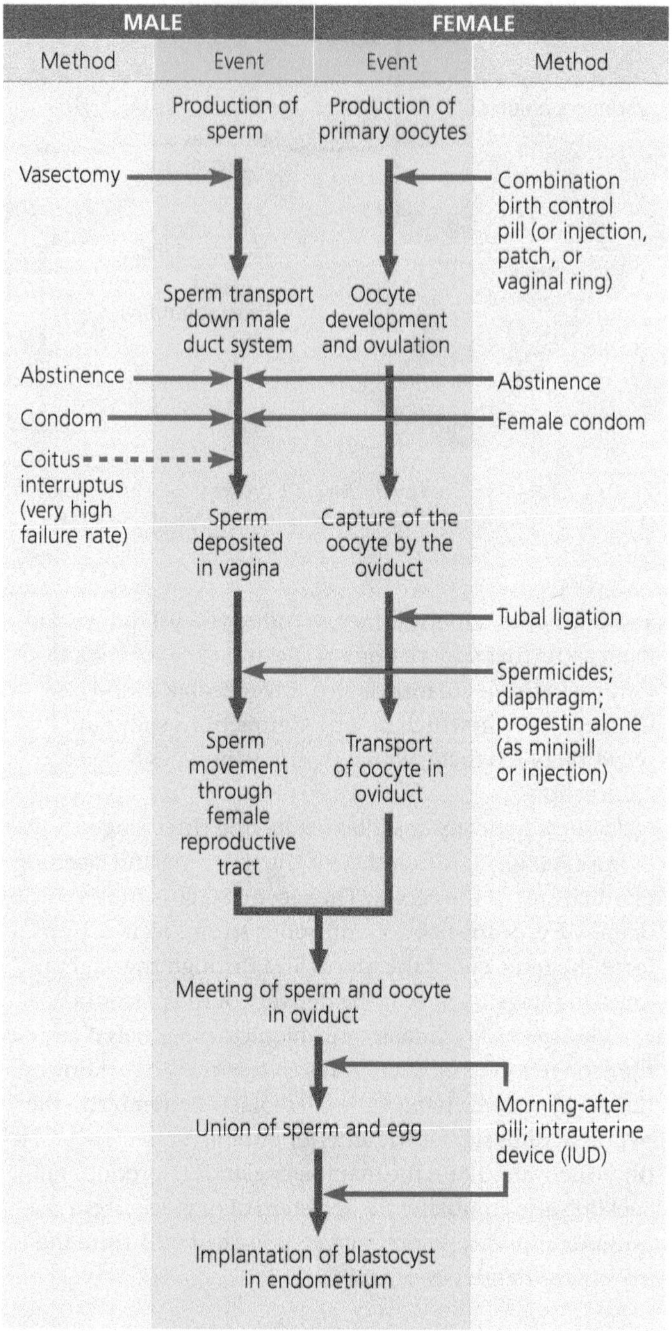

hormonal contraceptives. The IUD has a pregnancy rate of 1% or less and is the most commonly used reversible method of birth control outside the United States. Placed in the uterus by a doctor, the IUD interferes with fertilization and implantation. Hormonal contraceptives, most often in the form of **birth control pills**, also have pregnancy rates of 1% or less.

The most commonly prescribed hormonal contraceptives combine a synthetic estrogen and a synthetic progesterone-like hormone called progestin. This combination mimics negative feedback in the ovarian cycle, stopping the release of GnRH by the hypothalamus and thus of FSH and LH by the pituitary. The prevention of LH release blocks ovulation. In addition, the inhibition of FSH secretion by the low dose of estrogens in the pills prevents follicles from developing.

Another hormonal contraceptive with a very low pregnancy rate contains only progestin. Progestin causes thickening of a woman's cervical mucus so that it blocks sperm from entering the uterus. Progestin also decreases the frequency of ovulation and causes changes in the endometrium that may interfere with implantation if fertilization occurs. This contraceptive can be administered as injections that last for three months or as a tablet ("minipill") taken daily.

Hormonal contraceptives have both harmful and beneficial side effects. They increase the risk of some cardiovascular disorders slightly for nonsmokers and quite substantially (3- to 10-fold) for women who smoke regularly. At the same time, oral contraceptives eliminate the dangers of pregnancy; women on birth control pills have mortality rates about one-half those of pregnant women. Birth control pills also decrease the risk of ovarian and endometrial cancers. No hormonal contraceptives are available for men.

Sterilization is the permanent prevention of gamete production or release. For women, the most common method is **tubal ligation**, the sealing shut or tying off (ligating) of a section of each oviduct to prevent eggs from traveling into the uterus. Similarly, **vasectomy** in men is the cutting and tying off of each vas deferens to prevent sperm from entering the urethra. Sex hormone secretion and sexual function are unaffected by both procedures, with no change in menstrual cycles in females or ejaculate volume in males. Although tubal ligation and vasectomy are considered permanent, both procedures can in many cases be reversed by microsurgery.

The termination of a pregnancy in progress is called **abortion**. Spontaneous abortion, or *miscarriage*, is very common; it occurs in as many as one-third of all pregnancies, often before the woman is even aware she is pregnant. In addition, each year about 700,000 women in the United States choose to have an abortion performed by a physician.

A drug called mifepristone, or RU486, can terminate a pregnancy nonsurgically within the first 7 weeks. RU486 blocks progesterone receptors in the uterus, thus preventing progesterone from maintaining the pregnancy. It is taken with a small amount of prostaglandin to induce uterine contractions.

## Modern Reproductive Technologies

Recent scientific and technological advances have made it possible to address many reproductive problems, including genetic diseases and infertility.

### Detecting Disorders During Pregnancy

Many developmental problems and genetic diseases can now be diagnosed while the fetus is in the uterus. Ultrasound imaging, which generates images using sound frequencies above the normal hearing range, is commonly used to analyze the fetus's size and condition. In amniocentesis and chorionic villus sampling, a needle is used to obtain fetal cells from either fluid or tissue, respectively, surrounding the embryo; these cells then provide the basis for genetic analysis (see Figure 14.19).

A new reproductive technology makes use of a pregnant mother's blood to analyze the genome of her fetus. As discussed in Chapter 14, a pregnant woman's blood contains DNA from the growing embryo. How does it get there? The mother's blood reaches the embryo through the placenta. When cells produced by the embryo grow old, die, and break open within the placenta, the released DNA enters the mother's circulation. Although the blood also contains pieces of DNA from the mother, about 10–15% of the DNA circulating in the blood is from the fetus. Both the polymerase chain reaction (PCR) and high-throughput sequencing can convert the bits of fetal DNA into useful information.

Unfortunately, almost all detectable disorders remain untreatable in the uterus, and many cannot be corrected even after birth. Genetic testing may leave parents faced with difficult decisions about whether to terminate a pregnancy or to raise a child who may have profound defects and a short life expectancy. These are complex issues that demand careful, informed thought and competent genetic counseling.

Parents will be receiving even more genetic information and confronting further questions in the near future. Indeed, in 2012 we learned of the first infant whose entire genome was known before birth. Nevertheless, completing a genome sequence does not ensure complete information. Consider, for example, Klinefelter syndrome, in which males have an extra X chromosome. This disorder is quite common, affecting 1 in 1,000 men, and can cause reduced testosterone, a feminized appearance, and infertility. However, while some men with an extra X chromosome have a debilitating disorder, others have symptoms so mild that they are unaware of the condition. For other disorders, such as diabetes, heart disease, or cancer, a genome sequence may only indicate the degree of risk. How parents will use this and other information in having and raising children is a question with no clear answers.

### Infertility and In Vitro Fertilization

Infertility—an inability to conceive offspring—is quite common, affecting about one in ten couples in the United States and worldwide. The causes of infertility are varied, and the likelihood of a reproductive defect is nearly the same for men and women. For women, however, the risk of reproductive difficulties, as well as genetic abnormalities of the fetus, increases steadily past age 35. Evidence suggests that the prolonged period of time oocytes spend in meiosis is largely responsible for this increased risk.

Among preventable causes of infertility, STDs are the most significant. In women 15–24 years old, approximately 830,000 cases of chlamydia and gonorrhea are reported annually in the United States. The actual number of women infected with the chlamydia or gonorrhea bacterium is considerably higher because most women with these infections have no symptoms and are therefore unaware of their infection. Up to 40% of women who remain untreated for either chlamydia or gonorrhea develop an inflammatory disorder that can lead to infertility or to potentially fatal complications during pregnancy.

Some forms of infertility are treatable. Hormone therapy can sometimes increase sperm or egg production, and surgery can often correct ducts that formed improperly or have become blocked. In some cases, doctors recommend **in vitro fertilization (IVF)**, which involves combining oocytes and sperm in the laboratory. Fertilized eggs are incubated until they have formed at least eight cells and are then transferred to the woman's uterus for implantation. If mature sperm are defective or low in number, a whole sperm or a spermatid nucleus is injected directly into an oocyte (**Figure 46.21**). Though costly, IVF procedures have enabled more than a million couples to conceive children.

By whatever means fertilization occurs, a developmental program follows that transforms the single-celled zygote into

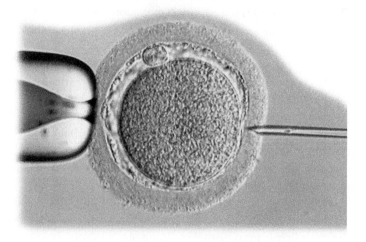

▼ **Figure 46.21** *In vitro* **fertilization (IVF).** In this form of IVF, a technician holds the egg in place with a pipette (left) and uses a very fine needle to inject one sperm into the egg cytoplasm (colorized LM).

a multicellular organism. The mechanisms of this remarkable program of development in humans and other animals are the subject of Chapter 47.

## CONCEPT CHECK 46.5

1. Why does testing for hCG (human chorionic gonadotropin) work as a pregnancy test early in pregnancy but not late in pregnancy? What is the function of hCG in pregnancy?

2. In what ways are tubal ligation and vasectomy similar?

3. **WHAT IF?** ➤ If a sperm nucleus is injected into an oocyte, what steps of gametogenesis and conception are bypassed?

*For suggested answers, see Appendix A.*

---

# 46 Chapter Review

 Go to **MasteringBiology**™ for Videos, Animations, Vocab Self-Quiz, Practice Tests, and more in the Study Area.

## SUMMARY OF KEY CONCEPTS

### CONCEPT 46.1

**Both asexual and sexual reproduction occur in the animal kingdom**
(pp. 1018–1020)

VOCAB SELF-QUIZ
goo.gl/6u55ks

- **Sexual reproduction** requires the fusion of male and female gametes, forming a diploid **zygote.**
  **Asexual reproduction** is the production of offspring without gamete fusion. Mechanisms of asexual reproduction include budding, **fission**, and fragmentation with regeneration. Variations on the mode of reproduction are achieved through **parthenogenesis, hermaphroditism**, and sex reversal. Hormones and environmental cues control reproductive cycles.

 *Would a pair of haploid offspring produced by parthenogenesis be genetically identical? Explain.*

### CONCEPT 46.2

**Fertilization depends on mechanisms that bring together sperm and eggs of the same species** (pp. 1020–1023)

- **Fertilization** occurs externally, when sperm and eggs are both released outside the body, or internally, when sperm deposited by the male fertilize an egg in the female reproductive system. In either case, fertilization requires coordinated timing, which may be mediated by environmental cues, pheromones, or courtship behavior. Internal fertilization is often associated with relatively fewer offspring and greater protection of offspring by the parents. Systems for gamete production and delivery range from undifferentiated cells in the body cavity to complex systems that include **gonads**, which produce gametes, and accessory tubes and glands that protect or transport gametes and embryos. Although sexual reproduction involves a partnership, it also provides an opportunity for competition between individuals and between gametes.

Complex reproductive systems in fruit flies

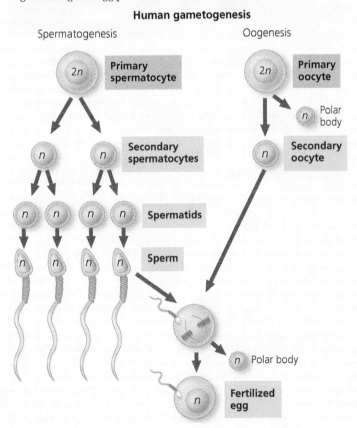

**Male fruit fly**

Testis
Vas deferens
Ejaculatory duct
Seminal vesicle
Penis and claspers

**Female fruit fly**

Ovary
Oviduct
Spermatheca
Accessory gland
Uterus
Vulva

**Key to labels:**
*Gamete production*
Gamete protection and transport

**?** *Identify which of the following, if any, are unique to mammals: a female uterus, a male vas deferens, extended internal development, and parental care of newborns.*

## CONCEPT 46.3

### Reproductive organs produce and transport gametes (pp. 1023–1027)

- In human males, **sperm** are produced in **testes**, which are suspended outside the body in the **scrotum**. Ducts connect the testes to internal accessory glands and to the **penis**. The reproductive system of the human female consists principally of the **labia** and the **glans** of the **clitoris** externally and the **vagina, uterus, oviducts**, and **ovaries** internally. **Eggs** are produced in the ovaries and upon fertilization develop in the uterus.
- **Gametogenesis**, or gamete production, consists of the processes of **spermatogenesis** in males and **oogenesis** in females. Human spermatogenesis is continuous and produces four sperm per meiosis. Human oogenesis is discontinuous and cyclic, generating one egg per meiosis.

**Human gametogenesis**

Spermatogenesis

2n — Primary spermatocyte
n / n — Secondary spermatocytes
n n n n — Spermatids
n n n n — Sperm

Oogenesis

2n — Primary oocyte
n — Polar body
n — Secondary oocyte
n — Polar body
n — Fertilized egg

**?** *How does the difference in size and cellular contents between sperm and eggs relate to their specific functions in reproduction?*

## CONCEPT 46.4

### The interplay of tropic and sex hormones regulates reproduction in mammals (pp. 1028–1032)

- In mammals, GnRH from the hypothalamus regulates the release of two hormones, **FSH** and **LH**, from the anterior pituitary. In males, FSH and LH control the secretion of androgens (chiefly **testosterone**) and sperm production. In females, cyclic secretion of FSH and LH orchestrates the **ovarian** and **uterine cycles** via estrogens (primarily **estradiol**) and **progesterone**. The developing **follicle** and the **corpus luteum** also secrete hormones, which help coordinate the uterine and ovarian cycles through positive and negative feedback.

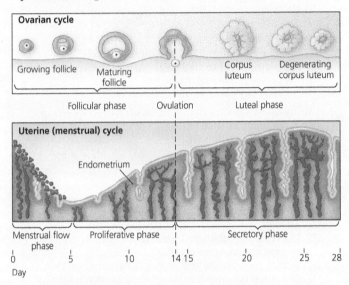

**Ovarian cycle**

Growing follicle
Maturing follicle
Corpus luteum
Degenerating corpus luteum

Follicular phase — Ovulation — Luteal phase

**Uterine (menstrual) cycle**

Endometrium

Menstrual flow phase | Proliferative phase | Secretory phase

Day: 0  5  10  14 15  20  25  28

- In **estrous cycles**, the lining of the **endometrium** is reabsorbed, and sexual receptivity is limited to a heat period. Reproductive structures with a shared origin in development underlie many features of human sexual arousal and orgasm common to males and females.

**?** *Why do anabolic steroids lead to reduced sperm counts?*

## CONCEPT 46.5

### In placental mammals, an embryo develops fully within the mother's uterus (pp. 1032–1038)

- After fertilization and the completion of meiosis in the oviduct, the zygote undergoes a series of cell divisions and develops into a **blastocyst** before implantation in the endometrium. All major organs start developing by 8 weeks. A pregnant woman's acceptance of her "foreign" offspring likely reflects partial suppression of the maternal immune response.
- **Contraception** may prevent release of mature gametes from the gonads, fertilization, or embryo implantation. **Abortion** is the termination of a pregnancy in progress.
- Reproductive technologies can help detect problems before birth and can assist infertile couples. Infertility may be treated through hormone therapy or *in vitro* fertilization.

**?** *What route would oxygen in the mother's blood follow to arrive at a body cell of the fetus?*

## Level 1: Knowledge/Comprehension

1. Which of the following characterizes parthenogenesis?
   - (A) An individual may change its sex during its lifetime.
   - (B) Specialized groups of cells grow into new individuals.
   - (C) An organism is first a male and then a female.
   - (D) An egg develops without being fertilized.

2. In male mammals, excretory and reproductive systems share
   - (A) the vas deferens.
   - (B) the urethra.
   - (C) the seminal vesicle.
   - (D) the prostate.

3. Which of the following is *not* properly paired?
   - (A) seminiferous tubule—cervix
   - (B) vas deferens—oviduct
   - (C) testosterone—estradiol
   - (D) scrotum—labia majora

4. Peaks of LH and FSH production occur during
   - (A) the menstrual flow phase of the uterine cycle.
   - (B) the beginning of the follicular phase of the ovarian cycle.
   - (C) the period just before ovulation.
   - (D) the secretory phase of the uterine cycle.

5. During human gestation, rudiments of all organs develop
   - (A) in the first trimester.
   - (B) in the second trimester.
   - (C) in the third trimester.
   - (D) during the blastocyst stage.

## Level 2: Application/Analysis

6. Which of the following is a true statement?
   - (A) All mammals have menstrual cycles.
   - (B) The endometrial lining is shed in menstrual cycles but reabsorbed in estrous cycles.
   - (C) Estrous cycles are more frequent than menstrual cycles.
   - (D) Ovulation occurs before the endometrium thickens in estrous cycles.

7. For which of the following is the number the same in human males and females?
   - (A) interruptions in meiotic divisions
   - (B) functional gametes produced by meiosis
   - (C) meiotic divisions required to produce each gamete
   - (D) different cell types produced by meiosis

8. Which statement about human reproduction is false?
   - (A) Fertilization occurs in the oviduct.
   - (B) Spermatogenesis and oogenesis require different temperatures.
   - (C) An oocyte completes meiosis after a sperm penetrates it.
   - (D) The earliest stages of spermatogenesis occur closest to the lumen of the seminiferous tubules.

## Level 3: Synthesis/Evaluation

9. **DRAW IT** In human spermatogenesis, mitosis of a stem cell gives rise to one cell that remains a stem cell and one cell that becomes a spermatogonium. (a) Draw four rounds of mitosis for a stem cell, and label the daughter cells. (b) For one spermatogonium, draw the cells it would produce from one round of mitosis followed by meiosis. Label the cells, and label mitosis and meiosis. (c) Explain what would happen if stem cells divided like spermatogonia.

10. **EVOLUTION CONNECTION** Hermaphroditism is often found in animals that are fixed to a surface. Motile species are less often hermaphroditic. Explain why.

11. **SCIENTIFIC INQUIRY** You discover a new egg-laying worm species. You dissect four adults and find both oocytes and sperm in each. Cells outside the gonad contain five chromosome pairs. Lacking genetic variants, explain how you would determine whether the worms can self-fertilize.

12. **WRITE ABOUT A THEME: ENERGY AND MATTER** In a short essay (100–150 words), discuss how different types of energy investment by females contribute to the reproductive success of a frog, a chicken, and a human.

13. **SYNTHESIZE YOUR KNOWLEDGE**

A female Komodo dragon (*Varanus komodoensis*) kept in isolation in a zoo had progeny. Each of the offspring had two identical copies of every gene in its genome. However, the offspring were not identical to one another. Based on your understanding of parthenogenesis and meiosis, propose a hypothesis to explain these observations.

*For selected answers, see Appendix A.*

 For additional practice questions, check out the **Dynamic Study Modules** in MasteringBiology. You can use them to study on your smartphone, tablet, or computer anytime, anywhere!

# Animal Development

47

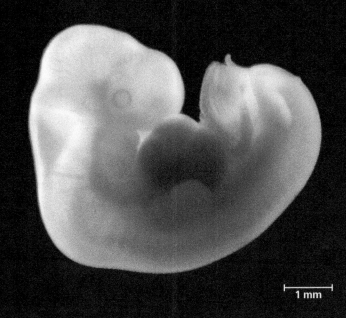

1 mm

▲ Figure 47.1 **How did a single cell develop into this intricately detailed embryo?**

## KEY CONCEPTS

**47.1** Fertilization and cleavage initiate embryonic development

**47.2** Morphogenesis in animals involves specific changes in cell shape, position, and survival

**47.3** Cytoplasmic determinants and inductive signals regulate cell fate

▽ **Chick embryo**

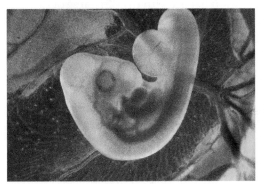

## A Body-Building Plan

The 5-week-old human embryo in **Figure 47.1** has already achieved a remarkable number of milestones in its development. Its heart—the red spot in the center—is beating, and a digestive tract traverses the length of its body. Its brain is forming (at the upper right in the photo), while the blocks of tissue that will give rise to the vertebrae are lined up along its back.

Examining embryos from different species, biologists have long noted common features of early stages, as evident for the human embryo and chick embryo shown here. More recently, experiments have demonstrated that specific patterns of gene expression in an embryo direct cells to adopt distinct functions during development. Furthermore, even animals that display widely differing body plans share many basic mechanisms of development and often use a common set of regulatory genes. For example, the gene that specifies where eyes form in a vertebrate embryo has a close counterpart with a nearly identical function in the fruit fly *Drosophila melanogaster*. Indeed, when the gene from a mouse is experimentally introduced into a fly embryo, the mouse gene directs eye formation wherever it is expressed.

Because the processes and mechanisms of embryonic development have many common features, lessons learned from studying a particular animal can often be applied quite broadly. For this reason, the study of development lends

When you see this blue icon, log in to **MasteringBiology** and go to the Study Area for digital resources.  Get Ready for This Chapter

itself well to the use of **model organisms**, species chosen for the ease with which they can be studied in the laboratory. *Drosophila melanogaster*, for example, is a useful model organism: Its life cycle is short, and mutants can be readily identified and studied (see Concepts 15.1 and 18.4). In this chapter, we will concentrate on four other model organisms: the sea urchin, the frog, the chick, and the nematode (roundworm). We will also explore some aspects of human embryonic development. Even though humans are not model organisms, we are, of course, intensely interested in our own species.

Regardless of the species being studied, development occurs at multiple points in the life cycle (**Figure 47.2**). In a frog, for example, a major developmental period is metamorphosis, when the larva (tadpole) undergoes sweeping changes in anatomy in becoming an adult. Development occurs in adult animals too, as when stem cells in the gonads produce sperm and eggs (gametes). In this chapter, however, our focus is on development in the embryonic stage.

Embryonic development in many animal species involves common stages that occur in a set order. The first is fertilization, the fusion of sperm and egg. Next is the cleavage stage, a series of cell divisions that divide, or cleave, the embryo into many cells. These cleavage divisions, which typically are rapid and lack accompanying cell growth, generate a hollow ball of cells called a blastula. The blastula then folds in on itself, rearranging into a multilayered embryo, the gastrula, in a process called gastrulation. During organogenesis, the last major stage of embryonic development, local changes in cell shape and large-scale changes in cell location generate the rudimentary organs from which adult structures grow.

▼ **Figure 47.2 Developmental events in the life cycle of a frog.**

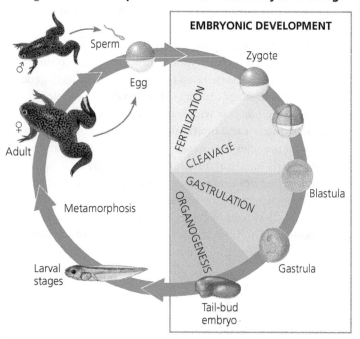

Our exploration of embryonic development will begin with a description of the basic stages common to most animals. We will then look at some of the cellular mechanisms that generate body form. Finally, we will consider how a cell becomes committed to a particular specialized role.

## CONCEPT 47.1
## Fertilization and cleavage initiate embryonic development

We'll begin our study of developmental stages with the events surrounding **fertilization**, the formation of a diploid zygote from a haploid egg and sperm.

### Fertilization

Molecules and events at the egg surface play a crucial role in each step of fertilization. First, sperm dissolve or penetrate any protective layer surrounding the egg to reach the plasma membrane. Next, molecules on the sperm surface bind to receptors on the egg surface, helping ensure that fertilization involves a sperm and egg of the same species. Finally, changes at the surface of the egg prevent **polyspermy**, the entry of multiple sperm nuclei into the egg. If polyspermy were to occur, the resulting abnormal number of chromosomes would be lethal for the embryo.

The cell-surface events that take place during fertilization have been studied most extensively in sea urchins, members of the phylum Echinodermata (see Figure 33.47). Sea urchin gametes are easy to collect, and fertilization occurs outside the animal body. As a result, researchers can observe fertilization and subsequent development simply by combining eggs and sperm in seawater in the laboratory.

### The Acrosomal Reaction

When sea urchins release their gametes into the water, the jelly coat of the egg exudes soluble molecules that attract the sperm, which swim toward the egg. As soon as a sperm head contacts the egg surface, molecules in the jelly coat trigger the **acrosomal reaction** in the sperm. As detailed in **Figure 47.3**, this reaction begins with the discharge of hydrolytic enzymes from the **acrosome**, a specialized vesicle at the tip of the sperm. These enzymes partially digest the jelly coat, enabling a sperm structure called the *acrosomal process* to form, elongate, and penetrate the coat. Protein molecules on the tip of the acrosomal process bind to specific receptor proteins in the egg plasma membrane. This "lock-and-key" recognition is especially important for sea urchins and other species with external fertilization because the water into which sperm and eggs are released may contain gametes of other species (see Figure 24.3g).

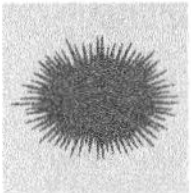

▼ **Figure 47.3 The acrosomal and cortical reactions during sea urchin fertilization.** The events following contact of a sperm and an egg ensure that the nucleus of only one sperm enters the egg cytoplasm.

The icon above is a simplified drawing of an adult sea urchin. Throughout the chapter, this icon and others representing an adult frog, chicken, nematode, and human indicate the animals whose embryos are featured in certain figures.

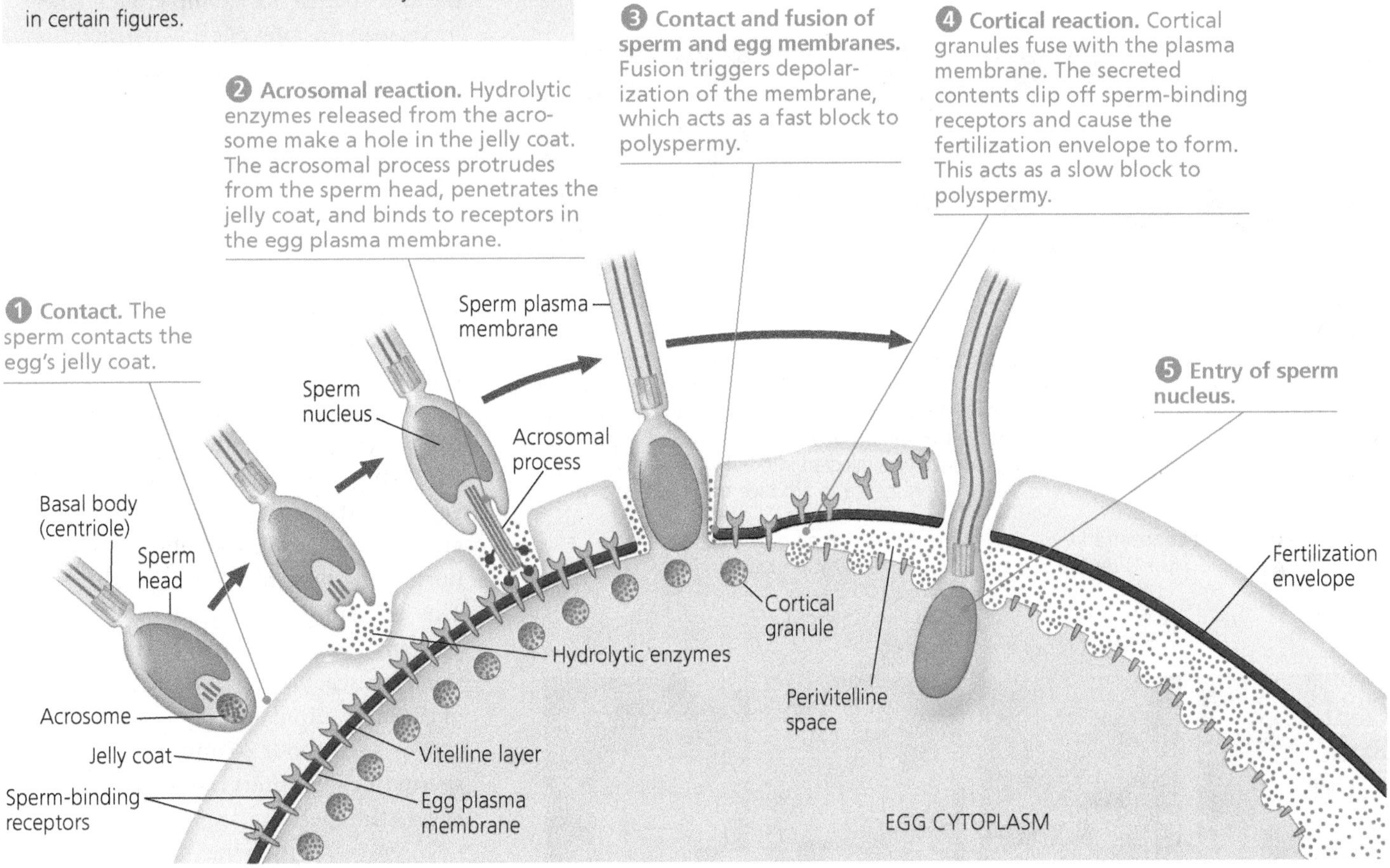

**2 Acrosomal reaction.** Hydrolytic enzymes released from the acrosome make a hole in the jelly coat. The acrosomal process protrudes from the sperm head, penetrates the jelly coat, and binds to receptors in the egg plasma membrane.

**3 Contact and fusion of sperm and egg membranes.** Fusion triggers depolarization of the membrane, which acts as a fast block to polyspermy.

**4 Cortical reaction.** Cortical granules fuse with the plasma membrane. The secreted contents clip off sperm-binding receptors and cause the fertilization envelope to form. This acts as a slow block to polyspermy.

**1 Contact.** The sperm contacts the egg's jelly coat.

**5 Entry of sperm nucleus.**

Sperm plasma membrane

Sperm nucleus

Acrosomal process

Basal body (centriole)

Sperm head

Fertilization envelope

Hydrolytic enzymes

Cortical granule

Acrosome

Perivitelline space

Jelly coat

Vitelline layer

Sperm-binding receptors

Egg plasma membrane

EGG CYTOPLASM

---

The recognition event between the sperm and egg triggers fusion of their plasma membranes. The sperm nucleus enters the egg cytoplasm as ion channels open in the egg's plasma membrane. Sodium ions diffuse into the egg and cause depolarization, a decrease in the membrane potential, the charge difference across the plasma membrane (see Concept 7.4). The depolarization occurs within about 1–3 seconds after a sperm binds to an egg. By preventing additional sperm from fusing with the egg's plasma membrane, this depolarization acts as the *fast block to polyspermy.*

## The Cortical Reaction

Although membrane depolarization in sea urchins lasts for only a minute or so, there is a longer-lasting change that prevents polyspermy. This *slow block to polyspermy* is established

by vesicles in the outer rim, or cortex, of the cytoplasm. Within seconds after a sperm binds to the egg, these vesicles, called cortical granules, fuse with the egg plasma membrane (see Figure 47.3, step 4). Contents of the cortical granules are released into the space between the plasma membrane and the surrounding vitelline layer, a structure formed by the egg's extracellular matrix. Enzymes and other granule contents then trigger a *cortical reaction*, which lifts the vitelline layer away from the egg and hardens the layer into a protective fertilization envelope.

Formation of the fertilization envelope requires a high concentration of calcium ions ($Ca^{2+}$) in the egg. Does a change in the $Ca^{2+}$ concentration trigger the cortical reaction? To answer this question, researchers used a calcium-sensitive dye to assess how $Ca^{2+}$ is distributed in the egg before and during fertilization. They found that $Ca^{2+}$ spread across the egg in

## ▼ Figure 47.4

### Inquiry  Does the distribution of Ca²⁺ in an egg correlate with formation of the fertilization envelope?

**Experiment**  Investigators mixed sea urchin eggs with sperm, waited 10–60 seconds, and then added a chemical fixative, freezing cellular structures in place. When photomicrographs of each sample are ordered according to the time of fixation, they illustrate the stages in the formation of a fertilization membrane for a single egg.

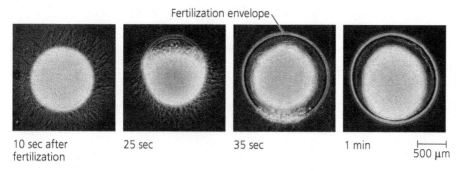

Fertilization envelope

10 sec after fertilization    25 sec    35 sec    1 min    500 μm

Calcium ion (Ca²⁺) signaling controls fusion of vesicles with the plasma membrane during neurotransmitter release, insulin secretion, and plant pollen tube formation. Researchers hypothesized calcium ion signaling plays a similar role in forming the fertilization envelope. To test this hypothesis, they tracked the release of free Ca²⁺ in sea urchin eggs after sperm binding. A fluorescent dye that glows when it binds free Ca²⁺ was injected into unfertilized eggs. The scientists then added sea urchin sperm and used a fluorescence to produce the results shown here.

**Results**  A rise in the concentration of Ca²⁺ in the cytosol began near where the sperm entered and spread in a wave. Soon after the wave passed, the fertilization envelope rose.

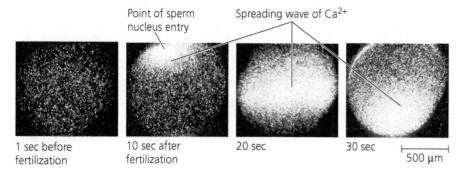

Point of sperm nucleus entry    Spreading wave of Ca²⁺

1 sec before fertilization    10 sec after fertilization    20 sec    30 sec    500 μm

**Conclusion**  Ca²⁺ release correlates with formation of the fertilization envelope, supporting the researchers' hypothesis that an increase in Ca²⁺ levels triggers cortical granule fusion.

**Data from** R. Steinhardt et al., Intracellular calcium release at fertilization in the sea urchin egg, *Developmental Biology* 58:185–197 (1977); M. Hafner et al., Wave of free calcium at fertilization in the sea urchin egg visualized with Fura-2, *Cell Motility and the Cytoskeleton* 9:271–277 (1988).

 **Instructors**: A related Experimental Inquiry Tutorial can be assigned in MasteringBiology.

**WHAT IF?** ➤ *Suppose a particular molecule could enter the egg and bind to Ca²⁺, blocking its function. How would you use this molecule to further test the hypothesis that a rise in Ca²⁺ level triggers cortical granule fusion?*

a wave that correlated with the appearance of the fertilization envelope, as described in **Figure 47.4**.

Further studies demonstrated that the binding of a sperm to the egg activates a signal transduction pathway that triggers release of Ca²⁺ into the cytosol from the endoplasmic reticulum. The resulting increase in Ca²⁺ levels causes cortical granules to fuse with the plasma membrane. A cortical reaction triggered by Ca²⁺ also occurs in vertebrates such as fishes and mammals.

### Egg Activation

Fertilization initiates and speeds up metabolic reactions that bring about the onset of embryonic development, "activating" the egg. There is, for example, a marked increase in the rates of cellular respiration and protein synthesis in the egg following the entry of the sperm nucleus. Soon thereafter, the egg and sperm nuclei fully fuse, and cycles of DNA synthesis and cell division begin.

What triggers activation of the egg? A major clue came from experiments demonstrating that the unfertilized eggs of sea urchins and many other species can be activated by an injection of Ca²⁺. Based on this discovery, researchers concluded that the rise in Ca²⁺ concentration that causes the cortical reaction also causes egg activation. Further experiments revealed that artificial activation is possible even if the nucleus has been removed from the egg. This further finding indicates that the proteins and mRNAs required for activation are already present in the cytoplasm of the unfertilized egg.

Not until about 20 minutes after the sperm nucleus enters the sea urchin egg do the sperm and egg nuclei fuse. DNA synthesis then begins. The first cell division, which occurs after about 90 minutes, marks the end of the fertilization stage.

Fertilization in other species shares many features with the process in sea urchins. However, there are differences, such as the stage of meiosis the egg has reached by the time it is fertilized. Sea urchin eggs have already completed meiosis when they are released from the female. In many other species, eggs are arrested at a specific stage of meiosis and do not complete the meiotic divisions until a sperm head enters. Human eggs, for example, are arrested at metaphase of meiosis II until sperm entry (see Figure 46.11).

### Fertilization in Mammals

Unlike sea urchins and most other marine invertebrates, terrestrial animals, including mammals, fertilize their eggs

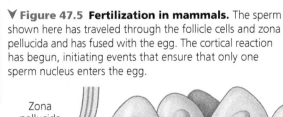

▼ **Figure 47.5 Fertilization in mammals.** The sperm shown here has traveled through the follicle cells and zona pellucida and has fused with the egg. The cortical reaction has begun, initiating events that ensure that only one sperm nucleus enters the egg.

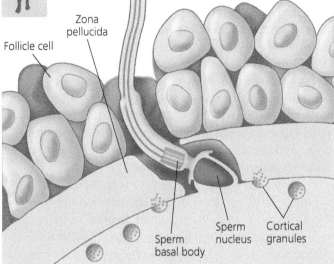

Zona pellucida

Follicle cell

Sperm basal body

Sperm nucleus

Cortical granules

internally. Support cells of the developing follicle surround the mammalian egg before and after ovulation. As shown in **Figure 47.5**, a sperm must travel through this layer of follicle cells before it reaches the **zona pellucida**, the extracellular matrix of the egg. There, the binding of a sperm to a sperm receptor induces an acrosomal reaction, facilitating sperm entry.

As in sea urchins, sperm binding triggers a cortical reaction, the release of enzymes from cortical granules to the outside of the cell. These enzymes catalyze changes in the zona pellucida, which then acts as the slow block to polyspermy. (No fast block to polyspermy is known in mammals.)

Overall, the process of fertilization is much slower in mammals than in sea urchins: The first cell division occurs within 12–36 hours after sperm binding in mammals, compared with about 1.5 hours in sea urchins. This cell division marks the end of fertilization and the beginning of the next stage of development, cleavage.

## Cleavage

The single nucleus in a newly fertilized egg has too little DNA to produce the amount of mRNA required to meet the cell's need for new proteins. Instead, initial development is carried out by mRNA and proteins deposited in the egg during oogenesis. There is still a need, however, to restore a balance between the cell's size and its DNA content. The process that addresses this challenge is **cleavage**, a series of rapid cell divisions during early development.

During cleavage, the cell cycle consists primarily of the S (DNA synthesis) and M (mitosis) phases (see Figure 12.6 for a review of the cell cycle). The $G_1$ and $G_2$ (gap) phases are essentially skipped, and little or no protein synthesis occurs. As a result, there is no increase in mass. Instead, cleavage partitions the cytoplasm of the large fertilized egg into many smaller cells called **blastomeres**. Because each blastomere is much smaller than the entire egg, its nucleus can make enough RNA to program further development.

The first five to seven cleavage divisions produce a hollow ball of cells, the **blastula**, surrounding a fluid-filled cavity called the **blastocoel**. In some species, including sea urchins and other echinoderms, the division pattern is uniform across the embryo (**Figure 47.6**). In others, including frogs,

▼ **Figure 47.6 Cleavage in an echinoderm embryo.** Cleavage is a series of mitotic cell divisions that transform the fertilized egg into a blastula, a hollow ball composed of cells called blastomeres. These light micrographs show the cleavage stages of a sand dollar embryo, which are virtually identical to those of a sea urchin. Each image is taken from above the embryo, with the focal plane, and hence the cells that are visible, at the equator.

 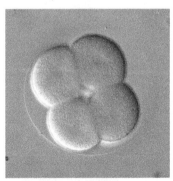 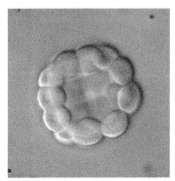 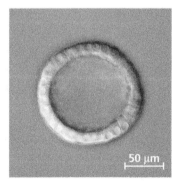

50 µm

**(a) Fertilized egg.** Shown here is the zygote shortly before the first cleavage division, surrounded by the fertilization envelope.

**(b) Four-cell stage.** Remnants of the mitotic spindle can be seen between the two pairs of cells that have just completed the second cleavage division.

**(c) Early blastula.** After further cleavage divisions, the embryo is a multicellular ball that is still surrounded by the fertilization envelope. The blastocoel has begun to form in the center.

**(d) Later blastula.** A single layer of cells surrounds a large blastocoel. (Although not visible here, the fertilization envelope is still present at this stage.)

**VISUAL SKILLS** ➤ *If the embryo in (c) or (d) were photographed at a focal plane midway from the equator to one of the poles, what visible features would change?*

 Video: Sea Urchin Fertilization and Cleavage

the pattern is asymmetric, with regions of the embryo differing in both the number and size of newly formed cells.

## Cleavage Pattern in Frogs

In the eggs of frogs (and many other animals), stored nutrients called **yolk** are concentrated toward one pole, called the **vegetal pole**, and away from the opposite or **animal pole**. This asymmetric distribution of yolk not only gives the two halves of the egg—the animal and vegetal hemispheres—different colors, but also influences the pattern of cleavage divisions, for reasons we will explore next

When an animal cell divides, an indentation called a *cleavage furrow* forms in the cell surface as cytokinesis divides the cell in half **(Figure 47.7)**. In the frog embryo, the first two cleavage furrows form parallel to the line (or meridian) connecting the two poles. During these divisions, the dense yolk slows completion of cytokinesis. As a result, the first cleavage furrow is still dividing the yolky cytoplasm in the vegetal hemisphere when the second cell division begins. Eventually, four blastomeres of equal size extend from the animal pole to the vegetal pole.

During the third division, the yolk begins to affect the relative size of cells produced in the two hemispheres. This division is equatorial (perpendicular to the line connecting the poles) and produces an eight-cell embryo. However, as each of the four blastomeres begins this division, yolk near the vegetal pole displaces the mitotic apparatus and the cleavage furrow from the egg equator toward the animal pole. The result is a smaller blastomere size in the animal hemisphere than in the vegetal hemisphere. The displacing effect of the yolk persists in subsequent divisions, causing the blastocoel to form entirely in the animal hemisphere (see Figure 47.7).

## Cleavage Patterns in Other Animals

Although yolk affects where division occurs in the eggs of frogs and other amphibians, the cleavage furrow still passes entirely through the egg. Cleavage in amphibian development is therefore said to be *holoblastic* (from the Greek *holos*, complete). Holoblastic cleavage is also seen in many other groups of animals, including echinoderms, mammals, and annelids. In those animals whose eggs contain relatively little yolk, the blastocoel forms centrally and the blastomeres are often of similar size, particularly during the

first few divisions of cleavage (see Figure 47.6). This is the case for humans.

Yolk is most plentiful and has its most pronounced effect on cleavage in the eggs of birds and other reptiles, many fishes, and insects. In these animals, the volume of yolk is so great that cleavage furrows cannot pass through it, and only the region of the egg lacking yolk undergoes cleavage. This incomplete cleavage of a yolk-rich egg is said to be *meroblastic* (from the Greek *meros*, partial).

For chickens and other birds, the part of the egg that we commonly call the yolk is actually the entire egg cell. Cell divisions are limited to a small whitish area at the animal pole. These divisions produce a cap of cells that sort into upper and lower layers. The cavity between these two layers is the avian version of the blastocoel.

In *Drosophila* and most other insects, yolk is found throughout the egg. Early in development, multiple rounds of mitosis occur without cytokinesis. In other words, no cell membranes form around the early nuclei. The first several hundred nuclei spread throughout the yolk and later migrate to the outer edge of the embryo. After several more rounds of mitosis, a plasma membrane forms around each nucleus, and the embryo, now the equivalent of a blastula, consists of a single layer of about 6,000 cells surrounding a mass of yolk (see Figure 18.22). Given that the number of cleavage divisions varies among animals, what determines the end of the cleavage stage? The **Scientific Skills Exercise** explores one of the landmark studies addressing this question.

▼ **Figure 47.7 Cleavage in a frog embryo.** The cleavage planes in the first and second divisions extend from the animal pole to the vegetal pole, but the third cleavage is perpendicular to the polar axis. In some species, the first division bisects the gray crescent, a lighter-colored region that appears opposite the site of sperm entry.

**Eight-cell stage (viewed from the animal pole).** The large amount of yolk displaces the third cleavage toward the animal pole, forming two tiers of cells. The four cells near the animal pole (closer, in this view) are smaller than the other four cells (colorized SEM).

**Blastula (at least 128 cells).** As cleavage continues, a fluid-filled cavity, the blastocoel, forms within the embryo. Because of unequal cell division, the blastocoel is located in the animal hemisphere. Both the drawing and the micrograph (assembled from fluorescence images) show cross sections of a blastula with about 4,000 cells.

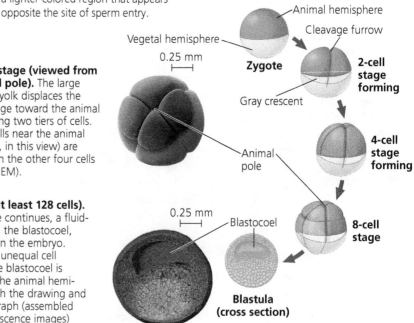

## Interpreting a Change in Slope

**What Causes the End of Cleavage in a Frog Embryo?** For a frog embryo in the cleavage stage, the cell cycle consists mainly of the S (DNA synthesis) and M (mitosis) phases. However, after the 12th cell division, $G_1$ and $G_2$ phases appear, and the cells grow, producing proteins and cytoplasmic organelles. What triggers this change?

**How the Experiments Were Done** Researchers tested the hypothesis that a mechanism for counting cell divisions determines when cleavage ends. They let frog embryos take up radioactively labeled nucleosides, either thymidine (to measure DNA synthesis) or uridine (to measure RNA synthesis). They then repeated the experiments in the presence of cytochalasin B, a chemical that prevents cell division by blocking cleavage furrow formation and cytokinesis.

**Data from the Experiments**

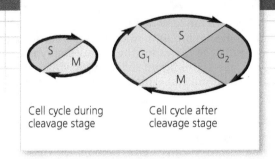

Cell cycle during cleavage stage  Cell cycle after cleavage stage

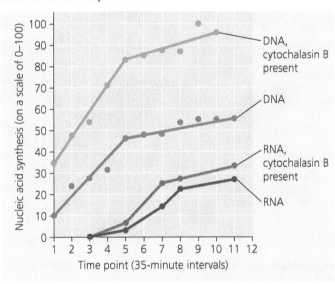

**INTERPRET THE DATA**

1. How does the use of particular labeled nucleosides allow independently measurement of DNA and RNA synthesis?
2. Describe the changes in synthesis that occur at the end of cleavage (time point 5 corresponds to cell division 12).
3. Comparing the rate of DNA synthesis with and without cytochalasin B, the researchers hypothesized that the toxin increases diffusion of thymidine into the embryos. Explain their logic.
4. Do the data support the hypothesis that the timing of the end of cleavage depends on counting cell divisions? Explain.
5. In a separate experiment, researchers disrupted the block to polyspermy, generating embryos with 7 to 10 sperm nuclei. At the end of cleavage, these embryos had the same nucleus-to-cytoplasm ratio as the wild-type embryos, but cleavage ended at the 10th cell division rather than the 12th cell division. What do these results indicate about the timing of the end of cleavage?

**Data from** J. Newport and M. Kirschner, A major developmental transition in early *Xenopus* embryos: I. Characterization and timing of cellular changes at the midblastula stage, *Cell* 30:675–686 (1982).

**Instructors**: A version of this Scientific Skills Exercise can be assigned in MasteringBiology.

---

## CONCEPT CHECK 47.1

1. How does the fertilization envelope form in sea urchins? What is its function?
2. **WHAT IF?** ➤ Predict what would happen if $Ca^{2+}$ was injected into an unfertilized sea urchin egg.
3. **MAKE CONNECTIONS** ➤ Review Figure 12.16 on cell cycle control. Would you expect MPF (maturation-promoting factor) activity to remain steady during cleavage? Explain.

*For suggested answers, see Appendix A.*

# CONCEPT 47.2

## Morphogenesis in animals involves specific changes in cell shape, position, and survival

The cellular and tissue-based processes that are called **morphogenesis** and by which the animal body takes shape occur over the last two stages of embryonic development.

During **gastrulation**, a set of cells at or near the surface of the blastula moves to an interior location, cell layers are established, and a primitive digestive tube is formed. Further transformation occurs during **organogenesis**, the formation of organs. We will discuss these two stages in turn.

## Gastrulation

Gastrulation is a dramatic reorganization of the hollow blastula into a two-layered or three-layered embryo called a **gastrula**. The embryos of all animals, and only animals, gastrulate. Cells move during gastrulation, taking up new positions and often acquiring new neighbors. **Figure 47.8** will help you visualize these complex three-dimensional changes. The cell layers produced are collectively called the embryonic **germ layers** (from the Latin *germen*, to sprout or germinate). In the late gastrula, **ectoderm** forms the outer layer and **endoderm** forms the lining of the digestive tract. In a few radially symmetric animals, only these two germ layers form during gastrulation. Such animals are called

## ▼ Figure 47.8 Visualizing Gastrulation

Gastrulation is a fundamental process in generating the animal body. Cells change position: Some are brought inside the embryo, and others spread over the surface. The net result is to rearrange the hollow embryo into two, or more commonly three, cell layers. This figure will help you visualize the basic choreography of gastrulation before you explore the specific steps in different types of animals.

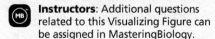 **Instructors**: Additional questions related to this Visualizing Figure can be assigned in MasteringBiology.

### Reorganizing the animal embryo in three dimensions

Gastrulation typically begins with invagination, the infolding of a sheet of cells, shown here in both surface view and cross section. The resulting changes to the epithelium covering the embryo resemble what happens if you push a finger into one end of a lightly inflated balloon.

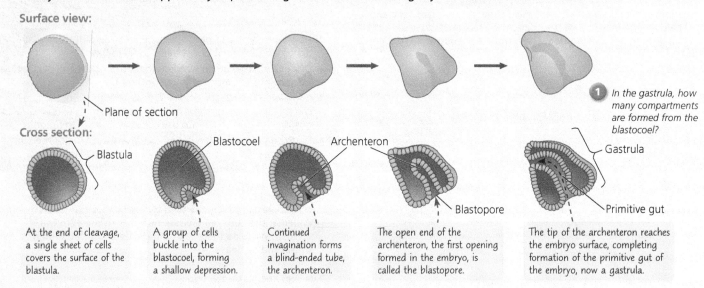

Surface view:

Plane of section

Cross section:

Blastula — Blastocoel — Archenteron — Blastopore — Gastrula — Primitive gut

**1** In the gastrula, how many compartments are formed from the blastocoel?

At the end of cleavage, a single sheet of cells covers the surface of the blastula.

A group of cells buckle into the blastocoel, forming a shallow depression.

Continued invagination forms a blind-ended tube, the archenteron.

The open end of the archenteron, the first opening formed in the embryo, is called the blastopore.

The tip of the archenteron reaches the embryo surface, completing formation of the primitive gut of the embryo, now a gastrula.

### Forming the primary cell layers of the animal body

In diploblasts, gastrulation forms two germ layers: ectoderm and endoderm. Triploblasts gain a third layer: mesoderm. At the end of embryogenesis, each germ layer gives rise to specific tissues and organs. To visualize this process, trace the fate of each germ layer in each row of drawings (all views other are cross sections except the sea urchin larva, which is a transparent surface view).

**Key**
Ectoderm
Mesoderm
Endoderm

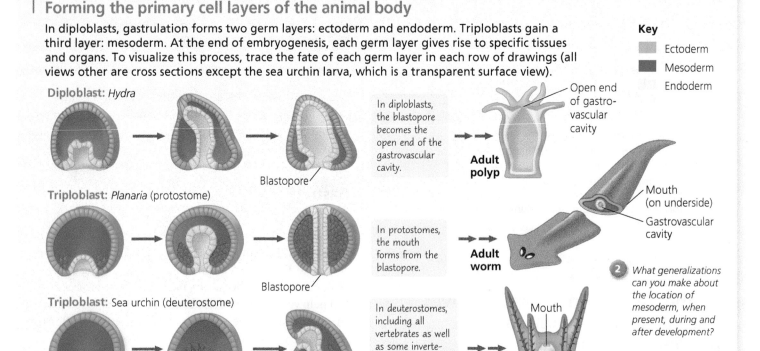

**Diploblast:** *Hydra*

Blastopore

In diploblasts, the blastopore becomes the open end of the gastrovascular cavity.

**Adult polyp**

Open end of gastrovascular cavity

**Triploblast:** *Planaria* (protostome)

Blastopore

In protostomes, the mouth forms from the blastopore.

**Adult worm**

Mouth (on underside)
Gastrovascular cavity

**Triploblast:** Sea urchin (deuterostome)

Blastopore

In deuterostomes, including all vertebrates as well as some invertebrates, the mouth forms *opposite* the blastopore.

Mouth
**Larva**
Anus

**2** What generalizations can you make about the location of mesoderm, when present, during and after development?

**Video: Sea Urchin Gastrulation**

diploblasts. In contrast, vertebrates and other bilaterally symmetric animals are triploblasts: In these animals, a third germ layer, the **mesoderm**, forms between the ectoderm and the endoderm.

## Gastrulation in Frogs

Each embryonic germ layer contributes to a distinct set of structures in the adult animal, as shown in **Figure 47.9**. The embryonic organization of the germ layers is often reflected in the adult: The ectoderm forms the nervous system and outer body layer, the mesoderm gives rise to muscles and skeleton, and the endoderm lines many organs and ducts. There are, however, numerous exceptions.

**Figure 47.10** depicts the details of gastrulation in a frog. The blastula of frogs and other triploblasts has a dorsal (top)

▼ **Figure 47.9 Major derivatives of the three embryonic germ layers in vertebrates.**

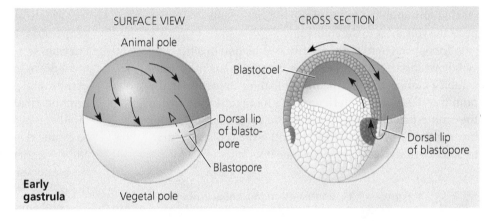

| ECTODERM (outer layer) | MESODERM (middle layer) | ENDODERM (inner layer) |
|---|---|---|
| • Epidermis of skin and its derivatives (including sweat glands, hair follicles) <br> • Nervous and sensory systems <br> • Pituitary gland, adrenal medulla <br> • Jaws and teeth | • Skeletal and muscular systems <br> • Circulatory and lymphatic systems <br> • Excretory and reproductive systems (except germ cells) <br> • Dermis of skin <br> • Adrenal cortex | • Epithelial lining of digestive tract and associated organs <br> • Epithelial lining of respiratory, excretory, and reproductive tracts and ducts <br> • Thymus, thyroid, and parathyroid glands |

 HHMI Video: Differentiation and the Fate of Cells

 ▼ **Figure 47.10 Gastrulation in a frog embryo.** In the frog blastula, the blastocoel is displaced toward the animal pole and is surrounded by a wall several cells thick.

**1** Gastrulation begins when cells on the dorsal side invaginate to form a small indented crease, the blastopore. The part above the crease is called the **dorsal lip**. As the blastopore is forming, a sheet of cells begins to spread out of the animal hemisphere, rolls inward over the dorsal lip (involution), and moves into the interior (shown by the dashed arrow). In the interior, these cells will form endoderm and mesoderm, with the endodermal layer on the inside. Meanwhile, cells at the animal pole change shape and begin spreading over the outer surface.

**2** The blastopore extends around both sides of the embryo as more cells invaginate. When the ends meet, the blastopore forms a circle that becomes smaller as ectoderm spreads downward over the surface. Internally, continued involution expands the endoderm and mesoderm; an archenteron forms and grows as the blastocoel shrinks and eventually disappears.

**3** Late in gastrulation, the cells remaining on the surface make up the ectoderm. The endoderm is the innermost layer, and the mesoderm lies between the ectoderm and endoderm. The circular blastopore surrounds a plug of yolk-filled cells.

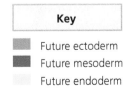

**Key**

- Future ectoderm
- Future mesoderm
- Future endoderm

SURFACE VIEW — CROSS SECTION

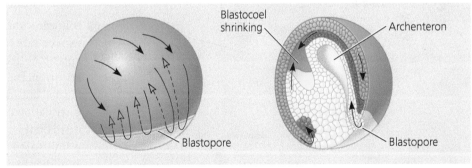

**Early gastrula** — Animal pole, Blastocoel, Dorsal lip of blastopore, Blastopore, Vegetal pole, Dorsal lip of blastopore

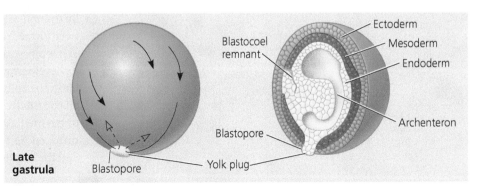

Blastocoel shrinking, Archenteron, Blastopore

**Late gastrula** — Blastocoel remnant, Ectoderm, Mesoderm, Endoderm, Blastopore, Archenteron, Yolk plug

and ventral (bottom) side, a left and right side, and an anterior (front) and posterior (back) end. As shown in ①, the cell movements that begin gastrulation occur on the dorsal side, opposite where the sperm entered the egg. The frog's anus develops from the blastopore, and the mouth eventually breaks through at the opposite end of the archenteron.

## Gastrulation in Chicks

At the onset of gastrulation in chicks, an upper and a lower layer of cells—the *epiblast* and *hypoblast*—lie atop a yolk mass. All the cells that will form the embryo come from the epiblast. During gastrulation, some epiblast cells move toward the midline, detach, and move inward toward the yolk **(Figure 47.11)**. The pileup of cells moving inward at the midline produces a visible thickening called the *primitive streak*. Some of these cells move downward and form endoderm, pushing aside the hypoblast cells, while others migrate laterally (sideways) and form mesoderm. The cells left behind on the surface at the end of gastrulation will become ectoderm. The hypoblast cells later segregate from the endoderm and eventually form part of the sac that surrounds the yolk and also part of the stalk that connects the yolk mass to the embryo.

Although different terms describe gastrulation in different vertebrate species, the rearrangements and movements of cells exhibit a number of fundamental similarities. In particular, the primitive streak, shown in Figure 47.11 for the chick embryo, is the counterpart of the blastopore lip, shown in Figure 47.10 for the frog embryo. Formation of a primitive streak is also central to human embryo gastrulation, our next topic.

▼ **Figure 47.11 Gastrulation in a chick embryo.** This is a cross section of a gastrulating embryo, looking toward the anterior end.

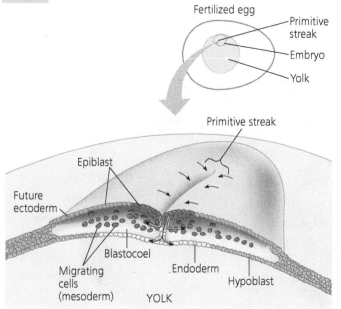

## Gastrulation in Humans

Unlike the large, yolky eggs of many vertebrates, human eggs are quite small, storing little in the way of food reserves. Fertilization takes place in the oviduct, and development begins while the embryo completes its journey down the oviduct to the uterus (see Figure 46.15).

**Figure 47.12** outlines the development of the human embryo, starting about 6 days after fertilization. This depiction is largely based on observations of embryos from other mammals, such as the mouse, and of very early human embryos following *in vitro* fertilization.

❶ At the end of cleavage, the embryo has more than 100 cells arranged around a central cavity and has reached the uterus. At this stage, the embryo is called a **blastocyst**, the mammalian version of a blastula. Clustered at one end of the blastocyst cavity is a group of cells called the **inner cell mass**, which will develop into the embryo proper. It is the cells of the inner cell mass that are the source of embryonic stem cell lines (see Concept 20.3).

❷ Implantation of the embryo is initiated by the **trophoblast**, the outer epithelium of the blastocyst. Enzymes secreted by the trophoblast during implantation break down molecules of the endometrium, the lining of the uterus, allowing invasion by the blastocyst. The trophoblast also extends finger-like projections that cause capillaries in the endometrium to spill out blood that can be captured by trophoblast tissues. Around the time the embryo undergoes implantation, the inner cell mass of the blastocyst forms a flat disk with an inner layer of cells, the *epiblast*, and an outer layer, the *hypoblast*. As is true for a bird embryo, the human embryo develops almost entirely from epiblast cells.

❸ Following implantation, the trophoblast continues to expand into the endometrium, and four new membranes appear. Although these **extraembryonic membranes** arise from the embryo, they enclose specialized structures located outside the embryo. As implantation is completed, gastrulation begins. Some epiblast cells remain as ectoderm on the surface, while others move inward through a primitive streak and form mesoderm and endoderm, just as in the chick (see Figure 47.11).

❹ By the end of gastrulation, the embryonic germ layers have formed. Extraembryonic mesoderm and four distinct extraembryonic membranes now surround the embryo. As development proceeds, cells of the invading trophoblast, the epiblast, and the adjacent endometrial tissue all contribute to the formation of the placenta. This vital organ mediates the exchange of nutrients, gases, and nitrogenous wastes between the developing embryo and the mother (see Figure 46.16).

 HHMI Video: Human Embryonic Development

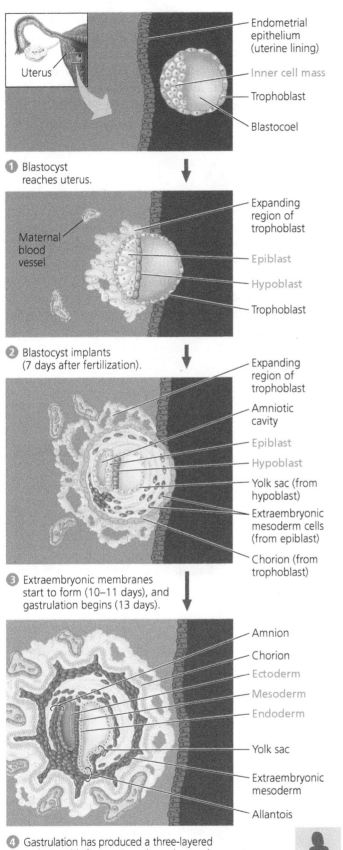

Endometrial epithelium (uterine lining)

Inner cell mass

Trophoblast

Blastocoel

Uterus

**1** Blastocyst reaches uterus.

Maternal blood vessel

Expanding region of trophoblast

Epiblast

Hypoblast

Trophoblast

**2** Blastocyst implants (7 days after fertilization).

Expanding region of trophoblast

Amniotic cavity

Epiblast

Hypoblast

Yolk sac (from hypoblast)

Extraembryonic mesoderm cells (from epiblast)

Chorion (from trophoblast)

**3** Extraembryonic membranes start to form (10–11 days), and gastrulation begins (13 days).

Amnion

Chorion

Ectoderm

Mesoderm

Endoderm

Yolk sac

Extraembryonic mesoderm

Allantois

**4** Gastrulation has produced a three-layered embryo with four extraembryonic membranes: the amnion, chorion, yolk sac, and allantois.

▲ **Figure 47.12 Four stages in the early embryonic development of a human.** The names of the tissues that develop into the embryo proper are printed in blue.

▼ **Figure 47.13 The shelled egg of reptiles.**

**(a) The four extraembryonic membranes in a reptile egg.**

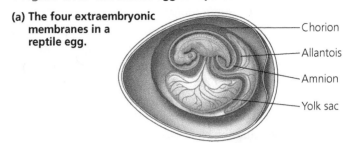

Chorion

Allantois

Amnion

Yolk sac

**(b) A baby red-tailed racer snake (*Gonyosoma oxycephala*) hatching from its protective egg.**

## Developmental Adaptations of Amniotes

**EVOLUTION** During embryonic development, mammals and reptiles (including birds) form four extraembryonic membranes: the chorion, allantois, amnion, and yolk sac **(Figure 47.13)**. In all these groups, such membranes provide a "life-support system" for further development. Why did this adaptation appear in the evolutionary history of reptiles and mammals, but not other vertebrates, such as fishes and amphibians? We can formulate a reasonable hypothesis by considering a few basic facts about embryonic development. All vertebrate embryos require an aqueous environment for their development. The embryos of fishes and amphibians usually develop in the surrounding sea or pond and need no specialized water-filled enclosure. However, the extensive colonization of land by vertebrates was possible only after the evolution of structures that would allow reproduction in dry environments. Two such structures exist today: (1) the shelled egg of birds and other reptiles as well as a few mammals (the monotremes) and (2) the uterus of marsupial and eutherian mammals. Inside the shell or uterus, the embryos of these animals are surrounded by fluid within a sac formed by one of the extraembryonic membranes, the amnion. Mammals and reptiles, including birds, are therefore called **amniotes** (see Concept 34.5).

For the most part, the extraembryonic membranes have similar functions in mammals and reptiles, consistent with a common evolutionary origin (see Figure 34.25). The chorion is the site of gas exchange, and the fluid within the amnion physically protects the developing embryo. (This amniotic fluid is released from the vagina when a pregnant woman's "water breaks" before childbirth.) The allantois, which disposes of wastes in the reptilian egg, is incorporated into the umbilical cord in mammals. There, it forms blood vessels that transport oxygen and nutrients from the placenta to the embryo and rid the embryo of carbon dioxide and nitrogenous wastes. The fourth extraembryonic membrane, the yolk sac, encloses yolk in the eggs of reptiles. In mammals it is a site of early formation of blood cells, which later migrate into the embryo proper. Thus, the extraembryonic membranes common to reptiles and mammals exhibit adaptations specific to development within a shelled egg or a uterus.

After gastrulation is complete and any extraembryonic membranes are formed, the next stage of embryonic development begins: organogenesis, the formation of organs.

## Organogenesis

During organogenesis, regions of the three embryonic germ layers develop into the rudiments of organs. Often, cells from two or three germ layers participate in forming a single organ, with interactions between cells of different germ layers helping to specify cell fates. Adopting particular developmental fates may in turn cause cells to change shape or, in certain circumstances, migrate to another location in the body. To see how these processes contribute to organogenesis, we'll consider *neurulation*, the early steps in the formation of the brain and spinal cord in vertebrates.

### Neurulation

Neurulation begins as cells from the dorsal mesoderm form the **notochord**, a rod that extends along the dorsal side of the chordate embryo, as seen for the frog in **Figure 47.14a**. Signaling molecules secreted by these mesodermal cells and other tissues cause the ectoderm above the notochord to become the *neural plate*. Formation of the neural plate is thus an example of **induction**, a process in which a group of cells or tissues influences the development of another group through close-range interactions (see Figure 18.17b).

▼ **Figure 47.14 Neurulation in a frog embryo.**

(MB) Video: Frog Development

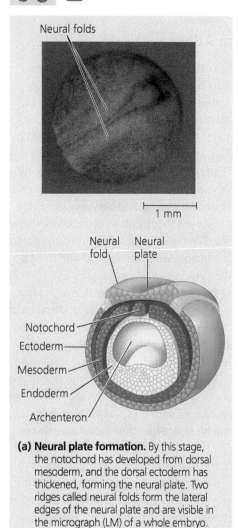

(a) **Neural plate formation.** By this stage, the notochord has developed from dorsal mesoderm, and the dorsal ectoderm has thickened, forming the neural plate. Two ridges called neural folds form the lateral edges of the neural plate and are visible in the micrograph (LM) of a whole embryo.

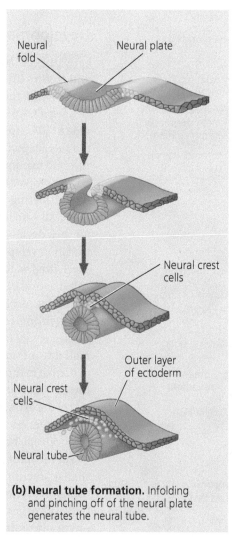

(b) **Neural tube formation.** Infolding and pinching off of the neural plate generates the neural tube.

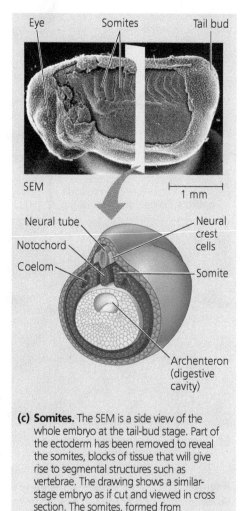

(c) **Somites.** The SEM is a side view of the whole embryo at the tail-bud stage. Part of the ectoderm has been removed to reveal the somites, blocks of tissue that will give rise to segmental structures such as vertebrae. The drawing shows a similar-stage embryo as if cut and viewed in cross section. The somites, formed from mesoderm, flank the notochord.

After the neural plate is formed, its cells change shape, curving the structure inward. In this way, the neural plate rolls itself into the **neural tube**, which runs along the anterior-posterior axis of the embryo (**Figure 47.14b**). The neural tube will become the brain in the head and the spinal cord along the rest of the body. In contrast, the notochord disappears before birth, although parts persist as the inner portions of the disks in the adult spine. (These are the disks that can herniate or rupture, causing back pain.)

Neurulation, like other stages of development, is sometimes imperfect. For example, *spina bifida*, the most common disabling birth defect in the United States, occurs when a portion of the neural tube fails to develop or close properly. The opening in the spinal column that remains causes nerve damage, resulting in varying degrees of leg paralysis. Although the opening can be surgically repaired shortly after birth, the nerve damage is permanent.

## Cell Migration in Organogenesis

During organogenesis, some cells undergo long-range migration, including two sets of cells that develop near the vertebrate neural tube. The first set is called the **neural crest**, a set of cells that develops along the borders where the neural tube pinches off from the ectoderm (see Figure 47.14b). Neural crest cells subsequently migrate to many parts of the embryo, forming a variety of tissues that include peripheral nerves as well as parts of the teeth and skull bones.

A second set of migratory cells is formed when groups of mesodermal cells lateral to the notochord separate into blocks called **somites (Figure 47.14c)**. Somites play a significant role in organizing the segmented structure of the vertebrate body. Parts of the somites dissociate

into mesenchyme cells. Some form the vertebrae; others form the muscles associated with the vertebral column and the ribs.

By contributing to the formation of vertebrae, ribs, and associated muscles, somites form repeated structures in the adult. Chordates, including ourselves, are thus segmented, although in the adult form the segmentation is much less obvious than in shrimp and other segmented invertebrates.

## Organogenesis in Chicks and Insects

Early organogenesis in the chick is quite similar to that in the frog. For example, the borders of the chick blastoderm fold downward and come together, pinching the embryo into a three-layered tube joined under the middle of the body to the yolk (**Figure 47.15a**). By the time the chick embryo is 3 days old, rudiments of the major organs, including the brain, eyes, and heart, are readily apparent (**Figure 47.15b**).

Comparing organogenesis in invertebrates with that in vertebrates often reveals fundamental similarities in mechanism that are masked by differences in pattern and appearance. For example, consider neurulation. In insects, tissues of the nervous system form on the ventral, not dorsal, side of the embryo. However, ectoderm along the anterior-posterior axis then rolls into a tube inside the embryo, just as in vertebrate neurulation. Furthermore, the molecular signaling pathways that bring about these similar events in different locations have many steps in common, underscoring a shared evolutionary history.

Like gastrulation, organogenesis in vertebrates and invertebrates relies substantially on changes in cell shape and location. We turn now to an exploration of how these changes take place.

▶ **Figure 47.15 Organogenesis in a chick embryo.**

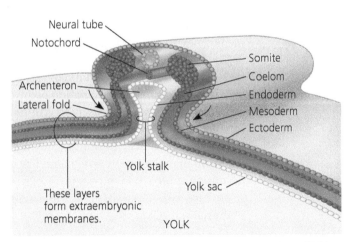

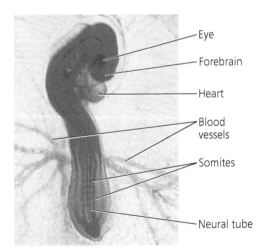

(a) **Early organogenesis.** The archenteron forms when lateral folds pinch the embryo away from the yolk. The embryo remains open to the yolk, attached by the yolk stalk, as shown in this cross section.

(b) **Late organogenesis.** Rudiments of most major organs have already formed in this 3-day old chick embryo. Blood vessels extending from the embryo supply the extraembryonic membranes, as seen in this light micrograph (LM).

# The Cytoskeleton in Morphogenesis

In animals, movement of parts of a cell can bring about changes in cell shape or enable a cell to migrate from one place to another within the embryo. One set of cellular components essential to these events is the collection of microtubules and microfilaments that make up the cytoskeleton (see Table 6.1).

## Cell Shape Changes in Morphogenesis

Reorganization of the cytoskeleton is a major force in changing cell shape during development. As an example, let's return to the topic of neurulation. At the onset of neural tube formation, microtubules oriented from dorsal to ventral in a sheet of ectodermal cells help lengthen the cells along that axis (Figure 47.16). At the apical end of each cell is a bundle of actin filaments (microfilaments) oriented crosswise. These actin filaments contract, giving the cells a wedge shape that bends the ectoderm layer inward.

The generation of wedge-shaped cells by apical constriction of actin filaments is a common mechanism in development for invaginating a cell layer. For instance, during gastrulation in the fruit fly *Drosophila melanogaster*, the formation of

▼ **Figure 47.16 Change in cell shape during morphogenesis.** Reorganization of the cytoskeleton is associated with morphogenetic changes in embryonic tissues, as shown here.

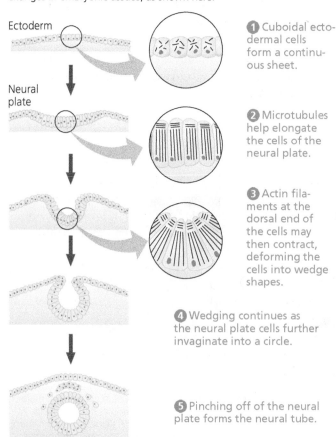

Ectoderm

Neural plate

❶ Cuboidal ectodermal cells form a continuous sheet.

❷ Microtubules help elongate the cells of the neural plate.

❸ Actin filaments at the dorsal end of the cells may then contract, deforming the cells into wedge shapes.

❹ Wedging continues as the neural plate cells further invaginate into a circle.

❺ Pinching off of the neural plate forms the neural tube.

wedge-shaped cells along the ventral surface drives generation of the tube of cells that forms the mesoderm.

Over the course of chick gastrulation, the primitive streak lengthens and narrows. This shape change results from a movement and sorting of cells called convergent extension. We'll explore the mechanism of this process shortly, when we examine how form and shape arise in development.

The cytoskeleton also directs a morphogenetic movement called **convergent extension**, a rearrangement that causes a sheet of cells to become narrower (converge) while it becomes longer (extends). This type of lengthening and narrowing of cells occurs often in gastrulation, including formation of the primitive streak in the fertilized chick egg (see Figure 47.11) and elongation of the archenteron in the sea urchin embryo (see Figure 47.8). Convergent extension is also important during involution in the frog gastrula. There, convergent extension changes the gastrulating embryo from a spherical shape to the rounded rectangular shape seen in Figure 47.14c.

The cell movements during convergent extension are quite simple: The cells elongate, with their ends pointing in the direction they will move, and then wedge between each other, forming fewer columns of cells (Figure 47.17). It's like a crowd of people about to enter a theater moving forward while also merging into a single-file line.

## Cell Migration in Morphogenesis

The cytoskeleton is responsible not only for cell shape changes but also for cell migration. During organogenesis in vertebrates, cells from the neural crest and from somites migrate to locations throughout the embryo. Cells "crawl" within the embryo by using cytoskeletal fibers to extend and retract cellular protrusions. This type of motility is akin to amoeboid movement (see Figure 6.26b). Transmembrane glycoproteins called *cell adhesion molecules* play a key role in cell migration by promoting interaction between pairs of cells. Cell migration also involves the *extracellular matrix* (*ECM*), the meshwork of secreted glycoproteins and other macromolecules lying outside the plasma membranes of cells (see Figure 6.28).

The ECM helps to guide cells in many types of movements, such as migration of individual cells and shape changes of cell sheets. Cells that line migration pathways regulate the movement of migrating cells by secreting specific molecules into the ECM. For these reasons, researchers are attempting to generate an artificial ECM that can serve as a scaffold for the repair or replacement of damaged tissues or organs. One promising approach involves the use of nanofiber fabrication to produce materials that mimic the essential properties of the natural ECM.

## Programmed Cell Death

Just as certain cells of the embryo are programmed to change shape or location, others are programmed to die. At various

> **Figure 47.17 Convergent extension of a sheet of cells.** In this simplified diagram, the cells elongate coordinately in a particular direction and crawl between each other (convergence) as the sheet becomes longer and narrower (extension).

**Convergence**
Cells elongate and crawl between each other.

**Extension**
The sheet of cells becomes longer and narrower.

times in development, individual cells, sets of cells, or whole tissues cease to develop, die, and are engulfed by neighboring cells. Thus, *programmed cell death*, also called **apoptosis**, is a common feature of animal development.

One circumstance for programmed cell death is when a structure functions only in a larval or other immature form of the organism. One familiar example is the tail of a tadpole, the free-swimming larval stage of a frog or toad. The tail forms during early development, enables locomotion during larval growth, and is then eliminated during metamorphosis into the adult form (see Figure 45.22).

Apoptosis may also occur when a large set of cells is formed, but only a subset has the properties required for further function. Such is the case in both nervous and immune system development. In the vertebrate nervous system, for instance, many more neurons are produced during development than exist in the adult. Neurons that make functional connections with other neurons typically survive; many of the rest undergo apoptosis. Similarly, in the adaptive immune system, self-reactive cells—cells with the potential to attack the animal itself rather than invading pathogens—are often eliminated by apoptosis.

Some cells that undergo apoptosis don't seem to have any function. Why do such cells form? The answer can be found by considering the evolution of amphibians, birds, and mammals. When these groups began to diverge during evolution, the basic developmental program for making a vertebrate body was already in place. The differences in present-day body forms arose through modification of that common developmental program. For example, the shared developmental program generates webbing between the embryonic digits, but in many birds and mammals, including humans, the webbing is eliminated by apoptosis (see Figure 11.21). This is one reason why such different adult forms arise from early vertebrate embryos that look so much alike.

As you have seen, cell behavior and the molecular mechanisms underlying it are crucial to the morphogenesis of the embryo. In the next section, you'll learn some ways in which shared cellular and genetic processes ensure that particular types of cells each end up in the right place.

**CONCEPT CHECK 47.2**

1. In the frog embryo, convergent extension elongates the notochord. Explain how the words *convergent* and *extension* apply to this process.

2. **WHAT IF?** ➤ Predict what would happen if, just before neural tube formation, you treated frog embryos with a drug that enters all the cells of the embryo and blocks the function of microfilaments.

3. **MAKE CONNECTIONS** ➤ Unlike some other types of birth defects, neural tube defects are largely preventable. Explain (see Figure 41.4).

*For suggested answers, see Appendix A.*

# CONCEPT 47.3

## Cytoplasmic determinants and inductive signals regulate cell fate

During embryonic development, cells arise by division, take up particular locations in the body, and become specialized in structure and function. Where a cell resides, how it appears, and what it together does define its development *fate*. Developmental biologists use the terms **determination** to refer to the process by which a cell or group of cells becomes committed to a particular fate and **differentiation** to refer to the resulting specialization in structure and function. You may find it a useful analogy to think about determination being equivalent to declaring a major in college and differentiation being comparable to taking the courses required by your major.

Every diploid cell formed during an animal's development has the same genome. With the exception of certain mature immune cells, the collection of genes present in a given cell is the same throughout the cell's life. How, then, do cells acquire different fates? As discussed in Concept 18.4, particular tissues, and often cells within a tissue, differ from one another by expressing distinct sets of genes from their shared genome.

A major focus of developmental biology is to uncover the mechanisms that direct the differences in gene expression underlying developmental fates. As one step toward this goal, scientists often seek to trace tissues and cell types back to their origins in the early embryo.

▼ **Figure 47.18 Fate mapping for two chordates.**

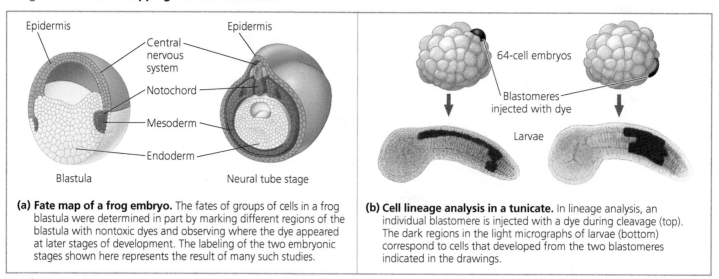

**(a) Fate map of a frog embryo.** The fates of groups of cells in a frog blastula were determined in part by marking different regions of the blastula with nontoxic dyes and observing where the dye appeared at later stages of development. The labeling of the two embryonic stages shown here represents the result of many such studies.

**(b) Cell lineage analysis in a tunicate.** In lineage analysis, an individual blastomere is injected with a dye during cleavage (top). The dark regions in the light micrographs of larvae (bottom) correspond to cells that developed from the two blastomeres indicated in the drawings.

# Fate Mapping

One way to trace the ancestry of embryonic cells is direct observation through the microscope. Such studies produced the first **fate maps**, diagrams showing the structures arising from each region of an embryo. In the 1920s, German embryologist Walther Vogt used this approach to determine where groups of cells from the blastula end up in the gastrula (**Figure 47.18a**). Later researchers developed techniques that allowed them to mark an individual blastomere during cleavage and then follow the marker as it was distributed to all the mitotic descendants of that cell (**Figure 47.18b**).

A much more comprehensive approach to fate mapping has been carried out on the soil-dwelling nematode *Caenorhabditis elegans*, as shown in **Figure 47.19**. This roundworm is about 1 mm long, has a simple, transparent body with only a few types of cells, and develops into a mature adult hermaphrodite in only 3.5 days in the laboratory. These attributes allowed Sydney Brenner, Robert Horvitz, and John Sulston to determine the complete developmental history, or *lineage*, of every cell in *C. elegans*. They found that every adult hermaphrodite has exactly 959 somatic cells, which arise from the

▼ **Figure 47.19 Cell lineage in *Caenorhabditis elegans*.** The *C. elegans* embryo is transparent, making it possible for researchers to trace the lineage of every cell, from the zygote to the adult worm (LM). The diagram shows a detailed lineage only for the intestine, which is derived exclusively from one of the first four cells formed from the zygote.

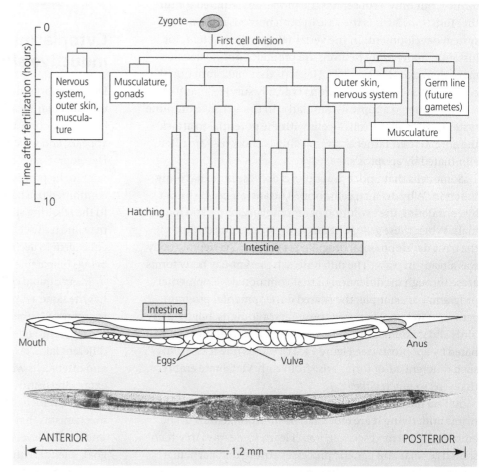

**VISUAL SKILLS ▶** *The pattern of divisions is exactly the same in every* C. elegans *embryo. How many divisions of the fertilized egg give rise to the intestinal cell closest to the worm's mouth?*

**▼ Figure 47.20 Determination of germ cell fate in *C. elegans*.** Labeling with a fluorescent antibody that is specific for a *C. elegans* P granule protein (green) reveals the incorporation of P granules into four cells of the newly hatched larva (two of the four cells are visible in this view).

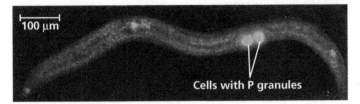

100 μm

Cells with P granules

fertilized egg in virtually the same way for every individual. Careful microscopic observations of worms at all stages of development, coupled with experiments in which particular cells or groups of cells were destroyed by a laser beam or through mutations, resulted in the cell lineage diagram shown in Figure 47.19. Using this cell lineage diagram, you can identify all of the progeny of a single cell, just as you would use a family history to trace the descendants of one great-great-grandparent.

As an example of a particular cell fate, let's consider *germ cells*, the specialized cells that give rise to eggs or sperm. In all animals studied, complexes of RNA and protein direct particular cells to become germ cells. In *C. elegans*, such complexes, called *P granules*, can be detected in four cells of the newly hatched larva **(Figure 47.20)** and, later, in the cells of the adult gonad that produce sperm or eggs.

Tracing the position of the P granules provides a dramatic illustration of how cells acquire a specific fate, during development. As shown in **Figure 47.21**, ❶ and ❷ the P granules are distributed throughout the newly fertilized egg but move to the posterior end of the zygote before the first cleavage division. ❸ As a result, only the posterior of the two cells formed by the first division contains P granules. ❹ The P granules continue to be asymmetrically partitioned during subsequent divisions. Thus, the P granules act as cytoplasmic determinants (see Concept 18.4), fixing germ cell fate at the earliest stage of *C. elegans* development.

Fate mapping in *C. elegans* paved the way for major discoveries about programmed cell death. Lineage analysis demonstrated that exactly 131 cells die during normal *C. elegans* development. In the 1980s, researchers found that a mutation inactivating a single gene allows all 131 cells to live. Further research revealed that this gene is part of a pathway that controls and carries out apoptosis in a wide range of animals, including humans. In 2002, Brenner, Horvitz, and Sulston shared a Nobel Prize for their use of the *C. elegans* fate map in studies of programmed cell death and organogenesis.

Having established fate maps for early development, scientists were positioned to answer questions about underlying

**▼ Figure 47.21 Partitioning of P granules during *C. elegans* development.** The differential interference contrast micrographs (left) highlight the boundaries of nuclei and cells through the first two cell divisions. The fluorescence micrographs (right) show identically staged embryos labeled with a fluorescent antibody specific for a P granule protein.

20 μm

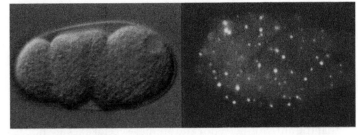

❶ Newly fertilized egg

❷ Zygote prior to first division

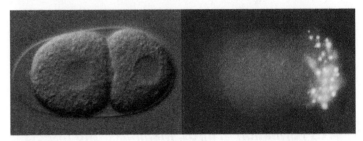

❸ Two-cell embryo

❹ Four-cell embryo

mechanisms, such as how the basic axes of the embryo are established, a process known as axis formation.

## Axis Formation

A body plan with bilateral symmetry is found across a range of animals, including nematodes, echinoderms, and vertebrates (see Concept 32.4). This body plan exhibits asymmetry along the dorsal-ventral and anterior-posterior axes, as shown for a frog tadpole in **Figure 47.22a**. The right-left axis is largely symmetrical, as the two sides are roughly mirror images. When and how are these three axes established? We'll begin answering this question by considering the frog.

## Axis Formation in the Frog

In the frog, the future position of the anterior-posterior axis is determined during oogenesis. Asymmetry in the egg is apparent in the formation of two distinct hemispheres: Dark melanin granules are embedded in the cortex of the animal hemisphere, whereas a yellow yolk fills the vegetal hemisphere. This animal-vegetal asymmetry dictates where the anterior-posterior axis forms in the embryo. Note, however, that the anterior-posterior and animal-vegetal axes are not the same; that is, the head of the embryo does not coincide with the animal pole.

Surprisingly, the dorsal-ventral axis of the frog embryo is determined at random. Specifically, wherever the sperm enters in the animal hemisphere determines where the dorsal-ventral axis forms. Once the sperm and egg have fused, the egg surface—the plasma membrane and associated cortex—rotates with respect to the inner cytoplasm, a movement called *cortical rotation*. From the perspective of the animal pole, this rotation is always toward the point of sperm entry (**Figure 47.22b**). The resulting interactions between molecules in the vegetal cortex and in the inner cytoplasm of the animal hemisphere activate regulatory proteins. Once activated, these proteins direct expression of one set of genes in dorsal regions and another set of genes in ventral regions.

## Axis Formation in Birds, Mammals, and Insects

It turns out that there are many different processes by which animal embryos establish their body axes. In mammals, the sperm appears to contribute to axis formation, but not in the same manner as in frogs. In particular, the orientation of the egg and sperm nuclei before they fuse influences the location of the first cleavage plane. In chicks, the anterior-posterior axis is established by the pull of gravity during the time when the soon-to-be-laid egg is traveling down the hen's oviduct. In zebrafish, signals within the embryo gradually establish the anterior-posterior axis over the course of a day. Still other mechanisms occur in insects, where gradients of active transcription factors across the body establish both the anterior-posterior and dorsal-ventral axes (see Concept 18.4).

Once the anterior-posterior and dorsal-ventral axes are established, the position of the left-right axis is fixed. Nevertheless, specific molecular mechanisms must establish which side is left and which is right. In vertebrates, there are marked left-right differences in the location of internal

**▼ Figure 47.22 The body axes and their establishment in an amphibian.** All three axes are established before the zygote begins to undergo cleavage.

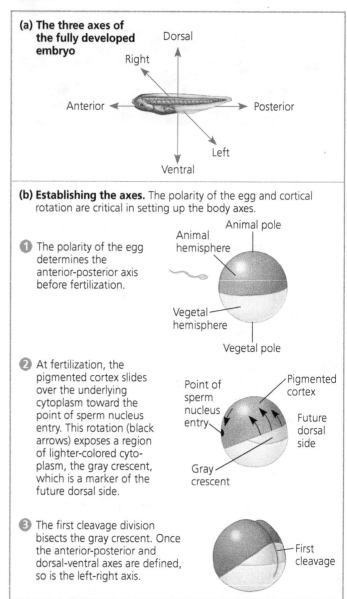

**(a) The three axes of the fully developed embryo**

Dorsal · Right · Anterior · Posterior · Left · Ventral

**(b) Establishing the axes.** The polarity of the egg and cortical rotation are critical in setting up the body axes.

❶ The polarity of the egg determines the anterior-posterior axis before fertilization.

Animal pole · Animal hemisphere · Vegetal hemisphere · Vegetal pole

❷ At fertilization, the pigmented cortex slides over the underlying cytoplasm toward the point of sperm nucleus entry. This rotation (black arrows) exposes a region of lighter-colored cytoplasm, the gray crescent, which is a marker of the future dorsal side.

Point of sperm nucleus entry · Pigmented cortex · Future dorsal side · Gray crescent

❸ The first cleavage division bisects the gray crescent. Once the anterior-posterior and dorsal-ventral axes are defined, so is the left-right axis.

First cleavage

**WHAT IF?** ➤ *When researchers allowed normal cortical rotation to occur and then forced the opposite rotation, the result was a two-headed embryo. How might you explain this finding, thinking about how cortical rotation influences body axis formation?*

organs as well as in the organization and structure of the heart and brain. Recent research has revealed a key role for cilia in setting up this left-right asymmetry, as we will discuss toward the end of this chapter.

## Restricting Developmental Potential

Earlier we described determination in terms of commitment to a particular cell fate. The fertilized egg gives rise to all cell fates. How long during development do cells retain this ability?

The German zoologist Hans Spemann addressed this question in 1938. By manipulating embryos to perturb normal development and then examining cell fate after the manipulation, he was able to assay a cell's *developmental potential*, the range of structures to which it can give rise **(Figure 47.23)**. The work of Spemann and others demonstrated that the first two blastomeres of the frog embryo are **totipotent**, meaning that they can each develop into all the different cell types of that species.

In mammals, embryonic cells remain totipotent through the eight-cell stage, much longer than in many other animals. Recent work, however, indicates that the very early cells (even the first two) are not actually equivalent in a normal embryo. Rather, their totipotency when isolated likely means that the cells can regulate their fate in response to their embryonic environment. Once the 16-cell stage is reached, mammalian cells are determined to form the trophoblast or the inner cell mass. Although the cells have a limited developmental potential from this point onward, their nuclei remain totipotent, as demonstrated in transplantation and cloning experiments (see Figures 20.17 and 20.18).

The totipotency of cells early in human embryogenesis is the reason why you or a classmate may have an identical twin. Identical (monozygotic) twins result when cells or groups of cells from a single embryo become separated. If the separation occurs before the trophoblast and inner cell mass become differentiated, two embryos grow, each with its own chorion and amnion. This is the case for about a third of identical twins. For the rest, the two embryos that develop share a chorion and, in very rare cases where separation is particularly late, an amnion as well.

Regardless of how uniform or varied early embryonic cells are in a particular species, the progressive restriction of developmental potential is a general feature of development in all animals. In general, the tissue-specific fates of cells are fixed in a late gastrula, but not always so in an early gastrula. For example, if the dorsal ectoderm of an early amphibian gastrula is experimentally replaced with ectoderm from some other location in the same gastrula, the transplanted tissue forms a neural plate. But if the same experiment is performed on a late-stage gastrula, the transplanted ectoderm does not respond to its new environment and does not form a neural plate.

## Cell Fate Determination and Pattern Formation by Inductive Signals

As embryonic development continues, cells influence each other's fates by induction. At the molecular level, the response to an inductive signal is usually to switch on a set of genes that make the receiving cells differentiate into a specific cell type or tissue. Here we will examine examples of this important

▼ **Figure 47.23**

**Inquiry** How does distribution of the gray crescent affect the developmental potential of the first two daughter cells?

**Experiment** Hans Spemann, at the University of Freiburg, Germany, carried out the following experiment in 1938 to test whether substances were located asymmetrically in the gray crescent.

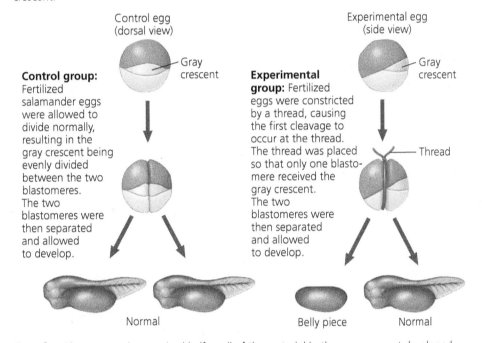

**Control group:** Fertilized salamander eggs were allowed to divide normally, resulting in the gray crescent being evenly divided between the two blastomeres. The two blastomeres were then separated and allowed to develop.

**Experimental group:** Fertilized eggs were constricted by a thread, causing the first cleavage to occur at the thread. The thread was placed so that only one blastomere received the gray crescent. The two blastomeres were then separated and allowed to develop.

**Results** Blastomeres that received half or all of the material in the gray crescent developed into normal embryos, but a blastomere that received none of the gray crescent gave rise to an abnormal embryo without dorsal structures. Spemann called it a "belly piece."

**Conclusion** The developmental potential of the two blastomeres normally formed during the first cleavage division depends on their acquisition of cytoplasmic determinants localized in the gray crescent.

**Data from** H. Spemann, *Embryonic Development and Induction*, Yale University Press, New Haven, CT (1938).

**DRAW IT ➤** *Draw lines to show the plane of the first cell division that would occur in the fertilized eggs above if no manipulations were done.*

**WHAT IF? ➤** *In a similar experiment 40 years earlier, embryologist Wilhelm Roux allowed the first cleavage to occur and then used a needle to kill just one blastomere. The embryo that developed from the remaining blastomere (plus remnants of the dead cell) was abnormal, resembling a half-embryo. How might the presence of molecules in the dead cell explain why Roux's result differed from the control result in Spemann's experiment?*

developmental process in organizing the basic body plan of an embryo and in directing the three-dimensional development of a vertebrate limb.

## The "Organizer" of Spemann and Mangold

Before his studies of totipotency in the fertilized frog egg, Spemann had investigated cell fate determination during gastrulation. In these experiments, he and his student Hilde Mangold transplanted tissues between early gastrulas. In their

▼ **Figure 47.24**

**Inquiry** Can the dorsal lip of the blastopore induce cells in another part of the amphibian embryo to change their developmental fate?

**Experiment** In 1924, Hans Spemann and Hilde Mangold, at the University of Freiburg, Germany, investigated the inductive ability of the dorsal lip of the gastrula. Using newts, they transplanted a piece of the dorsal lip from one gastrula to the ventral side of a second gastrula. Because the donor embryo was albino and thus lacked pigmentation, the researchers could visually follow how the transplanted material altered the fate of the recipient embryo.

**Results** The photograph in this figure documents a repeat of this classic experiment, using the frog *Xenopus laevis*. The tadpole at the top developed from a control gastrula. When an experimental gastrula received the transplant of a dorsal lip from an albino donor (lower left), the recipient embryo formed a second notochord and neural tube in the region of the transplant. Eventually most of a second embryo developed, producing a twinned tadpole (lower right).

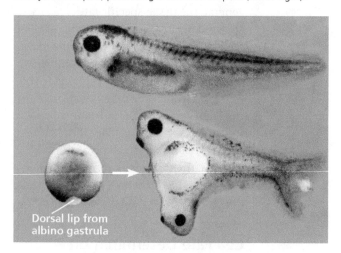

Dorsal lip from albino gastrula

**Conclusion** The transplanted dorsal lip was able to induce cells in a different region of the recipient to form structures different from their normal fate. In effect, the transplanted dorsal lip "organized" the later development of an entire extra embryo.

**Data from** H. Spemann and H. Mangold, Induction of embryonic primordia by implantation of organizers from a different species, Trans. V. Hamburger (1924). Reprinted in *International Journal of Developmental Biology* 45:13–38 (2001) and E. M. De Robertis and H. Kuroda, Dorsal-ventral patterning and neural induction in *Xenopus* embryos, *Ann. Rev. Cell Dev. Biol.* 20:285–308 (2004).

**WHAT IF?** ➤ *Because the transplant caused the recipient tissue to become something it would not have otherwise, a signal must have passed from the dorsal lip. If you identified a protein candidate for the signaling molecule, how would injecting it into ventral cells of a gastrula test its function?*

most famous such experiment, summarized in **Figure 47.24**, they made a remarkable discovery. Not only did a transplanted dorsal lip of the blastopore continue to be a blastopore lip, but it also triggered gastrulation of the surrounding tissue. They concluded that the dorsal lip of the blastopore in the early gastrula functions as an "organizer" of the embryo's body plan, inducing changes in surrounding tissue that direct formation of the notochord, the neural tube, and other organs.

Nearly a century later, developmental biologists are still studying the basis of induction by what is now called *Spemann's organizer*. An important clue has come from studies of a growth factor called bone morphogenetic protein 4 (BMP-4). One major function of the organizer seems to be to inactivate BMP-4 on the dorsal side of the embryo. Inactivating BMP-4 allows cells on the dorsal side to make dorsal structures, such as the notochord and neural tube. Proteins related to BMP-4 and its inhibitors are found as well in invertebrates such as the fruit fly, where they also function in regulating the dorsal-ventral axis.

## Formation of the Vertebrate Limb

Inductive signals play a major role in **pattern formation**, the process governing the arrangement of organs and tissues in their characteristic places in three-dimensional space. The molecular cues that control pattern formation, called **positional information**, tell a cell where it is with respect to the animal's body axes and help to determine how the cell and its descendants will respond to molecular signaling during embryonic development.

In Concept 18.4, we discussed pattern formation in the development of *Drosophila*. For the study of pattern formation in vertebrates, a classic model system has been limb development in the chick. The wings and legs of chicks, like all vertebrate limbs, begin as limb buds, bumps of mesodermal tissue covered by a layer of ectoderm **(Figure 47.25a)**. Each component of a chick limb, such as a specific bone or muscle, develops with a precise location and orientation relative to three axes: proximal-distal (shoulder to fingertip), anterior-posterior (thumb to little finger), and dorsal-ventral (knuckle to palm), as shown in **Figure 47.25b**.

Two regions in a limb bud have profound effects on its development. One such region is the **apical ectodermal ridge (AER)**, a thickened area of ectoderm at the tip of the bud (see Figure 47.25a). Surgically removing the AER blocks outgrowth of the limb along the proximal-distal axis. Why? The AER secretes a protein signal called fibroblast growth factor (FGF) that promotes limb-bud outgrowth. If the AER is replaced with beads soaked with FGF, a nearly normal limb develops.

The second major limb-bud regulatory region is the **zone of polarizing activity (ZPA)**, a specialized block of mesodermal tissue (see Figure 47.25a). The ZPA regulates

## Figure 47.25 Regulation of vertebrate limb development by organizer regions.

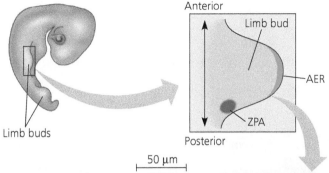

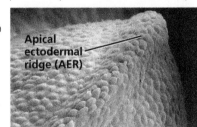

Anterior

Limb bud

AER

ZPA

Posterior

Limb buds

50 µm

**(a) Organizer regions.** Vertebrate limbs develop from protrusions called limb buds. Two regions in each limb bud, the apical ectodermal ridge (AER, shown in this SEM) and the zone of polarizing activity (ZPA), play key roles as organizers in limb pattern formation.

Apical ectodermal ridge (AER)

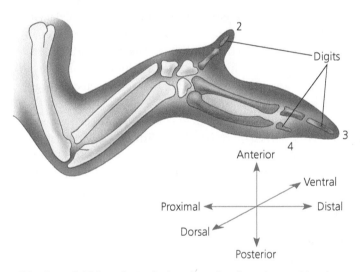

2

Digits

3

4

Anterior

Ventral

Proximal — Distal

Dorsal

Posterior

**(b) Wing of chick embryo.** Each embryonic cell receives positional information indicating location along the three axes of the limb. The AER and ZPA secrete molecules that help provide this information. (Numbers are assigned to the digits based on a convention established for vertebrate limbs. The chicken wing has only four digits; the first digit points backward and is not shown.)

development along the anterior-posterior axis of the limb. Cells nearest the ZPA form posterior structures, such as the most posterior of the chick's digits (equivalent to our little finger); cells farthest from the ZPA form anterior structures, including the most anterior digit (like our thumb). One key line of evidence for this model is the set of tissue transplantation experiments outlined in **Figure 47.26**.

Like the AER, the ZPA influences development by secreting a protein signal. The signal secreted by the ZPA is called

## Figure 47.26

**Inquiry** What role does the zone of polarizing activity (ZPA) play in limb pattern formation in vertebrates?

**Experiment** In 1985, researchers were eager to investigate the nature of the zone of polarizing activity. They transplanted ZPA tissue from a donor chick embryo under the ectoderm in the anterior margin of a limb bud in another chick (the host).

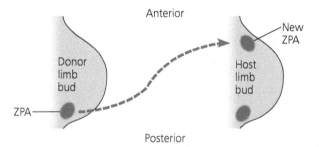

Anterior

New ZPA

Donor limb bud

Host limb bud

ZPA

Posterior

**Results** The host limb bud developed extra digits from host tissue in a mirror-image arrangement to the normal digits, which also formed (compare with Figure 47.26b, which shows a normal chick wing).

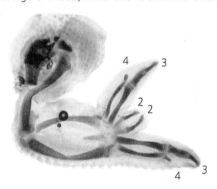

4 3

2 2

3

4

**Conclusion** The mirror-image duplication observed in this experiment suggests that ZPA cells secrete a signal that diffuses from its source and conveys positional information indicating "posterior." As the distance from the ZPA increases, the signal concentration decreases, and hence more anterior digits develop.

**Data from** L. S. Honig and D. Summerbell, Maps of strength of positional signaling activity in the developing chick wing bud, *Journal of Embryology and Experimental Morphology* 87:163–174 (1985).

**WHAT IF?** ➤ *Suppose you learned that the ZPA forms after the AER, leading you to develop the hypothesis that the AER is necessary for formation of the ZPA. If you removed the AER and looked for expression of Sonic hedgehog, how would that test your hypothesis?*

Sonic hedgehog, named after both a video game character and a similar protein in *Drosophila* that also regulates development. Implanting cells genetically engineered to produce Sonic hedgehog into the anterior region of a normal limb bud causes formation of a mirror-image limb—just as if a ZPA had been grafted there. Furthermore, experiments with mice reveal that production of Sonic hedgehog in part of the limb bud where it is normally absent can result in extra toes.

The AER and ZPA regulate the axes of a limb bud, but what determines whether the bud develops into a forelimb or hind limb? That information is provided by spatial patterns of *Hox* genes, which specify different developmental fates in particular body regions (see Figure 21.20).

BMP-4, FGF, Sonic hedgehog, and Hox proteins are examples of a much larger set of molecules that govern cell fates in animals. Having mapped out many of the basic functions of these molecules in embryonic development, researchers are now addressing their role in organogenesis, focusing in particular on the development of the brain.

## Cilia and Cell Fate

Recently, researchers found that the cellular organelles known as cilia are essential for specifying cell fate in human embryos. Like other mammals, humans have stationary and motile cilia (see Figure 6.24). Stationary primary cilia, or *monocilia*, jut from the surface of nearly all cells, one per cell. In contrast, motile cilia are restricted to cells that propel fluid over their surface, such as the epithelial cells of airways, and on sperm (as flagella that propel sperm movement). Both stationary and motile cilia have crucial roles in development.

Genetic studies provided vital clues to the developmental role of monocilia. In 2003, researchers discovered that certain mutations disrupting development of the mouse nervous system affect genes that function in the assembly of monocilia. Other geneticists found that mutations responsible for a severe kidney disease in mice alter a gene important for the transport of materials up and down monocilia. In addition, mutations in humans that block the function of monocilia were linked to cystic kidney disease.

How do monocilia function in development? Evidence indicates that monocilia act as antennae on the cell surface, receiving signals from multiple signaling proteins, including Sonic hedgehog. Mechanisms that regulate the set of receptor proteins that are present tune the cilium to particular signals. When the monocilia are defective, signaling is disrupted.

Insight into the role of motile cilia in development grew from studies of Kartagener's syndrome, a particular set of medical conditions that often appear together. These conditions include male infertility due to immotile sperm and infections of the nasal sinuses and bronchi in both males and females. However, by far the most intriguing feature of Kartagener's syndrome is *situs inversus*, a reversal of the normal left-right asymmetry of the organs in the chest and abdomen **(Figure 47.27)**. The heart, for example, is on the right side rather than the left. (By itself, situs inversus causes no significant medical problems.)

Scientists studying Kartagener's syndrome came to realize that all of the associated conditions result from a defect that makes cilia immotile. Without motility, sperm tails cannot beat and airway cells cannot sweep mucus and microbes out

▼ **Figure 47.27 Situs inversus, a reversal of normal left-right asymmetry in the chest and abdomen.**

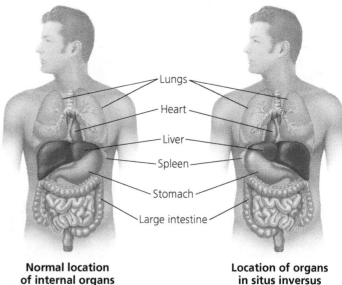

| | |
|---|---|
| **Normal location of internal organs** | **Location of organs in situs inversus** |

of the airway. But what causes situs inversus in these individuals? The current model proposes that ciliary motion in a particular part of the embryo is essential for normal development. Evidence indicates that movement of the cilia generates a leftward fluid flow, breaking the symmetry between left and right sides. Without that flow, asymmetry along the left-right axis arises randomly, and half of the affected embryos develop situs inversus.

If we consider development as a whole, we see a sequence of events marked by cycles of signaling and differentiation. Initial cell asymmetries allow different types of cells to influence each other, resulting in the expression of specific sets of genes. The products of these genes then direct cells to differentiate into specific types. Through pattern formation and morphogenesis, differentiated cells ultimately produce a complex arrangement of tissues and organs, each functioning in its appropriate location and in coordination with other cells, tissues, and organs throughout the organism.

## CONCEPT CHECK 47.3

1. How do axis formation and pattern formation differ?

2. MAKE CONNECTIONS ➤ How does a morphogen gradient differ from cytoplasmic determinants and inductive interactions with regard to the set of cells it affects (see Concept 18.4)?

3. WHAT IF? ➤ If the ventral cells of an early frog gastrula were experimentally induced to express large amounts of a protein that inhibits BMP-4, could a second embryo develop? Explain.

4. WHAT IF? ➤ If you removed the ZPA from a limb bud and then placed a bead soaked in Sonic hedgehog in the middle of the bud, what would be the most likely result?

*For suggested answers, see Appendix A.*

# 47 Chapter Review

 Go to **MasteringBiology**™ for Videos, Animations, Vocab Self-Quiz, Practice Tests, and more in the Study Area.

## SUMMARY OF KEY CONCEPTS

### CONCEPT 47.1

**Fertilization and cleavage initiate embryonic development** (pp. 1042–1047)

VOCAB
SELF-QUIZ
goo.gl/6u55ks

- **Fertilization** forms a diploid zygote and initiates embryonic development. The **acrosomal reaction** releases hydrolytic enzymes from the sperm head that digest material surrounding the egg.

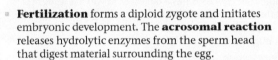

Sperm-egg fusion and depolarization of egg membrane (fast block to polyspermy)

↓

Cortical granule release (cortical reaction)

↓

Formation of fertilization envelope (slow block to polyspermy)

In mammalian fertilization, the cortical reaction modifies the **zona pellucida** as a slow block to polyspermy.

- Fertilization is followed by **cleavage**, a period of rapid cell division without growth, producing a large number of cells called **blastomeres**. The amount and distribution of **yolk** strongly influence the pattern of cleavage. In many species, the completion of the cleavage stage generates a **blastula** containing a fluid-filled cavity, the **blastocoel**.

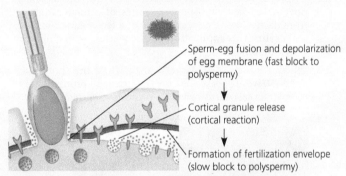

2-cell stage forming

**Animal pole**

8-cell stage

**Vegetal pole**

Blastula

Blastocoel

 *What cell-surface event would likely fail if a sperm contacted an egg of another species?*

### CONCEPT 47.2

**Morphogenesis in animals involves specific changes in cell shape, position, and survival** (pp. 1047–1055)

- **Gastrulation** converts the blastula to a **gastrula**, which has a primitive digestive cavity and three **germ layers: ectoderm** (blue), which forms the outer layer of the embryo, **mesoderm** (red), which forms the middle layer, and **endoderm** (yellow), which gives rise to the innermost tissues.

- Gastrulation and organogenesis in mammals resemble the processes in birds and other reptiles. After fertilization and early cleavage in the oviduct, the **blastocyst** implants in the uterus. The **trophoblast** initiates formation of the fetal portion of the placenta, and the embryo proper develops from a cell layer, the epiblast, within the blastocyst.

- The embryos of birds, other reptiles, and mammals develop within a fluid-filled sac that is contained within a shell or the uterus. In these organisms, the three germ layers produce four **extraembryonic membranes**: the amnion, chorion, yolk sac, and allantois.

- The organs of the animal body develop from specific portions of the three embryonic germ layers. Early events in **organogenesis** in vertebrates include neurulation: formation of the **notochord** by cells of the dorsal mesoderm and development of the **neural tube** from infolding of the ectodermal neural plate.

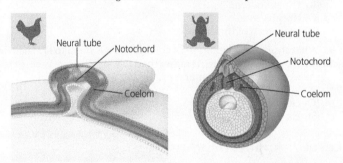

Neural tube — Notochord

Coelom

Neural tube — Notochord — Coelom

- Cytoskeletal rearrangements cause changes in the shape of cells that underlie cell movements in gastrulation and organogenesis, including invaginations and **convergent extension**. The cytoskeleton is also involved in cell migration, which relies on cell adhesion molecules and the extracellular matrix to help cells reach specific destinations. Migratory cells arise both from the neural crest and from **somites**.

- Some processes in animal development require **apoptosis**, programmed cell death.

 *What are some functions of apoptosis in development?*

### CONCEPT 47.3

**Cytoplasmic determinants and inductive signals regulate cell fate** (pp. 1055–1062)

- Experimentally derived **fate maps** of embryos show that specific regions of the zygote or blastula develop into specific parts of older embryos. The complete cell lineage has been worked out for *C. elegans*, revealing that programmed cell death contributes to animal development. In all species, the developmental potential of cells becomes progressively more limited as embryonic development proceeds.

- Cells in a developing embryo receive and respond to **positional information** that varies with location. This information is often in the form of signaling molecules secreted by cells in specific regions of the embryo, such as the dorsal lip of the blastopore in the amphibian gastrula and the **apical ectodermal ridge** and **zone of polarizing activity** of the vertebrate limb bud.

 *Suppose you found two classes of mouse mutations, one that affected limb development only and one that affected both limb and kidney development. Which class would be more likely to alter the function of monocilia? Explain.*

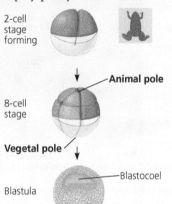

## Level 1: Knowledge/Comprehension

PRACTICE TEST
goo.gl/CUYGKD

1. The cortical reaction of sea urchin eggs functions directly in
   (A) the formation of a fertilization envelope.
   (B) the production of a fast block to polyspermy.
   (C) the generation of an electrical impulse by the egg.
   (D) the fusion of egg and sperm nuclei.

2. Which of the following is common to the development of both birds and mammals?
   (A) holoblastic cleavage
   (B) epiblast and hypoblast
   (C) trophoblast
   (D) gray crescent

3. The archenteron develops into
   (A) the mesoderm.
   (B) the endoderm.
   (C) the placenta.
   (D) the lumen of the digestive tract.

4. What structural adaptation in chickens allows them to lay their eggs in arid environments rather than in water?
   (A) extraembryonic membranes
   (B) yolk
   (C) cleavage
   (D) gastrulation

## Level 2: Application/Analysis

5. If an egg cell were treated with EDTA, a chemical that binds calcium and magnesium ions,
   (A) the acrosomal reaction would be blocked.
   (B) the fusion of sperm and egg nuclei would be blocked.
   (C) the fast block to polyspermy would not occur.
   (D) the fertilization envelope would not form.

6. In humans, identical twins are possible because
   (A) extraembryonic cells interact with the zygote nucleus.
   (B) convergent extension occurs.
   (C) early blastomeres can form a complete embryo if isolated.
   (D) the gray crescent divides the dorsal-ventral axis into new cells.

7. Cells transplanted from the neural tube of a frog embryo to the ventral part of another embryo develop into nervous system tissues. This result indicates that the transplanted cells were
   (A) totipotent.          (C) differentiated.
   (B) determined.          (D) mesenchymal.

8. **DRAW IT** Each blue circle in the figure below represents a cell in a cell lineage. Draw two modified versions of the cell lineage so that each version produces three cells. Use apoptosis in one of the versions, marking any dead cells with an X.

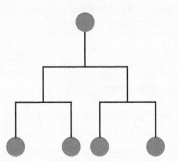

## Level 3: Synthesis/Evaluation

9. **EVOLUTION CONNECTION** Evolution in insects and vertebrates has involved the repeated duplication of body segments, followed by fusion of some segments and specialization of their structure and function. In vertebrates, what anatomical features reflect segmentation?

10. **SCIENTIFIC INQUIRY** The "snout" region of a salamander has a mustache-shaped structure called a balancer, whereas that of a frog tadpole does not. When you transplant tissue from the side of a young salamander embryo to the snout of a frog embryo, the tadpole that develops has a balancer. If you use a slightly older salamander embryo as the donor, no balancer forms. Propose a hypothesis to explain these results and explain how you might test your hypothesis.

11. **SCIENCE, TECHNOLOGY, AND SOCIETY** Scientists can now make identical copies, or clones, of animals ranging from dairy cows to pet cats. Propose a few arguments for and against this application of discoveries about embryonic development.

12. **WRITE ABOUT A THEME: ORGANIZATION** In a short essay (100–150 words), describe how the emergent properties of the cells of the gastrula direct embryonic development.

13. **SYNTHESIZE YOUR KNOWLEDGE**

Occasionally, two-headed animals such as this turtle are born. Thinking about the occurrence of identical twins and the property of totipotency, explain how this might happen.

*For selected answers, see Appendix A.*

 For additional practice questions, check out the **Dynamic Study Modules** in MasteringBiology. You can use them to study on your smartphone, tablet, or computer anytime, anywhere!

# Neurons, Synapses, and Signaling

▲ Figure 48.1 **What makes this snail such a deadly predator?**

## KEY CONCEPTS

**48.1** Neuron structure and organization reflect function in information transfer

**48.2** Ion pumps and ion channels establish the resting potential of a neuron

**48.3** Action potentials are the signals conducted by axons

**48.4** Neurons communicate with other cells at synapses

▼ Ribbon model of a toxic peptide from cone snail venom

## Lines of Communication

The tropical cone snail (*Conus geographus*) in **Figure 48.1** is small and slow moving, yet it is a dangerous hunter. A carnivore, this marine snail hunts, kills, and devours fish. Injecting venom with a hollow, harpoon-like tooth, the cone snail paralyzes its free-swimming prey almost instantaneously. The venom is so deadly that unlucky scuba divers have died from just a single injection. What makes it so fast acting and lethal? The answer is a mixture of toxin molecules: Each has a specific mechanism of disabling **neurons**, the nerve cells that transfer information within the body. Because the venom disrupts neuronal control of locomotion and respiration, an animal attacked by the cone snail cannot escape, defend itself, or otherwise survive.

Communication by neurons largely consists of long-distance electrical signals and short-distance chemical signals. The specialized structure of neurons allows them to use pulses of electrical current to receive, transmit, and regulate the flow of information over long distances within the body. In transferring information from one cell to another, neurons often rely on chemical signals that act over very short distances. Cone snail venom is particularly potent because it interferes with both electrical and chemical signaling by neurons.

 Interview: Baldomero Olivera: Developing drugs from research on cone snail venom

When you see this blue icon, log in to **MasteringBiology** and go to the Study Area for digital resources.

 Get Ready for This Chapter

All neurons transmit electrical signals within the cell in an identical manner. Thus a neuron that detects an odor transmits information along its length in the same way as a neuron that controls the movement of a body part. The particular connections made by the active neuron are what distinguish the type of information being transmitted. Interpreting nerve impulses therefore involves sorting neuronal paths and connections. In more complex animals, this processing is carried out largely in groups of neurons organized into a **brain** or into simpler clusters called **ganglia**.

In this chapter, we look closely at the structure of a neuron and explore the molecules and physical principles that govern signaling by neurons. In the remainder of this unit, we'll examine nervous, sensory, and motor systems before exploring how their functions are integrated in producing behavior.

# CONCEPT 48.1

## Neuron structure and organization reflect function in information transfer

Our starting point for exploring the nervous system is the neuron, a cell type exemplifying the close fit of form and function that often arises over the course of evolution.

## Neuron Structure and Function

The ability of a neuron to receive and transmit information is based on a highly specialized cellular organization **(Figure 48.2)**. Most of a neuron's organelles, including its nucleus, are located in the **cell body**. In a typical neuron, the cell body is studded with numerous highly branched extensions called **dendrites** (from the Greek *dendron*, tree). Together with the cell body, the dendrites *receive* signals from other neurons. A neuron also has a single **axon**, an extension that *transmits* signals to other cells. Axons are often much longer than dendrites, and some, such as those that reach from the spinal cord of a giraffe to the muscle cells in its feet, are over a meter long. The cone-shaped base of an axon, called the axon hillock, is typically where signals that travel down the axon are generated. Near its other end, an axon usually divides into many branches.

Each branched end of an axon transmits information to another cell at a junction called a **synapse**. The part of each axon branch that forms this specialized junction is a *synaptic terminal*. At most synapses, chemical messengers called **neurotransmitters** pass information from the transmitting neuron to the receiving cell (see Figure 48.2). In describing a synapse, we refer to the transmitting neuron as the *presynaptic cell* and the neuron, muscle, or gland cell that receives the signal as the *postsynaptic cell*.

The neurons of vertebrates and most invertebrates require supporting cells called **glial cells**, or **glia** (from a Greek word meaning "glue") **(Figure 48.3)**. Overall, glia outnumber neurons in the mammalian brain by 10- to 50-fold. Glia nourish neurons, insulate the axons of neurons, and regulate the extracellular fluid surrounding neurons. In addition, glia sometimes function in replenishing certain groups of neurons and in transmitting information (as we'll discuss later in this chapter and in Concept 49.1).

## Introduction to Information Processing

Information processing by a nervous system occurs in three stages: sensory input, integration, and motor output. As an example, let's consider the cone snail discussed earlier,

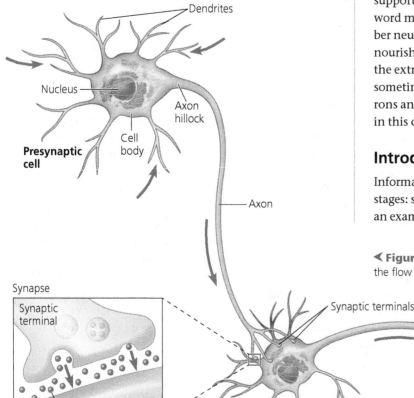

◄ **Figure 48.2 Neuron structure.** Arrows illustrate the flow of signals into, along, between, and out of neurons.

Dendrites

Nucleus

Axon hillock

Cell body

**Presynaptic cell**

Axon

Synapse

Synaptic terminal

Postsynaptic cell

Neurotransmitter

Synaptic terminals

Synaptic terminals

**Postsynaptic cell**

**▼ Figure 48.3 Glia in the mammalian brain.** This micrograph (a fluorescently labeled laser confocal image) shows a region of the rat brain packed with glia and interneurons. The glia are labeled red, the DNA in nuclei is labeled blue, and the dendrites of neurons are labeled green.

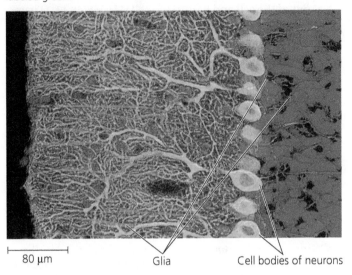

80 μm

Glia          Cell bodies of neurons

focusing on the steps involved in identifying and attacking its prey. To generate sensory input to the nervous system, the snail surveys its environment with its tubelike siphon, sampling scents that might reveal a nearby fish **(Figure 48.4)**. During the integration stage, networks of neurons process this information to determine if a fish is in fact present and, if so, where the fish is located. Motor output from the processing center then initiates attack, activating neurons that trigger release of the harpoon-like tooth toward the prey.

**▼ Figure 48.4 Summary of information processing.** The cone snail's siphon acts as a sensor, transferring information to the neuronal circuits in the snail's head. If prey is detected, these circuits issue motor commands, signals that control muscle activity, triggering release of a harpoon-like tooth from the proboscis.

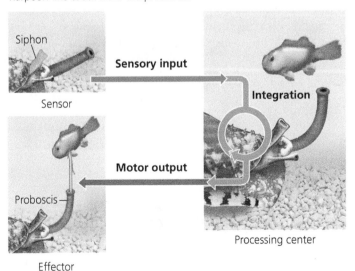

Siphon

Sensory input

Sensor

Integration

Motor output

Proboscis

Processing center

Effector

In all but the simplest animals, specialized populations of neurons handle each stage of information processing.

- **Sensory neurons**, like those in the snail's siphon, transmit information about external stimuli such as light, touch, or smell or internal conditions such as blood pressure or muscle tension.
- **Interneurons** form the local circuits connecting neurons in the brain or ganglia. Interneurons are responsible for the integration (analysis and interpretation) of sensory input.
- **Motor neurons** transmit signals to muscle cells, causing them to contract. Additional neurons that extend out of the processing centers trigger gland activity.

In many animals, the neurons that carry out integration are organized in a **central nervous system (CNS)**. The neurons that carry information into and out of the CNS constitute the **peripheral nervous system (PNS)**. When bundled together, the axons of neurons form **nerves**.

Depending on its role in information processing, the shape of a neuron can vary from simple to quite complex **(Figure 48.5)**. Neurons that have highly branched dendrites, such as some interneurons, can receive input through tens of thousands of synapses. Similarly, neurons that transmit information to many target cells do so through highly branched axons.

**▼ Figure 48.5 Structural diversity of neurons.** In these drawings of neurons, cell bodies and dendrites are black and axons are red.

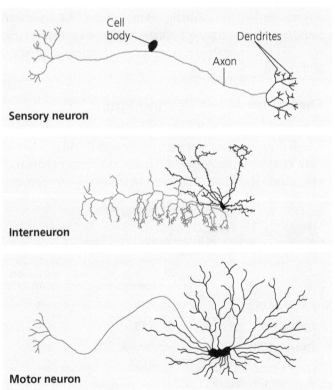

Cell body

Dendrites

Axon

**Sensory neuron**

**Interneuron**

**Motor neuron**

# CONCEPT 48.2

## Ion pumps and ion channels establish the resting potential of a neuron

We turn now to the essential role of ions in neuronal signaling. In neurons, as in other cells, ions are unequally distributed between the interior of cells and the surrounding fluid (see Concept 7.4). As a result, the inside of a cell is negatively charged relative to the outside. This charge difference, or *voltage*, across the plasma membrane is called the **membrane potential**, reflecting the fact that the attraction of opposite charges across the plasma membrane is a source of potential energy. For a resting neuron—one that is not sending a signal—the membrane potential is called the **resting potential** and is typically between −60 and −80 millivolts (mV).

When a neuron receives a stimulus, the membrane potential changes. Rapid shifts in membrane potential are what enable us to see the intricate structure of a spiderweb, hear a song, or ride a bicycle. These changes, which are known as *action potentials*, will be discussed in Concept 48.3. To understand how they convey information, we need to explore the ways in which membrane potentials are formed, maintained, and altered.

### Formation of the Resting Potential

Potassium ions ($K^+$) and sodium ions ($Na^+$) play an essential role in the formation of the resting potential. These ions each have a concentration gradient across the plasma membrane of a neuron **(Table 48.1)**. In most neurons, the concentration

of $K^+$ is higher inside the cell, while the concentration of $Na^+$ is higher outside. The $Na^+$ and $K^+$ gradients are maintained by the **sodium-potassium pump** (see Figure 7.15). This pump uses the energy of ATP hydrolysis to actively transport $Na^+$ out of the cell and $K^+$ into the cell **(Figure 48.6)**. (There are also concentration gradients for chloride ions ($Cl^-$) and other anions, as shown in Table 48.1, but we can ignore these for now.)

The sodium-potassium pump transports three $Na^+$ out of the cell for every two $K^+$ that it transports in. Although this pumping generates a net export of positive charge, the pump acts slowly. The resulting change in the membrane potential is therefore quite small—only a few millivolts. Why, then, is there a membrane potential of −60 to −80 mV in a resting neuron? The answer lies in ion movement through **ion channels**, pores formed by clusters of specialized proteins

▼ **Figure 48.6 The basis of the membrane potential.** The sodium-potassium pump generates and maintains the ionic gradients of $Na^+$ and $K^+$ shown in Table 48.1. The $Na^+$ gradient results in very little net diffusion of $Na^+$ in a resting neuron because very few sodium channels are open. In contrast, the many open potassium channels allow a significant net outflow of $K^+$. Because the membrane is only weakly permeable to chloride and other anions, this outflow of $K^+$ results in a net negative charge inside the cell.

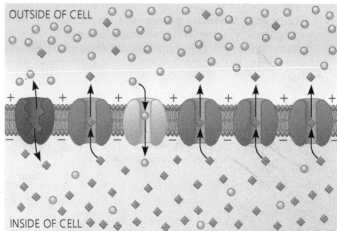

**Key**

- $Na^+$ — Sodium-potassium pump
- $K^+$ — Potassium channel — Sodium channel

**MB** BioFlix® Animation: Resting Potential

| Table 48.1 | Ion Concentrations Inside and Outside of Mammalian Neurons | |
|---|---|---|
| **Ion** | **Intracellular Concentration (m*M*)** | **Extracellular Concentration (m*M*)** |
| Potassium ($K^+$) | 140 | 5 |
| Sodium ($Na^+$) | 15 | 150 |
| Chloride ($Cl^-$) | 10 | 120 |
| Large anions ($A^-$), such as proteins, inside cell | 100 | Not applicable |

that span the membrane. Ion channels allow ions to diffuse back and forth across the membrane. As ions diffuse through channels, they carry with them units of electrical charge. Furthermore, ions can move quite rapidly through ion channels. When this occurs, the resulting current—a *net* movement of positive or negative charge—generates a membrane potential, or voltage across the membrane.

Concentration gradients of ions across a plasma membrane represent a chemical form of potential energy that can be harnessed for cellular processes (see Figure 44.17). In neurons, the ion channels that convert this chemical potential energy to electrical potential energy can do so because they have *selective permeability*, allowing only certain ions to pass. For example, a potassium channel allows $K^+$ to diffuse freely across the membrane, but not other ions, such as $Na^+$ or $Cl^-$.

Diffusion of $K^+$ through potassium channels that are always open (sometimes called *leak channels*) is critical for establishing the resting potential. The $K^+$ concentration is 140 millimolar (mM) inside the cell, but only 5 mM outside. The chemical concentration gradient thus favors a net outflow of $K^+$. Furthermore, a resting neuron has many open potassium channels, but very few open sodium channels. Because $Na^+$ and other ions can't readily cross the membrane, $K^+$ outflow leads to a net negative charge inside the cell. This buildup of negative charge within the neuron is the major source of the membrane potential.

What stops the buildup of negative charge? The excess negative charges inside the cell exert an attractive force that opposes the flow of additional positively charged potassium ions out of the cell. The separation of charge (voltage) thus results in an electrical gradient that counterbalances the chemical concentration gradient of $K^+$.

## Modeling the Resting Potential

The net flow of $K^+$ out of a neuron proceeds until the chemical and electrical forces are in balance. We can model this process by considering a pair of chambers separated by an artificial membrane. To begin, imagine that the membrane contains many open ion channels, all of which allow only $K^+$ to diffuse across (**Figure 48.7a**). To produce a $K^+$ concentration gradient like that of a mammalian neuron, we place a solution of 140 mM potassium chloride (KCl) in the inner chamber and 5 mM KCl in the outer chamber. The $K^+$ will diffuse down its concentration gradient into the outer chamber. But because the chloride ions ($Cl^-$) lack a means of crossing the membrane, there will be an excess of negative charge in the inner chamber.

When our model neuron reaches equilibrium, the electrical gradient will exactly balance the chemical gradient so that no further net diffusion of $K^+$ occurs across the membrane. The magnitude of the membrane voltage at equilibrium for a particular ion is called that ion's **equilibrium potential** ($E_{ion}$). For a membrane permeable to a single type of ion, $E_{ion}$ can be calculated using a formula called the *Nernst equation*. At human body temperature (37°C) and for an ion with a net charge of 1+, such as $K^+$ or $Na^+$, the Nernst equation is

$$E_{ion} = 62 \text{ mV}\left(\log \frac{[\text{ion}]_{\text{outside}}}{[\text{ion}]_{\text{inside}}}\right)$$

Plugging the $K^+$ concentrations into the Nernst equation reveals that the equilibrium potential for $K^+$ ($E_K$) is −90 mV (see Figure 48.7a). The minus sign indicates that $K^+$ is at equilibrium when the inside of the membrane is 90 mV more negative than the outside.

Whereas the equilibrium potential for $K^+$ is −90 mV, the resting potential of a mammalian neuron is somewhat less

➤ **Figure 48.7 Modeling a mammalian neuron.** In this model of the membrane potential of a resting neuron, an artificial membrane divides each container into two chambers. Ion channels allow free diffusion for particular ions, resulting in the net ion flow represented by arrows. **(a)** The presence of open potassium channels makes the membrane selectively permeable to $K^+$, and the inner chamber contains a 28-fold higher concentration of $K^+$ than the outer chamber; at equilibrium, the inside of the membrane is −90 mV relative to the outside. **(b)** The membrane is selectively permeable to $Na^+$, and the inner chamber contains a tenfold lower concentration of $Na^+$ than the outer chamber; at equilibrium, the inside of the membrane is +62 mV relative to the outside.

**WHAT IF?** ➤ *How would adding potassium or chloride channels to the membrane in (b) affect the membrane potential?*

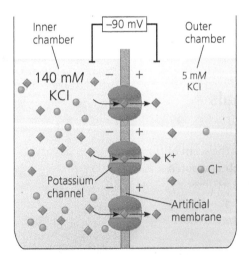

**(a) Membrane selectively permeable to $K^+$**

Nernst equation for $K^+$ equilibrium potential at 37°C:

$$E_K = 62 \text{ mV}\left(\log \frac{5 \text{ m}M}{140 \text{ m}M}\right) = -90 \text{ mV}$$

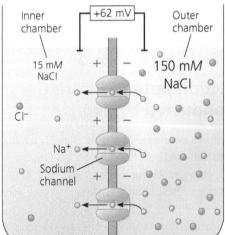

**(b) Membrane selectively permeable to $Na^+$**

Nernst equation for $Na^+$ equilibrium potential at 37°C:

$$E_{Na} = 62 \text{ mV}\left(\log \frac{150 \text{ m}M}{15 \text{ m}M}\right) = +62 \text{ mV}$$

negative. This difference reflects the small but steady movement of $Na^+$ across the few open sodium channels in a resting neuron. The concentration gradient of $Na^+$ has a direction opposite to that of $K^+$ (see Table 48.1). $Na^+$ therefore diffuses into the cell, making the inside of the cell less negative. If we model a membrane in which the only open channels are selectively permeable to $Na^+$, we find that a tenfold higher concentration of $Na^+$ in the outer chamber results in an equilibrium potential ($E_{Na}$) of +62 mV (**Figure 48.7b**). In an actual neuron, the resting potential (−60 to −80 mV) is much closer to $E_K$ than to $E_{Na}$ because there are many open potassium channels but only a small number of open sodium channels.

Because neither $K^+$ nor $Na^+$ is at equilibrium in a resting neuron, there is a net flow of each ion across the membrane. The resting potential remains steady, which means that these $K^+$ and $Na^+$ currents are equal and opposite. Ion concentrations on either side of the membrane also remain steady. Why? The resting potential arises from the net movement of far fewer ions than would be required to alter the concentration gradients.

If $Na^+$ is allowed to cross the membrane more readily, the membrane potential will move toward $E_{Na}$ and away from $E_K$. As you'll see, this happens in generation of a nerve impulse.

 Animation: Membrane Potentials

## CONCEPT CHECK 48.2

1. Under what circumstances could ions flow through an ion channel from a region of lower ion concentration to a region of higher ion concentration?

2. **WHAT IF?** ➤ Suppose a cell's membrane potential shifts from −70 mV to −50 mV. What changes in the cell's permeability to $K^+$ or $Na^+$ could cause such a shift?

3. **MAKE CONNECTIONS** ➤ Review Figure 7.10, which illustrates the diffusion of dye molecules across a membrane. Could diffusion eliminate the concentration gradient of a dye that has a net charge? Explain.

*For suggested answers, see Appendix A.*

# CONCEPT 48.3

## Action potentials are the signals conducted by axons

When a neuron responds to a stimulus, such as the scent of fish detected by a hunting cone snail, the membrane potential changes. Using intracellular recording, researchers can monitor these changes as a function of time (**Figure 48.8**). As you will see, such recordings have been central to the study of information transfer by neurons.

How does a stimulus bring about a change in the membrane potential? It turns out that some of the ion channels in a neuron are **gated ion channels**, ion channels that open or close in response to stimuli. When a gated ion channel opens or closes, it alters the membrane's permeability to particular ions (**Figure 48.9**). This change in permeability allows

**Research Method** Intracellular Recording

**Application** Electrophysiologists use intracellular recording to measure the membrane potential of neurons and other cells.

**Technique** A microelectrode is made from a glass capillary tube filled with an electrically conductive salt solution. One end of the tube tapers to an extremely fine tip (diameter < 1 μm). While looking through a microscope, the experimenter uses a micropositioner to insert the tip of the microelectrode into a cell. A voltage recorder (usually an oscilloscope or a computer-based system) measures the voltage between the microelectrode tip inside the cell and a reference electrode placed in the solution outside the cell.

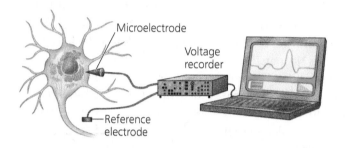

a rapid flow of ions across the membrane, altering the membrane potential.

Particular types of gated channels respond to different stimuli. For example, Figure 48.9 illustrates a **voltage-gated ion channel**, a channel that opens or closes in response to a shift in the voltage across the plasma membrane of the neuron. Later in this chapter, we will discuss gated channels in neurons that are regulated by chemical signals.

## Hyperpolarization and Depolarization

Let's consider now what happens in a neuron when a stimulus causes closed voltage-gated ion channels to open. If gated potassium channels in a resting neuron open, the membrane's

▼ Figure 48.9 **Voltage-gated ion channel.** A change in the membrane potential in one direction (solid arrow) opens the voltage-gated channel. The opposite change (dotted arrow) closes the channel.

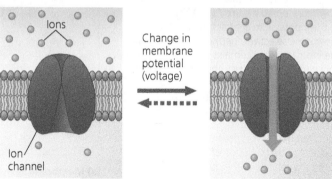

**Gate closed:** No ions flow across membrane.

**Gate open:** Ions flow through channel.

**VISUAL SKILLS** ➤ *Gated ion channels allow ion flow in either direction. Using visual information in this figure, explain why there is net ion movement when the channel opens.*

permeability to K⁺ increases. As a result, net diffusion of K⁺ out of the neuron increases, shifting the membrane potential toward $E_K$ (−90 mV at 37°C). This increase in the magnitude of the membrane potential, called a **hyperpolarization**, makes the inside of the membrane more negative **(Figure 48.10a)**. In a resting neuron, hyperpolarization results from any stimulus that increases the outflow of positive ions or the inflow of negative ions.

Although opening potassium channels in a resting neuron causes hyperpolarization, opening some other types of ion channels has an opposite effect, making the inside of the membrane less negative **(Figure 48.10b)**. A reduction in the magnitude of the membrane potential is a **depolarization**. In neurons, depolarization often involves gated sodium channels. If a stimulus causes gated sodium channels to open, the membrane's permeability to Na⁺ increases. Na⁺ diffuses into the cell along its concentration gradient, causing a depolarization as the membrane potential shifts toward $E_{Na}$ (+62 mV at 37°C).

## Graded Potentials and Action Potentials

Sometimes, the response to hyperpolarization or depolarization is simply a shift in the membrane potential. This shift, called a **graded potential**, has a magnitude that varies with the strength of the stimulus: A larger stimulus causes a greater change in the membrane potential (see Figure 48.10a and b). Graded potentials induce a small electrical current

that dissipates as it flows along the membrane. Graded potentials thus decay with time and with distance from their source.

If a depolarization shifts the membrane potential sufficiently, the result is a massive change in membrane voltage called an **action potential**. Unlike graded potentials, action potentials have a constant magnitude and can regenerate in adjacent regions of the membrane. Action potentials can therefore spread along axons, making them well suited for transmitting a signal over long distances.

Action potentials arise because some of the ion channels in neurons are voltage-gated (see Figure 48.9). If a depolarization increases the membrane potential to a level called **threshold**, the voltage-gated sodium channels open. The resulting flow of Na⁺ into the neuron results in further depolarization. Because the sodium channels are voltage gated, the increased depolarization causes more sodium channels to open, leading to an even greater flow of current. The result is a process of positive feedback that triggers a very rapid opening of many voltage-gated sodium channels and the marked temporary change in membrane potential that defines an action potential **(Figure 48.10c)**.

The positive-feedback loop of channel opening and depolarization triggers an action potential whenever the membrane potential reaches threshold, about −55 mV for many mammalian neurons. Once initiated, the action potential has a magnitude that is independent of the strength of the

▼ **Figure 48.10 Graded potentials and an action potential in a neuron.**

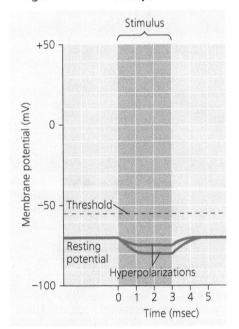

**(a) Graded hyperpolarizations produced by two stimuli that increase membrane permeability to K⁺.** The larger stimulus produces a larger hyperpolarization.

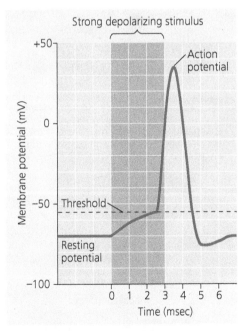

**(b) Graded depolarizations produced by two stimuli that increase membrane permeability to Na⁺.** The larger stimulus produces a larger depolarization.

**(c) Action potential triggered by a depolarization that reaches the threshold.**

**DRAW IT** ➤ *Redraw the graph in (c), extending the y-axis. Then label the positions of $E_K$ and $E_{Na}$.*

triggering stimulus. Because action potentials either occur fully or do not occur at all, they represent an *all-or-none* response to stimuli.

## Generation of Action Potentials: *A Closer Look*

The characteristic shape of the graph of an action potential reflects changes in membrane potential resulting from ion movement through voltage-gated sodium and potassium channels (**Figure 48.11**). Depolarization opens both types of channels, but they respond independently and sequentially. Sodium channels open first, initiating the action potential. As the action potential proceeds, sodium channels remain open but become *inactivated*: a portion of the channel protein called an inactivation loop blocks ion flow through the open channel. Sodium channels remain inactivated until after the membrane returns to the resting potential and the channels close. Potassium channels open more slowly than sodium channels, but remain open and functional until the end of the action potential.

▼ **Figure 48.11 The role of voltage-gated ion channels in the generation of an action potential.** The circled numbers on the graph in the center and the colors of the action potential phases correspond to the five diagrams showing voltage-gated sodium and potassium channels in a neuron's plasma membrane.

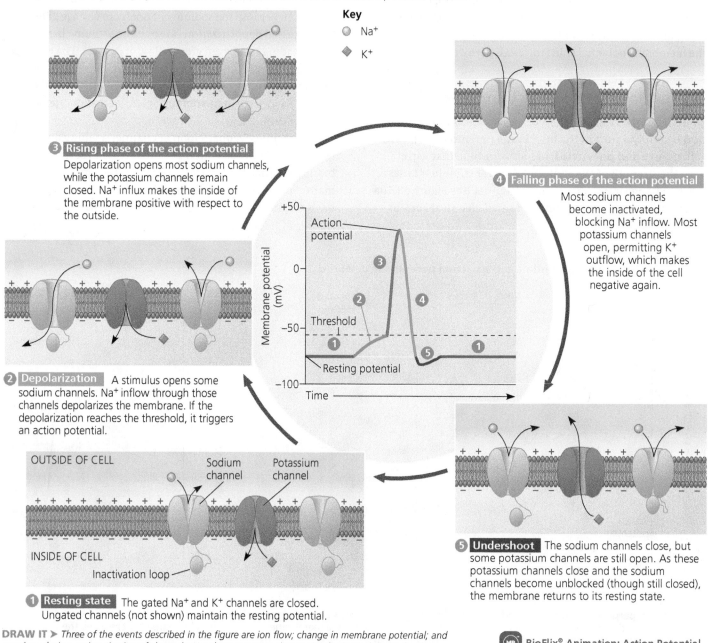

**Key**
- Na⁺
- K⁺

**3 Rising phase of the action potential** Depolarization opens most sodium channels, while the potassium channels remain closed. Na⁺ influx makes the inside of the membrane positive with respect to the outside.

**4 Falling phase of the action potential** Most sodium channels become inactivated, blocking Na⁺ inflow. Most potassium channels open, permitting K⁺ outflow, which makes the inside of the cell negative again.

**2 Depolarization** A stimulus opens some sodium channels. Na⁺ inflow through those channels depolarizes the membrane. If the depolarization reaches the threshold, it triggers an action potential.

**5 Undershoot** The sodium channels close, but some potassium channels are still open. As these potassium channels close and the sodium channels become unblocked (though still closed), the membrane returns to its resting state.

**1 Resting state** The gated Na⁺ and K⁺ channels are closed. Ungated channels (not shown) maintain the resting potential.

*Action potential*
*Threshold*
*Resting potential*
*Membrane potential (mV)*
*Time*
OUTSIDE OF CELL
Sodium channel
Potassium channel
INSIDE OF CELL
Inactivation loop

**DRAW IT ▶** *Three of the events described in the figure are ion flow; change in membrane potential; and opening, closing, or inactivation of channels. Use these events to draw a simple circuit diagram for the positive feedback that underlies the rising phase of the action potential.*

**MB** BioFlix® Animation: Action Potential

To understand further how voltage-gated channels shape the action potential, consider the process as a series of stages, as depicted in Figure 48.11. ❶ When the membrane of the axon is at the resting potential, most voltage-gated sodium channels are closed. Some potassium channels are open, but most voltage-gated potassium channels are closed. ❷ When a stimulus depolarizes the membrane, some gated sodium channels open, allowing more $Na^+$ to diffuse into the cell. If the stimulus is sufficiently strong, the $Na^+$ inflow persists, causing further depolarization, which opens more gated sodium channels, allowing even more $Na^+$ to diffuse into the cell. ❸ Once the threshold is crossed, the positive-feedback cycle then rapidly brings the membrane potential close to $E_{Na}$. This stage of the action potential is called the *rising phase*. ❹ Two events prevent the membrane potential from actually reaching $E_{Na}$: Voltage-gated sodium channels inactivate soon after opening, halting the flow of $Na^+$ into the cell, and most voltage-gated potassium channels open, causing a rapid outflow of $K^+$. Both events quickly bring the membrane potential back toward $E_K$. This stage is called the *falling phase*. ❺ In the final phase of an action potential, called the *undershoot*, the membrane's permeability to $K^+$ is higher than at rest, so the membrane potential is closer to $E_K$ than it is at the resting potential. The gated potassium channels eventually close, and the membrane potential returns to the resting potential.

Why is inactivation of channels required during an action potential? Because they are voltage gated, the sodium channels open when the membrane potential reaches the threshold of −55 mV and don't close until the resting potential is restored. They are therefore open throughout the action potential. However, the resting potential cannot be restored unless the flow of $Na^+$ into the cell stops. This is accomplished by inactivation. The sodium channels remain in the "open" state, but $Na^+$ cease flowing once inactivation occurs. The end of $Na^+$ inflow allows $K^+$ outflow to repolarize the membrane.

The sodium channels remain inactivated during the falling phase and the early part of the undershoot. As a result, if a second depolarizing stimulus occurs during this period, it will be unable to trigger an action potential. The "downtime" when a second action potential cannot be initiated is called the **refractory period**. Note that the refractory period is due to the inactivation of sodium channels, not to a change in the ion gradients across the plasma membrane. The flow of charged particles during an action potential involves far too few ions to change the concentration on either side of the membrane significantly.

## Conduction of Action Potentials

Having described the events of a single action potential, we'll explore next how a series of action potentials moves a signal along an axon. At the site where an action potential

is initiated (usually the axon hillock), $Na^+$ inflow during the rising phase creates an electrical current that depolarizes the neighboring region of the axon membrane (**Figure 48.12**).

▼ **Figure 48.12 Conduction of an action potential.** This figure shows events at three successive times as an action potential passes from left to right. At each point along the axon, voltage-gated ion channels go through the sequence of changes shown in Figure 48.11. Membrane colors correspond to the action potential phases in Figure 48.11.

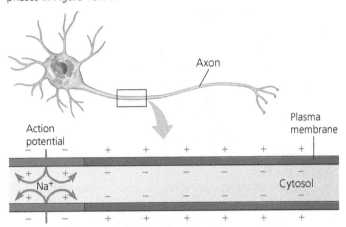

An action potential is generated as $Na^+$ flows inward across the membrane at one location.

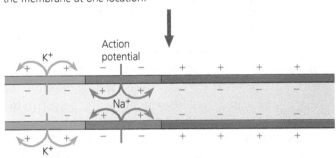

The depolarization of the membrane spreads to the neighboring region, reinitiating the action potential there. Where the action potential is already complete, the membrane is repolarizing as $K^+$ flows outward.

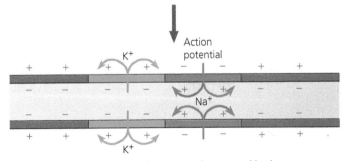

The depolarization-repolarization process is repeated in the next region of the membrane. In this way, local currents of ions *across* the plasma membrane cause the action potential to be propagated *along* the length of the axon.

**DRAW IT** ➤ *For the axon segment shown, consider a point at the left end, a point in the middle, and a point at the right end. Draw a graph for each point showing the change in membrane potential over time at that point as a single nerve impulse moves from left to right across the segment.*

 BioFlix® Animation: Conduction of an Action Potential

The depolarization is large enough to reach threshold, causing an action potential in the neighboring region. This process is repeated many times along the length of the axon. Because an action potential is an all-or-none event, the magnitude and duration of the action potential are the same at each position along the axon. The net result is the movement of a nerve impulse from the cell body to the synaptic terminals, much like the cascade of events triggered by knocking over the first domino in a line.

An action potential that starts at the axon hillock moves along the axon only toward the synaptic terminals. Why? Immediately behind the traveling zone of depolarization, the sodium channels remain inactivated, making the membrane temporarily refractory (not responsive) to further input. Consequently, the inward current that depolarizes the axon membrane *ahead* of the action potential cannot produce another action potential *behind* it. This is the reason action potentials do not travel back toward the cell body.

After the refractory period is complete, depolarization of the axon hillock to threshold will trigger a new action potential. In many neurons, action potentials last less than 2 milliseconds (msec), and the firing rate can thus reach hundreds of action potentials per second.

The frequency of action potentials conveys information: The rate at which action potentials are produced in a particular neuron is proportional to input signal strength. In hearing, for example, louder sounds result in more frequent action potentials in neurons connecting the ear to the brain. Similarly, increased frequency of action potentials in a neuron that stimulates skeletal muscle tissue will increase the tension in the contracting muscle. Differences in the number of action potentials in a given time are in fact the only variable in how information is encoded and transmitted along an axon.

Gated ion channels and action potentials have a central role in nervous system activity. As a consequence, mutations in genes that encode ion channel proteins can cause disorders affecting the nerves or brain—or the muscles or heart, depending largely on where in the body the gene for the ion channel protein is expressed. For example, mutations affecting voltage-gated sodium channels in skeletal muscle cells can cause myotonia, a periodic spasming of those muscles. Mutations affecting sodium channels in the brain can cause epilepsy, in which groups of nerve cells fire simultaneously and excessively, producing seizures.

## Evolutionary Adaptations of Axon Structure

**EVOLUTION** The rate at which the axons within nerves conduct action potentials governs how rapidly an animal can react to danger or opportunity. As a consequence, natural selection often results in anatomical adaptations that increase conduction speed. One such adaptation is a wider axon. In the same way that a wide hose offers less resistance to the flow of water than does a narrow hose, a wide axon provides less resistance to the current associated with an action potential than does a narrow axon.

In invertebrates, conduction speed varies from several centimeters per second in very narrow axons to approximately 30 m/sec in the giant axons of some arthropods and molluscs. These giant axons (up to 1 mm wide) function in rapid behavioral responses, such as the muscle contraction that propels a hunting squid toward its prey.

Vertebrate axons have narrow diameters but can still conduct action potentials at high speed. How is this possible? The evolutionary adaptation that enables fast conduction in vertebrate axons is electrical insulation, analogous to the plastic insulation that encases many electrical wires. Insulation causes the depolarizing current associated with an action potential to travel farther along the axon interior, bringing more distant regions to the threshold sooner.

The electrical insulation that surrounds vertebrate axons is called a **myelin sheath (Figure 48.13)**. Myelin sheaths

▼ **Figure 48.13 Schwann cells and the myelin sheath.** In the PNS, glia called Schwann cells wrap themselves around axons, forming layers of myelin. Gaps between adjacent Schwann cells are called nodes of Ranvier. The TEM shows a cross section through a myelinated axon.

0.1 µm

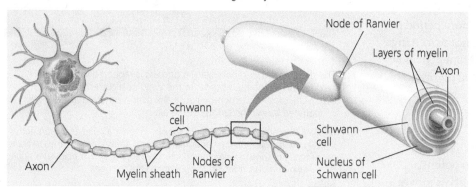

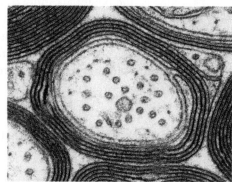

are produced by glia: **oligodendrocytes** in the CNS and **Schwann cells** in the PNS. During development, these specialized glia wrap axons in many layers of membrane. The membranes forming these layers are mostly lipid, which is a poor conductor of electrical current and thus a good insulator.

In myelinated axons, voltage-gated sodium channels are restricted to gaps in the myelin sheath called **nodes of Ranvier** (see Figure 48.13). Furthermore, the extracellular fluid is in contact with the axon membrane only at the nodes. As a result, action potentials are not generated in the regions between the nodes. Rather, the inward current produced during the rising phase of the action potential at a node travels within the axon all the way to the next node. There, the current depolarizes the membrane and regenerates the action potential **(Figure 48.14)**.

Action potentials propagate more rapidly in myelinated axons because the time-consuming process of opening and closing of ion channels occurs at only a limited number of positions along the axon. This mechanism for propagating action potentials is called **saltatory conduction** (from the Latin *saltare*, to leap) because the action potential appears to jump from node to node along the axon.

The major selective advantage of myelination is its space efficiency. A myelinated axon 20 μm in diameter has a conduction speed faster than that of a squid giant axon with a diameter 40 times greater. Consequently, more than 2,000 of those myelinated axons can be packed into the space occupied by just one giant axon.

For any axon, myelinated or not, the conduction of an action potential to the end of the axon sets the stage for the next step in neuronal signaling—the transfer of information to another cell. This information handoff occurs at synapses, our next topic.

## CONCEPT CHECK 48.3

1. How do action potentials and graded potentials differ?
2. In multiple sclerosis (from the Greek *skleros*, hard), a person's myelin sheaths harden and deteriorate. How would this affect nervous system function?
3. How do both negative and positive feedback contribute to the changes in membrane potential during an action potential?
4. **WHAT IF?** ➤ Suppose a mutation caused gated sodium channels to remain inactivated longer after an action potential. How would this affect the frequency at which action potentials could be generated? Explain.

*For suggested answers, see Appendix A.*

# CONCEPT 48.4

## Neurons communicate with other cells at synapses

Transmission of information from neurons to other cells occurs at synapses. Synapses are either electrical or chemical.

*Electrical synapses* contain gap junctions (see Figure 6.30) that allow electrical current to flow directly from one neuron to another. Such synapses often play a role in synchronizing the activity of neurons that direct rapid, unvarying behaviors. For example, electrical synapses associated with the giant axons of squids and lobsters facilitate swift escapes from danger. Electrical synapses are also found in the vertebrate heart and brain.

The majority of synapses are *chemical synapses*, which rely on the release of a chemical neurotransmitter by the presynaptic neuron to transfer information to the target cell. While at rest, the presynaptic neuron synthesizes the neurotransmitter at each synaptic terminal, packaging it in multiple membrane-enclosed compartments called *synaptic vesicles*.

▼ **Figure 48.14 Propagation of action potentials in myelinated axons.** In a myelinated axon, the depolarizing current during an action potential at one node of Ranvier spreads along the interior of the axon to the next node (blue arrows), where voltage-gated sodium channels enable reinitiation. Thus, the action potential appears to jump from node to node as it travels along the axon (red arrows).

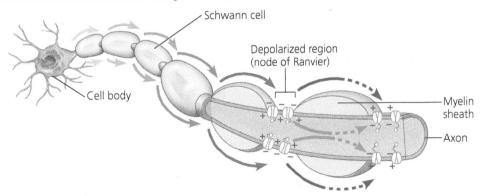

MB Animation: Propagation of an Action Potential in Unmyelinated and Myelinated Axons

When an action potential arrives at a chemical synapse, it depolarizes the plasma membrane at the synaptic terminal, opening voltage-gated channels that allow $Ca^{2+}$ to diffuse in (**Figure 48.15**). The $Ca^{2+}$ concentration in the terminal rises, causing synaptic vesicles to fuse with the terminal membrane and release the neurotransmitter.

Neurotransmitter released from the synaptic terminus diffuses across the *synaptic cleft*, the gap that separates the presynaptic neuron from the postsynaptic cell. Diffusion time is very short because the gap is less than 50 nm across. Upon reaching the postsynaptic membrane, the neurotransmitter binds to and activates a specific receptor in the membrane.

Information transfer at chemical synapses can be modified by altering either the amount of neurotransmitter that is released or the responsiveness of the postsynaptic cell. Such modifications underlie an animal's ability to alter its behavior in response to change and also form the basis for learning and memory, as you will read in Concept 49.4.

## Generation of Postsynaptic Potentials

At many chemical synapses, the receptor protein that binds and responds to neurotransmitters is a **ligand-gated ion channel**, often called an *ionotropic receptor*. These receptors are clustered in the membrane of the postsynaptic cell, directly opposite the synaptic terminal. Binding of the neurotransmitter (the receptor's ligand) to a particular part of the receptor opens the channel and allows specific ions to diffuse across the postsynaptic membrane. The result is a *postsynaptic potential*, a graded potential in the postsynaptic cell.

At some chemical synapses, the ligand-gated ion channels are permeable to both $K^+$ and $Na^+$ (see Figure 48.15). When these channels open, the membrane potential depolarizes toward a value roughly midway between $E_K$ and $E_{Na}$. Because such a depolarization brings the membrane potential toward threshold, it is called an **excitatory postsynaptic potential (EPSP)**.

▼ **Figure 48.15 A chemical synapse.** This figure illustrates the sequence of events that transmits a signal across a chemical synapse. In response to binding of neurotransmitter, ligand-gated ion channels in the postsynaptic membrane open (as shown here) or, less commonly, close. Synaptic transmission ends when the neurotransmitter diffuses out of the synaptic cleft, is taken up by the synaptic terminal or by another cell, or is degraded by an enzyme.

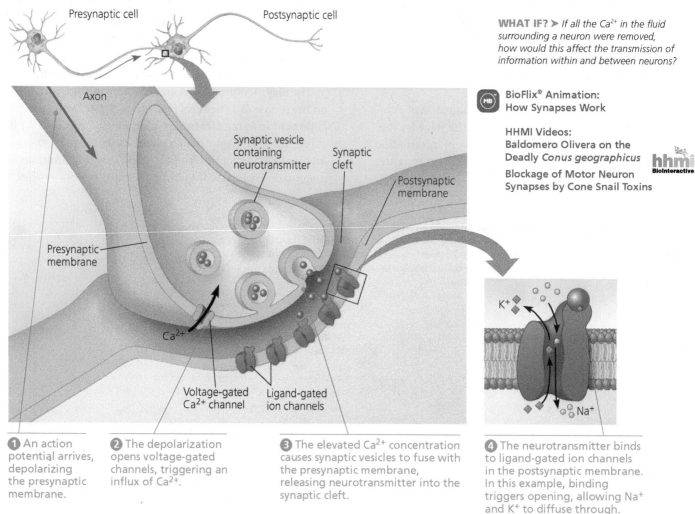

Presynaptic cell       Postsynaptic cell

**WHAT IF?** ➤ *If all the $Ca^{2+}$ in the fluid surrounding a neuron were removed, how would this affect the transmission of information within and between neurons?*

**MB** BioFlix® Animation: How Synapses Work

HHMI Videos:
Baldomero Olivera on the Deadly *Conus geographicus*
Blockage of Motor Neuron Synapses by Cone Snail Toxins

**hhmi** BioInteractive

Axon

Synaptic vesicle containing neurotransmitter

Synaptic cleft

Postsynaptic membrane

Presynaptic membrane

$Ca^{2+}$

$K^+$

$Na^+$

Voltage-gated $Ca^{2+}$ channel

Ligand-gated ion channels

❶ An action potential arrives, depolarizing the presynaptic membrane.

❷ The depolarization opens voltage-gated channels, triggering an influx of $Ca^{2+}$.

❸ The elevated $Ca^{2+}$ concentration causes synaptic vesicles to fuse with the presynaptic membrane, releasing neurotransmitter into the synaptic cleft.

❹ The neurotransmitter binds to ligand-gated ion channels in the postsynaptic membrane. In this example, binding triggers opening, allowing $Na^+$ and $K^+$ to diffuse through.

At other chemical synapses, the ligand-gated ion channels are selectively permeable for only K⁺ or Cl⁻. When such channels open, the postsynaptic membrane hyperpolarizes. A hyperpolarization produced in this manner is an **inhibitory postsynaptic potential (IPSP)** because it moves the membrane potential further from threshold.

## Summation of Postsynaptic Potentials

The interplay between multiple excitatory and inhibitory inputs is the essence of integration in the nervous system. The cell body and dendrites of a given postsynaptic neuron may receive inputs from chemical synapses formed with hundreds or even thousands of synaptic terminals (**Figure 48.16**). How do so many synapses contribute to information transfer?

The input from an individual synapse is typically insufficient to trigger a response in a postsynaptic neuron. To see why, consider an EPSP arising at a single synapse. As a graded potential, the EPSP becomes smaller as it spreads from the synapse. Therefore, by the time a particular EPSP reaches the axon hillock, it is usually too small to trigger an action potential (**Figure 48.17a**).

On some occasions, individual postsynaptic potentials combine to produce a larger postsynaptic potential, a process called **summation**. For instance, two EPSPs may occur at a single synapse in rapid succession. If the second EPSP arises before the postsynaptic membrane potential returns to its resting value, the EPSPs add together through *temporal*

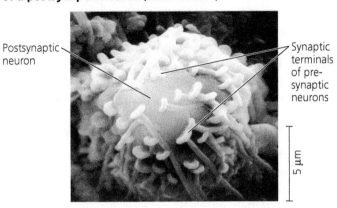

Postsynaptic neuron

Synaptic terminals of pre-synaptic neurons

5 μm

*summation*. If the summed postsynaptic potentials depolarize the membrane at the axon hillock to threshold, the result is an action potential (**Figure 48.17b**). Summation can also involve multiple synapses on the same postsynaptic neuron. If such synapses are active at the same time, the resulting EPSPs can add together through *spatial summation* (**Figure 48.17c**).

Summation applies as well to IPSPs: Two or more IPSPs occurring nearly simultaneously at synapses in the same region or in rapid succession at the same synapse have a larger hyperpolarizing effect than a single IPSP. Through summation, an IPSP can also counter the effect of an EPSP (**Figure 48.17d**).

▼ **Figure 48.17 Summation of postsynaptic potentials.** These graphs trace changes in the membrane potential at a postsynaptic neuron's axon hillock. The arrows indicate times when postsynaptic potentials occur at two excitatory synapses ($E_1$ and $E_2$, green in the diagrams above the graphs) and at one inhibitory synapse (I, red). Like most EPSPs, those produced at $E_1$ or $E_2$ do not reach the threshold at the axon hillock without summation.

 Animation: Action Potentials

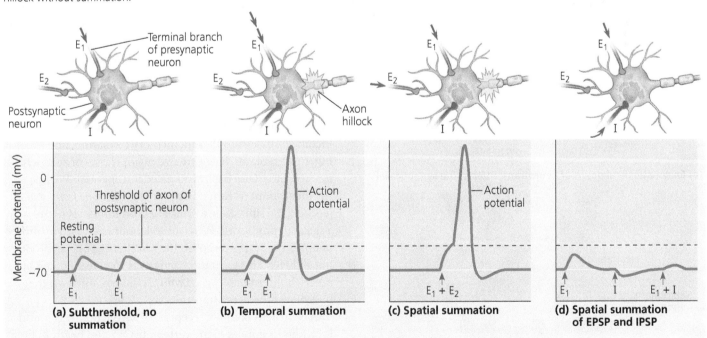

(a) Subthreshold, no summation

(b) Temporal summation

(c) Spatial summation

(d) Spatial summation of EPSP and IPSP

**VISUAL SKILLS ➤** *Using these drawings, propose an argument for all summation being in some sense temporal.*

The axon hillock is the neuron's integrating center, the region where the membrane potential at any instant represents the summed effect of all EPSPs and IPSPs. Whenever the membrane potential at the axon hillock reaches threshold, an action potential is generated and travels along the axon to its synaptic terminals. After the refractory period, the neuron may produce another action potential, provided the membrane potential at the axon hillock once again reaches threshold.

## Termination of Neurotransmitter Signaling

After a response is triggered, the chemical synapse returns to its resting state. How does this happen? The key step is clearing the neurotransmitter molecules from the synaptic cleft. Some neurotransmitters are inactivated by enzymatic hydrolysis (**Figure 48.18a**). Other neurotransmitters are recaptured into the presynaptic neuron (**Figure 48.18b**). After this reuptake occurs, neurotransmitters are repackaged in synaptic vesicles or transferred to glia for metabolism or recycling to neurons.

Clearing neurotransmitter from the synaptic cleft is an essential step in the transmission of information through the nervous system. Indeed, blocking this process can have severe consequences. For example, the nerve gas sarin triggers paralysis and death because it inhibits the enzyme that breaks down the neurotransmitter controlling skeletal muscles.

## Modulated Signaling at Synapses

So far, we have focused on synapses where a neurotransmitter binds directly to an ion channel, causing the channel

▼ **Figure 48.18  Two mechanisms of terminating neurotransmission.**

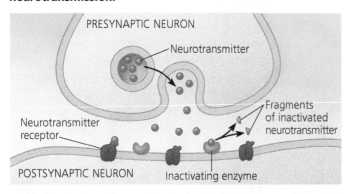

**(a) Enzymatic breakdown of neurotransmitter in the synaptic cleft**

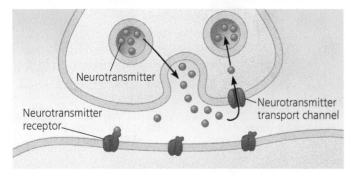

**(b) Reuptake of neurotransmitter by presynaptic neuron**

to open. However, there are also chemical synapses in which the receptor for the neurotransmitter is *not* part of an ion channel. At these synapses, the neurotransmitter binds to a G protein-coupled receptor, activating a signal transduction pathway in the postsynaptic cell involving a second messenger (see Concept 11.3). Because the resulting opening or closing of ion channels depends on one or more metabolic steps, these G protein-coupled receptors are also called *metabotropic receptors*.

G protein-coupled receptors modulate the responsiveness and activity of postsynaptic neurons in diverse ways. Consider, for example, the metabotropic receptor for the neurotransmitter norepinephrine. Binding of norepinephrine to its G protein-coupled receptor activates a G protein, which in turn activates adenylyl cyclase, the enzyme that converts ATP to cAMP (see Figure 11.11). Cyclic AMP activates protein kinase A, which phosphorylates specific ion channel proteins in the postsynaptic membrane, causing them to open or close. Because of the amplifying effect of the signal transduction pathway, the binding of one norepinephrine molecule can trigger the opening or closing of many channels.

Many neurotransmitters have both ionotropic and metabotropic receptors. Compared with the postsynaptic potentials produced by ligand-gated channels, the effects of G protein pathways typically have a slower onset but last longer.

## Neurotransmitters

Signaling at a synapse brings about a response that depends on both the neurotransmitter released from the presynaptic membrane and the receptor produced at the postsynaptic membrane. A single neurotransmitter may bind specifically to more than a dozen different receptors. Indeed, a particular neurotransmitter can excite postsynaptic cells expressing one receptor and inhibit postsynaptic cells expressing a different receptor. As an example, let's examine **acetylcholine**, a common neurotransmitter in both invertebrates and vertebrates.

### Acetylcholine

Acetylcholine is vital for nervous system functions that include muscle stimulation, memory formation, and learning. In vertebrates, there are two major classes of acetylcholine receptor. One is a ligand-gated ion channel. We know the most about its function at the vertebrate *neuromuscular junction*, the site where a motor neuron forms a synapse with a skeletal muscle cell. When acetylcholine released by motor neurons binds this receptor, the ion channel opens, producing an EPSP. This excitatory activity is soon terminated by acetylcholinesterase, an enzyme in the synaptic cleft that hydrolyzes the neurotransmitter.

A G protein-coupled receptor for acetylcholine is found at locations that include the vertebrate CNS and heart. In heart muscle, acetylcholine released by neurons activates a signal transduction pathway. The G proteins in the pathway inhibit adenylyl cyclase and open potassium channels in the muscle cell membrane. Both effects reduce the rate at which the heart pumps. Thus, the effect of acetylcholine in heart muscle is inhibitory rather than excitatory.

Several chemicals with profound effects on the nervous system mimic or alter the function of acetylcholine. Nicotine, a chemical found in tobacco and tobacco smoke, acts as a stimulant by binding to an ionotropic acetylcholine receptor in the CNS. As discussed earlier, the nerve gas sarin blocks enzymatic cleavage of acetylcholine. A third example is botulinum toxin, which inhibits presynaptic release of acetylcholine. The result is a form of food poisoning called botulism. Because muscles required for breathing fail to contract when acetylcholine release is blocked, untreated botulism is typically fatal. Today, injections of the botulinum toxin, known by the trade name Botox, are used cosmetically to minimize wrinkles around the eyes or mouth by inhibiting synaptic transmission to particular facial muscles.

Although acetylcholine has many roles, it is just one of more than 100 known neurotransmitters. As shown by the examples in **Table 48.2**, the rest fall into four classes: amino acids, biogenic amines, neuropeptides, and gases.

| Table 48.2 | Major Neurotransmitters |
|---|---|
| **Neurotransmitter** | **Structure** |
| *Acetylcholine* | |
| *Amino Acids*<br>Glutamate | |
| GABA (gamma-<br>aminobutyric acid) | $H_2N-CH_2-CH_2-CH_2-COOH$ |
| Glycine | $H_2N-CH_2-COOH$ |
| *Biogenic Amines*<br>Norepinephrine | |
| Dopamine | |
| Serotonin | |
| *Neuropeptides* (a very diverse group, only two of which are shown) | |
| Substance P | Arg—Pro—Lys—Pro—Gln—Gln—Phe—Phe—Gly—Leu—Met |
| Met-enkephalin (an endorphin) | Tyr—Gly—Gly—Phe—Met |
| *Gases* | |
| Nitric oxide | $N=O$ |

## Amino Acids

*Glutamate* is one of several amino acids that can act as a neurotransmitter. In invertebrates, glutamate, rather than acetylcholine, is the neurotransmitter at the neuromuscular junction. In vertebrates, glutamate is the most common neurotransmitter in the CNS. Synapses at which glutamate is the neurotransmitter have a key role in the formation of long-term memory, as you will see in Concept 49.4.

Two amino acids act as inhibitory neurotransmitters in the CNS. *Glycine* acts at inhibitory synapses in parts of the CNS that lie outside of the brain. Within the brain, the amino acid *gamma-aminobutyric acid (GABA)* is the neurotransmitter at most inhibitory synapses in the brain. Binding of GABA to receptors in postsynaptic cells increases membrane permeability to $Cl^-$, resulting in an IPSP. The widely prescribed drug diazepam (Valium) reduces anxiety through binding to a site on a GABA receptor.

## Biogenic Amines

The neurotransmitters grouped as *biogenic amines* are synthesized from amino acids and include *norepinephrine*, which is made from tyrosine. Norepinephrine is an excitatory neurotransmitter in the autonomic nervous system, a branch of the PNS. Outside the nervous system, norepinephrine has distinct but related functions as a hormone, as does the chemically similar biogenic amine *epinephrine* (see Concept 45.3).

The biogenic amines *dopamine* (made from tyrosine) and *serotonin* (made from tryptophan) are released at many sites in the brain and affect sleep, mood, attention, and learning. Some psychoactive drugs, including LSD and mescaline, apparently produce their hallucinatory effects by binding to brain receptors for these neurotransmitters.

Biogenic amines have a central role in a number of nervous system disorders and treatments (see Concept 49.5). The degenerative illness Parkinson's disease is associated with a lack of dopamine in the brain. In addition, depression is often treated with drugs that increase the brain concentrations of biogenic amines. Prozac, for instance, enhances the effect of serotonin by inhibiting its reuptake after release.

## Neuropeptides

Several **neuropeptides**, relatively short chains of amino acids, serve as neurotransmitters that operate via G protein-coupled receptors. Such peptides are typically produced by cleavage of much larger protein precursors. The neuropeptide *substance P* is a key excitatory neurotransmitter that mediates our perception of pain. Other neuropeptides, called **endorphins**, function as natural analgesics, decreasing pain perception.

Endorphins are produced in the brain during times of physical or emotional stress, such as childbirth. In addition to relieving pain, they reduce urine output, decrease respiration, and produce euphoria as well as other emotional effects. Because opiates (drugs such as morphine and heroin) bind

# Interpreting Data Values Expressed in Scientific Notation

**Does the Brain Have Specific Protein Receptors for Opiates?** Researchers were looking for opiate receptors in the mammalian brain. Knowing that the drug naloxone blocks the analgesic effect of opiates, they hypothesized that naloxone acts by binding tightly to brain opiate receptors without activating them. In this exercise, you will interpret the results of an experiment that the researchers conducted to test their hypothesis.

**How the Experiment Was Done** The researchers added radioactive naloxone to a protein mixture prepared from rodent brains. If the mixture contained opiate receptors or other proteins that could bind naloxone, the radioactivity would stably associate with the mixture. To determine whether the binding was due to specific opiate receptors, they tested other drugs, opiate and non-opiate, for their ability to block naloxone binding.

Radioactive naloxone

① Radioactive naloxone and a test drug are incubated with a protein mixture.

Drug

② Proteins are trapped on a filter. Bound naloxone is detected by measuring radioactivity.

**Data from the Experiment**

| Drug | Opiate | Lowest Concentration That Blocked Naloxone Binding |
|------|--------|---------------------------------------------------|
| Morphine | Yes | $6 \times 10^{-9}$ M |
| Methadone | Yes | $2 \times 10^{-8}$ M |
| Levorphanol | Yes | $2 \times 10^{-9}$ M |
| Phenobarbital | No | No effect at $10^{-4}$ M |
| Atropine | No | No effect at $10^{-4}$ M |
| Serotonin | No | No effect at $10^{-4}$ M |

**Data from** C. B. Pert and S. H. Snyder, Opiate receptor: demonstration in nervous tissue, *Science* 179:1011–1014 (1973).

**INTERPRET THE DATA**

1. The data above are expressed in scientific notation: a numerical factor times a power of 10. Remember that a negative power of 10 means a number less than 1. For example, $10^{-1}$ M (molar) can also be written as 0.1 M. Write the concentrations in the table above for morphine and atropine in this alternative format.

2. Compare the concentrations listed in the table for methadone and phenobarbital. Which concentration is higher? By how much?

3. Would phenobarbital, atropine, or serotonin have blocked naloxone binding at a concentration of $10^{-5}$ M? Explain why or why not.

4. Which drugs blocked naloxone binding in this experiment? What do these results indicate about the brain receptors for naloxone?

5. When the researchers instead used tissue from intestinal muscles rather than brains, they found no naloxone binding. What does that suggest about opiate receptors in mammalian muscle?

**MB** **Instructors:** A version of this Scientific Skills Exercise can be assigned in MasteringBiology.

---

to the same receptor proteins as endorphins, opiates mimic endorphins and produce many of the same physiological effects (see Figure 2.16). In the **Scientific Skills Exercise**, you can interpret data from an experiment designed to search for opiate receptors in the brain.

## Gases

Some vertebrate neurons release dissolved gases as neurotransmitters. In human males, for example, certain neurons release nitric oxide (NO) into the erectile tissue of the penis during sexual arousal. The resulting relaxation of smooth muscle in the blood vessel walls of the spongy erectile tissue allows the tissue to fill with blood, producing an erection. The erectile dysfunction drug Viagra works by inhibiting an enzyme that terminates the action of NO.

Unlike most neurotransmitters, NO is not stored in cytoplasmic vesicles but is instead synthesized on demand. NO diffuses into neighboring target cells, produces a change, and is broken down—all within a few seconds. In many of its targets, including smooth muscle cells, NO works like many

hormones, stimulating an enzyme to synthesize a second messenger that directly affects cellular metabolism.

Although the gas carbon monoxide (CO) is a deadly poison if inhaled, vertebrates produce small amounts of CO as a neurotransmitter. For example, CO synthesized in the brain regulates the release of hormones from the hypothalamus.

In the next chapter, we'll consider how the cellular and biochemical mechanisms we have discussed contribute to nervous system function on the system level.

**MB** The Virtual Brain: Neural Conduction and Synaptic Transmission

## CONCEPT CHECK 48.4

1. How is it possible for a particular neurotransmitter to produce opposite effects in different tissues?

2. Some pesticides inhibit acetylcholinesterase, the enzyme that breaks down acetylcholine. Explain how these toxins would affect EPSPs produced by acetylcholine.

3. **MAKE CONNECTIONS** ➤ Name one or more membrane activities that occur both in fertilization of an egg and in neurotransmission across a synapse (see Figure 47.3).

*For suggested answers, see Appendix A.*

# 48 Chapter Review

## SUMMARY OF KEY CONCEPTS

### CONCEPT 48.1

**Neuron structure and organization reflect function in information transfer** (pp. 1066–1068)

VOCAB
SELF-QUIZ
goo.gl/6u55ks

- Most **neurons** have branched **dendrites** that receive signals from other neurons and an **axon** that transmits signals to other cells at **synapses**. Neurons rely on **glia** for functions that include nourishment, insulation, and regulation.

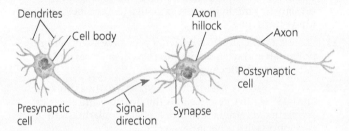

Dendrites  
Cell body  
Axon hillock  
Axon  
Postsynaptic cell  
Presynaptic cell  
Signal direction  
Synapse

- A **central nervous system (CNS)** and a **peripheral nervous system (PNS)** process information in three stages: sensory input, integration, and motor output to effector cells.

**?** *How would severing an axon affect the flow of information in a neuron?*

### CONCEPT 48.2

**Ion pumps and ion channels establish the resting potential of a neuron** (pp. 1068–1070)

- Ionic gradients generate a voltage difference, or **membrane potential**, across the plasma membrane of cells. The concentration of $Na^+$ is higher outside than inside; the reverse is true for $K^+$. In resting neurons, the plasma membrane has many open potassium channels but few open sodium channels. Diffusion of ions, principally $K^+$, through channels generates a **resting potential**, with the inside more negative than the outside.

**?** *Suppose you placed an isolated neuron in a solution similar to extracellular fluid and later transferred the neuron to a solution lacking any sodium ions. What change would you expect in the resting potential?*

### CONCEPT 48.3

**Action potentials are the signals conducted by axons** (pp. 1070–1075)

- Neurons have **gated ion channels** that open or close in response to stimuli, leading to changes in the membrane potential. An increase in the magnitude of the membrane potential is a **hyperpolarization**; a decrease is a **depolarization**. Changes in membrane potential that vary continuously with the strength of a stimulus are known as **graded potentials**.
- An **action potential** is a brief, all-or-none depolarization of a neuron's plasma membrane. When a graded depolarization brings the membrane potential to **threshold**, many **voltage-gated ion channels** open, triggering an inflow of $Na^+$ that rapidly brings the membrane potential to a positive value. A negative membrane

potential is restored by the inactivation of sodium channels and by the opening of many voltage-gated potassium channels, which increases $K^+$ outflow. A **refractory period** follows, corresponding to the interval when the sodium channels are inactivated.

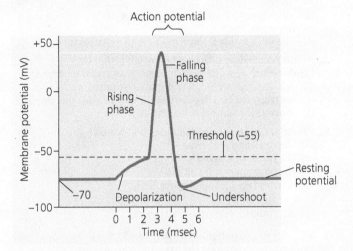

Action potential

Rising phase  
Falling phase  
Threshold (−55)  
Resting potential  
−70  
Depolarization  
Undershoot  
Membrane potential (mV)  
Time (msec)

- A nerve impulse travels from the axon hillock to the synaptic terminals by propagating a series of action potentials along the axon. The speed of conduction increases with the diameter of the axon and, in many vertebrate axons, with myelination. Action potentials in axons insulated by myelination appear to jump from one **node of Ranvier** to the next, a process called **saltatory conduction**.

**INTERPRET THE DATA ➤** *Assuming a refractory period equal in length to the action potential (see graph above), what is the maximum frequency per unit time at which a neuron could fire action potentials?*

### CONCEPT 48.4

**Neurons communicate with other cells at synapses** (pp. 1075–1080)

- In an electrical synapse, electrical current flows directly from one cell to another. In a chemical synapse, depolarization causes synaptic vesicles to fuse with the terminal membrane and release **neurotransmitter** into the synaptic cleft.
- At many synapses, the neurotransmitter binds to **ligand-gated ion channels** in the postsynaptic membrane, producing an **excitatory** or **inhibitory postsynaptic potential** (**EPSP** or **IPSP**). The neurotransmitter then diffuses out of the cleft, is taken up by surrounding cells, or is degraded by enzymes. A single neuron has many synapses on its dendrites and cell body. Temporal and spatial **summation** of EPSPs and IPSPs at the axon hillock determine whether a neuron generates an action potential.
- Different receptors for the same neurotransmitter produce different effects. Some neurotransmitter receptors activate signal transduction pathways, which can produce long-lasting changes in postsynaptic cells. Major neurotransmitters include **acetylcholine**; the amino acids GABA, glutamate, and glycine; biogenic amines; **neuropeptides**; and gases such as NO.

**?** *Why are many drugs that are used to treat nervous system diseases or to affect brain function targeted to specific receptors rather than particular neurotransmitters?*

## Level 1: Knowledge/Comprehension

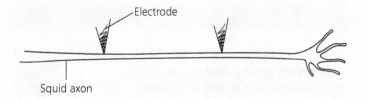

1. What happens when a resting neuron's membrane depolarizes?
   (A) There is a net diffusion of $Na^+$ out of the cell.
   (B) The equilibrium potential for $K^+$ ($E_K$) becomes more positive.
   (C) The neuron's membrane voltage becomes more positive.
   (D) The cell's inside is more negative than the outside.

2. A common feature of action potentials is that they
   (A) cause the membrane to hyperpolarize and then depolarize.
   (B) can undergo temporal and spatial summation.
   (C) are triggered by a depolarization that reaches threshold.
   (D) move at the same speed along all axons.

3. Where are neurotransmitter receptors located?
   (A) the nuclear membrane
   (B) the nodes of Ranvier
   (C) the postsynaptic membrane
   (D) synaptic vesicle membranes

## Level 2: Application/Analysis

4. Why are action potentials usually conducted in one direction?
   (A) Ions can flow along the axon in only one direction.
   (B) The brief refractory period prevents reopening of voltage-gated $Na^+$ channels.
   (C) The axon hillock has a higher membrane potential than the terminals of the axon.
   (D) Voltage-gated channels for both $Na^+$ and $K^+$ open in only one direction.

5. Which of the following is the most *direct* result of depolarizing the presynaptic membrane of an axon terminal?
   (A) Voltage-gated calcium channels in the membrane open.
   (B) Synaptic vesicles fuse with the membrane.
   (C) Ligand-gated channels open, allowing neurotransmitters to enter the synaptic cleft.
   (D) An EPSP or IPSP is generated in the postsynaptic cell.

6. Suppose a particular neurotransmitter causes an IPSP in postsynaptic cell X and an EPSP in postsynaptic cell Y. A likely explanation is that
   (A) the threshold value in the postsynaptic membrane is different for cell X and cell Y.
   (B) the axon of cell X is myelinated, but that of cell Y is not.
   (C) only cell Y produces an enzyme that terminates the activity of the neurotransmitter.
   (D) cells X and Y express different receptor molecules for this particular neurotransmitter.

## Level 3: Synthesis/Evaluation

7. **WHAT IF?** Ouabain, a plant substance used in some cultures to poison hunting arrows, disables the sodium-potassium pump. What change in the resting potential would you expect to see if you treated a neuron with ouabain? Explain.

8. **WHAT IF?** If a drug mimicked the activity of GABA in the CNS, what general effect on behavior might you expect? Explain.

9. **DRAW IT** Suppose a researcher inserts a pair of electrodes at two different positions along the middle of an axon dissected out of a squid. By applying a depolarizing stimulus, the researcher brings the plasma membrane at both positions to threshold. Using the drawing below as a model, create one or more drawings that illustrate where each action potential would terminate.

Electrode

Squid axon

10. **EVOLUTION CONNECTION** An action potential is an all-or-none event. This on/off signaling is an evolutionary adaptation of animals that must sense and act in a complex environment. It is possible to imagine a nervous system in which the action potentials are graded, with the amplitude depending on the size of the stimulus. Describe what evolutionary advantage on/off signaling might have over a graded (continuously variable) kind of signaling.

11. **SCIENTIFIC INQUIRY** From what you know about action potentials and synapses, propose two hypotheses for how various anesthetics might block pain.

12. **WRITE ABOUT A THEME: ORGANIZATION** In a short essay (100–150 words), describe how the structure and electrical properties of vertebrate neurons reflect similarities and differences with other animal cells.

13. **SYNTHESIZE YOUR KNOWLEDGE**

The rattlesnake alerts enemies to its presence with a rattle—a set of modified scales at the tip of its tail. Describe the distinct roles of gated ion channels in initiating and moving a signal along the nerve from the snake's head to its tail and then from that nerve to the muscle that shakes the rattle.

*For selected answers, see Appendix A.*

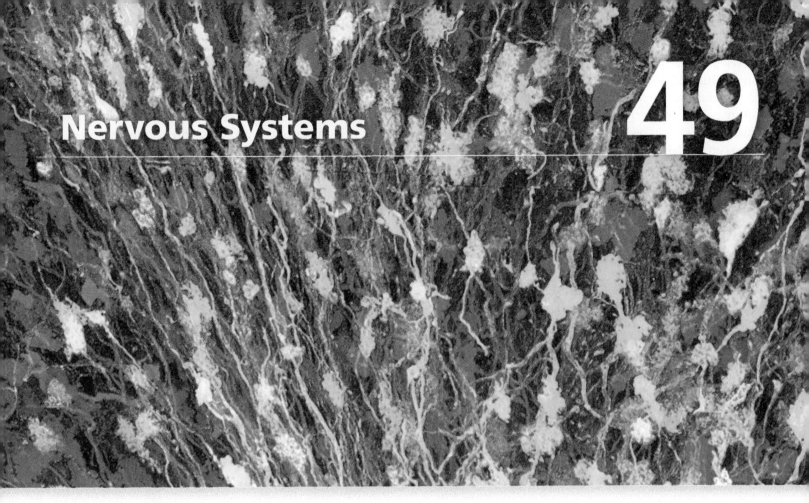

# Nervous Systems

## 49

▲ Figure 49.1 **How do scientists identify individual neurons in the brain?**

## KEY CONCEPTS

**49.1** Nervous systems consist of circuits of neurons and supporting cells

**49.2** The vertebrate brain is regionally specialized

**49.3** The cerebral cortex controls voluntary movement and cognitive functions

**49.4** Changes in synaptic connections underlie memory and learning

**49.5** Many nervous system disorders can now be explained in molecular terms

## Command and Control Center

What happens in your brain when you solve a math problem or listen to music? Answering such a question was for a long time nearly unimaginable. The human brain contains an estimated $10^{11}$ (100 billion) neurons organized into circuits more complex than those of even the most powerful supercomputers. However, thanks in part to several exciting new technologies, scientists have begun to sort out the cellular mechanisms for information processing in the brain, thus revealing the processes that underlie thought and emotion.

One breakthrough came with the development of powerful imaging techniques that reveal activity in the working brain. Researchers can monitor multiple areas of the human brain while a subject is performing various tasks, such as speaking, looking at pictures, or forming a mental image of a person's face. They then analyze these data to determine if there is a correlation between a particular task and activity in specific brain areas.

A more recent advance in exploring the brain relies on a method for expressing random combinations of colored proteins in brain cells—such that each cell shows up in a different color. The result is a "brainbow" like the one in **Figure 49.1**, which highlights neurons in the brain of a mouse. In this image, each neuron expresses one of more than 90 different color combinations of four fluorescent proteins.

When you see this blue icon, log in to **MasteringBiology** and go to the Study Area for digital resources.

 Get Ready for This Chapter

Using the brainbow technology, neuroscientists hope to develop detailed maps of the connections that transfer information between particular regions of the brain.

In this chapter, we'll discuss the structure and evolution of animal nervous systems, exploring how groups of neurons function in circuits dedicated to specific tasks. Next, we'll focus on specialization in regions of the vertebrate brain. We'll then turn to the ways in which the brain activity stores and organizes information. Finally, we'll consider recent findings regarding several nervous system disorders.

# CONCEPT 49.1

## Nervous systems consist of circuits of neurons and supporting cells

The ability to sense and react originated billions of years ago in prokaryotes, enhancing survival and reproductive success in changing environments. Later in evolution, modification of simple recognition and response processes provided a basis for communication between cells in an animal body. By the time of the Cambrian explosion, more than 500 million years ago (see Concept 32.2), specialized nervous systems had appeared that enable animals to sense their surroundings and respond rapidly.

Hydras, jellies, and other cnidarians are the simplest animals with nervous systems. In most cnidarians, interconnected neurons form a diffuse *nerve net* (Figure 49.2a), which controls the contraction and expansion of the gastrovascular cavity. In more complex animals, the axons of multiple neurons are often bundled together, forming **nerves**. These fibrous structures channel information flow along specific routes through the nervous system. For example, sea stars have a set of radial nerves connecting to a central nerve ring (Figure 49.2b). Within each arm of a sea star, the radial nerve is linked to a nerve net from which it receives input and to which it sends signals that control muscle contraction.

Animals with elongated, bilaterally symmetrical bodies have even more specialized nervous systems. In particular, they exhibit *cephalization*, an evolutionary trend toward a clustering of sensory neurons and interneurons at the anterior (front) end of the body. Nerves that extend toward the posterior (rear) end enable these anterior neurons to communicate with cells elsewhere in the body.

In many animals, neurons that carry out integration form a **central nervous system (CNS)**, and neurons that carry information into and out of the CNS form a **peripheral nervous system (PNS)**. In nonsegmented worms, such as the planarian in Figure 49.2c, a small brain and longitudinal nerve cords constitute the simplest clearly defined CNS. In

▼ **Figure 49.2 Nervous system organization. (a)** A hydra contains individual neurons (purple) organized in a diffuse nerve net. **(b–h)** Animals with more sophisticated nervous systems contain groups of neurons (blue) organized into nerves and often ganglia and a brain.

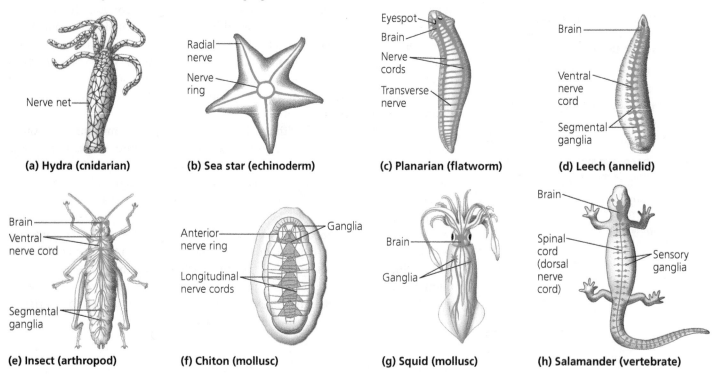

(a) Hydra (cnidarian)

(b) Sea star (echinoderm)

(c) Planarian (flatworm)

(d) Leech (annelid)

(e) Insect (arthropod)

(f) Chiton (mollusc)

(g) Squid (mollusc)

(h) Salamander (vertebrate)

certain nonsegmented worms, the entire nervous system is constructed from only a small number of cells, as in the case of the nematode *Caenorhabditis elegans*. In this species, an adult worm (hermaphrodite) has exactly 302 neurons, no more and no fewer. More complex invertebrates, such as segmented worms (**Figure 49.2d**) and arthropods (**Figure 49.2e**), have many more neurons. Their behavior is regulated by more complicated brains and by ventral nerve cords containing **ganglia**, segmentally arranged clusters of neurons that act as relay points in transmitting information.

Within an animal group, nervous system organization often correlates with lifestyle. Among the molluscs, for example, sessile and slow-moving species, such as clams and chitons, have relatively simple sense organs and little or no cephalization (**Figure 49.2f**). In contrast, active predatory molluscs, such as octopuses and squids (**Figure 49.2g**), have the most sophisticated nervous systems of any invertebrate. With their large, image-forming eyes and a brain containing millions of neurons, octopuses can learn to discriminate between visual patterns and to perform complex tasks, such as unscrewing a jar to feed on its contents.

In vertebrates (**Figure 49.2h**), the brain and the spinal cord form the CNS; nerves and ganglia are the key elements of the PNS. Regional specialization is a hallmark of both systems, as we will see throughout this chapter.

## Glia

As discussed in Concept 48.1, the nervous systems of vertebrates and most invertebrates include not only neurons but also **glial cells**, or **glia**. Examples of glia include the Schwann cells that produce the myelin sheaths surrounding axons in the PNS and oligodendrocytes, their counterparts in the CNS. **Figure 49.3** illustrates the major types of glia in the adult vertebrate and provides an overview of the ways in which they nourish, support, and regulate the functioning of neurons.

In embryos, two types of glia play essential roles in the development of the nervous system: radial glia and astrocytes. *Radial glia* form tracks along which newly formed neurons migrate from the neural tube, the structure that gives rise to the CNS (see Figure 47.14). Later, glia called *astrocytes* that are adjacent to brain capillaries participate in the formation of the *blood-brain barrier*, a physiological mechanism that restricts the entry of many substances from the blood into the CNS.

Both radial glia and astrocytes can act as stem cells, which undergo unlimited cell divisions to self-renew and to form more specialized cells. Studies with mice reveal that stem cells in the brain give rise to neurons that mature, migrate to particular locations, and become incorporated into the circuitry

▼ **Figure 49.3 Glia in the vertebrate nervous system.**

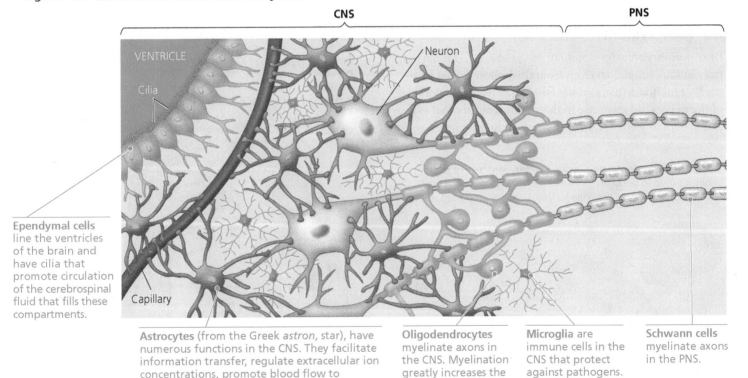

**Ependymal cells** line the ventricles of the brain and have cilia that promote circulation of the cerebrospinal fluid that fills these compartments.

**Astrocytes** (from the Greek *astron*, star), have numerous functions in the CNS. They facilitate information transfer, regulate extracellular ion concentrations, promote blood flow to neurons, help form the blood-brain barrier, and act as stem cells to replenish certain neurons.

**Oligodendrocytes** myelinate axons in the CNS. Myelination greatly increases the conduction speed of action potentials.

**Microglia** are immune cells in the CNS that protect against pathogens.

**Schwann cells** myelinate axons in the PNS.

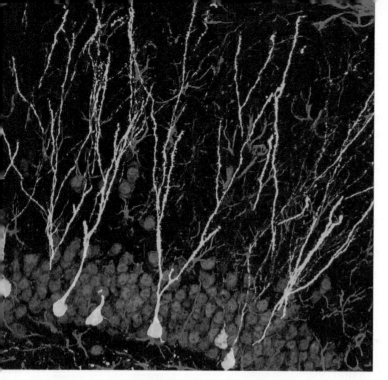

**▲ Figure 49.4 Newly born neurons in the brain of an adult mouse.** In this light micrograph, new neurons derived from adult stem cells are labeled with green fluorescent protein (GFP), and all neurons are labeled with a DNA-binding dye, colored red in this image.

of the adult nervous system **(Figure 49.4)**. Researchers are now exploring approaches to use these stem cells as a means of replacing brain tissue that has ceased to function properly.

## Organization of the Vertebrate Nervous System

During embryonic development in vertebrates, the central nervous system develops from the hollow dorsal nerve cord—a hallmark of chordates (see Figure 34.3). The cavity of the nerve cord gives rise to the narrow *central canal* of the spinal cord as well as the *ventricles* of the brain **(Figure 49.5)**.

**▼ Figure 49.5 Ventricles, gray matter, and white matter.** Ventricles deep in the brain's interior contain cerebrospinal fluid. Most of the gray matter is on the brain surface, surrounding the white matter.

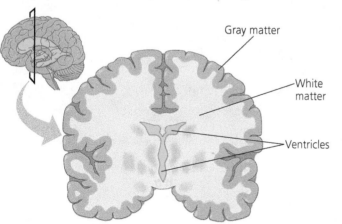

Gray matter

White matter

Ventricles

Both the canal and ventricles fill with *cerebrospinal fluid*, which is formed in the brain by filtering arterial blood. The cerebrospinal fluid supplies the CNS with nutrients and hormones and carries away wastes, circulating through the ventricles and central canal before draining into the veins.

In addition to fluid-filled spaces, the brain and spinal cord contain gray matter and white matter (see Figure 49.5). **Gray matter** is primarily made up of neuron cell bodies. **White matter** consists of bundled axons. In the spinal cord, white matter forms the outer layer, reflecting its role in linking the CNS to sensory and motor neurons of the PNS. In the brain, white matter is predominantly in the interior, where signaling between neurons functions in learning, feeling emotions, processing sensory information, and generating commands.

In vertebrates, the spinal cord runs lengthwise inside the vertebral column, known as the spine **(Figure 49.6)**. The spinal cord conveys information to and from the brain and generates basic patterns of locomotion. It also acts independently of the brain as part of the simple nerve circuits that produce **reflexes**, the body's automatic responses to certain stimuli.

**▼ Figure 49.6 The vertebrate nervous system.** The central nervous system consists of the brain and spinal cord (yellow). Left-right pairs of cranial nerves, spinal nerves, and ganglia make up most of the peripheral nervous system (dark gold).

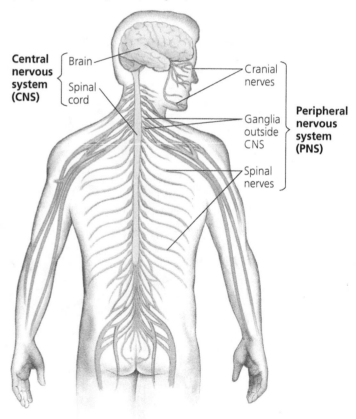

Central nervous system (CNS)
Brain
Spinal cord

Cranial nerves

Ganglia outside CNS

Spinal nerves

Peripheral nervous system (PNS)

> **Figure 49.7 The knee-jerk reflex.** Many neurons are involved in this reflex, but for simplicity only a few neurons are shown.

**MAKE CONNECTIONS** ➤ *Using the nerve signals to the hamstring and quadriceps in this reflex as an example, propose a model for regulation of smooth muscle activity in the esophagus during the swallowing reflex (see Figure 41.9).*

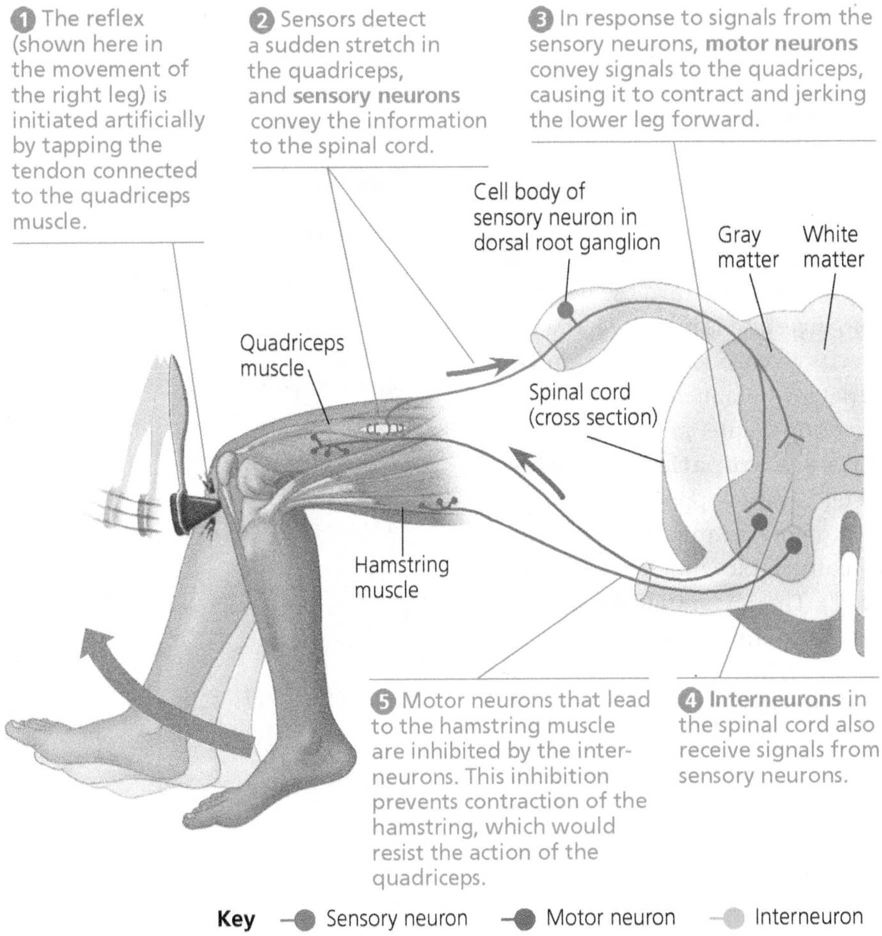

**1** The reflex (shown here in the movement of the right leg) is initiated artificially by tapping the tendon connected to the quadriceps muscle.

**2** Sensors detect a sudden stretch in the quadriceps, and **sensory neurons** convey the information to the spinal cord.

**3** In response to signals from the sensory neurons, **motor neurons** convey signals to the quadriceps, causing it to contract and jerking the lower leg forward.

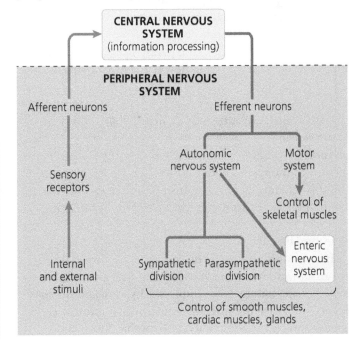

Cell body of sensory neuron in dorsal root ganglion

Gray matter

White matter

Quadriceps muscle

Spinal cord (cross section)

Hamstring muscle

**5** Motor neurons that lead to the hamstring muscle are inhibited by the interneurons. This inhibition prevents contraction of the hamstring, which would resist the action of the quadriceps.

**4** **Interneurons** in the spinal cord also receive signals from sensory neurons.

**Key** ──● Sensory neuron    ──● Motor neuron    ──● Interneuron

A reflex protects the body by providing a rapid, involuntary response to a particular stimulus. Reflexes are rapid because sensory information is used to activate motor neurons without the information first having to travel from the spinal cord to the brain and back. If you accidentally put your hand on a hot burner, a reflex begins to jerk your hand back before your brain processes any pain. Similarly, the knee-jerk reflex provides an immediate protective response when you pick up an unexpectedly heavy object. If your legs buckle, the tension across your knees triggers contraction of your thigh muscle (quadriceps), helping you stay upright and support the load. During a physical exam, your doctor may trigger the knee-jerk reflex with a triangular mallet to help assess nervous system function **(Figure 49.7).**

## The Peripheral Nervous System

The PNS transmits information to and from the CNS and plays a large role in regulating an animal's movement and its internal environment **(Figure 49.8)**. Sensory information reaches the CNS along PNS neurons designated as *afferent* (from the Latin, meaning "to carry toward"). Following information processing within the CNS, instructions then travel to muscles, glands, and endocrine cells along PNS neurons designated as *efferent* (from the Latin, meaning "to carry away"). Note that most nerves contain both afferent and efferent neurons.

The PNS has two efferent components: the motor system and the autonomic nervous system (see Figure 49.8). The neurons of the **motor system** carry signals to skeletal muscles. Motor control can be voluntary, as when you raise your hand to ask a question, or involuntary, as in the knee-jerk reflex controlled by the spinal cord. In contrast, regulation of smooth and cardiac muscles by the **autonomic nervous system** is generally involuntary. The sympathetic and parasympathetic divisions of the autonomic nervous system together regulate the organs of the digestive, cardiovascular, excretory, and endocrine systems. A distinct network of neurons now known as the **enteric nervous system** exerts direct and partially independent control over the digestive tract, pancreas, and gallbladder.

▼ **Figure 49.8 Functional hierarchy of the vertebrate peripheral nervous system.**

**CENTRAL NERVOUS SYSTEM** (information processing)

**PERIPHERAL NERVOUS SYSTEM**

Afferent neurons

Efferent neurons

Sensory receptors

Autonomic nervous system

Motor system

Control of skeletal muscles

Internal and external stimuli

Sympathetic division

Parasympathetic division

Enteric nervous system

Control of smooth muscles, cardiac muscles, glands

The sympathetic and parasympathetic divisions of the autonomic nervous system have largely antagonistic (opposite) functions in regulating organ function (**Figure 49.9**). Activation of the **sympathetic division** corresponds to arousal and energy generation (the "fight-or-flight" response). For example, the heart beats faster, digestion is inhibited, the liver converts glycogen to glucose, and the adrenal medulla increases secretion of epinephrine (adrenaline). Activation of the **parasympathetic division** generally causes opposite responses that promote calming and a return to self-maintenance functions ("rest and digest"). Thus, heart rate decreases, digestion is enhanced, and glycogen production increases. However, in regulating reproductive activity, a function that is not homeostatic, the parasympathetic division complements rather than antagonizes the sympathetic division, as shown at the bottom of Figure 49.9.

The two divisions differ not only in overall function but also in organization and signals released. Parasympathetic nerves exit the CNS at the base of the brain or spinal cord and form synapses in ganglia near or within an internal organ. In contrast, sympathetic nerves typically exit the CNS midway along the spinal cord and form synapses in ganglia located just outside of the spinal cord.

In both the sympathetic and parasympathetic divisions, the pathway for information flow frequently involves a preganglionic and a postganglionic neuron. The *preganglionic neurons*, those with cell bodies in the CNS, release acetylcholine as a neurotransmitter (see Concept 48.4). In the case of the *postganglionic neurons*, those of the parasympathetic division release acetylcholine, whereas nearly all their counterparts in the sympathetic division release norepinephrine. It is this difference in neurotransmitters that enables the sympathetic and parasympathetic divisions to bring about opposite effects in organs such as the lungs, heart, intestines, and bladder.

Homeostasis often relies on cooperation between the motor and autonomic nervous systems. In response to a drop in body temperature, for example, the hypothalamus signals the motor system to cause shivering, which increases heat production. At the same time, the hypothalamus signals the autonomic nervous system to constrict surface blood vessels, reducing heat loss.

▼ **Figure 49.9** **The parasympathetic and sympathetic divisions of the autonomic nervous system.** Most pathways in each division involve two neurons. The axon of the first neuron extends from a cell body in the CNS to a set of PNS neurons whose cell bodies are clustered into a ganglion (plural, *ganglia*). The axons of these PNS neurons transmit instructions to internal organs, where they form synapses with smooth muscle, cardiac muscle, or gland cells.

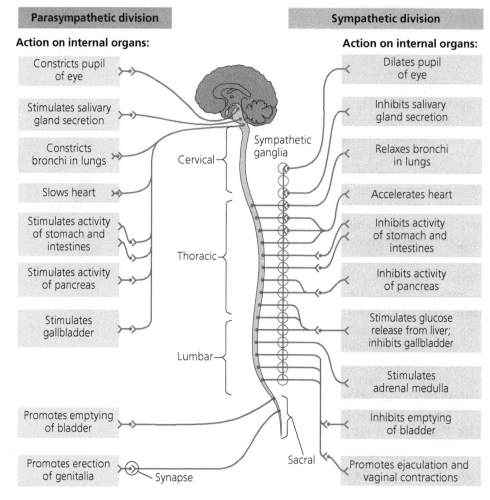

| Parasympathetic division | Sympathetic division |
|---|---|
| **Action on internal organs:** | **Action on internal organs:** |
| Constricts pupil of eye | Dilates pupil of eye |
| Stimulates salivary gland secretion | Inhibits salivary gland secretion |
| Constricts bronchi in lungs | Relaxes bronchi in lungs |
| Slows heart | Accelerates heart |
| Stimulates activity of stomach and intestines | Inhibits activity of stomach and intestines |
| Stimulates activity of pancreas | Inhibits activity of pancreas |
| Stimulates gallbladder | Stimulates glucose release from liver; inhibits gallbladder |
| | Stimulates adrenal medulla |
| Promotes emptying of bladder | Inhibits emptying of bladder |
| Promotes erection of genitalia | Promotes ejaculation and vaginal contractions |

Cervical, Thoracic, Lumbar, Sacral — Sympathetic ganglia — Synapse

## CONCEPT CHECK 49.1

1. Which division of the autonomic nervous system would likely be activated if a student learned that an exam she had forgotten about would start in 5 minutes? Explain your answer.

2. **WHAT IF?** ➤ Suppose a person had an accident that severed a small nerve required to move some of the fingers of the right hand. Would you also expect an effect on sensation from those fingers?

3. **MAKE CONNECTIONS** ➤ Most tissues regulated by the autonomic nervous system receive both sympathetic and parasympathetic input from postganglionic neurons. Responses are typically local. In contrast, the adrenal medulla receives input only from the sympathetic division and only from preganglionic neurons, yet responses are observed throughout the body. Explain why (see Figure 45.19).

*For suggested answers, see Appendix A.*

# CONCEPT 49.2

## The vertebrate brain is regionally specialized

We turn now to the vertebrate brain, which has three major regions: the forebrain, midbrain, and hindbrain (shown here for a ray-finned fish).

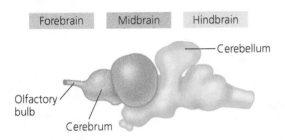

Each region is specialized in function. The **forebrain**, which contains the *olfactory bulb* and *cerebrum*, has activities that include processing of olfactory input (smells), regulation of sleep, learning, and any complex processing. The **midbrain**, located centrally in the brain, coordinates routing of sensory input. The **hindbrain**, part of which forms the *cerebellum*, controls involuntary activities, such as blood circulation, and coordinates motor activities, such as locomotion.

**EVOLUTION** Comparing vertebrates across a phylogenetic tree, we see that the relative sizes of particular brain regions vary **(Figure 49.10)**. Furthermore, these size differences reflect differences in the importance of particular brain functions. Consider, for example, ray-finned fishes, which explore their environment using olfaction, vision, and a lateral line system that detects water currents, electrical stimuli, and body position. The olfactory bulb, which detects scents in the water, is relatively large in these fishes. So is the midbrain, which processes input from the visual and lateral line systems. In contrast, the cerebrum, required for complex processing and learning, is relatively small. Evolution has thus resulted in a close match of structure to function, with the size of particular brain regions correlating with their importance for that species in nervous system function and, hence, species survival and reproduction.

The correlation between the size and function of brain regions can also be observed by considering the cerebellum. Free swimming ray-finned fishes, such as the tuna, control movement in three dimensions in the open water and have a relatively large cerebellum. In comparison, the cerebellum is much smaller in species that don't swim actively, such as the lamprey.

If one compares birds and mammals with groups that diverged from the common vertebrate ancestor earlier in evolution, two trends are apparent. First, the forebrain of birds and mammals occupies a larger fraction of the brain than it does in amphibians, fishes, and other vertebrates. Second, birds and mammals have much larger brains relative to body size than do other groups. Indeed, the ratio of brain size to body weight for birds and mammals is ten times larger than that for their evolutionary ancestors. These differences in both overall brain size and the relative size of the forebrain reflect the greater capacity of birds and mammals for cognition and higher-order reasoning, traits we will return to later in this chapter.

In the case of humans, the 100 billion neurons in the brain make 100 trillion connections. How are so many cells and links organized into circuits and networks that can perform highly sophisticated information processing, storage, and retrieval? In addressing this question, let's begin with **Figure 49.11**, which explores the overall architecture of the human brain. You can use this figure to trace how brain structures arise during embryonic development; as a reference for their size, shape, and location in the adult brain; and as an introduction to their best-understood functions.

To learn more about how particular brain structure and brain organization overall relate to brain function in humans, we'll first consider activity cycles of the brain and the physiological basis of emotion. Then, in Concept 49.3, we'll shift our attention to regional specialization within the cerebrum.

▼ **Figure 49.10 Vertebrate brain structure and evolution.** These examples of vertebrate brains are drawn to the same overall dimensions to highlight differences in the relative size of major structures. These differences in relative size, which arose over the course of vertebrate evolution, correlate with the importance of particular brain functions for particular vertebrate groups.

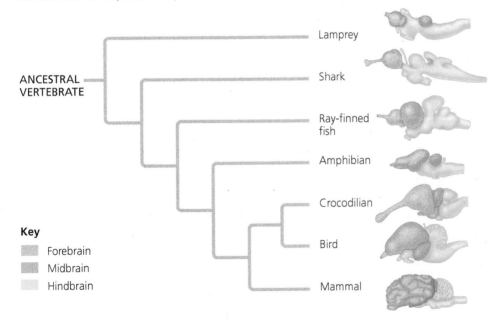

The brain is the most complex organ in the human body. Surrounded by the thick bones of the skull, the brain is divided into a set of distinctive structures, some of which are visible in the magnetic resonance image (MRI) of an adult's head shown at right. The diagram below traces the development of these structures in the embryo. Their major functions are explained in the main text of the chapter.

## Human Brain Development

As a human embryo develops, the neural tube forms three anterior bulges—the forebrain, midbrain, and hindbrain—that together produce the adult brain. The midbrain and portions of the hindbrain give rise to the **brainstem,** a stalk that joins with the spinal cord at the base of the brain. The rest of the hindbrain gives rise to the **cerebellum**, which lies behind the brainstem. Meanwhile, the forebrain develops into the diencephalon, including the neuroendocrine tissues of the brain, and the telencephalon, which becomes the **cerebrum**. Rapid, expansive growth of the telencephalon during the second and third months causes the outer portion, or cortex, of the cerebrum to extend over and around much of the rest of the brain.

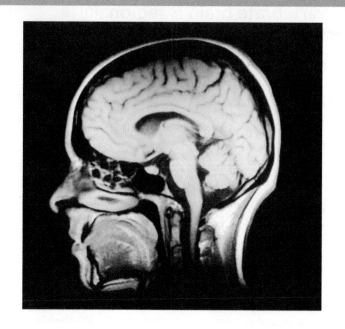

**Embryonic brain regions**

Forebrain → Telencephalon → Cerebrum (includes cerebral cortex, basal nuclei)

Forebrain → Diencephalon → Diencephalon (thalamus, hypothalamus, epithalamus)

Midbrain → Mesencephalon → Midbrain (part of brainstem)

Hindbrain → Metencephalon → Pons (part of brainstem), cerebellum

Hindbrain → Myelencephalon → Medulla oblongata (part of brainstem)

**Brain structures in child and adult**

Embryo at 1 month: Midbrain, Hindbrain, Forebrain

Embryo at 5 weeks: Mesencephalon, Metencephalon, Myelencephalon, Diencephalon, Telencephalon, Spinal cord

Child: Cerebrum, Diencephalon, Midbrain, Pons, Medulla oblongata, Cerebellum, Spinal cord, Brainstem

## The Cerebrum

The cerebrum controls skeletal muscle contraction and is the center for learning, emotion, memory, and perception. It is divided into right and left *cerebral hemispheres*. The outer layer of the cerebrum is called the **cerebral cortex** and is vital for perception, voluntary movement, and learning. The left side of the cerebral cortex receives information from, and controls the movement of, the right side of the body, and vice versa. A thick band of axons known as the **corpus callosum** enables the right and left cerebral cortices to communicate. Deep within the white matter, clusters of neurons called *basal nuclei* serve as centers for planning and learning movement sequences. Damage to these sites during fetal development can result in cerebral palsy, a disorder resulting from a disruption in the transmission of motor commands to the muscles.

## The Cerebellum

The cerebellum coordinates movement and balance and helps in learning and remembering motor skills. The cerebellum receives sensory information about the positions of the joints and the lengths of the muscles, as well as input from the auditory (hearing) and visual systems. It also monitors motor commands issued by the cerebrum. The cerebellum integrates this information as it carries out coordination and error checking during motor and perceptual functions. Hand-eye coordination is an example of cerebellar control; if the cerebellum is damaged, the eyes can follow a moving object, but they will not stop at the same place as the object. Hand movement toward the object will also be erratic.

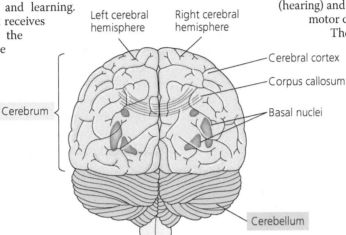

Left cerebral hemisphere — Right cerebral hemisphere — Cerebral cortex — Corpus callosum — Cerebrum — Basal nuclei — Cerebellum

**Adult brain viewed from the rear**

## The Diencephalon

The diencephalon gives rise to the thalamus, hypothalamus, and epithalamus. The **thalamus** is the main input center for sensory information going to the cerebrum. Incoming information from all the senses, as well as from the cerebral cortex, is sorted in the thalamus and sent to the appropriate cerebral centers for further processing. The thalamus is formed by two masses, each roughly the size and shape of a walnut. A much smaller structure, the **hypothalamus**, constitutes a control center that includes the body's thermostat as well as the central biological clock. Through its regulation of the pituitary gland, the hypothalamus regulates hunger and thirst, plays a role in sexual and mating behaviors, and initiates the fight-or-flight response. The hypothalamus is also the source of posterior pituitary hormones and of releasing hormones that act on the anterior pituitary. The *epithalamus* includes the pineal gland, the source of melatonin.

Diencephalon — Thalamus — Pineal gland — Hypothalamus — Pituitary gland — Spinal cord

**Adult brain viewed from the side (front at left)**

## The Brainstem

The brainstem consists of the midbrain, the **pons**, and the **medulla oblongata** (commonly called the *medulla*). The midbrain receives and integrates several types of sensory information and sends it to specific regions of the forebrain. All sensory axons involved in hearing either terminate in the midbrain or pass through it on their way to the cerebrum. In addition, the midbrain coordinates visual reflexes, such as the peripheral vision reflex: The head turns toward an object approaching from the side without the brain having formed an image of the object. A major function of the pons and medulla is to transfer information between the PNS and the midbrain and forebrain. Most of the axons that carry the instructions about large-scale body movements cross from one side of the CNS to the other side in the medulla. As a result, the right side of the brain controls much of the movement of the left side of the body, and vice versa. An additional function of the medulla is the control of several automatic, homeostatic functions, including breathing, heart and blood vessel activity, swallowing, vomiting, and digestion. The pons also participates in some of these activities; for example, it regulates the breathing centers in the medulla.

Brainstem — Midbrain — Pons — Medulla oblongata

 The Virtual Brain: Nervous System

## Arousal and Sleep

If you've ever drifted off to sleep while listening to a lecture (or reading a book), you know that your attentiveness and mental alertness can change rapidly. Such transitions are regulated by the brainstem and cerebrum, which control arousal and sleep. Arousal is a state of awareness of the external world. Sleep is a state in which external stimuli are received but not consciously perceived.

Contrary to appearances, sleep is an active state, at least for the brain. By placing electrodes at multiple sites on the scalp, we can record patterns of electrical activity called brain waves in an electroencephalogram (EEG). These recordings reveal that brain wave frequencies change as the brain progresses through distinct stages of sleep.

Although sleep is essential for survival, we still know very little about its function. One hypothesis is that sleep and dreams are involved in consolidating learning and memory. Evidence supporting this hypothesis includes the finding that test subjects who are kept awake for 36 hours have a reduced ability to remember when particular events occurred, even if they first "perk up" with caffeine. Other experiments show that regions of the brain that are activated during a learning task can become active again during sleep.

Arousal and sleep are controlled in part by the *reticular formation*, a diffuse network formed primarily by neurons in the midbrain and pons **(Figure 49.12)**. These neurons control the timing of sleep periods characterized by rapid eye movements (REMs) and by vivid dreams. Sleep is also regulated by the biological clock, discussed next, and by regions of the forebrain that regulate sleep intensity and duration.

 The Virtual Brain: Sleep and Waking

▼ **Figure 49.12 The reticular formation.** Once thought to consist of a single diffuse network of neurons, the reticular formation is now recognized as many distinct clusters of neurons. These clusters function in part to filter sensory input (blue arrows), blocking familiar and repetitive information that constantly enters the nervous system before sending the filtered input to the cerebral cortex (green arrows).

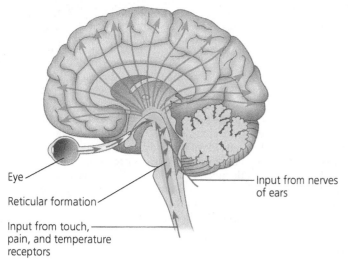

Eye
Reticular formation
Input from touch, pain, and temperature receptors
Input from nerves of ears

▼ **Figure 49.13 Dolphins can be asleep and awake at the same time.** EEG recordings were made separately for the two sides of a dolphin's brain. At each time point, low-frequency activity was recorded in one hemisphere while higher-frequency activity typical of being awake was recorded in the other hemisphere.

**Key**

ᴧᴧ Low-frequency waves characteristic of sleep

ᴡᴡ High-frequency waves characteristic of wakefulness

| Location | Time: 0 hours | Time: 1 hour |
|---|---|---|
| Left hemisphere | ᴧᴧᴧᴧᴧᴧ | ᴡᴡᴡᴡᴡᴡ |
| Right hemisphere | ᴡᴡᴡᴡᴡᴡ | ᴧᴧᴧᴧᴧᴧ |

Some animals have evolutionary adaptations that allow for substantial activity during sleep. Bottlenose dolphins, for example, swim while sleeping, rising to the surface to breathe air on a regular basis. How is this possible? As in other mammals, the forebrain is physically and functionally divided into two halves, the right and left hemispheres. Noting that dolphins sleep with one eye open and one closed, researchers hypothesized that only one side of the brain is asleep at a time. EEG recordings from each hemisphere of sleeping dolphins support this hypothesis **(Figure 49.13)**.

## Biological Clock Regulation

Cycles of sleep and wakefulness are an example of a circadian rhythm, a daily cycle of biological activity. Such cycles, which occur in organisms ranging from bacteria to humans, rely on a **biological clock**, a molecular mechanism that directs periodic gene expression and cellular activity. Although biological clocks are typically synchronized to the cycles of light and dark in the environment, they can maintain a roughly 24-hour cycle even in the absence of environmental cues (see Figure 40.9). For example, in a constant environment humans exhibit a sleep/wake cycle of 24.2 hours, with very little variation among individuals.

What normally links the biological clock to environmental cycles of light and dark in an animal's surroundings? In mammals, circadian rhythms are coordinated by clustered neurons in the hypothalamus (see Figure 49.11). These neurons form a structure called the **SCN**, which stands for **suprachiasmatic nucleus**. (Certain clusters of neurons in the CNS are referred to as "nuclei.") In response to sensory information from the eyes, the SCN acts as a pacemaker, synchronizing the biological clock in cells throughout the body to the natural cycles of day length. In the **Scientific Skills Exercise**, you can interpret

## Designing an Experiment Using Genetic Mutants

**Does the SCN Control the Circadian Rhythm in Hamsters?** By surgically removing the SCN from laboratory mammals, scientists demonstrated that the SCN is required for circadian rhythms. Those experiments did not, however, reveal whether circadian rhythms originate in the SCN. To answer this question, researchers performed an SCN transplant experiment on wild-type and mutant hamsters (*Mesocricetus auratus*). Whereas wild-type hamsters have a circadian cycle lasting about 24 hours in the absence of external cues, hamsters homozygous for the τ (tau) mutation have a cycle lasting only about 20 hours. In this exercise, you will evaluate the design of this experiment and propose additional experiments to gain further insight.

**How the Experiment Was Done** The researchers surgically removed the SCN from wild-type and τ hamsters. Several weeks later, each of these hamsters received a transplant of an SCN from a hamster of the opposite genotype. To determine the periodicity of rhythmic activity for the hamsters before the surgery and after the transplants, the researchers measured activity levels over a three-week period. They plotted the data collected for each day in the manner shown in Figure 40.9a and then calculated the circadian cycle period.

**Data from the Experiment** In 80% of the hamsters in which the SCN had been removed, transplanting an SCN from another hamster restored rhythmic activity. For hamsters in which an SCN transplant restored a circadian rhythm, the net effect of the two procedures (SCN removal and replacement) on the circadian cycle period is graphed at the upper right. Each red line connects the two data points for an individual hamster.

**INTERPRET THE DATA**

1. In a controlled experiment, researchers manipulate one variable at a time. What was the variable manipulated in this study? Why did the researchers use more than one hamster for each procedure? What traits of the individual hamsters would likely have been held constant among the treatment groups?

2. For the wild-type hamsters that received τ SCN transplants, what would have been an appropriate experimental control?

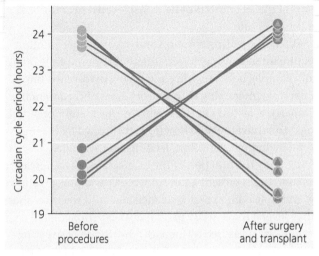

Legend: Wild-type hamster / Wild-type hamster with SCN from τ hamster / τ hamster / τ hamster with SCN from wild-type hamster

**Data from** M. R. Ralph et al., Transplanted suprachiasmatic nucleus determines circadian period, *Science* 247:975–978 (1990).

3. What general trends does the graph above reveal about the circadian cycle period of the transplant recipients? Do the trends differ for the wild-type and τ recipients? Based on these data, what can you conclude about the role of the SCN in determining the period of the circadian rhythm?

4. In 20% of the hamsters, there was no restoration of rhythmic activity following the SCN transplant. What are some possible reasons for this finding? Do you think you can be confident of your conclusion about the role of the SCN based on data from 80% of the hamsters?

5. Suppose that researchers identified a mutant hamster that lacked rhythmic activity; that is, its circadian activity cycle had no regular pattern. Propose SCN transplant experiments using such a mutant along with (a) wild-type and (b) τ hamsters. Predict the results of those experiments in light of your conclusion in question 3.

 **Instructors:** A version of this Scientific Skills Exercise can be assigned in MasteringBiology.

---

data from an experiment and propose experiments to test the role of the SCN in hamster circadian rhythms.

 HHMI Video: The Human Suprachiasmatic Nucleus

## Emotions

Whereas a single structure in the brain controls the biological clock, the generation and experience of emotions depend on many brain structures, including the amygdala, hippocampus, and parts of the thalamus. As shown in **Figure 49.14**, these structures border the brainstem in mammals and are therefore called the *limbic system* (from the Latin *limbus*, border).

One way the limbic system contributes to our emotions is by storing emotional experiences as memories that can be recalled by similar circumstances. This is why, for example, a situation that causes you to remember a frightening event can trigger a faster heart rate, sweating, or fear, even if there is

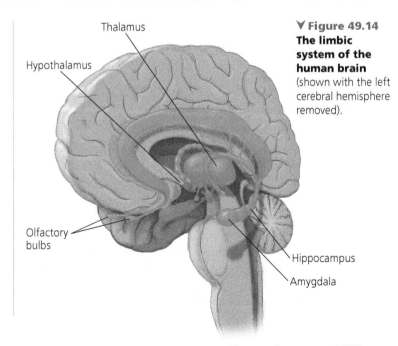

▼ **Figure 49.14 The limbic system of the human brain** (shown with the left cerebral hemisphere removed).

Labels: Thalamus, Hypothalamus, Olfactory bulbs, Hippocampus, Amygdala currently nothing scary or threatening in your surroundings. Such storage and recall of emotional memory are especially dependent on function of the **amygdala**, an almond-shaped mass of nuclei (clusters of neurons) located near the base of the cerebrum.

Often, generating emotion and experiencing emotion require interactions between different regions of the brain. For example, both laughing and crying involve the limbic system interacting with sensory areas of the forebrain. Similarly, structures in the forebrain attach emotional "feelings" to survival-related functions controlled by the brainstem, including aggression, feeding, and sexuality.

To study the function of the human amygdala, researchers sometimes present adult subjects with an image followed by an unpleasant experience, such as a mild electrical shock. After several trials, study participants experience *autonomic arousal*—as measured by increased heart rate or sweating— if they see the image again. Subjects with brain damage confined to the amygdala can recall the image because their explicit memory is intact. However, they do not exhibit autonomic arousal, indicating that damage to the amygdala has resulted in a reduced capacity for emotional memory.

## Functional Imaging of the Brain

In recent years, the amygdala and other brain structures have begun to be studied by functional imaging techniques. By scanning the brain while the subject performs a particular function, such as forming a mental image of a person's face, researchers can correlate particular functions with activity in specific brain areas.

Several approaches are available for functional imaging. The first widely used technique was positron-emission tomography (PET), in which injection of radioactive glucose enables a display of metabolic activity. Today, the most commonly used approach is functional magnetic resonance imaging (fMRI). In fMRI, a subject lies with his or her head in the center of a large, doughnut-shaped magnet. Brain activity is detected by an increase in the flow of oxygen-rich blood into a particular region.

In one experiment using fMRI, researchers mapped brain activity while subjects listened to music that they described as sad or happy (**Figure 49.15**). The findings were striking: Different regions of the brain were associated with the experience of each of these contrasting emotions. Subjects who heard sad music had increased activity in the amygdala. In contrast, listening to happy music led to increased activity in the *nucleus accumbens*, a brain structure important for the perception of pleasure.

As discussed at the beginning of the chapter, functional imaging methods have begun to transform our understanding of the brain. Furthermore, functional imaging has found widespread applications in medicine. Current applications of fMRI in hospitals include monitoring recovery from stroke,

▼ **Figure 49.15 Functional imaging in the working brain.** Here, fMRI was used to reveal brain activity associated with music that listeners described as happy or sad. (Each view shows activity in a single plane of the brain, as seen from above.)

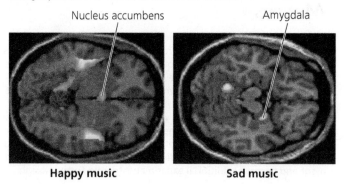

**Happy music**      **Sad music**

**VISUAL SKILLS ➤** *The two images reveal activity in different horizontal planes through the brain. How can you tell this from the two photographs? What can you conclude about the location of the nucleus accumbens and the amygdala?*

mapping abnormalities in migraine headaches, and increasing the effectiveness of brain surgery.

## CONCEPT CHECK 49.2

1. When you wave your right hand, what part of your brain initiates the action?
2. People who are inebriated have difficulty touching their nose with their eyes closed. Which brain region does this observation indicate is one of those impaired by alcohol?
3. **WHAT IF? ➤** Suppose you examine two groups of individuals with CNS damage. In one group, the damage has resulted in a coma (a prolonged state of unconsciousness). In the other group, it has caused paralysis (a loss of skeletal muscle function throughout the body). Relative to the position of the midbrain and pons, where is the likely site of damage in each group? Explain.

*For suggested answers, see Appendix A.*

# CONCEPT 49.3

## The cerebral cortex controls voluntary movement and cognitive functions

We turn now to the cerebrum, the part of the brain essential for language, cognition, memory, consciousness, and awareness of our surroundings. As shown in Figure 49.11, the cerebrum is the largest structure in the human brain. Like the brain overall, it exhibits regional specialization. For the most part, cognitive functions reside in the cortex, the outer layer of the cerebrum. Within this cortex, *sensory areas* receive and process sensory information, *association areas* integrate the information, and *motor areas* transmit instructions to other parts of the body.

In discussing the location of particular functions in the cerebral cortex, neurobiologists often use four regions, or *lobes*, as physical landmarks. Each lobe—frontal, temporal, occipital, and parietal—is named for a nearby bone of the skull, and each is the focus of specific brain activities (**Figure 49.16**).

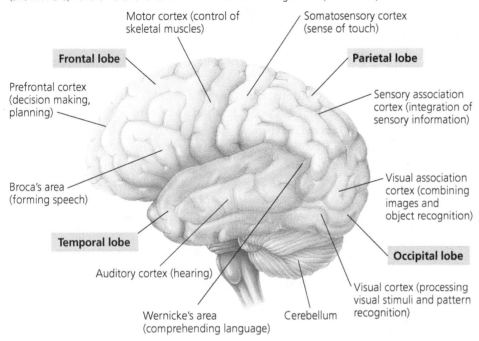

▼ **Figure 49.16 The human cerebral cortex.** Each of the four lobes of the cerebral cortex has specialized functions, some of which are listed here. Some areas on the left side of the brain (shown here) have different functions from those on the right side (not shown).

Motor cortex (control of skeletal muscles)

Somatosensory cortex (sense of touch)

**Frontal lobe**

**Parietal lobe**

Prefrontal cortex (decision making, planning)

Sensory association cortex (integration of sensory information)

Broca's area (forming speech)

Visual association cortex (combining images and object recognition)

**Temporal lobe**

**Occipital lobe**

Auditory cortex (hearing)

Visual cortex (processing visual stimuli and pattern recognition)

Wernicke's area (comprehending language)

Cerebellum

## Information Processing

Broadly speaking, the human cerebral cortex receives sensory information from two sources. Some sensory input originates in individual receptors in the hands, scalp, and elsewhere in the body. These somatic sensory, or *somatosensory*, receptors (from the Greek *soma*, body) provide information about touch, pain, pressure, temperature, and the position of muscles and limbs. Other sensory input comes from groups of receptors clustered in dedicated sensory organs, such as the eyes and nose.

Most sensory information coming into the cortex is directed via the thalamus to primary sensory areas within the brain lobes. Information received at the primary sensory areas is passed along to nearby association areas, which process particular features in the sensory input. In the occipital lobe, for instance, some groups of neurons in the primary visual area are specifically sensitive to rays of light oriented in a particular direction. In the visual association area, information related to such features is

combined in a region dedicated to recognizing complex images, such as faces.

Once processed, sensory information passes to the prefrontal cortex, which helps plan actions and movement. The cerebral cortex may then generate motor commands that cause particular behaviors—moving a limb or saying hello, for example. These commands consist of action potentials produced by neurons in the motor cortex, which lies at the rear of the frontal lobe (see Figure 49.16). The action potentials travel along axons to the brainstem and spinal cord, where they excite motor neurons, which in turn excite skeletal muscle cells.

In the somatosensory cortex and motor cortex, neurons are arranged according to the part of the body that generates the sensory input or receives the motor commands **(Figure 49.17).** For example, neurons that process sensory information from the legs and feet lie in the region of the somatosensory cortex closest to the midline. Neurons that control muscles in the legs and feet are located in the corresponding region of the motor cortex. Notice in Figure 49.17 that the cortical surface area devoted to each body part is not proportional to the size of the part.

▼ **Figure 49.17 Body part representation in the primary motor and primary somatosensory cortices.** In these cross-sectional maps of the cortices, the cortical surface area devoted to each body part is represented by the relative size of that part in the cartoons.

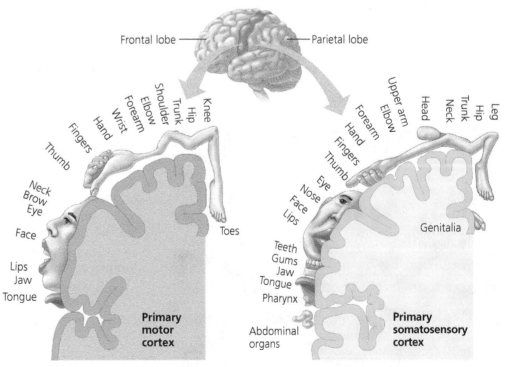

Frontal lobe

Parietal lobe

Shoulder
Elbow
Forearm
Wrist
Hand
Fingers
Thumb
Trunk
Hip
Knee

Neck
Brow
Eye
Face

Lips
Jaw
Tongue

Toes

**Primary motor cortex**

Upper arm
Elbow
Forearm
Hand
Fingers
Thumb
Eye
Nose
Face
Lips

Head
Neck
Trunk
Hip
Leg

Teeth
Gums
Jaw
Tongue
Pharynx

Genitalia

Abdominal organs

**Primary somatosensory cortex**

**VISUAL SKILLS** ➤ *Why is the hand larger than the forearm in both parts of this figure?*

Instead, surface area correlates with the extent of neuronal control needed (for the motor cortex) or with the number of sensory neurons that extend axons to that part (for the somatosensory cortex). Thus, the surface area of the motor cortex devoted to the face is much larger than that devoted to the trunk, reflecting the extensive involvement of facial muscles in communication.

Although our focus here is on humans, it is worth noting that the processing sites for sensory information vary among vertebrates. In ray-finned fishes, for example, the relatively large midbrain (see Figure 49.10) serves as the primary center for processing and responding to visual stimuli. Such differences reflect a recognizable evolutionary trend: Following the vertebrate phylogenetic tree from sharks to ray-finned fishes, amphibians, reptiles, and finally mammals, one observes a steadily increasing role for the forebrain in processing sensory information.

## Language and Speech

The mapping of cognitive functions within the cortex began in the 1800s when physicians studied the effects of damage to particular regions of the cortex by injuries, strokes, or tumors. Pierre Broca conducted postmortem (after death) examinations of patients who had been able to understand language but unable to speak. He discovered that many had defects in a small region of the left frontal lobe, now known as *Broca's area*. Karl Wernicke found that damage to a posterior portion of the left temporal lobe, now called *Wernicke's area*, abolished the ability to comprehend speech but not the ability to speak. PET studies have now confirmed activity in Broca's area during speech generation and Wernicke's area when speech is heard **(Figure 49.18)**.

▼ **Figure 49.18 Mapping language areas in the cerebral cortex.** These PET images show activity levels on the left side of one person's brain during four activities, all related to speech. Increases in activity are seen in Wernicke's area when hearing words, Broca's area when speaking words, the visual cortex when seeing words, and the prefrontal cortex when generating words (without reading them).

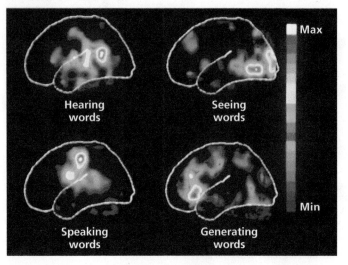

## Lateralization of Cortical Function

Both Broca's area and Wernicke's area are located in the left cortical hemisphere, reflecting a greater role in language for the left side of the cerebrum than for the right side. The left hemisphere is also more adept at math and logical operations. In contrast, the right hemisphere appears to dominate in the recognition of faces and patterns, spatial relations, and nonverbal thinking. This difference in function between the right and left hemispheres is called **lateralization**.

The two cortical hemispheres normally exchange information through the fibers of the corpus callosum (see Figure 49.11). Severing this connection (a treatment of last resort for the most extreme forms of epilepsy, a seizure disorder) results in a "split-brain" effect. In such patients, the two hemispheres function independently. For example, they cannot read even a familiar word that appears only in their left field of vision: The sensory information travels from the left field of vision to the right hemisphere, but cannot then reach the language centers in the left hemisphere.

## Frontal Lobe Function

In 1848, a horrific accident pointed to the role of the prefrontal cortex in temperament and decision-making. Phineas Gage was the foreman of a railroad construction crew when an explosion drove an iron rod through his head. The rod, which was more than 3 cm in diameter at one end, entered his skull just below his left eye and exited through the top of his head, damaging large portions of his frontal lobe **(Figure 49.19)**. Gage recovered, but his personality changed dramatically. He became emotionally detached, impatient, and erratic in his behavior.

▼ **Figure 49.19 Phineas Gage's skull injury.**

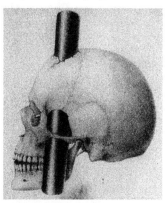

Two further sets of observations support the hypothesis that Gage's brain injury and personality change inform us about frontal lobe function. First, frontal lobe tumors cause similar symptoms: Intellect and memory seem intact, but decision making is flawed and emotional responses are diminished. Second, the same problems arise when the connection between the prefrontal cortex and the limbic system is surgically severed. (This procedure, called a frontal lobotomy, was once a common treatment for severe behavioral disorders but is no longer in use.) Together, these observations provide evidence that the frontal lobes have a substantial influence on what are called "executive functions."

## Evolution of Cognition in Vertebrates

**EVOLUTION** In nearly all vertebrates, the brain has the same basic structures (see Figure 49.10). Given this uniform organization, how did a capacity for advanced cognition, the perception and reasoning that constitute knowledge, evolve in certain species? For many years researchers favored the hypothesis that higher-order reasoning required evolution of an extensively convoluted cerebral cortex, as is found in humans, other primates, and cetaceans (whales, dolphins, and porpoises). Indeed, in humans the cerebral cortex accounts for about 80% of total brain mass.

Because birds lack a convoluted cerebral cortex, they were thought to have much lower intellectual capacity than primates and cetaceans. However, numerous experiments in recent years have refuted this idea: Western scrub jays (*Aphelocoma californica*) can remember which food items they hid first. New Caledonian crows (*Corvus moneduloides*) are highly skilled at making and using tools, an ability otherwise well documented only for humans and some other apes. African grey parrots (*Psittacus erithacus*) understand numerical and abstract concepts, such as "same" and "different" and "none."

The anatomical basis for sophisticated information processing in birds appears to be a clustered organization of neurons within the *pallium*, the top or outer portion of the brain (**Figure 49.20a**). This arrangement is different from that in the human cerebral cortex (**Figure 49.20b**), where six parallel layers of neurons are arranged tangential to the surface. Thus, evolution has resulted in two types of outer brain organization in vertebrates that support complex and flexible brain function.

How did the bird pallium and human cerebral cortex arise during evolution? The current consensus is that the common ancestor of birds and mammals had a pallium in which neurons were organized into nuclei, as is still found in birds. Early in mammalian evolution, this clustered organization was transformed into a layered one. However, connectivity was maintained such that, for example, the thalamus relays sensory input relating to sights, sounds, and touch to the pallium in birds and to the cerebral cortex in mammals.

Sophisticated information processing depends not only on the overall organization of a brain but also on the very small-scale changes that enable learning and encode memory. We'll turn to these changes in the context of humans in the next section.

### CONCEPT CHECK 49.3

1. How can studying individuals with damage to a particular brain region provide insight into the normal function of that region?
2. How do the functions of Broca's area and Wernicke's area each relate to the activity of the surrounding cortex?
3. **WHAT IF?** ➤ If a woman with a severed corpus callosum viewed a photograph of a familiar face, first in her left field of vision and then in her right field, why would she find it difficult to put a name to the face?

*For suggested answers, see Appendix A.*

## CONCEPT 49.4

### Changes in synaptic connections underlie memory and learning

Formation of the nervous system occurs stepwise. First, regulated gene expression and signal transduction determine where neurons form in the developing embryo. Next, neurons compete for survival. Every neuron requires growth-supporting factors, which are produced in limited quantities by tissues that direct neuron growth. Neurons that don't reach the proper locations fail to receive such factors and undergo programmed cell death. The net effect is the preferential survival of neurons that are in a proper location. The competition is so severe that half of the neurons formed in the embryo are eliminated.

In the final phase of organizing the nervous system, synapse elimination takes place. During development, each neuron forms numerous synapses, more than are required for its proper function. Once a neuron begins to function, its activity stabilizes some synapses and destabilizes others. By the time the embryo completes development, more than half of all synapses have been eliminated. In humans, this elimination of unnecessary connections, a process called synaptic pruning, continues after birth and throughout childhood.

▼ **Figure 49.20 Comparison of regions for higher cognition in avian and human brains.** Although structurally different, the **(a)** pallium of a songbird brain and the **(b)** cerebral cortex of the human brain play similar roles in higher cognitive activities and make many similar connections with other brain structures.

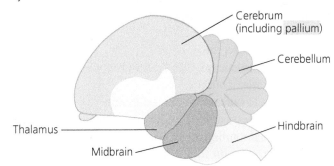

**(a) Songbird brain** (cross section)

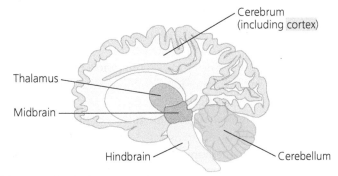

**(b) Human brain** (cross section)

Together, neuron development, neuron death, and synapse elimination establish the basic network of cells and connections within the nervous system required throughout life.

## Neuronal Plasticity

Although the overall organization of the CNS is established during embryonic development, the connections between neurons can be modified. This capacity for the nervous system to be remodeled, especially in response to its own activity, is called **neuronal plasticity**.

Much of the reshaping of the nervous system occurs at synapses. Synapses belonging to circuits that link information in useful ways are maintained, whereas those that convey bits of information lacking any context may be lost. Specifically, when the activity of a synapse coincides with that of other synapses, changes may occur that reinforce that synaptic connection. Conversely, when the activity of a synapse fails to coincide with that of other synapses, the synaptic connection sometimes becomes weaker.

**Figure 49.21a** illustrates how activity-dependent events can trigger the gain or loss of a synapse. If you think of signals in the nervous system as traffic on a highway, such changes are comparable to adding or removing an entrance ramp. The net effect is to increase signaling between particular pairs of neurons and decrease signaling between other pairs. Signaling at a synapse can also be strengthen or weakened, as shown in **Figure 49.21b**. In our traffic analogy, this would be equivalent to widening or narrowing an entrance ramp.

A defect in neuronal plasticity may underlie *autism*, a disorder that results in impaired communication and social interaction, as well as stereotyped and repetitive behaviors beginning in early childhood. There is now growing evidence that autism involves a disruption of activity-dependent remodeling at synapses.

Although the underlying causes of autism are unknown, there is a strong genetic contribution to this and related disorders. Extensive research has ruled out a link to vaccine preservatives, once proposed as a potential risk factor. Further understanding of the autism-associated disruption in synaptic plasticity may help efforts to better understand and treat this disorder.

## Memory and Learning

Neuronal plasticity is essential to the formation of memories. We are constantly checking what is happening against what just happened. We hold information for a time in **short-term memory** and then release it if it becomes irrelevant. If we wish to retain knowledge of a name, phone number, or other fact, the mechanisms of **long-term memory** are activated. If we later need to recall the name or number, we fetch it from long-term memory and return it to short-term memory.

Short-term and long-term memory both involve the storage of information in the cerebral cortex. In short-term memory, this information is accessed via temporary links formed in the hippocampus. When memories are made long-term, the links in the hippocampus are replaced by connections within the cerebral cortex itself. As discussed earlier, some of this consolidation of memory is thought to occur during sleep. Furthermore, the reactivation of the hippocampus that is required for memory consolidation likely forms the basis for at least some of our dreams.

According to our current understanding of memory, the hippocampus is essential for acquiring new long-term memories but not for maintaining them. This hypothesis readily explains the symptoms of some individuals who suffer damage to the hippocampus: They cannot form any new lasting memories but can freely recall events from before their injury. In effect, their lack of normal hippocampal function traps them in their past.

What evolutionary advantage might be offered by organizing short-term and long-term memories differently? One hypothesis is that the delay in forming connections in the cerebral cortex allows long-term memories to be integrated gradually into the existing store of knowledge and experience, providing a basis for more meaningful associations. Consistent with this hypothesis, the transfer of information from short-term to long-term memory is enhanced by the association of new data with data previously learned and stored in long-term

▼ **Figure 49.21  Neuronal plasticity.** Synaptic connections can change over time, strengthening or weakening in response to the level of activity at the synapse.

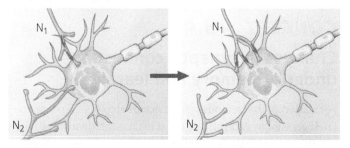

**(a)** Connections between neurons are strengthened or weakened in response to activity. High-level activity at the synapse of the post-synaptic neuron with presynaptic neuron $N_1$ leads to recruitment of additional axon terminals from that neuron. Lack of activity at the synapse with presynaptic neuron $N_2$ leads to loss of functional connections with that neuron.

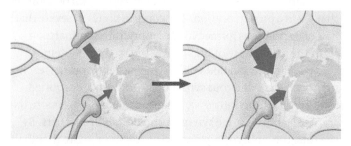

**(b)** If two synapses on the same postsynaptic cell are often active at the same time, the strength of the postsynaptic response may increase at both synapses.

memory. For example, it's easier to learn a new card game if you already have "card sense" from playing other card games.

Motor skills, such as tying your shoes or writing, are usually learned by repetition. You can perform these skills without consciously recalling the individual steps required to do these tasks correctly. Learning skills and procedures, such as those required to ride a bicycle, appears to involve cellular mechanisms very similar to those responsible for brain growth and development. In such cases, neurons actually make new connections. In contrast, memorizing phone numbers, facts, and places—which can be very rapid and may require only one exposure to the relevant item—may rely mainly on changes in the strength of existing neuronal connections. Next we will consider one way that such changes in strength can take place.

## Long-Term Potentiation

In searching for the physiological basis of memory, researchers have concentrated their attention on processes that can alter a synaptic connection, making the flow of communication either more efficient or less efficient. We will focus here on **long-term potentiation (LTP)**, a lasting increase in the strength of synaptic transmission.

First characterized in tissue slices from the hippocampus, LTP involves a presynaptic neuron that releases the excitatory neurotransmitter glutamate. For LTP to occur, there must be a high-frequency series of action potentials in this presynaptic neuron. In addition, these action potentials must arrive at the synaptic terminal at the same time that the postsynaptic cell receives a depolarizing stimulus at another synapse. The net effect is to strengthen a synapse whose activity coincides with that of another input (see Figure 48.17a).

LTP involves two types of glutamate receptors, each named for a molecule—NMDA or AMPA—that can be used to artificially activate that particular receptor. As shown in **Figure 49.22**, the set of receptors present on the postsynaptic membrane changes in response to an active synapse and a depolarizing stimulus. The result is LTP—a stable increase in the size of the postsynaptic potentials at the synapse. Because LTP can last for days or weeks in dissected tissue, it is thought to represent one of the fundamental processes by which memories are stored and learning takes place.

## CONCEPT CHECK 49.4

1. Outline two mechanisms by which information flow between two neurons in an adult can increase.

2. Individuals with localized brain damage have been very useful in the study of many brain functions. Why is this unlikely to be true for consciousness?

3. WHAT IF? ➤ Suppose that a person with damage to the hippocampus is unable to acquire new long-term memories. Why might the acquisition of short-term memories also be impaired?

*For suggested answers, see Appendix A.*

 The Virtual Brain: Learning and Memory

▼ **Figure 49.22 Long-term potentiation in the brain.**

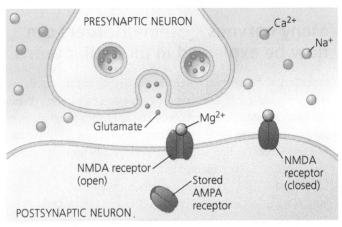

**(a) Synapse prior to long-term potentiation (LTP).** The NMDA glutamate receptors open in response to glutamate but are blocked by Mg²⁺.

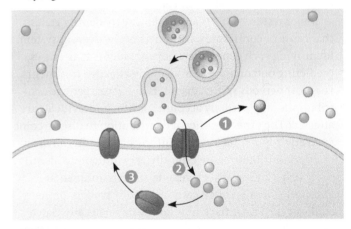

**(b) Establishing LTP.** Activity at nearby synapses (not shown) depolarizes the postsynaptic membrane, causing ❶ Mg²⁺ release from NMDA receptors. The unblocked receptors respond to glutamate by allowing ❷ an influx of Na⁺ and Ca²⁺. The Ca²⁺ influx triggers ❸ insertion of stored AMPA glutamate receptors into the postsynaptic membrane.

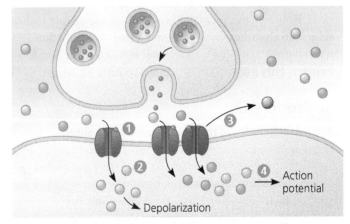

**(c) Synapse exhibiting LTP.** Glutamate release activates ❶ AMPA receptors that trigger ❷ depolarization. The depolarization unblocks ❸ NMDA receptors. Together, the AMPA and NMDA receptors trigger postsynaptic potentials strong enough to initiate ❹ action potentials without input from other synapses. Additional mechanisms (not shown) contribute to LTP, including receptor modification by protein kinases.

# CONCEPT 49.5

## Many nervous system disorders can now be explained in molecular terms

Disorders of the nervous system, including schizophrenia, depression, drug addiction, Alzheimer's disease, and Parkinson's disease, are a major public health problem. Together, they result in more hospitalizations in the United States than do heart disease or cancer. Until recently, hospitalization was typically the only available treatment, and many affected individuals were institutionalized for the rest of their lives. Today, many disorders that alter mood or behavior can be treated with medication, reducing average hospital stays for these disorders to only a few weeks. Nevertheless, many challenges remain with regard to preventing or treating nervous system disorders, especially Alzheimer's and other disorders that lead to nervous system degeneration.

Major research efforts are under way to identify genes that cause or contribute to disorders of the nervous system. Identifying such genes offers hope for identifying causes, predicting outcomes, and developing effective treatments. For most nervous system disorders, however, genetic contributions only partially account for which individuals are affected. The other significant contribution to disease comes from environmental factors. Unfortunately, such environmental contributions are typically very difficult to identify.

To distinguish between genetic and environmental variables, scientists often carry out family studies. In these studies, researchers track how family members are related genetically, which individuals are affected, and which family members grew up in the same household. These studies are especially informative when one of the affected individuals has either an adopted sibling who is genetically unrelated or an identical twin. In the case of schizophrenia, our next topic, family studies have revealed a very strong genetic component. However, as shown in **Figure 49.23**, the disease is also subject to environmental influences, since an individual who shares 100% of his or her genes with a schizophrenic twin has only a 48% chance of developing the disorder.

## Schizophrenia

Approximately 1% of the world's population suffers from **schizophrenia**, a severe mental disturbance characterized by psychotic episodes in which patients have a distorted perception of reality. People with schizophrenia typically experience hallucinations (such as "voices" that only they can hear) and delusions (for example, the idea that others are plotting to harm them). Despite the commonly held notion, schizophrenia does not necessarily result in multiple personalities. Rather, the name *schizophrenia* (from the Greek *schizo*, split, and *phren*, mind) refers to the fragmentation of what are normally integrated brain functions.

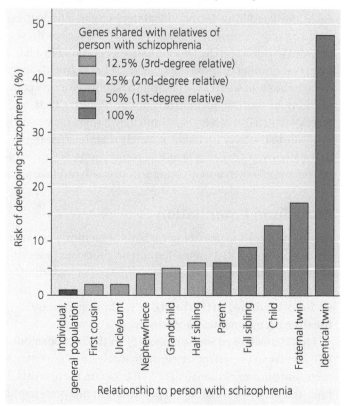

▼ **Figure 49.23 Genetic contribution to schizophrenia.** First cousins, uncles, and aunts of a person with schizophrenia have twice the risk of unrelated members of the population of developing the disease. The risks for closer relatives are many times greater.

**INTERPRET THE DATA** ➤ *What is the likelihood of a person developing schizophrenia if the disorder affects his or her fraternal twin? How would the likelihood change if DNA sequencing revealed that the twins shared the genetic variants that contribute to the disorder?*

One current hypothesis is that neuronal pathways that use dopamine as a neurotransmitter are disrupted in schizophrenia. Supporting evidence comes from the fact that many drugs that alleviate the symptoms of schizophrenia block dopamine receptors. In addition, the drug amphetamine ("speed"), which stimulates dopamine release, can produce the same set of symptoms as schizophrenia. Recent genetic studies suggest a link between schizophrenia and particular forms of the complement protein C4, an immune system component.

## Depression

Depression is a disorder characterized by depressed mood, as well as abnormalities in sleep, appetite, and energy level. Two broad forms of depressive illness are known: major depressive disorder and bipolar disorder. Individuals affected by **major depressive disorder** undergo periods—often lasting many months—during which once enjoyable activities provide no pleasure and provoke no interest. One of the most common nervous system disorders, major depression affects about one in every seven adults at some point, and twice as many women as men.

**Bipolar disorder**, or manic-depressive disorder, involves extreme swings of mood and affects about 1% of the world's population. The manic phase is characterized by high self-esteem, increased energy, a flow of ideas, over-talkativeness, and increased risk taking. In its milder forms, this phase is sometimes associated with great creativity, and some well-known artists, musicians, and literary figures (Vincent van Gogh, Robert Schumann, Virginia Woolf, and Ernest Hemingway, to name a few) have had productive periods during manic phases. The depressive phase comes with lessened motivation, sense of worth, and ability to feel pleasure, as well as sleep disturbances. These symptoms can be so severe that affected individuals attempt suicide.

Major depressive and bipolar disorders are among the nervous system disorders for which therapies are available. Many drugs used to treat depressive illness, including fluoxetine (Prozac), increase activity of biogenic amines in the brain.

## The Brain's Reward System and Drug Addiction

Emotions are strongly influenced by a neuronal circuit in the brain called the *reward system*. The reward system provides motivation for activities that enhance survival and reproduction, such as eating in response to hunger, drinking when thirsty, and engaging in sexual activity when aroused. As shown in **Figure 49.24**, inputs to the reward system are received by neurons in a region near the base of the brain called the *ventral tegmental area (VTA)*. When activated, these neurons release the neurotransmitter dopamine from their synaptic terminals within specific regions of the cerebrum. Targets of this dopamine signaling include the nucleus accumbens and the prefrontal cortex (see Figure 49.15 and 49.16).

The brain's reward system is dramatically affected by drug addiction, a disorder characterized by compulsive consumption of a drug and loss of control in limiting intake. Addictive drugs range from sedatives to stimulants and include alcohol, cocaine, nicotine, and heroin. All enhance the activity of the dopamine pathway (see Figure 49.24). As addiction develops, there are also long-lasting changes in the reward circuitry. The result is a craving for the drug independent of any pleasure associated with consumption.

Laboratory animals are highly valuable in modeling and studying addiction. Rats, for example, will provide themselves with heroin, cocaine, or amphetamine when given a dispensing system linked to a lever in their cage. Furthermore, they exhibit addictive behavior, continuing to self-administer the drug rather than seek food, even to the point of starvation.

 Interview with Ulrike Heberlein: Research with drunk flies

▼ **Figure 49.24 Effects of addictive drugs on the reward system of the mammalian brain.** Addictive drugs alter the transmission of signals in the pathway formed by neurons of the ventral tegmental area (VTA), a region located near the base of the brain.

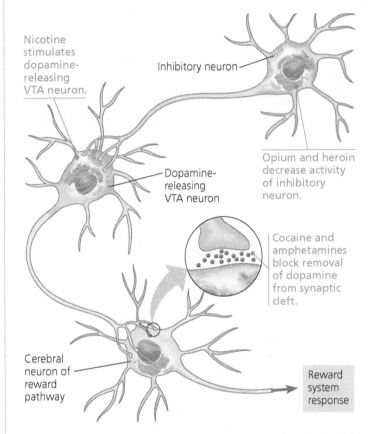

Nicotine stimulates dopamine-releasing VTA neuron.

Inhibitory neuron

Dopamine-releasing VTA neuron

Opium and heroin decrease activity of inhibitory neuron.

Cocaine and amphetamines block removal of dopamine from synaptic cleft.

Cerebral neuron of reward pathway

Reward system response

**MAKE CONNECTIONS** ➤ *What effect would you expect if you depolarized the neurons in the VTA (see Concept 48.3)? Explain.*

As scientists expand their knowledge about the brain's reward system and the various forms of addiction, there is hope that the insights will lead to more effective prevention and treatment.

## Alzheimer's Disease

The condition now known as **Alzheimer's disease** is a mental deterioration, or dementia, characterized by confusion and memory loss. Its incidence is age related, rising from about 10% at age 65 to about 35% at age 85. The disease is progressive, with patients gradually becoming less able to function and eventually needing to be dressed, bathed, and fed by others. Alzheimer's disease patients often lose their ability to recognize people and may treat even immediate family members with suspicion and hostility.

Examining the brains of individuals who have died of Alzheimer's disease reveals two characteristic features:

**▼ Figure 49.25 Microscopic signs of Alzheimer's disease.** A hallmark of Alzheimer's disease is the presence in brain tissue of neurofibrillary tangles surrounding plaques made of β-amyloid (LM).

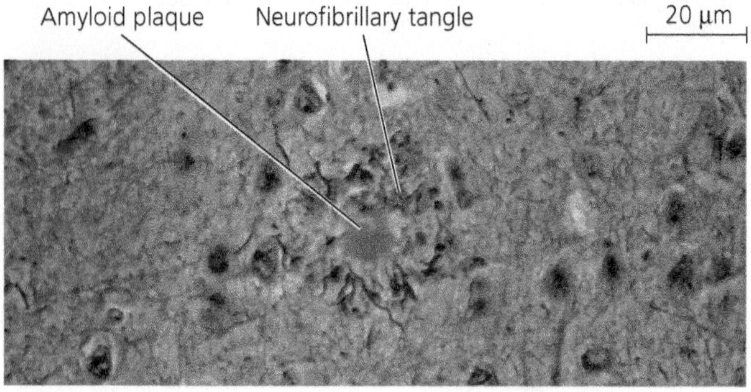

Amyloid plaque    Neurofibrillary tangle    20 μm

 BBC Video: Searching for a Cure for Alzheimer's

amyloid plaques and neurofibrillary tangles, as shown in **Figure 49.25.** There is also often massive shrinkage of brain tissue, reflecting the death of neurons in many areas of the brain, including the hippocampus and cerebral cortex.

The plaques are aggregates of β-amyloid, an insoluble peptide that is cleaved from the extracellular portion of a membrane protein found in neurons. Membrane enzymes, called secretases, catalyze the cleavage, causing β-amyloid to accumulate in plaques outside the neurons. It is these plaques that appear to trigger the death of surrounding neurons.

The neurofibrillary tangles observed in Alzheimer's disease are primarily made up of the tau protein. (This protein is unrelated to the tau mutation that affects circadian rhythm in hamsters.) The tau protein normally helps assemble and maintain microtubules that transport nutrients along axons. In Alzheimer's disease, tau undergoes changes that cause it to bind to itself, resulting in neurofibrillary tangles. There is evidence that changes in tau are associated with the appearance of early-onset Alzheimer's disease, a much less common disorder that affects relatively young individuals.

There is currently no cure for Alzheimer's disease, but recently developed drugs are partially effective in relieving some symptoms. Doctors are also beginning to use functional brain imaging to diagnose Alzheimer's disease in patients exhibiting early signs of dementia.

## Parkinson's Disease

Symptoms of **Parkinson's disease**, a motor disorder, include muscle tremors, poor balance, a flexed posture, and a shuffling gait. Facial muscles become rigid, limiting the ability of patients to vary their expressions. Cognitive defects may also develop. Like Alzheimer's disease, Parkinson's disease is a progressive brain illness and is more common with advancing age. The incidence of Parkinson's disease is about 1% at age 65 and about 5% at age 85. In the U.S. population, approximately 1 million people are afflicted.

Parkinson's disease involves the death of neurons in the midbrain that normally release dopamine at synapses in the basal nuclei. As with Alzheimer's disease, protein aggregates accumulate. Most cases of Parkinson's disease lack an identifiable cause; however, a rare form of the disease that appears in relatively young adults has a clear genetic basis. Molecular studies of mutations linked to this early-onset Parkinson's disease reveal disruption of genes required for certain mitochondrial functions. Researchers are investigating whether mitochondrial defects also contribute to the more common, later-onset form of the disease.

At present, Parkinson's disease can be treated, but not cured. Approaches used to manage the symptoms include brain surgery, deep-brain stimulation, and a dopamine-related drug, L-dopa. Unlike dopamine, L-dopa crosses the blood-brain barrier. Within the brain, the enzyme dopa decarboxylase converts the drug to dopamine, reducing the severity of Parkinson's disease symptoms:

L-dopa →(Dopa decarboxylase)→ Dopamine

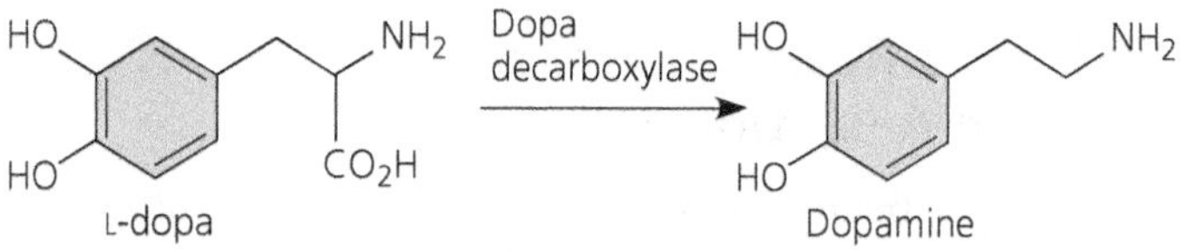

One potential cure for Parkinson's disease is to implant dopamine-secreting neurons in the midbrain or basal nuclei. Laboratory studies of this strategy show promise: In rats with an experimentally induced condition that mimics Parkinson's disease, implanting dopamine-secreting neurons can lead to a recovery of motor control. Whether this regenerative approach can also work in humans remains an important question.

## Future Directions

In 2014, the National Institutes of Health and other U.S. government agencies launched a bold 12-year project, the BRAIN (Brain Research through Advancing Innovative Neurotechnologies) Initiative. The objective is to drive scientific advances in much the same way as did past projects to land a person on the moon and to map the human genome. The overall plan of the initiative is to map brain circuits, measure the activity within those circuits, and discover how this activity is translated into thought and behavior. As with the moon landing and human genome projects, the development and application of innovative technologies will play a major role.

### CONCEPT CHECK 49.5

1. Compare Alzheimer's disease and Parkinson's disease.
2. How is dopamine activity related to schizophrenia, drug addiction, and Parkinson's disease?
3. **WHAT IF?** ➤ If you could detect early-stage Alzheimer's disease, would you expect to see brain changes that were similar to, although less extensive than, those seen in patients who have died of this disease? Explain.

*For suggested answers, see Appendix A.*

# 49 Chapter Review

Go to **MasteringBiology**™ for Videos, Animations, Vocab Self-Quiz, Practice Tests, and more in the Study Area.

## SUMMARY OF KEY CONCEPTS

### CONCEPT 49.1

**Nervous systems consist of circuits of neurons and supporting cells** *(pp. 1084–1088)*

VOCAB SELF-QUIZ goo.gl/6u55ks

- Invertebrate nervous systems range in complexity from simple nerve nets to highly centralized nervous systems having complicated brains and ventral nerve cords.

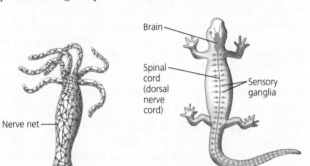

Hydra (cnidarian)    Salamander (vertebrate)

- In vertebrates, the **central nervous system (CNS)**, consisting of the brain and the spinal cord, integrates information, while the **nerves** of the **peripheral nervous system (PNS)** transmit sensory and motor signals between the CNS and the rest of the body. The simplest circuits control **reflex** responses, in which sensory input is linked to motor output without involvement of the brain.

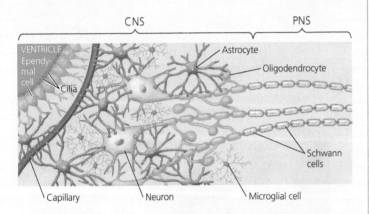

- Afferent neurons carry sensory signals to the CNS. Efferent neurons function in either the **motor system**, which carries signals to skeletal muscles, or the **autonomic nervous system**, which regulates smooth and cardiac muscles. The **sympathetic** and **parasympathetic divisions** of the autonomic nervous system have antagonistic effects on a diverse set of target organs, while the **enteric nervous system** controls the activity of many digestive organs.
- Vertebrate neurons are supported by **glia**, including astrocytes, oligodendrocytes, and Schwann cells. Some glia serve as stem cells that can differentiate into mature neurons.

**?** *How does the circuitry of a reflex facilitate a rapid response?*

### CONCEPT 49.2

**The vertebrate brain is regionally specialized** *(pp. 1089–1094)*

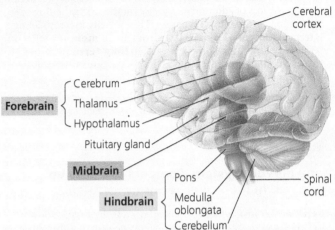

- The cerebrum has two hemispheres, each of which consists of cortical **gray matter** overlying **white matter** and basal nuclei. The basal nuclei are important in planning and learning movements. The **pons** and **medulla oblongata** are relay stations for information traveling between the PNS and the cerebrum. The reticular formation, a network of neurons within the **brainstem**, regulates sleep and arousal. The **cerebellum** helps coordinate motor, perceptual, and cognitive functions. The **thalamus** is the main center through which sensory information passes to the **cerebrum**. The **hypothalamus** regulates homeostasis and basic survival behaviors. Within the hypothalamus, a group of neurons called the **suprachiasmatic nucleus (SCN)** acts as the pacemaker for circadian rhythms. The **amygdala** plays a key role in recognizing and recalling a number of emotions.

**?** *What roles do the midbrain, cerebellum, thalamus, and cerebrum play in vision and responses to visual input?*

### CONCEPT 49.3

**The cerebral cortex controls voluntary movement and cognitive functions** *(pp. 1094–1097)*

- Each side of the **cerebral cortex** has four lobes—frontal, temporal, occipital, and parietal—that contain primary sensory areas and association areas. Association areas integrate information from different sensory areas. Broca's area and Wernicke's area are essential for generating and understanding language. These functions are concentrated in the left **cerebral hemisphere**, as are math and logic operations. The right hemisphere appears to be stronger at pattern recognition and nonverbal thinking.
- In the somatosensory cortex and the motor cortex, neurons are distributed according to the part of the body that generates sensory input or receives motor commands.
- Primates and cetaceans, which are capable of higher cognition, have an extensively convoluted cerebral cortex. In birds, a brain region called the pallium contains clustered nuclei that carry out functions similar to those performed by the cerebral cortex of mammals. Some birds can solve problems and understand abstractions in a manner indicative of higher cognition.

**?** *A patient has trouble with language and has paralysis on one side of the body. Which side would you expect to be paralyzed? Why?*

## CONCEPT 49.4

### Changes in synaptic connections underlie memory and learning (pp. 1097–1099)

- During development, more neurons and synapses form than will exist in the adult. The programmed death of neurons and elimination of synapses in embryos establish the basic structure of the nervous system. In the adult, reshaping of the nervous system can involve the loss or addition of synapses or the strengthening or weakening of signaling at synapses. This capacity for remodeling is termed **neuronal plasticity. Short-term memory** relies on temporary links in the hippocampus. In **long-term memory**, these temporary links are replaced by connections within the cerebral cortex.

 *Learning multiple languages is typically easier early in childhood than later in life. How does this fit with our understanding of neural development?*

## CONCEPT 49.5

### Many nervous system disorders can now be explained in molecular terms (pp. 1100–1102)

- **Schizophrenia**, which is characterized by hallucinations, delusions, and other symptoms, affects neuronal pathways that use dopamine as a neurotransmitter. Drugs that increase the activity of biogenic amines in the brain can be used to treat **bipolar disorder** and **major depressive disorder**. The compulsive drug use that characterizes addiction reflects altered activity of the brain's reward system, which normally provides motivation for actions that enhance survival or reproduction.
- **Alzheimer's disease** and **Parkinson's disease** are neurodegenerative and typically age related. Alzheimer's disease is a dementia in which neurofibrillary tangles and amyloid plaques form in the brain. Parkinson's disease is a motor disorder caused by the death of dopamine-secreting neurons and associated with the presence of protein aggregates.

 *The fact that both amphetamine and PCP have effects similar to the symptoms of schizophrenia suggests a potentially complex basis for this disease. Explain.*

## TEST YOUR UNDERSTANDING

### Level 1: Knowledge/Comprehension

1. Activation of the parasympathetic branch of the autonomic nervous system
   - (A) increases heart rate.
   - (B) enhances digestion.
   - (C) triggers release of epinephrine.
   - (D) causes conversion of glycogen to glucose.

2. Which of the following structures or regions is *incorrectly* paired with its function?
   - (A) limbic system—motor control of speech
   - (B) medulla oblongata—homeostatic control
   - (C) cerebellum—coordination of movement and balance
   - (D) amygdala—emotional memory

3. Patients with damage to Wernicke's area have difficulty
   - (A) coordinating limb movement.
   - (B) generating speech.
   - (C) recognizing faces.
   - (D) understanding language.

4. The cerebral cortex does *not* play a major role in
   - (A) short-term memory.
   - (B) long-term memory.
   - (C) circadian rhythm.
   - (D) breath holding.

PRACTICE TEST
goo.gl/CUYGKD

### Level 2: Application/Analysis

5. After suffering a stroke, a patient can see objects anywhere in front of him but pays attention only to objects in his right field of vision. When asked to describe these objects, he has difficulty judging their size and distance. What part of the brain was likely damaged by the stroke?
   - (A) the left frontal lobe
   - (B) the right frontal lobe
   - (C) the right parietal lobe
   - (D) the corpus callosum

6. Injury localized to the hypothalamus would most likely disrupt
   - (A) regulation of body temperature.
   - (B) short-term memory.
   - (C) executive functions, such as decision making.
   - (D) sorting of sensory information.

7. DRAW IT The reflex that pulls your hand away when you prick your finger on a sharp object relies on a neuronal circuit with two synapses in the spinal cord. (a) Using a circle to represent a cross section of the spinal cord, draw the circuit. Label the types of neurons, the direction of information flow in each, and the locations of synapses. (b) Draw a simple diagram of the brain indicating where pain would eventually be perceived.

### Level 3: Synthesis/Evaluation

8. EVOLUTION CONNECTION Scientists often use measures of "higher-order thinking" to assess intelligence in other animals. For example, birds are judged to have sophisticated thought processes because they can use tools and make use of abstract concepts. Identify problems you see in defining intelligence in these ways.

9. SCIENTIFIC INQUIRY Consider an individual who had been fluent in American Sign Language before suffering an injury to his left cerebral hemisphere. After the injury, he could still understand that sign language but could not readily generate sign language that represented his thoughts. Propose *two* hypotheses that could explain this finding. How might you distinguish between them?

10. SCIENCE, TECHNOLOGY, AND SOCIETY With increasingly sophisticated methods for scanning brain activity, scientists are developing the ability to detect an individual's particular emotions and thought processes from outside the body. What benefits and problems do you envision when such technology becomes readily available? Explain.

11. WRITE ABOUT A THEME: INFORMATION In a short essay (100–150 words), explain how specification of the adult nervous system by the genome is incomplete.

12. SYNTHESIZE YOUR KNOWLEDGE

Imagine you are standing at a microphone in front of a crowd. Checking your notes, you begin speaking. Using the information in this chapter, describe the series of events in particular regions of the brain that enabled you to say the very first word.

MB For additional practice questions, check out the **Dynamic Study Modules** in MasteringBiology. You can use them to study on your smartphone, tablet, or computer anytime, anywhere!

# Sensory and Motor Mechanisms

# 50

▲ Figure 50.1 **Of what use is a star-shaped nose?**

## KEY CONCEPTS

**50.1** Sensory receptors transduce stimulus energy and transmit signals to the central nervous system

**50.2** In hearing and equilibrium, mechanoreceptors detect moving fluid or settling particles

**50.3** The diverse visual receptors of animals depend on light-absorbing pigments

**50.4** The senses of taste and smell rely on similar sets of sensory receptors

**50.5** The physical interaction of protein filaments is required for muscle function

**50.6** Skeletal systems transform muscle contraction into locomotion

## Sense and Sensibility

Tunneling beneath the wetlands of eastern North America, the star-nosed mole (*Condylura cristata*) lives in almost total darkness. Virtually blind, the mole is nonetheless a remarkably deft predator, capable of detecting and eating its prey in as little as 120 milliseconds. Central to this hunting prowess are 11 pairs of appendages that protrude from its nose, forming a prominent pink star **(Figure 50.1)**. Although they look a bit like fingers, these appendages are not used in grasping. Nor are they used to detect odors. Instead, they are highly specialized to detect touch. Just below their surface lie 25,000 touch-sensitive receptors, more than are found in your whole hand. Over 100,000 neurons relay tactile information from these receptors to the mole's brain.

Detecting and processing sensory information and generating motor responses provide the physiological basis for all animal behavior. In this chapter, we'll explore the processes of sensing and acting in both vertebrates and invertebrates. We'll start with sensory processes that convey information about an animal's external and internal environment to its brain. We'll then consider the structure and function of muscles and skeletons that carry out movements as instructed by the brain and spinal cord. Finally, we'll investigate various mechanisms of animal movement. These topics will lead us naturally to our discussion of animal behavior in Chapter 51.

---

When you see this blue icon, log in to **MasteringBiology** and go to the Study Area for digital resources.

 Get Ready for This Chapter

# CONCEPT 50.1

## Sensory receptors transduce stimulus energy and transmit signals to the central nervous system

All sensory processes begin with stimuli, and all stimuli represent forms of energy. A sensory receptor converts stimulus energy to a change in membrane potential, thereby regulating the output of action potentials to the central nervous system (CNS). Decoding of this information within the CNS results in sensation.

When a stimulus is received and processed by the nervous system, a motor response may be generated. One of the simplest stimulus-response circuits is a reflex, such as the knee-jerk reflex shown in Figure 49.7. For many other behaviors, sensory input undergoes more elaborate processing. As an example, consider how the star-nosed mole searches for food, or forages, in a tunnel (**Figure 50.2**). When the mole's nose contacts an object, touch receptors in the nose are activated. These receptors transmit sensory information about the object, such as whether the object is moving, to the mole's brain. Circuits in the brain integrate the input and initiate one of two response pathways. If prey or other food is detected, the brain sends motor output commands to skeletal muscles that cause

the jaws to bite down. If no food is detected, the brain sends instructions to skeletal muscles to continue movement along the tunnel.

With this overview in mind, let's examine the general organization and activity of animal sensory systems. We'll focus on four basic functions common to sensory pathways: sensory reception, transduction, transmission, and perception.

## Sensory Reception and Transduction

A sensory pathway begins with **sensory reception**, the detection of a stimulus by sensory cells. Each sensory cell is either a specialized neuron or a non-neuronal cell that regulates a neuron (**Figure 50.3**). Some sensory cells exist singly; others are collected in sensory organs, such as the star-shaped nose of the mole in Figure 50.1.

The term **sensory receptor** describes a sensory cell or organ, as well as the subcellular structure that detects stimuli. Some sensory receptors respond to stimuli from within the body, such as blood pressure and body position. Others detect stimuli from outside the body, such as heat, light, pressure, or chemicals. Some of these receptors are sensitive to the smallest possible unit of stimulus. Most light receptors, for example, can detect a single quantum (photon) of light.

Although animals use a range of sensory receptors to detect widely varying stimuli, the effect in all cases is to open or close

▼ **Figure 50.2 A simple response pathway: foraging by a star-nosed mole.**

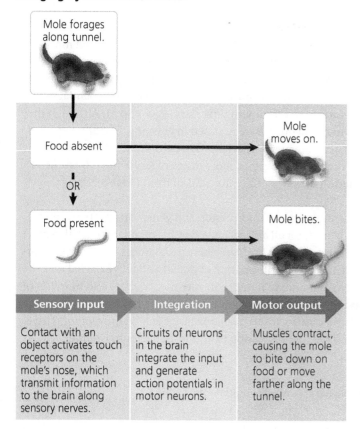

▼ **Figure 50.3 Categories of sensory receptors.**

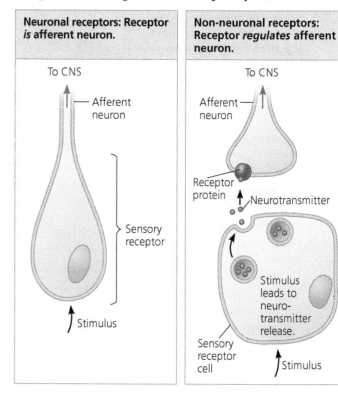

ion channels. The resulting change in the flow of ions across the membrane alters the membrane potential. The change in membrane potential is called a **receptor potential**, and conversion of the stimulus to a receptor potential is known as **sensory transduction**. Note that receptor potentials are graded potentials: Their magnitude varies with the strength of the stimulus.

## Transmission

Sensory information travels through the nervous system as action potentials. A sensory receptor that is also a neuron generates action potentials that travel along an axon extending into the CNS (see Figure 50.3). In contrast, a non-neuronal sensory receptor does not itself generate action potentials, but instead conveys information to sensory (afferent) neurons via chemical synapses. Because this chemical signaling alters the rate at which the afferent neurons produce action potentials, the sensory information generated also enters the CNS in the form of action potentials.

The size of a receptor potential increases with the intensity of the stimulus. If the receptor is a sensory neuron, a larger receptor potential results in more frequent action potentials **(Figure 50.4)**. If the receptor is not a sensory neuron, a larger receptor potential usually causes the receptor to release more neurotransmitter.

Many sensory neurons spontaneously generate action potentials at a low rate. In these neurons, a stimulus does not switch the production of action potentials on or off, but instead changes *how often* an action potential is produced, alerting the nervous system to changes in stimulus intensity.

Processing of sensory information can occur before, during, and after transmission of action potentials to the CNS. In many cases, the *integration* of sensory information begins as soon as the information is received. Receptor potentials produced by stimuli delivered to different parts of a sensory receptor cell are integrated through summation, as are postsynaptic potentials in sensory neurons that form synapses with multiple receptors (see Figure 48.17). As you'll see shortly, sensory structures such as eyes also provide higher levels of integration, and the brain further processes all incoming signals.

## Perception

When action potentials reach the brain via sensory neurons, circuits of neurons process this input, generating the **perception** of the stimulus. An action potential triggered by light striking the eye has the same properties as an action potential triggered by air vibrating in the ear. How, then, do we distinguish sights, sounds, and other stimuli? The answer lies in the connections that link sensory receptors to the brain. Action potentials from sensory receptors travel along neurons that are dedicated to a particular stimulus; these dedicated neurons form synapses with particular neurons in the brain or spinal cord. As a result, the brain distinguishes stimuli such as sight and sound solely by the path along which the action potentials have arrived.

Perceptions—such as colors, smells, sounds, and tastes—are constructions formed in the brain and do not exist outside it. So, if a tree falls and no animal is present to hear it, is there a sound? The falling tree certainly produces pressure waves in the air, but if sound is defined as a perception, then there is no sound unless an animal senses the waves and its brain perceives them.

## Amplification and Adaptation

The transduction of stimuli by sensory receptors is subject to two types of modification—amplification and adaptation. **Amplification** refers to the strengthening of a sensory signal during transduction. The effect of amplification can be considerable. For example, an action potential conducted from the eye to the human brain has about 100,000 times as much energy as the few photons of light that triggered it.

Amplification that occurs in sensory receptor cells often requires signal transduction that involves enzyme-catalyzed reactions (see Concept 11.3). Because a single enzyme molecule catalyzes the formation of many product molecules, these pathways amplify signal strength considerably. Amplification may also take place in accessory structures of a sense organ. For example, the lever system formed by three small bones in the ear enhances the pressure associated with sound waves more than 20-fold before the stimulus reaches receptors in the innermost part of the ear.

Upon continued stimulation, many receptors undergo a decrease in responsiveness known as **sensory adaptation** (not to be confused with the evolutionary term *adaptation*). Sensory adaptation has very important roles in our perception of ourselves and our surroundings. Without it, you

▼ Figure 50.4 **Coding of stimulus intensity by a single sensory receptor.**

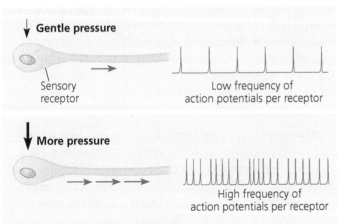

↓ **Gentle pressure**

Sensory receptor

Low frequency of action potentials per receptor

↓ **More pressure**

High frequency of action potentials per receptor

would feel each beat of your heart and be constantly aware of every bit of clothing on your body. Furthermore, adaptation is essential for you to see, hear, and smell changes in the environment that vary widely in stimulus intensity.

## Types of Sensory Receptors

Sensory receptors fall into five categories based on the nature of the stimuli they transduce: mechanoreceptors, chemoreceptors, electromagnetic receptors, thermoreceptors, and pain receptors.

### Mechanoreceptors

Our response to pressure, touch, stretch, motion, and sound relies on **mechanoreceptors**, which sense physical deformation caused by forms of mechanical energy. Mechanoreceptors typically consist of ion channels that are linked to structures that extend outside the cell, such as "hairs" (cilia), and also anchored to internal cell structures, such as the cytoskeleton. Bending or stretching of the external structure generates tension that alters the permeability of the ion channels. This change in ion permeability alters the membrane potential, resulting in a depolarization or hyperpolarization (see Concept 48.3).

The vertebrate stretch receptor, a mechanoreceptor that detects muscle movement, triggers the familiar knee-jerk reflex (see Figure 49.7). Vertebrate stretch receptors are dendrites of sensory neurons that spiral around the middle of certain small skeletal muscle fibers. When the muscle fibers are stretched, the sensory neurons depolarize, triggering nerve impulses that reach the spinal cord, activate motor neurons, and generate a reflex response.

Mechanoreceptors that are the dendrites of sensory neurons are also responsible for the mammalian sense of touch. Touch receptors are often embedded in layers of connective tissue. The structure of the connective tissue and the location of the receptors dramatically affect the type of mechanical energy (light touch, vibration, or strong pressure) that best stimulates them **(Figure 50.5)**. Receptors that detect a light touch or vibration are close to the surface of the skin; they transduce very slight inputs of mechanical energy into receptor potentials. Receptors that respond to stronger pressure and vibrations are in deep skin layers.

Some animals use mechanoreceptors to literally get a feel for their environment. For example, cats and many rodents have extremely sensitive mechanoreceptors at the base of their whiskers. Like the appendages on the face of the star-nosed mole, whiskers act as touch organs. Deflection of different whiskers triggers action potentials that reach different cells in the brain. As a result, an animal's whiskers enable the brain to assemble a "touch map" detailing the location of nearby objects such as food or obstacles.

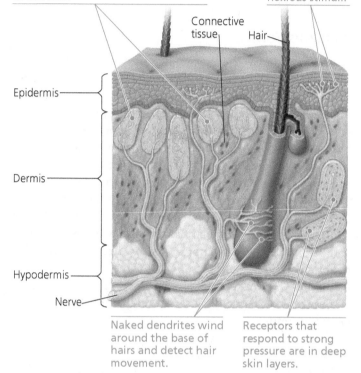

▼ **Figure 50.5 Sensory receptors in human skin.** Most receptors in the dermis are encapsulated by connective tissue. Receptors in the epidermis are naked dendrites, as are hair movement receptors that wind around the base of hairs in the dermis.

Receptors that detect gentle pressure and vibration are close to the surface of the skin.

Naked dendrites in the epidermis respond to temperature or noxious stimuli.

Connective tissue    Hair

Epidermis

Dermis

Hypodermis

Nerve

Naked dendrites wind around the base of hairs and detect hair movement.

Receptors that respond to strong pressure are in deep skin layers.

### Chemoreceptors

**Chemoreceptors** fall into two broad categories. Some transmit information about overall solute concentration. For example, osmoreceptors in the mammalian brain detect changes in the total solute concentration of the blood and stimulate thirst when osmolarity increases (see Figure 44.19). Other chemoreceptors respond to specific molecules, including glucose, oxygen, carbon dioxide, and amino acids.

The antennae of the male silkworm moth contain two of the most sensitive and specific chemoreceptors known **(Figure 50.6)**; these receptors can detect components of the sex pheromone released by a female moth several kilometers away. For pheromones and other molecules detected by chemoreceptors, the stimulus molecule binds to the specific receptor on the membrane of the sensory cell and initiates changes in ion permeability.

### Electromagnetic Receptors

**Electromagnetic receptors** detect forms of electromagnetic energy, such as light, electricity, and magnetism. For instance, the platypus has electroreceptors on its bill that can detect the electric field generated by the muscles of crustaceans, small fish, and other prey. In a few cases, the animal detecting the stimulus is also its source: Some fishes generate

V **Figure 50.6 Chemoreceptors in an insect.** The antennae of
the male silkworm moth *Bombyx mori* are covered with sensory hairs,
visible in the SEM enlargement. The hairs have chemoreceptors that
are highly sensitive to the sex pheromone released by the female.

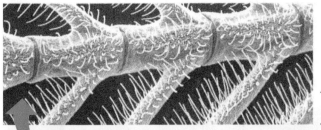

0.1 mm

**(a)** Some migrating animals, such as these beluga whales, apparently
sense Earth's magnetic field and use the information, along with
other cues, for orientation.

Eye

Heat-sensing
organ

**(b)** This rattlesnake and other pit vipers have a pair of heat-sensing pit
organs, one anterior to and just below each eye. These organs are
sensitive enough to detect the infrared radiation emitted by a
warm prey a meter away. The snake moves its head from side
to side until the radiation is detected equally by the two pit organs,
indicating that the prey is straight ahead.

electric currents and then use electroreceptors to locate prey
or other objects that disturb those currents.

Many animals can use Earth's magnetic field lines to orient
themselves as they migrate **(Figure 50.7a)**. In 2015, researchers identified a pair of proteins that appear to act as a sensor
for the Earth's magnetic field in many animals that can orient to it, including monarch butterflies, pigeons, and minke
whales. One of these proteins binds iron; the other belongs to
a family of receptors sensitive to electromagnetic radiation.

### Thermoreceptors

**Thermoreceptors** detect heat and cold. For example, certain venomous snakes rely on thermoreceptors to detect the
infrared radiation emitted by warm prey. These thermoreceptors are located in a pair of pit organs on the snake's head
**(Figure 50.7b)**. In humans, thermoreceptors are located in
the skin and in the anterior hypothalamus.

Recently, our understanding of thermoreception has
increased substantially, thanks to scientists with an appreciation for fiery foods. Jalapeno and cayenne peppers that
we describe as "hot" contain a substance called capsaicin.
Applying capsaicin to a sensory neuron causes an influx of
calcium ions. When scientists identified the receptor protein
in neurons that binds capsaicin, they made a fascinating
discovery: The receptor opens a calcium channel in response
not only to capsaicin but also to high temperatures (42°C or
higher). In essence, spicy foods taste "hot" because they activate the same receptors as hot soup and coffee.

Mammals have a variety of thermoreceptors, each specific
for a particular temperature range. The capsaicin receptor and
at least five other types of thermoreceptors belong to the TRP
(transient receptor potential) family of ion channel proteins.
Just as the TRP-type receptor specific for high temperature is
sensitive to capsaicin, the receptor for temperatures below
28°C can be activated by menthol, a plant product that we
perceive to have a "cool" flavor.

### Pain Receptors

Extreme pressure or temperature, as well as certain chemicals,
can damage animal tissues. To detect stimuli that reflect such
noxious (harmful) conditions, animals rely on **nociceptors**
(from the Latin *nocere*, to hurt), also called **pain receptors**.
By triggering defensive reactions, such as withdrawal from
danger, the perception of pain serves an important function.
The capsaicin receptor of mammals can detect dangerously
high temperatures, so it also functions as a pain receptor.

Chemicals produced in an animal's body sometimes
enhance the perception of pain. For example, damaged tissues produce prostaglandins, which act as local regulators
of inflammation (see Concept 45.1). Prostaglandins worsen

pain by increasing nociceptor sensitivity to noxious stimuli. Aspirin and ibuprofen reduce pain by inhibiting the synthesis of prostaglandins.

Next we'll turn our focus to sensory systems, beginning with systems for maintaining balance and detecting sound.

## CONCEPT CHECK 50.1

1. Which one of the five categories of sensory receptors is primarily dedicated to external stimuli?
2. Why can eating "hot" peppers cause a person to sweat?
3. **WHAT IF?** ➤ If you stimulated a sensory neuron electrically, how would that stimulation be perceived?

*For suggested answers, see Appendix A.*

# CONCEPT 50.2

## In hearing and equilibrium, mechanoreceptors detect moving fluid or settling particles

For most animals, the sense of hearing is closely related to the sense of balance, the perception of body equilibrium. For both senses, mechanoreceptor cells produce receptor potentials in response to deflection of cell-surface structures by settling particles or moving fluid.

### Sensing of Gravity and Sound in Invertebrates

To sense gravity and maintain equilibrium, most invertebrates rely on mechanoreceptors located in organs called **statocysts (Figure 50.8)**. In a typical statocyst, **statoliths**,

▼ **Figure 50.8 The statocyst of an invertebrate.** The settling of granules called statoliths to the low point in the chamber bends cilia on receptor cells in that location, providing the brain with information about the orientation of the body with respect to gravity.

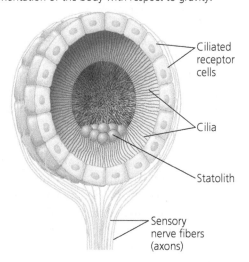

Ciliated receptor cells

Cilia

Statolith

Sensory nerve fibers (axons)

▼ **Figure 50.9 An insect's "ear"—on its leg.** The tympanic membrane, visible in this SEM of a cricket's front leg, vibrates in response to sound waves. The vibrations stimulate mechanoreceptors attached to the inside of the tympanic membrane.

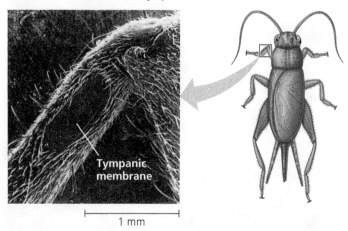

Tympanic membrane

1 mm

granules formed by grains of sand or other dense materials, sit freely in a chamber lined with ciliated cells. Each time an animal repositions itself, the statoliths resettle, stimulating mechanoreceptors at the low point in the chamber.

How did researchers test the hypothesis that resettling of statoliths provides information about body position relative to Earth's gravity? In one key experiment, statoliths were replaced with metal shavings. Researchers then "tricked" crayfish into swimming upside down by using magnets to pull the shavings to the upper end of statocysts at the base of their antennae.

Many (perhaps most) insects have body hairs that vibrate in response to sound waves. Hairs differing in stiffness and length vibrate at different frequencies. For example, fine hairs on the antennae of a male mosquito vibrate in a specific way in response to the hum produced by the beating wings of flying females. The importance of this sensory system in the attraction of males to a potential mate can be demonstrated very simply: A tuning fork vibrating at the same frequency as that of a female's wings will by itself attract males.

Many insects also detect sound by means of vibration-sensitive organs, which consist in some species of a tympanic membrane (eardrum) stretched over an internal air chamber **(Figure 50.9)**. Cockroaches lack such a tympanic membrane, but instead have vibration-sensitive organs that sense air movement, such as that caused by a descending human foot.

### Hearing and Equilibrium in Mammals

In mammals, as in most other terrestrial vertebrates, the sensory organs for hearing and equilibrium are closely associated. **Figure 50.10** explores the structure and function of these organs in the human ear.

## 1 Overview of Ear Structure

The **outer ear** consists of the external pinna and the auditory canal, which collect sound waves and channel them to the **tympanic membrane** (eardrum), a thin tissue that separates the outer ear from the **middle ear**. In the middle ear, three small bones—the malleus (hammer), incus (anvil), and stapes (stirrup)—transmit vibrations to the **oval window**, which is a membrane beneath the stapes. The middle ear also opens into the **Eustachian tube**, a passage that connects to the pharynx and equalizes pressure between the middle ear and the atmosphere. The **inner ear** consists of fluid-filled chambers, including the **semicircular canals**, which function in equilibrium, and the coiled **cochlea** (from the Latin meaning "snail"), a bony chamber that is involved in hearing.

 Animation: The Human Ear

## 2 The Cochlea

The cochlea has two large canals—an upper vestibular canal and a lower tympanic canal—separated by a smaller cochlear duct. Both canals are filled with fluid.

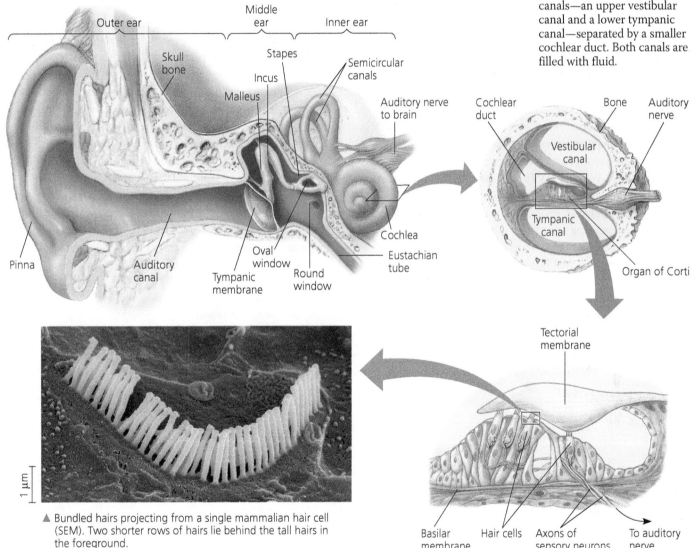

▲ Bundled hairs projecting from a single mammalian hair cell (SEM). Two shorter rows of hairs lie behind the tall hairs in the foreground.

## 4 Hair Cell

Projecting from each hair cell is a bundle of rod-shaped "hairs," within which lie a core of actin filaments. Vibration of the basilar membrane in response to sound raises and lowers the hair cells, bending the hairs against the surrounding fluid and the tectorial membrane. When the hairs are displaced, mechanoreceptors are activated, changing the membrane potential of the hair cell.

## 3 The Organ of Corti

The floor of the cochlear duct, the basilar membrane, bears the **organ of Corti**, which contains the mechanoreceptors of the ear—hair cells with hairs projecting into the cochlear duct. Many of the hairs are attached to the tectorial membrane, which hangs over the organ of Corti like an awning. Sound waves make the basilar membrane vibrate, which results in bending of the hairs and depolarization of the hair cells.

## Hearing

Vibrating objects, such as a plucked guitar string or the vocal cords of a person who is speaking, create pressure waves in the surrounding air. In *hearing*, the ear transduces this mechanical stimulus (pressure waves) into nerve impulses that the brain perceives as sound. To hear music, speech, or other sounds in our environment, we rely on **hair cells**, sensory cells with hairlike projections that detect motion.

Before vibration waves reach hair cells, they are amplified and transformed by accessory structures. The first steps involve structures in the ear that convert the vibrations of moving air to pressure waves in fluid. Moving air that reaches the outer ear causes the tympanic membrane to vibrate. The three bones of the middle ear transmit these vibrations to the oval window, a membrane on the cochlea's surface. When one of those bones, the stapes, vibrates against the oval window, it creates pressure waves in the fluid inside the cochlea.

Upon entering the vestibular canal, fluid pressure waves push down on the cochlear duct and basilar membrane. In response, the basilar membrane and attached hair cells vibrate up and down. The hairs projecting from the hair cells are deflected by the fixed tectorial membrane, which lies above (see Figure 50.10). With each vibration, the hairs bend first in one direction and then the other, causing ion channels in the hair cells to open or close. Bending in one direction depolarizes hair cells, increasing neurotransmitter release and the frequency of action potentials directed to the brain along the auditory nerve **(Figure 50.11)**. Bending the hairs in the other

direction hyperpolarizes hair cells, reducing neurotransmitter release and the frequency of auditory nerve sensations.

What prevents pressure waves from reverberating within the ear and causing prolonged sensation? After propagating through the vestibular canal, pressure waves pass around the apex (tip) of the cochlea and dissipate as they strike the **round window (Figure 50.12a)**. This damping of sound waves resets the apparatus for the next vibrations that arrive.

The ear captures information about two important sound variables: volume and pitch. *Volume* (loudness) is determined by the amplitude, or height, of the sound wave. A large-amplitude wave causes more vigorous vibration of the basilar membrane, greater bending of the hairs on hair cells, and more action potentials in the sensory neurons. *Pitch* is determined by a sound wave's frequency, the number of vibrations per unit time. The detection of sound wave frequency takes place in the cochlea and relies on the asymmetric structure of that organ.

The cochlea can distinguish pitch because the basilar membrane is not uniform along its length: It is relatively narrow and stiff near the oval window and wider and more flexible at the apex at the base of the cochlea. Each region of the basilar membrane is tuned to a different vibration frequency **(Figure 50.12b)**. Furthermore, each region is connected by axons to a different location in the cerebral cortex. Consequently, when a sound wave causes vibration of a particular region of the basilar membrane, nerve impulses are transduced to a specific site in our cortex and we perceive sound of a particular pitch.

▼ **Figure 50.11 Sensory reception by hair cells.** Vertebrate hair cells required for hearing and balance have "hairs" formed into a bundle that bends when surrounding fluid moves. Each hair cell releases an excitatory neurotransmitter at a synapse with a sensory neuron, which conducts action potentials to the CNS. Bending of the bundle in one direction depolarizes the hair cell, causing it to release more neurotransmitter and increasing the frequency of action potentials in the sensory neuron. Bending in the other direction has the opposite effect.

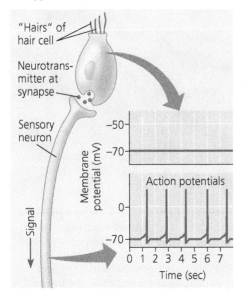

**(a) No bending of hairs**

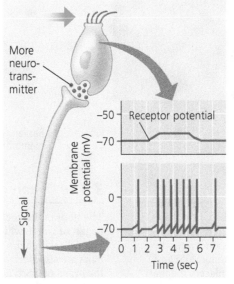

**(b) Bending of hairs in one direction**

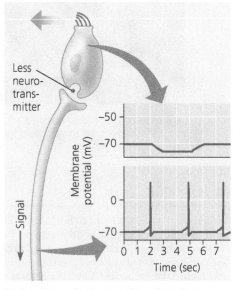

**(c) Bending of hairs in other direction**

▼ **Figure 50.12 Sensory transduction in the cochlea.**

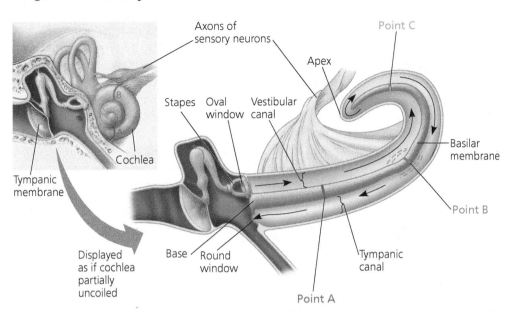

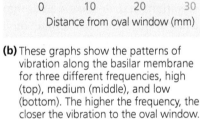

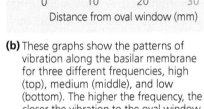

**(a)** Vibrations of the stapes against the oval window produce pressure waves (black arrows) in the fluid (perilymph; blue) of the cochlea. (For purposes of illustration, the cochlea on the right is drawn partially uncoiled.) The waves travel to the apex via the vestibular canal and back towards the base via the tympanic canal. The energy in the waves causes the basilar membrane (pink) to vibrate, stimulating hair cells (not shown). Because the basilar membrane varies in stiffness along its length, each point along the membrane vibrates maximally in response to waves of a particular frequency.

**INTERPRET THE DATA ➤** *A musical chord consists of several notes, each formed by a sound wave of different frequency. If a chord had notes with frequencies of 100, 1,000, and 6,000 Hz, what would happen to the basilar membrane? How would this result in your hearing a chord?*

**(b)** These graphs show the patterns of vibration along the basilar membrane for three different frequencies, high (top), medium (middle), and low (bottom). The higher the frequency, the closer the vibration to the oval window.

(MB) **Animation: Detecting Pitch**

## Equilibrium

Several organs in the inner ear of humans and most other mammals detect body movement, position, and equilibrium. For example, the chambers called the *utricle* and *saccule* allow us to perceive position with respect to gravity or linear movement **(Figure 50.13)**. Each of these chambers, which are situated in a vestibule behind the oval window, contains hair cells that project into a gelatinous material. Embedded in this gel are small calcium carbonate particles called *otoliths* ("ear stones"). When you tilt your head, the otoliths shift position, contacting a different set of hairs protruding into the gel. The hair cell receptors transform this deflection into a change in the output of sensory neurons, signaling the brain that your head is at an angle. The otoliths are also responsible for your

▼ **Figure 50.13 Organs of equilibrium in the inner ear.**

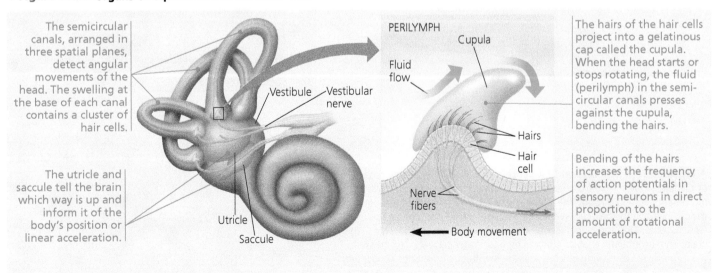

The semicircular canals, arranged in three spatial planes, detect angular movements of the head. The swelling at the base of each canal contains a cluster of hair cells.

The utricle and saccule tell the brain which way is up and inform it of the body's position or linear acceleration.

The hairs of the hair cells project into a gelatinous cap called the cupula. When the head starts or stops rotating, the fluid (perilymph) in the semi-circular canals presses against the cupula, bending the hairs.

Bending of the hairs increases the frequency of action potentials in sensory neurons in direct proportion to the amount of rotational acceleration.

ability to perceive acceleration, such as when a stationary car in which you are sitting pulls forward.

Three fluid-filled semicircular canals connected to the utricle detect turning of the head and other rotational acceleration. Within each canal, the hair cells form a cluster, with the hairs projecting into a gelatinous cap called a cupula (see Figure 50.13). Because the three canals are arranged in the three spatial planes, they can detect angular motion of the head in any direction. If you spin in place, the fluid in each canal eventually comes to equilibrium and remains in that state until you stop. At that point, the moving fluid encounters a stationary cupula, triggering the false sensation of angular motion that we call dizziness.

## Hearing and Equilibrium in Other Vertebrates

Fishes rely on several systems for detecting movement and vibrations in their aquatic environment. One system involves a pair of inner ears that contain otoliths and hair cells. Unlike the ears of mammals, these ears have no eardrum, cochlea, or opening to the outside of the body. Instead, the vibrations of the water caused by sound waves are conducted to the inner ear through the skeleton of the head. Some fishes also have a series of bones that conduct vibrations from the swim bladder to the inner ear.

Most fishes and aquatic amphibians are able to detect low-frequency waves by means of a **lateral line system** along each side of their body **(Figure 50.14)**. As in our semicircular canals, receptors are formed from a cluster of hair cells whose hairs are embedded in a cupula. Water entering the lateral line system through numerous pores bends the cupula, leading to depolarization of the hair cells and production of action potentials. In this way, the fish perceives its movement through water or the direction and velocity of water currents flowing over its body. The lateral line system also detects water movements or vibrations generated by prey, predators, and other moving objects.

In the ear of a frog or toad, sound vibrations in the air are conducted to the inner ear by a tympanic membrane on the body surface and a single middle ear bone. The same is true in birds and other reptiles, although they, like mammals, have a cochlea.

### CONCEPT CHECK 50.2

1. How are otoliths adaptive for burrowing mammals, such as the star-nosed mole?

2. **WHAT IF?** ➤ Suppose a series of pressure waves in your cochlea caused a vibration of the basilar membrane that moves gradually from the apex toward the base. How would your brain interpret this stimulus?

3. **WHAT IF?** ➤ If the stapes became fused to the other middle ear bones or to the oval window, how would this condition affect hearing? Explain.

4. **MAKE CONNECTIONS** ➤ Plants use statoliths to detect gravity (see Figure 39.22). How do plants and animals differ with regard to the type of compartment in which statoliths are found and the physiological mechanism for detecting their response to gravity?

*For suggested answers, see Appendix A.*

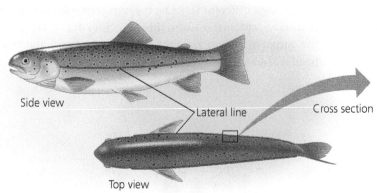
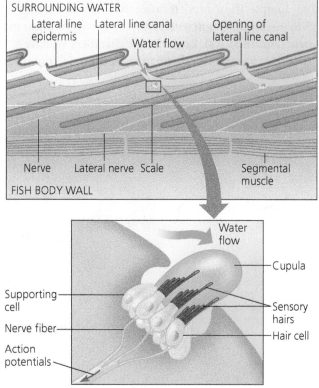

▲ **Figure 50.14 The lateral line system in a fish.** The sensory organs of the lateral line stretch from head to tail along each side of the fish. Water movement into and through the lateral line canals pushes on the gelatinous cupula, bending the hair cells within. In response, the hair cells generate receptor potentials, triggering action potentials that are conveyed to the brain. This information enables a fish to monitor water currents, any pressure waves produced by moving objects, and any low-frequency sounds conducted through the water.

# CONCEPT 50.3

## The diverse visual receptors of animals depend on light-absorbing pigments

The ability to detect light has a central role in the interaction of nearly all animals with their environment. Although the organs used for vision vary considerably among animals, the underlying mechanism for capturing light is the same, suggesting a common evolutionary origin.

### Evolution of Visual Perception

**EVOLUTION** Light detectors in the animal kingdom range from simple clusters of cells that detect only the direction and intensity of light to complex organs that form images. These diverse light detectors all contain **photoreceptors**, sensory cells that contain light-absorbing pigment molecules. Furthermore, the genes that specify where and when photoreceptors arise during embryonic development are shared among flatworms, annelids, arthropods, and vertebrates. It is thus very probable that the genetic underpinnings of all photoreceptors were already present in the earliest bilaterian animals.

 BBC Video: How Did Eyes Evolve?

### Light-Detecting Organs

Most invertebrates have some kind of light-detecting organ. One of the simplest is that of planarians (**Figure 50.15**).

▼ **Figure 50.15 Ocelli and orientation behavior of a planarian.**

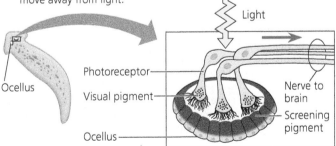

**(a)** The planarian's brain directs the body to turn until the sensations from the two ocelli are equal and minimal, causing the animal to move away from light.

**(b)** Whereas light striking the front of an ocellus excites the photoreceptors, light striking the back is blocked by the screening pigment. In this way, the ocelli indicate the direction of a light source, enabling the light avoidance behavior.

A pair of ocelli (singular, *ocellus*), sometimes called eyespots, are located in the head region. Photoreceptors in each ocellus receive light only through an opening where there are no pigmented cells. By comparing the rate of action potentials coming from the two ocelli, the planarian can move away from a light source until it reaches a shaded location, where the object providing the shade may hide it from predators.

### Compound Eyes

Insects, crustaceans, and some polychaete worms have **compound eyes**, each consisting of up to several thousand light detectors called **ommatidia** (**Figure 50.16**). Each of these "facets" of the eye has its own light-focusing lens that captures light from a tiny portion of the visual field (the total area seen when the eyes point forward). A compound eye is very effective at detecting movement, an important adaptation for flying insects and small animals constantly threatened with predation. Many compound eyes, including those of the fly in Figure 50.16, offer a very wide field of view.

Insects have excellent color vision, and some, such as bees, can see into the ultraviolet (UV) range of the electromagnetic spectrum. Because UV light is invisible to humans, we don't see differences in the environment that bees and

▼ **Figure 50.16 Compound eyes.**

**(a)** The faceted eyes on the head of a fly form a repeating pattern visible in this photomicrograph.

**(b)** The cornea and crystalline cone of each ommatidium together function as a lens that focuses light on the rhabdom, an organelle formed by and extending inward from a circle of photoreceptors. The rhabdom traps light, serving as the photosensitive part of the ommatidium. Information gathered from different intensities of light entering the many ommatidia from different angles is used to form a visual image.

other insects detect. In studying animal behavior, we cannot simply extrapolate our sensory world to other species; different animals have different sensitivities and different brain organizations.

### Single-Lens Eyes

Among invertebrates, **single-lens eyes** are found in some jellies and polychaete worms, as well as in spiders and many molluscs. A single-lens eye works somewhat like a camera.

The eye of an octopus or squid, for example, has a small opening, the **pupil**, through which light enters. Like a camera's adjustable aperture, the **iris** expands or contracts, changing the diameter of the pupil to let in more or less light. Behind the pupil, a single lens directs light on a layer of photoreceptors. Similar to a camera's focusing action, muscles in an invertebrate's single-lens eye move the lens forward or backward, focusing on objects at different distances.

▼ **Figure 50.17** **Exploring the Structure of the Human Eye**

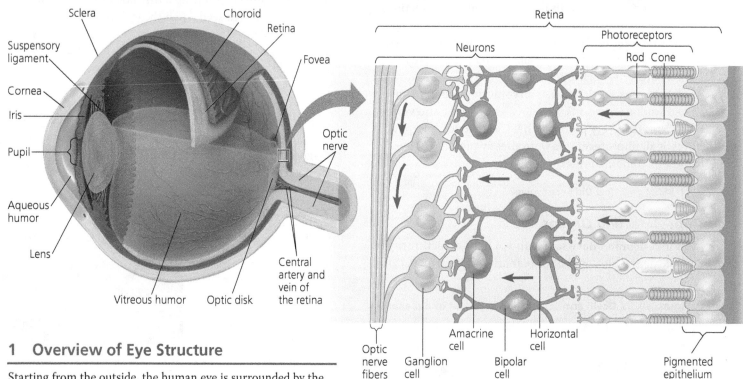

## 1   Overview of Eye Structure

Starting from the outside, the human eye is surrounded by the conjunctiva, a mucous membrane (not shown); the sclera, a connective tissue; and the choroid, a thin, pigmented layer. At the front, the sclera forms the transparent *cornea* and the choroid forms the colored *iris*. By changing size, the iris regulates the amount of light entering the pupil, the hole in the center of the iris. Just inside the choroid, the neurons and photoreceptors of the **retina** form the innermost layer of the eyeball. The optic nerve exits the eye at the optic disk.

The **lens**, a transparent disk of protein, divides the eye into two cavities. In front of the lens lies the *aqueous humor*, a clear watery substance. Blockage of ducts that drain this fluid can produce glaucoma, a condition in which increased pressure in the eye damages the optic nerve, causing vision loss. Behind the lens lies the jellylike *vitreous humor* (illustrated here in the lower portion of the eyeball).

 Animation: Structure and Function of the Eye

## 2   The Retina

Light (coming from left in the above view) strikes the retina, passing through largely transparent layers of neurons before reaching the rods and cones, two types of photoreceptors that differ in shape and in function. The neurons of the retina then relay visual information captured by the photo receptors to the optic nerve and brain along the pathways shown with red arrows. Each *bipolar cell* receives information from several rods or cones, and each *ganglion cell* gathers input from several bipolar cells. *Horizontal* and *amacrine cells* integrate information across the retina.

One region of the retina, the optic disk, lacks photoreceptors. As a result, this region forms a "blind spot" where light is not detected.

 Animation: Function of the Retina

The eyes of all vertebrates have a single lens. In fishes, focusing occurs as in invertebrates, with the lens moving forward or backward. In other species, including mammals, focusing is achieved by changing the shape of the lens.

## The Vertebrate Visual System

The human eye will serve as our model of vision in vertebrates. As described in **Figure 50.17**, vision begins when photons of light enter the eye and strike the rods and cones. There the energy of each photon is captured in retinal, the light-absorbing molecule in the visual pigment rhodopsin.

Although light detection in the eye is the first stage in vision, remember that it is actually the brain that "sees." Thus, to understand vision, we must examine how the capture of light by retinal changes the production of action potentials and then follow these signals to the visual centers of the brain, where images are perceived.

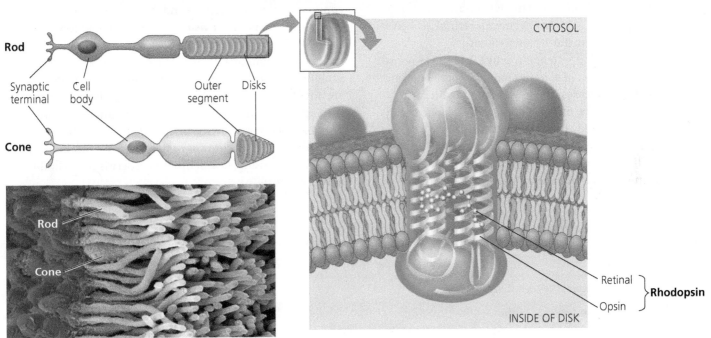

## 3  Photoreceptor Cells

Humans have two main types of photoreceptor cells: rods and cones. Within the outer segment of a rod or cone is a stack of membranous disks in which *visual pigments* are embedded. **Rods** are more sensitive to light than cones are, but they do not distinguish colors; rods enable us to see at night, but only in black and white. **Cones** provide color vision, but, being less sensitive, contribute very little to night vision. There are three types of cones. Each has a different sensitivity across the visible spectrum, providing an optimal response to red, green, or blue light.

In the colorized SEM shown above, cones (green), rods (light tan), and adjacent neurons (red) are visible. The pigmented epithelium, which was removed in this preparation, would be to the right.

Animation: Photoreception

## 4  Visual Pigments

Vertebrate visual pigments consist of a light-absorbing molecule called **retinal** (a derivative of vitamin A) bound to a membrane protein called an **opsin**. Seven α helices of each opsin molecule span the disk membrane. The visual pigment of rods, shown here, is called **rhodopsin**.

Retinal exists as two isomers. Absorption of light shifts one bond in retinal from a *cis* to a *trans* arrangement, converting the molecule from an angled shape to a straight shape. This change in configuration activates the opsin protein to which retinal is bound.

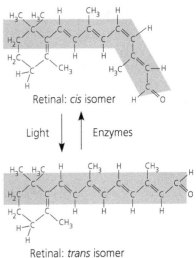

**VISUAL SKILLS ➤** *The isomers of retinal have the same number of atoms and bonds but differ in the spatial arrangement at one carbon-carbon double bond (C=C). In each isomer, circle that C=C. Looking at the atoms around that bond, to what atoms do the terms cis (same side) and trans (opposite side) refer?*

## Sensory Transduction in the Eye

The transduction of visual information to the nervous system begins with the light-induced conversion of *cis*-retinal to *trans*-retinal in rods and cones. Like other *cis-trans* pairs, these isomers of retinal differ only in the spatial arrangement of atoms at a carbon-carbon double bond (see Figure 4.7).

As shown in Figure 50.17, *trans*-retinal and *cis*-retinal differ in shape. This shift in shape activates the visual pigment (in rods, rhodopsin), which activates a G protein, which in turn activates the enzyme phosphodiesterase. The substrate for this enzyme in rods and cones is cyclic GMP, which in the dark binds to sodium ion (Na⁺) channels and keeps them open **(Figure 50.18a)**. When the enzyme hydrolyzes cyclic GMP, Na⁺ channels close, and the cell becomes hyperpolarized **(Figure 50.18b)**. The signal transduction pathway then shuts off as enzymes convert retinal back to the *cis* form, inactivating the visual pigment.

In bright light, rhodopsin remains active, and the response in the rods becomes saturated. If the amount of light entering the eyes abruptly decreases, the rods do not regain full responsiveness for several minutes. This is why you are briefly blinded if you pass quickly from bright sunshine into a dark movie theater. (Because light activation changes the color of rhodopsin from purple to yellow, rods in which the light response is saturated are often described as "bleached.")

## Processing of Visual Information in the Retina

The processing of visual information begins in the retina itself, where both rods and cones form synapses with bipolar cells (see Figure 50.17). In the dark, rods and cones are depolarized and continually release the neurotransmitter glutamate at these synapses **(Figure 50.19)**. When light strikes the rods and cones, they hyperpolarize, shutting off their release of glutamate. This decrease triggers a change in the membrane potential of the bipolar cells, altering their regulation of action potential transmission to the brain.

Processing of signals from rods and cones occurs via several different pathways in the retina. Some information passes directly from photoreceptors to bipolar cells to ganglion cells. In other cases, horizontal cells carry signals from one rod or cone to other photoreceptors and to several bipolar cells.

How is it adaptive for visual information to follow several paths? We'll consider one example. When an illuminated rod or cone stimulates a horizontal cell, the horizontal cell inhibits more distant photoreceptors and bipolar cells that are not illuminated. The result is that the region receiving light appears lighter and the dark surroundings even darker. This form of integration, called *lateral inhibition*, sharpens edges and enhances contrast in the image. An essential part of visual processing, lateral inhibition occurs in the brain as well as the retina.

▼ **Figure 50.18 Response of a photoreceptor cell to light.** Light triggers a receptor potential in a rod (shown here) or cone. Note that for photoreceptors this change in membrane potential is a hyperpolarization.

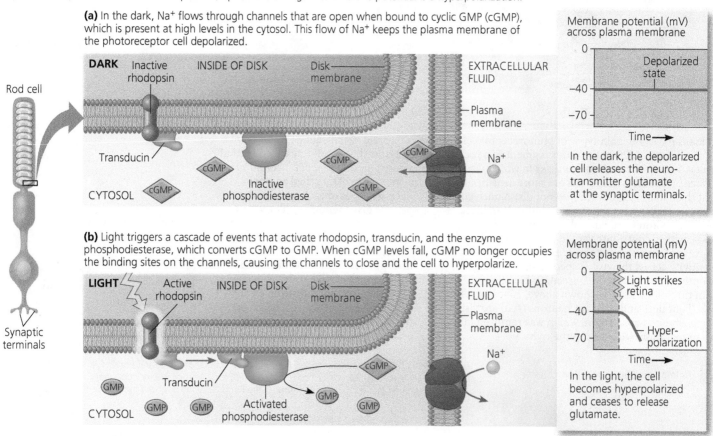

**(a)** In the dark, Na⁺ flows through channels that are open when bound to cyclic GMP (cGMP), which is present at high levels in the cytosol. This flow of Na⁺ keeps the plasma membrane of the photoreceptor cell depolarized.

Rod cell

DARK · Inactive rhodopsin · INSIDE OF DISK · Disk membrane · EXTRACELLULAR FLUID · Plasma membrane · Transducin · cGMP · cGMP · cGMP · cGMP · cGMP · Na⁺ · Inactive phosphodiesterase · CYTOSOL

Membrane potential (mV) across plasma membrane — Depolarized state — In the dark, the depolarized cell releases the neurotransmitter glutamate at the synaptic terminals.

**(b)** Light triggers a cascade of events that activate rhodopsin, transducin, and the enzyme phosphodiesterase, which converts cGMP to GMP. When cGMP levels fall, cGMP no longer occupies the binding sites on the channels, causing the channels to close and the cell to hyperpolarize.

Synaptic terminals

LIGHT · Active rhodopsin · INSIDE OF DISK · Disk membrane · EXTRACELLULAR FLUID · Plasma membrane · Transducin · Activated phosphodiesterase · GMP · GMP · GMP · GMP · cGMP · Na⁺ · CYTOSOL

Membrane potential (mV) across plasma membrane — Light strikes retina — Hyperpolarization — In the light, the cell becomes hyperpolarized and ceases to release glutamate.

**(MB)** Figure Walkthrough

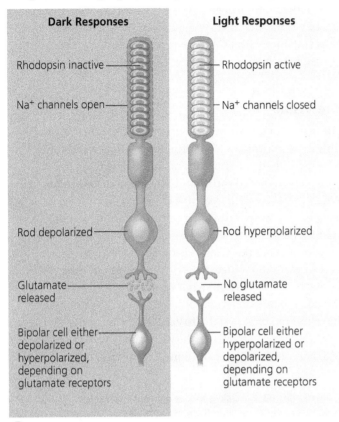

▼ **Figure 50.19 Synaptic activity of rod cells in light and dark.**

| Dark Responses | Light Responses |
|---|---|
| Rhodopsin inactive | Rhodopsin active |
| Na⁺ channels open | Na⁺ channels closed |
| Rod depolarized | Rod hyperpolarized |
| Glutamate released | No glutamate released |
| Bipolar cell either depolarized or hyperpolarized, depending on glutamate receptors | Bipolar cell either hyperpolarized or depolarized, depending on glutamate receptors |

**?** *Like rods, cone cells are depolarized when their opsin molecules are inactive. In the case of a cone, why might it be misleading to call this a dark response?*

A single ganglion cell receives information from an array of rods and cones, each of which responds to light coming from a particular location. Together, the rods and cones that are feeding information to one ganglion cell define a *receptive field*—the part of the visual field to which that ganglion cell can respond. The fewer rods or cones that supply a single ganglion cell, the smaller the receptive field. A smaller receptive field typically results in a sharper image because the information about where light has struck the retina is more precise.

## Processing of Visual Information in the Brain

Axons of ganglion cells form the optic nerves that transmit action potentials from the eyes to the brain **(Figure 50.20)**. The two optic nerves meet at the *optic chiasm* near the center of the base of the cerebral cortex. Axons in the optic nerves are routed at the optic chiasm such that sensations from the left visual field are transmitted to the right side of the brain, and sensations from the right visual field are transmitted to the left side of the brain. (Note that each visual field, whether right or left, involves input from both eyes.)

Within the brain, most ganglion cell axons lead to the *lateral geniculate nuclei*, which have axons that reach the *primary visual cortex* in the cerebrum. Additional neurons

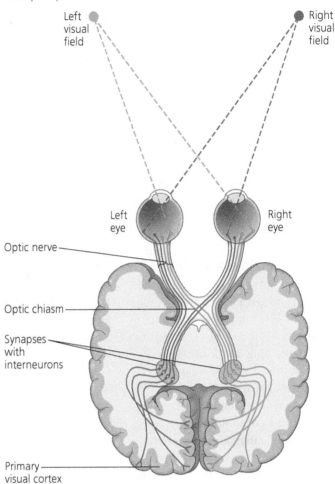

▼ **Figure 50.20 Neural pathways for vision.** Each optic nerve contains about a million axons that synapse with interneurons in the lateral geniculate nuclei. The nuclei relay sensations to the primary visual cortex, one of many brain centers that cooperate in constructing our visual perceptions.

Left visual field

Right visual field

Left eye

Right eye

Optic nerve

Optic chiasm

Synapses with interneurons

Primary visual cortex

carry the information to higher-order visual processing and integrating centers elsewhere in the cortex. Researchers estimate that at least 30% of the cerebral cortex, comprising hundreds of millions of neurons in perhaps dozens of integrating centers, takes part in formulating what we actually "see." Determining how these centers integrate such components of our vision as color, motion, depth, shape, and detail is the focus of much exciting research.

## Color Vision

Among vertebrates, most fishes, amphibians, and reptiles, including birds, have very good color vision. Humans and other primates also see color well, but are among the minority of mammals with this ability. For cats and other mammals that are most active at night, a high proportion of rods in the retina is an adaptation that provides keen night vision. Color vision among these nocturnal animals is limited, and they probably see a pastel world during the day.

In humans, the perception of color is based on three types of cones, each with a different visual pigment—red, green, or blue. The three visual pigments, called *photopsins*, are formed from the binding of retinal to three distinct opsin proteins. Slight differences in the opsin proteins cause each photopsin to absorb light optimally at a different wavelength. Although the visual pigments are designated as red, green, and blue, their absorption spectra in fact overlap. For this reason, the brain's perception of intermediate hues depends on the differential stimulation of two or more classes of cones. For example, if both red and green cones are stimulated, we see either yellow or orange, depending on which class of cones is more strongly stimulated.

Abnormal color vision typically results from mutations in the genes for one or more photopsin proteins. In humans, color blindness nearly always affects perception of red or green and is far more common in one gender than the other: 5–8% of males, fewer than 1% of females. Why? The human genes for both the red and green pigments are X-linked. Thus, males are affected by a single mutation, whereas females are color-blind only if both copies are mutant. (The human gene for the blue pigment is on chromosome 7.)

Experiments on color vision in the squirrel monkey (*Saimiri sciureus*) enabled a recent breakthrough in the field of gene therapy. These monkeys have only two opsin genes, one sensitive to blue light and the other sensitive to either red or green light, depending on the allele. Because the red/green opsin gene is X-linked, all males have only the red- or green-sensitive version and are red-green color-blind. When researchers injected a virus containing the gene for the missing version into the retina of adult male monkeys, evidence of full color vision was apparent after 20 weeks **(Figure 50.21)**.

The squirrel monkey gene therapy studies demonstrate that the neural circuits required to process visual information can be generated or activated even in adults, making it possible to treat a range of vision disorders. Indeed, gene therapy

▼ **Figure 50.21 Gene therapy for vision.** Once color-blind, this adult male monkey treated with gene therapy demonstrates his ability to distinguish red from green.

**MAKE CONNECTIONS** ➤ *Red-green color blindness is X-linked in squirrel monkeys and in humans (see Figure 15.7). Why is the inheritance pattern in humans not apparent in squirrel monkeys?*

has been used to treat Leber's congenital amaurosis (LCA), an inherited retinal degenerative disease that causes severe loss of vision. After using gene therapy to restore vision in dogs and mice with LCA, researchers successfully treated the disease in humans by injecting the functional LCA gene in a viral vector (see Figure 20.22).

## The Visual Field

The brain not only processes visual information but also controls what information is captured. One important control is focusing, which in humans occurs by changing the shape of the lens, as noted earlier and illustrated in **Figure 50.22**. When you focus your eyes on a close object, your lenses become almost spherical. When you view a distant object, your lenses are flattened.

Although our peripheral vision allows us to see objects over a nearly 180° range, the distribution of photoreceptors across the eye limits both what we see and how well we see it. Overall, the human retina contains about 125 million rods and 6 million cones. At the **fovea**, the center of the visual field, there are no rods but a very high density of cones—about 150,000 cones per square millimeter. The ratio of cones to rods

▼ **Figure 50.22 Focusing in the mammalian eye.** Ciliary smooth muscles control the shape of the lens, which bends light and focuses it on the retina. The thicker the lens, the more sharply the light is bent.

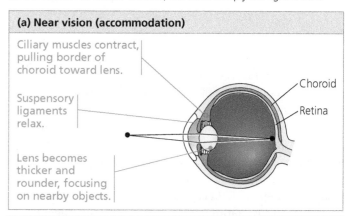

**(a) Near vision (accommodation)**

Ciliary muscles contract, pulling border of choroid toward lens.

Suspensory ligaments relax.

Lens becomes thicker and rounder, focusing on nearby objects.

Choroid

Retina

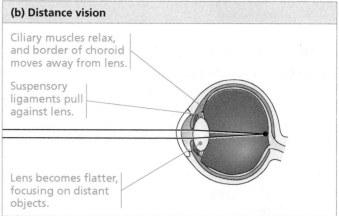

**(b) Distance vision**

Ciliary muscles relax, and border of choroid moves away from lens.

Suspensory ligaments pull against lens.

Lens becomes flatter, focusing on distant objects.

 Animation: Near and Distance Vision

falls with distance from the fovea, with the peripheral regions having only rods. In daylight, you achieve your sharpest vision by looking directly at an object, such that light shines on the tightly packed cones in your fovea. At night, looking directly at a dimly lit object is ineffective, since the rods—the more sensitive light receptors—are absent from the fovea. For this reason, you see a dim star best by focusing on a point just to one side of it.

## CONCEPT CHECK 50.3

1. Contrast the light-detecting organs of planarians and flies. How is each organ adaptive for the lifestyle of the animal?

2. In a condition called presbyopia, the eyes' lenses lose much of their elasticity and maintain a flat shape. How would you expect this condition to affect a person's vision?

3. **WHAT IF?** ➤ Our brain receives more action potentials when our eyes are exposed to light even though our photoreceptors release more neurotransmitter in the dark. Propose an explanation.

4. **MAKE CONNECTIONS** ➤ Compare the function of retinal in the eye with that of the pigment chlorophyll in a plant photosystem (see Concept 10.2).

*For suggested answers, see Appendix A.*

# CONCEPT 50.4

## The senses of taste and smell rely on similar sets of sensory receptors

Animals use their chemical senses for a wide range of purposes, including finding mates, recognizing marked territories, and helping navigate during migration. In addition, animals such as ants and bees that live in large social groups rely extensively on chemical "conversation."

In all animals, chemical senses are important for feeding behavior. The perceptions of **gustation** (taste) and **olfaction** (smell) both depend on chemoreceptors. In the case of terrestrial animals, taste is the detection of chemicals called **tastants** that are present in a solution, and smell is the detection of **odorants** that are carried through the air. There is no distinction between taste and smell in aquatic animals.

In insects, taste receptors are located within sensory hairs located on the feet and in mouthparts, where they are used to select food. A tasting hair contains several chemoreceptors, each especially responsive to a particular class of tastant, such as sugar or salt. Insects are also capable of smelling airborne odorants using olfactory hairs, usually located on their antennae (see Figure 50.6). The chemical DEET (*N,N*-diethyl-meta-toluamide), marketed as an insect "repellant," actually protects against bites by blocking the olfactory receptor in mosquitoes that detects human scent.

## Taste in Mammals

Humans and other mammals perceive five tastes: sweet, sour, salty, bitter, and umami. Umami (Japanese for "delicious") is elicited by the amino acid glutamate. Sometimes used as a flavor enhancer in the form of monosodium glutamate, or MSG, glutamate occurs naturally in meat, aged cheese, and other foods, to which it imparts a "savory" quality.

For decades, many researchers assumed that a taste cell could have more than one type of receptor. An alternative idea is that each taste cell has a single receptor type, programming the cell to recognize only one of the five tastes. To test this hypothesis, scientists used a cloned bitter taste receptor to genetically reprogram gustation in a mouse **(Figure 50.23)**. This reprogramming experiment, together with follow-up studies, revealed that an individual taste cell does in fact express a single receptor type and detects tastants representing only one of the five tastes.

▼ **Figure 50.23**

### Inquiry How do mammals detect different tastes?

**Experiment** To investigate the basis of mammalian taste perception, researchers used a chemical called phenyl-β-D-glucopyranoside (PBDG). Humans find PBDG extremely bitter. Mice, however, lack a receptor for PBDG. Mice avoid drinking water containing other bitter tastants but show no aversion to water that contains PBDG.

Using a molecular cloning strategy, the researchers generated mice that made the human PBDG receptor in cells that normally make either a sweet receptor or a bitter receptor. The mice were given a choice of two bottles, one filled with pure water and one filled with water containing PBDG at varying concentrations. The researchers then observed whether the mice had an attraction or an aversion to PBDG.

**Results**

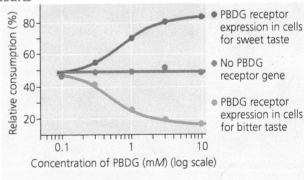

**Conclusion** The researchers found that the presence of a bitter receptor in sweet taste cells is sufficient to cause mice to be attracted to a bitter chemical. They concluded that the mammalian brain must therefore perceive sweet or bitter taste solely on the basis of which sensory neurons are activated.

**Data from** K. L. Mueller et al., The receptors and coding logic for bitter taste, *Nature* 434:225–229 (2005).

**WHAT IF?** ➤ *Suppose that instead of the PBDG receptor, the researchers had used a receptor specific for a sweetener that humans crave but mice ignore. How would the results of the experiment have differed?*

The receptor cells for taste in mammals are modified epithelial cells organized into **taste buds**, which are scattered in several areas of the tongue and mouth (**Figure 50.24**). Most taste buds on the tongue are associated with nipple-shaped projections called papillae. Any region of the tongue with taste buds can detect any of the five types of taste. (The frequently reproduced "taste maps" of the tongue are thus not accurate.)

Researchers have identified the receptor proteins for all five tastes. The sensations of sweet, umami, and bitter tastes each require one or more genes encoding a G protein-coupled receptor, or GPCR (see Figures 11.7 and 11.8). Humans have one type of sweet receptor and one type of umami receptor,

▼ Figure 50.24 **Human taste receptors.**

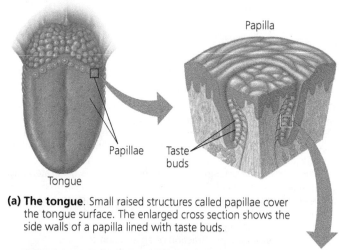

**(a) The tongue**. Small raised structures called papillae cover the tongue surface. The enlarged cross section shows the side walls of a papilla lined with taste buds.

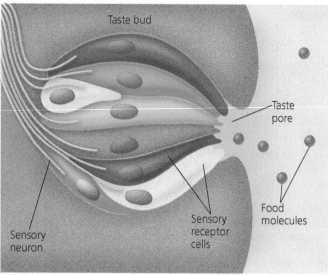

**Key**

■ Sweet  ■ Bitter  ■ Umami
■ Salty  □ Sour

**(b) A taste bud**. Taste buds in all regions of the tongue contain sensory receptor cells specific for each of the five taste types.

each assembled from a different pair of GPCR proteins. In contrast, humans have more than 30 different receptors for bitter taste, and each receptor is able to recognize multiple bitter tastants. GPCR proteins are also critical for the sense of smell, as will be discussed shortly.

The receptor for sour tastants belongs to the TRP family and is similar to the capsaicin receptor and other thermoreceptor proteins. In taste buds, the TRP proteins of the sour receptor assemble into an ion channel in the plasma membrane of the taste cell. Binding of an acid or other sour-tasting substance to the receptor triggers a change in the ion channel. Depolarization occurs, activating a sensory neuron.

The taste receptor for salt turns out to be a sodium channel. Not surprisingly, it specifically detects sodium salts, such as the NaCl that we use in cooking and flavoring.

## Smell in Humans

In olfaction, unlike gustation, the sensory cells are neurons. Olfactory receptor cells line the upper portion of the nasal cavity and send impulses along their axons to the olfactory bulb of the brain (**Figure 50.25**). The receptive ends of the cells contain cilia that extend into the layer of mucus coating the nasal cavity. When an odorant diffuses into this region, it binds to a specific GPCR protein called an olfactory receptor (OR) on the plasma membrane of the olfactory cilia. These events trigger signal transduction leading to the production of cyclic AMP. In olfactory cells, cyclic AMP opens channels in the plasma membrane that are permeable to both $Na^+$ and $Ca^{2+}$. The flow of these ions into the receptor cell leads to depolarization of the membrane, generating action potentials.

Mammals can distinguish thousands of different odors, each caused by a structurally distinct odorant. How is this remarkable sensory discrimination possible? Richard Axel and Linda Buck found the answer in mice—a family of 1,200 different OR genes—and were honored with a Nobel Prize in 2004. Humans have just 380 OR genes, far fewer than mice, but still nearly 2% of all the genes in our genome. Identification of particular odors relies on two basic properties of the olfactory system. First, each olfactory receptor cell expresses one OR gene. Second, those cells that express the same OR gene transmit action potentials to the same small region of the olfactory bulb.

After odorants are detected, information from olfactory receptors is collected and integrated. Genetic studies on mice, worms, and flies have shown that signals from the nervous system regulate this process, dialing the response to particular odorants up or down. As a result, animals can detect the location of food sources even if the concentration of a key odorant is particularly low or high.

**▼ Figure 50.25 Smell in humans.** Odorant molecules bind to specific chemoreceptor proteins in the plasma membrane of olfactory receptor cells, triggering action potentials. Each olfactory receptor cell has just one type of chemoreceptor. As shown, cells that express different chemoreceptors detect different odorants.

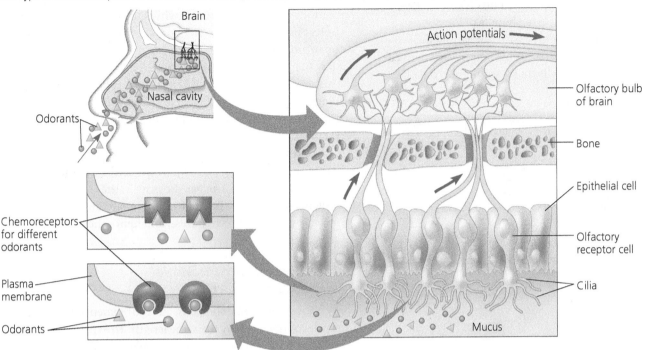

**WHAT IF?** ➤ *If you spray an "air freshener" in a musty room, would you be affecting detection, transmission, or perception of the odorants responsible for the musty smell?*

Studies of model organisms also reveal that complex mixtures of odorants are not processed as the simple sum of each input. Rather, the brain integrates olfactory information from different receptors into single sensations. These sensations contribute to the perception of the environment in the present and to the memory of events and emotions.

Although the receptors and neuronal pathways for taste and smell are independent, the two senses do interact. Indeed, much of the complex flavor humans experience when eating is due to our sense of smell. If the olfactory system is blocked, as occurs when you have a head cold, the perception of flavor is sharply reduced.

**CONCEPT CHECK 50.4**

1. Explain why some taste receptor cells and all olfactory receptor cells use G protein-coupled receptors, yet only olfactory receptor cells produce action potentials.

2. Pathways involving G proteins provide an opportunity for an increase in signal strength in the course of signal transduction, a change referred to as amplification. How might this be beneficial in olfaction?

3. **WHAT IF?** ➤ If you discovered a mutation in mice that disrupted the ability to taste sweet, bitter, and umami but not sour or salty, what might you predict about where this mutation acts in the signaling pathways used by these receptors?

*For suggested answers, see Appendix A.*

# CONCEPT 50.5

## The physical interaction of protein filaments is required for muscle function

In discussing sensory mechanisms, we have seen how sensory inputs to the nervous system can result in specific behaviors: the touch-guided foraging of a star-nosed mole, the upside-down swimming of a crayfish with manipulated statocysts, and the light-avoiding maneuvers of planarians. Underlying these diverse behaviors are common fundamental mechanisms: Feeding, swimming, and crawling all require muscle activity in response to nervous system motor output.

Muscle cell contraction relies on the interaction between protein structures called thin and thick filaments. The major component of **thin filaments** is the globular protein actin. In thin filaments, two strands of polymerized actin are coiled around one another; similar actin structures called microfilaments function in cell motility. The **thick filaments** are staggered arrays of myosin molecules. Muscle contraction is the result of filament movement powered by chemical energy; muscle extension occurs only passively. To understand how filaments bring about muscle contraction, we will begin by examining the skeletal muscle of vertebrates.

## Vertebrate Skeletal Muscle

Vertebrate **skeletal muscle**, which moves bones and body, has a hierarchy of smaller and smaller units (**Figure 50.26**). Within a typical skeletal muscle is a bundle of long fibers running along the length of the muscle. Each individual fiber is a single cell. Within are multiple nuclei, each derived from one of the embryonic cells that fused to form the fiber.

▼ **Figure 50.26 The structure of skeletal muscle.**

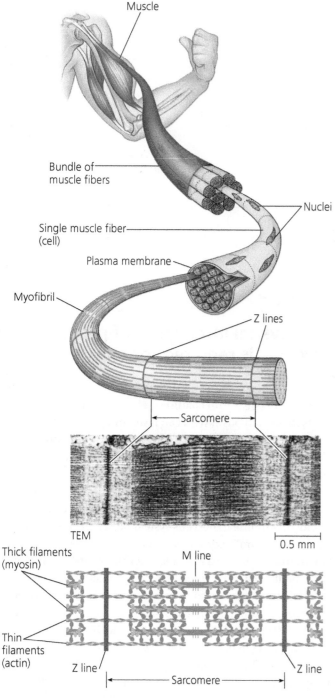

Muscle

Bundle of muscle fibers

Single muscle fiber (cell)

Plasma membrane

Myofibril

Nuclei

Z lines

Sarcomere

TEM

0.5 mm

Thick filaments (myosin)

M line

Thin filaments (actin)

Z line

Z line

Sarcomere

**VISUAL SKILLS** ➤ *Looking at this figure, would you say that there are multiple sarcomeres per myofibril or multiple myofibrils per sarcomere? Explain.*

Surrounding these nuclei are longitudinal **myofibrils**, which consist of bundles of thin and thick filaments.

The myofibrils in muscle fibers are made up of repeating sections called **sarcomeres**, which are the basic contractile units of skeletal muscle. The borders of the sarcomere line up in adjacent myofibrils, forming a pattern of light and dark bands (striations) visible with a light microscope. For this reason, skeletal muscle is also called *striated muscle*. Thin filaments attach at the Z lines at the sarcomere ends, while thick filaments are anchored in the middle of the sarcomere (M line).

In a resting (relaxed) myofibril, thick and thin filaments partially overlap. Near the edge of the sarcomere there are only thin filaments, whereas the zone in the center contains only thick filaments. This partially overlapping arrangement is the key to how the sarcomere, and hence the whole muscle, contracts.

### The Sliding-Filament Model of Muscle Contraction

A contracting muscle shortens, but the filaments that bring about contraction stay the same length. To explain this apparent paradox, we'll focus first on a single sarcomere. As shown in **Figure 50.27**, the filaments slide past each other, much like the segments of a telescoping support pole. According to the well-accepted **sliding-filament model**, the thin and thick filaments ratchet past each other, powered by myosin molecules.

**Figure 50.28** illustrates the cycles of change in the myosin molecule that convert the chemical energy of ATP into the longitudinal sliding of thick and thin filaments.

As shown in the figure, each myosin molecule has a long "tail" region and a globular "head" region. The tail adheres to the tails of other myosin molecules, binding together the thick filament. The head, jutting to the side, can bind ATP. Hydrolysis of bound ATP converts myosin to a high-energy form that binds to actin, forming a cross-bridge between the myosin and the thin filament. The myosin head then returns to its low-energy form as it helps to pull the thin filament toward the center of the sarcomere. When a new ATP molecule binds to the myosin head, the cross-bridge is disrupted, releasing the myosin head from the actin filament.

Muscle contraction requires repeated cycles of binding and release. During each cycle of each myosin head, the head is freed from a cross-bridge, cleaves the newly bound ATP, and binds again to actin. Because the thin filament moves toward the center of the sarcomere in each cycle, the myosin head now attaches to a binding site farther along the thin filament than in the previous cycle. Each end of a thick filament contains approximately 300 heads, each of which forms and re-forms about five cross-bridges per second, driving the thick and thin filaments past each other.

> **Figure 50.27 The sliding-filament model of muscle contraction.** The drawings on the left show that the lengths of the thick (myosin) filaments (purple) and thin (actin) filaments (orange) remain the same as a sarcomere shortens and a muscle fiber contracts.

**BioFlix® Animation: From Muscle Cells to Movement**

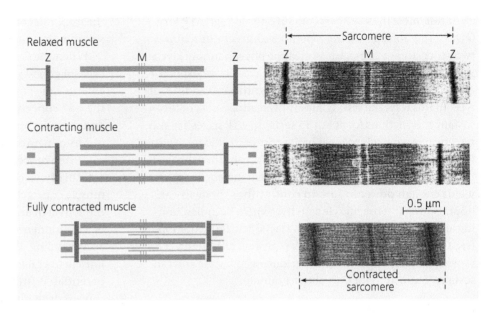

**▼ Figure 50.28 Myosin-actin interactions underlying muscle fiber contraction.**

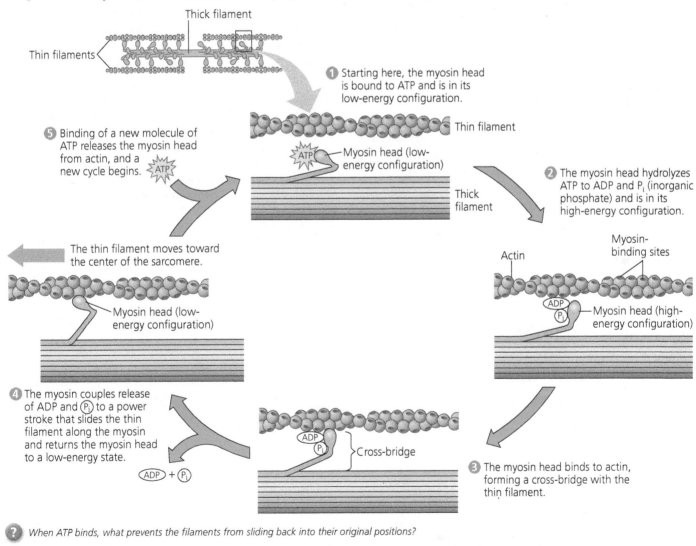

? *When ATP binds, what prevents the filaments from sliding back into their original positions?*

**BioFlix® Animation: Sliding-Filament Model of Muscle Contraction**

At rest, most muscle fibers contain only enough ATP for a few contractions. Powering repetitive contractions requires two other storage compounds: creatine phosphate and glycogen. Transfer of a phosphate group from creatine phosphate to ADP in an enzyme-catalyzed reaction synthesizes additional ATP. In this way, the resting supply of creatine phosphate can sustain contractions for about 15 seconds. ATP stores are also replenished when glycogen is broken down to glucose. During light or moderate muscle activity, this glucose is metabolized by aerobic respiration. This highly efficient metabolic process yields enough power to sustain contractions for nearly an hour. During intense muscle activity, oxygen becomes limiting and ATP is instead generated by lactic acid fermentation (see Concept 9.5). This anaerobic pathway, although very rapid, generates much less ATP per glucose molecule and can sustain contraction for only about 1 minute.

### The Role of Calcium and Regulatory Proteins

Proteins bound to actin play crucial roles in controlling muscle contraction. In a muscle fiber at rest, **tropomyosin**, a regulatory protein, and the **troponin complex**, a set of additional regulatory proteins, are bound to the actin strands of thin filaments. Tropomyosin covers the myosin-binding sites along the thin filament, preventing actin and myosin from interacting **(Figure 50.29a)**.

Motor neurons enable actin and myosin to interact by triggering a release of calcium ions ($Ca^{2+}$) into the cytosol. Once in the cytosol, $Ca^{2+}$ binds to the troponin complex, causing the myosin-binding sites on actin to be exposed **(Figure 50.29b)**. Note that the effect of $Ca^{2+}$ is indirect: Binding to $Ca^{2+}$ causes

the troponin complex to change shape, dislodging tropomyosin from the myosin-binding sites.

When the $Ca^{2+}$ concentration rises in the cytosol, the cycle of cross-bridge formation begins, the thin and thick filaments slide past each, and the muscle fiber contracts. When the $Ca^{2+}$ concentration falls, the binding sites are covered, and contraction stops.

Motor neurons cause muscle contraction through a multistep process triggering the movement of $Ca^{2+}$ into the cytosol of muscle cells **(Figure 50.30)**. The events in skeletal muscle contraction are summarized in **Figure 50.31**. First, the arrival of an action potential at the synaptic terminal of a motor neuron ❶ causes release of the neurotransmitter acetylcholine. Binding of acetylcholine to receptors on the muscle fiber leads to a depolarization that initiates an action potential. Within the muscle fiber, the action potential spreads deep into the interior, following infoldings of the plasma membrane called **transverse (T) tubules**. ❷ These make close contact with the **sarcoplasmic reticulum (SR)**, a specialized endoplasmic reticulum. As the action potential spreads along the T tubules, it triggers changes in the SR, opening $Ca^{2+}$ channels ❸. Calcium ions stored in the interior of the SR flow through open channels into the cytosol ❹ and bind to the troponin complex, ❺ initiating the muscle fiber contraction.

When motor neuron input stops, the filaments slide back to their starting position as the muscle relaxes. Relaxation begins as proteins in the SR pump $Ca^{2+}$ back into the SR ❻ from the

▼ **Figure 50.30 The roles of the sarcoplasmic reticulum and T tubules in muscle fiber contraction.** The synaptic terminal of a motor neuron releases acetylcholine, which depolarizes the plasma membrane of the muscle fiber. The depolarization causes action potentials (red arrows) to sweep across the muscle fiber and deep into it along the transverse (T) tubules. The action potentials trigger the release of calcium (green dots) from the sarcoplasmic reticulum into the cytosol. Calcium initiates the sliding of filaments by allowing myosin to bind to actin.

▼ **Figure 50.29 The role of regulatory proteins and calcium in muscle fiber contraction.** Each thin filament consists of two strands of actin, two long molecules of tropomyosin, and multiple copies of the troponin complex.

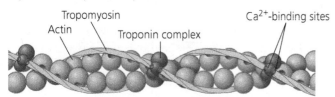

**(a) Myosin-binding sites blocked by tropomyosin**

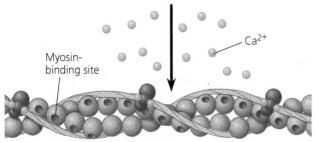

**(b) Myosin-binding sites exposed**

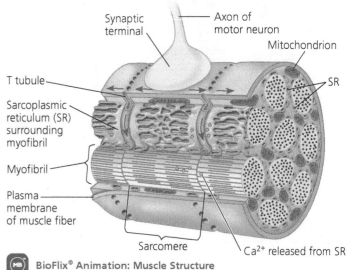

BioFlix® Animation: Muscle Structure

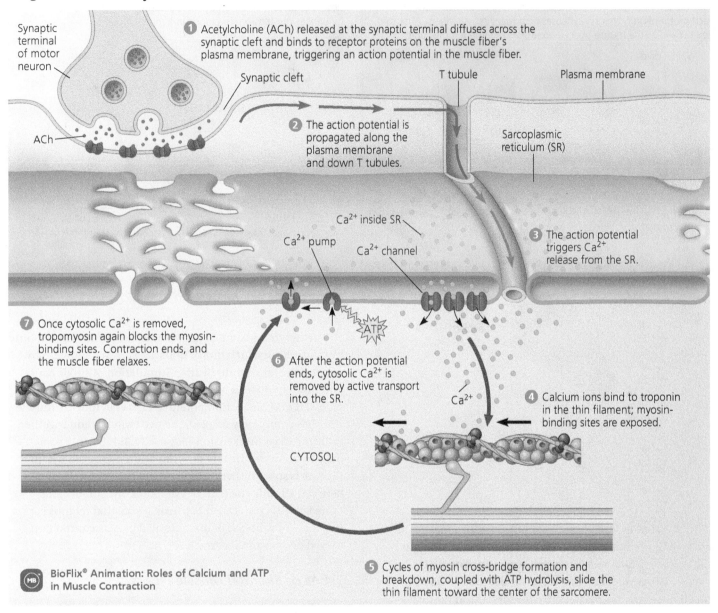

① Acetylcholine (ACh) released at the synaptic terminal diffuses across the synaptic cleft and binds to receptor proteins on the muscle fiber's plasma membrane, triggering an action potential in the muscle fiber.

Synaptic terminal of motor neuron

Synaptic cleft

T tubule

Plasma membrane

ACh

② The action potential is propagated along the plasma membrane and down T tubules.

Sarcoplasmic reticulum (SR)

$Ca^{2+}$ inside SR

$Ca^{2+}$ pump

$Ca^{2+}$ channel

③ The action potential triggers $Ca^{2+}$ release from the SR.

ATP

⑦ Once cytosolic $Ca^{2+}$ is removed, tropomyosin again blocks the myosin-binding sites. Contraction ends, and the muscle fiber relaxes.

⑥ After the action potential ends, cytosolic $Ca^{2+}$ is removed by active transport into the SR.

$Ca^{2+}$

④ Calcium ions bind to troponin in the thin filament; myosin-binding sites are exposed.

CYTOSOL

BioFlix® Animation: Roles of Calcium and ATP in Muscle Contraction

⑤ Cycles of myosin cross-bridge formation and breakdown, coupled with ATP hydrolysis, slide the thin filament toward the center of the sarcomere.

cytosol. When the $Ca^{2+}$ concentration in the cytosol drops to a low level, the regulatory proteins bound to the thin filament shift back to their starting position, ⑦ once again blocking the myosin-binding sites. At the same time, the $Ca^{2+}$ pumped from the cytosol accumulates in the SR, providing the stores needed to respond to the next action potential.

Several diseases cause paralysis by interfering with the excitation of skeletal muscle fibers by motor neurons. In amyotrophic lateral sclerosis (ALS), motor neurons in the spinal cord and brainstem degenerate, and muscle fibers atrophy. ALS is progressive and usually fatal within five years after symptoms appear. In myasthenia gravis, a person produces antibodies to the acetylcholine receptors of skeletal muscle. As the disease progresses and the number of receptors decreases, transmission between motor neurons and muscle fibers declines. Myasthenia gravis can generally be controlled with drugs that inhibit acetylcholinesterase or suppress the immune system.

### Nervous Control of Muscle Tension

Whereas contraction of a single skeletal muscle fiber is a brief all-or-none twitch, contraction of a whole muscle, such as the biceps in your upper arm, is graded; you can voluntarily alter the extent and strength of its contraction. The nervous system produces graded contractions of whole muscles by varying (1) the number of muscle fibers that contract and (2) the rate at which muscle fibers are stimulated. Let's consider each mechanism in turn.

## ▼ Figure 50.32 Motor units in a vertebrate skeletal muscle.
Each muscle fiber (cell) forms synapses with only one motor neuron, but each motor neuron typically synapses with many muscle fibers. A motor neuron and all the muscle fibers it controls constitute a motor unit.

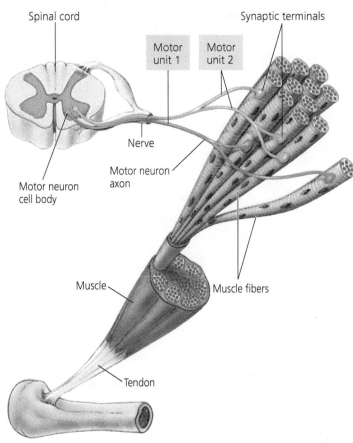

## ▼ Figure 50.33 Summation of twitches.
This graph illustrates how the number of action potentials during a short period of time influences the tension developed in a muscle fiber.

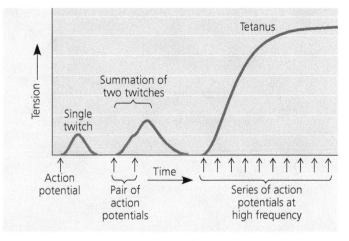

 *How could the nervous system cause a skeletal muscle to produce the most forceful contraction it is capable of?*

In vertebrates, each branched motor neuron may form synapses with many muscle fibers, although each fiber is controlled by only one motor neuron. A **motor unit** consists of a single motor neuron and all the muscle fibers it controls **(Figure 50.32)**. When a motor neuron produces an action potential, all the muscle fibers in its motor unit contract as a group. The strength of the resulting contraction depends on how many muscle fibers the motor neuron controls.

In the whole muscle, there may be hundreds of motor units. As more and more of the corresponding motor neurons are activated, a process called *recruitment*, the force (tension) developed by a muscle progressively increases. Depending on the number of motor neurons your brain recruits and the size of their motor units, you can lift a fork or something much heavier, like your biology textbook. Some muscles, especially those that hold up the body and maintain posture, are almost always partially contracted. In such muscles, the nervous system may alternate activation among the motor units, reducing the length of time any one set of fibers is contracted.

The nervous system regulates muscle contraction not only by controlling which motor units are activated but also by varying the rate of muscle fiber stimulation. A single action potential produces a twitch lasting about 100 milliseconds or less. If a second action potential arrives before the muscle fiber has completely relaxed, the two twitches add together, resulting in greater tension **(Figure 50.33)**. Further summation occurs as the rate of stimulation increases. When the rate is so high that the muscle fiber cannot relax at all between stimuli, the twitches fuse into one smooth, sustained contraction called **tetanus**. (Note that tetanus is also the name of a disease of uncontrolled muscle contraction caused by a bacterial toxin.)

## Types of Skeletal Muscle Fibers

Our discussion to this point has focused on the general properties of vertebrate skeletal muscles. There are, however, several distinct types of skeletal muscle fibers, each of which is adapted to a particular set of functions. We typically classify these varied fiber types both by the source of ATP used to power their activity and by the speed of their contraction **(Table 50.1)**.

**Oxidative and Glycolytic Fibers**   Fibers that rely mostly on aerobic respiration are called oxidative fibers. Such fibers are specialized in ways that enable them to make use of a steady energy supply: They have many mitochondria, a rich blood supply, and a large amount of an oxygen-storing protein called **myoglobin**. A brownish red pigment, myoglobin binds oxygen more tightly than does hemoglobin, enabling oxidative fibers to extract oxygen from the blood efficiently. In contrast, glycolytic fibers have

**Table 50.1  Types of Skeletal Muscle Fibers**

|  | Slow Oxidative | Fast Oxidative | Fast Glycolytic |
|---|---|---|---|
| Contraction speed | Slow | Fast | Fast |
| Major ATP source | Aerobic respiration | Aerobic respiration | Glycolysis |
| Rate of fatigue | Slow | Intermediate | Fast |
| Mitochondria | Many | Many | Few |
| Myoglobin content | High (red muscle) | High (red muscle) | Low (white muscle) |

▼ **Figure 50.34  Specialization of skeletal muscles.** The male toadfish (*Opsanus tau*) uses superfast muscles to produce its mating call.

a larger diameter and less myoglobin. Also, glycolytic fibers use glycolysis as their primary source of ATP and fatigue more readily than oxidative fibers. These two fiber types are readily apparent in the muscle of poultry and fish: The dark meat is made up of oxidative fibers rich in myoglobin, and the light meat is composed of glycolytic fibers.

**Fast-Twitch and Slow-Twitch Fibers**  Muscle fibers vary in the speed with which they contract: **Fast-twitch fibers** develop tension two to three times faster than **slow-twitch fibers**. Fast fibers enable brief, rapid, powerful contractions. Compared with a fast fiber, a slow fiber has less sarcoplasmic reticulum and pumps $Ca^{2+}$ more slowly. Because $Ca^{2+}$ remains in the cytosol longer, a muscle twitch in a slow fiber lasts about five times as long as one in a fast fiber.

The difference in contraction speed between slow-twitch and fast-twitch fibers mainly reflects the rate at which their myosin heads hydrolyze ATP. However, there isn't a one-to-one relationship between contraction speed and ATP source. Whereas all slow-twitch fibers are oxidative, fast-twitch fibers can be either glycolytic or oxidative.

Most human skeletal muscles contain both fast-twitch and slow-twitch fibers, although the muscles of the eye and hand are exclusively fast-twitch. In a muscle that has a mixture of fast and slow fibers, the relative proportions of each are genetically determined. However, if such a muscle is used repeatedly for activities requiring high endurance, some fast glycolytic fibers can develop into fast oxidative fibers. Because fast oxidative fibers fatigue more slowly than fast glycolytic fibers, the result will be a muscle that is more resistant to fatigue.

Some vertebrates have skeletal muscle fibers that twitch at rates far faster than any human muscle. For example, superfast muscles produce a rattlesnake's rattle and a dove's coo. Even faster are the muscles surrounding the gas-filled swim bladder of the male toadfish **(Figure 50.34)**.

In producing its "boat whistle" mating call, the toadfish can contract and relax these muscles more than 200 times per second!

## Other Types of Muscle

Although all muscles share the same fundamental mechanism of contraction—actin and myosin filaments sliding past each other—there are many different types of muscle. Vertebrates, for example, have cardiac muscle and smooth muscle in addition to skeletal muscle (see Figure 40.5).

Vertebrate **cardiac muscle** is found only in the heart and, like skeletal muscle, is striated. Unlike skeletal muscle fibers, cardiac muscle cells can initiate rhythmic depolarization and contraction without nervous system input. Normally, however, cells in one part of the heart act as a pacemaker to initiate contraction. Signals from the pacemaker spread throughout the heart because specialized regions called *intercalated disks* electrically couple each cardiac muscle cell to the adjacent cells. It is this coupling that enables action potentials generated in one part of the heart to trigger contraction throughout the organ. Although these action potentials last up to 20 times longer than those of skeletal muscle fibers, a long refractory period prevents summation and tetanus.

**Smooth muscle** in vertebrates is found in the walls of hollow organs, such as vessels and tracts of the circulatory, digestive and reproductive systems. Smooth muscle is also found in the eye, where its action controls focusing and pupil diameter. Smooth muscle cells lack striations because their actin and myosin filaments are not regularly arrayed along the length of the cell. Instead, the thick filaments are scattered throughout the cytoplasm, and the thin filaments are attached to structures called dense bodies, some of which are tethered to the plasma membrane. There is less myosin than in striated muscle fibers, and the myosin is not associated with specific actin strands. Some smooth muscle cells contract only when stimulated by neurons of the autonomic nervous system. Others are electrically coupled to one another and can generate action potentials without input from neurons. Smooth muscles contract and relax more slowly than striated muscles.

Although $Ca^{2+}$ regulates smooth muscle contraction, smooth muscle cells have no troponin complex or T tubules, and their sarcoplasmic reticulum is not well developed. During an action potential, $Ca^{2+}$ enters the cytosol mainly through the plasma membrane. Calcium ions cause contraction by binding to the protein calmodulin, which activates an enzyme that phosphorylates the myosin head, enabling cross-bridge activity.

Invertebrates have muscle cells similar to vertebrate skeletal and smooth muscle cells; in fact, arthropod skeletal muscles are nearly identical to those of vertebrates. However, because the flight muscles of insects contract in response to stretching, the wings of some insects can actually beat up and down faster than action potentials can arrive from the central nervous system. Another interesting evolutionary adaptation has been discovered in the muscles that hold a clam's shell closed. Modification of certain proteins in these muscles allows them to remain contracted for as long as a month with only a low rate of energy consumption.

## CONCEPT CHECK 50.5

1. Contrast the role of $Ca^{2+}$ in the contraction of a skeletal muscle fiber and a smooth muscle cell.

2. **WHAT IF?** ➤ Why are the muscles of an animal that has recently died likely to be stiff?

3. **MAKE CONNECTIONS** ➤ How does the activity of tropomyosin and troponin in muscle contraction compare with the activity of a competitive inhibitor in enzyme action? (See Figure 8.18b.)

*For suggested answers, see Appendix A.*

# CONCEPT 50.6

## Skeletal systems transform muscle contraction into locomotion

Converting muscle contraction to movement requires a skeleton—a rigid structure to which muscles can attach. An animal changes its shape or location by contracting muscles connecting two parts of its skeleton. Often muscles are anchored to bone indirectly via connective tissue formed into a tendon.

Because muscles exert force only during contraction, moving a body part back and forth typically requires two muscles

▼ **Figure 50.35 The interaction of muscles and skeletons in movement.** Back-and-forth movement of a body part is generally accomplished by antagonistic muscles. This arrangement works with either an internal skeleton, as in mammals, or an external skeleton, as in insects.

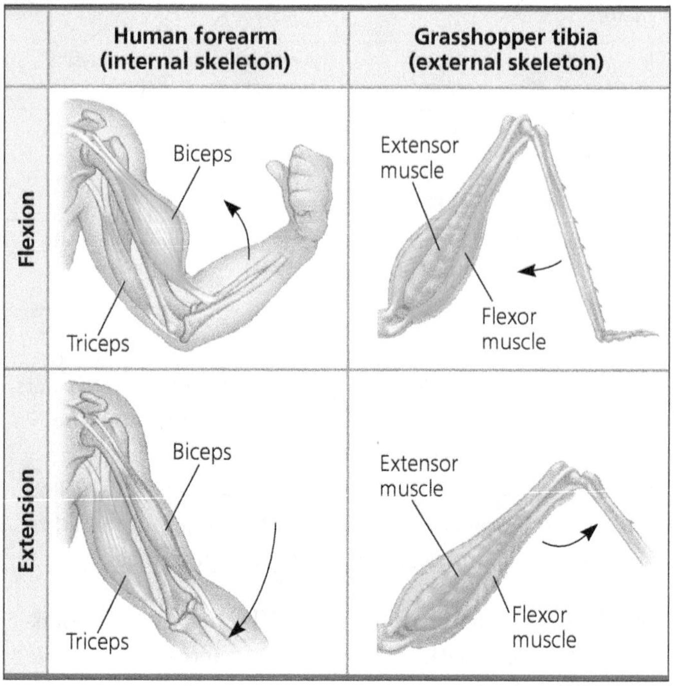

| Human forearm (internal skeleton) | Grasshopper tibia (external skeleton) |
|---|---|
| **Flexion** — Biceps / Triceps | Extensor muscle / Flexor muscle |
| **Extension** — Biceps / Triceps | Extensor muscle / Flexor muscle |

**Key** ▮ Contracting muscle ▮ Relaxing muscle

attached to the same section of the skeleton. We can see such an arrangement in the upper portion of a human arm or grasshopper leg **(Figure 50.35)**. Although we call such muscles an antagonistic pair, their function is actually cooperative, coordinated by the nervous system. For example, when you extend your arm, motor neurons trigger your triceps muscle to contract while the absence of neuronal input allows your biceps to relax.

Vital for movement, animal skeletons also function in support and protection. Most land animals would collapse if they had no skeleton to support their mass. Furthermore, an animal living in water would be formless without a framework to maintain its shape. In many animals, a hard skeleton also protects soft tissues. For example, the vertebrate skull protects the brain, and the ribs of terrestrial vertebrates form a cage around the heart, lungs, and other internal organs.

## Types of Skeletal Systems

Although we tend to think of skeletons only as interconnected sets of bones, skeletons come in many different forms. Hardened support structures can be external (as in exoskeletons), internal (as in endoskeletons), or even absent (as in fluid-based, or hydrostatic, skeletons).

## Hydrostatic Skeletons

A **hydrostatic skeleton** consists of fluid held under pressure in a closed body compartment. This is the main type of skeleton in most cnidarians, flatworms, nematodes, and annelids (see Figure 33.3). These animals control their form and movement by using muscles to change the shape of fluid-filled compartments. Among the cnidarians, for example, a hydra elongates by closing its mouth and constricting its central gastrovascular cavity using contractile cells in its body wall. Because water maintains its volume under pressure, the cavity must elongate when its diameter is decreased.

Worms carry out locomotion in a variety of ways. In planarians and other flatworms, body movement results mainly from muscles in the body wall exerting localized forces against the interstitial fluid. In nematodes (roundworms), longitudinal muscles contracting around the fluid-filled body cavity move the animal forward by wavelike motions called undulations. In earthworms and many other annelids, circular and longitudinal muscles act together to change the shape of individual fluid-filled segments, which are divided by septa. These shape changes bring about **peristalsis**, a movement produced by rhythmic waves of muscle contractions passing from front to back (**Figure 50.36**).

Hydrostatic skeletons are well suited for life in aquatic environments. On land, they provide support for crawling and burrowing and may cushion internal organs from shocks. However, a hydrostatic skeleton cannot support walking or running, in which an animal's body is held off the ground.

## Exoskeletons

The clam shell you find on a beach once served as an **exoskeleton**, a hard covering deposited on an animal's surface. The shells of clams and most other molluscs are made of calcium carbonate secreted by the mantle, a sheet-like extension of the body wall (see Figure 33.15). Clams and other bivalves close their hinged shell using muscles attached to the inside of this exoskeleton. As the animal grows, it enlarges its shell by adding to the outer edge.

Insects and other arthropods have a jointed exoskeleton called a *cuticle*, a coat secreted by the epidermis. About 30–50% of the arthropod cuticle consists of **chitin**, a polysaccharide similar to cellulose (see Figure 5.8). Fibrils of chitin are embedded in a protein matrix, forming a composite material that combines strength and flexibility. The cuticle may be hardened with organic compounds and, in some cases, calcium salts. In body parts that must be flexible, such as leg joints, the cuticle remains unhardened. Muscles are attached to knobs and plates of the cuticle that extend into the interior of the body. With each growth spurt, an

▼ **Figure 50.36 Crawling by peristalsis.** Contraction of the longitudinal muscles thickens and shortens the earthworm; contraction of the circular muscles constricts and elongates it.

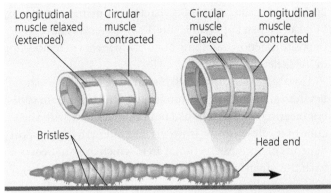

Longitudinal muscle relaxed (extended)   Circular muscle contracted   Circular muscle relaxed   Longitudinal muscle contracted

Bristles   Head end

**1** At the moment depicted, body segments at the earthworm's head end and just in front of the rear end are short and thick (longitudinal muscles contracted; circular muscles relaxed) and are anchored to the ground by bristles. The other segments are thin and elongated (circular muscles contracted; longitudinal muscles relaxed).

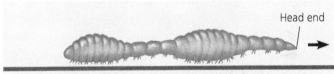

Head end

**2** The head has moved forward because circular muscles in the head segments have contracted. Segments behind the head and at the rear are now thick and anchored, thus preventing the worm from slipping backward.

Head end

**3** The head segments are thick again and anchored in their new positions. The rear segments have released their hold on the ground and have been pulled forward.

**MB**   Video: Earthworm Locomotion

arthropod must shed its exoskeleton (molt) and produce a larger one.

## Endoskeletons

Animals ranging from sponges to mammals have a hardened internal skeleton, or **endoskeleton**, buried within their soft tissues. In sponges, the endoskeleton consists of hard needle-like structures of inorganic material or fibers made of protein. Echinoderms' bodies are reinforced by ossicles, hard plates composed of magnesium carbonate and calcium carbonate crystals. Whereas the ossicles of sea urchins are tightly bound, the ossicles of sea stars are more loosely linked, allowing a sea star to change the shape of its arms.

Vertebrates have an endoskeleton consisting of cartilage, bone, or some combination of these materials (see Figure 40.5).

The mammalian skeleton contains more than 200 bones, some fused together and others connected at joints by ligaments that allow freedom of movement (**Figures 50.37** and **50.38**). Cells called *osteoblasts* secrete bone matrix and thereby build and repair bone (see Figure 40.5). *Osteoclasts* have an opposite function, resorbing bone components in remodeling of the skeleton.

How thick does an endoskeleton need to be? We can begin to answer this question by applying ideas from civil engineering. The weight of a building increases with the cube of its dimensions. However, the strength of a support depends on its cross-sectional area, which only increases with the square of its diameter. We can thus predict that if we scaled up a mouse to the size of an elephant, the legs of the giant mouse would be too thin to support its weight. Indeed, the body proportions of large animals are very different from those of small ones.

In applying the building analogy, we might also predict that the size of leg bones should be directly proportional to the strain imposed by body weight. Animal bodies, howevewr, are complex and nonrigid. In supporting body weight, it turns out that body posture—the position of the legs relative to the main body—is more important than leg size, at least in mammals and birds. In addition, muscles and tendons, which hold the legs of large mammals relatively strawight and positioned under the body, actually bear most of the load.

▼ **Figure 50.37 Bones and joints of the human skeleton.**

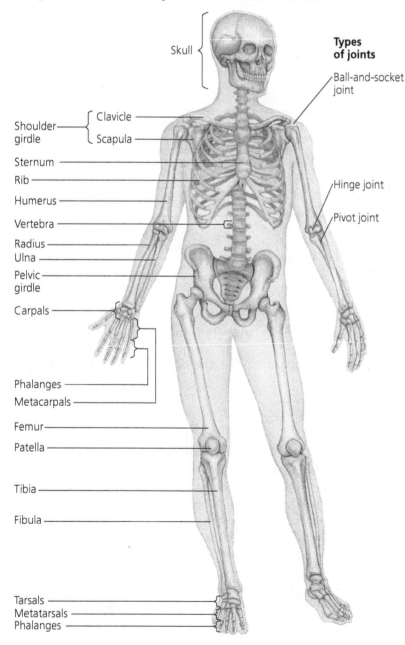

Skull

Shoulder girdle — Clavicle — Scapula

Sternum

Rib

Humerus

Vertebra

Radius

Ulna

Pelvic girdle

Carpals

Phalanges

Metacarpals

Femur

Patella

Tibia

Fibula

Tarsals

Metatarsals

Phalanges

**Types of joints**

Ball-and-socket joint

Hinge joint

Pivot joint

▼ **Figure 50.38 Types of joints.**

**Ball-and-socket joint**

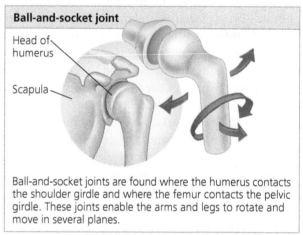

Head of humerus

Scapula

Ball-and-socket joints are found where the humerus contacts the shoulder girdle and where the femur contacts the pelvic girdle. These joints enable the arms and legs to rotate and move in several planes.

**Hinge joint**

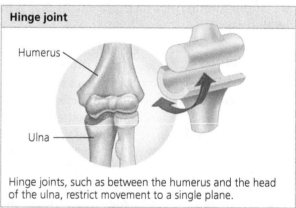

Humerus

Ulna

Hinge joints, such as between the humerus and the head of the ulna, restrict movement to a single plane.

**Pivot joint**

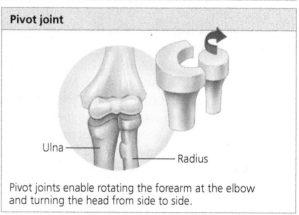

Ulna

Radius

Pivot joints enable rotating the forearm at the elbow and turning the head from side to side.

## Types of Locomotion

Movement is a hallmark of animals. Even animals fixed to a surface move their body parts: Sponges use beating flagella to generate water currents that draw and trap small food particles, and sessile cnidarians wave tentacles that capture prey. Most animals, however, are mobile and spend a considerable portion of their time and energy actively searching for food, escaping from danger, and seeking mates. These activities involve **locomotion**—active travel from place to place.

Friction and gravity tend to keep an animal stationary and therefore oppose locomotion. To move, an animal must expend energy to overcome these two forces. As we will see next, the amount of energy required to oppose friction or gravity is often reduced by an animal body plan adapted for movement in a particular environment.

▲ **Figure 50.39 Energy-efficient locomotion on land.** Members of the kangaroo family travel from place to place mainly by leaping on their large hind legs. Kinetic energy momentarily stored in tendons after each leap provides a boost for the next leap. In fact, a large kangaroo hopping at 30 km/hr uses no more energy per minute than it does at 6 km/hr. The large tail helps to balance the kangaroo when it leaps as well as when it sits.

 Interview with Terry Dawson: Kangaroos are "rule" breakers!

### Locomotion on Land

On land, a walking, running, hopping, or crawling animal must be able to support itself and move against gravity, but air poses relatively little resistance, at least at moderate speeds. When a land animal walks, runs, or hops, its leg muscles expend energy both to propel it and to keep it from falling down. With each step, the animal's leg muscles must overcome inertia by accelerating a leg from a standing start. For moving on land, powerful muscles and strong skeletal support are therefore more important than a streamlined shape.

Diverse adaptations for traveling on land have evolved in various vertebrates. For example, kangaroos have large, powerful muscles in their hind legs, suitable for locomotion by hopping **(Figure 50.39)**. As a kangaroo lands after each leap, tendons in its hind legs momentarily store energy. Much like the energy in a compressed spring, the energy stored in the tendons from one jump is released in the next jump, reducing the energy the animal must expend to travel. The legs of an insect, dog, or human also retain some energy during walking or running, although a considerably smaller share than those of a kangaroo.

Maintaining balance is another prerequisite for walking, running, or hopping. A cat, dog, or horse maintains balance by keeping three feet on the ground when walking. Illustrating the same principle, bipedal animals, such as humans and birds, keep part of at least one foot on the ground when walking. At running speeds, momentum more than foot contact keeps the body upright, enabling all the feet to be off the ground briefly. A kangaroo's large tail forms a stable tripod with its hind legs when the animal sits or moves slowly and helps balance its body during leaps. Recent studies reveal that the tail also generates significant force during hopping, helping to propel the kangaroo's forward movement.

Crawling poses a very different challenge. Having much of its body in contact with the ground, a crawling animal must exert considerable effort to overcome friction. As you have read, earthworms crawl by peristalsis. In contrast, many snakes crawl by undulating their entire body from side to side. Waves of bending propagate from head to tail, with each portion of the body eventually following the same undulating path as the head and neck. Some other snakes, such as boa constrictors and pythons, creep in a straight line, driven by muscles that lift belly scales off the ground, tilt the scales forward, and then push them backward against the ground.

### Swimming

Because most animals are reasonably buoyant in water, overcoming gravity is less of a problem for swimming animals than for species that move on land or through the air. On the other hand, water is a much denser and more viscous medium than air, and thus drag (friction) is a major problem for aquatic animals. A sleek, fusiform (torpedo-like) shape is a common adaptation of fast swimmers (see Figure 40.2).

Swimming occurs in diverse ways. Many insects and four-legged vertebrates use their legs as oars to push against the water. Sharks and bony fishes swim by moving their body and tail from side to side, while whales and dolphins move by undulating their body and tail up and down. Squids, scallops, and some cnidarians are jet-propelled, taking in water and squirting it out in bursts. In contrast, jellies appear to generate a region of low pressure in the water ahead of them such that they are pulled forward rather than pushed.

### Flying

Active flight (in contrast to gliding downward from a tree) has evolved in only a few animal groups: insects, reptiles (including birds), and, among the mammals, bats. One group of flying reptiles, the pterosaurs, died out millions of years ago, leaving birds and bats as the only flying vertebrates.

## Interpreting a Graph with Log Scales

**What Are the Energy Costs of Locomotion?** In the 1960s, animal physiologist Knut Schmidt-Nielsen, at Duke University, wondered whether general principles govern the energy costs of different forms of locomotion among diverse animal species. To answer this question, he drew on his own experiments as well as those of other researchers. In this exercise you will analyze the combined results of these studies and evaluate the rationale for plotting the experimental data on a graph with logarithmic scales.

**How the Experiments Were Done** Researchers measured the rate of oxygen consumption or carbon dioxide production in animals that ran on treadmills, swam in water flumes, or flew in wind tunnels. For example, a tube connected to a plastic face mask collected gases exhaled by a parakeet during flight (see photo). From these measurements, Schmidt-Nielsen calculated the amount of energy each animal used to transport a given amount of body mass over a given distance [calories/(kilogram · meter)].

**Data from the Experiments** Schmidt-Nielsen plotted the cost of running, flying, and swimming versus body mass on a single graph with logarithmic (log) scales for the axes. He then drew a best-fit straight line through the data points for each form of locomotion. (On the graph here, the individual data points are not shown.)

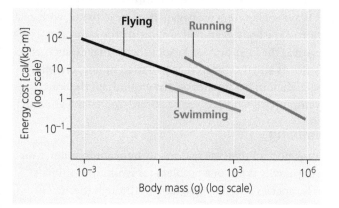

### INTERPRET THE DATA

1. The body masses of the animals used in these experiments ranged from about 0.001 g to 1,000,000 g, and their rates of energy use ranged from about 0.1 cal/(kg · m) to 100 cal/(kg · m). If you were to plot these data on a graph with linear instead of log scales for the axes, how would you draw the axes so that all of the data would be visible? What is the advantage of using log scales for plotting data with a wide range of values? (For additional information about graphs, see the Scientific Skills Review in Appendix F.)

2. Based on the graph, how much greater is the energy cost of flying for an animal that weighs $10^{-3}$ g than for an animal that weighs 1 g? For any given form of locomotion, which travels more efficiently, a larger animal or smaller animal?

3. The slopes of the flying and swimming lines are very similar. Based on your answer to question 2, if the energy cost of a 2-g swimming animal is 1.2 cal/(kg · m), what is the estimated energy cost of a 2-kg swimming animal?

4. Considering animals with a body mass of about 100 g, rank the three forms of locomotion from highest energy cost to lowest energy cost. Were these the results you expected, based on your own experience? What could explain the energy cost of running compared to that of flying or swimming?

5. Schmidt-Nielson calculated the swimming cost in a mallard duck and found that it was nearly 20 times as high as the swimming cost in a salmon of the same body mass. What could explain the greater swimming efficiency of salmon?

 **Instructors**: A version of this Scientific Skills Exercise can be assigned in MasteringBiology.

**Data from** K. Schmidt-Nielsen, Locomotion: Energy cost of swimming, flying, and running, *Science* 177:222–228 (1972). Reprinted with permission from AAAS.

---

 **Video: Soaring Hawk**

To fly, an animal's wings must develop enough lift to overcome gravity's downward force. The key to meeting this challenge is wing shape. All wings act as airfoils—structures whose shape alters air currents in a way that helps animals or airplanes stay aloft. As for the body to which the wings attach, a fusiform shape helps reduce drag in air as it does in water.

Flying animals are relatively light, with body masses ranging from less than a gram for some insects to about 20 kg for the largest flying birds. The low body mass of many flying animals is due to specialized structural adaptations. Birds, for example, have no urinary bladder or teeth and have relatively large bones with air-filled regions that help lessen the bird's weight (see Figure 34.30).

Flying, running, and swimming each impose different energetic demands on animals. In the **Scientific Skills Exercise**,

you can interpret a graph that compares the relative energy costs of these three forms of locomotion.

## CONCEPT CHECK 50.6

1. Contrast swimming and flying in terms of the main problems they pose and the adaptations that allow animals to overcome those problems.

2. **MAKE CONNECTIONS.** ➤ Peristalsis contributes to the locomotion of many annelids and to the movement of food in the digestive tract (see Concept 41.3). Using the muscles of your hand and a toothpaste tube as a model of peristalsis, how would your demonstration differ for the two processes?

3. **WHAT IF?** ➤ When using your arms to lower yourself into a chair, you bend your arms without using your biceps. Explain how this is possible. (Hint: Think about gravity as an antagonistic force.)

*For suggested answers, see Appendix A.*

# 50 Chapter Review

Go to **MasteringBiology**™ for Videos, Animations, Vocab Self-Quiz, Practice Tests, and more in the Study Area.

## SUMMARY OF KEY CONCEPTS

### CONCEPT 50.1

**Sensory receptors transduce stimulus energy and transmit signals to the central nervous system** (pp. 1106–1110)

VOCAB SELF-QUIZ
goo.gl/6u55ks

- The detection of a stimulus precedes **sensory transduction**, the change in the membrane potential of a **sensory receptor** in response to a stimulus. The resulting **receptor potential** controls transmission of action potentials to the CNS, where sensory information is integrated to generate **perceptions**. The frequency of action potentials in an axon and the number of axons activated determine stimulus strength. The identity of the axon carrying the signal encodes the nature or quality of the stimulus.
- **Mechanoreceptors** respond to stimuli such as pressure, touch, stretch, motion, and sound. **Chemoreceptors** detect either total solute concentrations or specific molecules. **Electromagnetic receptors** detect different forms of electromagnetic radiation. **Thermoreceptors** signal surface and core temperatures of the body. Pain is detected by a group of **nociceptors** that respond to excess heat, pressure, or specific classes of chemicals.

 *To simplify sensory receptor classification, why might it make sense to eliminate nociceptors as a distinct class?*

### CONCEPT 50.2

**In hearing and equilibrium, mechanoreceptors detect moving fluid or settling particles** (pp. 1110–1114)

- Most invertebrates sense their orientation with respect to gravity by means of **statocysts**. Specialized **hair cells** form the basis for hearing and balance in mammals and for detection of water movement in fishes and aquatic amphibians. In mammals, the **tympanic membrane** (eardrum) transmits sound waves to bones of the **middle ear**, which transmit the waves through the **oval window** to the fluid in the coiled **cochlea** of the **inner ear**. Pressure waves in the fluid vibrate the basilar membrane, depolarizing hair cells and triggering action potentials that travel via the auditory nerve to the brain. Receptors in the inner ear function in balance and equilibrium.

 *How are music volume and pitch encoded in signals to the brain?*

### CONCEPT 50.3

**The diverse visual receptors of animals depend on light-absorbing pigments** (pp. 1115–1121)

- Invertebrates have varied light detectors, including simple light-sensitive eyespots, image-forming **compound eyes**, and **single-lens eyes**. In the vertebrate eye, a single **lens** is used to focus light on **photoreceptors** in the **retina**. Both **rods** and **cones** contain a pigment, **retinal**, bonded to a protein (**opsin**). Absorption of light by retinal triggers a signal transduction pathway that hyperpolarizes the photoreceptors, causing them to release less neurotransmitter. Synapses transmit information from photoreceptors to cells that integrate information and convey it to the brain along axons that form the optic nerve.

 *How does processing of sensory information sent to the vertebrate brain in vision differ from that in hearing or olfaction?*

### CONCEPT 50.4

**The senses of taste and smell rely on similar sets of sensory receptors** (pp. 1121–1123)

- Taste (**gustation**) and smell (**olfaction**) depend on stimulation of chemoreceptors by small dissolved molecules. In humans, sensory cells in **taste buds** express a receptor type specific for one of the five taste perceptions: sweet, sour, salty, bitter, and umami (elicited by glutamate). Olfactory receptor cells line the upper part of the nasal cavity. More than 1,000 genes code for membrane proteins that bind to specific classes of **odorants**, and each receptor cell appears to express only one of those genes.

 *Why is the flavor of food less intense when you have a head cold?*

### CONCEPT 50.5

**The physical interaction of protein filaments is required for muscle function** (pp. 1123–1130)

- The muscle cells (fibers) of vertebrate **skeletal muscle** contain **myofibrils** composed of **thin filaments** of (mostly) actin and **thick filaments** of myosin. These filaments are organized into repeating units called **sarcomeres**. Myosin heads, energized by the hydrolysis of ATP, bind to the thin filaments, form cross-bridges, and then release upon binding ATP anew. As this cycle repeats, the thick and thin filaments slide past each other, shortening the sarcomere and contracting the muscle fiber.

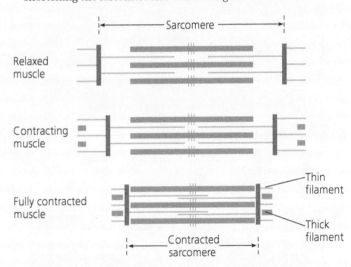

- Motor neurons release acetylcholine, triggering action potentials in muscle fibers that stimulate the release of $Ca^{2+}$ from the **sarcoplasmic reticulum**. When the $Ca^{2+}$ binds the **troponin complex, tropomyosin** moves, exposing the myosin-binding sites on actin and thus initiating cross-bridge formation. A **motor unit** consists of a motor neuron and the muscle fibers it controls. A twitch results from one action potential. Skeletal muscle fibers are **slow-twitch** or **fast-twitch** and oxidative or glycolytic.
- **Cardiac muscle**, found in the heart, consists of striated cells electrically connected by **intercalated disks**. Nervous system input controls the rate at which the heart contracts, but is not strictly required for cardiac muscle contraction. In **smooth muscles**, contractions are initiated by the muscles or by stimulation from neurons in the autonomic nervous system.

 *What are two major functions of ATP hydrolysis in skeletal muscle activity?*

## CONCEPT 50.6

### Skeletal systems transform muscle contraction into locomotion (pp. 1130–1134)

- Skeletal muscles, often in antagonistic pairs, contract and pull against the skeleton. Skeletons may be **hydrostatic** and maintained by fluid pressure, as in worms; hardened into **exoskeletons**, as in insects; or in the form of **endoskeletons**, as in vertebrates.
- Each form of **locomotion**—swimming, movement on land, or flying—presents a particular challenge. For example, swimmers need to overcome friction, but face less of a challenge from gravity than do animals that move on land or fly.

**?** *Explain how microscopic and macroscopic anchoring of muscle filaments enables you to bend your elbow.*

## TEST YOUR UNDERSTANDING

### Level 1: Knowledge/Comprehension

PRACTICE TEST
goo.gl/CUYGKD

1. Which of the following sensory receptors is *incorrectly* paired with its category?
   (A) hair cell—mechanoreceptor
   (B) snake pit organ—thermoreceptor
   (C) taste receptor—chemoreceptor
   (D) olfactory receptor—electromagnetic receptor

2. The middle ear converts
   (A) air pressure waves to fluid pressure waves.
   (B) air pressure waves to nerve impulses.
   (C) fluid pressure waves to nerve impulses.
   (D) pressure waves to hair cell movements.

3. During the contraction of a vertebrate skeletal muscle fiber, calcium ions
   (A) break cross-bridges as a cofactor in hydrolysis of ATP.
   (B) bind with troponin, changing its shape so that the myosin-binding sites on actin are exposed.
   (C) transmit action potentials from the motor neuron to the muscle fiber.
   (D) spread action potentials through the T tubules.

### Level 2: Application/Analysis

4. Which sensory distinction is *not* encoded by a difference in neuron identity?
   (A) white and red
   (B) red and green
   (C) loud and faint
   (D) salty and sweet

5. The transduction of sound waves into action potentials occurs
   (A) in the tectorial membrane as it is stimulated by hair cells.
   (B) when hair cells are bent against the tectorial membrane, causing them to depolarize and release neurotransmitter that stimulates sensory neurons.
   (C) as the basilar membrane vibrates at different frequencies in response to the varying volume of sounds.
   (D) within the middle ear as the vibrations are amplified by the malleus, incus, and stapes.

### Level 3: Synthesis/Evaluation

6. Although some sharks close their eyes just before they bite, their bites are on target. Researchers have noted that sharks often misdirect their bites at metal objects and that they can find batteries buried under sand. This evidence suggests that sharks keep track of their prey during the split second before they bite in the same way that
   (A) a rattlesnake finds a mouse in its burrow.
   (B) an insect avoids being stepped on.
   (C) a star-nosed mole locates its prey in tunnels.
   (D) a platypus locates its prey in a muddy river.

7. **DRAW IT** Based on the information in the text, fill in the following graph. Use one line for rods and another line for cones.

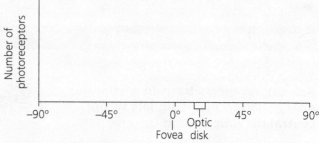

8. **EVOLUTION CONNECTION** In general, locomotion on land will require more energy than locomotion in water. By integrating what you learned about animal form and function in Unit 7, discuss some of the evolutionary adaptations of mammals that support the high energy requirements for moving on land.

9. **SCIENTIFIC INQUIRY: INTERPRET THE DATA** To help students appreciate how energy is stored in tendons during hopping, an instructor asked student volunteers to hop at a frequency that felt "natural" to them and then, after resting, to hop at exactly half that frequency. Hopping was done at a standard height and measurements were taken of mass, $O_2$ consumption, and $CO_2$ production. Here is a representative set of results calculated for one student.

| Frequency (hops/sec) | Energy used (joules/sec) |
|---|---|
| 1.85 | 735 |
| 0.92 | 716 |

The student consumed 159 joules/sec when standing. For each hop frequency, subtract this standing value from the energy used during hopping. Then divide by the hop frequency to calculate the energy cost per hop. How does the energy cost per hop differ at the two frequencies, and how might this be related to energy storage in tendons?

10. **WRITE ABOUT A THEME: ORGANIZATION** In a short essay (100–150 words), describe three ways in which the structure of the lens of the human eye is well adapted to its function in vision.

11. **SYNTHESIZE YOUR KNOWLEDGE**

Bloodhounds, which are adept at following a scent trail even days old, have no more olfactory receptor genes than other dogs. Predict how the sensory and nervous systems of bloodhounds differ from those of other dogs in ways that contribute to their tracking ability.

*For selected answers, see Appendix A.*

 For additional practice questions, check out the **Dynamic Study Modules** in MasteringBiology. You can use them to study on your smartphone, tablet, or computer anytime, anywhere!

# Animal Behavior

▲ Figure 51.1 **What prompts a male fiddler crab to display his giant claw?**

## KEY CONCEPTS

**51.1** Discrete sensory inputs can stimulate both simple and complex behaviors

**51.2** Learning establishes specific links between experience and behavior

**51.3** Selection for individual survival and reproductive success can explain diverse behaviors

**51.4** Genetic analyses and the concept of inclusive fitness provide a basis for studying the evolution of behavior

## The How and Why of Animal Activity

Unlike most animals, male fiddler crabs (genus *Uca*) are highly asymmetrical: One claw grows to giant proportions, up to half the mass of the entire body **(Figure 51.1)**. The name *fiddler* refers to the crab's behavior and appearance while feeding: As it grazes on algae, the crab moves the small claw to and from the mouth in front of the large claw, much like a musician playing a violin. However, at other times the male waves his large claw in the air. What triggers this behavior? What purpose does it serve?

Claw waving by a male fiddler crab has two functions. Waving the claw, which can be used as a weapon, helps the crab *repel* other males wandering too close to his burrow. Vigorous claw waving also helps him *attract* females, who wander through the crab colony in search of a mate. After the male fiddler crab lures a female to his burrow, he seals her in with mud or sand in preparation for mating.

Animal behavior, be it solitary or social, fixed or variable, is based on physiological systems and processes. An individual **behavior** is an action carried out by muscles under control of the nervous system. Examples include an animal using its throat muscles to produce a song, releasing a scent to mark its territory, or simply waving a claw. Behavior is an essential part of acquiring nutrients and finding a partner for sexual reproduction. Behavior also contributes to homeostasis, as when honeybees huddle to conserve heat (see Concept 40.3). In short, all of animal physiology contributes to behavior, and behavior influences all of physiology.

---

When you see this blue icon, log in to **MasteringBiology** and go to the Study Area for digital resources.

 Get Ready for This Chapter

Being essential for survival and reproduction, behavior is subject to substantial natural selection over time. This evolutionary process of selection also affects anatomy because the recognition and communication that underlie many behaviors depend on body form and appearance. Thus, the enlarged claw of the male fiddler crab is an adaptation that enables the display essential for recognition by other members of the species. Similarly, the positioning of the eyes on stalks held well above the crab's head enables him to see intruders from far off.

In this chapter, we'll examine how behavior is controlled, how it develops during an animal's life, and how it is influenced by genes and the environment. We'll also explore the ways in which behavior evolves over many generations. Shifting our focus from an animal's inner workings to its interactions with the outside world will set the stage for exploring ecology, the subject of Unit Eight.

# CONCEPT 51.1

## Discrete sensory inputs can stimulate both simple and complex behaviors

What approach do biologists use to determine how behaviors arise and what functions they serve? The Dutch scientist Niko Tinbergen, a pioneer in the study of animal behavior, suggested that understanding any behavior requires answering four questions, which can be summarized as follows:

1. What stimulus elicits the behavior, and what physiological mechanisms mediate the response?
2. How does the animal's experience during growth and development influence the response?
3. How does the behavior aid survival and reproduction?
4. What is the behavior's evolutionary history?

The first two questions ask about *proximate causation—how* a behavior occurs or is modified. The last two questions ask about *ultimate causation—why* a behavior occurs in the context of natural selection.

Studies on proximate causation by Tinbergen earned him a share of a Nobel Prize awarded in 1973. We'll consider those and related experiments in the early part of the chapter. The concept of ultimate causation is central to **behavioral ecology**, the study of the ecological and evolutionary basis for animal behavior. We'll explore this vibrant area of modern biological research in the rest of the chapter.

## Fixed Action Patterns

In addressing Tinbergen's first question, the nature of the stimuli that trigger behavior, we'll begin with behavioral responses to well-defined stimuli, starting with an example from one of Tinbergen's own experiments.

▼ **Figure 51.2 Sign stimuli in a classic fixed action pattern.** A male stickleback fish attacks other male sticklebacks that invade its nesting territory. The red belly of the intruding male (left) acts as a sign stimulus that releases the aggressive behavior.

? *Suggest an explanation for why this behavior evolved (its ultimate causation).*

As part of his research, Tinbergen kept fish tanks containing three-spined sticklebacks (*Gasterosteus aculeatus*), a species in which males, but not females, have red bellies. Male sticklebacks attack other males that invade their nesting territories **(Figure 51.2)**. Tinbergen noticed that his male sticklebacks also behaved aggressively when a red truck passed within view of their tank. Inspired by this chance observation, he carried out experiments showing that the red color of an intruder's underside is the proximate cause of the attack behavior. A male stickleback will not attack a fish lacking red coloration, but will attack even unrealistic models if they contain areas of red color.

The territorial response of male sticklebacks is an example of a **fixed action pattern**, a sequence of unlearned acts directly linked to a simple stimulus. Fixed action patterns are essentially unchangeable and, once initiated, are usually carried to completion. The trigger for the behavior is an external cue called a **sign stimulus**, such as a red object that prompts the male stickleback's aggressive behavior.

## Migration

Environmental stimuli not only trigger behaviors but also provide cues that animals use to carry out those behaviors. For example, a wide variety of birds, fishes, and other animals use environmental cues to guide **migration**—a regular, long-distance change in location **(Figure 51.3)**. In the course of migration, many animals pass through environments they have not previously encountered. How, then, do they find their way in these foreign settings?

Some migrating animals track their position relative to the sun, even though the sun's position relative to Earth changes throughout the day. Animals can adjust for these changes by means of a *circadian clock*, an internal mechanism that maintains a 24-hour activity rhythm or cycle (see Concept 49.2). For example, experiments have shown that migrating birds orient differently relative to the sun at distinct times of the day. Nocturnal animals can instead use the North Star, which has a constant position in the night sky.

**Figure 51.3 Migration.** Wildebeest herds migrate long distances twice each year, changing their feeding grounds in coordination with the dry and rainy seasons.

Although the sun and stars can provide useful clues for navigation, clouds can obscure these landmarks. How do migrating animals overcome this problem? A simple experiment with homing pigeons provided one answer. On an overcast day, placing a small magnet on the head of a homing pigeon prevented it from returning efficiently to its roost. Researchers concluded that pigeons sense their position relative to Earth's magnetic field and can thereby navigate without solar or celestial cues.

## Behavioral Rhythms

Although the circadian clock plays a small but significant role in navigation by some migrating species, it has a major role in the daily activity of all animals. As discussed in Concepts 40.2 and 49.2, the clock is responsible for a circadian rhythm, a daily cycle of rest and activity. The clock is normally synchronized with the light and dark cycles of the environment but can maintain rhythmic activity even under constant environmental conditions, such as during hibernation.

Some behaviors, such as migration and reproduction, reflect biological rhythms with a longer cycle, or period, than the circadian rhythm. Behavioral rhythms linked to the yearly cycle of seasons are called *circannual rhythms*. Although migration and reproduction typically correlate with food availability, these behaviors are not a direct response to changes in food intake. Instead, circannual rhythms, like circadian rhythms, are influenced by the periods of daylight

and darkness in the environment. For example, studies with several bird species have shown that an artificial environment with extended daylight can induce out-of-season migratory behavior.

Not all biological rhythms are linked to the light and dark cycles in the environment. Consider, for instance, the fiddler crab shown in Figure 51.1. The male's claw-waving courtship behavior is linked to the timing of the new and full moon. This timing helps the development of offspring. Fiddler crabs begin their lives as larvae settling in the mudflats. The tides disperse larvae to deeper waters, where they complete early development in relative safety before returning to the tidal flats. By courting at the time of the new or full moon, crabs link their reproduction to the times of greatest tidal movement.

## Animal Signals and Communication

Claw waving by fiddler crabs during courtship is an example of one animal (the male crab) generating the stimulus that guides the behavior of another animal (the female crab). A stimulus transmitted from one organism to another is called a **signal**. The transmission and reception of signals between animals constitute **communication**, which often has a role in the proximate causation of behavior.

 Video: Albatross Courtship Ritual
Video: Giraffe Courtship Ritual

### Forms of Animal Communication

Let's consider the courtship behavior of the fruit fly, *Drosophila melanogaster*, as an introduction to the four common modes of animal communication: visual, chemical, tactile, and auditory.

Fruit fly courtship constitutes a *stimulus-response chain*, in which the response to each stimulus is itself the stimulus for the next behavior. In the first step, a male detects a female in his field of vision and orients his body toward hers. To confirm she belongs to his species, he uses his olfactory system to detect chemicals she releases into the air. The male then approaches and touches the female with a foreleg **(Figure 51.4)**. This touching, or tactile communication, alerts the female to the male's presence.

**▼ Figure 51.4**
**Male fruit fly tapping female with foreleg.**

In the third stage of courtship, the male extends and vibrates one wing, producing a courtship song. This auditory communication informs the female whether he is of the same species. Only if all of these forms of communication are successful will the female allow the male to attempt copulation.

In general, the form of communication that evolves is closely related to an animal's lifestyle and environment. For example, most terrestrial mammals are nocturnal, which makes visual displays relatively ineffective. Instead, these species use olfactory and auditory signals, which work as well in the dark as in the light. In contrast, most birds are diurnal (active mainly in daytime) and communicate primarily by visual and auditory signals. Humans are also diurnal and, like birds, use primarily visual and auditory communication. We can thus detect and appreciate the songs and bright colors used by birds to communicate but miss many chemical cues on which other mammals base their behavior.

The information content of animal communication varies considerably. One of the most remarkable examples is the symbolic language of the European honeybee (*Apis mellifera*), discovered in the early 1900s by Austrian researcher Karl von Frisch. Using glass-walled observation hives, he and his students spent several decades observing honeybees. Methodical recordings of bee movements enabled von Frisch to decipher a "dance language" that returning foragers use to inform other bees about the distance and direction of travel to a source of nectar.

When a successful forager returns to the hive, its movements, as well as sounds and odors, quickly become the center of attention for other bees, called followers (Figure 51.5). Moving along the vertical wall of the honeycomb, the forager performs a "waggle dance" that communicates to the follower bees both the direction and distance of the food source in relation to the hive. In performing the dance, the bee follows a half-circle swing in one direction, a straight run during which it waggles its abdomen, and a half-circle swing in the other direction. What von Frisch and colleagues deduced was that the angle of the straight run relative to the hive's vertical surface indicates the horizontal angle of the food in relation to the sun. Thus, if the returning bee runs at a 30° angle to

the right of vertical, the follower bees leaving the hive fly 30° to the right of the horizontal direction of the sun.

How does the waggle dance communicate distance to the nectar source? It turns out that a dance with a longer straight run, and therefore more abdominal waggles per run, indicates a greater distance to the food found by the forager. As follower bees exit the hive, they fly almost directly to the area indicated by the waggle dance. By using flower odor and other clues, they locate the source of nectar within this area.

If the food source is close to the hive (less than 50 m away), the waggle dance takes a slightly different form that primarily advertises the availability of nectar nearby. In this form of the waggle dance, which von Frisch called "round," the returning bee moves in tight circles while moving its abdomen from side to side. In response, the follower bees leave the hive and search in all directions for nearby flowers rich in nectar.

▼ **Figure 51.5 Honeybee dance language.** Honeybees returning to the hive communicate the location of food sources through the symbolic language of a dance.

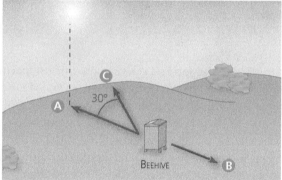

Worker bees cluster around a recently returned bee.

Location **A**: Food source is in same direction as sun.

Location **B**: Food source is in direction opposite sun.

Location **C**: Food source is 30° to right of sun.

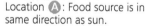

**The waggle dance performed when food is distant.** The waggle dance resembles a figure eight. Distance is indicated by the number of abdominal waggles performed in the straight-run part of the dance. Direction is indicated by the angle (in relation to the vertical surface of the hive) of the straight run.

**VISUAL SKILLS** ➤ *What information, if any, might be conveyed by the portions of the waggle dance between the straight runs? Explain.*

### Pheromones

Animals that communicate through odors or tastes emit chemical substances called **pheromones**. Pheromones are especially common among mammals and insects and often relate to reproductive behavior. For example, pheromones are the basis for the chemical communication in fruit fly courtship (see Figure 51.4). Pheromones are not limited to short-distance signaling, however. Male silkworm moths have receptors that can detect the pheromone from a female moth from several kilometers away (see Figure 50.6).

In a honeybee colony, pheromones produced by the queen and her daughters, the workers, maintain the hive's complex social order. One pheromone (once called the queen substance) has a particularly wide range of effects. It attracts workers to the queen, inhibits development of ovaries in workers, and attracts males (drones) to the queen during her mating flights out of the hive.

Pheromones can also serve as alarm signals. For example, when a minnow or catfish is injured, a substance released from the fish's skin disperses in the water, inducing a fright response in other fish. These nearby fish become more vigilant and often form tightly packed schools near the river or lake bottom, where they are safer from attack **(Figure 51.6)**. Pheromones can be very effective at remarkably low concentrations. For instance, just 1 cm$^2$ of skin from a fathead minnow contains sufficient alarm substance to induce a reaction in 58,000 L of water.

So far in this chapter, we have explored the types of stimuli that elicit behaviors—the first part of Tinbergen's first question. The second part of that question—the physiological mechanisms that mediate responses—involves the nervous, muscular, and skeletal systems: Stimuli activate sensory systems, are processed in the central nervous system, and result in motor outputs that constitute behavior. Thus, we are ready to focus on Tinbergen's second question—how experience influences behavior.

▼ **Figure 51.6 Minnows responding to the presence of an alarm substance.**

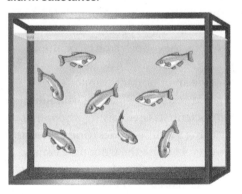

**1** Minnows are widely dispersed in an aquarium before an alarm substance is introduced.

**2** Within seconds of the alarm substance being introduced, minnows aggregate near the bottom of the aquarium and reduce their movement.

### CONCEPT CHECK 51.1

1. If an egg rolls out of the nest, a mother greylag goose will retrieve it by nudging it with her beak and head. If researchers remove the egg or substitute a ball during this process, the goose continues to bob her beak and head while she moves back to the nest. Explain how and why this behavior occurs.

2. **WHAT IF?** ➤ Suppose you exposed various fish species from the minnows' environment to the alarm substance from minnows. Thinking about natural selection, suggest why some species might respond like minnows, some might increase their activity, and some might show no change.

3. **MAKE CONNECTIONS** ➤ How is the lunar-linked rhythm of fiddler crab courtship similar in mechanism and function to the seasonal timing of plant flowering? (See Concept 39.3.)

*For suggested answers, see Appendix A.*

## CONCEPT 51.2

# Learning establishes specific links between experience and behavior

For some behaviors—such as a fixed action pattern, a courtship stimulus-response chain, or pheromone signaling—nearly all individuals in a population behave alike. Behavior that is developmentally fixed in this way is known as **innate behavior**. Other behaviors, however, vary with experience and thus differ between individuals.

## Experience and Behavior

Tinbergen's second question asks how an animal's experiences during growth and development influence the response to stimuli. One informative approach to this question is a **cross-fostering study**, in which the young of one species are placed in the care of adults from another species in the same or a similar environment. The extent to which the offspring's behavior changes in such a situation provides a measure of how the social and physical environment influences behavior.

Certain mouse species have behaviors well suited for cross-fostering studies. Male California mice (*Peromyscus*

**Table 51.1   Influence of Cross-Fostering on Male Mice***

| Species | Aggression Toward an Intruder | Aggression In Neutral Situation | Paternal Behavior |
|---|---|---|---|
| California mice fostered by white-footed mice | Reduced | No difference | Reduced |
| White-footed mice fostered by California mice | No difference | Increased | No difference |

*Comparisons are with mice raised by parents of their own species.

*californicus*) are highly aggressive toward other mice and provide extensive parental care. In contrast, male white-footed mice (*Peromyscus leucopus*) are less aggressive and engage in little parental care. When the pups of each species were placed in the nests of the other species, the cross-fostering altered some behaviors of both species **(Table 51.1)**. For instance, male California mice raised by white-footed mice were less aggressive toward intruders. Thus, experience during development can strongly influence aggressive behavior in these rodents.

One of the most important findings of the cross-fostering experiments with mice was that the influence of experience on behavior can be passed on to progeny: When the cross-fostered California mice became parents, they spent less time retrieving offspring who wandered off than did California mice raised by their own species. Thus, experience during development can modify physiology in a way that alters parental behavior, extending the influence of environment to a subsequent generation.

For humans, the influence of genetics and environment on behavior can be explored by a **twin study**, in which researchers compare the behavior of identical twins raised apart with the behavior of those raised in the same household. Twin studies have been instrumental in studying disorders that alter human behavior, such as anxiety disorders, schizophrenia, and alcoholism.

▼ **Identical twins who were raised separately.**

## Learning

One powerful way that an animal's environment can influence its behavior is through **learning**, the modification of behavior as a result of specific experiences. The capacity for learning depends on nervous system organization established during development following instructions encoded in the genome. Learning itself involves the formation of memories by specific changes in neuronal connectivity (see Concept 49.4). Therefore, the essential challenge for research into learning is not to decide between nature (genes) and nurture (environment), but rather to explore the contributions of *both* nature and nurture in shaping learning and, more generally, behavior.

### *Imprinting*

In some species, the ability of offspring to recognize and be recognized by a parent is essential for survival. In the young, this learning often takes the form of **imprinting**, the establishment of a long-lasting behavioral response to a particular individual or object. Imprinting can take place only during a specific time period in development, called the **sensitive period**. Among gulls, for instance, the sensitive period for a parent to bond with its young lasts one to two days. During the sensitive period, the young imprint on their parent and learn basic behaviors, while the parent learns to recognize its offspring. If bonding does not occur, the parent will not care for the offspring, leading to the death of the offspring and a decrease in the reproductive success of the parent.

How do the young know on whom—or what—to imprint? Experiments with many species of waterfowl indicate that young birds have no innate recognition of "mother." Rather, they identify with the first object they encounter that has certain key characteristics. In the 1930s, experiments showed that the principal imprinting stimulus in greylag geese (*Anser anser*) is a nearby object that is moving away from the young. When incubator-hatched goslings spent their first few hours with a person rather than with a goose, they imprinted on the human and steadfastly followed that person from then on **(Figure 51.7)**. Furthermore, they showed no recognition of their biological mother.

Imprinting has become an important component of efforts to save endangered species, such as the whooping crane (*Grus americana*). Scientists tried raising whooping cranes in captivity by using sandhill cranes (*Grus canadensis*) as foster parents. However, because the whooping cranes imprinted on their foster parents, none formed a *pair-bond* (strong attachment) with a whooping crane mate. To avoid such problems, captive breeding programs now isolate young cranes, exposing them to the sights and sounds of members of their own species.

Until recently, scientists made further use of imprinting to teach cranes born in captivity to migrate along safe routes. Young whooping cranes were imprinted on humans in "crane suits" and then allowed to follow these "parents" as they flew ultralight aircraft along selected migration routes. Beginning in 2016, efforts shifted to a focus on minimizing human intervention as part of an overall strategy aimed at fostering self-sustaining crane populations.

## Figure 51.7 **Imprinting.** Young graylag geese imprinted on a man.

WHAT IF? ➤ *Suppose the geese shown in (a) were bred to each other. How might their imprinting on a human affect their offspring? Explain.*

 Video: Ducklings

## Spatial Learning and Cognitive Maps

Every natural environment has spatial variation, as in locations of nest sites, hazards, food, and prospective mates. Therefore, an organism's fitness may be enhanced by the capacity for **spatial learning**, the establishment of a memory that reflects the environment's spatial structure.

The idea of spatial learning intrigued Tinbergen while he was a graduate student in the Netherlands. At that time, he was studying females of a digger wasp species (*Philanthus triangulum*) that nests in small burrows dug into sand dunes. When a wasp leaves her nest to go hunting, she hides the entrance from potential intruders by covering it with sand. When she returns, however, she flies directly to her hidden nest, despite the presence of hundreds of other burrows in the area. How does she accomplish this feat? Tinbergen hypothesized that a wasp locates her nest by learning its position relative to visible landmarks. To test his hypothesis, he carried out an experiment in the wasps' natural habitat **(Figure 51.8)**. By manipulating objects around nest entrances, he demonstrated that digger wasps engage in spatial learning. This experiment was so simple and

## Figure 51.8

### Inquiry Does a digger wasp use landmarks to find her nest?

**Experiment** A female digger wasp covers the entrance to her nest while foraging for food, but finds the correct wasp nest reliably upon her return 30 minutes or more later. Niko Tinbergen wanted to test the hypothesis that a wasp learns visual landmarks that mark her nest before she leaves on hunting trips. First, he marked one nest with a ring of pinecones while the wasp was in the burrow. After leaving the nest to forage, the wasp returned to the nest successfully.

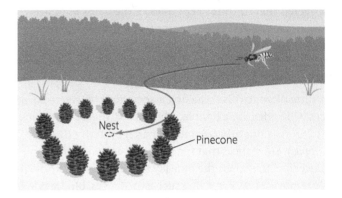

Two days later, after the wasp had again left, Tinbergen shifted the ring of pinecones away from the nest. Then he waited to observe the wasp's behavior.

**Results** When the wasp returned, she flew to the center of the pinecone circle instead of to the nearby nest. Repeating the experiment with many wasps, Tinbergen obtained the same results.

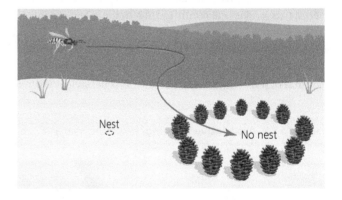

**Conclusion** The experiment supported the hypothesis that digger wasps use visual landmarks to keep track of their nests.

**Data from** N. Tinbergen, *The Study of Instinct,* Clarendon Press, Oxford (1951).

WHAT IF? ➤ *Suppose the digger wasp had returned to her original nest site, despite the pinecones having been moved. What alternative hypotheses might you propose regarding how the wasp finds her nest and why the pinecones didn't misdirect the wasp?*

 Animation: Digger Wasps and Landmarks

informative that it could be summarized very concisely. In fact, at 32 pages, Tinbergen's Ph.D. thesis from 1932 is still the shortest ever approved at Leiden University.

In some animals, spatial learning involves formulating a **cognitive map**, a representation in an animal's nervous system of the spatial relationships between objects in its surroundings. One striking example is found in the Clark's nutcracker (*Nucifraga columbiana*), a relative of ravens, crows, and jays. In the fall, nutcrackers hide pine seeds for retrieval during the winter. By experimentally varying the distance between landmarks in the birds' environment, researchers discovered that the birds kept track of the halfway point between landmarks, rather than a fixed distance, to find their hidden food stores.

### Associative Learning

Learning often involves making associations between experiences. Consider, for example, a blue jay (*Cyanocitta cristata*) that ingests a brightly colored monarch butterfly (*Danaus plexippus*). Substances that the monarch accumulates from milkweed plants cause the blue jay to vomit almost immediately **(Figure 51.9)**. Following such experiences, blue jays avoid attacking monarchs and similar-looking butterflies. The ability to associate one environmental feature (such as a color) with another (such as a foul taste) is called **associative learning**.

Associative learning is well suited to study in the laboratory. Such studies typically involve either classical conditioning or operant conditioning. In *classical conditioning*, an arbitrary stimulus becomes associated with a particular outcome. Russian physiologist Ivan Pavlov carried out early experiments in classical conditioning, demonstrating that if he always rang a bell just before feeding a dog, the dog would eventually salivate when the bell sounded, anticipating food. In *operant conditioning*, also called trial-and-error learning, an animal first learns to associate one of its behaviors with a

▼ **Figure 51.9 Associative learning.** Having ingested and vomited a monarch butterfly, a blue jay has probably learned to avoid this species.

reward or punishment and then tends to repeat or avoid that behavior (see Figure 51.9). B. F. Skinner, an American pioneer in the study of operant conditioning, explored this process in the laboratory by, for example, having a rat learn through trial and error to obtain food by pressing a lever.

Studies reveal that animals can learn to link many pairs of features of their environment, but not all. For example, pigeons can learn to associate danger with a sound but not with a color. However, they can learn to associate a color with food. What does this mean? The development and organization of the pigeon's nervous system apparently restrict the associations that can be formed. Moreover, such restrictions are not limited to birds. Rats, for example, can learn to avoid illness-inducing foods on the basis of smells, but not on the basis of sights or sounds.

If we consider how behavior evolves, the fact that some animals can't learn to make particular associations appears logical. The associations an animal can readily form typically reflect relationships likely to occur in nature. Conversely, associations that can't be formed are those unlikely to be of selective advantage in a native environment. In the case of a rat's diet in the wild, for example, a harmful food is far more likely to have a certain odor than to be associated with a particular sound.

### Cognition and Problem Solving

The most complex forms of learning involve **cognition**—the process of knowing that involves awareness, reasoning, recollection, and judgment. Although it was once argued that only primates and certain marine mammals have high-level thought processes, many other groups of animals, including insects, appear to exhibit cognition in controlled laboratory studies. For example, an experiment using Y-shaped mazes provided evidence for abstract thinking in honeybees. One maze had different colors, and one had different black-and-white striped patterns, either vertical or horizontal bars. Two groups of honeybees were trained in the color maze. Upon entering, a bee would see a sample color and could then choose between an arm of the maze with the same color or an arm with a different color. Only one arm contained a food reward. The first group of bees were rewarded for flying into the arm with the *same* color as the sample **(Figure 51.10, ❶)**; the second group were rewarded for choosing the arm with the *different* color. Next, bees from each group were tested in the bar maze, which had no food reward. After encountering a sample black-and-white pattern of bars, a bee could choose an arm with the same pattern or an arm with a different pattern. The bees in the first group most often chose the arm with the same pattern **(Figure 51.10, ❷)**, whereas those in the second group typically chose the arm with the different pattern.

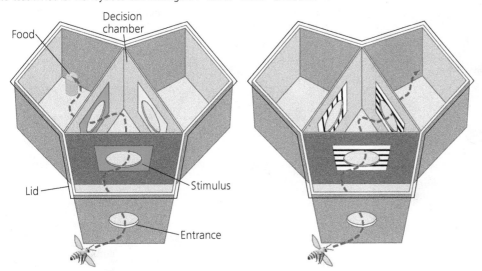

▼ **Figure 51.10 A maze test of abstract thinking by honeybees.** These mazes are designed to test whether honeybees can distinguish "same" from "different."

Food

Decision chamber

Lid

Stimulus

Entrance

**❶ Bees were trained in a color maze.** As shown here, one group were rewarded for choosing the same color as the stimulus.

**❷ Bees were tested in a pattern maze.** If previously rewarded for choosing the same color, bees most often chose lines oriented the same way as the stimulus.

**VISUAL SKILLS ➤** *Describe how you would set up the pattern maze to control for an inherent preference for or against a particular orientation of the black bars.*

The maze experiments provide strong experimental support for the hypothesis that honeybees can distinguish on the basis of "same" and "different." Remarkably, research published in 2010 indicates that honeybees can also learn to distinguish between human faces.

The information-processing ability of a nervous system can also be revealed in **problem solving**, the cognitive activity of devising a method to proceed from one state to another in the face of real or apparent obstacles. For example, if a chimpanzee is placed in a room with several boxes on the floor and a banana hung high out of reach, the chimpanzee can assess the situation and stack the boxes, enabling it to reach the food. Problem-solving behavior is highly developed in some mammals, especially primates and dolphins. Notable examples have also been observed in some bird species, especially corvids. In one study, ravens were confronted with food hanging from a branch by a string. After failing to grab the food in flight, one raven flew to the branch and alternately pulled up and stepped on the string until the food was within reach. A number of other ravens eventually arrived at similar solutions. Nevertheless, some ravens failed to solve the problem, indicating that problem-solving success in this species, as in others, varies with individual experience and abilities.

### Development of Learned Behaviors

Most of the learned behaviors we have discussed develop over a relatively short time. Some behaviors develop more gradually. For example, some bird species learn songs in stages.

In the case of the white-crowned sparrow (*Zonotrichia leucophrys*), the first stage of song learning takes place early in life, when the fledgling sparrow first hears the song. If a fledgling is prevented from hearing real sparrows or recordings of sparrow songs during the first 50 days of its life, it fails to develop the adult song of its species. Although the young bird does not sing during the sensitive period, it memorizes the song of its species by listening to other white-crowned sparrows sing. During the sensitive period, fledglings chirp more in response to songs of their own species than to songs of other species. Thus, when young white-crowned sparrows learn the songs they will sing later on, that learning appears to be bounded by genetically controlled preferences.

The sensitive period when a white-crowned sparrow memorizes its species' song is followed by a second learning phase when the juvenile bird sings tentative notes called a subsong. The juvenile bird hears its own singing and compares it with the song memorized during the sensitive period. Once a sparrow's own song matches the one it memorized, the song "crystallizes" as the final song, and the bird sings only this adult song for the rest of its life.

The song-learning process can be quite different in other bird species. Canaries, for example, do not have a single sensitive period for song learning. A young canary begins with a subsong, but the full song does not crystallize in the same way as in white-crowned sparrows. Between breeding seasons, the song becomes flexible again, and an adult male may learn new song "syllables" each year, adding to the song it already sings.

Song learning is one of many examples of how animals learn from other members of their species. In finishing our exploration of learning, we'll look at several more examples that reflect the more general phenomenon of social learning.

### Social Learning

Many animals learn to solve problems by observing the behavior of other individuals. This type of learning through observing others is called **social learning**. Young wild chimpanzees, for example, learn how to crack open oil

**▼ Figure 51.11 A young chimpanzee learning to crack oil palm nuts by observing an experienced elder.**

 Video: Chimp Cracking Nut

palm nuts with two stones by copying experienced chimpanzees (**Figure 51.11**).

Another example of how social learning can modify behavior comes from studies of the vervet monkeys (*Chlorocebus pygerythrus*) in Amboseli National Park, Kenya. Vervet monkeys, which are about the size of a domestic cat, produce a complex set of alarm calls. Amboseli vervets give distinct alarm calls for leopards, eagles, and snakes. When a vervet sees a leopard, it gives a loud barking sound; when it sees an eagle, it gives a short double-syllable cough; and the snake alarm call is a "chutter." Upon hearing a particular alarm call, other vervets in the group behave in an appropriate way: They run up a tree on hearing the alarm for a leopard (vervets are nimbler than leopards in the trees); look up on hearing the alarm for an eagle; and look down on hearing the alarm for a snake (**Figure 51.12**).

Infant vervet monkeys give alarm calls, but in a relatively undiscriminating way. For example, they give the "eagle" alarm on seeing any bird, including harmless birds such as bee-eaters. With age, the monkeys improve their accuracy. In fact, adult vervet monkeys give the eagle alarm only on seeing an eagle belonging to either of the two species that eat vervets. Infants probably learn how to give the right call by observing other members of the group and receiving social confirmation. For instance, if the infant gives the call on the right occasion—say, an eagle alarm when there is an eagle overhead—another member of the group will also give the eagle call. But if the infant gives the call when a bee-eater flies by, the adults in the group are silent. Thus, vervet monkeys have an initial, unlearned tendency to give calls upon seeing potentially threatening objects in the environment. Learning fine-tunes the call so that adult vervets give calls only in response to genuine danger and can fine-tune the alarm calls of the next generation.

Social learning forms the roots of **culture**, a system of information transfer through social learning or teaching

**▼ Figure 51.12 Vervet monkeys learning correct use of alarm calls.** On seeing a python (foreground), vervet monkeys give a distinct "snake" alarm call (inset), and the members of the group stand upright and look down.

that influences the behavior of individuals in a population. Cultural transfer of information can alter behavioral phenotypes and thereby influence the fitness of individuals.

Changes in behavior that result from natural selection occur on a much longer time scale than does learning. In Concept 51.3, we'll examine the relationship between particular behaviors and the processes of selection related to survival and reproduction.

### CONCEPT CHECK 51.2

1. How might associative learning explain why different species of distasteful or stinging insects have similar colors?

2. **WHAT IF?** ➤ How might you position and manipulate a few objects in a lab to test whether an animal can use a cognitive map to remember the location of a food source?

3. **MAKE CONNECTIONS** ➤ How might a learned behavior contribute to speciation? (See Concept 24.1.)

*For suggested answers, see Appendix A.*

## CONCEPT 51.3

# Selection for individual survival and reproductive success can explain diverse behaviors

**EVOLUTION** We turn now to Tinbergen's third question—how behavior enhances survival and reproduction in a population. The focus thus shifts from proximate causation—the "how" questions—to ultimate causation—the "why" questions. We'll begin by considering the activity of gathering food. Food-obtaining behavior, or **foraging**, includes not only eating but also any activities an animal uses to search for, recognize, and capture food items.

## Evolution of Foraging Behavior

The fruit fly allows us to examine one way that foraging behavior might have evolved. Variation in a gene called *forager* (*for*) dictates how far *Drosophila* larvae travel when foraging. On average, larvae carrying the *for*$^R$ ("Rover") allele travel nearly twice as far while foraging as do larvae with the *for*$^s$ ("sitter") allele.

Both the *for*$^R$ and *for*$^s$ alleles are present in natural populations. What circumstances might favor one or the other allele? The answer became apparent in experiments that maintained flies at either low or high population densities for many generations. Larvae in populations kept at a low density foraged over shorter distances than those in populations kept at high density **(Figure 51.13)**. Furthermore, the *for*$^s$ allele increased in frequency in the low-density populations, whereas the *for*$^R$ allele increased in frequency in the high-density group. These changes make sense. At a low population density, short-distance foraging yields sufficient food, while long-distance foraging would result in unnecessary energy expenditure. Under crowded conditions, long-distance foraging could enable larvae to move beyond areas depleted of food. Thus, an interpretable evolutionary change in behavior occurred in the course of the experiment.

▼ **Figure 51.13 Evolution of foraging behavior by laboratory populations of *Drosophila melanogaster*.** After 74 generations of living at low population density, *Drososphila* larvae (populations R1–R3) followed foraging paths significantly shorter than those of *Drososphila* larvae that had lived at high density (populations K1–K3).

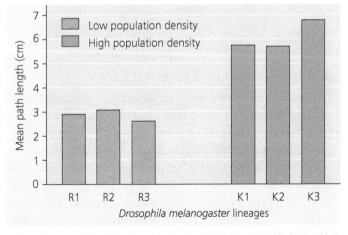

**INTERPRET THE DATA** ➤ *What alternative hypothesis is made far less likely by having three R and K lines, rather than one of each?*

### Optimal Foraging Model

To study the ultimate causation of foraging strategies, biologists sometimes apply a type of cost-benefit analysis used in economics. This idea proposes that foraging behavior is a compromise between the benefits of nutrition and the costs of obtaining food. These costs might include the energy expenditure of foraging as well as the risk of being eaten while foraging. According to this **optimal foraging model**, natural selection should favor a foraging behavior that minimizes the costs of foraging and maximizes the benefits. The **Scientific Skills Exercise** provides an example of how this model can be applied to animals in the wild.

### Balancing Risk and Reward

One of the most significant potential costs to a forager is risk of predation. Maximizing energy gain and minimizing energy costs are of little benefit if the behavior makes the forager a likely meal for a predator. It seems logical, therefore, that predation risk would influence foraging behavior. Such appears to be the case for the mule deer (*Odocoileus hemionus*), which lives in the mountains of western North America. Researchers found that the food available for mule deer was fairly uniform across the potential foraging areas, although somewhat lower in open, nonforested areas. In contrast, the risk of predation differed greatly; mountain lions (*Puma concolor*), the major predator, killed large numbers of mule deer at forest edges and only a small number in open areas and forest interiors.

How does mule deer foraging behavior reflect the differences in predation risk in particular areas? Mule deer feed predominantly in open areas. Thus, it appears that mule deer foraging behavior reflects the large variation in predation risk and not the smaller variation in food availability. This result underscores the point that behavior typically reflects a compromise between competing selective pressures.

## Mating Behavior and Mate Choice

Just as foraging is crucial for individual survival, mating behavior and mate choice play a major role in determining reproductive success. These behaviors include seeking or attracting mates, choosing among potential mates, competing for mates, and caring for offspring.

### Mating Systems and Sexual Dimorphism

Although we tend to think of mating simply as the union of a male and female, species vary greatly with regard to *mating systems*, the length and number of relationships between males and females. In some animal species, mating is *promiscuous*, with no strong pair-bonds. In others, mates form a relationship of some duration that is **monogamous** (one male mating

## Testing a Hypothesis with a Quantitative Model

**Do Crows Display Optimal Foraging Behavior?** On islands off British Columbia, Canada, Northwestern crows (*Corvus caurinus*) search rocky tide pools for sea snails called whelks. After spotting a whelk, the crow picks it up in its beak, flies upward, and drops the whelk onto the rocks. If the drop is successful, the shell breaks and the crow can dine on the whelk's soft parts. If not, the crow flies up and drops the whelk again and again until the shell breaks. What determines how high the crow flies? If energetic considerations dominated selection for the crow's foraging behavior, the average drop height might reflect a trade-off between the cost of flying higher and the benefit of more frequent success. In this exercise you'll test how well this optimal foraging model predicts the average drop height observed in nature.

**How the Experiments Were Done** The height of drops made by crows in the wild was measured by referring to a marked pole erected nearby. In the test, the crow's behavior was simulated using a device that dropped a whelk onto the rocks from a fixed platform. The average number of drops required to break whelks from various platform heights was recorded and averaged over many trials with the device. Combining the data for each platform height, total "flight" height was calculated by multiplying the height times the average number of drops required.

### Data from the Experiment

The graph summarizes the results of the experiment.

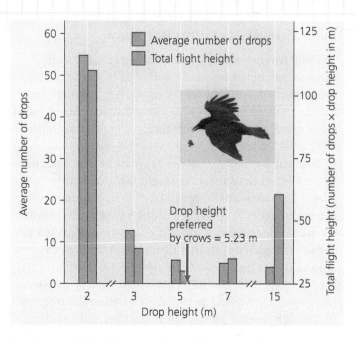

Data from R. Zach, Shell-dropping: Decision-making and optimal foraging in northwestern crows, *Behavior* 68:106–117 (1979).

### INTERPRET THE DATA

1. How does the average number of drops required to break open a whelk depend on platform height for a drop of 5 meters or less? For drops of more than 5 meters?

2. Total flight height can be considered to be a measure of the total energy required to break open a whelk. Why is this value lower for a platform set at 5 meters than for one at 2 or 15 meters?

3. Compare the drop height preferred by crows with the graph of total flight height for the platform drops. Are the data consistent with the hypothesis of optimal foraging? Explain.

4. In testing the optimal foraging model, it was assumed that changing the height of the drop only changed the total energy required. Do you think this is a realistic limitation, or might other factors than total energy be affected by height?

5. Researchers observed that the crows only gather and drop the largest whelks. What are some reasons crows might favor larger whelks?

6. It turned out that the probability of a whelk breaking was the same for a whelk dropped for the first time as for an unbroken whelk dropped several times previously. If the probability of breaking instead increased, what change might you predict in the crow's behavior?

**Instructors:** A version of this Scientific Skills Exercise can be assigned in MasteringBiology.

---

with one female) or **polygamous** (an individual of one sex mating with several of the other). Polygamous relationships involve either *polygyny*, a single male and many females, or *polyandry*, a single female and multiple males.

The extent to which males and females differ in appearance, a characteristic known as *sexual dimorphism*, typically varies with the type of mating system (**Figure 51.14**). Among monogamous species, males and females often look very similar. In contrast, among polygamous species, the sex that attracts multiple mating partners is typically showier and larger than the opposite sex. We'll discuss the evolutionary basis of these differences shortly.

## Mating Systems and Parental Care

The needs of the young are an important factor constraining the evolution of mating systems. Most newly hatched birds, for instance, cannot care for themselves. Rather, they require a large, continuous food supply, a need that is difficult for a single parent to meet. In such cases, a male that stays with and helps a single mate may ultimately have more viable offspring than it would by going off to seek additional mates. This may explain why many birds are monogamous. In contrast, for birds with young that can feed and care for themselves almost immediately after hatching, the males derive less benefit from staying

## Figure 51.14 Relationship between mating system and male and female forms.

### (a) Monogamy (one male, one female)

In monogamous species, such as these western gulls (*Larus occidentalis*), males and females are often difficult to distinguish using external characteristics only.

### (b) Polygyny (one male, multiple females)

Among polygynous species, such as elk (*Cervus canadensis*), the male (right) is often highly ornamented.

### (c) Polyandry (one female, multiple males)

In polyandrous species, such as these red-necked phalaropes (*Phalaropus lobatus*), females (right) are generally more ornamented than males.

with their partner. Males of these species, such as pheasants and quail, can maximize their reproductive success by seeking other mates, and polygyny is relatively common in such birds. In the case of mammals, the lactating female is often the only food source for the young, and males usually play no role in raising the young. In mammalian species where males protect the females and young, such as lions, a male or small group of males typically cares for a harem of many females.

Another factor influencing mating behavior and parental care is *certainty of paternity*. Young born to or eggs laid by a female definitely contain that female's genes. However, even within a normally monogamous relationship, a male other than the female's usual mate may have fathered that female's offspring. The certainty of paternity is relatively low in most species with internal fertilization because the acts of mating and birth (or mating and egg laying) are separated over time. This could explain why exclusively male parental care is rare in bird and mammal species. However, the males of many species with internal fertilization engage in behaviors that appear to increase their certainty of paternity. These behaviors include guarding females, removing any sperm from the female reproductive tract before copulation, and introducing large quantities of sperm that displace the sperm of other males.

Certainty of paternity is high when egg laying and mating occur together, as in external fertilization. This may explain why parental care in aquatic invertebrates, fishes, and amphibians, when it occurs at all, is at least as likely to be by males as by females (**Figure 51.15**; see also Figure 46.6). Among fishes and amphibians, parental care occurs in fewer than 10% of species with internal fertilization but in more than half of species with external fertilization.

It is important to point out that certainty of paternity does not mean that animals are aware of those factors when they behave a certain way. Parental behavior correlated with

## Figure 51.15 Paternal care by a male jawfish.

The male jawfish, which lives in tropical marine environments, holds the eggs it has fertilized in its mouth, keeping them aerated and protecting them from egg predators until the young hatch.

certainty of paternity exists because it has been reinforced over generations by natural selection. The intriguing relationship between certainty of paternity and male parental care remains an area of active research.

## Sexual Selection and Mate Choice

Sexual dimorphism results from sexual selection, a form of natural selection in which differences in reproductive success among individuals are a consequence of differences in mating success (see Concept 23.4). Sexual selection can take the form of *intersexual selection*, in which members of one sex choose mates on the basis of characteristics of the other sex, such as courtship songs, or *intrasexual selection*, which involves competition between members of one sex for mates.

**Mate Choice by Females**  Mate preferences of females may play a central role in the evolution of male behavior and anatomy through intersexual selection. Consider, for example, the courtship behavior of stalk-eyed flies. The eyes of these insects are at the tips of stalks, which are longer in males than in females. During courtship, a male approaches the female headfirst. Researchers have shown that females are more likely to mate with males that have relatively long eyestalks. Why would females favor this seemingly arbitrary trait? Ornaments such as long eyestalks in these flies and bright coloration in birds correlate in general with health and vitality. A female whose mate choice is a healthy male is likely to produce more offspring that survive to reproduce. As a result, males may compete with each other in ritualized contests to attract female attention **(Figure 51.16)**. In faceoffs between male stalkeyed flies, the male whose eyestalk length is smaller usually retreats peacefully.

◀ **Figure 51.17 Appearance of zebra finches in nature.** The male zebra finch (left) is more highly patterned and colorful than the female zebra finch.

Mate choice can also be influenced by imprinting, as revealed by experiments carried out with zebra finches (*Taeniopygia guttata*). Both male and female zebra finches normally lack any feather crest on their head **(Figure 51.17)**. To explore whether parental appearance affects mate preference in offspring independent of any genetic influence, researchers provided zebra finches with artificial ornamentation. A 2.5-cm-long red feather was taped to the forehead feathers of either or both zebra finch parents when their chicks were 8 days old, approximately 2 days before they opened their eyes. A control group of zebra finches was raised by unadorned parents. When the chicks matured, they were presented with prospective mates that were either artificially ornamented with a red feather or non-ornamented **(Figure 51.18)**. Males showed

▼ **Figure 51.16 A face-off between male stalk-eyed flies competing for female attention.**

▼ **Figure 51.18 Sexual selection influenced by imprinting.** Experiments demonstrated that female zebra finch chicks that had imprinted on artificially ornamented fathers preferred ornamented males as adult mates. For all experimental groups, male offspring showed no preference for either ornamented or non-ornamented female mates.

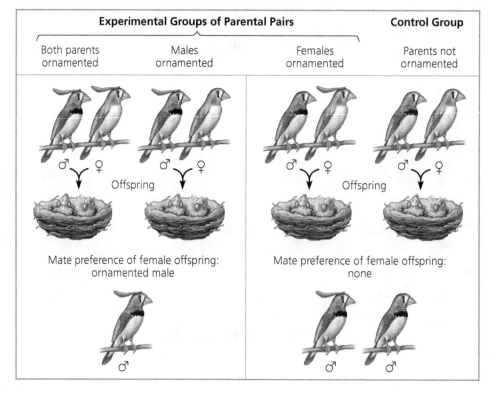

no preference. Females raised by a male parent that was not ornamented also showed no preference. However, females raised by an ornamented male parent preferred ornamented males as their own mates. Thus, female finches apparently take cues from their fathers in choosing mates.

**Mate-choice copying**, a behavior in which individuals in a population copy the mate choice of others, has been studied in the guppy, *Poecilia reticulata*. When a female guppy chooses between males with no other females present, the female almost always chooses the male with more orange coloration. To explore if the behavior of other females could influence this preference, an experiment was set up using both living females and artificial model females **(Figure 51.19)**. If a female guppy observed the model "courting" a male with less extensive orange markings, she often copied the preference of the model female. That is, the female chose the male that had been presented in association with a model female rather than a more orange alternative. The exceptions were also informative. Mate-choice behavior typically did not change when the difference in coloration was particularly large. Mate-choice copying can thus mask genetically controlled female preference below a certain threshold of difference, in this case for male color.

Mate-choice copying, a form of social learning, has also been observed in several other fish and bird species. What is the selective pressure for such a mechanism? One possibility is that a female that mates with males that are attractive to other females increases the probability that her male offspring will also be attractive and have high reproductive success.

**Male Competition for Mates**   The previous examples show how female choice can select for one best type of male in a given situation, resulting in low variation among males. Similarly, male competition for mates can reduce variation among males. Such competition may involve *agonistic behavior*, an often-ritualized contest that determines which competitor gains access to a resource, such as food or a mate **(Figure 51.20**; see also Figure 51.16).

Despite the potential for male competition to select for reduced variation, behavioral and morphological variation in males is extremely high in some vertebrate species,

▼ **Figure 51.19 Mate choice copying by female guppies (*Poecilia reticulata*).** In the absence of other females (control group), female guppies generally choose males with more orange coloration. However, when a female model is placed near one of the males (experimental group), female guppies often copy the apparent mate choice of the model, even if the male is less colorful than others. Guppy females ignored the mate choice of the model only if an alternative male had much more orange coloration.

### Control Sample

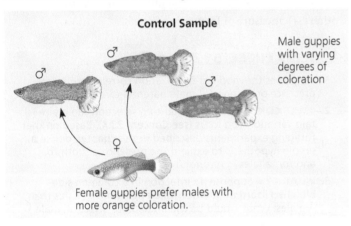

Male guppies with varying degrees of coloration

Female guppies prefer males with more orange coloration.

### Experimental Sample

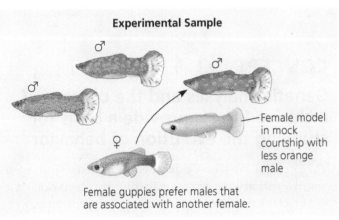

Female model in mock courtship with less orange male

Female guppies prefer males that are associated with another female.

▼ **Figure 51.20 Agonistic interaction.** Male eastern grey kangaroos (*Macropus giganteus*) often "box" in contests that determine which male is most likely to mate with an available female. Typically, one male snorts loudly and strikes the other with his forelimbs. If the male under attack does not retreat, the fight may escalate into grappling or the two males balancing on their tails while attempting to kick each other with the sharp toenails of their hind feet.

Video: Agonistic Behavior in Wolves
Video: Snake Ritual Wrestling

including species of fish and deer, as well as in a wide variety of invertebrates. In some species, sexual selection has led to the evolution of alternative male mating behavior and morphology. How do scientists analyze situations where more than one mating behavior can result in successful reproduction? One approach relies on the rules that govern games.

## Applying Game Theory

Often, the fitness of a particular behavioral phenotype is influenced by other behavioral phenotypes in the population. In studying such situations, behavioral ecologists use a range of tools, including game theory. Developed by American mathematician John Nash and others to model human economic behavior, **game theory** evaluates alternative strategies in situations where the outcome depends on the strategies of all the individuals involved.

As an example of applying game theory to mating behavior, let's consider the side-blotched lizard (*Uta stansburiana*) of California. Genetic variations give rise to males with orange, blue, or yellow throats **(Figure 51.21)**. One would expect that natural selection would favor one of the three color types, yet all three persist. Why? The answer appears to lie in the fact that each throat color is associated with a different pattern of behavior: Orange-throat males are the most aggressive and defend large territories that contain many females. Blue-throat males are also territorial but defend smaller territories and fewer females. Yellow-throats are nonterritorial males that mimic females and use "sneaky" tactics to gain the chance to mate.

Evidence indicates that the mating success of each male lizard type is influenced by the relative abundance of the other types, an example of frequency-dependent selection. In one study population, the most frequent throat coloration changed over a period of several years from blue to orange to yellow and back to blue.

▼ **Figure 51.21 Male polymorphism in the side-blotched lizard (*Uta stansburiana*).** An orange-throat male, left; a blue-throat male, center; a yellow-throat male, right.

By comparing the competition between common side-blotched lizard males to the children's game of rock-paper-scissors, scientists devised an explanation for the cycles of variation in the lizard population. In the game, paper defeats rock, rock defeats scissors, and scissors defeats paper. Each hand symbol thus wins one matchup but loses the other. Similarly, each type of male lizard has an advantage over one of the other two types. When blue-throats are abundant, they can defend the few females in their territories from the advances of the sneaky yellow-throat males. However, blue-throats cannot defend their territories against the hyperaggressive orange-throats. Once the orange-throats become the most abundant, the larger number of females in each territory provides the opportunity for the yellow-throats to have greater mating success. The yellow-throats become more frequent, but then give way to the blue-throats, whose tactic of guarding small territories once again allows them the most success. Thus, following the population over time, one sees a persistence of all three color types and a periodic shift in which type is most prevalent.

Game theory provides a way to think about complex evolutionary problems in which relative performance (reproductive success relative to other phenotypes), not absolute performance, is the key to understanding the evolution of behavior. This makes game theory an important tool because the relative performance of one phenotype compared with others is a measure of Darwinian fitness.

### CONCEPT CHECK 51.3

1. Why does the mode of fertilization correlate with the presence or absence of male parental care?
2. **MAKE CONNECTIONS** ➤ Balancing selection can maintain variation at a locus (see Concept 23.4). Based on the foraging experiments described in this chapter, devise a simple hypothesis to explain the presence of both *for*$^R$ and *for*$^s$ alleles in natural fly populations.
3. **WHAT IF?** ➤ Suppose an infection in a common side-blotched lizard population killed many more males than females. What would be the immediate effect on male competition for reproductive success?

*For suggested answers, see Appendix A.*

# CONCEPT 51.4

## Genetic analyses and the concept of inclusive fitness provide a basis for studying the evolution of behavior

**EVOLUTION** We'll now explore issues related to Tinbergen's fourth question—the evolutionary history of behaviors. We will first look at the genetic control of a behavior. Next, we will examine the genetic variation underlying the evolution of particular behaviors. Finally, we will see how expanding the definition of fitness beyond individual survival can help explain "selfless" behavior.

## Genetic Basis of Behavior

In exploring the genetic basis of behavior, we'll begin with the courtship behavior of the male fruit fly (see Figure 51.4). During courtship, the male fly carries out a complex series of actions in response to multiple sensory stimuli. Genetic studies have revealed that a single gene called *fru* controls this entire courtship ritual. If the *fru* gene is mutated to an inactive form, males do not court or mate with females. (The name *fru* is short for *fruitless*, reflecting the absence of offspring from the mutant males.) Normal male and female flies express distinct forms of the *fru* gene. When females are genetically manipulated to express the male form of *fru*, they court other females, performing the role normally played by the male.

How does the *fru* gene control so many different actions? Experiments carried out cooperatively in several laboratories demonstrated that *fru* is a master regulatory gene that directs the expression and activity of many genes with narrower functions. Together, genes that are controlled by the *fru* gene bring about sex-specific development of the fly nervous system. In effect, *fru* programs the fly for male courtship behavior by overseeing a male-specific wiring of the central nervous system.

In many cases, differences in behavior arise not from gene inactivation, but from variation in the activity or amount of a gene product. One striking example comes from the study of two related species of voles, which are small, mouse-like rodents. Male meadow voles (*Microtus pennsylvanicus*) are solitary and do not form lasting relationships with mates. Following mating, they pay little attention to their pups. In contrast, male prairie voles (*Microtus ochrogaster*) form a pair-bond with a single female after they mate (**Figure 51.22**). Male prairie voles provide care for their young pups, hovering over them, licking them, and carrying them, while acting aggressively toward intruders.

A peptide neurotransmitter is critical for the partnering and parental behavior of male voles. Known as **antidiuretic hormone (ADH)** or **vasopressin** (see Concept 44.5), this peptide is released during mating and binds to a specific receptor in the central nervous system. When male prairie voles are given a drug that inhibits the receptor in the brain that detects vasopressin, the male voles fail to form pair-bonds after mating.

The vasopressin receptor gene is much more highly expressed in the brain of prairie voles than in the brain of meadow voles. Testing the hypothesis that vasopressin

▼ **Figure 51.22 A pair of prairie voles (*Microtus ochrogaster*) huddling.** Male North American prairie voles associate closely with their mates, as shown here, and contribute substantially to the care of young.

receptor levels in the brain regulate postmating behavior, researchers inserted the vasopressin receptor gene from prairie voles into the genome of meadow voles. The male meadow voles carrying this gene not only developed brains with higher levels of the vasopressin receptor but also showed many of the same mating behaviors as male prairie voles, such as pair-bonding. Thus, although many genes influence pair-bonding and parenting in male voles, a change in the level of expression of the vasopressin receptor is sufficient to alter the development of these behaviors.

## Genetic Variation and the Evolution of Behavior

Behavioral differences between closely related species, such as meadow and prairie voles, are common. Significant differences in behavior can also be found *within* a species but are often less obvious. When behavioral variation between populations of a species correlates with variation in environmental conditions, it may reflect natural selection.

### Case Study: *Variation in Prey Selection*

An example of genetically based behavioral variation within a species involves prey selection by the western garter snake (*Thamnophis elegans*). The natural diet of this species differs widely across its range in California. Coastal

▼ **Figure 51.23 Western garter snake from a coastal habitat eating a banana slug.** Experiments indicate that the preference of these snakes for banana-slugs may be influenced more by genetics than by environment.

populations feed predominantly on banana slugs (*Ariolimax californicus*) **(Figure 51.23).** Inland populations feed on frogs, leeches, and fish, but not banana slugs. In fact, banana slugs are rare or absent in the inland habitats.

When researchers offered banana slugs to snakes collected from each wild population, most coastal snakes readily ate them, whereas inland snakes tended to refuse. To what extent does genetic variation among snake species contribute to a fondness for banana slugs? To answer this question, researchers collected pregnant snakes from the wild coastal and inland populations and then housed these females in separate cages in the laboratory. While the offspring were still very young, they were each offered a small piece of banana slug on ten successive days. More than 60% of the young snakes from coastal mothers ate banana slugs on eight or more of the ten days. In contrast, fewer than 20% of the young snakes from inland mothers ate a piece of banana slug even once. Perhaps not surprisingly, banana slugs thus appear to be a genetically acquired taste.

How did a genetically determined difference in feeding preference come to match the snakes' habitats so well? It turns out that the coastal and inland populations also vary with respect to their ability to recognize and respond to odor molecules produced by banana slugs. Researchers hypothesize that when inland snakes colonized coastal habitats more than 10,000 years ago, some of them could recognize banana slugs by scent. Because these snakes took advantage of this food source, they had higher fitness than snakes in the population that ignored the slugs. Over hundreds or thousands of generations, the capacity to recognize the slugs as prey increased in frequency in the coastal population.

The marked variation in behavior observed today between the coastal and inland populations may be evidence of this past evolutionary change.

## Case Study: *Variation in Migratory Patterns*

Another species suited to the study of behavioral variation is the blackcap (*Sylvia atricapilla*), a small migratory warbler. Blackcaps that breed in Germany generally migrate southwest to Spain and then south to Africa for the winter. In the 1950s, a few blackcaps began to spend their winters in Britain, and over time the population of blackcaps wintering in Britain grew to many thousands. Leg bands showed that some of these birds had migrated westward from central Germany. Was this change in the pattern of migration the outcome of natural selection? If so, the birds wintering in Britain must have a heritable difference in migratory behavior. To test this hypothesis, researchers at the Max Planck Institute for Ornithology in Radolfzell, Germany, devised a strategy to study migratory orientation in the laboratory **(Figure 51.24).** The results demonstrated that the two patterns of migration— to the west and to the southwest—do in fact reflect genetic differences between the two populations.

The study of western European blackcaps indicated that the change in their migratory behavior occurred both recently and rapidly. Before the year 1950, there were no known westward-migrating blackcaps in Germany. By the 1990s, westward migrants made up 7–11% of the blackcap populations of Germany. Once westward migration began, it persisted and increased in frequency, perhaps due to the widespread use of winter bird feeders in Britain, as well as shorter migration distances.

## Altruism

We typically assume that behaviors are selfish; that is, they benefit the individual at the expense of others, especially competitors. For example, superior foraging ability by one individual may leave less food for others. The problem comes with "unselfish" behaviors. How can such behaviors arise through natural selection? To answer this question, let's look more closely at some examples of unselfish behavior and consider how they might arise.

In discussing selflessness, we will use the term **altruism** to describe a behavior that reduces an animal's individual fitness but increases the fitness of other individuals in the population. Consider, for example, the Belding's ground squirrel, which lives in the western United States and is vulnerable to predators such as coyotes and hawks. A squirrel that sees a predator approach often gives a high-pitched alarm call that alerts unaware individuals to retreat to their burrows. Note that for the squirrel that warns others, the conspicuous alarm behavior increases the risk of being killed because it brings attention to the caller's location.

## Figure 51.24

### Inquiry  Are differences in migratory orientation within a species genetically determined?

**Experiment**  Birds known as blackcaps that live in Germany winter elsewhere. Most migrate to Spain and Africa, but a few fly to Britain, where they find food left out by city dwellers. German scientist Peter Berthold and colleagues wondered if this change had a genetic basis. To test this hypothesis, they captured blackcaps wintering in Britain and bred them in Germany in an outdoor cage. They also collected young blackcaps from nests in Germany and raised them in cages. In the autumn, the blackcaps captured in Britain and the birds raised in cages were placed in large, glass-covered funnel cages. When the funnels were lined with carbon-coated paper and placed outside at night, the birds moved around, making marks on the paper that indicated the direction in which they were trying to "migrate."

Scratch marks

**Results**  The wintering adult birds captured in Britain and their laboratory-raised offspring both attempted to migrate to the west. In contrast, the young birds collected from nests in southern Germany attempted to migrate to the southwest.

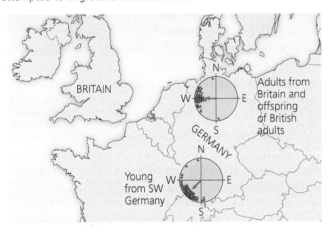

BRITAIN

Adults from Britain and offspring of British adults

GERMANY

Young from SW Germany

**Conclusion**  The young of the British blackcaps and the young birds from Germany (the control group) were raised under similar conditions but showed very different migratory orientations, indicating that their migratory orientation has a genetic basis.

**Data from**  P. Berthold et al., Rapid microevolution of migratory behavior in a wild bird species, *Nature* 360:668–690 (1992).

**WHAT IF?** ➤ *Suppose the birds had not shown a difference in orientation in these experiments. Could you conclude that the behavior was not genetically based? Explain.*

Another example of altruistic behavior occurs in honeybee societies, in which the workers are sterile. The workers themselves never reproduce, but they labor on behalf of a single fertile queen. Furthermore, the workers sting intruders, a behavior that helps defend the hive but results in the death of those workers.

Altruism is also observed in naked mole rats (*Heterocephalus glaber*), highly social rodents that live in underground chambers and tunnels in southern and northeastern Africa. The naked mole rat, which is almost hairless and nearly blind, lives in colonies of 20 to 300 individuals (**Figure 51.25**). Each colony has only one reproducing female, the queen, who mates with one to three males, called kings. The rest of the colony consists of nonreproductive females and males who at times sacrifice themselves to protect the queen or kings from snakes or other predators that invade the colony.

## Inclusive Fitness

With these examples from ground squirrels, honeybees, and mole rats in mind, let's return to the question of how altruistic behavior arises during evolution. The easiest case to consider is that of parents sacrificing for their offspring. When parents sacrifice their own well-being to produce and aid offspring, this act actually increases the fitness of the parents because it maximizes their genetic representation in the population. By this logic, altruistic behavior can be maintained by evolution even though it does not enhance the survival and reproductive success of the self-sacrificing individuals.

What about circumstances when individuals help others who are not their offspring? By considering a broader group of relatives than just parents and offspring, Biologist William Hamilton found an answer. He began by proposing that an animal could increase its genetic representation in the next generation by helping close relatives other than its

## ▼ Figure 51.25  Naked mole rats, a species of colonial mammal that exhibits altruistic behavior. Pictured here is a queen nursing offspring while surrounded by other members of the colony.

own offspring. Like parents and offspring, full siblings have half their genes in common. Therefore, selection might also favor helping siblings or helping one's parents produce more siblings. This thinking led Hamilton to the idea of **inclusive fitness**, the total effect an individual has on proliferating its genes by producing its own offspring *and* by providing aid that enables other close relatives to produce offspring.

### Hamilton's Rule and Kin Selection

The power of Hamilton's hypothesis was that it provided a way to measure, or quantify, the effect of altruism on fitness. According to Hamilton, the three key variables in an act of altruism are the benefit to the recipient, the cost to the altruist, and the coefficient of relatedness. The benefit, $B$, is the average number of *extra* offspring that the recipient of an altruistic act produces. The cost, $C$, is how many *fewer* offspring the altruist produces. The **coefficient of relatedness**, $r$, equals the fraction of genes that, on average, are shared. Natural selection favors altruism when the benefit to the recipient multiplied by the coefficient of relatedness exceeds the cost to the altruist—in other words, when $rB > C$. This statement is called **Hamilton's rule**.

To better understand Hamilton's rule, let's apply it to a human population in which the average individual has two children. We'll imagine that a young man is close to drowning in heavy surf, and his sister risks her life to swim out and pull her sibling to safety. If the young man had drowned, his reproductive output would have been zero; but now, if we use the average, he can father two children. The benefit to the man is thus two offspring ($B = 2$). What cost does his sister incur? Let's say that she has a 25% chance of drowning in attempting the rescue. The cost of the altruistic act to the sister is then 0.25 times 2, the number of offspring she would be expected to have if she had stayed on shore ($C = 0.25 \times 2 = 0.5$). Finally, we note that a brother and sister share half their genes on average ($r = 0.5$). One way to see this is in terms of the separation of homologous chromosomes that occurs during meiosis of gametes (**Figure 51.26**; see also Figure 13.7).

We can use our values of $B$, $C$, and $r$ to evaluate whether natural selection would favor the altruistic act in our imaginary scenario. For the surf rescue, $rB = 0.5 \times 2 = 1$, whereas $C = 0.5$. Because $rB$ is greater than $C$, Hamilton's rule is satisfied; thus, natural selection would favor this altruistic act.

Averaging over many individuals and generations, any particular gene in a sister faced with the situation described will be passed on to more offspring if she risks the rescue than if she does not. Among the genes propagated in this way may be some that contribute to altruistic behavior. Natural

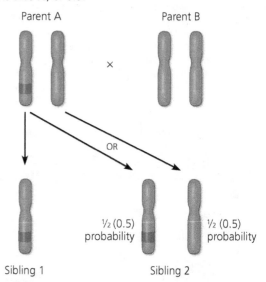

**▼ Figure 51.26 The coefficient of relatedness between siblings.** The red band indicates a particular allele (version of a gene) present on one chromosome, but not its homolog, in parent A. Sibling 1 has inherited the allele from parent A. There is a probability of ½ that sibling 2 will also inherit this allele from parent A. Any allele present on one chromosome of either parent will behave similarly. The coefficient of relatedness between the two siblings is thus ½, or 0.5.

Parent A          Parent B

½ (0.5) probability          ½ (0.5) probability

Sibling 1          Sibling 2

**WHAT IF?** ➤ *The coefficient of relatedness of an individual to a full (nontwin) sibling or to either parent is the same: 0.5. Does this value also hold true in cases of polyandry and polygyny?*

selection that thus favors altruism by enhancing the reproductive success of relatives is called **kin selection**.

Kin selection weakens with hereditary distance. Siblings have an $r$ of 0.5, but between an aunt and her niece, $r = 0.25$ (¼), and between first cousins, $r = 0.125$ (⅛). Notice that as the degree of relatedness decreases, the $rB$ term in the Hamilton inequality also decreases. Would natural selection favor rescuing a cousin? Not unless the surf were less treacherous. For the original conditions, $rB = 0.125 \times 2 = 0.25$, which is only half the value of $C$ (0.5). British geneticist J. B. S. Haldane appears to have anticipated these ideas when he jokingly stated that he would not lay down his life for one brother, but would do so for two brothers or eight cousins.

If kin selection explains altruism, then the examples of unselfish behavior we observe among diverse animal species should involve close relatives. This is apparently the case, but often in complex ways. Like most mammals, female Belding's ground squirrels settle close to their site of birth, whereas males settle at distant sites (**Figure 51.27**). Since nearly all alarm calls are given by females, they are most likely aiding close relatives. In the case of worker bees, who are all sterile, anything they do to help the entire hive benefits the only permanent member who is reproductively active—the queen, who is their mother.

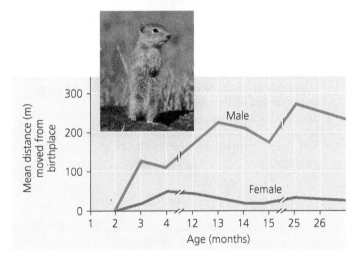

**▼ Figure 51.27 Kin selection and altruism in Belding's ground squirrels.** This graph helps explain the male-female difference in altruistic behavior of ground squirrels. Once weaned (pups are nursed for about one month), females are more likely than males to live near close relatives. Alarm calls that warn these relatives increase the inclusive fitness of the female altruist.

In the case of naked mole rats, DNA analyses have shown that all the individuals in a colony are closely related. Genetically, the queen appears to be a sibling, daughter, or mother of the kings, and the nonreproductive mole rats are the queen's direct descendants or her siblings. Therefore, when a nonreproductive individual enhances a queen's or king's chances of reproducing, the altruist increases the chance that some genes identical to its own will be passed to the next generation.

## Reciprocal Altruism

Some animals occasionally behave altruistically toward others who are not relatives. A baboon may help an unrelated companion in a fight, or a wolf may offer food to another wolf even though they share no kinship. Such behavior can be adaptive if the aided individual returns the favor in the future. This sort of exchange of aid, called **reciprocal altruism**, is commonly invoked to explain altruism that occurs between unrelated humans. Reciprocal altruism is rare in other animals; it is limited largely to species (such as chimpanzees) with social groups stable enough that individuals have many chances to exchange aid. It is generally thought to occur when individuals are likely to meet again and when there would be negative consequences associated with not returning favors to individuals who had been helpful in the past, a pattern of behavior that behavioral ecologists refer to as "cheating."

Since cheating may benefit the cheater substantially, how could reciprocal altruism evolve? Game theory provides a possible answer in the form of a behavioral strategy called *tit for tat*. In the tit-for-tat strategy, an individual treats another in the same way it was treated the last time they met. Individuals adopting this behavior are always altruistic, or cooperative, on the first encounter with another individual and will remain so as long as their altruism is reciprocated. When their cooperation is not reciprocated, however, individuals employing tit for tat will retaliate immediately but return to cooperative behavior as soon as the other individual becomes cooperative. The tit-for-tat strategy has been used to explain the few apparently reciprocal altruistic interactions observed in animals—ranging from blood sharing between nonrelated vampire bats to social grooming in primates.

## Evolution and Human Culture

As animals, humans behave (and, sometimes, misbehave). Just as humans vary extensively in anatomical features, we display substantial variations in behavior. Environment intervenes in the path from genotype to phenotype for physical traits, but does so much more profoundly for behavioral traits. Furthermore, as a consequence of our marked capacity for learning, humans are probably more able than any other animal to acquire new behaviors and skills **(Figure 51.28)**.

Some human activities have a less easily defined function in survival and reproduction than do, for example, foraging or courtship. One of these activities is play, which is sometimes defined as behavior that appears purposeless. We recognize play in children and what we think is play in the young of other vertebrates. Behavioral biologists describe "object play," such as chimpanzees playing with leaves, "locomotor play," such as the acrobatics of an antelope, and "social play," such as the interactions and antics of lion cubs. These categories, however, do little to inform us about the function of play. One idea is that, rather than generating specific skills or experience, play serves as preparation for unexpected events and for circumstances that cannot be controlled.

Human behavior and culture are related to evolutionary theory in the discipline of **sociobiology**. The main premise of sociobiology is that certain behavioral characteristics exist because they are expressions of genes that have been perpetuated by

**▲ Figure 51.28 Learning a new behavior.**

natural selection. In his seminal 1975 book *Sociobiology: The New Synthesis,* E. O. Wilson speculated about the evolutionary basis of certain kinds of social behavior. By including a few examples from human culture, he sparked a debate that continues today.

Over our recent evolutionary history, we have built up structured societies with governments, laws, cultural values, and religions that define what is acceptable behavior and what is not, even when unacceptable behavior might enhance an individual's Darwinian fitness. Perhaps it is our social and cultural institutions that make us distinct and that provide those qualities that at times make less apparent the continuum between humans and other animals. One such quality, our considerable capacity for reciprocal altruism, will be essential as we tackle current challenges, including global climate change, in which individual and collective interests often appear to be in conflict.

 Interview with E. O. Wilson: Pioneering the field of sociobiology

## CONCEPT CHECK 51.4

1. Explain why geographic variation in garter snake prey choice might indicate that the behavior evolved by natural selection.

2. Suppose an individual organism aids the survival and reproductive success of the offspring of its sibling. How might this behavior result in indirect selection for certain genes carried by that individual?

3. **WHAT IF?** ➤ Suppose you applied Hamilton's logic to a situation in which one individual is past reproductive age. Could there still be selection for an altruistic act?

*For suggested answers, see Appendix A.*

# 51 Chapter Review

 Go to **MasteringBiology**™ for Videos, Animations, Vocab Self-Quiz, Practice Tests, and more in the Study Area.

## SUMMARY OF KEY CONCEPTS

### CONCEPT 51.1

**Discrete sensory inputs can stimulate both simple and complex behaviors** (pp. 1138–1141)

VOCAB SELF-QUIZ
goo.gl/6u55ks

- **Behavior** is the sum of an animal's responses to external and internal stimuli. In behavior studies, proximate, or "how," questions focus on the stimuli that trigger a behavior and on genetic, physiological, and anatomical mechanisms underlying a behavioral act. Ultimate, or "why," questions address evolutionary significance.

- A **fixed action pattern** is a largely invariant behavior triggered by a simple cue known as a **sign stimulus**. **Migratory** movements involve navigation, which can be based on orientation relative to the sun, the stars, or Earth's magnetic field. Animal behavior is often synchronized to the circadian cycle of light and dark in the environment or to cues that cycle over the seasons.

- The transmission and reception of **signals** constitute animal **communication**. Animals use visual, auditory, chemical, and tactile signals. Chemical substances called **pheromones** transmit species-specific information between members of a species in behaviors ranging from foraging to courtship.

❓ *How is migration based on circannual rhythms poorly suited for adaptation to global climate change?*

### CONCEPT 51.2

**Learning establishes specific links between experience and behavior** (pp. 1141–1146)

- **Cross-fostering studies** can be used to measure the influence of social environment and experience on behavior.

- **Learning**, the modification of behavior as a result of experience, can take many forms:

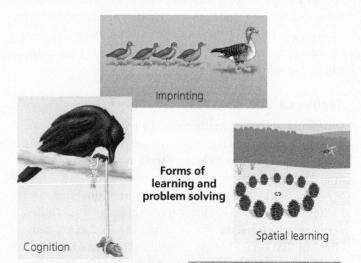

Imprinting

Forms of learning and problem solving

Spatial learning

Cognition

Associative learning

Social learning

❓ *How do imprinting in geese and song development in sparrows differ with regard to the resulting behavior?*

## CONCEPT 51.3

### Selection for individual survival and reproductive success can explain diverse behaviors (pp. 1146–1152)

- Controlled experiments in the laboratory can give rise to interpretable evolutionary changes in behavior.
- An **optimal foraging model** is based on the idea that natural selection should favor **foraging** behavior that minimizes the costs of foraging and maximizes the benefits.
- Sexual dimorphism correlates with the types of mating relationship, which include **monogamous** and **polygamous** mating systems. Variations in mating system and mode of fertilization affect certainty of paternity, which in turn has a significant influence on mating behavior and parental care.
- **Game theory** provides a way of thinking about evolution in situations where the fitness of a particular behavioral phenotype is influenced by other behavioral phenotypes in the population.

? *In some spider species, the female eats the male immediately after copulation. How might you explain this behavior from an evolutionary perspective?*

## CONCEPT 51.4

### Genetic analyses and the concept of inclusive fitness provide a basis for studying the evolution of behavior (pp. 1152–1158)

- Genetic studies in insects have revealed the existence of master regulatory genes that control complex behaviors. Within the underlying hierarchy, multiple genes influence specific behaviors, such as a courtship song. Research on voles illustrates how variation in a single gene can determine differences in complex behaviors.
- Behavioral variation within a species that corresponds to environmental variation may be evidence of past evolution.
- **Altruism** can be explained by the concept of **inclusive fitness**, the effect an individual has on proliferating its genes by producing its own offspring *and* by providing aid that enables close relatives to reproduce. The **coefficient of relatedness** and **Hamilton's rule** provide a way of measuring the strength of the selective forces favoring altruism against the potential cost of the "selfless" behavior. **Kin selection** favors altruistic behavior by enhancing the reproductive success of relatives.

? *What insight about the genetic basis of behavior emerges from studying the effects of courtship mutations in fruit flies and of pair-bonding in voles?*

## TEST YOUR UNDERSTANDING

### Level 1: Knowledge/Comprehension

PRACTICE TEST
goo.gl/CUYGKD

1. Which of the following is true of innate behaviors?
    (A) Their expression is only weakly influenced by genes.
    (B) They occur with or without environmental stimuli.
    (C) They are expressed in most individuals in a population.
    (D) They occur in invertebrates and some vertebrates but not mammals.

2. According to Hamilton's rule,
    (A) natural selection does not favor altruistic behavior that causes the death of the altruist.
    (B) natural selection favors altruistic acts when the resulting benefit to the recipient, corrected for relatedness, exceeds the cost to the altruist.
    (C) natural selection is more likely to favor altruistic behavior that benefits an offspring than altruistic behavior that benefits a sibling.
    (D) the effects of kin selection are larger than the effects of direct natural selection on individuals.

3. Female spotted sandpipers aggressively court males and, after mating, leave the clutch of young for the male to incubate. This sequence may be repeated several times with different males until no available males remain, forcing the female to incubate her last clutch. Which of the following terms best describes this behavior?
    (A) polygyny
    (B) polyandry
    (C) promiscuity
    (D) certainty of paternity

### Level 2: Application/Analysis

4. A region of the canary forebrain shrinks during the nonbreeding season and enlarges when breeding season begins. This change is probably associated with the annual
    (A) addition of new syllables to a canary's song repertoire.
    (B) crystallization of subsong into adult songs.
    (C) sensitive period in which canary parents imprint on new offspring.
    (D) elimination of the memorized template for songs sung the previous year.

5. Although many chimpanzees live in environments with oil palm nuts, members of only a few populations use stones to crack open the nuts. The likely explanation is that
    (A) the behavioral difference is caused by genetic differences between populations.
    (B) members of different populations have different nutritional requirements.
    (C) the cultural tradition of using stones to crack nuts has arisen in only some populations.
    (D) members of different populations differ in learning ability.

6. Which of the following is *not* required for a behavioral trait to evolve by natural selection?
    (A) In each individual, the form of the behavior is determined entirely by genes.
    (B) The behavior varies among individuals.
    (C) An individual's reproductive success depends in part on how the behavior is performed.
    (D) Some component of the behavior is genetically inherited.

### Level 3: Synthesis/Evaluation

7. **DRAW IT** You are considering two optimal foraging models for the behavior of a mussel-feeding shorebird, the oystercatcher. In model A, the energetic reward increases solely with mussel size. In model B, you take into consideration that larger mussels are more difficult to open. Draw a graph of reward (energy benefit on a scale of 0–10) versus mussel length (scale of 0–70 mm) for each model. Assume that mussels under 10 mm provide no benefit and are ignored by the birds. Also assume that mussels start becoming difficult to open when they reach 40 mm in length and impossible to open when 70 mm long. Considering the graphs you have drawn, indicate what observations and measurements you would want to make in this shorebird's habitat to help determine which model is more accurate.

8. **EVOLUTION CONNECTION** We often explain our behavior in terms of subjective feelings, motives, or reasons, but evolutionary explanations are based on reproductive fitness. Discuss the relationship between the two kinds of explanation. For instance, is an explanation for behavior such as "falling in love" incompatible with an evolutionary explanation?

9. **SCIENTIFIC INQUIRY** Scientists studying scrub jays found that "helpers" often assist mated pairs of birds by gathering food for their offspring.

   (A) Propose a hypothesis to explain what advantage there might be for the helpers to engage in this behavior instead of seeking their own territories and mates.

   (B) Explain how you would test your hypothesis. If it is correct, what results would you expect your tests to yield?

10. **SCIENCE, TECHNOLOGY, AND SOCIETY** Researchers are very interested in studying identical twins separated at birth and raised apart. So far, the data reveal that such twins frequently have similar personalities, mannerisms, habits, and interests. What general question do you think researchers hope to answer by studying such twins? Why do identical twins make good subjects for this research? What are the potential pitfalls of this research? What abuses might occur if the studies are not evaluated critically? Explain your thinking.

11. **WRITE ABOUT A THEME: INFORMATION** Learning is defined as a change in behavior as a result of experience. In a short essay (100–150 words), describe how heritable information contributes to the acquisition of learning, using some examples from imprinting and associative learning.

12. **SYNTHESIZE YOUR KNOWLEDGE**

Acorn woodpeckers (*Melanerpes formicivorus*) stash acorns in storage holes they drill in trees. When these woodpeckers breed, the offspring from previous years often help with parental duties. Activities of these nonbreeding helpers include incubating eggs and defending stashed acorns. Propose some questions about the proximate and ultimate causation of these behaviors that a behavioral biologist could ask.

*For selected answers, see Appendix A.*

 For additional practice questions, check out the **Dynamic Study Modules** in MasteringBiology. You can use them to study on your smartphone, tablet, or computer anytime, anywhere!

## Chapter 35

### Figure Questions

**Figure 35.11**

(1)

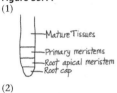

— Mature Tissues
— Primary meristems
— Root apical meristem
— Root cap

(2)

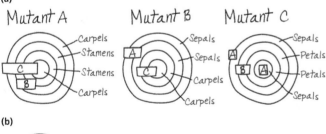

As a result of the addition of secondary xylem cells, the vascular cambium is pushed farther to the outside.

**Figure 35.15**

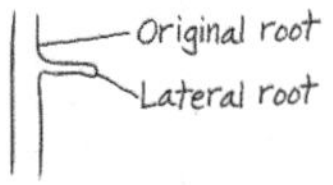

— Original root
— Lateral root

**Figure 35.17** Pith and cortex are defined, respectively, as ground tissue that is internal and ground tissue that is external to vascular tissue. Since vascular bundles of monocot stems are scattered throughout the ground tissue, there is no clear distinction between internal and external relative to the vascular tissue.
**Figure 35.19** The vascular cambium produces growth that increases the diameter of a stem or root. The tissues that are exterior to the vascular cambium cannot keep pace with the growth because their cells no longer divide. As a result, these tissues rupture.    **Figure 35.23** Periderm (mainly cork and cork cambium), primary phloem, secondary phloem, vascular cambium, secondary xylem (sapwood and heartwood), primary xylem, and pith. At the base of ancient redwood that is many centuries old, the remnants of primary growth (primary phloem, primary xylem and pith would be quite insignificant.    **Figure 35.33** Every root epidermal cell would develop a root hair.    **Figure 35.35** Another example of homeotic gene mutation is the mutation in a *Hox* gene that causes legs to form in place of antennae in *Drosophila* (see Figure 18.20).
**Figure 35.36**
**(a)**

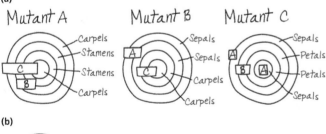

**(b)**

### Concept Check 35.1

**1.** The vascular tissue system connects leaves and roots, allowing sugars to move from leaves to roots in the phloem and allowing water and minerals to move to the leaves in the xylem.    **2.** To get sufficient energy from photosynthesis, we would need lots of surface area exposed to the sun. This large surface-to-volume ratio, however, would create a new problem—evaporative water loss. We would have to be permanently connected to a water source—the soil, also our source of minerals. In short, we would probably look and behave very much like plants.
**3.** As plant cells enlarge, they typically form a huge central vacuole that contains a dilute, watery sap. Central vacuoles enable plant cells to become large with only a minimal investment of new cytoplasm. The orientation of the cellulose microfibrils in plant cell walls affects the growth pattern of cells.

### Concept Check 35.2

**1.** Yes. In a woody plant, secondary growth is occurring in the older parts of the stem and root, while primary growth is occurring at the root and shoot tips.

**2.** The largest, oldest leaves would be lowest on the shoot. Since they would probably be heavily shaded, they would not photosynthesize much regardless of their size. Determinate growth benefits the plant by keeping it from investing an ever-increasing amount of resources into organs that provide little photosynthetic product.
**3.** No. The carrot roots will probably be smaller at the end of the second year because the food stored in the roots will be used to produce flowers, fruits, and seeds.

### Concept Check 35.3

**1.** In roots, primary growth occurs in three successive stages, moving away from the tip of the root: the zones of cell division, elongation, and differentiation. In shoots, it occurs at the tip of apical buds, with leaf primordia arising along the sides of an apical meristem. Most growth in length occurs in older internodes below the shoot tip.    **2.** No. Because vertically oriented leaves, such as those of maize, can capture light equally well on both sides of the leaf, you would expect them to have mesophyll cells that are not differentiated into palisade and spongy layers. This is typically the case. Also, vertically oriented leaves usually have stomata on both leaf surfaces.    **3.** Root hairs are cellular extensions that increase the surface area of the root epidermis, thereby enhancing the absorption of minerals and water. Microvilli are extensions that increase the absorption of nutrients by increasing the surface area of the gut.

### Concept Check 35.4

**1.** The sign will still be 2 m above the ground because this part of the tree is no longer growing in length (primary growth); it is now growing only in thickness (secondary growth).    **2.** Stomata must be able to close because evaporation is much more intensive from leaves than from the trunks of woody trees as a result of the higher surface-to-volume ratio in leaves.    **3.** Since there is little seasonal temperature variation in the tropics, the growth rings of a tree from the tropics would be difficult to discern unless the tree came from an area that had pronounced wet and dry seasons.    **4.** The tree would die slowly. Girdling removes an entire ring of secondary phloem (part of the bark), completely preventing transport of sugars and starches from the shoots to the roots. After several weeks, the roots would have used all of their stored carbohydrate reserves and would die.

### Concept Check 35.5

**1.** Although all the living vegetative cells of a plant have the same genome, they develop different forms and functions because of differential gene expression.
**2.** Plants show indeterminate growth; juvenile and mature phases are found on the same individual plant; and cell differentiation in plants is more dependent on final position than on lineage.    **3.** One hypothesis is that tepals arise if *B* gene activity is present in all three of the outer whorls of the flower.

### Summary of Key Concepts Questions

**35.1** Here are a few examples: The cuticle of leaves and stems protects these structures from desiccation. Collenchyma and sclerenchyma cells have thick walls that provide support for plants. Strong, branching root systems help anchor plants in the soil.    **35.2** Primary growth arises from apical meristems and involves production and elongation of organs. Secondary growth arises from lateral meristems and adds to the diameter of roots and stems.    **35.3** Lateral roots emerge from the pericycle and destroy plant cells as they emerge. In stems, branches arise from axillary buds and do not destroy any cells.    **35.4** With the evolution of secondary growth, plants were able to grow taller and shade competitors.    **35.5** The orientation of cellulose microfibrils in the innermost layers of the cell wall causes growth along one axis. Microtubules in the cell's outermost cytoplasm play a key role in regulating the axis of cell expansion because it is their orientation that determines the orientation of cellulose microfibrils.

### Test Your Understanding

**1.** D    **2.** C    **3.** C    **4.** A    **5.** B    **6.** D    **7.** D
**8.**

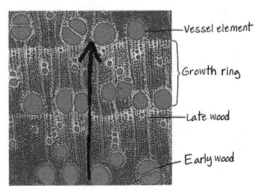

— Vessel element
— Growth ring
— Late wood
— Early wood

# Chapter 36

## Figure Questions

**Figure 36.2** Cellular respiration is occurring in all parts of a growing plant at all times, with mitochondria continuously releasing $CO_2$ and consuming $O_2$. In photosynthetic cells, the $CO_2$ produced by mitochondria during the day is consumed by chloroplasts, which also consume $CO_2$ from the air. Meanwhile, the mitochondria obtain $O_2$ from the chloroplasts, which also release $O_2$ into the air. At night, when photosynthesis does not occur, the mitochondria must exchange gases with the air rather than with the chloroplasts. As a result, at night photosynthetic cells are *releasing* $CO_2$ into the air and *consuming* $O_2$ from the air, the opposite of what happens during the day. **Figure 36.3** The leaves are being produced in a counterclockwise spiral. The next leaf primordium will emerge approximately between and to the inside of leaves 8 and 13. **Figure 36.4** A higher leaf area index will not necessarily increase photosynthesis because of upper leaves shading lower leaves. **Figure 36.6** A proton pump inhibitor would depolarize (increase) the membrane potential because fewer hydrogen ions would be pumped out across the plasma membrane. The immediate effect of an inhibitor of the $H^+$/sucrose transporter would be to hyperpolarize (decrease) the membrane potential because fewer hydrogen ions would be leaking back into the cell through these cotransporters. An inhibitor of the $H^+/NO_3^-$ cotransporter would have no effect on the membrane potential because the simultaneous cotransport of a positively charged ion and a negatively charged ion has no net effect on charge difference across the membrane. An inhibitor of the potassium ion channels would decrease the membrane potential because additional positively charged ions would not be accumulating outside the cell. **Figure 36.8** Few, if any, mesophyll cells are more than three cells from a vein. **Figure 36.9** The Casparian strip blocks water and minerals from moving between endodermal cells or moving around an endodermal cell via the cell's wall. Therefore, water and minerals must pass through an endodermal cell's plasma membrane. **Figure 36.18** Because the xylem is under negative pressure (tension), excising a stylet that had been inserted into a tracheid or vessel element would probably introduce air into the cell. No xylem sap would exude unless positive root pressure was predominant.

## Concept Check 36.1

**1.** Vascular plants must transport minerals and water absorbed by the roots to all the other parts of the plant. They must also transport sugars from sites of production to sites of use. **2.** Increased stem elongation would raise the plant's upper leaves. Erect leaves and reduced lateral branching would make the plant less subject to shading by the encroaching neighbors. **3.** Pruning shoot tips removes apical dominance, resulting in lateral shoots (branches) growing from axillary buds (see Concept 35.3). This branching produces a bushier plant with a higher leaf area index.

## Concept Check 36.2

**1.** The cell's $\Psi_P$ is 0.7 MPa. In a solution with a $\Psi$ of $^-$0.4 MPa, the cell's $\Psi_P$ at equilibrium would be 0.3 MPa. **2.** The cell would still adjust to changes in its osmotic environment, but its responses would be slower. Although aquaporins do not affect the water potential gradient across membranes, they allow for more rapid osmotic adjustments. **3.** If tracheids and vessel elements were alive at maturity, their cytoplasm would impede water movement, preventing rapid long-distance transport. **4.** The protoplasts would burst. Because the cytoplasm has many dissolved solutes, water would enter the protoplast continuously without reaching equilibrium. (When present, the cell wall prevents rupturing by limiting expansion of the protoplast.)

## Concept Check 36.3

**1.** At dawn, a drop is exuded from the rooted stump because the xylem is under positive pressure due to root pressure. At noon, the xylem is under negative pressure (tension) when it is cut, and the xylem sap is pulled back into the rooted stump. Root pressure cannot keep pace with the increased rate of transpiration at noon. **2.** Perhaps greater root mass helps compensate for the lower water permeability of the plasma membranes. **3.** The Casparian strip and tight junctions both prevent movement of fluid between cells.

## Concept Check 36.4

**1.** Stomatal opening at dawn is controlled mainly by light, $CO_2$ concentration, and a circadian rhythm. Environmental stresses such as drought, high temperature, and wind can stimulate stomata to close during the day. Water deficiency during the peak of the day can trigger release of the plant hormone abscisic acid, which signals guard cells to close stomata. **2.** The activation of the proton pumps of stomatal cells would cause the guard cells to take up $K^+$. The increased turgor of the guard cells would lock the stomata open and lead to extreme evaporation from the leaf. **3.** After the flowers are cut, transpiration from any leaves and from the petals (which are modified leaves) will continue to draw water up the xylem. If cut flowers are transferred directly to a vase, air pockets in xylem vessels prevent delivery of water from the vase to the flowers. Cutting stems again underwater, a few centimeters from the original cut, will sever the xylem above the air pocket. The water droplets prevent another air pocket from forming while the flowers are transferred to a vase. **4.** Water molecules are in constant motion, traveling at different speeds. If water molecules gain enough energy, the most energetic molecules near the liquid's surface will have sufficient speed, and therefore sufficient kinetic energy, to leave the liquid in the form of gaseous molecules (water vapor). As the molecules with the highest kinetic energy leave the liquid, the average kinetic energy of the remaining liquid decreases. Because a liquid's temperature is directly related to the average kinetic energy of its molecules, the temperature drops as evaporation proceeds.

## Concept Check 36.5

**1.** In both cases, the long-distance transport is a bulk flow driven by a pressure difference at opposite ends of tubes. Pressure is generated at the source end of a sieve tube by the loading of sugar and resulting osmotic flow of water into the phloem, and this pressure *pushes* sap from the source end to the sink end of the tube. In contrast, transpiration generates a negative pressure potential (tension) that *pulls* the ascent of xylem sap. **2.** The main sources are fully grown leaves (producing sugar by photosynthesis) and fully developed storage organs (producing sugar by breakdown of starch). Roots, buds, stems, expanding leaves, and fruits are powerful sinks because they are actively growing. A storage organ may be a sink in the summer when accumulating carbohydrates but a source in the spring when breaking down starch into sugar for growing shoot tips. **3.** Positive pressure, whether it be in the xylem when root pressure predominates or in the sieve-tube elements of the phloem, requires active transport. Most long-distance transport in the xylem depends on bulk flow driven by the negative pressure potential generated ultimately by the evaporation of water from the leaf and does not require living cells. **4.** The spiral slash prevents optimal bulk flow of the phloem sap to the root sinks. Therefore, more phloem sap can move from the source leaves to the fruit sinks, making them sweeter.

## Concept Check 36.6

**1.** Plasmodesmata, unlike gap junctions, have the ability to pass RNA, proteins, and viruses from cell to cell. **2.** Long-distance signaling is critical for the integrated functioning of all large organisms, but the speed of such signaling is much less critical to plants because their responses to the environment, unlike those of animals, do not typically involve rapid movements. **3.** Although this strategy would eliminate the systemic spread of viral infections, it would also severely impact the development of the plants.

## Summary of Key Concepts Questions

**36.1** Plants with tall shoots and elevated leaf canopies generally had an advantage over shorter competitors. A consequence of the selective pressure for tall shoots was the further separation of leaves from roots. This separation created problems for the transport of materials between root and shoot systems. Plants with xylem cells were more successful at supplying their shoot systems with soil resources (water and minerals). Similarly, those with phloem cells were more successful at supplying sugar sinks with carbohydrates. **36.2** Xylem sap is pulled up the plant by transpiration much more often than it is pushed up the plant by root pressure. **36.3** Hydrogen bonds are necessary for the cohesion of water molecules to each other and for the adhesion of water to other materials, such as cell walls. Both adhesion and cohesion of water molecules are involved in the ascent of xylem sap under conditions of negative pressure. **36.4** Although stomata account for most of the water lost from plants, they are necessary for exchange of gases—for example, for the uptake of carbon dioxide needed for photosynthesis. The loss of water through stomata also drives the long-distance transport of water that brings soil nutrients from roots to the rest of the plant. **36.5** Although the movement of phloem sap depends on bulk flow, the pressure gradient that drives phloem transport depends on the osmotic uptake of water in response to the loading of sugars into sieve-tube elements at sugar sources. Phloem loading depends on $H^+$ cotransport processes that ultimately depend on $H^+$ gradients established by active $H^+$ pumping. **36.6** Electrical signaling, cytoplasmic pH, cytoplasmic $Ca^{2+}$ concentration, and viral movement proteins all affect symplastic communication, as do developmental changes in the number of plasmodesmata.

## Test Your Understanding

**1.** A  **2.** B  **3.** B  **4.** C  **5.** B  **6.** C  **7.** A  **8.** D

# Chapter 37

## Figure Questions

**Figure 37.3** Cations. At low pH, there would be more protons ($H^+$) to displace mineral cations from negatively charged soil particles into the soil solution. **Figure 37.4** The A horizon, which consists of the topsoil. **Table 37.1** During photosynthesis, $CO_2$ is fixed into carbohydrates, which contribute to the dry mass. In cellular respiration, $O_2$ is reduced to $H_2O$ and does not contribute to the dry mass. **Figure 37.10** Some other examples of mutualism are the following relationships. *Flashlight fish and bioluminescent bacteria:* The bacteria gain nutrients and protection from the fish, while the bioluminescence attracts prey and mates for the fish. *Flowering plants and pollinators:* Animals distribute the pollen and are rewarded by a meal of nectar or pollen. *Vertebrate herbivores and some bacteria in the digestive system:* Microorganisms in the alimentary canal break down cellulose to glucose and, in some cases, provide the animal with vitamins or amino acids. Meanwhile, the microorganisms have a steady supply of food and a warm environment. *Humans and some bacteria in the digestive system:* Some bacteria provide humans with vitamins, while the bacteria get nutrients from the digested food. **Figure 37.12** Both ammonium and nitrate. A decomposing animal would release amino acids into the soil that would be converted into ammonium by ammonifying bacteria. Some of this ammonium could be used directly by the plant. A large part of the ammonium, however, would be converted by nitrifying bacteria to form nitrate ions that could also be absorbed by the plant root system. **Figure 37.13** The legume plants benefit because the bacteria fix nitrogen that is absorbed by their roots. The bacteria benefit because they acquire photosynthetic products from the plants. **Figure 37.14** All three plant tissue systems are affected. Root hairs (dermal tissue) are modified to allow *Rhizobium* penetration. The cortex (ground tissue) and pericycle (vascular tissue) proliferate during nodule formation. The vascular tissue of the nodule connects to the vascular cylinder of the root to allow for efficient nutrient exchange.

## Concept Check 37.1

**1.** Overwatering deprives roots of oxygen. Overfertilizing is wasteful and can lead to soil salinization and water pollution.   **2.** As lawn clippings decompose, they restore mineral nutrients to the soil. If they are removed, the minerals lost from the soil must be replaced by fertilization.   **3.** Because of their small size and negative charge, clay particles would increase the number of binding sites for cations and water molecules and would therefore increase cation exchange and water retention in the soil.   **4.** Due to hydrogen bonding between water molecules, water expands when it freezes, and this causes mechanical fracturing of rocks. Water also coheres to many objects, and this cohesion combined with other forces, such as gravity, can help tug particles from rock. Finally, water, because it is polar, is an excellent solvent that allows many substances, including ions, to become dissolved in solution.

## Concept Check 37.2

**1.** No. Even though macronutrients are required in greater amounts, all essential elements are necessary for the plant to complete its life cycle.   **2.** No. The fact that the addition of an element results in an increase in the growth rate of a crop does not mean that the element is strictly required for the plant to complete its life cycle.   **3.** Inadequate aeration of the roots of hydroponically grown plants would promote alcohol fermentation, which uses more energy and may lead to the accumulation of ethanol, a toxic by-product of fermentation.

## Concept Check 37.3

**1.** The rhizosphere is the zone in the soil immediately adjacent to living roots. It harbors many rhizobacteria with which the root systems form beneficial mutualisms. Some rhizobacteria produce antibiotics that protect roots from disease. Others absorb toxic metals or make nutrients more available to roots. Still others convert gaseous nitrogen into forms usable by the plant or produce chemicals that stimulate plant growth.   **2.** Soil bacteria and mycorrhizae enhance plant nutrition by making certain minerals more available to plants. For example, many types of soil bacteria are involved in the nitrogen cycle, and the hyphae of mycorrhizae provide a large surface area for the absorption of nutrients, particularly phosphate ions.   **3.** Mixotrophy refers to the strategy of using photosynthesis and heterotrophy for nutrition. Euglenids are well-known mixotrophic protists.   **4.** Saturating rainfall may deplete the soil of oxygen. A lack of soil oxygen would inhibit nitrogen fixation by the peanut root nodules and decrease the nitrogen available to the plants. Alternatively, heavy rain may leach nitrate from the soil. A symptom of nitrogen deficiency is yellowing of older leaves.

## Summary of Key Concepts Questions

**37.1** The term *ecosystem* refers to the communities of organisms within a given area and their interactions with the physical environment around them. Soil is teeming with many communities of organisms, including bacteria, fungi, animals, and the root systems of plants. The vigor of these individual communities depends on nonliving factors in the soil environment, such as minerals, oxygen, and water, as well as on interactions, both positive and negative, between different communities of organisms.   **37.2** No. Plants can complete their life cycle when grown hydroponically, that is, in aerated salt solutions containing the proper ratios of all the minerals needed by plants.   **37.3** No. Some parasitic plants obtain their energy by siphoning off carbon nutrients from other organisms.

## Test Your Understanding

**1.** B   **2.** B   **3.** A   **4.** D   **5.** B   **6.** B   **7.** D   **8.** C   **9.** D
**10.**

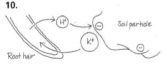

# Chapter 38

## Figure Questions

**Figure 38.4** Having a specific pollinator is more efficient because less pollen gets delivered to flowers of the wrong species. However, it is also a risky strategy: If the pollinator population suffers to an unusual degree from predation, disease, or climate change, then the plant may not be able to produce seeds.   **Figure 38.6** The part of the angiosperm life cycle characterized by the most mitotic divisions is the step between seed germination and the mature sporophyte.   **Figure 38.8 Make Connections** In addition to having a single cotyledon, monocots have leaves with parallel leaf venation, scattered vascular bundles in their stems, a fibrous root system, floral parts in threes or multiples of threes, and pollen grains with only one opening. In contrast, dicots have two cotyledons, netlike leaf venation, vascular bundles in a ring, taproots, floral parts in fours or fives or multiples thereof, and pollen grains with three openings.   **Figure 38.8 Visual Skills** The mature garden bean seed lacks an endosperm at maturity. Its endosperm was consumed during seed development, and its nutrients were stored anew in the cotyledons.   **Figure 38.9** Beans use a hypocotyl hook to push through the soil. The delicate leaves and shoot apical meristem are also protected by being sandwiched between two large cotyledons. The coleoptile of maize seedlings helps protect the emerging leaves.

## Concept Check 38.1

**1.** In angiosperms, pollination is the transfer of pollen from an anther to a stigma. Fertilization is the fusion of the egg and sperm to form the zygote; it cannot occur until after the growth of the pollen tube from the pollen grain.   **2.** Long styles help to weed out pollen grains that are genetically inferior and not capable of successfully growing long pollen tubes.   **3.** No. The haploid (gametophyte) generation of plants is multicellular and arises from spores. The haploid phase of the animal life cycles is a single-celled gamete (egg or sperm) that arises directly from meiosis: There are no spores.

## Concept Check 38.2

**1.** Flowering plants can avoid self-fertilization by self-incompatibility, having male and female flowers on separate plants (dioecious species), or having stamens and styles of different heights on separate plants ("pin" and "thrum" flowers).   **2.** Asexually propagated crops lack genetic diversity. Genetically diverse populations are less likely to become extinct in the face of an epidemic because there is a greater likelihood that a few individuals in the population are resistant.   **3.** In the short term, selfing may be advantageous in a population that is so dispersed and sparse that pollen delivery is unreliable. In the long term, however, selfing is an evolutionary dead end because it leads to a loss of genetic diversity that may preclude adaptive evolution.

## Concept Check 38.3

**1.** Traditional breeding and genetic engineering both involve artificial selection for desired traits. However, genetic engineering techniques facilitate faster gene transfer and are not limited to transferring genes between closely related varieties or species.   **2.** *Bt* maize suffers less insect damage; therefore, *Bt* maize plants are less likely to be infected by fumonisin-producing fungi that infect plants through wounds.   **3.** In such species, engineering the transgene into the chloroplast DNA would not prevent its escape in pollen; such a method requires that the chloroplast DNA be found only in the egg. An entirely different method of preventing transgene escape would therefore be needed, such as male sterility, apomixis, or self-pollinating closed flowers.

## Summary of Key Concepts Questions

**38.1** After pollination and fertilization, a flower changes into a fruit. The petals, sepals, and stamens typically fall off the flower. The stigma of the pistil withers, and the ovary begins to swell. The ovules (embryonic seeds) inside the ovary begin to mature.   **38.2** Asexual reproduction can be advantageous in a stable environment because individual plants that are well suited to that environment pass on all their genes to offspring. Also, asexual reproduction generally results in offspring that are less fragile than the seedlings produced by sexual reproduction. However, sexual reproduction offers the advantage of dispersal of tough seeds. Moreover, sexual reproduction produces genetic variety, which may be advantageous in an unstable environment. The likelihood is better that at least one offspring of sexual reproduction will survive in a changed environment.   **38.3** "Golden Rice," although not yet in commercial production, has been engineered to produce more vitamin A, thereby raising the nutritional value of rice. A protoxin gene from a soil bacterium has been engineered into *Bt* maize. This protoxin is lethal to invertebrates but harmless to vertebrates. *Bt* crops require less pesticide spraying and have lower levels of fungal infection and fungal toxins. The nutritional value of cassava is being increased in many ways by genetic engineering. Enriched levels of iron and beta-carotene (a vitamin A precursor) have been achieved, and cyanide-producing chemicals have been almost eliminated from the roots.

## Test Your Understanding

**1.** A   **2.** C   **3.** C   **4.** C   **5.** D   **6.** D   **7.** D
**8.**

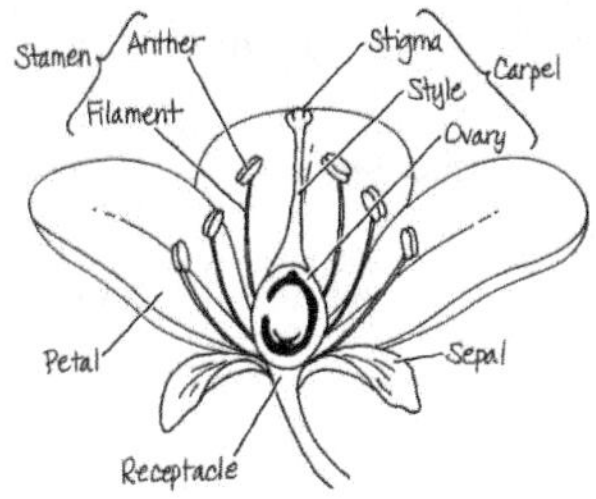

Stamen   Anther   Stigma   Carpel
Filament   Style   Ovary
Petal   Sepal
Receptacle

# Chapter 39

## Figure Questions

**Figure 39.4** Panel B in Figure 11.17 shows a branching signal transduction pathway that resembles the branching phytochrome-dependent pathway involved in de-etiolation.   **Figure 39.5** To determine which wavelengths of light are most effective in phototropism, you could use a glass prism to split white light into its component colors and see which colors cause the quickest bending (the answer is blue; see Figure 39.15).   **Figure 39.6** No. Polar auxin transport depends on the distribution of auxin transport proteins at the basal ends of cells.   **Figure 39.12** No. Since the *ein* mutation renders the seedling "blind" to ethylene, enhancing ethylene production by adding an *eto* mutation would have no effect on phenotype compared with the *ein* mutation alone.   **Figure 39.16** Yes. The white light, which contains red light, would stimulate seed germination in all treatments.   **Figure 39.20** Since far-red light, like darkness, causes an accumulation of the red-absorbing form ($P_r$) of phytochrome, single flashes of far-red light at night would have no effect on flowering beyond what the dark periods alone would have.   **Figure 39.21** If this were true, florigen would be an inhibitor of flowering, not an inducer.   **Figure 39.27** Photosynthetic adaptations can occur at the molecular level, as is apparent in the fact that $C_3$ plants use rubisco to fix carbon dioxide initially, whereas $C_4$ and CAM plants use PEP carboxylase. An adaptation at the tissue level is that plants have different stomatal densities based on their genotype and environmental conditions. At the organismal level, plants alter their shoot architectures to make photosynthesis more efficient. For example, self-pruning removes branches and leaves that respire more than they photosynthesize.

## Concept Check 39.1

**1.** Dark-grown seedlings are etiolated: They have long stems, underdeveloped root systems, and unexpanded leaves, and their shoots lack chlorophyll. Etiolated growth is beneficial to seeds sprouting under the dark conditions they would encounter underground. By devoting more energy to stem elongation and less to leaf expansion and root growth, a plant increases the likelihood that the shoot will reach the sunlight before its stored foods run out. **2.** Cycloheximide should inhibit de-etiolation by preventing the synthesis of new proteins necessary for de-etiolation. **3.** No. Applying Viagra, like injecting cyclic GMP as described in the text, should cause only a partial de-etiolation response. Full de-etiolation would require activation of the calcium branch of the signal transduction pathway.

## Concept Check 39.2

**1.** Fusicoccin's ability to cause an increase in plasma $H^+$ pump activity has an auxin-like effect and promotes stem cell elongation. **2.** The plant will exhibit a constitutive triple response. Because the kinase that normally prevents the triple response is dysfunctional, the plant will undergo the triple response regardless of whether ethylene is present or the ethylene receptor is functional. **3.** Since ethylene often stimulates its own synthesis, it is under positive-feedback regulation.

## Concept Check 39.3

**1.** Not necessarily. Many environmental factors, such as temperature and light, change over a 24-hour period in the field. To determine whether the enzyme is under circadian control, a scientist would have to demonstrate that its activity oscillates even when environmental conditions are held constant. **2.** It is impossible to say. To establish that this species is a short-day plant, it would be necessary to establish the critical night length for flowering and that this species only flowers when the night is longer than the critical night length. **3.** According to the action spectrum of photosynthesis, red and blue light are the most effective in photosynthesis. Thus, it is not surprising that plants assess their light environment using blue- and red-light-absorbing photoreceptors.

## Concept Check 39.4

**1.** A plant that overproduces ABA would undergo less evaporative cooling because its stomata would not open as widely. **2.** Plants close to the aisles may be more subject to mechanical stresses caused by passing workers and air currents. The plants nearer the center of the bench may also be taller as a result of shading and less evaporative stress. **3.** No. Because root caps are involved in sensing gravity, roots that have their root caps removed are almost completely insensitive to gravity.

## Concept Check 39.5

**1.** Some insects increase plants' productivity by eating harmful insects or aiding in pollination. **2.** Mechanical damage breaches a plant's first line of defense against infection, its protective dermal tissue. **3.** No. Pathogens that kill their hosts would soon run out of victims and might themselves go extinct. **4.** Perhaps the breeze dilutes the local concentration of a volatile defense compound that the plants produce.

## Summary of Key Concepts Questions

**39.1** Signal transduction pathways often activate protein kinases, enzymes that phosphorylate other proteins. Protein kinases can directly activate certain preexisting enzymes by phosphorylating them, or they can regulate gene transcription (and enzyme production) by phosphorylating specific transcription factors. **39.2** Yes, there is truth to the old adage that one bad apple spoils the whole bunch. Ethylene, a gaseous hormone that stimulates ripening, is produced by damaged, infected, or overripe fruits. Ethylene can diffuse to healthy fruit in the "bunch" and stimulate their rapid ripening. **39.3** Plant physiologists proposed the existence of a floral-promoting factor (florigen) based on the fact that a plant induced to flower could induce flowering in a second plant to which it was grafted, even though the second plant was not in an environment that would normally induce flowering in that species. **39.4** Plants subjected to drought stress are often more resistant to freezing stress because the two types of stress are quite similar. Freezing of water in the extracellular spaces causes free water concentrations outside the cell to decrease. This, in turn, causes free water to leave the cell by osmosis, leading to the dehydration of cytoplasm, much like what is seen in drought stress. **39.5** Chewing insects make plants more susceptible to pathogen invasion by disrupting the waxy cuticle of shoots, thereby creating an opening for infection. Moreover, substances released from damaged cells can serve as nutrients for the invading pathogens.

## Test Your Understanding

**1.** B **2.** C **3.** D **4.** C **5.** B **6.** B **7.** C
**8.**

# Chapter 40

## Figure Questions

**Figure 40.4** Such exchange surfaces are internal in the sense that they are inside the body. However, they are also continuous with openings on the external body surface that contact the environment. **Figure 40.6** Signals in the nervous system always travel on a direct route between the sending and receiving cell. In contrast, hormones that reach target cells can have an effect regardless of the path by which they arrive or how many times they travel through the circulatory system. **Figure 40.8** The stimuli (gray boxes) are the room temperature increasing in the top loop or decreasing in the bottom loop. The responses could include the heater turning off and the temperature decreasing in the top loop and the heater turning on and the temperature increasing in the bottom loop. The sensor/control center is the thermostat. The air conditioner would form a second control circuit, cooling the house when air temperature exceeded the set point. Such opposing, or antagonistic, pairs of control circuits increase the effectiveness of a homeostatic mechanism. **Figure 40.12** The conduction arrows would be in the opposite direction, transferring heat from the walrus to the ice because the walrus is warmer than the ice. **Figure 40.17** If a female Burmese python were not incubating eggs, her oxygen consumption would decrease with decreasing temperature, as for any other ectotherm. **Figure 40.18** The ice water would cool tissues in your head, including blood that would then circulate throughout your body. This effect would accelerate the return to a normal body temperature. If, however, the ice water reached the eardrum and cooled the blood vessel that supplies the hypothalamus, the hypothalamic thermostat would respond by inhibiting sweating and constricting blood vessels in the skin, slowing cooling elsewhere in the body. **Figure 40.19** The transport of nutrients across membranes and the synthesis of RNA and protein are coupled to ATP hydrolysis. These processes proceed spontaneously because there is an overall drop in free energy, with the excess energy given off as heat. Similarly, less than half of the free energy in glucose is captured in the coupled reactions of cellular respiration. The remainder of the energy is released as heat. **Figure 40.22** Nothing. Although genes that show a circadian variation in expression during euthermia exhibit constant RNA levels during hibernation, a gene that shows constant expression during hibernation might also show constant expression during euthermia. **Figure 40.23** In hot environments, both plants and animals experience evaporative cooling as a result of transpiration (in plants) or bathing, sweating, and panting (in animals); both plants and animals synthesize heat-shock proteins, which protect other proteins from heat stress; and animals also use various behavioral responses to minimize heat absorption. In cold environments, both plants and animals increase the proportion of unsaturated fatty acids in their membrane lipids and use antifreeze proteins that prevent or limit the formation of intracellular ice crystals; plants increase cytoplasmic levels of specific solutes that help reduce the loss of intracellular water during extracellular freezing; and animals increase metabolic heat production and use insulation, circulatory adaptations such as countercurrent exchange, and behavioral responses to minimize heat loss.

## Concept Check 40.1

**1.** All types of epithelia consist of cells that line a surface, are tightly packed, are situated on top of a basal lamina, and form an active and protective interface with the external environment. **2.** An oxygen molecule must cross a plasma membrane when entering the body at an exchange surface in the respiratory system, in both entering and exiting the circulatory system, and in moving from the interstitial fluid to the cytoplasm of the body cell. **3.** You need the nervous system to perceive the danger and provoke a split-second muscular response to keep from falling. The nervous system, however, does not make a direct connection with blood vessels or glucose-storing cells in the liver. Instead, the nervous system triggers the release of a hormone (called epinephrine, or adrenaline) by the endocrine system, bringing about a change in these tissues in just a few seconds.

## Concept Check 40.2

**1.** In thermoregulation, the product of the pathway (a change in temperature) decreases pathway activity by reducing the stimulus. In an enzyme-catalyzed biosynthetic process, the product of the pathway (in this case, isoleucine) inhibits the pathway that generated it. **2.** You would want to put the thermostat close to where you would be spending time, where it would be protected from environmental perturbations, such as direct sunshine, and not right in the path of the output of the heating system. Similarly, the sensors for homeostasis located in the human brain are separated from environmental influences and can monitor conditions in a vital and sensitive tissue. **3.** In convergent evolution, the same biological trait arises independently in two or more species. Gene analysis can provide evidence for an independent origin. In particular, if the genes responsible for the trait in one species lack significant sequence similarity to the corresponding genes in another species, scientists conclude that there is a separate genetic basis for the trait in the two species and thus an independent origin. In the case of circadian rhythms, the clock genes in cyanobacteria appear unrelated to those in humans.

## Concept Check 40.3

**1.** "Wind chill" involves heat loss through convection, as the moving air contributes to heat loss from the skin surface. **2.** The hummingbird, being a very small endotherm, has a very high metabolic rate. If by absorbing sunlight certain flowers warm their nectar, a hummingbird feeding on these flowers is saved the metabolic expense of warming the nectar to its body temperature. **3.** To raise its body temperature to the higher range of fever, the hypothalamus triggers heat generation by muscular contractions, or shivering. The person with a fever may in fact say that they feel cold, even though their body temperature is above normal.

## Concept Check 40.4

**1.** The mouse would consume oxygen at a higher rate because it is an endotherm, so its basal metabolic rate is higher than the ectothermic lizard's standard metabolic rate. **2.** The house cat; smaller animals have a higher metabolic rate per unit body mass and a greater demand for food per unit body mass. **3.** The alligator's body temperature would decrease along with the air temperature. Its metabolic rate would therefore also decrease as chemical reactions slowed. In contrast, the lion's body temperature would not change. Its metabolic rate would increase as it shivered and produced heat to keep its body temperature constant.

### Summary of Key Concepts Questions

**40.1** Animals exchange materials with their environment across their body surface, and a spherical shape has the minimum surface area per unit volume. As body size increases, the ratio of surface area to body volume decreases. **40.2** No; an animal's internal environment fluctuates slightly around set points or within normal ranges. Homeostasis is a dynamic state. Furthermore, there are sometimes programmed changes in set points, such as those resulting in radical increases in hormone levels at particular times in development. **40.3** Heat exchange across the skin is a primary mechanism for the regulation of body core temperature, with the result that the skin is cooler than the body core. **40.4** Small animals have a higher BMR per unit mass and therefore consume more oxygen per unit mass than large animals. A higher breathing rate is required to support this increased oxygen consumption.

### Test Your Understanding

**1.** B **2.** C **3.** A **4.** B **5.** C **6.** B **7.** D
**8.**

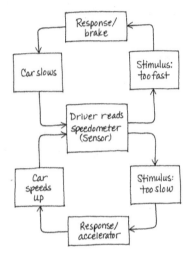

## Chapter 41

### Figure Questions

**Figure 41.6** Your diagram should show food entering through the hydra's mouth and being digested into nutrients in the large portion of the gastrovascular cavity. The nutrients then diffuse into the extensions of that cavity that reach into the tentacles. There, nutrients would be absorbed by cells of the gastrodermis and transported to cells of the epidermis of a tentacle. **Figure 41.9** The airway must be open for exhaling to occur. If the epiglottis is up, milk entered the throat from the mouth encounters air forced out of the lungs and is carried along into the nasal cavity and out the nose. **Figure 41.11** Since enzymes are proteins, and proteins are hydrolyzed in the small intestine, the digestive enzymes in that compartment need to be resistant to enzymatic cleavage other than the cleavage required to activate them. **Figure 41.12** None. Since digestion is completed in the small intestine, tapeworms simply absorb predigested nutrients through their large body surface. **Figure 41.13** Yes. The exit of the chylomicrons involves exocytosis, an active process that consumes energy in the form of ATP. In contrast, the entry of monoglycerides and fatty acids into the cell by diffusion is a passive process that does not consume energy. **Figure 41.21** Both insulin and glucagon are involved in negative feedback circuits.

### Concept Check 41.1

**1.** The only essential amino acids are those that an animal cannot synthesize from other molecules. **2.** Many vitamins serve as enzyme cofactors, which, like enzymes themselves, are unchanged by the chemical reactions in which they participate. Therefore, only very small amounts of vitamins are needed. **3.** To identify the essential nutrient missing from an animal's diet, a researcher could supplement the diet with individual nutrients one at a time and determine which nutrient eliminates the signs of malnutrition.

### Concept Check 41.2

**1.** A gastrovascular cavity is a digestive pouch with a single opening that functions in both ingestion and elimination; an alimentary canal is a digestive tube with a separate mouth and anus at opposite ends. **2.** As long as nutrients are within the cavity of the alimentary canal, they are in a compartment that is continuous with the outside environment via the mouth and anus and have not yet crossed a membrane to enter the body. **3.** In both cases, high-energy fuels are consumed, complex molecules are broken down into simpler ones, and waste products are

eliminated. In addition, gasoline, like food, is broken down in a specialized compartment, so that surrounding structures are protected from disassembly. Finally, just as food and wastes remain outside the body in a digestive tract, neither gasoline nor its waste products enter the passenger compartment of the automobile.

### Concept Check 41.3

**1.** Because parietal cells in the stomach pump hydrogen ions into the stomach lumen where they combine with chloride ions to form HCl, a proton pump inhibitor reduces the acidity of chyme and thus the irritation that occurs when chyme enters the esophagus. **2.** By releasing sugars from starch or glycogen in the mouth, amylase might allow us to recognize foods that provide a ready source of energy. **3.** Proteins would be denatured and digested into peptides. Further digestion, to individual amino acids, would require enzymatic secretions found in the small intestine. No digestion of carbohydrates or lipids would occur.

### Concept Check 41.4

**1.** The increased time for transit through the alimentary canal allows for more extensive processing, and the increased surface area of the canal provides greater opportunity for absorption. **2.** A mammal's digestive system provides mutualistic microorganisms with an environment that is protected against other microorganisms by saliva and gastric juice, that is held at a constant temperature conducive to enzyme action, and that provides a steady source of nutrients. **3.** For the yogurt treatment to be effective, the bacteria from yogurt would have to establish a mutualistic relationship with the small intestine, where disaccharides are broken down and sugars are absorbed. Conditions in the small intestine are likely to be very different from those in a yogurt culture. The bacteria might be killed before they reach the small intestine, or they might not be able to grow there in sufficient numbers to aid in digestion.

### Concept Check 41.5

**1.** Over the long term, the body stores excess calories in fat, whether those calories come from fat, carbohydrate, or protein in food. **2.** In normal individuals, leptin levels decline during fasting. Individuals in the group with low levels of leptin are likely to be defective in leptin production, so leptin levels would remain low regardless of food intake. Individuals in the group with high leptin levels are likely to be defective in responding to leptin, but they still should shut off leptin production as fat stores are used up. **3.** The excess production of insulin will cause blood glucose levels to decrease below normal physiological levels. It will also trigger glycogen synthesis in the liver, further decreasing blood glucose levels. However, low blood glucose levels will stimulate the release of glucagon from alpha cells in the pancreas, which will trigger glycogen breakdown. Thus, there will be antagonistic effects in the liver.

### Summary of Key Concepts Questions

**41.1** Since the cofactor is necessary in all animals, those animals that do not require it in their diet must be able to synthesize it from other organic molecules. **41.2** A liquid diet containing glucose, amino acids, and other building blocks could be ingested and absorbed without the need for mechanical or chemical digestion. **41.3** The small intestine has a much larger surface area than the stomach. **41.4** The assortment of teeth in our mouth and the short length of our cecum suggest that our ancestors' digestive systems were not specialized for digesting plant material. **41.5** When mealtime arrives, nervous inputs from the brain signal the stomach to prepare to digest food through secretions and churning.

### Test Your Understanding

**1.** B **2.** A **3.** B **4.** C **5.** B **6.** D **7.** B
**8.**

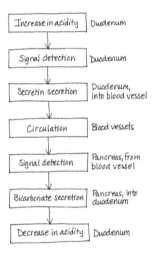

## Chapter 42

### Figure Questions

**Figure 42.2** Although gas exchange might be improved by a steady, one-way flow of fluid, there would likely be inadequate time for food to be digested and nutrients absorbed if fluid flowed through the cavity in this manner. **Figure 42.5** Two capillary beds. The molecule of carbon dioxide would need to enter a capillary bed in the thumb before returning to the right atrium and ventricle, then travel to the lung and enter a capillary from which it could diffuse into an alveolus and be available to be exhaled.   **Figure 42.8** Each feature of the ECG recording, such as the sharp upward spike, occurs once per cardiac cycle. Using the *x*-axis to measure the time in seconds between successive spikes and dividing that number by 60 would yield the heart rate as the number of cycles per minute.   **Figure 42.25** The reduction in surface tension results from the presence of surfactant. Therefore, for all the infants who had died of RDS, you would expect the amount of surfactant to be near zero. For infants who had died of other causes, you would expect the amount of surfactant to be near zero for body masses less than 1,200 g but much greater than zero for body masses above 1,200 g.   **Figure 42.27** Since exhalation is largely passive, the recoil of the elastic fibers in alveoli helps force air out of the lungs. When alveoli lose their elasticity, as occurs in the disease emphysema, less air is exhaled. Because more air is left in the lungs, less fresh air can be inhaled. With a smaller volume of air exchanged, there is a decrease in the partial pressure gradient that drives gas exchange.   **Figure 42.28** Breathing at a rate greater than that needed to meet metabolic demand (hyperventilation) would lower blood $CO_2$ levels. Sensors in major blood vessels and the medulla would signal the breathing control center to decrease the rate of contraction of the diaphragm and rib muscles, decreasing the breathing rate and restoring normal $CO_2$ levels in the blood and other tissues.   **Figure 42.29** The resulting increase in tidal volume would enhance ventilation within the lungs, increasing $P_{O_2}$ and decreasing $P_{CO_2}$ in the alveoli.

### Concept Check 42.1

**1.** In both an open circulatory system and a fountain, fluid is pumped through a tube and then returns to the pump after collecting in a pool.   **2.** The ability to shut off blood supply to the lungs when the animal is submerged   **3.** The $O_2$ content would be abnormally low because some oxygen-depleted blood returned to the right atrium from the systemic circuit would mix with the oxygen-rich blood in the left atrium.

### Concept Check 42.2

**1.** The pulmonary veins carry blood that has just passed through capillary beds in the lungs, where it accumulated $O_2$. The venae cavae carry blood that has just passed through capillary beds in the rest of the body, where it lost $O_2$ to the tissues.   **2.** The delay allows the atria to empty completely, filling ventricles fully before they contract.   **3.** The heart, like any other muscle, becomes stronger through regular exercise. You would expect a stronger heart to have a greater stroke volume, which would allow for the decrease in heart rate.

### Concept Check 42.3

**1.** The large total cross-sectional area of the capillaries   **2.** An increase in blood pressure and cardiac output combined with the diversion of more blood to the skeletal muscles would increase the capacity for action by increasing the rate of blood circulation and delivering more $O_2$ and nutrients to the skeletal muscles.   **3.** Additional hearts could be used to improve blood return from the legs. However, it might be difficult to coordinate the activity of multiple hearts and to maintain adequate blood flow to hearts far from the gas exchange organs.

### Concept Check 42.4

**1.** An increase in the number of white blood cells (leukocytes) may indicate that the person is combating an infection.   **2.** Clotting factors do not initiate clotting but are essential steps in the clotting process.   **3.** The chest pain results from inadequate blood flow in coronary arteries. Vasodilation promoted by nitric oxide from nitroglycerin increases blood flow, providing the heart muscle with additional oxygen and thus relieving the pain.   **4.** Embryonic stem cells are pluripotent rather than multipotent, meaning that they can give rise to many rather than a few different cell types.

### Concept Check 42.5

**1.** Their interior position helps gas exchange tissues stay moist. If the respiratory surfaces of lungs extended out into the terrestrial environment, they would quickly dry out, and diffusion of $O_2$ and $CO_2$ across these surfaces would stop.   **2.** Earthworms need to keep their skin moist for gas exchange, but they need air outside this moist layer. If they stay in their waterlogged tunnels after a heavy rain, they will suffocate because they cannot get as much $O_2$ from water as from air.   **3.** In fish, water passes over the gills in the direction opposite to that of blood flowing through the gill capillaries, maximizing the extraction of oxygen from the water along the length of the exchange surface. Similarly, in the extremities of some vertebrates, blood flows in opposite directions in neighboring veins and arteries; this countercurrent arrangement maximizes the recapture of heat from blood leaving the body core in arteries, which is important for thermoregulation in cold environments.

### Concept Check 42.6

**1.** An increase in blood $CO_2$ concentration causes an increase in the rate of $CO_2$ diffusion into the cerebrospinal fluid, where the $CO_2$ combines with water to form carbonic acid. Dissociation of carbonic acid releases hydrogen ions, decreasing the pH of the cerebrospinal fluid.   **2.** Increased heart rate increases the rate at which $CO_2$-rich blood is delivered to the lungs, where $CO_2$ is removed.   **3.** A hole would allow air to enter the space between the inner and outer layers of the double membrane, resulting in a condition called a pneumothorax. The two layers would no longer stick together, and the lung on the side with the hole would collapse and cease functioning.

### Concept Check 42.7

**1.** Differences in partial pressure between the capillaries and the surrounding tissues or medium; the net diffusion of a gas occurs from a region of higher partial pressure to a region of lower partial pressure.   **2.** The Bohr shift causes

hemoglobin to release more $O_2$ at a lower pH, such as found in the vicinity of tissues with high rates of cellular respiration and $CO_2$ release.   **3.** The doctor is assuming that the rapid breathing is the body's response to low blood pH. Metabolic acidosis, the lowering of blood pH as a result of metabolism, can have many causes, including complications of certain types of diabetes, shock (extremely low blood pressure), and poisoning.

### Summary of Key Concepts Questions

**42.1** In a closed circulatory system, an ATP-driven muscular pump generally moves fluids in one direction on a scale of millimeters to meters. Exchange between cells and their environment relies on diffusion, which involves random movements of molecules. Concentration gradients of molecules across exchange surfaces can drive rapid net diffusion on a scale of 1 mm or less.   **42.2** Replacement of a defective valve would increase stroke volume. A lower heart rate would therefore be sufficient to maintain the same cardiac output.   **42.3** Blood pressure in the arm would fall by 25–30 mm Hg, the same difference as is normally seen between your heart and your brain.   **42.4** One microliter of blood contains about 5 million erythrocytes and 5,000 leukocytes, so leukocytes make up only about 0.1% of the cells in the absence of infection.   **42.5** Because $CO_2$ is such a small fraction of atmospheric gas (0.29 mm Hg/760 mm Hg, or less than 0.04%), the partial pressure gradient of $CO_2$ between the respiratory surface and the environment always strongly favors the release of $CO_2$ to the atmosphere.   **42.6** Because the lungs do not empty completely with each breath, incoming and outgoing air mix. Lungs thus contain a mixture of fresh and stale air.   **42.7** An enzyme speeds up a reaction without changing the equilibrium and without being consumed. Similarly, a respiratory pigment speeds up the exchange of gases between the body and the external environment without changing the equilibrium state and without being consumed.

### Test Your Understanding

**1.** C   **2.** A   **3.** D   **4.** C   **5.** C   **6.** A   **7.** A
**8.**

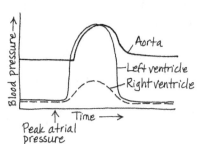

# Chapter 43

### Figure Questions

**Figure 43.4** Dicer-2 binds double-stranded RNA without regard to size or sequence and then cuts that RNA into fragments, each 21 base pairs long. The Argo complex binds to double-stranded RNA fragments that are each 21 base pairs long, displaces one strand, and then uses the remaining strand to match to a particular target sequence in a single-stranded mRNA.   **Figure 43.5** Cell-surface TLRs recognize molecules on the surface of pathogens, whereas TLRs in vesicles recognize internal molecules of pathogens after the pathogens are broken down.   **Figure 43.7** Because the pain of a splinter stops almost immediately when you remove it from the skin, you can correctly deduce that the signals that mediate the inflammatory response are quite short-lived.   **Figure 43.10** Part of the enzyme or antigen receptor provides a structural "backbone" that maintains overall shape, while interaction occurs at a surface with a close fit to the substrate or antigen. The combined effect of multiple noncovalent interactions at the active site or binding site is a high-affinity interaction of tremendous specificity.   **Figure 43.13** After gene rearrangement, a lymphocyte and its daughter cells make a single version of the antigen receptor. In contrast, alternative splicing is not heritable and can give rise to diverse gene products in a single cell.   **Figure 43.14** A single B cell has more than 100,000 identical antigen receptors on its surface, not four, and there are more than 1 million B cells differing in their antigen specificity, not three.   **Figure 43.17** These receptors enable memory cells to present antigen on their cell surface to a helper T cell. This presentation of antigen is required to activate memory cells in a secondary immune response.
**Figure 43.22** Primary response: arrows extending from Antigen (1st exposure), Antigen-presenting cell, Helper T cell, B cell, Plasma cells, Cytotoxic T cell, and Active cytotoxic T cells; secondary response: arrows extending from Antigen (2nd exposure), Memory helper T cells, Memory B cells, Memory cytotoxic T cells, Plasma cells, and Active cytotoxic T cells.   **Figure 43.24** There would be no change in the results. Because the two antigen binding sites of an antibody have identical specificity, the two bacteriophages bound would have to display the same viral peptide.

### Concept Check 43.1

**1.** Because pus contains white blood cells, fluid, and cell debris, it indicates an active and at least partially successful inflammatory response against invading pathogens.   **2.** Whereas the ligand for the TLR receptor is a foreign molecule, the ligand for many signal transduction pathways is a molecule produced by the organism itself.   **3.** Mounting an immune response would require recognition of some molecular feature of the wasp egg not found in the host. It might be that only some potential hosts have a receptor with the necessary specificity.

## Concept Check 43.2

**1.** See Figure 43.9. The transmembrane regions lie within the C regions, which also form the disulfide bridges. In contrast, the antigen-binding sites are in the V regions. **2.** Generating memory cells ensures both that a receptor specific for a particular epitope will be present and that there will be more lymphocytes with this specificity than in a host that had never encountered the antigen. **3.** If each B cell produced two different light and heavy chains for its antigen receptor, different combinations would make four different receptors. If any one were self-reactive, the lymphocyte would be eliminated in the generation of self-tolerance. For this reason, many more B cells would be eliminated, and those that could respond to a foreign antigen would be less effective at doing so due to the variety of receptors (and antibodies) they express.

## Concept Check 43.3

**1.** A child lacking a thymus would have no functional T cells. Without helper T cells to help activate B cells, the child would be unable to produce antibodies against extracellular bacteria. Furthermore, without cytotoxic T cells or helper T cells, the child's immune system would be unable to kill virus-infected cells. **2.** Since the antigen-binding site is intact, the antibody fragments could neutralize viruses and opsonize bacteria. **3.** If the handler developed immunity to proteins in the antivenin, another injection could provoke a severe immune response.

## Concept Check 43.4

**1.** Myasthenia gravis is considered an autoimmune disease because the immune system produces antibodies against self molecules (certain receptors on muscle cells). **2.** A person with a cold is likely to produce oral and nasal secretions that facilitate viral transfer. In addition, since sickness can cause incapacitation or death, a virus that is programmed to exit the host when there is a physiological stress has the opportunity to find a new host at a time when the current host may cease to function. **3.** A person with a macrophage deficiency would have frequent infections. The causes would be poor innate responses, due to diminished phagocytosis and inflammation, and poor adaptive responses, due to the lack of macrophages to present antigens to helper T cells.

## Summary of Key Concepts Questions

**43.1** Lysozyme in saliva destroys bacterial cell walls; the viscosity of mucus helps trap bacteria; acidic pH in the stomach kills many bacteria; and the tight packing of cells lining the gut provides a physical barrier to infection. **43.2** Sufficient numbers of cells to mediate an innate immune response are always present, whereas an adaptive response requires selection and proliferation of an initially very small cell population specific for the infecting pathogen. **43.3** No. Immunological memory after a natural infection and that after vaccination are very similar. There may be minor differences in the particular antigens that can be recognized in a subsequent infection. **43.4** No. AIDS refers to a loss of immune function that can occur over time in an individual infected with HIV. However, certain multidrug combinations ("cocktails") or rare genetic variations usually prevent progression to AIDS in HIV-infected individuals.

## Test Your Understanding

**1.** B **2.** C **3.** C **4.** B **5.** B **6.** B **7.** C **8.** One possible answer:

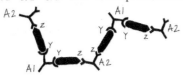

# Chapter 44

## Figure Questions

**Figure 44.13** You would expect to find these cells lining tubules where they pass through the renal medulla. Because the extracellular fluid of the renal medulla has a very high osmolarity, production of organic solutes by tubule cells in this region keeps intracellular osmolarity high, with the result that these cells maintain normal volume. **Figure 44.14** Furosemide increases urine volume. The absence of ion transport in the ascending limb leaves the filtrate too concentrated for substantial volume reduction in the distal tubule and collecting duct. **Figure 44.17** When the concentration of an ion differs across a plasma membrane, the difference in the concentration of ions inside and outside represents chemical potential energy, while the resulting difference in charge inside and outside represents electrical potential energy. **Figure 44.20** The ADH levels would likely be elevated in both sets of patients with mutations because either defect prevents the recapture of water that restores blood osmolarity to normal levels. **Figure 44.21** Arrows that would be labeled "Secretion" are the arrows indicating secretion of aldosterone, angiotensinogen, and renin.

## Concept Check 44.1

**1.** Because the salt is moved against its concentration gradient, from low concentration (fresh water) to high concentration (blood) **2.** A freshwater osmoconformer would have body fluids too dilute to carry out life's processes. **3.** Without a layer of insulating fur, the camel must use the cooling effect of evaporative water loss to maintain body temperature, thus linking thermoregulation and osmoregulation.

## Concept Check 44.2

**1.** Because uric acid is largely insoluble in water, it can be excreted as a semisolid paste, thereby reducing an animal's water loss. **2.** Humans produce uric acid from purine breakdown, and reducing purines in the diet often lessens the severity of gout. Birds, however, produce uric acid as a waste product of general nitrogen metabolism. They would therefore need a diet low in all nitrogen-containing compounds, not just purines.

## Concept Check 44.3

**1.** In flatworms, ciliated cells draw interstitial fluids containing waste products into protonephridia. In earthworms, waste products pass from interstitial fluids into the coelom. From there, cilia move the wastes into metanephridia via a funnel surrounding an internal opening to the metanephridia. In insects, the Malpighian tubules pump fluids from the hemolymph, which receives waste products during exchange with cells in the course of circulation. **2.** Filtrate is formed when the glomerulus filters blood from the renal artery within Bowman's capsule. Some of the filtrate contents are recovered, enter capillaries, and exit in the renal vein; the rest remain in the filtrate and pass out of the kidney in the ureter. **3.** The presence of $Na^+$ and other ions (electrolytes) in the dialysate would limit the extent to which they would be removed from the filtrate during dialysis. Adjusting the electrolytes in the starting dialysate can thus lead to the restoration of proper electrolyte concentrations in the plasma. Similarly, the absence of urea and other waste products in the starting dialysate facilitates their removal from the filtrate.

## Concept Check 44.4

**1.** The numerous nephrons and well-developed glomeruli of freshwater fishes produce urine at a high rate, while the small numbers of nephrons and smaller glomeruli of marine fishes produce urine at a low rate. **2.** The kidney medulla would absorb less water; thus, the drug would increase the amount of water lost in the urine. **3.** A decline in blood pressure in the afferent arteriole would reduce the rate of filtration by moving less material through the vessels.

## Concept Check 44.5

**1.** Alcohol inhibits the release of ADH, causing an increase in urinary water loss and increasing the chance of dehydration. **2.** The consumption of a very large amount of water in a short period of time, coupled with an absence of solute intake, can reduce sodium levels in the blood below tolerable levels. This condition, called hyponatremia, leads to disorientation and, sometimes, respiratory distress. It has occurred in some marathon runners who drink water rather than sports drinks. (It has also caused the death of a fraternity pledge as a consequence of a water hazing ritual and the death of a contestant in a water-drinking competition.) **3.** High blood pressure

## Summary of Key Concepts Questions

**44.1** Water moves into a cell by osmosis when the fluid outside the cells is hypoosmotic (has a lower solute concentration than the cytosol).
**44.2**

| Waste Attribute | Ammonia | Urea | Uric Acid |
|---|---|---|---|
| Toxicity | High | Very low | Low |
| Energy cost to produce | Low | Moderate | High |
| Water loss to excretion | High | Moderate | Low |

**44.3** Filtration produces a fluid for exchange processes that is free of cells and large molecules, which are of benefit to the animal and could not readily be reabsorbed. **44.4** Both types of nephrons have proximal tubules that can reabsorb nutrients, but only juxtamedullary nephrons have loops of Henle that extend deep into the renal medulla. Thus, only kidneys containing juxtamedullary nephrons can produce urine that is more concentrated than the blood. **44.5** Patients who don't produce ADH have symptoms relieved by treatment with the hormone, but many patients with diabetes insipidus lack functional receptors for ADH.

## Test Your Understanding

**1.** C **2.** A **3.** C **4.** D **5.** C **6.** B

# Chapter 45

## Figure Questions

**Figure 45.4**

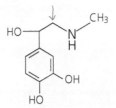

Epinephrine

**Figure 45.5** The hormone is water-soluble and has a cell-surface receptor. Such receptors, unlike those for lipid-soluble hormones, can cause observable changes in cells without hormone-dependent gene transcription. **Figure 45.6** ATP is enzymatically converted to cAMP. The other steps represent binding reactions. **Figure 45.21** The embryonic gonad can become either a testis or an ovary. In contrast, the ducts either form a particular structure or degenerate, and the bladder forms in both males and females.

## Concept Check 45.1

**1.** Water-soluble hormones, which cannot penetrate the plasma membrane, bind to cell-surface receptors. This interaction triggers an intracellular signal transduction pathway that ultimately alters the activity of a preexisting protein in the cytoplasm and/or changes transcription of specific genes in the nucleus. Steroid hormones are lipid-soluble and can cross the plasma membrane into the cell interior, where they bind to receptors located in the cytosol or nucleus. The hormone-receptor complex then functions directly as a transcription factor that changes transcription of specific genes. **2.** An exocrine gland, because pheromones are not secreted into interstitial fluid, but instead are typically released onto a body surface or into the environment **3.** Because receptors for water-soluble hormones are located on the cell surface, facing the extracellular space, injecting the hormone into the cytosol would not trigger a response.

## Concept Check 45.2

**1.** Prolactin regulates milk production, and oxytocin regulates milk release. **2.** The posterior pituitary, an extension of the hypothalamus that contains the axons of neurosecretory cells, is the storage and release site for two neurohormones, oxytocin and antidiuretic hormone (ADH). The anterior pituitary contains endocrine cells that make at least six different hormones. Secretion of anterior pituitary hormones is controlled by hypothalamic hormones that travel via blood vessels to the anterior pituitary. **3.** The hypothalamus and pituitary glands function in many different endocrine pathways. Many defects in these glands, such as those affecting growth or organization, would therefore disrupt many hormone pathways. Only a very specific defect, such as a mutation affecting a particular hormone receptor, would alter just one endocrine pathway. The situation is quite different for the final gland in a pathway, such as the thyroid gland. In this case, a wide range of defects that disrupt gland function would disrupt only the one pathway or small set of pathways in which that gland functions. **4.** Both diagnoses could be correct. In one case, the thyroid gland may produce excess thyroid hormone despite normal hormonal input from the hypothalamus and anterior pituitary. In the other, abnormally elevated hormonal input (elevated TSH levels) may be the cause of the overactive thyroid gland.

## Concept Check 45.3

**1.** If the function of the pathway is to provide a transient response, a short-lived stimulus would be less dependent on negative feedback. **2.** You would be exploiting the anti-inflammatory activity of glucocorticoids. Local injection avoids the effects on glucose metabolism that would occur if glucocorticoids were taken orally and transported throughout the body in the bloodstream. **3.** Both hormones produce opposite effects in different target tissues. In the fight-or-flight response, epinephrine increases blood flow to skeletal muscles and reduces blood flow to smooth muscles in the digestive system. In establishing apical dominance, auxin promotes the growth of apical buds and inhibits the growth of lateral buds.

## Summary of Key Concepts Questions

**45.1** As shown in Figure 43.16, helper T cell activation by cytokines acting as local regulators involves both autocrine and paracrine signaling. **45.2** The pancreas, parathyroid glands, and pineal gland **45.3** Both the pituitary and the adrenal glands are formed by fusion of neural and nonneural tissue. ADH is secreted by the neurosecretory portion of the pituitary gland, and epinephrine is secreted by the neurosecretory portion of the adrenal gland.

## Test Your Understanding

**1.** C **2.** D **3.** D **4.** B **5.** B **6.** B **7.** A
**8.**

Prolactin-releasing hormone
circulates in body via blood
↓
Anterior pituitary
secretes prolactin(o)
Prolactin circulates
in body via blood
↓
Mammary glands
↓
Milk production

# Chapter 46

## Figure Questions

**Figure 46.7** Newly formed sperm enter the seminal vesicle from the testis and exit via the ejaculatory duct during intercourse. Sperm enter the spermatheca after intercourse and, after storage, are released into the oviduct to fertilize an egg moving into the uterus. **Figure 46.8** When successfully courted by a second male, regardless of his genotype, about one-third of the females rid themselves of all sperm from the first mating. Thus, two-thirds retained some sperm from the first mating. We would therefore predict that two-thirds of those females would have some offspring exhibiting the small-eye phenotype of the dominant mutation carried by the males with which the females mated first. **Figure 46.11** The analysis would be informative because the polar bodies contain all of the maternal chromosomes that don't end up in the mature egg. For example, finding two copies of the disease gene in the polar bodies would indicate its absence in the egg. This method of genetic testing is sometimes carried out when oocytes collected from a female are fertilized with sperm in a laboratory dish. **Figure 46.15** The embryo normally implants about a week after conception, but it spends several days in the uterus before implanting, receiving nutrients from the endometrium. Therefore, the fertilized egg should be cultured for several days in liquid that is at normal body temperature and contains the same nutrients as those provided by the endometrium before implantation. **Figure 46.16** Testosterone can pass from fetal blood to maternal blood via the placental circulation, temporarily upsetting the hormonal balance in the mother. **Figure 46.18** Oxytocin would most likely induce labor, starting a positive-feedback loop that would direct labor to completion. Synthetic oxytocin is in fact frequently used to induce labor when prolonged pregnancy might endanger the mother or fetus.

## Concept Check 46.1

**1.** The offspring of sexual reproduction are more genetically diverse. However, asexual reproduction can produce more offspring over multiple generations. **2.** Unlike other forms of asexual reproduction, parthenogenesis involves gamete production. By controlling whether or not haploid eggs are fertilized, species such as honeybees can readily switch between asexual and sexual reproduction. **3.** No. Owing to random assortment of chromosomes during meiosis, the offspring may receive the same copy or different copies of a particular parental chromosome from the sperm and the egg. Furthermore, genetic recombination during meiosis will result in reassortment of genes between pairs of parental chromosomes. **4.** Fragmentation occurs in both plants and animals. Also, budding in animals and the growth of adventitious from plant roots both involve emergence of new individuals from outgrowths of the parent.

## Concept Check 46.2

**1.** Internal fertilization allows sperm to reach the egg without either gamete drying out. **2.** (a) Animals with external fertilization tend to release many gametes at once, resulting in the production of enormous numbers of zygotes. This increases the chances that some will survive to adulthood. (b) Animals with internal fertilization produce fewer offspring but generally exhibit greater care of the embryos and the young. **3.** Like the uterus of an insect, the ovary of a plant is the site of fertilization. Unlike the plant ovary, the uterus is not the site of egg production, which occurs in the insect ovary. In addition, the fertilized insect egg is expelled from the uterus, whereas the plant embryo develops within a seed in the ovary.

## Concept Check 46.3

**1.** Spermatogenesis occurs normally only when the testicles are cooler than normal body temperature. Extensive use of a hot tub (or of very tight-fitting underwear) can cause a decrease in sperm quality and number. **2.** In humans, the secondary oocyte combines with a sperm before it finishes the second meiotic division. Thus, oogenesis is completed after, not before, fertilization. **3.** The only effect of sealing off each vas deferens is an absence of sperm in the ejaculate. Sexual response and ejaculate volume are unchanged. The cutting and sealing off of these ducts, a *vasectomy*, is a common surgical procedure for men who do not wish to produce any (more) offspring.

## Concept Check 46.4

**1.** In the testis, FSH stimulates the Sertoli cells, which nourish developing sperm. LH stimulates the production of androgens (mainly testosterone), which in turn stimulate sperm production. In both females and males, FSH encourages the growth of cells that support and nourish developing gametes (follicle cells in females and Sertoli cells in males), and LH stimulates the production of sex hormones that promote gametogenesis (estrogens, primarily estradiol, in females and androgens, especially testosterone, in males). **2.** In estrous cycles, which occur in most female mammals, the endometrium is reabsorbed (rather than shed) if fertilization does not occur. Estrous cycles often occur just once or a few times a year, and the female is usually receptive to copulation only during the period around ovulation. Menstrual cycles are found only in humans and some other primates. They control the buildup and breakdown of the uterine lining, but not sexual receptivity. **3.** The combination of estradiol and progesterone would have a negative-feedback effect on the hypothalamus, blocking release of GnRH. This would interfere with LH secretion by the pituitary, thus preventing ovulation. This is in fact one basis of action of the most common hormonal contraceptives. **4.** In the viral replicative cycle, the production of new viral genomes is coordinated with capsid protein expression and with the production of phospholipids for viral coats. In the reproductive cycle of a human female, there is hormonally based coordination of egg maturation with the development of support tissues of the uterus.

## Concept Check 46.5

**1.** The secretion of hCG by the early embryo stimulates the corpus luteum to make progesterone, which helps maintain the pregnancy. During the second trimester, however, hCG production drops, the corpus luteum disintegrates, and the placenta completely takes over progesterone production. **2.** Both tubal ligation and vasectomy block the movement of gametes from the gonads to a site where fertilization could take place. **3.** The introduction of a sperm nucleus directly into an oocyte bypasses the sperm's acquisition of motility in the epididymis, its swimming to meet the egg in the oviduct, and its fusion with the egg.

## Summary of Key Concepts Questions

**46.1** No. Because parthenogenesis involves meiosis, the mother would pass on to each offspring a random and therefore typically distinct combination of the chromosomes she inherited from her mother and father. **46.2** None **46.3** The small size and lack of cytoplasm characteristic of a sperm are adaptations well suited to its function as a delivery vehicle for DNA. The large size and rich cytoplasmic contents of eggs support the growth and development of the embryo. **46.4** Circulating anabolic steroids mimic the feedback regulation of testosterone, turning off pituitary signaling to the testes and thereby blocking the release of signals required for spermatogenesis. **46.5** Oxygen in maternal blood diffuses from pools in the endometrium into fetal capillaries in the chorionic villi of the placenta, and from there travels throughout the circulatory system of the fetus.

### Test Your Understanding

**1.** D **2.** B **3.** A **4.** C **5.** A **6.** B **7.** C **8.** D
**9.**

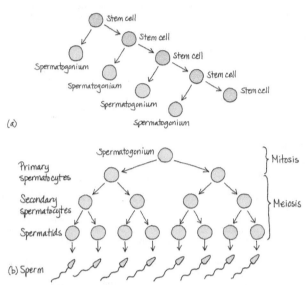

(c) The supply of stem cells would be used up, and spermatogenesis would not be able to continue.

## Chapter 47

### Figure Questions

**Figure 47.4** You could inject the compound into an unfertilized egg, expose the egg to sperm, and see whether the fertilization envelope forms.
**Figure 47.6** There would be fewer cells and they would be closer together.
**Figure 47.8** (1) The blastocoel forms a single compartment that surrounds the gut, much like a doughnut surrounds a hole. (2) Ectoderm forms the outer covering of the animal, and endoderm lines the internal organs, such as the digestive tract. Mesoderm fills much of the space between these two layers.
**Figure 47.19** Eight cell divisions are required to give rise to the intestinal cell closest to the mouth. **Figure 47.22** When the researchers allowed normal cortical rotation to occur, the "back-forming" determinants were activated. When they then forced the opposite rotation to occur, the back was established on the opposite side as well. Because the molecules on the normal side were already activated, forcing the opposite rotation apparently did not "cancel out" the establishment of the back side by the first rotation.
**Figure 47.23 Draw It**

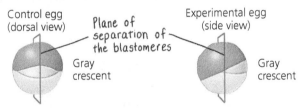

**What If?** In Spemann's control, the two blastomeres were physically separated, and each grew into a whole embryo. In Roux's experiment, remnants of the dead blastomere were still contacting the live blastomere, which developed into a half-embryo. Therefore, molecules present in the dead cell's remnants may have been signaling to the live cell, inhibiting it from making all the embryonic structures. **Figure 47.24** You could inject the isolated protein (or an mRNA encoding it) into ventral cells of an earlier gastrula. If dorsal structures form on the ventral side, that would support the idea that the protein is the signaling molecule secreted or presented by the dorsal lip. You should also do a control experiment to make sure the injection process alone did not cause dorsal

structures to form. **Figure 47.26** Either Sonic hedgehog mRNA or protein can serve as a marker of the ZPA. The absence of either one after removal of the AER would support your hypothesis. You could also block FGF function and see whether the ZPA formed (by looking for Sonic hedgehog).

### Concept Check 47.1

**1.** The fertilization envelope forms after cortical granules release their contents outside the egg, causing the vitelline membrane to rise and harden. The fertilization envelope serves as a barrier to fertilization by more than one sperm. **2.** The increased $Ca^{2+}$ concentration in the egg would cause the cortical granules to fuse with the plasma membrane, releasing their contents and causing a fertilization envelope to form, even though no sperm had entered. This would prevent fertilization. **3.** You would expect it to fluctuate. The fluctuation of MPF drives the transition between DNA replication (S phase) and mitosis (M phase), which is still required in the abbreviated cleavage cell cycle.

### Concept Check 47.2

**1.** The cells of the notochord migrate toward the midline of the embryo (converge), rearranging themselves so there are fewer cells across the notochord, which thus becomes longer overall (extends; see Figure 47.17). **2.** Because microfilaments would not be able to contract and decrease the size of one end of the cell, both the inward bending in the middle of the neural tube and the outward bending of the hinge regions at the edges would be blocked. Therefore, the neural tube probably would not form. **3.** Dietary intake of the vitamin folic acid dramatically reduces the frequency of neural tube defects.

### Concept Check 47.3

**1.** Axis formation establishes the location and polarity of the three axes that provide the coordinates for development. Pattern formation positions particular tissues and organs in the three-dimensional space defined by those coordinates. **2.** Morphogen gradients act by specifying cell fates across a field of cells through variation in the level of a determinant. Morphogen gradients thus act more globally than cytoplasmic determinants or inductive interactions between pairs of cells. **3.** Yes, a second embryo could develop because inhibiting BMP-4 activity would have the same effect as transplanting an organizer. **4.** The limb that developed probably would have a mirror-image duplication, with the most posterior digits in the middle and the most anterior digits at either end.

### Summary of Key Concepts Questions

**47.1** The binding of a sperm to a receptor on the egg surface is very specific and likely would not occur if the two gametes were from different species. Without sperm binding, the sperm and egg membranes would not fuse. **47.2** Apoptosis functions to eliminate structures required only in an immature form, nonfunctional cells from a pool larger than the number required, and tissues formed by a developmental program that is not adaptive for the organism as it has evolved. **47.3** Mutations that affected both limb and kidney development would be more likely to alter the function of monocilia because these organelles are important in several signaling pathways. Mutations that affected limb development but not kidney development would more likely alter a single pathway, such as Hedgehog signaling.

### Test Your Understanding

**1.** A **2.** B **3.** D **4.** A **5.** D **6.** C **7.** B
**8.**

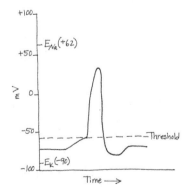

## Chapter 48

### Figure Questions

**Figure 48.7** Adding chloride channels would make the membrane potential less positive. Adding potassium channels would have no effect because there are no potassium ions present. **Figure 48.9** In the absence of other forces, chemical concentration gradients govern net diffusion. In this case, ions are more concentrated outside of the cell and move in when the channel opens.
**Figure 48.10**

**Figure 48.11**

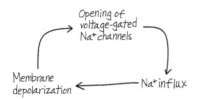

**Figure 48.12**

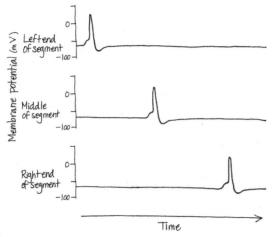

**Figure 48.15** The production and transmission of action potentials would be unaffected. However, action potentials arriving at chemical synapses would be unable to trigger release of neurotransmitter. Signaling at such synapses would thus be blocked. **Figure 48.17** Summation only occurs if inputs occur simultaneously or nearly so. Thus, spatial summation, in which input is received from two different sources, is in effect also temporal summation.

## Concept Check 48.1

**1.** Axons and dendrites extend from the cell body and function in information flow. Dendrites transfer information to the cell body, whereas axons transmit information from the cell body. A typical neuron has multiple dendrites and one axon. **2.** Sensors in your ear transmit information to your brain. There, the activity of interneurons in processing centers enables you to recognize your name. In response, signals transmitted via motor neurons cause contraction of muscles that turn your neck. **3.** Increased branching would allow control of a greater number of postsynaptic cells, enhancing coordination of responses to nervous system signals.

## Concept Check 48.2

**1.** Ions can flow against a chemical concentration gradient if there is an opposing electrical gradient of greater magnitude. **2.** A decrease in permeability to $K^+$, an increase in permeability to $Na^+$, or both **3.** Charged dye molecules could equilibrate only if other charged molecules could also cross the membrane. If not, a membrane potential would develop that would counterbalance the chemical gradient.

## Concept Check 48.3

**1.** A graded potential has a magnitude that varies with stimulus strength, whereas an action potential has an all-or-none magnitude that is independent of stimulus strength. **2.** Loss of the insulation provided by myelin sheaths leads to a disruption of action potential propagation along axons. Voltage-gated sodium channels are restricted to the nodes of Ranvier, and without the insulating effect of myelin, the inward current produced at one node during an action potential cannot depolarize the membrane to the threshold at the next node. **3.** Positive feedback is responsible for the rapid opening of many voltage-gated sodium channels, causing the rapid outflow of sodium ions responsible for the rising phase of the action potential. As the membrane potential becomes positive, voltage-gated potassium channels open in a form of negative feedback that helps bring about the falling phase of the action potential. **4.** The maximum frequency would decrease because the refractory period would be extended.

## Concept Check 48.4

**1.** It can bind to different types of receptors, each triggering a specific response in postsynaptic cells. **2.** These toxins would prolong the EPSPs that acetylcholine produces because the neurotransmitter would remain longer in the synaptic cleft. **3.** Membrane depolarization, exocytosis, and membrane fusion each occur in fertilization and in neurotransmission.

## Summary of Key Concepts Questions

**48.1** It would prevent information from being transmitted away from the cell body along the axon. **48.2** There are very few open sodium channels in a resting

neuron, so the resting potential either would not change or would become slightly more negative (hyperpolarization). **48.4** A given neurotransmitter can have many receptors that differ in their location and activity. Drugs that target receptor activity rather than neurotransmitter release or stability are therefore likely to exhibit greater specificity and potentially have fewer undesirable side effects.

## Test Your Understanding

**1.** C **2.** C **3.** C **4.** B **5.** A **6.** D
**7.** The activity of the sodium-potassium pump is essential to maintain the resting potential. With the pump inactivated, the sodium and potassium concentration gradients would gradually disappear, resulting in a greatly reduced resting potential. **8.** Since GABA is an inhibitory neurotransmitter in the CNS, this drug would be expected to decrease brain activity. A decrease in brain activity might be expected to slow down or reduce behavioral activity. Many sedative drugs act in this fashion. **9.** As shown in this pair of drawings, a pair of action potentials would move outward in both directions from each electrode. (Action potentials are unidirectional only if they begin at one end of an axon.) However, because of the refractory period, the two action potentials between the electrodes both stop where they meet. Thus, only one action potential reaches the synaptic terminals.

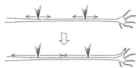

# Chapter 49

## Figure Questions

**Figure 49.7** During swallowing, muscles along the esophagus alternately contract and relax, resulting in peristalsis. One model to explain this alternation is that each section of muscle receives nerve impulses that alternate between excitation and inhibition, just as the quadriceps and hamstring receive opposing signals in the knee-jerk reflex. **Figure 49.15** The gray areas have a different shape and pattern, indicating different planes through the brain. This fact indicates that the nucleus accumbens and the amygdala are in different planes. **Figure 49.17** The hand is shown larger than the forearm because the hand receives more innervation than the forearm for sensory input to the brain and motor output from the brain. **Figure 49.24** If the depolarization brings the membrane potential to or past threshold, it should initiate action potentials that cause dopamine release from the VTA neurons. This should mimic natural stimulation of the brain reward system, resulting in positive and perhaps pleasurable sensations.

## Concept Check 49.1

**1.** The sympathetic division would likely be activated. It mediates the "fight-or-flight" response in stressful situations. **2.** Nerves contain bundles of axons, some that belong to motor neurons, which send signals outward from the CNS, and some that belong to sensory neurons, which bring signals into the CNS. Therefore, you would expect effects on both motor control and sensation. **3.** Neurosecretory cells of the adrenal medulla secrete the hormones epinephrine and norepinephrine in response to preganglionic input from sympathetic neurons. These hormones travel in the circulation throughout the body, triggering responses in many tissues.

## Concept Check 49.2

**1.** The cerebral cortex on the left side of the brain initiates voluntary movement of the right side of the body. **2.** Alcohol diminishes function of the cerebellum. **3.** A coma reflects a disruption in the cycles of sleep and arousal regulated by communication between the midbrain and pons (reticular formation) and the cerebrum. You would expect this group to have damage to the midbrain, the pons, the cerebrum, or any part of the brain between these structures. Paralysis reflects an inability to carry out motor commands transmitted from the cerebrum to the spinal cord. You would expect this group to have damage to the portion of the CNS extending from the spinal cord up to but not including the midbrain and pons.

## Concept Check 49.3

**1.** Brain damage that disrupts behavior, cognition, memory, or other functions provides evidence that the portion of the brain affected by the damage is important for the normal activity that is blocked or altered. **2.** Broca's area, which is active during the generation of speech, is located near the motor cortex, which controls skeletal muscles, including those in the face. Wernicke's area, which is active when speech is heard, is located in the posterior part of the temporal lobe, which is involved in hearing. **3.** Each cerebral hemisphere is specialized for different parts of this task—the right for face recognition and the left for language. Without an intact corpus callosum, neither hemisphere can take advantage of the other's processing abilities.

## Concept Check 49.4

**1.** There can be an increase in the number of synapses between the neurons or an increase in the strength of existing synaptic connections. **2.** If consciousness is an emergent property resulting from the interaction of many different regions of the brain, then it is unlikely that localized brain damage will have a discrete effect on consciousness.   **3.** The hippocampus is responsible for organizing newly acquired information. Without hippocampal function, the links necessary to retrieve information from the cerebral cortex will be lacking, and no functional memory, short- or long-term, will be formed.

### Concept Check 49.5

**1.** Both are progressive brain diseases whose risk increases with advancing age. Both result from the death of brain neurons and are associated with the accumulation of peptide or protein aggregates.   **2.** The symptoms of schizophrenia can be mimicked by a drug that stimulates dopamine-releasing neurons. The brain's reward system, which is involved in drug addiction, is composed of dopamine-releasing neurons that connect the ventral tegmental area to regions in the cerebrum. Parkinson's disease results from the death of dopamine-releasing neurons.   **3.** Not necessarily. It might be that the plaques, tangles, and missing regions of the brain seen at death reflect secondary effects, the consequence of other unseen changes that are actually responsible for the alterations in brain function.

### Summary of Key Concepts Questions

**49.1** Because reflex circuits involve only a few neurons—the simplest consist of a sensory neuron and a motor neuron—the path for information transfer is short and simple, increasing the speed of the response.   **49.2** The midbrain coordinates visual reflexes; the cerebellum controls coordination of movement that depends on visual input; the thalamus serves as a routing center for visual information; and the cerebrum is essential for converting visual input to a visual image.   **49.3** You would expect the right side of the body to be paralyzed because it is controlled by the left cerebral hemisphere, where language generation and interpretation are localized.   **49.4** Learning a new language likely requires the maintenance of synapses that are formed during early development but are otherwise lost prior to adulthood.   **49.5** Whereas amphetamine stimulates dopamine release, PCP blocks glutamate receptors, suggesting that schizophrenia does not reflect a defect in the function of just one neurotransmitter.

### Test Your Understanding

**1.** B   **2.** B   **3.** D   **4.** C   **5.** C   **6.** A
**7.**

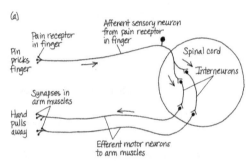

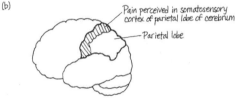

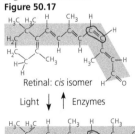

## Chapter 50

### Figure Questions

**Figure 50.17** The hydrogen (H) atoms are on the same side of the carbon-carbon double bond in the *cis* isomer and the opposite side in the *trans* isomer.

Retinal: *cis* isomer

Light ↓ ↑ Enzymes

Retinal: *trans* isomer

**Figure 50.19** Each of the three types of cones is most sensitive to a different wavelength of light. A cone might be fully depolarized when there is light present if

the light is of a wavelength far from its optimum.   **Figure 50.21** In humans, an X chromosome with a defect in the red or green opsin gene is much less common than a wild-type X chromosome. Color blindness therefore typically skips a generation as the defective allele passes from an affected male to a carrier daughter and back to an affected grandson. In squirrel monkeys, no X chromosome can confer full color vision. As a result, all males are color-blind and no unusual inheritance pattern is observed.   **Figure 50.23** The results of the experiment would have been identical. What matters is the activation of particular sets of neurons, not the manner in which they are activated. Any signal from a bitter cell will be interpreted by the brain as a bitter taste, regardless of the nature of the compound and the receptor involved.   **Figure 50.25** Only perception. Binding of an odorant to its receptor will cause action potentials to be sent to the brain. Although an excess of that odorant might cause a diminished response through adaptation, another odorant can mask the first only at the level of perception in the brain. **Figure 50.26** Both. A muscle fiber contains many myofibrils bundled together and divided lengthwise into many sarcomeres. A sarcomere is a contractile unit made up of portions of many myofibrils, and each myofibril is a part of many sarcomeres.   **Figure 50.28** Hundreds of myosin heads participate in sliding each pair of thick and thin filaments past each other. Because cross-bridge formation and breakdown are not synchronized, many myosin heads are exerting force on the thin filaments at all times during muscle contraction.   **Figure 50.33** By causing all of the motor neurons that control the muscle to generate action potentials at a rate high enough to produce tetanus in all of the muscle fibers.

### Concept Check 50.1

**1.** Electromagnetic receptors in general detect only external stimuli. Nonelectromagnetic receptors, such as chemoreceptors or mechanoreceptors, can act as either internal or external sensors.   **2.** The capsaicin present in the peppers activates the thermoreceptor for high temperatures. In response to the perceived high temperature, the nervous system triggers sweating to achieve evaporative cooling.   **3.** You would perceive the electrical stimulus as if the sensory receptors that regulate that neuron had been activated. For example, electrical stimulation of the sensory neuron controlled by the thermoreceptor activated by menthol would likely be perceived as a local cooling.

### Concept Check 50.2

**1.** Otoliths detect the animal's orientation with respect to gravity, providing information that is essential in environments such as the tunnel habitat of the star-nosed mole, where light cues are absent.   **2.** As a sound that changes gradually from a very low to a very high pitch   **3.** The stapes and the other middle ear bones transmit vibrations from the tympanic membrane to the oval window. Fusion of these bones (as occurs in a disease called otosclerosis) would block this transmission and result in hearing loss.   **4.** In animals, the statoliths are extracellular. In contrast, the statoliths of plants are found within an intracellular organelle. The methods for detecting their location also differ. In animals, detection is by means of mechanoreceptors on ciliated cells. In plants, the mechanism appears to involve calcium signaling.

### Concept Check 50.3

**1.** Planarians have ocelli that cannot form images but can sense the intensity and direction of light, providing enough information to enable the animals to find protection in shaded places. Flies have compound eyes that form images and excel at detecting movement.   **2.** The person can focus on distant objects but not close objects (without glasses) because close focusing requires the lens to become almost spherical. This problem is common after age 50.   **3.** The signal produced by rod and cone cells is glutamate, and their release of glutamate decreases upon exposure to light. However, a decrease in glutamate production causes other retinal cells to increase the rate at which action potentials are sent to the brain, so that the brain receives more action potentials in light than in dark.   **4.** Absorption of light by retinal converts retinal from its *cis* isomer to its *trans* isomer, initiating the process of light detection. In contrast, a photon absorbed by chlorophyll does not bring about isomerization, but instead boosts an electron to a higher energy orbital, initiating the electron flow that generates ATP and NADPH.

### Concept Check 50.4

**1.** Both taste cells and olfactory cells have receptor proteins in their plasma membrane that bind certain substances, leading to membrane depolarization through a signal transduction pathway involving a G protein. However, olfactory cells are sensory neurons, whereas taste cells are not.   **2.** Since animals rely on chemical signals for behaviors that include finding mates, marking territories, and avoiding dangerous substances, it is adaptive for the olfactory system to have a robust response to a very small number of molecules of a particular odorant.   **3.** Because the sweet, bitter, and umami tastes involve GPCR proteins but the sour taste does not, you might predict that the mutation is in a molecule that acts in the signal transduction pathway common to the different GPCRs.

### Concept Check 50.5

**1.** In a skeletal muscle fiber, $Ca^{2+}$ binds to the troponin complex, which moves tropomyosin away from the myosin-binding sites on actin and allows crossbridges to form. In a smooth muscle cell, $Ca^{2+}$ binds to calmodulin, which activates an enzyme that phosphorylates the myosin head and thus enables cross-bridge formation.   **2.** *Rigor mortis*, a Latin phrase meaning "stiffness of death," results from the complete depletion of ATP in skeletal muscle. Since ATP is required to release myosin from actin and to pump $Ca^{2+}$ out of the cytosol, muscles become chronically contracted beginning about 3–4 hours after death.   **3.** A competitive inhibitor binds to the same site as the substrate for the enzyme. In contrast, the troponin and tropomyosin complex masks, but does not bind to, the myosin-binding sites on actin.

### Concept Check 50.6

**1.** The main problem in swimming is drag; a fusiform body minimizes drag. The main problem in flying is overcoming gravity; wings shaped like airfoils provide lift, and adaptations such as air-filled bones reduce body mass.   **2.** In modeling peristalsis you would constrict the toothpaste tube at different points along its length, using your hand to encircle the tube and squeeze concentrically. To demonstrate movement of food through the digestive tract you would want the cap off the toothpaste tube, whereas you would want the cap on to show how peristalsis contributes to worm locomotion.   **3.** When you grasp the sides of the chair, you are using a contraction of the triceps to keep your arms extended against the pull of gravity on your body. As you lower yourself slowly into the chair, you gradually decrease the number of motor units in the triceps that are contracted. Contracting your biceps would jerk you down, since you would no longer be opposing gravity.

### Summary of Key Concepts Questions

**50.1** Nociceptors overlap with other classes of receptors in the type of stimulus they detect. They differ from other receptors only in how a particular stimulus is perceived.   **50.2** Volume is encoded by the frequency of action potentials transmitted to the brain; pitch is encoded by which axons are transmitting action potentials.   **50.3** The major difference is that neurons in the retina integrate information from multiple sensory receptors (photoreceptors) before transmitting information to the central nervous system.   **50.4** Our olfactory sense is responsible for most of what we describe as distinct tastes. A head cold or other source of congestion blocks odorant access to receptors lining portions of the nasal cavity.   **50.5** Hydrolysis of ATP is required to convert myosin to a high-energy configuration for binding to actin and to power the $Ca^{2+}$ pump that removes cytosolic $Ca^{2+}$ during muscle relaxation.   **50.6** Human body movements rely on the contraction of muscles anchored to a rigid endoskeleton. Tendons attach muscles to bones, which in turn are composed of fibers built up from a basic organizational unit, the sarcomere. The thin and thick filaments have separate points of attachment within the sarcomere. In response to nervous system motor output, the formation and breakdown of cross-bridges between myosin heads and actin ratchet the thin and thick filaments past each other. Because the filaments are anchored, this sliding movement shortens the muscle fibers. Furthermore, because the fibers themselves are part of the muscles attached at each end to bones, muscle contraction moves bones of the body relative to each other. In this way, the structural anchoring of muscles and filaments enables muscle function, such as the bending of an elbow by contraction of the biceps.

### Test Your Understanding

**1.** D   **2.** A   **3.** B   **4.** C   **5.** B   **6.** D
**7.**

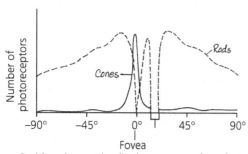

Fovea
Position along retina (in degrees away from fovea)

The answer shows the actual distribution of rods and cones in the human eye. Your graph may differ, but should have the following properties: only cones at the fovea; fewer cones and more rods at both ends of the *x*-axis; no photoreceptors in the optic disk.

## Chapter 51

### Figure Questions

**Figure 51.2** The fixed action pattern based on the sign stimulus of a red belly ensures that the male will chase away any invading males of his species. By chasing away such males, the defender decreases the chance that another male will fertilize eggs laid in his nesting territory.   **Figure 51.5** The straight-run portion conveys two pieces of information: direction, via the angle of that run relative to the wall of the hive, and distance, via the number of waggles performed during the straight run. At a minimum, the portions between the straight runs identify the activity as a waggle dance. Since they also provide contact with workers to

one side and then the other, they may ensure transmission of information to a larger number of other bees.   **Figure 51.7** There should be no effect. Imprinting is an innate behavior that is carried out anew in each generation. Assuming the nest was not disturbed, the offspring of the geese imprinted on a human would imprint on the mother goose.   **Figure 51.8** Perhaps the wasp doesn't use visual cues. It might also be that wasps recognize objects native to their environment, but not foreign objects, such as the pinecones. Tinbergen addressed these ideas before carrying out the pinecone study. When he swept away the pebbles and sticks around the nest, the wasps could no longer find their nests. If he shifted the natural objects in their natural arrangement, the shift in the landmarks caused a shift in the site to which the wasps returned. Finally, if natural objects around the nest site were replaced with pinecones while the wasp was in the burrow, the wasp nevertheless found her way back to the nest site.   **Figure 51.10** Switching the orientations of all three grids would control for an inherent preference for or against a particular orientation. If there were no inherent preference or bias, the experiment should work equally well after the switch.   **Figure 51.24** It might be that the birds require stimuli during flight to exhibit their migratory preference. If this were true, the birds would show the same orientation in the funnel experiment despite their distinct genetic programming.   **Figure 51.26** It holds true for some, but not all individuals. If a parent has more than one reproductive partner, the offspring of different partners will have a coefficient of relatedness less than 0.5.

### Concept Check 51.1

**1.** The proximate explanation for this fixed action pattern might be that nudging and rolling are released by the sign stimulus of an object outside the nest, and the behavior is carried to completion once initiated. The ultimate explanation might be that ensuring that eggs remain in the nest increases the chance of producing healthy offspring.   **2.** There might be selective pressure for other prey fish to detect an injured fish because the source of the injury might threaten them as well. Among predators, there might be selection for those that are attracted to the alarm substance because they would be more likely to encounter crippled prey. Fish with adequate defenses might show no change because they have a selective advantage if they do not waste energy responding to the alarm substance.   **3.** In both cases, the detection of periodic variation in the environment results in a reproductive cycle timed to environmental conditions that optimize the opportunity for success.

### Concept Check 51.2

**1.** Natural selection would tend to favor convergence in color pattern because a predator learning to associate a pattern with a sting or bad taste would avoid all other individuals with that same color pattern, regardless of species.   **2.** You might move objects around to establish an abstract rule, such as "past landmark A, the same distance as A is from the starting point," while maintaining a minimum of fixed metric relationships, that is, avoiding having the food directly adjacent to or a set distance from a landmark. As you might surmise, designing an informative experiment of this kind is not easy.   **3.** Learned behavior, just like innate behavior, can contribute to reproductive isolation and thus to speciation. For example, learned bird songs contribute to species recognition during courtship, thereby helping ensure that only members of the same species mate.

### Concept Check 51.3

**1.** Certainty of paternity is higher with external fertilization.   **2.** Balancing selection could maintain the two alleles at the *forager* locus if population density fluctuated from one generation to another. At times of low population density, the energy-conserving sitter larvae (carrying the $for^s$ allele) would be favored, while at higher population density, the more mobile Rover larvae ($for^R$ allele) would have a selective advantage.   **3.** Because females would now be present in much larger numbers than males, all three types of males should have some reproductive success. Nevertheless, since the advantage that the blue-throats rely on—a limited number of females in their territory—will be absent, the yellow-throats are likely to increase in frequency in the short term.

### Concept Check 51.4

**1.** Because this geographic variation corresponds to differences in prey availability between two garter snake habitats, it seems likely that snakes with characteristics enabling them to feed on the abundant prey in their locale would have had increased survival and reproductive success. In this way, natural selection would have resulted in the divergent foraging behaviors.   **2.** The fact that the individual shares some genes with the offspring of its sibling (in the case of humans, with the individual's niece or nephew) means that the reproductive success of that niece or nephew increases the representation of those genes in the population (selects for them).   **3.** The older individual cannot be the beneficiary because he or she cannot have extra offspring. However, the cost is low for an older individual performing the altruistic act because that individual has already reproduced (but perhaps is still caring for a child or grandchild). There can therefore be selection for an altruistic act by a postreproductive individual that benefits a young relative.

### Summary of Key Concepts Questions

**51.1** Circannual rhythms are typically based on the cycles of light and dark in the environment. As the global climate changes, animals that migrate in response to these rhythms may shift to a location before or after local environmental conditions are optimal for reproduction and survival.   **51.2** For the goose, all that is acquired is an object at which the behavior is directed. In the case of the sparrow, learning takes place that will give shape to the behavior itself.   **51.3** Because feeding the female is likely to improve her reproductive success, the genes from the sacrificed male are likely to appear in a greater number of progeny.   **51.4** Studying the genetic basis of these behaviors reveals that changes in a single gene can have large-scale effects on even complex behaviors.

**Test Your Understanding**
1. C   2. B   3. B   4. A   5. C   6. A

7.

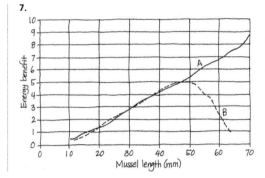

You could measure the size of mussels that oystercatchers successfully open and compare that with the size distribution in the habitat.

# Credits

## Photo Credits

**42.19** Image Source/Exactostock.1598/SuperStock; **42 Scientific Skills Exercise** Fotolia; **42.21a** Peter Batson/Image Quest Marine; **42.21b** Olgysha/Shutterstock; **42.21c** Jez Tryner/Image Quest Marine; **42.23** Hong Y. Yan, University of Kentucky and Peng Chai, University of Texas; **42.24** Motta/Macchiarelli, Anatomy Dept./Univ. La Sapienza, Rome/SPL/Science Source; **42.26** Hans-Rainer Duncker, Institute of Anatomy and Cell Biology, Justus-Liebig-University Giessen; **p. 947** Doug Allan/Nature Picture Library; **p. 949** Stefan Hetz/WENN.com/Newscom

Chapter 43 **43.1** SPL/Science Source; **p. 950 bottom** Juergen Berger/Science Source; **p. 962** Steve Gschmeissner/Science Source; **43.26** CNRI/Science Source; **43 Scientific Skills Exercise** Eye of Science/Science Source; **43.28** Stephen Č. Harrison/The Laboratory of Structural Cell Biology/Harvard Medical School; **p. 974** Tatan YUFLANA/AP Images

Chapter 44 **44.1** David Wall/Alamy Stock Photo; **p. 975 bottom** David Wall/Alamy Stock Photo; **44.3** Mark Conlin/Image Quest Marine; **44.5 left** Eye of Science/Science Source; **right** Eye of Science/Science Source; **44 Scientific Skills Exercise** Jiri Lochman/Lochman Transparencies; **44.7 left** GeorgePeters/E+/Getty Images; **center** Eric Isselée/Fotolia; **right** Maksym Gorpenyuk/Shutterstock; **44.12 right** Steve Gschmeissner/Science Source; **44.15** Michael Lynch/Shutterstock; **44.16** v_blinov/Fotolia; **44.17 cod** Roger Steene/Image Quest Marine; **frog** F. Rauschenbach/F1online digitale Bildagentur GmbH/Alamy Stock Photo; **stomata** Power and Syred/Science Source; **bacteria** Eye of Science/Science Source; **p. 996** Steven A. Wasserman

Chapter 45 **45.1** Phillip Colla/Oceanlight.com; **p. 997 bottom** Craig K. Lorenz/Science Source; **45.3** Volker Witte/Ludwig-Maximilians-Universitat Munchen; **45.11** Cathy Keifer/123RF; **p. 1008** angellodeco/Fotolia; **45.17** AP Images; **45.22 left** Blickwinkel/Alamy Stock Photo; **45.22 right** Jurgen and Christine Sohns/Frank Lane Picture Agency Limited; **p. 1016** Eric Roubos

Chapter 46 **46.1** Auscape/UIG/Getty Images; **46.2** Colin Marshall/Frank Lane Picture Agency; **46.3** P. de Vries; **46.5** Andy Sands/Nature Picture Library; **46.6** John Cancalosi/Alamy Stock Photo; **46 Scientific Skills Exercise** Tierbild Okapia/Science Source; **46.12** Design Pics Inc./Alamy Stock Photo; **46.17ab** Lennart Nilsson/Scanpix; **46.21** Phanie/SuperStock; **p. 1040** Dave Thompson/AP Images

Chapter 47 **47.1** Brad Smith/Stamps School of Art & Design, University of Michigan; **p. 1041 bottom** Oxford Scientific/Getty Images; **47.4abcd** From: Methods for quantitating sea urchin sperm-egg binding. V D Vacquier and J E Payne. *Exp Cell Res.* 1973 Nov; 82(1):227-35.; **47.4efgh** From: Wave of Free Calcium at Fertilization in the Sea Urchin Egg Visualized with Fura-2. M. Hafner et al. *Cell Motil. Cytoskel.*, 1988; 9:271-277; **47.6a-d** George von Dassow; **47.7 top** Jurgen Berger; **bottom** Andrew J. Ewald; **47.8a** Charles A. Ettensohn; **47.13b** Alejandro Díaz Díez/AGE Fotostock/Alamy Stock Photo; **47.14 left** Huw Williams; **right** Thomas Poole; **47.15b** Keith Wheeler/Science Source; **47.18b left** Hiroki Nishida; **right** Hiroki Nishida; **47.19** Medical Research Council; **47.20 & 21** MDC Biology Sinsheimer Labs; **47.24** From: Dorsal-ventral patterning and neural induction in *Xenopus* embryos. E. M. De Robertis and H. Kuroda. *Annu Rev Cell Dev Biol.* 2004;20:285-308. Fig. 1.; **47.25a** Kathryn W. Tosney; **47.26** Dennis Summerbell; **p. 1064** James Gerholdt/Getty Images

Chapter 48 **48.1** Franco Banfi/Science Source; **48.3** Thomas Deerinck; **48.13** Alan Peters; **48.16** Edwin R. Lewis, Y. Y. Zeevi and T. E, Everhart, University of California, Berkeley; **p. 1082** B.A.E. Inc./Alamy Stock Photo

Chapter 49 **49.1** Tamily Weissman; **49.4** Image by Sebastian Jessberger. Fred H. Gage, Laboratory of Genetics LOG-G, The Salk Institute for Biological Studies; **49.11** Larry Mulvehill/Corbis; **49.15ab** From: A functional MRI study of happy and sad affective states induced by classical music, M. T. Mitterschiffthaler et al. *Hum Brain Mapp.* 2007 Nov;28(11):1150-62. Fig. 1.; **49.18**, Marcus E Raichle; **49.19** From: Dr. Harlow's Case of Recovery from the passage of an Iron Bar through the Head, H. Bigelow. *Am. J of the Med. Sci.* July 1850;XXXIX. Images from the History of Medicine (NLM).; **49.25** Martin M. Rotker/Science Source; **p. 1104** Eric Delmar/Getty Images

Chapter 50 **50.1** Kenneth Catania; **50.6 top** CSIRO Publishing; **bottom** R. A. Steinbrecht; **50.7a** Michael Nolan/Robert Harding World Imagery; **50.7b** Grischa Georgiew/AGE Fotostock; **50.9** Richard Elzinga; **50.10** SPL//Science Source; **50.16a** USDA/APHIS Animal and Plant Health Inspection Service; **50.17** Steve Gschmeissner/Science Source; **50.21** Neitz Laboratory, University of Washington Medical School, Seattle; **50.26** Clara Franzini-Armstrong; **50.27** H. E. Huxley; **50.34** George Cathcart Photography; **50.39** Dave Watts/NHPA/Science Source; **50 Scientific Skills Exercise** Vance A. Tucker; **p. 1136** Dogs/Fotolia

Chapter 51 **51.1** Manamana/Shutterstock; **p. 1137 bottom** Ivan Kuzmin/Alamy Stock Photo; **51.2** Martin Harvey/Photolibrary/Getty Images; **51.3** Denis-Huot/Hemis/Alamy Stock Photo; **51.5** Kenneth Lorenzen; **p. 1142** Dustin Finkelstein/Getty Images; **51.7** Thomas D. McAvoy/The LIFE Picture Collection/Getty Images; **51.9** Lincoln Brower/Sweet Briar College; **51.11** Clive Bromhall/Oxford Scientific/Getty Images; **51.12** Richard Wrangham; **inset** Alissa Crandall/Encyclopedia/Corbis; **51 Scientific Skills Exercise** Matt Goff; **51.14a** Matt T. Lee; **51.14b** David Osborn/Alamy Stock Photo; **51.14c** David Tipling/Frank Lane Picture Agency Limited; **51.15** James D Watt/Image Quest Marine; **51.16** Gerald S. Wilkinson; **51.17** Cyril Laubscher/Dorling Kindersley, Ltd.; **51.20** Martin Harvey/Photolibrary/Getty Images; **51.21** Erik Svensson/Lund University, Sweden; **51.22** Lowell Getz; **51.23** Rory Doolin; **51.25** Jennifer Jarvis; **51.27** Marie Read/NHPA/Photoshot; **51.28** Jupiterimages/Creatas/Thinkstock/Getty Images; **p. 1160** William Leaman/Alamy Stock Photo

Appendix A **p. A-1 right 01** From: Anatomy of the vessel network within and between tree rings of *Fraxinus lanuginosa* (Oleaceae). Peter B. Kitin, Tomoyuki Fujii, Hisashi Abe and Ryo Funada. *American Journal of Botany.* 2004;91:779-788.

## Illustration and Text Credits

Chapter 35 **35 Scientific Skills Exercise** Data from D. L. Royer et al., Phenotypic Plasticity of Leaf Shape Along a Temperature Gradient in *Acer rubrum, PLOS ONE* 4(10):e7653 (2009); **35.21** Data from "Mongolian Tree Rings and 20th-Century Warming" by Gordon C. Jacoby, et al., from *Science*, August 9, 1996, Volume 273(5276): 771–773.

Chapter 36 **36 Scientific Skills Exercise** Data from J. D. Murphy and D. L. Noland, Temperature Effects on Seed Imbibition and Leakage Mediated by Viscosity and Membranes, *Plant Physiology* 69:428–431 (1982); **36.18** Data from S. Rogers and A. J. Peel, Some Evidence for the Existence of Turgor Pressure in the Sieve Tubes of Willow (*Salix*), *Planta* 126:259–267 (1975).

Chapter 37 **37.11b** Data from D.S. Lundberg et al., Defining the Core *Arabidopsis thaliana* Root Microbiome, *Nature* 488:86–94 (2012).

Chapter 38 **38 Scientific Skills Exercise** Data from S. Sutherland and R. K. Vickery, Jr. Trade-offs between Sexual and Asexual Reproduction in the Genus *Mimulus. Oecologia* 76:330–335 (1998).

Chapter 39 **39.5** Data from C. R. Darwin, *The Power of Movement in Plants*, John Murray, London (1880). P. Boysen-Jensen, Concerning the Performance of Phototropic Stimuli on the Avenacoleoptile, *Berichte der Deutschen Botanischen Gesellschaft (Reports of the German Botanical Society)* 31:559–566 (1913); **39.6** Data from L. Gälweiler et al., Regulation of Polar Auxin Transport by AtPIN1 in *Arabidopsis* Vascular Tissue, *Science* 282:2226–2230 (1998); **39.15a** Based on *Plantwatching: How Plants Remember, Tell Time, Form Relationships and More* by Malcolm Wilkins. Facts on File, 1988; **39.16** Data from H. Borthwick et al., A Reversible Photo Reaction Controlling Seed Germination, *Proceedings of the National Academy of Sciences USA* 38:662–666 (1952); **39 Problem-Solving Exercise** Map data from Camilo Mora et al. Days for Plant Growth Disappear under Projected Climate Change: Potential Human and Biotic Vulnerability. *PLoS Biol.* 13(6): e1002167 (2015); **39 Scientific Skills Exercise** Data from O. Falik et al., Rumor Has It ...: Relay Communication of Stress Cues in Plants, *PLoS ONE* 6(11):e23625 (2011).

Chapter 40 **40.17** Data from V. H. Hutchison, H. G. Dowling, and A. Vinegar, Thermoregulation in a Brooding Female Indian Python, *Python molurus bivittatus, Science* 151:694–696 (1966); **40 Scientific Skills Exercise** Based on the data from M. A. Chappell et al., Energetics of Foraging in Breeding Adélie Penguins, *Ecology* 74:2450–2461 (1993); M. A. Chappell et al., Voluntary Running in Deer Mice: Speed, Distance, Energy Costs, and Temperature Effects, *Journal of Experimental Biology* 207:3839–3854 (2004); T. M. Ellis and M. A. Chappell, Metabolism, Temperature Relations, Maternal Behavior, and Reproductive Energetics in the Ball Python (*Python regius), Journal of Comparative Physiology B* 157:393–402 (1987); **40.22** Data from F. G. Revel et al., The Circadian Clock Stops Ticking During Deep Hibernation in the European Hamster, *Proceedings of the National Academy of Sciences USA* 104:13816–13820 (2007).

Chapter 41 **41.4** Data from R. W. Smithells et al., Possible Prevention of Neural-Tube Defects by Periconceptional Vitamin Supplementation, *Lancet* 315:339–340 (1980);**41.8** Adapted from Marieb, Elaine; Hoehn, Katja, *Human Anatomy and Physiology*, 8th Edition, 2010, p. 852, Reprinted and electronically reproduced by permission of Pearson Education, Upper Saddle River, New Jersey; **41.17** Adapted from Ottman N., Smidt H., de Vos W.M. and Belzer C. (2012) The function of our microbiota: who is out there and what do they do? *Front. Cell. Inf. Microbiol.* 2:104. doi: 10.3389/fcimb.2012.00104; **41.22** Republished with permission of American Association for the Advancement of Science, from Cellular Warriors at the Battle of the Bulge by Kathleen Sutliff and Jean Marx, from *Science*, February 2003, Volume 299(5608); permission conveyed through Copyright Clearance Center, Inc.; **41 Scientific Skills Exercise** Based on the data from D. L. Coleman, Effects of Parabiosis of Obese Mice with Diabetes and Normal Mice, *Diabetologia* 9:294–298 (1973).

Chapter 42 **42 Scientific Skills Exercise** Data from J. C. Cohen et al., Sequence Variations in PCSK9, Low LDL, and Protection Against Coronary Heart Disease, *New England Journal of Medicine* 354:1264–1272 (2006); **42.25** Data from M. E. Avery and J. Mead, Surface Properties in Relation to Atelectasis and Hyaline Membrane Disease, *American Journal of Diseases of Children* 97:517–523 (1959).

Chapter 43 **43.6** Adapted from Marieb, Elaine N.; Hoehn, Katja, *Human Anatomy and Physiology*, 8th Ed., © 2010. Reprinted and electronically reproduced by permission of Pearson Education, Inc., Upper Saddle River, New Jersey; **43.7**Adapted from *Microbiology: An Introduction*, 11th Edition, by Gerard J. Tortora, Berdell R. Funke, and Christine L. Case. Pearson Education, Inc.; **43.23** Based on multiple sources: *WHO/UNICEF Coverage Estimates 2014 Revision.* July 2015. Map Production: Immunization Vaccines and Biologicals (IVB). World Health Organization, 16 July 2015; *Our Progress Against Polio*, May 1, 2014. Centers for Disease Control and Prevention; **43 Scientific Skills Exercise** Data from sources: L. J. Morrison et al., Probabilistic Order in Antigenic Variation of *Trypanosoma brucei, International Journal for Parasitology* 35:961-972 (2005); and L. J. Morrison et al., Antigenic Variation in the African Trypanosome: Molecular Mechanisms and Phenotypic Complexity, *Cellular Microbiology* 1: 1724–1734 (2009).

Chapter 44 **44 Scientific Skills Exercise** Data from R. E. MacMillen et al., Water Economy and Energy Metabolism of the Sandy Inland Mouse, *Leggadina hermannsburgensis, Journal of Mammalogy* 53:529–539 (1972); **44.7** Adapted from Mitchell, Lawrence G., *Zoology*, © 1998. Reprinted and electronically reproduced by permission of Pearson Education, Inc., Upper Saddle River, New Jersey; **44.12 Kidney structure** Adapted from Marieb, Elaine N.; Hoehn, Katja, *Human Anatomy and Physiology*, 8th Ed., 2010. Reprinted and electronically reproduced by permission of Pearson Education, Inc., Upper Saddle River, New Jersey; **44.13a Kidney structure** Adapted from Marieb, Elaine N.; Hoehn, Katja, *Human Anatomy and Physiology*, 8th Ed., 2010. Reprinted and electronically reproduced by permission of Pearson Education, Inc., Upper Saddle River, New Jersey; **44.20** Data in tables from P. M. Deen et al., Requirement of Human Renal Water Channel Aquaporin-2 for Vasopressin-Dependent Concentration of Urine, *Science* 264:92–95 (1994); **44 Summary Figure** Adapted from Beck, *Life: An Introduction to Biology*, 3rd Ed., ©1991, p. 643. Reprinted and electronically reproduced by permission of Pearson Education, Inc., Upper Saddle River, New Jersey; **44 Test Your Understanding Question 7** Data for kangaroo rat from *Animal Physiology: Adaptation and Environment* by Knut Schmidt-Nielsen. Cambridge University Press, 1991.

Chapter 45 **45 Scientific Skills Exercise** Data from J. Born et al., Timing the End of Nocturnal Sleep, *Nature* 397:29–30 (1999).

Chapter 46 **46.8** Data from R. R. Snook and D. J. Hosken, Sperm Death and Dumping in *Drosophila, Nature* 428:939–941 (2004); **46 Scientific Skills Exercise** Data from

A. Jost, *Recherches Sur la Differenciation Sexuelle de l'embryon de Lapin* (Studies on the Sexual Differentiation of the Rabbit Embryo), *Archives d'Anatomie Microscopique et de Morphologie Experimentale* 36:271–316 (1947); **46.16** Adapted from Marieb, Elaine N., Hoehn, Katja, *Human Anatomy and Physiology*, 8th Ed., 2010. Reprinted and electronically reproduced by permission of Pearson Education, Inc., Upper Saddle River, New Jersey.

**Chapter 47** **47.4** Data from "Intracellular Calcium Release at Fertilization in the Sea Urchin Egg" by R. Steinhardt et al., from *Developmental Biology*, July 1977, Volume 58(1); **47 Scientific Skills Exercise** Data from J. Newport and M. Kirschner, A Major Developmental Transition in Early *Xenopus* Embryos: I. Characterization and Timing of Cellular Changes at the Midblastula Stage, *Cell* 30:675–686 (1982); **47.10** Adapted from Keller, R. E. 1986. The Cellular Basis of Amphibian Gastrulation. In L. Browder (ed.), *Developmental Biology: A Comprehensive Synthesis*, Vol. 2. Plenum, New York, pp. 241–327; **47.14** Based on "Cell Commitment and Gene Expression in the Axolotl Embryo" by T. J. Mohun et al., from *Cell*, November 1980, Volume 22(1); **47.17** *Principles of Development*, 2nd Edition by Wolpert (2002), Fig. 8.26, p. 275. By permission of Oxford University Press; **47.19** Republished with permission of Garland Science, Taylor & Francis Group, from *Molecular Biology of the Cell*, Bruce Alberts et al., 4th Edition, ©2002; permission conveyed through Copyright Clearance Center, Inc.; **47.23** Data from H. Spemann, *Embryonic Development and Induction*, Yale University Press, New Haven, CT (1938); **47.24** Data from H. Spemann and H. Mangold, Induction of Embryonic Primordia by Implantation of Organizers from a Different Species, Trans. V. Hamburger (1924). Reprinted in *International Journal of Developmental Biology* 45:13–38 (2001); **47.26** Data from L. S. Honig and D. Summerbell, Maps of strength of positional signaling activity in the developing chick wing bud, *Journal of Embryology and Experimental Morphology* 87:163–174 (1985); **47.27** Adapted from Marieb, Elaine N.; Hoehn, Katja, *Human Anatomy and Physiology*, 8th Edition, 2010. Reprinted and electronically reproduced by permission of Pearson Education, Inc., Upper Saddle River, New Jersey.

**Chapter 48** **48.11 Graph** Based on Figure 6-2d from *Cellular Physiology of Nerve and Muscle*, 4th Edition by Gary G. Matthews. Wiley-Blackwell, 2003; **48 Scientific Skills Exercise** Data from C. B. Pert and S. H. Snyder, Opiate Receptor: Demonstration in Nervous Tissue, *Science* 179:1011–1014 (1973).

**Chapter 49** **49.9** Adapted from Marieb, Elaine N.; Hoehn, Katja, *Human Anatomy and Physiology*, 8th Ed., © 2010. Reprinted and electronically reproduced by permission of Pearson Education, Inc., Upper Saddle River, New Jersey; **49.13** Based on "Sleep in Marine Mammals" by L. M. Mukhametov, from *Sleep Mechanisms*, edited by Alexander A. Borberly and J. L. Valatx. Springer; **49 Scientific Skills Exercise** Data from M. R. Ralph et al., Transplanted Suprachiasmatic Nucleus Determines Circadian Period, *Science* 247:975–978 (1990); **49.20** Adaptation of Figure 1c from "Avian Brains and a New Understanding of Vertebrate Brain Evolution" by Erich D. Jarvis et al., from *Nature Reviews Neuroscience*, February 2005, Volume 6(2);

**49.23** Adaptation of Figure 10 from *Schizophrenia Genesis: The Origins of Madness* by Irving I. Gottesman. Worth Publishers.

**Chapter 50** **50.12a** Adapted from Marieb, Elaine N; Hoehn, Katja, *Human Anatomy and Physiology*, 8th Ed., © 2010 Reprinted and electronically reproduced by Permission of Pearson Education, Inc., Upper Saddle River, New Jersey; **50.13** Adapted from Marieb, Elaine N; Hoehn, Katja, *Human Anatomy and Physiology*, 8th Ed., © 2010 Reprinted and electronically reproduced by Permission of Pearson Education, Inc., Upper Saddle River, New Jersey; **50.17 Eye structure** Adapted from Marieb, Elaine N; Hoehn, Katja, *Human Anatomy and Physiology*, 8th Ed., © 2010 Reprinted and electronically reproduced by Permission of Pearson Education, Inc., Upper Saddle River, New Jersey; **50.23** Data from K. L. Mueller et al., The receptors and coding logic for bitter taste, *Nature* 434:225–229 (2005); **50.24a** Adapted from Marieb, Elaine N; Hoehn, Katja, *Human Anatomy and Physiology*, 8th Ed., © 2010 Reprinted and electronically reproduced by Permission of Pearson Education, Inc., Upper Saddle River, New Jersey; **50.26** Adapted from Marieb, Elaine N; Hoehn, Katja, *Human Anatomy and Physiology*, 8th Ed., © 2010 Reprinted and electronically reproduced by Permission of Pearson Education, Inc., Upper Saddle River, New Jersey; **50.31** Adapted from Marieb, Elaine N; Hoehn, Katja, *Human Anatomy and Physiology*, 8th Ed., © 2010 Reprinted and electronically reproduced by Permission of Pearson Education, Inc., Upper Saddle River, New Jersey; **50.35 Grasshopper** Based on Hickman et al., *Integrated Principles of Zoology*, 9th ed., p. 518, Fig. 22.6, McGraw-Hill Higher Education, NY (1993); **50 Scientific Skills Exercise** Data from K. Schmidt-Nielsen, Locomotion: Energy Cost of Swimming, Flying, and Running, *Science* 177:222–228 (1972).

**Chapter 51** **51.4** Based on "*Drosophila*: Genetics Meets Behavior" by Marla B. Sokolowski, from *Nature Reviews: Genetics*, November 2001, Volume 2(11); **51.8** Data from *The Study of Instinct*, N. Tinbergen, Clarendon Press, Oxford (1951); **51.10** Adapted from "Prospective and Retrospective Learning in Honeybees" by Martin Giurfa and Julie Bernard, from *International Journal of Comparative Psychology*, 2006, Volume 19(3); **51.13** Adapted from Evolution of Foraging Behavior in *Drosophila* by Density Dependent Selection by Maria B. Sokolowski et al., from *Proceedings of the National Academy of Sciences USA*, July 8, 1997, Volume 94(14); **51 Scientific Skills Exercise** Data from Shell Dropping: Decision-Making and Optimal Foraging in North-western Crows by Reto Zach, from *Behaviour*, 1979, Volume 68(1–2); 51; **51.18** Reprinted by permission from Klaudia Witte; **51.24 Illustration** Adaptations of photograph by Jonathan Blair, Figure/PhotoID: 3.14, as appeared in *Animal Behavior: An Evolutionary Approach*, 8th Edition, Editor: John Alcock, p. 88. Reprinted by permission; **51.24 Map** Data from "Rapid Microevolution of Migratory Behaviour in a Wild Bird Species" by P. Berthold et al., from *Nature*, December 1992, Volume 360(6405); **51 Art for Concept 51.2 Summary:** Data from *The Study of Instinct*, N. Tinbergen, Clarendon Press, Oxford (1951).

# Glossary

## Pronunciation Key

| | |
|---|---|
| ā | ace |
| a/ah | ash |
| ch | chose |
| ē | meet |
| e/eh | bet |
| g | game |
| ī | ice |
| i | hit |
| ks | box |
| kw | quick |
| ng | song |
| ō | robe |
| o | ox |
| oy | boy |
| s | say |
| sh | shell |
| th | thin |
| ū | boot |
| u/uh | up |
| z | zoo |

′ = primary accent

′ = secondary accent

**5′ cap** A modified form of guanine nucleotide added onto the 5′ end of a pre-mRNA molecule.

**ABC hypothesis** A model of flower formation identifying three classes of organ identity genes that direct formation of the four types of floral organs.

**abiotic** (ā′-bī-ot′-ik) Nonliving; referring to the physical and chemical properties of an environment.

**abortion** The termination of a pregnancy in progress.

**abscisic acid (ABA)** (ab-sis′-ik) A plant hormone that slows growth, often antagonizing the actions of growth hormones. Two of its many effects are to promote seed dormancy and facilitate drought tolerance.

**absorption** The third stage of food processing in animals: the uptake of small nutrient molecules by an organism's body.

**absorption spectrum** The range of a pigment's ability to absorb various wavelengths of light; also a graph of such a range.

**abyssal zone** (uh-bis′-ul) The part of the ocean's benthic zone between 2,000 and 6,000 m deep.

**acanthodian** (ak′-an-thō′-dē-un) Any of a group of ancient jawed aquatic vertebrates from the Silurian and Devonian periods.

**accessory fruit** A fruit, or assemblage of fruits, in which the fleshy parts are derived largely or entirely from tissues other than the ovary.

**acclimatization** (uh-klī′-muh-tī-zā′-shun) Physiological adjustment to a change in an environmental factor.

**acetyl CoA** Acetyl coenzyme A; the entry compound for the citric acid cycle in cellular respiration, formed from a two-carbon fragment of pyruvate attached to a coenzyme.

**acetylcholine** (as′-uh-til-kō′-lēn) One of the most common neurotransmitters; functions by binding to receptors and altering the permeability of the postsynaptic membrane to specific ions, either depolarizing or hyperpolarizing the membrane.

**acid** A substance that increases the hydrogen ion concentration of a solution.

**acoelomate** (uh-sē′-lō-māt) A solid-bodied animal lacking a cavity between the gut and outer body wall.

**acquired immunodeficiency syndrome (AIDS)** The symptoms and signs present during the late stages of HIV infection, defined by a specified reduction in the number of T cells and the appearance of characteristic secondary infections.

**acrosomal reaction** (ak′-ruh-sōm′-ul) The discharge of hydrolytic enzymes from the acrosome, a vesicle in the tip of a sperm, when the sperm approaches or contacts an egg.

**acrosome** (ak′-ruh-sōm) A vesicle in the tip of a sperm containing hydrolytic enzymes and other proteins that help the sperm reach the egg.

**actin** (ak′-tin) A globular protein that links into chains, two of which twist helically about each other, forming microfilaments (actin filaments) in muscle and other kinds of cells.

**action potential** An electrical signal that propagates (travels) along the membrane of a neuron or other excitable cell as a nongraded (all-or-none) depolarization.

**action spectrum** A graph that profiles the relative effectiveness of different wavelengths of radiation in driving a particular process.

**activation energy** The amount of energy that reactants must absorb before a chemical reaction will start; also called free energy of activation.

**activator** A protein that binds to DNA and stimulates gene transcription. In prokaryotes, activators bind in or near the promoter; in eukaryotes, activators generally bind to control elements in enhancers.

**active immunity** Long-lasting immunity conferred by the action of B cells and T cells and the resulting B and T memory cells specific for a pathogen. Active immunity can develop as a result of natural infection or immunization.

**active site** The specific region of an enzyme that binds the substrate and that forms the pocket in which catalysis occurs.

**active transport** The movement of a substance across a cell membrane against its concentration or electrochemical gradient, mediated by specific transport proteins and requiring an expenditure of energy.

**adaptation** Inherited characteristic of an organism that enhances its survival and reproduction in a specific environment.

**adaptive evolution** Evolution that results in a better match between organisms and their environment.

**adaptive immunity** A vertebrate-specific defense that is mediated by B lymphocytes (B cells) and T lymphocytes (T cells) and that exhibits specificity, memory, and self-nonself recognition; also called acquired immunity.

**adaptive radiation** Period of evolutionary change in which groups of organisms form many new species whose adaptations allow them to fill different ecological roles in their communities.

**addition rule** A rule of probability stating that the probability of any one of two or more mutually exclusive events occurring can be determined by adding their individual probabilities.

**adenosine triphosphate** *See* ATP (adenosine triphosphate).

**adenylyl cyclase** (uh-den′-uh-lil) An enzyme that converts ATP to cyclic AMP in response to an extracellular signal.

**adhesion** The clinging of one substance to another, such as water to plant cell walls by means of hydrogen bonds.

**adipose tissue** A connective tissue that insulates the body and serves as a fuel reserve; contains fat-storing cells called adipose cells.

**adrenal gland** (uh-drē′-nul) One of two endocrine glands located adjacent to the kidneys in mammals. Endocrine cells in the outer portion (cortex) respond to adrenocorticotropic hormone (ACTH) by secreting steroid hormones that help maintain homeostasis during long-term stress. Neurosecretory cells in the central portion (medulla) secrete epinephrine and norepinephrine in response to nerve signals triggered by short-term stress.

**aerobic respiration** A catabolic pathway for organic molecules, using oxygen ($O_2$) as the final electron acceptor in an electron transport chain and ultimately producing ATP. This is the most efficient catabolic pathway and is carried out in most eukaryotic cells and many prokaryotic organisms.

**age structure** The relative number of individuals of each age in a population.

**aggregate fruit** A fruit derived from a single flower that has more than one carpel.

**AIDS (acquired immunodeficiency syndrome)** The symptoms and signs present during the late stages of HIV infection, defined by a specified reduction in the number of T cells and the appearance of characteristic secondary infections.

**alcohol fermentation** Glycolysis followed by the reduction of pyruvate to ethyl alcohol, regenerating NAD$^+$ and releasing carbon dioxide.

**alga** (plural, **algae**) A general term for any species of photosynthetic protist, including both unicellular and multicellular forms. Algal species are included in three eukaryote supergroups (Excavata, SAR, and Archaeplastida).

**alimentary canal** (al'-uh-men'-tuh-rē) A complete digestive tract, consisting of a tube running between a mouth and an anus.

**alkaline vent** A deep-sea hydrothermal vent that releases water that is warm (40–90°C) rather than hot and that has a high pH (is basic). These vents consist of tiny pores lined with iron and other catalytic minerals that some scientists hypothesize might have been the location of the earliest abiotic synthesis of organic compounds.

**allele** (uh-lē'-ul) Any of the alternative versions of a gene that may produce distinguishable phenotypic effects.

**allopatric speciation** (al'-uh-pat'-rik) The formation of new species in populations that are geographically isolated from one another.

**allopolyploid** (al'-ō-pol'-ē-ployd) A fertile individual that has more than two chromosome sets as a result of two different species interbreeding and combining their chromosomes.

**allosteric regulation** The binding of a regulatory molecule to a protein at one site that affects the function of the protein at a different site.

**alpha (α) helix** (al'-fuh hē'-liks) A coiled region constituting one form of the secondary structure of proteins, arising from a specific pattern of hydrogen bonding between atoms of the polypeptide backbone (not the side chains).

**alternation of generations** A life cycle in which there is both a multicellular diploid form, the sporophyte, and a multicellular haploid form, the gametophyte; characteristic of plants and some algae.

**alternative RNA splicing** A type of eukaryotic gene regulation at the RNA-processing level in which different mRNA molecules are produced from the same primary transcript, depending on which RNA segments are treated as exons and which as introns.

**altruism** (al'-trū-iz-um) Selflessness; behavior that reduces an individual's fitness while increasing the fitness of another individual.

**alveolates** (al-vē'-uh-lets) One of the three major subgroups for which the SAR eukaryotic supergroup is named. This clade arose by secondary endosymbiosis, and its members have membrane-enclosed sacs (alveoli) located just under the plasma membrane.

**alveolus** (al-vē'-uh-lus) (plural, **alveoli**) One of the dead-end air sacs where gas exchange occurs in a mammalian lung.

**Alzheimer's disease** (alts'-hī-merz) An age-related dementia (mental deterioration) characterized by confusion and memory loss.

**amino acid** (uh-mēn'-ō) An organic molecule possessing both a carboxyl and an amino group. Amino acids serve as the monomers of polypeptides.

**amino group** (uh-mēn'-ō) A chemical group consisting of a nitrogen atom bonded to two hydrogen atoms; can act as a base in solution, accepting a hydrogen ion and acquiring a charge of 1 + .

**aminoacyl-tRNA synthetase** An enzyme that joins each amino acid to the appropriate tRNA.

**ammonia** A small, toxic molecule ($NH_3$) produced by nitrogen fixation or as a metabolic waste product of protein and nucleic acid metabolism.

**ammonite** A member of a group of shelled cephalopods that were important marine predators for hundreds of millions of years until their extinction at the end of the Cretaceous period (65.5 million years ago).

**amniocentesis** (am'-nē-ō-sen-tē'-sis) A technique associated with prenatal diagnosis in which amniotic fluid is obtained by aspiration from a needle inserted into the uterus. The fluid and the fetal cells it contains are analyzed to detect certain genetic and congenital defects in the fetus.

**amniote** (am'-nē-ōt) A member of a clade of tetrapods named for a key derived character, the amniotic egg, which contains specialized membranes, including the fluid-filled amnion, that protect the embryo. Amniotes include mammals as well as birds and other reptiles.

**amniotic egg** An egg that contains specialized membranes that function in protection, nourishment, and gas exchange. The amniotic egg was a major evolutionary innovation, allowing embryos to develop on land in a fluid-filled sac, thus reducing the dependence of tetrapods on water for reproduction.

**amoeba** (uh-mē'-buh) A protist characterized by the presence of pseudopodia.

**amoebocyte** (uh-mē'-buh-sīt') An amoeba-like cell that moves by pseudopodia and is found in most animals. Depending on the species, it may digest and distribute food, dispose of wastes, form skeletal fibers, fight infections, or change into other cell types.

**amoebozoan** (uh-mē'-buh-zō'-an) A protist in a clade that includes many species with lobe- or tube-shaped pseudopodia.

**amphibian** A member of the clade of tetrapods that includes salamanders, frogs, and caecilians.

**amphipathic** (am'-fē-path'-ik) Having both a hydrophilic region and a hydrophobic region.

**amplification** The strengthening of stimulus energy during transduction.

**amygdala** (uh-mig'-duh-luh) A structure in the temporal lobe of the vertebrate brain that has a major role in the processing of emotions.

**amylase** (am'-uh-lās') An enzyme that hydrolyzes starch (a glucose polymer from plants) and glycogen (a glucose polymer from animals) into smaller polysaccharides and the disaccharide maltose.

**anabolic pathway** (an'-uh-bol'-ik) A metabolic pathway that consumes energy to synthesize a complex molecule from simpler molecules.

**anaerobic respiration** (an-er-ō'-bik) A catabolic pathway in which inorganic molecules other than oxygen accept electrons at the "downhill" end of electron transport chains.

**analogous** Having characteristics that are similar because of convergent evolution, not homology.

**analogy** (an-al'-uh-jē) Similarity between two species that is due to convergent evolution rather than to descent from a common ancestor with the same trait.

**anaphase** The fourth stage of mitosis, in which the chromatids of each chromosome have separated and the daughter chromosomes are moving to the poles of the cell.

**anatomy** The structure of an organism.

**anchorage dependence** The requirement that a cell must be attached to a substratum in order to initiate cell division.

**androgen** (an'-drō-jen) Any steroid hormone, such as testosterone, that stimulates the development and maintenance of the male reproductive system and secondary sex characteristics.

**aneuploidy** (an'-yū-ploy'-dē) A chromosomal aberration in which one or more chromosomes are present in extra copies or are deficient in number.

**angiosperm** (an'-jē-ō-sperm) A flowering plant, which forms seeds inside a protective chamber called an ovary.

**anhydrobiosis** (an-hī'-drō-bī-ō'-sis) A dormant state involving loss of almost all body water.

**animal pole** The point at the end of an egg in the hemisphere where the least yolk is concentrated; opposite of vegetal pole.

**anion** (an'-ī-on) A negatively charged ion.

**anterior** Pertaining to the front, or head, of a bilaterally symmetrical animal.

**anterior pituitary** A portion of the pituitary gland that develops from nonneural tissue; consists of endocrine cells that synthesize and secrete several tropic and nontropic hormones.

**anther** In an angiosperm, the terminal pollen sac of a stamen, where pollen grains containing sperm-producing male gametophytes form.

**antheridium** (an-thuh-rid'-ē-um) (plural, **antheridia**) In plants, the male gametangium, a moist chamber in which gametes develop.

**anthropoid** (an'-thruh-poyd) A member of a primate group made up of the monkeys and the apes (gibbons, orangutans, gorillas, chimpanzees, bonobos, and humans).

**antibody** A protein secreted by plasma cells (differentiated B cells) that binds to a particular antigen; also called immunoglobulin. All antibodies have the same Y-shaped structure and in their monomer form consist of two identical heavy chains and two identical light chains.

**anticodon** (an'-tī-kō'-don) A nucleotide triplet at one end of a tRNA molecule that base-pairs with a particular complementary codon on an mRNA molecule.

**antidiuretic hormone (ADH)** (an'-tī-dī-yū-ret'-ik) A peptide hormone, also called vasopressin, that promotes water retention by the kidneys. Produced in the hypothalamus and released from the posterior pituitary, ADH also functions in the brain.

**antigen** (an'-ti-jen) A substance that elicits an immune response by binding to receptors of B or T cells.

**antigen presentation** (an'-ti-jen) The process by which an MHC molecule binds to a fragment of an intracellular protein antigen and carries it to the cell surface, where it is displayed and can be recognized by a T cell.

**antigen-presenting cell** (an'-ti-jen) A cell that upon ingesting pathogens or internalizing pathogen proteins generates peptide fragments that are bound by class II MHC molecules and subsequently displayed on the cell surface to T cells. Macrophages, dendritic cells, and B cells are the primary antigen-presenting cells.

**antigen receptor** (an'-ti-jen) The general term for a surface protein, located on B cells and T cells, that binds to antigens, initiating adaptive immune responses. The antigen receptors on B cells are called B cell receptors, and the antigen receptors on T cells are called T cell receptors.

**antiparallel** Referring to the arrangement of the sugar-phosphate backbones in a DNA double helix (they run in opposite 5′ S 3′ directions).

**aphotic zone** (ā'-fō'-tik) The part of an ocean or lake beneath the photic zone, where light does not penetrate sufficiently for photosynthesis to occur.

**apical bud** (ā'-pik-ul) A bud at the tip of a plant stem; also called a terminal bud.

**apical dominance** (ā'-pik-ul) Tendency for growth to be concentrated at the tip of a plant shoot because the apical bud partially inhibits axillary bud growth.

**apical ectodermal ridge (AER)** (ā'-pik-ul) A thickened area of ectoderm at the tip of a limb bud that promotes outgrowth of the limb bud.

**apical meristem** (ā'-pik-ul mār'-uh-stem) A localized region at a growing tip of a plant body where one or more cells divide repeatedly. The dividing cells of an apical meristem enable the plant to grow in length.

**apicomplexan** (ap'-ē-kom-pleks'-un) A group of alveolate protists, this clade includes many species that parasitize animals. Some apicomplexans cause human disease.

**apomixis** (ap'-uh-mik'-sis) The ability of some plant species to reproduce asexually through seeds without fertilization by a male gamete.

**apoplast** (ap'-ō-plast) Everything external to the plasma membrane of a plant cell, including cell walls, intercellular spaces, and the space within dead structures such as xylem vessels and tracheids.

**apoptosis** (ā-puh-tō'-sus) A type of programmed cell death, which is brought about by activation of enzymes that break down many chemical components in the cell.

**aposematic coloration** (ap'-ō-si-mat'-ik) The bright warning coloration of many animals with effective physical or chemical defenses.

**appendix** A small, finger-like extension of the vertebrate cecum; contains a mass of white blood cells that contribute to immunity.

**aquaporin** A channel protein in a cellular membrane that specifically facilitates osmosis, the diffusion of free water across the membrane.

**aqueous solution** (ā'-kwē-us) A solution in which water is the solvent.

**arachnid** A member of a subgroup of the major arthropod clade Chelicerata. Arachnids have six pairs of appendages, including four pairs of walking legs, and include spiders, scorpions, ticks, and mites.

**arbuscular mycorrhiza** (ar-bus'-kyū-lur mī'-kō-rī'-zuh) Association of a fungus with a plant root system in which the fungus causes the invagination of the host (plant) cells' plasma membranes.

**arbuscular mycorrhizal fungus** (ar-bus'-kyū-lur) A symbiotic fungus whose hyphae grow through the cell wall of plant roots and extend into the root cell (enclosed in tubes formed by invagination of the root cell plasma membrane).

**arbuscules** Specialized branching hyphae that are found in some mutualistic fungi and exchange nutrients with living plant cells.

**Archaea** (ar'-kē'-uh) One of two prokaryotic domains, the other being Bacteria.

**Archaeplastida** (ar'-kē-plas'-tid-uh) One of four supergroups of eukaryotes proposed in a current hypothesis of the evolutionary history of eukaryotes. This monophyletic group, which includes red algae, green algae, and plants, descended from an ancient protistan ancestor that engulfed a cyanobacterium. *See also* Excavata, SAR, and Unikonta.

**archegonium** (ar-ki-gō'-nē-um) (plural, **archegonia**) In plants, the female gametangium, a moist chamber in which gametes develop.

**archenteron** (ar-ken'-tuh-ron) The endoderm-lined cavity, formed during gastrulation, that develops into the digestive tract of an animal.

**archosaur** (ar'-kō-sōr) A member of the reptilian group that includes crocodiles, alligators and dinosaurs, including birds.

**arteriole** (ar-ter'-ē-ōl) A vessel that conveys blood between an artery and a capillary bed.

**artery** A vessel that carries blood away from the heart to organs throughout the body.

**arthropod** A segmented ecdysozoan with a hard exoskeleton and jointed appendages. Familiar examples include insects, spiders, millipedes, and crabs.

**artificial selection** The selective breeding of domesticated plants and animals to encourage the occurrence of desirable traits.

**ascocarp** The fruiting body of a sac fungus (ascomycete).

**ascomycete** (as'-kuh-mī'-sēt) A member of the fungal phylum Ascomycota, commonly called sac fungus. The name comes from the saclike structure in which the spores develop.

**ascus** (plural, **asci**) A saclike spore capsule located at the tip of a dikaryotic hypha of a sac fungus.

**asexual reproduction** The generation of offspring from a single parent that occurs without the fusion of gametes. In most cases, the offspring are genetically identical to the parent.

**A site** One of a ribosome's three binding sites for tRNA during translation. The A site holds the tRNA carrying the next amino acid to be added to the polypeptide chain. (A stands for aminoacyl tRNA.)

**assisted migration** The translocation of a species to a favorable habitat beyond its native range for the purpose of protecting the species from human-caused threats.

**associative learning** The acquired ability to associate one environmental feature (such as a color) with another (such as danger).

**atherosclerosis** A cardiovascular disease in which fatty deposits called plaques develop in the inner walls of the arteries, obstructing the arteries and causing them to harden.

**atom** The smallest unit of matter that retains the properties of an element.

**atomic mass** The total mass of an atom, numerically equivalent to the mass in grams of 1 mole of the atom. (For an element with more than one isotope, the atomic mass is the average mass of the naturally occurring isotopes, weighted by their abundance.)

**atomic nucleus** An atom's dense central core, containing protons and neutrons.

**atomic number** The number of protons in the nucleus of an atom, unique for each element and designated by a subscript.

**ATP (adenosine triphosphate)** (a-den'-ō-sēn trī-fos'-fāt) An adenine-containing nucleoside triphosphate that releases free energy when its phosphate bonds are hydrolyzed. This energy is used to drive endergonic reactions in cells.

**ATP synthase** A complex of several membrane proteins that functions in chemiosmosis with adjacent electron transport chains, using the energy of a hydrogen ion (proton) concentration gradient to make ATP. ATP synthases are found in the inner mitochondrial membranes of eukaryotic cells and in the plasma membranes of prokaryotes.

**atrial natriuretic peptide (ANP)** (ā'-trē-ul na'-trē-yū-ret'-ik) A peptide hormone secreted by cells of the atria of the heart in response to high blood pressure. ANP's effects on the kidney alter ion and water movement and reduce blood pressure.

**atrioventricular (AV) node** A region of specialized heart muscle tissue between the left and right atria where electrical impulses are delayed for about 0.1 second before spreading to both ventricles and causing them to contract.

**atrioventricular (AV) valve** A heart valve located between each atrium and ventricle that prevents a backflow of blood when the ventricle contracts.

**atrium** (ā'-trē-um) (plural, **atria**) A chamber of the vertebrate heart that receives blood from the veins and transfers blood to a ventricle.

**autocrine** Referring to a secreted molecule that acts on the cell that secreted it.

**autoimmune disease** An immunological disorder in which the immune system turns against self.

**autonomic nervous system** (ot'-ō-nom'-ik) An efferent branch of the vertebrate peripheral nervous system that regulates the internal environment; consists of the sympathetic, parasympathetic, and enteric divisions.

**autopolyploid** (ot'-ō-pol'-ē-ployd) An individual that has more than two chromosome sets that are all derived from a single species.

**autosome** (ot'-ō-sōm) A chromosome that is not directly involved in determining sex; not a sex chromosome.

**autotroph** (ot'-ō-trōf) An organism that obtains organic food molecules without eating other organisms or substances derived from other organisms. Autotrophs use energy from the sun or from oxidation of inorganic substances to make organic molecules from inorganic ones.

**auxin** (ôk'-sin) A term that primarily refers to indoleacetic acid (IAA), a natural plant hormone that has a variety of effects, including cell elongation, root formation, secondary growth, and fruit growth.

**axillary bud** (ak´-sil-ār-ē) A structure that has the potential to form a lateral shoot, or branch. The bud appears in the angle formed between a leaf and a stem.

**axon** (ak´-son) A typically long extension, or process, of a neuron that carries nerve impulses away from the cell body toward target cells.

**B cells** The lymphocytes that complete their development in the bone marrow and become effector cells for the humoral immune response.

**Bacteria** One of two prokaryotic domains, the other being Archaea.

**bacteriophage** (bak-tēr´-ē-ō-fāj) A virus that infects bacteria; also called a phage.

**bacteroid** A form of the bacterium *Rhizobium* contained within the vesicles formed by the root cells of a root nodule.

**balancing selection** Natural selection that maintains two or more phenotypic forms in a population.

**bar graph** A graph in which the independent variable represents groups or nonnumerical categories and the values of the dependent variable(s) are shown by bars.

**bark** All tissues external to the vascular cambium, consisting mainly of the secondary phloem and layers of periderm.

**Barr body** A dense object lying along the inside of the nuclear envelope in cells of female mammals, representing a highly condensed, inactivated X chromosome.

**basal angiosperm** A member of one of three clades of early-diverging lineages of extant flowering plants. Examples are *Amborella*, water lilies, and star anise and its relatives.

**basal body** (bā´-sul) A eukaryotic cell structure consisting of a "9 + 0" arrangement of microtubule triplets. The basal body may organize the microtubule assembly of a cilium or flagellum and is structurally very similar to a centriole.

**basal metabolic rate (BMR)** The metabolic rate of a resting, fasting, and nonstressed endotherm at a comfortable temperature.

**basal taxon** In a specified group of organisms, a taxon whose evolutionary lineage diverged early in the history of the group.

**base** A substance that reduces the hydrogen ion concentration of a solution.

**basidiocarp** Elaborate fruiting body of a dikaryotic mycelium of a club fungus.

**basidiomycete** (buh-sid´-ē-ō-mī´-sēt) A member of the fungal phylum Basidiomycota, commonly called club fungus. The name comes from the club-like shape of the basidium.

**basidium** (plural, **basidia**) (buh-sid´-ē-um, buh-sid´-ē-ah) A reproductive appendage that produces sexual spores on the gills of mushrooms (club fungi).

**Batesian mimicry** (bāt´-zē-un mim´-uh-krē) A type of mimicry in which a harmless species resembles an unpalatable or harmful species to which it is not closely related.

**behavior** Individually, an action carried out by muscles or glands under control of the nervous system in response to a stimulus; collectively, the sum of an animal's responses to external and internal stimuli.

**behavioral ecology** The study of the evolution of and ecological basis for animal behavior.

**benign tumor** A mass of abnormal cells with specific genetic and cellular changes such that the cells are not capable of surviving at a new site and generally remain at the site of the tumor's origin.

**benthic zone** The bottom surface of an aquatic environment.

**benthos** (ben´-thōz) The communities of organisms living in the benthic zone of an aquatic biome.

**beta (β) pleated sheet** One form of the secondary structure of proteins in which the polypeptide chain folds back and forth. Two regions of the chain lie parallel to each other and are held together by hydrogen bonds between atoms of the polypeptide backbone (not the side chains).

**beta oxidation** A metabolic sequence that breaks fatty acids down to two-carbon fragments that enter the citric acid cycle as acetyl CoA.

**bicoid** A maternal effect gene that codes for a protein responsible for specifying the anterior end in *Drosophila melanogaster*.

**bilateral symmetry** Body symmetry in which a central longitudinal plane divides the body into two equal but opposite halves.

**bilaterian** (bī´-luh-ter´-ē-uhn) A member of a clade of animals with bilateral symmetry and three germ layers.

**bile** A mixture of substances that is produced in the liver and stored in the gallbladder; enables formation of fat droplets in water as an aid in the digestion and absorption of fats.

**binary fission** A method of asexual reproduction in single-celled organisms in which the cell grows to roughly double its size and then divides into two cells. In prokaryotes, binary fission does not involve mitosis, but in single-celled eukaryotes that undergo binary fission, mitosis is part of the process.

**binomial** A common term for the two-part, latinized format for naming a species, consisting of the genus and specific epithet; also called a binomen.

**biodiversity hot spot** A relatively small area with numerous endemic species and a large number of endangered and threatened species.

**bioenergetics** (1) The overall flow and transformation of energy in an organism. (2) The study of how energy flows through organisms.

**biofilm** A surface-coating colony of one or more species of prokaryotes that engage in metabolic cooperation.

**biofuel** A fuel produced from biomass.

**biogeochemical cycle** Any of the various chemical cycles, which involve both biotic and abiotic components of ecosystems.

**biogeography** The scientific study of the past and present geographic distributions of species.

**bioinformatics** The use of computers, software, and mathematical models to process and integrate biological information from large data sets.

**biological augmentation** An approach to restoration ecology that uses organisms to add essential materials to a degraded ecosystem.

**biological clock** An internal timekeeper that controls an organism's biological rhythms. The biological clock marks time with or without environmental cues but often requires signals

from the environment to remain tuned to an appropriate period. *See also* circadian rhythm.

**biological magnification** A process in which retained substances become more concentrated at each higher trophic level in a food chain.

**biological species concept** Definition of a species as a group of populations whose members have the potential to interbreed in nature and produce viable, fertile offspring but do not produce viable, fertile offspring with members of other such groups.

**biology** The scientific study of life.

**biomanipulation** An approach that applies the top-down model of community organization to alter ecosystem characteristics. For example, ecologists can prevent algal blooms and eutrophication by altering the density of higher-level consumers in lakes instead of by using chemical treatments.

**biomass** The total mass of organic matter comprising a group of organisms in a particular habitat.

**biome** (bī´-ōm) Any of the world's major ecosystem types, often classified according to the predominant vegetation for terrestrial biomes and the physical environment for aquatic biomes and characterized by adaptations of organisms to that particular environment.

**bioremediation** The use of organisms to detoxify and restore polluted and degraded ecosystems.

**biosphere** The entire portion of Earth inhabited by life; the sum of all the planet's ecosystems.

**biotechnology** The manipulation of organisms or their components to produce useful products.

**biotic** (bī-ot´-ik) Pertaining to the living factors—the organisms—in an environment.

**bipolar disorder** A depressive mental illness characterized by swings of mood from high to low; also called manic-depressive disorder.

**birth control pill** A hormonal contraceptive that inhibits ovulation, retards follicular development, or alters a woman's cervical mucus to prevent sperm from entering the uterus.

**blade** (1) A leaflike structure of a seaweed that provides most of the surface area for photosynthesis. (2) The flattened portion of a typical leaf.

**blastocoel** (blas´-tuh-sēl) The fluid-filled cavity that forms in the center of a blastula.

**blastocyst** (blas´-tuh-sist) The blastula stage of mammalian embryonic development, consisting of an inner cell mass, a cavity, and an outer layer, the trophoblast. In humans, the blastocyst forms 1 week after fertilization.

**blastomere** An early embryonic cell arising during the cleavage stage of an early embryo.

**blastopore** (blas´-tō-pōr) In a gastrula, the opening of the archenteron that typically develops into the anus in deuterostomes and the mouth in protostomes.

**blastula** (blas´-tyū-luh) A hollow ball of cells that marks the end of the cleavage stage during early embryonic development in animals.

**blood** A connective tissue with a fluid matrix called plasma in which red blood cells, white blood cells, and cell fragments called platelets are suspended.

**blue-light photoreceptor** A type of light receptor in plants that initiates a variety of responses, such as phototropism and slowing of hypocotyl elongation.

**body cavity** A fluid- or air-filled space between the digestive tract and the body wall.

**body plan** In multicellular eukaryotes, a set of morphological and developmental traits that are integrated into a functional whole—the living organism.

**Bohr shift** A lowering of the affinity of hemoglobin for oxygen, caused by a drop in pH. It facilitates the release of oxygen from hemoglobin in the vicinity of active tissues.

**bolus** A lubricated ball of chewed food.

**bone** A connective tissue consisting of living cells held in a rigid matrix of collagen fibers embedded in calcium salts.

**book lung** An organ of gas exchange in spiders, consisting of stacked plates contained in an internal chamber.

**bottleneck effect** Genetic drift that occurs when the size of a population is reduced, as by a natural disaster or human actions. Typically, the surviving population is no longer genetically representative of the original population.

**bottom-up model** A model of community organization in which mineral nutrients influence community organization by controlling plant or phytoplankton numbers, which in turn control herbivore numbers, which in turn control predator numbers.

**Bowman's capsule** (bō'-munz) A cup-shaped receptacle in the vertebrate kidney that is the initial, expanded segment of the nephron, where filtrate enters from the blood.

**brachiopod** (bra'-kē-uh-pod') A marine lophophorate with a shell divided into dorsal and ventral halves; also called lamp shells.

**brain** Organ of the central nervous system where information is processed and integrated.

**brainstem** A collection of structures in the vertebrate brain, including the midbrain, the pons, and the medulla oblongata; functions in homeostasis, coordination of movement, and conduction of information to higher brain centers.

**branch point** The representation on a phylogenetic tree of the divergence of two or more taxa from a common ancestor. A branch point is usually shown as a dichotomy in which a branch representing the ancestral lineage splits (at the branch point) into two branches, one for each of the two descendant lineages.

**brassinosteroid** A steroid hormone in plants that has a variety of effects, including inducing cell elongation, retarding leaf abscission, and promoting xylem differentiation.

**breathing** Ventilation of the lungs through alternating inhalation and exhalation.

**bronchiole** (brong'-kē-ōl') A fine branch of the bronchi that transports air to alveoli.

**bronchus** (brong'-kus) (plural, **bronchi**) One of a pair of breathing tubes that branch from the trachea into the lungs.

**brown alga** A multicellular, photosynthetic protist with a characteristic brown or olive color that results from carotenoids in its plastids. Most brown algae are marine, and some have a plantlike body.

**bryophyte** (brī'-uh-fīt) An informal name for a moss, liverwort, or hornwort; a nonvascular plant that lives on land but lacks some of the terrestrial adaptations of vascular plants.

**buffer** A solution that contains a weak acid and its corresponding base. A buffer minimizes changes in pH when acids or bases are added to the solution.

**bulk feeder** An animal that eats relatively large pieces of food.

**bulk flow** The movement of a fluid due to a difference in pressure between two locations.

**bundle-sheath cell** In $C_4$ plants, a type of photosynthetic cell arranged into tightly packed sheaths around the veins of a leaf.

**$C_3$ plant** A plant that uses the Calvin cycle for the initial steps that incorporate $CO_2$ into organic material, forming a three-carbon compound as the first stable intermediate.

**$C_4$ plant** A plant in which the Calvin cycle is preceded by reactions that incorporate $CO_2$ into a four-carbon compound, the end product of which supplies $CO_2$ for the Calvin cycle.

**calcitonin** (kal'-si-tō'-nin) A hormone secreted by the thyroid gland that lowers blood calcium levels by promoting calcium deposition in bone and calcium excretion from the kidneys; nonessential in adult humans.

**callus** A mass of dividing, undifferentiated cells growing at the site of a wound or in culture.

**calorie (cal)** The amount of heat energy required to raise the temperature of 1 g of water by 1°C; also the amount of heat energy that 1 g of water releases when it cools by 1°C. The Calorie (with a capital C), usually used to indicate the energy content of food, is a kilocalorie.

**Calvin cycle** The second of two major stages in photosynthesis (following the light reactions), involving fixation of atmospheric $CO_2$ and reduction of the fixed carbon into carbohydrate.

**Cambrian explosion** A relatively brief time in geologic history when many present-day phyla of animals first appeared in the fossil record. This burst of evolutionary change occurred about 535–525 million years ago and saw the emergence of the first large, hard-bodied animals.

**CAM plant** A plant that uses crassulacean acid metabolism, an adaptation for photosynthesis in arid conditions. In this process, $CO_2$ entering open stomata during the night is converted to organic acids, which release $CO_2$ for the Calvin cycle during the day, when stomata are closed.

**canopy** The uppermost layer of vegetation in a terrestrial biome.

**capillary** (kap'-il-ār'-ē) A microscopic blood vessel that penetrates the tissues and consists of a single layer of endothelial cells that allows exchange between the blood and interstitial fluid.

**capillary bed** (kap'-il-ār'-ē) A network of capillaries in a tissue or organ.

**capsid** The protein shell that encloses a viral genome. It may be rod-shaped, polyhedral, or more complex in shape.

**capsule** (1) In many prokaryotes, a dense and well-defined layer of polysaccharide or protein that surrounds the cell wall and is sticky, protecting the cell and enabling it to adhere to substrates or other cells. (2) The sporangium of a bryophyte (moss, liverwort, or hornwort).

**carbohydrate** (kar'-bō-hī'-drāt) A sugar (monosaccharide) or one of its dimers (disaccharides) or polymers (polysaccharides).

**carbon fixation** The initial incorporation of carbon from $CO_2$ into an organic compound by an autotrophic organism (a plant, another photosynthetic organism, or a chemoautotrophic prokaryote).

**carbonyl group** (kar'-buh-nil) A chemical group present in aldehydes and ketones and consisting of a carbon atom double-bonded to an oxygen atom.

**carboxyl group** (kar-bok'-sil) A chemical group present in organic acids and consisting of a single carbon atom double-bonded to an oxygen atom and also bonded to a hydroxyl group.

**cardiac cycle** (kar'-dē-ak) The alternating contractions and relaxations of the heart.

**cardiac muscle** (kar'-dē-ak) A type of striated muscle that forms the contractile wall of the heart. Its cells are joined by intercalated disks that relay the electrical signals underlying each heartbeat.

**cardiac output** (kar'-dē-ak) The volume of blood pumped per minute by each ventricle of the heart.

**cardiovascular system** A closed circulatory system with a heart and branching network of arteries, capillaries, and veins. The system is characteristic of vertebrates.

**carnivore** An animal that mainly eats other animals.

**carotenoid** (kuh-rot'-uh-noyd') An accessory pigment, either yellow or orange, in the chloroplasts of plants and in some prokaryotes. By absorbing wavelengths of light that chlorophyll cannot, carotenoids broaden the spectrum of colors that can drive photosynthesis.

**carpel** (kar'-pul) The ovule-producing reproductive organ of a flower, consisting of the stigma, style, and ovary.

**carrier** In genetics, an individual who is heterozygous at a given genetic locus for a recessively inherited disorder. The heterozygote is generally phenotypically normal for the disorder but can pass on the recessive allele to offspring.

**carrying capacity** The maximum population size that can be supported by the available resources, symbolized as $K$.

**cartilage** (kar'-til-ij) A flexible connective tissue with an abundance of collagenous fibers embedded in chondroitin sulfate.

**Casparian strip** (ka-spār'-ē-un) A water-impermeable ring of wax in the endodermal cells of plants that blocks the passive flow of water and solutes into the stele by way of cell walls.

**catabolic pathway** (kat'-uh-bol'-ik) A metabolic pathway that releases energy by breaking down complex molecules to simpler molecules.

**catalysis** (kuh-ta'-luh-sis) A process by which a chemical agent called a catalyst selectively increases the rate of a reaction without being consumed by the reaction.

**catalyst** (kat'-uh-list) A chemical agent that selectively increases the rate of a reaction without being consumed by the reaction.

**cation** (cat'-ī-on) A positively charged ion.

**cation exchange** (cat'-ī'-on) A process in which positively charged minerals are made available to a plant when hydrogen ions in the soil displace mineral ions from the clay particles.

**cecum** (sē'-kum) (plural, **ceca**) The blind pouch forming one branch of the large intestine.

**cell** Life's fundamental unit of structure and function; the smallest unit of organization that can perform all activities required for life.

**cell body** The part of a neuron that houses the nucleus and most other organelles.

**cell cycle** An ordered sequence of events in the life of a cell, from its origin in the division of a parent cell until its own division into two. The eukaryotic cell cycle is composed of interphase (including G₁, S, and G₂ phases) and M phase (including mitosis and cytokinesis).

**cell cycle control system** A cyclically operating set of molecules in the eukaryotic cell that both triggers and coordinates key events in the cell cycle.

**cell division** The reproduction of cells.

**cell fractionation** The disruption of a cell and separation of its parts by centrifugation at successively higher speeds.

**cell-mediated immune response** The branch of adaptive immunity that involves the activation of cytotoxic T cells, which defend against infected cells.

**cell plate** A membrane-bounded, flattened sac located at the midline of a dividing plant cell, inside which the new cell wall forms during cytokinesis.

**cellular respiration** The catabolic pathways of aerobic and anaerobic respiration, which break down organic molecules and use an electron transport chain for the production of ATP.

**cellulose** (sel'-yū-lōs) A structural polysaccharide of plant cell walls, consisting of glucose monomers joined by β glycosidic linkages.

**cell wall** A protective layer external to the plasma membrane in the cells of plants, prokaryotes, fungi, and some protists. Polysaccharides such as cellulose (in plants and some protists), chitin (in fungi), and peptidoglycan (in bacteria) are important structural components of cell walls.

**central nervous system (CNS)** The portion of the nervous system where signal integration occurs; in vertebrate animals, the brain and spinal cord.

**central vacuole** In a mature plant cell, a large membranous sac with diverse roles in growth, storage, and sequestration of toxic substances.

**centriole** (sen'-trē-ōl) A structure in the centrosome of an animal cell composed of a cylinder of microtubule triplets arranged in a "9 + 0" pattern. A centrosome has a pair of centrioles.

**centromere** (sen'-trō-mēr) In a duplicated chromosome, the region on each sister chromatid where it is most closely attached to its sister chromatid by proteins that bind to the centromeric DNA. Other proteins condense the chromatin in that region, so it appears as a narrow "waist" on the duplicated chromosome. (An unduplicated chromosome has a single centromere, identified by the proteins bound there.)

**centrosome** (sen'-trō-sōm) A structure present in the cytoplasm of animal cells that functions as a microtubule-organizing center and is important during cell division. A centrosome has two centrioles.

**cercozoan** An amoeboid or flagellated protist that feeds with threadlike pseudopodia.

**cerebellum** (sār'-ruh-bel'-um) Part of the vertebrate hindbrain located dorsally; functions in unconscious coordination of movement and balance.

**cerebral cortex** (suh-rē'-brul) The surface of the cerebrum; the largest and most complex part of the mammalian brain, containing nerve cell bodies of the cerebrum; the part of the vertebrate brain most changed through evolution.

**cerebrum** (suh-rē'-brum) The dorsal portion of the vertebrate forebrain, composed of right and left hemispheres; the integrating center for memory, learning, emotions, and other highly complex functions of the central nervous system.

**cervix** (ser'-viks) The neck of the uterus, which opens into the vagina.

**chaparral** A scrubland biome of dense, spiny evergreen shrubs found at midlatitudes along coasts where cold ocean currents circulate offshore; characterized by mild, rainy winters and long, hot, dry summers.

**chaperonin** (shap'-er-ō'-nin) A protein complex that assists in the proper folding of other proteins.

**character** An observable heritable feature that may vary among individuals.

**character displacement** The tendency for characteristics to be more divergent in sympatric populations of two species than in allopatric populations of the same two species.

**checkpoint** A control point in the cell cycle where stop and go-ahead signals can regulate the cycle.

**chelicera** (kē-lih'-suh-ruh) (plural, **chelicerae**) One of a pair of clawlike feeding appendages characteristic of chelicerates.

**chelicerate** (kē-lih-suh'-rāte) An arthropod that has chelicerae and a body divided into a cephalothorax and an abdomen. Living chelicerates include sea spiders, horseshoe crabs, scorpions, ticks, and spiders.

**chemical bond** An attraction between two atoms, resulting from a sharing of outer-shell electrons or the presence of opposite charges on the atoms. The bonded atoms gain complete outer electron shells.

**chemical energy** Energy available in molecules for release in a chemical reaction; a form of potential energy.

**chemical equilibrium** In a chemical reaction, the state in which the rate of the forward reaction equals the rate of the reverse reaction, so that the relative concentrations of the reactants and products do not change with time.

**chemical reaction** The making and breaking of chemical bonds, leading to changes in the composition of matter.

**chemiosmosis** (kem'-ē-oz-mō'-sis) An energy-coupling mechanism that uses energy stored in the form of a hydrogen ion gradient across a membrane to drive cellular work, such as the synthesis of ATP. Under aerobic conditions, most ATP synthesis in cells occurs by chemiosmosis.

**chemoautotroph** (kē'-mō-ot'-ō-trōf) An organism that obtains energy by oxidizing inorganic substances and needs only carbon dioxide as a carbon source.

**chemoheterotroph** (kē'-mō-het'-er-ō-trōf) An organism that requires organic molecules for both energy and carbon.

**chemoreceptor** A sensory receptor that responds to a chemical stimulus, such as a solute or an odorant.

**chiasma** (plural, **chiasmata**) (kī-az'-muh, kī-az'-muh-tuh) The X-shaped, microscopically visible region where crossing over has occurred earlier in prophase I between homologous nonsister chromatids. Chiasmata become visible after synapsis ends, with the two homologs remaining associated due to sister chromatid cohesion.

**chitin** (kī'-tin) A structural polysaccharide, consisting of amino sugar monomers, found in many fungal cell walls and in the exoskeletons of all arthropods.

**chlorophyll** (klōr'-ō-fil) A green pigment located in membranes within the chloroplasts of plants and algae and in the membranes of certain prokaryotes. Chlorophyll *a* participates directly in the light reactions, which convert solar energy to chemical energy.

**chlorophyll *a*** (klōr'-ō-fil) A photosynthetic pigment that participates directly in the light reactions, which convert solar energy to chemical energy.

**chlorophyll *b*** (klōr'-ō-fil) An accessory photosynthetic pigment that transfers energy to chlorophyll *a*.

**chloroplast** (klōr'-ō-plast) An organelle found in plants and photosynthetic protists that absorbs sunlight and uses it to drive the synthesis of organic compounds from carbon dioxide and water.

**choanocyte** (kō-an'-uh-sīt) A flagellated feeding cell found in sponges. Also called a collar cell, it has a collar-like ring that traps food particles around the base of its flagellum.

**cholesterol** (kō-les'-tuh-rol) A steroid that forms an essential component of animal cell membranes and acts as a precursor molecule for the synthesis of other biologically important steroids, such as many hormones.

**chondrichthyan** (kon-drik'-thē-an) A member of the clade Chondrichthyes, vertebrates with skeletons made mostly of cartilage, such as sharks and rays.

**chordate** A member of the phylum Chordata, animals that at some point during their development have a notochord; a dorsal, hollow nerve cord; pharyngeal slits or clefts; and a muscular, post-anal tail.

**chorionic villus sampling (CVS)** (kōr'-ē-on'-ik vil'-us) A technique associated with prenatal diagnosis in which a small sample of the fetal portion of the placenta is removed for analysis to detect certain genetic and congenital defects in the fetus.

**chromatin** (krō'-muh-tin) The complex of DNA and proteins that makes up eukaryotic chromosomes. When the cell is not dividing, chromatin exists in its dispersed form, as a mass of very long, thin fibers that are not visible with a light microscope.

**chromosome** (krō'-muh-sōm) A cellular structure consisting of one DNA molecule and associated protein molecules. (In some contexts, such as genome sequencing, the term may refer to the DNA alone.) A eukaryotic cell typically has multiple, linear chromosomes, which are located in the nucleus. A prokaryotic cell often has a single, circular chromosome, which is found in the nucleoid, a region that is not enclosed by a membrane. *See also* chromatin.

**chromosome theory of inheritance** (krō'-muh-sōm) A basic principle in biology stating that genes are located at specific positions (loci) on chromosomes and that the behavior of chromosomes during meiosis accounts for inheritance patterns.

**chylomicron** (kī'-lō-mī'-kron) A lipid transport globule composed of fats mixed with cholesterol and coated with proteins.

**chyme** (kīm) The mixture of partially digested food and digestive juices formed in the stomach.

**chytrid** (kī'-trid) A member of the fungal phylum Chytridiomycota, mostly aquatic fungi with flagellated zoospores that represent an early-diverging fungal lineage.

**ciliate** (sil'-ē-it) A type of protist that moves by means of cilia.

**cilium** (sil'-ē-um) (plural, **cilia**) A short appendage containing microtubules in eukaryotic cells. A motile cilium is specialized for locomotion or moving fluid past the cell; it is formed from a core of nine outer doublet microtubules and two inner single microtubules (the "9 + 2" arrangement) ensheathed in an extension of the plasma membrane. A primary cilium is usually nonmotile and plays a sensory and signaling role; it lacks the two inner microtubules (the "9 + 0" arrangement).

**circadian rhythm** (ser-kā'-dē-un) A physiological cycle of about 24 hours that persists even in the absence of external cues.

***cis-trans* isomer** One of several compounds that have the same molecular formula and covalent bonds between atoms but differ in the spatial arrangements of their atoms owing to the inflexibility of double bonds; formerly called a geometric isomer.

**citric acid cycle** A chemical cycle involving eight steps that completes the metabolic breakdown of glucose molecules begun in glycolysis by oxidizing acetyl CoA (derived from pyruvate) to carbon dioxide; occurs within the mitochondrion in eukaryotic cells and in the cytosol of prokaryotes; together with pyruvate oxidation, the second major stage in cellular respiration.

**clade** (klād) A group of species that includes an ancestral species and all of its descendants. A clade is equivalent to a monophyletic group.

**cladistics** (kluh-dis'-tiks) An approach to systematics in which organisms are placed into groups called clades based primarily on common descent.

**class** In Linnaean classification, the taxonomic category above the level of order.

**cleavage** (1) The process of cytokinesis in animal cells, characterized by pinching of the plasma membrane. (2) The succession of rapid cell divisions without significant growth during early embryonic development that converts the zygote to a ball of cells.

**cleavage furrow** The first sign of cleavage in an animal cell; a shallow groove around the cell in the cell surface near the old metaphase plate.

**climate** The long-term prevailing weather conditions at a given place.

**climate change** A directional change in temperature, precipitation, or other aspect of the global climate that lasts for three decades or more.

**climograph** A plot of the temperature and precipitation in a particular region.

**clitoris** (klit'-uh-ris) An organ at the upper intersection of the labia minora that engorges with blood and becomes erect during sexual arousal.

**cloaca** (klō-ā'-kuh) A common opening for the digestive, urinary, and reproductive tracts found in many nonmammalian vertebrates but in few mammals.

**clonal selection** The process by which an antigen selectively binds to and activates only those lymphocytes bearing receptors specific for the antigen. The selected lymphocytes proliferate and differentiate into a clone of effector cells and a clone of memory cells specific for the stimulating antigen.

**clone** (1) A lineage of genetically identical individuals or cells. (2) In popular usage, an individual that is genetically identical to another individual. (3) As a verb, to make one or more genetic replicas of an individual or cell. *See also* gene cloning.

**cloning vector** In genetic engineering, a DNA molecule that can carry foreign DNA into a host cell and replicate there. Cloning vectors include plasmids and bacterial artificial chromosomes (BACs), which move recombinant DNA from a test tube back into a cell, and viruses that transfer recombinant DNA by infection.

**closed circulatory system** A circulatory system in which blood is confined to vessels and is kept separate from the interstitial fluid.

**cnidocyte** (nī'-duh-sīt) A specialized cell unique to the phylum Cnidaria; contains a capsule-like organelle housing a coiled thread that, when discharged, explodes outward and functions in prey capture or defense.

**cochlea** (kok'-lē-uh) The complex, coiled organ of hearing that contains the organ of Corti.

**coding strand** Nontemplate strand of DNA, which has the same sequence as the mRNA except it has thymine (T) instead of uracil (U).

**codominance** The situation in which the phenotypes of both alleles are exhibited in the heterozygote because both alleles affect the phenotype in separate, distinguishable ways.

**codon** (kō'-don) A three-nucleotide sequence of DNA or mRNA that specifies a particular amino acid or termination signal; the basic unit of the genetic code.

**coefficient of relatedness** The fraction of genes that, on average, are shared by two individuals.

**coelom** (sē'-lōm) A body cavity lined by tissue derived only from mesoderm.

**coelomate** (sē'-lō-māt) An animal that possesses a true coelom (a body cavity lined by tissue completely derived from mesoderm).

**coenocytic fungus** (sē'-no-si'-tic) A fungus that lacks septa and hence whose body is made up of a continuous cytoplasmic mass that may contain hundreds or thousands of nuclei.

**coenzyme** (kō-en'-zīm) An organic molecule serving as a cofactor. Most vitamins function as coenzymes in metabolic reactions.

**coevolution** The joint evolution of two interacting species, each in response to selection imposed by the other.

**cofactor** Any nonprotein molecule or ion that is required for the proper functioning of an enzyme. Cofactors can be permanently bound to the active site or may bind loosely and reversibly, along with the substrate, during catalysis.

**cognition** The process of knowing that may include awareness, reasoning, recollection, and judgment.

**cognitive map** A neural representation of the abstract spatial relationships between objects in an animal's surroundings.

**cohesion** The linking together of like molecules, often by hydrogen bonds.

**cohesion-tension hypothesis** The leading explanation of the ascent of xylem sap. It states that transpiration exerts pull on xylem sap, putting the sap under negative pressure, or tension, and that the cohesion of water molecules transmits this pull along the entire length of the xylem from shoots to roots.

**cohort** A group of individuals of the same age in a population.

**coleoptile** (kō'-lē-op'-tul) The covering of the young shoot of the embryo of a grass seed.

**coleorhiza** (kō'-lē-uh-rī'-zuh) The covering of the young root of the embryo of a grass seed.

**collagen** A glycoprotein in the extracellular matrix of animal cells that forms strong fibers, found extensively in connective tissue and bone; the most abundant protein in the animal kingdom.

**collecting duct** The location in the kidney where processed filtrate, called urine, is collected from the renal tubules.

**collenchyma cell** (kō-len'-kim-uh) A flexible plant cell type that occurs in strands or cylinders that support young parts of the plant without restraining growth.

**colon** (kō'-len) The largest section of the vertebrate large intestine; functions in water absorption and formation of feces.

**commensalism** (kuh-men'-suh-lizm) A +/0 ecological interaction in which one organism benefits but the other is neither helped nor harmed.

**communication** In animal behavior, a process involving transmission of, reception of, and response to signals. The term is also used in connection with other organisms, as well as individual cells of multicellular organisms.

**community** All the organisms that inhabit a particular area; an assemblage of populations of different species living close enough together for potential interaction.

**community ecology** The study of how interactions between species affect community structure and organization.

**companion cell** A type of plant cell that is connected to a sieve-tube element by many plasmodesmata and whose nucleus and ribosomes may serve one or more adjacent sieve-tube elements.

**competition** A −/− interaction that occurs when individuals of different species compete for a resource that limits the survival and reproduction of each species.

**competitive exclusion** The concept that when populations of two similar species compete for the same limited resources, one population will use the resources more efficiently and have a reproductive advantage that will eventually lead to the elimination of the other population.

**competitive inhibitor** A substance that reduces the activity of an enzyme by entering the active site in place of the substrate, whose structure it mimics.

**complement system** A group of about 30 blood proteins that may amplify the inflammatory response, enhance phagocytosis, or directly lyse extracellular pathogens.

**complementary DNA (cDNA)** A double-stranded DNA molecule made *in vitro* using mRNA as a template and the enzymes reverse transcriptase and DNA polymerase. A cDNA molecule corresponds to the exons of a gene.

**complete dominance** The situation in which the phenotypes of the heterozygote and dominant homozygote are indistinguishable.

**complete flower** A flower that has all four basic floral organs: sepals, petals, stamens, and carpels.

**complete metamorphosis** The transformation of a larva into an adult that looks very different, and often functions very differently in its environment, than the larva.

**compound** A substance consisting of two or more different elements combined in a fixed ratio.

**compound eye** A type of multifaceted eye in insects and crustaceans consisting of up to several thousand light-detecting, focusing ommatidia.

**concentration gradient** A region along which the density of a chemical substance increases or decreases.

**conception** The fertilization of an egg by a sperm in humans.

**cone** A cone-shaped cell in the retina of the vertebrate eye, sensitive to color.

**conformer** An animal for which an internal condition conforms to (changes in accordance with) changes in an environmental variable.

**conidium** (plural, **conidia**) A haploid spore produced at the tip of a specialized hypha in ascomycetes during asexual reproduction.

**conifer** A member of the largest gymnosperm phylum. Most conifers are cone-bearing trees, such as pines and firs.

**conjugation** (kon′-jū-gā′-shun) (1) In prokaryotes, the direct transfer of DNA between two cells that are temporarily joined. When the two cells are members of different species, conjugation results in horizontal gene transfer. (2) In ciliates, a sexual process in which two cells exchange haploid micronuclei but do not reproduce.

**connective tissue** Animal tissue that functions mainly to bind and support other tissues, having a sparse population of cells scattered through an extracellular matrix.

**conodont** An early, soft-bodied vertebrate with prominent eyes and dental elements.

**conservation biology** The integrated study of ecology, evolutionary biology, physiology, molecular biology, and genetics to sustain biological diversity at all levels.

**consumer** An organism that feeds on producers, other consumers, or nonliving organic material.

**contraception** The deliberate prevention of pregnancy.

**contractile vacuole** A membranous sac that helps move excess water out of certain freshwater protists.

**control element** A segment of noncoding DNA that helps regulate transcription of a gene by serving as a binding site for a transcription factor. Multiple control elements are present in a eukaryotic gene's enhancer.

**control group** In a controlled experiment, a set of subjects that lacks (or does not receive) the specific factor being tested. Ideally, the control group should be identical to the experimental group in other respects.

**controlled experiment** An experiment designed to compare an experimental group with a control group; ideally, the two groups differ only in the factor being tested.

**convergent evolution** The evolution of similar features in independent evolutionary lineages.

**convergent extension** A process in which the cells of a tissue layer rearrange themselves in such a way that the sheet of cells becomes narrower (converges) and longer (extends).

**cooperativity** A kind of allosteric regulation whereby a shape change in one subunit of a protein caused by substrate binding is transmitted to all the other subunits, facilitating binding of additional substrate molecules to those subunits.

**coral reef** Typically a warm-water, tropical ecosystem dominated by the hard skeletal structures secreted primarily by corals. Some coral reefs also exist in cold, deep waters.

**corepressor** A small molecule that binds to a bacterial repressor protein and changes the protein's shape, allowing it to bind to the operator and switch an operon off.

**cork cambium** (kam′-bē-um) A cylinder of meristematic tissue in woody plants that replaces the epidermis with thicker, tougher cork cells.

**corpus callosum** (kor′-pus kuh-lō′-sum) The thick band of nerve fibers that connects the right and left cerebral hemispheres in mammals, enabling the hemispheres to process information together.

**corpus luteum** (kor′-pus lū′-tē-um) A secreting tissue in the ovary that forms from the collapsed follicle after ovulation and produces progesterone.

**cortex** (1) The outer region of cytoplasm in a eukaryotic cell, lying just under the plasma membrane, that has a more gel-like consistency than the inner regions due to the presence of multiple microfilaments. (2) In plants, ground tissue that is between the vascular tissue and dermal tissue in a root or eudicot stem.

**cortical nephron** In mammals and birds, a nephron with a loop of Henle located almost entirely in the renal cortex.

**cotransport** The coupling of the "downhill" diffusion of one substance to the "uphill" transport of another against its own concentration gradient.

**cotyledon** (kot′-uh-lē′-dun) A seed leaf of an angiosperm embryo. Some species have one cotyledon, others two.

**countercurrent exchange** The exchange of a substance or heat between two fluids flowing in opposite directions. For example, blood in a fish gill flows in the opposite direction of water passing over the gill, maximizing diffusion of oxygen into and carbon dioxide out of the blood.

**countercurrent multiplier system** A countercurrent system in which energy is expended in active transport to facilitate exchange of materials and generate concentration gradients.

**covalent bond** (kō-vā′-lent) A type of strong chemical bond in which two atoms share one or more pairs of valence electrons.

**crassulacean acid metabolism (CAM)** (crass-yū-lā′-shen) An adaptation for photosynthesis in arid conditions, first discovered in the family Crassulaceae. In this process, a plant takes up $CO_2$ and incorporates it into a variety of organic acids at night; during the day, $CO_2$ is released from organic acids for use in the Calvin cycle.

**CRISPR-Cas9 system** A technique for editing genes in living cells, involving a bacterial protein called Cas9 associated with a guide RNA complementary to a gene sequence of interest.

**crista** (plural, **cristae**) (kris′-tuh, kris′-tē) An infolding of the inner membrane of a mitochondrion. The inner membrane houses electron transport chains and molecules of the enzyme catalyzing the synthesis of ATP (ATP synthase).

**critical load** The amount of added nutrient, usually nitrogen or phosphorus, that can be absorbed by plants without damaging ecosystem integrity.

**crop rotation** The practice of growing different crops in succession on the same land chiefly to preserve the productive capacity of the soil.

**cross-fostering study** A behavioral study in which the young of one species are placed in the care of adults from another species.

**crossing over** The reciprocal exchange of genetic material between nonsister chromatids during prophase I of meiosis.

**cross-pollination** In angiosperms, the transfer of pollen from an anther of a flower on one plant to the stigma of a flower on another plant of the same species.

**cryptic coloration** Camouflage that makes a potential prey difficult to spot against its background.

**culture** A system of information transfer through social learning or teaching that influences the behavior of individuals in a population.

**cuticle** (kyū′-tuh-kul) (1) A waxy covering on the surface of stems and leaves that prevents desiccation in terrestrial plants. (2) A tough coat that covers the body of a nematode.

**cyclic AMP (cAMP)** Cyclic adenosine monophosphate, a ring-shaped molecule made from ATP that is a common intracellular signaling molecule (second messenger) in eukaryotic cells. It is also a regulator of some bacterial operons.

**cyclic electron flow** A route of electron flow during the light reactions of photosynthesis that involves only one photosystem and that produces ATP but not NADPH or $O_2$.

**cyclin** (sī'-klin) A cellular protein that occurs in a cyclically fluctuating concentration and that plays an important role in regulating the cell cycle.

**cyclin-dependent kinase (Cdk)** (sī'-klin) A protein kinase that is active only when attached to a particular cyclin.

**cyclostome** (sī'-cluh-stōm) Member of one of the two main clades of vertebrates; cyclostomes lack jaws and include lampreys and hagfishes. *See also* gnathostome.

**cystic fibrosis** (sis'-tik fī-brō'-sis) A human genetic disorder caused by a recessive allele for a chloride channel protein; characterized by an excessive secretion of mucus and consequent vulnerability to infection; fatal if untreated.

**cytochrome** (sī'-tō-krōm) An iron-containing protein that is a component of electron transport chains in the mitochondria and chloroplasts of eukaryotic cells and the plasma membranes of prokaryotic cells.

**cytokinesis** (sī'-tō-kuh-nē'-sis) The division of the cytoplasm to form two separate daughter cells immediately after mitosis, meiosis I, or meiosis II.

**cytokinin** (sī'-tō-kī'-nin) Any of a class of related plant hormones that retard aging and act in concert with auxin to stimulate cell division, influence the pathway of differentiation, and control apical dominance.

**cytoplasm** (sī'-tō-plaz-um) The contents of the cell bounded by the plasma membrane; in eukaryotes, the portion exclusive of the nucleus.

**cytoplasmic determinant** A maternal substance, such as a protein or RNA, that when placed into an egg influences the course of early development by regulating the expression of genes that affect the developmental fate of cells.

**cytoplasmic streaming** A circular flow of cytoplasm, involving interactions of myosin and actin filaments, that speeds the distribution of materials within cells.

**cytoskeleton** A network of microtubules, microfilaments, and intermediate filaments that extend throughout the cytoplasm and serve a variety of mechanical, transport, and signaling functions.

**cytosol** (sī'-tō-sol) The semifluid portion of the cytoplasm.

**cytotoxic T cell** A type of lymphocyte that, when activated, kills infected cells as well as certain cancer cells and transplanted cells.

**dalton** A measure of mass for atoms and subatomic particles; the same as the atomic mass unit, or amu.

**data** Recorded observations.

**day-neutral plant** A plant in which flower formation is not controlled by photoperiod or day length.

**decomposer** An organism that absorbs nutrients from nonliving organic material such as corpses, fallen plant material, and the wastes of living organisms and converts them to inorganic forms; a detritivore.

**deductive reasoning** A type of logic in which specific results are predicted from a general premise.

**de-etiolation** The changes a plant shoot undergoes in response to sunlight; also known informally as greening.

**dehydration reaction** A chemical reaction in which two molecules become covalently bonded to each other with the removal of a water molecule.

**deletion** (1) A deficiency in a chromosome resulting from the loss of a fragment through breakage. (2) A mutational loss of one or more nucleotide pairs from a gene.

**demographic transition** In a stable population, a shift from high birth and death rates to low birth and death rates.

**demography** The study of changes over time in the vital statistics of populations, especially birth rates and death rates.

**denaturation** (dē-nā'-chur-ā'-shun) In proteins, a process in which a protein loses its native shape due to the disruption of weak chemical bonds and interactions, thereby becoming biologically inactive; in DNA, the separation of the two strands of the double helix. Denaturation occurs under extreme (noncellular) conditions of pH, salt concentration, or temperature.

**dendrite** (den'-drīt) One of usually numerous, short, highly branched extensions of a neuron that receive signals from other neurons.

**dendritic cell** An antigen-presenting cell, located mainly in lymphatic tissues and skin, that is particularly efficient in presenting antigens to helper T cells, thereby initiating a primary immune response.

**density** The number of individuals per unit area or volume.

**density dependent** Referring to any characteristic that varies with population density.

**density-dependent inhibition** The phenomenon observed in normal animal cells that causes them to stop dividing when they come into contact with one another.

**density independent** Referring to any characteristic that is not affected by population density.

**deoxyribonucleic acid (DNA)** (dē-ok'-sē-rī'-bō-nū-klā'-ik) A nucleic acid molecule, usually a double-stranded helix, in which each polynucleotide strand consists of nucleotide monomers with a deoxyribose sugar and the nitrogenous bases adenine (A), cytosine (C), guanine (G), and thymine (T); capable of being replicated and determining the inherited structure of a cell's proteins.

**deoxyribose** (dē-ok'-si-rī'-bōs) The sugar component of DNA nucleotides, having one fewer hydroxyl group than ribose, the sugar component of RNA nucleotides.

**dependent variable** A factor whose value is measured during an experiment or other test to see whether it is influenced by changes in another factor (the independent variable).

**depolarization** A change in a cell's membrane potential such that the inside of the membrane is made less negative relative to the outside. For example, a neuron membrane is depolarized if a stimulus decreases its voltage from the resting potential of $-70\,mV$ in the direction of zero voltage.

**dermal tissue system** The outer protective covering of plants.

**desert** A terrestrial biome characterized by very low precipitation.

**desmosome** A type of intercellular junction in animal cells that functions as a rivet, fastening cells together.

**determinate cleavage** A type of embryonic development in protostomes that rigidly casts the developmental fate of each embryonic cell very early.

**determinate growth** A type of growth characteristic of most animals and some plant organs, in which growth stops after a certain size is reached.

**determination** The progressive restriction of developmental potential in which the possible fate of each cell becomes more limited as an embryo develops. At the end of determination, a cell is committed to its fate.

**detritivore** (deh-trī'-tuh-vōr) A consumer that derives its energy and nutrients from nonliving organic material such as corpses, fallen plant material, and the wastes of living organisms; a decomposer.

**detritus** (di-trī'-tus) Dead organic matter.

**deuteromycete** (dū'-tuh-rō-mī'-sēt) Traditional classification for a fungus with no known sexual stage.

**deuterostome development** (dū'-tuh-rō-stōm') In animals, a developmental mode distinguished by the development of the anus from the blastopore; often also characterized by radial cleavage and by the body cavity forming as outpockets of mesodermal tissue.

**Deuterostomia** (dū'-tuh-rō-stōm'-ē-uh) One of the three main lineages of bilaterian animals. *See also* Ecdysozoa and Lophotrochozoa.

**development** The events involved in an organism's changing gradually from a simple to a more complex or specialized form.

**diabetes mellitus** (dī'-uh-bē'-tis mel'-uh-tus) An endocrine disorder marked by an inability to maintain glucose homeostasis. The type 1 form results from autoimmune destruction of insulin-secreting cells; treatment usually requires daily insulin injections. The type 2 form most commonly results from reduced responsiveness of target cells to insulin; obesity and lack of exercise are risk factors.

**diacylglycerol (DAG)** (dī-a'-sil-glis'-er-ol) A second messenger produced by the cleavage of the phospholipid $PIP_2$ in the plasma membrane.

**diaphragm** (dī'-uh-fram') (1) A sheet of muscle that forms the bottom wall of the thoracic cavity in mammals. Contraction of the diaphragm pulls air into the lungs. (2) A dome-shaped rubber cup fitted into the upper portion of the vagina before sexual intercourse. It serves as a physical barrier to the passage of sperm into the uterus.

**diapsid** (dī-ap'-sid) A member of an amniote clade distinguished by a pair of holes on each side of the skull. Diapsids include the lepidosaurs and archosaurs.

**diastole** (dī-as'-tō-lē) The stage of the cardiac cycle in which a heart chamber is relaxed and fills with blood.

**diastolic pressure** Blood pressure in the arteries when the ventricles are relaxed.

**diatom** Photosynthetic protist in the stramenopile clade; diatoms have a unique glass-like wall made of silicon dioxide embedded in an organic matrix.

**dicot** A term traditionally used to refer to flowering plants that have two embryonic seed leaves, or cotyledons. Recent molecular evidence indicates that dicots do not form a clade; species once classified as dicots are now grouped into eudicots, magnoliids, and several lineages of basal angiosperms.

**differential gene expression** The expression of different sets of genes by cells with the same genome.

**differentiation** The process by which a cell or group of cells becomes specialized in structure and function.

**diffusion** The random thermal motion of particles of liquids, gases, or solids. In the presence of a concentration or electrochemical gradient, diffusion results in the net movement of a substance from a region where it is more concentrated to a region where it is less concentrated.

**digestion** The second stage of food processing in animals: the breaking down of food into molecules small enough for the body to absorb.

**dihybrid** (dī′-hī′-brid) An organism that is heterozygous with respect to two genes of interest. All the offspring from a cross between parents doubly homozygous for different alleles are dihybrids. For example, parents of genotypes *AABB* and *aabb* produce a dihybrid of genotype *AaBb*.

**dihybrid cross** (dī′-hī′-brid) A cross between two organisms that are each heterozygous for both of the characters being followed (or the self-pollination of a plant that is heterozygous for both characters).

**dikaryotic** (dī′-kār-ē-ot′-ik) Referring to a fungal mycelium with two haploid nuclei per cell, one from each parent.

**dinoflagellate** (dī′-nō-flaj′-uh-let) A member of a group of mostly unicellular photosynthetic algae with two flagella situated in perpendicular grooves in cellulose plates covering the cell.

**dinosaur** A member of an extremely diverse clade of reptiles varying in body shape, size, and habitat. Birds are the only extant dinosaurs.

**dioecious** (dī-ē′-shus) In plant biology, having the male and female reproductive parts on different individuals of the same species.

**diploblastic** Having two germ layers.

**diploid cell** (dip′-loyd) A cell containing two sets of chromosomes (2n), one set inherited from each parent.

**diplomonad** A protist that has modified mitochondria, two equal-sized nuclei, and multiple flagella.

**directional selection** Natural selection in which individuals at one end of the phenotypic range survive or reproduce more successfully than do other individuals.

**disaccharide** (dī-sak′-uh-rīd) A double sugar, consisting of two monosaccharides joined by a glycosidic linkage formed by a dehydration reaction.

**dispersal** The movement of individuals or gametes away from their parent location. This movement sometimes expands the geographic range of a population or species.

**dispersion** The pattern of spacing among individuals within the boundaries of a population.

**disruptive selection** Natural selection in which individuals on both extremes of a phenotypic range survive or reproduce more successfully than do individuals with intermediate phenotypes.

**distal tubule** In the vertebrate kidney, the portion of a nephron that helps refine filtrate and empties it into a collecting duct.

**disturbance** A natural or human-caused event that changes a biological community and usually removes organisms from it. Disturbances, such as fires and storms, play a pivotal role in structuring many communities.

**disulfide bridge** A strong covalent bond formed when the sulfur of one cysteine monomer bonds to the sulfur of another cysteine monomer.

**DNA (deoxyribonucleic acid)** (dē-ok′-sē-rī′-bō-nū-klā′-ik) A nucleic acid molecule, usually a double-stranded helix, in which each polynucleotide strand consists of nucleotide monomers with a deoxyribose sugar and the nitrogenous bases adenine (A), cytosine (C), guanine (G), and thymine (T); capable of being replicated and determining the inherited structure of a cell's proteins.

**DNA cloning** The production of multiple copies of a specific DNA segment.

**DNA ligase** (lī′-gās) A linking enzyme essential for DNA replication; catalyzes the covalent bonding of the 3′ end of one DNA fragment (such as an Okazaki fragment) to the 5′ end of another DNA fragment (such as a growing DNA chain).

**DNA methylation** The presence of methyl groups on the DNA bases (usually cytosine) of plants, animals, and fungi. (The term also refers to the process of adding methyl groups to DNA bases.)

**DNA microarray assay** A method to detect and measure the expression of thousands of genes at one time. Tiny amounts of a large number of single-stranded DNA fragments representing different genes are fixed to a glass slide and tested for hybridization with samples of labeled cDNA.

**DNA polymerase** (puh-lim′-er-ās) An enzyme that catalyzes the elongation of new DNA (for example, at a replication fork) by the addition of nucleotides to the 3′ end of an existing chain. There are several different DNA polymerases; DNA polymerase III and DNA polymerase I play major roles in DNA replication in *E. coli*.

**DNA replication** The process by which a DNA molecule is copied; also called DNA synthesis.

**DNA sequencing** Determining the complete nucleotide sequence of a gene or DNA segment.

**DNA technology** Techniques for sequencing and manipulating DNA.

**domain** (1) A taxonomic category above the kingdom level. The three domains are Archaea, Bacteria, and Eukarya. (2) A discrete structural and functional region of a protein.

**dominant allele** An allele that is fully expressed in the phenotype of a heterozygote.

**dominant species** A species with substantially higher abundance or biomass than other species in a community. Dominant species exert a powerful control over the occurrence and distribution of other species.

**dormancy** A condition typified by extremely low metabolic rate and a suspension of growth and development.

**dorsal** Pertaining to the top of an animal with radial or bilateral symmetry.

**dorsal lip** The region above the blastopore on the dorsal side of the amphibian embryo.

**double bond** A double covalent bond; the sharing of two pairs of valence electrons by two atoms.

**double circulation** A circulatory system consisting of separate pulmonary and systemic circuits, in which blood passes through the heart after completing each circuit.

**double fertilization** A mechanism of fertilization in angiosperms in which two sperm cells unite with two cells in the female gametophyte (embryo sac) to form the zygote and endosperm.

**double helix** The form of native DNA, referring to its two adjacent antiparallel polynucleotide strands wound around an imaginary axis into a spiral shape.

**Down syndrome** A human genetic disease usually caused by the presence of an extra chromosome 21; characterized by developmental delays and heart and other defects that are generally treatable or non-life-threatening.

**Duchenne muscular dystrophy** (duh-shen′) A human genetic disease caused by a sex-linked recessive allele; characterized by progressive weakening and a loss of muscle tissue.

**duodenum** (dū′-uh-dēn′-um) The first section of the small intestine, where chyme from the stomach mixes with digestive juices from the pancreas, liver, and gallbladder as well as from gland cells of the intestinal wall.

**duplication** An aberration in chromosome structure due to fusion with a fragment from a homologous chromosome, such that a portion of a chromosome is duplicated.

**dynein** (dī′-nē-un) In cilia and flagella, a large motor protein extending from one microtubule doublet to the adjacent doublet. ATP hydrolysis drives changes in dynein shape that lead to bending of cilia and flagella.

**E site** One of a ribosome's three binding sites for tRNA during translation. The E site is the place where discharged tRNAs leave the ribosome. (E stands for exit.)

**Ecdysozoa** (ek′-dē-sō-zō′-uh) One of the three main lineages of bilaterian animals; many ecdysozoans are molting animals. *See also* Deuterostomia and Lophotrochozoa.

**echinoderm** (i-kī′-nō-derm) A slow-moving or sessile marine deuterostome with a water vascular system and, in larvae, bilateral symmetry. Echinoderms include sea stars, brittle stars, sea urchins, feather stars, and sea cucumbers.

**ecological footprint** The aggregate land and water area required by a person, city, or nation to produce all of the resources it consumes and to absorb all of the waste it generates.

**ecological niche** (nich) The sum of a species' use of the biotic and abiotic resources in its environment.

**ecological species concept** Definition of a species in terms of ecological niche, the sum of how members of the species interact with the nonliving and living parts of their environment.

**ecological succession** Transition in the species composition of a community following a disturbance; establishment of a community in an area virtually barren of life.

**ecology** The study of how organisms interact with each other and their environment.

**ecosystem** All the organisms in a given area as well as the abiotic factors with which they interact; one or more communities and the physical environment around them.

**ecosystem ecology** The study of energy flow and the cycling of chemicals among the various biotic and abiotic components in an ecosystem.

**ecosystem engineer** An organism that influences community structure by causing physical changes in the environment.

**ecosystem service** A function performed by an ecosystem that directly or indirectly benefits humans.

**ecotone** The transition from one type of habitat or ecosystem to another, such as the transition from a forest to a grassland.

**ectoderm** (ek′-tō-durm) The outermost of the three primary germ layers in animal embryos; gives rise to the outer covering and, in some phyla, the nervous system, inner ear, and lens of the eye.

**ectomycorrhiza** (plural, **ectomycorrhizae**) (ek′-tō-mī′-kō-rī′-zuh, ek′-tō-mī′-kō-rī′-zē) Association of a fungus with a plant root system in which the fungus surrounds the roots but does not cause invagination of the host (plant) cell's plasma membrane.

**ectomycorrhizal fungus** A symbiotic fungus that forms sheaths of hyphae over the surface of plant roots and also grows into extracellular spaces of the root cortex.

**ectoparasite** A parasite that feeds on the external surface of a host.

**ectopic** Occurring in an abnormal location.

**ectoproct** A sessile, colonial lophophorate; also called a bryozoan.

**ectothermic** Referring to organisms for which external sources provide most of the heat for temperature regulation.

**Ediacaran biota** (ē′-dē-uh-keh′-run bī-ō′-tuh) An early group of macroscopic, soft-bodied, multicellular eukaryotes known from fossils that range in age from 635 million to 535 million years old.

**effective population size** An estimate of the size of a population based on the numbers of females and males that successfully breed; generally smaller than the total population.

**effector** A pathogen-encoded protein that cripples the host's innate immune system.

**effector cell** (1) A muscle cell or gland cell that carries out the body's response to stimuli as directed by signals from the brain or other processing center of the nervous system. (2) A lymphocyte that has undergone clonal selection and is capable of mediating an adaptive immune response.

**egg** The female gamete.

**ejaculation** The propulsion of sperm from the epididymis through the muscular vas deferens, ejaculatory duct, and urethra.

**electrocardiogram (ECG or EKG)** A record of the electrical impulses that travel through heart muscle during the cardiac cycle.

**electrochemical gradient** The diffusion gradient of an ion, which is affected by both the concentration difference of an ion across a membrane (a chemical force) and the ion's tendency to move relative to the membrane potential (an electrical force).

**electrogenic pump** An active transport protein that generates voltage across a membrane while pumping ions.

**electromagnetic receptor** A receptor of electromagnetic energy, such as visible light, electricity, or magnetism.

**electromagnetic spectrum** The entire spectrum of electromagnetic radiation, ranging in wavelength from less than a nanometer to more than a kilometer.

**electron** A subatomic particle with a single negative electrical charge and a mass about 1/2,000 that of a neutron or proton. One or more electrons move around the nucleus of an atom.

**electron microscope (EM)** A microscope that uses magnets to focus an electron beam on or through a specimen, resulting in a practical resolution that is 100-fold greater than that of a light microscope using standard techniques. A transmission electron microscope (TEM) is used to study the internal structure of thin sections of cells. A scanning electron microscope (SEM) is used to study the fine details of cell surfaces.

**electron shell** An energy level of electrons at a characteristic average distance from the nucleus of an atom.

**electron transport chain** A sequence of electron carrier molecules (membrane proteins) that shuttle electrons down a series of redox reactions that release energy used to make ATP.

**electronegativity** The attraction of a given atom for the electrons of a covalent bond.

**electroporation** A technique to introduce recombinant DNA into cells by applying a brief electrical pulse to a solution containing the cells. The pulse creates temporary holes in the cells' plasma membranes, through which DNA can enter.

**element** Any substance that cannot be broken down to any other substance by chemical reactions.

**elimination** The fourth and final stage of food processing in animals: the passing of undigested material out of the body.

**embryo sac** (em′-brē-ō) The female gametophyte of angiosperms, formed from the growth and division of the megaspore into a multicellular structure that typically has eight haploid nuclei.

**embryonic lethal** A mutation with a phenotype leading to death of an embryo or larva.

**embryophyte** Alternate name for land plants that refers to their shared derived trait of multicellular, dependent embryos.

**emergent properties** New properties that arise with each step upward in the hierarchy of life, owing to the arrangement and interactions of parts as complexity increases.

**emigration** The movement of individuals out of a population.

**enantiomer** (en-an′-tē-ō-mer) One of two compounds that are mirror images of each other and that differ in shape due to the presence of an asymmetric carbon.

**endangered species** A species that is in danger of extinction throughout all or a significant portion of its range.

**endemic** (en-dem′-ik) Referring to a species that is confined to a specific geographic area.

**endergonic reaction** (en′-der-gon′-ik) A nonspontaneous chemical reaction in which free energy is absorbed from the surroundings.

**endocrine gland** (en′-dō-krin) A ductless gland that secretes hormones directly into the interstitial fluid, from which they diffuse into the bloodstream.

**endocrine system** (en′-dō-krin) In animals, the internal system of communication involving hormones, the ductless glands that secrete hormones, and the molecular receptors on or in target cells that respond to hormones; functions in concert with the nervous system to effect internal regulation and maintain homeostasis.

**endocytosis** (en′-dō-sī-tō′-sis) Cellular uptake of biological molecules and particulate matter via formation of vesicles from the plasma membrane.

**endoderm** (en′-dō-durm) The innermost of the three primary germ layers in animal embryos; lines the archenteron and gives rise to the liver, pancreas, lungs, and the lining of the digestive tract in species that have these structures.

**endodermis** In plant roots, the innermost layer of the cortex that surrounds the vascular cylinder.

**endomembrane system** The collection of membranes inside and surrounding a eukaryotic cell, related either through direct physical contact or by the transfer of membranous vesicles; includes the plasma membrane, the nuclear envelope, the smooth and rough endoplasmic reticulum, the Golgi apparatus, lysosomes, vesicles, and vacuoles.

**endometriosis** (en′-dō-mē-trē-ō′-sis) The condition resulting from the presence of endometrial tissue outside of the uterus.

**endometrium** (en′-dō-mē′-trē-um) The inner lining of the uterus, which is richly supplied with blood vessels.

**endoparasite** A parasite that lives within a host.

**endophyte** A harmless fungus, or occasionally another organism, that lives between cells of a plant part or multicellular alga.

**endoplasmic reticulum (ER)** (en′-dō-plaz′-mik ruh-tik′-yū-lum) An extensive membranous network in eukaryotic cells, continuous with the outer nuclear membrane and composed of ribosome-studded (rough) and ribosome-free (smooth) regions.

**endorphin** (en-dōr′-fin) Any of several hormones produced in the brain and anterior pituitary that inhibit pain perception.

**endoskeleton** A hard skeleton buried within the soft tissues of an animal.

**endosperm** In angiosperms, a nutrient-rich tissue formed by the union of a sperm with two polar nuclei during double fertilization. The endosperm provides nourishment to the developing embryo in angiosperm seeds.

**endospore** A thick-coated, resistant cell produced by some bacterial cells when they are exposed to harsh conditions.

**endosymbiont theory** The theory that mitochondria and plastids, including chloroplasts, originated as prokaryotic cells engulfed by a host cell. The engulfed cell and its host cell then evolved into a single organism. *See also* endosymbiosis.

**endosymbiosis** A relationship between two species in which one organism lives inside the cell or cells of another organism. *See also* endosymbiont theory.

**endothelium** (en'-dō-thē'-lē-um) The simple squamous layer of cells lining the lumen of blood vessels.

**endothermic** Referring to organisms that are warmed by heat generated by their own metabolism. This heat usually maintains a relatively stable body temperature higher than that of the external environment.

**endotoxin** A toxic component of the outer membrane of certain gram-negative bacteria that is released only when the bacteria die.

**energetic hypothesis** The concept that the length of a food chain is limited by the inefficiency of energy transfer along the chain.

**energy** The capacity to cause change, especially to do work (to move matter against an opposing force).

**energy coupling** In cellular metabolism, the use of energy released from an exergonic reaction to drive an endergonic reaction.

**enhancer** A segment of eukaryotic DNA containing multiple control elements, usually located far from the gene whose transcription it regulates.

**enteric nervous system** A distinct network of neurons that exerts direct and partially independent control over the digestive tract, pancreas, and gallbladder.

**entropy** A measure of molecular disorder, or randomness.

**enzyme** (en'-zīm) A macromolecule serving as a catalyst, a chemical agent that increases the rate of a reaction without being consumed by the reaction. Most enzymes are proteins.

**enzyme-substrate complex** (en'-zīm) A temporary complex formed when an enzyme binds to its substrate molecule(s).

**epicotyl** (ep'-uh-kot'-ul) In an angiosperm embryo, the embryonic axis above the point of attachment of the cotyledon(s) and below the first pair of miniature leaves.

**epidemic** A widespread outbreak of a disease.

**epidermis** (1) The dermal tissue system of nonwoody plants, usually consisting of a single layer of tightly packed cells. (2) The outermost layer of cells in an animal.

**epididymis** (ep'-uh-did'-uh-mus) A coiled tubule located adjacent to the mammalian testis where sperm are stored.

**epigenetic inheritance** Inheritance of traits transmitted by mechanisms that do not involve the nucleotide sequence.

**epinephrine** (ep'-i-nef'-rin) A catecholamine that, when secreted as a hormone by the adrenal medulla, mediates "fight-or-flight" responses to short-term stresses; also released by some neurons as a neurotransmitter; also called adrenaline.

**epiphyte** (ep'-uh-fīt) A plant that nourishes itself but grows on the surface of another plant for support, usually on the branches or trunks of trees.

**epistasis** (ep'-i-stā'-sis) A type of gene interaction in which the phenotypic expression of one gene alters that of another independently inherited gene.

**epithelial tissue** (ep'-uh-thē'-lē-ul) Sheets of tightly packed cells that line organs and body cavities as well as external surfaces.

**epithelium** An epithelial tissue.

**epitope** A small, accessible region of an antigen to which an antigen receptor or antibody binds.

**equilibrium potential** ($E_{\text{ion}}$) The magnitude of a cell's membrane voltage at equilibrium; calculated using the Nernst equation.

**erythrocyte** (eh-rith'-ruh-sīt) A blood cell that contains hemoglobin, which transports oxygen; also called a red blood cell.

**erythropoietin (EPO)** (eh-rith'-rō-poy'-uh-tin) A hormone that stimulates the production of erythrocytes. It is secreted by the kidney when body tissues do not receive enough oxygen.

**esophagus** (eh-sof'-uh-gus) A muscular tube that conducts food, by peristalsis, from the pharynx to the stomach.

**essential amino acid** An amino acid that an animal cannot synthesize itself and must be obtained from food in prefabricated form.

**essential element** A chemical element required for an organism to survive, grow, and reproduce.

**essential fatty acid** An unsaturated fatty acid that an animal needs but cannot make.

**essential nutrient** A substance that an organism cannot synthesize from any other material and therefore must absorb in preassembled form.

**estradiol** (es'-truh-dī'-ol) A steroid hormone that stimulates the development and maintenance of the female reproductive system and secondary sex characteristics; the major estrogen in mammals.

**estrogen** (es'-trō-jen) Any steroid hormone, such as estradiol, that stimulates the development and maintenance of the female reproductive system and secondary sex characteristics.

**estrous cycle** (es'-trus) A reproductive cycle characteristic of female mammals except humans and certain other primates, in which the endometrium is reabsorbed in the absence of pregnancy and sexual response occurs only during a mid-cycle point known as estrus.

**estuary** The area where a freshwater stream or river merges with the ocean.

**ethylene** (eth'-uh-lēn) A gaseous plant hormone involved in responses to mechanical stress, programmed cell death, leaf abscission, and fruit ripening.

**etiolation** Plant morphological adaptations for growing in darkness.

**euchromatin** (yū-krō'-muh-tin) The less condensed form of eukaryotic chromatin that is available for transcription.

**eudicot** (yū-dī'-kot) A member of a clade that contains the vast majority of flowering plants that have two embryonic seed leaves, or cotyledons.

**euglenid** (yū'-glen-id) A protist, such as *Euglena* or its relatives, characterized by an anterior pocket from which one or two flagella emerge.

**euglenozoan** A member of a diverse clade of flagellated protists that includes predatory heterotrophs, photosynthetic autotrophs, and pathogenic parasites.

**Eukarya** (yū-kar'-ē-uh) The domain that includes all eukaryotic organisms.

**eukaryotic cell** (yū'-ker-ē-ot'-ik) A type of cell with a membrane-enclosed nucleus and membrane-enclosed organelles. Organisms with eukaryotic cells (protists, plants, fungi, and animals) are called eukaryotes.

**eumetazoan** (yū'-met-uh-zō'-un) A member of a clade of animals with true tissues. All animals except sponges and a few other groups are eumetazoans.

**eurypterid** (yur-ip'-tuh-rid) An extinct carnivorous chelicerate; also called a water scorpion.

**Eustachian tube** (yū-stā'-shun) The tube that connects the middle ear to the pharynx.

**eutherian** (yū-thēr'-ē-un) Placental mammal; mammal whose young complete their embryonic development within the uterus, joined to the mother by the placenta.

**eutrophic lake** (yū-trōf'-ik) A lake that has a high rate of biological productivity supported by a high rate of nutrient cycling.

**eutrophication** A process by which nutrients, particularly phosphorus and nitrogen, become highly concentrated in a body of water, leading to increased growth of organisms such as algae or cyanobacteria.

**evaporative cooling** The process in which the surface of an object becomes cooler during evaporation, a result of the molecules with the greatest kinetic energy changing from the liquid to the gaseous state.

**evapotranspiration** The total evaporation of water from an ecosystem, including water transpired by plants and evaporated from a landscape, usually measured in millimeters and estimated for a year.

**evo-devo** Evolutionary developmental biology; a field of biology that compares developmental processes of different multicellular organisms to understand how these processes have evolved and how changes can modify existing organismal features or lead to new ones.

**evolution** Descent with modification; the idea that living species are descendants of ancestral species that were different from the present-day ones; also defined more narrowly as the change in the genetic composition of a population from generation to generation.

**evolutionary tree** A branching diagram that reflects a hypothesis about evolutionary relationships among groups of organisms.

**Excavata** (ex'-kuh-vah'-tuh) One of four supergroups of eukaryotes proposed in a current hypothesis of the evolutionary history of eukaryotes. Excavates have unique cytoskeletal features, and some species have an "excavated" feeding groove on one side of the cell body. *See also* SAR, Archaeplastida, and Unikonta.

**excitatory postsynaptic potential (EPSP)** An electrical change (depolarization) in the membrane of a postsynaptic cell caused by the binding of an excitatory neurotransmitter from a presynaptic cell to a postsynaptic receptor; makes it more likely for a postsynaptic cell to generate an action potential.

**excretion** The disposal of nitrogen-containing metabolites and other waste products.

**exergonic reaction** (ek'-ser-gon'-ik) A spontaneous chemical reaction in which there is a net release of free energy.

**exocytosis** (ek'-sō-sī-tō'-sis) The cellular secretion of biological molecules by the fusion of vesicles containing them with the plasma membrane.

**exon** A sequence within a primary transcript that remains in the RNA after RNA processing; also refers to the region of DNA from which this sequence was transcribed.

**exoskeleton** A hard encasement on the surface of an animal, such as the shell of a mollusc or the cuticle of an arthropod, that provides protection and points of attachment for muscles.

**exotoxin** (ek'-sō-tok'-sin) A toxic protein that is secreted by a prokaryote or other pathogen and that produces specific symptoms, even if the pathogen is no longer present.

**expansin** Plant enzyme that breaks the cross-links (hydrogen bonds) between cellulose microfibrils and other cell wall constituents, loosening the wall's fabric.

**experiment** A scientific test. Often carried out under controlled conditions that involve manipulating one factor in a system in order to see the effects of changing that factor.

**experimental group** A set of subjects that has (or receives) the specific factor being tested in a controlled experiment. Ideally, the experimental group should be identical to the control group for all other factors.

**exploitation** A +/− ecological interaction in which one species benefits by feeding on the other species, which is harmed. Exploitative interactions include predation, herbivory, and parasitism.

**exponential population growth** Growth of a population in an ideal, unlimited environment, represented by a J-shaped curve when population size is plotted over time.

**expression vector** A cloning vector that contains a highly active bacterial promoter just upstream of a restriction site where a eukaryotic gene can be inserted, allowing the gene to be expressed in a bacterial cell. Expression vectors are also available that have been genetically engineered for use in specific types of eukaryotic cells.

**extinction vortex** A downward population spiral in which inbreeding and genetic drift combine to cause a small population to shrink and, unless the spiral is reversed, become extinct.

**extracellular matrix (ECM)** The meshwork surrounding animal cells, consisting of glycoproteins, polysaccharides, and proteoglycans synthesized and secreted by cells.

**extraembryonic membrane** One of four membranes (yolk sac, amnion, chorion, and allantois) located outside the embryo that support the developing embryo in reptiles and mammals.

**extreme halophile** An organism that lives in a highly saline environment, such as the Great Salt Lake or the Dead Sea.

**extreme thermophile** An organism that thrives in hot environments (often 60–80°C or hotter).

**extremophile** An organism that lives in environmental conditions so extreme that few other species can survive there. Extremophiles include extreme halophiles ("salt lovers") and extreme thermophiles ("heat lovers").

**F₁ generation** The first filial, hybrid (heterozygous) offspring arising from a parental (P generation) cross.

**F₂ generation** The offspring resulting from interbreeding (or self-pollination) of the hybrid F₁ generation.

**facilitated diffusion** The passage of molecules or ions down their electrochemical gradient across a biological membrane with the assistance of specific transmembrane transport proteins, requiring no energy expenditure.

**facultative anaerobe** (fak'-ul-tā'-tiv an'-uh-rōb) An organism that makes ATP by aerobic respiration if oxygen is present but that switches to anaerobic respiration or fermentation if oxygen is not present.

**family** In Linnaean classification, the taxonomic category above genus.

**fast-twitch fiber** A muscle fiber used for rapid, powerful contractions.

**fat** A lipid consisting of three fatty acids linked to one glycerol molecule; also called a triacylglycerol or triglyceride.

**fate map** A territorial diagram of embryonic development that displays the future derivatives of individual cells and tissues.

**fatty acid** A carboxylic acid with a long carbon chain. Fatty acids vary in length and in the number and location of double bonds; three fatty acids linked to a glycerol molecule form a fat molecule, also called triacylglycerol or triglyceride.

**feces** (fē'-sēz) The wastes of the digestive tract.

**feedback inhibition** A method of metabolic control in which the end product of a metabolic pathway acts as an inhibitor of an enzyme within that pathway.

**feedback regulation** The regulation of a process by its output or end product.

**fermentation** A catabolic process that makes a limited amount of ATP from glucose (or other organic molecules) without an electron transport chain and that produces a characteristic end product, such as ethyl alcohol or lactic acid.

**fertilization** (1) The union of haploid gametes to produce a diploid zygote. (2) The addition of mineral nutrients to the soil.

**fetus** (fē'-tus) A developing mammal that has all the major structures of an adult. In humans, the fetal stage lasts from the 9th week of gestation until birth.

**F factor** In bacteria, the DNA segment that confers the ability to form pili for conjugation and associated functions required for the transfer of DNA from donor to recipient. The F factor may exist as a plasmid or be integrated into the bacterial chromosome.

**fiber** A lignified cell type that reinforces the xylem of angiosperms and functions in mechanical support; a slender, tapered sclerenchyma cell that usually occurs in bundles.

**fibroblast** (fī'-brō-blast) A type of cell in loose connective tissue that secretes the protein ingredients of the extracellular fibers.

**fibronectin** An extracellular glycoprotein secreted by animal cells that helps them attach to the extracellular matrix.

**filament** In an angiosperm, the stalk portion of the stamen, the pollen-producing reproductive organ of a flower.

**filter feeder** An animal that feeds by using a filtration mechanism to strain small organisms or food particles from its surroundings.

**filtrate** Cell-free fluid extracted from the body fluid by the excretory system.

**filtration** In excretory systems, the extraction of water and small solutes, including metabolic wastes, from the body fluid.

**fimbria** (plural, **fimbriae**) A short, hairlike appendage of a prokaryotic cell that helps it adhere to the substrate or to other cells.

**first law of thermodynamics** The principle of conservation of energy: Energy can be transferred and transformed, but it cannot be created or destroyed.

**fission** The separation of an organism into two or more individuals of approximately equal size.

**fixed action pattern** In animal behavior, a sequence of unlearned acts that is essentially unchangeable and, once initiated, usually carried to completion.

**flaccid** (flas'-id) Limp. Lacking turgor (stiffness or firmness), as in a plant cell in surroundings where there is a tendency for water to leave the cell. (A walled cell becomes flaccid if it has a higher water potential than its surroundings, resulting in the loss of water.)

**flagellum** (fluh-jel'-um) (plural, **flagella**) A long cellular appendage specialized for locomotion. Like motile cilia, eukaryotic flagella have a core with nine outer doublet microtubules and two inner single microtubules (the "9 + 2" arrangement) ensheathed in an extension of the plasma membrane. Prokaryotic flagella have a different structure.

**florigen** A flowering signal, probably a protein, that is made in leaves under certain conditions and that travels to the shoot apical meristems, inducing them to switch from vegetative to reproductive growth.

**flower** In an angiosperm, a specialized shoot with up to four sets of modified leaves, bearing structures that function in sexual reproduction.

**fluid feeder** An animal that lives by sucking nutrient-rich fluids from another living organism.

**fluid mosaic model** The currently accepted model of cell membrane structure, which envisions the membrane as a mosaic of protein molecules drifting laterally in a fluid bilayer of phospholipids.

**follicle** (fol'-uh-kul) A microscopic structure in the ovary that contains the developing oocyte and secretes estrogens.

**follicle-stimulating hormone (FSH)** (fol'-uh-kul) A tropic hormone that is produced and secreted by the anterior pituitary and that stimulates the production of eggs by the ovaries and sperm by the testes.

**food chain** The pathway along which food energy is transferred from trophic level to trophic level, beginning with producers.

**food vacuole** A membranous sac formed by phagocytosis of microorganisms or particles to be used as food by the cell.

**food web** The interconnected feeding relationships in an ecosystem.

**foot** (1) The portion of a bryophyte sporophyte that gathers sugars, amino acids, water, and minerals from the parent gametophyte via transfer cells. (2) One of the three main parts of a mollusc; a muscular structure usually used for movement. *See also* mantle and visceral mass.

**foraging** The seeking and obtaining of food.

**foram (foraminiferan)** An aquatic protist that secretes a hardened shell containing calcium carbonate and extends pseudopodia through pores in the shell.

**forebrain** One of three ancestral and embryonic regions of the vertebrate brain; develops into the thalamus, hypothalamus, and cerebrum.

**fossil** A preserved remnant or impression of an organism that lived in the past.

**founder effect** Genetic drift that occurs when a few individuals become isolated from a larger population and form a new population whose gene pool composition is not reflective of that of the original population.

**fovea** (fō′-vē-uh) The place on the retina at the eye's center of focus, where cones are highly concentrated.

**F plasmid** The plasmid form of the F factor.

**fragmentation** A means of asexual reproduction whereby a single parent breaks into parts that regenerate into whole new individuals.

**frameshift mutation** A mutation occurring when nucleotides are inserted in or deleted from a gene and the number inserted or deleted is not a multiple of three, resulting in the improper grouping of the subsequent nucleotides into codons.

**free energy** The portion of a biological system's energy that can perform work when temperature and pressure are uniform throughout the system. The change in free energy of a system ($\Delta G$) is calculated by the equation $\Delta G = \Delta H - T\Delta S$, where $\Delta H$ is the change in enthalpy (in biological systems, equivalent to total energy), $\Delta T$ is the absolute temperature, and $\Delta S$ is the change in entropy.

**frequency-dependent selection** Selection in which the fitness of a phenotype depends on how common the phenotype is in a population.

**fruit** A mature ovary of a flower. The fruit protects dormant seeds and often functions in their dispersal.

**functional group** A specific configuration of atoms commonly attached to the carbon skeletons of organic molecules and involved in chemical reactions.

**fusion** In evolutionary biology, a process in which gene flow between two species that can form hybrid offspring weakens barriers to reproduction between the species. This process causes their gene pools to become increasingly alike and can cause the two species to fuse into a single species.

**G₀ phase** A nondividing state occupied by cells that have left the cell cycle, sometimes reversibly.

**G₁ phase** The first gap, or growth phase, of the cell cycle, consisting of the portion of interphase before DNA synthesis begins.

**G₂ phase** The second gap, or growth phase, of the cell cycle, consisting of the portion of interphase after DNA synthesis occurs.

**gallbladder** An organ that stores bile and releases it as needed into the small intestine.

**game theory** An approach to evaluating alternative strategies in situations where the outcome of a particular strategy depends on the strategies used by other individuals.

**gametangium** (gam′-uh-tan′-jē-um) (plural, **gametangia**) Multicellular plant structure in which gametes are formed. Female gametangia are called archegonia, and male gametangia are called antheridia.

**gamete** (gam′-ēt) A haploid reproductive cell, such as an egg or sperm, that is formed by meiosis or is the descendant of cells formed by meiosis. Gametes unite during sexual reproduction to produce a diploid zygote.

**gametogenesis** (guh-mē′-tō-gen′-uh-sis) The process by which gametes are produced.

**gametophore** (guh-mē′-tō-fōr) The mature gamete-producing structure of a moss gametophyte.

**gametophyte** (guh-mē′-tō-fīt) In organisms (plants and some algae) that have alternation of generations, the multicellular haploid form that produces haploid gametes by mitosis. The haploid gametes unite and develop into sporophytes.

**ganglion** (gan′-glē-uhn) (plural, **ganglia**) A cluster (functional group) of nerve cell bodies.

**gap junction** A type of intercellular junction in animal cells, consisting of proteins surrounding a pore that allows the passage of materials between cells.

**gas exchange** The uptake of molecular oxygen from the environment and the discharge of carbon dioxide to the environment.

**gastric juice** A digestive fluid secreted by the stomach.

**gastrovascular cavity** A central cavity with a single opening in the body of certain animals, including cnidarians and flatworms, that functions in both the digestion and distribution of nutrients.

**gastrula** (gas′-trū-luh) An embryonic stage in animal development encompassing the formation of three layers: ectoderm, mesoderm, and endoderm.

**gastrulation** (gas′-trū-lā′-shun) In animal development, a series of cell and tissue movements in which the blastula-stage embryo folds inward, producing a three-layered embryo, the gastrula.

**gated channel** A transmembrane protein channel that opens or closes in response to a particular stimulus.

**gated ion channel** A gated channel for a specific ion. The opening or closing of such channels may alter a cell's membrane potential.

**gel electrophoresis** (ē-lek′-trō-fōr-ē′-sis) A technique for separating nucleic acids or proteins on the basis of their size and electrical charge, both of which affect their rate of movement through an electric field in a gel made of agarose or another polymer.

**gene** A discrete unit of hereditary information consisting of a specific nucleotide sequence in DNA (or RNA, in some viruses).

**gene annotation** Analysis of genomic sequences to identify protein-coding genes and determine the function of their products.

**gene cloning** The production of multiple copies of a gene.

**gene drive** A process that biases inheritance such that a particular allele is more likely to be inherited than are other alleles, causing the favored allele to spread (be "driven") through the population.

**gene expression** The process by which information encoded in DNA directs the synthesis of proteins or, in some cases, RNAs that are not translated into proteins and instead function as RNAs.

**gene flow** The transfer of alleles from one population to another, resulting from the movement of fertile individuals or their gametes.

**gene pool** The aggregate of all copies of every type of allele at all loci in every individual in a population. The term is also used in a more restricted sense as the aggregate of alleles for just one or a few loci in a population.

**gene therapy** The introduction of genes into an afflicted individual for therapeutic purposes.

**genetic drift** A process in which chance events cause unpredictable fluctuations in allele frequencies from one generation to the next. Effects of genetic drift are most pronounced in small populations.

**genetic engineering** The direct manipulation of genes for practical purposes.

**genetic map** An ordered list of genetic loci (genes or other genetic markers) along a chromosome.

**genetic profile** An individual's unique set of genetic markers, detected most often today by PCR or, previously, by electrophoresis and nucleic acid probes.

**genetic recombination** General term for the production of offspring with combinations of traits that differ from those found in either parent.

**genetic variation** Differences among individuals in the composition of their genes or other DNA segments.

**genetically modified organism (GMO)** An organism that has acquired one or more genes by artificial means; also called a transgenic organism.

**genetics** The scientific study of heredity and hereditary variation.

**genome** (jē′-nōm) The genetic material of an organism or virus; the complete complement of an organism's or virus's genes along with its noncoding nucleic acid sequences.

**genome-wide association study** (jē′-nōm) A large-scale analysis of the genomes of many people having a certain phenotype or disease, with the aim of finding genetic markers that correlate with that phenotype or disease.

**genomic imprinting** (juh-nō′-mik) A phenomenon in which expression of an allele in offspring depends on whether the allele is inherited from the male or female parent.

**genomics** (juh-nō′-miks) The systematic study of whole sets of genes (or other DNA) and their interactions within a species, as well as genome comparisons between species.

**genotype** (jē′-nō-tīp) The genetic makeup, or set of alleles, of an organism.

**genus** (jē′-nus) (plural, **genera**) A taxonomic category above the species level, designated by the first word of a species' two-part scientific name.

**geologic record** A standard time scale dividing Earth's history into time periods, grouped into four eons—Hadean, Archaean, Proterozoic, and Phanerozoic—and further subdivided into eras, periods, and epochs.

**germ layer** One of the three main layers in a gastrula that will form the various tissues and organs of an animal body.

**gestation** (jes-tā′-shun) See pregnancy.

**gibberellin** (jib′-uh-rel′-in) Any of a class of related plant hormones that stimulate growth in the stem and leaves, trigger the germination of seeds and breaking of bud dormancy, and (with auxin) stimulate fruit development.

**glans** The rounded structure at the tip of the clitoris or penis that is involved in sexual arousal.

**glia (glial cells)** Cells of the nervous system that support, regulate, and augment the functions of neurons.

**global ecology** The study of the functioning and distribution of organisms across the biosphere and how the regional exchange of energy and materials affects them.

**glomeromycete** (glō′-mer-ō-mī′-sēt) A member of the fungal phylum Glomeromycota, characterized by a distinct branching form of mycorrhizae called arbuscular mycorrhizae.

**glomerulus** (glō-mār′-yū-lus) A ball of capillaries surrounded by Bowman's capsule in the nephron and serving as the site of filtration in the vertebrate kidney.

**glucocorticoid** A steroid hormone that is secreted by the adrenal cortex and that influences glucose metabolism and immune function.

**glucagon** (glū′-kuh-gon) A hormone secreted by the pancreas that raises blood glucose levels. It promotes glycogen breakdown and release of glucose by the liver.

**glyceraldehyde 3-phosphate (G3P)** (glis′-er-al′-de-hīd) A three-carbon carbohydrate that is the direct product of the Calvin cycle; it is also an intermediate in glycolysis.

**glycogen** (glī′-kō-jen) An extensively branched glucose storage polysaccharide found in the liver and muscle of animals; the animal equivalent of starch.

**glycolipid** A lipid with one or more covalently attached carbohydrates.

**glycolysis** (glī-kol′-uh-sis) A series of reactions that ultimately splits glucose into pyruvate. Glycolysis occurs in almost all living cells, serving as the starting point for fermentation or cellular respiration.

**glycoprotein** A protein with one or more covalently attached carbohydrates.

**glycosidic linkage** A covalent bond formed between two monosaccharides by a dehydration reaction.

**gnathostome** (na′-thu-stōm) Member of one of the two main clades of vertebrates; gnathostomes have jaws and include sharks and rays, ray-finned fishes, coelacanths, lungfishes, amphibians, reptiles, and mammals. See also cyclostome.

**golden alga** A biflagellated, photosynthetic protist named for its color, which results from its yellow and brown carotenoids.

**Golgi apparatus** (gol′-jē) An organelle in eukaryotic cells consisting of stacks of flat membranous sacs that modify, store, and route products of the endoplasmic reticulum and synthesize some products, notably non-cellulose carbohydrates.

**gonad** (gō′-nad) A male or female gamete-producing organ.

**G protein** A GTP-binding protein that relays signals from a plasma membrane signal receptor, known as a G protein-coupled receptor, to other signal transduction proteins inside the cell.

**G protein-coupled receptor (GPCR)** A signal receptor protein in the plasma membrane that responds to the binding of a signaling molecule by activating a G protein. Also called a G protein-linked receptor.

**graded potential** In a neuron, a shift in the membrane potential that has an amplitude proportional to signal strength and that decays as it spreads.

**Gram stain** A staining method that distinguishes between two different kinds of bacterial cell walls; may be used to help determine medical response to an infection.

**gram-negative** Describing the group of bacteria that have a cell wall that is structurally more complex and contains less peptidoglycan than the cell wall of gram-positive bacteria. Gram-negative bacteria are often more toxic than gram-positive bacteria.

**gram-positive** Describing the group of bacteria that have a cell wall that is structurally less complex and contains more peptidoglycan than the cell wall of gram-negative bacteria. Gram-positive bacteria are usually less toxic than gram-negative bacteria.

**granum** (gran′-um) (plural, **grana**) A stack of membrane-bounded thylakoids in the chloroplast. Grana function in the light reactions of photosynthesis.

**gravitropism** (grav′-uh-trō′-pizm) A response of a plant or animal to gravity.

**gray matter** Regions of clustered neuron cell bodies within the CNS.

**green alga** A photosynthetic protist, named for green chloroplasts that are similar in structure and pigment composition to the chloroplasts of plants. Green algae are a paraphyletic group; some members are more closely related to plants than they are to other green algae.

**greenhouse effect** The warming of Earth due to the atmospheric accumulation of carbon dioxide and certain other gases, which absorb reflected infrared radiation and reradiate some of it back toward Earth.

**gross primary production (GPP)** The total primary production of an ecosystem.

**ground tissue system** Plant tissues that are neither vascular nor dermal, fulfilling a variety of functions, such as storage, photosynthesis, and support.

**growth factor** (1) A protein that must be present in the extracellular environment (culture medium or animal body) for the growth and normal development of certain types of cells. (2) A local regulator that acts on nearby cells to stimulate cell proliferation and differentiation.

**growth hormone (GH)** A hormone that is produced and secreted by the anterior pituitary and that has both direct (nontropic) and tropic effects on a wide variety of tissues.

**guard cells** The two cells that flank the stomatal pore and regulate the opening and closing of the pore.

**gustation** The sense of taste.

**guttation** The exudation of water droplets from leaves, caused by root pressure in certain plants.

**gymnosperm** (jim′-nō-sperm) A vascular plant that bears naked seeds—seeds not enclosed in protective chambers.

**hagfish** Marine jawless vertebrates that have highly reduced vertebrae and a skull made of cartilage; most hagfishes are bottom-dwelling scavengers.

**hair cell** A mechanosensory cell that alters output to the nervous system when hairlike projections on the cell surface are displaced.

**half-life** The amount of time it takes for 50% of a sample of a radioactive isotope to decay.

**halophile** See extreme halophile.

**Hamilton's rule** The principle that for natural selection to favor an altruistic act, the benefit to the recipient, devalued by the coefficient of relatedness, must exceed the cost to the altruist.

**haploid cell** (hap′-loyd) A cell containing only one set of chromosomes (n).

**Hardy-Weinberg equilibrium** The state of a population in which frequencies of alleles and genotypes remain constant from generation to generation, provided that only Mendelian segregation and recombination of alleles are at work.

**heart** A muscular pump that uses metabolic energy to elevate the hydrostatic pressure of the circulatory fluid (blood or hemolymph). The fluid then flows down a pressure gradient through the body and eventually returns to the heart.

**heart attack** The damage or death of cardiac muscle tissue resulting from prolonged blockage of one or more coronary arteries.

**heart murmur** A hissing sound that most often results from blood squirting backward through a leaky valve in the heart.

**heart rate** The frequency of heart contraction (in beats per minute).

**heat** Thermal energy in transfer from one body of matter to another.

**heat of vaporization** The quantity of heat a liquid must absorb for 1 g of it to be converted from the liquid to the gaseous state.

**heat-shock protein** A protein that helps protect other proteins during heat stress. Heat-shock proteins are found in plants, animals, and microorganisms.

**heavy chain** One of the two types of polypeptide chains that make up an antibody molecule and B cell receptor; consists of a variable region, which contributes to the antigen-binding site, and a constant region.

**helicase** An enzyme that untwists the double helix of DNA at replication forks, separating the two strands and making them available as template strands.

**helper T cell** A type of T cell that, when activated, secretes cytokines that promote the response of B cells (humoral response) and cytotoxic T cells (cell-mediated response) to antigens.

**hemoglobin** (hē′-mō-glō′-bin) An iron-containing protein in red blood cells that reversibly binds oxygen.

**hemolymph** (hē′-mō-limf′) In invertebrates with an open circulatory system, the body fluid that bathes tissues.

**hemophilia** (hē′-muh-fil′-ē-uh) A human genetic disease caused by a sex-linked recessive allele resulting in the absence of one or more blood-clotting proteins; characterized by excessive bleeding following injury.

**hepatic portal vein** A large vessel that conveys nutrient-laden blood from the small intestine to the liver, which regulates the blood's nutrient content.

**herbivore** (hur′-bi-vōr′) An animal that mainly eats plants or algae.

**herbivory** An interaction in which an organism eats part of a plant or alga.

**heredity** The transmission of traits from one generation to the next.

**hermaphrodite** (hur-maf′-ruh-dīt′) An individual that functions as both male and female in sexual reproduction by producing both sperm and eggs.

**hermaphroditism** (hur-maf′-rō-dī-tizm) A condition in which an individual has both female and male gonads and functions as both a male and a female in sexual reproduction by producing both sperm and eggs.

**heterochromatin** (het′-er-ō-krō′-muh-tin) Eukaryotic chromatin that remains highly compacted during interphase and is generally not transcribed.

**heterochrony** (het′-uh-rok′-ruh-nē) Evolutionary change in the timing or rate of an organism's development.

**heterocyst** (het′-er-ō-sist) A specialized cell that engages in nitrogen fixation in some filamentous cyanobacteria; also called a heterocyte.

**heterokaryon** (het′-er-ō-kār′-ē-un) A fungal mycelium that contains two or more haploid nuclei per cell.

**heteromorphic** (het′-er-ō-mōr′-fik) Referring to a condition in the life cycle of plants and certain algae in which the sporophyte and gametophyte generations differ in morphology.

**heterosporous** (het-er-os′-pōr-us) Referring to a plant species that has two kinds of spores: microspores, which develop into male gametophytes, and megaspores, which develop into female gametophytes.

**heterotroph** (het′-er-ō-trōf) An organism that obtains organic food molecules by eating other organisms or substances derived from them.

**heterozygote** An organism that has two different alleles for a gene (encoding a character).

**heterozygote advantage** Greater reproductive success of heterozygous individuals compared with homozygotes; tends to preserve variation in a gene pool.

**heterozygous** (het′-er-ō-zī′-gus) Having two different alleles for a given gene.

**hibernation** A long-term physiological state in which metabolism decreases, the heart and respiratory system slow down, and body temperature is maintained at a lower level than normal.

**high-density lipoprotein (HDL)** A particle in the blood made up of thousands of cholesterol molecules and other lipids bound to a protein. HDL scavenges excess cholesterol.

**hindbrain** One of three ancestral and embryonic regions of the vertebrate brain; develops into the medulla oblongata, pons, and cerebellum.

**histamine** (his′-tuh-mēn) A substance released by mast cells that causes blood vessels to dilate and become more permeable in inflammatory and allergic responses.

**histogram** A variant of a bar graph that is made for numeric data by first grouping, or "binning," the variable plotted on the x-axis into intervals of equal width. The "bins" may be integers or ranges of numbers. The height of each bar shows the percent or number of experimental subjects whose characteristics can be described by one of the intervals plotted on the x-axis.

**histone** (his′-tōn) A small protein with a high proportion of positively charged amino acids that binds to the negatively charged DNA and plays a key role in chromatin structure.

**histone acetylation** (his′-tōn) The attachment of acetyl groups to certain amino acids of histone proteins.

**HIV (human immunodeficiency virus)** The infectious agent that causes AIDS. HIV is a retrovirus.

**holdfast** A rootlike structure that anchors a seaweed.

**homeobox** (hō′-mē-ō-boks′) A 180-nucleotide sequence within homeotic genes and some other developmental genes that is widely conserved in animals. Related sequences occur in plants and yeasts.

**homeostasis** (hō′-mē-ō-stā′-sis) The steady-state physiological condition of the body.

**homeotic gene** (hō-mē-o′-tik) Any of the master regulatory genes that control placement and spatial organization of body parts in animals, plants, and fungi by controlling the developmental fate of groups of cells.

**hominin** (hō′-mi-nin) A group consisting of humans and the extinct species that are more closely related to us than to chimpanzees.

**homologous chromosomes (or homologs)** (hō-mol′-uh-gus) A pair of chromosomes of the same length, centromere position, and staining pattern that possess genes for the same characters at corresponding loci. One homologous chromosome is inherited from the organism's father, the other from the mother. Also called a homologous pair.

**homologous pair** *See* homologous chromosomes.

**homologous structures** (hō-mol′-uh-gus) Structures in different species that are similar because of common ancestry.

**homologs** *See* homologous chromosomes.

**homology** (hō-mol′-ō-jē) Similarity in characteristics resulting from a shared ancestry.

**homoplasy** (hō′-muh-play′-zē) A similar (analogous) structure or molecular sequence that has evolved independently in two species.

**homosporous** (hō-mos′-puh-rus) Referring to a plant species that has a single kind of spore, which typically develops into a bisexual gametophyte.

**homozygote** An organism that has a pair of identical alleles for a gene (encoding a character).

**homozygous** (hō′-mō-zī′-gus) Having two identical alleles for a given gene.

**horizontal gene transfer** The transfer of genes from one genome to another through mechanisms such as transposable elements, plasmid exchange, viral activity, and perhaps fusions of different organisms.

**hormone** In multicellular organisms, one of many types of secreted chemicals that are formed in specialized cells, travel in body fluids, and act on specific target cells in other parts of the organism, changing the target cells' functioning.

**hornwort** A small, herbaceous, nonvascular plant that is a member of the phylum Anthocerophyta.

**host** The larger participant in a symbiotic relationship, often providing a home and food source for the smaller symbiont.

**host range** The limited number of species whose cells can be infected by a particular virus.

**Human Genome Project** An international collaborative effort to map and sequence the DNA of the entire human genome.

**human immunodeficiency virus (HIV)** The infectious agent that causes AIDS (acquired immunodeficiency syndrome). HIV is a retrovirus.

**humoral immune response** (hyū′-mer-ul) The branch of adaptive immunity that involves the activation of B cells and that leads to the production of antibodies, which defend against bacteria and viruses in body fluids.

**humus** (hyū′-mus) Decomposing organic material that is a component of topsoil.

**Huntington's disease** A human genetic disease caused by a dominant allele; characterized by uncontrollable body movements and degeneration of the nervous system; usually fatal 10 to 20 years after the onset of symptoms.

**hybrid** Offspring that results from the mating of individuals from two different species or from two true-breeding varieties of the same species.

**hybrid zone** A geographic region in which members of different species meet and mate, producing at least some offspring of mixed ancestry.

**hybridization** In genetics, the mating, or crossing, of two true-breeding varieties.

**hydration shell** The sphere of water molecules around a dissolved ion.

**hydrocarbon** An organic molecule consisting only of carbon and hydrogen.

**hydrogen bond** A type of weak chemical bond that is formed when the slightly positive hydrogen atom of a polar covalent bond in one molecule is attracted to the slightly negative atom of a polar covalent bond in another molecule or in another region of the same molecule.

**hydrogen ion** A single proton with a charge of $1+$. The dissociation of a water molecule ($H_2O$) leads to the generation of a hydroxide ion ($OH^-$) and a hydrogen ion ($H^+$); in water, $H^+$ is not found alone but associates with a water molecule to form a hydronium ion.

**hydrolysis** (hī-drol′-uh-sis) A chemical reaction that breaks bonds between two molecules by the addition of water; functions in disassembly of polymers to monomers.

**hydronium ion** A water molecule that has an extra proton bound to it; $H_3O^+$, commonly represented as $H^+$.

**hydrophilic** (hī′-drō-fil′-ik) Having an affinity for water.

**hydrophobic** (hī′-drō-fō′-bik) Having no affinity for water; tending to coalesce and form droplets in water.

**hydrophobic interaction** (hī′-drō-fō′-bik) A type of weak chemical interaction caused when molecules that do not mix with water coalesce to exclude water.

**hydroponic culture** A method in which plants are grown in mineral solutions rather than in soil.

**hydrostatic skeleton** A skeletal system composed of fluid held under pressure in a closed body compartment; the main skeleton of most cnidarians, flatworms, nematodes, and annelids.

**hydrothermal vent** An area on the seafloor where heated water and minerals from Earth's interior gush into the seawater, producing a dark, hot, oxygen-deficient environment. The producers in a hydrothermal vent community are chemoautotrophic prokaryotes.

**hydroxide ion** A water molecule that has lost a proton; $OH^-$.

**hydroxyl group** (hī-drok′-sil) A chemical group consisting of an oxygen atom joined to a hydrogen atom. Molecules possessing this group are soluble in water and are called alcohols.

**hyperpolarization** A change in a cell's membrane potential such that the inside of the membrane becomes more negative relative to the outside. Hyperpolarization reduces the chance that a neuron will transmit a nerve impulse.

**hypersensitive response** A plant's localized defense response to a pathogen, involving the death of cells around the site of infection.

**hypertension** A disorder in which blood pressure remains abnormally high.

**hypertonic** Referring to a solution that, when surrounding a cell, will cause the cell to lose water.

**hypha** (plural, **hyphae**) (hī′-fuh, hī′-fē) One of many connected filaments that collectively make up the mycelium of a fungus.

**hypocotyl** (hī′-puh-cot′-ul) In an angiosperm embryo, the embryonic axis below the point of attachment of the cotyledon(s) and above the radicle.

**hypothalamus** (hī′-pō-thal′-uh-mus) The ventral part of the vertebrate forebrain; functions in maintaining homeostasis, especially in coordinating the endocrine and nervous systems; secretes hormones of the posterior pituitary and releasing factors that regulate the anterior pituitary.

**hypothesis** (hī-poth′-uh-sis) A testable explanation for a set of observations based on the available data and guided by inductive reasoning. A hypothesis is narrower in scope than a theory.

**hypotonic** Referring to a solution that, when surrounding a cell, will cause the cell to take up water.

**imbibition** The uptake of water by a seed or other structure, resulting in swelling.

**immigration** The influx of new individuals into a population from other areas.

**immune system** An organism's system of defenses against agents that cause disease.

**immunization** The process of generating a state of immunity by artificial means. In vaccination, an inactive or weakened form of a pathogen is administered, inducing B and T cell responses and immunological memory. In passive immunization, antibodies specific for a particular pathogen are administered, conferring immediate but temporary protection.

**immunoglobulin (Ig)** (im′-yū-nō-glob′-yū-lin) *See* antibody.

**imprinting** In animal behavior, the formation at a specific stage in life of a long-lasting behavioral response to a specific individual or object. *See also* genomic imprinting.

**inclusive fitness** The total effect an individual has on proliferating its genes by producing its own offspring and by providing aid that enables other close relatives to increase production of their offspring.

**incomplete dominance** The situation in which the phenotype of heterozygotes is intermediate between the phenotypes of individuals homozygous for either allele.

**incomplete flower** A flower in which one or more of the four basic floral organs (sepals, petals, stamens, or carpels) are either absent or nonfunctional.

**incomplete metamorphosis** A type of development in certain insects, such as grasshoppers, in which the young (called nymphs) resemble adults but are smaller and have different body proportions. The nymph goes through a series of molts, each time looking more like an adult, until it reaches full size.

**independent variable** A factor whose value is manipulated or changed during an experiment to reveal possible effects on another factor (the dependent variable).

**indeterminate cleavage** A type of embryonic development in deuterostomes in which each cell produced by early cleavage divisions retains the capacity to develop into a complete embryo.

**indeterminate growth** A type of growth characteristic of plants, in which the organism continues to grow as long as it lives.

**induced fit** Caused by entry of the substrate, the change in shape of the active site of an enzyme so that it binds more snugly to the substrate.

**inducer** A specific small molecule that binds to a bacterial repressor protein and changes the repressor's shape so that it cannot bind to an operator, thus switching an operon on.

**induction** A process in which a group of cells or tissues influences the development of another group through close-range interactions.

**inductive reasoning** A type of logic in which generalizations are based on a large number of specific observations.

**inflammatory response** An innate immune defense triggered by physical injury or infection of tissue involving the release of substances that promote swelling, enhance the infiltration of white blood cells, and aid in tissue repair and destruction of invading pathogens.

**inflorescence** A group of flowers tightly clustered together.

**ingestion** The first stage of food processing in animals: the act of eating.

**ingroup** A species or group of species whose evolutionary relationships are being examined in a given analysis.

**inhibitory postsynaptic potential (IPSP)** An electrical change (usually hyperpolarization) in the membrane of a postsynaptic neuron caused by the binding of an inhibitory neurotransmitter from a presynaptic cell to a postsynaptic receptor; makes it more difficult for a postsynaptic neuron to generate an action potential.

**innate behavior** Animal behavior that is developmentally fixed and under strong genetic control. Innate behavior is exhibited in virtually the same form by all individuals in a population despite internal and external environmental differences during development and throughout their lifetimes.

**innate immunity** A form of defense common to all animals that is active immediately upon exposure to a pathogen and that is the same whether or not the pathogen has been encountered previously.

**inner cell mass** An inner cluster of cells at one end of a mammalian blastocyst that subsequently develops into the embryo proper and some of the extraembryonic membranes.

**inner ear** One of the three main regions of the vertebrate ear; includes the cochlea (which in turn contains the organ of Corti) and the semicircular canals.

**inositol trisphosphate (IP₃)** (in-ō′-suh-tol) A second messenger that functions as an intermediate between certain signaling molecules and a subsequent second messenger, $Ca^{2+}$, by causing a rise in cytoplasmic $Ca^{2+}$ concentration.

**inquiry** The search for information and explanation, often focusing on specific questions.

**insertion** A mutation involving the addition of one or more nucleotide pairs to a gene.

***in situ* hybridization** A technique using nucleic acid hybridization with a labeled probe to detect the location of a specific mRNA in an intact organism.

**insulin** (in′-suh-lin) A hormone secreted by pancreatic beta cells that lowers blood glucose levels. It promotes the uptake of glucose by most body cells and the synthesis and storage of glycogen in the liver and also stimulates protein and fat synthesis.

**integral protein** A transmembrane protein with hydrophobic regions that extend into and often completely span the hydrophobic interior of the membrane and with hydrophilic regions in contact with the aqueous solution on one or both sides of the membrane (or lining the channel in the case of a channel protein).

**integrin** (in′-tuh-grin) In animal cells, a transmembrane receptor protein with two subunits that interconnects the extracellular matrix and the cytoskeleton.

**integument** (in-teg′-yū-ment) Layer of sporophyte tissue that contributes to the structure of an ovule of a seed plant.

**integumentary system** The outer covering of a mammal's body, including skin, hair, and nails, claws, or hooves.

**interferon** (in′-ter-fēr′-on) A protein that has antiviral or immune regulatory functions. For example, interferons secreted by virus-infected cells help nearby cells resist viral infection.

**intermediate disturbance hypothesis** The concept that moderate levels of disturbance can foster greater species diversity than low or high levels of disturbance.

**intermediate filament** A component of the cytoskeleton that includes filaments intermediate in size between microtubules and microfilaments.

**interneuron** An association neuron; a nerve cell within the central nervous system that forms synapses with sensory and/or motor neurons and integrates sensory input and motor output.

**internode** A segment of a plant stem between the points where leaves are attached.

**interphase** The period in the cell cycle when the cell is not dividing. During interphase, cellular metabolic activity is high, chromosomes and organelles are duplicated, and cell size may increase. Interphase often accounts for about 90% of the cell cycle.

**intersexual selection** A form of natural selection in which individuals of one sex (usually the females) are choosy in selecting their mates from the other sex; also called mate choice.

**interspecific interaction** A relationship between individuals of two or more species in a community.

**interstitial fluid** The fluid filling the spaces between cells in most animals.

**intertidal zone** The shallow zone of the ocean adjacent to land and between the high- and low-tide lines.

**intrasexual selection** A form of natural selection in which there is direct competition among individuals of one sex for mates of the opposite sex.

**intrinsic rate of increase ($r$)** In population models, the per capita rate at which an exponentially growing population increases in size at each instant in time.

**introduced species** A species moved by humans, either intentionally or accidentally, from its native location to a new geographic region; also called non-native or exotic species.

**intron** (in′-tron) A noncoding, intervening sequence within a primary transcript that is removed from the transcript during RNA processing; also refers to the region of DNA from which this sequence was transcribed.

**invasive species** A species, often introduced by humans, that takes hold outside its native range.

**inversion** An aberration in chromosome structure resulting from reattachment of a chromosomal fragment in a reverse orientation to the chromosome from which it originated.

**invertebrate** An animal without a backbone. Invertebrates make up 95% of animal species.

***in vitro* fertilization (IVF)** (vē′-trō) Fertilization of oocytes in laboratory containers followed by artificial implantation of the early embryo in the mother's uterus.

***in vitro* mutagenesis** A technique used to discover the function of a gene by cloning it, introducing specific changes into the cloned gene's sequence, reinserting the mutated gene into a cell, and studying the phenotype of the mutant.

**ion** (ī′-on) An atom or group of atoms that has gained or lost one or more electrons, thus acquiring a charge.

**ion channel** (ī′-on) A transmembrane protein channel that allows a specific ion to diffuse across the membrane down its concentration or electrochemical gradient.

**ionic bond** (ī-on′-ik) A chemical bond resulting from the attraction between oppositely charged ions.

**ionic compound** (ī-on′-ik) A compound resulting from the formation of an ionic bond; also called a salt.

**iris** The colored part of the vertebrate eye, formed by the anterior portion of the choroid.

**isomer** (ī′-sō-mer) One of two or more compounds that have the same numbers of atoms of the same elements but different structures and hence different properties.

**isomorphic** Referring to alternating generations in plants and certain algae in which the sporophytes and gametophytes look alike, although they differ in chromosome number.

**isotonic** (ī′-sō-ton′-ik) Referring to a solution that, when surrounding a cell, causes no net movement of water into or out of the cell.

**isotope** (ī′-sō-tōp′) One of several atomic forms of an element, each with the same number of protons but a different number of neutrons, thus differing in atomic mass.

**iteroparity** Reproduction in which adults produce offspring over many years; also called repeated reproduction.

**jasmonate** Any of a class of plant hormones that regulate a wide range of developmental processes in plants and play a key role in plant defense against herbivores.

**joule (J)** A unit of energy: 1 J = 0.239 cal; 1 cal = 4.184 J.

**juxtaglomerular apparatus (JGA)** (juks′-tuh-gluh-mār′-yū-ler) A specialized tissue in nephrons that releases the enzyme renin in response to a drop in blood pressure or volume.

**juxtamedullary nephron** In mammals and birds, a nephron with a loop of Henle that extends far into the renal medulla.

**karyogamy** (kār′-ē-og′-uh-mē) In fungi, the fusion of haploid nuclei contributed by the two parents; occurs as one stage of sexual reproduction, preceded by plasmogamy.

**karyotype** (kār′-ē-ō-tīp) A display of the chromosome pairs of a cell arranged by size and shape.

**keystone species** A species that is not necessarily abundant in a community yet exerts strong control on community structure by the nature of its ecological role or niche.

**kidney** In vertebrates, one of a pair of excretory organs where blood filtrate is formed and processed into urine.

**kilocalorie (kcal)** A thousand calories; the amount of heat energy required to raise the temperature of 1 kg of water by 1°C.

**kinetic energy** (kuh-net′-ik) The energy associated with the relative motion of objects. Moving matter can perform work by imparting motion to other matter.

**kinetochore** (kuh-net′-uh-kōr) A structure of proteins attached to the centromere that links each sister chromatid to the mitotic spindle.

**kinetoplastid** A protist, such as a trypanosome, that has a single large mitochondrion that houses an organized mass of DNA.

**kingdom** A taxonomic category, the second broadest after domain.

**kin selection** Natural selection that favors altruistic behavior by enhancing the reproductive success of relatives.

***K*-selection** Selection for life history traits that are sensitive to population density; also called density-dependent selection.

**labia majora** A pair of thick, fatty ridges that encloses and protects the rest of the vulva.

**labia minora** A pair of slender skin folds that surrounds the openings of the vagina and urethra.

**lacteal** (lak′-tē-ul) A tiny lymph vessel extending into the core of an intestinal villus and serving as the destination for absorbed chylomicrons.

**lactic acid fermentation** Glycolysis followed by the reduction of pyruvate to lactate, regenerating NAD⁺ with no release of carbon dioxide.

**lagging strand** A discontinuously synthesized DNA strand that elongates by means of Okazaki fragments, each synthesized in a $5′ \rightarrow 3′$ direction away from the replication fork.

**lamprey** Any of the jawless vertebrates with highly reduced vertebrae that live in freshwater and marine environments. Almost half of extant lamprey species are parasites that feed by clamping their round, jawless mouth onto the flank of a live fish; nonparasitic lampreys are suspension feeders that feed only as larvae.

**lancelet** A member of the clade Cephalochordata, small blade-shaped marine chordates that lack a backbone.

**landscape** An area containing several different ecosystems linked by exchanges of energy, materials, and organisms.

**landscape ecology** The study of how the spatial arrangement of habitat types affects the distribution and abundance of organisms and ecosystem processes.

**large intestine** The portion of the vertebrate alimentary canal between the small intestine and the anus; functions mainly in water absorption and the formation of feces.

**larva** (lar′-vuh) (plural, **larvae**) A free-living, sexually immature form in some animal life cycles that may differ from the adult animal in morphology, nutrition, and habitat.

**larynx** (lār′-inks) The portion of the respiratory tract containing the vocal cords; also called the voice box.

**lateralization** Segregation of functions in the cortex of the left and right cerebral hemispheres.

**lateral line system** A mechanoreceptor system consisting of a series of pores and receptor units along the sides of the body in fishes and aquatic amphibians; detects water movements made by the animal itself and by other moving objects.

**lateral meristem** (mār′-uh-stem) A meristem that thickens the roots and shoots of woody plants. The vascular cambium and cork cambium are lateral meristems.

**lateral root** A root that arises from the pericycle of an established root.

**law of conservation of mass** A physical law stating that matter can change form but cannot be created or destroyed. In a closed system, the mass of the system is constant.

**law of independent assortment** Mendel's second law, stating that each pair of alleles segregates, or assorts, independently of each other pair during gamete formation; applies when genes for two characters are located on different pairs of homologous chromosomes or when they are far enough apart on the same chromosome to behave as though they are on different chromosomes.

**law of segregation** Mendel's first law, stating that the two alleles in a pair segregate (separate from each other) into different gametes during gamete formation.

**leading strand** The new complementary DNA strand synthesized continuously along the template strand toward the replication fork in the mandatory $5' \rightarrow 3'$ direction.

**leaf** The main photosynthetic organ of vascular plants.

**leaf primordium** (plural, **primordia**) A finger-like projection along the flank of a shoot apical meristem, from which a leaf arises.

**learning** The modification of behavior as a result of specific experiences.

**lens** The structure in an eye that focuses light rays onto the photoreceptors.

**lenticel** (len'-ti-sel) A small raised area in the bark of stems and roots that enables gas exchange between living cells and the outside air.

**lepidosaur** (leh-pid'-uh-sōr) A member of the reptilian group that includes lizards, snakes, and two species of New Zealand animals called tuataras.

**leukocyte** (lū'-kō-sīt') A blood cell that functions in fighting infections; also called a white blood cell.

**lichen** The mutualistic association between a fungus and a photosynthetic alga or cyanobacterium.

**life cycle** The generation-to-generation sequence of stages in the reproductive history of an organism.

**life history** The traits that affect an organism's schedule of reproduction and survival.

**life table** A summary of the age-specific survival and reproductive rates of individuals in a population.

**ligament** A fibrous connective tissue that joins bones together at joints.

**ligand** (lig'-und) A molecule that binds specifically to another molecule, usually a larger one.

**ligand-gated ion channel** (lig'-und) A transmembrane protein containing a pore that opens or closes as it changes shape in response to a signaling molecule (ligand), allowing or blocking the flow of specific ions; also called an ionotropic receptor.

**light chain** One of the two types of polypeptide chains that make up an antibody molecule and B cell receptor; consists of a variable region, which contributes to the antigen-binding site, and a constant region.

**light-harvesting complex** A complex of proteins associated with pigment molecules (including chlorophyll *a*, chlorophyll *b*, and carotenoids) that captures light energy and transfers it to reaction-center pigments in a photosystem.

**light microscope (LM)** An optical instrument with lenses that refract (bend) visible light to magnify images of specimens.

**light reactions** The first of two major stages in photosynthesis (preceding the Calvin cycle). These reactions, which occur on the thylakoid membranes of the chloroplast or on

membranes of certain prokaryotes, convert solar energy to the chemical energy of ATP and NADPH, releasing oxygen in the process.

**lignin** (lig'-nin) A strong polymer embedded in the cellulose matrix of the secondary cell walls of vascular plants that provides structural support in terrestrial species.

**limiting nutrient** An element that must be added for production to increase in a particular area.

**limnetic zone** In a lake, the well-lit, open surface waters far from shore.

**linear electron flow** A route of electron flow during the light reactions of photosynthesis that involves both photosystems (I and II) and produces ATP, NADPH, and $O_2$. The net electron flow is from $H_2O$ to $NADP^+$.

**line graph** A graph in which each data point is connected to the next point in the data set with a straight line.

**linkage map** A genetic map based on the frequencies of recombination between markers during crossing over of homologous chromosomes.

**linked genes** Genes located close enough together on a chromosome that they tend to be inherited together.

**lipid** (lip'-id) Any of a group of large biological molecules, including fats, phospholipids, and steroids, that mix poorly, if at all, with water.

**littoral zone** In a lake, the shallow, well-lit waters close to shore.

**liver** A large internal organ in vertebrates that performs diverse functions, such as producing bile, maintaining blood glucose level, and detoxifying poisonous chemicals in the blood.

**liverwort** A small, herbaceous, nonvascular plant that is a member of the phylum Hepatophyta.

**loam** The most fertile soil type, made up of roughly equal amounts of sand, silt, and clay.

**lobe-fin** Member of a clade of osteichthyans having rod-shaped muscular fins. The group includes coelacanths, lungfishes, and tetrapods.

**local regulator** A secreted molecule that influences cells near where it is secreted.

**locomotion** Active motion from place to place.

**locus** (lō'-kus) (plural, **loci**) (lō'-sī) A specific place along the length of a chromosome where a given gene is located.

**logistic population growth** Population growth that levels off as population size approaches carrying capacity.

**long-day plant** A plant that flowers (usually in late spring or early summer) only when the light period is longer than a critical length.

**long noncoding RNA (lncRNA)** An RNA between 200 and hundreds of thousands of nucleotides in length that does not code for protein but is expressed at significant levels.

**long-term memory** The ability to hold, associate, and recall information over one's lifetime.

**long-term potentiation (LTP)** An enhanced responsiveness to an action potential (nerve signal) by a receiving neuron.

**loop of Henle** (hen'-lē) The hairpin turn, with a descending and ascending limb, between the proximal and distal tubules of the vertebrate kidney; functions in water and salt reabsorption.

**lophophore** (lof'-uh-fōr) In some lophotrochozoan animals, including brachiopods, a crown of ciliated tentacles that surround the mouth and function in feeding.

**Lophotrochozoa** (lo-phah'-truh-kō-zō'-uh) One of the three main lineages of bilaterian animals; lophotrochozoans include organisms that have lophophores or trochophore larvae. *See also* Deuterostomia and Ecdysozoa.

**low-density lipoprotein (LDL)** A particle in the blood made up of thousands of cholesterol molecules and other lipids bound to a protein. LDL transports cholesterol from the liver for incorporation into cell membranes.

**lung** An infolded respiratory surface of a terrestrial vertebrate, land snail, or spider that connects to the atmosphere by narrow tubes.

**luteinizing hormone (LH)** (lū'-tē-uh-nī'-zing) A tropic hormone that is produced and secreted by the anterior pituitary and that stimulates ovulation in females and androgen production in males.

**lycophyte** (lī'-kuh-fīt) An informal name for a member of the phylum Lycophyta, which includes club mosses, spike mosses, and quillworts.

**lymph** The colorless fluid, derived from interstitial fluid, in the lymphatic system of vertebrates.

**lymph node** An organ located along a lymph vessel. Lymph nodes filter lymph and contain cells that attack viruses and bacteria.

**lymphatic system** A system of vessels and nodes, separate from the circulatory system, that returns fluid, proteins, and cells to the blood.

**lymphocyte** A type of white blood cell that mediates immune responses. The two main classes are B cells and T cells.

**lysogenic cycle** (lī'-sō-jen'-ik) A type of phage replicative cycle in which the viral genome becomes incorporated into the bacterial host chromosome as a prophage, is replicated along with the chromosome, and does not kill the host.

**lysosome** (lī'-suh-sōm) A membrane-enclosed sac of hydrolytic enzymes found in the cytoplasm of animal cells and some protists.

**lysozyme** (lī'-sō-zīm) An enzyme that destroys bacterial cell walls; in mammals, it is found in sweat, tears, and saliva.

**lytic cycle** (lit'-ik) A type of phage replicative cycle resulting in the release of new phages by lysis (and death) of the host cell.

**macroevolution** Evolutionary change above the species level. Examples of macroevolutionary change include the origin of a new group of organisms through a series of speciation events and the impact of mass extinctions on the diversity of life and its subsequent recovery.

**macromolecule** A giant molecule formed by the joining of smaller molecules, usually by a dehydration reaction. Polysaccharides, proteins, and nucleic acids are macromolecules.

**macronutrient** An essential element that an organism must obtain in relatively large amounts. *See also* micronutrient.

**macrophage** (mak'-rō-fāj) A phagocytic cell present in many tissues that functions in innate immunity by destroying microbes and in acquired immunity as an antigen-presenting cell.

**magnoliid** A member of the angiosperm clade that is most closely related to the combined eudicot and monocot clades. Extant examples are magnolias, laurels, and black pepper plants.

**major depressive disorder** A mood disorder characterized by feelings of sadness, lack of self-worth, emptiness, or loss of interest in nearly all things.

**major histocompatibility complex (MHC) molecule** A host protein that functions in antigen presentation. Foreign MHC molecules on transplanted tissue can trigger T cell responses that may lead to rejection of the transplant.

**malignant tumor** A cancerous tumor containing cells that have significant genetic and cellular changes and are capable of invading and surviving in new sites. Malignant tumors can impair the functions of one or more organs.

**Malpighian tubule** (mal-pig′-ē-un) A unique excretory organ of insects that empties into the digestive tract, removes nitrogenous wastes from the hemolymph, and functions in osmoregulation.

**mammal** A member of the clade Mammalia, amniotes that have hair and mammary glands (glands that produce milk).

**mammary gland** An exocrine gland that secretes milk for nourishing the young. Mammary glands are characteristic of mammals.

**mantle** One of the three main parts of a mollusc; a fold of tissue that drapes over the mollusc's visceral mass and may secrete a shell. *See also* foot and visceral mass.

**mantle cavity** A water-filled chamber that houses the gills, anus, and excretory pores of a mollusc.

**map unit** A unit of measurement of the distance between genes. One map unit is equivalent to a 1% recombination frequency.

**marine benthic zone** The ocean floor.

**mark-recapture method** A sampling technique used to estimate the size of animal populations.

**marsupial** (mar-sū′-pē-ul) A mammal, such as a koala, kangaroo, or opossum, whose young complete their embryonic development inside a maternal pouch called the marsupium.

**mass extinction** The elimination of a large number of species throughout Earth, the result of global environmental changes.

**mass number** The total number of protons and neutrons in an atom's nucleus.

**mate-choice copying** Behavior in which individuals in a population copy the mate choice of others, apparently as a result of social learning.

**maternal effect gene** A gene that, when mutant in the mother, results in a mutant phenotype in the offspring, regardless of the offspring's genotype. Maternal effect genes, also called egg-polarity genes, were first identified in *Drosophila melanogaster*.

**matter** Anything that takes up space and has mass.

**maximum likelihood** As applied to DNA sequence data, a principle that states that when considering multiple phylogenetic hypotheses, one should take into account the hypothesis that reflects the most likely sequence of evolutionary events, given certain rules about how DNA changes over time.

**maximum parsimony** A principle that states that when considering multiple explanations for an observation, one should first investigate the simplest explanation that is consistent with the facts.

**mean** The sum of all data points in a data set divided by the number of data points.

**mechanoreceptor** A sensory receptor that detects physical deformation in the body's environment associated with pressure, touch, stretch, motion, or sound.

**medulla oblongata** (meh-dul′-uh ob′-long-go′-tuh) The lowest part of the vertebrate brain, commonly called the medulla; a swelling of the hindbrain anterior to the spinal cord that controls autonomic, homeostatic functions, including breathing, heart and blood vessel activity, swallowing, digestion, and vomiting.

**medusa** (plural, **medusae**) (muh-dū′-suh) The floating, flattened, mouth-down version of the cnidarian body plan. The alternate form is the polyp.

**megapascal (MPa)** (meg′-uh-pas-kal′) A unit of pressure equivalent to about 10 atmospheres of pressure.

**megaphyll** (meh′-guh-fil) A leaf with a highly branched vascular system, found in almost all vascular plants other than lycophytes. *See also* microphyll.

**megaspore** A spore from a heterosporous plant species that develops into a female gametophyte.

**meiosis** (mī-ō′-sis) A modified type of cell division in sexually reproducing organisms consisting of two rounds of cell division but only one round of DNA replication. It results in cells with half the number of chromosome sets as the original cell.

**meiosis I** (mī-ō′-sis) The first division of a two-stage process of cell division in sexually reproducing organisms that results in cells with half the number of chromosome sets as the original cell.

**meiosis II** (mī-ō′-sis) The second division of a two-stage process of cell division in sexually reproducing organisms that results in cells with half the number of chromosome sets as the original cell.

**melanocyte-stimulating hormone (MSH)** A hormone produced and secreted by the anterior pituitary with multiple activities, including regulating the behavior of pigment-containing cells in the skin of some vertebrates.

**melatonin** A hormone that is secreted by the pineal gland and that is involved in the regulation of biological rhythms and sleep.

**membrane potential** The difference in electrical charge (voltage) across a cell's plasma membrane due to the differential distribution of ions. Membrane potential affects the activity of excitable cells and the transmembrane movement of all charged substances.

**memory cell** One of a clone of long-lived lymphocytes, formed during the primary immune response, that remains in a lymphoid organ until activated by exposure to the same antigen that triggered its formation. Activated memory cells mount the secondary immune response.

**menopause** The cessation of ovulation and menstruation marking the end of a human female's reproductive years.

**menstrual cycle** (men′-strū-ul) In humans and certain other primates, the periodic growth and shedding of the uterine lining that occurs in the absence of pregnancy.

**menstruation** The shedding of portions of the endometrium during a uterine (menstrual) cycle.

**meristem** (mār′-uh-stem) Plant tissue that remains embryonic as long as the plant lives, allowing for indeterminate growth.

**meristem identity gene** (mār′-uh-stem) A plant gene that promotes the switch from vegetative growth to flowering.

**mesoderm** (mez′-ō-derm) The middle primary germ layer in a triploblastic animal embryo; develops into the notochord, the lining of the coelom, muscles, skeleton, gonads, kidneys, and most of the circulatory system in species that have these structures.

**mesohyl** (mez′-ō-hīl) A gelatinous region between the two layers of cells of a sponge.

**mesophyll** (mez′-ō-fil) Leaf cells specialized for photosynthesis. In $C_3$ and CAM plants, mesophyll cells are located between the upper and lower epidermis; in $C_4$ plants, they are located between the bundle-sheath cells and the epidermis.

**messenger RNA (mRNA)** A type of RNA, synthesized using a DNA template, that attaches to ribosomes in the cytoplasm and specifies the primary structure of a protein. (In eukaryotes, the primary RNA transcript must undergo RNA processing to become mRNA.)

**metabolic pathway** A series of chemical reactions that either builds a complex molecule (anabolic pathway) or breaks down a complex molecule to simpler molecules (catabolic pathway).

**metabolic rate** The total amount of energy an animal uses in a unit of time.

**metabolism** (muh-tab′-uh-lizm) The totality of an organism's chemical reactions, consisting of catabolic and anabolic pathways, which manage the material and energy resources of the organism.

**metagenomics** The collection and sequencing of DNA from a group of species, usually an environmental sample of microorganisms. Computer software sorts partial sequences and assembles them into genome sequences of individual species making up the sample.

**metamorphosis** (met-uh-mōr′-fuh-sis) A developmental transformation that turns an animal larva into either an adult or an adult-like stage that is not yet sexually mature.

**metanephridium** (met′-uh-nuh-frid′-ē-um) (plural, **metanephridia**) An excretory organ found in many invertebrates that typically consists of tubules connecting ciliated internal openings to external openings.

**metaphase** The third stage of mitosis, in which the spindle is complete and the chromosomes, attached to microtubules at their kinetochores, are all aligned at the metaphase plate.

**metaphase plate** An imaginary structure located at a plane midway between the two poles of a cell in metaphase on which the centromeres of all the duplicated chromosomes are located.

**metapopulation** A group of spatially separated populations of one species that interact through immigration and emigration.

**metastasis** (muh-tas'-tuh-sis) The spread of cancer cells to locations distant from their original site.

**methanogen** (meth-an'-ō-jen) An organism that produces methane as a waste product of the way it obtains energy. All known methanogens are in domain Archaea.

**methyl group** A chemical group consisting of a carbon bonded to three hydrogen atoms. The methyl group may be attached to a carbon or to a different atom.

**microbiome** The collection of microorganisms living in or on an organism's body, along with their genetic material.

**microclimate** Climate patterns on a very fine scale, such as the specific climatic conditions underneath a log.

**microevolution** Evolutionary change below the species level; change in the allele frequencies in a population over generations.

**microfilament** A cable composed of actin proteins in the cytoplasm of almost every eukaryotic cell, making up part of the cytoskeleton and acting alone or with myosin to cause cell contraction; also called an actin filament.

**micronutrient** An essential element that an organism needs in very small amounts. *See also* macronutrient.

**microphyll** (mī'-krō-fil) A small, usually spine-shaped leaf supported by a single strand of vascular tissue, found only in lycophytes.

**micropyle** A pore in the integuments of an ovule.

**microRNA (miRNA)** A small, single-stranded RNA molecule, generated from a double-stranded RNA precursor. The miRNA associates with one or more proteins in a complex that can degrade or prevent translation of an mRNA with a complementary sequence.

**microspore** A spore from a heterosporous plant species that develops into a male gametophyte.

**microtubule** A hollow rod composed of tubulin proteins that makes up part of the cytoskeleton in all eukaryotic cells and is found in cilia and flagella.

**microvillus** (plural, **microvilli**) One of many fine, finger-like projections of the epithelial cells in the lumen of the small intestine that increase its surface area.

**midbrain** One of three ancestral and embryonic regions of the vertebrate brain; develops into sensory integrating and relay centers that send sensory information to the cerebrum.

**middle ear** One of three main regions of the vertebrate ear; in mammals, a chamber containing three small bones (the malleus, incus, and stapes) that convey vibrations from the eardrum to the oval window.

**middle lamella** (luh-mel'-uh) In plants, a thin layer of adhesive extracellular material, primarily pectins, found between the primary walls of adjacent young cells.

**migration** A regular, long-distance change in location.

**mineral** In nutrition, a simple nutrient that is inorganic and therefore cannot be synthesized in the body.

**mineralocorticoid** A steroid hormone secreted by the adrenal cortex that regulates salt and water homeostasis.

**minimum viable population (MVP)** The smallest population size at which a species is able to sustain its numbers and survive.

**mismatch repair** The cellular process that uses specific enzymes to remove and replace incorrectly paired nucleotides.

**missense mutation** A nucleotide-pair substitution that results in a codon that codes for a different amino acid.

**mitochondrial matrix** The compartment of the mitochondrion enclosed by the inner membrane and containing enzymes and substrates for the citric acid cycle, as well as ribosomes and DNA.

**mitochondrion** (mī'-tō-kon'-drē-un) (plural, **mitochondria**) An organelle in eukaryotic cells that serves as the site of cellular respiration; uses oxygen to break down organic molecules and synthesize ATP.

**mitosis** (mī-tō'-sis) A process of nuclear division in eukaryotic cells conventionally divided into five stages: prophase, prometaphase, metaphase, anaphase, and telophase. Mitosis conserves chromosome number by allocating replicated chromosomes equally to each of the daughter nuclei.

**mitotic (M) phase** The phase of the cell cycle that includes mitosis and cytokinesis.

**mitotic spindle** An assemblage of microtubules and associated proteins that is involved in the movement of chromosomes during mitosis.

**mixotroph** An organism that is capable of both photosynthesis and heterotrophy.

**model** A physical or conceptual representation of a natural phenomenon.

**model organism** A particular species chosen for research into broad biological principles because it is representative of a larger group and usually easy to grow in a lab.

**molarity** A common measure of solute concentration, referring to the number of moles of solute per liter of solution.

**mold** Informal term for a fungus that grows as a filamentous fungus, producing haploid spores by mitosis and forming a visible mycelium.

**mole (mol)** The number of grams of a substance that equals its molecular or atomic mass in daltons; a mole contains Avogadro's number of the molecules or atoms in question.

**molecular clock** A method for estimating the time required for a given amount of evolutionary change, based on the observation that some regions of genomes evolve at constant rates.

**molecular mass** The sum of the masses of all the atoms in a molecule; sometimes called molecular weight.

**molecule** Two or more atoms held together by covalent bonds.

**molting** A process in ecdysozoans in which the exoskeleton is shed at intervals, allowing growth by the production of a larger exoskeleton.

**monilophyte** An informal name for a member of the phylum Monilophyta, which includes ferns, horsetails, and whisk ferns and their relatives.

**monoclonal antibody** (mon'-ō-klōn'-ul) Any of a preparation of antibodies that have been produced by a single clone of cultured cells and thus are all specific for the same epitope.

**monocot** A member of a clade consisting of flowering plants that have one embryonic seed leaf, or cotyledon.

**monogamous** (muh-nog'-uh-mus) Referring to a type of relationship in which one male mates with just one female.

**monohybrid** An organism that is heterozygous with respect to a single gene of interest. All the offspring from a cross between parents homozygous for different alleles are monohybrids. For example, parents of genotypes *AA* and *aa* produce a monohybrid of genotype *Aa*.

**monohybrid cross** A cross between two organisms that are heterozygous for the character being followed (or the self-pollination of a heterozygous plant).

**monomer** (mon'-uh-mer) The subunit that serves as the building block of a polymer.

**monophyletic** (mon'-ō-fī-let'-ik) Pertaining to a group of taxa that consists of a common ancestor and all of its descendants. A monophyletic taxon is equivalent to a clade.

**monosaccharide** (mon'-ō-sak'-uh-rīd) The simplest carbohydrate, active alone or serving as a monomer for disaccharides and polysaccharides. Also called simple sugars, monosaccharides have molecular formulas that are generally some multiple of $CH_2O$.

**monosomic** Referring to a diploid cell that has only one copy of a particular chromosome instead of the normal two.

**monotreme** An egg-laying mammal, such as a platypus or echidna. Like all mammals, monotremes have hair and produce milk, but they lack nipples.

**morphogen** A substance, such as Bicoid protein in *Drosophila*, that provides positional information in the form of a concentration gradient along an embryonic axis.

**morphogenesis** (mōr'-fō-jen'-uh-sis) The development of the form of an organism and its structures.

**morphological species concept** Definition of a species in terms of measurable anatomical criteria.

**moss** A small, herbaceous, nonvascular plant that is a member of the phylum Bryophyta.

**motor neuron** A nerve cell that transmits signals from the brain or spinal cord to muscles or glands.

**motor protein** A protein that interacts with cytoskeletal elements and other cell components, producing movement of the whole cell or parts of the cell.

**motor system** An efferent branch of the vertebrate peripheral nervous system composed of motor neurons that carry signals to skeletal muscles in response to external stimuli.

**motor unit** A single motor neuron and all the muscle fibers it controls.

**movement corridor** A series of small clumps or a narrow strip of quality habitat (usable by organisms) that connects otherwise isolated patches of quality habitat.

**MPF** Maturation-promoting factor (or M-phase-promoting factor); a protein complex required for a cell to progress from late interphase to mitosis. The active form consists of cyclin and a protein kinase.

**mucus** A viscous and slippery mixture of glyco-proteins, cells, salts, and water that moistens and protects the membranes lining body cavities that open to the exterior.

**Müllerian mimicry** (myū-lār′-ē-un mim′-uh-krē) Reciprocal mimicry by two unpalatable species.

**multifactorial** Referring to a phenotypic character that is influenced by multiple genes and environmental factors.

**multigene family** A collection of genes with similar or identical sequences, presumably of common origin.

**multiple fruit** A fruit derived from an entire inflorescence.

**multiplication rule** A rule of probability stating that the probability of two or more independent events occurring together can be determined by multiplying their individual probabilities.

**muscle tissue** Tissue consisting of long muscle cells that can contract, either on its own or when stimulated by nerve impulses.

**mutagen** (myū′-tuh-jen) A chemical or physical agent that interacts with DNA and can cause a mutation.

**mutation** (myū-tā′-shun) A change in the nucleotide sequence of an organism's DNA or in the DNA or RNA of a virus.

**mutualism** (myū′-chū-ul-izm) A +/+ ecological interaction that benefits each of the interacting species.

**mycelium** (mī-sē′-lē-um) The densely branched network of hyphae in a fungus.

**mycorrhiza** (plural, **mycorrhizae**) (mī′-kō-rī′-zuh, mī′-kō-rī′-zē) A mutualistic association of plant roots and fungus.

**mycosis** (mī-kō′-sis) General term for a fungal infection.

**myelin sheath** (mī′-uh-lin) Wrapped around the axon of a neuron, an insulating coat of cell membranes from Schwann cells or oligodendrocytes. It is interrupted by nodes of Ranvier, where action potentials are generated.

**myofibril** (mī′-ō-fī′-bril) A longitudinal bundle in a muscle cell (fiber) that contains thin filaments of actin and regulatory proteins and thick filaments of myosin.

**myoglobin** (mī′-uh-glō′-bin) An oxygen-storing, pigmented protein in muscle cells.

**myosin** (mī′-uh-sin) A type of motor protein that associates into filaments that interact with actin filaments to cause cell contraction.

**myriapod** (mir′-ē-uh-pod′) A terrestrial arthropod with many body segments and one or two pairs of legs per segment. Millipedes and centipedes are the two major groups of living myriapods.

**NAD⁺** The oxidized form of nicotinamide adenine dinucleotide, a coenzyme that can accept electrons, becoming NADH. NADH temporarily stores electrons during cellular respiration.

**NADH** The reduced form of nicotinamide adenine dinucleotide that temporarily stores electrons during cellular respiration. NADH acts as an electron donor to the electron transport chain.

**NADP⁺** The oxidized form of nicotinamide adenine dinucleotide phosphate, an electron carrier that can accept electrons, becoming NADPH. NADPH temporarily stores energized electrons produced during the light reactions.

**NADPH** The reduced form of nicotinamide adenine dinucleotide phosphate; temporarily stores energized electrons produced during the light reactions. NADPH acts as "reducing power" that can be passed along to an electron acceptor, reducing it.

**natural killer cell** A type of white blood cell that can kill tumor cells and virus-infected cells as part of innate immunity.

**natural selection** A process in which individuals that have certain inherited traits tend to survive and reproduce at higher rates than other individuals because of those traits.

**negative feedback** A form of regulation in which accumulation of an end product of a process slows the process; in physiology, a primary mechanism of homeostasis, whereby a change in a variable triggers a response that counteracts the initial change.

**negative pressure breathing** A breathing system in which air is pulled into the lungs.

**nematocyst** (nem′-uh-tuh-sist′) In a cnidocyte of a cnidarian, a capsule-like organelle containing a coiled thread that when discharged can penetrate the body wall of the prey.

**nephron** (nef′-ron) The tubular excretory unit of the vertebrate kidney.

**neritic zone** The shallow region of the ocean overlying the continental shelf.

**nerve** A fiber composed primarily of the bundled axons of neurons.

**nervous system** In animals, the fast-acting internal system of communication involving sensory receptors, networks of nerve cells, and connections to muscles and glands that respond to nerve signals; functions in concert with the endocrine system to effect internal regulation and maintain homeostasis.

**nervous tissue** Tissue made up of neurons and supportive cells.

**net ecosystem production (NEP)** The gross primary production of an ecosystem minus the energy used by all autotrophs and heterotrophs for respiration.

**net primary production (NPP)** The gross primary production of an ecosystem minus the energy used by the producers for respiration.

**neural crest** In vertebrates, a region located along the sides of the neural tube where it pinches off from the ectoderm. Neural crest cells migrate to various parts of the embryo and form pigment cells in the skin and parts of the skull, teeth, adrenal glands, and peripheral nervous system.

**neural tube** A tube of infolded ectodermal cells that runs along the anterior-posterior axis of a vertebrate, just dorsal to the notochord. It will give rise to the central nervous system.

**neurohormone** A molecule that is secreted by a neuron, travels in body fluids, and acts on specific target cells, changing their functioning.

**neuron** (nyūr′-on) A nerve cell; the fundamental unit of the nervous system, having structure and properties that allow it to conduct signals by taking advantage of the electrical charge across its plasma membrane.

**neuronal plasticity** The capacity of a nervous system to change with experience.

**neuropeptide** A relatively short chain of amino acids that serves as a neurotransmitter.

**neurotransmitter** A molecule that is released from the synaptic terminal of a neuron at a chemical synapse, diffuses across the synaptic cleft, and binds to the postsynaptic cell, triggering a response.

**neutral variation** Genetic variation that does not provide a selective advantage or disadvantage.

**neutron** A subatomic particle having no electrical charge (electrically neutral), with a mass of about $1.7 \times 10^{-24}$g, found in the nucleus of an atom.

**neutrophil** The most abundant type of white blood cell. Neutrophils are phagocytic and tend to self-destruct as they destroy foreign invaders, limiting their life span to a few days.

**nitric oxide (NO)** A gas produced by many types of cells that functions as a local regulator and as a neurotransmitter.

**nitrogen cycle** The natural process by which nitrogen, either from the atmosphere or from decomposed organic material, is converted by soil bacteria to compounds assimilated by plants. This incorporated nitrogen is then taken in by other organisms and subsequently released, acted on by bacteria, and made available again to the nonliving environment.

**nitrogen fixation** The conversion of atmospheric nitrogen ($N_2$) to ammonia ($NH_3$). Biological nitrogen fixation is carried out by certain prokaryotes, some of which have mutualistic relationships with plants.

**nociceptor** (nō′-si-sep′-tur) A sensory receptor that responds to noxious or painful stimuli; also called a pain receptor.

**node** A point along the stem of a plant at which leaves are attached.

**node of Ranvier** (ron′-vē-ā′) Gap in the myelin sheath of certain axons where an action potential may be generated. In saltatory conduction, an action potential is regenerated at each node, appearing to "jump" along the axon from node to node.

**nodule** A swelling on the root of a legume. Nodules are composed of plant cells that contain nitrogen-fixing bacteria of the genus *Rhizobium*.

**noncompetitive inhibitor** A substance that reduces the activity of an enzyme by binding to a location remote from the active site, changing the enzyme's shape so that the active site no longer effectively catalyzes the conversion of substrate to product.

**nondisjunction** An error in meiosis or mitosis in which members of a pair of homologous chromosomes or a pair of sister chromatids fail to separate properly from each other.

**nonequilibrium model** A model that maintains that communities change constantly after being buffeted by disturbances.

**nonpolar covalent bond** A type of covalent bond in which electrons are shared equally between two atoms of similar electronegativity.

**nonsense mutation** A mutation that changes an amino acid codon to one of the three stop codons, resulting in a shorter and usually nonfunctional protein.

**norepinephrine** A catecholamine that is chemically and functionally similar to epinephrine and acts as a hormone or neurotransmitter; also called noradrenaline.

**northern coniferous forest** A terrestrial biome characterized by long, cold winters and dominated by cone-bearing trees.

**no-till agriculture** A plowing technique that minimally disturbs the soil, thereby reducing soil loss.

**notochord** (nō′-tuh-kord′) A longitudinal, flexible rod made of tightly packed mesodermal cells that runs along the anterior-posterior axis of a chordate in the dorsal part of the body.

**nuclear envelope** In a eukaryotic cell, the double membrane that surrounds the nucleus, perforated with pores that regulate traffic with the cytoplasm. The outer membrane is continuous with the endoplasmic reticulum.

**nuclear lamina** A netlike array of protein filaments that lines the inner surface of the nuclear envelope and helps maintain the shape of the nucleus.

**nucleariid** A member of a group of unicellular, amoeboid protists that are more closely related to fungi than they are to other protists.

**nuclease** An enzyme that cuts DNA or RNA, either removing one or a few bases or hydrolyzing the DNA or RNA completely into its component nucleotides.

**nucleic acid** (nū-klā′-ik) A polymer (polynucleotide) consisting of many nucleotide monomers; serves as a blueprint for proteins and, through the actions of proteins, for all cellular activities. The two types are DNA and RNA.

**nucleic acid hybridization** (nū-klā′-ik) The base pairing of one strand of a nucleic acid to the complementary sequence on a strand from *another* nucleic acid molecule.

**nucleic acid probe** (nū-klā′-ik) In DNA technology, a labeled single-stranded nucleic acid molecule used to locate a specific nucleotide sequence in a nucleic acid sample. Molecules of the probe hydrogen-bond to the complementary sequence wherever it occurs; radioactive, fluorescent, or other labeling of the probe allows its location to be detected.

**nucleoid** (nū′-klē-oyd) A non-membrane-enclosed region in a prokaryotic cell where its chromosome is located.

**nucleolus** (nū-klē′-ō-lus) (plural, **nucleoli**) A specialized structure in the nucleus, consisting of chromosomal regions containing ribosomal RNA (rRNA) genes along with ribosomal proteins imported from the cytoplasm; site of rRNA synthesis and ribosomal subunit assembly. *See also* ribosome.

**nucleosome** (nū′-klē-ō-sōm′) The basic, bead-like unit of DNA packing in eukaryotes, consisting of a segment of DNA wound around a protein core composed of two copies of each of four types of histone.

**nucleotide** (nū-klē-ō-tīd′) The building block of a nucleic acid, consisting of a five-carbon sugar covalently bonded to a nitrogenous base and one to three phosphate groups.

**nucleotide excision repair** (nū′-klē-ō-tīd′) A repair system that removes and then correctly replaces a damaged segment of DNA using the undamaged strand as a guide.

**nucleotide-pair substitution** (nū′-klē-ō-tīd′) A type of point mutation in which one nucleotide in a DNA strand and its partner in the complementary strand are replaced by another pair of nucleotides.

**nucleus** (1) An atom's central core, containing protons and neutrons. (2) The organelle of a eukaryotic cell that contains the genetic material in the form of chromosomes, made up of chromatin. (3) A cluster of neurons.

**nutrition** The process by which an organism takes in and makes use of food substances.

**obligate aerobe** (ob′-lig-et ār′-ōb) An organism that requires oxygen for cellular respiration and cannot live without it.

**obligate anaerobe** (ob′-lig-et an′-uh-rōb) An organism that carries out only fermentation or anaerobic respiration. Such organisms cannot use oxygen and in fact may be poisoned by it.

**ocean acidification** The process by which the pH of the ocean is lowered (made more acidic) when excess $CO_2$ dissolves in seawater and forms carbonic acid ($H_2CO_3$).

**oceanic pelagic zone** Most of the ocean's waters far from shore, constantly mixed by ocean currents.

**odorant** A molecule that can be detected by sensory receptors of the olfactory system.

**Okazaki fragment** (ō′-kah-zah′-kē) A short segment of DNA synthesized away from the replication fork on a template strand during DNA replication. Many such segments are joined together to make up the lagging strand of newly synthesized DNA.

**olfaction** The sense of smell.

**oligodendrocyte** A type of glial cell that forms insulating myelin sheaths around the axons of neurons in the central nervous system.

**oligotrophic lake** A nutrient-poor, clear lake with few phytoplankton.

**ommatidium** (ōm′-uh-tid′-ē-um) (plural, **ommatidia**) One of the facets of the compound eye of arthropods and some polychaete worms.

**omnivore** An animal that regularly eats animals as well as plants or algae.

**oncogene** (on′-kō-jēn) A gene found in viral or cellular genomes that is involved in triggering molecular events that can lead to cancer.

**oocyte** (ō′-uh-sīt) A cell in the female reproductive system that differentiates to form an egg.

**oogenesis** (ō′-uh-jen′-uh-sis) The process in the ovary that results in the production of female gametes.

**oogonium** (ō′-uh-gō′-nē-em) (plural, **oogonia**) A cell that divides mitotically to form oocytes.

**open circulatory system** A circulatory system in which fluid called hemolymph bathes the tissues and organs directly and there is no distinction between the circulating fluid and the interstitial fluid.

**operator** In bacterial and phage DNA, a sequence of nucleotides near the start of an operon to which an active repressor can attach. The binding of the repressor prevents RNA polymerase from attaching to the promoter and transcribing the genes of the operon.

**operculum** (ō-per′-kyuh-lum) In aquatic osteichthyans, a protective bony flap that covers and protects the gills.

**operon** (op′-er-on) A unit of genetic function found in bacteria and phages, consisting of a promoter, an operator, and a coordinately regulated cluster of genes whose products function in a common pathway.

**opisthokont** (uh-pis′-thuh-kont′) A member of an extremely diverse clade of eukaryotes that includes fungi, animals, and several closely related groups of protists.

**opposable thumb** A thumb that can touch the ventral surface (fingerprint side) of the fingertip of all four fingers of the same hand with its own ventral surface.

**opsin** A membrane protein bound to a light-absorbing pigment molecule.

**optimal foraging model** The basis for analyzing behavior as a compromise between feeding costs and feeding benefits.

**oral cavity** The mouth of an animal.

**orbital** The three-dimensional space where an electron is found 90% of the time.

**order** In Linnaean classification, the taxonomic category above the level of family.

**organ** A specialized center of body function composed of several different types of tissues.

**organelle** (ōr-guh-nel′) Any of several membrane-enclosed structures with specialized functions, suspended in the cytosol of eukaryotic cells.

**organic chemistry** The study of carbon compounds (organic compounds).

**organ identity gene** A plant homeotic gene that uses positional information to determine which emerging leaves develop into which types of floral organs.

**organism** An individual living thing, consisting of one or more cells.

**organismal ecology** The branch of ecology concerned with the morphological, physiological, and behavioral ways in which individual organisms meet the challenges posed by their biotic and abiotic environments.

**organ of Corti** (kor′-tē) The actual hearing organ of the vertebrate ear, located in the floor of the cochlear duct in the inner ear; contains the receptor cells (hair cells) of the ear.

**organogenesis** (ōr-gan′-ō-jen′-uh-sis) The process in which organ rudiments develop from the three germ layers after gastrulation.

**organ system** A group of organs that work together in performing vital body functions.

**origin of replication** Site where the replication of a DNA molecule begins, consisting of a specific sequence of nucleotides.

**orthologous genes** Homologous genes that are found in different species because of speciation.

**osculum** (os′-kyuh-lum) A large opening in a sponge that connects the spongocoel to the environment.

**osmoconformer** An animal that is isoosmotic with its environment.

**osmolarity** (oz′-mō-lār′-uh-tē) Solute concentration expressed as molarity.

**osmoregulation** Regulation of solute concentrations and water balance by a cell or organism.

**osmoregulator** An animal that controls its internal osmolarity independent of the external environment.

**osmosis** (oz-mō′-sis) The diffusion of free water across a selectively permeable membrane.

**osteichthyan** (os′-tē-ik′-thē-an) A member of a vertebrate clade with jaws and mostly bony skeletons.

**outer ear** One of the three main regions of the ear in reptiles (including birds) and mammals; made up of the auditory canal and, in many birds and mammals, the pinna.

**outgroup** A species or group of species from an evolutionary lineage that is known to have diverged before the lineage that contains the group of species being studied. An outgroup is selected so that its members are closely related to the group of species being studied, but not as closely related as any study-group members are to each other.

**oval window** In the vertebrate ear, a membrane-covered gap in the skull bone, through which sound waves pass from the middle ear to the inner ear.

**ovarian cycle** (ō-vār′-ē-un) The cyclic recurrence of the follicular phase, ovulation, and the luteal phase in the mammalian ovary, regulated by hormones.

**ovary** (ō′-vuh-rē) (1) In flowers, the portion of a carpel in which the egg-containing ovules develop. (2) In animals, the structure that produces female gametes and reproductive hormones.

**oviduct** (ō′-vuh-duct) A tube passing from the ovary to the vagina in invertebrates or to the uterus in vertebrates, where it is also called a fallopian tube.

**oviparous** (ō-vip′-uh-rus) Referring to a type of development in which young hatch from eggs laid outside the mother's body.

**ovoviviparous** (ō′-vō-vī-vip′-uh-rus) Referring to a type of development in which young hatch from eggs that are retained in the mother's uterus.

**ovulation** The release of an egg from an ovary. In humans, an ovarian follicle releases an egg during each uterine (menstrual) cycle.

**ovule** (o′-vyūl) A structure that develops within the ovary of a seed plant and contains the female gametophyte.

**oxidation** The complete or partial loss of electrons from a substance involved in a redox reaction.

**oxidative phosphorylation** (fos′-fōr-uh-lā′-shun) The production of ATP using energy derived from the redox reactions of an electron transport chain; the third major stage of cellular respiration.

**oxidizing agent** The electron acceptor in a redox reaction.

**oxytocin** (ok′-si-tō′-sen) A hormone produced by the hypothalamus and released from the posterior pituitary. It induces contractions of the uterine muscles during labor and causes the mammary glands to eject milk during nursing.

**p53 gene** A tumor-suppressor gene that codes for a specific transcription factor that promotes the synthesis of proteins that inhibit the cell cycle.

**paedomorphosis** (pē′-duh-mōr′-fuh-sis) The retention in an adult organism of the juvenile features of its evolutionary ancestors.

**pain receptor** A sensory receptor that responds to noxious or painful stimuli; also called a nociceptor.

**paleoanthropology** The study of human origins and evolution.

**paleontology** (pā′-lē-un-tol′-ō-jē) The scientific study of fossils.

**pancreas** (pan′-krē-us) A gland with exocrine and endocrine tissues. The exocrine portion functions in digestion, secreting enzymes and an alkaline solution into the small intestine via a duct; the ductless endocrine portion functions in homeostasis, secreting the hormones insulin and glucagon into the blood.

**pancrustacean** A member of a diverse arthropod clade that includes lobsters, crabs, barnacles and other crustaceans, as well as insects and their six-legged terrestrial relatives.

**pandemic** A global epidemic.

**Pangaea** (pan-jē′-uh) The supercontinent that formed near the end of the Paleozoic era, when plate movements brought all the landmasses of Earth together.

**parabasalid** A protist, such as a trichomonad, with modified mitochondria.

**paracrine** Referring to a secreted molecule that acts on a neighboring cell.

**paralogous genes** Homologous genes that are found in the same genome as a result of gene duplication.

**paraphyletic** (pār′-uh-fī-let′-ik) Pertaining to a group of taxa that consists of a common ancestor and some, but not all, of its descendants.

**parareptile** A basal group of reptiles, consisting mostly of large, stocky quadrupedal herbivores. Parareptiles died out in the late Triassic period.

**parasite** (pār′-uh-sīt) An organism that feeds on the cell contents, tissues, or body fluids of another species (the host) while in or on the host organism. Parasites harm but usually do not kill their host.

**parasitism** (pār′-uh-sit-izm) A +/− ecological interaction in which one organism, the parasite, benefits by feeding upon another organism, the host, which is harmed; some parasites live within the host (feeding on its tissues), while others feed on the host's external surface.

**parasympathetic division** One of three divisions of the autonomic nervous system; generally enhances body activities that gain and conserve energy, such as digestion and reduced heart rate.

**parathyroid gland** One of four small endocrine glands, embedded in the surface of the thyroid gland, that secrete parathyroid hormone.

**parathyroid hormone (PTH)** A hormone secreted by the parathyroid glands that raises blood calcium level by promoting calcium release from bone and calcium retention by the kidneys.

**parenchyma cell** (puh-ren′-ki-muh) A relatively unspecialized plant cell type that carries out most of the metabolism, synthesizes and stores organic products, and develops into a more differentiated cell type.

**parental type** An offspring with a phenotype that matches one of the true-breeding parental (P generation) phenotypes; also refers to the phenotype itself.

**Parkinson's disease** A progressive brain disease characterized by difficulty in initiating movements, slowness of movement, and rigidity.

**parthenogenesis** (par′-thuh-nō′-jen′-uh-sis) A form of asexual reproduction in which females produce offspring from unfertilized eggs.

**partial pressure** The pressure exerted by a particular gas in a mixture of gases (for instance, the pressure exerted by oxygen in air).

**passive immunity** Short-term immunity conferred by the transfer of antibodies, as occurs in the transfer of maternal antibodies to a fetus or nursing infant.

**passive transport** The diffusion of a substance across a biological membrane with no expenditure of energy.

**pathogen** An organism or virus that causes disease.

**pathogen-associated molecular pattern (PAMP)** A molecular sequence that is specific to a certain pathogen.

**pattern formation** The development of a multicellular organism's spatial organization, the arrangement of organs and tissues in their characteristic places in three-dimensional space.

**peat** Extensive deposits of partially decayed organic material often formed primarily from the wetland moss *Sphagnum*.

**pedigree** A diagram of a family tree with conventional symbols, showing the occurrence of heritable characters in parents and offspring over multiple generations.

**pelagic zone** The open-water component of aquatic biomes.

**penis** The copulatory structure of male mammals.

**PEP carboxylase** An enzyme that adds $CO_2$ to phosphoenolpyruvate (PEP) to form oxaloacetate in mesophyll cells of $C_4$ plants. It acts prior to photosynthesis.

**pepsin** An enzyme present in gastric juice that begins the hydrolysis of proteins.

**pepsinogen** The inactive form of pepsin secreted by chief cells located in gastric pits of the stomach.

**peptide bond** The covalent bond between the carboxyl group on one amino acid and the amino group on another, formed by a dehydration reaction.

**peptidoglycan** (pep′-tid-ō-glī′-kan) A type of polymer in bacterial cell walls consisting of modified sugars cross-linked by short polypeptides.

**perception** The interpretation of sensory system input by the brain.

**pericycle** The outermost layer in the vascular cylinder, from which lateral roots arise.

**periderm** (pār′-uh-derm′) The protective coat that replaces the epidermis in woody plants during secondary growth, formed of the cork and cork cambium.

**peripheral nervous system (PNS)** The sensory and motor neurons that connect to the central nervous system.

**peripheral protein** A protein loosely bound to the surface of a membrane or to part of an integral protein and not embedded in the lipid bilayer.

**peristalsis** (pār′-uh-stal′-sis) (1) Alternating waves of contraction and relaxation in the smooth muscles lining the alimentary canal that push food along the canal. (2) A type of movement on land produced by rhythmic waves of muscle contractions passing from front to back, as in many annelids.

**peristome** (pār'-uh-stōme') A ring of interlocking, tooth-like structures on the upper part of a moss capsule (sporangium), often specialized for gradual spore discharge.

**peritubular capillary** One of the tiny blood vessels that form a network surrounding the proximal and distal tubules in the kidney.

**peroxisome** (puh-rok'-suh-sōm') An organelle containing enzymes that transfer hydrogen atoms from various substrates to oxygen ($O_2$), producing and then degrading hydrogen peroxide ($H_2O_2$).

**petal** A modified leaf of a flowering plant. Petals are the often colorful parts of a flower that advertise it to insects and other pollinators.

**petiole** (pet'-ē-ōl) The stalk of a leaf, which joins the leaf to a node of the stem.

**P generation** The true-breeding (homozygous) parent individuals from which $F_1$ hybrid offspring are derived in studies of inheritance; P stands for "parental."

**pH** A measure of hydrogen ion concentration equal to $-\log[H^+]$ and ranging in value from 0 to 14.

**phage** (fāj) A virus that infects bacteria; also called a bacteriophage.

**phagocytosis** (fag'-ō-sī-tō'-sis) A type of endocytosis in which large particulate substances or small organisms are taken up by a cell. It is carried out by some protists and by certain immune cells of animals (in mammals, mainly macrophages, neutrophils, and dendritic cells).

**pharyngeal cleft** (fuh-rin'-jē-ul) In chordate embryos, one of the grooves that separate a series of arches along the outer surface of the pharynx and may develop into a pharyngeal slit.

**pharyngeal slit** (fuh-rin'-jē-ul) In chordate embryos, one of the slits that form from the pharyngeal clefts and open into the pharynx, later developing into gill slits in many vertebrates.

**pharynx** (făr'-inks) (1) An area in the vertebrate throat where air and food passages cross. (2) In flatworms, the muscular tube that protrudes from the ventral side of the worm and ends in the mouth.

**phase change** (1) A shift from one developmental phase to another. (2) In plants, a morphological change that arises from a transition in shoot apical meristem activity.

**phenotype** (fē'-nō-tīp) The observable physical and physiological traits of an organism, which are determined by its genetic makeup.

**pheromone** (făr'-uh-mōn) In animals and fungi, a small molecule released into the environment that functions in communication between members of the same species. In animals, it acts much like a hormone in influencing physiology and behavior.

**phloem** (flō'-em) Vascular plant tissue consisting of living cells arranged into elongated tubes that transport sugar and other organic nutrients throughout the plant.

**phloem sap** (flō'-em) The sugar-rich solution carried through a plant's sieve tubes.

**phosphate group** A chemical group consisting of a phosphorus atom bonded to four oxygen atoms; important in energy transfer.

**phospholipid** (fos'-fō-lip'-id) A lipid made up of glycerol joined to two fatty acids and a phosphate group. The hydrocarbon chains of the fatty acids act as nonpolar, hydrophobic tails, while the rest of the molecule acts as a polar, hydrophilic head. Phospholipids form bilayers that function as biological membranes.

**phosphorylated intermediate** (fos'-fōr-uh-lā'-ted) A molecule (often a reactant) with a phosphate group covalently bound to it, making it more reactive (less stable) than the unphosphorylated molecule.

**phosphorylation cascade** (fos'-fōr-uh-lā'-shun) A series of chemical reactions during cell signaling mediated by enzymes (kinases), in which each kinase in turn phosphorylates and activates another, ultimately leading to phosphorylation of many proteins.

**photic zone** (fō'-tic) The narrow top layer of an ocean or lake, where light penetrates sufficiently for photosynthesis to occur.

**photoautotroph** (fō'-tō-ot'-ō-trōf) An organism that harnesses light energy to drive the synthesis of organic compounds from carbon dioxide.

**photoheterotroph** (fō'-tō-het'-er-ō-trōf) An organism that uses light to generate ATP but must obtain carbon in organic form.

**photomorphogenesis** Effects of light on plant morphology.

**photon** (fō'-ton) A quantum, or discrete quantity, of light energy that behaves as if it were a particle.

**photoperiodism** (fō'-tō-pēr'-ē-ō-dizm) A physiological response to photoperiod, the interval in a 24-hour period during which an organism is exposed to light. An example of photoperiodism is flowering.

**photophosphorylation** (fō'-tō-fos'-fōr-uh-lā'-shun) The process of generating ATP from ADP and phosphate by means of chemiosmosis, using a proton-motive force generated across the thylakoid membrane of the chloroplast or the membrane of certain prokaryotes during the light reactions of photosynthesis.

**photoreceptor** An electromagnetic receptor that detects the radiation known as visible light.

**photorespiration** A metabolic pathway that consumes oxygen and ATP, releases carbon dioxide, and decreases photosynthetic output. Photorespiration generally occurs on hot, dry, bright days, when stomata close and the $O_2/CO_2$ ratio in the leaf increases, favoring the binding of $O_2$ rather than $CO_2$ by rubisco.

**photosynthesis** (fō'-tō-sin'-thi-sis) The conversion of light energy to chemical energy that is stored in sugars or other organic compounds; occurs in plants, algae, and certain prokaryotes.

**photosystem** A light-capturing unit located in the thylakoid membrane of the chloroplast or in the membrane of some prokaryotes, consisting of a reaction-center complex surrounded by numerous light-harvesting complexes. There are two types of photosystems, I and II; they absorb light best at different wavelengths.

**photosystem I (PS I)** A light-capturing unit in a chloroplast's thylakoid membrane or in the membrane of some prokaryotes; it has two molecules of P700 chlorophyll *a* at its reaction center.

**photosystem II (PS II)** One of two light-capturing units in a chloroplast's thylakoid membrane or in the membrane of some prokaryotes; it has two molecules of P680 chlorophyll *a* at its reaction center.

**phototropism** (fō'-tō-trō'-pizm) Growth of a plant shoot toward or away from light.

**phyllotaxy** (fil'-uh-tak'-sē) The pattern of leaf attachment to the stem of a plant.

**phylogenetic tree** A branching diagram that represents a hypothesis about the evolutionary history of a group of organisms.

**phylogeny** (fī-loj'-uh-nē) The evolutionary history of a species or group of related species.

**phylum** (fī'-lum) (plural, **phyla**) In Linnaean classification, the taxonomic category above class.

**physiology** The processes and functions of an organism.

**phytochrome** (fī'-tuh-krōm) A type of light receptor in plants that mostly absorbs red light and regulates many plant responses, such as seed germination and shade avoidance.

**phytoremediation** An emerging technology that seeks to reclaim contaminated areas by taking advantage of some plant species' ability to extract heavy metals and other pollutants from the soil and to concentrate them in easily harvested portions of the plant.

**pilus** (plural, **pili**) (pī'-lus, pī'-lī) In bacteria, a structure that links one cell to another at the start of conjugation; also called a sex pilus or conjugation pilus.

**pineal gland** (pī'-nē-ul) A small gland on the dorsal surface of the vertebrate forebrain that secretes the hormone melatonin.

**pinocytosis** (pī'-nō-sī-tō'-sis) A type of endocytosis in which the cell ingests extracellular fluid and its dissolved solutes.

**pistil** A single carpel (a simple pistil) or a group of fused carpels (a compound pistil).

**pith** Ground tissue that is internal to the vascular tissue in a stem; in many monocot roots, parenchyma cells that form the central core of the vascular cylinder.

**pituitary gland** (puh-tū'-uh-tār'-ē) An endocrine gland at the base of the hypothalamus; consists of a posterior lobe, which stores and releases two hormones produced by the hypothalamus, and an anterior lobe, which produces and secretes many hormones that regulate diverse body functions.

**placenta** (pluh-sen'-tuh) A structure in the uterus of a pregnant eutherian mammal that nourishes the fetus with the mother's blood supply; formed from the uterine lining and embryonic membranes.

**placoderm** A member of an extinct group of fishlike vertebrates that had jaws and were enclosed in a tough outer armor.

**planarian** A free-living flatworm found in ponds and streams.

**plasma** (plaz'-muh) The liquid matrix of blood in which the blood cells are suspended.

**plasma membrane** (plaz'-muh) The membrane at the boundary of every cell that acts as a selective barrier, regulating the cell's chemical composition.

**plasmid** (plaz'-mid) A small, circular, double-stranded DNA molecule that carries accessory genes separate from those of a bacterial chromosome; in DNA cloning, plasmids are used as vectors carrying up to about 10,000 base pairs (10 kb) of DNA. Plasmids are also found in some eukaryotes, such as yeasts.

**plasmodesma** (plaz'-mō-dez'-muh) (plural, **plasmodesmata**) An open channel through the cell wall that connects the cytoplasm of adjacent plant cells, allowing water, small solutes, and some larger molecules to pass between the cells.

**plasmogamy** (plaz-moh'-guh-mē) In fungi, the fusion of the cytoplasm of cells from two individuals; occurs as one stage of sexual reproduction, followed later by karyogamy.

**plasmolysis** (plaz-mol'-uh-sis) A phenomenon in walled cells in which the cytoplasm shrivels and the plasma membrane pulls away from the cell wall; occurs when the cell loses water to a hypertonic environment.

**plastid** One of a family of closely related organelles that includes chloroplasts, chromoplasts, and amyloplasts. Plastids are found in cells of photosynthetic eukaryotes.

**plate tectonics** The theory that the continents are part of great plates of Earth's crust that float on the hot, underlying portion of the mantle. Movements in the mantle cause the continents to move slowly over time.

**platelet** A pinched-off cytoplasmic fragment of a specialized bone marrow cell. Platelets circulate in the blood and are important in blood clotting.

**pleiotropy** (plī'-o-truh-pē) The ability of a single gene to have multiple effects.

**pluripotent** Describing a cell that can give rise to many, but not all, parts of an organism.

**point mutation** A change in a single nucleotide pair of a gene.

**polar covalent bond** A covalent bond between atoms that differ in electronegativity. The shared electrons are pulled closer to the more electronegative atom, making it slightly negative and the other atom slightly positive.

**polar molecule** A molecule (such as water) with an uneven distribution of charges in different regions of the molecule.

**polarity** A lack of symmetry; structural differences in opposite ends of an organism or structure, such as the root end and shoot end of a plant.

**pollen grain** In seed plants, a structure consisting of the male gametophyte enclosed within a pollen wall.

**pollen tube** A tube that forms after germination of the pollen grain and that functions in the delivery of sperm to the ovule.

**pollination** (pol-uh-nā'-shun) The transfer of pollen to the part of a seed plant containing the ovules, a process required for fertilization.

**poly-A tail** A sequence of 50–250 adenine nucleotides added onto the 3' end of a pre-mRNA molecule.

**polygamous** Referring to a type of relationship in which an individual of one sex mates with several of the other.

**polygenic inheritance** (pol'-ē-jen'-ik) An additive effect of two or more genes on a single phenotypic character.

**polymer** (pol'-uh-mer) A long molecule consisting of many similar or identical monomers linked together by covalent bonds.

**polymerase chain reaction (PCR)** (puh-lim'-uh-rās) A technique for amplifying DNA *in vitro* by incubating it with specific primers, a heat-resistant DNA polymerase, and nucleotides.

**polynucleotide** (pol'-ē-nū'-klē-ō-tīd) A polymer consisting of many nucleotide monomers in a chain. The nucleotides can be those of DNA or RNA.

**polyp** The sessile variant of the cnidarian body plan. The alternate form is the medusa.

**polypeptide** (pol'-ē-pep'-tīd) A polymer of many amino acids linked together by peptide bonds.

**polyphyletic** (pol'-ē-fī-let'-ik) Pertaining to a group of taxa that includes distantly related organisms but does not include their most recent common ancestor.

**polyploidy** (pol'-ē-ploy'-dē) A chromosomal alteration in which the organism possesses more than two complete chromosome sets. It is the result of an accident of cell division.

**polyribosome (polysome)** (pol'-ē-rī'-buh-sōm') A group of several ribosomes attached to, and translating, the same messenger RNA molecule.

**polysaccharide** (pol'-ē-sak'-uh-rīd) A polymer of many monosaccharides, formed by dehydration reactions.

**polyspermy** The fertilization of an egg by more than one sperm.

**polytomy** (puh-lit'-uh-mē) In a phylogenetic tree, a branch point from which more than two descendant taxa emerge. A polytomy indicates that the evolutionary relationships between the descendant taxa are not yet clear.

**pons** A portion of the brain that participates in certain automatic, homeostatic functions, such as regulating the breathing centers in the medulla.

**population** A group of individuals of the same species that live in the same area and interbreed, producing fertile offspring.

**population dynamics** The study of how complex interactions between biotic and abiotic factors influence variations in population size.

**population ecology** The study of populations in relation to their environment, including environmental influences on population density and distribution, age structure, and variations in population size.

**positional information** Molecular cues that control pattern formation in an animal or plant embryonic structure by indicating a cell's location relative to the organism's body axes. These cues elicit a response by genes that regulate development.

**positive feedback** A form of regulation in which an end product of a process speeds up that process; in physiology, a control mechanism in which a change in a variable triggers a response that reinforces or amplifies the change.

**positive interaction** A +/+ or +/0 ecological interaction in which at least one of the interacting species benefits and neither is harmed; positive interactions include mutualism and commensalism.

**positive pressure breathing** A breathing system in which air is forced into the lungs.

**posterior** Pertaining to the rear, or tail end, of a bilaterally symmetrical animal.

**posterior pituitary** An extension of the hypothalamus composed of nervous tissue that secretes oxytocin and antidiuretic hormone made in the hypothalamus; a temporary storage site for these hormones.

**postzygotic barrier** (pōst'-zī-got'-ik) A reproductive barrier that prevents hybrid zygotes produced by two different species from developing into viable, fertile adults.

**potential energy** The energy that matter possesses as a result of its location or spatial arrangement (structure).

**predation** An interaction between species in which one species, the predator, eats the other, the prey.

**prediction** In deductive reasoning, a forecast that follows logically from a hypothesis. By testing predictions, experiments may allow certain hypotheses to be rejected.

**pregnancy** The condition of carrying one or more embryos in the uterus; also called gestation.

**prepuce** (prē'-pyūs) A fold of skin covering the head of the clitoris or penis.

**pressure potential ($\psi_P$)** A component of water potential that consists of the physical pressure on a solution, which can be positive, zero, or negative.

**prezygotic barrier** (prē'-zī-got'-ik) A reproductive barrier that impedes mating between species or hinders fertilization if interspecific mating is attempted.

**primary cell wall** In plants, a relatively thin and flexible layer that surrounds the plasma membrane of a young cell.

**primary consumer** An herbivore; an organism that eats plants or other autotrophs.

**primary electron acceptor** In the thylakoid membrane of a chloroplast or in the membrane of some prokaryotes, a specialized molecule that shares the reaction-center complex with a pair of chlorophyll *a* molecules and that accepts an electron from them.

**primary growth** Growth produced by apical meristems, lengthening stems and roots.

**primary immune response** The initial adaptive immune response to an antigen, which appears after a lag of about 10–17 days.

**primary meristems** The three meristematic derivatives (protoderm, procambium, and ground meristem) of an apical meristem.

**primary oocyte** (ō'-uh-sīt) An oocyte prior to completion of meiosis I.

**primary producer** An autotroph, usually a photosynthetic organism. Collectively, autotrophs make up the trophic level of an ecosystem that ultimately supports all other levels.

**primary production** The amount of light energy converted to chemical energy (organic compounds) by the autotrophs in an ecosystem during a given time period.

**primary structure** The level of protein structure referring to the specific linear sequence of amino acids.

**primary succession** A type of ecological succession that occurs in an area where there were originally no organisms present and where soil has not yet formed.

**primary transcript** An initial RNA transcript from any gene; also called pre-mRNA when transcribed from a protein-coding gene.

**primase** An enzyme that joins RNA nucleotides to make a primer during DNA replication, using the parental DNA strand as a template.

**primer** A short polynucleotide with a free 3′ end, bound by complementary base pairing to the template strand and elongated with DNA nucleotides during DNA replication.

**prion** An infectious agent that is a misfolded version of a normal cellular protein. Prions appear to increase in number by converting correctly folded versions of the protein to more prions.

**problem solving** The cognitive activity of devising a method to proceed from one state to another in the face of real or apparent obstacles.

**producer** An organism that produces organic compounds from $CO_2$ by harnessing light energy (in photosynthesis) or by oxidizing inorganic chemicals (in chemosynthetic reactions carried out by some prokaryotes).

**product** A material resulting from a chemical reaction.

**production efficiency** The percentage of energy stored in assimilated food that is not used for respiration or eliminated as waste.

**progesterone** A steroid hormone that contributes to the menstrual cycle and prepares the uterus for pregnancy; the major progestin in mammals.

**progestin** Any steroid hormone with progesterone-like activity.

**prokaryotic cell** (prō′-kār′-ē-ot′-ik) A type of cell lacking a membrane-enclosed nucleus and membrane-enclosed organelles. Organisms with prokaryotic cells (bacteria and archaea) are called prokaryotes.

**prolactin** A hormone produced and secreted by the anterior pituitary with a great diversity of effects in different vertebrate species. In mammals, it stimulates growth of and milk production by the mammary glands.

**prometaphase** The second stage of mitosis, in which the nuclear envelope fragments and the spindle microtubules attach to the kinetochores of the chromosomes.

**promoter** A specific nucleotide sequence in the DNA of a gene that binds RNA polymerase, positioning it to start transcribing RNA at the appropriate place.

**prophage** (prō′-fāj) A phage genome that has been inserted into a specific site on a bacterial chromosome.

**prophase** The first stage of mitosis, in which the chromatin condenses into discrete chromosomes visible with a light microscope, the mitotic spindle begins to form, and the nucleolus disappears but the nucleus remains intact.

**prostaglandin** (pros′-tuh-glan′-din) One of a group of modified fatty acids that are secreted by virtually all tissues and that perform a wide variety of functions as local regulators.

**prostate gland** (pros′-tāt) A gland in human males that secretes an acid-neutralizing component of semen.

**protease** (prō′-tē-āz) An enzyme that digests proteins by hydrolysis.

**protein** (prō′-tēn) A biologically functional molecule consisting of one or more polypeptides folded and coiled into a specific three-dimensional structure.

**protein kinase** (prō′-tēn kī′-nās) An enzyme that transfers phosphate groups from ATP to a protein, thus phosphorylating the protein.

**protein phosphatase** (prō′-tēn fos′-fuh-tās) An enzyme that removes phosphate groups from (dephosphorylates) proteins, often functioning to reverse the effect of a protein kinase.

**proteoglycan** (prō′-tē-ō-gli′-kan) A large molecule consisting of a small core protein with many carbohydrate chains attached, found in the extracellular matrix of animal cells. A proteoglycan may consist of up to 95% carbohydrate.

**proteome** The entire set of proteins expressed by a given cell, tissue, or organism.

**proteomics** (prō′-tē-ō′-miks) The systematic study of sets of proteins and their properties, including their abundance, chemical modifications, and interactions.

**protist** An informal term applied to any eukaryote that is not a plant, animal, or fungus. Most protists are unicellular, though some are colonial or multicellular.

**protocell** An abiotic precursor of a living cell that had a membrane-like structure and that maintained an internal chemistry different from that of its surroundings.

**proton** (prō′-ton) A subatomic particle with a single positive electrical charge, with a mass of about $1.7 \times 10^{-24}$g, found in the nucleus of an atom.

**protonema** (prō′-tuh-nē′-muh) (plural, **protonemata**) A mass of green, branched, one-cell-thick filaments produced by germinating moss spores.

**protonephridium** (prō′-tō-nuh-frid′-ē-um) (plural, **protonephridia**) An excretory system, such as the flame bulb system of flatworms, consisting of a network of tubules lacking internal openings.

**proton-motive force** (prō′-ton) The potential energy stored in the form of a proton electrochemical gradient, generated by the pumping of hydrogen ions ($H^+$) across a biological membrane during chemiosmosis.

**proton pump** (prō′-ton) An active transport protein in a cell membrane that uses ATP to transport hydrogen ions out of a cell against their concentration gradient, generating a membrane potential in the process.

**proto-oncogene** (prō′-tō-on′-kō-jēn) A normal cellular gene that has the potential to become an oncogene.

**protoplast** The living part of a plant cell, which also includes the plasma membrane.

**protostome development** In animals, a developmental mode distinguished by the development of the mouth from the blastopore; often also characterized by spiral cleavage and by the body cavity forming when solid masses of mesoderm split.

**provirus** A viral genome that is permanently inserted into a host genome.

**proximal tubule** In the vertebrate kidney, the portion of a nephron immediately

downstream from Bowman's capsule that conveys and helps refine filtrate.

**pseudocoelomate** (sū-dō-sē′-lō-māt) An animal whose body cavity is lined by tissue derived from mesoderm and endoderm.

**pseudogene** (sū′-dō-jēn) A DNA segment that is very similar to a real gene but does not yield a functional product; a DNA segment that formerly functioned as a gene but has become inactivated in a particular species because of mutation.

**pseudopodium** (sū′-dō-pō′-dē-um) (plural, **pseudopodia**) A cellular extension of amoeboid cells used in moving and feeding.

**P site** One of a ribosome's three binding sites for tRNA during translation. The P site holds the tRNA carrying the growing polypeptide chain. (P stands for peptidyl tRNA.)

**pterosaur** Winged reptile that lived during the Mesozoic era.

**pulse** The rhythmic bulging of the artery walls with each heartbeat.

**punctuated equilibria** In the fossil record, long periods of apparent stasis, in which a species undergoes little or no morphological change, interrupted by relatively brief periods of sudden change.

**Punnett square** A diagram used in the study of inheritance to show the predicted genotypic results of random fertilization in genetic crosses between individuals of known genotype.

**pupil** The opening in the iris, which admits light into the interior of the vertebrate eye. Muscles in the iris regulate its size.

**purine** (pyū′-rēn) One of two types of nitrogenous bases found in nucleotides, characterized by a six-membered ring fused to a five-membered ring. Adenine (A) and guanine (G) are purines.

**pyrimidine** (puh-rim′-uh-dēn) One of two types of nitrogenous bases found in nucleotides, characterized by a six-membered ring. Cytosine (C), thymine (T), and uracil (U) are pyrimidines.

**quantitative character** A heritable feature that varies continuously over a range rather than in an either-or fashion.

**quaternary structure** (kwot′-er-nār′-ē) The particular shape of a complex, aggregate protein, defined by the characteristic three-dimensional arrangement of its constituent subunits, each a polypeptide.

**radial cleavage** A type of embryonic development in deuterostomes in which the planes of cell division that transform the zygote into a ball of cells are either parallel or perpendicular to the vertical axis of the embryo, thereby aligning tiers of cells one above the other.

**radial symmetry** Symmetry in which the body is shaped like a pie or barrel (lacking a left side and a right side) and can be divided into mirror-imaged halves by any plane through its central axis.

**radicle** An embryonic root of a plant.

**radioactive isotope** An isotope (an atomic form of a chemical element) that is unstable; the nucleus decays spontaneously, giving off detectable particles and energy.

**radiolarian** A protist, usually marine, with a shell generally made of silica and pseudopodia that radiate from the central body.

**radiometric dating** A method for determining the absolute age of rocks and fossils, based on the half-life of radioactive isotopes.

**radula** A straplike scraping organ used by many molluscs during feeding.

***ras* gene** A gene that codes for Ras, a G protein that relays a growth signal from a growth factor receptor on the plasma membrane to a cascade of protein kinases, ultimately resulting in stimulation of the cell cycle.

**ratite** (rat′-īt) A member of the group of flightless birds.

**ray-finned fish** A member of the clade Actinopterygii, aquatic osteichthyans with fins supported by long, flexible rays, including tuna, bass, and herring.

**reabsorption** In excretory systems, the recovery of solutes and water from filtrate.

**reactant** A starting material in a chemical reaction.

**reaction-center complex** A complex of proteins associated with a special pair of chlorophyll *a* molecules and a primary electron acceptor. Located centrally in a photosystem, this complex triggers the light reactions of photosynthesis. Excited by light energy, the pair of chlorophylls donates an electron to the primary electron acceptor, which passes an electron to an electron transport chain.

**reading frame** On an mRNA, the triplet grouping of ribonucleotides used by the translation machinery during polypeptide synthesis.

**receptacle** The base of a flower; the part of the stem that is the site of attachment of the floral organs.

**reception** In cellular communication, the first step of a signaling pathway in which a signaling molecule is detected by a receptor molecule on or in the cell.

**receptor-mediated endocytosis** (en′-dō-sī-tō′-sis) The movement of specific molecules into a cell by the infolding of vesicles containing proteins with receptor sites specific to the molecules being taken in; enables a cell to acquire bulk quantities of specific substances.

**receptor potential** An initial response of a receptor cell to a stimulus, consisting of a change in voltage across the receptor membrane proportional to the stimulus strength.

**receptor tyrosine kinase (RTK)** A receptor protein spanning the plasma membrane, the cytoplasmic (intracellular) part of which can catalyze the transfer of a phosphate group from ATP to a tyrosine on another protein. Receptor tyrosine kinases often respond to the binding of a signaling molecule by dimerizing and then phosphorylating a tyrosine on the cytoplasmic portion of the other receptor in the dimer.

**recessive allele** An allele whose phenotypic effect is not observed in a heterozygote.

**reciprocal altruism** Altruistic behavior between unrelated individuals, whereby the altruistic individual benefits in the future when the beneficiary reciprocates.

**recombinant chromosome** A chromosome created when crossing over combines DNA from two parents into a single chromosome.

**recombinant DNA molecule** A DNA molecule made *in vitro* with segments from different sources.

**recombinant type (recombinant)** An offspring whose phenotype differs from that of the true-breeding P generation parents; also refers to the phenotype itself.

**rectum** The terminal portion of the large intestine, where the feces are stored prior to elimination.

**red alga** A photosynthetic protist, named for its color, which results from a red pigment that masks the green of chlorophyll. Most red algae are multicellular and marine.

**redox reaction** (rē′-doks) A chemical reaction involving the complete or partial transfer of one or more electrons from one reactant to another; short for **red**uction-**ox**idation reaction.

**reducing agent** The electron donor in a redox reaction.

**reduction** The complete or partial addition of electrons to a substance involved in a redox reaction.

**reflex** An automatic reaction to a stimulus, mediated by the spinal cord or lower brain.

**refractory period** (rē-frakt′-ōr-ē) The short time immediately after an action potential in which the neuron cannot respond to another stimulus, owing to the inactivation of voltage-gated sodium channels.

**regulator** An animal for which mechanisms of homeostasis moderate internal changes in a particular variable in the face of external fluctuation of that variable.

**regulatory gene** A gene that codes for a protein, such as a repressor, that controls the transcription of another gene or group of genes.

**reinforcement** In evolutionary biology, a process in which natural selection strengthens prezygotic barriers to reproduction, thus reducing the chances of hybrid formation. Such a process is likely to occur only if hybrid offspring are less fit than members of the parent species.

**relative abundance** The proportional abundance of different species in a community.

**relative fitness** The contribution an individual makes to the gene pool of the next generation, relative to the contributions of other individuals in the population.

**renal cortex** The outer portion of the vertebrate kidney.

**renal medulla** The inner portion of the vertebrate kidney, beneath the renal cortex.

**renal pelvis** The funnel-shaped chamber that receives processed filtrate from the vertebrate kidney's collecting ducts and is drained by the ureter.

**renin-angiotensin-aldosterone system (RAAS)** A hormone cascade pathway that helps regulate blood pressure and blood volume.

**repetitive DNA** Nucleotide sequences, usually noncoding, that are present in many copies in a eukaryotic genome. The repeated units may be short and arranged tandemly (in series) or long and dispersed in the genome.

**replication fork** A Y-shaped region on a replicating DNA molecule where the parental strands are being unwound and new strands are being synthesized.

**repressor** A protein that inhibits gene transcription. In prokaryotes, repressors bind to the DNA in or near the promoter. In eukaryotes, repressors may bind to control elements within enhancers, to activators, or to other proteins in a way that blocks activators from binding to DNA.

**reproductive isolation** The existence of biological factors (barriers) that impede members of two species from producing viable, fertile offspring.

**reptile** A member of the clade of amniotes that includes tuataras, lizards, snakes, turtles, crocodilians, and birds.

**reservoir** In biogeochemical cycles, location of a chemical element, consisting of either organic or inorganic materials that are either available for direct use by organisms or unavailable as nutrients.

**residual volume** The amount of air that remains in the lungs after forceful exhalation.

**resource partitioning** The division of environmental resources by coexisting species such that the niche of each species differs by one or more significant factors from the niches of all coexisting species.

**respiratory pigment** A protein that transports oxygen in blood or hemolymph.

**response** (1) In cellular communication, the change in a specific cellular activity brought about by a transduced signal from outside the cell. (2) In feedback regulation, a physiological activity triggered by a change in a variable.

**resting potential** The membrane potential characteristic of a nonconducting excitable cell, with the inside of the cell more negative than the outside.

**restriction enzyme** An endonuclease (type of enzyme) that recognizes and cuts DNA molecules foreign to a bacterium (such as phage genomes). The enzyme cuts at specific nucleotide sequences (restriction sites).

**restriction fragment** A DNA segment that results from the cutting of DNA by a restriction enzyme.

**restriction site** A specific sequence on a DNA strand that is recognized and cut by a restriction enzyme.

**retina** (ret′-i-nuh) The innermost layer of the vertebrate eye, containing photoreceptor cells (rods and cones) and neurons; transmits images formed by the lens to the brain via the optic nerve.

**retinal** The light-absorbing pigment in rods and cones of the vertebrate eye.

**retrotransposon** (re′-trō-trans-pō′-zon) A transposable element that moves within a genome by means of an RNA intermediate, a transcript of the retrotransposon DNA.

**retrovirus** (re′-trō-vī′-rus) An RNA virus that replicates by transcribing its RNA into DNA and then inserting the DNA into a cellular chromosome; an important class of cancer-causing viruses.

**reverse transcriptase** (tran-skrip′-tās) An enzyme encoded by certain viruses (retroviruses) that uses RNA as a template for DNA synthesis.

**reverse transcriptase–polymerase chain reaction (RT-PCR)** A technique for determining expression of a particular gene. It uses reverse transcriptase and DNA polymerase to synthesize cDNA from all the mRNA in a sample and then subjects the cDNA to PCR amplification using primers specific for the gene of interest.

**rhizarians** (rī-za′-rē-uhns) One of the three major subgroups for which the SAR eukaryotic supergroup is named. Many species in this clade are amoebas characterized by threadlike pseudopodia.

**rhizobacterium** A soil bacterium whose population size is much enhanced in the rhizosphere, the soil region close to a plant's roots.

**rhizoid** (rī'-zoyd) A long, tubular single cell or filament of cells that anchors bryophytes to the ground. Unlike roots, rhizoids are not composed of tissues, lack specialized conducting cells, and do not play a primary role in water and mineral absorption.

**rhizosphere** The soil region close to plant roots and characterized by a high level of microbiological activity.

**rhodopsin** (rō-dop'-sin) A visual pigment consisting of retinal and opsin. Upon absorbing light, the retinal changes shape and dissociates from the opsin.

**ribonucleic acid (RNA)** (rī'-bō-nū-klā'-ik) A type of nucleic acid consisting of a polynucleotide made up of nucleotide monomers with a ribose sugar and the nitrogenous bases adenine (A), cytosine (C), guanine (G), and uracil (U); usually single-stranded; functions in protein synthesis, in gene regulation, and as the genome of some viruses.

**ribose** The sugar component of RNA nucleotides.

**ribosomal RNA (rRNA)** (rī'-buh-sō'-mul) RNA molecules that, together with proteins, make up ribosomes; the most abundant type of RNA.

**ribosome** (rī'-buh-sōm) A complex of rRNA and protein molecules that functions as a site of protein synthesis in the cytoplasm; consists of a large and a small subunit. In eukaryotic cells, each subunit is assembled in the nucleolus. *See also* nucleolus.

**ribozyme** (rī'-buh-zīm) An RNA molecule that functions as an enzyme, such as an intron that catalyzes its own removal during RNA splicing.

**RNA interference (RNAi)** A mechanism for silencing the expression of specific genes. In RNAi, double-stranded RNA molecules that match the sequence of a particular gene are processed into siRNAs that either block translation or trigger the degradation of the gene's messenger RNA. This happens naturally in some cells, and can be carried out in laboratory experiments as well.

**RNA polymerase** An enzyme that links ribonucleotides into a growing RNA chain during transcription, based on complementary binding to nucleotides on a DNA template strand.

**RNA processing** Modification of RNA primary transcripts, including splicing out of introns, joining together of exons, and alteration of the 5' and 3' ends.

**RNA sequencing (RNA-seq)** (RNA-sēk) A method of analyzing large sets of RNAs that involves making cDNAs and sequencing them.

**RNA splicing** After synthesis of a eukaryotic primary RNA transcript, the removal of portions of the transcript (introns) that will not be included in the mRNA and the joining together of the remaining portions (exons).

**rod** A rodlike cell in the retina of the vertebrate eye, sensitive to low light intensity.

**root** An organ in vascular plants that anchors the plant and enables it to absorb water and minerals from the soil.

**root cap** A cone of cells at the tip of a plant root that protects the apical meristem.

**root hair** A tiny extension of a root epidermal cell, growing just behind the root tip and increasing surface area for absorption of water and minerals.

**root pressure** Pressure exerted in the roots of plants as the result of osmosis, causing exudation from cut stems and guttation of water from leaves.

**root system** All of a plant's roots, which anchor it in the soil, absorb and transport minerals and water, and store food.

**rooted** Describing a phylogenetic tree that contains a branch point (often, the one farthest to the left) representing the most recent common ancestor of all taxa in the tree.

**rough ER** That portion of the endoplasmic reticulum with ribosomes attached.

**round window** In the mammalian ear, the point of contact where vibrations of the stapes create a traveling series of pressure waves in the fluid of the cochlea.

**R plasmid** A bacterial plasmid carrying genes that confer resistance to certain antibiotics.

*r*-**selection** Selection for life history traits that maximize reproductive success in uncrowded environments; also called density-independent selection.

**rubisco** (rū-bis'-kō) Ribulose bisphosphate (RuBP) carboxylase-oxygenase, the enzyme that normally catalyzes the first step of the Calvin cycle (the addition of $CO_2$ to RuBP). When excess $O_2$ is present or $CO_2$ levels are low, rubisco can bind oxygen, resulting in photorespiration.

**ruminant** (rūh'-muh-nent) A cud-chewing animal, such as a cow or sheep, with multiple stomach compartments specialized for an herbivorous diet.

**salicylic acid** (sal'-i-sil'-ik) A signaling molecule in plants that may be partially responsible for activating systemic acquired resistance to pathogens.

**salivary gland** A gland associated with the oral cavity that secretes substances that lubricate food and begin the process of chemical digestion.

**salt** A compound resulting from the formation of an ionic bond; also called an ionic compound.

**saltatory conduction** (sol'-tuh-tōr'-ē) Rapid transmission of a nerve impulse along an axon, resulting from the action potential jumping from one node of Ranvier to another, skipping the myelin-sheathed regions of membrane.

**SAR** One of four supergroups of eukaryotes proposed in a current hypothesis of the evolutionary history of eukaryotes. This supergroup contains a large, extremely diverse collection of protists from three major subgroups: stramenopiles, alveolates, and rhizarians. *See also* Excavata, Archaeplastida, and Unikonta.

**sarcomere** (sar'-kō-mēr) The fundamental, repeating unit of striated muscle, delimited by the Z lines.

**sarcoplasmic reticulum (SR)** (sar'-kō-plaz'-mik ruh-tik'-yū-lum) A specialized endoplasmic reticulum that regulates the calcium concentration in the cytosol of muscle cells.

**saturated fatty acid** A fatty acid in which all carbons in the hydrocarbon tail are connected by single bonds, thus maximizing the number of hydrogen atoms that are attached to the carbon skeleton.

**savanna** A tropical grassland biome with scattered individual trees and large herbivores and maintained by occasional fires and drought.

**scaffolding protein** A type of large relay protein to which several other relay proteins are simultaneously attached, increasing the efficiency of signal transduction.

**scanning electron microscope (SEM)** A microscope that uses an electron beam to scan the surface of a sample, coated with metal atoms, to study details of its topography.

**scatter plot** A graph in which each piece of data is represented by a point. A scatter plot is used when the data for all variables are numerical and continuous.

**schizophrenia** (skit'-suh-frē'-nē-uh) A severe mental disturbance characterized by psychotic episodes in which patients have a distorted perception of reality.

**Schwann cell** A type of glial cell that forms insulating myelin sheaths around the axons of neurons in the peripheral nervous system.

**science** An approach to understanding the natural world.

**scion** (sī'-un) The twig grafted onto the stock when making a graft.

**sclereid** (sklār'-ē-id) A short, irregular sclerenchyma cell in nutshells and seed coats. Sclereids are scattered throughout the parenchyma of some plants.

**sclerenchyma cell** (skluh-ren'-kim-uh) A rigid, supportive plant cell type usually lacking a protoplast and possessing thick secondary walls strengthened by lignin at maturity.

**scrotum** A pouch of skin outside the abdomen that houses the testes; functions in maintaining the testes at the lower temperature required for spermatogenesis.

**second law of thermodynamics** The principle stating that every energy transfer or transformation increases the entropy of the universe. Usable forms of energy are at least partly converted to heat.

**second messenger** A small, nonprotein, water-soluble molecule or ion, such as a calcium ion ($Ca^{2+}$) or cyclic AMP, that relays a signal to a cell's interior in response to a signaling molecule bound by a signal receptor protein.

**secondary cell wall** In plant cells, a strong and durable matrix that is often deposited in several laminated layers around the plasma membrane and provides protection and support.

**secondary consumer** A carnivore that eats herbivores.

**secondary endosymbiosis** A process in eukaryotic evolution in which a heterotrophic eukaryotic cell engulfed a photosynthetic eukaryotic cell, which survived in a symbiotic relationship inside the heterotrophic cell.

**secondary growth** Growth produced by lateral meristems, thickening the roots and shoots of woody plants.

**secondary immune response** The adaptive immune response elicited on second or subsequent exposures to a particular antigen. The secondary immune response is more rapid, of greater magnitude, and of longer duration than the primary immune response.

**secondary oocyte** (ō′-uh-sīt) An oocyte that has completed meiosis I.

**secondary production** The amount of chemical energy in consumers' food that is converted to their own new biomass during a given time period.

**secondary structure** Regions of repetitive coiling or folding of the polypeptide backbone of a protein due to hydrogen bonding between constituents of the backbone (not the side chains).

**secondary succession** A type of succession that occurs where an existing community has been cleared by some disturbance that leaves the soil or substrate intact.

**secretion** (1) The discharge of molecules synthesized by a cell. (2) The active transport of wastes and certain other solutes from the body fluid into the filtrate in an excretory system.

**seed** An adaptation of some terrestrial plants consisting of an embryo packaged along with a store of food within a protective coat.

**seed coat** A tough outer covering of a seed, formed from the outer coat of an ovule. In a flowering plant, the seed coat encloses and protects the embryo and endosperm.

**seedless vascular plant** An informal name for a plant that has vascular tissue but lacks seeds. Seedless vascular plants form a paraphyletic group that includes the phyla Lycophyta (club mosses and their relatives) and Monilophyta (ferns and their relatives).

**selective permeability** A property of biological membranes that allows them to regulate the passage of substances across them.

**self-incompatibility** The ability of a seed plant to reject its own pollen and sometimes the pollen of closely related individuals.

**semelparity** (seh′-mel-pār′-i-tē) Reproduction in which an organism produces all of its offspring in a single event; also called big-bang reproduction.

**semen** (sē′-mun) The fluid that is ejaculated by the male during orgasm; contains sperm and secretions from several glands of the male reproductive tract.

**semicircular canals** A three-part chamber of the inner ear that functions in maintaining equilibrium.

**semiconservative model** Type of DNA replication in which the replicated double helix consists of one old strand, derived from the parental molecule, and one newly made strand.

**semilunar valve** A valve located at each exit of the heart, where the aorta leaves the left ventricle and the pulmonary artery leaves the right ventricle.

**seminal vesicle** (sem′-i-nul ves′-i-kul) A gland in males that secretes a fluid component of semen that lubricates and nourishes sperm.

**seminiferous tubule** (sem′-i-nif′-er-us) A highly coiled tube in the testis in which sperm are produced.

**senescence** (se-nes′-ens) The growth phase in a plant or plant part (as a leaf) from full maturity to death.

**sensitive period** A limited phase in an animal's development when learning of particular behaviors can take place; also called a critical period.

**sensor** In homeostasis, a receptor that detects a stimulus.

**sensory adaptation** The tendency of sensory neurons to become less sensitive when they are stimulated repeatedly.

**sensory neuron** A nerve cell that receives information from the internal or external environment and transmits signals to the central nervous system.

**sensory reception** The detection of a stimulus by sensory cells.

**sensory receptor** A specialized structure or cell that responds to a stimulus from an animal's internal or external environment.

**sensory transduction** The conversion of stimulus energy to a change in the membrane potential of a sensory receptor cell.

**sepal** (sē′-pul) A modified leaf in angiosperms that helps enclose and protect a flower bud before it opens.

**septum** (plural, **septa**) One of the cross-walls that divide a fungal hypha into cells. Septa generally have pores large enough to allow ribosomes, mitochondria, and even nuclei to flow from cell to cell.

**serial endosymbiosis** A hypothesis for the origin of eukaryotes consisting of a sequence of endosymbiotic events in which mitochondria, chloroplasts, and perhaps other cellular structures were derived from small prokaryotes that had been engulfed by larger cells.

**set point** In homeostasis in animals, a value maintained for a particular variable, such as body temperature or solute concentration.

**seta** (sē′-tuh) (plural, **setae**) The elongated stalk of a bryophyte sporophyte.

**sex chromosome** A chromosome responsible for determining the sex of an individual.

**sex-linked gene** A gene located on either sex chromosome. Most sex-linked genes are on the X chromosome and show distinctive patterns of inheritance; there are very few genes on the Y chromosome.

**sexual dimorphism** (dī-mōr′-fizm) Differences between the secondary sex characteristics of males and females of the same species.

**sexual reproduction** Reproduction arising from fusion of two gametes.

**sexual selection** A process in which individuals with certain inherited characteristics are more likely than other individuals of the same sex to obtain mates.

**Shannon diversity** An index of community diversity symbolized by $H$ and represented by the equation $H = -(p_A \ln p_A + p_B \ln p_B + p_C \ln p_C + \cdots)$, where A, B, C … are species, $p$ is the relative abundance of each species, and ln is the natural logarithm.

**shared ancestral character** A character, shared by members of a particular clade, that originated in an ancestor that is not a member of that clade.

**shared derived character** An evolutionary novelty that is unique to a particular clade.

**shoot system** The aerial portion of a plant body, consisting of stems, leaves, and (in angiosperms) flowers.

**short tandem repeat (STR)** Simple sequence DNA containing multiple tandemly repeated units of two to five nucleotides. Variations in STRs act as genetic markers in STR analysis, used to prepare genetic profiles.

**short-day plant** A plant that flowers (usually in late summer, fall, or winter) only when the light period is shorter than a critical length.

**short-term memory** The ability to hold information, anticipations, or goals for a time and then release them if they become irrelevant.

**sickle-cell disease** A recessively inherited human blood disorder in which a single nucleotide change in the α-globin gene causes hemoglobin to aggregate, changing red blood cell shape and causing multiple symptoms in afflicted individuals.

**sieve plate** An end wall in a sieve-tube element, which facilitates the flow of phloem sap in angiosperm sieve tubes.

**sieve-tube element** A living cell that conducts sugars and other organic nutrients in the phloem of angiosperms; also called a sieve-tube member. Connected end to end, they form sieve tubes.

**sign stimulus** An external sensory cue that triggers a fixed action pattern by an animal.

**signal** In animal behavior, transmission of a stimulus from one animal to another. The term is also used in the context of communication in other kinds of organisms and in cell-to-cell communication in all multicellular organisms.

**signal peptide** A sequence of about 20 amino acids at or near the leading (amino) end of a polypeptide that targets it to the endoplasmic reticulum or other organelles in a eukaryotic cell.

**signal-recognition particle (SRP)** A protein-RNA complex that recognizes a signal peptide as it emerges from a ribosome and helps direct the ribosome to the endoplasmic reticulum (ER) by binding to a receptor protein on the ER.

**signal transduction** The linkage of a mechanical, chemical, or electromagnetic stimulus to a specific cellular response.

**signal transduction pathway** A series of steps linking a mechanical, chemical, or electrical stimulus to a specific cellular response.

**silent mutation** A nucleotide-pair substitution that has no observable effect on the phenotype; for example, within a gene, a mutation that results in a codon that codes for the same amino acid.

**simple fruit** A fruit derived from a single carpel or several fused carpels.

**simple sequence DNA** A DNA sequence that contains many copies of tandemly repeated short sequences.

**single bond** A single covalent bond; the sharing of a pair of valence electrons by two atoms.

**single circulation** A circulatory system consisting of a single pump and circuit, in which blood passes from the sites of gas exchange to the rest of the body before returning to the heart.

**single-lens eye** The camera-like eye found in some jellies, polychaete worms, spiders, and many molluscs.

**single nucleotide polymorphism (SNP)** (snip) A single base-pair site in a genome where nucleotide variation is found in at least 1% of the population.

**single-strand binding protein** A protein that binds to the unpaired DNA strands during DNA replication, stabilizing them and holding them apart while they serve as templates for the synthesis of complementary strands of DNA.

**sinoatrial (SA) node** (sī'-nō-ā'-trē-uhl) A region in the right atrium of the heart that sets the rate and timing at which all cardiac muscle cells contract; the pacemaker.

**sister chromatids** Two copies of a duplicated chromosome attached to each other by proteins at the centromere and, sometimes, along the arms. While joined, two sister chromatids make up one chromosome. Chromatids are eventually separated during mitosis or meiosis II.

**sister taxa** Groups of organisms that share an immediate common ancestor and hence are each other's closest relatives.

**skeletal muscle** A type of striated muscle that is generally responsible for the voluntary movements of the body.

**sliding-filament model** The idea that muscle contraction is based on the movement of thin (actin) filaments along thick (myosin) filaments, shortening the sarcomere, the basic unit of muscle organization.

**slow-twitch fiber** A muscle fiber that can sustain long contractions.

**small interfering RNA (siRNA)** One of multiple small, single-stranded RNA molecules generated by cellular machinery from a long, linear, double-stranded RNA molecule. The siRNA associates with one or more proteins in a complex that can degrade or prevent translation of an mRNA with a complementary sequence.

**small intestine** The longest section of the alimentary canal, so named because of its small diameter compared with that of the large intestine; the principal site of the enzymatic hydrolysis of food macromolecules and the absorption of nutrients.

**smooth ER** That portion of the endoplasmic reticulum that is free of ribosomes.

**smooth muscle** A type of muscle lacking the striations of skeletal and cardiac muscle because of the uniform distribution of myosin filaments in the cells; responsible for involuntary body activities.

**social learning** Modification of behavior through the observation of other individuals.

**sociobiology** The study of social behavior based on evolutionary theory.

**sodium-potassium pump** A transport protein in the plasma membrane of animal cells that actively transports sodium out of the cell and potassium into the cell.

**soil horizon** A soil layer with physical characteristics that differ from those of the layers above or beneath.

**solute** (sol'-yūt) A substance that is dissolved in a solution.

**solute potential (ψS)** A component of water potential that is proportional to the molarity of a solution and that measures the effect of solutes on the direction of water movement; also called osmotic potential, it can be either zero or negative.

**solution** A liquid that is a homogeneous mixture of two or more substances.

**solvent** The dissolving agent of a solution. Water is the most versatile solvent known.

**somatic cell** (sō-mat'-ik) Any cell in a multicellular organism except a sperm or egg or their precursors.

**somite** One of a series of blocks of mesoderm that exist in pairs just lateral to the notochord in a vertebrate embryo.

**soredium** (suh-rē'-dē-um) (plural, **soredia**) In lichens, a small cluster of fungal hyphae with embedded algae.

**sorus** (plural, **sori**) A cluster of sporangia on a fern sporophyll. Sori may be arranged in various patterns, such as parallel lines or dots, which are useful in fern identification.

**spatial learning** The establishment of a memory that reflects the environment's spatial structure.

**speciation** (spē'-sē-ā'-shun) An evolutionary process in which one species splits into two or more species.

**species** (spē'-sēz) A population or group of populations whose members have the potential to interbreed in nature and produce viable, fertile offspring but do not produce viable, fertile offspring with members of other such groups.

**species-area curve** (spē'-sēz) The biodiversity pattern that shows that the larger the geographic area of a community is, the more species it has.

**species diversity** (spē'-sēz) The number and relative abundance of species in a biological community.

**species richness** (spē'-sēz) The number of species in a biological community.

**specific heat** The amount of heat that must be absorbed or lost for 1 g of a substance to change its temperature by 1°C.

**spectrophotometer** An instrument that measures the proportions of light of different wavelengths absorbed and transmitted by a pigment solution.

**sperm** The male gamete.

**spermatheca** (sper'-muh-thē'-kuh) (plural, **spermathecae**) In many insects, a sac in the female reproductive system where sperm are stored.

**spermatogenesis** (sper-ma'-tō-gen'-uh-sis) The continuous and prolific production of mature sperm in the testis.

**spermatogonium** (sper-ma'-tō-gō'-nē-um) (plural, **spermatogonia**) A cell that divides mitotically to form spermatocytes.

**S phase** The synthesis phase of the cell cycle; the portion of interphase during which DNA is replicated.

**sphincter** (sfink'-ter) A ringlike band of muscle fibers that controls the size of an opening in the body, such as the passage between the esophagus and the stomach.

**spiral cleavage** A type of embryonic development in protostomes in which the planes of cell division that transform the zygote into a ball of cells are diagonal to the vertical axis of the embryo. As a result, the cells of each tier sit in the grooves between cells of adjacent tiers.

**spliceosome** (splī'-sō-sōm) A large complex made up of proteins and RNA molecules that splices RNA by interacting with the ends of an RNA intron, releasing the intron and joining the two adjacent exons.

**spongocoel** (spon'-jō-sēl) The central cavity of a sponge.

**spontaneous process** A process that occurs without an overall input of energy; a process that is energetically favorable.

**sporangium** (spōr-an'-jē-um) (plural, **sporangia**) A multicellular organ in fungi and plants in which meiosis occurs and haploid cells develop.

**spore** (1) In the life cycle of a plant or alga undergoing alternation of generations, a haploid cell produced in the sporophyte by meiosis. A spore can divide by mitosis to develop into a multicellular haploid individual, the gametophyte, without fusing with another cell. (2) In fungi, a haploid cell, produced either sexually or asexually, that produces a mycelium after germination.

**sporocyte** (spō'-ruh-sīt) A diploid cell within a sporangium that undergoes meiosis and generates haploid spores; also called a spore mother cell.

**sporophyll** (spō'-ruh-fil) A modified leaf that bears sporangia and hence is specialized for reproduction.

**sporophyte** (spō-ruh-fīt·) In organisms (plants and some algae) that have alternation of generations, the multicellular diploid form that results from the union of gametes. Meiosis in the sporophyte produces haploid spores that develop into gametophytes.

**sporopollenin** (spōr-uh-pol'-eh-nin) A durable polymer that covers exposed zygotes of charophyte algae and forms the walls of plant spores, preventing them from drying out.

**stability** In evolutionary biology, a term referring to a hybrid zone in which hybrids continue to be produced; this causes the hybrid zone to be "stable" in the sense of persisting over time.

**stabilizing selection** Natural selection in which intermediate phenotypes survive or reproduce more successfully than do extreme phenotypes.

**stamen** (stā'-men) The pollen-producing reproductive organ of a flower, consisting of an anther and a filament.

**standard deviation** A measure of the variation found in a set of data points.

**standard metabolic rate (SMR)** Metabolic rate of a resting, fasting, and nonstressed ectotherm at a particular temperature.

**starch** A storage polysaccharide in plants, consisting entirely of glucose monomers joined by glycosidic linkages.

**start point** In transcription, the nucleotide position on the promoter where RNA polymerase begins synthesis of RNA.

**statocyst** (stat'-uh-sist') A type of mechanoreceptor that functions in equilibrium in invertebrates by use of statoliths, which stimulate hair cells in relation to gravity.

**statolith** (stat'-uh-lith') (1) In plants, a specialized plastid that contains dense starch grains and may play a role in detecting gravity. (2) In invertebrates, a dense particle that settles in response to gravity and is found in sensory organs that function in equilibrium.

**stele** (stēl) The vascular tissue of a stem or root.

**stem** A vascular plant organ consisting of an alternating system of nodes and internodes that support the leaves and reproductive structures.

**stem cell** Any relatively unspecialized cell that can produce, during a single division, two identical daughter cells or two more specialized daughter cells that can undergo further differentiation, or one cell of each type.

**steroid** A type of lipid characterized by a carbon skeleton consisting of four fused rings with various chemical groups attached.

**sticky end** A single-stranded end of a double-stranded restriction fragment.

**stigma** (plural, **stigmata**) The sticky part of a flower's carpel, which receives pollen grains.

**stimulus** In feedback regulation, a fluctuation in a variable that triggers a response.

**stipe** A stemlike structure of a seaweed.

**stock** The plant that provides the root system when making a graft.

**stoma** (stō'-muh) (plural, **stomata**) A microscopic pore surrounded by guard cells in the epidermis of leaves and stems that allows gas exchange between the environment and the interior of the plant.

**stomach** An organ of the digestive system that stores food and performs preliminary steps of digestion.

**Stramenopiles** (strah'-men-ō'-pē-lēs) One of the three major subgroups for which the SAR eukaryotic supergroup is named. This clade arose by secondary endosymbiosis and includes diatoms and brown algae.

**stratum** (strah'-tum) (plural, **strata**) A rock layer formed when new layers of sediment cover older ones and compress them.

**strigolactone** Any of a class of plant hormones that inhibit shoot branching, trigger the germination of parasitic plant seeds, and stimulate the association of plant roots with mycorrhizal fungi.

**strobilus** (strō-bī'-lus) (plural, **strobili**) The technical term for a cluster of sporophylls known commonly as a cone, found in most gymnosperms and some seedless vascular plants.

**stroke** The death of nervous tissue in the brain, usually resulting from rupture or blockage of arteries in the head.

**stroke volume** The volume of blood pumped by a heart ventricle in a single contraction.

**stroma** (strō'-muh) The dense fluid within the chloroplast surrounding the thylakoid membrane and containing ribosomes and DNA; involved in the synthesis of organic molecules from carbon dioxide and water.

**stromatolite** Layered rock that results from the activities of prokaryotes that bind thin films of sediment together.

**structural isomer** One of two or more compounds that have the same molecular formula but differ in the covalent arrangements of their atoms.

**style** The stalk of a flower's carpel, with the ovary at the base and the stigma at the top.

**substrate** The reactant on which an enzyme works.

**substrate feeder** An animal that lives in or on its food source, eating its way through the food.

**substrate-level phosphorylation** The enzyme-catalyzed formation of ATP by direct transfer of a phosphate group to ADP from an intermediate substrate in catabolism.

**sugar sink** A plant organ that is a net consumer or storer of sugar. Growing roots, shoot tips, stems, and fruits are examples of sugar sinks supplied by phloem.

**sugar source** A plant organ in which sugar is being produced by either photosynthesis or the breakdown of starch. Mature leaves are the primary sugar sources of plants.

**sulfhydryl group** A chemical group consisting of a sulfur atom bonded to a hydrogen atom.

**summation** A phenomenon of neural integration in which the membrane potential of the postsynaptic cell is determined by the combined effect of EPSPs or IPSPs produced in rapid succession at one synapse or simultaneously at different synapses.

**suprachiasmatic nucleus (SCN)** (sūp'-ruh-kē'-as-ma-tik) A group of neurons in the hypothalamus of mammals that functions as a biological clock.

**surface tension** A measure of how difficult it is to stretch or break the surface of a liquid. Water has a high surface tension because of the hydrogen bonding of surface molecules.

**surfactant** A substance secreted by alveoli that decreases surface tension in the fluid that coats the alveoli.

**survivorship curve** A plot of the number of members of a cohort that are still alive at each age; one way to represent age-specific mortality.

**suspension feeder** An animal that feeds by removing suspended food particles from the surrounding medium by a capture, trapping, or filtration mechanism.

**sustainable agriculture** Long-term productive farming methods that are environmentally safe.

**sustainable development** Development that meets the needs of people today without limiting the ability of future generations to meet their needs.

**swim bladder** In aquatic osteichthyans, an air sac that enables the animal to control its buoyancy in the water.

**symbiont** (sim'-bē-ont) The smaller participant in a symbiotic relationship, living in or on the host.

**symbiosis** An ecological relationship between organisms of two different species that live together in direct and intimate contact.

**sympathetic division** One of three divisions of the autonomic nervous system; generally increases energy expenditure and prepares the body for action.

**sympatric speciation** (sim-pat'-rik) The formation of new species in populations that live in the same geographic area.

**symplast** In plants, the continuum of cytoplasm connected by plasmodesmata between cells.

**synapse** (sin'-aps) The junction where a neuron communicates with another cell across a narrow gap via a neurotransmitter or an electrical coupling.

**synapsid** (si-nap'-sid) A member of an amniote clade distinguished by a single hole on each side of the skull. Synapsids include the mammals.

**synapsis** (si-nap'-sis) The pairing and physical connection of one duplicated chromosome to its homolog during prophase I of meiosis.

**synaptonemal** (si-nap'-tuh-nē'-muhl) **complex** A zipper-like structure composed of proteins, which connects a chromosome to its homolog tightly along their lengths during part of prophase I of meiosis.

**systematics** A scientific discipline focused on classifying organisms and determining their evolutionary relationships.

**systemic acquired resistance** A defensive response in infected plants that helps protect healthy tissue from pathogenic invasion.

**systemic circuit** The branch of the circulatory system that supplies oxygenated blood to and carries deoxygenated blood away from organs and tissues throughout the body.

**systems biology** An approach to studying biology that aims to model the dynamic behavior of whole biological systems based on a study of the interactions among the system's parts.

**systole** (sis'-tō-lē) The stage of the cardiac cycle in which a heart chamber contracts and pumps blood.

**systolic pressure** Blood pressure in the arteries during contraction of the ventricles.

**taproot** A main vertical root that develops from an embryonic root and gives rise to lateral (branch) roots.

**tastant** Any chemical that stimulates the sensory receptors in a taste bud.

**taste bud** A collection of modified epithelial cells on the tongue or in the mouth that are receptors for taste in mammals.

**TATA box** A DNA sequence in eukaryotic promoters crucial in forming the transcription initiation complex.

**taxis** (tak'-sis) An oriented movement toward or away from a stimulus.

**taxon** (plural, **taxa**) A named taxonomic unit at any given level of classification.

**taxonomy** (tak-son'-uh-mē) A scientific discipline concerned with naming and classifying the diverse forms of life.

**Tay-Sachs disease** A human genetic disease caused by a recessive allele for a dysfunctional enzyme, leading to accumulation of certain lipids in the brain. Seizures, blindness, and degeneration of motor and mental performance usually become manifest a few months after birth, followed by death within a few years.

**T cells** The class of lymphocytes that mature in the thymus; they include both effector cells for the cell-mediated immune response and helper cells required for both branches of adaptive immunity.

**technology** The application of scientific knowledge for a specific purpose, often involving industry or commerce but also including uses in basic research.

**telomere** (tel'-uh-mēr) The tandemly repetitive DNA at the end of a eukaryotic chromosome's DNA molecule. Telomeres protect the organism's genes from being eroded during successive rounds of replication. *See also* repetitive DNA.

**telophase** The fifth and final stage of mitosis, in which daughter nuclei are forming and cytokinesis has typically begun.

**temperate broadleaf forest** A biome located throughout midlatitude regions where there is sufficient moisture to support the growth of large, broadleaf deciduous trees.

**temperate grassland** A terrestrial biome that exists at midlatitude regions and is dominated by grasses and forbs.

**temperate phage** A phage that is capable of replicating by either a lytic or lysogenic cycle.

**temperature** A measure in degrees of the average kinetic energy (thermal energy) of the atoms and molecules in a body of matter.

**template strand** The DNA strand that provides the pattern, or template, for ordering, by complementary base pairing, the sequence of nucleotides in an RNA transcript.

**tendon** A fibrous connective tissue that attaches muscle to bone.

**terminator** In bacteria, a sequence of nucleotides in DNA that marks the end of a gene and signals RNA polymerase to release the newly made RNA molecule and detach from the DNA.

**territoriality** A behavior in which an animal defends a bounded physical space against encroachment by other individuals, usually of its own species.

**tertiary consumer** (ter'-shē-ār'-ē) A carnivore that eats other carnivores.

**tertiary structure** (ter'-shē-ār'-ē) The overall shape of a protein molecule due to interactions of amino acid side chains, including hydrophobic interactions, ionic bonds, hydrogen bonds, and disulfide bridges.

**test** In foram protists, a porous shell that consists of a single piece of organic material hardened with calcium carbonate.

**testcross** Breeding an organism of unknown genotype with a homozygous recessive individual to determine the unknown genotype. The ratio of phenotypes in the offspring reveals the unknown genotype.

**testis** (plural, **testes**) The male reproductive organ, or gonad, in which sperm and reproductive hormones are produced.

**testosterone** A steroid hormone required for development of the male reproductive system, spermatogenesis, and male secondary sex characteristics; the major androgen in mammals.

**tetanus** (tet'-uh-nus) The maximal, sustained contraction of a skeletal muscle, caused by a very high frequency of action potentials elicited by continual stimulation.

**tetrapod** A vertebrate clade whose members have limbs with digits. Tetrapods include mammals, amphibians, and birds and other reptiles.

**thalamus** (thal'-uh-mus) An integrating center of the vertebrate forebrain. Neurons with cell bodies in the thalamus relay neural input to specific areas in the cerebral cortex and regulate what information goes to the cerebral cortex.

**theory** An explanation that is broader in scope than a hypothesis, generates new hypotheses, and is supported by a large body of evidence.

**thermal energy** Kinetic energy due to the random motion of atoms and molecules; energy in its most random form. *See also* heat.

**thermocline** A narrow stratum of abrupt temperature change in the ocean and in many temperate-zone lakes.

**thermodynamics** (ther'-mō-dī-nam'-iks) The study of energy transformations that occur in a collection of matter. *See also* first law of thermodynamics and second law of thermodynamics.

**thermophile** *See* extreme thermophile.

**thermoreceptor** A receptor stimulated by either heat or cold.

**thermoregulation** The maintenance of internal body temperature within a tolerable range.

**theropod** A member of a group of dinosaurs that were bipedal carnivores.

**thick filament** A filament composed of staggered arrays of myosin molecules; a component of myofibrils in muscle fibers.

**thigmomorphogenesis** (thig'-mō-mor'-phō-gen'-uh-sis) A response in plants to chronic mechanical stimulation, resulting from increased ethylene production. An example is thickening stems in response to strong winds.

**thigmotropism** (thig-mō'-truh-pizm) A directional growth of a plant in response to touch.

**thin filament** A filament consisting of two strands of actin and two strands of regulatory protein coiled around one another; a component of myofibrils in muscle fibers.

**threatened species** A species that is considered likely to become endangered in the foreseeable future.

**threshold** The potential that an excitable cell membrane must reach for an action potential to be initiated.

**thrombus** A fibrin-containing clot that forms in a blood vessel and blocks the flow of blood.

**thylakoid** (thī'-luh-koyd) A flattened, membranous sac inside a chloroplast. Thylakoids often exist in stacks called grana that are interconnected; their membranes contain molecular "machinery" used to convert light energy to chemical energy.

**thymus** (thī'-mus) A small organ in the thoracic cavity of vertebrates where maturation of T cells is completed.

**thyroid gland** An endocrine gland, located on the ventral surface of the trachea, that secretes two iodine-containing hormones, triiodothyronine ($T_3$) and thyroxine ($T_4$), as well as calcitonin.

**thyroid hormone** Either of two iodine-containing hormones (triiodothyronine and thyroxine) that are secreted by the thyroid gland and that help regulate metabolism, development, and maturation in vertebrates.

**thyroxine ($T_4$)** One of two iodine-containing hormones that are secreted by the thyroid gland and that help regulate metabolism, development, and maturation in vertebrates.

**tidal volume** The volume of air a mammal inhales and exhales with each breath.

**tight junction** A type of intercellular junction between animal cells that prevents the leakage of material through the space between cells.

**tissue** An integrated group of cells with a common structure, function, or both.

**tissue system** One or more tissues organized into a functional unit connecting the organs of a plant.

**Toll-like receptor (TLR)** A membrane receptor on a phagocytic white blood cell that recognizes fragments of molecules common to a set of pathogens.

**tonicity** The ability of a solution surrounding a cell to cause that cell to gain or lose water.

**top-down model** A model of community organization in which predation influences community organization by controlling herbivore numbers, which in turn control plant or phytoplankton numbers, which in turn control nutrient levels; also called the trophic cascade model.

**topoisomerase** A protein that breaks, swivels, and rejoins DNA strands. During DNA replication, topoisomerase helps to relieve strain in the double helix ahead of the replication fork.

**topsoil** A mixture of particles derived from rock, living organisms, and decaying organic material (humus).

**torpor** A physiological state in which activity is low and metabolism decreases.

**totipotent** (tō'-tuh-pōt'-ent) Describing a cell that can give rise to all parts of the embryo and adult, as well as extraembryonic membranes in species that have them.

**trace element** An element indispensable for life but required in extremely minute amounts.

**trachea** (trā'-kē-uh) The portion of the respiratory tract that passes from the larynx to the bronchi; also called the windpipe.

**tracheal system** In insects, a system of branched, air-filled tubes that extends throughout the body and carries oxygen directly to cells.

**tracheid** (trā'-kē-id) A long, tapered water-conducting cell found in the xylem of nearly all vascular plants. Functioning tracheids are no longer living.

**trait** One of two or more detectable variants in a genetic character.

*trans* **fat** An unsaturated fat, formed artificially during hydrogenation of oils, containing one or more *trans* double bonds.

**transcription** The synthesis of RNA using a DNA template.

**transcription factor** A regulatory protein that binds to DNA and affects transcription of specific genes.

**transcription initiation complex** The completed assembly of transcription factors and RNA polymerase bound to a promoter.

**transcription unit** A region of DNA that is transcribed into an RNA molecule.

**transduction** A process in which phages (viruses) carry bacterial DNA from one bacterial cell to another. When these two cells are members of different species, transduction results in horizontal gene transfer. *See also* signal transduction.

**transfer RNA (tRNA)** An RNA molecule that functions as a translator between nucleic acid and protein languages by picking up a specific amino acid and carrying it to the ribosome, where the tRNA recognizes the appropriate codon in the mRNA.

**transformation** (1) The process by which a cell in culture acquires the ability to divide indefinitely, similar to the division of cancer cells. (2) A change in genotype and phenotype due to the assimilation of external DNA by a cell. When the external DNA is from a member of a different species, transformation results in horizontal gene transfer.

**transgenic** Pertaining to an organism whose genome contains DNA introduced from another organism of the same or a different species.

**translation** The synthesis of a polypeptide using the genetic information encoded in an mRNA molecule. There is a change of "language" from nucleotides to amino acids.

**translocation** (1) An aberration in chromosome structure resulting from attachment of a chromosomal fragment to a nonhomologous chromosome. (2) During protein synthesis, the third stage in the elongation cycle, when the RNA carrying the growing polypeptide moves from the A site to the P site on the ribosome. (3) The transport of organic nutrients in the phloem of vascular plants.

**transmission electron microscope (TEM)** A microscope that passes an electron beam through very thin sections stained with metal atoms and is primarily used to study the internal structure of cells.

**transpiration** The evaporative loss of water from a plant.

**transport epithelium** One or more layers of specialized epithelial cells that carry out and regulate solute movement.

**transport protein** A transmembrane protein that helps a certain substance or class of closely related substances to cross the membrane.

**transport vesicle** A small membranous sac in a eukaryotic cell's cytoplasm carrying molecules produced by the cell.

**transposable element** A segment of DNA that can move within the genome of a cell by means of a DNA or RNA intermediate; also called a transposable genetic element.

**transposon** A transposable element that moves within a genome by means of a DNA intermediate.

**transverse (T) tubule** An infolding of the plasma membrane of skeletal muscle cells.

**triacylglycerol** (trī-as′-ul-glis′-uh-rol) A lipid consisting of three fatty acids linked to one glycerol molecule; also called a fat or triglyceride.

**trichome** An epidermal cell that is a highly specialized, often hairlike outgrowth on a plant shoot.

**triple response** A plant growth maneuver in response to mechanical stress, involving slowing of stem elongation, thickening of the stem, and a curvature that causes the stem to start growing horizontally.

**triplet code** A genetic information system in which a series of three-nucleotide-long words specifies a sequence of amino acids for a polypeptide chain.

**triploblastic** Possessing three germ layers: the endoderm, mesoderm, and ectoderm. All bilaterian animals are triploblastic.

**trisomic** Referring to a diploid cell that has three copies of a particular chromosome instead of the normal two.

**trochophore larva** (trō′-kuh-fōr) Distinctive larval stage observed in some lophotrochozoan animals, including some annelids and molluscs.

**trophic efficiency** The percentage of production transferred from one trophic level to the next higher trophic level.

**trophic structure** The different feeding relationships in an ecosystem, which determine the route of energy flow and the pattern of chemical cycling.

**trophoblast** The outer epithelium of a mammalian blastocyst. It forms the fetal part of the placenta, supporting embryonic development but not forming part of the embryo proper.

**tropical dry forest** A terrestrial biome characterized by relatively high temperatures and precipitation overall but with a pronounced dry season.

**tropical rain forest** A terrestrial biome characterized by relatively high precipitation and temperatures year-round.

**tropics** Latitudes between 23.5° north and south.

**tropism** A growth response that results in the curvature of whole plant organs toward or away from stimuli due to differential rates of cell elongation.

**tropomyosin** The regulatory protein that blocks the myosin-binding sites on actin molecules.

**troponin complex** The regulatory proteins that control the position of tropomyosin on the thin filament.

**true-breeding** Referring to organisms that produce offspring of the same variety over many generations of self-pollination.

**tubal ligation** A means of sterilization in which a woman's two oviducts (fallopian tubes) are tied closed and a segment of each is removed to prevent eggs from reaching the uterus.

**tube foot** One of numerous extensions of an echinoderm's water vascular system. Tube feet function in locomotion and feeding.

**tumor-suppressor gene** A gene whose protein product inhibits cell division, thereby preventing the uncontrolled cell growth that contributes to cancer.

**tundra** A terrestrial biome at the extreme limits of plant growth. At the northernmost limits, it is called arctic tundra, and at high altitudes, where plant forms are limited to low shrubby or matlike vegetation, it is called alpine tundra.

**tunicate** A member of the clade Urochordata, sessile marine chordates that lack a backbone.

**turgid** (ter′-jid) Swollen or distended, as in plant cells. (A walled cell becomes turgid if it has a lower water potential than its surroundings, resulting in entry of water.)

**turgor pressure** The force directed against a plant cell wall after the influx of water and swelling of the cell due to osmosis.

**turnover** The mixing of waters as a result of changing water-temperature profiles in a lake.

**twin study** A behavioral study in which researchers compare the behavior of identical twins raised apart with that of identical twins raised in the same household.

**tympanic membrane** Another name for the eardrum, the membrane between the outer and middle ear.

**Unikonta** (yū′-ni-kon′-tuh) One of four supergroups of eukaryotes proposed in a current hypothesis of the evolutionary history of eukaryotes. This clade, which is supported by studies of myosin proteins and DNA, consists of amoebozoans and opisthokonts. *See also* Excavata, SAR, and Archaeplastida.

**unsaturated fatty acid** A fatty acid that has one or more double bonds between carbons in the hydrocarbon tail. Such bonding reduces the number of hydrogen atoms attached to the carbon skeleton.

**urban ecology** The study of organisms and their environment in urban and suburban settings.

**urea** A soluble nitrogenous waste produced in the liver by a metabolic cycle that combines ammonia with carbon dioxide.

**ureter** (yū-rē′-ter) A duct leading from the kidney to the urinary bladder.

**urethra** (yū-rē′-thruh) A tube that releases urine from the mammalian body near the vagina in females and through the penis in males; also serves in males as the exit tube for the reproductive system.

**uric acid** A product of protein and purine metabolism and the major nitrogenous waste product of insects, land snails, and many reptiles. Uric acid is relatively nontoxic and largely insoluble in water.

**urinary bladder** The pouch where urine is stored prior to elimination.

**uterine cycle** The cyclic changes in the endometrium (uterine lining) of mammals that occur in the absence of pregnancy. In certain primates, including humans, the uterine cycle is a menstrual cycle.

**uterus** A female organ where eggs are fertilized and/or development of the young occurs.

**vaccine** A harmless variant or derivative of a pathogen that stimulates a host's immune system to mount defenses against the pathogen.

**vacuole** (vak′-yū-ōl′) A membrane-bounded vesicle whose specialized function varies in different kinds of cells.

**vagina** Part of the female reproductive system between the uterus and the outside opening; the birth canal in mammals. During copulation, the vagina accommodates the male's penis and receives sperm.

**valence** The bonding capacity of a given atom; the number of covalent bonds that an atom can form, which usually equals the number of unpaired electrons in its outermost (valence) shell.

**valence electron** An electron in the outermost electron shell.

**valence shell** The outermost energy shell of an atom, containing the valence electrons involved in the chemical reactions of that atom.

**van der Waals interactions** Weak attractions between molecules or parts of molecules that result from transient local partial charges.

**variable** A factor that varies in an experiment.

**variation** Differences between members of the same species.

**vas deferens** In mammals, the tube in the male reproductive system in which sperm travel from the epididymis to the urethra.

**vasa recta** The capillary system in the kidney that serves the loop of Henle.

**vascular cambium** A cylinder of meristematic tissue in woody plants that adds layers of secondary vascular tissue called secondary xylem (wood) and secondary phloem.

**vascular plant** A plant with vascular tissue. Vascular plants include all living plant species except liverworts, mosses, and hornworts.

**vascular tissue** Plant tissue consisting of cells joined into tubes that transport water and nutrients throughout the plant body.

**vascular tissue system** A transport system formed by xylem and phloem throughout a vascular plant. Xylem transports water and minerals; phloem transports sugars, the products of photosynthesis.

**vasectomy** The cutting and sealing of each vas deferens to prevent sperm from entering the urethra.

**vasoconstriction** A decrease in the diameter of blood vessels caused by contraction of smooth muscles in the vessel walls.

**vasodilation** An increase in the diameter of blood vessels caused by relaxation of smooth muscles in the vessel walls.

**vasopressin** *See* antidiuretic hormone (ADH).

**vector** An organism that transmits pathogens from one host to another.

**vegetal pole** The point at the end of an egg in the hemisphere where most yolk is concentrated; opposite of animal pole.

**vegetative propagation** Asexual reproduction in plants that is facilitated or induced by humans.

**vegetative reproduction** Asexual reproduction in plants.

**vein** (1) In animals, a vessel that carries blood toward the heart. (2) In plants, a vascular bundle in a leaf.

**ventilation** The flow of air or water over a respiratory surface.

**ventral** Pertaining to the underside, or bottom, of an animal with radial or bilateral symmetry.

**ventricle** (ven′-tri-kul) (1) A heart chamber that pumps blood out of the heart. (2) A space in the vertebrate brain, filled with cerebrospinal fluid.

**venule** (ven′-yūl) A vessel that conveys blood between a capillary bed and a vein.

**vernalization** The use of cold treatment to induce a plant to flower.

**vertebrate** A chordate animal with vertebrae, the series of bones that make up the backbone.

**vesicle** (ves′-i-kul) A membranous sac in the cytoplasm of a eukaryotic cell.

**vessel** A continuous water-conducting micropipe found in most angiosperms and a few nonflowering vascular plants.

**vessel element** A short, wide water-conducting cell found in the xylem of most angiosperms and a few nonflowering vascular plants. Dead at maturity, vessel elements are aligned end to end to form micropipes called vessels.

**vestigial structure** A feature of an organism that is a historical remnant of a structure that served a function in the organism's ancestors.

**villus** (plural, **villi**) (1) A finger-like projection of the inner surface of the small intestine. (2) A finger-like projection of the chorion of the mammalian placenta. Large numbers of villi increase the surface areas of these organs.

**viral envelope** A membrane, derived from membranes of the host cell, that cloaks the capsid, which in turn encloses a viral genome.

**virulent phage** A phage that replicates only by a lytic cycle.

**virus** An infectious particle incapable of replicating outside of a cell, consisting of an RNA or DNA genome surrounded by a protein coat (capsid) and, for some viruses, a membranous envelope.

**visceral mass** One of the three main parts of a mollusc; the part containing most of the internal organs. *See also* foot and mantle.

**visible light** That portion of the electromagnetic spectrum that can be detected as various colors by the human eye, ranging in wavelength from about 380 nm to about 750 nm.

**vital capacity** The maximum volume of air that a mammal can inhale and exhale with each breath.

**vitamin** An organic molecule required in the diet in very small amounts. Many vitamins serve as coenzymes or parts of coenzymes.

**viviparous** (vī-vip′-uh-rus) Referring to a type of development in which the young are born alive after having been nourished in the uterus by blood from the placenta.

**voltage-gated ion channel** A specialized ion channel that opens or closes in response to changes in membrane potential.

**vulva** Collective term for the female external genitalia.

**water potential** (ψ) The physical property predicting the direction in which water will flow, governed by solute concentration and applied pressure.

**water vascular system** A network of hydraulic canals unique to echinoderms that branches into extensions called tube feet, which function in locomotion and feeding.

**wavelength** The distance between crests of waves, such as those of the electromagnetic spectrum.

**wetland** A habitat that is inundated by water at least some of the time and that supports plants adapted to water-saturated soil.

**white matter** Tracts of axons within the CNS.

**whole-genome shotgun approach** Procedure for genome sequencing in which the genome is randomly cut into many overlapping short segments that are sequenced; computer software then assembles the complete sequence.

**wild type** The phenotype most commonly observed in natural populations; also refers to the individual with that phenotype.

**wilting** The drooping of leaves and stems as a result of plant cells becoming flaccid.

**wobble** Flexibility in the base-pairing rules in which the nucleotide at the 5′ end of a tRNA anticodon can form hydrogen bonds with more than one kind of base in the third position (3′ end) of a codon.

**xerophyte** (zir′-ō-fīt′) A plant adapted to an arid climate.

**X-linked gene** A gene located on the X chromosome; such genes show a distinctive pattern of inheritance.

**X-ray crystallography** A technique used to study the three-dimensional structure of molecules. It depends on the diffraction of an X-ray beam by the individual atoms of a crystallized molecule.

**xylem** (zī′-lum) Vascular plant tissue consisting mainly of tubular dead cells that conduct most of the water and minerals upward from the roots to the rest of the plant.

**xylem sap** (zī′-lum) The dilute solution of water and minerals carried through vessels and tracheids.

**yeast** Single-celled fungus. Yeasts reproduce asexually by binary fission or by the pinching of small buds off a parent cell. Many fungal species can grow both as yeasts and as a network of filaments; relatively few species grow only as yeasts.

**yolk** Nutrients stored in an egg.

**zero population growth (ZPG)** A period of stability in population size, when additions to the population through births and immigration are balanced by subtractions through deaths and emigration.

**zona pellucida** The extracellular matrix surrounding a mammalian egg.

**zoned reserve** An extensive region that includes areas relatively undisturbed by humans surrounded by areas that have been changed by human activity and are used for economic gain.

**zone of polarizing activity (ZPA)** A block of mesoderm located just under the ectoderm where the posterior side of a limb bud is attached to the body; required for proper pattern formation along the anterior-posterior axis of the limb.

**zoonotic pathogen** A disease-causing agent that is transmitted to humans from other animals.

**zoospore** Flagellated spore found in chytrid fungi and some protists.

**zygomycete** (zī′-guh-mī′-sēt) A member of the fungal phylum Zygomycota, characterized by the formation of a sturdy structure called a zygosporangium during sexual reproduction.

**zygosporangium** (zī′-guh-spōr-an′-jē-um) (plural, **zygosporangia**) In zygomycete fungi, a sturdy multinucleate structure in which karyogamy and meiosis occur.

**zygote** (zī′-gōt) The diploid cell produced by the union of haploid gametes during fertilization; a fertilized egg.

# H

as energy for life, 145, 150
global energy budget and, 1239
latitudinal variation in intensity of, 1164f
in photosynthesis, 187f, 206, 207f
primary production in aquatic ecosystems and
limitations of, 1240
properties of, 192f
species distributions and availability of, 1184f
Supercontinent, 536, 537f
Supergroups, protist, 592–593, 594f–595f
Superimposed electron orbitals model, 35f
Supernatural vs. natural explanations, 18
Super-resolution microscopy, 95f, 96
Super weeds, 436–437
Suprachiasmatic nucleus (SCN), 891f, 1013,
**1092**–1093
Surface area
calculating cell volume and, 99
leaf, 629f
maximizing, by animals, 693f
Surface area-volume relationships, 98f
Surface tension, **45**, 46f
Surfactants, **941**
Surroundings, systems and, 145
Survival
adaptations, natural selection, and, 473f, 474
gecko appearance and, 27
life histories and, 1198, 1199f–1200f
Survivorship curves, **1191**, 1192f
Suspension feeding, 719f, 725, 901f
Suspensor cells, 826f
Sustainability, 1281
Sustainable agriculture, **806**
in Costa Rica zoned reserves, 1271
soil conservation in, 805f–807f
Sustainable development, **1281**f–1282f
Sutherland, Earl W., 216f, 217f, 223
Sutton, Walter S., 294
Swallowing reflex, 904f
Sweden, 1206
Sweet potatoes, 649
Sweet tastes, 1121f–1122f
Swim bladders, **726**
Swimming, 1133
Swine flu, 408, 1232–1233
Switchgrass, 836
Symbionts, **586**
Symbiosis, **586**, 1254f. See also Commensalism;
Mutualism; Parasitism
in flower pollination, 820–821
fungal, 659f, 660, 665f–667f
protist, 612f
sym genes, 658
Symmetry
animal body, 677f, 678
body, 1057–1058, 1062f
flower, 642f, 647f
plant cell division, 774, 775f–776f
Sympathetic division, peripheral nervous system,
926f, 1087f–**1088**f
Sympatric populations, character displacement in,
1214, 1215f
Sympatric speciation, **511**, 512f–513f, 514
Symplast, **785**, 786f
Symplastic communication, 799, 800f
Symplastic domains, 800
Symplastic route, 786f, 791f
Synapses, **1066**
electrical and chemical, 1075, 1076f
generation of postsynaptic potentials and,
1076–1077
in memory and learning, 1097, 1098f–1099f
modulated signaling at, 1078
neurotransmitters and, 1075, 1076f, 1078f,
1079t, 1080
in regulation of muscle contraction, 1126,
1127f, 1128
scaffolding proteins and, 228f, 229
summation of postsynaptic potentials and, 1077f
Synapsids, 529f, **739**f, 740
Synapsis, 262f
Synaptic cleft, 1076
Synaptic signaling, 215f, 216, 998f, **999**
Synaptic terminals, 1066
Synaptic vesicles, 1075
Synaptonemal complex, **262**f
Syndermata, 685f

Syndromes, 308
Synthesis stage, phage lytic cycle, 400f
Synthetases, 349f
Syphilis, 583f
Systematics, **552**, 680, 681f, 682. See also Cladistics;
Molecular systematics; Taxonomy
Systemic acquired resistance, 864, 865f
Systemic circuit, 922f, 923
Systemic inflammatory response, 955
Systemic lupus erythematosus, 969
Systemic mycoses, 668
Systems
systems biology and biological, 5–6
thermodynamics and isolated vs. open, 145,
149f–150f
Systems biology, **6**, 444, **445**f–446f
Systole phase, **925**f
Systolic pressure, **928**, 929f
Szostak, Jack, 465f, 526

T
T2 phage. See Sodium chloride
Table salt. See Sodium chloride
Tables in Scientific Skills Exercises, 58, 89, 157, 179,
205, 264, 304, 318, 456, 491, 511, 568, 588,
593, 627, 637, 655, 676, 749, 760, 788, 832,
916, 936, 971, 979, 1012, 1028, 1047, 1080,
1184, 1215, 1245, 1276
TACK supergroup, 585
Tactile communication, 1139f
Tadpoles, 379f, 730f
Taiga, 1173f
Tail, muscular post-anal, 718f
Tails, histone, 330f, 369f
Takahe bird, 1252f
TAL protein, 334
Tamiflu, 412
Tamoxifen, 250, 391f
tangled-1 mutant, 774
Tannins, 1218
Tansley, A. G., 1226
Tapeworms, 685f, 694, 695f
Tappania fossil, 527f
Tapping, in fruit fly courtship, 1139f, 1140
Taproots, **757**f–758f
Taq polymerase, 419, 1261
Tardigrades, 687f, 978f
Target cells, hormone, 998, 1000f–1001f, 1002
Tarsiers, 744
Tar spot fungus, 667f
Tasmania, 1183f
Tastants, **1121**f–1122f
Taste, 233, 1121f–1122f
Taste buds, **1122**f
TATA boxes, 343f, **344**, 371
Tatum, Edward, 336f–337f, 338
Tau protein, 1102
Taxis, **574**
Taxol, 249
Taxon, **552**, 553f–554f, 558
Taxonomy, **552**, E-2-E-3. See also Cladistics;
Phylogenies; Systematics
early schemes of, 468
grouping of species in, 12f–13f
mammalian, 742f–743f
phyla of extant plants, 621t
phylogenies and, 552, 553f–554f
possible plant kingdoms, 617f
three-domain system of, 12f, 13, 566, 567f
tree of life of, 15f–16f
Tay-Sachs disease, **280**
allele dominance and, 280
fetal testing for, 288, 289f
as lysosomal storage disease, 108
recessive alleles in, 285
T cells, **956**
antigen recognition by, 957f–958f
cell-mediated immune response and, 961
clonal selection of, 960, 961f
development of, 958, 959f–961f
diversity of, 958, 959f
DNA of, 974
immunological memory, 960, 961f
proliferation of, 960f
regulatory, 969
Tea, 649
Teal, John, 1245

Technology, **23**, 24f
DNA. See Biotechnology; DNA technology
global carrying capacity and, 1209
prokaryotes in research and, 587, 588f–589f
Tectonic plates, 536f–537f
Teeth
conodont mineralized dental elements, 722f
diet and adaptations of, 909f, 910
mammalian, 528, 529f, 739
origins of, 723
Teixobactin, 476
Telomerase, 329
Telomeres, **328**, 329f, 450
Telomeric DNA, 450
Telophase (mitosis), **237**, 239f, 243f, 252, 263f
Telophase I, 260f, 263f
Telophase II, 261f
Temperate broadleaf forests, **1174**f
Temperate forests, decomposition in, 1246
Temperate grasslands, **1173**f
Temperate phages, **400**, 401f
Temperature, **46**
aquatic biomes and, 1175, 1176f
climographs of, 1169f
coefficients in Scientific Skills Exercise, 788
correlation of atmospheric carbon dioxide with
global, 1275f–1279f
decomposition rates and, 1246f
effects of transpiration on leaf, 796
enzymatic catalysis and, 157, 158f
global, and extinction rates, 539f, 540
heat vs., 46
membrane proteins and, 128f
moderation by water, 46, 47f
plant response to stress of, 863
primary production in terrestrial biomes and,
1241, 1242f, 1243
protein denaturation and, 82f, 83
regulation of body. See Thermoregulation
species distributions and, 1183f
Templates, viral DNA and RNA, 403f, 404t
Template strands, DNA, 320, 321f–322f, 324f–327f, **340**
Tempo, speciation, 518f–519f
Temporal fenestra, 529f, 739
Temporal isolation, 506f
Temporal lobe, 1095f
Temporal summation, 1077f
Tendons, **876**f, 1136
Tendrils, 760f
Tentacles, invertebrate, 684, 689f, 699, 701f
Terminal cells, 826f
Termination, neurotransmission, 1078f
Termination codons, 341f
Termination stage
transcription, 343f, 344
translation, 353f
Terminators, **342**, 343f
Termites, 612f, 653
Terns, 1236f
Terpenoids, 866f
Terrestrial adaptations
mycorrhizae as plant, 815
seed plant, 635f–636f, 637
Terrestrial biomes
animal osmoregulation in, 978–979
biodiversity hot spots in, 1270f
biomass pyramids in, 1245f
chaparral, 1172f
climate and, 1168, 1169f
climate change effects on, 1242f, 1243
decomposition in, 1246
deserts, 1171f
disturbance in, 1170
food chains in, 1222f
general features of, 1169, 1170f
global distribution of, 1169f
habitat loss in, 1262
locomotion in, 1133f
northern coniferous forests, 1173f
nutrient cycling in, 1248f–1249f
plant adaptations to, 203
primary production in, 1241, 1242f, 1243
savannas, 1172f
temperate broadleaf forests, 1174f
temperate grasslands, 1173f
tropical forests, 1171f
tundra, 1174f, 1254f–1255f